How to use your Connected Casebook

Step 1: Go to **www.CasebookConnect.com** and redeem your access code to get started.

Access Code: STXT99849464417

Step 2: Go to your **BOOKSHELF** and select your Connected Casebook to start reading, highlighting, and taking notes in the margins of your e-book.

Step 3: Select the **STUDY** tab in your toolbar to access a variety of practice materials designed to help you master the course material. These materials may include explanations, videos, multiple-choice questions, flashcards, short answer, essays, and issue spotting.

Step 4: Select the **OUTLINE** tab in your toolbar to access chapter outlines that automatically incorporate your highlights and annotations from the e-book. Use the My Notes area for copying, pasting, and editing your book notes or creating new notes.

Step 5: If your professor has enrolled your class, you can select the **CLASS INSIGHTS** tab and compare your own study center results against the average of your classmates.

Is this a used casebook? Access code already scratched off?

You can purchase the Digital Version and still access all of the powerful tools listed above. Please visit CasebookConnect.com and select Catalog to learn more.

PLEASE NOTE: Each access code can only be used once. This access code will expire one year after the discontinuation of the corresponding print title and must be redeemed before then. CCH reserves the right to discontinue this program at any time for any business reason. For further details, please see the Casebook Connect End User Agreement.

PIN: 9111149549

22165

Torts

ASPEN CASEBOOK SERIES

Torts
Cases and Materials

Fourth Edition

Aaron D. Twerski

Irwin and Jill Cohen Professor of Law
Brooklyn Law School

James A. Henderson, Jr.

Frank B. Ingersoll Professor of Law, Emeritus
Cornell Law School

W. Bradley Wendel

Professor of Law
Cornell Law School

Published by Wolters Kluwer in New York.

Wolters Kluwer Legal & Regulatory U.S. serves customers worldwide with CCH, Aspen Publishers, and Kluwer Law International products. (www.WKLegaledu.com)

To contact Customer Service, e-mail customer.service@wolterskluwer.com, call 1-800-234-1660, fax 1-800-901-9075, or mail correspondence to:

Wolters Kluwer
Attn: Order Department
PO Box 990
Frederick, MD 21705

Printed in the United States of America.

2 3 4 5 6 7 8 9 0

ISBN 978-1-4548-7575-8

Names: Twerski, Aaron D., author. | Henderson, James A., 1938- author. |
     Wendel, W. Bradley, 1969- author.
Title: Torts : cases and materials / Aaron D. Twerski, Irwin and Jill Cohen
     Professor of Law, Brooklyn Law School; James A. Henderson, Jr. Frank B.
     Ingersoll Professor of Law, Emeritus Cornell Law School; W. Bradley
     Wendel, Professor of Law, Cornell Law School.
Description: Fourth edition. | New York : Wolters Kluwer, [2017]
Identifiers: LCCN 2016056655 | ISBN 9781454875758
Subjects: LCSH: Torts — United States. | LCGFT: Casebooks.
Classification: LCC KF1250 .T93 2017 | DDC 346.7303 — dc23
LC record available at https://lccn.loc.gov/2016056655

From Aaron
to
Kreindel

From Jim
to
Marcie

From Brad
to my father, Harry W. Wendel,
and to the memory of my mother,
Barbara J. Wendel

Summary of Contents

Contents

chapter 2

Privileges/Defenses   77

chapter **3**

Negligence

chapter 4

Actual Causation   239

chapter 5

Proximate Causation

chapter **6**

Nonliability for Foreseeable Consequences (Limited Duty Rules)   375

chapter **7**

Owners and Occupiers of Land   459

chapter **8**

Affirmative Defenses 493

chapter **9**

Joint Tortfeasors

chapter **10**

Strict Liability

chapter **11**

Products Liability

chapter **12**

Trespass to Land and Nuisance   713

chapter **15**

Privacy   887

Preface

We continue to hear from students that they find the book both accessible and rigorous. Features like the hypotheticals and authors' dialogues highlight areas of uncertainty or genuine disagreement among courts and scholars. At the same time, however, we have striven to avoid the "hide the ball" approach that afflicts far too many casebooks. Where a clear explanation is possible, we have given it, rather than trying to obscure the matter. If something remains murky, it may be due to an error on our parts, in which case we'd appreciate hearing about it. But it may simply be that the issue in question is genuinely difficult.

It is tempting to let a torts casebook rest on a foundation of great cases from the past, and not do too much updating. While the American Law Institute Third Restatement of Torts projects continue to generate a great deal of energy, tort doctrine overall has been relatively stable in recent years. However, in planning for the fourth edition of this book, we committed ourselves to a comprehensive revision, pruning out deadwood cases and adding in new ones as needed. The result is a book that varies quite a bit from the third edition. We know this can be a bit of a headache for instructors who have prepared syllabi and class notes based on the last edition, but we hope the improvement makes the additional preparation worthwhile. We noticed, by the way, that many of the new cases involve various types of sexual misconduct. This was not due to our prurient interests. Tort law is an arena for social conflict, and these cases reflect the disputes that people are bringing to the courts today. Many of the cases are also good teaching tools, for reasons that we are hopeful will be apparent when you read through them.

Brad Wendel joined the book for the third edition, initially because of his expertise in legal ethics. However, Brad is also an enthusiastic teacher of torts and products liability and has expanded his role as editor for this edition. All three of us love the subject of torts, have had a lot of fun working on this book, and hope you will find the study of torts as stimulating and enjoyable as we do.

A.D.T., J.A.H., Jr., and W.B.W.

Acknowledgments

We thank Golda Lawrence at Brooklyn Law School, who helped to prepare the manuscript. We could not have seen this through without her.

Research assistants provided invaluable help in assembling these materials. Helder Agostinho (Cornell '09), Josh Chandler (Cornell '04), M. Ryan Farabough (Cornell '04), Daniel Hendrick (Cornell '09), Ledra Horowitz (Brooklyn '04), Julie Levine (Brooklyn '09), John Marston (Cornell '04), Rebekah Rollo (Brooklyn '04), Kristopher Rossfeld (Cornell '04), Michael Siegel (Cornell '09), Shimon Sternhell (Brooklyn '12), Stephen Sternschein (Brooklyn '09), Skyler Tanner (Cornell '09), Greg Wicker (Brooklyn '04), and Melissa Y. Wu (Brooklyn '08) helped us meet extremely tight deadlines. We are indebted to them for their contributions.

Deans Eduardo Peñalver and Stewart J. Schwab at Cornell and Michael Gerber and Joan Wexler at Brooklyn also deserve thanks for their generous support.

We thank the authors and publishers of the following works for permitting us to include excerpts from these works:

American Law Institute, Restatement of Torts, Second, § 13; § 18; § 21; § 35; § 58 comment a, illustration 1; § 59 comment a, illustrations 1 and 2; § 63; § 65; § 222A; § 291; § 310; § 311; § 339; § 402A and comment i; § 402B; § 431; § 442; § 524; § 542(2); § 559; § 652D; § 652E; § 821B; § 821C; § 876 and comment a, illustration 2, comment d, and illustrations 9 and 11; § 892. Copyright © 1965 The American Law Institute. Reprinted by permission. All rights reserved.

American Law Institute, Restatement of Torts, Third: Liability for Physical and Emotional Harm, § 3 and comment e; § 5; § 8; § 10; § 12 and comment b; 14 and comment c and illustration 1; § 17 and comment a; § 20; § 26 comment n; § 27; 29 and comment d and Reporters' Notes p. 517; § 34; § 35; § 42; § 45 illustration 6; § 46. Copyright © 2011 The American Law Institute. Reprinted by permission. All rights reserved.

American Law Institute, Restatement of Torts, Third: Apportionment of Liability, § 8 and comments b and c; § 14; § 22. Copyright © 2000 The American Law Institute. Reprinted by permission. All rights reserved.

American Law Institute, Restatement of Torts, Third: Products Liability § 1; § 2 and comments f and i; § 3. Copyright © 1998 The American Law Institute. Reprinted by permission. All rights reserved.

Torts

Introduction

The observations and comments that follow address subjects that you should know something about as you set out on your study of tort law. Although these topics are not taken up separately in the course, they will be relevant throughout the materials. None of the comments should be taken as authoritative or exhaustive. Rather, they are aimed at giving you a bit of a head-start in your journey through the rich and provocative — and occasionally confounding — world of torts.

WHAT THIS COURSE IS ABOUT

The term "torts" connotes civil (rather than criminal) wrongs for which the victims (the plaintiffs) have causes of action against the wrongdoers (the defendants) to recover money judgments. The term traces its origins to the Norman French word for "twisted," or "crooked." It shares the same root in modern English with "tortuous" and "torture." Torts include punching someone in the face without just cause; driving an automobile negligently so as to cause harm to others; and commercially distributing a defective, harmful product. The three major areas of tort that this book explores, reflected in these examples, are intentional torts, negligence, and strict liability. Tort law is often characterized as private law. Tort actions are typically brought by private persons who either claim themselves to be victims of wrongdoing or who claim to represent such victims. Criminal law is the public-law counterpart to tort. Crimes are prosecuted by officers of the state, to protect and vindicate essentially public interests. Many torts have parallels in criminal law, and the terminology is quite similar in both the private (tort) and public (criminal) contexts.

In addition to learning about tort law, you will also be learning about the processes by which tort claims get resolved in our system. Formal adjudication, which takes place in both state and federal trial courts, is the subject of a separate first-year law course unto itself — civil procedure. In this torts course you will also consider the appellate phase of adjudication, whereby one or the other side takes the case to a higher court. And you will be introduced to the settlement process whereby the parties agree outside of court to terms that resolve the claim once and for all. Most tort claims are resolved via settlement — it is too costly to take very many cases to full-blown trial. Settlement agreements are formal contracts that must conform to the requirements you will be studying in your course on contract law.

More than any other course in your first year of law school, torts has been the subject of public controversy in recent years. Massive class actions have sought to vindicate the rights of hundreds of thousands of injured victims. Tort liabilities that run in the hundreds of billions of dollars have forced entire industries into bankruptcy. Perhaps most directly relevant to those of you who may eventually go into trial practice on the civil side, lawyers and law firms for both tort plaintiffs and defendants have prospered financially from all of this legal activity. Some observers applaud these developments, believing that America is a better, safer place for all of it. Other observers are appalled at what they view to be excesses that threaten our national welfare. Obviously, it is premature for you to form firm opinions one way or the other, given that your study of tort law has only just begun. However, these issues will not go away any time soon; and before we are finished with this course you should be in a better position to decide where you stand.

SOME PRELIMINARY THOUGHTS REGARDING THE SOCIAL OBJECTIVES OF TORT LAW

In order to understand tort law it is useful, as a general matter, to appreciate what tort law is trying to accomplish. Of course, sometimes the rules of tort law are so clear and precise that the proper liability outcome in a given case is obvious regardless of what the underlying objectives of the system may be. Thus, the intentional tort of battery requires that the defendant's intentional act cause a harmful or offensive contact with the plaintiff's person. In the absence of such contact the defendant has not committed a battery regardless of how deliberately wrongful the defendant's conduct has been. Even if tort law is assumed to be aimed at discouraging intentionally wrongful conduct, without a harmful or offensive contact with the plaintiff the defendant has not committed a battery, and that is that. But inevitably (and more often than you might think) cases arise in which the contact requirement for battery is not so clear. For example, will kicking a park bench on which the plaintiff is sitting suffice? Is a sharp tap on a stranger's shoulder to get her attention an "offensive" (and therefore wrongful) contact within the rules governing battery? In these instances, reasonable minds may differ on whether the contact requirement is satisfied. In determining the appropriate outcomes in these cases, an appreciation of the underlying objectives of tort certainly helps.

Current thinking about the objectives of our tort system falls into two main camps. Many observers believe that tort law exists to correct wrongs — injustices — that have occurred in the course of human interactions. In determining whether a tort remedy is appropriate, courts look backward at past events and ask if a wrong has been committed. If it has, the court so declares and enters its declaration in the public record that the defendant has wronged the plaintiff. On the assumption that the payment of money damages by the defendant to the plaintiff will make the injured plaintiff whole again (or as nearly whole as possible), the court achieves corrective justice by ordering such payment. On this widely shared view, tort law's primary objective is to achieve fairness for its own sake. The other major view concerning the objectives of tort is instrumental — tort remedies are justified because they create incentives for actors to behave more carefully in the future. The emphasis from this second perspective is not to correct past wrongs but to deter future losses. Unlike the corrective justice perspective, in which tort judgments are ends in themselves, from the instrumental viewpoint tort judgments are means to the end that really matters: achieving a less dangerous (and thus more prosperous) society.

If the truth be told, these two contrasting views regarding the underlying objectives of tort will, in many, if not most, instances, explain and justify the same outcomes on the same facts. The question raised earlier concerning whether a sharp tap on a stranger's shoulder is, or is not, offensive to reasonable sensibilities should probably be decided in the same way from either a fairness/corrective-justice or an instrumental/safety perspective. But situations arise in which one's choice of a worldview makes a difference in how actual cases get decided. For example, debate continues currently on the issue of whether a product manufacturer's duty to warn consumers of nonobvious risks is based solely on reducing future injuries or is also based on maintaining respect for the dignitary values that inhere in consumers being allowed to make fully informed choices regarding product use and consumption. Depending on the view one adopts, certain kinds of warnings will, or will not, be required from manufacturers, and the tort liabilities will vary accordingly.

As you work through the appellate decisions in this book, you should ask yourself whether a particular court's rationale seems to reflect corrective justice or instrumental perspectives, or perhaps a combination of the two. And where no view of underlying objectives is evident from the opinion, you should ask yourself how the case on appeal might have been argued for each side, using one or the other perspective. This is a course on tort *law,* not tort *policy.* But sometimes the two cannot easily be separated.

ETHICAL RESPONSIBILITIES OF LAWYERS

Cases do not make their way through the litigation system all by themselves. Most plaintiffs and defendants in tort lawsuits are represented by lawyers. In an adversarial system of adjudication as we have in the United States (as in other countries sharing the heritage of the English common law, such as the United Kingdom, Canada, Australia, and New Zealand), it is up to the parties themselves, with the assistance of their lawyers, to decide what claims and defenses to assert. The parties and their lawyers also investigate incidents to determine the facts; largely control the process of pretrial discovery, where plaintiffs and defendants learn information in the possession of the other party; and have significant latitude to decide what evidence to introduce at trial. The practice in adversarial systems is in contrast with so-called civil law systems, often based on the French or German civil code, in which judges exercise greater control over the processes of investigation, discovery, and presentation of evidence at trial. It is true, as you will see, that American judges do have the authority to manage trial and pretrial litigation to some extent, but the parties and their lawyers nevertheless play a central role in the justice system in the United States.

Lawyers are not merely cogs in the machinery of the justice system, but play a vital, creative role as representatives of clients. Lawyers make countless decisions in the course of a lawsuit, concerning matters such as which parties to sue, what claims or defenses to assert, what avenues of investigation and discovery to pursue, whether to recommend that their client settle a case or go to trial, and how to conduct the trial. In making these decisions, lawyers are guided and constrained by obligations they owe both to their client and to the justice system. American lawyers like to describe themselves as "zealous advocates within the bounds of the law," capturing both of these duties — to clients, to be dedicated, loyal, competent representatives, and to courts, to ensure that their own actions and those of their clients remain lawful. These general ethical ideals are fleshed out as more specific, legally enforceable obligations. For example, lawyers are prohibited from disclosing confidential information related to their representation of clients, and may not represent other parties whose interests conflict with those of a client. Lawyers also may not knowingly introduce false evidence or fail to correct the false testimony of a witness. Violations of these duties may subject a lawyer to professional discipline, meted out by the court of the jurisdiction in which the lawyer is admitted to practice law. Alternatively, a lawyer may be subject to a lawsuit by a client for malpractice or breach of fiduciary duty, or may be sanctioned or held in contempt by a tribunal before which the lawyer is appearing.

Legal ethics is an ambiguous term. It may refer to general ideals, such as being a loyal representative of clients or an "officer of the court." Lawyers may also be subject to criticism by others in ethical terms for doing things that appear to be improper by the standards of ordinary morality. The academic discipline of legal ethics is concerned, among other things, with working out the right way to understand the relationship between the professional obligations of lawyers and the values and principles that guide people in their everyday lives. As often as not, however, when lawyers talk about legal ethics they mean the rules of professional conduct under which they practice and other aspects of the law governing lawyers. Almost every state in the United States (with California as the sole holdout, and even it appears to be changing soon) has adopted rules of conduct based on Model Rules prepared by the American Bar Association (ABA). The ABA does not have authority to regulate the profession — it is really only a trade association of lawyers — but its model professional standards have proved to be very influential, and state courts have generally adopted conduct rules based closely on the ABA's models. In addition to these rules of professional conduct, the violation of which can subject the lawyer to sanctions including reprimand, suspension, or disbarment, lawyers must conform their conduct to applicable legal standards set out in tort, contract, agency, criminal, constitutional, and procedural law.

At various points in this book we will consider some of the ethical issues that arise for lawyers in tort litigation. Although some of these issues, such as conflicts of interest and confidentiality, are complex and technical, it is never too early to start spotting the issues, as lawyers like to say, and becoming aware of when you might need to think like a lawyer about your own duties and liabilities. It is also never too early to think more broadly, in ethical terms, about the role of the legal profession in society and whether lawyers are justified in doing things that sometimes seem ethically troubling. There is really no way to separate ethical issues from the contexts in which lawyers practice, so we hope to offer some food for thought along the way while you are learning torts.

MEASURES OF RECOVERY IN TORT: THE RULES GOVERNING DAMAGES

In all of the cases we will consider in these materials, and in almost all of the tort cases brought to court, plaintiffs seek to recover money damages from defendants. When a plaintiff is successful, the court enters a *judgment* against the defendant, in favor of the plaintiff. If a jury is involved, the jury will have returned a *verdict* for the plaintiff, upon which the court enters judgment. The judgment is an order by the court to the defendant to pay the plaintiff a specified amount of money, together with interest from the date of judgment, within a certain time. (When the judgment is for defendant, the court simply enters an order to that effect.) If the defendant does not satisfy the judgment by paying as ordered, the plaintiff may seek the court's assistance in employing governmental officers to force payment, sometimes by a court-supervised sale of the defendant's reachable assets.

For what elements of loss may successful tort plaintiffs recover? Measured by what standards? In some cases successful plaintiffs are entitled to *nominal damages* — a token amount awarded simply to commemorate the plaintiff's vindication in court. At early common law in England, nominal damages often took the form of defendant's payment of a peppercorn. Today, for some intentional torts that do not involve physical harm or outrageous behavior, courts award nominal damages — one dollar, perhaps — to successful plaintiffs. Courts award *compensatory damages* to compensate the plaintiff for losses caused by the defendant's tortious conduct. In personal injury cases, compensatory damages include economic losses such as lost earnings and reduced future earning capacity. Economic losses for personal injury also include medical and rehabilitation expenses, both past and future. Plaintiffs may also recover for intangible, *noneconomic losses,* including pain and suffering and mental upset past, present, and future.

In connection with claims for property damage, the successful plaintiff recovers an amount representing the extent by which the market value of the plaintiff's property has been diminished because of the defendant's tortious conduct.

Special rules apply when the defendant's tortious conduct causes death. For one thing, the action is brought by surviving next of kin or by a legal representative on behalf of the decedent's estate. *Wrongful death statutes* authorize recovery for the death itself. *Survival statutes* authorize recovery for losses incurred by the victim between the time of injury and the subsequent death. Compensatory damages in wrongful death cases track those awarded in personal injury cases not involving death, and include funeral and burial costs. The major element of economic recovery in these cases is destruction of the decedent's earning capacity. Damages do not, of course, include the elements of future medical expenses and pain and suffering, allowed in non-death cases. Jurisdictions vary with respect to whether surviving family members are allowed to recover for their own grief and emotional upset brought on by the death. A majority of American jurisdictions allow such recovery.

In addition to nominal and compensatory damages, American courts award *punitive damages* when the defendant's tortious conduct is especially outrageous. Jurisdictions vary in their descriptions of the sort of tortious conduct that justifies punitive damages. In theory, the amount of the award should be great enough, in relation to both the defendant's conduct and the defendant's net economic worth, to teach the defendant a lesson. The United States Supreme Court has begun to monitor the size of punitive damage awards in state courts on the grounds that awards that are too great violate the rights of defendants to due process of law under the Fourteenth Amendment to the United States Constitution.

TIME LIMITATIONS ON THE BRINGING OF TORT ACTIONS

When someone discovers that she has been harmed by another's conduct, she (the plaintiff) has a fixed period of time within which to commence a legal action against the other (the defendant) by filing a complaint in court. Actions commenced after the time period has expired are dismissed as being time barred. Statutes of limitations establish these time periods in every jurisdiction, with different periods applicable to different causes of action. Claims for intentional torts have the shortest limitations periods — typically, one year from the time that the plaintiff discovers the injury. Unintentional, fault-based tort claims have somewhat longer limitations periods — typically two years from the discovery of injury. The rationale behind these statutes of limitations is that when claims are allowed into court years after the events giving rise to the plaintiff's claim, the relevant evidence is likely to be stale and untrustworthy, or unavailable. Placing reasonable time pressures on plaintiffs reduces these difficulties, while being fair to the injured victims of wrongful conduct.

Jurisdictions differ regarding exactly what events start the limitations period running. A majority of states start running their limitations periods from the time the plaintiff discovers — or should reasonably discover — that the defendant has caused her to suffer injury. Some jurisdictions start the period at discovery of the injury even if its cause is unknown; and a few start the period at the time of injury whether or not discovered. The limitations period begins to run in almost all states even if the plaintiff does not yet realize that the defendant has acted tortiously. When the victim of tortious conduct is under a legal disability when the statutory limitations period would ordinarily start to run, the statute is *tolled* — does not start to run — until the disability has ended.

In addition to these statutes of limitations, some jurisdictions have *statutes of repose* that impose time periods — typically four to six years — that begin to run upon occurrence of an event other than discovery of injury to the plaintiff. For example, some states have enacted statutes that bar products liability actions from being brought more than six years after original sale or distribution of the defective product regardless of when the product causes injury. These repose statutes have been the object of attack under various state constitutional provisions.

HOW TO READ AN APPELLATE DECISION

Your torts instructor may have his or her preferred way for you to summarize, or "brief," the appellate decisions in this book, and you are advised to follow those directions. But it will help you get started if we share our own insights regarding how to read an appellate decision. The first thing you should understand is that every appeal involves a review by a higher court of a decision reached by a lower court, usually the court that tried the case in the first instance. Trial courts hear evidence, including testimony from witnesses who are sworn to tell the truth. Throughout the trial, the judge makes rulings on a number of issues raised on motions by the lawyers for both sides — whether to dismiss the complaint, whether to admit certain evidence, how to instruct the jury, whether to enter judgment on the jury's verdict, and the like. The trial judge's responses to all these requests take the form of legal rulings, the correctness of which is reviewable on appeal. Of the relatively few tort cases that actually reach trial, only a small proportion get appealed.

The appeal, brought by the party who lost at trial, asks the appellate court to review a limited number of the rulings of law by the trial court to determine whether error was committed. The findings of fact by the jury at trial, assuming the judge did not commit error in giving the case to the jury, are not reviewable on appeal. The appellate court may review only issues of law that were implicitly resolved for the winning side in the trial court's legal rulings. In performing this review, the appellate court does not admit evidence or hear testimony. Instead, the appellate court is limited to the written record from the trial, including pleadings, motions, transcripts of testimony, the trial court's legal rulings, and final judgment.

Because every torts trial begins with the plaintiff's written complaint and ends with the trial court's written judgment, every summary of the case on appeal could begin with a description of the trial. For example, in connection with the first appellate decision in this book, *Garratt v. Dailey*, which starts on page 9, a summary of the trial below might begin by stating that the plaintiff brought an action against the defendant in battery. The summary could then describe the trial, perhaps by stating that "[i]t appears to have been undisputed that . . . ," with a description of the relevant testimony. Next, the summary might state that "at the close of testimony the trial court, sitting without a jury, found that . . . ," with a description of the judge's fact findings relevant to the issue of intent. Then the summary might state that the trial court entered judgment on the findings for the defendant, Brian Dailey, and that the plaintiff appealed. There might follow a description of the issue on appeal (did the trial court err in entering judgment for defendant without making a finding on what Brian Dailey knew when he moved the chair), together with the Supreme Court's resolution of that issue and its disposition of the case: "The Supreme Court found error, reversed the entry of judgment for the defendant, and remanded the case to the trial court for clarification on the factual issue of . . . ."

Of course, these are only suggestions, offered as a beginning to guide your own thinking about appellate decisions. Your professor will no doubt guide you through the process of understanding and assimilating the materials in this course.

chapter 1

Intentional Torts: Interference with Persons and Property

A. INTENT

Intentional torts are the first of three major categories of tort liability we will consider in this course. One might think that the law of intentional torts would be easy to understand. It does not take an Einstein to conclude that, if Jones intentionally and with no provocation punches Smith and bloodies Smith's face, Jones will have to pay for the damages he causes. But as we shall see, Jones's state of mind when he intentionally contacts another can range from the most evil intent to cause serious harm to an innocent intent to cause trivial contact with Smith's person. Where along the spectrum of intentional contacts tort liability should be imposed will require considerable thought. A word of caution is in order before we embark on the study of intentional torts. The word "intent" is an everyday street word. In the cases that follow, it will be given rather precise definition. As you read the cases in this chapter, ask yourself whether the courts are imposing liability because they disapprove of the conduct of the defendant, because they disapprove of what the defendant was thinking while engaging in the conduct in question, or both.

GARRATT v. DAILEY
279 P.2d 1091 (Wash. 1955)

HILL, Justice.

The liability of an infant for an alleged battery is presented to this court for the first time. Brian Dailey (age five years, nine months) was visiting with Naomi Garratt, an adult and a sister of the plaintiff, Ruth Garratt, likewise an adult, in the backyard of the plaintiff's home, on July 16, 1951. It is plaintiff's contention that she came out into the backyard to talk with Naomi and that, as she started to sit down in a wood and canvas lawn chair, Brian deliberately pulled it out from under her. The only one of the three persons present so testifying was Naomi

Garratt. (Ruth Garratt, the plaintiff, did not testify as to how or why she fell.) The trial court, unwilling to accept this testimony, adopted instead Brian Dailey's version of what happened, and made the following findings:

> III. . . . that while Naomi Garratt and Brian Dailey were in the back yard the plaintiff, Ruth Garratt, came out of her house into the back yard. Some time subsequent thereto defendant, Brian Dailey, picked up a lightly built wood and canvas lawn chair which was then and there located in the back yard of the above described premises, moved it sideways a few feet and seated himself therein, at which time he discovered the plaintiff, Ruth Garratt, about to sit down at the place where the lawn chair had formerly been, at which time he hurriedly got up from the chair and attempted to move it toward Ruth Garratt to aid her in sitting down in the chair; that due to the defendant's small size and lack of dexterity he was unable to get the lawn chair under the plaintiff in time to prevent her from falling to the ground. That plaintiff fell to the ground and sustained a fracture of her hip, and other injuries and damages as hereinafter set forth.
>
> IV. That the preponderance of the evidence in this case establishes that when the defendant, Brian Dailey, moved the chair in question *he did not have any wilful or unlawful purpose in doing so; that he did not have any intent to injure the plaintiff, or any intent to bring about any unauthorized or offensive contact with her person* or any objects appurtenant thereto; that the circumstances which immediately preceded the fall of the plaintiff established that the defendant, *Brian Dailey, did not have purpose, intent or design to perform a prank or to effect an assault and battery upon the person of the plaintiff.* (Italics ours, for a purpose hereinafter indicated.)

It is conceded that Ruth Garratt's fall resulted in a fractured hip and other painful and serious injuries. To obviate the necessity of a retrial in the event this court determines that she was entitled to a judgment against Brian Dailey, the amount of her damage was found to be eleven thousand dollars. Plaintiff appeals from a judgment dismissing the action and asks for the entry of a judgment in that amount or a new trial.

The authorities generally, but with certain notable exceptions . . . state that, when a minor has committed a tort with force, he is liable to be proceeded against as any other person would be. . . .

In our analysis of the applicable law, we start with the basic premise that Brian, whether five or fifty-five, must have committed some wrongful act before he could be liable for appellant's injuries. . . .

It is urged that Brian's action in moving the chair constituted a battery. A definition (not all-inclusive but sufficient for our purpose) of a battery is the intentional infliction of a harmful bodily contact upon another. The rule that determines liability for battery is given in 1 Restatement, Torts, 29, § 13, as:

> An act which, directly or indirectly, is the legal cause of a harmful contact with another's person makes the actor liable to the other, if
>> (a) the act is done with the intention of bringing about a harmful or offensive contact or an apprehension thereof to the other or a third person, and
>> (b) the contact is not consented to by the other or the other's consent thereto is procured by fraud or duress, and
>> (c) the contact is not otherwise privileged.

We have in this case no question of consent or privilege. We therefore proceed to an immediate consideration of intent and its place in the law of battery. In the comment on clause (a), the Restatement says:

> *Character of actor's intention.* In order that an act may be done with the intention of bringing about a harmful or offensive contact or an apprehension thereof to a particular person, either the other or a third person, the act must be done for the purpose of causing the contact or apprehension or with knowledge on the part of the actor that such contact or apprehension is substantially certain to be produced.

We have here the conceded volitional act of Brian, i.e., the moving of a chair. Had the plaintiff proved to the satisfaction of the trial court that Brian moved the chair while she was in the act of sitting down, Brian's action would patently have been for the purpose or with the intent of causing the plaintiff's bodily contact with the ground, and she would be entitled to a judgment against him for the resulting damages. . . .

The plaintiff based her case on that theory, and the trial court held that she failed in her proof and accepted Brian's version of the facts rather than that given by the eyewitness who testified for the plaintiff. After the trial court determined that the plaintiff had not established her theory of a battery (i.e., that Brian had pulled the chair out from under the plaintiff while she was in the act of sitting down), it then became concerned with whether a battery was established under the facts as it found them to be.

In this connection, we quote another portion of the comment on the "Character of actor's intention," relating to clause (a) of the rule from the Restatement heretofore set forth:

> It is not enough that the act itself is intentionally done and this, even though the actor realizes or should realize that it contains a very grave risk of bringing about the contact or apprehension. Such realization may make the actor's conduct negligent or even reckless but unless he realizes that to a substantial certainty, the contact or apprehension will result, the actor has not that intention which is necessary to make him liable under the rule stated in this Section.

A battery would be established if, in addition to plaintiff's fall, it was proved that, when Brian moved the chair, he knew with substantial certainty that the plaintiff would attempt to sit down where the chair had been. If Brian had any of the intents which the trial court found, in the italicized portions of the findings of fact quoted above, that he did not have, he would of course have had the knowledge to which we have referred. The mere absence of any intent to injure the plaintiff or to play a prank on her or to embarrass her, or to commit an assault and battery on her would not absolve him from liability if in fact he had such knowledge. . . . Without such knowledge, there would be nothing wrongful about Brian's act in moving the chair, and, there being no wrongful act, there would be no liability.

While a finding that Brian had no such knowledge can be inferred from the findings made, we believe that before the plaintiff's action in such a case should be dismissed there should be no question but that the trial court had passed upon that issue; hence, the case should be remanded for clarification of the findings to specifically cover the question of Brian's knowledge, because intent could be inferred therefrom. If the court finds that he had such knowledge, the necessary intent will be established and the plaintiff will be entitled to recover, even though there was no purpose to injure or embarrass the plaintiff. . . . If Brian did not have such knowledge, there was no wrongful act by him, and the basic premise of liability on the theory of a battery was not established.

It will be noted that the law of battery as we have discussed it is the law applicable to adults, and no significance has been attached to the fact that Brian was a child less than six years of age when the alleged battery occurred. The only circumstance where Brian's age is of any consequence is in determining what he knew, and there his experience, capacity, and understanding are of course material.

From what has been said, it is clear that we find no merit in plaintiff's contention that we can direct the entry of a judgment for eleven thousand dollars in her favor on the record now before us.

Nor do we find any error in the record that warrants a new trial. . . .

The cause is remanded for clarification, with instructions to make definite findings on the issue of whether Brian Dailey knew with substantial certainty that the plaintiff would attempt to sit down where the chair which he moved had been, and to change the judgment if the findings warrant it. . . .

Remanded for clarification.

THE RESTATEMENTS, SECOND AND THIRD, OF TORTS

Throughout this book, both cases and text will refer to the Restatements, Second and Third, of Torts. In your other courses you will also find references to Restatement sections on various subject matters. It is important to understand what Restatements are and what weight is to be given to them. First, Restatements are not statutes. Stylistically they consist of black letter rules (that often sound like statutes) and more expansive comments to the black letter rules (that don't sound like statutes) but they are not legislative. Instead, they emanate from a private not-for-profit organization, the American Law Institute (ALI). The ALI consists of approximately 4,000 members drawn from the bench, the practicing bar, and academia. Its governing body is the Council, which consists of close to 70 members—all of them highly prestigious judges, lawyers, and law professors. Over seven decades the ALI has produced Restatements in a host of areas of the law. Reporters are chosen by the ALI to work on a discrete area of the law. They are charged with the task of synthesizing the work product of the state and federal courts and discerning what is the best governing rule. The reporters create tentative drafts that are reviewed and critiqued by several advisory groups, the Council, and finally by the entire membership. After numerous iterations and drafts, the ALI approves the final draft for publication.

Restatements are not primary authority. Courts are not bound to accept the Restatement view. But, they are often highly persuasive and the frequency with which they are cited gives evidence to the fact that courts take them seriously. The

Restatement of Torts has gone through three iterations. The Restatement, First, of Torts was completed in 1939. The Restatement, Second, of Torts was completed in 1964. The reporter for the Second Restatement was the legendary William L. Prosser, one of the most influential figures in American tort law. The process of drafting the Restatement, Third, of Torts began in 1992. However, this time rather than attempting to draft an entire Restatement for all of tort law, the ALI decided to break torts down into several discrete subject matters. The first project was the Restatement of Products Liability for which two of the co-authors of this book (Twerski and Henderson) served as reporters. That project was completed in 1998. The second project was the Restatement, Third, of Torts: Apportionment of Liability (1999) (Reporters Professors William C. Powers, Jr. and Michael D. Green). The third project was the Restatement, Third of Torts, Liability for Physical and Emotional Harm (2012) (Reporters Professors Michael D. Green and William C. Powers, Jr.). The last two projects in progress are the Restatement, Third, of Torts: Intentional Torts to Persons (Reporters Professors Kenneth W. Simons and W. Jonathan Cardi) and Restatement, Third, of Torts: The Law of Economic Harm (Reporter Professor Ward Farnsworth).

Since the Restatement, Third, of Torts addresses discrete subject matters and leaves many sections of the Second Restatement as authoritative, you will find references to both the Second and Third Restatements throughout this book. For example, the section on "Intent" has been reworked and now can be found in § 1 of Restatement, Third, of Torts, Vol. 1 (2010). Thus § 1 of the Third Restatement is in agreement with the First and Second Restatements that one acts with intent when one acts with the purpose to produce that consequence or when one knows with substantial certainty that the consequence will result. However, the sections dealing with the individual intentional torts, i.e., battery, assault, false imprisonment, trespass to land and trespass to chattels, are to be found in the Second Restatement and in tentative drafts of the Third Restatement. On the other hand, the tort of intentional infliction of emotional distress is taken up in § 45 of the Restatement, Third, of Torts, Vol. 2 (2012). This back and forth between the Second and Third Restatements is simply a product of the ongoing revision process.

FOOD FOR THOUGHT

Why did the appellate court in *Garratt* send the case back to the trial court? Consider the following possibilities: (1) The appellate court believed that to make out a battery it was sufficient if Brian knew that Ruth Garratt would sit where the chair had been and the court was not certain that the trial judge considered such knowledge sufficient to establish battery; (2) the appellate court believed that in order to make out a battery it was sufficient that Brian Dailey knew that he was going to bring about a contact that would be harmful or offensive and the court was concerned that the trial judge focused only on whether Brian acted with the desire or purpose of bringing about a harmful or offensive contact;

or (3) the appellate court believed that it was not necessary to determine whether Brian subjectively knew that he would cause either (1) or (2) but that it was sufficient if a reasonable child of Brian's age would know that his conduct would bring about a harmful or offensive contact.

On remand the trial judge, after reviewing the evidence, concluded that Brian knew with substantial certainty that the plaintiff would sit where the chair had been, since she was in the act of seating herself when Brian removed the chair. At least that is what the Washington Supreme Court, on a second appeal, believed had happened on remand. *See* Garratt v. Dailey, 304 P.2d 681 (Wash. 1956). Several scholars who have reviewed the trial judge's second decision are not sure that the Washington Supreme Court's characterization of what the trial judge held on remand was correct. In their view the trial judge found for the plaintiff because he held that constructive intent was sufficient to establish a battery. Apparently the trial judge held that a battery could be established if a reasonable child of Brian's age would know that an offensive or harmful contact was certain to occur. *See* Walter Probert, *A Case Study in Interpretation in Torts:* Garratt v. Dailey, 19 Toledo L. Rev. 73 (1987); *and* David J. Jung & David I. Levine, *Whence Knowledge Intent? Whither Knowledge Intent?*, 20 U.C. Davis L. Rev. 551, 559-565 (1987).

In *Garratt*, plaintiff's lawyer clearly sought to establish through questioning of Brian that he knew that pulling a chair out from under someone would be an unpleasant experience. What if, however, Brian were to testify that he and his friends do it all the time to each other and that it's great fun? No one ever gets hurt and everyone enjoys the game. If Brian acted believing that Ruth would be neither injured nor offended, would his state of mind meet the requisites for battery as set forth in the Restatement?

In any event, even if a plaintiff must establish subjective intent, the trier of fact, be it judge or jury, is not required to believe a child's testimony that he did not know that his conduct would cause a harmful or offensive contact. It could conclude that the child was bright and mature and did actually know that his act would bring about undesired consequences. *See* Prosser and Keeton on the Law of Torts § 8 (5th ed. 1984).

INTENT AND DIMINISHED CAPACITY

Children of Brian Dailey's tender age are routinely held liable for their intentional torts. *See, e.g.,* Bailey v. C.S., 12 S.W.3d 159 (Tex. App. 2000) (four-year-old became angry at a baby sitter and struck her in the throat); Jorgensen v. Nudelman, 195 N.E.2d 422 (Ill. App. Ct. 1963) (six-year-old held liable for throwing a stone, injuring playmate). Adults of diminished capacity have also been held liable based on intent. Thus, persons with mental retardation and insane persons are held liable based on intent as long as they are capable of formulating in their mind the intent set forth in the Restatement. *See, e.g.,* Polmatier v. Russ, 537 A.2d 468 (Conn. 1988) (defendant adjudged not guilty of murder on grounds of insanity is civilly liable for intentionally causing the decedent's death).

INTENT TO OFFEND OR INTENT TO CONTACT?

In White v. Muniz, 999 P.2d 814, 815 (Colo. 2000), defendant, a patient suffering from Alzheimer's disease, struck the plaintiff caregiver on the jaw when the plaintiff attempted to change defendant's adult diaper. The trial judge instructed the jury as follows:

> The fact that a person may suffer from Dementia, Alzheimer type, does not prevent a finding that she acted intentionally. You may find that she acted intentionally, if she intended to do what she did even though her reasons and motives were entirely irrational. However, she must have appreciated the offensiveness of her conduct.

Based on this instruction, the jury found for the defendant and the plaintiff appealed. In affirming, the Colorado Supreme Court held that a battery cannot be established by simply proving that the defendant intended a contact with the plaintiff's body that turns out to be offensive. The plaintiff must prove that the defendant intended the contact be harmful or offensive to the other person. The court noted that other courts disagree and require only that the defendant intend contact with another and that the contact result in a touching that would be offensive to a reasonable person.

On similar facts the Utah Supreme Court in Wagner v. State of Utah, 122 P.3d 599 (Utah 2005), held that "mere intent to contact" was sufficient to trigger an action for battery if the contact was offensive to a reasonable person. Plaintiff was standing in a customer service area at a Kmart store when a mentally disabled mental patient who was under the supervision of the Utah State Development Center suddenly and inexplicably attacked her. Plaintiff sued the State of Utah for negligently failing to supervise the mental patient, who had a history of violent behavior. Under Utah law the state is immunized against negligence if the action arises out of an assault or battery. Plaintiff, seeking to avoid being barred by the immunity, argued that the action of the mental patient could not legally constitute a battery since she was mentally incompetent to intend to cause "harmful or offensive contact." The state argued that the "only intent required ... is simply the intent to make contact." The Utah court agreed with the state and barred the action.

Citing to the Restatement sections set forth in *Garratt* the court said:

> If a physician who has performed a life-saving act of assistance upon an unconsenting patient with the hope of making that patient whole is liable for battery under the express terms of the Restatement, and a practical joker who makes a contact which he thinks will be taken as a joke or to which he thinks his victim has actually given consent is likewise liable, we cannot then say that other actors must intend harm in order to perfect a battery. *Id.* at 605.

Accord White v. University of Idaho, 797 P.2d 108 (Idaho 1990) (piano teacher who approached student from behind and ran his fingers over her back to demonstrate the light touch that a pianist should have when running his hands over the

authors' dialogue 1

JIM: Aaron, I'm troubled by the text that you drafted following the *Garratt* case. It doesn't take a rocket scientist to realize that you believe that in order to be liable for a battery, the defendant must have intended to harm or offend the plaintiff. Now, I agree that the contact should be one that would be offensive to a reasonable, normal person. If I tap you gently on the elbow to get your attention and you suffer some gosh-awful, unexpected reaction, I shouldn't be liable. But why should it be necessary that the defendant intend that the contact be harmful or offensive? Why should Ruth Garratt have to prove that Brian Dailey intended to do something bad? Why isn't it enough that Brian knew that she would suffer a contact that normal people would find harmful or offensive?

AARON: Let's get this straight. Do you agree that in order to make out a case in battery you have to prove that the defendant subjectively desired to cause contact?

JIM: Of course not. It's enough to establish that the defendant knew that a contact was substantially certain to result. Ruth Garratt must show that the defendant himself knew she would fall.

AARON: Fair enough. But once we take the trouble to delve into Brian Dailey's five-year-old mind to determine what he knew when he moved the chair, what if we

keyboard committed the tort of battery even though he had not intended to injure or offend the plaintiff); Kelley v. County of Monmouth, 883 A.2d 411. 552 (N.J. Super. Ct. App. Div. 2005) (defendant's claim that he intended "horseplay" does not absolve him for liability for battery). *But see* Walters v. Soriano, 706 N.W.2d 702 (Wis. Ct. App. 2005) (physician doing a medical evaluation to discover whether patient was malingering in order to receive worker's compensation benefits accused patient of not trying to bend over as far as she could and thus pulled her backward causing her injury; held not liable for battery since he did not act for the purpose of causing bodily harm nor of causing offensive contact but rather for the purpose of performing a medical evaluation).

The First and Second Restatement of Torts appear to require that to be liable for battery that the defendant acts intending to cause a harmful or offensive contact (dual intent). The Tentative Draft No. 1 of the Restatement, Third of Torts: Intentional Torts to Persons, Sections 101 and 102 (April 8, 2015) require only that the "actor intends to cause contact with another" and the "contact (i) causes bodily harm or (ii) is offensive" (to a reasonable sense of personal dignity). Whether it is sufficient that an actor intend physical contact with the person of the plaintiff (single intent) or the actor must also intend to offend or cause bodily harm (dual intent) is a matter of controversy both in the case law and between scholars. See Nancy Moore, *Intent and Consent in the Tort of Battery, Confusion and Controversy,* 61 Am. Univ. L. Rev. 1585, 1612-1617 (2013). For an exhaustive review of

discover that he did not intend to harm or offend? His mind on that aspect of the case is pure as driven snow. For that we are going to hold him liable like he was a mugger?

JIM: You're missing the point. If Brian subjectively knows Ruth will hit the ground that should be sufficient. He has presented Ruth Garratt with an unwanted contact.

AARON: As Perry Mason would say, "Your answer is non-responsive." The question is why are you holding him liable for his subjective knowledge when he did not subjectively desire to offend or harm? Brian may not know that it was unwanted. As I say in the notes, Brian may have thought it was good fun and that she would sit down on the ground and laugh, as did all his friends. He may not have known that older people are more fragile and react differently than his playmates.

JIM: It seems to me rather elementary, at least from Ruth Garratt's point of view. All of us, especially as we get on in years, should be able to go through life without being messed with intentionally by other people, even youngsters. Once the defendant decides to cause another person to fall on the ground, the show is over. Yes, the contact must be objectively offensive to a reasonable person. But the defendant need not intend more than to cause such a contact.

---

the case law supporting the single intent or dual intent rule. See Restatement (Third) of Torts; Intentional Torts to Persons, Section 102, Tentative Draft No. 1 (April 8, 2015), Reporters' Notes. For recent cases, *see, e.g.,* Sutton v. Tacoma School District. No. 10, 324 P.3d 763 (2014) ("requisite intent for battery is the intent to cause the contact not the intent to cause injury) (single intent). Carlsen v. Koivuumaki, 227 Cal. App. 4th 879 (2014) (to make out battery requires proof that "the defendant touched the plaintiff or caused the plaintiff to be touched with the intent to harm or offend the plaintiff.") (dual intent). Consider whether the ABC Construction Co. building a 100-floor skyscraper with knowledge to substantial certainty that at least three workers will fall to their death over the five years it takes to construct the building should be liable under the "single intent" rule. See Kenneth W. Simons, *Statistical Knowledge Deconstructed*, 92 B.U. L. Rev. 1 (2012).

hypo 1

A, an immigrant from country *X,* is visiting America for the first time. In *X,* when taking leave from a friend or acquaintance, it is customary for the parties to kiss. *A* met *B,* a stranger in a bar, and chatted amicably for half an hour. When *B* got up to leave, *A* planted a kiss on *B*'s cheek. *B* was so taken aback that he fell backward and injured himself. Has *A* committed a battery?

hypo 2

In March 2015 Jennifer Cleary, age 50, was injured when her 8 year-old nephew jumped into her arms welcoming her to his birthday party ("I love you, Aunt Jennifer"), causing her to fall and break her wrist. She subsequently sued her nephew for $127,000 for medical bills and pain and suffering. She hoped that if her nephew were found liable the insurer would foot the bill. What result?

hypo 3

Adam, a long-distance truck driver, develops lung cancer after driving for ten years with a co-worker who was a chain smoker of XYZ cigarettes. Doctors are prepared to testify that his cancer was caused by exposure to second-hand smoke. Adam sues the XYZ Tobacco Co. for battery claiming that it knew with substantial certainty that people would be exposed to second-hand smoke and thus suffer injury. Is XYZ liable for battery?

WHO PAYS THE BILL?

However one formulates the rule that subjects children to liability for their intentional torts, the question arises as to why an injured plaintiff would take the trouble to sue minors who have no assets. Some infants are born with silver spoons in their mouths. But not many — most children have no property of their own with which to satisfy a judgment. Parents and caretakers are generally not liable for the acts of minors or incompetents unless they themselves were negligent for failing to supervise or watch over their charges. *See, e.g.,* Dinsmore-Poff v. Alvord, 972 P.2d 978 (Alaska 1999) (thorough review of the case law establishing that, unless parent had reason to know with specificity of a present need to restrain a child to prevent imminently foreseeable harm, the general knowledge of child's past misconduct is not sufficient to impose liability on the parent for the acts of the child).

Many claims based on the intentional torts of a child are brought with the hope of recovering against the parents' homeowner's insurance policy. Although homeowner's policies provide very broad coverage, they generally exclude liability for intentional torts. Whether the exclusion bars recovery for the intentional torts of a child is a matter of some controversy. *See Intent in Other Contexts, infra,* p. 24.

More than a dozen states have enacted statutes imposing liability on nonnegligent parents for the malicious or willful acts of their offspring. Most of these statutes limit liability. *See, e.g.,* Ala. Code § 6-5-380 (2016) ($1,000 and court costs); Ariz. Rev. Stat. Ann. § 12-661(B) (2016) ($10,000); Cal. Civ. Code § 1714.1 (West 1998) ($25,000); Cal. Civ. Code § 1714.3 (West 2016) (capping parental firearm liability at $25,000 per death or injury, not exceeding $60,000 per occurrence); Miss. Code Ann. § 93-13-2(1) (West 2016) ($5,000) (limited to property damage); W. Va. Code Ann. § 55-7A-2 (LexisNexis 2016) ($5,000).

GARRATT *IN THE CLASSROOM*

The ghost of *Garratt* came back to haunt a law professor. On June 26, 2001, the *New York Post* ran a front page story entitled "Class Action — Student Files $5M Suit Against Her Own Law Prof." The crux of the story was that a law professor teaching *Garratt v. Dailey* called the plaintiff, a 30-year-old female student, to the front of the class. He pointed out a chair and asked her to sit down. As she was sitting down he pulled the chair out from under her. She fell and claimed she hurt her back. The lawyer representing her in a battery action against the professor said, "It was humiliating. There she was in front of all her peers with her dress up around her waist and injured." The lawyer suggested that the professor may have singled her out because she had sent him an e-mail saying that she was not prepared for class that day. The lawyer further claimed that his client had an "eggshell body" because she had undergone a back operation shortly before her fall and thus sustained serious injuries to her back. Assume that the professor never read the student's e-mail and had not singled her out, but merely wanted to demonstrate the *Garratt* story. Can he successfully defend a battery claim?

RANSON v. KITNER
31 Ill. App. 241 (1888)

CONGER, Justice.

This was an action brought by appellee against appellants to recover the value of a dog killed by appellants, and a judgment rendered for $50.

The defense was that appellants were hunting for wolves, that appellee's dog had a striking resemblance to a wolf, that they in good faith believed it to be one, and killed it as such.

Many points are made, and a lengthy argument failed to show that error in the trial below was committed, but we are inclined to think that no material error occurred to the prejudice of appellants.

The jury held them liable for the value of the dog, and we do not see how they could have done otherwise under the evidence. Appellants are clearly liable for the damages caused by their mistake, notwithstanding they were acting in good faith.

We see no reason for interfering with the conclusion reached by the jury, and the judgment will be affirmed.

TALMAGE v. SMITH
59 N.W. 656 (Mich. 1894)

MONTGOMERY, Justice.

The plaintiff recovered in an action of trespass. The case made by plaintiff's proofs was substantially as follows: . . . Defendant had on his premises certain sheds. He came up to the vicinity of the sheds, and saw six or eight boys on the roof of one of them. He claims that he ordered the boys to get down, and they at once did so. He then passed around to where he had a view of the roof of another shed, and saw two boys on the roof. The defendant claims that he did not see the plaintiff, and the proof is not very clear that he did, although there was some testimony from which it might have been found that plaintiff was within his view. Defendant ordered the boys in sight to get down, and there was testimony tending to show that the two boys in defendant's view started to get down at once. Before they succeeded in doing so, however, defendant took a stick, which is described as being two inches in width and of about the same thickness and about 16 inches long, and threw it in the direction of the boys; and there was testimony tending to show that it was thrown at one of the boys in view of the defendant. The stick missed him, and hit the plaintiff just above the eye with such force as to inflict an injury which resulted in the total loss of the sight of the eye.

Counsel for the defendant contends that the undisputed testimony shows that defendant threw the stick without intending to hit anybody, and that under the circumstances, if it in fact hit the plaintiff, — defendant not knowing that he was on the shed, — he was not liable. We cannot understand why these statements should find a place in the brief of defendant's counsel. George Talmage, the plaintiff's father, testifies that defendant said to him that he threw the stick, intending it for Byron Smith, — one of the boys on the roof, — and this is fully supported by the circumstances of the case. It is hardly conceivable that this testimony escaped the attention of defendant's counsel.

The circuit judge charged the jury as follows:

> If you conclude that Smith did not know the Talmage boy was on the shed, and that he did not intend to hit Smith, or the young man that was with him, but simply, by throwing the stick, intended to frighten Smith and the other young man that was there, and the club hit Talmage, and injured him, as claimed, then the plaintiff could not recover. If you conclude that Smith threw the stick or club at Smith, or the young man that was with Smith, — intended to hit one or the other of them, — and you also conclude that the throwing of the stick or club was, under the circumstances, reasonable, and not excessive, force to use towards Smith and the other young man, then there would be no recovery by this plaintiff. But if you conclude from the evidence in the case that he threw the stick, intending to hit Smith, or the young man with him, — to hit one of them — and that that force was unreasonable force, under all the circumstances, then Smith, . . . (the defendant), would be doing an unlawful act, if the force was unreasonable, because he had no right to use it; then he would be doing an unlawful act. He would be liable, then, for the injury done to this boy with the stick, if he threw it intending to hit the young man Smith, or the young man that was with Smith on the roof, and the force that he was using, by the throwing of the club, was excessive and unreasonable, under all the circumstances of the case. . . .

We think the charge a very fair statement of the law of the case. The doctrine of contributory negligence could have no place in the case. The plaintiff, in climbing upon the shed, could not have anticipated the throwing of the missile, and the fact that he was a trespasser did not place him beyond the pale of the law. The right of the plaintiff to recover was made to depend upon an intention on the part of the defendant to hit somebody, and to inflict an unwarranted injury upon someone.

Under these circumstances, the fact that the injury resulted to another than was intended does not relieve the defendant from responsibility. . . .

The judgment will be affirmed, with costs.

TRANSFERRED INTENT

In *Talmage* the court "transferred the intent" to batter one person to establish a battery against another whom the defendant did not intend to hit. This illustrates the "unintended victim" category of transferred intent cases. *See, e.g.,* Baska v. Scherzer, 156 P.3d 617 (Kan. 2007) (plaintiff recovered for battery when she intervened in a fist fight and was punched); Hall v. McBryde, 919 P.2d 910 (Col. Ct. App. 1996) (defendant liable for battery to neighbor injured during defendant's gunfire with drive-by shooters). *See also* Restatement (Third) of Torts: Intentional Torts to Persons § 110 cmt. *b* (Tentative Draft No. 1 April 8, 2015). The second category arises where a defendant has the intent to commit assault, battery, false imprisonment, trespass to land, or trespass to chattels and harm results to another's person or property. Restatement (Third) of Torts, Intentional Torts to Persons § 110 cmt. *b* (Id.). Intent to commit any one of the five torts will suffice to make out the intent for any of the others. *See* Manning v. Grimsley, 643 F.2d 20 (1st Cir. 1981) (Baltimore Oriole pitcher liable for battery to plaintiff hit by 80 mile-per-hour ball meant to scare hecklers); People v. Washington, 222 N.E.2d 378 (N.Y. 1966) (stating in dictum that defendant who threw a trash can at plaintiff that hit plaintiff's car was liable for trespass to chattel). In the third category, the defendant mistakenly believes the plaintiff is another person that he intended to harm. *See* Am. Family Mut. Ins. Co. v. Johnson, 816 P.2d 952 (Colo. 1991) (defendant liable for battery to woman he mistook for his wife and kicked). *See also* Restatement (Third) of Torts, Intentional Torts to Persons § 110 cmt. *b* (Id.). The classic article on the subject is William L. Prosser, *Transferred Intent,* 45 Tex. L. Rev. 650 (1967). Three law review articles question the necessity for, and the wisdom of, the transferred intent doctrine. *See* Osborne N. Reynolds, *Transferred Intent: Should Its "Curious Survival" Continue?,* 50 Okla. L. Rev. 529 (1997); Vincent R. Johnson, *Transferred Intent in American Tort Law,* 87 Marq. L. Rev. 903 (2004); Peter B. Kutner, *The Prosser Myth of Transferred Intent,* 91 Ind. L J. 1105 (2016) (arguing that transferred intent between the five categories of intentional torts unnecessarily broadens the scope of liability).

hypo 4

A mugs *B* to steal his Rolex watch. Unbeknownst to *A*, *C* watches the mugging in horror. *C* remains hidden behind some trees, fearful that if he comes out *A* will mug him as well. The tort of false imprisonment requires that the defendant intentionally restrict the plaintiff's freedom of movement. Has *A* falsely imprisoned *C*?

hypo 5

A shot a gun over the head of *B* intending to frighten him. The bullet ricocheted off a telephone pole and killed a bird flying by. The bird fell onto the hood of a passing car. Two miles later the bird slipped onto the windshield and obstructed the driver's vision, causing him to collide with *C*. Is *A* liable to *C* under transferred intent?

THE LAWYER WHISPERED SWEET NOTHINGS IN MY EAR

It would certainly be convenient if a lawyer's client were able to recall helpful factual details that fit nicely into a narrative supporting the client's position. In *Ranson*, the defendant sought to avoid liability by stating the crucial fact that the plaintiff's dog looked just like a wolf. As in the author's dialogue, it might have been useful to Brian's defense if he had testified that he and his friends thought it was a riot to pull chairs out from under each other. Given the importance of facts to the outcome of cases (something lawyers quickly come to appreciate in practice), you might be wondering whether there are limits on what lawyers can do to prepare clients and other witnesses to testify. Professional disciplinary rules forbid lawyers to "falsify evidence, [or] counsel or assist a witness to testify falsely." Model Rules of Professional Conduct, Rule 3.4(b). But what if the lawyer reasonably believes it is true that Brian and his friends played the chair game, or the defendant in *Ranson* mistook the plaintiff's dog for a wolf? Imagine the conversation between the defendant in *Ranson* and his lawyer:

Lawyer: Tell me what happened.

Defendant: Well, we were out hunting wolves. They're a real menace, you know? Always taking our sheep.

Lawyer: What do you do when you hunt wolves?

Defendant: That's a pretty dumb question. We shoot them.

Lawyer: What I mean is, wolves are dangerous animals. I imagine you don't get too close to them. How far away are you when you shoot?

Defendant: I would never get closer than 50 yards, but mostly I'm about 100 yards away — I'm a good shot.

Lawyer: From that far away, how can you be sure what you're shooting is a wolf and not something else?

Defendant: I've been hunting wolves for 25 years. I know a wolf when I see it.

Lawyer: So you would never shoot without first making absolutely sure it was a wolf?

Defendant: That's right.

Lawyer: When you shot the dog owned by the plaintiff, what did you see?

Defendant: That dog looked just like a wolf.

Lawyer: You wouldn't have shot if it were a dog, right?

Defendant: No way — I don't shoot dogs.

There is no express prohibition in the disciplinary rules on this kind of suggestive interview, using leading questions to steer the client into telling a story that would be helpful from the point of view of the client's case. Many lawyers believe they are justified in working out the details of their clients' stories, because people tend to get confused and forget important details, and therefore may not be as effective as witnesses at trial. At some point, however, witness "preparation" can turn into a charade, with the lawyer effectively planting facts in the mind of the witness. A law firm representing plaintiffs in product liability lawsuits against asbestos manufacturers was criticized for doing just that when an internal memo was discovered entitled "Preparing for Your Deposition." The memo included advice such as:

> Remember to say you saw the NAMES [of the asbestos-containing products] on the BAGS. . . . The more often you were around the product, the better for your case. . . . It is important to emphasize that you had NO IDEA ASBESTOS WAS DANGEROUS when you were working around it. . . . It is important to maintain that you NEVER saw any labels on asbestos products that said WARNING or DANGER.

See Roger C. Cramton, *Lawyer Ethics on the Lunar Landscape of Asbestos Litigation*, 31 Pepp. L. Rev. 175, 185-188 (2003).

Is this taking things a bit too far? Even though there is no rule directly on point, one might argue that the purpose of adversarial litigation is to enable both parties to tell their stories. Lawyers are permitted to assist their clients in telling a coherent, persuasive story, but fundamentally they are not playwrights — their job is to work with the raw materials of a narrative as they actually exist. Of course, figuring out where the line is between assisting a client in telling her story and scripting the client's testimony requires judgment, and the fact that witness preparation usually takes place in a confidential setting might tempt lawyers to take a more active role than they would if their activities were exposed to scrutiny. Do you think the plaintiffs' lawyers in the asbestos case would have written the memo if they had known it would be disclosed publicly?

There is one very clear limitation on the way lawyers use witnesses and evidence at trial. Under no circumstances may a lawyer introduce false evidence or permit a witness to testify falsely. Model Rule 3.3(a) prohibits the knowing introduction of false evidence and, if a lawyer subsequently comes to learn that a witness she called has given material false evidence, the lawyer has an obligation to rectify the perjury including, if necessary, disclosing it to the court. Model Rule 3.3(a)(3). For a fascinating civil case in which lawyers came to suspect that one of their party's witnesses had introduced false evidence, but did not take sufficient vigorous remedial measures, see United States v. Shaffer Equipment Co., 11 F.3d 450 (4th Cir. 1993). The duty to take corrective action applies only when the lawyer knows the evidence is false, but *Shaffer Equipment*, along with many other cases involving civil litigation, takes a dim view of lawyers who claim that there was some uncertainty about the truth.

INTENT IN OTHER CONTEXTS

Heretofore, we have focused on the kind of intent necessary to establish the tort of battery (*Garratt* and *Talmage*) or torts involved in damaging the property of another (*Ranson*). However, the concept of intent rears its ugly head in a host of other tort-related areas. For example, many liability insurance policies exclude coverage for intentional torts. We have already established that Brian Dailey was liable for battery based on his knowledge to substantial certainty that he would cause an offensive contact. Would a liability insurance policy that excludes coverage for harms caused intentionally necessarily exclude coverage for the conduct of a five-year-old who did not act for the purpose of causing harm? *See, e.g.,* Baldinger v. Consol. Mut. Insurance Co., 222 N.Y.S.2d 736, *aff'd*, 183 N.E.2d 908 (1962) (insurance policy covered injury caused by a six-year-old boy who pushed a little girl to get her to move; although the boy's act may have been tortious under the knowledge rule in *Garratt*, the boy did not act for the purpose of injuring the girl). *See also* Cynthia A. Muse, *Homeowners Insurance: A Way to Pay for Children's Intentional — and Often Violent — Acts?*, 33 Ind. L. Rev. 665 (2000); Erik S. Knutsen *Fortuity Victims and the Compensation Gap: Re-Envisioning Liability Insurance Coverage for Intentional and Criminal Conduct,* 21 Conn. Ins. L.J. 209, 219-222 (2014-15). Does a liability insurance policy that excludes coverage for liability arising from an assault or battery exclude coverage of a defendant who claims that he committed the battery in self-defense? *See* Mouton v. Thomas, 924 So. 2d 394 (La. Ct. App. 2006) (though self-defense justifies a battery, the insured intended to harm the plaintiff and therefore the exclusion applies).

All states have statutorily mandated workers' compensation systems that provide benefits to employees injured on the job without regard to whether the employer was at fault. These compensation systems generally provide for recovery of a percentage of lost earnings (typically one-half to two-thirds), and medical expenses, but do not allow recovery for pain and suffering. An employee covered under workers' compensation forfeits her right to a common law negligence action against the employer. Thus, the workers' compensation remedy is exclusive of fault-based tort remedies. However, when an employer acts intentionally to injure an employee, the question of whether the employer still enjoys immunity from tort liability is more complex. Courts are in agreement that an employer who in a fit of anger strikes an employee is not entitled to the immunity of workers' compensation. However, how far one can push the "intentional tort" exception to workers' compensation is a matter of some controversy. An employer may be aware that its conduct would be substantially certain to bring about employee injury yet not have acted with the purpose of doing so. Removing safety guards or ordering an employee to repeatedly engage in highly risky activity may lead an employer to believe that an employee will, in the future, be substantially certain to suffer injury; yet an employer would certainly disavow that it acted with the purpose of causing injury. Some courts utilize the Restatement dual definition of intent but others allow a tort action only if the employer acts with the purpose of causing harm. *See, e.g.,* Laidlow v. Hariton Machin. Co., 790 A.2d 884 (N.J. 2002) (applying the substantial certainty test in a case where an employer removed a safety guard in a rolling mill and employee's left hand was mangled); *but see* Grillo v. National Bank of Washington, 540 A.2d 743 (D.C. 1988) (specific intent to injure necessary to remove case from workers' compensation immunity).

In Helf v. Chevron U.S.A. Inc., 203 P.3d 962 (Utah 2009), the court forged a middle ground between the purpose and the knowledge approaches to intent. The plaintiff in that case alleged her injuries were caused by a chemical reaction that occurred when her supervisors directed her to neutralize toxic sludge through a chemical reaction in an open-air pit. She claimed that several hours before she was directed to initiate the reaction, several workers got ill from an identical reaction in the same open-air pit. Consequently, she argued that her injuries fell within the intentional injury exception to the Workers' Compensation Act because her supervisors directed her to initiate a chemical process that they knew, with substantial certainty, would result in the same dangerous conditions that occurred earlier that day and would injure whoever initiated the chemical reaction.

The court held that "a plaintiff may not demonstrate intent by showing merely that some injury was substantially certain to occur at some time. For a workplace injury to qualify as an intentional injury under the Act, the employer or supervisor must know or expect that the assigned task will injure the particular employee that undertakes it. In other words, the employer must know or expect that a specific employee will be injured doing a specific task." Only such knowledge, the court held, "robs an injury of its accidental character."

Strange as it may seem, on occasion a plaintiff may allege negligence and defendant will be tempted to argue, "No, I was not negligent, I intended the harm." What might explain this odd reaction? Well, intentional torts generally have shorter statutes of limitations than do actions grounded in negligence. When the short statute of limitations has run, the defendant may be tempted to insist that he acted intentionally rather than negligently. Of course, if liability insurance applies, coverage may be jeopardized by such an argument. (*See* above.) In that case, it will likely be the insurance company who will argue that the defendant intended to cause harm. This argument has been received with mixed success in several cases. In Spivey v. Battaglia, 258 So. 2d 815 (Fla. 1972), defendant tried to tease the plaintiff whom he knew to be shy and gave her a "friendly, unsolicited hug." The joke turned ugly when, as a result, plaintiff suffered paralysis on the left side of her face and mouth. The court held that there was no battery since defendant could not have known with substantial certainty that such devastating harm would take place. It allowed the plaintiff to go forward under the longer negligent statute of limitations even though the action would have been barred by the shorter statute of limitations that governed assault and battery. In Baska v. Scherzer, 156 P.3d 617 (Kan. 2007), plaintiff had a party at her home for her daughter's friends. During the party, a fight broke out between two boys. "Plaintiff placed herself between the boys and was punched in the face, losing several teeth and receiving injuries to her neck and jaw." Plaintiff filed suit just short of two years after the incident, alleging that she was injured by the defendants' negligence. The defendants moved for summary judgment based on the one-year statute of limitations for assault and battery. The trial court granted the motion holding that the doctrine of transferred intent applied. The intermediate appellate court reversed,

ling that the case was one of negligence "because the plaintiff was unin-
ially struck by the defendants." Thus, the sole issue on appeal before the
s Supreme Court was whether the action was governed by the one-year
e of limitations for assault and battery or the two-year statute of limitations
rning negligence. Relying on the doctrine of transferred intent, the Supreme
rt held that "the defendants' acts of throwing punches in this case were *inten-
ial* actions. . . . The fact that the punches in question hit the plaintiff rather than
the defendants is immaterial to the analysis. Because the defendants' actions were
intentional the substance of Baska's action is one for assault and battery. Failure to
initiate her action within 1 year of the fight bars her action by reason of the 1-year
statute of limitations."

The long and short of the above discussion is that when one asks whether an
actor intended the consequences of his conduct, one must follow with the
question — why do you want to know? What may be deemed intentional for
one purpose may not be for another.

B. BATTERY

In the previous section we focused on the general nature of the intent that a
defendant must harbor in order to make out an intentional tort. In this and in
the ensuing sections we examine the elements of each of the traditional intentional
torts. In addition to establishing the defendant's intent the plaintiff must establish
that the interest protected by law was, in fact, invaded.

The elements of battery are set out in the Restatement, Third, of Torts. Intentional Torts to Persons §§ 101-03 (Tentative Draft No. 1 (April 8, 2015):

§ 101. Battery: General Definition

An actor is subject to liability to another for battery if:

(a) the actor intends to cause a contact with the person of the other, as
provided in § 102, or the actor's intent is sufficient under § 110 (transferred
intent);

(b) the actor's affirmative conduct causes such a contact;

(c) the contact (i) causes bodily harm to the other or (ii) is offensive, as
provided in § 103; and

(d) the other does not effectively consent to the otherwise tortious
conduct of the actor, as provided in § 111.

§ 102. Battery: Required Intent

The intent required for battery is the intent to cause a contact with the person
of another. The actor need not intend to cause harm or offense to the other.

§ 103. Battery: Definition of Offensive Contact

A contact is offensive within the meaning of § 101(c)(ii) if:

(a) the contact offends a reasonable sense of personal dignity; or

(b) the contact is highly offensive to the other's unusually sensitive sense of personal dignity, and the actor knows that the contact will be highly offensive to the other

Liability under (b) shall not be imposed if the court determines that such liability would violate public policy or that requiring the actor to avoid the contact would be unduly burdensome.

BRZOSKA v. OLSON
668 A.2d 1355 (Del. 1995)

WALSH, Justice . . .

In this appeal from the Superior Court, we confront the question of whether a patient may recover damages for treatment by a health care provider afflicted with Acquired Immunodeficiency Syndrome ("AIDS") absent a showing of a resultant physical injury or exposure to disease. The appellants, plaintiffs below, are 38 former patients of Dr. Raymond P. Owens, a Wilmington dentist who died of AIDS on March 1, 1991. In an action brought against Edward P. Olson, the administrator of Dr. Owens' estate, the plaintiffs sought recovery [for] . . . battery. . . . After limited discovery, the Superior Court granted summary judgment in favor of Dr. Owens' estate, ruling that, in the absence of a showing of physical harm, plaintiffs were not entitled to recover. . . .

Prior to his death, Dr. Owens had been engaged in the general practice of dentistry in the Wilmington area for almost 30 years. Although plaintiffs have alleged that Dr. Owens was aware that he had AIDS for at least ten years, it is clear from the record that it was in March, 1989, that Dr. Owens was advised by his physician that he was HIV-positive. Dr. Owens continued to practice, but his condition had deteriorated by the summer of 1990. Toward the end of 1990, he exhibited open lesions, weakness, and memory loss. In February, 1991, his physician recommended that Dr. Owens discontinue his practice because of deteriorating health. Shortly thereafter, on February 23, Dr. Owens was hospitalized. He remained hospitalized until his death on March 1, 1991.

Shortly after Dr. Owens' death, the Delaware Division of Public Health (the "Division") undertook an evaluation of Dr. Owens' practice and records, in part to determine if his patients had been placed at risk through exposure to HIV. The Division determined that Dr. Owens' equipment, sterilization procedures and precautionary methods were better than average and that he had ceased doing surgery since being diagnosed as HIV-positive in 1989. Although the Division determined that the risk of patient exposure was "very small," it notified all patients treated by Dr. Owens from the time of his 1989 diagnosis until his death that their dentist had died from AIDS and that there was a possibility that they were exposed to HIV. The Division also advised the former patients that they could participate in a free program of HIV testing and counseling. Some patients availed themselves of the Division's testing while others secured independent testing. Of the 630 former patients of Dr. Owens who have been tested, none have tested positive for HIV. . . .

In their Superior Court action, the plaintiffs alleged that each of them had been patients of Dr. Owens in 1990 or 1991. Each claimed to have received treatment, including teeth extraction, reconstruction and cleaning, during which their gums bled. The plaintiffs alleged that Dr. Owens was HIV-positive and that he exhibited open lesions and memory loss at the time of such treatment. The plaintiffs did not allege the contraction of any physical ailment or injury as a result of their treatment, but claimed to have suffered "mental anguish" from past and future fear of contracting AIDS. . . .

Our review of the Superior Court's grant of summary judgment is plenary. We consider *de novo* the factual record before the trial court and examine anew the legal conclusions to determine whether error occurred in applying pertinent legal standards. . . .

In essence, the tort of battery is the intentional, unpermitted contact upon the person of another which is harmful or offensive. . . . The intent necessary for battery is the intent to make contact with the person, not the intent to cause harm. . . . In addition, the contact need not be harmful, it is sufficient if the contact offends the person's integrity. . . . "Proof of the technical invasion of the integrity of the plaintiff's person by even an entirely harmless, yet offensive, contact entitles the plaintiff to vindication of the legal right by the award of nominal damages." [*See* Prosser and Keeton on the Law of Torts § 9 (5th ed. 1984).] The fact that a person does not discover the offensive nature of the contact until after the event does not, *ipso facto*, preclude recovery. *See* Restatement (Second) of Torts § 18, cmt. *d* (1965).

Although a battery may consist of any unauthorized touching of the person which causes offense or alarm, the test for whether a contact is "offensive" is not wholly subjective. The law does not permit recovery for the extremely sensitive who become offended at the slightest contact. Rather, for a bodily contact to be offensive, it must offend a *reasonable* sense of personal dignity. Restatement (Second) of Torts § 19 (1965).

> In order that a contact be offensive to a reasonable sense of personal dignity, it must be one which would offend the ordinary person and as such one not unduly sensitive as to his personal dignity. It must, therefore, be a contact which is unwarranted by the social usages prevalent at the time and place at which it is inflicted.

Restatement (Second) of Torts § 19, cmt. *a*; Prosser and Keeton § 9 at 42. The propriety of the contact is therefore assessed by an objective "reasonableness" standard.

Plaintiffs contend that the "touching" implicit in the dental procedures performed by Dr. Owens was offensive because he was HIV-positive. We must therefore determine whether the performance of dental procedures by an HIV-infected dentist, standing alone, may constitute offensive bodily contact for purposes of battery, i.e., would such touching offend a *reasonable* sense of personal dignity?

. . . HIV is transmitted primarily through direct blood-to-blood contact or by the exchange of bodily fluids with an infected individual. In a dental setting, the most probable means of transmission is through the exchange of bodily fluids between the dentist and patient by percutaneous (through the skin) contact, by way of an open wound, non-intact skin or mucous membrane, with infected blood or blood-contaminated bodily fluids. During invasive dental procedures, such as teeth extraction, root canal and periodontal treatments, there is a risk that the dentist may suffer a percutaneous injury to the hands, such as a puncture wound caused by a sharp instrument or object during treatment, and expose the dentist and patient to an exchange of blood or other fluids. . . . Although the use of gloves as a protective barrier during invasive dental procedures reduces the risk of exposure of HIV, their use cannot prevent piercing injuries to the hands caused by needles, sharp instruments or patient biting. . . .

The risk of HIV transmission from a health care worker to a patient during an invasive medical procedure is very remote. In fact, even a person who is *exposed to* HIV holds a slim chance of infection. The CDC has estimated that the theoretical risk of HIV transmission from an HIV-infected health care worker to patient following actual percutaneous exposure to HIV-infected blood is, by any measure, less than one percent.

As earlier noted, the offensive character of a contact in a battery case is assessed by a "reasonableness" standard. In a "fear of AIDS" case in which battery is alleged, therefore, we examine the overall reasonableness of the plaintiffs' fear in contracting the disease to determine whether the contact or touching was offensive. Since HIV causes AIDS, any assessment of the fear of contracting AIDS must, ipso facto, relate to the exposure to HIV. Moreover, because HIV is transmitted only through fluid-to-fluid contact or exposure, the reasonableness of a plaintiff's fear of AIDS should be measured by whether or not there was a channel of infection or actual exposure of the plaintiff to the virus.

It is unreasonable for a person to fear infection when that person has not been exposed to a disease. In the case of AIDS, actual exposure to HIV may escalate the threat of infection from a theoretical, remote risk to a real and grave possibility if the person exposed is motivated by speculation unrelated to the objective setting. Such fear is based on uninformed apprehension, not reality. In such circumstances, the fear of contracting AIDS is per se unreasonable without proof of actual exposure to HIV.[9] In our view, the mere fear of contracting AIDS, in the absence of actual exposure to HIV, is not sufficient to impose liability on a health care provider. AIDS phobia, standing alone, cannot form the basis for recovery of damages, even under a battery theory because the underlying causation/harm nexus is not medically supportable.

AIDS is a disease that spawns widespread public misperception based upon the dearth of knowledge concerning HIV transmission. Indeed, plaintiffs rely upon the degree of public misconception about AIDS to support their claim that their fear was reasonable. To accept this argument is to contribute to the phobia. Were we to recognize a claim for the fear of contracting AIDS based upon a mere allegation that one may have been exposed to HIV, totally unsupported by any medical

---

9. In this holding, we recognize that the issue of reasonableness is ordinarily a question of fact for the trier of fact. . . . Nevertheless, this Court will decide an issue *as a matter of law* in those circumstances where only one conclusion can be reached from the application of the legal standard to the undisputed facts. . . .

evidence or factual proof, we would open a Pandora's Box of "AIDS-phobia" claims by individuals whose ignorance, unreasonable suspicion or general paranoia cause them apprehension over the slightest of contact with HIV-infected individuals or objects. Such plaintiffs would recover for their fear of AIDS, no matter how irrational. . . .

In sum, we find that, without actual exposure to HIV, the risk of its transmission is so minute that any fear of contracting AIDS is per se unreasonable. We therefore hold, *as a matter of law,* that the incidental touching of a patient by an HIV-infected dentist while performing ordinary, consented-to dental procedures is insufficient to sustain a battery claim in the absence of a channel for HIV infection. In other words, such contact is "offensive" only if it results in actual exposure to the HIV virus. . . .

In this case, the material facts are not in dispute. Even viewing the facts from plaintiffs' vantage point, the record fails to establish actual exposure to HIV. Plaintiffs argue to the contrary, noting that Dr. Owens exhibited lesions on his arms, legs, and elbow, and that he was known to have cut himself on at least one occasion while working on a patient. They have not, however, averred that the wound or lesions of Dr. Owens ever came into contact with the person of any of the plaintiffs, nor have they identified which patient was present during Dr. Owens' injury or even whether that patient was a plaintiff in this action. In fact, nothing in this record suggests any bleeding from Dr. Owens or that any wound or lesions ever came into contact with a break in the skin or mucous membrane of any of the plaintiffs. Plaintiffs have failed to demonstrate any evidence of actual exposure to potential HIV transmission beyond mere unsupported supposition. . . .

In conclusion, the tort of battery requires a harmful or offensive contact, and "offensive" conduct is tested by a reasonableness standard. We hold that the fear of contracting a disease without exposure to a disease-causing agent is per se unreasonable. Thus, absent actual exposure to HIV, plaintiffs cannot recover for fear of contracting AIDS. . . .

The judgment of the Superior Court is AFFIRMED IN PART, REVERSED IN PART [based on other issues omitted from the discussion] and REMANDED for proceedings consistent with this opinion.

[Dissent omitted.]

FOOD FOR THOUGHT

Based on similar reasoning, the West Virginia Supreme Court refused to recognize a claim by a mortician who sought to assert a battery claim against a hospital for failing to inform him that a body given over for embalming was AIDS infected. The mortician could not establish that he had, in fact, come in contact with the AIDS virus since he had used surgical gloves during the embalming. He claimed that, had he known that the body was AIDS infected, he would have utilized special barrier techniques to assure that he did not contract AIDS. Funeral Services By Gregory v. Bluefield Community Hospital, 413 S.E.2d 79 (W. Va. 1991). *Accord* Majca v. Beekil, 701 N.E.2d 1084 (Ill. 1998).

A minority of courts allow recovery without actual exposure to the AIDS virus. Recovery is limited to the distress suffered during the "window of anxiety" period, that is, the time between the possible exposure to HIV and the receipt of negative test results. *See, e.g.,* South Central Regional Medical Center v. Pickering, 749 So. 2d 95 (Miss. 1999); Hartwig v. Oregon Trail Eye Clinic, 580 N.W.2d 86 (Neb. 1998).

Do you have any doubt that the plaintiffs in *Brzoska* believed that they had suffered an offensive contact when they learned that they had been treated by a dentist who was suffering from an advanced stage of AIDS? Was it for naught that the Delaware Division of Public Health offered AIDS testing to all of Dr. Owens' patients? Why must the contact be offensive to some hypothetical reasonable person? If the contact is manifestly unwanted, doesn't the plaintiff have a right to be supersensitive?

Perhaps the plaintiff was not supersensitive, but was wrongly susceptible to the fear of contracting HIV, albeit no more fearful than many other people during the late 1980s. Panic over the outbreak of AIDS was similar to the more recent hysteria over Ebola, although longer-lasting and with greater social consequences:

> The first decade of the AIDS epidemic spawned a similar kind of hysteria. . . . Various politicians called for quarantining of anyone who tested positive for HIV, and commentator William F. Buckley infamously penned an op-ed in the New York Times saying that "everyone detected with AIDS should be tattooed." There was an AIDS-quarantine ballot initiative in California, and various states threatened or passed conditional quarantine measures. . . . People living with HIV-AIDS in the 1980s and 1990s also faced other kinds of discrimination, including the loss of employment and housing, as well as outright violence, including assault and murder. Some HIV-positive children were excluded from school; two such cases — those of the three Ray brothers in Arcadia, Florida, and of Ryan White in Kokomo, Indiana — received national attention.

Gregg Gonsalves & Peter Staley, *Panic, Paranoia, and Public Health — The AIDS Epidemic's Lessons for Ebola*, N. Engl. J. Med. 2014; 371:2348-2349 (Dec. 18, 2014). The court in *Brzoska* refers to AIDS panic as "based on uniformed apprehension, not reality" and deems per se unreasonable an offensive battery claim founded in "ignorance, unreasonable suspicion, or general paranoia." This case illustrates an important point about objective standards, particularly the ubiquitous reasonable person standard we will encounter throughout tort law. An objectively reasonable belief is not necessarily one which is widely shared. It is possible to criticize a generally held belief as based on "uninformed apprehension, not reality," as the Delaware Supreme Court says regarding AIDS phobia. What is objectively reasonable cannot be settled by public-opinion polling. It is, instead, a normative conclusion reached after full consideration of whether a belief is sufficiently well grounded in fact.

ANOTHER CLASSROOM SIMULATION GONE SOUR

While pondering these questions, consider the following story that appeared in a newspaper. During an introductory program for first-year law students, a nationally prominent professor was teaching his students the case of Vosburg v. Putney, 50 N.W. 403 (Wis. 1891). In that case plaintiff, a 14-year-old boy, was sitting across the aisle from the defendant, an 11-year-old. The defendant gave the plaintiff a slight kick in his leg. The slight kick precipitated severe swelling of the leg and damage to the bone. The injury was so serious that the plaintiff never recovered use of the limb. In teaching the case the professor made the point that once a prima facie case for battery was established, the defendant was liable for all the ensuing damages. If one batters a plaintiff with an "eggshell skull" (i.e., a peculiar vulnerability to injury), the plaintiff may recover all his damages notwithstanding the lack of foreseeability of the ultimate injury. After announcing his intention to show the class how a slight contact could be actionable, the professor then touched a student on her fully clothed shoulder. The student brought suit against the professor seeking $25,000 in compensatory damages and $10,000 in punitive damages. She said that the tap on her shoulder flooded her with memories of being terrorized, raped, and molested when she was 11 years old and living in her native land of Panama. "What some would characterize as mere touching, to this victim was an extreme event," said her lawyer. "What makes it different is that she was the victim at the hands of men in the past." Does she have a case for battery?

hypo **6**

A sends B a box of chocolates knowing that one out of every six chocolates is poisoned with arsenic. B eats several of the non-poisoned chocolates and is unaware that poisoned chocolates are in the box. Later A informs B that poisoned chocolates were in the box. Has A battered B?

hypo **7**

Rabbi S negotiated a contract with caterer X for his daughter's wedding. He insisted that the food be kosher. X prepared sushi dishes that contained shrimp (non-kosher), which X knew to be non-kosher. Rabbi S ate from some food platters at the wedding but is not certain that he ate shrimp sushi. Rabbi S sues X for battery. Has X battered Rabbi S?

FISHER v. CARROUSEL MOTOR HOTEL, INC.
424 S.W.2d 627 (Tex. 1967)

Greenhill, Justice.

This is a suit for actual and exemplary damages growing out of an alleged assault and battery. The plaintiff Fisher was a mathematician with the Data Processing Division of the Manned Spacecraft Center, an agency of the National Aeronautics and Space Agency, . . . (NASA). The defendants were the Carrousel Motor Hotel, Inc., located in Houston, the Brass Ring Club, which is located in the

Carrousel, and Robert W. Flynn, who as an employee of the Carrousel was the manager of the Brass Ring Club. . . . Trial was to a jury which found for the plaintiff Fisher. The trial court rendered judgment for the defendants notwithstanding the verdict. The Court of Civil Appeals affirmed. The questions before this Court are whether there was evidence that an actionable battery was committed, . . .

The plaintiff Fisher had been invited by Ampex Corporation and Defense Electronics to a one day's meeting regarding telemetry equipment at the Carrousel. The invitation included a luncheon. The luncheon was buffet style, and Fisher stood in line with others and just ahead of a graduate student of Rice University who testified at the trial. As Fisher was about to be served, he was approached by Flynn, who snatched the plate from Fisher's hand and shouted that he, a Negro, could not be served in the club. Fisher testified that he was not actually touched, and did not testify that he suffered fear or apprehension of physical injury; but he did testify that he was highly embarrassed and hurt by Flynn's conduct in the presence of his associates.

The jury found that Flynn "forcibly dispossessed plaintiff of his dinner plate" and "shouted in a loud and offensive manner" that Fisher could not be served there, thus subjecting Fisher to humiliation and indignity. It was stipulated that Flynn was an employee of the Carrousel Hotel and as such, managed the Brass Ring Club. The jury . . . found that Flynn acted maliciously and awarded Fisher $400 actual damages for his humiliation and indignity and $500 exemplary damages for Flynn's malicious conduct.

The Court of Civil Appeals held that there was no assault because there was no physical contact and no evidence of fear or apprehension of physical contact. However, it has long been settled that there can be a battery without an assault, and that actual physical contact is not necessary to constitute a battery, so long as there is contact with clothing or an object closely identified with the body. 1 Harper & James, The Law of Torts 216 (1956); Restatement of Torts 2d, §§ 18 and 19.

Under the facts of this case, we have no difficulty in holding that the intentional grabbing of plaintiff's plate constituted a battery. The intentional snatching of an object from one's hand is as clearly an offensive invasion of his person as would be an actual contact with the body. "To constitute an assault and battery, it is not necessary to touch the plaintiff's body or even his clothing; knocking or snatching anything from plaintiff's hand or touching anything connected with his person, when, done in an offensive manner, is sufficient." . . .

The rationale for holding an offensive contact with such an object to be a battery is explained in 1 Restatement of Torts 2d § 18 (Comment p. 31) as follows:

> Since the essence of the plaintiff's grievance consists in the offense to the dignity involved in the unpermitted and intentional invasion of the inviolability of his person and not in any physical harm done to his body, it is not necessary that the plaintiff's actual body be disturbed. Unpermitted and intentional contacts with anything so connected with the body as to be customarily regarded as part of the other's person and therefore as partaking of its inviolability is actionable as an offensive contact with his person. There are some things such as clothing or a cane or, indeed, anything directly grasped by the hand which are so intimately connected with one's body as to be universally regarded as part of the person.

We hold, therefore, that the forceful dispossession of plaintiff Fisher's plate in an offensive manner was sufficient to constitute a battery, and the trial court erred in granting judgment notwithstanding the verdict on the issue of actual damages.

We now turn to the question of the liability of the corporations for exemplary damages. In this regard, the jury found that Flynn was acting within the course and scope of his employment on the occasion in question; that Flynn acted maliciously and with a wanton disregard of the rights and feelings of plaintiff on the occasion in question. There is no attack upon these jury findings. The jury further found that the defendant Carrousel did not authorize or approve the conduct of Flynn.

The rule in Texas is that a principal or master is liable for exemplary or punitive damages because of the acts of his agent, but only if:

(a) the principal authorized the doing and the manner of the act, or
(b) the agent was unfit and the principal was reckless in employing him, or
(c) the agent was employed in a managerial capacity and was acting in the scope of employment, or
(d) the employer or a manager of the employer ratified or approved the act.

The above test is set out in the Restatement of Torts § 909 and was adopted in King v. McGuff, . . . 234 S.W.2d 403 (1950). . . .

The rule of the Restatement of Torts adopted in the *King* case set out above has four separate and disjunctive categories as a basis of liability. They are separated by the word "or." As applicable here, there is liability if (a) the act is authorized, or (b) the act is ratified or approved, or (c) the agent was employed in a managerial capacity and was acting in the scope of his employment. Since it was established that the agent was employed in a managerial capacity and was in the scope of his employment, the finding of the jury that the Carrousel did not authorize or approve Flynn's conduct became immaterial. . . .

The judgments of the courts below are reversed, and judgment is here rendered for the plaintiff for $900 with interest from the date of the trial court's judgment, and for costs of this suit.

OBJECTIVE STANDARDS AGAIN

The court in *Fisher* holds that the forceful disposition of the plaintiff's plate in an offensive manner is an actionable battery. Contact with the plaintiff's body, or some object closely identified with the body, may be a battery if it offends a reasonable sense of personal dignity. From the vantage point of 2016, we have no difficulty in perceiving the offensiveness of the manager's conduct. In the mid-1960's, however, the manager's actions might not have seemed unusual to the majority of white residents of Texas, and the plaintiff's emotional injury might be seen as something he simply had to deal with. Again, the important point is that objective standards do not make reference only to majority sentiment or beliefs. A court or jury applying an objective reasonableness test may determine, as here, that the plaintiff's harm is objectively genuine, and the manager's conduct is objectively awful, even if a majority of one's fellow citizens feel differently. Reasonable behavior, reasonable belief, a reasonable sense of personal dignity, and similar concepts are constructive ethical ideals that may be informed by empirical evidence, but are not completely determined by facts about what people actually believe.

RESPONDEAT SUPERIOR

Fisher is the first case where we encounter the liability of an employer for the tortious conduct of an employee. This form of vicarious liability goes under the Latin name of respondeat superior — "let the employer answer" (for damages). An employer (formerly labeled in the law as a master) is generally liable for the tortious conduct of its employee (formerly, the servant) that is within the scope of employment. Although it is essential to the law of torts, vicarious liability is really a part of the law of agency — that body of law that deals with grants of authority to act on behalf of another. Agency law has also been restated three times, and the current Restatement has a seemingly straightforward rule of vicarious liability:

> An employer is subject to liability for torts committed by employees while acting within the scope of their employment.

Restatement (Third) of Agency § 2.04. The seemingly simple formulation of the Restatement conceals some complexities you should be aware of.

The first issue is whether the individual defendant who committed the wrong (the "tortfeasor") is actually an employee or is instead an independent contractor. Vicarious liability follows only from an actual or apparent agency relationship (more on apparent agency in a moment). An agency relationship requires that the person acting for the other (the agent) be subject to *control* by the other (the principal). Restatement (Third) of Agency § 1.01, cmt. *f.* An agent is different from an independent contractor. If *A* hires *B* to paint *A*'s house, and on the way to the job *B* gets into a car accident, *A* is most likely not vicariously liable for *B*'s tort. House painters are ordinarily independent contractors. In agency-law terms, *A* probably did not assert a right to control the way in which *B* performed the job, did not provide tools and supplies to *B*, and was not involved in training and supervising *B*. In addition, *B* is engaged in a recognized trade or occupation, and likely paints houses for people other than *A*. On the other hand, if *C* owns a trucking company and one of *C*'s drivers, *D*, gets into an accident, *C* would be vicariously liable if, as is generally the case, *C* controls the way in which drivers perform their duties (e.g. by having safety procedures in place, training and supervising drivers, and so on). Truck driving is also not a recognized independent trade or business; most truck drivers are employees and provide services only for one employer. This is merely a rough description of the tests used by courts for determining whether someone is an employee or an independent contractor. The IRS, for example, uses a 20-factor test to determine whether employment taxes must be paid when a person is compensated for providing services. While the details may vary, the important thing to keep in mind is that, in general, the right to control the way someone provides services is the hallmark of an employment relationship.

An important exception to this principle is the doctrine of apparent authority. An actor who ordinarily would be deemed an independent contractor might be treated as an agent if the would-be principal does something that a reasonable person would understand to be a manifestation of intent that the actor have authority to act on the principal's behalf. Restatement (Third) of Agency § 2.03. A context in which this issue arises frequently is the liability of hospitals for malpractice committed by physicians with whom the hospital has an independent-contractor relationship. A physician may have "privileges" to practice at the hospital, but is not a hospital employee; the hospital exercises no control, beyond the initial grant of privileges, and the physician bills separately for his or her services. Nevertheless, a patient may come to the reasonable belief that Dr. X is actually an employee of the hospital. If that belief is based on communications or other signals by the hospital that patients should regard Dr. X as an employee, the hospital may be liable for malpractice committed by Dr. X. For example, where services were provided by a radiologist who had offices only at the hospital, without giving the patient an opportunity to select a radiologist but instead accepted the one provided by the hospital, it was a question of fact for the jury whether the radiologist had apparent authority. Roessler v. Novak, 858 So. 2d 1158 (Fla. Ct. App. 2003). On the other hand, if the plaintiff could not reasonably believe that the would-be agent was not, in fact, an independent contractor, the doctrine of apparent agency does not apply. *See, e.g.,* Smolnikar v. Royal Caribbean Cruises, Ltd., 787 F. Supp. 2d 1308,1324 (S.D. Fla. 2011) (plaintiff could not reasonably believe that independently operated on-shore zipline excursion was an agent of cruise line, when cruise line repeatedly advised passengers that on-shore tour operators were independent contractors).

The second issue under the Restatement of Agency test is whether the agent is acting within the scope of employment. Of course no one, except maybe Tony Soprano, hires employees to commit torts, so the question cannot be whether the precise act is within the scope of employment. Rather, it is whether the tortfeasor was going about the employer's business at the time of the accident or whether, instead, the tortfeasor was off on a "frolic of his own," as old cases amusingly describe it. The Third Restatement's test is fairly broad: "If an employee commits a tort while performing work assigned by the employer or while acting within a course of conduct subject to the employer's control, the employee's conduct is within the scope of employment unless the employee was engaged in an independent course of conduct not intended to further any purpose of the employer." Restatement (Third) of Agency § 7.07, cmt. *c.* In Taber v. Maine, 67 F.3d 1029 (2d Cir. 1995), a sailor on active duty in the Navy went on shore leave and, as sailors sometimes do, started to drink with his buddies. As the evening went on he decided to go off base to get something to eat, where he crashed into another driver, causing serious injuries. Applying California law, Judge Calabresi distinguished an older conception of *respondeat superior,* in which the employee's actions had to confer some benefit on the employer. He noted that off-base drinking is a customary incident of the Navy-sailor employment relationship and the risk of resulting damage is certainly foreseeable. Vicarious liability is intended to hold employers liable for injuries that may fairly be regarded as costs of its business. Given the well-known propensity of sailors on shore leave to drink to excess, it is fair to regard the accident as a cost of the Navy's activities.

PUNITIVE DAMAGES IN INTENTIONAL TORTS

When a defendant's conduct is particularly egregious — that is, when the defendant acts either with intent to harm or with willful or wanton disregard of whether harm will occur — most courts allow a jury to assess punitive damages. Numerous reasons have been offered by courts and scholars in justification of punitives. Some justify them on the ground that compensatory damages alone may not sufficiently deter bad actors from engaging in nefarious conduct. Many cases are not brought by plaintiffs either because they are not aware of their legal rights or because the cases may not generate sufficient damages to make them worthwhile for a lawyer to prosecute. For others, punitives allow society to express its sense of outrage against the defendant's conduct. Still others justify punitives as compensating the plaintiff for legal fees she had to pay out in order to prevail in the case. Commentators have written extensively, examining the various justifications for punitive damages. *See, e.g.,* A. Mitchell Polinsky & Steven Shavell, *Punitive Damages: An Economic Analysis,* 111 Harv. L. Rev. 869, 890-891 (1998); Marc Galanter, Introduction, *Shadow Play: The Fabled Menace of Punitive Damages,* 1998 Wis. L. Rev. 1 (1998); David G. Owen, *The Moral Foundations of Punitive Damages,* 40 Ala. L. Rev. 705 (1989); Anthony J. Sebok, *Punitive Damages: From Myth to Theory,* 92 Iowa L. Rev. 957 (2007).

Punitive damages have become the subject of intense political debate. The tort reform movement has targeted punitive damages as one of the ills that beset the American tort litigation system. In response to the demand of corporate defendants who argue that the threat of huge punitive damages not only deters bad conduct but discourages innovation, many states have imposed significant limits on punitive damages. Some states cap the dollar amount of damages and others limit punitives to some multiple of compensatory damages. Many states demand that there be clear and convincing evidence of the egregious nature of the defendant's conduct. And a host of procedural devices have been put in place to assure that punitive damages don't get out of hand. In recent years the United States Supreme Court has held that the imposition of punitive damages that are significant multiples of compensatory damages may violate the due process clause of the constitution. *See* Chapter 13.

In *Fisher,* Robert W. Flynn was an employee and was acting within the scope of his employment. The defendant employer was, without question, liable for compensatory damages. The question before the court was whether punitive damages should be vicariously assessed against an employer for the acts of the employee. The court cited § 909 of the Restatement, Second, of Torts setting forth the special circumstances in which an employer would be vicariously liable for punitive damages.

C. ASSAULT

Unlike battery, in which the defendant causes physical contact with the plaintiff, the tort of assault involves a defendant who "touches the mind" of the plaintiff. In considering the following materials, ask yourself what does the defendant have to intend and what must the plaintiff actually suffer to make out the tort. The Restatement, Second, of Torts § 21 (1965), sets out the elements for assault.

§ 21. Assault

(1) An actor is subject to liability to another for assault if

(a) he acts intending to cause a harmful or offensive contact with the person of the other or a third person, or an imminent apprehension of such a contact, and

(b) the other is thereby put in such imminent apprehension.

WESTERN UNION TELEGRAPH CO. v. HILL
150 So. 709 (Ala. Ct. App. 1933)

[Action for damages for assault against Western Union Telegraph Co. Defendant appeals from a judgment for plaintiff.]

SAMFORD, Judge.

The action in this case is based upon an alleged assault on the person of plaintiff's wife by one Sapp, an agent of defendant in charge of its office in Huntsville, Ala. The assault complained of consisted of an attempt on the part of Sapp to put his hand on the person of plaintiff's wife coupled with a request that she come behind the counter in defendant's office, and that, if she would come and allow Sapp to love and pet her, he "would fix her clock."

The first question that addresses itself to us is, Was there such an assault as will justify an action for damages? . . .

While every battery includes an assault, an assault does not necessarily require a battery to complete it. What it does take to constitute an assault is an unlawful attempt to commit a battery, incomplete by reason of some intervening cause; or, to state it differently, to constitute an actionable assault there must be an intentional, unlawful, offer to touch the person of another in a rude or angry manner under such circumstances as to create in the mind of the party alleging the assault a well-founded fear of an imminent battery, coupled with the apparent present ability to effectuate the attempt, if not prevented.

Solicitation by a man to a woman for intercourse unaccompanied by an assault is not actionable. . . . Insulting words used when not accompanied by an assault are not the subject of an action for damages.

What are the facts here? Sapp was the agent of defendant and the manager of its telegraph office in Huntsville. Defendant was under contract with plaintiff to keep in repair and regulated an electric clock in plaintiff's place of business. When the clock needed attention, that fact was to be reported to Sapp, and he in turn would report to a special man, whose duty it was to do the fixing. At 8:13 o'clock p.m. plaintiff's wife reported to Sapp over the phone that the clock needed attention, and, no one coming to attend to the clock, plaintiff's wife went to the office of defendant about 8:30 p.m. There she found Sapp in charge and behind a desk or counter, separating the public from the part of the room in which defendant's operator worked. The counter is four feet and two inches high, and so wide that, Sapp standing on the floor, leaning against the counter and stretching his arm and hand to the full length, the end of his fingers reaches just to the outer edge of the counter. The photographs in evidence show that the counter was as high as Sapp's armpits. Sapp had had two or three drinks and was "still slightly feeling the effects of whisky; I felt all right; I felt good and amiable." When plaintiff's wife came into the office, Sapp came towards the rear of the room and asked what he could do for her. She replied: "I asked him if he understood over the phone that my clock was out of order and when he was going to fix it. He stood there and looked at me a few minutes and said: 'If you will come back here and let me love and pet you, I will fix your clock.' This he repeated and reached for me with his hand, he extended his hand toward me, he did not put it on me; I jumped back. I was in his reach as I stood there. He reached for me right along here (indicating her left shoulder and arm)." The foregoing is the evidence offered by plaintiff tending to prove an assault. Per contra, aside from the positive denial by Sapp of any effort to touch Mrs. Hill, the physical surroundings as evidenced by the photographs of the locus tend to rebut any evidence going to prove that Sapp could have touched plaintiff's wife across that counter even if he had reached his hand in her direction unless she was leaning against the counter or Sapp should have stood upon something so as to elevate him and allow him to reach beyond the counter. However, there is testimony tending to prove that, notwithstanding the width of the counter and the height of Sapp, Sapp could have reached from six to eighteen inches beyond the desk in an effort to place his hand on Mrs. Hill. The evidence as a whole presents a question for the jury. This was the view taken by the trial judge, and in the several rulings bearing on this question there is no error.

The next question is, was the act of Sapp towards Mrs. Hill, plaintiff's wife, such as to render this defendant liable under the doctrine of respondeat superior? It is admitted that at the time of the alleged assault Sapp was the manager of defendant's office in Huntsville; that he was in and about his master's business incident to that office; that a part of the business of defendant was the regulation and keeping in repair an electric clock in the store of plaintiff. . . .

The defendant is a public service corporation, maintaining open offices for the transaction of its business with the public. In these offices are placed managers, who, within the line and scope of their authority, are the alter ego of the corporation. People entering these offices are entitled to courteous treatment, and if, while transacting the business of the corporation with the agent, an assault is made growing out of, or being related to, the business there in hand, the corporation would be liable. . . . But the assault in this case, if committed, was clearly from a motive or purpose solely and alone to satisfy the sensuous desires of Sapp, and not in furtherance of the business of defendant. In such case the liability rests with the agent and not the master. . . . The rules of law governing cases of this nature are perfectly clear and well defined. The confusion arises now and then from a failure to keep in mind the distinction between the act done by the servant within the scope of, and the act done during, his employment. The act charged in this case is clearly personal to Sapp and not referable to his employer. . . .

The rulings of the trial court with reference to this question were erroneous. Reversed and remanded.

FOOD FOR THOUGHT

Might the defendant have been able to defend this case on the ground that he did not intend to put the plaintiff in imminent apprehension of contact to her body? Is it necessary that the plaintiff reasonably believe that the defendant was about to touch her? What if she is unusually fearful? How important is the size of the counter?

CONDITIONAL THREATS

Cases agree with the Restatement that, to make out an assault, one must put the plaintiff in imminent apprehension of bodily contact. This requisite is satisfied when the defendant makes a conditional threat. ("Your money or your life.") Assuming the defendant has no privilege to take the plaintiff's money, the immediate threat of force is sufficient to make out an assault. Bear in mind that the apprehended contact must be imminent; conditional threats about doing something in the future won't do. *See, e.g.,* Dickens v. Puryear, 276 S.E.2d 325 (N.C. 1981) (defendant threatened to kill plaintiff if he did not return home, pull his telephone off the wall, pack his clothes, and leave North Carolina; held not actionable as assault). It is suggested that threats might make out the tort of intentional infliction of emotional distress. When we take up that tort, consider whether that tort will sufficiently cover threats of future physical harm. In any event, why should I be able to scare the living daylights out of you by threatening future harm? Why does such a threat not constitute an independent tort on its own bottom?

CIVIL OR CRIMINAL ASSAULT

Firing a loaded gun at a sleeping victim who did not know that she was being shot at does not make out a civil assault even if she later learns that she was shot at. However, a defendant who engaged in such conduct could be prosecuted for criminal assault. *See, e.g.,* Harris v. State, 970 So. 2d 151 (Miss. 2007) (defendant appealed conviction of aggravated assault on the grounds that the intended victims never apprehended any danger because they never saw him point or fire a weapon). The court held that the defendant "confused the common law definition of assault in tort which requires the element of apprehension" with the criminal definition of assault. The common law tort cause of action "protects a person's interest in being free from imminent apprehension of harmful or offensive bodily contact. . . . The criminal statute, on the other hand, does not require an apprehension of danger. . . ." Why the difference?

ANOTHER RESPONDEAT SUPERIOR ISSUE

We noted after *Fisher* that an employer may be liable for torts committed by an employee within the scope and course of employment. In *Hill* the court said the harassment of the plaintiff was not in furtherance of the business of Western Union, the employer. The Restatement (Third) of Agency §7.07, comment *c*, clarifies that intentional torts may be within the scope of employment if the course of conduct in which the tort occurred is within the scope of employment. In *Hill*, the course of conduct was interacting with a customer alone in the store at night, which was clearly within the scope of Sapp's employment-related duties. *See, e.g.,* GTE Southwest, Inc. v. Bruce, 998 S.W.2d 605 (Tex. 1999) (employer vicariously liable for manager's harassment and bullying of employees, which constituted intentional infliction of emotional distress).

D. FALSE IMPRISONMENT

The following are the elements of false imprisonment as set forth in Restatement, Second, of Torts §35 (1965):

> §35. False Imprisonment
>> (1) An actor is subject to liability to another for false imprisonment if
>>> (a) he acts intending to confine the other or a third person within boundaries fixed by the actor, and
>>> (b) his act directly or indirectly results in such a confinement of the other, and
>>> (c) the other is conscious of the confinement or is harmed by it.

Claims of false imprisonment arise in a host of settings. The elderly complain that they have been involuntarily confined in nursing homes. *See, e.g.,* Pounders v. Trinity Court Nursing Home, Inc., 576 S.W.2d 934 (Ark. 1979) (elderly woman brought an action for false imprisonment against both the individual who arranged for her admission to a nursing home and the nursing home itself); Antoine v. New York City Health & Hospitals Corp., 800 N.Y.S.2d 341 (N.Y. Sup. Ct. 2005) (plaintiff brought an action for false imprisonment claiming that she was retained under involuntary commitment to Bellevue Hospital for an unreasonable period of time based on an erroneous diagnosis of her mental status). Debtors allege that they have been detained until they pay their bills. *See, e.g.,* Vahlsing v. Commercial Union Insurance Co., Inc., 928 F.2d 486 (1st Cir. 1991) (plaintiff debtor brought an action for false imprisonment after creditor had him arrested for contempt of order requiring debtor to pay judgment, despite the fact that debtor had filed for bankruptcy). However, by far the most frequently litigated cases arise from

mers or employees who are detained for questioning because they are sus-
d of shoplifting.

/e have deferred consideration of possible defenses (privileges) to intentional
until the next chapter. In the instance of false imprisonment, however, we
nt in this chapter the "shopkeeper's defense" together with the case dealing
with the prima facie tort of false imprisonment. Common law rules and statutes
giving merchants special privileges to detain suspected shoplifters are pervasive
throughout the United States and are raised in most of the cases by shopkeepers as
a defense to false imprisonment charges. To take up the problem of false imprisonment without considering these rules and statutes makes little sense. In the next
chapter we shall briefly revisit these statutes in the context of the broader privilege
of the right of the owner of chattels to recapture stolen property.

GRANT v. STOP-N-GO MARKET OF TEXAS, INC.
994 S.W.2d 867 (Tex. App. 1999)

MICHOL O'CONNOR, J.

Gerald Grant, the appellant, sued Stop-N-Go Market of Texas, Inc., the appellee, for false imprisonment. . . . The trial court granted summary judgment in favor
of Stop-N-Go. We reverse and remand to the trial court for further proceedings.

. . . False Imprisonment

In point of error one, Grant claims the trial court erred in granting the motion
because there are genuine issues of material fact regarding each element of the false
imprisonment claim. The elements of false imprisonment are (1) a willful detention,
(2) without consent, and (3) without authority of law. Stop-N-Go argues it negated
the first two elements of Grant's claim because it established Grant was not willfully
detained without his consent. Stop-N-Go argues Grant chose to remain in the store,
and he could have left if he so desired. In the alternative, Stop-N-Go argues it
negated the third element of a false imprisonment claim because its actions were
authorized by law under Chapter 124 of the Civil Practice and Remedies Code.

1. The Summary Judgment Evidence

As evidence to support its motion, Stop-N-Go presented the trial court with an
affidavit from Gerald Calhoun, the store manager, and excerpts from Grant's
deposition. Grant responded to Stop-N-Go's motion for summary judgment
with excerpts from his deposition, Stop-N-Go's responses to interrogatories, the
police report, and Stop-N-Go's response to a request for production. The summary judgment evidence is summarized as follows.

a. Grant's Deposition Testimony

In his deposition, Grant said he went to the Stop-N-Go store with his girlfriend.
His girlfriend stayed in the car, which was parked in front of the door to the store.

Grant paid for a can of beer, and then decided he wanted to buy some potato chips. He left the bag with the can of beer on the counter, and picked out two bags of potato chips which were marked on sale, two for 99 cents. Grant returned to the clerk and laid both bags of potato chips on the counter along with a one dollar bill.

The store clerk rang up the chips at 69 cents each. Grant told the clerk that the chips were on sale. The store clerk said something to Grant, but Grant did not understand what was said because the clerk spoke with a heavy foreign accent. The store clerk and Grant went back to the chip display. The clerk told Grant that the chips he selected were not on sale, but that another brand was on sale. Although Grant thought the clerk was wrong, he decided to buy the brand that the clerk said was on sale because he was in a hurry.

As the clerk began to total the price for the two bags of chips, Grant noticed someone leaning through the window of his car and apparently talking to his girlfriend. The appellant became concerned for his girlfriend because he did not recognize the person. He went to the door to make sure she was alright. As Grant walked to the door, he picked up the one dollar bill which he had previously laid on the counter. Grant opened the door to the store with his right hand and held the dollar bill in his left hand. After determining that the person leaning on his car was an acquaintance, Grant returned to the counter, paid for the two bags of chips, and began to walk out of the store. As he walked away from the counter, Grant told the clerk that he (the clerk) needed to learn his job better, a reference to the verbal altercation concerning the price of the chips.

Just as Grant reached the door, the store manager, Calhoun, came from the back of the store, grabbed him by the arm, and said words to the effect, "he (the clerk) is doing his job well, let's talk about the cigarettes that you stole." Grant said he was pulled back when Calhoun grabbed his arm. When Calhoun made the accusation against Grant, his voice was loud enough that all the patrons in the store heard what he was saying. Calhoun said words to the effect, "everything was on a surveillance videotape and there is nothing to talk about."

Grant said Calhoun went behind the counter and asked the store clerk three times what it was that Grant had stolen. The clerk did not respond until Calhoun asked if a pack of cigarettes was on the counter, to which the clerk responded affirmatively. Calhoun repeated his accusation that Grant stole a pack of cigarettes and passed them through the door.

Grant tried to explain to Calhoun that he did not steal any cigarettes. Grant said Calhoun told him to shut up. Grant said he got real quiet after Calhoun told him to shut up because he was afraid. After Calhoun grabbed him and accused him of stealing, Grant felt he could not leave. He thought if he did leave, the police would come looking for him.

b. Calhoun's Affidavit

In his affidavit, Calhoun said he was in the back room of the store where a monitor for the store's surveillance camera was located. On the monitor, he saw Grant pick up something from the counter which appeared to him to be a pack of cigarettes.

Calhoun said Grant went to the door and stepped at least part way outside, while still holding the object in his hand. Calhoun said a car was parked directly in front of the door to the store. He then saw Grant return to the counter and complete his purchase. However, Calhoun did not see Grant return the item that he picked up from the counter.

Calhoun said he left the back room and approached Grant as he was leaving the store because, after watching the monitor, he believed Grant had passed a pack of cigarettes out the door. He put his hand on Grant's arm to get his attention, and then he asked Grant about the cigarettes he thought were stolen. Calhoun said his hand was only on Grant's arm for a few seconds because, as soon as Grant turned around, Calhoun quit touching his arm.

According to Calhoun's affidavit, Grant denied stealing any cigarettes. Calhoun thought Grant's attitude was hostile and somewhat threatening, and so he decided to call the police to investigate the matter. He said he feared a confrontation with Grant. Calhoun said that when he told Grant he was going to call the police, Grant responded by saying to go ahead and call the police.

The police arrived within 15 to 20 minutes. Calhoun said Grant and the officer viewed the surveillance video. He said Grant told the officer he had picked up a dollar before stepping out the door. Calhoun told the officer he thought the object Grant picked up looked like a pack of cigarettes. According to Calhoun, the officer said he would take Grant in, but Calhoun never asked or directed the officer to do so. Calhoun gave the officer the surveillance video, and then the officer left the store with Grant.

Calhoun said he had no physical contact with Grant other than the initial touching to get Grant's attention. Once he got his attention, Calhoun said he and Grant remained on opposite sides of the counter while they waited for the police. Calhoun said a woman, perhaps Grant's girlfriend, came into the store and waited with Grant. Calhoun said nobody threatened Grant, nobody told Grant he could not leave, nobody prevented Grant from leaving, and nobody told Grant he was under arrest. According to Calhoun, Grant had a clear path to the door, nothing prevented Grant from leaving the store, Grant was never directed to remain in the store, and Grant was not put in or asked to go to a back room.

c. The Surveillance Videotape

Grant claims the surveillance videotape is the best evidence to determine the reasonableness of Calhoun's belief that he stole cigarettes and of Calhoun's actions. However, Stop-N-Go did not produce it. Grant presented the trial court with the police report and Stop-N-Go's responses to discovery requests, which all address the location of the videotape.

The police report and the discovery requests are all inconsistent. The police report states the videotape was returned to Stop-N-Go. In a response to interrogatories, Stop-N-Go said the videotape was at the corporate office of the Risk Management Department of National Convenience Stores. However, in a response to a request to produce the surveillance videotape, Stop-N-Go said, "none." During oral argument before this Court, Stop-N-Go said the tape was lost.[1]

2. Willful Detention Without Consent

Stop-N-Go ... argues [that] Grant was not detained because he was not restrained from moving from one place to another. Although physical restraint is one way to establish a willful detention, it is not the only way. ... A willful detention may also be accomplished by violence, threats, or any other means that restrains a person from moving from one place to another. ... When, as here, a plaintiff alleges the detention was effected by a threat, the plaintiff must demonstrate the threat was such as would inspire a just fear of injury to his person, reputation, or property. ...

Grant met this burden with his summary judgment evidence that raised genuine issues of material fact. According to Grant, Calhoun told Grant he could not leave and that he (Calhoun) was calling the police. This contradicts Calhoun's affidavit, in which Calhoun said he did not tell Grant that he could not leave. This raises a genuine issue of material fact concerning whether Grant was detained, and whether he consented to stay in the store. ...

Stop-N-Go also argues that threats of future actions, such as to call the police, are not sufficient to constitute false imprisonment. However, Calhoun did more than threaten to call the police; he actually called the police. Grant said he was afraid of what was going to happen; he had never been in trouble with the police before. He was afraid to try and leave the store because Calhoun had already grabbed him and told him not to leave. ...

... [W]e conclude Grant raised fact issues concerning whether he was willfully detained without his consent.

3. The Shopkeeper's Privilege

In its motion for summary judgment, Stop-N-Go claimed its actions were authorized by law under Civil Practice and Remedies Code *section 124.001,* the shopkeeper's privilege. If this is true, then Stop-N-Go would have negated the third element of Grant's false imprisonment claim. Grant argues he raised genuine issues of material fact regarding whether Stop-N-Go established this privilege as a matter of law. ...

---

1. In issue three, Grant argues the trial court erred in granting summary judgment because it should have presumed the missing videotape was unfavorable to Stop-N-Go. Stop-N-Go argues Grant was not entitled to this presumption because he has not shown the videotape was intentionally destroyed. Although we need not decide this issue (we sustain issues one and two), we note that Grant may be entitled to a jury instruction on this presumption. See Trevino v. Ortega, 969 S.W.2d 950, 953 (Tex., 1998) (explaining the trial court has the discretion to allow a jury instruction or sanction parties for spoliation of evidence); Watson v. Brazos Elec. Power Co-op., Inc., 918 S.W.2d 639, 643 (Tex. App. — Waco, 1996, *writ denied*) (stating the presumption arises whenever the party not in possession of the evidence has introduced evidence harmful to the party who had control of the evidence).

authors' dialogue 2

From: aaron.twerski@brooklaw.edu
To: henderson@postoffice.law.cornell.edu
Subject: False Imprisonment

Jim, I'm puzzled by the false imprisonment–shoplifter cases. Am I missing something or are the lawyers who defend these cases overlooking a solid argument? In almost every case I can remember, the defendant argues that the suspected shoplifter remained on the premises not because of the defendant's coercion, but rather because the plaintiff voluntarily agreed to stick around to eliminate suspicion. The question always seems to be whether the plaintiff subjectively felt coerced to stay. If a jury believes that the plaintiff remained because she believed that she was not free to go, she wins. Why doesn't anyone raise the question of whether the defendant had the requisite subjective intent to detain the plaintiff? Very simply, if the defendant subjectively believes that the plaintiff is willing to stay, then the defendant may not intend to deprive the plaintiff of her freedom of movement, regardless of whether the plaintiff is or is not, in fact, intimidated by the circumstances. In most shoplifter cases the intimidation is not overt, but rather subtle. A plaintiff might well believe that she is not free to go but the defendant may not for a moment realize that his actions are creating that perception in the mind of the plaintiff.

Henderson's Reply

I need to think about this. But here are two quick reactions. As a practical matter it seems to me that if a jury is convinced that a reasonable person in the plaintiff's position would have felt coerced to stay, the same jury will almost certainly conclude

The shopkeeper's privilege provides that a person who reasonably believes another person has stolen, or is attempting to steal property, is privileged to detain that person in a reasonable manner and for a reasonable time to investigate ownership of the property. Tex. Civ. Prac. & Rem. Code § 124.001; Wal-Mart v. Resendez, 962 S.W.2d 539, 540 (Tex. 1998). Thus, there are three components to the shopkeeper's privilege: (1) a reasonable belief a person has stolen or is attempting to steal; (2) detention for a reasonable time; and (3) detention in a reasonable manner. *Id.* at 540.

. . . The test of liability is not based on the store patron's guilt or innocence, but instead on the reasonableness of the store's action under the circumstances; the trier of fact usually determines whether reasonable belief is established. *Id.* Whether Calhoun was reasonable in believing Grant had committed a theft, or reasonable in detaining Grant, is a question to be determined by the jury. See *id.*

Stop-N-Go relies on *Resendez* to argue that a ten to 15 minute detention is reasonable as a matter of law. This is a true statement of the law in *Resendez. See* 962

that the defendant actually intended that the plaintiff would not feel free to go. But I must admit that the defendant is entitled to have the jury instructed that if the defendant believed he was not coercing the plaintiff, false imprisonment is not made out.

At the tactical level, however, it may be that defendants may believe that making a big to-do about intent is unwise. If the plaintiff's feeling of imprisonment is reasonable, it is only because the actions of the defendant were perceived by the plaintiff as coercive. For the defendant to argue that, even if the plaintiff felt coerced because of defendant's actions, "let me off the hook because I didn't mean it" may get the jury hopping mad. Sometimes a litigant may argue in the alternative. But, for defendant to argue to the jury that (1) plaintiff was not coerced but willingly stayed on to clear her name and (2) even if she was coerced, liability should not attach because the defendant did not intend to coerce her, may result in a jury rejecting both contentions out of hand. Sometimes you have to pick your most effective argument and stick with it even though you have a legitimate right to an alternative argument.

Twerski's Reply

That's not half bad, Jim. I just had another thought. When a defendant argues that he did not intend to imprison because he thought plaintiff was willing to stay, he is basically saying he did not commit a tort because he thought plaintiff consented to stay. Rather than focusing on whether plaintiff actually did consent, defendant turns the tables and says, "I'm not liable because I thought she consented." Maybe the courts don't want to allow such a neat way of bypassing proof of consent.

Henderson's Reply

Aaron, it's 11:20 p.m. and I'm dog tired. We don't take up consent until next week. I'll think about this consent business then. As a long-time Boston Red Sox fan, I'm used to saying "there's always tomorrow."

S.W.2d at 540. While *Resendez* held a ten to 15 minute detention was reasonable as a matter of law, it so held, "*without deciding the outer parameters* of a permissible period of time under section 124.001 . . ." *Id.* (emphasis added).

Resendez does not support Stop-N-Go's position, because Grant was detained for more than ten to 15 minutes. According to Calhoun, the police arrived 15 to 20 minutes after they were called. Once the police arrived, they viewed the tape at the store, and then they took Grant to the police station and viewed the tape again. Grant said he spent approximately an hour in police custody. Thus, Grant's detention lasted for more than an hour and 20 minutes.

4. Conclusion

Stop-N-Go did not negate any element of Grant's false imprisonment claim as a matter of law, and Grant raised genuine issues of material fact on each element. Therefore, summary judgment on this claim was improper.

---

authors' dialogue 3

AARON: Jim and Brad. I ask you both. Did the plaintiff in *Grant* stay on willingly to clear his name or did the defendant force him to stay to wait for the police?

BRAD: Aaron, read the case more carefully. Grant said that Calhoun told him he could not leave. Calhoun's affidavit states that he did not tell Grant that he could not leave. So we have an issue of fact for the jury.

AARON: Look, guys. In an essay authored by myself and a colleague, Nina Farber, we argue that in the shoplifter cases the issue of consent is impossible to untangle. The plaintiff does not leave for several reasons; (1) he is afraid to confront the security officer who he believes will stop him and (2) he also wants to clear his reputation. The security office wants the suspected shoplifter to stay because he wants (1) to wrangle a confession from him and (2) he wants him to stay until the police come. It is hard to figure out the motives. At trial plaintiff says he was coerced and defendant says that the plaintiff was free to go.

JIM: Ok. Then we have a question of fact for the jury.

We reverse the trial court's judgment and remand to the trial court for further proceedings.

In Riley v. Wilbanks, 2013 WL 1767785 (E.D. Tex. April 24, 2013) plaintiff was making use of a self-checkout register at Wal-Mart. A security officer noticed plaintiff intentionally placing her fingers over merchandise bar codes for various items. She passed all point of sales without paying for eleven items of merchandise. The security officer brought her back to the "asset protection office" to determine which items had been taken and their value. The event was videotaped. The court reviewed the tape and said that he "can see how an untrained eye may not be able to tell whether Plaintiff was intentionally taking the merchandise." The shopkeepers statute was identical to that in the Grant case. In denying the defendant's motion for summary judgment the court held that reasonable persons could differ as to whether the defendant had reasonable grounds to believe that the plaintiff had stolen property. The fact that the plaintiff had actually stolen eleven items that were not paid for "was immaterial to the question as to whether defendant had reasonable grounds to believe that the plaintiff had stolen the items." This seems clearly wrong. Even absent the statute an owner of a chattel has a common law right to recover his chattel from a thief if he acts promptly after his dispossession. See Restatement, Second, of Torts Sections 102-104 (1964).

STATUTORY OR COMMON LAW PRIVILEGE

Many states have statutes similar to that of Texas allowing a shopkeeper to detain a subject for investigation. *See, e.g.,* N.Y. Gen. Bus. Law § 218 (McKinney 2004); Wis.

AARON: The jury will simply be confused. They might as well toss a coin.

BRAD: You have something up your sleeve. What does your article say to do about it?

AARON: We suggest that both parties are at fault for the ambiguity and we should use comparative fault to determine damages for false imprisonment.

BRAD: That is pretty revolutionary. Comparative fault to decide whether consent was or was not given to false imprisonment? We generally don't apply comparative fault to intentional torts.

AARON: We have not lost our marbles. Read our essay. It goes into considerable depth on the issue of utilizing comparative fault in apparent and implied consent cases.

BRAD: Where can we find this article?

AARON: Thought you'd never ask. It's entitled "Extending Comparative Fault to Apparent and Implied Consent Cases". It will appear in the 81 Brook. L. Rev. ___ (Issue No. 1 Winter 2016).

Stat. Ann. § 943.50 (West 2005). Even in the absence of a statute, the Restatement, Second, of Torts § 120A suggests that courts should adopt a special privilege to allow shopkeepers to detain a suspected shoplifter for reasonable investigation.

THE SHOPKEEPER'S DILEMMA

In the absence of a statute or special common law rule allowing a shopkeeper to detain a suspected shoplifter for questioning, the shopkeeper is placed in a dilemma. Most shoplifters are guilty only of petty larceny — a crime that is almost always a misdemeanor. Citizens are not permitted to make a citizen's arrest in most jurisdictions unless the crime was committed in the presence of the person making the arrest and the suspect was, in fact, guilty of the crime. Even if the security guard making the arrest saw the suspect through mirrors set up to detect shoplifting, and would be entitled to arrest the suspected shoplifter if the shoplifter was, in fact, guilty, the problem is that if the guard misjudged and the suspect was not guilty, the store will face a false imprisonment action. If the shopkeeper argues that he only stopped the shoplifter to prevent his property walking out the door, never to be seen again, and thus invokes a common law privilege to recover stolen chattels, the shopkeeper is faced with the same dilemma. The privilege works only when the suspect, in fact, had the stolen property on him. If the guard guesses wrong, the employer will face a false imprisonment action since the employee was clearly acting within the scope of his employment. The special statutes or common law rules designed to protect shopkeepers clearly help. But, as the main case demonstrates, they provide no guarantee that successful actions cannot be brought for detaining the suspected shoplifter.

By the way, how comfortable are you with these statutes? Tens of thousands of private security guards now police commercial establishments. Is it wise to give the power to detain suspects set forth in these statutes to private security guards who are not subject to the constitutional restraints imposed on police officers? Parenthetically, can these statutes be interpreted to give the security guard a <u>privilege to search</u> the suspect? What if a security guard finds marijuana on a suspect and turns it over to the police? What if plaintiff who suffers from hypoglycemia (low blood sugar) is detained for an hour until the police arrive and is denied access to food or drink that will raise the blood sugar to normal levels? *See, e.g.,* Forgie-Buccioni v. Hannaford Bros., Inc., 413 F.3d 175 (1st Cir. 2005) (plaintiff's jury verdict for $100,000 upheld on appeal because jury could have concluded that defendant did not have probable cause to believe that plaintiff was shoplifting but instead was just exchanging an item; the high damage award reflected the fact that plaintiff nearly went into hypoglycemic shock while waiting 40 minutes for the police officer to arrive).

LEANING ON EMPLOYEES

In cases involving employees suspected of stealing, the defendant often threatens that if the plaintiff does not agree to stay and answer questions with regard to the alleged theft, the employee will be fired. Most such cases do not constitute grounds for false imprisonment. *See, e.g.,* Lopez v. Winchell's Donut House, 466 N.E.2d 1309 (Ill. App. Ct. 1984); Shannon v. Office Max of North America, 662 S.E.2d 885 (Ga. Ct. App. 2008). Frequently, however, the employee is brought into a closed room with security guards present and the atmosphere may become sufficiently coercive that the employee stays on because she believes that she cannot leave. These cases are fact-sensitive and usually the issue of whether or not the plaintiff was coerced is for the jury. *See, e.g.,* Dupler v. Seubert, 230 N.W.2d 626 (Wis. 1975); Foley v. Polaroid Corp., 508 N.E.2d 72 (Mass. 1987). Should courts have to sort out these cases to determine the degree of coercion?

hypo **8**

Mrs. *A* gave birth to a baby boy, *B*, at *X* hospital. Two days later, prior to discharge, *X* insisted that Mrs. *A* pay the $500 differential between her insurance coverage and the actual bill. The hospital refused to discharge *B*. Mrs. *A* left the hospital without *B*. Next day she paid her bill and got her baby back. Mrs. *A* sues on behalf of *B* alleging false imprisonment. If Mrs. *A* stayed in the hospital lobby for several hours after the hospital refused to discharge the baby so that she could nurse her baby, does she have a case for false imprisonment of her baby? Of herself?

E. INTENTIONAL INFLICTION OF EMOTIONAL DISTRESS (IIED)

All the intentional torts that we have encountered to this point in our materials have an ancient lineage. They date back as many as 700 years. The tort of intentional infliction of emotional distress (IIED) is relatively new — a little more than 50 years old. Recovery for emotional distress arising from battery, assault, and false imprisonment was always allowed. Indeed, emotional distress accounts for the lion's share of the damages in these actions. But, courts were always reluctant to recognize a free-standing action for intentional infliction of emotional distress. They expressed concern that such an action might provide an avenue for all sorts of crank claims and flood the courts with cases that had little merit.

The common law developed incrementally. First, courts recognized a cause of action for intentional infliction of emotional distress when the actor should have foreseen that the emotional distress would lead to physical harm. *See* Restatement, Second, of Torts § 312 (1964). Predictably, plaintiffs would allege such physical harm in order to comport with the elements of the tort. All plaintiffs in such cases seemed to suffer from severe stomach upset and all would allege that they vomited as a result of the emotional distress. In a famous case authored by one of the country's most illustrious appellate court judges, the California court crossed the bridge and said it was time to give intentional infliction of emotional distress the dignity of its own cause of action. In State Rubbish Collectors Assn. v. Siliznoff, 240 P.2d 282 (Cal. 1952), Judge Robert Traynor was faced with the following story. The plaintiff, Siliznoff, had the poor judgment to collect trash in a neighborhood that the defendant Association considered to be its exclusive territory. A representative of the Association visited Siliznoff and told him that if he did not make an arrangement to pay the Association the monies he had collected from the trash business in their neighborhood, they would beat him up, cut the tires of his truck (or in the alternative, burn his truck), or otherwise put him out of business. Siliznoff dutifully alleged that he became ill and vomited several times and had to remain home from work for several days as a result of his emotional upset arising from the threats.

The defendant contended that plaintiff did not make out an assault. (Why not?) The court took no issue with the defendant on that score and went on to say that California had already recognized a cause of action for intentional infliction of emotional distress resulting in foreseeable physical harm. But, instead of grappling with the question of whether the plaintiff's vomiting was sufficient to make out the requisite physical harm, Judge Traynor held that defendant had caused the plaintiff to suffer severe fright and that was quite enough to make out a tort. Sixty years later the tort of intentional infliction of emotional distress has come to be widely recognized. Nonetheless, as the following case demonstrates, the elements of this tort are demanding.

NAGATA v. QUEST DIAGNOSTICS INC.
303 F. Supp. 2d 1121 (D. Hawaii 2004)

On January 19, 1999, Plaintiff provided a urine sample to his employer, Garden Isle Telecommunications ("Garden Isle"), pursuant to Garden Isle's drug-testing policy. Defendant tested the sample and reported to Garden Isle's Medical Review Officer ("Dr. Lam") that the sample was inconsistent with human urine. Garden Isle subsequently terminated Plaintiff from his job on January 25, 1999.

Plaintiff bargained for his job back from Garden Isle with no success. Plaintiff also requested that his urine sample be retested. Dr. Lam informed Plaintiff that, under Department of Transportation ("DOT") regulations, Plaintiff's sample could not be retested. See Defendant Quest Diagnostics Clinical Laboratories, Inc.'s Separate and Concise Statement of Material Facts in Support of Its Motion for Summary Judgment (Count IV), filed June 19, 2003 ("Defendant Quest's Facts"), Ex. G.

On January 10, 2001, Defendant informed Dr. Lam that it "did not measure the creatinine concentration of specimens to at least one decimal place" between January 4, 1999 and February 2, 1999. See id., Ex. H. Consequently, Defendant did not know whether Plaintiff's urine sample actually met the Department of Health and Human Services' criteria for determining whether a specimen was substituted. Id. Accordingly, Defendant canceled Plaintiff's test and instructed Dr. Lam to inform Garden Isle that "any personnel action taken with respect to the donor on the basis of the canceled test no longer has a basis in DOT regulations." Id.

On January 25, 2001, Plaintiff was notified by mail of Defendant's error and was offered his job back. . . . [Plaintiff brought suit for mental distress against Quest. Def. moved for summary judgment on plaintiff's claim of intentional inflection of emotional distress]

The court determined that Plaintiff's IIED claim arose out of Defendant's alleged intentional withholding of information from Plaintiff from when it found out about the error in February of 1999 until it informed Dr. Lam on January 10, 2001. . . .

Discussion

. . .

In Hawai'i, the elements of a claim for intentional infliction of emotional distress ("IIED") are:

1) that the conduct allegedly causing the harm was intentional or reckless,
2) that the conduct was outrageous, and
3) that the conduct caused
4) extreme emotional distress to another.

Hac v. Univ. of Hawai'i, 102 Hawai'i 92, 73 P.3d 46, 60–61 (2003). In the instant case, Defendant argues that "Plaintiff cannot meet his burden of establishing one or more essential elements of his claim for intentional infliction of emotional distress." . . . The court will address each element in turn.

A. Intentional or Reckless Conduct

In Hawai'i, a plaintiff must establish "that the act allegedly causing the harm was intentional or reckless," in order to prevail with his IIED claim. *Hac*, 73 P.3d at 60. . . .

In *Hac*, the court altered the elements of the tort of IIED to more accurately reflect the language in the Second Restatement. [Sec. 46]. See *Hac*, 73 P.3d at 60. In arriving at its decision to reformulate the elements of the tort, the court focused on the fact that likelihood of illness, usually evidenced by bodily injury, should no longer be a required element. Id.

The court in *Hac* does not, however, specifically address the implications of the addition of the term reckless to the first element. While there are no Hawai'i cases following the *Hac* decision that discuss the effect of the inclusion of the term reckless on an IIED claim, this court has previously articulated a standard similar to the one in *Hac*, which includes the term reckless. In *Nelsen v. Research Corp. of the University*, the court stated that an IIED claim required that (1) the conduct be intentional or reckless; (2) the conduct be extreme and outrageous; (3) there be a causal connection between the wrongful conduct and the emotional distress; and (4) the emotional distress be severe. 805 F.Supp. 837, 851–52 (D.Haw.1992). In *Nelsen*, the court stated, "[r]ecklessness requires that defendant must know, or have reason to know, the facts which create the risk." Id. (citing Restatement, Torts, 2d § 500, comment *a*). Accordingly, the court holds that the scope of the first element of a claim for IIED is now broadened to include the definition of reckless as articulated in *Nelsen*. Id.

In the instant case, Defendant argues that it did not intend to cause Plaintiff to suffer emotional distress. Defendant claims that it did not withhold information from Plaintiff, but rather, it "timely communicated such information when it became obligated to do so." . . . at 11. Plaintiff argues, however, that Defendant's two-year delay in disclosure represents an intentional concealment of information. . . . In addition, Plaintiff claims that Defendant was aware of the consequences which followed its report of test results, yet disregarded the affect that its failure to disclose would have on the person whose test results could not be validated. . . .

The court finds that issues of material fact exist as to whether Defendant intended to cause or recklessly caused Plaintiff to suffer emotional distress. Defendant began fulfilling its requirement to analyze creatinine concentration to one decimal place in February 1999, but did not inform Dr. Lam of this until January 2001. While Defendant may not have known Plaintiff's identity beyond his sample's control number, reasonable jurors could find that Defendant knew that the person whose control number they had could be negatively impacted as a result of its delay in disclosure. A jury could find that Defendant had reason to know that there was a high degree of risk that its delay in disclosure would cause serious harm to Plaintiff, and that they disregarded that risk. Accordingly, a reasonable jury could find that Defendant's conduct was intentional or reckless, thereby satisfying the first element of Plaintiff's IIED claim.

B. Outrageous Conduct

In Hawai'i, a plaintiff must establish that the defendant's alleged conduct was "outrageous," as defined by the Restatement (Second) of Torts, in order to prevail with his IIED claim. Hac, 73 P.3d at 60; *Shoppe v. Gucci America, Inc.*, 94 Hawai'i 368, 14 P.3d 1049, 1068 (2000). The Restatement provides:

> The cases thus far decided have found liability only where the defendant's conduct has been extreme and outrageous. It has not been enough that the defendant has acted with an intent which is tortious or even criminal, or that he has intended to

inflict emotional distress, or even that his conduct has been characterized by "malice," or a degree of aggravation which would entitle the plaintiff to punitive damages for another tort. Liability has been found only where the conduct has been so outrageous in character, and so extreme in degree, as to go beyond all possible bounds of decency, and to be regarded as atrocious, and utterly intolerable in a civilized community. Generally, the case is one in which the recitation of the facts to an average member of the community would arouse his resentment against the actor, and lead him to exclaim, "Outrageous!"

Restatement (Second) of Torts § 46, cmt. *d* (1965). "The question whether the actions of the alleged tortfeasor are . . . outrageous is for the court in the first instance, although where reasonable persons may differ on that question it should be left to the jury." *Shoppe*, 14 P.3d at 1068.

Defendant argues that, as a matter of law, its alleged conduct is not "outrageous" enough to support a claim for IIED. . . . Defendant contends that, pursuant to DOT regulations at the time, Plaintiff's urine sample could not be retested once it had been deemed "substituted." . . . Additionally, Defendant argues that "Plaintiff made no inquiry with Defendant QDCL and therefore cannot establish any outrageous, intolerable or indecent conduct on the part of QDCL in responding or failing to respond to such an inquiry."

In Hawai'i, courts have generally been reluctant to define conduct as outrageous. See *Shoppe*, 14 P.3d at 1068 (where the court found that abusive verbal attacks by an employer directed at an employee did not rise to the level of outrageous conduct as a matter of law); *Keiter v. Penn Mutual Ins. Co.*, 900 F. Supp. 1339 (D.Haw.1995) (where the court found that the defendant's conduct which resulted in a significant increase in the premium payment on plaintiffs' life insurance policy was not outrageous conduct as a matter of law); and *Lapinad v. Pacific Oldsmobile–GMC, Inc.*, 679 F. Supp. 991, 996 (D. Haw.1988) (where the court stated that an employer must have engaged in conduct beyond merely firing an employee for unfair reasons in order for the conduct to possibly be considered outrageous).

The court has found, however, that sexually harassing behavior, racial slurs, and accusations of criminal conduct could all possibly be considered outrageous conduct. See *Lapinad*, 679 F. Supp. at 996. In addition, in *Kalawe v. KFC Nat. Mgmt. & Co.*, the court found outrageous behavior may exist where a plaintiff claimed her supervisor used plaintiff's work injury as a pretext for wrongfully discharging her in retaliation and response to a personal dislike for her. . . . 1991 WL 338566 at *5 (D. Haw. July 16, 1991).

The court finds that issues of material fact exist as to whether Defendant's delay in disclosure rose to the level of outrageous conduct. Construing the evidence in the light most favorable to Plaintiff, the court determines that a reasonable juror could find that Defendant's failure to provide information about Plaintiff's urine test to Plaintiff in a timely manner, which resulted in him losing his job for two years and allegedly caused Plaintiff's depression, is "so outrageous in character, and so extreme in degree, as to go beyond all possible bounds of decency, and to be regarded as atrocious, and utterly intolerable in a civilized community." See Restatement (Second) of Torts § 46, cmt. *d.* Accordingly, material facts exist as to whether Defendant's conduct was outrageous.

C. Causation

In order to pursue his IIED claim, Plaintiff must prove that Defendant's intentional conduct "must have actually caused the plaintiff to suffer severe emotional distress." *Hac*, 73 P.3d at 59. Plaintiff alleges that he suffered the following injuries: contemplation of suicide, depression, substance abuse, shame, and confusion. . . . Plaintiff states that these symptoms arose after he lost his job, which resulted from Defendant's inaccurate report that his urine specimen had been substituted. . . .

Defendant argues that "[t]here is no evidence that any subsequent withholding of information by Defendant QDCL legally caused emotional distress to Plaintiff." Motion, at 12. Furthermore, Defendant argues that evidence presented by Plaintiff "actually confirms that Plaintiff's emotional distress resulted from other causes." . . . Specifically, Defendant provides evidence that Plaintiff's drug use and long-standing depression were the sources of the extreme emotional distress Plaintiff alleges he suffered as a result of Defendant's conduct.

Although the evidence presented by Defendant may support its position about causation, they do not, as a matter of law, establish that position. To the contrary, the court finds that genuine issues of material fact exist as to whether Defendant's alleged withholding of the information caused Plaintiff's emotional distress. . . .

D. Extreme Emotional Distress

"[M]ental distress may be found where a reasonable [person], normally constituted, would be unable to adequately cope with the mental stress engendered by the circumstances of the case." *Shoppe*, 14 P.3d at 1068. The Hawai'i Supreme Court recently recognized that "the likelihood of illness is no longer a necessary element of the tort," and defined "severe emotional distress" as "'mental suffering, mental anguish, mental or nervous shock and including all highly unpleasant mental reactions, such as fright, horror, grief, shame, humiliation, embarrassment, anger, chagrin, disappointment, worry and nausea.'" *Hac*, 73 P.3d at 59. Defendant argues that Plaintiff does not allege any severe emotional distress, but "asserts only that [he] suffered from depression, shame and confusion, became withdrawn, had no self-esteem and lost trust in people."

At the summary judgment stage, the court construes the facts in the light most favorable to Plaintiff. See *Anderson v. Liberty Lobby, Inc.*, 106 S. Ct. 2505. Thus, accepting as true Plaintiff's claim that he contemplated suicide and suffered from depression, substance abuse, shame, and confusion, the court concludes that a trier of fact could find that Plaintiff suffered "mental suffering, mental anguish, mental or nervous shock and including all highly unpleasant mental reactions, such as fright, horror, grief, shame, humiliation, embarrassment, anger, chagrin, disappointment, worry and nausea," all of which the Hawai'i Supreme Court recognizes as symptoms of severe emotional distress. *Hac*, 73 P.3d at 59.

Conclusion

Given that genuine issues of material fact exists as to every element of Plaintiff's claim of intentional infliction of emotional distress, the court DENIES Defendant's Motion for Summary Judgement.

THE RESTATEMENT, THIRD, AND IIED

The Restatement, Third, of Torts § 45 (2012) is virtually identical with § 46 of the Second Restatement as set forth in the elements of IIED listed in *Nagata*. The Third Restatement does, however, add something new to IIED. Traditionally, transferred intent applied only to the five traditional intentional torts set forth at p. 11. In § 45, comment *h*, the Restatement takes the position that transferred intent also applies, at least in part, to IIED. Illustration 6 provides:

> Caryn, desiring to obtain revenge on her ex-boyfriend, Mike, calls his home one night with an untrue story about the death of his daughter, employing horrific descriptions of her rape, torture, and ultimate death. Unknown to Caryn, Mike's roommate, Bill, who has a very close relationship with Mike's daughter, answers her call and hears the story. Caryn is subject to liability under this Section even though she acted with a purpose to cause emotional harm to Mike and not to Bill.

By the way—was it necessary that the story was untrue? Would transferred intent apply if *A* battered *B* and caused emotional distress to *C* whose presence was not known to *A*?

FOOD FOR THOUGHT

Note that a plaintiff must establish both "extreme and outrageous conduct" and "severe emotional distress." Several commentators believe that this dual requirement is unwarranted. *See* Willard H. Pedrick, *Intentional Infliction: Should Section 46 Be Revised?*, 13 Pepp. L. Rev. 1 (1985); Regina Austin, *Employer Abuse, Worker Resistance and the Tort of Intentional Infliction of Emotional Distress*, 41 Stan. L. Rev. 1 (1988).

EXTREME AND OUTRAGEOUS CONDUCT

Courts can be very demanding as to whether the conduct was extreme and outrageous. The Sixth Circuit has described this requirement as an "exacting standard which provides the primary safeguard against fraudulent and trivial claims." MacDermid v. Discover Fin. Servs., 488 F.3d 721, 732 (6th Cir. 2007) (applying Tennessee law) (quoting Miller v. Willbanks, 8 S.W.3d 607, 614 (Tenn. 1999)). Abusive language and insults generally do not qualify as the kind of conduct to support the tort. Thus, a seventh-grade girl with special education needs who alleged that she experienced depression and suicidal thoughts when her band teacher continually called her "retarded," "stupid," and "dumb" in front of her classmates did not sufficiently allege outrageousness. *See* Costello v. Mitchell Pub. Sch. Dist. 79, 266 F.3d 916 (8th Cir. 2001). *See also* Spence v. Donahoe, 515 F. App'x 561 (6th Cir. 2013) (supervisor's references to employee as a "piece of sh*t" and "useless" did not satisfy outrageousness requirement); Cavazos v. Edgewood Indep. Sch. Dist., 210 F. App'x 414 (5th Cir. 2006) (school board members' repeated threats to fire a high school principal did not constitute extreme and outrageous conduct); Stevenson v. Bluhm, 2006 WL 3096688 (D.D.C. 2006) (insurance agent suggested to family of child killed in automobile accident that the child committed suicide; court dismissed plaintiff's IIED claim because, though unkind, the statements were not outrageous). *But see* Fox v. Hayes, 600 F.3d 819, 842-843 (7th Cir. 2010) (a jury could find that a police officer's conduct was extreme and outrageous when he screamed "your husband's a f***** murderer. He never loved you or your f***** daughter" at wife of husband accused of raping and killing their daughter); Macdermid *supra* (credit card company's threat of criminal prosecution for failure to pay account knowing of customer's fragile mental status and leading to her suicide was sufficient on the issue of "outrageous conduct" to withstand motion to dismiss).

Although insults generally don't qualify, it is hard to generalize as to what conduct will meet a court's minimum standard for extreme and outrageous conduct. In Moore v. Solar Group, 311 F. App'x 722 (5th Cir. 2009), a supervisor fired an employee, then "zig-zagged" a small flashlight in the employee's eyes, and then followed the employee while riding an adult tricycle "in a menacing fashion" as she left the building. The appellate court stated that the facts simply did not constitute "intolerable, outrageous, or revolting" conduct and affirmed summary judgment for the employer. *Id.* at 724. However, in Perk v. Worden, 475 F. Supp. 2d 565 (E.D. Va. 2007), an attorney who was hired to collect a debt from plaintiff agreed to postponement of a trial date but showed up on the original trial date and received a default judgment against the plaintiff. The court held that a jury could find the attorney's conduct in obtaining a default judgment when he knew the plaintiff was contesting the debt amounted to outrageous conduct. Several recent cases demonstrate the wide variance of opinion as to what kind of conduct constitutes extreme and outrageous conduct. Factors that bear on a court's determination of the "extreme and outrageous" requirement include: (1) the actor's position of authority; and (2) the actor's awareness of the victim's particular vulnerability to emotional distress. For example, in *Fox v. Hayes, supra,* the wife of a man accused of raping and killing the couple's daughter brought an IIED claim against the detective in charge of the husband's interrogation. Denying summary judgment, the court stated that the detective's supervisory role in the interrogation, as well as his knowledge of the wife's particular vulnerability under such emotional circumstances "boosts what otherwise might be characterized as a particularly ugly insult across the threshold into a valid IIED claim." Hayes, 600 F.3d at 842. For more cases illustrating this element, see Restatement (Third) of Torts, Liability for Physical and Emotional Harm § 46 cmt. *d* (2005).

hypo 9

An elderly woman shopping at Food Flop (a bargain supermarket) suffered a heart attack when after inquiring about the cost of a jar of instant coffee was told by a clerk that she would have to find out by herself because "You stink to me." What result? If the elderly woman were shopping at Tiffany's would that make a difference?

---

authors' dialogue 4

AARON: I have never quite made peace with the requirement in emotional distress cases that plaintiff establish not only extreme and outrageous conduct but also severe emotional distress. In the text we cite Professor Regina Austin's article dealing with employer abuse. She argues that, in the employment setting, the requirement that severe emotional distress be proven allows employers to get away with conduct that is quite outrageous simply because plaintiffs cannot make out severe emotional distress. Take a look at Restatement § 46, comment *j*, dealing with the requirement of severe emotional distress. It offers no explanation other than the lame statement that "[c]omplete emotional tranquility is seldom attainable in this world and some degree of transient and trivial emotional distress is part of the price of living among people." Give me a break! If the defendant's intentional conduct is truly outrageous — for example, deliberately telling a mother that her young child has been killed, while flinging blood-soaked clothing at her feet — why shouldn't that be tortious conduct even if the parent happens to be a stoic who suffers less-than-extreme upset? I can understand why we require that the defendant's conduct be extreme and outrageous. We want to allow people — even mean-spirited so-and-sos — to engage in conduct that is less than polite or nice. The world does come with rough edges, and I can live with that. But, what explains the necessity that the victim suffer "big time" in order to have a remedy?

JIM: Aaron! Has Kreindel been lacing your corn flakes with Ecstasy pills? For good reasons, tort law looks skeptically on claims of emotional upset. Even when the

---

Courts were initially reluctant to recognize a tort remedy for intentional infliction of emotional distress that took place within the marriage, but they have recently been more willing to consider such tort actions. In *Feltmeier v. Feltmeier*, 798 N.E.2d 75 (Ill. 2003), the court said it would join the national trend toward giving such actions recognition. The court noted that "special caution" is required in dealing with actions for intentional infliction of emotional distress arising from conduct within the marital setting. Other states have come to similar conclusions. *See, e.g., McCulloh v. Drake*, 24 P.3d 1162 (Wyo. 2001); *Christians v. Christians*, 637 N.W. 2d 377 (S.D. 2001). For a discussion of the history of spousal immunity and the difficulties presented by *McCulloh*, see Brandi Monger, *Family Law — Wyoming's Adoption of Intentional Infliction of Emotional Distress in the Marital Context. McCulloh v. Drake*, 24 P.3d 1162 (Wyo. 2001), 2 Wyo. L. Rev. 563 (2002). *Also see* Benjamin Shmueli, *Tort Litigation Between Spouses: Let's Meet Somewhere in the Middle*, 15 Harv. Negot. L. Rev. 195 (2010).

SEVERE EMOTIONAL DISTRESS

As to what constitutes severe emotional distress, some courts are very demanding. Courts typically require that the distress be such that "no reasonable person could

upset is real, it is never really as bad as it seems when dramatized in court. Heck, some psychologists even argue that occasional emotional upheavals are good for us — they make us appreciate the good things in life more. The parent in your example may appreciate her child even more when she learns that he's alive, after all. And purely emotional upset is too easily faked and exaggerated. My amazement is not that courts set the "upset" bar high for claimants, but that they allow these claims at all.

AARON: Jim! Has Marcie been putting nails in your breakfast porridge? I can't believe your reaction to my bloody clothes hypothetical! Do you really mean what you just said?

JIM: Come on, now, Aaron, don't you go and get emotionally upset with me! (Have I committed a tort?) To answer what I assume to have been a rhetorical question, "Yes, I really *do* mean what I just said." If the plaintiff in your hypothetical is upset enough to hire a lawyer, she will claim in court that she was extremely upset by what the defendant did to her. And given the outrageous conduct of that jerk, she'll reach the jury with her claim. And my hunch is that the jury will share your feelings, not mine, and reward her generously. (I would go so far as to say that her extreme upset is genuine — which it very probably is.) So she is going to win, and win big. The tort claims that the "severe upset" requirement will (hopefully) prevent are the ones closer to what Professor Austin is stumping for: punishing corporate conduct that, while antisocial and clearly actionable for any provable economic harm caused to individuals against whom it is aimed, probably does not (and, I think, clearly should not) qualify for big-bucks recoveries on the "emotional upset" side of the aisle.

---

be expected to endure it." *See, e.g.,* Lawler v. Montblanc N. Am., LLC, 704 F.3d 1235, 1246 (9th Cir. 2013); Smith v. Amedisys, Inc., 298 F.3d 434, 449 (5th Cir. 2002). *See also* Restatement (Second) of Torts § 46 cmt. *j* (1965). In *Lawler v. Montblanc,* the Ninth Circuit applied California law and held that an employee failed to sufficiently allege severe emotional distress. 704 F.3d at 1246. The employee alleged that she suffered "[a]nxiety, sleeplessness, upset stomach, [and] sometimes muscle twitches" after the employer made intimidating and insulting remarks about the employee's job performance. *Id. See also* Garay v. Liriano, 943 F. Supp. 2d 1, 23 (D.D.C. 2013) (allegations of "depression, nervousness, lack of sleep, and loss of appetite" did not constitute severe emotional distress). Similarly in Alderson v. Bonner, 132 P.3d 1261 (Idaho Ct. App. 2006), defendant who videotaped a 16-year-old girl through the gaps in the window blades while she was in various states of undress was entitled to a judgment n.o.v. The court acknowledged that the defendant's conduct was extreme and outrageous but concluded that plaintiff's claim that she had suffered embarrassment, lost trust in men, and would dress only in a windowless room, did not constitute severe emotional distress.

WHO DECIDES: JUDGE OR JURY?

With regard to any element of a cause of action in torts, the court must decide whether the plaintiff has produced sufficient evidence to make out her claim. If reasonable persons can differ as to the adequacy of the proof, the issue should be submitted to the jury; if no reasonable jury could find otherwise, the court should direct a verdict for the defendant. Nonetheless, judicial scrutiny of the factual basis for a claim varies depending on the issue to be decided. We shall see, for example, that in negligence claims, courts generally defer to juries in deciding whether the conduct of the defendant was reasonable. In the case of the tort of intentional infliction of emotional stress, courts are not shy in directing verdicts for a defendant on the grounds that either the conduct was not "extreme and outrageous" or the emotional distress suffered was not "severe." *See, e.g.,* Harris v. Kreutzer, 624 S.E.2d 24 (Va. 2006) ("It is for the court to determine in the first instance whether the defendant's conduct may reasonably be regarded as so extreme and outrageous as to permit recovery . . ."); Richard Rosen, Inc. v. Mendivil, 225 S.W.3d 181 (Tex. App. 2005) (an employee who had a claim for defamation of character arising from statements about him after he resigned from his position did not have a claim for intentional infliction of emotional distress; statements by defendant were not so outrageous in the context of an employment dispute as to warrant the emotional distress claim). The Restatement, Third, of Torts: Liability for Physical and Emotional Harm, § 45, comment *g* (2010), supports the heightened scrutiny by courts on the grounds that a "broad application of this tort poses concerns that it could interfere with the exercise of legal rights; deter socially useful conduct that nevertheless causes emotional harm; impinging on free speech or target conduct that is 'different' rather than particularly reprehensible."

YOU ARE INSURED TO GET A RAW DEAL

In several cases courts have found that insurance companies may be held liable for IIED for canceling the policies of their insureds. In Liberty Mutual Insurance Co. v. Steadman, 968 So. 2d 592 (Fla. Dist. Ct. App. 2007), the court held that a health insurer who delayed authorizing approval for a lung transplant for nine months in the hope that the patient would die before it had to pay for the surgery would be liable for IIED. The court found that as a matter of law the conduct of the insurer was outrageous. Similarly, in Hailey v. California Physicians' Service, 69 Cal. Rptr. 3d 789 (Cal. Ct. App. 2007), an insurer who delayed canceling a health insurance policy because of misrepresentation by the insured until after the insured incurred over $450,000 in medical bills following an automobile accident was held subject to liability for intentional infliction of emotional distress. The court denied summary judgment to the insurer, finding that the facts raised the specter that the insurer's final decision to rescind "may not have come about because of omissions in the application, but because of the substantial medical bills resulting from [the] automobile accident."

SPECIAL RULE FOR COMMON CARRIERS AND INNKEEPERS

The demanding requisites for imposing liability for emotional distress are relaxed when the defendant is either a common carrier or an innkeeper. For centuries courts have held these two enterprises to a very high standard of care. A classic example is Lipman v. Atlantic Coast Line R. Co., 93 S.E. 714 (S.C. 1917). In that case a conductor told a passenger he was a lunatic who belonged in a "lunatic asylum" and that he would be glad to give him two black eyes if he were off duty. Given the status of the defendant as a common carrier, the insult was sufficient to make out a cause of action even though the conduct did not amount to more than a gross insult. Restatement, Second, of Torts § 48 endorses this exception. In recent years some courts have rejected the rule imposing a higher duty of care on common carriers. *See, e.g.,* Bethel v. N.Y.C. Transit Authority, 703 N.E.2d 1214 (N.Y. 1998). It remains to be seen whether this reduction of duty on common carriers will cause courts to treat them differently than other defendants when they subject their patrons to insults.

THE FIRST AMENDMENT AND IIED

Many IIED cases involve hurtful speech. When does such speech come under the protection of the First Amendment? In Snyder v. Phelps, 131 S. Ct. 1207 (2011), the United States Supreme Court struggled with the issue. The defendant, the Westboro Baptist Church and its members, picketed the funeral of Marine Corporal Matthew Snyder, who was killed in Iraq in the line of duty. The picketers peacefully displayed signs stating, "Thank God for Dead Soldiers," "America Is Doomed," "Priests Rape Boys," "You're Going to Hell." Matthew's father sued the church and its members who picketed the funeral for IIED, alleging that the conduct was "extreme and outrageous" and caused him "severe emotional" distress. At trial, a Maryland jury found for Snyder and awarded him $2.9 million in compensatory damages and $8 million in punitive damages. The Fourth Circuit reversed the verdict on constitutional grounds. In an 8-1 decision affirming the court of appeals, the Supreme Court said that "whether the First Amendment prohibits holding Westboro liable for its speech in this case turns largely on whether the speech is of public or private concern as determined by all the circumstances of the case." The Court went on to say that speech deals with matters of public concern when it can "be fairly considered as relating to any matter of political, social, or other concern to the community." In applying that test to the Westboro picketing, the court found that the pickets addressed the political and moral conduct of the United States and its citizens, homosexuality in the military, and scandals involving the Catholic clergy — all matters of public import.

After *Snyder*, if the defendant, restaurant manager, in *Fisher v. Carrousel Motor Hotel,* discussed earlier, had uttered his racial slur without snatching the plate from the plaintiff's hand, would the plaintiff be able to make out a case for IIED?

F. TRESPASS TO LAND

A possessor of real property has a right to exclusive possession. One who intentionally enters land in the possession of another has committed the tort of trespass to land. Even one who mistakenly steps on another's property, believing it to be his own, commits the tort. (Remember *Ranson v. Kitner.*) However, if someone loses control of his car and ends up in your living room, he has not committed a trespass to land. (Why?) In this world where airwaves and pollutants make their way onto another's property, plaintiffs have sought to push the tort of trespass to seek damages or injunctions against those responsible for such environmental torts. In these cases, trespass nudges up very close to the tort of nuisance that deals with the right of a possessor of land to be free from unreasonable interference with the use and enjoyment of her property. We will explore this topic briefly in Chapter 12.

Although trespass to land is generally a pretty straightforward tort, occasionally cases arise where it is not so clear that a trespass has been committed.

ROGERS v. KENT COUNTY BOARD OF ROAD COMMISSIONERS
30 N.W.2d 358 (Mich. 1948)

REID, Justice.

Plaintiff instituted this suit to recover damages because of the death of her husband, Theodore Rogers, which plaintiff claims was caused by the trespass and negligence of the defendant board of county road commissioners. Defendant filed a motion to dismiss, based on the pleadings and on the ground of governmental immunity. The lower court granted defendant's motion and dismissed the cause. Plaintiff appeals from the judgment of dismissal of her cause.

Plaintiff claims that for two winter seasons previous to the date of the fatal injury to her husband the defendant board of road commissioners had obtained a license to place a snow fence in decedent's field parallel to the roadway past decedent's farm. Plaintiff claims in her declaration that the placing of the snow fence there was with the distinct understanding and agreement between the defendant and decedent that all of the fence together with the anchor posts should be removed by defendant at the end of each winter season, when the necessity for snow fences for that season no longer existed. Plaintiff claims that such was the arrangement for the winter season of 1943-1944, that the arrangement was renewed for the winter season of 1944-1945, and that in the spring of 1945 the defendant's agents and employees removed the snow fence but did not remove a steel anchor post which protruded from 6 to 8 inches above the ground. Plaintiff further claims that the place where the post was located was a meadow where the grass grew to a considerable height so that the anchor post was entirely hidden, and that . . . after decedent's husband had mowed several swaths around the field where the snow fence had been, with his mowing machine attached to his neighbor's tractor, and without any negligence or want of proper method of operation on his part, the mowing bar struck the steel stake and as a result of the impact,

decedent was forcibly thrown from the seat of the mowing machine to and u̱
the wheels of the mowing machine and upon the ground. By reason of the acci
decedent received severe injuries which caused his death on October 25, 19̱

Plaintiff based her suit upon trespass and negligence of defendant, clai̱
that the accident was the result of the trespass and negligence by the defendant in
leaving the stake after the license to have the snow fence in place had expired, and
the rest of the snow fence had been removed. . . .

The court dismissed plaintiff's cause of action, ruling that the action was
plainly an action based upon negligence, that there was no basis for any finding
of trespass and that the defense of governmental immunity applied to the facts set
forth in plaintiff's declaration.

Failure to remove the anchor stake upon expiration of the license to have it on
plaintiff's land was a continuing trespass and is alleged by plaintiff to have been a
proximate cause of the damage which she seeks to recover.

§ 160. Failure to Remove a Thing Placed on the Land Pursuant to a License or Other Privilege

A trespass, actionable under the rule stated in section 158, may be committed
by the continued presence on the land of a structure, chattel or other thing which
the actor or his predecessor in legal interest therein has placed thereon

(a) with the consent of the person then in possession of the land, if the
actor fails to remove it after the consent has been effectively terminated, or

(b) pursuant to a privilege conferred on the actor irrespective of the
possessor's consent, if the actor fails to remove it after the privilege has been
terminated, by the accomplishment of its purpose or otherwise. 1 Restatement, Torts, p. 368. . . .

[The court found that governmental immunity did not apply to counties and sent
the case back for trial on both negligence and trespass to land.] . . .

The judgment of the court dismissing the cause of action is reversed and the
cause remanded for such further proceedings as shall be found necessary.

FOOD FOR THOUGHT

Trespass to land is an intentional tort. Did the defendant deliberately decide to
leave the stake in the ground? If not, isn't he simply negligent for failing to remove
the stake? Why are we talking trespass?

hypo 10

Garp operates a commercial hog farm on his 150-acre tract of land. He dumps
the waste into Irving Creek, which runs through Garp's tract and onto Jenny's
tract. One of Jenny's cows, valued at $5,000, dies from drinking the contam-
inated creek water. Has Garp committed a tort?

G. TRESPASS TO CHATTELS AND CONVERSION

The twin torts of trespass to chattels and conversion deal with intentional inter-ferences with the personal property of others. The difference between the two depends on the seriousness of the interference. Where the interference is minor, the tort is trespass to chattels and the defendant pays only the value of the harm caused to the chattel. Where the interference is serious and constitutes a conver-sion, the law gives the plaintiff the option of retaining the chattel and recovering the value of the harm from the defendant or relinquishing the chattel to the defendant and recovering its fair market value. If a classmate mistakenly picks up your Torts casebook believing it to be hers, and discovers her mistake shortly thereafter and returns the book, there is no tort. Without some damage to the chattel there is no cause of action for trespass to chattels. If she takes the book, goes down to the cafeteria for five minutes and spills some coffee on the book, the defendant is liable for the harm caused. However, if she keeps the book for two months, never noticing that it is not hers, and returns it when she discovers her error, she has converted the book. The interference with the chattel is of sufficient severity that she is required to pay the full value of the book. And if your classmate knowingly takes your book because she needs the casebook for class, she has converted the book to her own use. The intent to appropriate the book for even an hour renders the interference so serious that the plaintiff has the option to demand payment of its full value.

The Restatement, Second, of Torts § 222A defines conversion as follows:

> (1) Conversion is an intentional exercise of dominion or control over a chattel which so seriously interferes with the right of another to control it that the actor may justly be required to pay the other the full value of the chattel.
> (2) In determining the seriousness of the interference and the justice of requiring the actor to pay the full value, the following factors are important:
> (a) the extent and duration of the actor's exercise of dominion or control;
> (b) the actor's intent to assert a right in fact inconsistent with the other's right of control;
> (c) the actor's good faith;
> (d) the extent and duration of the resulting interference with the other's right of control;
> (e) the harm done to the chattel;
> (f) the inconvenience and expense caused to the other.

hypo 11

A and *B,* wealthy roommates in college, own expensive watches. *A* by mistake puts on *B*'s Patek Philippe worth $5,000. Later in the day *A* is involved in an auto accident. *B*'s watch is damaged in the crash. It can be repaired at the cost of $500. Is *A* liable for conversion?

hypo **12**

Same as above, except that *A* takes *B*'s watch as a prank for the day. Is *A* liable for conversion?

hypo **13**

Dumbo parallel parks his car on a hill, taking up two spots. Rob, searching for a parking spot, sees that Dumbo has left the window down. Rob gets into Dumbo's car, slowly releases the parking brake, and allows the car to roll four feet into the proper parking space. He then puts the brake back on, gets out of the car, and parks his own car in the open spot. Has Rob committed a tort?

With the advent of computer technology the old tort of trespass to chattels has found new utility. Consider the following case.

INTEL CORP. v. HAMIDI
71 P.3d 296 (Cal. 2003)

WERDEGAR, J. . . .

Hamidi, a former Intel engineer, together with others, formed an organization named Former and Current Employees of Intel (FACE-Intel) to disseminate information and views critical of Intel's employment and personnel policies and practices. FACE-Intel maintained a Web site (which identified Hamidi as Webmaster and as the organization's spokesperson) containing such material. In addition, over a 21-month period Hamidi, on behalf of FACE-Intel, sent six mass e-mails to employee addresses on Intel's electronic mail system. The messages criticized Intel's employment practices, warned employees of the dangers those practices posed to their careers, suggested employees consider moving to other companies, solicited employees' participation in FACE-Intel, and urged employees to inform themselves further by visiting FACE-Intel's Web site. The messages stated that recipients could, by notifying the sender of their wishes, be removed from FACE-Intel's mailing list; Hamidi did not subsequently send messages to anyone who requested removal.

Each message was sent to thousands of addresses (as many as 35,000 according to FACE-Intel's Web site), though some messages were blocked by Intel before reaching employees. Intel's attempt to block internal transmission of the messages succeeded only in part; Hamidi later admitted he evaded blocking efforts by using different sending computers. When Intel, in March 1998, demanded in writing that Hamidi and FACE-Intel stop sending e-mails to Intel's computer system, Hamidi asserted the organization had a right to communicate with willing Intel employees; he sent a new mass mailing in September 1998. . . .

Intel sued Hamidi and FACE-Intel, pleading causes of action for trespass to chattels and nuisance, and seeking both actual damages and an injunction against further e-mail messages. Intel later voluntarily dismissed its nuisance claim and waived its demand for damages. The trial court entered default against FACE-Intel upon that organization's failure to answer. The court then granted Intel's motion for summary judgment, permanently enjoining Hamidi, FACE-Intel, and their agents "from sending unsolicited e-mail to addresses on Intel's computer systems." Hamidi appealed.

The Court of Appeal, with one justice dissenting, affirmed the grant of injunctive relief. The majority took the view that the use of or intermeddling with another's personal property is actionable as a trespass to chattels without proof of any actual injury to the personal property; even if Intel could not show any damages resulting from Hamidi's sending of messages, "it showed he was disrupting its business by using its property and therefore is entitled to injunctive relief based on a theory of trespass to chattels." The dissenting justice warned that the majority's application of the trespass to chattels tort to "unsolicited electronic mail that causes no harm to the private computer system that receives it" would "expand the tort of trespass to chattel in untold ways and to unanticipated circumstances."

We granted Hamidi's petition for review.

I.

Dubbed by Prosser the "little brother of conversion," the tort of trespass to chattels allows recovery for interferences with possession of personal property "not sufficiently important to be classed as conversion, and so to compel the defendant to pay the full value of the thing with which he has interfered." (Prosser & Keeton, Torts (5th ed. 1984) § 14, pp. 85-86.)

Though not amounting to conversion, the defendant's interference must, to be actionable, have caused some injury to the chattel or to the plaintiff's rights in it. Under California law, trespass to chattels "lies where an intentional interference with the possession of personal property *has proximately caused injury.* . . ." In modern American law generally, "[t]respass remains as an occasional remedy for minor interferences, *resulting in some damage,* but not sufficiently serious or sufficiently important to amount to the greater tort" of conversion. (Prosser & Keeton, Torts, *supra,* § 15, p. 90, italics added.)

The Restatement, too, makes clear that some actual injury must have occurred in order for a trespass to chattels to be actionable. Under *section 218 of the Restatement Second of Torts,* dispossession alone, without further damages, is actionable (see *id.,* par. (a) & *com. d,* pp. 420-421), but other forms of interference require some additional harm to the personal property or the possessor's interests in it. (*Id.,* pars. (b)-(d).) "The interest of a possessor of a chattel in its inviolability, unlike the similar interest of a possessor of land, is not given legal protection by an action for nominal damages for harmless intermeddlings with the chattel. In order that an actor who interferes with another's chattel may be liable, his conduct must affect some other and more important interest of the possessor. *Therefore, one who intentionally intermeddles with another's chattel is subject to liability only if his intermeddling is harmful to the possessor's materially valuable interest in the physical* *condition, quality, or value of the chattel, or if the possessor is deprived of the use of the chattel for a substantial time, or some other legally protected interest of the possessor is affected as stated in Clause (c).*Sufficient legal protection of the possessor's interest in the mere inviolability of his chattel is afforded by his privilege to use reasonable force to protect his possession against even harmless interference." (*Id., com. e*, pp. 421-422, italics added.) . . .

In this respect, as Prosser explains, modern day trespass to chattels differs both from the original English writ and from the action for trespass to land: "Another departure from the original rule of the old writ of trespass concerns the necessity of some actual damage to the chattel before the action can be maintained. Where the defendant merely interferes without doing any harm — as where, for example, he merely lays hands upon the plaintiff's horse, or sits in his car — there has been a division of opinion among the writers, and a surprising dearth of authority. *By analogy to trespass to land there might be a technical tort in such a case. . . . Such scanty authority as there is, however, has considered that the dignitary interest in the inviolability of chattels, unlike that as to land, is not sufficiently important to require any greater defense than the privilege of using reasonable force when necessary to protect them. Accordingly it has been held that nominal damages will not be awarded, and that in the absence of any actual damage the action will not lie."* (Prosser & Keeton, Torts, *supra*, § 14, p. 87, italics added, fns. omitted.) . . .

The dispositive issue in this case, therefore, is whether the undisputed facts demonstrate Hamidi's actions caused or threatened to cause damage to Intel's computer system, or injury to its rights in that personal property, such as to entitle Intel to judgment as a matter of law. To review, the undisputed evidence revealed no actual or threatened damage to Intel's computer hardware or software and no interference with its ordinary and intended operation. Intel was not dispossessed of its computers, nor did Hamidi's messages prevent Intel from using its computers for any measurable length of time. Intel presented no evidence its system was slowed or otherwise impaired by the burden of delivering Hamidi's electronic messages. Nor was there any evidence transmission of the messages imposed any marginal cost on the operation of Intel's computers. In sum, no evidence suggested that in sending messages through Intel's Internet connections and internal computer system Hamidi used the system in any manner in which it was not intended to function or impaired the system in any way. Nor does the evidence show the request of any employee to be removed from FACE-Intel's mailing list was not honored. The evidence did show, however, that some employees who found the messages unwelcome asked management to stop them and that Intel technical staff spent time and effort attempting to block the messages. A statement on the FACE-Intel Web site, moreover, could be taken as an admission that the messages had caused "[e]xcited and nervous managers" to discuss the matter with Intel's human resources department.

Relying on a line of decisions, most from federal district courts, applying the tort of trespass to chattels to various types of unwanted electronic contact between computers, Intel contends that, while its computers were not damaged by receiving Hamidi's messages, its interest in the "physical condition, quality or value" (*Rest. 2d Torts, § 218, com. e*, p. 422) of the computers was harmed. We disagree. The cited line of decisions does not persuade us that the mere sending of electronic communications that assertedly cause injury only because of their contents constitutes an actionable trespass to a computer system through which the messages are transmitted. Rather, the decisions finding electronic contact to be a trespass to computer systems have generally involved some actual or threatened interference with the computers' functioning.

In *Thrifty-Tel, Inc. v. Bezenek, supra,* . . . 54 Cal. Rptr. 2d 468 (*Thrifty-Tel*), the California Court of Appeal held that evidence of automated searching of a telephone carrier's system for authorization codes supported a cause of action for trespass to chattels. The defendant's automated dialing program "overburdened the [plaintiff's] system, denying some subscribers access to phone lines" (*id.* . . . 54 Cal. Rptr. 2d 468), showing the requisite injury.

Following *Thrifty-Tel,* a series of federal district court decisions held that sending UCE [unsolicited commercial bulk e-mail] through an ISP's [internet service provider] equipment may constitute trespass to the ISP's computer system. The lead case, *CompuServe, Inc. v. Cyber Promotions, Inc., supra,* 962 F. Supp. 1015, 1021-1023 (*CompuServe*), was followed by *Hotmail Corp. v. Van$ Money Pie, Inc.* (N.D. Cal., Apr. 16, 1998, No. C 98-20064 JW) 1998 U.S. Dist. LEXIS 10729, page *7, *America Online, Inc. v. IMS* (E.D. Va. 1998) 24 F. Supp. 2d 548, 550-551, and *America Online, Inc. v. LCGM, Inc.* (E.D. Va. 1998) 46 F. Supp. 2d 444, 451-452.

In each of these spamming cases, the plaintiff showed, or was prepared to show, some interference with the efficient functioning of its computer system. In *CompuServe,* the plaintiff ISP's mail equipment monitor stated that mass UCE mailings, especially from nonexistent addresses such as those used by the defendant, placed "a tremendous burden" on the ISP's equipment, using "disk space and drain[ing] the processing power," making those resources unavailable to serve subscribers. (*CompuServe, supra,* 962 F. Supp. at p. 1022.) Similarly, in *Hotmail Corp. v. Van$ Money Pie, Inc., supra,* 1998 U.S. Dist. LEXIS 10729 at page *7, the court found the evidence supported a finding that the defendant's mailings "fill[ed] up Hotmail's computer storage space and threaten[ed] to damage Hotmail's ability to service its legitimate customers. . . ."

In addition to impairment of system functionality, *CompuServe* and its progeny also refer to the ISP's loss of business reputation and customer goodwill, resulting from the inconvenience and cost that spam causes to its members, as harm to the ISP's legally protected interests in its personal property. (See *CompuServe, supra,* 962 F. Supp. 2d at p. 1023; *Hotmail Corp. v. Van$ Money Pie, Inc., supra,* 1998 U.S. Dist. LEXIS 10729 at p. *7; *America Online, Inc. v. IMS, supra,* 24 F. Supp. 2d at p. 550.) Intel argues that its own interest in employee productivity, assertedly disrupted by Hamidi's messages, is a comparable protected interest in its computer system. We disagree. . . .

CompuServe's customers were annoyed because the system was inundated with unsolicited commercial messages, making its use for personal communication more difficult and costly. (*CompuServe, supra,* 962 F. Supp. at p. 1023.) Their complaint, which allegedly led some to cancel their CompuServe service, was about *the functioning of CompuServe's electronic mail service.* Intel's workers, in contrast, were allegedly distracted from their work not because of the frequency or quantity of Hamidi's messages, but because of assertions and opinions the messages conveyed. Intel's complaint is thus about *the contents of the messages* rather than the functioning of the company's e-mail system. Even accepting *CompuServe's* economic injury rationale, therefore, Intel's position represents a further extension of the trespass to chattels tort, fictionally recharacterizing the allegedly injurious effect of a communication's *contents* on recipients as an impairment to the device which transmitted the message. . . .

Nor may Intel appropriately assert a *property* interest in its employees' time. "The Restatement test clearly speaks in the first instance to the impairment of the chattel. . . . But employees are not chattels (at least not in the legal sense of the term)." (Burk, *The Trouble with Trespass, supra,* 4 J. Small & Emerging Bus. L. at p. 36.) Whatever interest Intel may have in preventing its employees from receiving disruptive communications, it is not an interest in personal property, and trespass to chattels is therefore not an action that will lie to protect it. Nor, finally, can the fact Intel staff spent time attempting to block Hamidi's messages be bootstrapped into an injury to Intel's possessory interest in its computers. To quote, again, from the dissenting opinion in the Court of Appeal: "[I]t is circular to premise the damage element of a tort solely upon the steps taken to prevent the damage. Injury can only be established by the completed tort's consequences, not by the cost of the steps taken to avoid the injury and prevent the tort; otherwise, we can create injury for every supposed tort."

Intel connected its e-mail system to the Internet and permitted its employees to make use of this connection both for business and, to a reasonable extent, for their own purposes. In doing so, the company necessarily contemplated the employees' receipt of unsolicited as well as solicited communications from other companies and individuals. That some communications would, because of their contents, be unwelcome to Intel management was virtually inevitable. Hamidi did nothing but use the e-mail system for its intended purpose — to communicate with employees. The system worked as designed, delivering the messages without any physical or functional harm or disruption. These occasional transmissions cannot reasonably be viewed as impairing the quality or value of Intel's computer system. We conclude, therefore, that Intel has not presented undisputed facts demonstrating an injury to its personal property, or to its legal interest in that property, that support, under California tort law, an action for trespass to chattels. . . .

Writing on behalf of several industry groups appearing as amici curiae, Professor Richard A. Epstein of the University of Chicago urges us to excuse the required showing of injury to personal property in cases of unauthorized electronic contact between computers, "extending the rules of trespass to real property to all interactive Web sites and servers." The court is thus urged to recognize, for owners of a particular species of personal property, computer servers, the same interest in inviolability as is generally accorded a possessor of land. In effect, Professor Epstein suggests that a company's server should be its castle, upon which any unauthorized intrusion, however harmless, is a trespass.

Epstein's argument derives, in part, from the familiar metaphor of the Internet as a physical space, reflected in much of the language that has been used to describe it: "cyberspace," "the information superhighway," e-mail "addresses," and the like.

---

authors' dialogue 5

JIM: Aaron, the *Intel* case is a very close call. Both the majority and dissent lay claim to a correct reading of the Restatement §218. Yet, there is something off-putting about the case. I can't put my finger on it.

AARON: I think that you are right. Something is wrong with this case. Section 218 is an historical relic that works very well when I lean on your car for five minutes and cause no damage. Unlike trespass to real property, there is no action for nominal damages for trivial interference with a chattel. But, to draw the analogy from §218 to heavy, nontrivial use of an in-house computer system is more than a little strained. We have today found ways to make pests of ourselves using technological devices that don't belong to us. I spend about 15 minutes each day erasing spam.

JIM: But, Aaron, that just makes the defendant's point. You have to put up with plenty of junk e-mail — one more or less won't break the bank.

AARON: But, why should the employer have to provide the vehicle for the delivery of mail that he believes to be unproductive or harmful? It's his computer system and

---

Of course, the Internet is also frequently called simply the "Net," a term, Hamidi points out, "evoking a fisherman's chattel." A major component of the Internet is the World Wide "Web," a descriptive term suggesting neither personal nor real property, and "cyberspace" itself has come to be known by the oxymoronic phrase "virtual reality," which would suggest that any real property "located" in "cyberspace" must be "virtually real" property. Metaphor is a two-edged sword. . . .

More substantively, Professor Epstein argues that a rule of computer server inviolability will, through the formation or extension of a market in computer-to-computer access, create "the right social result." In most circumstances, he predicts, companies with computers on the Internet will continue to authorize transmission of information through e-mail, Web site searching, and page linking because they benefit by that open access. When a Web site owner does deny access to a particular sending, searching, or linking computer, a system of "simple one-on-one negotiations" will arise to provide the necessary individual licenses.

Other scholars are less optimistic about such a complete propertization of the Internet. Professor Mark Lemley of the University of California, Berkeley, writing on behalf of an amici curiae group of professors of intellectual property and computer law, observes that under a property rule of server inviolability, "each of the hundreds of millions of [Internet] users must get permission in advance from anyone with whom they want to communicate and anyone who owns a server through which their message may travel." The consequence for e-mail could be a substantial reduction in the freedom of electronic communication, as the owner of each computer through which an electronic message passes could impose its own limitations on message content or source. As Professor Dan Hunter of the University of Pennsylvania asks rhetorically: "Does this mean that one must read the 'Terms of Acceptable Email Usage' of every email system that one emails in the

he should have final say as to how it can be used. There is nothing wrong if an employer places a spam filter on his system to prevent junk e-mail from distracting his employees. Why can't he screen by employer edict? In any event, Restatement §218 needs to be supplemented with a new section dealing with unauthorized use of computer systems. When old authority is not relevant, it should be junked and the problem faced anew without the heavy hand of history being used as support.

BRAD: Aaron, you can't actually mean the last thing you said. Authority is never irrelevant to common law reasoning. It's fine to recognize that technology has changed and the law needs to adapt, but it has to adapt incrementally, with due regard for existing authority. The *Intel* case doesn't just come out of the blue. It follows other cases, like *Thrifty-Tel*, which apply trespass law to the case of interference with computer systems. The court here distinguished *Thrifty-Tel* but maybe in a different case it would say that excessive spamming would interfere with the physical condition, quality, or value of the plaintiff's network. I don't see why we have to chuck the old law out the window and reason from the ground up about what rights a computer owner ought to have, without the benefit of the guidance of precedent.

---

course of an ordinary day? If the University of Pennsylvania had a policy that sending a joke by email would be an unauthorized use of its system, then under the logic of [the lower court decision in this case], you would commit 'trespass' if you emailed me a . . . cartoon." (Hunter, *Cyberspace as Place and the Tragedy of the Digital Anticommons* (2003) 91 Cal. L. Rev. 439, 508-509.)

The judgment of the Court of Appeals is reversed.

Dissenting Opinion by Mosk, J.

The majority hold that the California tort of trespass to chattels does not encompass the use of expressly unwanted electronic mail that causes no physical damage or impairment to the recipient's computer system. They also conclude that because a computer system is not like real property, the rules of trespass to real property are also inapplicable to the circumstances in this case. Finally, they suggest that an injunction to preclude mass, noncommercial, unwelcome e-mails may offend the interests of free communication.

I respectfully disagree and would affirm the trial court's decision. In my view, the repeated transmission of bulk e-mails by appellant Kourosh Kenneth Hamidi (Hamidi) to the employees of Intel Corporation (Intel) on its proprietary confidential e-mail lists, despite Intel's demand that he cease such activities, constituted an actionable trespass to chattels. The majority fail to distinguish open communication in the public "commons" of the Internet from unauthorized intermeddling on a private, proprietary intranet. Hamidi is not communicating in the equivalent of a town square or of an unsolicited "junk" mailing through the United States Postal Service. His action, in crossing from the public Internet into a private intranet, is more like intruding into a private office mailroom, commandeering the mail cart, and dropping off unwanted broadsides on 30,000 desks. Because Intel's security measures have been circumvented by Hamidi, the majority leave Intel, which has exercised all reasonable self-help efforts, with no recourse unless he causes a malfunction or systems "crash." Hamidi's repeated intrusions did more than merely "prompt[] discussions between '[e]xcited and nervous managers' and the company's human resources department" (maj. opn., *ante*, at p. 1349); they also constituted a misappropriation of Intel's private computer system contrary to its intended use and against Intel's wishes.

The law of trespass to chattels has not universally been limited to physical damage. I believe it is entirely consistent to apply that legal theory to these circumstances—that is, when a proprietary computer system is being used contrary to its owner's purposes and expressed desires, and self-help has been ineffective. Intel correctly expects protection from an intruder who misuses its proprietary system, its nonpublic directories, and its supposedly controlled connection to the Internet to achieve his bulk mailing objectives—incidentally, without even having to pay postage. . . .

The Restatement Second of Torts explains that a trespass to a chattel occurs if "the chattel is impaired as to its *condition, quality, or value*" or if "harm is caused to some . . . thing in which the possessor has a legally protected interest." (*Rest. 2d Torts, §218*, subds. (b) & (d), p. 420, italics added.) As to this tort, a current prominent treatise on the law of torts explains that "[t]he defendant may interfere with the chattel by interfering with the plaintiff's access or use" and observes that the tort has been applied so as "to protect computer systems from electronic invasions by way of unsolicited email or the like." (1 Dobbs, The Law of Torts (2001) §60, pp. 122-123.) Moreover, "[t]he harm necessary to trigger liability for trespass to chattels can be . . . harm to something other than the chattel itself." (*Id.* at pp. 124-125; see also 1 Harper et al., The Law of Torts (3d ed. 1996 & 2003 supp.) §2.3, pp. 2:14-2:18.) The Restatement points out that, unlike a possessor of land, a possessor of a chattel is not given legal protection from harmless invasion, but the "actor" may be liable if the conduct affects "some other and more important *interest* of the possessor." (*Rest. 2d Torts, §218, com. (e)*, p. 421, italics added.)

The Restatement explains that the rationale for requiring harm for trespass to a chattel but not for trespass to land is the availability and effectiveness of self-help in the case of trespass to a chattel. "Sufficient legal protection of the possessor's interest in the mere inviolability of his chattel is afforded by his privilege to use reasonable force to protect his possession against even harmless interference." (*Rest. 2d Torts, §218, com. (e)*, p. 422.) Obviously, "force" is not available to prevent electronic trespasses. As shown by Intel's inability to prevent Hamidi's intrusions, self-help is not an adequate alternative to injunctive relief. . . .

IV.

The trial court granted an injunction to prevent threatened injury to Intel. That is the purpose of an injunction. . . . Intel should not be helpless in the face of repeated and threatened abuse and contamination of its private computer system. The undisputed facts, in my view, rendered Hamidi's conduct legally actionable. Thus, the trial court's decision to grant a permanent injunction was not "a clear abuse of discretion" that may be "disturbed on appeal."[citations omitted]

The injunction issued by the trial court simply required Hamidi to refrain from further trespassory conduct, drawing no distinction based on the content of his e-mails. Hamidi remains free to communicate with Intel employees and others outside the walls — both physical and electronic — of the company.

For these reasons, I respectfully dissent.

In Universal Tube & Rollform Equipment Corp. v. YouTube, Inc., 504 F. Supp. 2d 260 (N.D. Ohio 2007), Universal, a used tube and pipe mill supplier, owned the website domain name "www.utube.com." Following the launch of the well-known video website, "www.youtube.com," Universal alleged a massive increase in traffic on its website from visitors intending to access YouTube's website. *Universal,* 504 F. Supp. 2d at 263. Universal claimed its traffic increased from a "few thousand" visits per month to "approximately 70,000 visits *per day.*" As a result, Universal claimed that its web servers had crashed multiple times, which impeded customers' access to the website and made the business lose sales. Universal brought a trespass to chattels claim against YouTube, arguing that its chattels — the website and its computer server hosts — were damaged due to YouTube's actions. *Id.* at 268. Citing CompuServe, Inc. v. Cyber Promotions, Inc., 952 F. Supp. 1015 (S.D. Ohio 1997) for the requirement that a chattel be a physical object capable of being physically contacted, the court held that a website domain is intangible and therefore is not a chattel. While the computers hosting Universal's website were physical objects, Universal did not have a possessory interest in them because it had hired a third party to host the website. *Id.* at 269. Moreover, even if Universal did have the requisite interest in the computer hosts, the trespass to chattels claim would nonetheless fail because it was the thousands of mistaken visitors, and not YouTube itself, that contacted the computer hosts. *Id.*

For more on the application of trespass to chattels to Internet-era problems, see Susan M. Ballantine, *Computer Network Trespasses: Solving New Problems with Old Solutions,* 57 Wash. & Lee L. Rev. 209 (2000). For a full-blown treatment of the nuances of the torts of trespass to chattels and conversions, see Dan B. Dobbs, The Law of Torts, §§ 59-67 (2000).

hypo 14

Andy, a collector of ancient Chinese vases, purchased a magnificent vase for which he paid $100,000. In order to protect the vase he ordered a custom-made glass case with a lock into which he placed the vase. On the outside of the glass case he placed a sign that read: "THIS VASE IS FOR VIEWING ONLY: NO ONE IS TO TOUCH THIS VASE WITHOUT THE EXPRESS CONSENT OF THE OWNER." Alice came to visit Andy one day and had a yearning to lift the vase. She wanted the feel of holding something worth $100,000 in her hands. A few minutes earlier Andy had opened the glass case and left the key to the glass case on the dining room table. While Andy was out of the room Alice took the key, opened the case and removed the vase. She held it for a minute and then replaced the vase in the case. Andy walked into the room and saw her replace the vase in the case. Andy was furious. He ordered Alice out of his house and said that he would see her in court. Can Alice be held liable for trespass to chattels?

H. AN UMBRELLA INTENTIONAL TORT

The recently drafted Restatement, Third, of Torts (2010) includes the following section:

§ 5. Liability for Intentional Physical Harms

An actor who intentionally causes physical harm is subject to liability for that harm.

Comment:

a. *An umbrella rule.* The rule of liability in § 5 provides a framework that encompasses many of the specific torts described in much more detail in the Restatement, Second, of Torts. Among these specific torts in the Restatement, Second, are harmful battery (§ 13), trespass on land (§ 158), trespass to chattels (§ 217), and conversion by destruction or alteration (§ 226).

The general statement of liability in this section highlights the point that tort law treats the intentional infliction of physical harm differently than it treats the intentional causation of economic loss or the intentional infliction of emotional distress. In cases involving physical harm, proof of intent provides a basic case for liability, although various affirmative defenses may be available. However, as the focus shifts from physical harm to other forms of harm, the intent to cause harm may be an important but not a sufficient condition for liability. For example, . . . [w]hen the defendant either intentionally or recklessly causes the plaintiff to suffer emotional distress, to justify a recovery the plaintiff must further establish that the defendant's conduct is "extreme and outrageous" and that the plaintiff's emotional distress is "severe." See Restatement, Second, Torts § 46.

Is there value in having a broad umbrella rule? Can you think of physical harms that are not sufficiently covered by the existing intentional torts that we have studied? Is there any downside to the adoption of an umbrella intentional tort rule?

hypo 15

A, involved in a bitter argument with *B,* says, "I hope you drop dead." Upset by *A*'s words, *B* suffers a heart attack and dies. Has *A* committed an intentional tort?

hypo 16

A suffers from a heart condition and frequently takes nitroglycerin pills to open his arteries and relieve angina pain. *B*, *A*'s attendant, seeking to hasten *A*'s death, places a book on *A*'s night table blocking *A*'s view so that he cannot easily find his nitro pills. *A* awakes in the middle of the night suffering chest pain and cannot locate his pills. Minutes later he suffers a heart attack and dies. Has *B* committed an intentional tort?

I. THE MONSTER INTENTIONAL TORT

If you think you have seen everything in intentional torts, you are wrong. Litigation under the Alien Tort Statute (ATS) 28 U.S.C. § 1350 provides a forum for aliens to sue for what we can only label as monster intentional torts. Enacted in 1789 as part of the Judiciary Act, the entire ATS is only one cryptic sentence: "[t]he district courts shall have original jurisdiction of any civil action by an alien for a tort only, committed in violation of the law of nations or a treaty of the United States." While the ATS lay practically dormant for nearly two centuries — only two cases found ATS jurisdiction in 191 years after its enactment — in the last several decades courts have gradually expanded its scope. Abdullahi v. Pfizer, Inc., 562 F.3d 163 (2d Cir. 2009). The seminal Supreme Court case on the subject is Sosa v. Alvarez-Machain, 542 U.S. 692 (2004). Under *Sosa*, an alleged violation of the law of nations invokes ATS jurisdiction only if: 1) the action involves one of the three traditional law of nations violations that was recognized when the ATS was enacted — piracy, offenses against ambassadors, and violations of safe conducts; or 2) the action involves a present-day law of nations violation, which the Court defined as one that "rest[s] on a norm of international character accepted by the civilized world and defined with a specificity comparable to the features of the [aforementioned] 18th-century paradigms." *Sosa*, 542 U.S. at 724-725. The Court called for "judicial caution" in determining whether an action satisfies the latter category. In *Sosa*, the Court held that the illegal detention and transfer of a Mexican national from Mexico to the United States for prosecution did not violate a present-day law of nations and therefore the ATS did not confer jurisdiction over the alien's claim. For other claims that failed to establish ATS jurisdiction, *see* Kiobel v. Royal Dutch Petroleum Co., 621 F.3d 111 (2d Cir. 2010) (ATS did not authorize jurisdiction over claims against corporations, as customary international law rejects the notion of corporate liability); Taveras v. Taveraz, 477 F.3d 767 (6th Cir. 2007) (cross-border parental child abduction did not violate the law of nations). *But see* Romero v. Drummond Co., 552 F.3d 1303 (11th Cir. 2008) (recognizing ATS jurisdiction over a claim against a corporation). For an argument proposing liberal construction of the scope of the ATS's jurisdictional grant, *see* William R. Casto, *The Federal Courts' Protective Jurisdiction over Torts Committed in Violation of the Law of Nations*, 18 Conn. L. Rev. 467 (1986).

chapter 2

Privileges/Defenses

In Chapter 1, we considered the various intentional torts involving interference with persons and property, focusing on the elements that the plaintiff must prove to establish a claim. Many observers refer to the elements in Chapter 1 as making up the plaintiff's "prima facie case." Now we turn attention to special circumstances in which a defendant may escape liability for what would otherwise be a valid case for the plaintiff. The defenses that these circumstances provide are referred to as "privileges." In the eyes of the law, one is privileged to act in a certain way when one owes no legal duty to refrain from so acting. Strictly speaking, a person is legally privileged to eat cereal for breakfast, or to study torts in the evening. However, to use privilege this way seems odd. By common consent, the term "privilege" refers to conduct that would normally be prohibited, but, under the circumstances, is permitted. Thus, it is not peculiar to say that a particular actor was, under the circumstances, "privileged" to punch another in the nose, because normally one owes a duty to refrain from such acts of violence.

Treating privileges as affirmative defenses in connection with intentional torts helps to emphasize that they come into play at a second logical stage in the liability sequence, after the plaintiff has shown a prima facie entitlement at the first stage. Thus, for example, if a plaintiff claims that the defendant shot and wounded him (a battery) the defendant may assert the privilege of self-defense. The one exception to this neat compartmentalization is found in the first privilege we consider — consent. It will be recalled that some batteries are offensive in nature. When an actor kisses a stranger, for example, the intended contact may be offensive when judged against community mores. But when the stranger knowingly and freely consents, the contact no longer is offensive. In that instance, consent operates to eliminate the plaintiff's prima facie case — the offensiveness of the contact — rather than operating as a logically separate affirmative defense. In most jurisdictions the plaintiff bears the burden of proof to persuade the trier of fact of her nonconsent. Apart from that one exception, however, the privileges considered in this chapter function exclusively as affirmative defenses.

A. CONSENT

THE CORE CONCEPT OF CONSENT

At its core, the legal concept of consent is the same as the one we use in everyday life — one consents to the acts of another, or to the consequences of those acts, if one is subjectively willing for that conduct or those consequences to occur. Generally, a person communicates his consent. For instance, if *A* refrains from acting for fear of being liable for interfering with *B*'s legally protected interests, *B* may communicate his consent in order to induce *A* to act. But even if one's consent is not communicated, if a defendant can prove that the willing state of mind, in fact, existed at the time he acted, then the conduct may be legally privileged. The normative principle underlying consent-based privilege is *volenti non fit injuria*: to one who consents, no wrong is done. To some extent, the concept of consent in tort law merges with the notion that competent adults may enter contracts that diminish or eliminate legal rights they would otherwise enjoy. As you react to the cases in this section, ask yourself if the court could have reached the same result via the law of contracts.

O'BRIEN v. CUNARD STEAMSHIP CO.
28 N.E. 266 (Mass. 1891)

[The plaintiff brought an action against the defendant steamship company for harm allegedly caused in transit from Ireland to Boston by the wrongful acts of the defendant's servant, the ship's surgeon. Plaintiff's claim consisted of two counts, the first count for battery (the court uses the term "assault") and the second count for negligence. The court's treatment of the negligence count, which rested on allegations that the surgeon had employed substandard technique in performing a smallpox vaccination on the plaintiff, is not reproduced. At trial, plaintiff produced credible, though disputed, evidence that the vaccination had caused her to suffer skin eruptions and sickness. The trial court directed a verdict for the defendant steamship company and the plaintiff appealed.]

KNOWLTON, J.

This [appeal] presents [the] question [of] whether there was any evidence to warrant the jury in finding that the defendant, by any of its servants or agents, committed an assault on the plaintiff. . . . To sustain the first count, which was for an alleged assault, the plaintiff relied on the fact that the surgeon who was employed by the defendant vaccinated her on ship-board, while she was on her passage from Queenstown to Boston. On this branch of the case the question is whether there was any evidence that the surgeon used force upon the plaintiff against her will. In determining whether the act was lawful or unlawful, the surgeon's conduct must be considered in connection with the surrounding circumstances. If the plaintiff's behavior was such as to indicate consent on her part, he was justified in his act, whatever her unexpressed feelings may have been. In determining whether she consented, he could be guided only by her overt acts and the manifestations of her feelings. It is undisputed that at Boston there are strict quarantine regulations in regard to the examination of emigrants [sic], to see that they are protected from small-pox by vaccination, and that only those persons who hold a certificate from the medical officer of the steam-ship, stating that they are so protected, are permitted to land without detention in quarantine, or vaccination by the port physician. It appears that the defendant is accustomed to have its surgeons vaccinate all emigrants who desire it, and who are not protected by previous vaccination, and give them a certificate which is accepted at quarantine as evidence of their protection. Notices of the regulations at quarantine, and of the willingness of the ship's medical officer to vaccinate such as needed vaccination, were posted about the ship in various languages, and on the day when the operation was performed the surgeon had a right to presume that she and the other women who were vaccinated understood the importance and purpose of vaccination for those who bore no marks to show that they were protected. By the plaintiff's testimony, which, in this particular, is undisputed, it appears that about 200 women passengers were assembled below, and she understood from conversation with them that they were to be vaccinated; that she stood about 15 feet from the surgeon, and saw them form in a line, and pass in turn before him; that he "examined their arms, and, passing some of them by, proceeded to vaccinate those that had no mark;" that she did not hear him say anything to any of them; that upon being passed by they each received a card, and went on deck; that when her turn came she showed him her arm; he looked at it, and said there was no mark, and that she should be vaccinated; that she told him she had been vaccinated before, and it left no mark; "that he then said nothing; that he should vaccinate her again;" that she held up her arm to be vaccinated; that no one touched her; that she did not tell him she did not want to be vaccinated; and that she took the ticket which he gave her, certifying that he had vaccinated her, and used it at quarantine. She was one of a large number of women who were vaccinated on that occasion, without, so far as appears, a word of objection from any of them. They all indicated by their conduct that they desired to avail themselves of the provisions made for their benefit. There was nothing in the conduct of the plaintiff to indicate to the surgeon that she did not wish to obtain a card which would save her from detention at quarantine, and to be vaccinated, if necessary, for that purpose. Viewing his conduct in the light of the surrounding circumstances, it was lawful; and there was no evidence tending to show that it was not. The ruling of the court on this part of the case was correct. [The court never reached the negligence count, ruling that the surgeon's negligence, if any, could not be attributed to defendant Cunard. The judgment for the defendant was affirmed.]

hypo **17**

A, expecting to meet *B*, his wife, at a particular street corner, arrives to find *C* standing at the corner with her back turned toward him. *C* bears an incredibly close resemblance to *B*, even wearing a bright blue sports jacket exactly like the one that *B* often wears. *A* walks up behind *C* and kisses her on the back of the neck, believing her to be *B. C* screams and falls off the curb, suffering harm. If a jury finds *A*'s mistaken belief that he was kissing *B* to have been reasonable, has *A* committed a battery on *C?* Does the answer to this question depend on whether we follow the single or dual intent rule?

hypo 18

A is standing in line at a health clinic with *B*, his son, to have *B* vaccinated for chicken pox. As a result of a city-wide epidemic, the City Board of Health recommended that all persons who have never had chicken pox be vaccinated. *A* told his wife earlier in the day that it might not be a bad idea for him to be vaccinated as well since he never had chicken pox as a child and the same virus that causes chicken pox in children can cause shingles, a painful affliction, in adults. *C,* the clinic nurse administering vaccinations, quickly vaccinated both *A* and *B. A* gave no indication whatever to *C* that he wanted to be vaccinated. *C* admits that he vaccinated *A* without thinking about it. *A* admits that he wanted to be vaccinated, but had planned to ask *C* to do it after *C* vaccinated *B*. As a result of the vaccination, *A* has a serious allergic reaction resulting in paralysis. Does *A* have an action for battery against *C?*

APPEARANCES DO MATTER

While many cases involve the issue of whether a person subjectively consents in that the person desires that conduct, or consequences, occur, many involve the issue of whether a plaintiff's words or conduct reasonably caused a defendant to understand that the plaintiff consented. The Restatement, Second, of Torts § 892 affords the latter, apparent consent, the same weight as the former, actual consent. The Restatement, Second, of Torts defines consent in this way:

> ### § 892. Meaning of Consent
>
> (1) Consent is willingness in fact. It may be manifested by action or inaction and need not be communicated to the actor.
>
> (2) If words or conduct are reasonably understood by another to be intended as consent, they constitute apparent consent and are as effective as consent in fact.

Whether a party's conduct may reasonably be taken for consent depends on a case-by-case analysis of the context. In *Reavis v. Slominski*, for example, the plaintiff-employee claimed that her employer sexually assaulted her shortly after a New Year's Eve work party. 551 N.W.2d 528 (Neb. 1996). Defendant claimed that plaintiff apparently consented as a matter of law when she began to disrobe at his request. The Supreme Court of Nebraska upheld the jury verdict for the plaintiff, arguing that disrobing does not constitute apparent consent to sexual intercourse as a matter of law, where plaintiff initially said "No" to sexual advances and all other conduct suggested submission, rather than consent. In *Wulf v. Kunnath*, the same Nebraska court upheld a jury verdict in favor of the defendant-doctor who swatted a nurse on the back of the head. 827 N.W.2d 248 (Neb. 2013). As the court noted, "the conduct occurred over the noon hour while doctors and nurses were joking around," and the plaintiff and defendant had a "familial-like relationship." Id. at 254. These circumstances, as well as the fact that the defendant had thumped the nurse on prior occasions without offending her, were enough for the court to uphold the verdict that the nurse consented to the swat.

HACKBART v. CINCINNATI BENGALS, INC.
601 F.2d 516 (10th Cir. 1979)

WILLIAM E. DOYLE, Circuit Judge.

The question in this case is whether in a regular season professional football game an injury which is inflicted by one professional football player on an opposing player can give rise to liability in tort where the injury was inflicted by the intentional striking of a blow during the game.

The injury occurred in the course of a game between the Denver Broncos and the Cincinnati Bengals, which game was being played in Denver in 1973. The Broncos' defensive back, Dale Hackbart, was the recipient of the injury and the Bengals' offensive back, Charles "Booby" Clark, inflicted the blow which produced it.

By agreement the liability question was determined by the United States District Court for the District of Colorado without a jury. The judge resolved the liability issue in favor of the Cincinnati team and Charles Clark. Consistent with this result, final judgment was entered for Cincinnati and the appeal challenges this judgment. In essence the trial court's reasons for rejecting plaintiff's claim were that professional football is a species of warfare and that so much physical force is tolerated and the magnitude of the force exerted is so great that it renders injuries not actionable in court; that even intentional batteries are beyond the scope of the judicial process.

Clark was an offensive back and just before the injury he had run a pass pattern to the right side of the Denver Broncos' end zone. The injury flowed indirectly from this play. The pass was intercepted by Billy Thompson, a Denver free safety, who returned it to mid-field. The subject injury occurred as an aftermath of the pass play. As a consequence of the interception, the roles of Hackbart and Clark suddenly changed. Hackbart, who had been defending, instantaneously became an offensive player. Clark, on the other hand, became a defensive player. Acting as an offensive player, Hackbart attempted to block Clark by throwing his body in front of him. He thereafter remained on the ground. He turned, and with one knee on the ground, watched the play following the interception.

The trial court's finding was that Charles Clark, "acting out of anger and frustration, but without a specific intent to injure . . . stepped forward and struck a blow with his right forearm to the back of the kneeling plaintiff's head and neck with sufficient force to cause both players to fall forward to the ground." Both players, without complaining to the officials or to one another, returned to their respective sidelines since the ball had changed hands and the offensive and defensive teams of each had been substituted. Clark testified at trial that his frustration was brought about by the fact that his team was losing the game.

Due to the failure of the officials to view the incident, a foul was not called. However, the game film showed very clearly what had occurred. Plaintiff did not at the time report the happening to his coaches or to anyone else during the game. However, because of the pain which he experienced he was unable to play golf the next day. He did not seek medical attention, but the continued pain caused him to report this fact and the incident to the Bronco trainer who gave him treatment. Apparently he played on the specialty teams for two successive Sundays, but after that the Broncos released him on waivers. (He was in his thirteenth year as a player.) He sought medical help and it was then that it was discovered by the physician that he had a serious neck fracture injury.

Despite the fact that the defendant Charles Clark admitted that the blow which had been struck was not accidental, that it was intentionally administered, the trial court ruled as a matter of law that the game of professional football is basically a business which is violent in nature, and that the available sanctions are imposition of penalties and expulsion from the game. Notice was taken of the fact that many fouls are overlooked; that the game is played in an emotional and noisy environment; and that incidents such as that here complained of are not unusual.

The trial court spoke as well of the unreasonableness of applying the laws and rules which are a part of injury law to the game of professional football, noting the unreasonableness of holding that one player has a duty of care for the safety of others. He also talked about the concept of assumption of risk and contributory fault as applying and concluded that Hackbart had to recognize that he accepted the risk that he would be injured by such an act, . . .

The evidence at the trial uniformly supported the proposition that the intentional striking of a player in the head from the rear is not an accepted part of either the playing rules or the general customs of the game of professional football. The trial court, however, believed that the unusual nature of the case called for the consideration of underlying policy which it defined as common law principles which have evolved as a result of the case to case process and which necessarily affect behavior in various contexts. From these considerations the belief was expressed that even intentional injuries incurred in football games should be outside the framework of the law. The court recognized that the potential threat of legal liability has a significant deterrent effect, and further said that private civil actions constitute an important mechanism for societal control of human conduct. Due to the increase in severity of human conflicts, a need existed to expand the body of governing law more rapidly and with more certainty, but that this had to be accomplished by legislation and administrative regulation. The judge compared football to coal mining and railroading insofar as all are inherently hazardous. Judge Matsch said that in the case of football it was questionable whether social values would be improved by limiting the violence. Thus the district court's assumption was that Clark had inflicted an intentional blow which would ordinarily generate civil liability and which might bring about a criminal sanction as well, but that since it had occurred in the course of a football game, it should not be subject to the restraints of the law; that if it were it would place unreasonable impediments and restraints on the activity. The judge also pointed out that courts are ill-suited to decide the different social questions and to administer conflicts on what is much like a battlefield where the restraints of civilization have been left on the sidelines. . . .

Plaintiff, of course, maintains that tort law applicable to the injury in this case applies on the football field as well as in other places. On the other hand, plaintiff does not rely on the theory of negligence being applicable. This is in recognition of the fact that subjecting another to unreasonable risk of harm, the essence of negligence, is inherent in the game of football, for admittedly it is violent. Plaintiff maintains that in the area of contributory fault, a vacuum exists in relationship to intentional infliction of injury. Since negligence does not apply, contributory negligence is inapplicable. Intentional or reckless contributory fault could theoretically at least apply to infliction of injuries in reckless disregard of the rights of others. This has some similarity to contributory negligence and undoubtedly it would apply if the evidence would justify it. But it is highly questionable whether a professional football player consents or submits to injuries caused by conduct not within the rules, and there is no evidence which we have seen which shows this. However, the trial court did not consider this question and we are not deciding it.

Contrary to the position of the court then, there are no principles of law which allow a court to rule out certain tortious conduct by reason of general roughness of the game or difficulty of administering it.

Indeed, the evidence shows that there are rules of the game which prohibit the intentional striking of blows. Thus, Article 1, Item 1, Subsection C, provides that:

> All players are prohibited from striking on the head, face or neck with the heel, back or side of the hand, wrist, forearm, elbow or clasped hands.

Thus the very conduct which was present here is expressly prohibited by the rule which is quoted above.

The general customs of football do not approve the intentional punching or striking of others. That this is prohibited was supported by the testimony of all of the witnesses. They testified that the intentional striking of a player in the face or from the rear is prohibited by the playing rules as well as the general customs of the game. Punching or hitting with the arms is prohibited. Undoubtedly these restraints are intended to establish reasonable boundaries so that one football player cannot intentionally inflict a serious injury on another. Therefore, the notion is not correct that all reason has been abandoned, whereby the only possible remedy for the person who has been the victim of an unlawful blow is retaliation. . . .

In sum, having concluded that the trial court did not limit the case to a trial of the evidence bearing on defendant's liability but rather determined that as a matter of social policy the game was so violent and unlawful that valid lines could not be drawn, we take the view that this was not a proper issue for determination and that plaintiff was entitled to have the case tried on an assessment of his rights and whether they had been violated.

The trial court has heard the evidence and has made findings. The findings of fact based on the evidence presented are not an issue on this appeal. Thus, it would not seem that the court would have to repeat the areas of evidence that have already been fully considered. The need is for a reconsideration of that evidence in the light of that which is taken up by this court in its opinion. We are not to be understood as limiting the trial court's consideration of supplemental evidence if it deems it necessary.

The cause is reversed and remanded for a new trial in accordance with the foregoing views.

DIFFERENT VISIONS OF THE ROLE OF TORT LAW

As reflected in the decision of the court of appeals, the trial court in *Hackbart* had held that it was inappropriate for tort law to attempt to regulate the on-the-field behavior of professional football players, as violence is an integral part of the game to which players impliedly consent when they step onto the field. The trial judge, sitting as trier of fact, found that players are conditioned to maximize their violent inclinations, noting the testimony of one witness "that the pre-game psychological preparation should be designed to generate an emotion equivalent to that which would be experienced by a father whose family had been endangered by another driver who had attempted to force the family car off the edge of a mountain road. The precise pitch of motivation for players . . . should be the feeling of that father when . . . he is about to open the door to take revenge upon the person of the other driver." 435 F. Supp. 352, 355 (D. Colo. 1977). Acknowledging this pervasive culture of violence in professional football, the trial court determined as a matter of law that it would be very difficult for courts to differentiate between on-the-field incidents that are "fair play" and those that merit legal sanctions. In effect, according to the trial judge, when a player steps onto the field he consents as a matter of law to all violent contact that could be construed as part of the physical struggle commonly referred to as "professional football." Tort law should not second-guess the customs of that "sport."

The court of appeals held that the trial court went too far in deferring to the customs in the NFL, but it is unclear just how much weight should be given to the "professional sports" aspect on remand. Is that aspect of the case simply one factor to be weighed in the balance? Or should it be given no independent weight at all? One need not buy into the district judge's battlefield metaphor ("courts are ill-suited to decide the different social questions and to administer conflicts on what is much like a battlefield where the restraints of civilization have been left on the sidelines") to believe that courts are not in a good position to differentiate between permitted, or at least expected, contact, and actionable batteries. Considering a different sport, baseball fans know there are numerous unwritten rules of baseball, some of which make the violator liable to retaliation. "Don't show up the pitcher" is one of those rules. When Jose Bautista flipped his bat in triumph after a game-winning home run to win a tied playoff series between the Toronto Blue Jays and the Texas Rangers in 2015, it was widely expected that he had exposed himself to getting hit by a pitcher from the Rangers the next time the two teams faced each other. Should an intentional hit to enforce the unwritten "code" of baseball constitute a tort? Is tort law needed to prevent the vengeance used to enforce unwritten codes from spiraling out of control? When the Rangers and Blue Jays played again in 2016, Bautista was hit by a pitch, as expected. But in retaliation for this (which, arguably, he had coming to him), he slid hard into Rangers second baseman Roughned Odor. Odor then punched Bautista and set off a bench-clearing brawl. Tort law may be imperfect, but honor codes and blood feuds are also imperfect means of social control.

SHOULD THE TEAMS, THEMSELVES, BE LIABLE?

Violence in sports continues to be as problematic today as when *Hackbart* was decided. An especially troubling incident occurred in February 2000 when Boston Bruins hockey player Marty McSorley deliberately struck Vancouver Canucks player Donald Brashear in the temple with his stick, knocking Brashear unconscious. McSorley was eventually found guilty of criminal assault by a court in British Columbia, a rare example of criminal law intervening in sports altercations. As the owners and coaches of professional teams often encourage such violent behavior in their players — and derive a financial benefit from doing so — one commentator has suggested that the teams themselves should be held liable for torts committed by players during the course of a game. *See* Steven I. Rubin, Note, *The Vicarious Liability of Professional Sports Teams for on-the-Field Assaults Committed by Their Players,* 1 Va. J. Sports & L. 266 (1999).

AMATEUR AND RECREATIONAL SPORTS

The issue of implied consent exemplified by *Hackbart* plays a role not only in the highly structured and intense setting of professional sports, but also in the context of amateur sports activities — indeed, even in presumably friendly backyard games. However persuasive one finds the notion that professional athletes impliedly consent to a host of violent acts when they step onto the field, as the trial court in *Hackbart* did (and perhaps the Court of Appeals, as well, at least to some extent), one might wonder whether there doesn't remain an important place for tort law in nonprofessional sporting contexts. For example, should the rules and customs of the game override potential tort liability to any extent in college football? What about high school? Athletes at these levels are similarly encouraged and rewarded for their aggressiveness. Should the fact that they are not playing for a paycheck make a significant difference? For example, in Avila v. Citrus Community College District, 131 P.3d 383 (Cal. 2006), plaintiff claimed that in a college baseball game the opposing pitcher intentionally threw a "beanball" at him, hitting him in the head. The provocation for this was to get back for a ball thrown at a teammate in

---

authors' dialogue 6

AARON: After reading the notes you drafted after the *Hackbart* case I sense that you agree with the court's decision. Am I reading you right?

JIM: I'm not sure that you are. I am ambivalent about *Hackbart*. The defendant's hit on the plaintiff just after the whistle had blown leaves me uneasy. But, I do agree that pulling a knife on an opponent is not covered by implied consent. There have to be some limitations on craziness.

AARON: Come on, Jim. This is no different than the arena in Rome with the gladiators and the lions. The folks come out to see a good brawl. If they don't see at least one good one in a game they believe they've been cheated and should get their money back. Violent sports appeal to blood lust and the players that indulge in them get paid good money to put on the show. I wouldn't be surprised if some of the brawls are actually staged for the benefit of the patrons.

JIM: You're wrong, they are not staged. The anger is very real and the players get out of control. Somebody must put the brakes on them.

AARON: But why should courts have to draw the line of what is or is not appropriate behavior? These are professionals who know the nature of the game. Let them

---

the previous inning. Intentionally throwing at a batter's head violates both Major League Baseball rules and those of the National Collegial Athletic Association. The California Supreme Court reversed its intermediate appellate court and affirmed the decision of the trial court dismissing the plaintiff's claim of battery. The court recounted the history of the "beanball" as a tactic to retaliate and to upset opposing hitters and opined that the dangers of being hit by a pitch often thrown at speeds approaching 100 miles per hour are well known. It then concluded that "the baseball player who steps to the plate consents to the possibility the opposing pitcher may throw near or at him. The complaint established Avila voluntarily participated in the baseball game; as such his consent would bar any battery claim as a matter of law." Can *Avila* be reconciled with *Hackbart*?

At the far end of the spectrum of relative professionalism lie cases in which the sporting participants are neither professionals nor systematically conditioned for aggressiveness — games among friends. Should courts in these contexts hold that the participants impliedly consent to a range of violent contact, even if that range is narrower than the one in *Hackbart*? In Knight v. Jewett, 834 P.2d 696 (Cal. 1992), the Supreme Court of California held such backyard games to the same basic standard as *Hackbart*, holding that participants in a pickup touch football game impliedly consent to violent contact when they step onto the field — but not to "conduct [that is] so reckless as to be totally outside the range of the ordinary activity involved in the sport." *Id.* at 712. The question left to the courts is whether and to what extent to include increasingly violent levels of conduct within the "ordinary activity" of a sport as one moves from case to case across the spectrum of professionalism.

decide in advance, by contract, the kinds of behavior that are out of bounds and then provide for appropriate sanctions. They could establish a schedule of damages when a player has violated the stated norms. Why should courts be put upon to straighten out the mess? From my point of view, I would say a plague on both their houses. Keep these rotten cases out of the court system. It is like asking the court to decide what is appropriate behavior in an insane asylum filled to the brim with psychotics.

JIM: Aaron, transferring the responsibility for working out the details of acceptable conduct to the football industry will not work. I would much rather have some societal input into the decision making than abdicate all the line-drawing to an interest group.

BRAD: I think both of you are wrong. There is a gray area where Aaron's argument is convincing. But I don't think we need extreme conduct to justify non-consent. I admit that the defendant's conduct in *Hackbart* is close question. But I would not lose sleep if Bobby Clark has to face the music. The analogy to bench clearing brawls does not work. They usually invoke some pushing and shoving. Slamming *Hackbart* from behind and causing serious neck injury may be beyond the pale. Let the jury decide.

The issue in many sports-related and recreation-related injury cases is whether the defendant intentionally or unintentionally caused the injuries. Plaintiffs often sue under both battery and negligence theories of recovery. For example, the plaintiff in *Knight* claimed that the defendant intentionally injured her, thus suing under battery; but she also claimed under negligence, arguing that even if the defendant unintentionally injured her he should be liable for acting unreasonably. Courts dealing with the negligence issue often consider whether the injured person assumed the risks of possible injuries by agreeing to participate. Courts apply this "assumption of the risk" doctrine, in sports and recreation cases, which you will learn more about in Chapter 8, much as courts apply the consent concept in connection with intentional tort claims.

hypo **19**

Sam Spot, a pitcher for the St. Louis Blues, a major league baseball team, has had an ongoing feud with Bobby Batt, an outfielder with the Cincinnati Greens. Batt has consistently bad-mouthed Spot to the press, saying, among other things, that Spot's fastball travels so slow that he could autograph it on the way to the plate. The day before the game in question Batt told a reporter that Spot was a crybaby always seeking to make an excuse every time he loses a game. The story was featured on sports pages throughout the country. Spot had enough. The inning before he was to face Batt in a game against the Greens, Spot told a teammate, "I am going to hit Batt straight between the eyes. That should put an end to his filthy mouth." Spot threw a very accurate beanball that hit Batt smack in the face. Batt suffered a brain concussion and multiple broken bones in his face. The beanball put an end to Batt's career. Does Batt have an action in battery against Spot?

Watch the video of Pittsburgh Steelers wide receiver Antonio Brown inflicting what some have classified as a karate kick on Cleveland Browns punter Spencer Lanning: http://www.nfl.com/videos/cleveland-browns/0ap3000000390434/Antonio-Brown-kicks-Spencer-Lanning-in-the-face. The NFL fined Brown $8,200 for "unnecessary roughness" following this event. Under *Hackbart*, has Brown committed a tort against Lanning?

CHRISTMAN v. DAVIS
889 A.2d 746 (Vt. 2005)

DOOLEY, J.

Plaintiff Paul Christman appeals a superior court order granting defendants summary judgment on his claim of medical battery. Plaintiff claims . . . that defendant periodontist performed a surgical procedure for which plaintiff did not consent and therefore defendant committed a battery. We affirm.

Plaintiff consulted defendant Gordon Davis, a periodontist, to treat his gum recession and root exposure. Defendant discussed procedures to obtain root coverage including a tissue graft, and plaintiff consented to this procedure. A tissue graft involves making vertical incisions around the exposed root; the incision is made to free gingival tissue and then donor tissue from the palate is grafted onto the root. After administering a local anaesthetic, defendant began the procedure and determined that instead he would perform a flap procedure. This procedure follows the same preliminary step as the graft, but after incision, the periodontist applies a protein, Emdogain, to the gum to help it adhere to the tooth, and no graft is made. After surgery, plaintiff was surprised that he did not receive a graft. He was upset to learn later that the procedure did not achieve full results and that he would need to undergo a tissue graft.

Plaintiff sued defendants for dental malpractice, lack of informed consent, and battery. Plaintiff eventually dismissed the malpractice and lack of informed consent claims, and proceeded solely on the battery claim. . . . The court concluded, however, that defendant performed surgery on an area of the body to which plaintiff consented, and choosing to perform a less-invasive procedure did not constitute battery. . . .

Plaintiff bases his . . . claim in battery, which is an intentional act that results in harmful contact with another. Restatement (Second) of Torts § 13 (1965) [hereinafter Restatement]; Kent v. Katz, 146 F. Supp. 2d 450, 463 (D. Vt. 2001). In a medical context, a health care provider commits battery if the provider performs a procedure for which the patient has not given consent. Duncan v. Scottsdale Med. Imaging, Ltd., . . . 70 P.3d 435, 438-39, (Ariz. 2003). Generally, consent to particular conduct, or "substantially the same conduct," bars recovery for a harmful invasion. Restatement § 892A(2)(b); Godwin v. Danbury Eye Physicians & Surgeons, P.C., . . . 757 A.2d 516, 520 (Conn. 2000) (quoting Restatement § 892A(2)(b)). . . .

At the outset, it is important to distinguish between cases involving no consent and those involving a lack of informed consent. Generally, battery occurs only when a physician performs an operation for which there was no consent. If the patient does provide consent for the procedure employed, but receives inadequate disclosures of the alternatives and foreseeable risks and benefits of the alternatives, liability must be based on lack of informed consent, and a claim of medical malpractice in failing to provide the necessary disclosures . . . . This difference, however, can be "slippery." D. Dobbs, The Law of Torts § 103, at 243 (2001). The California Supreme Court explained the requirements of each claim well in *Cobbs v. Grant*:

> The battery theory should be reserved for those circumstances when a doctor performs an operation to which the patient has not consented. When the patient gives permission to perform one type of treatment and the doctor performs another, the requisite element of deliberate intent to deviate from the consent given is present. However, when the patient consents to certain treatment and the doctor performs that treatment but an undisclosed inherent complication with a low probability occurs, no intentional deviation from the consent given appears; rather, the doctor in obtaining consent may have failed to meet his due care duty to disclose pertinent information. In that situation the action should be pleaded in negligence. . . . 502 P.2d 1, 8 (1972).

[The court's discussion of informed consent is omitted. The court concludes that the plaintiff's claim for battery is not governed by the Vermont statute dealing with informed consent.]

Having determined that plaintiff's battery claim is not preempted by statute, we consider whether defendants are entitled to summary judgment in this case, as the superior court held. In analyzing this question, we note the parties substantially disagreed as to what disclosures defendant made to plaintiff. Plaintiff's theory is, as he expressed in his affidavit, that defendant "did not discuss with me any other or different procedure" than the tissue graft procedure and plaintiff consented only to the tissue graft procedure. Defendant disputes this recitation of events.

Based on defendant's statement of undisputed facts and plaintiff's response to the statement, the parties are in agreement on certain key factual issues. In defendant's first statement of undisputed material facts, defendant stated that "the coronally repositioned flap is a less invasive procedure," and plaintiff did not dispute that statement. In fact, plaintiff stated in his affidavit that he would not have consented to the flap procedure "because I was more interested in the likelihood of a successful outcome than I was in the degree of invasiveness of the procedure." In his second statement of undisputed material facts, defendant stated "[a] periodontist must perform the steps of a flap procedure in order to determine whether there is sufficient tissue of adequate quality to perform the graft." Although plaintiff answered that the statement "does not concern the treatment to which Plaintiff gave his consent," he added that he didn't dispute the defendant's statement "as a matter of general periodontics."

Based on the undisputed facts in the record, plaintiff's claim is that defendant did less than he promised — that is, defendant did not go further and do the tissue graft — and that was why the procedure was unsuccessful. We agree with the trial court that plaintiff does not have a battery claim and conclude that summary judgment was properly granted for defendant.

The central issue is whether plaintiff consented to the procedure that was performed so that he cannot prove an essential element of battery. Effective consent must be "to the particular conduct, or to substantially the same conduct." Restatement § 892A(2)(b). Consequently, "where a doctor obtains consent of the patient to perform one type of treatment and subsequently performs a substantially different treatment for which consent was not obtained, there is a clear case of battery."

In essence, this is a case in which the medical professional did a less-extensive operation than that to which the patient consented, taking steps the professional would have taken in the more extensive operation. Under the elements of battery described above, courts have dismissed medical battery claims where a surgeon chooses to perform a less-extensive operation than that discussed with the patient. . . . *Conte v. Girard Orthopaedic Surgeons Med. Group, Inc.*, 132 Cal. Rptr. 2d 855, 860-61 (Ct. App. 2003) (concluding that where doctor decided during surgery not to repair patient's shoulder, no battery occurred because he did less than he was authorized to do); . . . . In doing so, one court explained: "We see no policy reason to extend the law of battery to these circumstances where the treatment was within the bounds of [the patient's] consent. . . . If doctors were subject to liability for battery in such situations, it would deter them from freely exercising their medical judgment." *Conte*, 132 Cal. Rptr. 2d at 860-61. We agree with the rationale of these decisions. . . .

Affirmed.

FOOD FOR THOUGHT

Assuming that a jury in *Christman* were to believe plaintiff's version of the facts, i.e., that he consented only to the more extensive "tissue graft procedure" and that he was not concerned that it was a highly invasive procedure, why is the "half measure" operation not an unconsented-to battery? For a case finding battery against a surgeon where patient agreed to a "total hip replacement" but the surgeon merely inserted a pin in the patient's femur, *see* Cathemer v. Hunter, 558 P.2d 975 (Ariz. Ct. App. 1976).

The classic case of overreaching is Mohr v. Williams, 104 N.W. 12 (Minn. 1905). Plaintiff agreed to surgery on her right ear. While the patient was under anesthesia the surgeon discovered that the right ear did not require surgery but the left ear did. Without waking the patient, the doctor performed the necessary surgery. Plaintiff sued for battery and won. On appeal the court affirmed the judgment for plaintiff. *But see* Kennedy v. Parrott, 90 S.E.2d 754 (N.C. 1956). In that case plaintiff agreed to undergo an appendectomy. While the surgeon was operating, he found an enlarged ovarian cyst, which he punctured. It seems that when puncturing the cyst the surgeon inadvertently (not negligently) cut a blood vessel causing the plaintiff to develop phlebitis in her left leg. The court was not sympathetic to the plaintiff's claim that the surgeon had exceeded his consent by operating on the cyst. The doctor had no reason to expect to find the cyst and it would have been foolhardy not to puncture the cyst, which was directly in sight. Exposing the patient to a second surgery would have created unwarranted risk. Can you reconcile Mohr and Kennedy?

Murphy v. Implicito, M.D., 920 A.2d 678 (N.J. Super. Ct. App. Div. 2007), raises a novel question as to the damages to be assessed when a defendant exceeds his consent. In that case plaintiff underwent an operation on his spine but told the doctor that under no circumstances was the doctor to implant cadaver bone in his spine. The surgery was unsuccessful and the implanted bone did not graft. Later x-rays revealed that the doctor had implanted cadaver bone. No expert opined that the use of cadaver bone caused the failure of the graft. On appeal from the trial judge's finding that plaintiff was only entitled to damages related to use of the cadaver bone, the New Jersey Superior Court agreed that plaintiff was clearly entitled to damages for battery arising from use of the cadaver bone and was not entitled to recovery for all damages arising from the failed surgery. However, the burden of segregating the battery damages from the failed surgery damages was on the defendant-surgeon.

DID I REALLY CONSENT?

In Perry v. Shaw, 106 Cal. Rptr. 2d 70 (Cal. Ct. App. 2001), a patient who had lost a significant amount of weight went to the defendant-doctor to have excess loose skin removed from her thighs, back, arms, and stomach. At the first visit, the defendant discussed a breast enlargement procedure whereby he would take the excess skin from the aforementioned areas and increase the bust size. Plaintiff told the defendant that she did not want a breast enlargement. In a follow-up visit, the defendant again discussed a breast procedure (this time a breast lift), and the plaintiff again declined. On the day of the surgery, the doctor presented the plaintiff with a consent form that included consent to a breast enlargement. She had refused to sign the consent form on two separate occasions. However, after being heavily medicated, she ultimately signed the form. The doctor performed the breast enlargement, along with surgical procedures expressly requested. Both the jury and the appellate court rejected the defendant's consent defense.

Similarly, in Hensley v. Scokin, 148 S.W.3d 352 (Tenn. Ct. App. 2003), plaintiff who had to undergo a hysterectomy informed her anesthesiologist, Dr. Scokin, that because of a preexisting problem with her temporomandibular joint (TMJ), he should use nasal intubation instead of oral intubation. She provided Dr. Scokin with x-rays demonstrating her TMJ problem. She informed her gynecologist and two hospital employees that only nasal intubation should be used. While she was on the gurney in her hospital gown, she gave the x-rays to Dr. Scokin and explained that she would need nasal intubation. Scokin cast the x-rays aside and told her that he would decide what type of intubation she would receive. Scokin gave her oral intubation and plaintiff suffered serious injuries to her lower teeth, facial pain, and damages to the bone structure of the TMJ. At trial Scokin moved for summary judgment because plaintiff had proffered no expert testimony that he had deviated from accepted standards of medical care. Plaintiff's contention was that her claim was predicated on a theory of battery and that no expert testimony was necessary to support that claim. The trial court disagreed and granted the defendant's motion for summary judgment. On appeal the court held that the fact that the plaintiff did not abort the surgery when lying on the gurney after the defendant told her that he would decide how to intubate her was not dispositive on the issue of her consent. The court reversed the summary judgment saying that there was a material issue of fact to whether the oral intubation amounted to an unconsented-to battery.

Many health care providers address the issue of informed consent by requiring patients to sign written consent forms that outline the risks associated with proposed treatments. By signing the contract, the patient agrees to undergo the procedure and acknowledges that he is aware of the risks associated therewith. Accordingly, the realm of informed consent offers one of the starkest examples of overlap between tort and contract jurisprudence. Courts frequently must determine the weight that should be afforded such contracts: Does the existence of such an agreement conclusively bar all claims on the part of the patient for lack of informed consent, or is the contract merely one factor for the court to consider in determining whether the patient's consent to treatment was truly informed? Most courts adopt the latter approach, refusing to give effect to such contracts where evidence indicates that they were accompanied by less than adequate oral disclosure by the physician dealing one-on-one with the patient. For example, in Hondroulis v. Schumacher, 553 So. 2d 398 (La. 1988), the Supreme Court of Louisiana held that a patient-physician contract creates a presumption of informed consent, which can be rebutted at trial via evidence that the doctor failed adequately to disclose to the patient the risks associated with treatment.

The plaintiff did not fare so well in Bundrick v. Stewart, 114 P.3d 1204 (Wash. Ct. App. 2005). Plaintiff, Lori Bundrick, had undergone a tubal ligation to prevent pregnancy. When she and her second husband wished to conceive a child, she attempted to reverse the tubal ligation through a procedure called tubal reanastomosis. Dr. Stewart was to perform the surgery at Swedish Hospital. About a week before the operation, Bundrick met with Stewart, who told her that a resident would be present during the surgery. Bundrick asked, "They [the residents] are not going to do my surgery, are they?" and Stewart responded, "[N]o, I will do it all. They are just here to observe." Bundrick then signed a consent form. It did not indicate that a resident would participate in the surgery. It did, however, contain the following statement:

> I, the undersigned, hereby *consent to all medical treatment or hospital services performed or prescribed by/or at the direction of the attending physician.* . . .

During the surgery Dr. Stewart was assisted by Tarun Jain, a third-year resident at the hospital. Jain performed several tasks during the surgery at Dr. Stewart's direction and under his supervision. It turned out that Bundrick's fallopian tubes could not be reattached and with the agreement of Bundrick's husband, the rea-nastomosis was aborted. However, during surgery Stewart discovered a tear in the mesentery lining of Bundrick's bowel, which he and the resident Jain attempted to repair. The repair job did not go well and Bundrick suffered massive infections in her bowels and had to undergo several painful surgeries. Stewart and Bundrick settled their lawsuit but Bundrick sued Swedish Hospital and the University of Washington (who supervised the resident Tarun Jain). The claim was for outright battery since Stewart had promised that no resident would operate on Bundrick. The court found that Bundrick had signed the broad consent form allowing ser-vices to be performed by or at the direction of the attending physician. Once broad consent is given, the patient must communicate her limitation. *But see* Perna v. Pirozzi, M.D., 457 A.2d 431 (N.J. 1983) (patient specified one member of a medical group to do his surgery but surgery was performed by another member of the group; court reversed jury verdict and remanded to try the case on grounds of medical battery). The issue of "ghost surgery" arises with some frequency. In teaching hospitals with strong residency programs it is common for residents to assist in surgery under supervision of the experienced surgeon. Consent forms (rarely read carefully by patients) often provide that the primary surgeon may be "assisted" by others.

DE MAY v. ROBERTS
9 N.W. 146 (Mich. 1881)

MARSTON, C.J.

The declaration in this case in the first count sets forth that the plaintiff was at a time and place named a poor married woman, and being confined in child-bed and a stranger, employed in a professional capacity defendant De May who was a physician; that defendant visited the plaintiff as such, and against her desire and intending to deceive her wrongfully, etc., introduced and caused to be present at the house and lying-in room of the plaintiff and while she was in the pains of parturition the defendant Scattergood, who intruded upon the privacy of the plaintiff, indecently, wrongfully and unlawfully laid hands upon and assaulted her, the said Scattergood, which was well known to defendant De May, being a young unmarried man, a stranger to the plaintiff and utterly ignorant of the practice of medicine, while the plaintiff believed that he was an assistant physician, a competent and proper person to be present and to aid her in her extremity.

The second and third counts while differing in form set forth a similar cause of action. [The case was tried to a jury, who returned a verdict for the plaintiff. The trial court entered judgment on the verdict and the defendant appealed.]

The evidence on the part of the plaintiff tended to prove the allegations of the declaration. On the part of the defendants evidence was given tending to prove that Scattergood very reluctantly accompanied Dr. De May at the urgent request of the latter; that the night was a dark and stormy one, the roads over which they had to travel in getting to the house of the plaintiff were so bad that a horse could not be rode or driven over them; that the doctor was sick and very much fatigued from overwork, and therefore asked the defendant Scattergood to accompany and assist him in carrying a lantern, umbrella and certain articles deemed necessary upon such occasions; that upon arriving at the house of the plaintiff the doctor knocked, and when the door was opened by the husband of the plaintiff, De May said to him, "that I had fetched a friend along to help carry my things;" he, plaintiff's husband, said all right, and seemed to be perfectly satisfied. They were bid to enter, treated kindly and no objection whatever made to the presence of defendant Scattergood. That while there Scattergood, at Dr. De May's request, took hold of plaintiff's hand and held her during a paroxysm of pain, and that both of the defendants in all respects throughout acted in a proper and becoming manner actuated by a sense of duty and kindness.

Some preliminary questions were raised during the progress of the trial which may first be considered. The plaintiff when examined as a witness was asked, what idea she entertained in reference to Scattergood's character and right to be in the house during the time he was there, and answered that she thought he was a student or a physician. To this there could be no good legal objection. It was not only important to know the character in which Scattergood went there, but to learn what knowledge the plaintiff had upon that subject. It was not claimed that the plaintiff or her husband, who were strangers in that vicinity, had ever met Scattergood before this time or had any knowledge or information concerning him beyond what they obtained on that evening, and it was claimed by the defendant that both the plaintiff and her husband must have known, from certain ambiguous expressions used, that he was not a physician. We are of opinion that the plaintiff and her husband had a right to presume that a practicing physician would not, upon an occasion of that character, take with him and introduce into the house, a young man in no way, either by education or otherwise, connected with the medical profession; and that something more clear and certain as to his non-professional character would be required to put the plaintiff and her husband upon their guard, or remove such presumption, than the remark made by De May that he had brought a friend along to help carry his things. . . .

A few facts which were undisputed may assist in more clearly presenting the remaining question. Upon the morning of January 3d Dr. De May was called to visit the plaintiff professionally which he did at her house. This house was 14 by 16 feet. A partition ran partly across one end thus forming a place for a bed or bedroom, but there was no door to this bedroom. Next to this so-called bedroom, and between the partition and side of the house, there was what is known and designated as a bed sink, here there was a bed with a curtain in front of it, and it was in this bed the doctor found Mrs. Roberts when he made his first visit. On their way to the house that night De May told Scattergood, who knew that the plaintiff was about to be confined, "how the house was; that she was in the bed sink lock, and there was a curtain in front of her, and told him he need not see her at all." When the defendants got to the house they found Mrs. Roberts "had moved from the bed sink and was lying on the lounge near the stove." I now quote further from the testimony of Dr. De May as to what took place: "I made an examination of Mrs. Roberts and found no symptoms of labor at all, any more than there was the previous morning. I told them that I had been up several nights and was tired and would like to lie down awhile; previous to this, however, some one spoke about supper, and supper was got and Scattergood and myself eat supper, and then went to bed. I took off my pants and had them hung up by the stove to dry; Scattergood also laid down with his clothes on. We lay there an hour or more, and Scattergood shook me and informed me that they had called me and wanted me. Scattergood got my pants and then went and sat down by the stove and placed his feet on a pile of wood that lay beside the stove, with his face towards the wall of the house and his back partially toward the couch on which Mrs. Roberts was lying. I made an examination and found that the lady was having labor pains. Her husband stood at her head to assist her; Mrs. Parks upon one side, and I went to the foot of the couch. During her pains Mrs. Roberts had kicked Mrs. Parks in the pit of the stomach, and Mrs. Parks got up and went out doors, and while away and about the time she was coming in, Mrs. Roberts was subjected to another labor pain and commenced rocking herself and throwing her arms, and I said catch her, to Scattergood, and he jumped right up and came over to her and caught her by the hand and staid there a short time, and then Mrs. Parks came up and took her place again, and Scattergood got up and went and took his place again, back by the stove. In a short time the child was born. Scattergood took no notice of her while sitting by the stove. The child was properly cared for; Mrs. Roberts was properly cared for, dressed and carried and placed in bed. I left some medicine to be given her in case she should suffer from pains."

Dr. De May therefore took an unprofessional young unmarried man with him, introduced and permitted him to remain in the house of the plaintiff, when it was apparent that he could hear at least, if not see all that was said and done, and as the jury must have found, under the instructions given, without either the plaintiff or her husband having any knowledge or reason to believe the true character of such third party. It would be shocking to our sense of right, justice and propriety to doubt even but that for such an act the law would afford an ample remedy. To the plaintiff the occasion was a most sacred one and no one had a right to intrude unless invited or because of some real and pressing necessity which it is not pretended existed in this case. The plaintiff had a legal right to the privacy of her apartment at such a time, and the law secures to her this right by requiring others to observe it, and to abstain from its violation. The fact that at the time, she consented to the presence of Scattergood supposing him to be a physician, does not preclude her from maintaining an action and recovering substantial damages upon afterwards ascertaining his true character. In obtaining admission at such a time and under such circumstances without fully disclosing his true character, both parties were guilty of deceit, and the wrong thus done entitles the injured party to recover the damages afterwards sustained, from shame and mortification upon discovering the true character of the defendants. . . .

It follows therefore that the judgment must be affirmed with costs.

CONSENT INVALIDATED BY FRAUD

The *De May* court held that the defendants procured the plaintiff's consent by means of fraudulent, deceitful conduct. However, this nineteenth-century court's decision holding the good-natured doctor and his well-meaning companion liable for deceit may strike some contemporary students as unduly harsh. Comfort may be found in the realization that most examples of deceit-induced consent are more clear cut than that found in *De May*. For example, in Bowman v. Home Life Insurance Co., 243 F.2d 331 (3d Cir. 1957), an insurance company employee falsely represented himself to be a physician and conducted intimate medical examinations of two women seeking to purchase life insurance. On appeal, the court determined that the women's consent to this examination was vitiated because the defendant had procured their acquiescence through fraudulent misrepresentations concerning his status as a doctor. *See also* Sanchez-Scott v. Alza Pharmaceuticals, 103 Cal. Rptr. 2d 410 (Cal. Ct. App. 2001) (pharmaceutical salesman could be held liable for invasion of privacy for assisting doctor in a breast exam). According to the Restatement, Second, of Torts § 892B(2), the misrepresentation must be about something that affects the intrinsic nature and quality of the invasion or the harm. Misrepresentations about collateral facts will not invalidate consent. For instance, if a researcher falsely promises a patient that the patient will be paid $20 to be part of a medical experiment, but in fact he is paid nothing, most courts will not invalidate consent. Should courts require a doctor to notify patients that he suffers from a cocaine addiction? No, according to Albany Urology Clinic, P.C. v. Cleveland, 528 S.E.2d 777 (Ga. 2000); Rice v. Brakel, M.D., 310 P.3d 16 (Ariz. Ct. App. 2013) (same). Both of these cases rejected the plaintiffs' claims of medical battery. *But see* Hidding v. Williams, 578 So. 2d 1192 (La. Appt. Ct.) (1991) (failure to inform patient that surgeon was an alcoholic supported trial judges finding of lack of informed consent).

Related issues arise when news reporters misrepresent their intentions in order to gain access to, and film, a person's property. In one such case, a plaintiff sued for trespass after employees of a media corporation falsified employment applications to gain access and film plaintiff's food handling practices. Food Lion v. Capital Cities, 194 F.3d 505 (4th Cir. 1999). After the trial court dismissed the claim, the court of appeals ruled that plaintiff stated a cause of action. *See contra* Desnick v. American Broadcasting Co., 44 F.3d 1345 (7th Cir. 1995) (producer who told plaintiff that he would not use hidden cameras or ambush interviewees, but decided to do both, did not commit trespass because there was not an interference with land); Am. Transmission, Inc. v. Channel 7 of Detroit, Inc., 609 N.W.2d 607 (Mich. Ct. App. 2000) (journalist who posed as a customer while secretly recording a transmission repair shop's vehicle assessment in order to expose the shop charging customers for unnecessary repairs did not commit trespass because the journalist did not invade the shop's property interest).

hypo **20**

A, knowing he has a sexually transmitted disease, has mutually consented-to sex with *B* after telling her, in response to her query, that he does not have a sexually transmitted disease. Both *A* and *B* are in their mid-20s. *B* does not contract the disease, but, upon learning of *A*'s lie, sues *A* for battery. *B* argues that *A* fraudulently induced her to consent. Would a court invalidate the consent? Has *A* committed a battery on *B*?

hypo 21

Rose, who is very particular about who cuts her hair, will only go to stylists who have been certified as "Grade A." Grade A means the stylist scored in the top 10% of his/her certification class. Roger advertises himself as Grade A, although he actually scored in the bottom 10% of his certification class. Rose gets a haircut from Roger because she believes he is Grade A. She later learns that he is not. Is Roger liable for battery? What if he had butchered the haircut, and his poor performance could be traced to his low certification scores?

CONSENT INVALIDATED BY DURESS

That consent should be invalidated by duress is fairly straightforward and intuitively satisfying, certainly in cases in which defendants threaten their victims with physical harm. Consider a situation in which *A*, holding a gun to *B*'s head, tells *B* that, unless *B* submits to a certain contract, *A* will shoot him. *B* is a sober, reasonable adult who fully understands the consequences of consenting. Courts (rightly) invalidate such consent, even though it is offered by an otherwise reliable, competent person. Indeed, courts also reasonably invalidate consent given in order to protect a loved one from physical harm. *See* Restatement, Second, of Torts § 58 cmt. *a*, illus. 1 (1965) ("*A* points a revolver which *B* believes to be loaded at *C*, *B*'s child, and threatens to shoot *C* if *B* does not submit to degrading familiarities. *B* submits thereto to save her child. *A* is subject to liability to *B*."). However, questions do arise as to exactly which sorts of pressure courts will recognize as giving rise to duress such as will vitiate consent.

Determining whether a defendant's conduct constitutes legal duress can be challenging. What kind of threatening conduct on the part of the aggressor is sufficient to cause a court to take notice? In Hutchison v. Brookshire Bros., Ltd., 205 F. Supp. 2d 629 (E.D. Tex. 2002), a customer of a gas station brought an action, inter alia, against a police officer for intentional infliction of emotional distress and assault and battery after the officer refused to let the plaintiff leave the gas station until he siphoned, by sucking through one end of a garden hose, ten gallons of gasoline from his car. (The plaintiff had received more gasoline than he asked for, and lacked funds to pay for the overage.) The police officer allegedly placed his hand over his gun holster as he told the plaintiff that he'd better suck and siphon $10.63 worth of gasoline or come with him. The district court rejected the defendant's consent-based motion for summary judgment, holding that a jury could find that the customer acted under duress.

Courts, however, have not been willing to find duress in cases of more subtle forms of pressure. For example, in Wende C. v. United Methodist Church, 776 N.Y.S.2d 390 (N.Y. App. Div. 2004), aff'd 827 N.E.2d 265 (2005), plaintiff and her husband were receiving pastoral counseling from their minister. During the period that the counseling was going on, the minister and Wende C. had numerous sexual encounters. The trial court granted the defendant's motion for summary judgment on plaintiff's claim of sexual battery even though she averred that the unwanted sexual contact "occurred at a time when she was unable to fully consent because of the defendant'[s] control and influence over her as her counselor." In affirming the judgment for defendant, the court found that there was ample evidence that the romantic attachment between the plaintiff and defendant was mutual and the sexual contact consensual. The court also refused to find the minister liable for clergy malpractice or breach of fiduciary duty since New York does not recognize these causes of action against clergy.

Whether threatening conduct will vitiate consent becomes even more difficult to determine when economic pressure is exerted. An employer, for example, might threaten to fire an employee unless she consents to sexually offensive contact. If the employee consents, should a court disregard that consent by reason of duress? What if she consented in the absence of an explicit threat because she believed that she would be fired if she did not consent? *See* Reavis v. Slominski, 551 N.W.2d 528, 542 (Neb. 1996) (failure to give instruction that economic duress does not vitiate consent is reversible error); Lucas v. Redig, 2004 WL 1700517 (Cal. Ct. App.) (July 2004) (mere belief on the part of sexual partner that failure to acquiesce to sexual relations would lead to termination of employment does not vitiate consent). Do plaintiffs in such situations have a meaningful choice in the matter? What if, instead of threatening dismissal, the defendant promises a promotion in exchange for sexual advances?

One would think that duress either is or is not made out under the facts of a case. When duress is present, consent is vitiated. But the following case puts a different slant on this issue.

GRAGER v. SCHUDAR
770 N.W.2d 692 (N.D. 2009)

KAPSNER, Justice.

Michele Grager appeals from a judgment and from an order denying her motion for a new trial in her action against Barnes County and Kevin Schudar, a jailer at the Barnes County Jail, stemming from Schudar's sexual act with Grager while she was a prisoner at the Barnes County Jail. A jury found that Barnes County was not negligent in supervising Schudar and that Grager consented to Schudar's sexual act. Grager argues the district court erred in instructing the jury that consent was a complete defense to her tort and constitutional claims, the court failed to properly instruct the jury on scope of employment, the court erred in instructing the jury on judicial notice, and the court erred in several evidentiary rulings. We hold the court erred in instructing the jury that Grager's consent to or participation in Schudar's conduct was a complete defense to her claims for assault, battery, intentional infliction of emotional distress, and civil rights violations, and we reverse and remand for further proceedings.

I

Grager sued Barnes County and Schudar, individually and as an employee of Barnes County, alleging that while Grager was incarcerated in the Barnes County

Jail in November 2004, Schudar sexually assaulted her. As a result of the incident, Schudar pled guilty to sexual abuse of a ward under N.D.C.C. § 12.1-20-06, which proscribes a jailer's sexual act with a prisoner regardless of the prisoner's consent. In this civil action, Grager sued Schudar for assault, battery, intentional infliction of emotional distress, and a violation of her civil rights, and she also sued Barnes County for negligent supervision of Schudar and for a violation of her civil rights. A jury found that Barnes County was not at fault in supervising Schudar and that Grager consented to Schudar's conduct. A judgment was entered dismissing Grager's civil action, and the district court thereafter denied Grager's motion for a new trial. . . .

IV

Grager argues the district court erred in instructing the jury that consent was a complete defense to her tort and constitutional claims. She contends the Legislature has determined that consent is not a defense to the criminal charge of sexual abuse of a ward under N.D.C.C. § 12.1-20-06, and an inmate is not legally capable of consenting to sexual assault by a jailer. She asserts it is incongruous for Schudar to be strictly liable in a criminal prosecution for the sexual offense, but for consent to be a complete defense in a civil action. . . .

Generally, one who consents to conduct that would otherwise be an intentional tort cannot recover damages for that conduct. Daniel B. Dobbs, The Law of Torts, § 95 (2001); see Restatement (2nd) of Torts, § 892A (1979) ("One who effectively consents to conduct of another intended to invade his interests cannot recover in an action of tort for the conduct or for harm resulting from it."); N.D.C.C. § 31-11-05(6) ("One who consents to an act is not wronged by it."). . . .

Professor Dobbs . . . explains that . . . consent is not a defense if it was obtained by duress, or by an abuse of power, and an abuse of power includes sexual demands by employers, or by others in special positions of power. Dobbs, The Law of Torts, at §§ 95, 101-02. See also Restatement (2nd) of Torts, §§ 892B (1979) (consent is not effective if given under duress) and 892C (1979) (consent effective to bar recovery in tort action although conduct consented to is crime, but if conduct is made criminal in order to protect certain class of persons irrespective of their consent, consent of members of that class to conduct is not effective to bar tort action).

Some courts have recognized that a prisoner's consent to sexual conduct with a prison official is a defense to a civil lawsuit for damages. See Freitas v. Ault, 109 F.3d 1335, 1338-39 (8th Cir.1997); Robins v. Harris, 769 N.E.2d 586, 587 (Ind. 2002); Pritchett v. Heil, 756 N.E.2d 561, 566-67 (Ind. Ct. App. 2001).

In Freitas, 109 F.3d at 1338, the Eighth Circuit Court of Appeals said prisoners could state a cause of action for sexual harassment or abuse under 42 U.S.C. § 1983. The court said a corrections officer's sexual harassment or abuse of a prisoner can never serve a legitimate penological purpose and may result in unnecessary and wanton infliction of pain under the Eighth Amendment. Id. The court concluded, however, the trial court did not clearly err in finding the relationship between the corrections officer and the prisoner was "consensual in the freest sense of the word" and welcomed by the prisoner. Id. at 1338-39. The court of appeals held that "[w]ithout deciding at what point unwelcome sexual advances become serious enough to constitute 'pain,' . . . at the very least, welcome and voluntary sexual interactions, no matter how inappropriate, cannot as a matter of law constitute 'pain'" under the Eighth Amendment. Id. at 1339. . . .

Section 12.1-20-06, N.D.C.C., criminalizes a jailer's sexual act with a prisoner regardless of whether the prisoner consents to the act:

> A person who engages in a sexual act with another person, or any person who causes another to engage in a sexual act is guilty of a class C felony if the other person is in official custody or detained in a hospital, prison, or other institution and the actor has supervisory or disciplinary authority over the other person.

For purposes of criminal liability, N.D.C.C. § 12.1-20-06 protects a class of persons regardless of their consent and reflects a policy of this state under our criminal laws to provide prisoners protection from sexual acts by persons who have supervisory or disciplinary authority over the prisoners regardless of the prisoners' consent. See also N.D.C.C. § 12.1-20-07(1)(d) (proscribing sexual contact with person in official custody or detained in prison if actor has supervisory or disciplinary authority over other person); N.D.C.C. § 25-03.3-01(9)(a)(6) (defining sexual predatory conduct as conduct involving sexual act or contact with victim in official custody in correctional facility and under supervisory authority, disciplinary control, or care of actor). The issue in this case is the impact of those statutes on tort liability.

In 1987, the North Dakota Legislature enacted the modified comparative fault provisions of N.D.C.C. ch. 32-03.2, see 1987 N.D. Sess. Laws ch. 404, which significantly revised tort liability in North Dakota and shifted the focus from traditional tort doctrines to the singular inclusive concept of "fault." See Rodenburg v. Fargo-Moorhead YMCA, 2001 ND 139, ¶ 25, 632 N.W.2d 407. "As used in [N.D.C.C. ch. 32-03.2], 'fault' includes acts or omissions that are in any measure negligent or reckless towards the person or property of the actor or others, or that subject a person to tort liability or dram shop liability." N.D.C.C. § 32-03.2-01. The term fault "also includes strict liability for product defect, breach of warranty, negligence or assumption of risk, misuse of a product for which the defendant otherwise would be liable, and failure to exercise reasonable care to avoid an injury or to mitigate damages." Id.; see also N.D.C.C. § 32-03.2-02 ("fault includes negligence, malpractice, absolute liability, dram shop liability, failure to warn, reckless or willful conduct, assumption of risk, misuse of product, failure to avoid injury, and product liability, including product liability involving negligence or strict liability or breach of warranty for product defect"). Under N.D.C.C. § 32-03.2-02, contributory fault does not bar recovery in an action by any person to recover damages for injury unless the fault was as great as the combined fault of all other persons who contribute to the injury. One of the underlying purposes of N.D.C.C. ch. 32-03.2 is to allocate fault for tortious conduct and to replace joint and several liability with several allocation of damages among those who commit torts in proportion to the fault of those who contributed to an injury. Rodenburg, at ¶ 25. Those statutory provisions for allocating comparative fault include voluntary conduct. See N.D.C.C. §§ 32-03.2-01 and 32-03.2-02. . . .

Construing our comparative fault statutes in conjunction with our criminal statutes and N.D.C.C. § 31-11-05(6), we conclude an adult prisoner's apparent consent to or participation in sexual conduct with a jailer imposes neither absolute liability on the jailer nor a complete bar to the prisoner's recovery in a civil action premised upon the sexual conduct. When the statutory provisions for comparative fault are considered together with N.D.C.C. §§ 12.1-20-06, 12.1-20-07, 25-03.3-01(9)(a)(6) and 31-11-05(6), and the Restatement (2nd) of Torts § 892C, we believe those provisions preclude consent as a complete defense to a civil action for damages, but do not prevent a trier-of-fact from considering consent in allocating fault or determining the existence and extent of damages. We conclude that when consent to a sexual act by a person in official custody or detained in a treatment facility, prison, or other institution is at issue in a situation where the actor has supervisory authority, disciplinary control or care over the detained person, the jury must be instructed that it must consider all of the factors limiting the detained person's ability to control the situation or to give consent in deciding whether the detained person effectively consented to the sexual act. Each case must be decided on its own factual circumstances, including the age, sex, mental capacity, and relative positions of the parties. . . .

We hold the district court's instruction that Grager's consent to or participation in Schudar's conduct was a complete defense is not a correct statement of the law. The instruction was incorrect because mere participation in the conduct does not automatically signify consent. The instructions were further inadequate. For purposes of finding consent in the context of an institutionalized person, the jury must be instructed to consider the factors previously discussed. We therefore conclude the court erred in instructing the jury that if Grager consented to or participated in Schudar's conduct, her consent or participation was a complete defense to her claims for assault, battery, intentional infliction of emotional distress, and civil rights violations. . . .

We reverse the judgment and the order denying the motion for a new trial, and we remand for further proceedings.

Gerald W. Vande Walle, C.J., Mary Muehlen Maring, Daniel D. Crothers and Dale V. Sandstrom, JJ., concur.

Assuming that a jury were to find 30% duress on the part of defendant should any duress to engage in sex reduce a plaintiff's recovery. For discussion of this issue, *see* Aaron D. Twerski and Nina Farber, *Extending Comparative Fault to Apparent and Implied Consent Cases*, 81 Bklyn L. Rev. (Issue No. 1 Winter 2016).

CONSENT INVALIDATED BY LACK OF CAPACITY

What should courts do when presented with a plaintiff who in fact consciously desired — and voluntarily agreed to — contact from another, and yet claims that the court should disregard it because the plaintiff is somehow incapable of giving valid consent? Courts invalidate voluntary, actual consent on grounds of incapacity primarily when that consent is offered by adults obviously suffering from some form of temporary or permanent diminished mental ability, or by minors who consent to potentially harmful contact. Consent offered by one adult to another, by individuals on putatively equal footing, can be deemed invalid by reason of incapacity when, for example, the person consenting is intoxicated. *See* Restatement, Second, of Torts § 59 cmt. *a*, illus. 2 (1965) ("*B* is so drunk as to be incapable of appreciating the consequences of what he is doing. *A* induces *B* to drink more whiskey in such quantities as to cause him a serious illness. *A* is subject to liability to *B*."). *See, e.g.,* Miller v. Rhode Island Hospital, 625 A.2d 778, 785-786 (R.I. 1993) (doctors who ignored an intoxicated plaintiff's objections to an emergency surgical procedure did not commit a battery where the plaintiff was not of "sufficient mind to reasonably understand the condition, the nature and effect of the proposed treatment, and the attendant risks in pursuing the treatment, and not pursuing the treatment"); *and* Reavis v. Slominski, 551 N.W.2d 528 (Neb. 1996) (case remanded for new trial with the instructions that a plaintiff's claim that her consent was ineffective because childhood sexual abuse prevented her from refusing sexual advances could only be upheld if she could prove that the incapacity prevented her from weighing the consequences of intercourse and that the defendant had knowledge of that incapacity). What degree of validity should courts afford the consent offered by a person who is developmentally disabled?

While instances of courts invalidating the freely given consent of an otherwise competent adult may sometimes appear suspect, particularly in cases of voluntary intoxication, setting aside a child's consent to harmful contact seems a lot less questionable. Courts reasonably view consent offered by young children with a suspicious eye, especially when those children consent to conduct that carries a substantial risk of injury. *See* Restatement, Second, of Torts § 59 cmt. *a*, illus. 1 (1965) ("*A*, a boy of seven, consents to an operation, the serious character of which a child of his age could not appreciate. *B*, the surgeon, performs the operation. *B* is subject to liability to *A*.").

However, whether a court will allow a child to consent to contact that does not carry a risk of substantial injury depends on the context. For example, most courts would validate a 17-year-old's consent to contact during a friendly game of tackle football and to medical treatment for a broken ankle received during that game. What if the 17-year-old consented to a boxing match or an abortion? Courts also wrestle with when a child becomes old enough to consent. Many states have adopted a common law "mature minor" doctrine, whereby courts measure a child's age, ability, experience, education, training, and degree of maturity or judgment to determine if she has the capacity to consent. *See, e.g.,* Belcher v. Charleston Area Medical Center, 422 S.E.2d 827 (W. Va. 1992). Other state courts have followed legislatively established guidelines of adulthood, requiring children to be the prescribed age of consent. *See, e.g.,* Commonwealth v. Nixon, 761 A.2d 1151 (Pa. 2000) (age of consent is 18).

Occasionally, a court must confront the issue of whether a minor has legally consented to sexual intercourse. The child, or more likely the child's parents, on behalf of the child, may bring an action in tort, claiming that the consent was invalid. While the criminal statutory rape statutes establish bright-line rules whereby such consent is necessarily invalid, courts hearing claims in tort sometimes leave this issue for a case-by-case determination. Thus, in McNamee v. A.J.W., 519 S.E.2d 298 (Ga. Ct. App. 1999), the court declined to preclude evidence that a 15-year-old girl consented to sexual relations with a 16-year-old boy even though consent was not a defense to statutory rape of a minor under the age of 16. *See also* Doe v. Mama Taori's Premium Pizza, LLC, 2001 Tenn. App. LEXIS 224 (Tenn. Ct. App. 2001) (defendant may raise a defense at trial that a 16-year-old consented to homosexual acts with an older man). Other courts hold that minors are legally incapable of giving consent to sexual intercourse. *See, e.g.,* C.C.H. v. Philadelphia Phillies, Inc., 940 A.2d 336 (Pa. 2008) (where the victim is less than 13 years of age, evidence of the victim's consent to sexual contact, as in criminal proceedings, is not available as a defense in determining a defendant's civil liability). *Accord* Bjerke v. Johnson, 727 N.W.2d 183 (Minn. Ct. App. 2007). *See also* Restatement, Second, of Torts § 892C(2) (1965) (conduct made criminal to protect persons irrespective of their consent is not effective to bar a tort action).

INFORMED CONSENT

SCOTT v. BRADFORD
606 P.2d 554 (Okla. 1980)

Doolin, Justice.

This appeal is taken by plaintiffs, from a judgment in favor of defendant rendered on a jury verdict in a medical malpractice action.

Mrs. Scott's physician advised her she had several fibroid tumors on her uterus. He referred her to defendant surgeon. Defendant admitted her to the hospital where she signed a routine consent form prior to defendant's performing a hysterectomy. After surgery, Mrs. Scott experienced problems with incontinence. She visited another physician who discovered she had a vesico-vaginal fistula which permitted urine to leak from her bladder into the vagina. This physician referred her to an urologist who, after three surgeries, succeeded in correcting her problems.

Mrs. Scott, joined by her husband, filed the present action alleging medical malpractice, claiming defendant failed to advise her of the risks involved or of available alternatives to surgery. She further maintained had she been properly informed she would have refused the surgery.

The case was submitted to the jury with instructions to which plaintiffs objected. The jury found for defendant and plaintiffs appeal. . . .

Plaintiffs complain of three instructions and submit the following instruction should have been given:

> The law requires physician to disclose to his patient the material risks of a proposed treatment, the material risks of foregoing any treatment, the existence of any alternatives and the material risks of choosing these alternatives. The failure to disclose these things is negligence.

A risk is "material" when a reasonable person, in what the physician knows or should know to be the patient's position, would be likely to attach significance to the risk or cluster of risks in deciding whether or not to forego the proposed therapy.

If you find from the evidence in this case that the defendant failed to make disclosures to the plaintiff, Norma Jo Scott, as required by law, then your verdict would be for the plaintiffs, for the amount of their damages proximately caused thereby.

This instruction refers to the doctrine of "informed consent."

The issue involved is whether Oklahoma adheres to the doctrine of informed consent as the basis of an action for medical malpractice, and if so did the present instructions adequately advise the jury of defendant's duty.

Anglo-American law starts with the premise of thoroughgoing self-determination, each man considered to be his own master. This law does not permit a physician to substitute his judgment for that of the patient by any form of artifice. The doctrine of informed consent arises out of this premise.

Consent to medical treatment, to be effective, should stem from an understanding decision based on adequate information about the treatment, the available alternatives, and the collateral risks. This requirement, labeled "informed consent," is, legally speaking, as essential as a physician's care and skill in the performance of the therapy. The doctrine imposes a duty on a physician or surgeon to inform a patient of his options and their attendant risks. If a physician breaches this duty, patient's consent is defective, and physician is responsible for the consequences.

If treatment is completely unauthorized and performed without any consent at all, there has been a battery. However, if the physician obtains a patient's consent but has breached his duty to inform, the patient has a cause of action sounding in negligence for failure to inform the patient of his options, regardless of the due care exercised at treatment, assuming there is injury.

Until today, Oklahoma has not officially adopted this doctrine. In [an earlier case], this Court discussed a physician's duty in this area but reversed the trial court on other grounds. It impliedly approved the doctrine and stated its basic principles but left its adoption until a later time. . . .

More recently, in perhaps one of the most influential informed consent decisions, Canterbury v. Spence, . . . 464 F.2d 772 (D.C. Cir. 1972), cert. den. 409 U.S. 1064, . . . the doctrine received perdurable impetus. Judge Robinson observed that suits charging failure by a physician adequately to disclose risks and alternatives of proposed treatment were not innovative in American law. He emphasized the fundamental concept in American jurisprudence that every human being of adult years and sound mind has a right to determine what shall be done with his own body. True consent to what happens to one's self is the informed exercise of a choice. This entails an opportunity to evaluate knowledgeably the options available and the risks attendant upon each. It is the prerogative of every patient to chart his own course and determine which direction he will take.

The decision in *Canterbury* recognized the tendency of some jurisdictions to turn this duty on whether it is the custom of physicians practicing in the community to make the particular disclosure to the patient. That court rejected this standard and held the standard measuring performance of the duty of disclosure is conduct which is reasonable under the circumstances: "(We can not) ignore the fact that to bind disclosure obligations to medical usage is to arrogate the decision on revelation to the physician alone." We agree. A patient's right to make up his mind whether to undergo treatment should not be delegated to the local medical group. What is reasonable disclosure in one instance may not be reasonable in another. We decline to adopt a standard based on the professional standard. We, therefore, hold the scope of a physician's communications must be measured by his patient's need to know enough to enable him to make an intelligent choice. In other words, full disclosure of all material risks incident to treatment must be made. There is no bright line separating the material from the immaterial; it is a question of fact. A risk is material if it would be likely to affect patient's decision. When non-disclosure of a particular risk is open to debate, the issue is for the finder of facts.

This duty to disclose is the first element of the cause of action in negligence based on lack of informed consent. However, there are exceptions creating a privilege of a physician not to disclose. There is no need to disclose risks that either ought to be known by everyone or are already known to the patient. Further, the primary duty of a physician is to do what is best for his patient and where full disclosure would be detrimental to a patient's total care and best interests a physician may withhold such disclosure, for example, where disclosure would alarm an emotionally upset or apprehensive patient. Certainly too, where there is an emergency and the patient is in no condition to determine for himself whether treatment should be administered, the privilege may be invoked.

The patient has the burden of going forward with evidence tending to establish prima facie the essential elements of the cause of action. The burden of proving an exception to his duty and thus a privilege not to disclose, rests upon the physician as an affirmative defense.

The cause of action, based on lack of informed consent, is divided into three elements: the duty to inform being the first, the second is causation, and the third is injury. The second element, that of causation, requires that plaintiff patient would have chosen no treatment or a different course of treatment had the alternatives and material risks of each been made known to him. If the patient would have elected to proceed with treatment had he been duly informed of its risks, then the element of causation is missing. In other words, a causal connection exists between physician's breach of the duty to disclose and patient's injury when and only when disclosure of material risks incidental to treatment would have resulted in a decision against it. A patient obviously has no complaint if he would have submitted to the treatment if the physician had complied with his duty and informed him of the risks. . . . This fact decision raises the difficult question of the correct standard on which to instruct the jury.

The court in *Canterbury v. Spence, supra,* although emphasizing principles of self-determination permits liability only if non-disclosure would have affected the decision of a fictitious "reasonable patient," even though [the] actual patient testifies he would have elected to forego therapy had he been fully informed.

Decisions discussing informed consent have emphasized the disclosure element but paid scant attention to the consent element of the concept, although this is the root of causation. Language in some decisions suggest the standard to be applied is a subjective one, i.e., whether that particular patient would still have consented to the treatment, reasonable choice or otherwise. . . .

Although the *Canterbury* rule is probably that of the majority, its "reasonable man" approach has been criticized by some commentators as backtracking on its own theory of self-determination. The *Canterbury* view certainly severely limits the protection granted an injured patient. To the extent the plaintiff, given an adequate disclosure, would have declined the proposed treatment, and a reasonable person in similar circumstances would have consented, a patient's right of self-determination is irrevocably lost. This basic right to know and decide is the reason for the full-disclosure rule. Accordingly, we decline to jeopardize this right by the imposition of the "reasonable man" standard.

If a plaintiff testifies he would have continued with the proposed treatment had he been adequately informed, the trial is over. . . . If he testifies he would not, then the causation problem must be resolved by examining the credibility of plaintiff's testimony. The jury must be instructed that it must find plaintiff would have refused the treatment if he is to prevail.

Although it might be said this approach places a physician at the mercy of a patient's hindsight, a careful practitioner can always protect himself by insuring that he has adequately informed each patient he treats. If he does not breach this duty, a causation problem will not arise. . . .

In summary, in a medical malpractice action a patient suing under the theory of informed consent must allege and prove:

1) defendant physician failed to inform him adequately of a material risk before securing his consent to the proposed treatment;
2) if he had been informed of the risks he would not have consented to the treatment;
3) the adverse consequences that were not made known did in fact occur and he was injured as a result of submitting to the treatment.

As a defense, a physician may plead and prove plaintiff knew of the risks, full disclosure would be detrimental to patient's best interests or that an emergency existed requiring prompt treatment and patient was in no condition to decide for himself.

Because we are imposing a new duty on physicians, we hereby make this opinion prospective only, affecting those causes of action arising after the date this opinion is promulgated.

The trial court in the case at bar gave rather broad instructions upon the duty of a physician to disclose. The instructions objected to did instruct that defendant should have disclosed material risks of the hysterectomy and feasibility of alternatives. Instructions are sufficient when considered as a whole they present the law applicable to the issues. Jury found for defendant. We find no basis for reversal.

Affirmed.

The subject of informed consent has attracted great interest among academic commentators. *See, e.g.,* Marjorie Maguire Shultz, *From Informed Consent to Patient Choice: A New Protected Interest,* 95 Yale L.J. 219 (1985); P. Appelbaum, C. Lidz & A. Meisel, *Informed Consent: Legal Theory and Clinical Practice* (1987); Aaron D. Twerski & Neil B. Cohen, *Informed Decision Making and the Law of Torts: The Myth of Justiciable Causation,* 1988 U. Ill. L. Rev. 607 (1988); Dayna Bowen Matthew, *Race, Religion, and Informed Consent-Lessons from Social Science,* 36 J.L. Med. & Ethics 150 (2008); Russell Korobkin, *Autonomy and Informed Consent in Nontherapeutic Biomedical Research,* 54 UCLA L. Rev. 605 (2007). Anna B. Leakman, *When Should Physicians be Liable for Innovation?,* 36 Cardozo L. Rev. 913 (2015).

How far must a doctor go in revealing matters that could be of interest to a patient before undergoing a medical procedure? There is no bright line defining the scope of information that need be disclosed.

In Moore v. Regents of the University of California, 793 P.2d 479 (Cal. 1990), the plaintiff filed multiple claims against doctors, researchers, and a university after the plaintiff learned that his entire spleen and samples of his blood, blood serum, skin, bone marrow aspirate, and sperm had been used to create a cell line worth over $3 billion. The plaintiff claimed that doctors told him that the removal of his spleen and tissue samples were necessary aspects of his medical treatment. No mention was made of the possibility of using the tissue commercially. Based on these representations, the plaintiff consented to the procedures. In reversing the trial court's dismissal of plaintiff's claims, the California Supreme Court ruled that to satisfy the informed consent doctrine, the doctor must disclose any personal interest he may have that is unrelated to the patient's health that may affect his professional judgment. More recently in Shapira v. Health Christiana Care Health Care Services, Inc., 99 A.3d 217 (Del. 2014) the defendant physician had failed to obtain informed consent when he did not reveal his business relationship with the manufacturer of a catheter used for the "On-Q procedure." In upholding a jury verdict for the plaintiff the court said the doctor "was . . . earning money by promoting the On-Q Procedure and gathering data about the procedure's efficacy." *Id.* at 99 A.3d 222.

hypo **22**

Dr. *A* encourages *B* to consider undergoing open-heart surgery. *A* tells *B* that *A* can treat *B*'s heart condition with medication alone, but that *B* will have a better quality of life with surgery. *A* tells *B* that it is a close call. *A* performs the surgery with *B*'s consent. *A* performs the surgery competently, but *B* nevertheless suffers harm as a result of the surgery. Can *B* reach the jury in an action against *A* predicated on lack of informed consent because *A* did not tell *B* that, given the applicable health insurance, *A* benefited much more monetarily by doing the surgery than he would have from administering the drug therapy?

---

authors' dialogue 7

AARON: Brad, I just got finished teaching *Scott v. Bradford* and I am truly puzzled by something. In its summary of the elements that a plaintiff must establish to make out an informed consent case the court says that plaintiff must show that: (1) the defendant failed to inform the plaintiff about a material risk; (2) the plaintiff, if informed, would not have consented to the therapy utilized by the doctor; and (3) the adverse consequences that were not made known actually occurred and the plaintiff was injured as a result of submitting to the treatment.

BRAD: Those elements make sense to me. What troubles you?

AARON: I understand how the court concludes that the plaintiff in *Scott* made out the first two elements. Plaintiff was not informed of material risks and she almost certainly testified that she would not have undergone the surgery had she known of the risk of becoming incontinent. But how do we assume that the surgery caused the injury?

BRAD: Do you have any doubt that the surgery caused her to become incontinent?

AARON: No, I agree that without the surgery she would not have become incontinent. But, consider this, Brad. Mrs. Scott came to the doctor with fibroid tumors. The doctor was not negligent in recommending a hysterectomy. Had his advice been negligent she would be suing for negligent malpractice, not informed consent. Well, what would have happened had she not undergone the surgery? She might not have been incontinent but she might have died from internal bleeding. In other words, tort law provides for damages that compare the plaintiff in the uninjured state and in the injured state and compensate for the difference. In almost every informed consent case, excluding cosmetic surgery, the plaintiff would have suffered from the malady that brought her to the doctor in the first

---

hypo 23

Dr. *A* performed laparoscopic gall bladder surgery on Mrs. *B*. He failed to inform her that he was scheduled the next day to undergo triple bypass surgery on his heart. In the process of performing the surgery, Dr. *A* severed the common bile duct of Mrs. *B*. Prior to the surgery Dr. *A* informed Mrs. *B* that this was a risk that sometimes occurs during gall bladder surgery. There is no evidence that Dr. *A* was negligent in performing the surgery. Does Mrs. *B* have an action based on informed consent against Dr. *A*?

---

hypo 24

A was delivered without a heartbeat. Dr. *B* took charge of resuscitation and continued his effort for 24 minutes after birth, at which time *A*'s heart began to beat. As a result of the lack of heartbeat for such a prolonged period of time, *A* suffers from severe cerebral palsy and a host of other serious diseases. *A*'s

place. Even if Mrs. Scott would not have chosen to undergo the hysterectomy, the alternative therapy was not risk free. In short, I am thinking that Mrs. Scott should not receive full value for the damages she suffered as a result of her incontinence.

BRAD: I see where you are going but I think you are wrong. Once the doctor decides to go it alone and not consult the patient, and the doctor-chosen therapy causes the very harm that the doctor had a duty to tell the patient about, causation is established. Any attempt to speculate about the risks attached to no therapeutic intervention or to an alternative therapy is unfair to the plaintiff. She was deprived of her right to make an informed choice and the very idea that we need to conjure up a risk scenario to compare with the one actually suffered seems harsh. We don't know and will never know what would have happened in that hypothetical setting, and we won't know because the doctor deprived the plaintiff of the right to choose.

AARON: It seems to me that you are arguing that plaintiff ought to recover full damages because the doctor is guilty of a dignitary tort — he insulted the plaintiff's personal dignity. Once her right to choose was offended, the doctor is liable for all the harm that follows from the failure to disclose. But why should substantial tort damages be awarded for a dignitary tort? Why not compensate the plaintiff for the insult to her dignity and then inquire as to whether she suffered any real tort damages?

BRAD: You are missing the point. She suffered real damages from her incontinence. That was the very risk she was not warned about. If plaintiff was warned about the risk of bleeding to death if she did not undergo surgery, and she believes that she would be better risking death than risking incontinence, it is not our business to second-guess that decision and limit her damages by comparing her postsurgical status with some hypothetical alternative. That's not what informed consent is all about.

---

parents C and D sue Dr. B for failing to inform them that continual resuscitation after 10 minutes was certain to result in permanent injury to A. C and D were present in a room adjacent to the delivery room.

Informed consent is also a key concept in the law governing lawyers and was expressly incorporated into that body of law from torts. Many duties owed to clients, such as the duty of confidentiality and the obligation to refrain from representing other clients with conflicting interests, can be waived with the informed consent of the affected client or clients. *See, e.g.,* ABA Model Rules of Professional Conduct, Rule 1.2(c) (limitation on scope of representation), Rule 1.6(a) (confidentiality), Rule 1.7(b) (conflicts of interest). Informed consent is defined as "the agreement by a person to a proposed course of conduct after the lawyer has communicated adequate information and explanation about the material risks of and reasonably available alternatives to the proposed course of conduct." *Id.,* Rule 1.0(e). That is pretty much exactly the way the term is defined in the preceding case.

LEGISLATING INFORMED CONSENT

A fair number of states have passed statutes dealing with this issue of informed consent. Some agree with *Canterbury v. Spence* and *Scott v. Bradford* and apply a reasonable patient test as the standard for what risks should be communicated to the patient. *See, e.g.,* Haw. Rev. Stat. § 671-3 (2005); Wash. Rev. Code Ann. § 7.70.050 (2016). However, most states that have enacted legislation have adopted the reasonable doctor test. The New York statute reflects this view. N.Y. Pub. Health Law § 2805-d provides:

1. Lack of informed consent means the failure of the person providing the professional treatment or diagnosis to disclose to the patient such alternatives thereto and the reasonably foreseeable risks and benefits involved as a reasonable medical, dental or podiatric practitioner under similar circumstances would have disclosed, in a manner permitting the patient to make a knowledgeable evaluation.
2. The right of action to recover for medical, dental or podiatric malpractice based on a lack of informed consent is limited to those cases involving either (a) non-emergency treatment, procedure or surgery, or (b) a diagnostic procedure which involved invasion or disruption of the integrity of the body.
3. For a cause of action therefore it must also be established that a reasonably prudent person in the patient's position would not have undergone the treatment or diagnosis if he had been fully informed and that the lack of informed consent is a proximate cause of the injury or condition for which recovery is sought.

Accord Ky. Rev. Stat. Ann. § 304.40-320 (2016).

RICE v. BRAKEL, M.D.
310 P.3d 16 (Ariz. App. Ct. 2013)

Howard, Chief Judge.

. . . On July 30, 2007, Jay Rice ("Rice") underwent spinal surgery on his S1 and L5 nerve roots in an attempt to relieve pain in his right leg. Rice also was experiencing pain in his left leg before the surgery. Arlo Brakel ("Brakel"), a neurosurgeon, performed the surgery. The procedure successfully relieved pain in his right leg, but Rice experienced increasing pain in his left leg after the surgery.

Other doctors in Brakel's practice group, the Center for Neurosciences ("Center"), provided follow-up care. Initially the follow-up exams indicated Rice probably was experiencing some nerve irritation as a result of the surgery. However, an MRI from 2010 indicated that Rice had scar tissue surrounding one nerve root, and an exam in March of that year showed fibrillation and insertion potentials consistent with L5 or S1 radiculopathy on the left side. After an exam in October 2011, one of Rice's doctors concluded there was "[p]robable operative injury to S1 nerve root and postoperative scar affecting L5 nerve root."

In July 2010, Rice read a newspaper article about how to use the Board of Medical Examiners' website to check the disciplinary history of a doctor licensed in the state. He decided to use the site to look into Brakel's history. Upon doing so, he discovered that Brakel had a dependency on unprescribed prescription drugs including morphine, Dilaudid, and Percocet around the time of Rice's July 2007 surgery, and that sometime after the surgery Brakel had been reprimanded by the board and placed on probation for five years. Brakel obtained some of these drugs by stealing them from his patients.

Rice sued Brakel and the Center for battery, negligence, and breach of contract in September 2010. Rice moved for partial summary judgment on the issues of battery and negligent supervision. Claiming Rice had failed to adduce evidence to establish a prima facie case for any of the claims against him, Brakel moved for summary judgment, and the Center moved for partial summary judgment on the issue of negligent supervision. The trial court denied Rice's motion, granted Brakel and the Center's motions, and awarded the successful parties their costs. Rice moved for a new trial, which the court denied. Rice appeals.

Discussion

... Rice first argues the trial court erred while applying the law of medical battery to his case. He reasons that under Duncan v. Scottsdale Med. Imaging, Ltd., 205 Ariz. 306, 70 P.3d 435 (2003), consent is not valid when the surgeon is suffering from an undisclosed drug dependency at the time consent is given, because it effectively revokes the patient's right to choose his surgeon and exposes the patient to much greater risk than he anticipated — essentially, that he received a different surgeon than the one to whom he consented. Brakel responds that Duncan stands only for the proposition that a medical battery exists if a patient receives a procedure to which he did not consent. Because Rice consented to the procedure he received, Brakel argues, Rice has no claim for battery.

The elements of common law battery consist of an intentional act by one person that "results in harmful or offensive contact with the person of another. . . . [A] health care provider commits a common law battery on a patient if a medical procedure is performed without the patient's consent." Duncan, 70 P.3d at 438 (citations omitted). In Duncan, our supreme court clarified the distinction between "lack of consent" and "lack of informed consent." Id. In so doing, the court adopted the reasoning of the California Supreme Court case Cobbs v. Grant, 502 P.2d 1 (1972), which stated that "'[t]he battery theory should be reserved for those circumstances when a doctor performs an operation to which the patient has not consented. When the patient gives permission to perform one type of treatment and the doctor performs another, the requisite element of deliberate intent to deviate from the consent given is present.'" Id. In choosing to classify a lack of informed consent cause of action under a negligence theory, the California court also relied on several public policy considerations: (1) battery does not require expert testimony on community standards; (2) punitive damages are available under battery; and (3) malpractice insurance may not cover intentional torts like battery. . . . Based on this reasoning, our supreme court held that "claims involving lack of consent, i.e., the doctor's failure to operate within the limits of the patient's consent, may be brought as battery actions. In contrast, true 'informed consent' claims, i.e., those involving the doctor's obligation to provide information, must be brought as negligence actions." 70 P.3d at 439.

. . . Second, Rice has an available cause of action for any damages caused by Brakel's failure to disclose, because the duty to disclose relevant risks already exists under the informed consent theory of medical malpractice. Gorney v. Meaney, . . . 150 P.3d 799, 804 (App. 2007). Under this doctrine, a causal nexus must exist between the patient's consent to treatment, an undisclosed negative influence, and the injury the patient claims. Id. The doctrine prevents liability where such a nexus remains speculative or nonexistent. See id. (plaintiff must show "adequate disclosure would have caused the plaintiff to decline the treatment"); Cobbs, 502 P.2d at 11. The doctrine thus strikes a balance between the patient's right of self-determination and the doctor's exposure to liability that we see no reason to disrupt. . . .

. . . To expand the disclosure requirements under a battery theory . . . could require doctors to volunteer personal information on the off chance that a patient might later be able to claim it was important to effective consent generally — as judged by a lay person. Patients would not have to prove that the information actually was relevant to them, that the doctor had breached the relevant standard of care in failing to disclose the information, or that they actually had sustained a medical injury. Instead, they would have to establish only that the absence of disclosure created a mistake of fact or could be considered a misrepresentation that would void their consent as a matter of law.

. . . Rice next argues that a genuine dispute of material fact exists about whether he gave informed consent, and that it is up to the jury to determine "whether the increased risk contributed to [his] injury." Brakel responds that Rice has failed to establish a breach of the standard of care or causation and therefore his claim must fail.

Medical malpractice is established by showing a breach of the applicable standard of care and that the breach caused the plaintiff's injuries. See Seisinger v. Siebel, . . . 203 P.3d 483, 492 (2009); Plaintiffs alleging lack of informed consent must show two types of causation: (1) the plaintiff would have declined the treatment with adequate disclosure; and (2) the treatment proximately caused injury to the plaintiff. Gorney, 150 P.3d at 804.

Here, Rice failed to adduce evidence that he would have declined the treatment had Brakel's status been disclosed. Additionally, he has not established that Brakel's acts about which he complains proximately caused his injury. He therefore failed to establish the essential elements of this claim. The court did not err in granting summary judgment to Brakel on this issue.

Why didn't plaintiff's lawyer aggressively pursue informed consent? Do you have any doubt that plaintiff would have testified that if informed he would not have agreed to have his neurological surgery performed by a doctor who was dependent on potent pain killers? Assume that plaintiff cannot prove that the injury to his nerve roots were due to the negligence of the surgeon. But, the fact remains that he is suffering from nerve root problems and the surgeon who performed the surgery on those nerve roots was high on potent pain killers. Why is that not enough?

INFORMED CONSENT: DOCTORS BUT NOT HOSPITALS?

Whereas *DeMay v. Roberts* deals with consent to medical treatment procured through deceit, *Scott v. Bradford* concerns consent founded upon inadequate information regarding attendant risks — consent that was not adequately informed. Although there is close to unanimity that doctors are to be held liable for failure to provide informed consent, courts have generally rejected attempts to hold hospitals liable when physicians who have staff privileges fail to obtain informed consent prior to a surgical procedure. *See, e.g.,* Newell v. Trident Medical Center, 597 S.E.2d 776, 777 (S.C. 2004) ("It is not the responsibility of hospital personnel to undertake to inform the patient. This remains the responsibility of the attending physician or surgeon."); Foster v. Traul, 120 P.3d 278 (Idaho 2005) (hospital not liable for failure of a nurse to obtain informed consent; the responsibility devolves on the treating physician). The failure to impose any duty on hospitals to monitor informed consent is roundly criticized in Robert Gatter, *The Mysterious Survival of the Policy Against Informed Consent Liability for Hospitals*, 81 Notre Dame L. Rev. 1203 (2006). Gatter notes that courts have recognized two situations where the hospital will be liable for the failure of the physician to provide informed consent: (1) when the doctor is an employee of the hospital, liability may attach under the doctrine of respondeat superior, and (2) when the hospital acting as a research institution conducts clinical testing on human beings. *But see* Magana v. Elie, 439 N.E.2d 1319 (Ill. App. Ct. 1982) (hospital may have a duty to see to it that its physicians obtain informed consent; it is for the factfinder to determine whether the hospital met the standard of reasonable care); Rogers v. T.J. Samson Community Hospital, 276 F.3d 228 (6th Cir. 2002) (applying Kentucky law) (hospital as a "health care provider" under Kentucky law has a statutory duty to secure patient's informed consent to surgical procedure); Salandy v. Bryk, 864 N.Y.S.2d 46 (N.Y. App. Div. 2008) (if hospital either "knew or should have known" that a private physician was acting or would act without the patient's informed consent, it may be held liable.)

SOME RADICAL IDEAS: BROADENING INFORMED CONSENT

Scholars have suggested some rather radical proposals for broadening the action for informed consent. Professors Twerski and Cohen argue that courts should recognize a duty on the part of hospitals or physicians to reveal to patients statistical information regarding the relative risks associated with individual medical providers. Such information has recently become available in some states, thereby enabling patients to compare the "track records" of various doctors and hospitals. The authors argue that if such provider-specific risk information is not afforded to patients before treatment then a cause of action for lack of informed consent should be available to the patient. They cite to Johnson v. Kokemoor, 545 N.W.2d 495 (Wis. 1996), as a case that indicates that courts may require physicians to reveal their experience and "success ratio" to patients. If they do not, they may be held liable for failing to provide informed consent. *See* Aaron D. Twerski & Neil B. Cohen, *The Second Revolution in Informed Consent: Comparing Physicians to Each Other*, 94 Nw. U. L. Rev. 1 (1999). *See also* Howard v. University of Medicine and Dentistry of New Jersey, 800 A.2d 73 (N.J. 2002) (physician's material misrepresentations of credentials are grounds for informed consent action); Goldberg v. Boone, 912 A.2d 698 (Md. Ct. App. 2006) (surgeon's lack of experience gave rise to duty to inform the patient that a more experienced surgeon could better perform the surgery); Housel v. W. James, 172 P.3d 712, 716 (Wash. Ct. App. 2007) ("[t]here may well be situations where evidence of a physician's experience would be a significant factor in a patient's decision to undertake a particular course of treatment"). *But see* Duttry v. Patterson, 771 A.2d 1255 (Pa. 2001) (a patient could not recover for lack of informed consent against a doctor who performed a resection of her esophagus and stomach, causing injuries, even though the doctor told the plaintiff that he performed the procedure once a month, when, in fact, he had performed the surgery only nine times in the past five years).

Other commentators have voiced growing concern about managed care. As the court in Moore expressed concern with a doctor's financial interest interfering with her patient responsibilities, Professor Grant H. Morris expresses concern over the emergence of managed care. He argues that the current informed consent doctrine defers too much to doctors and is inadequate to protect patients from doctors who refuse to disclose clinically appropriate, but uninsured, alternatives to the doctor's treatment recommendations. In fact, Professor Morris finds that many contracts that physicians sign with HMO companies expressly prohibit the doctors from informing patients about medically appropriate treatments that the HMO does not cover. He concludes that courts should expand the informed consent doctrine to require doctors to inform patients about alternatives treatment beyond those recommended by managed care insurers. If courts are reluctant to do this, then Morris recommends that courts create a new tort that would adequately protect plaintiffs. Grant H. Morris, *Dissing Disclosure: Just What the Doctor Ordered*, 44 Ariz. L. Rev. 313 (2002).

Finally, two authors have surveyed empirical research as to how informed consent actually works in practice. They find that whether courts utilize the "reasonable doctor" test or "reasonable patient" test in deciding the question of how much information is to be communicated to the patient, there is little reason to have confidence that courts and juries can adequately assess the issue. Their surveys show that there is wide disagreement among physicians as to what risks should be disclosed and equally divergent views by patients as to which risks they would want to learn about before undergoing a medical procedure. The authors advocate a process of shared decision making to replace the present order. To make such a scheme workable, modules for hundreds of procedures would have to be created that would provide the basic risk information to patients. Physicians would then sit down with patients and learn about their value preferences with regard to the already disclosed risks. *See* Jaime Staples King & Benjamin W. Moulton, *Rethinking Informed Consent: The Case for Shared Medical Decision Making,* 32 Am J. L. & Med. 429 (2006). The authors concede that their proposal would require a heavy investment of physician time to make the process work.

B. SELF-DEFENSE

HATTORI v. PEAIRS
662 So.2d 509 (La. Ct. App. 1995)

Lottinger, Chief Judge.

This is a wrongful death and survival action filed by the parents of a 16-year old Japanese exchange student who was shot and killed by a homeowner. From a judgment in favor of the parents, the homeowner has appealed.

In the fall of 1992, Yoshihiro Hattori (Yoshi) was a foreign exchange student from Nagoya, Japan living with the Richard Haymaker family at their home in Baton Rouge. Yoshi had come to the United States in August, and attended McKinley High School with the Haymakers' son, Webb. Both boys were nearly seventeen years of age and members of the senior class at McKinley.

A few weeks prior to the incident in question, the boys learned through an acquaintance that another Japanese exchange student was living in the Baton Rouge area. She and Yoshi later spoke over the telephone, and the boys were subsequently invited to a Halloween costume party to be held for area exchange students at the home of the girl's host parents, Frank and Connie Pitre. On the evening of the party, Saturday, October 17, 1992, Webb's father allowed him to drive the family's car and provided him with directions to the Pitre home which was located in Central, an unincorporated community north of Baton Rouge.

Not being familiar with the Central area, Webb experienced some difficulty in finding the Pitre home which was situated at 10131 East Brookside. When Webb and Yoshi finally found East Brookside, Webb proceeded slowly down the street whereupon he observed various Halloween decorations at the third house on the right. Because the house bore a similar number, 10311 East Brookside, and had three cars parked in the driveway, the boys thought they had found the party. Having driven past the house, Webb turned the car around, and returned to park in front of the house.

As this was to have been a costume party, the boys were dressed up. Because Webb wore a soft cervical collar as a result of an earlier diving accident, his costume was that of an accident victim. Dressed in shorts and tennis shoes, Webb had a bandage around his head, a hand splint and an ace bandage around his knee. He wore no makeup or fake blood. Yoshi loved to dance and had decided to go as John Travolta's character from the movie "Saturday Night Fever". He rented a white tuxedo jacket, black pants and a ruffled white shirt of which he had unbuttoned the top three buttons. He also carried a camera. Neither boy wore a mask.

At approximately 8:15 P.M., the boys walked up the driveway, and rang the front doorbell. No one answered the front door; however, the boys heard the clinking of window blinds emanating from the rear of the carport area to the left of where they stood. Webb, followed by Yoshi to his left, proceeded around the corner, under the carport, toward the carport door. As the boys turned the corner, Webb observed a small boy, approximately eight or nine years of age, peering through the blinds of the carport door. A moment later, the door was opened by a woman wearing a bathrobe and glasses. As Webb attempted to speak to the woman, she slammed the door.

At this point, the boys turned around and walked down the driveway towards the sidewalk. Webb was fairly certain they had stopped at the wrong house, and attempted to communicate this fact to Yoshi. As they stood on the sidewalk near a streetlamp, the carport door opened again, and Webb observed a man standing in the doorway with a large handgun. At that point, Yoshi moved towards the house exclaiming enthusiastically, "We're here for the party!"

Webb, immediately grasping the seriousness of the situation, pleaded with his friend to come back; however, Yoshi, who was not wearing his contact lenses that evening, continued towards the man smiling and explaining several times that he had come for the party. As Yoshi reached the carport, Webb heard the man in the doorway yell, "Freeze"; however, Yoshi continued to move towards the man. From Webb's vantage point, Yoshi was adjacent to the rear-view mirror of the Toyota station wagon parked on the right of the double carport, when the man in the doorway fired. The bullet struck Yoshi in the chest, causing him to fall to the ground on his back, with his head about a foot from the carport door.

At this point, Webb ran to the house next door, and screamed for the residents inside to call 911. The homeowner, Stan Lucky, answered the door and advised that his wife was calling the emergency number at that moment. Mr. Lucky then returned with Webb to the house next door, the home of Rodney and Bonnie Peairs, to render aid to Yoshi. Mr. Lucky elevated Yoshi's feet and instructed Webb to apply pressure to the wound in Yoshi's chest. The two labored until relieved by personnel from the Central Volunteer Fire Department who administered treatment while sheriff's deputies secured the scene. E.M.S. technicians arrived on the scene a short while later at 8:39 P.M. Sometime between 8:48 and 8:49 P.M., while en route to the hospital, Yoshi stopped breathing.

The homeowners, Rodney and Bonnie Peairs, testified that upon hearing the doorbell that evening, Rodney sent his stepson to answer the carport door. Not wanting her son to answer the door after dark, Bonnie Peairs stopped him and answered the door herself. Upon opening the door, she observed a person in bandages standing near a pillar of the porch at the end of the carport. A moment later, she observed an oriental person taller than she, with a small build, come quickly around the corner toward the door. Startled, Bonnie slammed the door, locked it, and yelled for her husband to, "Get the gun."

Stating that he had never seen his wife so frightened, Rodney Peairs ran to the master bedroom, followed by Bonnie and their three children. There he retrieved the .44 magnum Smith & Wesson revolver equipped with a scope which he kept loaded in a suitcase situated on the top shelf of his closet. Now armed, Rodney raced to the carport door and peered through the blinds. Not seeing anything, and without seeking an explanation for his wife's startled behavior, Rodney flung open the carport door.

With Bonnie behind him to his right, Rodney positioned himself in the doorway. After observing movement at the rear of the Dodge vehicle parked in the driveway behind his pick-up truck, Rodney, moments later, was confronted by a figure to the rear of the Toyota station wagon which was parked on the right side of the carport. In the carport light, Rodney was able to discern an approaching oriental male approximately 5'7" in height wearing a white jacket who appeared to be laughing and carrying an object in his left hand. Raising his weapon with both *513 hands, Rodney shouted for the individual to "Freeze"; however, the stranger continued towards him uttering something unintelligible.

Several seconds later, Yoshi came alongside the right passenger mirror of the Toyota station wagon, Rodney, from the doorway of his home, fired his weapon striking Yoshi in the chest. Rodney immediately closed the door and locked it, instructing his wife to call 911. The family then proceeded to close open windows throughout the house and gathered around the kitchen table blocking out the plaintive cries emanating from the carport and the flashing lights of emergency vehicles.

The shooting attracted national, as well as international attention. Following a four-day trial on September 12-15, 1994, the trial judge rendered judgment in favor of Yoshi's parents, Masaichi and Mieko Hattori (the Hattoris) finding Rodney Peairs to be solidarily liable with his homeowner's insurer, Louisiana Farm Bureau Mutual Insurance Company (Farm Bureau), in the amount of $653,077.85 together with legal interest and costs. Farm Bureau's liability was subject to the $100,000.00 coverage limitations of its policy.

Farm Bureau subsequently tendered its policy limits plus interest; Rodney Peairs has appealed. . . .

[The discussion of first assignment of error concerning the refusal to admit their testimony of an expert is omitted.]

The second assignment of error raised by Rodney Peairs is that the trial court was manifestly erroneous in determining that the shooting was not justified under the circumstances presented by this case. With regard to this issue, the trial judge found:

The law in Louisiana is that the standard in determining when a homicide is justified is found in La.R.S. 14:20. This is a criminal statute, but it is applicable to civil cases. The jurisprudence in Louisiana is well-settled that resort to the use of a dangerous weapon to repel an attack is not justified except in exceptional cases where the actor's fear of danger is not only genuine but is founded upon facts that would likely produce similar emotions in men of reasonable prudence.

There was absolutely no need to resort to the use of a dangerous weapon to repel an attack, as, in fact there would have been no fear of an attack if Rodney had summoned help or simply stayed within his home. Rodney Peairs' statement, "I was scared to death." [sic] We have no explanation why. No other reason than he heard his wife slam a door and say, "Get the gun."

The court believes very sincerely that a reasonable person would have responded with "Why do I need [sic] gun? What did you see, Bonnie?" Further, Rodney Peairs saw Yoshi at the back of the Toyota. He had sufficient time to shut the door, which Bonnie had done earlier. The court inquired as to why he did not shut the door. The excuse, well, the second time the door was open wider. So what? We know that when Rodney Peairs first saw Yoshi, he was further away than when Bonnie had seen him, and she was able to shut the door.

Self defense is not acceptable. There was no justification whatsoever that a killing was necessary for Rodney Peairs to save himself and/or to protect his family.

After a thorough review of the record, we must agree with the trial court. In brief, Rodney Peairs similarly relies upon La.R.S. 14:20[1] and asserts that at the time he shot Yoshi he reasonably believed that he was in imminent danger of losing his life or receiving great bodily harm and that the use of deadly force was necessary to save himself and his family. Rodney Peairs also cites Duplechain v. Turner, 444 So. 2d 1322, 1326 (La. App. 4th Cir.), writ denied, 448 So.2d 114 (La. 1984), and a number of other cases for the proposition that the danger itself need not be real, if the actor reasonably believes that the threat of great bodily harm or death is imminent. Upon review of the cases cited by Rodney Peairs, we find same to be inapposite as the intruders were either armed or engaged in surreptitious activity on the defendant's property.

While we do not doubt that Rodney Peairs' fear of impending bodily harm was genuine, we nevertheless find nothing within the record to support his assertion that such fear was reasonable. Prior to the shooting, Yoshi and Webb had announced their presence by ringing the doorbell of the Peairs' home. Testifying that he believed Yoshi to be armed, Rodney Peairs conceded that he did not see a gun, a knife, a stick, or a club—only an object which he later ascertained to be a camera. In the well-lit carport, Rodney Peairs stated that he observed an oriental person proceeding towards him and that he appeared to be laughing. We have no

---

1. A homicide is justifiable:

(1) When committed in self-defense by one who reasonably believes that he is in imminent danger of losing his life or receiving great bodily harm and that the killing is necessary to save himself from that danger.

(2) When committed for the purpose of preventing a violent or forcible felony involving danger to life or of great bodily harm by one who reasonably believes that such an offense is about to be committed and that such action is necessary for its prevention. The circumstances must be sufficient to excite the fear of a reasonable person that there would be serious danger to his own life or person if he attempted to prevent the felony without the killing.

(3) When committed against a person whom one reasonably believes to be likely to use any unlawful force against a person present in a dwelling or a place of business while committing or attempting to commit a burglary or robbery of such dwelling or business. The homicide shall be justifiable even though the person does not retreat from the encounter.

(4) When committed by a person lawfully inside a dwelling or a place of business against a person who is attempting to make an unlawful entry into the dwelling or place of business, or who has made an unlawful entry into the dwelling or place of business, and the person committing the homicide reasonably believes that the use of deadly force is necessary to prevent the entry or to compel the intruder to leave the premises. The homicide shall be justifiable even though the person committing the homicide does not retreat from the encounter.

idea why Yoshi failed to heed Rodney Peairs' order to "Freeze," or grasp the danger posed by the gun, but can only speculate that the answer stems from cultural differences and an unfamiliarity with American slang. Under the circumstances of this case, we cannot say that it was either reasonable or necessary for Rodney Peairs to resort to the use of deadly force in order to protect himself and his family. This assignment of error is without merit.

The next assignment of error raised by Rodney Peairs is that the trial court was manifestly erroneous in its determination that the shooting of Yoshi was an intentional act. In support of this assignment, Rodney Peairs cites Bazley v. Tortorich, 397 So. 2d 475 (La.1981) for the proposition that an act is intentional "only where the actor entertained a desire to bring about the consequences that followed or where the actor believed that the result was substantially certain to follow." Rodney Peairs claims that while he intended to prevent an intruder from injuring himself or his family, he did not intend to kill a sixteen-year-old exchange student, and relying on *Bazley*, contends that his shooting of Yoshi does not constitute an intentional tort. We believe Rodney Peairs has misconstrued the holding of *Bazley*, and therefore his reliance thereon is misplaced.

It is clear from the testimony elicited at trial that Rodney Peairs intended to shoot the individual who was proceeding under the carport towards him. At the time he fired the .44 magnum revolver, Rodney Peairs knew or should have known that serious injury or death were reasonably certain to result from this act, As our supreme court stated in *Bazley*, "[i]ntent is not, however, limited to consequences which are desired. If the actor knows that the consequences are certain, or substantially certain, to result from his act, and still goes ahead, he is treated by the law as if he had in fact desired to produce the result." *Bazley*, 397 So. 2d 475, 482 (La.1981).

Because Rodney Peairs, at the time he pulled the trigger, clearly intended to harm the individual we now know to be Yoshi, in the mistaken belief that he was an intruder, his mistake is no defense. Rodney Peairs clearly intended to harm someone. See, 12 F. Stone, Louisiana Civil Law Treatise-Tort Doctrine § 130(2) (1977). The trial court did not err in its determination that the shooting of Yoshi was an intentional act.

In brief, Rodney Peairs inexplicably asserts that if we uphold the trial court's determination that the shooting was an intentional act, then we must address the issue of whether an exclusion within the Farm Bureau policy operates to exclude coverage. Because Farm Bureau has previously paid its policy limits to the Hattoris, together with accrued interest thereon, and has subsequently failed to appeal, the question of whether the exclusion applies is not an issue in this appeal.

For the foregoing reasons, this assignment of error is without merit.

In his fourth assignment of error, Rodney Peairs asserts that the trial court misinterpreted Louisiana law by not apportioning fault to the other parties involved in this incident. Specifically, Rodney Peairs contends that both boys — Yoshi and Webb — were at fault in this matter and that their actions contributed to the cause of this incident.

In brief, Rodney Peairs alleges that Yoshi caused or contributed to his death by failing to realize he had reached the wrong house, ignoring calls from Webb to return, failing to heed the directive to "Freeze," and finally, by failing to comprehend the danger posed by the gun. Similarly, Rodney Peairs also contends that Webb was at fault in bringing Yoshi to the wrong house, and thereafter, failing to adequately explain this fact to Yoshi. Rodney Peairs further asserts that it was foreseeable that Yoshi could have been injured in trespassing at night on property to which he had not been invited and at which he was not expected.

In his reasons for judgment, the trial judge stated that the actions of Webb did not constitute fault, and based upon our review of the record in this matter, we find no error in this determination.

The trial judge further found that "Rodney Peairs' conduct was intentional. That finding means the court will not make an inquiry as to whether there was any fault on behalf of Yoshi Hattori." Rodney Peairs argues that this is an incorrect application of Louisiana law, and cites Harris v. Pineset, 499 So.2d 499 (La. App. 2nd Cir. 1986), writs denied, 502 So.2d 114, 117 (La. 1987), and cases cited therein which hold that where a battery has been committed, the victim's conduct which helps to create the circumstances causing the injury can be taken into account in mitigating damages or apportioning fault.

Upon reviewing the cases cited by Rodney Peairs, we find that in each case, the plaintiff-victim initially provoked the difficulty in which he was injured; however, the defendant retaliated with more force than was necessary to repel the aggression. Because the victim voluntarily participated in the confrontation which resulted in his injuries, his damages were reduced accordingly. In the instant case, there has been no showing that Yoshi provoked the shooting, and for this reason, we find these cases to be inapposite.

As we have stated, the trial judge found the actions of Rodney Peairs to be intentional, and for this reason, declined to make a determination of whether Yoshi's actions that evening constituted fault on his part. Plaintiffs correctly point out that until recently, the general rule in Louisiana has been that contributory or comparative negligence is not a defense to an intentional tort. Broussard v. Lovelace, 610 So. 2d 159, 162 (La. App. 3rd Cir. 1992), writ denied, 615 So. 2d 343 (La.1993).

Following the trial of this case, our supreme court in Veazey v. Elmwood Plantation Associates, Ltd., 93-2818 (La. 11/30/94); 650 So. 2d 712, examined the concept of comparative fault as it exists in Louisiana today, and whether this theory could be extended to encompass harms caused by intentional torts. The court noted that while several Louisiana appellate courts have recently applied comparative fault to intentional torts, other circuits, including this court, have declined to do so.

Holding that while Louisiana law is broad enough to allow a comparison of fault between intentional tortfeasors and negligent tortfeasors, the court in *Veazey* cautioned that the question of whether such a comparison should be made, must be determined by the trial court on a case by case basis in light of public policy concerns. The court in *Veazey* declined to "express any opinion . . . as to whether, or in what situations, if any, victim fault should be compared to the fault of an intentional tortfeasor." *Veazey*, 650 So.2d at 719 n.10.

In the instant case, the trial court declined to make a determination of whether fault on Yoshi's part contributed to his injuries. We find no error in this determination.

Under the facts before us, there can be no reasonable or rational explanation which would justify the use of deadly force by Rodney Peairs that evening. Because his actions were so extreme, we believe it would be poor public policy to compare fault in this situation. We similarly find this assignment of error to be without merit.

SELF-DEFENSE IN THE RESTATEMENT, SECOND, OF TORTS

Self-defense is the most significant nonconsensual privilege in tort law. It is also the most intuitively satisfying privilege; one is surely justified in using force to defend oneself. The test as set forth in *Hattori* is whether a reasonable person would have perceived danger to his life. Courts continue to apply this doctrine. Thus, in Ashford v. Betleyoun, 2006 WL 1409793 (Ohio Ct. App.), plaintiff's decedent was shot when he brandished an air pistol at defendant in a robbery attempt. Defendant, who was licensed to carry a firearm, shot his assailant three times and killed him. In upholding summary judgment in favor of the defendant, the court held that defendant's reasonable belief that the gun was not fake gave him the right to respond in self-defense. Similarly, a third-party bystander was entitled to use reasonable force when he believed that the plaintiff, who initiated a barroom brawl, was acting in a wild and uncontrollable manner and was concerned that the plaintiff, while fighting with his opponent, might hit him. Flanagan v. The Grill, LLC, 2006 WL 494647 (Conn. Super. Ct.). The rules governing self-defense in tort are more complex and nuanced than may at first appear. The Restatement, Second, of Torts reflects this reality in its two main sections dealing with self-defense:

§ 63. Self-Defense by Force Not Threatening Death or Serious Bodily Harm

(1) An actor is privileged to use reasonable force, not intended or likely to cause death or serious bodily harm, to defend himself against unprivileged harmful or offensive contact or other bodily harm which he reasonably believes that another is about to inflict intentionally upon him.

(2) Self-defense is privileged under the conditions stated in Subsection (1), although the actor correctly or reasonably believes that he can avoid the necessity of so defending himself,

(a) by retreating or otherwise giving up a right or privilege, or

(b) by complying with a command with which the actor is under no duty to comply or which the other is not privileged to enforce by the means threatened.

§ 65. Self-Defense by Force Threatening Death or Serious Bodily Harm

(1) Subject to the statement in Subsection (3), an actor is privileged to defend himself against another by force intended or likely to cause death or serious bodily harm, when he reasonably believes that

(a) the other is about to inflict upon him an intentional contact or other bodily harm, and that

(b) he is thereby put in peril of death or serious bodily harm or ravishment, which can safely be prevented only by the immediate use of such force.

(2) The privilege stated in Subsection (1) exists although the actor correctly or reasonably believes that he can safely avoid the necessity of so defending himself by

(a) retreating if he is attacked within his dwelling place, which is not also the dwelling place of the other, or

(b) permitting the other to intrude upon or dispossess him of his dwelling place, or

(c) abandoning an attempt to effect a lawful arrest.

(3) The privilege stated in Subsection (1) does not exist if the actor correctly or reasonably believes that he can with complete safety avoid the necessity of so defending himself by

(a) retreating if attacked in any place other than his dwelling place, or in a place which is also the dwelling of the other, or

(b) relinquishing the exercise of any right or privilege other than his privilege to prevent intrusion upon or dispossession of his dwelling place or to effect a lawful arrest.

Sections 70 and 71 of the Restatement, Second, go on to address the issue of excessive force, limiting the self-defense privilege to that amount of force that the actor correctly or reasonably believes to be necessary to protect himself, and holding the actor who uses excessive force liable only for so much of the force as is excessive. Why doesn't the distinction between force that threatens death or serious bodily harm, and force that does not, adequately address the excessive force issue? Assuming in a given case that deadly force is justified, how can what the defendant did ever constitute "excessive force"?

Can a person claim self-defense against a police officer who attempts to unlawfully arrest her? In White v. Morris, 345 So. 2d 461 (La. 1977), the court rejected a police officer's battery claim where the defendant struck the officer in the face, causing injuries, in an attempt to flee unlawful arrest. The Supreme Court of Louisiana upheld the trial court's determination that the police officer lacked reasonable suspicion to arrest the defendant and determined that a person in Louisiana has a privilege to resist an unlawful arrest. The majority of states today, however, have abrogated the common law right to resist unlawful arrest. *See, e.g.,* State v. Hobson, 577 N.W.2d 825, 837 (Wis. 1998) ("we hold that Wisconsin has recognized a privilege to forcibly resist an unlawful arrest, but based on public policy concerns, we hereby abrogate that privilege"); State v. Clavette, 969 So. 2d 463, 466 (Fla. Dist. Ct. App. 2007) ("it is well established that a person is not entitled to use force to resist even an illegal arrest."). Other states have overturned by statute the common law right to resist an unlawful arrest. *See, e.g.,* Ala. Code § 13A-3-28 (2016). For an argument that courts should revive the right, *see* Craig Hemmens & Daniel Levin, *"Not a Law at All": A Call for a Return to the Common Law Right to Resist Unlawful Arrest,* 29 Sw. U. L. Rev. 1 (1999).

---

authors' dialogue 8

JIM: A couple of things about self-defense bother me. The first one is doctrinal. Tort law says that, in order to use deadly force in self-defense, a defendant's belief that he is being attacked with deadly force must be reasonable. If the defendant's belief is unreasonable, he loses the privilege and is liable to the plaintiff. Why isn't that simply liability for negligence? If the defendant acts unreasonably, he's negligent. What has battery got to do with it?

AARON: Well, who has the burden of proving that the defendant's belief was reasonable?

JIM: The defendant — it's an affirmative defense.

AARON: And who has to prove negligence in a negligence case?

JIM: The plaintiff. OK, but is that the only difference? The burden of proof?

AARON: You said something else was bothering you about self-defense.

JIM: Yeah. It seems to me that when a defendant mistakenly but reasonably believes that a completely innocent plaintiff is threatening him, and intentionally harms the plaintiff to protect himself, the defendant should pay the plaintiff for the plaintiff's well-being that the defendant has deliberately taken for his (the defendant's) own benefit. The defendant hasn't committed a battery; he acted reasonably, in self-defense. But there should be some other basis — implied contract? unjust enrichment? deliberate appropriation? — on which the innocent plaintiff can recover for what he "gave" to the defendant.

AARON: I tend to agree, at least philosophically. But why do you suppose the courts haven't come up with something?

BRAD: Let me jump in. Self-defense always has been and always will be an absolute privilege. One does not fool with absolutes.

YOU STARTED THE FIGHT

Does the privilege of self-defense operate in favor of a defendant who provoked the fight? In some jurisdictions a defendant who provoked the fight may find his right to self-defense curtailed. In Root v. Saul, 718 N.W.2d 197 (Wis. Ct. App. 2006), Root and Saul were watching a football game with others at a friend's house. Saul asked Root numerous times not to smoke his cigar. After exchanging insults Saul slapped Root "across the cheek and lips." Root then came after Saul. Saul put Root in a headlock. Saul testified, "The reason I put him in a headlock right away is because I felt, first of all, threatened or the possibility existed that something was going to happen to escalate it. And secondly, my thought was somebody is going to get hurt here and I tried to restrain him." Root suffered a torn ligament in his knee, which required surgery, and sued Saul for battery. The jury found that Saul's action was taken in self-defense. The appellate court reversed, finding that the trial judge had refused to give the jury an instruction to the effect that the defendant (Saul) lost the right to the privilege of self-defense if he provoked the attack. The

Wisconsin court concluded that "a defendant, who is the initial aggressor, can lose the right to claim self-defense, unless the defendant abandons the fight and gives notice to his adversary that he has done so." *Id.* at 204. *See generally* 6 Am. Jur. 2d Assault and Battery § 135. Louisiana, a state that had long followed the "aggressor doctrine," abandoned it after adopting pure comparative fault. Henceforth, the conduct of both the plaintiff and the defendant will be apportioned even when the conduct of both parties is intentional. Landry v. Bellanger, 851 So. 2d 943 (La. 2003).

hypo 25

A tells B that he is about to punch B in the face. B pulls out a knife and threatens A in order to protect himself. A pulls out a gun and shoots B to protect himself. Has A committed a battery against B?

hypo 26

A attacks B with a knife. B pulls out a gun to defend himself and fires at A. The bullet misses A and hits C, an innocent bystander. Has B committed a battery against C?

C. DEFENSE OF OTHERS

ARE WOULD-BE RESCUERS PRIVILEGED TO INTERVENE?

PAGES v. SELIMAN–TAPIA
134 So. 3d 536 (Fla. App. Ct. 2014)

On December 27, 2009, Dr. and Mrs. Pages were in the parking lot of the Dolphin Mall when they were confronted by Tapia, who accused Dr. Pages of parking too close to his car, causing it to become inoperable. According to witnesses who testified at an evidentiary hearing, Dr. Pages became very agitated, and was acting in an aggressive and confrontational manner toward Tapia, who had his hands in his pockets and was backing away from Dr. Pages. Dr. Pages continued to be confrontational and was bumping into Tapia with his chest. Mrs. Pages got between her husband and Tapia. At some point, Dr. Pages turned toward Tapia's wife, Ms. Singer, who was telling Dr. Pages to calm down. Dr. Pages then rushed toward Ms. Singer in an aggressive manner. At this point Tapia became worried about his wife, who was disabled, and Tapia rushed toward Dr. Pages and pushed him down, causing Dr. Pages to hit his head. . . .

Tapia was later charged by information with felony battery on Dr. Pages and misdemeanor battery on Mrs. Pages. Pursuant to a negotiated plea, Tapia pled guilty to the misdemeanor battery, was adjudicated guilty, and the State entered a nolle prosequi to the felony battery charge.

The Pages filed a civil lawsuit against Tapia, and in the complaint asserted two counts — assault and battery against Dr. Pages and loss of consortium on Mrs. Pages' behalf. The complaint was later amended to include an additional count of assault and battery upon Mrs. Pages.

Tapia asserted entitlement to immunity based on Florida's Stand Your Ground laws. The issue of immunity was referred to a general magistrate, who conducted an evidentiary hearing on June 14, 2012. The general magistrate found that Tapia had established his entitlement to immunity under section 776.032, Florida Statutes (2009). . . .

On appeal, we apply a mixed standard of review: "The trial court's legal conclusion[s are] reviewed de novo, but its findings of fact are presumed correct and can be reversed only if not supported by competent substantial evidence." . . .

Chapter 776, Florida Statutes, encompasses what is referred to as Florida's "Stand Your Ground" law. Under section 776.032(1):

> A person who uses force as permitted in s.776.012, s.776.013, or s.776.031 is justified in using such force and is immune from criminal prosecution and civil action for the use of such force, unless the person against whom force was used is a law enforcement officer. . . .

Section 776.012 ("Use of force in defense of person") provides in pertinent part:

> A person is justified in using force, except deadly force, against another when and to the extent that the person reasonably believes that such conduct is necessary to defend himself or herself or another against the other's imminent use of unlawful force.

Section 776.013, titled "Home protection; use of deadly force; presumption of fear of death or great bodily harm," provides, inter alia:

> A person who is not engaged in an unlawful activity and who is attacked in any other place where he or she has a right to be has no duty to retreat and has the right to stand his or her ground and meet force with force, including deadly force if he or she reasonably believes it is necessary to do so to prevent death or great bodily harm to himself or herself or another. . . .

§ 776.013(3).

Dr. and Mrs. Pages assert that Tapia was not entitled to immunity because, under section 776.013(3), he was "engaged in unlawful activity" when he pushed Dr. Pages. As evidence that Tapia was "engaged in unlawful activity," Dr. and Mrs. Pages point to Tapia's plea of guilty to the misdemeanor battery charge on Mrs. Pages. In other words, Dr. and Mrs. Pages argue, Tapia's guilty plea and adjudication of guilt for a battery upon Mrs. Pages established, as a matter of law, that Tapia was "engaged in unlawful activity" when he pushed Dr. Pages, barring Tapia from seeking immunity under section 776.032.

Even if we were to find that the guilty plea to misdemeanor battery upon Mrs. Pages established as a matter of law that Tapia was "engaged in criminal activity" under section 776.013, it is beside the point: Tapia was entitled to, and did, assert immunity not only under section 776.013, but under section 776.012 as well. Under section 776.012, Tapia would be justified in using non-deadly force against Dr. Pages if he reasonably believed such force was necessary to defend himself or Ms. Singer (Tapia's disabled wife) against Dr. Pages' imminent use of unlawful force.

It is true that under section 776.013(3), a person may "meet force with force, including deadly force" (emphasis supplied), which on its face appears to contemplate the use of both deadly and non-deadly force. We also acknowledge that the person seeking immunity under section 776.013(3) must establish that he was "not engaged in unlawful activity." However, this "not engaged in unlawful activity" language is not present in the applicable portion of section 776.012, which unambiguously provides for the justified use of non-deadly force. Section 776.032, by its express language, provides immunity for a person "who uses force as permitted in sections 776.012, 776.013 or 776.031." This language evidences a clear legislative intent to provide alternative bases for asserting immunity under the Stand Your Ground Law.[2]

Therefore, even if Tapia was determined to have been "engaged in unlawful activity" (the misdemeanor battery upon Mrs. Pages) at the time of his use of force upon Dr. Pages, it is of no moment because the force used by Tapia upon Dr. Pages was non-deadly force and, under the relevant portion of section 776.012, Tapia need not establish that he was not engaged in unlawful activity.

Following an evidentiary hearing, the magistrate issued a detailed fourteen-page report and recommendation with factual findings, credibility assessments,

---

2. Appellant's argument would require us to conclude that the Legislature, in enacting section 776.013(3), abolished the long-recognized and near-universal common-law concept that there is no duty to retreat when using non-deadly force in defense of self or others. *See* Weiand v. State, 732 So. 2d 1044, 1049 n.4 (Fla.1999) (observing there is no duty to retreat when using non-deadly force in self-defense); Redondo v. State, 380 So. 2d 1107, 1110 n.1 (Fla. 3d DCA 1980), quashed in part on other grounds, 403 So.2d 954 (Fla.1981) (recognizing there is "no duty to retreat when the defender uses non-deadly force to defend himself against an unlawful assault. 'It seems everywhere agreed that one who can safely retreat need not do so before using non-deadly force.' W. LaFave & A. Scott, Jr., Criminal Law 395 (1972). 'If he does not resort to a deadly force, one who is assailed may hold his ground whether the attack upon him be of a deadly or some lesser character. Although it might be argued that a safe retreat should be taken if thereby the use of any force could be avoided, yet . . . the logic of this position never has been accepted when moderate force is used in self-defense.' State v. Abbott, 36 N.J. 63, 174 A.2d 881, 885 (1961). Indeed all the duty to retreat cases in Florida have involved homicides in which deadly force was employed by the person asserting self defense. 16 Fla. Jur. 'Homicide' s 60 (1957)").

There is nothing in the language of the Stand Your Ground Law, or its legislative history, evidencing an intent to effectuate such a change. *See* Fla. S. Comm. on CJ, CS for SB 436 (2005). To the contrary, the Stand Your Ground Law *expanded* the circumstances in which one using *deadly force* has *no* duty to retreat and may stand his or her ground (hence the name of the law) and meet force with force. The creation of a duty to retreat before using non-deadly force in defense of self or others would require express legislative language. *See* Thornber v. City of Ft. Walton Beach, 568 So.2d 914, 918 (Fla.1990) (recognizing that "[t]he presumption is that no change in the common law is intended unless the statute is explicit and clear in that regard. Unless a statute unequivocally states that it changes the common law, or is so repugnant to the common law that the two cannot coexist, the statute will not be held to have changed the common law") (internal citations omitted).

and a conclusion that Tapia established by a preponderance of that evidence that he "had a reasonable fear for the safety of his wife, Ms. Singer, given Dr. Pages' immediate and continuing aggressive behavior and, based on this reasonable fear, Thus, because a determination was made that Tapia reasonably believed he had to act to defend against Pages' imminent use of "unlawful force" upon Tapia's wife, Tapia was justified in the use of non-deadly force under section 776.012, rendering unnecessary any further discussion of the alternative provisions or requirements of section 776.013(3).

We conclude that there is competent substantial evidence to support the magistrate's findings, and the trial court properly adopted the Report and Recommendation and dismissed the claims against Tapia.

Affirmed.

American courts have extended a privilege to actors who intervene and use force to protect and defend others from threats and attacks by third persons. In general, the privilege is the same as that of self-defense — the intervening actor is privileged to the same extent that the one threatened by the third person would be privileged to defend himself. Thus, for example, the use of deadly force requires greater justification than does the use of non-deadly force. *See, e.g.,* McCullough v. McAnnelly, 248 So. 2d 7 (La. Ct. App. 1971) (holding that the defendant was privileged to use deadly force to defend a third party, who was being viciously beaten by three assailants). And force in excess of what is reasonably required is not privileged. Most often, courts invoke the privilege when the defendant acts to protect family members and acquaintances against third-person threats. *See, e.g., McCullough, supra* (holding that the defendant was privileged to use deadly force to defend his son). But courts also extend the privilege to those defending strangers. *See, e.g.,* Beavers v. Calloway, 61 N.Y.S.2d 804 (N.Y. Sup. Ct.), *aff'd by* 66 N.Y.S.2d 613 (N.Y. App. Div. 1946) (holding that a female bar patron was privileged to intervene in an altercation between two band members).

OOPS! I THOUGHT YOU NEEDED HELP

The most interesting and difficult cases arise when the actor intervenes to protect another and it turns out the actor is mistaken — when it turns out, for example, that the other individual was not being attacked at all, but was actually being helped by a well-meaning, innocent third person. (Or even worse, when our hero mistakenly helps the wrongdoer instead of the victim.) Some courts allow the privilege if the mistaken belief regarding the need to intervene was reasonable under the circumstances. *See, e.g.,* Sloan v. Pierce, 85 P. 812 (Kan. 1906) (endorsing the reasonableness approach to the mistaken defense of third parties, while affirming the verdict against the defendant because the jury had determined that the defendant had made an unreasonable mistake when he intervened to protect his father by shooting the plaintiff); *cf.* Bell v. Smith, 488 S.E.2d 91 (Ga. Ct. App. 1997) (holding that the defendant could not invoke the privilege of defense of others because it was not reasonable for him to believe that his brother was in danger at the time that he shot the plaintiff's decedent); *see also* Restatement, Second, of Torts § 76 (1965). Other courts refuse to extend the defense-of-others privilege when the intervenor/defendant's belief was mistaken, even if the belief was sincere and reasonable. *See, e.g.,* State v. Wenger, 390 N.E.2d 801, 803 (Ohio 1979) ("A person who intervenes in a struggle and has no duty to do so, acts at his own peril . . ."). Which approach to mistaken defense of others strikes you as more sensible?

D. DEFENSE OF PROPERTY

KATKO v. BRINEY
183 N.W.2d 657 (Iowa 1971)

MOORE, Chief Justice.

Plaintiff's action is for damages resulting from serious injury caused by a shot from a 20-gauge spring shotgun set by defendants in a bedroom of an old farm house which had been uninhabited for several years. Plaintiff and his companion, Marvin McDonough, had broken and entered the house to find and steal old bottles and dated fruit jars which they considered antiques.

At defendants' request plaintiff's action was tried to a jury consisting of residents of the community where defendants' property was located. The jury returned a verdict for plaintiff and against defendants for $20,000 actual and $10,000 punitive damages.

After careful consideration of defendants' motions for judgment notwithstanding the verdict and for new trial, the experienced and capable trial judge overruled them and entered judgment on the verdict. Thus we have this appeal by defendants. . . .

II. Most of the facts are not disputed. In 1957 defendant Bertha L. Briney inherited her parents' farm land in Mahaska and Monroe Counties. Included was an 80-acre tract in southwest Mahaska County where her grandparents and parents had lived. No one occupied the house thereafter. Her husband, Edward, attempted to care for the land. He kept no farm machinery thereon. The outbuildings became dilapidated.

For about 10 years, 1957 to 1967, there occurred a series of trespassing and housebreaking events with loss of some household items, the breaking of windows and "messing up of the property in general." The latest occurred June 8, 1967, prior to the event on July 16, 1967 herein involved.

Defendants through the years boarded up the windows and doors in an attempt to stop the intrusions. They had posted "no trespass" signs on the land several years before 1967. The nearest one was 35 feet from the house. On June 11, 1967 defendants set "a shotgun trap" in the north bedroom. After Mr. Briney cleaned and oiled his 20-gauge shotgun, the power of which he was well aware, defendants took it to the old house where they secured it to an iron bed with the barrel pointed at the bedroom door. It was rigged with wire from the doorknob to the gun's trigger so it would fire when the door was opened. Briney first pointed the gun so an intruder would be hit in the stomach but at Mrs Briney's suggestion it was lowered to hit the legs. He admitted he did so "because I was mad and tired of being tormented" but "he did not intend to injure anyone." He gave no explanation of why he used a loaded shell and set it to hit a person already in the house. Tin was nailed over the bedroom window. The spring gun could not be seen from the outside. No warning of its presence was posted.

Plaintiff lived with his wife and worked regularly as a gasoline station attendant in Eddyville, seven miles from the old house. He had observed it for several years while hunting in the area and considered it as being abandoned. He knew it had long been uninhabited. In 1967 the area around the house was covered with high weeds. Prior to July 16, 1967 plaintiff and McDonough had been to the premises and found several old bottles and fruit jars which they took and added to their collection of antiques. On the latter date about 9:30 p.m. they made a second trip to the Briney property. They entered the old house by removing a board from a porch window which was without glass. While McDonough was looking around the kitchen area plaintiff went to another part of the house. As he started to open the north bedroom door the shotgun went off striking him in the right leg above the ankle bone. Much of his leg, including part of the tibia, was blown away. Only by McDonough's assistance was plaintiff able to get out of the house and after crawling some distance was put in his vehicle and rushed to a doctor and then to a hospital. He remained in the hospital 40 days. . . .

There was undenied medical testimony plaintiff had a permanent deformity, a loss of tissue, and a shortening of the leg.

The record discloses plaintiff to trial time had incurred $710 medical expense, $2056.85 for hospital service, $61.80 for orthopedic service and $750 as loss of earnings. In addition thereto the trial court submitted to the jury the question of damages for pain and suffering and for future disability.

III. Plaintiff testified he knew he had no right to break and enter the house with intent to steal bottles and fruit jars therefrom. He further testified he had entered a plea of guilty to larceny in the nighttime of property of less than $20 value from a private building. He stated he had been fined $50 and costs and paroled during good behavior from a 60-day jail sentence. Other than minor traffic charges this was plaintiff's first brush with the law. On this civil case appeal it is not our prerogative to review the disposition made of the criminal charge against him.

IV. The main thrust of defendants' defense in the trial court and on this appeal is that "the law permits use of a spring gun in a dwelling or warehouse for the purpose of preventing the unlawful entry of a burglar or thief." They repeated this contention in their exceptions to the trial court's instructions 2, 5 and 6. They took no exception to the trial court's statement of the issues or to other instructions.

In the statement of issues the trial court stated plaintiff and his companion committed a felony when they broke and entered defendants' house. In instruction 2 the court referred to the early case history of the use of spring guns and stated under the law their use was prohibited except to prevent the commission of felonies of violence and where human life is in danger. The instruction included a statement [that] breaking and entering is not a felony of violence.

Instruction 5 stated: "You are hereby instructed that one may use reasonable force in the protection of his property, but such right is subject to the qualification that one may not use such means of force as will take human life or inflict great bodily injury. Such is the rule even though the injured party is a trespasser and is in violation of the law himself."

Instruction 6 stated: "An owner of premises is prohibited from willfully or intentionally injuring a trespasser by means of force that either takes life or inflicts great bodily injury; and therefore a person owning a premise is prohibited from setting out 'spring guns' and like dangerous devices which will likely take life or inflict great bodily injury, for the purpose of harming trespassers. The fact that the trespasser may be acting in violation of the law does not change the rule. The only time when such conduct of setting a 'spring gun' or a like dangerous device is justified would be when the trespasser was committing a felony of violence or a felony punishable by death, or where the trespasser was endangering human life by his act."

Instruction 7, to which defendants made no objection or exception, stated: "To entitle the plaintiff to recover for compensatory damages, the burden of proof is upon him to establish by a preponderance of the evidence each and all of the following propositions:

1. That defendants erected a shotgun trap in a vacant house on land owned by defendant, Bertha L. Briney, on or about June 11, 1967, which fact was known only by them, to protect household goods from trespassers and thieves.
2. That the force used by defendants was in excess of that force reasonably necessary and which persons are entitled to use in the protection of their property.
3. That plaintiff was injured and damaged and the amount thereof.
4. That plaintiff's injuries and damages resulted directly from the discharge of the shotgun trap which was set and used by defendants.

The overwhelming weight of authority, both textbook and case law, supports the trial court's statement of the applicable principles of law.

Prosser on Torts, Third Edition, pages 116-118, states:

> . . . the law has always placed a higher value upon human safety than upon mere rights in property, it is the accepted rule that there is no privilege to use any force calculated to cause death or serious bodily injury to repel the threat to land or chattels, unless there is also such a threat to the defendant's personal safety as to justify a self-defense. . . . spring guns and other mankilling devices are not justifiable against a mere trespasser, or even a petty thief. They are privileged only against those upon whom the landowner, if he were present in person would be free to inflict injury of the same kind. . . .

In Hooker v. Miller, 37 Iowa 613, we held defendant vineyard owner liable for damages resulting from a spring gun shot although plaintiff was a trespasser and there to steal grapes. At pages 614, 615, this statement is made: "This court has held that a mere trespass against property other than a dwelling is not a sufficient justification to authorize the use of a deadly weapon by the owner in its defense; and that if death results in such a case it will be murder, though the killing be actually necessary to prevent the trespass. The State v. Vance, 17 Iowa 138." At page 617 this court said: "(T)respassers and other inconsiderable violators of the law are not to be visited by barbarous punishments or prevented by inhuman inflictions of bodily injuries."

The facts in Allison v. Fiscus, . . . 110 N.E.2d 237, . . . decided in 1951, are very similar to the case at bar. There plaintiff's right to damages was recognized for injuries received when he feloniously broke a door latch and started to enter defendant's warehouse with intent to steal. As he entered a trap of two sticks of dynamite buried under the doorway by defendant owner was set off and plaintiff seriously injured. The court held the question whether a particular trap was justified as a use of reasonable and necessary force against a trespasser engaged in the commission of a felony should have been submitted to the jury. The Ohio Supreme Court recognized plaintiff's right to recover punitive or exemplary damages in addition to compensatory damages. . . .

The legal principles stated by the trial court . . . are well established and supported by the authorities cited and quoted *supra*. There is no merit in defendants' objections and exceptions thereto. Defendants' various motions based on the same reasons stated in exceptions to instructions were properly overruled.

Study and careful consideration of defendants' contentions on appeal reveal no reversible error.

Affirmed.

All Justices concur except LARSON, J., who dissents.

LARSON, Justice.

I respectfully dissent, first, because the majority wrongfully assumes that by installing a spring gun in the bedroom of their unoccupied house the defendants intended to shoot any intruder who attempted to enter the room. Under the record presented here, that was a fact question. Unless it is held that these property owners are liable for any injury to a intruder from such a device regardless of the intent with which it is installed, liability under these pleadings must rest upon two definite issues of fact, i.e., did the defendants intend to shoot the invader, and if so, did they employ unnecessary and unreasonable force against him? . . .

Unless, then, we hold for the first time that liability for death or injury in such cases is absolute, the matter should be remanded for a jury determination of defendant's intent in installing the device under instructions usually given to a jury on the issue of intent.

I personally have no objection to this court's determination of the public policy of this state in such a case to ban the use of such devices in all instances where there is no intruder threat to human life or safety, but I do say we have never done so except in the case of a mere trespasser in a vineyard. Hooker v. Miller, 37 Iowa 613 (1873). To that extent, then, this is a case of first impression, and in any opinion we should make the law in this jurisdiction crystal clear. Although the legislature could pronounce this policy, as it has in some states, since we have entered this area of the law by the Hooker decision, I believe it proper for us to declare the applicable law in cases such as this for the guidance of the bench and bar hereafter. The majority opinion utterly fails in this regard. It fails to recognize the problem where such a device is installed in a building housing valuable property to ward off criminal intruders, and to clearly place the burden necessary to establish liability. . . .

I feel the better rule is that an owner of buildings housing valuable property may employ the use of spring guns or other devices intended to repel but not seriously injure an intruder who enters his secured premises with or without a criminal intent, but I do not advocate its general use, for there may also be liability for negligent installation of such a device. What I mean to say is that under such circumstances as we have here the issue as to whether the set was with an intent to seriously injure or kill an intruder is a question of fact that should be left to the jury under proper instructions, that the mere setting of such a device with a resultant serious injury should not as a matter of law establish liability. . . .

Although I am aware of the often-repeated statement that personal rights are more important than property rights, where the owner has stored his valuables representing his life's accumulations, his livelihood business, his tools and implements, and his treasured antiques as appears in the case at bar, and where the evidence is sufficient to sustain a finding that the installation was intended only as a warning to ward off thieves and criminals, I can see no compelling reason why the use of such a device alone would create liability as a matter of law. . . .

In the case at bar, as I have pointed out, there is a sharp conflict in the evidence. The physical facts and certain admissions as to how the gun was aimed would tend to support a finding of intent to injure, while the direct testimony of both defendants was that the gun was placed so it would "hit the floor eventually" and that it was set "low so it couldn't kill anybody." Mr. Briney testified, "My purpose in setting up the gun was not to injure somebody. I thought more or less that the gun would be at a distance of where anyone would grab the door, it would scare them," and in setting the angle of the gun to hit the lower part of the door, he said, "I didn't think it would go through quite that hard."

If the law in this jurisdiction permits, which I think it does, an explanation of the setting of a spring gun to repel invaders of certain private property, then the intent with which the set is made is a vital element in the liability issue.

In view of the failure to distinguish and clearly give the jury the basis upon which it should determine that liability issue, I would reverse and remand the entire case for a new trial. . . .

FOOD FOR THOUGHT

The *Katko* decision generated considerable disagreement among legal scholars. While commentators who believe that the primary purpose of tort law is to promote fairness values are able to defend the *Katko* court's reasoning that the law should place a higher value upon human life than upon mere property rights, commentators who see tort law as promoting efficiency-based instrumentalism question the accuracy of such a blanket assertion. For example, Professor (now

Judge) Posner argues that courts adjudicating defense-of-property matters should rely upon case-by-case cost-benefit analysis, Richard A. Posner, *Killing or Wounding to Protect a Property Interest*, 14 J.L. & Econ. 201, 214, 225 (1971):

> [N]either blanket permission nor blanket prohibition of spring guns and other methods of using deadly force to protect property interests is likely to be the rule of liability that minimizes the relevant costs. What is needed is a standard of reasonableness that permits the court to weigh such considerations as the value of property at stake, its location (which bears not only on the difficulty of protecting it by other means but also on the likelihood of innocent trespass), what kind of warning was given, the deadliness of the device (there is no reason to recognize a privilege to kill when adequate protection can be assured by a device that only wounds), the character of the conflicting activities, the trespasser's care or negligence, and the cost of avoiding interference by other means (including storing the property elsewhere). . . .
>
> All things considered, the approach to tort questions sketched here seems decidedly superior to the "method of maxims" — the pseudo-logical deduction of rules from essentially empty formulas such as "no man should be permitted to do indirectly what he would be forbidden to do directly" or "the interest in property can never outweigh the value of human life" — that plays so large a role in certain kinds of legal scholarship.

hypo **27**

At a 9/11 Memorial erected in the State of New California, a wealthy donor commissioned a statue of a fireman. The statue was to honor the memory of the brave men and women who lost their lives to save the victims of the Twin Tower collapse after being struck by airplanes hijacked by terrorists. The statue was sculpted by Aristo Clavy, a world-renowned artist. Newspapers reported that the cost of the statue was $2 million. On the first day that the memorial was open to the public, Jack Crazy, an anarchist, came to the memorial and raised his gun to shoot at and damage the Clavy statue. He screamed, "Down with the statue that honors the pigs." A state police officer, Jane LaBrave, drew her gun and shot Crazy dead. She explained that it was either the statue or Crazy. "Those were my choices. I did not have the luxury of trying to aim so as not to kill him. There was no time to take a more careful aim." Crazy's wife brings a wrongful death action against the State of New California. What result?

E. RECOVERY OF PROPERTY

HEY! THAT'S MY BRIEFCASE!

In general, one who has lost rightful possession of a chattel to another must resort to legal redress to recover the property. The specter of two competing parties, each seeking forcibly to take control of the property, militates against self-help as an appropriate remedy. Nonetheless, the courts have had to make some accommodation for the reality that one who discovers that another has absconded with her property will instinctively move quickly to regain the lost property. Hence, courts came to recognize a privilege to use reasonable force to regain a chattel tortiously taken by another so long as the rightful possessor acted promptly in "hot pursuit" after dispossession or after timely discovery of it. *See* Restatement, Second, of Torts §§ 100-106. Thus, a shopkeeper who learns that she was paid with a counterfeit bill or a bogus check may, upon discovery, use self-help to recover the chattel. *See* Hodgeden v. Hubbard, 18 Vt. 504 (1846).

LIMITS ON SELF-HELP PRIVILEGES

The privilege to take self-help measures is limited. The possessor must act promptly to recover the chattel. Once the sense of immediacy has passed, the self-help privilege is lost. Only reasonable force may be used. Force likely to cause death or serious bodily harm is never permitted to recapture property. The party seeking to recapture the chattel must be in the right. If, in fact, the possessor seeking to recapture her chattel was mistaken, the privilege is not available. Thus, if a shopkeeper reasonably, but erroneously, believes that a check is bogus and uses reasonable force to recapture the chattel taken by the customer who wrote the check, the shopkeeper has no privilege, and any force used against the customer to retrieve the chattel constitutes a battery. Recall that, in Chapter 1, in discussing the dilemma of a shopkeeper who seeks to recover property from a shoplifter, we noted that in the absence of a special rule giving the shopkeeper a privilege to recover property from a suspected shoplifter, the shopkeeper acts at his peril. If, in fact, the shoplifter takes the property, then the privilege to recapture the stolen goods would protect her from a battery or false imprisonment claim. However, if the suspected shoplifter was innocent, then the shopkeeper may be held liable. Special shopkeeper statutes and the common law in some states (*see* § 120A of the Restatement, Second, of Torts) allow the shopkeeper to use reasonable force to detain the suspected shoplifter based on reasonable suspicion that goods have been taken, even if it turns out the shopkeeper was mistaken. In Guijosa v. Wal-Mart Stores, Inc., 6 P.3d 583 (Wash. Ct. App. 2000), *aff'd*, 32 P.3d 250 (Wash. 2001), a store surveillance clerk believed that the plaintiffs entered the store without hats, selected some hats, then left without paying for the hats that they put on their heads. The surveillance clerk questioned the salesman, who said that the men did not pay for the hats on their heads. Based on these incorrect beliefs, the surveillance clerk detained and held the three plaintiffs for 20 to 30 minutes before the police arrived. The appellate court sustained a jury verdict for Wal-Mart, finding that reasonable suspicion existed and the clerk detained plaintiffs for a reasonable time.

REPO MAN STRIKES AGAIN

Buyers who purchase goods under conditional sales contracts and who are in default on their payments are frequently confronted with sellers who seek to repossess goods under specific terms of the sales contract that allow such repossession. (The agents who do the repossessing are commonly referred to as "repo men.") The right of sellers to repossess is governed by Section 9-503 of the Uniform Commercial Code. That section states that "unless otherwise agreed a secured party has on default the right to take possession of the collateral. In taking possession a secured party may proceed without judicial process if this can be done without breach of the peace." Courts are not in agreement as to what constitutes a breach of the peace in the repo context. Some courts find any action by the seller against the consent of the buyer to constitute a breach of the peace, whereas others adopt a standard very much like the common law privilege allowing the repossessor to use reasonable force.

F. NECESSITY

VINCENT v. LAKE ERIE TRANSPORTATION CO.
124 N.W. 221 (Minn. 1910)

Action in the district court for St. Louis County to recover $1,200 for damage to plaintiffs' wharf, caused by defendant negligently keeping its vessel tied to it. The defendant in its answer alleged that a portion of the cargo was consigned to the plaintiffs' dock and on November 27, 1905, its vessel was placed alongside at the place and in the manner designated by plaintiffs and the discharge of cargo continued until ten o'clock that night, that by the time the discharge of cargo was completed the wind had attained so great a velocity the master and crew were powerless to move the vessel. The case was tried before Ensign, J., who denied the defendant's motion to direct a verdict in its favor, and a jury which rendered a verdict in favor of plaintiffs for $500. From an order denying defendant's motion for judgment notwithstanding the verdict or for a new trial, it appealed. Affirmed.

O'BRIEN, J.
The steamship Reynolds, owned by the defendant, was for the purpose of discharging her cargo on November 27, 1905, moored to plaintiff's dock in Duluth. While the unloading of the boat was taking place a storm from the northeast developed, which at about 10 o'clock p.m., when the unloading was completed, had so grown in violence that the wind was then moving at 50 miles per hour and continued to increase during the night. There is some evidence that one, and perhaps two, boats were able to enter the harbor that night, but it is plain that navigation was practically suspended from the hour mentioned until the morning of the 29th, when the storm abated, and during that time no master would have been justified in attempting to navigate his vessel, if he could avoid doing so. After the discharge of the cargo the Reynolds signaled for a tug to tow her from the dock, but none could be obtained because of the severity of the storm. If the lines holding the ship to the dock had been cast off, she would doubtless have drifted away; but, instead, the lines were kept fast, and as soon as one parted or chafed it was replaced, sometimes with a larger one. The vessel lay upon the outside of the dock, her bow

to the east, the wind and waves striking her starboard quarter with such force that she was constantly being lifted and thrown against the dock, resulting in its damage, as found by the jury, to the amount of $500.

We are satisfied that the character of the storm was such that it would have been highly imprudent for the master of the Reynolds to have attempted to leave the dock or to have permitted his vessel to drift away from it. One witness testified upon the trial that the vessel could have been warped into a slip, and that, if the attempt to bring the ship into the slip had failed, the worst that could have happened would be that the vessel would have been blown ashore upon a soft and muddy bank. The witness was not present in Duluth at the time of the storm, and, while he may have been right in his conclusions, those in charge of the dock and the vessel at the time of the storm were not required to use the highest human intelligence, nor were they required to resort to every possible experiment which could be suggested for the preservation of their property. Nothing more was demanded of them than ordinary prudence and care, and the record in this case fully sustains the contention of the appellant that, in holding the vessel fast to the dock, those in charge of her exercised good judgment and prudent seamanship.

It is claimed by the respondent that it was negligence to moor the boat at an exposed part of the wharf, and to continue in that position after it became apparent that the storm was to be more than usually severe. We do not agree with this position. The part of the wharf where the vessel was moored appears to have been commonly used for that purpose. It was situated within the harbor at Duluth, and must, we think, be considered a proper and safe place, and would undoubtedly have been such during what would be considered a very severe storm. The storm which made it unsafe was one which surpassed in violence any which might have reasonably been anticipated.

The appellant contends by ample assignments of error that, because its conduct during the storm was rendered necessary by prudence and good seamanship under conditions over which it had no control, it cannot be held liable for any injury resulting to the property of others, and claims that the jury should have been so instructed. An analysis of the charge given by the trial court is not necessary, as in our opinion the only question for the jury was the amount of damages which the plaintiffs were entitled to recover, and no complaint is made upon that score.

The situation was one in which the ordinary rules regulating property rights were suspended by forces beyond human control, and if, without the direct intervention of some act by the one sought to be held liable, the property of another was injured, such injury must be attributed to the act of God, and not to the wrongful act of the person sought to be charged. If during the storm the Reynolds had entered the harbor, and while there had become disabled and been thrown against the plaintiffs' dock, the plaintiffs could not have recovered. Again, if while attempting to hold fast to the dock the lines had parted, without any negligence, and the vessel carried against some other boat or dock in the harbor, there would be no liability upon her owner. But here those in charge of the vessel deliberately and by their direct efforts held her in such a position that the damage to the dock resulted, and, having thus preserved the ship at the expense of the dock, it seems to us that her owners are responsible to the dock owners to the extent of the injury inflicted.

In Depue v. Flatau, . . . 111 N.W. 1 [(Minn. 1907)], this court held that where the plaintiff, while lawfully in the defendants' house, became so ill that he was incapable of traveling with safety, the defendants were responsible to him in damages for compelling him to leave the premises. If, however, the owner of the premises had furnished the traveler with proper accommodations and medical attendance, would he have been able to defeat an action brought against him for their reasonable worth?

In Ploof v. Putnam [71 A. 188 (Vt. 1908)], the Supreme Court of Vermont held that where, under stress of weather, a vessel was without permission moored to a private dock at an island in Lake Champlain owned by the defendant, the plaintiff was not guilty of trespass, and that the defendant was responsible in damages because his representative upon the island unmoored the vessel, permitting it to drift upon the shore, with resultant injuries to it. If, in that case, the vessel had been permitted to remain, and the dock had suffered an injury, we believe the shipowner would have been held liable for the injury done.

Theologians hold that a starving man may, without moral guilt, take what is necessary to sustain life; but it could hardly be said that the obligation would not be upon such person to pay the value of the property so taken when he became able to do so. And so public necessity, in times of war or peace, may require the taking of private property for public purposes; but under our system of jurisprudence compensation must be made.

Let us imagine in this case that for the better mooring of the vessel those in charge of her had appropriated a valuable cable lying upon the dock. No matter how justifiable such appropriation might have been, it would not be claimed that, because of the overwhelming necessity of the situation, the owner of the cable could not recover its value.

This is not a case where life or property was menaced by any object or thing belonging to the plaintiff, the destruction of which became necessary to prevent the threatened disaster. Nor is it a case where, because of the act of God, or unavoidable accident, the infliction of the injury was beyond the control of the defendant, but is one where the defendant prudently and advisedly availed itself of the plaintiffs' property for the purpose of preserving its own more valuable property, and the plaintiffs are entitled to compensation for the injury done.

Order affirmed.

Lewis, J.

I dissent. It was assumed on the trial before the lower court that appellant's liability depended on whether the master of the ship might, in the exercise of reasonable care, have sought a place of safety before the storm made it impossible to leave the dock. The majority opinion assumes that the evidence is conclusive that appellant moored its boat at respondent's dock pursuant to contract, and that the vessel was lawfully in position at the time the additional cables were fastened to the dock, and the reasoning of the opinion is that, because appellant made use of the stronger cables to hold the boat in position, it became liable under the rule that it had voluntarily made use of the property of another for the purpose of saving its own.

In my judgment, if the boat was lawfully in position at the time the storm broke, and the master could not, in the exercise of due care, have left that position without subjecting his vessel to the hazards of the storm, then the damage to the dock, caused by the pounding of the boat, was the result of an inevitable accident. If the master was in the exercise of due care, he was not at fault. The reasoning of the opinion admits that if the ropes, or cables, first attached to the dock had not parted, or if, in the first instance, the master had used the stronger cables, there would be no liability. If the master could not, in the exercise of reasonable care, have anticipated the severity of the storm and sought a place of safety before it became impossible, why should he be required to anticipate the severity of the storm, and, in the first instance, use the stronger cables?

I am of the opinion that one who constructs a dock to the navigable line of waters, and enters into contractual relations with the owner of a vessel to moor at the same, takes the risk of damage to his dock by a boat caught there by a storm, which event could not have been avoided in the exercise of due care, and further, that the legal status of the parties in such a case is not changed by renewal of cables to keep the boat from being cast adrift at the mercy of the tempest.

JAGGARD, J., concurs herein.

FOOD FOR THOUGHT

You will recall that in the text following the *Scott* case, *supra,* dealing with informed consent to medical treatment, we considered the possibility that the doctor and patient might agree ahead of time, via contract, regarding the rights and responsibilities of each. Would not the same possibility also exist in connection with the *Vincent* decision? Indeed, in this context, one might expect courts to be more receptive to the idea of deferring to contract, since the parties to such an agreement would, in contrast to the medical situation, presumably be business entities dealing with each other at arm's length. Moreover, even if the shipowner and the dockowner in *Vincent* had not actually agreed ahead of time regarding who should pay for damage to the dock, might not the court frame the issue by asking what reasonable persons in such a situation would have agreed to, if they had thought of it ahead of time? If such a framing of the issue makes sense in *Vincent,* would it make sense in other situations we have considered thus far in this course? In *O'Brien,* the shipboard vaccination case involving apparent consent? In *Hackbart,* the professional football case involving implied consent? In connection with self-defense based on appearances, would not reasonable people agree ahead of time to allow one person, who reasonably believes he is about to be killed, to shoot the would-be perpetrator, but then to ask the shooter to pay the victim for his injuries if the shooter is mistaken, through no fault of the injured party, as to the other's intentions? Reconsider Authors' Dialogue #6, p. 86, *supra*.

CRITIQUES OF VINCENT

The privilege of necessity that emerges from *Vincent* is not without its critics. For example, Professor George Christie argues that this privilege, which is endorsed by the Restatement, Second, of Torts § 263, is based upon an erroneous reading of the relevant case law. Indeed, Christie argues that the *Vincent* court did not actually hold that the defendant was privileged by necessity to keep his ship tied to the plaintiff's dock for the duration of the storm; instead, the court merely held that the defendant was liable for damage to the dock because he had knowingly caused such damage by reattaching the ship's mooring lines after the storm had snapped them. While Christie agrees with the holding of the court in *Ploof v. Putnam*, a Vermont case discussed in *Vincent,* that an actor is privileged to damage the private property of another in order to save human life, he concludes that it is contrary to the principles of both law and morality to privilege one person to harm another's property so as merely to safeguard his own possessions. *See generally* George C. Christie, *The Defense of Necessity Considered from the Legal and Moral Points of View*, 48 Duke L.J. 975 (1999).

SACRIFICING PROPERTY TO SAVE ENTIRE COMMUNITIES

Less controversial, perhaps, are those cases in which the actor sought to be held liable destroys the property of another not to save his own private property but to save an entire town from destruction or to prevent the loss of life. For example, in Surocco v. Geary, 3 Cal. 69 (Cal. 1853), the defendant, a public official in San Francisco, ordered the destruction of the plaintiff's home so as to create a firebreak and prevent the spread of a vast inferno that was threatening to engulf the city. The plaintiff sued for the damage caused by the intentional destruction of his home, but the Supreme Court of California held that the necessity created by the impending destruction of the entire city of San Francisco privileged the defendant to act as he did. Accordingly, the plaintiff was not entitled to any compensation for the property loss that he suffered. In Brewer v. State of Alaska, 341 P.3d 1107 (Alaska 2014) fire-fighters acting under state authority set fire to the plaintiffs' vegetation in order to deprive a raging fire of fuel. The plaintiffs argued that the fire-fighters could have burned state property rather than waiting and causing the destruction of his private property. The court invoked the doctrine of public necessity and held that the state was not liable to pay damages for eminent domain under the "takings clause" of the Alaska or federal constitution. But what if the defendant in *Surocco* had destroyed the plaintiff's home merely to protect his own house from burning, not to save an entire city? Would the plaintiff then be entitled to compensation? What if the defendant had saved two homes? Three?

Similarly, in *Mouse's Case* (1609), an English decision relied on in *Ploof v. Putnam*, the defendant, a ferry passenger, threw a fellow-passenger's casket overboard to prevent the boat upon which they were crossing from capsizing during a storm. The court held that the plaintiff was not entitled to compensation in tort, because the destruction of his property was necessary to save the lives of all those aboard. However, the court also stated that the property owner could recover his losses from the operator of the ferry if he could prove that the ferryman had overloaded the boat, thereby creating the life-threatening situation and the necessity for discarding the plaintiff's casket into the river. *See also* Seavey v. Preble, 64 Me. 120 (1874) (holding that a doctor was privileged by necessity to order the destruction of wallpaper in rooms where smallpox victims were treated, so as to prevent the spread of the disease).

INJURING, MAIMING, OR KILLING TO SAVE LIVES

hypo 28

A is driving his car and sees a manhole cover that just exploded spewing forth fire. If he continues straight ahead he is certain to be killed as well as his wife and daughter, who are sitting in the car. If he veers to the right he will hit *B*, a young boy, either seriously injuring or more likely killing him. *A* decides to save three lives at the cost of *B*. *A* kills *B*. Is *A* liable for the death of *B*?

This problem, writ small in the hypo set forth above, takes on mega proportions when the question is posed with the regard to torturing terror suspects in what has come to be known as the "ticking bomb" problem. You have a suspect in custody who, you believe, has information about a bomb that will explode in hours, killing thousands of people. Do you have a privilege of necessity to torture the suspect to extract the desired information? If *Vincent* stands for the proposition that the boat owner is best situated to make a risk-utility decision as to whether the ship or the dock will suffer more damage and we thus grant him a conditional privilege to take another's property, should not a government agent be allowed to make a similar decision when confronted with a choice of taking another's liberty or life to accomplish a greater good? For fascinating discussions of the legal and ethical questions surrounding the defense of necessity when confronting terrorism, *see* John Alan Cohan, *Torture and the Necessity Doctrine*, 41 Val. L. Rev. 1587 (2007); Christopher Kutz, *Torture, Necessity and Existential Politics*, 95 Cal. L. Rev. 235 (2007); Jens David Ohlin, *The Torture Lawyers*, 51 Harv. Int'l L. J. 193 (2010); Alan M. Dershowitz, *Why Terrorism Works: Understanding the Threat, Responding to the Challenge* (2002). An early classic article struggling with the necessity defense in the case of explorers marooned in a cave who killed and cannibalized a cohort to save themselves from death is *The Case of the Speluncean Explorers*, authored by Professor Lon Fuller, 62 Harv. L. Rev. 616 (1949). It is a must-read for every law student.

G. LEGAL AUTHORITY

STOP, IN THE NAME OF THE LAW!

In an important sense, all of the privileges discussed in this chapter are exercised under the authority of law, inasmuch as they are sanctioned by courts as exceptions to what otherwise would be tortious conduct. This section, however, gives a special meaning to the phrase "legal authority." Here, we consider privileges retained by public officials. When such officials act within the limits of their predefined roles, exercising the power and authority that those roles afford them, such officials are not subject to liability for those actions. We are not here concerned with governmental immunities, which assume the underlying breach of duty but bar liability in order to protect the governmental fisc. Privileges based on legal authority render the conduct of officials lawful and appropriate.

A core example of the exercise of legal authority is the privilege of a police officer to arrest someone. While the average citizen is authorized, under very limited circumstances, to temporarily detain another, a police officer is officially authorized by the state to arrest and detain suspects for a much wider range of reasons. Of course, even police officers must act within reasonable limits. As noted in *Cartnail v. State*, "[n]o right is held more sacred, or is more carefully guarded by the common law, than the right of every individual to the possession and control of his own person, free from all restraint or interference of others, unless by clear and unquestionable authority of law." 753 A.2d 519, 525 (Md. 2000) (quoting Terry v. Ohio, 392 U.S. 1, 9 (1968)). Police officers must act, therefore, within "the reasonableness requirement of the Fourth Amendment" when effecting an arrest. Richardson v. McGriff, 762 A.2d 48, 73 (Md. 2000) (holding that the defendant-officer used reasonable force in shooting the plaintiff when the officer found the plaintiff hiding in a closet and mistook a vacuum cleaner for a gun). In addition, a police officer must afford the arrestee due process of law. If an officer unlawfully arrests without a warrant or probable cause, he may be liable for a variety of torts. *See, e.g.,* Pahle v. Colebrookdale Township, 227 F. Supp. 2d 361 (E.D. Pa. 2002) (a jury could hold a police officer liable for assault, battery, and false imprisonment when she injured a man with disabilities by pulling his arm behind his back, throwing him to the ground, kicking him, and handcuffing him, if the jury finds that the officer did not have probable cause for the arrest). *Accord* Lee v. City of South Charleston, 668 F. Supp. 2d 763 (S.D. W. Va. 2009) (question of fact for jury whether officer had grounds to detain and "strip search" plaintiff; summary judgment for defendant on claims of battery not warranted).

In addition to the privilege to effect lawful arrests, police officers are privileged to enter private property under legal authority without being deemed trespassers. However, if the police officers cause harm to a person's property while carrying out their official duties, such as effecting a lawful arrest, the government may be liable to the plaintiff for that harm under the federal Constitution's takings clause that prohibits the government from taking personal property without just compensation. *See, e.g.,* Wegner v. Milwaukee Mutual Insurance Co., 479 N.W.2d 38 (Minn.

1991) (plaintiff could recover against the city after police damaged plaintiff's house attempting to arrest a suspect who fled there). *But see* Kelley v. Story County Sheriff, 611 N.W.2d 475 (Iowa 2000) (plaintiff could not recover for damage done to two of his front doors by police officers executing an arrest warrant of a fleeing suspect).

H. DISCIPLINING CHILDREN

SPARE THE ROD AND SPOIL THE CHILD

The utilization of corporal punishment to discipline children is deeply rooted in American culture. The Bible itself repeatedly sanctions the use of physical force as a means of controlling wayward children. Thus, it should come as no surprise that the law privileges parents to use reasonable physical force in disciplining their children. Custodians who are in loco parentis may have a right to use corporal punishment on a child; a baby sitter does not qualify for this privilege. *See* McReynolds v. State, 901 N.E.2d 1149 (Ind. Ct. App. 2009). Teachers and other school officials also possess a similar privilege to inflict reasonable corporal punishment upon students. *Compare* Roy v. Continental Insurance Co., 313 So. 2d 349 (La. Ct. App. 1975) (four or five paddle strokes to student's buttocks is reasonable punishment), *and* O'Rourke v. Walker, 128 A. 25 (Conn. 1925) (eight strokes on each of student's hands could be found to be reasonable punishment), *with* Baikie v. Luther High School S., 366 N.E.2d 542 (Ill. App. Ct. 1977) (forcibly thrusting a student into a locker could be found to be unreasonable punishment), *and* Neal v. Fulton Cty. Board, 229 F.3d 1069 (11th Cir. 2000) (hitting a student in the eye with a metal lock could be found to be unreasonable punishment). Some courts consider this privilege on the part of teachers to be derived from that possessed by parents, as educators are considered to stand in loco parentis during school hours; other courts have held that a teacher's privilege is independent of a parent's and instead is derived from society's interest in maintaining order and discipline in schools.

hypo **29**

A and *B* divorce. The court awards *A* sole custody of their ten-year-old child, *C,* while *B* is given biweekly visitation rights. During a biweekly visit with *B, C* refuses to go to bed. As punishment, *B* strikes *C* with a belt. *A* brings suit against *B,* on behalf of *C,* for assault and battery. Has *B* committed a battery on *C*?

TEACHER'S PRIVILEGE: THE CONSTITUTIONAL DIMENSION

Courts have been reluctant to abridge the disciplinary privilege afforded to parents and teachers. In Ingraham v. Wright, 430 U.S. 651 (1977), the United States Supreme Court held that the infliction of corporal discipline in schools contravenes neither the Eighth Amendment prohibition on cruel and unusual punishment nor the due process clause of the Fourteenth Amendment. However, the Court held that the punishment itself must be reasonable in light of the "seriousness of the offense, the attitude and past behavior of the child, the nature and severity of the punishment, the age and strength of the child, and the availability of less severe but equally effective means of discipline." *Id.* at 662. If a teacher inflicts excessive physical discipline upon a student, he is subject to both civil and criminal sanctions. For a harsh criticism of the *Ingraham* decision, arguing that it was a decision based on tradition rather than modern due process law, *see* C.C. Swisher, *Constitutional Abuse of Public School Students: An Argument for Overruling* Ingraham v. Wright, 8 Whittier J. Child & Fam. Advoc. 3 (2008).

CRITIQUES OF SUCH AUTHORIZED PUNISHMENT

Although parents and teachers have inflicted corporal punishment upon generations of American children, contemporary legal scholars and social commentators have harshly criticized the continued utilization of physical discipline and the approbation that the law affords such practices. For example, Professor Bitensky asserts that corporal punishment violates international law, and she compares the physical punishment of children to slavery and wife beating, arguing that "children in this country hold an anachronistic subhuman status insofar as they alone may legally be made the object of violence. . . ." Susan H. Bitensky, *Spare the Rod, Embrace Our Humanity: Toward a New Legal Regime Prohibiting Corporal Punishment of Children,* 31 U. Mich. J.L. Reform 353, 473-474 (1998). *See also* Deana Pollard Sacks, *State Actors Beating Children: A Call for Judicial Relief,* 42 U.C. Davis L. Rev. 1165 (2009). Other critics allege that the use of corporal punishment is an ineffective disciplinary tool that actually encourages future incidents of violence on the part of children. *See generally* Leonard P. Edwards, *Corporal Punishment and the Legal System,* 36 Santa Clara L. Rev. 983 (1996). For an argument that the roots of violence against children began and continue to thrive under religious traditions, *see* Barbara Finkelstein, *A Crucible of Contradictions: Historical Roots of Violence Against Children in the United States,* 40 Hist. Educ. Q. 1 (2000).

While courts have continued to uphold the teacher's privilege to punish students, state legislatures have not been able to withstand the critics' pressure. The vast majority of states now either strongly discourage or completely prohibit corporal punishment in schools. *See, e.g.,* Mich. Comp. Laws § 380.1312 (2016) ("a person employed by or engaged as a volunteer or contractor by a local or intermediate school board or public school academy shall not inflict or cause to be inflicted corporal punishment upon any pupil under any circumstances"). Thirteen states expressly permit a teacher to physically punish a student. *See, e.g.,* Okla. Stat. tit. 21, § 844 (2016) ("parent, teacher or other person [may use] ordinary force as a means of discipline, including but not limited to spanking, switching or paddling"). However, even those states that prohibit corporal punishment recognize that in some situations, a teacher must be permitted to contact a student. *See, e.g.,* Mich. Comp. Laws § 380.1312 (2016) (a teacher "may use reasonable physical force upon a pupil as necessary to maintain order and control in a school or school-related setting for the purpose of providing an environment conducive to safety and learning"). Michigan and other states distinguish between force used to subdue and force used to punish a student; most permit the former, but not the latter. For more on this distinction, *see* Kathryn R. Urbonya, *Determining Reasonableness Under the Fourth Amendment: Physical Force to Control and Punish Students*, 10 Cornell J.L. & Pub. Pol'y 397 (2001).

Corporal punishment of children is not without its defenders. For example, Richard Garner, *Fundamentally Speaking: Application of Ohio's Domestic Abuse Violence Law in Parental Discipline Cases: A Parental Perspective*, 30 U. Tol. L. Rev. 1, 28 (1998), argues that states should not undermine what he views as fundamental family privacy values. He concludes:

> Spanking, slapping, and other forms of physical discipline still retain widespread acceptance for one simple reason: they tend to be viewed as effective where nothing else works. In general, parents understand their responsibilities to their children and take them seriously. Nothing can be more aggravating to a parent than someone else telling him or her the best way to handle his or her children. This is because every child and every disciplinary situation is different. One size does not fit all.

For a similar view that corporal punishment is sometimes beneficial, *see* Jason Fuller, *Corporal Punishment and Child Development*, 44 Akron L. Rev. 537 (2010).

I. AN UMBRELLA JUSTIFICATION DEFENSE

SINDLE v. NEW YORK CITY TRANSIT AUTHORITY
307 N.E.2d 245 (N.Y. 1973)

JASEN, Judge.

At about noon on June 20, 1967, the plaintiff, then 14 years of age, boarded a school bus owned by the defendant, New York City Transit Authority, and driven by its employee, the defendant Mooney. It was the last day of the term . . . and the 65 to 70 students on board the bus were in a boisterous and exuberant mood. Some of this spirit expressed itself in vandalism, a number of students breaking dome lights, windows, ceiling panels and advertising poster frames. There is no evidence that the plaintiff partook in this destruction.

The bus made several stops at appointed stations. On at least one occasion, the driver admonished the students about excessive noise and damage to the bus. When he reached the Annadale station, the driver discharged several more passengers, went to the rear of the bus, inspected the damage and advised the students that he was taking them to the St. George police station.

The driver closed the doors of the bus and proceeded, bypassing several normal stops. As the bus slowed to turn onto Woodrow Road, several students jumped without apparent injury from a side window at the rear of the bus. Several more followed, again without apparent harm, when the bus turned onto Arden Avenue.

At the corner of Arden Avenue and Arthur Kill Road, departing from its normal route, the bus turned right in the general direction of the St. George police station. The plaintiff, intending to jump from the bus, had positioned himself in a window on the right-rear side. Grasping the bottom of the window sill with his hands, the plaintiff extended his legs (to mid-thigh), head and shoulders out of the window. As the bus turned right, the right rear wheels hit the curb and the plaintiff either jumped or fell to the street. The right rear wheels then rolled over the midsection of his body, causing serious personal injuries.

The plaintiff, joined with his father, then commenced an action to recover damages for negligence and false imprisonment. At the outset of the trial, the negligence cause was waived and plaintiffs proceeded on the theory of false imprisonment. At the close of the plaintiffs' case, the court denied defendants' motion to amend their answers to plead the defense of justification. The court also excluded all evidence bearing on the justification issue.

We believe that it was an abuse of discretion for the trial court to deny the motion to amend and to exclude the evidence of justification. It was the defendants' burden to prove justification — a defense that a plaintiff in an action for false imprisonment should be prepared to meet — and the plaintiffs could not have been prejudiced by the granting of the motion to amend. The trial court's rulings precluded the defendants from introducing any evidence in this regard and were manifestly unfair. Accordingly, the order of the Appellate Division must be reversed and a new trial granted.

In view of our determination, it would be well to outline some of the considerations relevant to the issue of justification. In this regard, we note that, generally, restraint or detention, reasonable under the circumstances and in time and manner, imposed for the purpose of preventing another from inflicting personal injuries or interfering with or damaging real or personal property in one's lawful possession or custody is not unlawful. Also, a parent, guardian or teacher entrusted with the care or supervision of a child may use physical force reasonably necessary to maintain discipline or promote the welfare of the child.

Similarly, a bus driver, entrusted with the care of his student-passengers and the custody of public property, has the duty to take reasonable measures for the safety and protection of both — the passengers and the property. In this regard, the reasonableness of his actions — as bearing on the defense of justification — is to be determined from a consideration of all the circumstances. At a minimum, this would seem to import, a consideration of the need to protect the persons and property in his charge, the duty to aid the investigation and apprehension of those inflicting damage, the manner and place of the occurrence, and the feasiblity [sic] and practicality of other alternative courses of action. . . .

For the reasons stated, the order of the Appellate Division should be reversed and the case remitted for a new trial.

Why did the New York Court of Appeals create a new "justification" privilege? Why aren't the classic privileges to intentional torts set forth in this chapter perfectly adequate to the task of protecting the defendant in this case?

FOOD FOR THOUGHT

In Rodriguez v. Johnson, 504 N.Y.S.2d 379 (N.Y. Civ. Ct. 1986), a school bus matron slapped a child who, along with other passengers, was "noisy and troublesome." However, unlike *Sindle,* the court rejected the defendant's justification defense. In a decision broadly rejecting corporal punishment of children in general, the court reasoned that "[t]he tort of battery, which once protected only the bodily integrity of men, must now protect all persons, be they adults or children, from unauthorized physical contact. Physical abuse in even the slightest degree seriously harms children." *Id.* at 383. Can *Rodriguez* be reconciled with *Sindle?* What if the child was not only talking loudly, but also hitting other children? Are babysitters privileged to discipline children in their charge? In what other contexts might a justification defense apply?

chapter 3

Negligence

A. INTRODUCTION

Negligence as a separate action in tort dates back to the early nineteenth century. Why it emerged as a separate tort has engaged the interest of historians. But this much is certain. At the beginning of the twenty-first century, negligence is the dominant theory under which the overwhelming majority of tort actions are brought. Unlike the intentional torts, in which each category was carefully defined (e.g., assault, battery, false imprisonment), negligence is an all-purpose cause of action that can be tailored to fit almost every kind of human activity imaginable. It is breathtaking in its scope. A theory of law that judges almost all conduct as to whether it meets the standard of what a "reasonable person" would do under similar circumstances provides enormous latitude to injured persons seeking redress for harm done to them.

Notwithstanding the broad scope of negligence law, it is not entirely given over to intuition. To establish a cause of action in negligence, a plaintiff must prove facts that establish each of the following five elements:

(1) **Duty.** In general, members of society owe a duty to act reasonably to avoid causing physical harm to each other. However, exceptional situations arise where courts will question whether such an underlying obligation exists. For example, assume you are walking along the street and a stranger asks you to call 911 from your cell phone because he is having severe chest pains, and you refuse to do so. The law recognizes no duty to rescue a total stranger from injury. Thus, even if we were all to agree that your conduct was not reasonable, liability will not attach.

(2) **Breach of Duty.** Once a duty has been established, plaintiff must establish that the defendant failed to act reasonably. To do so, the finder of fact must first decide what constitutes reasonable care under the circumstances and then find that the defendant failed to meet that standard.

(3) **Cause-in-Fact.** The mere fact that the defendant breached a standard of reasonable care is not itself sufficient. Plaintiff must prove a connection between the defendant's negligent conduct and the harm suffered.

(4) **Proximate Cause.** A single negligent act may produce untold and unforeseeable consequences. A driver in midtown Chicago speeding ten miles per hour over the limit rear-ends an unmarked truck loaded with dynamite. The truck explodes and causes severe damage to the first 50 floors of the Sears Tower. The defendant speeder is not liable for the millions of dollars of damages caused by the explosion. The driver is not the proximate cause of all the harm done to the Sears Tower.

(5) **Harm.** Unlike the law of intentional torts, where a plaintiff need not suffer tangible harm and can recover nominal damages for the defendant's intentional invasion of her rights (even if wholly intangible), it is necessary for a plaintiff to suffer actual, tangible harm in order to make out a prima facie tort of negligence.

A noted torts scholar agrees with this way of parsing the elements of the negligence tort. *See* David G. Owen, *The Five Elements of Negligence*, 35 Hofstra L. Rev. 1671, 1673, 1686 (2007):

> Disputes over how the elements of negligence should be formulated arise every generation or so. . . . Normally, most courts and commentators have other (arguably more important) fish to fry and little interest in trifling with how one element or another should be conceived or phrased. Yet the outline of a tort structures how lawyers frame specific issues, which affects how scholars conceive and critique the law and how judges apply it to cases they decide. Thus, how the components of negligence are formulated is important to an elemental understanding of the nature of [the negligence] tort and how it properly should be applied. . . .
>
> Five is the number of negligence elements here endorsed, rather than the usual four. The five-element approach permits the division of the conventional, two-pronged element of "causation" (or "proximate causation") into its separate components, cause in fact and proximate cause, in recognition of the distinctions and complexity of issues embraced by each. Cause in fact requires a determination of cause and effect, which involves a sometimes rigorous comparison of physical, historical facts in the actual universe with those in a hypothetical universe from which the defendant's negligence is removed. Actual causation thus logically precedes and usually has little to do with the proximate cause inquiry into the array of fairness and justice considerations bearing on the propriety of imposing negligence responsibility on a person whose wrongdoing actually, though remotely, caused the plaintiff's harm.

A tort does not take place in five neatly defined stages. The elements set forth above are constructs that help us discuss discrete aspects of a negligence case. But once we have been through the entire prima facie case and the affirmative defenses that can be raised to a negligence action, we shall come to see that the elements and defenses are not totally separate. They create a seamless web, in which the elements are often related and intertwined.

It is worthwhile pausing briefly to consider the duty element of the negligence action set forth above. We begin with the assumption that in the overwhelming majority of tort cases an actor has a duty to exercise reasonable care when the actor's conduct creates a risk of physical harm. As we shall see in Chapters 6 and 7, in some cases courts decline to impose a duty of reasonable care. One instance was noted above. The law imposes no legal obligation to come to the rescue of a stranger even though we all might agree that calling 911 to help someone who is suffering severe chest pains is the reasonable thing to do. But now it gets tricky. Assume that we all agree that a defendant has a duty to act reasonably. For example, a landlord must act reasonably to keep the hallways of an apartment well lit. Assume further that she changed the bulb one hour before a tenant fell in the darkened hallway. The light bulb went out five minutes before the accident because some teenager threw a pebble at the bulb and broke it. Though the defendant has a duty to act reasonably, she almost certainly did so. She simply has not breached the duty. Some courts will say that the defendant had no duty to the plaintiff. However, the defendant escapes liability because it would be unreasonable to ask her to check the lights in the hallways every few minutes. She has met the standard of reasonable care. No reasonable jury could find otherwise. The court will find for the defendant as a matter of law. To say that defendant had no duty may suggest that she had no duty whatever to check the light bulbs in the hallway. She did owe such a duty, but she didn't breach it. Failure to breach a duty should not be confused with "no duty."

Finally, as we shall see in Chapter 5, tort law limits liability based on the notion of proximate cause. In our Sears Tower example it simply was not foreseeable that speeding ten miles per hour over the limit would cause such damage to the Tower. Once again, courts will often say that the speeding driver had no duty to the owners of the Tower. The driver did owe a duty of reasonable care and breached it but the consequences were so out of proportion to the negligent act that liability will not attach. For an exhaustive and stimulating discussion of the role of duty in negligence law critical of the Third Restatement, *see* John C. P. Goldberg and Benjamin C. Zipursky, *The Restatement (Third) and the Place of Duty in Negligence Law*, 54 Vand. L. Rev. 657 (2001). The Third Restatement's duty formulation has subtly removed power from trial courts to deny liability on no-duty grounds and allows juries to decide more cases based on whether they believe the defendant acted reasonably. *See* W. Jonathan Cardi, *Purging Foreseeability: The New Vision of Duty and Judicial Power in the Proposed Restatement (Third) of Torts*, 58 Vand. L. Rev. 739 (2005).

B. THE GENERAL STANDARD OF CARE: NEGLIGENCE BALANCING

LUBITZ v. WELLS
113 A.2d 147 (Conn. Super. Ct. 1955)

TROLAND, Justice.

The complaint alleges that James Wells was the owner of a golf club and that he left it for some time lying on the ground in the backyard of his home. That thereafter his son, the defendant James Wells, Jr., aged eleven years, while playing in the yard with plaintiff, Judith Lubitz, aged nine years, picked up the golf club and proceeded to swing at a stone lying on the ground. In swinging the golf club, James Wells, Jr., caused the club to strike the plaintiff about the jaw and chin.

Negligence alleged against the young Wells boy is that he failed to warn his little playmate of his intention to swing the club and that he did swing the club when he knew she was in a position of danger.

In an attempt to hold the boy's father, James Wells, liable for his son's action, it is alleged that James Wells was negligent because although he knew the golf club was on the ground in his backyard and that his children would play with it, and that although he knew or "should have known" that the negligent use of the golf club by children would cause injury to a child, he neglected to remove the golf club from the backyard or to caution James Wells, Jr., against the use of the same.

The demurrer challenges the sufficiency of the allegations of the complaint to state a cause of action or to support a judgment against the father, James Wells.

It would hardly be good sense to hold that this golf club is so obviously and intrinsically dangerous that it is negligence to leave it lying on the ground in the yard. The father cannot be held liable on the allegations of this complaint. . . .

The demurrer is sustained.

FOOD FOR THOUGHT

Why was it so clear to the trial judge that the allegations of the complaint could not support a cause of action for negligence? What if, just prior to leaving the golf club in the backyard, James Sr. had given James Jr. his first golf lesson and Junior was practicing his golf swing just the way his daddy had shown him? Shouldn't James Sr. have foreseen the danger of Judith getting hit by the backswing? What if there were half a dozen little boys and girls in the backyard when James Sr. left the scene?

What do you make of the judge's statement that it would not be good sense to hold a parent liable for leaving a golf club lying on the ground because it was not "obviously and intrinsically dangerous"? Can one extract a general rule of law that one who leaves common objects in his backyard will not be held liable for injuries caused by such objects? If so, what constitutes a common object? A baseball bat? A hockey stick? A kitchen knife left out on the picnic table? A rake left out on the lawn after removing the leaves in the fall? And what qualifies as an intrinsically dangerous object? An ice pick? A battery-operated hedge clipper?

In Thompson v. Kaczinski, 774 N.W.2d 829 (Iowa 2009), the defendants left a disassembled trampoline in their backyard and the wind carried it onto a nearby highway where it helped cause an accident in which the plaintiff suffered injury. The Iowa high court reversed the trial court's judgment for defendants as a matter of law, ruling that plaintiff's claim was for the trier of fact. Reading torts cases is an art form. In general, whether under a given set of circumstances conduct is negligent is for the trier of fact. Most often a jury decides whether the defendant's conduct was unreasonable and hence negligent. However, occasionally the trial judge concludes that "reasonable persons cannot differ" simply meaning that no reasonable jury could reach the conclusion that the jury did. When this happens the judge sits as a super jury with the power to decide that, under a given set of circumstances, negligence has not been or cannot be established.

Courts, however, are also empowered to establish rules of law as to whether given categories of conduct can serve as a predicate for a negligence cause of action. It is not always clear as to when courts are speaking in the echo chamber voice of lawmakers or when they are sitting as super juries policing the fact-finding role of juries. In *Lubitz*, the court might have been saying that it would not give the case to a jury to decide because no reasonable jury could find for the plaintiff on any set of facts arising from this complaint. Or it might have been articulating (clumsily to be sure) a general rule that a defendant has no duty to prevent common objects from lying around in his backyard.

It is not certain that all courts would agree with *Lubitz*. In Killeen v. Harmon Grain Products, Inc., 413 N.E.2d 767 (Mass. App. Ct. 1980), the court upheld a directed verdict for the manufacturer of a cinnamon-flavored toothpick that punctured the lip of a ten-year-old who fell, face down, while sucking the toothpick. Plaintiff claimed, in part, that the manufacturer of the toothpick was negligent because it was "pointed at both ends, rather than being somewhat rounded at one end." *Id.* at 769-770. The court noted that the toothpick, an "everyday item," was "exactly what it was represented to be, neither more nor less, with no hidden dangers or unpredictable propensities," and that such an everyday item could not be deemed "unreasonably dangerous" merely because it might foreseeably cause injuries. *Id.* The court stated (*id.* at 770):

> Toothpicks, like pencils, pins, needles, knives, razor blades, nails, tools of most kinds, bottles and other objects made of glass, present obvious dangers to users, but they are not unreasonably dangerous, in part because the very obviousness of the danger puts the user on notice. It is part of normal upbringing that one learns in childhood to cope with the dangers posed by such useful everyday items. It is foreseeable that some will be careless in using such items and will be injured, but the policy of our law in such cases is not to shift the loss from the careless user to a blameless manufacturer or supplier.

Although the manufacturer of the cinnamon-flavored toothpicks was not subject to liability, in an abrupt turnaround the court held that it was a jury question as to whether the retailer who sold the toothpicks to young children was negligent. The manufacturer, unlike the retailer, did not target youngsters in its sale or promotion of the toothpicks. If the retailer may be found negligent in *Killeen*, why is the father's possible negligence in *Lubitz* not a jury issue?

UNITED STATES v. CARROLL TOWING CO.
159 F.2d 169 (2d Cir. 1947)

[A barge, the "Anna C," was moored in a busy part of New York Harbor. The bargee — an employee hired to safeguard the barge — went ashore after checking the fasts to make sure they were tight. A tugboat, trying to clear an obstruction in the area, refastened the moorings of the Anna C and several neighboring barges.

After the tug moved away, the Anna C broke free and crashed into a nearby tanker, springing a leak. The Anna C filled with water, careened, and sank, spilling her cargo of flour. Anna C's owner contended that the owner and charterer of the tug were fully responsible for the incident. One issue that arose in the case was whether the bargee's absence constituted negligence. The court reasoned that if the bargee had been on board, he might have prevented the Anna C from going down, saving the cargo and avoiding "sinking damages." If the bargee's absence was negligent, the barge owner could not recover fully from the defendants for the loss of the boat and cargo. His contributory negligence would reduce the recovery.]

L. HAND, J. . . .

It appears . . . that there is no general rule to determine when the absence of a bargee or other attendant will make the owner of the barge liable for injuries to other vessels if she breaks away from her moorings. However, in any cases where he would be so liable for injuries to others, obviously he must reduce his damages proportionately, if the injury is to his own barge. It becomes apparent why there can be no such general rule, when we consider the grounds for such a liability. Since there are occasions when every vessel will break from her moorings, and since, if she does, she becomes a menace to those about her; the owner's duty, as in other similar situations, to provide against resulting injuries is a function of three variables: (1) The probability that she will break away; (2) the gravity of the resulting injury, if she does; (3) the burden of adequate precautions. Possibly it serves to bring this notion into relief to state it in algebraic terms: if the probability be called P; the injury L; and the burden, B; liability depends upon whether B is less than L multiplied by P: i.e., whether $B < PL$. Applied to the situation at bar, the likelihood that a barge will break from her fasts and the damage she will do, vary with the place and time; for example, if a storm threatens, the danger is greater; so it is, if she is in a crowded harbor where moored barges are constantly being shifted about. On the other hand, the barge must not be the bargee's prison, even though he lives aboard; he must go ashore at times. We need not say whether, even in such crowded waters as New York Harbor a barge must be aboard at night at all; it may be that the custom is otherwise . . . and that, if so, the situation is one where custom should control. We leave that question open; but we hold that it is not in all cases a sufficient answer to a bargee's absence without excuse, during working hours, that he has properly made fast his barge to a pier, when he leaves her. In the case at bar the bargee left at five o'clock in the afternoon of January 3rd, and the flotilla broke away at about two o'clock in the afternoon of the following day, twenty-one hours afterwards. The bargee had been away all the time, and we hold that his fabricated story was affirmative evidence that he had no excuse for his absence. The locus in quo — especially during the short January days and in the full tide of war activity — barges were being constantly "drilled" in and out. Certainly it was not beyond reasonable expectation that, with the inevitable haste and bustle, the work might not be done with adequate care. In such circumstances we hold — and it is all that we do hold — that it was a fair requirement that [the owner of the barge] should have a bargee aboard (unless he had some excuse for his absence), during the working hours of daylight. . . .

FOOD FOR THOUGHT

What kind of excuse would suffice to make the defendant bargee non-negligent and hence the owner of the barge not vicariously liable?

(1) He left for an hour to visit his sick mother.
(2) He went to the doctor because he had a fever and was away from the barge for two hours.
(3) He went to the rescue of another bargee who was drowning.
(4) He had a heart attack and was taken to the hospital. No one notified the owner of the barge that the bargee was incapacitated.

Should any of the excuses set forth exonerate the owner of the barge from his own negligence in not having a backup in place in the event of an emergency?

WASHINGTON v. LOUISIANA POWER & LIGHT CO.
555 So. 2d 1350 (La. 1990)

DENNIS, Justice.

We granted certiorari in this power line accident case to review the Court of Appeal's judgment setting aside a jury award to the adult children of a man who was electrocuted when he accidentally allowed a citizens band radio antenna to come into contact with an uninsulated 8000 volt electrical wire that spanned the backyard of his residence. We affirm. The jury verdict for the plaintiffs was manifestly erroneous. . . .

[Defendant owned an uninsulated high-voltage electrical wire that stretched over decedent's property. Decedent was a CB radio hobbyist who had an antenna which was designed to be raised or lowered in a part of the yard parallel to the wire and at a safe distance. The antenna was difficult to move under the wire without making contact. Five years before the event giving rise to this suit, decedent and his son, while attempting to move the antenna, made contact with the electrical wire; the son was thrown to the ground, and both father's and son's hands were burned. The father repeatedly contacted the electric company, which offered to bury the wire, but only on the condition that the father pay the cost. The father refused, but took special precautions after the first incident not to bring the antenna near the wire. Nevertheless, five years after the first incident, the father and a friend touched the wire while moving the antenna and the father died.]

After a trial on the merits, a jury found LP&L at fault in the accident and awarded plaintiffs $500,000 for pain and suffering and the loss of life of the decedent and $75,000 for each plaintiff's loss of love, affection and support. LP&L appealed suspensively. The Court of Appeal, noting that the decedent had five years earlier received an electrical shock when he touched the antenna to the same line, and had since that time been extremely careful to never move the antenna alone or toward the line until the day of the fatal accident, reversed, concluding that LP&L did not breach any duty owed to the decedent. . . .

When the evidence is clear, as in the present case, that the power company either knew or should have known of the possibility of an accident that materialized in the decedent's electrocution, the remaining negligence issue is whether the possibility of such injury or loss constituted an unreasonable risk of harm. . . . Such a case invites "a sharp focus upon the essential balancing process that lies at the heart of negligence." Malone, *Work of Appellate Courts*, 29 La. L. Rev. 212, 212 (1969). In this regard, we recently held that the power company's duty to provide against resulting injuries, as in similar situations, is a function of three variables: (1) the possibility that the electricity will escape; (2) the gravity of the resulting injury, if it does; (3) the burden of taking adequate precautions that would avert the accident. When the product of the possibility of escape multiplied times the gravity of the harm, if it happens, exceeds the burden of precautions, the risk is unreasonable and the failure to take those precautions is negligence. [The court referred to other cases, including United States v. Carroll Towing Co., 159 F.2d 169, 173 (2d Cir. 1947).]

Applying the negligence balancing process, we conclude that although there was a cognizable risk that the antenna stationed in the corner of Mr. Washington's backyard could be lowered and moved to within a dangerous proximity of the power line, that possibility could not be characterized as an unreasonable risk and the power company's failure to take additional precautions against it was not negligence.

Under the circumstances, there was not a significant possibility before the accident that Mr. Washington or anyone acting for him would detach the antenna and attempt to carry it under or dangerously near the power line. Standing alone, Mr. Washington's 1980 accident might have caused an objective observer to increase his estimate of the chances that this particular antenna might be handled carelessly. The other surrounding circumstances, however, overwhelmingly erase any pre-accident enlargement of the risk at that site. Except for the single occasion of the 1980 accident, the antenna was stationed safely in the corner of the backyard for many years, one to three years before the 1980 mishap and five years afterwards. Most of that time it was maintained safely in the pipe receptacle which, by Mr. Washington's design, allowed it to be lowered only in a safe direction. Between his close call in 1980 and his fatal accident in 1985, Mr. Washington had never been known to handle the antenna carelessly. Indeed, after he and his son narrowly escaped death or serious injury in 1980, his remarks to friends and relatives indicated that the experience had convinced him to keep the antenna far away from the power line. That he continued to be aware of the danger and take exemplary precautions to avoid it until his fatal accident was further illustrated by the care that he and his friend took when they lowered and laid it next to the fence several days before the accident.

The likelihood that the antenna in this case would be brought into contact with the power line was not as great as the chances of an electrical accident in situations creating significant potential for injuries to victims who may contact or come into dangerous proximity with the power line due to their unawareness of or inadvertence to the charged wire. . . .

Prior to the accident, the anticipated gravity of the loss if the risk were to take effect was, of course, of a very high degree. The deaths and serious injuries in this and other electrical accidents verify that the weight of the loss threatened by a power line accident is not trivial. While some accidents, such as Mr. Washington's 1980 mishap, do not lead to dire consequences, a consideration of all losses resulting from this type of risk indicates that the gravity of the loss if it occurs is usually extreme.

Yet when this high degree of gravity of loss is multiplied by the very small possibility of the accident occurring in this case, we think it is clear that the product does not outweigh the burdens or costs of the precautions of relocating or insulating the power line. This does not mean, of course, that it would not have been worth what it would have cost to place the line underground or to insulate it in order to save the decedent's life if it had been known that the accident would happen or even if the chance of it occurring had been greater. Nor does it mean, on the other hand, that we stop with a consideration of only the burden of an effective precaution in this single case. Common knowledge indicates that within any power company's territory there probably are a great number of situations involving antennas that have been safely installed, but which conceivably could be detached and carelessly moved about dangerously near a power line. In fairness, in this case, in which the coexistence of the powerline and the safely installed antenna was no riskier than countless other similar coexistences not considered to involve negligence, the burden to the company of taking precautions against all such slight possibilities of harm should be balanced against the total magnitude of all these risks, including the relatively few losses resulting from the total of all those insignificant risks. Just as single case applications of the Hand formula can understate the benefits of accident prevention by overlooking all other accidents that could be avoided by the same safety expenditures, the burdens of taking precautions in all similar cases may be depreciated by single case consideration here.

The foregoing, of course, is merely a shorthand expression of the mental processes involved in such considerations. We cannot mathematically or mechanically quantify, multiply or weigh risks, losses and burdens of precautions. As many scholars have noted, the formula is primarily helpful in keeping in mind the relationship of the factors involved and in centering attention upon which of them may be determinative in any given situation. . . .[1] Nevertheless, the formula would seem to be of greater assistance in cases of the present type, in which the power company's ability to perceive risks is superior and its duty is utmost, than other notions, such as "reasonable man," "duty" or "foreseeability," for example, which

---

1. As Professor Epstein has observed, Judge Hand himself stated it well only two years after *Carroll Towing* was decided: "But of these factors care [or precaution] is the only one ever susceptible of quantitative estimate, and often that is not. The injuries are always a variable within limits, which do not admit of even approximate ascertainment; and although probability might theoretically be estimated, if any statistics were available, they never are; and, besides, probability varies with the severity of the injuries. It follows that all such attempts are illusory, and, if serviceable at all, are so only to center attention upon which one of the factors may be determinative in any given situation." Moisan v. Loftus, 178 F.2d 148, 149 (2d Cir. 1949).

be little more than labels to be applied after some sort of balancing or
ling that the formula attempts to describe. In the present case, the balancing
ess focuses our attention on the fact that the possibility of an accident
eared to be slight beforehand and on the reality that precautions against
h slight risks would be costly and burdensome because they exist in great
imber and have not usually been considered unreasonable or intolerable. . . .

For the reasons assigned, the judgment of the court of appeal is affirmed.

RESTATEMENTS, SECOND AND THIRD, OF TORTS ON RISK-UTILITY BALANCING

The Restatement, Second, of Torts (1965) defines negligence as follows:

§ 291. Unreasonableness; How Determined; Magnitude of Risk and Utility of Conduct

Where an act is one which a reasonable man would recognize as involving a
risk of harm to another, the risk is unreasonable and the act is negligent if the risk
is of such magnitude as to outweigh what the law regards as the utility of the act or
of the particular manner in which it is done.

The Restatement, Third, of Torts retains the same basic framework as Restatement, Second, but expresses it in a manner that more closely tracks Judge Learned
Hand's formulation in *Carroll Towing*:

§ 3. Negligence

A person acts negligently if the person does not exercise reasonable care under
all the circumstances. Primary factors to consider in ascertaining whether the
person's conduct lacks reasonable care are the foreseeable likelihood that the
person's conduct will result in harm, the foreseeable severity of any harm that
may ensue, and the burden of precautions to eliminate or reduce the risk of harm.

Comment *e* to § 3 explains the balancing approach:

e. Balancing risks and benefits. Insofar as this Section identifies primary factors
for ascertaining negligence, it can be said to suggest a "risk-benefit test" for negligence, where the "risk" is the overall level of the foreseeable risk created by the
actor's conduct and the "benefit" is the advantages that the actor or others gain if
the actor refrains from taking precautions. The test can also be called a "cost-
benefit test," where "cost" signifies the cost of precautions and the "benefit" is the
reduction in risk those precautions would achieve. . . .

The balancing approach rests on and expresses a simple idea. Conduct is
negligent if its disadvantages outweigh its advantages, while conduct is not negligent if its advantages outweigh its disadvantages. The disadvantage in question is
the magnitude of risk that the conduct occasions: as noted, the phrase "magnitude
of the risk" includes both the foreseeable likelihood of harm and the foreseeable
severity of harm that might ensue. The "advantages" of the conduct relate to the
burden or risk prevention that is avoided when the actor declines to incorporate

some precaution. The actor's conduct is hence negligent if the magnitude of the risk outweighs the burden of risk prevention. The burden of precautions can take a very wide variety of forms. In many cases it is a financial burden borne originally by the actor, although likely passed on, to a substantial extent, to the actor's customers. In highway cases, the burden can be the delays experienced by motorists in driving more slowly, and the greater level of exertion motorists must make in maintaining a constant lookout. In cases in which a gun owner is held liable for negligently storing a gun, thereby giving access to people who might use the gun improperly, the burden is the greater inconvenience the owner incurs in storing the gun in a more secure way. . . . In certain situations, if the actor takes steps to reduce one set of injury risks, this would involve the burden of disadvantage of creating a different set of injury risks, and these other risks are included within the burden of precautions. . . .

LIABILITY FOR FORESEEABLE RISKS

All of the factors set forth in the Restatement sections are assessed from the vantage point of the actor prior to engaging in the questionable conduct. Where the actor has arguably inadequate data about either the probability or gravity of a bad result, the question then becomes whether a reasonable person should have invested more resources to learn about potential risks before acting. The question is usually phrased as to whether defendant acted reasonably because she "knew or should have known" about a given risk. It is important not to jump to the conclusion that an actor should have known about a risk. As you all know by the size of your tuition bill in law school, the cost of acquiring information can be very high. Thus, for example, the cost to society of demanding that a drug manufacturer conduct additional testing before it brings a drug to market may be unacceptable. Not only might additional testing for what appears to be a remote risk be terribly costly, it may delay the introduction of a valuable drug to society for years, thus denying its benefits to thousands who might benefit from a cure. Thus, the burden of precaution against the foreseeably remote risk may be too high. After the fact, we might learn that what appeared to be a remote risk was not so remote, and indeed much more serious than anyone originally contemplated. However, such after-acquired knowledge does not render the defendant negligent.

THE (NEAR TO) ALMIGHTY JURY

In the *Washington* case, the court found that the jury's evaluation of negligence was manifestly erroneous; i.e., reasonable persons could not differ that the conduct of the electric company was not negligent. Although courts can and do overturn jury verdicts on the grounds that reasonable persons cannot differ, it is a relatively rare occurrence. Defendants regularly importune them to do so but, in general, the determination of negligence is for the jury. Negligence cases are very fact sensitive and a jury's commonsense assessment as to whether the defendant's conduct was reasonable or not is rarely disturbed by appellate courts. In finding a defendant

---

authors' dialogue 9

AARON: I must tell you that the Learned Hand B $<$ PL test and Posner's gloss that risk-utility balancing leads to the conclusion that it is economically efficient not to invest in safer conduct sends a cold shudder down my spine. Are judges to be heartless, ruthless machines ready to sacrifice life and limb because economic efficiency theory dictates that it is cheaper to have the accident rather than spend money to avoid harms?

JIM: Aaron, you're taking this way too seriously. The footnote in the *Washington* case indicates that Learned Hand himself knew that one could not calculate the probability and gravity of the harm with any exactitude and that his formula was just an aid in thinking about reasonable conduct.

AARON: I take little solace from that fact. First, Judge Posner's view that the Learned Hand test is a test based on economic efficiency is dead serious; and courts that rely on his interpretation of Hand's formula seem to be trying their darnedest to decide the case based on their best assessment of risk-utility. Second, risk-utility assessment is getting better every day. We live in a world where we are flooded with statistical data. Third, just look at the *Washington* case. The court acknowledges that there is a risk of electrocution from uninsulated wires and that this is not the first, nor will it be the last, case where through inadvertence someone is going to get killed. In fact, the plaintiff in *Washington* was as sensitive to the risk as anyone could be. He was almost electrocuted several years before and took extensive precautions to avoid it ever happening again. Nonetheless, as careful as he was, something happened. He either lost his footing or was distracted when moving the radio antenna and got killed. If the court had just asked whether the defendant acted as a reasonable *mensch*, the jury verdict would have stood. In fact, a jury faced with just that question found for plaintiff. It is only when the court started acting like Alan Greenspan doing economic balancing that it found for the defendant.

JIM: All right, Aaron, have it your way. Would you prefer that judges put blinders on and not articulate their reasons for finding a defendant not negligent as a matter

---

negligent on a given set of facts, the jury is making law for the particular case. If another case with almost the same exact set of historical facts were tried in the same jurisdiction and a jury were to find for the defendant, both a pro-plaintiff and a pro-defendant verdict could withstand appellate review. A court on appeal could reach the conclusion that reasonable persons could differ as to the appropriate standard of reasonable care and how to apply it. That two juries did so on the same day in different courtrooms in the same jurisdiction, and reached opposite conclusions, makes no difference. *See* Restatement, Third, of Torts § 8b and comment *c.* For an interesting debate on appellate review of jury decision making, *see* David W. Robertson, *Allocating Authority Among Institutional Decision Makers in Louisiana State-Court Negligence and Strict Liability Cases*, 57 La. L. Rev. 1079 (1997); *and* Thomas C. Galligan, Jr., *Revisiting the Patterns of Negligence: Some Ramblings Inspired by Robertson*, 57 La. L. Rev. 1119 (1997).

of law? You just can't avoid the reality that a court must consider the factors captured by the B < PL formula. Those are the factors that anyone who is to judge whether an activity is negligent must take into account.

AARON: It's one thing to take them into account and another to make them dispositive. The reasonable person is not the same as the reasonable economist.

JIM: Two final thoughts: first, factors only "count" when they have the potential of being dispositive; and second, you are wrong — economists *are* persons. Most appellate courts review a trial court's finding of negligence and make no explicit reference to risk-utility balancing. They ask only whether a jury's conclusion that the actor's conduct was reasonable or not was justified by the evidence. *See, e.g.,* White River Rural Water District v. Moon, 839 S.W.2d 211, 212 (Ark. 1992) ("reasonably careful person"); Hennessy v. Pyne, 694 A.2d 691, 698 (R.I. 1997) ("reasonable care").

BRAD: I think both of you guys are reading too much into this case. You can balance risks and benefits without doing the kind of economic cost-benefit analysis that sends chills down Aaron's spine. The question in *Washington* is whether the power company didn't do enough to keep people safe. It's tempting to turn that question into an economic one by asking whether it was "worth it" to insulate the wires. That's what sounds so cold, because it implies that Mr. Washington's life was merely a cost to be factored into the power company's economic decision making. But there are all sorts of accidents that might result from having power lines strung up around the state. Airplanes and helicopters might crash into them, workers with cherry-pickers might make contact with them, and CB radio hobbyists might have to maneuver their antennas around the wires. In light of all of those risks, and knowing that perfect safety is an unattainable goal, how much are we going to ask the power company to do? I see the court here as saying only that the jury was asking too much of them by holding them liable for not insulating the wires, without evoking any kind of chilling cost-benefit analysis. I think cost-benefit analysis is a chimera here, at least in the form that would be recognizable to economists and regulators.

FORMAL BALANCING? OR INTUITION?

Some courts refer explicitly to the Learned Hand balancing test for negligence. In a case factually similar to *Carroll Towing*, federal judge Edward Korman relied on the Learned Hand formula. The case arose when the Staten Island Ferry *Andrew K. Barberi* collided with a pier, killing 11 passengers and injuring a score of others. The collision was brought about when the assistant captain, who was piloting the ship, fell asleep due to extreme fatigue. The captain was at another part of the ship and thus unavailable to avert the accident. In holding the city liable, Judge Korman said that under "the test formulated by Judge Hand, operating a large ferry carries with it a risk of great harm. Certainly one such foreseeable risk is that the pilot would become incapacitated and the boat would crash, with the consequent loss of life and physical injury. Requiring that a second pilot be in the pilothouse is a simple, practical and cost-effective way to counter this risk." In Matter of the Complaint of the City of New York, as Owner and Operator of the M/V Andrew J. Barberi, 475 F. Supp. 2d 235, 250 (E.D.N.Y. 2007). *Also see, e.g.,* Halek v. United States, 178 F.3d 481, 484 (7th Cir. 1999) ("[n]egligence is a function of the likelihood of an accident as well as of its gravity if it occurs and of the ease of preventing it"); Gailey v. Barnett, 106 So.3d 625 (La. Ct. App. 2012) (whether injuries, sustained by a repairman who fell through a skylight while working on a roof, were the result of unreasonable maintenance by the owner of the building depended on such factors as the probability of the risk occurring, the gravity of the consequences, the burden of adequate precautions, individual and societal rights and obligations, and the social utility involved).

Note that even courts committed to formal risk-utility balancing utilize the Learned Hand formula only in order to decide whether it is appropriate to direct a verdict. In only very rare cases are juries told anything about risk-utility trade-offs. Jury instructions typically ask only whether the defendant acted as a reasonable person under the circumstances. Why this is so is examined in depth by Stephen G. Gilles, *The Invisible Hand Formula*, 80 Va. L. Rev. 1015 (1994). *Also see* Patrick J. Kelley & Laurel A. Wendt, *What Judges Tell Juries About Negligence: A Review of Pattern Jury Instructions*, 77 Chi.-Kent L. Rev. 587 (2002) (article reviews all state jury instructions on negligence and finds that few states allude to risk-utility balancing in their jury instructions); Ronald J. Allen & Ross M. Rosenberg, *Legal Phenomena, Knowledge, and Theory: A Cautionary Tale of Hedgehogs and Foxes*, 77 Chi.-Kent L. Rev. 683 (2002) (article argues that overarching theories such as risk-utility balancing are not reflected in judicial decisions).

Perhaps this is as it should be. One of us (Brad) sees torts as an area of law that is very much permeated by everyday, informal notions of responsibility. Judges have often talked about the negligence standard as personified, as in the English example of the man on the Clapham omnibus (Clapham at the time being a working-class suburb of London, so the American equivalent would be something like Joe Six-Pack). Brad has asked his students over the years what real or fictional person best embodies the qualities of prudence, level-headedness, and moderate safety consciousness — not a worrywart but not a thrill-seeker. Students have usually come up with popular culture examples like Ned Flanders from *The Simpsons* or Hank Hill from *King of the Hill*. In all seriousness, there are some black letter doctrines and many results in cases that can be explained by asking about the content of the everyday ethics of Ned Flanders or Hank Hill. Some of the duty cases we will consider in a subsequent chapter, for example, direct judges to consider the moral blame attached to the defendant's conduct as a factor in determining whether the defendant owes the plaintiff a legal duty. In the context of the reasonable person standard, the law means what it says, and the legal test for negligence really is supposed to track this kind of folk morality. If Hank Hill is an insufficiently impressive citation, the basic idea here is that legal officials ought to express the appropriate moral attitudes toward persons, such as condemnation or praise, and is considered in articles such as Elizabeth S. Anderson & Richard H.

Pildes, *Expressive Theories of Law: A General Restatement,* 148 U. Pa. L. Rev. 1503 (2000).

AN ECONOMIST'S VIEW OF RISK-UTILITY BALANCING

A leading guru of the law and economics movement, Judge Richard A. Posner, believes that the Learned Hand formula is in lock-step with an economist's test for negligence. In a landmark article, Posner argues that the Learned Hand formula stands for the following proposition (Richard A. Posner, *A Theory of Negligence,* 1 J. Legal Stud. 29, 32 (1972)):

> Discounting (multiplying) the cost of an accident if it occurs by the probability of occurrence yields a measure of the economic benefit to be anticipated from incurring the costs necessary to prevent the accident. The cost of prevention is what Hand meant by the burden of taking precautions against the accident. It may be the cost of installing safety equipment or otherwise making the activity safer, or the benefit forgone by curtailing or eliminating the activity. If the cost of safety measures or of curtailment — whichever cost is lower — exceeds the benefit in accident avoidance to be gained by incurring that cost, society would be better off, in economic terms, to forgo accident prevention. A rule making the enterprise liable for the accidents that occur in such cases cannot be justified on the ground that it will induce the enterprise to increase the safety of its operations. When the cost of accidents is less than the cost of prevention, a rational profit-maximizing enterprise will pay tort judgments to the accident victims rather than incur the larger cost of avoiding liability. Furthermore, overall economic value or welfare would be diminished rather than increased by incurring a higher accident-prevention cost in order to avoid a lower accident cost. If, on the other hand, the benefits in accident avoidance exceed the costs of prevention, society is better off if those costs are incurred and the accident averted, and so in this case the enterprise is made liable, in the expectation that self-interest will lead it to adopt the precautions in order to avoid a greater cost in tort judgments.

IS THE DEFENDANT'S POVERTY RELEVANT?

In Bodin v. City of Stanwood, 927 P.2d 240, 244-245 (Wash. 1996), the court made explicit reference to the factors to be taken into account in risk-utility balancing. The trial court allowed the defendant-municipality to introduce evidence that it sought unsuccessfully to obtain state and federal funds to raise the level of the dikes so as to prevent flooding of plaintiff's land. After a defense verdict, the plaintiff appealed, claiming that such evidence was not relevant to the issue of the defendant's negligence. The appellate court held that the evidence was allowable because it demonstrated that the defendant had undertaken reasonable efforts to prevent the flooding problem. The dissent bitterly complained that the introduction of the evidence concerning attempts to obtain funding permitted a defendant to argue poverty as a defense to negligence. Who had it right?

---

authors' dialogue 10

BRAD: I have a gripe about the editing of cases.

JIM: The editing? Seriously? That's what you worry about?

BRAD: Hear me out. We've included this little snippet of *Carroll Towing* that has the B<PL formula, but in the context of the full opinion, it's clear that was just a throwaway comment by Learned Hand. The bulk of the opinion is taken up with good old-fashioned common-law analysis. For example, he spends a lot of time distinguishing cases on the facts, like one where the bargee was sleeping, or another case where the boat was maliciously set adrift by hooligans.

AARON: Do you disagree that the Hand formula is a useful way to summarize the cost-benefit analysis that is part of the negligence standard? We don't expect the barge owner to take every possible precaution, and considering the expected costs of accidents if a precaution is not taken is a halfway decent way to get a handle on the standard of care.

BRAD: I'm okay with using B<PL as a heuristic, but I'm worried we're inadvertently training a bunch of Posner-bots who reduce the reasonable person standard to economic cost-benefit analysis. Courts don't actually use the Hand formula that way, and I think the full *Carroll Towing* opinion makes that point nicely.

---

hypo 30

X and *Y* both manufacture hot water vaporizers. As a result of accidents to children who inadvertently are scalded when the vaporizers tip over, the companies are faced with numerous lawsuits. It is possible to secure the top of the vaporizer by instituting a screw-on cap. This new design would increase the cost of the vaporizer by $10 per unit for *X* and $15 for *Y* because the cost of retooling is greater in *Y*'s locale. Should *Y*'s additional cost of retooling be taken into account under the Learned Hand formula?

RISK-UTILITY BALANCING FOR THOSE WHO LIKE IT AND THOSE WHO DON'T

Not everyone is enamored with what courts have done with the Learned Hand formula. In debating whether a tortfeasor should have to pay for conduct that creates a risk of harm, commentators tend to fall into two camps. Instrumentalists — many of them utilitarians — focus on the broad social picture, often claiming that tort law should try to maximize utility or overall wealth. They believe that the calculus should hinge on whether the defendant made a choice that tends to increase the overall level of social well-being. By contrast, no instrumentalists claim that the role of torts should be to punish individuals for their wrongdoing. This "fairness" or "corrective justice" approach worries less about maximizing wealth or deterring future tortious conduct and more about making sure actors are brought to account for behaving badly. Professor Gary T. Schwartz finds support for both views in case law. *Mixed Theories of Tort Law: Affirming Both Deterrence and Corrective Justice*, 75 Tex. L. Rev. 1801 (1997). *See* Lawrence A. Cunningham, *Traditional Versus Economic Analysis: Evidence from Cardozo and Posner Torts Opinions*, 62 Fla. L. Rev. 667, 672 (2010) ("traditional legal analysis promotes comprehending complex human reality that contemporary economic analysis oversimplifies").

A recent critic of the instrumental approach to liability has argued that, quite apart from the normative question of whether negligence law should seek to promote efficiency, it is empirically impossible for tort to accomplish that objective. Thus, in Ronen Perry, *Re-Torts*, 59 Ala. L. Rev. 987 (2008), the author argues that a number of factors prevent the tort system from sending appropriate signals to harm-causing actors. For starters, the negligence concept is too indeterminate either for courts to reach consistent outcomes or for actors to predict their exposures to liability. And even if courts and actors could make the necessary determinations of past or future liability, insurance serves to blunt the effects of the liability signals as guides to behavior. And many would-be defendants are judgment-proof and thus indifferent to threats of future liability. Adding to these difficulties facing instrumentalists, the efficiency norms of negligence are systematically underenforced. Often the victims do not realize they have been injured by the actors who should be held liable; or the victims cannot prove otherwise valid claims; or the costs of going through trial to judgment force settlements that are significantly less than they should be. So even if efficiency is a legitimate theoretical objective, it cannot be reached as a practical matter by threatening actors with fault-based liability. For writers concerned about the normative legitimacy of the efficiency objective, the B < PL formula distracts courts from the bedrock question of the value of human life and safety. In *Defense of Deterrence*, Andrew F. Popper, 75 Alb. L. Rev. 181, 189 (2011-2012), takes an opposing view, claiming that the argument that civil liability in negligence cases does not have a deterrent effect is at tension with common understanding of how society reacts to the potential of punishment. Tort cases often create public dialogue about what is and is not socially acceptable behavior and society adjusts their actions accordingly. And even if the articulation of norms is not always clear or certain, it is evident that courts have the ability to set forth norms that have a powerful deterrent effect. Also, "were insurance free to the insured, premiums unaffected by civil judgments, and the history of American tort law to reflect that the presence of insurance increases the likelihood of misconduct, the argument [that insurance hinders the effect of liability] might merit consideration." Last, those who assess that the unpredictability in punitive damages lessen the deterrence effect of liability "assume without questioning that uncertainty in sanctions is undesirable."

One notable salvo in the normative battle against economic efficiency arguments is made by Professor Steven Kelman in *Cost-Benefit Analysis: An Ethical Critique*, 5 Reg.; AEI J. on Govt. & Socy. 33-40 (Jan.-Feb. 1981). Professor Kelman believes that those gauging whether the benefits of an activity outweigh the costs often ignore pressing human rights concerns. Rights and duties of individuals, he says, may have such moral importance that whether an actor managed an eco-nomically rational net savings has no bearing on whether he is morally culpable. Professor William Rodgers offers another normative critique of the instrumentalist view. Rodgers suggests that the goal of tort law should be "zero injury," and that tort rules should respect people and assign liability based on "what people deserve." He discusses a model of "rational decisionmaking" that treats actors differently according to the level of conscious choice that goes into their risky conduct. Those who opt to engage in activity that is foreseeably dangerous should assume the burden of any injury their conduct causes. *See* William H. Rodgers, Jr., *Negligence Reconsidered: The Role of Rationality in Tort Theory*, 54 So. Cal. L. Rev. 1 (1980). Does this kind of strict liability for rational actors make sense? Should a home-owner, aware that glass windows can shatter, be strictly liable if a neighborhood kid hits a baseball through the window and cuts himself trying to come in to fetch the ball? Every decision a person makes involves risks. At what point might we say it's not morally wrong to stop worrying about it?

Most thinkers acknowledge that it is impossible for a court to make sophis-ticated torts decisions without weighing the social interests of encouraging certain activities against the risk of harm to others that those activities entail. Some writers have tried to split the difference between Posner and the corrective justice enthu-siasts by offering ways to use cost-benefit analysis without letting people off the hook for proceeding on a risky course of action when the benefits equal or just barely outweigh the costs. For instance, Professor Geistfeld argues that lawmakers can apply the B < PL formula while still placing a high value on safety.

> An equitable concern about protecting potential victims is the most plausible justification for the safety principle, and altering the . . . rule to give safety inter-ests greater weight than economic interests defensibly redresses the distributive inequity characteristic of certain cost-benefit outcomes. Cost-benefit methodol-ogy therefore provides a good reason for accepting the safety principle rather than being fundamentally inconsistent with it.

Mark Geistfeld, *Reconciling Cost-Benefit Analysis with the Principle That Safety Matters More than Money*, 76 N.Y.U. L. Rev. 114, 185 (2001).

Another line of inquiry in the search for an appropriate standard of care comes from several feminist writers who question whether the "reasonable person" standard is really just a cloaked form of the "reasonable man" standard. Professor Leslie Bender argues that the masculine values embodied in traditional standards for negligence — culminating in the Learned Hand formula — ought to be reworked to accommodate a different value system, featuring "the feminine voice's ethic of care — a premise that no one should be hurt." Leslie Bender, *A Lawyer's Primer on Feminist Theory and Tort*, 38 J. Legal Educ. 3, 31-32 (1988). Several writers continue to look at the possibility of a "reasonable woman standard." *See, e.g.*, Margo Schlanger, *Gender Matters: Teaching a Reasonable Woman Standard in Personal Injury Law*, 45 St. Louis U. L.J. 769 (2001) (arguing that some courts covertly applied a reasonable woman standard in traditional tort law); *but see* Gary T. Schwartz, *Feminist Approaches to Tort Law*, 2 Theoretical Inquiries L. 175 (2001) (criticizing some feminist writers for overstating the case law and failing to

---

authors' dialogue 11

AARON: You know, Jim, it's interesting that all this attention is paid to risk-utility balancing but it is kept a deep dark secret from the jury.

JIM: What do you mean?

AARON: Tell me. Have you ever seen a jury instruction that says that in deciding whether the defendant acted as a reasonable person they are to decide whether the burden of precaution is less than the risk of harm?

JIM: You are right. But that is the way it should be. The risk-utility test is for the judge so that she can decide whether to direct a verdict. We don't need juries trying to do economic balancing. Once the judge has decided that the issue of reasonable care is one upon which reasonable persons can differ, the case is for the jury to use their common sense.

AARON: Now I get it. We trust juries to decide multimillion-dollar cases but we keep them in the dark as to the fundamentals of the underlying legal issue. I can point to lots of places in negligence law where we hide the ball from the jury.

JIM: Like what?

AARON: Well, in many states we don't tell the jury about the role of emergencies in deciding whether a defendant is negligent. We never explain basic principles of causation to a jury. We just tell them a bunch of mumbo jumbo and hope for the best.

JIM: Aaron. It's a sensitive balance. Lawmaking is for the judge and factfinding is for the jury. Whenever we get skittish that we will get the jury into the business of lawmaking by overinstructing them, we opt for mumbo jumbo.

AARON: My guess is that the degree of instruction has more to do with plaintiff or defense bias on the trial judge's part. Law is the defendant's friend; defendants want juries to know more about the law. Facts are the plaintiff's friend; they want to keep the law as general and vague as possible.

---

consider the effects of juries on shaping standards with respect to gender); and Assaf Jacob, *Feminist Approaches to Tort Law Revisited — A Reply to Professor Schwartz*, 2 Theoretical Inquiries L. 211 (2001).

For articles exploring the various interpretations that scholars have given to risk-utility balancing and the Learned Hand formula, *see* 54 Vand. L. Rev. 813-939 (2001). The articles challenge the Posnerian view that risk-utility balancing and/or the reasonable person formula reflect a desire by courts to maximize wealth to the actor in monetary terms and explore a wide range of alternate views both utilitarian and nonutilitarian that are consistent with general risk-utility balancing.

C. THE QUALITIES OF THE REASONABLE PERSON

The general negligence balancing formula judges the actor by the standard of what a reasonable person would have done under the same or similar circumstances. But how broad a reading do we give to the concept of "same or similar circumstances" and how much is governed by the "reasonable person" concept? For example, is a person's ability to make good judgments a circumstance which may be taken into account in setting the standard of care? Age? Superior or inferior skills? Quickness of reaction time in emergencies? Physical or mental disabilities?

The dilemma is real. On the one hand, if negligence is a fact-sensitive balancing test, we ought to take into account the varying circumstances in which the actor finds herself and then ask whether the actor made a judgment that comports with what society views to be a reasonable judgment. On the other hand, if we subjectify the negligence test too much, we destroy the test as a standard for judging human conduct. The case law has rather ingeniously worked out these tensions. In the cases that follow, courts apply the reasonable person test to a host of situations. When we have made our way through the cases, we will see that there is a method to the madness.

AN OLDIE BUT GOODIE: VAUGHN v. MENLOVE

Before tackling the more recent cases, mention should be made of one of the old chestnuts that makes a rather important point. In Vaughn v. Menlove, 132 Eng. Rep. 490 (1837), defendant built a hayrick on his land not far removed from his neighbor's cottages. He was repeatedly warned that the hayrick could catch fire by spontaneous combustion and endanger the nearby cottages. The defendant said he would "chance it" and then undertook to make a chimney in the hayrick which he thought would reduce the risk of fire. The court noted that in spite, or perhaps in consequence, of the chimney, the spontaneous heating of the hay caused the hayrick to burst into flames, ultimately destroying the plaintiff's cottages. The trial court instructed the jury that the defendant "was bound to proceed with such reasonable caution as a prudent man would have exercised under such circumstances." *Id.* at 492. The defendant complained that the jury should have been asked "whether the [d]efendant has acted honestly and bona fide to the best of his own judgment." *Id.* at 493.

In rejecting the defendant's argument, the court held that instead of saying "the liability for negligence should be co-extensive with the judgment of each individual, which would be as variable as the length of the foot of each individual, we ought to adhere to the rule which requires in all cases a regard to caution such as a man of ordinary prudence would observe." *Id.*

One can have sympathy with a defendant who exercises his best judgment and gets bad results. The defendant apparently thought that building the chimney in a hayrick would reduce the likelihood of spontaneous combustion. In fact, his actions may have made things worse. But the court was right. If we are to do risk-utility balancing, the question must be did the actor balance in a way that reflects society's view of what is reasonable? To say that an actor used his best judgment misses the point by the proverbial country mile. Bad judgment is not only a matter of low I.Q. It is also a result of poor values. If I am too lazy to take the trouble to find out that building a chimney in a hay rick makes things worse, then society correctly censures me for my indolence.

1. What the Reasonable Person Knows

BREWER v. MURRAY
292 P.3d 41 (Okla. Civ. App. 2012)

[Ashley] Brewer was thirteen years old at the time the incident occurred on which her claim is based. Jackson's daughter was fourteen. Brewer was invited to spend the night in Jackson's home. Brewer's mother contacted Jackson to confirm the invitation and to provide certain rules that her daughter was to follow. From this conversation, Brewer's mother understood that Jackson agreed to those rules and would be at home to supervise the girls. After Brewer's father dropped her off at the Jackson home, Jackson went to the lake and decided to remain there overnight, leaving the two girls alone and unsupervised. Jackson did not inform Brewer's parents that she decided to leave the girls alone. Later in the evening, Jackson's daughter called her mother and confirmed that Jackson would not return home that night. The girls then drank alcohol that they found in Jackson's home and made plans to invite some older male acquaintances of Jackson's daughter to come over. The young men, who were in their late teens and early twenties, brought more alcohol to the home. The girls became inebriated and had sexual intercourse with two of the men. Jerry Murray, the man with whom Brewer had intercourse, was nineteen at the time and was subsequently convicted of statutory rape.

Within one year of turning eighteen, Brewer sued Murray and Jackson. Brewer alleged three theories of recovery against Murray based on the sexual assault. In her claim against Jackson, Brewer alleged that Jackson "was grossly negligent" in leaving Brewer and Jackson's daughter "completely unsupervised." She further alleged that Jackson's conduct "put [Brewer] at risk and was a direct cause of her sexual assault and resulting damages which could have been prevented by Jackson's timely intervention."

Jackson sought summary judgment arguing, in essence, that she did not have a duty to protect Brewer from criminal conduct and that Brewer's injuries were caused by her own intentional conduct and Murray's criminal conduct rather than by any of Jackson's acts or omissions. The district court found in favor of Jackson in both respects. Brewer appeals that ruling. . . .

Most of the material facts in this case are not disputed. Brewer was invited by Jackson's daughter to spend the night at Jackson's home. Jackson knew of and approved the invitation. Brewer's parents instructed her not to spend the night at a friend's house unless a parent was present, not to stay in a home where boys were present without adult supervision and not to drink alcohol. Brewer's parents had no knowledge of any prior incident when Brewer violated these rules. Brewer's mother conveyed these rules to Jackson, who agreed the rules would be followed while Brewer was in her custody. Prior to this incident, Jackson had no knowledge that her daughter had drunk alcohol or was sexually active. Prior to this incident, Jackson did not know her daughter had any interest in boys, other than a crush on a boy her age, and did not know her daughter knew any older men. Jackson was present when Brewer was dropped off but left later that evening and spent the night at her lake house without telling Brewer's parents that she was leaving the girls alone. Jackson was available by cell phone and could have called a neighbor or relative living nearby to check on the girls. There was alcohol in Jackson's liquor cabinet that the girls consumed, and as a result became intoxicated. During the evening, Jackson's daughter called to make sure Jackson would not be returning home and told Jackson everything was fine. After this call, Jackson's daughter called a twenty-year-old male she knew and invited him over. He and several friends arrived, including Murray, and provided the girls more alcohol. After drinking this alcohol, the girls went into the back yard and jumped on a trampoline while topless. Later, both girls had sexual intercourse.

The dispositive issues in this case are whether a person who takes temporary custody of a child has any duty to protect that child from the wrongful conduct of third parties and, if so, the scope of that duty. The Oklahoma Supreme Court has not previously decided these issues. Nonetheless, it has decided issues sufficiently similar to convince us that the answer to the first question is yes. For the reasons discussed in this Opinion, we find that Jackson was not entitled to judgment as a matter of law based on either the lack of duty regarding a third party's wrongful conduct or the lack of a special relationship with Brewer.

. . . Brewer's theory of recovery against Jackson is based on negligence. Any claim of negligence depends on the existence of a duty and the breach of that duty.

[In a lengthy discussion the court held that Jackson had a duty to exercise reasonable care to Brewer.]

Although we find that the district court erred in concluding that Jackson owed no duty to Brewer, Jackson is still entitled to judgment if she was not negligent. Negligence is conduct that fails to meet the standard of care.

The standard of care required in this case is what a reasonable person in Jackson's position would have done to prevent the harm to Brewer. See Restatement (Second) of Torts § 283. . . . (explaining that no instruction should be given regarding the care required by an automobile driver for the safety of a child because the "essence of the [ordinary care] instruction is that one must anticipate the ordinary behavior of children and exercise greater care for their protection"). "The standard of care is ordinary care, and anticipation of the behavior of children is one circumstance as to what constitutes ordinary care in the situation." Id. In determining the ordinary care required in this case, Jackson either knows or is charged with knowing the general qualities and habits of human beings, the common law and any community customs. See Restatement (Second) of Torts § 290. "The recognition of the propensities of children is within the common knowledge of the ordinary juror. . . . It is readily apparent that ordinary care, insofar as young children are concerned, involves the exercise of greater care." . . . As a result, Jackson is charged with knowing that teenagers are "particularly prone" to careless and reckless behavior, Restatement (Second) of Torts § 290 cmt. k, that a child is generally incapable of exercising the same judgment and prudence exercised by adults, id. § 283A, and that third persons may take advantage of situations created by her conduct to commit crimes, id. § 290 cmt. m. Jackson's brief in support of her motion for summary judgment confirms that she actually had this knowledge concerning the behavior of teenagers. "Adolescents have been breaking rules, sneaking out, sneaking around, deceiving parents, etc. since the beginning of time." . . .

Viewing the facts in this case in the light most favorable to Brewer, we conclude that determination of whether Jackson breached her duty to Brewer and was negligent in leaving the girls unsupervised cannot be determined as a matter of law, depends on facts which are in dispute and must be made by the trier of fact. . . .

The district court erred in granting Jackson's motion for summary judgment, and the order granting that motion is reversed. As a matter of law, Jackson owed Brewer a duty to protect her when she assumed custody of Brewer for the evening. Whether Jackson's allegedly negligent conduct was a breach of that duty when she left her daughter and Brewer alone overnight, without adult supervision, is an issue of fact that remains unresolved. Whether Jackson's conduct was the proximate cause of Brewer's injury is an issue for determination by a jury.

Reversed and remanded for further proceedings.

FOOD FOR THOUGHT

In an old casebook favorite, Delair v. McAdoo, 188 A.181 (Pa. 1936) plaintiff was injured when defendant lost control of his car when his left tire blew out and collided with plaintiff's car. The tire was worn down to its fabric. In upholding a jury verdict for the plaintiff the court said, "Any ordinary individual, whether a car owner or not knows that when a tire is worn through to the fabric, its further use is dangerous and should be removed. When worn through several plys, it is very dangerous for further use. All drivers must be held to a knowledge of these facts. An owner or operator cannot escape simply because he says he does not know. He must know." *Id.* at 184.

What if the tires were not worn through to the fabric but instead had very little tread left on them and were dangerous? The owner, being an absent-minded law professor who has no appreciation for cars, tires, brakes, etc., asks his mechanic to check out the car. The mechanic tells him that his tires are fine for at least another 6,000 miles. The next day a tire blows out. Are all car owners required to know that tires with very little tread are dangerous? If so, how much of the *Encyclopedia Britannica* is supposed to reside in the mind of the reasonable person?

hypo **31**

Twerski and Dale Earnhardt, Jr. (a nationally known stock car driver who has twice won the Daytona 500) are traveling in their own cars on a wet slick road and see an object 200 feet ahead. Twerski and Earnhardt both begin braking at 100 feet. Assume that Earnhardt, because of his vast knowledge of driving and braking, knows that if he begins braking at 100 feet there is 1 in 5 chance that he will hit the object. Twerski (ignorant as he is) believes that he will stop 20 feet in front of the object. Is it possible that Earnhardt is negligent and Twerski is not?

THE RESTATEMENT AND CASE LAW

The Restatement, Third, of Torts takes the following position regarding the characteristics of the reasonable person:

§ 12. Knowledge and Skills

If an actor has skills or knowledge that exceed those possessed by most others, these skills or knowledge are circumstances to be taken into account in determining whether the actor has behaved as a reasonably careful person.

Comment *b* to § 12 then notes:

... As far as actors with below-average knowledge and skills are concerned, to the extent their conduct can be explained only in terms of their below-average knowledge and skills, it is evident that this conduct is distinctly substandard in terms of its risky character; moreover, the acquisition of knowledge and skills is a process that is generally within a person's control. Accordingly, it is appropriate to impose liability on persons for the harmful consequences of substandard conduct that is due to their below-average knowledge or skills.

Where a defendant holds herself out to have expertise and another relies on such representation, there is no question that she is held to the general knowledge and skill of that field of expertise (e.g., doctor, orthopedist, engineer). *See, e.g.,* Jackson v. Axelrad, 221 S.W.3d 650 (Tex. 2007), in which a patient, himself a physician, brought a malpractice action against a treating physician for negligent failure to diagnose a colon condition. The jury assessed 51 percent fault to plaintiff and the trial court entered judgment for defendant. The Supreme Court of Texas held that reasonable jurors could infer, based on plaintiff's skill and experience as a physician, that he knew or should have known the significance of where in his abdomen his own pain started. The question becomes more difficult in the hypothetical posed above where an actor has knowledge that others don't have and absent that knowledge he would otherwise not be negligent. The Restatement position finds support in LaVine v. Clear Creek Skiing Corp., 557 F.2d 730 (10th Cir. 1977) (the expertise of a skiing instructor who collided with another skier is a relevant circumstance that may be taken into account in deciding whether he acted reasonably); Dakter v. Cavallino, 866 N.W.2d 656 (Wis. 2015) (court citing to Restatement § 12 held truck driver's superior knowledge and skills were relevant in evaluating whether he acted as a reasonable person). Harvey v. Palumbo, 2015 WL 7573371 (Pa. Sup. Ct. 2015) (same). *But see* Heath v. Swift Wings, Inc., 252 S.E.2d 526 (N.C. Ct. App. 1979).

hypo **32**

X, aged 67, retired two years ago as a health inspector for public restaurants. At a private barbecue that *X* attended, he saw the host, *Y*, open a dented can of mushrooms. It is not general knowledge that damaged cans containing mushrooms can be dangerous, but from his previous experience as a food inspector, *X* had known that such damaged cans may result in food poisoning. *X* saw *Y* pouring mushrooms from the dented can on top of barbecued steaks but said nothing. *X* ate the steaks and suffered food poisoning. Should *X*'s conduct be considered negligent and thus affect his ability to recover fully for his injuries?

hypo **33**

A, at the age of 30, decides to learn how to drive. He hires *B*, a licensed driving instructor, to teach him. During his second lesson *A* makes a left turn and collides with *C*. A more experienced driver would not have made the turn and would have avoided the accident. *B* is seriously injured in the collision. Is the fact that *A* is just learning how to drive a relevant factor in deciding whether *A* is liable to *B*?

2. How the Reasonable Person Responds to Emergencies

CORDAS v. PEERLESS TRANSPORTATION CO.
27 N.Y.S.2d 198 (N.Y. City Ct. 1941)

CARLIN, Justice.

This case presents the ordinary man — that problem child of the law — in a most bizarre setting. As a lowly chauffeur in defendant's employ he became in a trice the protagonist in a breath-bating drama with a denouement almost tragic. It appears that a man, whose identity it would be indelicate to divulge was feloniously relieved of his portable goods by two nondescript highwaymen in an alley near 26th Street and Third Avenue, Manhattan; they induced him to relinquish his possessions by a strong argument ad hominem couched in the convincing cant of the criminal and pressed at the point of a most persuasive pistol. Laden with their loot, but not thereby impeded, they took an abrupt departure and he, shuffling off the coil of that discretion which enmeshed him in the alley, quickly gave chase through 26th Street toward 2d Avenue, whither they were resorting "with expedition swift as thought" for most obvious reasons. Somewhere on that thoroughfare of escape they indulged the stratagem of separation ostensibly to disconcert their pursuer and allay the ardor of his pursuit. He then centered on for capture the man with the pistol whom he saw board defendant's taxicab, which quickly veered south toward 25th Street on 2d Avenue where he saw the chauffeur jump out while the cab, still in motion, continued toward 24th Street; after the chauffeur relieved himself of the cumbersome burden of his fare the latter also is said to have similarly departed from the cab before it reached 24th Street.

The chauffeur's story is substantially the same except that he states that his uninvited guest boarded the cab at 25th Street while it was at a standstill waiting for a less colorful fare; that his "passenger" immediately advised him "to stand not upon the order of his going but to go at once" and added finality to his command by an appropriate gesture with a pistol addressed to his sacroiliac. The chauffeur in reluctant acquiescence proceeded about fifteen feet, when his hair, like unto the quills of the fretful porcupine, was made to stand on end by the hue and cry of the man despoiled accompanied by a clamorous concourse of the law-abiding which paced him as he ran; the concatenation of "stop thief," to which the patter of persistent feet did maddingly beat time, rang in his ears as the pursuing posse all the while gained on the receding cab with its quarry therein contained. The hold-up man sensing his insecurity suggested to the chauffeur that in the event there was the slightest lapse in obedience to his curt command that he, the chauffeur, would suffer the loss of his brains, a prospect as horrible to an humble chauffeur as it undoubtedly would be to one of the intelligentsia. The chauffeur . . . quickly threw his car out of first speed in which he was proceeding, pulled on the emergency, jammed on his brakes and, although he thinks the motor was still running, swung open the door to his left and jumped out of his car. He confesses that the only act that smacked of intelligence was that by which he jammed the brakes in order to throw off balance the hold-up man who was half-standing and half-sitting with his pistol menacingly poised. Thus abandoning his car and passenger the chauffeur sped toward 26th Street and then turned to look; he saw the cab proceeding south toward 24th Street where it mounted the sidewalk. The plaintiff-mother and her two infant children were there injured by the cab which, at the time, appeared to be also minus its passenger who, it appears, was apprehended in the cellar of a local hospital where he was pointed out to a police officer by a remnant of the posse, hereinbefore mentioned. He did not appear at the trial. The three aforesaid plaintiffs and the husband-father sue the defendant for damages predicating their respective causes of action upon the contention that the chauffeur was negligent in abandoning the cab under the aforesaid circumstances. Fortunately the injuries sustained were comparatively slight. . . .

Negligence has been variously defined but the common legal acceptation is the failure to exercise that care and caution which a reasonable and prudent person ordinarily would exercise under like conditions or circumstances. . . . Negligence is "not absolute or intrinsic," but "is always relevant to some circumstances of time, place or person." In slight paraphrase of the world's first bard it may be truly observed that the expedition of the chauffeur's violent love of his own security outran the pauser, reason, when he was suddenly confronted with unusual emergency which "took his reason prisoner." The learned attorney for the plaintiffs concedes that the chauffeur acted in an emergency but claims a right to recovery upon the following proposition taken verbatim from his brief: "It is respectfully submitted that the value of the interests of the public at large to be immune from being injured by a dangerous instrumentality such as a car unattended while in motion is very superior to the right of a driver of a motor vehicle to abandon same while it is in motion even when acting under the belief that his life is in danger and by abandoning same he will save his life." To hold thus under the facts adduced herein would be tantamount to a repeal by implication of the primal law of nature written in indelible characters upon the fleshy tablets of sentient creation by the Almighty Law-giver, "the supernal Judge who sits on high."

There are those who stem the turbulent current for bubble fame, or who bridge the yawning chasm with a leap for the leap's sake or who "outstare the sternest eyes that look outbrave the heart most daring on the earth, pluck the young sucking cubs from the she-bear, yea, mock the lion when he roars for prey" to win a fair lady and these are the admiration of the generality of men; but they are made of sterner stuff than the ordinary man upon whom the law places no duty of emulation. The law would indeed be fond if it imposed upon the ordinary man the obligation to so demean himself when suddenly confronted with a danger, not of his creation, disregarding the likelihood that such a contingency may darken the intellect and palsy the will of the common legion of the earth, the fraternity of ordinary men, — whose acts or omissions under certain conditions or circumstances make the yardstick by which the law measures culpability or innocence, negligence or care. If a person is placed in a sudden peril from which death might ensue, the law does not impel another to the rescue of the person endangered nor does it condemn him for his unmoral failure to rescue when he can; this is in recognition of the immutable law written in frail flesh.

Returning to our chauffeur. If the philosophic Horatio and the martial companions of his watch were "distilled almost to jelly with the act of fear" when they beheld "in the dead vast and middle of the night" the disembodied spirit of Hamlet's father stalk majestically by "with a countenance more in sorrow than in anger" was not the chauffeur, though unacquainted with the example of these eminent men-at-arms, more amply justified in his fearsome reactions when he was more palpably confronted by a thing of flesh and blood bearing in its hand an engine of destruction which depended for its lethal purpose upon the quiver of a hair? . . . Kolanka v. Erie Railroad Co., 212 N.Y.S. 714, 717, says: "The law in this state does not hold one in an emergency to the exercise of that mature judgment required of him under circumstances where he has an opportunity for deliberate action. He is not required to exercise unerring judgment, which would be expected of him, were he not confronted with an emergency requiring prompt action." . . . If under normal circumstances an act is done which might be considered negligent it does not follow as a corollary that a similar act is negligent if performed by a person acting under an emergency, not of his own making, in which he suddenly is faced with a patent danger with a moment left to adopt a means of extrication. The chauffeur — the ordinary man in this case — acted in a split second in a most harrowing experience. To call him negligent would be to brand him coward; the court does not do so in spite of what those swaggering heroes, "whose valor plucks dead lions by the beard," may bluster to the contrary. Judgment for defendant against plaintiffs dismissing their complaint upon the merits. . . .

TO TELL OR NOT TO TELL

No one doubts that one who acts in an emergency is entitled to have the jury consider the emergency as one of the circumstances to be taken into account in deciding whether the defendant acted reasonably. *See* Restatement, Third, of Torts § 9; Restatement, Second, of Tort § 296. Conduct that might otherwise be considered negligent may be reasonable given the short amount of time in which the actor must make a decision. The issue that has divided the courts is whether the jury should be given an "emergency instruction." Should a jury be specifically told that they are to take into account that the actor was faced with an emergency or should the jury be simply instructed that an actor must behave reasonably under the circumstances and leave it to the lawyers to bring to the attention of the jurors that the emergency is a factor that they may take into account in deciding whether the actor was negligent? A majority favor the special instruction. *See, e.g.*, Whittaker v. Coca-Cola, 812 So. 2d 1252 (Ala. Civ. App. 2001); Desrosiers v. Flight International of Florida Inc., 156 F.3d 952 (9th Cir. 1998) (applying California law); Hagenow v. Schmidt, 842 N.W.2d 661 (Iowa 2014); Pazienza v. Reader, 717 A.2d 644 (R.I. 1998); Rivera v. New York City Transit Authority, 569 N.E.2d 432 (N.Y. 1991); Kappelman v. Lutz, 217 P.3d 286 (Wash. 2009). A minority would abolish the special instruction. *See, e.g.*, Knapp v. Stanford, 392 So. 2d 196, 198 (Miss. 1980) ("The hazard of relying on the doctrine of 'sudden emergency' is the tendency to elevate its principles above what is required to be proven in a negligence action. Even the wording of a well-drawn instruction intimates that ordinary rules of negligence do not apply to the circumstances constituting the claimed 'sudden emergency.'"); Lyons v. Midnight Sun Transportation Services, Inc., 928 P.2d 1202 (Alaska 1996); Wiles v. Webb, 946 S.W.2d 685 (Ark. 1997); Bjorndal v. Weitman, 184 P.3d 1115 (Or. 2008).

Even states that allow for an emergency instruction must grapple with the question of what constitutes an emergency. In Herr v. Wheeler, 634 S.E.2d 317 (Va. 2006), defendant was operating her vehicle in a downpour when her vehicle hydroplaned and hit another car, causing that car to cross the center line and injure the plaintiff. The trial granted the defendant an emergency instruction on the basis that the weather conditions constituted an emergency. The jury returned a verdict for the defendant. On appeal, the court reversed, saying that "[T]he issue for the jury . . . was not whether hydroplaning on an obviously wet road constitutes a sudden emergency. Once a vehicle becomes involved in hydroplaning, the driver has little, if any, control of the vehicle. The issue was whether [the defendant] exercised reasonable care in the operation of her vehicle under the prevailing conditions prior to the hydroplaning of her vehicle so as to avoid the collision." The same high court of Virginia held that the emergency doctrine was not available when a defendant driver experienced a sudden loss of consciousness. *See* Hancock-Underwood v. Knight, 670 S.E.2d 720 (Va. 2009). In a questionable decision the Minnesota Court of Appeals in Barnes v. Dees, 2007 Minn. App. Unpub. LEXIS 15, reversed a jury finding for defendant because the trial court gave an emergency instruction. The defendant, after coming out of an S-curve, began sneezing and continued to sneeze until he ran a red light and collided with the plaintiff. The defendant admitted that he did not take his foot off the accelerator though he was aware of the upcoming intersection. Have you not had the problem of sudden sneezing that diverts your attention? Why does sneezing not constitute an emergency?

Even courts that routinely give the special emergency instruction will not do so when the actor's prior negligence created the emergency. This is akin to killing one's parents so as to attend the orphan's picnic. *See, e.g.*, Posas v. Horton, 228 P.3d 457 (Nev. 2010); Mitchell v. Johnson, 641 So. 2d 238 (Ala. 1994). *See also*

Restatement, Third, of Torts §9 and comment *d*; Restatement, Second of Torts §296 and comment *d*.

GETTING IT WRONG

In Hargrove v. McGinley, 766 A.2d 587 (Me. 2001), a defendant was found not negligent for rear-ending cars that had just been involved in a sudden collision. The trial judge had given an emergency instruction stating that one "who is confronted with an emergency situation is not to be held to the same standard of conduct normally applied to one who is in no such situation." *Id.* at 589. The plaintiff did not claim the instruction was incorrect but argued that the defendant, by following too closely and not paying attention, was not entitled to the emergency instruction. Wasn't the instruction flat-out wrong?

hypo 34

X, a school crossing guard in a high-crime neighborhood, hears a car backfire and she believes that it is the sound of gunfire. She runs behind a building for cover, abandoning her crossing post. *Y,* a child, crosses the street unescorted and is hit by a car in the crosswalk. In the suit *Y* v. *X,* may *X* raise the "emergency" defense?

3. Does the Reasonable Person Follow Customary Practice?

TRIMARCO v. KLEIN
436 N.E.2d 502 (N.Y. 1982)

FUCHSBERG, Judge.

After trial by jury in a negligence suit for personal injuries, the plaintiff, Vincent N. Trimarco, recovered a judgment of $240,000. A sharply divided Appellate Division having reversed on the law and dismissed the complaint, our primary concern on this appeal is with the role of the proof plaintiff produced on custom and usage. The ultimate issue is whether he made out a case.

The controversy has its genesis in the shattering of a bathtub's glass enclosure door in a multiple dwelling in July, 1976. . . . According to the trial testimony, at the time of the incident plaintiff, the tenant of the apartment in which it happened, was in the process of sliding the door open so that he could exit the tub. It is undisputed that the occurrence was sudden and unexpected and the injuries he received from the lacerating glass most severe. . . .

As part of his case, plaintiff, with the aid of expert testimony, developed that, since at least the early 1950's, a practice of using shatterproof glazing materials for bathroom enclosures had come into common use, so that by 1976 the glass door here no longer conformed to accepted safety standards. This proof was reinforced by a showing that over this period bulletins of nationally recognized safety and consumer organizations along with official Federal publications had joined in warning of the dangers that lurked when plain glass was utilized in "hazardous locations," including "bathtub enclosures." . . . On examination of the defendants' managing agent, who long had enjoyed extensive familiarity with the management of multiple dwelling units in the New York City area, plaintiff's counsel elicited agreement that, since at least 1965, it was customary for landlords who had occasion to install glass for shower enclosures, whether to replace broken glass or to comply with the request of a tenant or otherwise, to do so with "some material such as plastic or safety glass." . . .

Our analysis may well begin by rejecting defendants' contention that the shower door was not within the compass of *section 78* of the Multiple Dwelling Law. From early on, it was understood that this statute was enacted in recognition of the reality that occupants of tenements in apartment houses, notwithstanding their control of the rented premises, as a practical matter looked to their landlords for the safe maintenance of the tenanted quarters as well. The result was that, if responsibility for keeping "every part thereof . . . in good repair" was not placed on the landlords, defects would remain unremedied. . . .

Which brings us to the well-recognized and pragmatic proposition that when "certain dangers have been removed by a customary way of doing things safely, this custom may be proved to show that [the one charged with the dereliction] has fallen below the required standard." . . . Such proof, of course, is not admitted in the abstract. It must bear on what is reasonable conduct under all the circumstances, the quintessential test of negligence.

It follows that, when proof of an accepted practice is accompanied by evidence that the defendant conformed to it, this may establish due care . . . and, contrariwise, when proof of a customary practice is coupled with a showing that it was ignored and that this departure was a proximate cause of the accident, it may serve to establish liability. . . . Put more conceptually, proof of a common practice aids in "[formulating] the general expectation of society as to how individuals will act in the course of their undertakings, and thus to guide the common sense or expert intuition of a jury or commission when called on to judge of particular conduct under particular circumstances" (Pound, *Administrative Application of Legal Standards*, 44 ABA Rep. 445, 456-457).

The source of the probative power of proof of custom and usage is described differently by various authorities, but all agree on its potency. Chief among the rationales offered is, of course, the fact that it reflects the judgment and experience and conduct of many. . . . Support for its relevancy and reliability comes too from the direct bearing it has on feasibility, for its focusing is on the practicality of a precaution in actual operation and the readiness with which it can be employed (Morris, *Custom and Negligence*, 42 Colum. L. Rev. 1147, 1148). Following in the train of both of these boons is the custom's exemplification of the opportunities it provides to others to learn of the safe way, if that the customary one be. (*See* Restatement of Torts 2d, § 295A, Comments *a, b.*)

From all this it is not to be assumed customary practice and usage need be universal. It suffices that it be fairly well defined and in the same calling or business so that "the

---

authors' dialogue **12**

JIM: If I read you correctly, you believe that the fact that an actor's conduct took place under emergency circumstances is merely one factor to weigh in risk-utility balancing to determine whether the actor was behaving as a reasonable person. Even in emergency situations, an actor can be found negligent if it is found that, even taking the short time span to make a decision into consideration, the defendant made a bad choice. On the other hand, a defendant may be found not to be negligent because he made a reasonable choice given the time constraints.

AARON: That's fair.

JIM: Well, then I have a bone to pick with you. I don't think that *Cordas* can be read to say that the defendant taxi driver was relieved of liability because he made a good decision under the circumstances. It seems to me that the court is saying that where his life is threatened, the cabbie is not required to be a hero and take a chance of sacrificing his life in order to prevent risk of harm to others. This has nothing to do with emergency. He could have had ten minutes to contemplate his decision. According to the court he's entitled to invoke the first law of nature — self-preservation.

AARON: I'm not so sure. At points the court does seem to be saying that the cabbie need not be a hero. But, there is plenty of language that places emphasis on the suddenness of the decision-making. Anyway, Jim, if you are right, then I have another problem. If the court is saying that one is permitted to place another's life in jeopardy in order to save one's own skin, then I don't see the difference between *Cordas* and *Vincent v. Lake Erie Transport Co.* that we took up in Chapter 2. In that case the court held that there was a privilege to take another's property in order to save one's own. The decision to do so may have been reasonable but the defendant must pay for the damage to the plaintiff's property. Here the defendant consciously decided to put people at risk when he jumped out of the cab to avoid being shot. Why does he get off the hook entirely? Why should this not be like the privilege of necessity?

JIM: You can't make the necessity argument in the context of risk-taking activity. All human activity, even if done reasonably, puts people at risk. If the necessity privilege is taken beyond intentional torts, you will destroy the idea that there ought to be no liability for non-negligent conduct. You must tame the beast.

---

actor may be charged with knowledge of it or negligent ignorance" (Prosser, Torts [4th ed.], § 33, p. 168; Restatement, Torts 2d, § 295A, p. 62, Comment *a*).

However, once its existence is credited, a common practice or usage is still not necessarily a conclusive or even a compelling test of negligence. . . . Before it can be, the jury must be satisfied with its reasonableness, just as the jury must be satisfied with the reasonableness of the behavior which adhered to the custom or the unreasonableness of that which did not. . . . After all, customs and usages run the gamut of merit like everything else. That is why the question in each instance is whether it meets the test of reasonableness. As Holmes' now classic statement on this subject expresses it, "[what] usually is done may be evidence of what ought to be done, but what ought to be done is fixed by a standard of reasonable prudence, whether it usually is complied with or not" (Texas & Pacific Ry. Co. v. Behymer, 189 U.S. 468, 470).

So measured, the case the plaintiff presented . . . was enough to send it to the jury and to sustain the verdict reached. The expert testimony, the admissions of the defendant's manager, the data on which the professional and governmental bulletins were based, the evidence of how replacements were handled by at least the local building industry for the better part of two decades, these in the aggregate easily filled that bill. Moreover, it was also for the jury to decide whether, at the point in time when the accident occurred, the modest cost and ready availability of safety glass and the dynamics of the growing custom to use it for shower enclosures had transformed what once may have been considered a reasonably safe part of the apartment into one which, in the light of later developments, no longer could be so regarded. . . .

[Nonetheless, the court reversed and ordered a new trial because the trial judge permitted the jury to consider a statute relating to the use of safety materials that the court ruled was not applicable to the defendant.]

FOOD FOR THOUGHT

Was the court right in allowing into evidence the industry custom for replacement of shower doors? The custom that the plaintiff sought to introduce was that landlords generally replaced shower doors that had been broken, or substituted shatterproof glass when refurbishing apartments. In *Trimarco* the shower door had not broken nor was the landlord refurbishing all his apartments. Thus, the contention of the plaintiff was that all glass shower doors should have been replaced throughout the state. If the landlord had to replace the shower door in question, he would also have had to replace all the glass shower doors in all of his apartments. Would that not incur very substantial immediate costs far greater than piecemeal replacement of shower doors over a multiyear period?

THE EVIDENTIARY POWER OF CUSTOM

Evidence of customary practice is powerful. Although the black letter rule is that departure from industry custom is relevant but does not require a finding that the actor was negligent, *see* Restatement, Third, of Torts § 13, the reality is that a defendant who is in violation of a widely recognized industry practice is dead in the water. It is unlikely that a jury will find in favor of a defendant who has violated industry standards. Where an actor conforms to industry standards, the rule once again is that such conformance is relevant to, but does not require, a finding that the actor was non-negligent. In the famous *T.J. Hooper* case, 60 F.2d 737 (2d Cir. 1932), the question arose as to whether the customary practice of tug owners not to equip tugs with radio equipment constituted negligence. The tug owners were sued for the value of two barges and their cargoes, which were lost at sea during a coastal storm. The basis of the claim was that the tug was negligently unseaworthy in that it was not equipped with a radio receiver, and thus could not receive weather reports of an impending storm. In responding to the argument that it was not the custom of the industry to equip tugs with radio receivers, Judge Learned Hand made the following pronouncement which has been oft repeated by courts through the years (*id.* at 740):

> There are yet no doubt, cases where courts seem to make the general practice of the calling the standard of proper diligence. . . . Indeed in most cases reasonable prudence is in fact common prudence; but strictly it is never its measure; a whole calling may have unduly lagged in the adoption of new and available devices. It may never set its own tests, however persuasive be its usages. Courts must in the end say what is required; there are precautions so imperative that even their universal disregard will not excuse their omission.

A respected scholar has recently observed that torts teachers and scholars tend to exaggerate the power over juries of evidence of custom and noncustomary common practice and urges the more liberal admission of the latter as a means of reducing jury speculation about how firms in a particular industry actually behave. *See* Kenneth S. Abraham, *Essay: Custom, Noncustomary Practice, and Negligence,* 109 Colum. L. Rev. 1784 (2009).

DOES JUDICIAL DEFERENCE TO INDUSTRY CUSTOM AFFECT TECHNOLOGICAL INNOVATION?

Whenever a firm departs from safety-related industry custom and introduces new ways of doing business, it runs the risk that its departure will support an inference of negligence; after all, an entire industry is unlikely to have been negligent. (The same increase in liability exposure is created when a firm departs from its own "customary" practices even if no industry custom is involved, is it not?) And although compliance with custom is not a bar to liability, it comes into evidence and benefits the defendant. Don't these treatments of custom tend to stifle innovation, much of which is socially beneficial? Coauthors have arrived at this conclusion. *See* Gideon Parchomovsky & Alex Stein, *Torts and Innovation,* 107 Mich. L. Rev. 285 (2008). The authors propose two solutions: either evidence of industry custom and all inferences based on that evidence should not be allowed in fault-based tort litigation; or a nonjudicial administrative agency should determine, ahead of time, the net social benefits of technological innovations, and those determinations should have binding effects in any subsequent fault-based tort litigation. Administratively approved innovations would be entitled to the same deference as customary technologies, and disapproved innovations would thereafter be treated as unreasonably unsafe. Do you accept the authors' assessment of an unfortunate judicial bias against innovation? Do their proposed solutions seem plausible? For a pushback on this, *see* James A. Henderson, Jr., *Tort vs. Technology: Accommodating Disruptive Innovation,* 47 Ariz. St. L.J. 1145 (2015) (arguing that the American tort system accommodates technological innovation).

Another author invokes a different dynamic regarding judicial deference to custom in the context of medical malpractice litigation. *See* James Gibson, *Doctrinal Feedback and (Un)Reasonable Care*, 94 Va. L. Rev. 1641 (2008). Referring to the "doctrinal feedback" phenomenon, the author explains that health care providers will tend to overinvest in precautions in attempting to give themselves a cushion against subsequently being found to have provided too little care, and that courts will adopt such marginal overinvestment as the customary professional standard without independently assessing its reasonableness. And then providers will invest even further in precautions in trying to maintain a cushion, and that new (and even more socially wasteful) level of cautionary overinvestment will become the new professional standard, and so on. Over time, this "doctrinal feedback" process will move the health care community to absurdly elevated, grossly wasteful levels of care. The author suggests that the remedy for this destructive feedback phenomenon is to abandon fault-based liability altogether.

The two analyses just summarized reach the same conclusion—that judicial deference to custom leads to overinvestment in care—but they rely on different dynamics. The first analysis suggests that deference to industry custom pressures firms to "stay put" in wastefully cautious technologies. The second analysis suggests that deference to custom will drive medical providers *away from* customary patterns of behavior and toward wasteful overinvestments in care. Is there a way to reconcile the two analyses?

SUMMING UP

It seems to come down to this. If an actor departs from safety-related industry custom, she has little hope of prevailing before a jury. The only real way to beat the rap is to argue that the custom speaks to a practice that is not directly on point with the case at bar. Before admitting evidence of custom, courts should be clear that the conduct in question lines up with the custom. Where the custom is not directly on point, as was the case in *Trimarco*, one can question the propriety of admitting the custom into evidence. Plaintiff is, of course, free to present testimony as to the feasibility and cost of replacing all shower doors. But stigmatizing the defendant with a custom that is not on all fours dooms the defendant.

Where the actor is in conformance with custom, the problem is more complex. Evidence of conformance is relevant, but not binding, on the issue of negligence. However, Learned Hand was right when he said that "in most cases reasonable prudence is, in fact, common prudence." The tough question is when does a judge direct a verdict in favor of defendant because she complied with the custom and when is the case for the jury? Where there is a firmly entrenched custom, the party challenging the custom bears a significant burden in presenting evidence that the custom is ill conceived. In short, customs are not sacrosanct. On the other hand, they are not to be thrown to the wind. For a general survey of the development of custom, *see* Richard A. Epstein, *The Path to* The T.J. Hooper: *The Theory and History of Custom in the Law of Tort*, 21 J. Legal Stud. 1 (1992). *Also see* James A. Henderson, Jr., *Learned Hand's Paradox: An Essay on Custom in Negligence Law*,

---

authors' dialogue 13

JIM: Your critique of *Trimarco* is not well founded, Aaron. The custom of the industry to replace regular glass with shatterproof glass for shower doors was clearly relevant to whether the defendant should have replaced the shower door in the plaintiff's apartment. The custom shows that the harm was foreseeable, that replacement was technologically feasible, and that replacement with shatterproof glass was not prohibitively expensive.

AARON: I disagree. When the plaintiff introduces evidence of departure from custom, the jury is being told that the defendant is basically a bum. Everybody in the industry is following a custom and "you Mr. Defendant" can't keep up with even the minimal standards of what all responsible people are doing. A defendant who is in violation of a custom does not have a prayer to win his case. If, in *Trimarco*, there was evidence that building owners were replacing regular glass shower doors with the shatterproof doors as a matter of course, then custom evidence should have come in. But that was not the case. The custom was that such replacements took place only where the old shower door broke or when a landlord was refurbishing an entire building. There was no evidence of wholesale, across-the-board replacement of glass shower doors with the shatterproof kind. Perhaps there was no such custom because to do so would be prohibitively expensive.

JIM: What's the big deal? If, in fact, across-the-board replacement is expensive, let the defendant present evidence to that effect to the jury. Let the defendant convince the jury that the custom is not on all fours.

AARON: You can't be serious. Evidence of violation of custom is devastating to the defendant. It portrays him as sleazy. Now you tell me that the defendant is not prejudiced because he can argue to the jury that "I'm not quite as sleazy as you might imagine." No, Jim, if the custom is not on point, it is the task of the trial judge to keep it out of the case. Plaintiff is free to present all the evidence concerning the cost of shatterproof shower doors and ease of replacement. Let the jury decide whether the defendant acted reasonably.

JIM: I believe that you are placing too heavy a burden on plaintiff. When a custom is close to the conduct in question, it should come in. It provides valuable data to the jury and lets them know that with that data in hand, the custom is to behave otherwise. Defendant can tell his story and try to convince them that he has acted reasonably. Plaintiffs should not be hamstrung by requiring that a custom precisely fit the conduct in question.

___ Cal. L.Rev. ___ (2017) (safety-related custom should be given substantial weight except where courts, in a manner analogous to judicial reviewed administrative action, perceive that the custom is part of a drift to under or over-investment in safety by industrial or professional defendants).

hypo 35

X was suspected of shoplifting and was detained by *Y*, a security guard, for 30 minutes to investigate whether *X* took the store's property. A statute provides that a suspected shoplifter may be detained "for a reasonable amount of time" to determine whether property was in fact stolen. *Y*'s employer, *Z*, provided all security guards with a handbook of procedures to be followed with regard to suspected shoplifters. The handbook provides that suspected shoplifters should not be detained for longer than 15 minutes to investigate whether property was taken. Is the handbook admissible against *Z* as an internal custom of the employer?

4. The Physical and Mental Attributes of the Reasonable Person

ROBERTS v. STATE OF LOUISIANA
396 So. 2d 566 (La. Ct. App. 1981)

LABORDE, Justice.

In this tort suit, William C. Roberts sued to recover damages for injuries he sustained in an accident in the lobby of the U.S. Post Office Building in Alexandria, Louisiana. Roberts fell after being bumped into by Mike Burson, the blind operator of the concession stand located in the building.

Plaintiff sued the State of Louisiana, through the Louisiana Health and Human Resources Administration, advancing two theories of liability: respondeat superior and negligent failure by the State to properly supervise and oversee the safe operation of the concession stand. The stand's blind operator, Mike Burson, is not a party to this suit although he is charged with negligence.

The trial court ordered plaintiff's suit dismissed holding that there is no respondeat superior liability without an employer-employee relationship and that there is no negligence liability without a cause in fact showing.

We affirm the trial court's decision for the reasons which follow.

On September 1, 1977, at about 12:45 in the afternoon, operator Mike Burson left his concession stand to go to the men's bathroom located in the building. As he was walking down the hall, he bumped into plaintiff who fell to the floor and injured his hip. Plaintiff was 75 years old, stood 5′6″ and weighed approximately 100 pounds. Burson, on the other hand, was 25 to 26 years old, stood approximately 6′ and weighed 165 pounds.

At the time of the incident, Burson was not using a cane nor was he utilizing the technique of walking with his arm or hand in front of him.

Even though Burson was not joined as a defendant, his negligence or lack thereof is crucial to a determination of the State's liability. Because of its importance, we begin with it.

Plaintiff contends that operator Mike Burson traversed the area from his concession stand to the men's bathroom in a negligent manner. To be more specific, he focuses on the operator's failure to use his cane even though he had it with him in his concession stand.

In determining an actor's negligence, various courts have imposed differing standards of care to which handicapped persons are expected to perform. Professor William L. Prosser expresses one generally recognized modern standard of care as follows:

> As to his physical characteristics, the reasonable man may be said to be identical with the actor. The man who is blind . . . is entitled to live in the world and to have allowance made by others for his disability, and he cannot be required to do the impossible by conforming to physical standards which he cannot meet. . . . At the same time, the conduct of the handicapped individual must be reasonable in the light of his knowledge of his infirmity, which is treated merely as one of the circumstances under which he acts. . . . It is sometimes said that a blind man must use a greater degree of care than one who can see; but it is now generally agreed that as a fixed rule this is inaccurate, and that the correct statement is merely that he must take the precautions, be they more or less, which the ordinary reasonable man would take if he were blind. W. Prosser, The Law of Torts, Section 32, at Page 151–52 (4th ed. 1971).

A careful review of the record in this instance reveals that Burson was acting as a reasonably prudent blind person would under these particular circumstances. . . .

On the date of the incident in question, Mike Burson testified that he left his concession stand and was on his way to the men's bathroom when he bumped into plaintiff. He, without hesitancy, admitted that at the time he was not using his cane, explaining that he relies on his facial sense which he feels is an adequate technique for short trips inside the familiar building. Burson testified that he does use a cane to get to and from work.

Plaintiff makes much of Burson's failure to use a cane when traversing the halls of the post office building. Yet, our review of the testimony received at trial indicates that it is not uncommon for blind people to rely on other techniques when moving around in a familiar setting. For example George Marzloff, the director of the Division of Blind Services, testified that he can recommend to the blind operators that they should use a cane but he knows that when they are in a setting in which they are comfortable, he would say that nine out of ten will not use a cane and in his personal opinion, if the operator is in a relatively busy area, the cane can be more of a hazard than an asset. . . .

The only testimony in the record that suggests that Burson traversed the halls in a negligent manner was that elicited from plaintiff's expert witness, William Henry Jacobson. Jacobson is an instructor in peripathology, which he explained as the science of movement within the surroundings by visually impaired individuals. Jacobson, admitting that he conducted no study or examination of Mike Burson's mobility skills and that he was unfamiliar with the State's vending program, nonetheless testified that he would require a blind person to use a cane in traversing the areas outside the concession stand. . . . He added that a totally blind individual probably should use a cane under any situation where . . . in an unfamiliar environment or where a familiar environment involves a change, whether it be people moving through that environment or strangers moving through that environment or just a heavy traffic within that environment. . . .

Upon our review of the record, we feel that plaintiff has failed to show that Burson was negligent. Burson testified that he was very familiar with his surroundings, having worked there for three and a half years. He had special mobility training and his reports introduced into evidence indicate good mobility skills. He explained his decision to rely on his facial sense instead of his cane for these short trips in a manner which convinces us that it was a reasoned decision. Not only was Burson's explanation adequate, there was additional testimony from other persons indicating that such a decision is not an unreasonable one. Also important is the total lack of any evidence in the record showing that at the time of the incident, Burson engaged in any acts which may be characterized as negligence on his part. For example, there is nothing showing that Burson was walking too fast, not paying attention, et cetera. Under all of these circumstances, we conclude that Mike Burson was not negligent.

Our determination that Mike Burson was not negligent disposes of our need to discuss liability on the part of the State.

For the above and foregoing reasons, the judgment of the trial court dismissing plaintiff's claims against defendant is affirmed and all costs of this appeal are assessed against the plaintiff-appellant.

Affirmed.

FOOD FOR THOUGHT

Is the following a fair statement? A person with physical disabilities may have to be more careful due to his disability, but he is not held to a higher standard of care. Negligence is determined by what is reasonable conduct under the circumstances and one of the circumstances that must be taken into account is the physical disability. This is no different than saying that reasonable care when driving may have to take into account that the weather is foggy and the visibility is poor. Think about the range of possibilities that we might impose on the blind when crossing the street. The law could require (1) use of a red and white cane; (2) wearing an iridescent jacket; (3) special sensory training; (4) a seeing eye dog; (5) a human companion. Where along the continuum do we stop?

For an interesting analysis as to the reasons for differing standards of care for children and persons with physical and mental disabilities, *see* Anita Bernstein, *The Communities That Make Standards of Care Possible*, 77 Chi.-Kent L. Rev. 735 (2002).

PHYSICAL DISABILITIES

The cases appear unanimous in the view that physical attributes are one of the circumstances to be considered in deciding whether an actor was negligent. *See, e.g.*, Shepherd v. Gardner Wholesale, Inc., 256 So. 2d 877 (Ala. 1972) (poor vision due to cataracts); Hodges v. Jewel Cos. 390 N.E.2d 930 (whether polio victim who used crutches was contributorily negligent in negotiating dangerous steps). (Ill. App. Ct. 1979) *Accord* Restatement, Third, of Torts § 11(a). An interesting question arises when the actor suffers sudden incapacitation, such as a heart attack or a stroke, when driving a car or engaging in some other activity that can pose a serious danger to others. If the condition is one that the actor could not have foreseen, he is not negligent. Kellog v Finnegan, 823 N.W.2d 454 (Minn. Ct. App. (2012) (driver with no history of seizures had a seizure while driving) Cincinnati Ins. Co. v. Allen, 2008 WL 286 1670 (Ohio Ct. App. 2008) (driver whose physician told him that he was cleared to drive despite occasional lightheadedness suffered sudden blackout). *Accord* Restatement, Third, of Torts § 11(b). What rule would you apply to a driver who has a known condition such as epilepsy that is being treated by medication that kept epilepsy generally under control? Assume that there exists a small risk of experiencing a seizure without advance notice. In the event of the sudden onset of a seizure, should the driver be held negligent?

MENTAL INCAPACITY OR MENTAL ILLNESS

With regard to mental incapacity or illness the question cannot be whether the incapacity or illness should be one of the circumstances to be taken into account in deciding whether one's conduct was reasonable. Since the actor by definition suffers from a mental deficiency that may not permit him to make reasonable judgments, the law must make a hard choice as to whether or not it wishes to hold him liable for failing to meet normal societal standards. Not surprisingly the case law gives no quarter for mental disability. In Creasy v. Rusk, 730 N.E.2d 659 (Ind. 2000), the court identified five reasons why American courts have refused to take into consideration mental incapacity in implementing the reasonable person standard: (1) As between two innocent parties the loss should be allocated to the one who occasioned the loss; (2) the imposition of liability provides incentives to those responsible for the mentally ill and who have interest in their estates to prevent harm by restraining those who are potentially dangerous; (3) to allow for mental incapacity defense might induce tortfeasors to fake mental disability to avoid tort liability; (4) court administration of a mental incapacity defense would be onerous because it is difficult to draw a satisfactory line between mental deficiency and a host of variations of temperament, intelligence, and emotional balance; (5) the liability rule forces persons with mental disabilities to pay for the damage they do if they are to live in the world as ordinary citizens. The Restatement, Third, of Torts § 11(c) agrees. It provides: "An actor's mental or emotional disability is not considered in determining whether conduct is negligent, unless the actor is a child." Though the court in *Creasy* adopted the rule imposing liability on the mentally ill, it found that, in the case of an institutionalized Alzheimer's patient who negligently injured a nurse, liability would not attach. The court reviewed the reasons for the general rule imposing liability against the mentally ill and found that they did not apply to a patient who committed harm to a caregiver in an institutional setting. The court reasoned that the patient owed no duty of reasonable care to the caregiver because caregivers are hired for the specific purpose of aiding patients who pose particular dangers and "by accepting such employment assume the risks associated with their respective occupations." Id. at 668. *Accord* Berberian v. Lynn, 845 A.2d 122 (N.J. 2004); Gregory v. Cott, 331 P.3d 179 (Cal. 2014) (court expanded rule that caregivers for Alzheimer patients cannot recover for otherwise tortious conduct of the patient to in-home caregivers; limiting the immunity from liability to institutional caregivers would encourage institutionalizing Alzheimer patients).

In one way the law concerning the liability of the mentally ill, at first, appears unusually harsh, in not providing an exception for injuries caused by the sudden onset of a mental illness without prior notice. *See, e.g.*, Bashi v. Wodarz, 53 Cal. Rptr. 2d 635 (Cal. Ct. App. 1996); Kuhn v. Zabotsky, 224 N.E.2d 137 (Ohio 1967). One frequently cited case, Breunig v. American Family Insurance Co., 173 N.W.2d 619 (Wis. 1970), held that there ought to be a "sudden mental illness" defense to a negligence case but only where there was an "absence of notice or forewarning to the person that he may be suddenly subject to such a type of insanity or mental illness." *Id.* at 623. In Ramey v. Knorr, 124 P.3d 314 (Wash. Ct. App. 2005), defendant, while in a delusional state, turned her car around toward oncoming traffic and drove head on into plaintiff's car for the purpose of committing suicide. Defendant raised the *Breunig* defense but the court found that she had ongoing symptoms of serious mental illness and that she did not suffer "sudden mental incapacity." As noted earlier, the Restatement, Third, of Torts § 11(b) and (c) recognizes a defense of sudden physical incapacity but does not recognize a defense of sudden mental incapacity. It appears that the Reporters believe that mental incapacity is never sudden and thus need not be considered.

CONTRIBUTORY FAULT AND MENTAL INCAPACITY OR ILLNESS

The one issue on which there is serious debate is whether an actor's mental incapacity or illness should be taken into account when deciding whether he has been contributorily negligent. It is one thing to hold a mentally ill person or one with diminished capacity liable when he acts to cause harm to others, but quite another to bar him from recovering from a negligent defendant because he has not taken reasonable care for himself. Where his conduct endangers others, we may be willing to impose liability to protect innocent victims from the harms done to them by mentally ill injurers. But, when the defendant was a competent negligent wrongdoer and the mentally ill plaintiff failed to act reasonably with regard to his own safety, there is good reason to allow him to recover. The courts are split on the issue. Some apply a subjective standard. *See, e.g.*, Cowan v. Doering, 545 A.2d 159 (N.J. 1988). Others opt for the objective standard. *See, e.g.*, Galindo v. TMT Transport, Inc., 733 P.2d 631 (Ariz. Ct. App. 1986). For an exhaustive discussion of the pros and cons of adopting an objective or subjective standard for the contributory negligence of plaintiffs suffering from mental illness, *see* Jankee v. Clark County, 612 N.W.2d 297 (Wis. 2000). The recent Restatement, Third, of Torts § 11, comment *e*, suggests that with the advent of comparative fault, juries are likely to reduce the percentage of fault they attribute to the plaintiff when the plaintiff is mentally ill, thus allowing him to recover a larger share of his damages.

RELIGIOUS BELIEFS: G-D TOLD ME TO DO IT

A fascinating question has arisen in a number of cases as to whether courts should deem a person unreasonable when he acts in a manner required by his religious beliefs. These cases center around situations where an injured person refuses medical treatment after being negligently injured by the defendant and suffers aggravated injuries as a result. A plaintiff who fails to undertake reasonable medical treatment cannot recover for injuries that could have been reasonably avoided. Courts typically refuse to regard an actor's choice as reasonable simply because his or her religion compels a given course of action. In Williams v. Bright, 632 N.Y.S.2d 760 (N.Y. Sup. Ct. 1995), a Jehovah's Witness suffered severe injuries when her rental car went off the road because her father fell asleep at the wheel. For a full recovery she needed to undergo several surgeries that would have involved blood transfusions, a procedure that she refused because, under the tenets of her faith, she would be "[deprived] of entry into the Kingdom of Heaven for all eternity." *Id.* at 763. The trial court refused to pass judgment on the soundness of her religious convictions. The court instead charged the jury to consider only whether her belief was reasonable within the context of her religion. The jury found that she had a right to refuse treatment and declined to reduce her recovery.

On appeal the case was reversed. Williams v. Bright, 658 N.Y.S.2d 910 (N.Y. App. Div. 1997), *appeal dismissed,* 686 N.E.2d 1368 (N.Y. 1997). The appeals court found that in asking the jury to consider the reasonableness of plaintiff's religiously motivated actions, the trial court did not treat the issue of her beliefs neutrally, but instead implicitly endorsed plaintiff's religion. The *Williams* court ultimately held that to avoid a purely objective or subjective standard in assessing the reasonableness of a failure to mitigate medical damages on religious grounds, the jury should be instructed to consider subjective beliefs only as a factor in risk-utility balancing. *See also* Christiansen v. Hollings, 112 P.2d 723, 729-730 (Cal. Ct. App. 1941) (upholding instruction that in determining whether a decedent suffering acute peritonitis after an accident was a "reasonably prudent person" in failing to have appendix surgery, jury was entitled to consider "conscientious belief in methods of treatment" prescribed by Christian Science Church); Munn v. Algee, 924 F.2d 568 (5th Cir. 1991) (upholding charge that jury may consider religious beliefs of Jehovah's Witness as well as known medical risks in determining whether refusal of blood transfusion was reasonable). Does the charge that allows the jury to consider religion as a factor avoid the problem of endorsing the religious practice of a plaintiff? For a general discussion of the possible standards courts may apply in these cases, *see* Jeremy Pomeroy, *Reason, Religion, and Avoidable Consequences: When Faith and the Duty to Mitigate Collide,* 67 N.Y.U. L. Rev. 1111 (1992).

For an argument that a plaintiff's preexisting religious beliefs should be treated the same as preexisting physical conditions, and that no reduction in recovery should be allowed when a plaintiff refuses medical care because of religious convictions, *see* Anne C. Loomis, *Thou Shalt Take Thy Victim as Thou Findest Him: Religious Convictions as a Pre-Existing State Not Subject to the Avoidable Consequences Doctrine*, 14 Geo. Mason L. Rev. 473 (2007).

5. To What Standard of Conduct Is a Child Held?

STEVENS v. VEENSTRA
573 N.W.2d 341 (Mich. Ct. App. 1998)

MURPHY, Justice.

Plaintiff appeals as of right from a jury verdict of no cause of action in favor of defendant. We reverse and remand.

As a fourteen-year-old, defendant Aaron Veenstra took a driver's education course offered through the Calumet Public School system. Veenstra had skipped four grades in elementary school and graduated from high school early. He was taking driver's education so that he would have transportation to college. Before the driver's education course, Veenstra had never driven an automobile on a public road in a developed area. On the first day of the driving portion of the class, Veenstra stopped the automobile he was driving at an intersection. When the traffic cleared, Veenstra made a right turn. However, Veenstra turned too sharply and headed at plaintiff who was getting out of his parked automobile. Both Veenstra and the driving instructor attempted to turn Veenstra's automobile away from plaintiff. Veenstra testified that as he was heading for plaintiff, he may have hit the accelerator instead of the brake. As a result, Veenstra's automobile struck plaintiff.

At trial, over plaintiff's objection, the trial court gave the following instruction:

> A minor is not held to the same standard of conduct as an adult. When I use the words "ordinary care" with respect to the minor, Aaron S. Veenstra, I mean the degree of care which a reasonably careful minor of age, mental capacity and experience of Aaron S. Veenstra would use under the circumstances which you find existed in this case. It is for you to decide what a reasonably careful minor would do or would not do under such circumstances.

Utilizing this instruction, the jury found that Veenstra was not negligent. . . .

On appeal, plaintiff claims that the trial court's instruction was improper and mandates reversal. We agree.

Generally, in the context of negligence actions, the capability of minors, seven years of age or older, is not determined on the basis of an adult standard of conduct, but rather is determined on the basis of how a minor of similar age, mental capacity, and experience would conduct himself. *See* Fire Insurance Exchange v. Diehl, 520 N.W.2d 675 (Mich. Ct. App. 1994). However, Michigan "has a longstanding policy of holding all drivers, even minors, to an adult standard of care." . . . A minor who engages in an adult activity that is dangerous, e.g., driving an automobile, is charged with the same standard of conduct as an adult. . . . Osner v. Boughner, 446 N.W.2d 873 (Mich. Ct. App. 1989).

Plaintiff argued below and argues on appeal that this black-letter law applies to this case and that, although Veenstra was a minor, because he was engaged in the adult activity of driving an automobile, he should be held to the same standard of conduct as an adult. Veenstra and the trial court consider this case to be distinguishable from prior cases holding that minors driving automobiles are held to an adult standard of conduct and call for an exception to that rule. In denying plaintiff's motion for a new trial, the trial court stated that, although driving an automobile is an adult activity, "[d]riving a motor vehicle as a student driver under the supervision of a driver's training teacher during the course of a school driver's training program" is not an adult activity. Veenstra argues that, because he was participating in a minor-oriented driver training program, he was not engaged in an adult activity and attempts to bolster this argument by referring to M.C.L. § 257.811(6); M.S.A. § 9.2511(6), which states that an operator's license shall not be issued to a person under eighteen years of age unless that person passes a driver's education course. In essence, Veenstra defines the activity he was involved in as not simply driving an automobile, but driving an automobile as part of a driver's education course to satisfy the legislative requirements placed upon those under eighteen years of age seeking to obtain an operator's license, and claims that because he was engaged in an activity, which by definition is limited to minors, he was not engaged in an adult activity and should not be held to an adult standard of conduct. We disagree.

One rationale behind holding a minor driving an automobile to an adult standard of conduct is that, because of the frequency and sometimes catastrophic results of automobile accidents, it would be unfair to the public to permit a minor operating an automobile to observe any standard of care other than that expected of all others operating automobiles. *See* Dellwo v. Pearson, 107 N.W.2d 859 (Minn. 1961). It would seem illogical to think that the dangers associated with driving are lessened when the activity is undertaken by a minor with little or no experience. While we concede that Veenstra was attempting to satisfy requirements placed only upon minors, we do not think that changes the nature of, or danger associated with, driving an automobile. In our opinion, defendant defines the activity he was engaged in too narrowly. Veenstra was engaged in the adult activity of driving an automobile, and we do not consider the reasons behind his undertaking the activity to justify departure from the general rule that all drivers, even minors, are held to an adult standard of care. . . .

While the process of learning involves unique dangers, for which some allowance may be justified for beginners undertaking some activities, when the probability of, or potential harm associated with, a particular activity is great, anyone engaged in the activity must be held to a certain minimum level of competence, even though that level may lie beyond the capability of a beginner. *See* Restatement, Second, of Torts, § 299, comment *d*. In other words, some activities are so dangerous that the risk must be borne by the beginner rather than the innocent victims, and lack of competence is no excuse. *Id.* We believe that driving an automobile is such an activity, and that anyone driving an automobile, regardless of age, must be held to the same standard of competence and conduct.

Reversed and remanded for a new trial. . . .

THE RESTATEMENT, THIRD, AND CASE LAW

The Restatement, Third, of Torts § 10 sets forth the following rule with regard to children:

§ 10. Children

(a) A child's conduct is negligent if it does not conform to that of a reasonably careful person of the same age, intelligence, and experience, except as provided in subsection (b) or (c).

(b) A child less than five years of age is incapable of negligence.

(c) The special rule in Subsection (a) does not apply when the child is engaging in a dangerous activity that is characteristically undertaken by adults.

Most states follow the Restatement formulation. *See, e.g.,* Ruiz v. Faulkner, 470 P.2d 500 (Ariz. Ct. App. 1970); Lester v. Sayles, 850 S.W.2d 858 (Mo. 1993); Nielsen ex rel. C.N. v. Bell ex rel. B.B. 2016 WL 1178392 (Utah 2016). A sizable minority follows what has come to be known as the Illinois rule. Under this approach, if the child is above the age of 14, there is a rebuttable presumption that the child is able to meet the adult reasonable person standard, in which no allowance is made for age, intelligence, and experience. Between the ages of 7 and 14, the presumption is that the child is incapable of meeting the adult standard. Below the age of 7, the child cannot be found negligent. For decisions that still follow the "Rule of Sevens," *see, e.g.,* Savage Industries, Inc. v. Duke, 598 So. 2d 856 (Ala. 1992); Chu v. Bowers, 656 N.E.2d 436 (Ill. App. Ct. 1995).

With regard to adults, no allowance is made for age, intelligence, and experience. These factors are generally swallowed into the objective reasonable person standard. For children, evidence may be introduced on each of these factors to either raise or lower the standard of care. *See, e.g.,* Mathis v. Massachusetts Electric Co., 565 N.E.2d 1180 (Mass. 1991). Note, however, once allowance is made for age, intelligence, and experience, the question is whether a reasonable child with similar qualities would have so acted. The test is thus partially subjective and partially objective. It is interesting that Australia and England take age into account in setting the standard of care for children but do not make allowance for intelligence and experience. Would it be wise for us to adopt the Australian-English approach?

WHY THE SPECIAL RULE FOR CHILDREN?

The *Stevens* case tests the fairness of the rule that a child who indulges in adult activities should be judged by adult standards. If the rule is justified because third persons cannot protect themselves against children who engage in adult activities, whereas they are better able to do so when children engage in more youthful type conduct, e.g., bicycle riding, then *Stevens* makes sense. If, however, the adult activities rule is based on a notion that by indulging in adult activities the child has moved himself out of the world of children and has achieved adult-like status, then the *Stevens* holding is less compelling. The defendant-driver was indulging in behavior that the statute tailor-made for children seeking to learn to drive.

WHAT IS AN ADULT ACTIVITY?

For the most part, courts have not had a difficult time identifying what is adult activity. *See, e.g.*, Medina v. McAllister, 202 So. 2d 755 (Fla. 1967) (operating motor scooter); Robinson v. Lindsay, 598 P.2d 392 (Wash. 1979) (driving snowmobile). But some activities are less clear. Some courts apply the child standard to the use of firearms. *See, e.g.*, Purtle v. Shelton, 474 S.W.2d 123 (Ark. 1971). Others apply the adult standard. *See, e.g.*, Huebner v. Koelfgren, 519 N.W.2d 488 (Minn. Ct. App. 1994). Golfing was held to require application of the adult standard in Neumann v. Shlansky, 294 N.Y.S.2d 628 (Co. Ct. 1968), but the child standard in Gremillion v. State Farm Mutual Insurance Co., 331 So. 2d 130 (La. Ct. App. 1976). For a thorough discussion of the "adult activity" exception to special rules dealing with the liability of children for negligence *see*, Dan B. Dobbs, Paul T. Hayden & Ellen M. Burlick, The Law of Torts § 137.

hypo **36**

X, a precocious nine-year-old, took the keys to his father's car out of his jacket pocket and took the car for a spin. Not surprisingly, he wasn't good at driving and he struck another car, injuring a passenger, *Y*. In *Y*'s action against *X* for negligent driving, is *X* held to an adult standard?

6. The Standard of Care for Professionals

One who represents herself to be a physician, cardiac surgeon, accountant, lawyer, or electrical engineer is held to the standard of knowledge and skill normally possessed by members of that profession. The question is then asked whether, under the circumstances of the particular case, the actor exercised reasonable judgment. Perhaps the better way of explaining the rule is that a professional who holds herself out as competent to practice in a field cannot argue that she acted reasonably based on the knowledge and skill that she actually had. In this case, the "should have known" is taken for granted. Having held herself out as a professional, she has a clear obligation to acquire the requisite knowledge.

Professional malpractice cases do raise some special problems. First, in the overwhelming majority of professional malpractice cases, juries are incapable of determining the professional standard of care without the aid of expert witnesses from that specialty. Juries cannot rely on common experience to guide them as to what is reasonable conduct. They do not have a frame of reference to make these decisions. Experts will thus testify as to whether they believe the defendant's

---

authors' dialogue 14

AARON: I understand the reason for holding minors who are not involved in adult activities to a standard that is more subjective, based on reasonable conduct of children of like age, intelligence, and experience. Children have more limited knowledge upon which to exercise judgment and they have not developed the judgment capabilities of adults. But why doesn't the very same argument apply to those suffering from various forms of mental illness?

JIM: Elementary, my dear Watson. Part of the normal maturation process of children is that they grow more knowledgeable and develop better judgment skills as they grow older. All of us were once children. We can't lock them up until adulthood and we can't saddle them when they become adults with judgments that were taken out against them for actions they did when they were kids. But, if the mentally ill cannot conform to normal societal standards, then those responsible for caring for them ought to keep them from harm's way.

AARON: I believe you're wrong on all counts. First, in the vast majority of cases the liability of the children will be covered under homeowner liability policies. Second, at one time in our history we used to put mentally ill persons who just didn't measure up into institutions. Involuntary confinement was the norm. Today, involuntary commitment is limited to cases where the mentally ill person is dangerous to himself or others. The decision now is to have the mentally ill become an integral part of society. If kids are part of our world and don't have to measure up to adult standards, then the mentally ill should not have to measure up either.

JIM: Well, then let me turn the tables. If society has decided to deinstitutionalize the mentally ill and integrate them into our world, then they should be treated as all other members of society. No special breaks. As to the special rule for minors — maybe it is because they are not given full entree into the adult world. They are, in fact, kept at bay. Proof of this is the fact that once they fully enter the adult world by engaging in adult activities, we hold them to the adult standard.

AARON: I don't know. Maybe this gets us beyond the law of torts. It seems to me we have deinstitutionalized the mentally ill and have not provided them with the supervision and other resources necessary to cope. Then when they turn out to be tortfeasors, we ask them to adhere to a standard that they cannot meet. Maybe what it boils down to is this: if the mentally ill have financial resources, those caring for them will manage their lives so that they do not commit torts. Informally they will see to it that their activities are curtailed, even if it means depriving them of being full members of society. As to the ones who have no resources, they won't be sued anyway.

---

conduct conformed to how a reasonable profession would have behaved. They will, in a very real way, be invading the province of the jury. In the run-of-the-mill negligence case, a jury hears the facts and decides what is reasonable conduct. In the professional malpractice cases, the jury will typically hear from experts on both sides opining as to whether the defendant acted reasonably. They will then have to choose which expert to believe.

Second, the judge will not give the jury a simple "reasonable person" instruction but will instead ask the jury whether the defendant acted with the skill and knowledge normal to the profession. Some courts have said that professionals are not liable for a "mere error in judgment." *See, e.g.*, Hodges v. Carter, 80 S.E.2d 144, 146 (N.C. 1954) (in an action for attorney malpractice defendant is not liable if he "acts in good faith and in an honest belief that his advice and acts are well founded and in the best interests of his client"). But, this view is clearly not correct. Professionals are not excepted from the general reasonableness standard. In Ziegelheim v. Apollo, 607 A.2d 1298 (N.J. 1992), an attorney advised his client to settle a lawsuit rather than proceeding to trial, reasoning that she was not likely to do much better than the settlement offer if she went to trial. While acknowledging that in general the decision whether to advise a client to settle a case is a matter of judgment, in this case a jury could have found that the lawyer's decision was ill informed because it did not adequately account for several features of the client's case that might have enabled her to do unusually well at trial. What can be said is that a professional faced with two reasonable choices is not liable if the reasonable choice she made turns out badly. *See, e.g.*, Cosgrove v. Grimes, 774 S.W.2d 662, 664-665 (Tex. 1989); Clark County Fire District No. 5 v. Bullivant Houser Bailey PC, 324 P.3d 743 (Wash. Ct. App. 2014).

The highest-profile judicial delegations of standard-setting responsibility occur in medical malpractice cases. A leading decision is Boyce v. Brown, 77 P.2d 455 (Ariz. 1938), in which a wife and her husband sought to recover from a surgeon for alleged negligence in treating the wife's fractured ankle. Seven years after what appeared to have been successful surgery by the defendant surgeon, the wife began to experience pain and returned to the defendant surgeon, who made minor adjustments to an arch support but did not order that x-rays be taken. After two more years of increasing pain, the wife went to another surgeon, who x-rayed the ankle, detected necrosis, and removed the surgical screws that the defendant surgeon had used in the original fracture repair. The patient thereafter experienced no further fracture-related problems with her ankle. The plaintiffs brought actions against the defendant surgeon for medical malpractice in connection with the wife's second, and last, visit to the defendant. The plaintiffs based their claims mainly on the defendant's failure to have x-rays taken. Their medical expert, the second surgeon who x-rayed the ankle and removed the surgical screws, would not testify that the defendant's failure to order an x-ray violated recognized medical treatment standards; but the plaintiffs argued that the need for an x-ray was so obvious that even a layman knows that it was required for proper medical treatment. The trial court directed a verdict for the defendant. The Supreme Court of Arizona affirmed.

The opinion in *Boyce* considers that in some jurisdictions the judge instructs the jury that a physician is presumed to possess the skill of the "average physician." In other jurisdictions such an instruction may well be reversible error. As the court noted in Hall v. Hilbun, 466 So. 2d 856, 871 (Miss. 1985), such an instruction implies "that the lower 50 percent of our physicians regularly engage in medical malpractice." *Accord* Nowatske v. Osterloh, 543 N.W.2d 265, 273 (Wis. 1996).

The requirement in *Boyce* that in order to be liable for malpractice the doctor must have violated the "recognized standard of good medical practice in the community in which he is practicing" adopts a rule for physicians that differs from that applicable to all other persons. You will recall that in our discussion of custom in section 3, *supra*, we set forth the prevailing rule that compliance with custom is relevant but not dispositive as to whether an actor was negligent. The almost universal rule with regard to physicians is that compliance with medical custom exonerates the defendant from liability. Why does the medical profession get a special break? For some interesting insights on this question, *see* Richard N. Pearson, *The Role of Custom in Medical Malpractice Cases*, 51 Ind. L.J. 528 (1976).

The court's pronouncement that a physician is held to the standard of good medical practice "in the community in which he is practicing" reflects a view that has been trashed by courts in recent years. The trend has been to depart from the "locality rule" and to hold physicians to what is good medical practice nationally. *See, e.g.,* Brune v. Belinkoff, 235 N.E.2d 793 (Mass. 1968); Morrison v. MacNamara, 407 A.2d 555 (D.C. 1979). With the advent of the Internet and instant communication, it is unlikely that the "locality rule" will continue to have any credence whatsoever. In legal malpractice cases, however, courts are more inclined to apply a locality-based standard of care, because attorney's possess knowledge of state law, local rules and practices of courts, and even the characteristics of judges and juries in the community. Many courts do admit expert testimony based on a statewide standard of care. *See, e.g.,* Russo v. Griffin, 510 A.2d 436 (Vt. 1986). It seems unlikely that this limitation will be further relaxed, except in areas of legal practice that are truly national in scope, particularly those governed by federal law such as patent, antitrust, and securities cases.

For a physician to owe a duty of reasonable care to a patient, a physician-patient relationship between the two must exist at the time of the alleged negligence. Thus, in Jennings v. Badgett, 230 P.3d 861 (Okla. 2010), the plaintiff's treating physician sought and received — and relied upon — a medical opinion over the telephone from the defendant nontreating physician. The defendant knew that the treating physician would rely on the opinion, which the plaintiff claimed was negligently reached, but the defendant insisted that the final decision regarding treatment was that of the treating physician. The defendant never saw the plaintiff; nor did he receive any payment for giving his opinion. The Supreme Court of Oklahoma reinstated the trial court's summary judgment in defendant's favor, holding that the defendant owed no duty of care to the plaintiff in the absence of a physician-patient relationship between them.

In legal malpractice cases, the existence of an attorney-client relationship can sometimes be a question of fact for the jury. In the well-known case of Togstad v. Vesely, Otto, Miller & Keefe, 291 N.W.2d 686 (Minn. 1980), a woman came to a lawyer's office to talk about a possible medical malpractice case against the neurosurgeon who had operated on her husband. As the lawyer remembered the conversation, he told Mrs. Togstad that she did have a case that his firm would be interested in taking on. Mrs. Togstad remembered that the lawyer said simply that she "did not have a case." Attorneys are free to decline to represent a client for many reasons, including lack of competence in a specialized area of law (like medical malpractice), conflicts of interest, insufficient staffing to handle a complex case, or even the belief that taking the case would not make economic sense for the firm. Given the divergence in the parties' testimony, however, a trier of fact might conclude that the lawyer considered the facts and gave Mrs. Togstad the advice that her medical malpractice claim was no good. The law firm might then become liable for the damages proximately caused by the lawyer's negligent advice, which caused Mrs. Togstad to take no action against the neurosurgeon before the statute of limitations ran on her medical malpractice cause of action. Observing the impact of cases like *Togstad* on law firms' liability, legal malpractice insurers advise lawyers who decline a prospective client's case to clearly advise the would-be client in writing that the lawyer is not representing her, advise her of the desirability of consulting with another lawyer and inform her that statutes of limitations make it imperative to take these actions expeditiously.

The need to adduce expert testimony to make out a malpractice case is widely recognized. *See, e.g.*, Brannon v. Wood, 444 P.2d 558 (Or. 1968). If, however, a surgeon leaves a sponge in a patient's innards, thus necessitating subsequent surgery to remove it, expert testimony is not necessary to establish negligence. *See, e.g.*, Coleman v. Rice, 706 So. 2d 696 (Miss. 1997); Fessenden v. Robert Packer Hospital, 97 A.3d 1225 (Pa. Super. Ct. 2014). One does not have to be a brain surgeon to figure out that such conduct is negligent. Same story for a lawyer who blows an obvious filing deadline. *See* discussion, *infra*, section E (res ipsa loquitur).

The FDA has approved a radiofrequency identification (RFID) microchip that attaches to each sponge. Upon completion of the surgery the surgeon uses a hand held wand-scanning device that signals that a sponge was left in the patient's body. What are the implications for liability if a hospital does not utilize the RFID and a sponge is left in a patient's body?

HELLING v. CAREY
519 P.2d 981 (Wash. 1974)

HUNTER, Associate Justice.

This case arises from a malpractice action instituted by the plaintiff (petitioner), Barbara Helling.

The plaintiff suffers from primary open angle glaucoma. Primary open angle glaucoma is essentially a condition of the eye in which there is an interference in the ease with which the nourishing fluids can flow out of the eye. Such a condition results in pressure gradually rising above the normal level to such an extent that damage is produced to the optic nerve and its fibers with resultant loss in vision. The first loss usually occurs in the periphery of the field of vision. The disease usually has few symptoms and, in the absence of a pressure test, is often undetected until the damage has become extensive and irreversible.

The defendants (respondents), Dr. Thomas F. Carey and Dr. Robert C. Laughlin, are partners who practice the medical specialty of ophthalmology. . . .

The plaintiff first consulted the defendants for myopia, nearsightedness, in 1959. At that time she was fitted with contact lenses. She next consulted the defendants in September, 1963, concerning irritation caused by the contact lenses. Additional consultations occurred in October 1963; February 1967; September 1967; October 1967; May 1968; July 1968; August 1968; September 1968; and October 1968. Until the October 1968 consultation, the defendants considered the plaintiff's visual problems to be related solely to complications associated with her contact lenses. On that occasion, the defendant, Dr. Carey, tested the plaintiff's eye pressure and field of vision for the first time. This test indicated that the plaintiff had glaucoma. The plaintiff, who was then 32 years of age, had essentially lost her peripheral vision and her central vision was reduced to approximately 5 degrees vertical by 10 degrees horizontal.

Thereafter, in August of 1969, after consulting other physicians, the plaintiff filed a complaint against the defendants alleging, among other things, that she sustained severe and permanent damage to her eyes as a proximate result of the defendants' negligence. During trial, the testimony of the medical experts for both the plaintiff and the defendants established that the standards of the profession for that specialty in the same or similar circumstances do not require routine pressure tests for glaucoma upon patients under 40 years of age. The reason the pressure test for glaucoma is not given as a regular practice to patients under the age of 40 is that the disease rarely occurs in this age group. Testimony indicated, however, that the standards of the profession do require pressure tests if the patient's complaints and symptoms reveal to the physician that glaucoma should be suspected.

The trial court entered judgment for the defendants following a defense verdict. The plaintiff . . . appealed to the Court of Appeals which affirmed the judgment of the trial court. . . . The plaintiff then petitioned the court for review, which was granted.

We find this to be a unique case. The testimony of the medical experts is undisputed concerning the standard of the profession for the specialty of ophthalmology. . . . The issue is whether the defendants' compliance with the standard of the profession of ophthalmology, which does not require the giving of a routine pressure test to persons under 40 years of age, should insulate them from liability under the facts in this case where the plaintiff has lost a substantial amount of her vision due to the failure of the defendants to timely give the pressure test to the plaintiff.

The incidence of glaucoma in one out of 25,000 persons under the age of 40 may appear quite minimal. However, that one person, the plaintiff in this instance, is entitled to the same protection, as afforded persons over 40, essential for timely detection of the evidence of glaucoma where it can be arrested to avoid the grave and devastating result of this disease. The test is a simple pressure test, relatively inexpensive. There is no judgment factor involved, and there is no doubt that by giving the test the evidence of glaucoma can be detected. The giving of the test is harmless if the physical condition of the eye permits. The testimony indicates that although the condition of the plaintiff's eyes might have at times prevented the defendants from administering the pressure test, there is an absence of evidence in the record that the test could not have been timely given.

Justice Holmes stated in Texas & Pac. Ry. v. Behymer, 189 U.S. 468, 470 . . . (1903):

> What usually is done may be evidence of what ought to be done, but what ought to be done is fixed by a standard of reasonable prudence whether it usually is complied with or not. . . .

Under the facts of this case reasonable prudence required the timely giving of the pressure test to this plaintiff. The precaution of giving this test to detect the incidence of glaucoma to patients under 40 years of age is so imperative that irrespective of its disregard by the standards of the ophthalmology profession, it is the duty of the courts to say what is required to protect patients under 40 from the damaging results of glaucoma.

We therefore hold, as a matter of law, that the reasonable professional standard that should have been followed under the undisputed facts of this case was the timely giving of this simple, harmless pressure test to this plaintiff and that, in failing to do so, the defendants were negligent, which proximately resulted in the blindness sustained by the plaintiff for which the defendants are liable. . . .

The judgment of the trial court and the decision of the Court of Appeals is reversed, and the case is remanded for a new trial on the issue of damages only. . . .

FOOD FOR THOUGHT

Helling took two rather unorthodox positions. First, the court did not defer to medical custom as controlling in a case alleging medical malpractice. *See* pp. 191-194, *supra.* Second, it established a rule of law governing malpractice without expert testimony, supporting the position that the standard the court adopted was reasonable for the medical profession.

Was the court right in holding that ophthalmologists must test for rare occurrences? Must a doctor give a urine test to every patient to test for diabetes even absent any symptoms of the disease? Must blood pressure be tested at every visit? Examination of the eyes to see whether there is evidence of a brain tumor? All of these tests are relatively cheap to perform and can be done quickly and without undue effort.

Shortly after *Helling* was decided, the Washington legislature passed a statute requiring that to recover in a malpractice action the plaintiff must prove "that the defendant or defendants failed to exercise that degree of skill, care, and learning possessed at that time by other persons in the same profession. . . ." Wash. Rev. Code § 4.24.290 (2007). In Gates v. Jensen, 595 P.2d 919 (Wash. 1979), the court held that this statute did not alter the *Helling* rule. In *Gates*, as in *Helling*, the alleged negligence was the defendants' failure to test the plaintiff for glaucoma. In ruling that the trial judge improperly refused to instruct the jury that it was not bound by medical custom, the court stated that liability can be imposed if the defendant failed to exercise the "skill, care and learning *possessed* by others in the profession," whether customarily used or not in similar circumstances.

MEDICAL MALPRACTICE CRISIS: MYTH OR REALITY?

Concern that malpractice claims were getting out of hand and imposing huge insurance costs on the medical profession have spurred state legislatures to curb what they considered excesses in this genre of claims. As of 2016, 38 states have imposed caps on damages that can be recovered. In some states, malpractice caps have been upheld by the courts. *See, e.g.,* Fein v. Permanente Medical Group, 695 P.2d 665 (Cal. 1985) ($250,000); Butler v. Flint Goodrich Hospital of Dillard

University, 607 So. 2d 517 (La. 1992) ($500,000); Kirkland by & ex rel. Kirkland v. Blaine County Med. Ctr., 4 P.3d 1115 (Idaho 2000) ($400,000). Others have found such caps to be unconstitutional. *See, e.g.,* Carson v. Maurer, 424 A.2d 825 (N.H. 1980); Arneson v. Olson, 270 N.W.2d 125 (N.D. 1978); Atlanta Oculoplastic Surgery, P.C. v. Nestlehutt, 691 S.E.2d 218 (Ga. 2010); Lebron v. Gottlieb Mem. Hosp., 930 N.E.2d 895 (Ill. 2010); Estate of McCall v. United States, 134 So.3d 894 (Fla. 2014). Most states have shortened the statute of limitations in which a malpractice action can be brought (*e.g.,* Tenn. Code Ann. § 29-26-116 (1975) (one year); Ga. Code. Ann. § 9-3-71 (1985) (two years); N.Y. C.P.L.R. § 214-a (McKinney 1990) (two years six months)). Each state's law must be carefully examined. You can't tell a player without a scorecard.

In a provocative book, *The Medical Malpractice Myth* (2005), Professor Tom Baker makes a strong case that the medical malpractice crisis is simply trumped up and has little basis in fact. Independent studies have demonstrated that most medical malpractice claims are not frivolous. Indeed, Baker argues that highly respected researchers have shown that the vast majority of legitimate medical malpractice claims are never pursued by victims. Baker admits that doctors are often subject to radical increases in their insurance premiums but places the blame on insurance companies for under-reserving for future claims. He further finds little evidence to support the contention that doctors practice defensive medicine and insist on medically unnecessary tests and procedures. Baker believes that medical malpractice litigation serves as a deterrent against the negligent practice of medicine. He notes that in the 1980s anesthesiologists were faced with extremely high premiums. Rather than blame the lawyers, they undertook a painstaking analysis of practices that contributed to the large number of negligence claims against them and instituted safety practices that sharply reduced the number of claims. As a result, insurance rates dropped dramatically. For an incisive analysis of Professor Baker's book, *see* Anthony J. Sebok, *Dispatches from the Tort Wars*, 85 Tex. L. Rev. 1465 (2007). Building on Professor Baker's book Marc A. Rodwin, Justin Silverman and David Merfield in *Why the Medical Malpractice Crisis Persists Even When Malpractice Insurance Premiums Fall*, 25 Heath Matrix 163 (2015) support the thesis that the crisis is a myth with elaborate statistics. At least one of the authors (Twerski) remains unconvinced. For an argument that medical malpractice reform reduces patient safety, while malpractice litigation increases transparent discussion of errors and reveals valuable information about the areas of weakness in the medical practice, *see* Joanna C. Schwartz, *A Dose of Reality for Medical Malpractice Reform*, 88 N.Y.U. L. Rev. 1224 (2013).

hypo **37**

Parents concerned about their 16-year-old daughter's mood swings asked their congregation's rabbi to talk with her. The rabbi counseled her and told the parents that he believed that her moods were transitory and would blow over. One week later, the young girl committed suicide. If the parents seek to bring a negligence action for their daughter's death, to what standard of care is the rabbi held?

D. JUDICIALLY-DETERMINED STANDARDS OF CARE

1. Courts Utilizing Risk-Utility Balancing to Decide Cases as a Matter of Law

In most negligence cases, juries perform two functions. First, they resolve factual conflicts between the parties as to what occurred. Did the pedestrian cross against the light? Did the carpet on which the plaintiff tripped and fell become loose two hours, four hours, or two days before the fall? Second, they set the legal standard of reasonable care under the circumstances. If, for example, the carpet in an apartment house became loose two hours before the plaintiff fell, is the two-hour interval sufficient time to put the owner on notice to have repaired the condition? It is hornbook law that, where reasonable persons cannot differ, the judge should direct a verdict. Thus, if the evidence showed that the superintendent of the apartment checked each stairway twice a day, a court might find that the care taken by defendant was sufficient and that no jury could find the defendant negligent. Using the Learned Hand formula, a court might hold that to impose hourly inspection of the stairways would be far too costly given the likelihood and gravity of any potential harm. What if the issue of the loose carpet wound its way up to the Supreme Court of State X and in a 4-3 decision the court found that twice daily inspections were sufficient? The three dissenters took the position that whether such conduct constituted negligence was for the jury to decide. Would the four-member majority be telling their three brethren or sisters on the court that they are not reasonable persons? What gives?

Assume that a court dismisses the loose carpet case and says that twice daily inspections of carpeted steps in apartment houses are sufficient as a matter of law. Assume further that the case in which they made the pronouncement dealt with an apartment house that had 20 units. Is the law still good for a 40-unit apartment? From time to time, courts express their findings on standard of care in ways that are overbroad and likely to make mischief. The problem is that negligence cases are very fact-sensitive and what may be a sensible judicial finding of negligence or non-negligence in one case may be of questionable merit in another. The best-known all-time goof on this issue came from no less a source than Justice Oliver Wendell Holmes while sitting on the United States Supreme Court. In Baltimore & Ohio R.R. v. Goodman, 275 U.S. 66 (1927), plaintiff was struck by a train at a railroad crossing. Under the facts of the case, plaintiff was contributorily negligent since he should have seen the train coming. It would have been enough if the court had said that plaintiff was negligent for failing to look and see. But, Holmes went further and sought to set forth a rule that would govern future railroad crossing cases. He said:

> In such circumstances it seems to us that if a driver cannot be sure otherwise whether a train is dangerously near he must stop and get out of his vehicle, although obviously he will not often be required to do more than to stop and look.

In a later case, Pokora v. Wabash Ry., 292 U.S. 98 (1934), plaintiff, driving a truck, approached a railroad crossing. He was unable to get a good view of the tracks to the north because boxcars were blocking his vision. He stopped, looked, and listened for bells or whistles of an oncoming train. He then proceeded onto the track and was hit by a passenger train coming from the north. Both the trial court and the circuit court of appeals directed a verdict for the defendant on the ground that the plaintiff was contributorily negligent as a matter of law, citing to Holmes's statement as a binding ruling. If the plaintiff could not get a good view, he had to get out of the truck and look. In a hard-hitting opinion, Justice Cardozo made short shrift of Holmes's "stop and get out of the vehicle" rule. Cardozo acknowledged that, perhaps under the facts of the case reviewed by Holmes, that rule might have been proper. But to say that when you can't see from the truck, you always, have to get out and look is just nonsense. In the *Pokora* case, if the plaintiff had followed the Holmes rule, he would have been in greater danger. By the time he got back into the truck, another train might have been bearing down at the crossing.

Cardozo cautions that courts should be careful before they declare rules of law in fact-sensitive negligence cases. The next case that comes along with slightly different facts may require a fresh look at the question of whether the actor behaved reasonably. The judge trying the second case should not be hamstrung by a judicial pronouncement that conduct either is or is not negligent as a matter of law but should be free to send the case to the jury.

TIMPTE INDUSTRIES INC. v. GISH
286 S.W.3d 306 (Tex. 2009)

Justice MEDINA delivered the opinion of the Court.

Robert Gish was seriously injured when he fell from the top of a trailer into which he was attempting to load fertilizer. He sued Timpte Industries, the manufacturer of the trailer, alleging, among other things, that several features of the trailer were negligently designed, rendering the trailer unreasonably dangerous.[2] The trial court granted a no-evidence summary judgment in Timpte's favor, but the court of appeals reversed.

Finding no negligence in design, we reverse the court of appeals' judgment and render judgment reinstating the trial court's summary judgment.

I

On the morning of June 19, 2002, Robert Gish, a long haul trucker for Scott Hinde Trucking, arrived at the Martin Resources plant in Plainview, Texas, to pick up a load of ammonium sulfate fertilizer. Gish was familiar with the plant, as he had picked up fertilizer there once or twice a week for approximately the past year. That morning Gish checked his trailer, weighed it, and waited for another customer to finish loading.

---

2. The court refers in its opinion to the central issue as one of "defective design." Given that the term "defective" is the same as "negligent," the editors have taken the liberty of substituting the latter term for the former throughout.

Gish's Peterbilt truck was hauling a forty-eight-foot Super Hopper trailer manufactured by Timpte Inc., a subsidiary of Timpte Industries. The Super Hopper trailer is a standard open-top, twin hopper trailer, which is loaded from above through use of a downspout or other device and is emptied through two openings on its bottom. Once the trailer is loaded, a tarp is rolled over the top to protect its contents. A ladder and an observation platform are attached to the front and rear of the trailer to allow the operator to view its contents.

After the truck ahead of him finished loading, Gish backed his trailer under the downspout attached to the fertilizer plant and yelled to a Martin employee to begin loading. In a typical delivery, an employee inside the Martin plant uses a front-end loader to drop fertilizer into a hopper. The fertilizer is then dropped onto a conveyor system that moves it to the downspout outside the plant and into the waiting trailer.

To prevent the granulated fertilizer from being blown away during the loading process, Gish attempted to lower the downspout by using a rope attached to it. The rope was attached to the downspout for that purpose, but Gish could not get it to work. He had previously complained to Martin employees about problems lowering the downspout, but he did not do so again that morning. Instead, using the ladder attached to the front of the trailer, Gish climbed atop the trailer (as he had on several other occasions when the downspout would not lower) and attempted to lower the downspout by hand while standing on the trailer's top rail. This top rail is also the top of the trailer's side wall. It is made of extruded aluminum, is between 5 and 5.66 inches wide, and is nine-and-a-half feet above the ground.

While Gish was standing on the top rail working with the downspout, a gust of wind hit him from the back, causing him to fall. This fall fractured his legs, broke his ankles, and ruptured an Achilles tendon. Gish was in a wheelchair for six months, and he still has difficulty walking and standing.

Gish sued Martin and Timpte, asserting a cause of action for premises liability against Martin and causes of action for marketing, manufacturing, and negligent design . . . against Timpte. Specifically, Gish asserted that the Super Hopper trailer [was negligently designed in several respects:]

- The top two rungs of the ladders attached to the front and rear of the trailer allow a person to climb atop the trailer; and
- The top rail of the trailer is too narrow and slippery and contains too many tripping hazards for a person to walk safely along it. . . .
- To remedy these alleged [negligent aspects of] design, . . . Gish's expert witness proposed three design changes [that a reasonable person would have adopted:]
- Remove the top two rungs of the ladders attached to the trailer to make it impossible for a person to climb atop the trailer;
- Provide an adequate foothold and handhold at the top of the trailer so that a user on top of the trailer can maintain three-point contact with the trailer at all times; and
- If an adequate handhold cannot be provided, then widen the side rail to at least 12 inches to provide an adequate foothold.

Timpte moved for a . . . summary judgment, which the trial court granted. . . . The court of appeals [reversed,] concluding that there was "some evidence upon which reasonable factfinders could disagree as to whether the trailer's design was . . . unreasonably dangerous. . . ."

III

Gish alleges that the Super Hopper trailer was [negligently] designed in two ways: (1) the top rail of the trailer was too narrow and presented tripping hazards; and (2) the top two rungs of the ladders mounted on the trailer were unnecessary and allowed the operator to climb to the top of the trailer. Essentially, Gish complains that the trailer's design failed to prevent him from climbing atop the trailer and then, once he was up there, failed to protect him from the risk of falling.

There is no evidence, however, that the top rail of the trailer is unreasonably dangerous in light of its use and purpose. As already noted, the top rail from which Gish fell is only 5 to 5.66 inches wide and made of extruded aluminum, an extremely slippery surface. Timpte's executive vice president of manufacturing and engineering, Jeffrey Thompson, testified that the top rail was designed this way for two reasons: (1) the width of the top rail is only as wide as necessary to support the front end of the trailer; and (2) the top rail is made of extruded aluminum and slants slightly towards the inside of the trailer so that any commodity that spills onto the top rail will slide into the trailer. Thompson testified that, were the top rail to be widened, it would add to the total weight of the trailer thereby reducing the weight of the commodity that the trailer would be permitted to carry. The utility of this design — maximizing the amount of commodity that the trailer can haul while keeping the structure of the trailer sound — is undeniably very high.

The corresponding risk of someone being injured the way Gish was is extremely low. The risk of falling while trying to balance on a 5 inch wide strip of extruded aluminum nearly ten feet above the ground is an obvious risk that is certainly "within the ordinary knowledge common to the community." . . .

The risk of falling from the top of the trailer while trying to balance on a five-inch strip of extruded aluminum is equally obvious to an average user of the Super Hopper trailer.

The focus of a [negligent] defect claim, . . . is whether there was a reasonable alternative design that, at a reasonable cost, would have reduced a foreseeable risk of harm. Thus, if it is reasonable for a product's designer to incorporate a design that eliminates an open and obvious risk, the product reaches a more optimum level of safety by incorporating the safer design than by keeping the current design with the open and obvious risk. We see no reason to discard the risk-utility analysis that Texas courts have long-applied to encourage manufacturers to reach an optimum level of safety in designing their products.

Nevertheless, the risk-utility factors here confirm that the . . . Super Hopper trailer was not [negligently designed] as a matter of law. Timpte warned users to always maintain three-point contact with the trailer, which is impossible for a user standing on the top rail. Had Gish adhered to this warning, his accident would not have happened. Additionally, widening the side walls of the trailer so as to convert the top rail into a safe walkway, as Gish's expert proposed, would have increased the cost and weight of the trailer while decreasing its utility. The Federal Highway Administration generally limits the gross vehicle weight of a commercial motor vehicle to 80,000 pounds; therefore, any increase in the unloaded weight of the trailer results in a decrease of the amount of commodity the trailer can haul, thus reducing its overall utility to users. The width of the top rail of the Super Hopper trailer is therefore not a design defect that renders the trailer unreasonably dangerous.

There is also no evidence that the top two rungs of the ladder . . . render the trailer unreasonably dangerous. Thompson testified that the top two rungs are necessary to maintain the structure and stability of the ladder when the side rails are under pressure; without them, the ladder could twist or bend. Additionally, even though Timpte warned users to use the side rails of the ladder as a handhold when climbing the ladder, were a user's hands to slip, the additional rungs provided additional handholds and an additional measure of safety. Thus, the utility of the ladder as constructed is high.

Conversely, the risk of injury from the use of the ladder is very slight. Gish's injury is only remotely related to the ladder's top two rungs: they allowed him to climb atop the trailer, where he was subsequently injured. Timpte warned users not to use the ladder to climb into the trailer itself, and the obvious nature of the risk of climbing onto the top rail negates the need for any additional warning. Therefore, any risk from the ladder itself stems only from the risk that a user will ignore both Timpte's warnings and open and obvious dangers.

Additionally, as noted above, removal of the top two rungs, although it might have prevented Gish's injury, might also increase the risk of injury to others who might need those rungs as a failsafe handhold. Removing the top two rungs could also cause the ladder to bend or become unstable under pressure, thereby increasing the risk of danger from its use. The inclusion of the top two rungs of the ladder [was not, therefore, negligent as a matter of law.]

[W]e reverse the court of appeals' judgment and render judgment reinstating the trial court's summary judgment.

2. Courts Utilizing Safety Statutes to Set Specific Standards of Care: Negligence Per Se

In the last section, we observed that courts can judicially set the standard of care when they conclude that reasonable persons cannot differ as to what are the appropriate risk-utility tradeoffs. In most instances, when a court directs a verdict on standard of care, the holding has limited precedential value. As we noted, negligence cases are fact-sensitive. What may support a directed verdict on one set of facts will not necessarily support a directed verdict when the facts are somewhat different. However, as we saw in *Helling*, courts may be willing to generalize and speak in more sweeping terms, setting the standard of conduct for all patients who visit an ophthalmologist for an eye examination.

The most significant manner in which courts can move away from case-by-case fact-sensitive standard-setting is through their use of statutes and regulations to establish the standard of reasonable care. The party (either plaintiff or defendant) whose conduct falls below the statutory standard of care is held to be negligent per se. The issue of what constitutes reasonable conduct is not for the jury to decide. The judge "imports" the statutory standard as the minimum standard of care to which an actor must conform. It is imperative that we realize that though most of the time the statutory standard governs, there are instances when it does not. Courts have a vital role to play in deciding when it is appropriate to utilize the statutory standard as the tort standard of reasonable care. This area is tricky but it will help to keep in mind that ultimately the judge who utilizes a statute as the governing standard of care is utilizing judicial discretion to direct a verdict. The judge is not an automaton merely feeding a criminal statute or other state regulation into the tort system.

Perhaps the best starting place in understanding this area of the law is the Restatement, Third, of Torts: Liability for Physical Harm:

§ 14. Statutory Violations as Negligence Per Se

An actor is negligent if, without excuse, the actor violates a statute that is designed to protect against the type of accident the actor's conduct causes, and if the accident victim is within the class of persons the statute is designed to protect.

Comment:

c. Rationale. The rule in this section presupposes a statute that declares conduct unlawful but which is silent as to civil liability and which cannot be readily interpreted as to impliedly creating a private right of action. The section hence acknowledges that the statute may not itself provide civil liability. The section nevertheless concludes that courts, exercising their common-law authority to develop tort doctrine, not only should regard the actor's statutory violation as evidence admissible against the actor, but should treat that violation as actually determining the actor's negligence. An unexcused violation of the statute is thus negligence per se.

There are several rationales for this common-law practice. First, even when the legislature has not chosen to attach a liability provision to the prohibition it has imposed, as a matter of institutional comity it would be awkward for a court in a tort case to commend as reasonable that behavior which the legislature has already condemned as unlawful. Second, in ordinary tort cases, so long as reasonable minds can differ, the responsibility for determining whether a person's conduct is negligent is vested in the jury. One major reason for this is to take advantage of community assessments in making the negligence determination. Yet when the legislature has addressed the issue of what conduct is appropriate, the judgment of the legislature, as the authoritative representative of the community, takes precedence over the views of any one jury.

Third, it must be recognized that the negligence standard encounters difficulty in dealing with problems of recurring conduct. When each jury makes up its own mind as to the negligence of that conduct, there are serious disadvantages in terms of inequality, high litigation costs, and failing to provide clear guidance to persons engaged in primary activity. Because . . . courts on their own can only occasionally take negligence determinations away from the jury, these disadvantages of case-by-case decisionmaking remain. In general, statutes address conduct that conspicuously recurs in a way that brings it to the attention of the legislature. Negligence per se hence replaces decisionmaking by juries in categories of cases where the operation of the latter may be least satisfactory. . . .

Illustration:

1. A state statute requires that the operator of a vehicle that becomes disabled on a highway promptly put out a warning sign at least 100 feet behind the vehicle. When a deflated tire disables Carl's truck, he places a warning sign right next to the truck. Ann, approaching Carl's truck from behind, does not see Carl's warning sign until it is too late for her to stop. Her car strikes the rear of Carl's truck, and she is injured in the collision. Ann would have been able to stop in time had the warning sign been set at the 100-foot distance. In the suit brought by Ann against Carl, Carl's violation of the statute is negligence per se; the basic purpose of the statute is to prevent accidents of this type. In the absence of the statute, Carl's failure to place a warning sign at least 100 feet away from the truck would merely raise a jury question as to Carl's possible negligence.

MARTIN v. HERZOG
126 N.E. 814 (N.Y. 1920)

CARDOZO, Justice.

The action is one to recover damages for injuries resulting in death.

Plaintiff and her husband, while driving toward Tarrytown in a buggy on the night of August 21, 1915, were struck by the defendant's automobile coming in the opposite direction. They were thrown to the ground, and the man was killed. At the point of the collision the highway makes a curve. The car was rounding the curve when suddenly it came upon the buggy, emerging, the defendant tells us, from the gloom. Negligence is charged against the defendant, the driver of the car, in that he did not keep to the right of the center of the highway. . . . Negligence is charged against the plaintiff's intestate, the driver of the wagon, in that he was traveling without lights. . . . There is no evidence that the defendant was moving at an excessive speed. There is none of any defect in the equipment of his car. The beam of light from his lamps pointed to the right as the wheels of his car turned along the curve toward the left; and looking in the direction of the plaintiff's approach, he was peering into the shadow. The case against him must stand, therefore, if at all, upon the divergence of his course from the center of the highway. The jury found him delinquent and his victim blameless. The Appellate Division reversed, and ordered a new trial.

We agree with the Appellate Division that the charge to the jury was erroneous and misleading. . . . In the body of the charge the trial judge said that the jury could consider the absence of light "in determining whether the plaintiff's intestate was guilty of contributory negligence in failing to have a light upon the buggy as provided by law. I do not mean to say that the absence of light necessarily makes him negligent, but it is a fact for your consideration." The defendant requested a ruling that the absence of a light on the plaintiff's vehicle was "prima facie evidence of contributory negligence." This request was refused, and the jury were again instructed that they might consider the absence of lights as some evidence of negligence, but that it was not conclusive evidence. The plaintiff then requested a charge that "the fact that the plaintiff's intestate was driving without a light is not negligence in itself," and to this the court acceded. The defendant saved his rights by appropriate exceptions.

We think the unexcused omission of the statutory signals is more than some evidence of negligence. It *is* negligence in itself. Lights are intended for the guidance and protection of other travelers on the highway (Highway Law, sec. 329a). By the very terms of the hypothesis, to omit, willfully or heedlessly, the safeguards prescribed by law for the benefit of another that he may be preserved in life or limb, is to fall short of the standard of diligence to which those who live in organized society are under a duty to conform. That, we think, is now the established rule in this state. . . . In the case at hand, we have an instance of the admitted violation of a statute intended for the protection of travelers on the highway, of whom the defendant at the time was one. Yet the jurors were instructed in effect that they were at liberty in their discretion to treat the omission of lights either as innocent or as culpable. They were allowed to "consider the default as lightly or gravely" as they would (Thomas, J., in the court below). They might as well have been told that they could use a like discretion in holding a master at fault for the omission of a safety appliance prescribed by positive law for the protection of a workman. . . . Jurors have no dispensing power by which they may relax the duty that one traveler on the highway owes under the statute to another. It is error to tell them that they have. The omission of these lights was a wrong, and being wholly unexcused was also a negligent wrong. No license should have been conceded to the triers of the facts to find it anything else.

We must be on our guard, however, against confusing the question of negligence with that of the causal connection between the negligence and the injury. A defendant who travels without lights is not to pay damages for his fault unless the absence of lights is the cause of the disaster. A plaintiff who travels without them is not to forfeit the right to damages unless the absence of lights is at least a contributing cause of the disaster. To say that conduct is negligence is not to say that it is always contributory negligence. "Proof of negligence in the air, so to speak, will not do." . . . We think, however, that evidence of a collision occurring more than an hour after sundown between a car and an unseen buggy, proceeding without lights, is evidence from which a causal connection may be inferred between the collision and the lack of signals. . . . If nothing else is shown to break the connection, we have a case, prima facie sufficient, of negligence contributing to the result. There may indeed be times when the lights on a highway are so many and so bright that lights on a wagon are superfluous. If that is so, it is for the offender to go forward with the evidence, and prove the illumination as a kind of substituted performance. . . .

We are persuaded that the tendency of the charge and of all the rulings following it, was to minimize unduly, in the minds of the triers of the facts, the gravity of the decedent's fault. Errors may not be ignored as unsubstantial when they tend to such an outcome. A statute designed for the protection of human life is not to be brushed aside as a form of words, its commands reduced to the level of cautions, and the duty to obey attenuated into an option to conform.

The order of the Appellate Division should be affirmed, and judgment absolute directed on the stipulation in favor of the defendant, with costs in all courts.

[Dissenting opinion omitted.]

This case interestingly sets forth three views as to the role a statute may play in negligence litigation. Since the issue in the case dealt with the contributory negligence of the plaintiff, the question was whether the plaintiff's conduct in driving his buggy at night without lights was negligent per se. Plaintiff argued that the statute should be only evidence of negligence. The defendant countered that it should create a prima facie case of negligence. The court went one better and held that the unexcused failure to comply with a statute was negligence per se. Each one of the following views has been adopted in some jurisdictions:

VIOLATION OF STATUTE AS NEGLIGENCE PER SE

The strong majority view follows *Martin v. Herzog,* that violation of a statute is negligence per se. The judge decides whether the statute is applicable to the case at bar and then directs a verdict on standard of care. The only role for the jury is to decide whether the actor did, in fact, violate the statute and whether the negligence had a causal relation to the harm suffered. *See, e.g.,* Ferrell v. Baxter, 484 P.2d 250 (Alaska 1971); Schlimmer v. Poverty Hunt Club, 597 S.E.2d 43 (Va. 2004).

VIOLATION OF STATUTE AS EVIDENCE OF NEGLIGENCE

A fair number of states take the position that violation of statute is some evidence of negligence. The jury hears the evidence of the allegedly negligent conduct and takes the statute into account in deciding what the appropriate standard of care should be. *See, e.g.,* Hansen v. Friend, 824 P.2d 483 (Wash. 1992); Braitman v. Overlook Terrace Corp., 346 A.2d 76 (N.J. 1975). This view treats violation of statute no different than custom. You will recall that violation of custom is relevant but not binding on the issue of the appropriate standard of care. However, telling a jury that there is a statute that may govern the standard of care and that it is up to them to decide if it does seems very strange. One would think that deciding whether the statutory standard applies to a particular fact pattern is peculiarly a judicial function.

VIOLATION OF STATUTE AS A PRESUMPTION OF NEGLIGENCE

Finally, a handful of states say that the violation of a statute creates a prima facie case of negligence or presumption of negligence that can be rebutted by proof that a reasonable person would have acted as did the person whose conduct is in question. *See, e.g.,* Waugh v. Traxler, 412 S.E.2d 756 (W. Va. 1991) (applying Vermont law). It would appear that under this view, if a defendant comes forth with evidence that her conduct was reasonable, the jury will be deciding the reasonableness of the actor's conduct and the statute will not play a significant role in the final resolution of the case.

If you are wondering what Justice Cardozo meant when he said that a statute might not constitute negligence per se if it were "excused," stay tuned. It will be the subject of discussion shortly. But, first we must deal with the question as to when a statute is at all relevant to the question of an actor's negligence.

REQUE v. MILWAUKEE & SUBURBAN TRANSPORT CORP.
97 N.W.2d 182 (Wis. 1959)

CURRIE, Justice.

[Plaintiff was injured when she fell alighting from a bus that was parked more than 12 inches from the curb. The plaintiff contended that the defendant violated Sec. 85.19(2) of the Wisconsin Statutes, which requires a parked vehicle to be within 12 inches from the curb. The trial court in its memorandum opinion held that violation of the statute did not constitute negligence per se.

In affirming the trial court that sustained the defendants' demurrer to the complaint the court said:]

In our original opinion we held that the allegations of the complaint, when liberally construed, were sufficient to charge a violation by the defendant of Sec. 85.19(2)(a), Stats., 1955. We are now satisfied that a violation of such statute by the defendant did not constitute negligence per se as to the plaintiff passenger.

Such statute was enacted as a rule of the road for the purpose of insuring sufficient adequate usable highway space to vehicles traveling in the same direction as was the stopped or parked vehicle, and to prevent a collision occurring between such moving vehicle and the one stopped or parked. By the observance of the statute on the part of the operator of the stopped vehicle, such moving vehicles would not be put under the necessity of diverging from their own traffic lane in order to avoid a collision. We can perceive no legislative purpose in such statute to protect passengers in a public conveyance such as defendant's bus from any hazard other than that arising from a collision between a moving vehicle and the stopped bus. Not every violation of a statute constitutes negligence per se.

Sec. 288 . . . of [the] Restatement, Torts, provides as follows:

> The court will not adopt as the standard of conduct of a reasonable man the requirements of a legislative enactment or an administrative regulation whose purpose is found to be exclusively

(a) To protect the interests of state or any subdivision of it as such; or

(b) To secure to individuals the enjoyment of rights or privileges to which they are entitled only as members of the public; or

(c) To impose upon the actor the performance of a service which the state or any subdivision of it undertakes to give to the public; or

(d) To protect a class of persons other than the one whose interests are invaded; or

(e) To protect an interest other than the one invaded; or

(f) To protect against other harm than that which has resulted; or

(g) To protect against other hazards than that from which the harm has resulted. . . .

We consider that subparagraph (g) of . . . Sec. 288 rules the instant appeal. . . .

The demurrer to the complaint was properly sustained by the trial court because the complaint failed to allege any causal negligence on the part of the defendant. . . .

FOOD FOR THOUGHT

It is the task of the court to decide whether the hazard was the one that the legislature intended to protect against and whether the victim is within the class of persons the statute is designed to protect. Presumably a court would utilize the classic tools of statutory construction in making these determinations. The court could be expected to consult legislative history and committee reports. Is it not possible, however, that a statute created for one purpose takes on a secondary meaning? Given that buses normally park within 12 inches of the curb, might not riders, when stepping down, expect to step onto a curb that is 4 or 5 inches higher than the level ground? Should such a claim be grounded in negligence per se or common law negligence? Consider that even if a statute is not directly applicable, the plaintiff is always free to portray the conduct of the defendant as negligent because it does not comport with the reasonable person standard.

In Leizerman v. Kanous, 910 N.E.2d 26 (Ohio Ct. App. 2009), the plaintiff was riding a bicycle on a sidewalk and suffered injury when he was struck by an automobile exiting a driveway. The plaintiff argued that a statute that prohibited adults from riding bicycles on sidewalks was intended to protect pedestrians, not bicyclists, and was therefore irrelevant in judging plaintiff's contributory negligence. The appellate court held that the statute was also aimed at protecting bicyclists and that the plaintiff was therefore contributorily negligent per se. By contrast, in Maver v. Speedway, LLC, 714 F.3d 1132 (7th Cir. 2014) (applying Indiana Law) the court held that a municipal ordinance mandating access walkways to stores must have a minimum width of 36 inches was designed to provide wheelchair access by the handicapped but was not relevant to a healthy plaintiff. Her claim that a 24 inch walkway constituted negligence *per se* was rejected since she was not in the class of persons the ordinance intended to protect.

Courts often have considerable difficulty in deciding whether a statute should be used to direct a verdict on standard of care by declaring the conduct negligence per se. The so-called key statutes have provided a fertile ground for controversy. In

Ney v. Yellow Cab Co., 117 N.E.2d 74 (Ill. 1954), the court considered whether a taxi driver who left the key in his cab was liable to a pedestrian injured by a thief that had stolen it. The statute provided that

> [n]o person driving or in charge of a motor vehicle shall permit it to stand unattended without first stopping the engine, locking the ignition and removing the key, or when standing upon any perceptible grade, without effectively setting the brake thereon and turning the front wheels to the curb or side of the highway.

Id. at 76. The majority held that the statute could be construed to seek to protect citizens from the negligent driving of a getaway thief. The dissent thought otherwise. As they read the statute, its purpose was to prevent inadvertent or negligent movement of a parked vehicle or to prevent youngsters in a car from starting the car.

The majority opinion suggests that certain factual variations on how the story unfolded might create a jury question as to liability. They raise the following scenarios:

> Assume a defendant violates the statute in question, yet before leaving the vehicle he secures the doors and windows. Or assume he has a reliable or an unreliable person nearby watching the vehicle for him. Or assume he leaves his car within view of a police officer who knows defendant and is acquainted with his habit of so leaving his car.

Id. at 83. Does it make any sense to tell the jury that the statute governs but leave to them the question of whether the hazard or class of persons is within the protection of the statute? If the court does not know, how should the jury? As noted earlier, most courts arrogate such questions to themselves in deciding whether to declare the defendant's conduct negligence per se.

In Mest v. Cabot Corp., 449 F.3d 502 (3d Cir. 2006) (applying Pennsylvania law), plaintiffs (dairy farmers) alleged that their cows suffered from fluorosis, a disease caused by fluoride poisoning that resulted from the defendant's systematic release of hydrogen fluoride from its factory over decades. The disease not only reduced the milk production of the cows but also caused a host of other ailments. Plaintiffs predicated their claim in part on the doctrine of negligence per se based on the defendant's violation of the Pennsylvania Air Pollution Control Act (PAPCA). In upholding the district court's dismissal of the negligence per se claim, the court held that to "assert a claim for negligence per se . . . the statute's purpose is, at least in part, to protect the interest of the plaintiff individually, as opposed to the public." *Id.* at 518. The court concluded that the PAPCA "is an environmental statute governing air quality with the purpose of protecting the general public rather than the plaintiffs in particular." *Id.*

STACHNIEWICZ v. MAR-CAM CORP.
488 P.2d 436 (Or. 1971)

HOLMAN, Justice.

The patron of a drinking establishment seeks to recover against the operator for personal injuries allegedly inflicted by other customers during a barroom brawl. The jury returned a verdict for defendant. Plaintiff appealed.

From the evidence introduced, the jury could find as follows:

A fight erupted in a bar between a group of persons of American Indian ancestry, who were sitting in a booth, and other customers who were at an adjacent table with plaintiff. One of plaintiff's friends had refused to allow a patron from the booth to dance with the friend's wife because the stranger was intoxicated. Thereafter, such threats as, "Hey, Whitey, how big are you?" were shouted from the booth at plaintiff and his companions. One of the persons at the table, after complaining to the bartender, was warned by him, "Don't start trouble with those guys." Soon thereafter, those individuals who had been sitting in the booth approached the table and one of them knocked down a person who was talking to a member of plaintiff's party. With that, the brawl commenced.

After a short melee, someone shouted "Fuzz!" and those persons who had been sitting in the booth ran out a door and into the parking lot, with one of plaintiff's friends in hot pursuit. Upon reaching the door, the friend discovered plaintiff lying just outside with his feet wedging the door open.

Plaintiff suffered retrograde amnesia and could remember nothing of the events of the evening. No one could testify to plaintiff's whereabouts at the time the band in the booth went on the warpath or to the cause of the vicious head injuries which plaintiff displayed when the brawl was ended.

The customers in the booth had been drinking in defendant's place of business for approximately two and one-half hours before the affray commenced.

The principal issue is whether, as plaintiff contends, violations of ORS 471.410 (3) and of Oregon Liquor Control Regulation No. 10-065 (2) constitute negligence as a matter of law. The portion of the statute relied on by plaintiff reads as follows:

> (3) No person shall give or otherwise make available any alcoholic liquor to a person visibly intoxicated. . . .

The portion of the regulation to which plaintiff points provides:

> (2) No licensee shall permit or suffer any loud, noisy, disorderly or boisterous conduct, or any profane or abusive language, in or upon his licensed premises, or permit any visibly intoxicated person to enter or remain upon his licensed premises.

The trial court held that a violation of either the statute or the regulation did not constitute negligence per se. It refused requested instructions and withdrew allegations of negligence which were based on their violation.

A violation of a statute or regulation constitutes negligence as a matter of law when the violation results in injury to a member of the class of persons intended to be protected by the legislation and when the harm is of the kind which the statute or regulation was enacted to prevent. . . . The reason behind the rule is that when a legislative body has generalized a standard from the experience of the community and prohibits conduct that is likely to cause harm, the court accepts the formulation. Justice Traynor in Clinkscales v. Carver, . . . 136 P.2d 777 (1943).

However, in addition, it is proper for the court to examine preliminarily the appropriateness of the standard as a measure of care for civil litigation under the circumstances presented. F. James, Jr., "Statutory Standards and Negligence in

Accident Cases," 11 La. L. Rev. 95, 111-12 (1950-51); Restatement (Second) of Torts § 286, comment *d.* (1965). The statute in question prevents making available alcohol to a person who is *already visibly intoxicated*. This makes the standard particularly inappropriate for the awarding of civil damages because of the extreme difficulty, if not impossibility, of determining whether a third party's injuries would have been caused, in any event, by the already inebriated person. Unless we are prepared to say that an alcoholic drink given after visible intoxication is the cause of a third party's injuries as a matter of law, a concept not advanced by anyone, the standard would be one almost impossible of application by a factfinder in most circumstances. . . .

The regulation promulgated by the commission is an altogether different matter. The regulation requires certain conduct of licensees in the operation of bars. The regulation was issued under ORS 471.730(5) which provides:

> The function, duties and powers of the commission include the following:
> . . .
>> (5) To adopt such regulations as are necessary and feasible for carrying out the provisions of this chapter and to amend or repeal such regulations. When such regulations are adopted they shall have the full force and effect of law.

ORS 471.030, entitled "Purpose of Liquor Control Act," provides, in part, as follows:

>> (1) The Liquor Control Act shall be liberally construed so as:
>>> (a) To prevent the recurrence of abuses associated with saloons or resorts for the consumption of alcoholic beverages.
> . . .

An examination of the regulation discloses that it concerns matters having a direct relation to the creation of physical disturbances in bars which would, in turn, create a likelihood of injury to customers. A common feature of our western past, now preserved in story and reproduced on the screen hundreds of times, was the carnage of the barroom brawl. No citation of authority is needed to establish that the "abuses associated with saloons," which the Liquor Control Act seeks to prevent, included permitting on the premises profane, abusive conduct and drunken clientele (now prohibited by the regulation) which results in serious personal injuries to customers in breach of the bar owner's duty to protect his patrons from harm. We find it reasonable to assume that the commission, in promulgating the regulation, intended to prevent these abuses, and that they had in mind the safety of patrons of bars as well as the general peace and quietude of the community. In view of the quoted purpose of the Act and of the history of injury to innocent patrons of saloons, we cannot assume otherwise.

In addition, we see no reason why the standard is not an appropriate one for use in the awarding of civil damages. Because plaintiff was within the class of persons intended to be protected by the regulation and the harm caused to him was the kind intended to be prevented by the statute, we hold that the trial court erred in not treating the alleged violations of the regulation as negligence as a matter of law. . . .

The judgment of the trial court is reversed and the case is remanded for a new trial.

FOOD FOR THOUGHT

Justice Holman's refusal to treat the statute prohibiting sale of liquor to a person visibly intoxicated as negligence per se suggests that a judge has the discretion to refuse to apply the per se rule when to do so would be inappropriate in the litigation of a negligence case. Holman's conclusion that it would be "extremely difficult, if not impossible," to determine whether a third party's injuries would have been caused in any event by the inebriated person is open to question. Some courts disagree and would allow a jury to pass on whether the defendant's conduct was causal. *See* El Chico Corp. v. Poole, 732 S.W.2d 306 (Tex. 1987). But, we give Justice Holman high marks for his thoughtful opinion. Holman was not prepared to take a statute and simply plug it into a negligence case without questioning whether utilization of the statutory standard of care would help facilitate the litigation. Having concluded that the causation issue could not be fairly litigated, he decided that using the statutory standard was inappropriate. He may have been wrong on the causation issue but he was right in taking into consideration the difficulty in determining causation in deciding whether the statute should provide the governing standard of care.

STATUTES THAT SET AMORPHOUS STANDARDS

An excellent example of a court taking a host of considerations into account and deciding that a criminal statute should not be imported into a civil negligence case is provided by Perry v. S.N., 973 S.W.2d 301 (Tex. 1998). In that case plaintiff sought to use the failure of the defendant to comply with the statutory requirement to report sexual abuse of a child as negligence per se. A Texas statute required "any person having cause to believe a child is being abused to report the abuse to state authorities." *Id.* at 302. Knowing failure to make such a report constituted a misdemeanor. Parents of abused children brought a negligence action against the defendants, whose failure to report allowed the sexual abuse to continue and resulted in serious psychological harm to their children.

The court found that several factors militated against use of the reporting statute as setting the standard of care. First, tort law in general does not impose a duty to protect another from the criminal acts of a third person. The statute would not simply be giving substantive content to any already recognized tort duty but would be creating a new duty to rescue an innocent person from the clutches of an evildoer. Second, the language of the statute was vague and did not clearly set forth the standard of conduct. If a defendant has "cause to believe" that sexual abuse "may be" taking place, there is a duty to report. In most negligence per se cases, the statute sets forth a clear definitive rule which substitutes for the more amorphous negligence standard. No such definitive rule was provided by the statute in question. Third, the court noted that a sexual abuser can be imprisoned from 5 to 95 years. Those who fail to report are subject to a maximum of six months imprisonment and a $2,000 fine. The legislature clearly wished to treat nonreporters far less harshly than the sexual abuser. Should the court adopt the criminal standard for civil liability and the defendant nonreporter be held liable, a judgment could run into the millions of dollars. Liability for the nonreporter would not be far different from that for the abuser himself. The court found the specter of such disproportionate liability very troubling. *But see* Grimm v. Summit County Children Services Bd., 2006 Ohio App. LEXIS 2304 (2006), in which a hospital's failure to immediately report its suspicions that a 17-year-old girl, who was admitted to deliver a baby, had been an abused child resulted in damages against the hospital in the amount of $224,000. During the two-day interim before the hospital reported its suspicions to the state child-care agency, the father of the newborn (who had raped the young girl) was present in the delivery room and saw her naked in her hospital room. The plaintiff suffered nightmares of her rape and physical abuse. The fact that there were no clear standards as to what constituted grounds for suspicion did not deter the court from finding that the violation of the reporting statute was negligence per se.

In Chadbourne v. Kappaz, 779 A.2d 293, 295 n.1 (D.C. 2001), a law provided that "[n]o owner of an animal shall allow the animal to go at large." Plaintiff, who was injured by defendant's dog who had escaped the house, sought to have defendant's conduct be declared negligence per se. The court refused, holding that liability would be imposed only if the defendant acted intentionally or without exercising reasonable care. The statute did not prescribe a specific standard of care and was thus of no value in deciding whether the defendant acted reasonably.

LICENSING STATUTES

Violations of licensing statutes have been particularly troublesome. In some cases it is clear that the violation of a licensing statute ought not to be negligence per se. If a driver who holds a Pennsylvania driver's license moves and establishes residency in New York, she is required to obtain a New York driver's license within 30 days of moving to the state. If the driver fails to do so, she is in violation of the statute. If she has an accident, the driver's license statute does not set a standard of care and does not speak to whether defendant acted negligently. *See, e.g.,* Fielding v. Driggers, 190 S.E.2d 601 (Ga. Ct. App. 1972). Similarly, the mere fact that a nurse not licensed to perform surgical procedures did so does not support a negligence per se claim when the plaintiff did not allege that she suffered injuries as a result of improper treatment. Turek v. Saint Elizabeth Community Health Center, 488 N.W.2d 567 (Neb. 1992). Whether one articulates the finding that the licensing statute does not provide a standard of care against which to measure the defendant's conduct, or that the violation of the licensing statute was not the cause of the plaintiff's injury, is of little moment. Plaintiff simply cannot prevail on negligence per se grounds.

A more difficult question arises when an unlicensed medical practitioner performs a procedure and the claim is that the practitioner was negligent in that she did not have the skills necessary to perform the procedure. Or that a motorist who failed her driving test had an accident because she was inept in steering her car. A leading case has taken the position that the failure to have obtained a license does not constitute negligence per se and it is error to suggest to the jury that they should take into account the lack of license in determining negligence. In Brown v. Shyne, 151 N.E. 197 (N.Y. 1926), defendant, a chiropractor who did not have a license to practice medicine, yet held himself out as being able to diagnose and treat disease, was found negligent in bringing about the paralysis of the plaintiff. On appeal the defendant argued that the trial judge improperly instructed the jury that the defendant's practice of medicine without a license was "some evidence" of negligence that they might consider in deciding whether the defendant failed to exercise reasonable care. The court reversed the judgment for plaintiff holding that (*id.* at 198):

> Proper formulation of general standards of preliminary education and proper examination of the particular applicant should serve to raise the standards of skill and care generally possessed by members of the profession in this State; but the license to practice medicine confers no additional skill upon the practitioner; nor does it confer immunity from physical injury upon a patient if the practitioner fails to exercise care. Here, injury may have been caused by lack of skill or care; it would not have been obviated if the defendant had possessed a license yet failed to exercise the skill and care required of one practicing medicine. True, if the defendant had not practiced medicine in this State, he could not have injured the plaintiff, but the protection which the statute was intended to provide was against risk of injury by the unskilled or careless practitioner, and unless the plaintiff's injury was caused by carelessness or lack of skill, the defendant's failure to obtain a license was not connected with the injury.

The court in *Brown* concedes that plaintiff may introduce evidence as to the requisite skill and knowledge that are required in order to procure a license. If defendant did not have that skill and knowledge and the lack thereof was the proximate cause of plaintiff's harm, then liability will ensue. But whether the defendant did or did not have a license does not constitute negligence per se. After *Brown* was decided, the New York legislature enacted the following statute (N.Y. C.P.L.R. §4504(d) (2007):

> **Proof of negligence: unauthorized practice of medicine.** In any action for damages for personal injuries or death against a person not authorized to practice medicine under article 131 of the education law for any act or acts constituting the practice of medicine, when such act or acts were a competent producing proximate or contributing cause of such injuries or death, the fact that such person practiced medicine without being so authorized shall be deemed prima facie evidence of negligence.

The rule that the violation of a licensing statute does not constitute negligence per se applies to other categories of licensed activities as well, *see, e.g.,* Klinkenstein v. Third Ave. Ry. Co., 158 N.E. 886 (N.Y. 1927) (bus operated without a common-carrier license); Corbett v. Scott, 152 N.E. 467 (N.Y. 1926) (motorcycle driven without a license); Haliburton v. General Hospital Soc., 48 A.2d 261 (Conn. 1946) (dentistry performed without a license); Riddell v. Little, 488 S.W.2d 34 (Ark. 1972) (unlicensed operation of aircraft); Kronzer v. First National Bank, 235 N.W.2d 187 (Minn. 1975) (dispensing legal advice without a license).

IMPSON v. STRUCTURAL METALS, INC.
487 S.W.2d 694 (Tex. 1972)

GREENHILL, Justice.

This action for damages arose out of a tragic highway accident between a truck owned and operated by the defendants, Structural Metals and Joe Polanco respectively, and an automobile in which three people were killed, including Mrs. Impson, and two others were injured. The truck attempted to pass the car within a prohibited distance of a highway intersection. The car turned left into the intersection and was struck by the truck which was attempting to pass the car in the left hand lane. The interests represented by the plaintiffs are those of the passengers in the back seat of the car. No issues of contributory negligence are before us.

A criminal statute prohibits drivers from driving their vehicles on the left hand side of a highway within 100 feet of an intersection. The jury found that the defendant driver did this, and that such action was a proximate cause. No issue of negligence was submitted, and this creates the problem before us.

The trial court viewed the violation of the statute, intended as a highway safety measure, as negligence per se; and under the above findings, it entered judgment for the plaintiffs. The Court of Civil Appeals agreed that violation of the statute was negligence per se; but the majority of that court held that since evidence of justification or excuse was introduced, it became the duty of the trial court to submit (and the duty of the plaintiffs to request) a special issue on negligence. In doing so, it followed the rationale of the opinions in Hammer v. Dallas Transit Co., 400 S.W.2d 885 (Tex. 1966) and Phoenix Refining Co. v. Powell, 251 S.W.2d 892 (Tex. 1952). . . .

Under the *Hammer* and *Phoenix* rule, . . . the party violating the statute must present some legally substantial excuse or justification. As stated by Dean Page Keeton, mere "[o]rdinary care does not necessarily constitute one of the excuses ingrafted by the courts to the legislative standard. Otherwise, the doctrine is meaningless; it would simply be another way of saying that the violation of a statute is negligence per se when the violation would constitute the failure to exercise ordinary care." [citation omitted]

So the problem here is to decide what excuses or justifications are legally acceptable. In *Phoenix*, the excuse was a tire blowout. In *Hammer*, it was that because of the wet streets, the defendant's bus unavoidably skidded out of control. . . . In none of these cases has this court addressed itself to the legal sufficiency of the excuse.

The Restatement of Torts, Second (1965), deals with this problem in a new section, 288A. It states that an *excused* violation of a legislative enactment is not negligence. While the section expressly says that the list of excusable situations given is not intended to be exclusive, it lists five categories. They are:

(a) the violation is reasonable because of the actor's incapacity;
(b) he neither knows nor should know of the occasion for compliance;
(c) he is unable after reasonable diligence or care to comply;
(d) he is confronted by an emergency not due to his own misconduct;
(e) compliance would involve a greater risk of harm to the actor or to others.

Under category (a), "incapacity," could come cases where the violator was too young, or did not have the mental capacity, to be charged with negligence. It might include a blind man who unknowingly walks a red light (though he may be contributorily negligent for other reasons), or a driver who is rendered physically incapable because of a heart attack. Under category (b) could come cases where a night driver has a tail light go out unexpectedly and without his knowledge. Under category (c), "unable after reasonable diligence or care to comply," could come cases involving impossibility. . . . Under category (d), "emergency not due to his own misconduct," could come cases in which there is an unexpected failure in the steering or braking system; a blowout of a tire which is reasonably thought to be in good condition; a sudden confrontation with blinding dust or smoke on the highway. It could include driving on the left side of the highway to avoid striking a darting child, and similar situations. Finally, the illustration given by the Restatement for category (e), "greater risk of harm," is one in which the law requires people to walk facing traffic, but due to particular circumstances, it would involve greater risk to walk upon that side. The above are intended merely as illustrations of a principle and are recognized to be dictum here. But we do approve of the general treatment of legally acceptable excuses as set out in the Restatement, Second.

None of the excuses offered by the truck driver here are within the classes of excuse set out in the Restatement, Second, or are even close thereto. . . . The driver admitted that he was familiar with the law which prohibits the passing of vehicles within the prohibited area; he admitted that he knew about the intersection in question, having driven that way before, — though he momentarily forgot about the particular location at the time. It was at night, and the sign was small, — but the sign was the same size as others of its kind and was not concealed. There was some testimony that some trees or houses obscured the intersection; and there was testimony that there was no dashed or solid line in the road to indicate "no passing." The driver relied on the fact that as the two vehicles left the town of Tynan, the road narrowed from four lanes to two lanes; i.e., only one lane each way. The car the truck driver intended to pass was being driven partially on the right hand shoulder, and it speeded up as the truck began to pass. The car accelerated from about 35 miles per hour to 40 miles per hour, while the truck was going 40 to 50 miles per hour. There was no testimony that the truck driver could not have dropped back of the car. The matter seems to come down to one or more errors of judgment and the belief that the truck driver could, by sounding his horn, make it safely. The driver said he was watching the car to be passed rather than watching for the sign warning of the intersection, — which he did not see; and he did not anticipate soon enough the left hand turn of the driver of the car.

All of the above matters fall within the realm of ordinary care, — or lack of care. The driver made his move deliberately, with knowledge of the law and with at least notice of the presence of the highway intersection. There was no impossibility, no reason for any particular hurry, no emergency, and no incapacity. The problem of greater risk of harm is not involved. If there was an emergency, it was only after the statutory violation had begun, and was due in large part to his own deliberate conduct.

In view of the evidence offered, the trial court correctly determined that there was no evidence offered of any legally acceptable excuse or justification. It was, in law, an unexcused violation. The finding, therefore, that the driver violated the statute intended as a safety measure and the finding of proximate cause entitled the plaintiffs to a judgment.

The judgment of the Court of Civil Appeals is reversed, and the judgment of the trial court is affirmed.

CAN I TELL MY BRAKES TO STOP?

Actors who violate auto equipment statutes often seek to absolve themselves from negligence per se on the grounds that they have legitimate excuses for their violations. *See, e.g.,* Freund v. De Buse, 506 P.2d 491 (Or. 1973). Such statutes typically provide that brakes and tail lights should be in good working order. Do these statutes set a standard of care? If the statute were to say that brakes must be inspected four times a year, then an actor who fails to comply is negligent per se. But if the statute says that brakes should be in good working order, the statute does not tell the actor how to do it. As a car owner, I can't tell my brakes to stop. I can only use reasonable care in seeing to it that my brakes are inspected or not drive when I know that the brakes are not working properly. If a statute does not speak to the standard of care, why is it in the case in the first place? Is resort to excused violation necessary?

I THOUGHT I WAS COMPLYING

In Moore v. K & J Enterprises, 856 So. 2d 621 (Miss. Ct. App. 2003), a group of teenagers entered a bar. As they entered, their hands were stamped with an "X" to show that they were underage and were not to be served intoxicating beverages. One of the teenagers presented a driver's license with a picture that resembled him. Since the driver's license resembled him and confirmed that he was over the age of 21, he was permitted to purchase liquor. As it turned out the imposter ordered multiple drinks, which he shared with his teenage compatriots. After imbibing for an hour, one of the teenagers (who was presumed to be most sober) was designated the driver. Shortly after, while driving, she injured the plaintiff, causing a head injury resulting in brain damage. Relying on Restatement, Third, of Torts (Tent.

Draft No. 1, 2001) § 15, the court found that the sale to the imposter was not negligent per se since the owner had reasonably relied on the false identification. Relying on language of the statute that prohibits "furnishing" of intoxicating liquor to minors, the court said that, depending on the facts, a jury might find that selling the liquor to the imposter with actual or constructive knowledge that it was being served to minors might well violate the statute. It thus reversed the trial court's grant of directed verdict in favor of the bar and sent the case back for trial to determine whether the bar owner knew or should have known that by serving the imposter multiple drinks he was in fact furnishing intoxicants to minors. The Third Restatement section on excused violation with minor variations tracks § 288A of the Second Restatement as set forth in *Impson. See* Restatement, Third, of Torts § 15.

I COMPLIED WITH THE LAW

Heretofore we have focused on violations of safety statutes. What about an actor's compliance with such a statute? Should such compliance be dispositive on the actor's non-negligence? The law is clear that in most instances compliance is relevant evidence that a jury may consider as to whether the defendant acted reasonably but does not preclude a finding of negligence. *See, e.g.,* Huntwork v. Voss, 525 N.W.2d 632 (Neb. 1995); Miller v. Warren, 390 S.E.2d 207 (W. Va. 1990). Traux v. Roulhac, 126 A.3d 991, 1001 (Pa. Super. 2015). The rule reflects a belief that statutes often reflect minimum standards of care but that reasonable persons might well take additional precautions. In some instances, the statute simply does not provide for all contingencies. Thus, for example, a 50-mph speed limit might be appropriate when the roads are dry, but one who drives at the posted speed limit in snowy or icy conditions might be negligent. Courts occasionally do find an actor's compliance with a statute to be non-negligent as a matter of law. When a statute or regulation gives evidence of not being a minimum standard, speaks directly to the conduct in question, and there are no unusual circumstances which suggest that the actor should have been more careful, a court may find that compliance with the statute demands a finding of non-negligence. *See, e.g.,* Deshotels v. Southern Farm Bureau Casualty Insurance Co., 164 So. 2d 688 (La. Ct. App. 1964); Fowler v. Smith, 213 A.2d 549 (Md. 1965).

hypo **38**

State of Bliss has a statute mandating that medical interns or residents may not work more than 12 hours per day. Dr. *X*, a resident, worked 15 hours per day on three successive days. At the end of her last stint, she improperly inserted a feeding tube into the stomach of Mr. *Y*, an 80-year-old patient. The improper insertion caused a serious infection, resulting in the death of Mr. *Y*. In a malpractice action, is the violation of the Bliss statute negligence per se?

3. Statutory Private Rights of Action: Express or Implied

In the previous section, we focused on the role of courts in setting the standard of care by borrowing the governing rule from either criminal statutes or administrative regulations. On rare occasions, courts need not borrow or import the statutory standard to support a tort claim. Some statutes directly provide a private cause of action and others are so structured that courts can imply a private cause of action. The Consumer Product Safety Act, 15 U.S.C. § 2072 (2000), is an example of the former. It provides that anyone who sustains personal injury "by reason of any knowing . . . violation of a consumer product safety rule . . . shall recover damages sustained. . . ." In Baas v. Hoye, 766 F.2d 1190 (8th Cir. 1985), a pharmacist who knowingly violated a rule requiring that a prescription drug be dispensed in a childproof container was held liable for the death of a child who swallowed several tablets of the drug from the non-childproof container. Recovery was not dependent on the reasonableness of the pharmacist's conduct. If the terms of the statute were violated, the civil cause of action is directly conferred by the statute. In Cort v. Ash, 422 U.S. 66 (1975), the United States Supreme Court set forth a four-step test as to when a court would infer a private right of action from a federal criminal statute: (1) the plaintiff must be a member of the class for whose special benefit the statute was enacted; (2) there must be indication of legislative intent to create a private right of action; (3) the private right of action must be consistent with the underlying purpose of the statute; and (4) the plaintiff's cause of action must be one that is not traditionally relegated to state law. Some subsequent cases have modified the *Cort* test a bit, effectively making the question of whether or not there was legislative intent to create a private right of action dispositive. *See, e.g.,* Touche Ross & Co. v. Redington, 442 U.S. 560, 575-576 (1979); Thompson v. Thompson, 484 U.S. 174, 188-191 (1988) (J. Scalia, dissenting). Though express and implied private rights of action are relatively rare phenomena, when they exist tort actions can be brought without struggling with the problem of the appropriate standard of care that serves as a predicate for the cause of action. The statute sets the standard. *See* Restatement, Third, of Torts § 14, comment *b*.

In an interesting twist in Vanderwerf v. SmithKlineBeecham Corp., 414 F. Supp. 2d 1023 (D. Kan. 2006), a decedent's estate and his widow sued several drug companies that manufactured antidepressants, claiming the drugs caused the decedent to commit suicide. Plaintiff alleged that defendants had violated a provision of the Food, Drug and Cosmetic Act and that, although Congress had not expressly recognized a private right of action, Kansas should do so. The court declined the invitation, saying the Food, Drug and Cosmetic Act provided for criminal and administrative remedies for the violation of its provisions and it would not infer a private right of action where there was no evidence Congress intended to do so.

E. PROOF OF NEGLIGENCE: RES IPSA LOQUITUR

If you look at your contracts casebook, you will not find a section entitled proof of contract. Nor will you find in your property book a section entitled proof of adverse possession. Why is it that, in your torts book, smack in the middle of a chapter dealing with the elements of a negligence cause of action, we find a section entitled proof of negligence? Why aren't evidentiary matters left to the course devoted to those arcane questions? As you read the materials dealing with res ipsa loquitur, ponder these questions.

We begin this discussion with some observations as to how most negligence cases are litigated. In the main, plaintiffs are able to allege and prove the negligence of the defendant with considerable specificity. The driver was speeding and lost control of her car. The doctor misread an x-ray and did not diagnose cancer in a timely fashion. The engineer miscalculated the load on a beam and was responsible for the collapse of the building. But, on occasion, the evidence as to what went wrong is just not there. An airplane suddenly falls out of the sky and crashes, and even after months of investigation by the National Transportation Safety Board, the answer is we just don't know what caused the accident. Perhaps a flock of birds flew into the engine; the engine may have been poorly maintained; the pilot may have misread weather maps. What, however, if we can generalize and say that although we can't tell what happened, when we consider all the possibilities of what might have happened, the most probable explanation is that the airline was negligent? In case of such indeterminacy, can the plaintiff make out a prima facie case to take to the jury?

THE GRANDFATHER CASE: BYRNE v. BOADLE

Courts, faced with the unpleasant alternative of sending a plaintiff home without a remedy if she cannot spell out in detail the defendant's negligence, fashioned a doctrine to allow a direct inference of negligence, bypassing the need to tell the defendant the exact nature of the negligent conduct responsible for the plaintiff's harm.

The first articulation of the res ipsa loquitur ("the thing speaks for itself") doctrine stems from Baron Pollock in Byrne v. Boadle, 159 Eng. Rep. 299 (Ex. 1863). In that case, a plaintiff was injured by a barrel of flour that had fallen from a window in the defendant's warehouse. At the trial, the only evidence put in by either party was by the plaintiff, and he made no attempt to show how the barrel fell from the window. On this state of the evidence, the trial judge granted the defendant's motion for a nonsuit. In the course of argument on appeal, the defendant's attorney made this point: "Surmise ought not to be substituted for strict proof. . . . The plaintiff was bound to give affirmative proof of negligence." *Id.* at 300. To which Baron Pollock replied: "There are certain cases of which it may be said res ipsa loquitur and this seems one of them. In some cases the Court has held that the mere fact of the accident having occurred is evidence of negligence. . . ." *Id.* Two years later, in Scott v. London & St. Katherine Docks Co., 159 Eng. Rep. 665, 667 (Ex. 1865), Chief Justice Erle supplied what is generally recognized as the first formulation of the res ipsa loquitur doctrine:

> There must be reasonable evidence of negligence. But where the thing is shown to
> be under the management of the defendant or his servants, and the accident is

such as in the ordinary course of things does not happen if those who have the management use proper care, it affords reasonable evidence, in the absence of explanation by the defendants, that the accident arose from want of care.

Falling objects continue to support giving a res ipsa instruction to a jury. *See* e.g. Gillespie v. Ruby Tuesday Inc., 861 F. Supp. 2d 637 (D. Md. 2012) (applying Maryland law) (shade from light fixture fell from the ceiling of a restaurant and struck plaintiff on the head while she was eating lunch). MacClatchey v. JCA Health Services of Florida, 139 So.3d 970 (Fla. Ct. App. 2014) (framed piece of artwork fell on the head of a visitor to a patient in hospital). In both cases defendant argued that they did not have exclusive control of the instrumentality of the harm and there was no evidence to support an inference of negligence. In both, the court found that a common sense inference of negligence against the defendant was sufficient to send the case to the jury.

Some judges believe that res ipsa loquitur is not a special doctrine but merely a recognition that, where no specific evidence is available, a jury may rely on circumstantial evidence to conclude that the defendant's conduct was negligent. But the overwhelming majority of courts recognize that res ipsa cases are a separate genre. Where circumstantial evidence is available, a jury is able, from the bits and pieces of evidence, to construct a scenario of what went wrong and then conclude that the conduct in question was negligent. In res ipsa cases we have nothing more than a generalization. We admit we don't know what went wrong, but are willing to conclude that whatever went wrong was more likely than not the result of negligent conduct. One may concede that a generalization about the behavior of airplanes may be of value to the National Transportation Safety Board if they are doing a study of airplane crashes between the years of 1950 and 2000. But a lawsuit is about a defendant's behavior on a given day, and generalizations are not necessarily probative as to what actually occurred on that day. Ultimately, courts have developed a doctrine in these nonevidence cases to allow plaintiffs to recover but they have set forth some rather rigid requirements before plaintiff can make out a prima facie case. Now let's have a look at the case law.

LAMPRECHT v. SCHLUNTZ
870 N.W. 2d 646 (Neb. 2015)

BISHOP, Judge.

Arthur Lamprecht and his wife, Linda Lamprecht, brought this action against Brent Schluntz and his brother, Gerald Schluntz, seeking compensation for property damage that the Lamprechts sustained from a fire that originated on Brent's farm during a wheat harvest. The Lamprechts' sole theory of recovery was premised on the doctrine of res ipsa loquitur. The district court for Furnas County granted summary judgment in favor of the Schluntzes, and the Lamprechts now appeal. We affirm. . . .

On a hot and windy day in June 2012, Brent, Gerald, and their employee, Christopher Joppa, were harvesting wheat on Brent's real property in Furnas

County. As part of the harvesting operation, Joppa was operating a Case 9260 tractor with a grain cart attached. Brent and Gerald were operating combines. Brent and Gerald jointly owned the wheat, tractor, and combines, and Gerald was the sole owner of the grain cart.

According to Brent, he, Gerald, and Joppa were doing "back-landing" in the wheatfield; Brent was operating a combine and was heading west, Gerald was in a combine heading east, and Joppa was in the tractor with the attached grain cart heading to unload Gerald's combine. Brent testified that "as soon as the grain cart pulled up," he saw a "flash . . . underneath the tractor." Brent testified that he "pulled out and tried to wave at those guys, because they couldn't see it, to get out and try to stomp it out or get out of there, but it just exploded." Brent called the fire department immediately, and he, Gerald, and Joppa drove their respective pieces of farm equipment to the road. Brent testified the fire spread "like gasoline" although they attempted to "disk" the fields to create firebreaks to stop the fire. Several firefighters and other personnel responded to the fire around 3:30 p.m. Joe Kresser, the Stamford, Nebraska, fire chief, testified that when he arrived on the scene, the fire was in the wheatfield east of Brent's house.

Brent's property was located approximately 2 miles south and half a mile west of the Lamprechts' farm in Oxford, Nebraska, where Arthur raised corn, wheat, beans, and cattle. On the day of the fire, Arthur and his son were harvesting on Arthur's property and had gone to Holdrege, Nebraska, to pick up Arthur's truck from the repair shop. When they returned to Arthur's farm around 4:30 p.m., Arthur saw smoke coming in their direction from the south. When Arthur got to where the fire was located, his wheat stubble was on fire and it had burned through a couple neighboring fields. Arthur attempted to shred his crops to make a fire-break or "disk out the fire." Arthur testified that the fire came so fast he "couldn't get in front of it" and that it went into his pasture. Arthur continued to disk lengthwise to the fire so it would not burn sideways, and one of his neighbors also helped disk with his tractor. Arthur testified that there were "lots of people there from the fire departments and the neighbors" trying to put the fire out.

Kresser testified that when he first arrived at Brent's property to put out the fire, he spoke to Brent to get his opinion about what caused the fire. Kresser testified that a field fire can sometimes start when a "bearing" "go[es] out or get[s] hot or something of that sort, and somebody can drive in a field, an exhaust pipe can start it." Kresser recalled that Brent at that time thought the fire was caused by an electrical short on the tractor. Kresser did not examine the tractor because by the time the fire was under control enough to where he felt comfortable leaving the scene, the tractor was no longer in the field and Brent "wasn't around."

Kresser authored a fire log the day after the fire. According to the fire log, the fire burned approximately 1,200 acres and was driven by high winds from the south and temperatures in excess of 100 degrees Fahrenheit. The fire log notes that the property owner, Brent, suspected the cause of the fire was an electrical short on the tractor pulling the grain cart and that upon inspection there was a "burnt wire" on the tractor.

According to Brent, he asked Joppa what started the fire, but "[h]e didn't know, either." Brent told Joppa he saw "[the fire] come down from underneath the tractor." Brent recalled that he told Kresser that he saw a "burnt wire" underneath the tractor, but he did not know "if it was from the fire coming up on it." None of the farm equipment, including the tractor, were "burn[ed] up" in the fire. . . .

Joppa testified that he grew up in North Dakota on a farm and that during his life, he had seen two wildfires start during harvest; Joppa testified that one of those fires was started by a bearing that "went out in the combine" and "[o]verheated and started the fire." Joppa agreed that fires in wheatfields are not normal occurrences, although "they do have spontaneous combustions" caused by too much heat. However, Joppa then testified, "I know that didn't happen that day," followed by his statement that "it could have happened that day, I guess. I mean, I don't think it would have. I know it was really hot."

Although Joppa is not a mechanic and has no training as a mechanic, he has experience changing oil and filters, and greasing farm equipment, and he testified that he had previously changed the oil and greased the tractor at issue. Joppa testified that their farm equipment is "serviced every morning." Joppa stated that he had no reason to believe that the tractor he was driving was dangerous or unsafe on the day of the fire and that he had no reason to believe there was a mechanical defect in the tractor he was driving.

The district court in the instant case concluded that based upon the evidence received, there was "not sufficient evidence from which reasonable persons could find it more likely than not that there was negligence on the part of the [Schluntzes]." The court found that no genuine issue of material fact existed and that the Schluntzes were entitled to judgment as a matter of law. Summary judgment was granted in favor of the Schluntzes; the district court dismissed the Lamprechts' second amended complaint.

The Lamprechts now appeal.

The Lamprechts initially alleged two theories of recovery: (1) negligence for failure to properly maintain and repair the farming machinery and (2) res ipsa loquitur. The Lamprechts subsequently abandoned their negligence theory and amended their complaint to proceed solely on the theory of res ipsa loquitur. The doctrine of res ipsa loquitur is an exception to the general rule that negligence cannot be presumed. McLaughlin Freight Lines v. Gentrup, 798 N.W.2d 386 (2011). Res ipsa loquitur is a procedural tool that, if applicable, allows an inference of a defendant's negligence to be submitted to the fact finder, where it may be accepted or rejected. Id. The essence of res ipsa loquitur is that the facts speak for themselves and lead to a proper inference of negligence by the fact finder without further proof. Swierczek v. Lynch, 466 N.W.2d 512 (1991).

There are three elements that must be met for res ipsa loquitur to apply: (1) The occurrence must be one which would not, in the ordinary course of things, happen in the absence of negligence; (2) the instrumentality which produces the occurrence must be under the exclusive control and management of the alleged wrongdoer; and (3) there must be an absence of explanation by the alleged wrong-doer. *McLaughlin Freight Lines, supra.*

When deciding whether res ipsa loquitur applies, a court must determine whether evidence exists from which reasonable persons can say that it is more likely than not that the three elements of res ipsa loquitur have been met. Id. If such evidence is presented, then there exists an inference of negligence which presents a question of material fact, and summary judgment is improper. Id. The court should not weigh the evidence to determine whether res ipsa loquitur applies. Id. Instead, the court must determine whether there is sufficient evidence from which reasonable persons could find that it is more likely than not that the three elements of res ipsa loquitur have been proved and that it is therefore more likely than not that there was negligence associated with the event. Id.

Our analysis turns on the first element of res ipsa loquitur, that the occurrence must be one which would not, in the ordinary course of things, happen in the absence of negligence. *See McLaughlin Freight Lines, supra.* Our Supreme Court has stated that this element "'is of course only another way of stating an obvious principle of circumstantial evidence: that the event must be such that in the light of ordinary experience it gives rise to an inference that someone must have been negligent.'" Anderson v. Service Merchandise Co., . . . 485 N.W.2d 170, 175 (1992).

As a general rule, the mere occurrence of a fire, with resultant damage, does not raise a presumption of negligence, although the circumstances under which a fire occurs may sometimes be such as to justify the application of the doctrine res ipsa loquitur and impose upon the defendant the burden of proving his freedom from fault. *See* Security Ins. Co. v. Omaha Coca–Cola Bottling Co., . . . 62 N.W.2d 127 (1954). In Security Ins. Co., the Nebraska Supreme Court affirmed a directed verdict in favor of the defendant bottling company, concluding that res ipsa loquitur did not apply to the plaintiff-insurer's claim that the bottling company had negligently permitted its vending machine to catch fire. At some point during a day when no one was in the building, a fire broke out in the lunchroom where the vending machine was located. The evening janitor found the building filled with smoke and damage, but did not see a fire, and noticed the vending machine and adjacent wooden pop cases had been completely burned, leaving only the metal shell of the machine. Nothing else in the lunchroom had caught fire. The court in Security Ins. Co. concluded that the doctrine of res ipsa loquitur was of limited and restricted scope and should ordinarily be applied sparingly, and the court considered the doctrine inapplicable to the case before it, finding no precedent wherein a party had even attempted to apply the doctrine to a like situation.

Our research has revealed no Nebraska cases wherein the doctrine of res ipsa loquitur was utilized against a defendant in an action for damages resulting from a field fire allegedly caused by the defendant's tractor or other farm equipment where the exact cause of the fire was unknown. . . .

We note that there are cases where res ipsa loquitur has been applied to vehicles alleged to have started a fire. In one case, for example, a truck backed into a barn filled with hay and allegedly caused a fire from its hot exhaust gas and sparks; the court found that fires do not ordinarily occur during the loading or unloading of bales of hay in a barn absent someone's negligence. *See* Seeley v. Combs, . . . 416 P.2d 810, 578 (1966). In another case where a vehicle was alleged to have started a forest fire, Roddiscraft, Inc. v. Skelton Logging Co., . . . 28 Cal. Rptr. 277 (1963), a logging tractor that had been used in proximity to the fire had not been equipped with a spark arrester and had been smoking excessively. The court concluded that this supported an inference of negligence because as a matter of common knowledge, forest fires do not occur, other than perhaps from lightning, unless someone has been negligent, and therefore the cause of this forest fire was more likely than not from the negligence of the logging tractor owner.

In the instant case, the only evidence presented with respect to the fire's cause was that Brent saw a "flash" underneath the tractor and that he found a "burnt wire" under the tractor. Kresser testified that a field fire can start when a bearing goes out or gets hot or that an exhaust pipe can start a fire, and Brent thought the fire could have been caused by an electrical short on the tractor. However, none of those explanations are ones which are more likely than not explained by negligence; and the mere fact that a fire started under Brent's tractor does not lead to an inference that there was negligence. Even though a fire in a wheatfield may not ordinarily happen, such an occurrence is not so unusual as to justify an inference of negligence based upon an alleged lack of due care by the owner and/or operator of a tractor or other equipment being used to harvest the wheat. Further as. . . . even when the facts may raise a presumption that the vehicle caused the fire, that mere presumption cannot support a further inference that the vehicle was defective or improperly maintained or operated.

. . .

Because the Lamprechts cannot establish the first element of res ipsa loquitur, we agree with the district court that the doctrine of res ipsa loquitur is inapplicable as a matter of law, and affirm summary judgment in favor of the Schluntzes . . .

On facts not dissimilar, other courts have denied summary judgment to defendant. *See, e.g.,* Terry v. Carnival Corp., 3 F. Supp. 3d 1363 (U.S.S.D. Fla. 2014) (federal admiralty). Plaintiff alleged emotional distress arising from a fire that originated in the engine room of a ship when a flexible fuel hose leaked fuel. Carnival argued that the fuel hose had been replaced six months prior to the incident and that it had been inspected as part of overall maintenance. The court denied summary judgment, saying that "Carnival offers no feasible explanation for the fire absent lack of due care."

Unlike *Lamprecht,* when a plaintiff sues the manufacturer of a product under strict liability if the plaintiff can establish the origin of the defect, a res ipsa inference can be drawn against the manufacturer. *See* Speller v. Sears, Roebuck & Co., 790 N.E.2d 352 (N.Y 2003) (a fire originated from a refrigerator causing injury to the plaintiff; it was not necessary to establish that defendant was negligent, only that a defect was the cause of the fire). *See* Restatement, Third, of Products Liability, § 3 (1998).

In some cases, trial courts deny plaintiff's request to instruct the jury that they may draw on inference of negligence in the absence of direct evidence. The failure to give a res ipsa instruction when appropriate is grounds for reversal. *See, e.g.,* Eaton v. Eaton, 575 A.2d 858 (N.J. 1990); Banea D. Roma v. Mutual Life of Am. Insurance Co., 793 N.Y.S. 2d 341 (N.Y. App. Div. 2005).

RES IPSA AND PROBABILITY

The res ipsa requirement that an event be of a kind that does not ordinarily occur in the absence of negligence may be, and usually is, taken to mean simply that an event must more probably than not be the result of negligence. If so, this is just a way of establishing circumstantial proof from a showing that it is more likely than not that an event resulted from negligence. A broader, and more problematic, reading of "does not ordinarily occur in the absence of negligence" would regard an event as grounds for a res ipsa inference merely because it rarely happens. One problem with the proposition that an occurrence may create a res ipsa inference simply from the great unlikelihood of its happening is that something which happens very rarely may nevertheless be more likely to occur non-negligently rather than negligently. Imagine that an event, on average, takes place only 3 times for every 1,000 times it might happen. Assume that it will happen in two of those instances even though an actor takes every reasonable precaution, and will happen once due to an actor's negligence. Even though it is twice as likely to happen non-negligently as negligently, because it is such a rare occurrence, a court might say it supported a res ipsa inference. Does it seem fitting to punish an actor, even though there is no evidence of wrongdoing, when statistically the chances are better that she acted reasonably? *See* David Kaye, *Probability Theory Meets Res Ipsa Loquitur*, 77 Mich. L. Rev. 1456 (1979), for an examination of the problems of misusing res ipsa loquitur in this way.

THE THIRD RESTATEMENT FORMULATION OF RES IPSA LOQUITUR

The formulation of the elements of a res ipsa case as set forth in *Lamprecht* can be found in a multitude of cases. The Restatement, Third, of Torts: Liability for Physical Harm has attempted to streamline the elements and clear up some ambiguities:

§ 17. Res Ipsa Loquitur

The factfinder may infer that the defendant has been negligent when the accident causing the plaintiff's physical harm is a type of accident that ordinarily happens as a result of the negligence of a class of actors of which the defendant is the relevant member.

a. Background. Res ipsa loquitur is an appropriate form of circumstantial evidence enabling the plaintiff in particular cases to establish the defendant's likely negligence. . . .

However, res ipsa loquitur is circumstantial evidence of a quite distinctive form. The doctrine implies that the court does not know, and cannot find out, what actually happened in the individual case. Instead, the finding of likely negligence is derived from knowledge of the causes of the type or category of accidents involved. Assume, for example, that a car driven by the defendant runs off the road, injuring a pedestrian. In considering this category of accidents — cars that run off the road — several possible causes can be identified, including motorist negligence; some mechanical problem with the car; some defect in the roadway; and very adverse weather conditions. If the jury can reasonably believe that motorist negligence is most often the cause when cars run off the road, then, absent further evidence about the particular incident, the jury can reason from the general to the particular and hence properly infer that the defendant motorist was probably negligent.

USE OF EXPERT TESTIMONY TO SUPPORT A RES IPSA INFERENCE

In some cases expert testimony may be necessary to establish a res ipsa case. In Mireles v. Broderick, 872 P.2d 863 (N.M. 1994), the plaintiff developed numbness in her right arm shortly after undergoing a bilateral mastectomy. The numbness was diagnosed as ulnar neuropathy that resulted in degenerative nerve damage to several fingers in her right hand. A jury could not, from its own experience, decide whether damage to the ulnar nerve was a complication from non-negligently performed surgery. Plaintiff introduced testimony of a physician who opined that the injury to the ulnar nerve was preventable by proper care by the anesthesiologist. Thus the res ipsa inference was not predicated on the jury's commonsense inference but rather on the inference of the expert. Note that the expert himself did not know what went wrong but concluded that whatever went wrong was more probably than not the result of negligence. On rare occasions, malpractice may be so clear that a jury can draw a res ipsa inference without expert testimony. If a surgeon leaves an eight-inch piece of wire in the patient's innards, it does not take a genius to figure out that the doctor's performance leaves something to be desired. *See, e.g.,* Hyder v. Weilbaecher, 283 S.E.2d 426 (N.C. Ct. App. 1981).

RES IPSA AND SPECIFIC ACTS OF NEGLIGENCE

Plaintiffs often seek to go to the jury with a double-barreled attack. First, they seek the res ipsa inference. Second, they introduce evidence to support specific acts of negligence. Courts are in a dither as to whether it is appropriate to allow a jury to draw a res ipsa inference and also to consider specific evidence of negligence. A leading hornbook, *Prosser and Keeton on Torts*, § 40 (5th ed. 1984), explains it this way:

> Plaintiff is . . . bound by his own evidence; but proof of some specific facts does not necessarily exclude inferences of others. When the plaintiff shows that the railway car in which he was a passenger was derailed, there is an inference that the defendant railroad has somehow been negligent. When the plaintiff goes further and shows that the derailment was caused by an open switch, the plaintiff destroys any inference of other causes; but the inference that the defendant has not used proper care in looking after its switches is not destroyed, but considerably strengthened. If the plaintiff goes further still and shows that the switch was left open by a drunken switchman on duty, there is nothing left to infer; and if

the plaintiff shows that the switch was thrown by an escaped convict with a grudge against the railroad, the plaintiff has proven himself out of court. It is only in this sense that when the facts are known there is no inference, and res ipsa loquitur simply vanishes from the case. On the basis of reasoning such as this, it is quite generally agreed that the introduction of some evidence which tends to show specific acts of negligence on the part of the defendant, but which does not purport to furnish a full and complete explanation of the occurrence, does not destroy the inferences which are consistent with the evidence, and so does not deprive the plaintiff of the benefit of res ipsa loquitur.

Also see Restatement, Third, of Torts: Liability for Physical Harm § 17, comment *g.*

EXCLUSIVE CONTROL: PINNING THE TAIL ON THE DONKEY

The second res ipsa factor requires that the instrumentality or agent that caused the accident had been under the "exclusive control" of the defendant. Whoever first gave voice to the exclusive control articulation should be shot at sunrise. It has caused untold mischief in the courts. Consider the case of a plaintiff who purchased a hot water heater and had it installed in his basement. Two years later, the boiler exploded, causing serious injury to the plaintiff. The evidence establishes that the boiler was properly installed and that the plaintiff had not touched the boiler since the date of its installation. If defect must have arisen while in control of M, why not? Was the boiler manufacturer in exclusive control of the instrumentality of the harm? The answer is no. Nonetheless, it is clear that in this instance it is appropriate to draw a res ipsa inference against the manufacturer. *See, e.g.*, Brumburg v. Cipriani 973 N.Y.S. 2d (N.Y. App. Div. 2013), Smith v. Consolidated Edison Co. of NY, 961 N.Y.S. 2d 73 (N.Y. App. Div 2015). The true issue is whether there is sufficient evidence to support the proposition that the negligence that caused the harm points to the defendant. Where the defendant can point to an alternative cause that is equally probable to have been the cause of the harm, the judge cannot submit the res ipsa case to the jury. *See, e.g.*, Larson v. St. Francis Hotel, 188 P.2d 513 (Cal. Ct. App. 1948) (res ipsa does not apply against hotel when chair flew out of a window injuring passerby, since the cause of the harm may have been any of the hotel occupants); Ebanks v. New York City Transit Authority, 512 N.E.2d 297 (N.Y. 1987) (res ipsa instruction is not called for in a case where plaintiff got his shoe caught in a damaged escalator in a subway station, since the damage to the escalator could have been caused by acts of vandalism or by a user permitting an object, such as a hand truck, to become lodged in the space between the step and the sidewall).

Under the Restatement, Third, formulation the "exclusive control" element is no longer required and instead an inference of negligence is proper when the "accident causing the harm . . . ordinarily happens because of the negligence of the class of actors of which the defendant is the relevant member."

hypo **39**

X purchased a new car manufactured by *ABC*. While driving in a torrential rainstorm, *X* attempted to brake her car. The car veered to the right and hit a car driven by *D. X*'s car was demolished in the accident and its parts cannot be tested for defects. It is not clear whether the car veered to the right due to the negligent driving of *X*, the seepage of a huge amount of rain into the brake system, or a defect in the brakes. May the trial judge submit the case to the jury on a res ipsa instruction against *X* or *ABC*?

YBARRA v. SPANGARD
154 P.2d 687 (Cal. 1944)

GIBSON, Justice.

This is an action for damages for personal injuries alleged to have been inflicted on plaintiff [Ybarra] by defendants [Spangard and others] during the course of a surgical operation. The trial court entered judgments of nonsuit as to all defendants and plaintiff appealed.

On October 28, 1939, plaintiff consulted defendant Dr. Tilley, who diagnosed his ailment as appendicitis, and made arrangements for an appendectomy to be performed by defendant Dr. Spangard at a hospital owned and managed by defendant Dr. Swift. Plaintiff entered the hospital, was given a hypodermic injection, slept, and later was awakened by Doctors Tilley and Spangard and wheeled into the operating room by a nurse whom he believed to be defendant Gisler, an employee of Dr. Swift. Defendant Dr. Reser, the anesthetist, also an employee of Dr. Swift, adjusted plaintiff for the operation, pulling his body to the head of the operating table and, according to plaintiff's testimony, laying him back against two hard objects at the top of his shoulders, about an inch below his neck. Dr. Reser then administered the anesthetic and plaintiff lost consciousness. When he awoke early the following morning he was in his hospital room attended by defendant Thompson, the special nurse, and another nurse who was not made a defendant.

Plaintiff testified that prior to the operation he had never had any pain in, or injury to, his right arm or shoulder, but that when he awakened he felt a sharp pain about half way between the neck and the point of the right shoulder. He complained to the nurse, and then to Dr. Tilley, who gave him diathermy treatments while he remained in the hospital. The pain did not cease, but spread down to the lower part of his arm, and after his release from the hospital the condition grew worse. He was unable to rotate or lift his arm, and developed paralysis and atrophy of the muscles around the shoulder. He received further treatments from Dr. Tilley until March, 1940, and then returned to work, wearing his arm in a splint on the advice of Dr. Spangard.

Plaintiff also consulted Dr. Wilfred Sterling Clark, who had X-ray pictures taken which showed an area of diminished sensation below the shoulder and atrophy and wasting away of the muscles around the shoulder. In the opinion of Dr. Clark, plaintiff's condition was due to trauma or injury by pressure or strain, applied between his right shoulder and neck.

Plaintiff was also examined by Dr. Fernando Garduno, who expressed the opinion that plaintiff's injury was a paralysis of traumatic origin, not arising from pathological causes, and not systemic, and that the injury resulted in atrophy, loss of use and restriction of motion of the right arm and shoulder.

Plaintiff's theory is that the foregoing evidence presents a proper case for the application of the doctrine of res ipsa loquitur, and that the inference of negligence arising therefrom makes the granting of a nonsuit improper. Defendants take the position that, assuming that plaintiff's condition was in fact the result of an injury, there is no showing that the act of any particular defendant, nor any particular instrumentality, was the cause thereof. They attack plaintiff's action as an attempt to fix liability "en masse" on various defendants, some of whom were not responsible for the acts of others; and they further point to the failure to show which defendants had control of the instrumentalities that may have been involved. Their main defense may be briefly stated in two propositions: (1) that where there are several defendants, and there is a division of responsibility in the use of an instrumentality causing the injury, and the injury might have resulted from the separate act of either one of two or more persons, the rule of res ipsa loquitur cannot be invoked against any one of them; and (2) that where there are several instrumentalities, and no showing is made as to which caused the injury or as to the particular defendant in control of it, the doctrine cannot apply. We are satisfied, however, that these objections are not well taken in the circumstances of this case. . . .

The present case is of a type which comes within the reason and spirit of the doctrine more fully perhaps than any other. The passenger sitting awake in a railroad car at the time of a collision, the pedestrian walking along the street and struck by a falling object or the debris of an explosion, are surely not more entitled to an explanation than the unconscious patient on the operating table. Viewed from this aspect, it is difficult to see how the doctrine can, with any justification, be so restricted in its statement as to become inapplicable to a patient who submits himself to the care and custody of doctors and nurses, is rendered unconscious, and receives some injury from instrumentalities used in his treatment. Without the aid of the doctrine a patient who received permanent injuries of a serious character, obviously the result of someone's negligence, would be entirely unable to recover unless the doctors and nurses in attendance voluntarily chose to disclose the identity of the negligent person and the facts establishing liability. . . . If this were the state of the law of negligence, the courts, to avoid gross injustice, would be forced to invoke the principles of absolute liability, irrespective of negligence, in actions by persons suffering injuries during the course of treatment under anesthesia. But we think this juncture has not yet been reached, and that the doctrine of res ipsa loquitur is properly applicable to the case before us. . . .

The argument of defendants is simply that plaintiff has not shown an injury caused by an instrumentality under a defendant's control, because he has not shown which of the several instrumentalities that he came in contact with while in the hospital caused the injury; and he has not shown that any one defendant or his servants had exclusive control over any particular instrumentality. Defendants assert that some of them were not the employees of other defendants, that some did not stand in any permanent relationship from which liability in tort would follow, and that in view of the nature of the injury, the number of defendants and the different functions performed by each, they could not all be liable for the wrong, if any.

We have no doubt that in a modern hospital a patient is quite likely to come under the care of a number of persons in different types of contractual and other relationships with each other. For example, in the present case it appears that Doctors Smith, Spangard and Tilley were physicians or surgeons commonly placed in the legal category of independent contractors; and Dr. Reser, the anesthetist, and defendant Thompson, the special nurse, were employees of Dr. Swift and not of the other doctors. But we do not believe that either the number or relationship of the defendants alone determines whether the doctrine of res ipsa loquitur applies. Every defendant in whose custody the plaintiff was placed for any period was bound to exercise ordinary care to see that no unnecessary harm came to him and each would be liable for failure in this regard. Any defendant who negligently injured him, and any defendant charged with his care who so neglected him as to allow injury to occur, would be liable. The defendant employers would be liable for the neglect of their employees; and the doctor in charge of the operation would be liable for the negligence of those who became his temporary servants for the purpose of assisting in the operation. . . .

It may appear at the trial that, consistent with the principles outlined above, one or more defendants will be found liable and others absolved, but this should not preclude the application of the rule of res ipsa loquitur. The control, at one time or another, of one or more of the various agencies or instrumentalities which might have harmed the plaintiff was in the hands of every defendant or of his employees or temporary servants. This, we think, places upon them the burden of initial explanation. Plaintiff was rendered unconscious for the purpose of undergoing surgical treatment by the defendants; it is manifestly unreasonable for them to insist that he identify any one of them as the person who did the alleged negligent act.

The other aspect of the case which defendants so strongly emphasize is that plaintiff has not identified the instrumentality any more than he has the particular guilty defendant. Here, again, there is a misconception which, if carried to the extreme for which defendants contend, would unreasonably limit the application of the res ipsa loquitur rule. It should be enough that the plaintiff can show an injury resulting from an external force applied while he lay unconscious in the hospital; this is as clear a case of identification of the instrumentality as the plaintiff may ever be able to make.

An examination of the recent cases, particularly in this state, discloses that the test of actual exclusive control of an instrumentality has not been strictly followed, but exceptions have been recognized where the purpose of the doctrine of res ipsa loquitur would otherwise be defeated. Thus, the test has become one of right of control rather than actual control. *See* Metz v. Southern Pac. Co., . . . 124 P.2d 6701. In the bursting bottle cases where the bottler has delivered the instrumentality to a retailer and thus has given up actual control, he will nevertheless be subject to the doctrine where it is shown that no change in the condition of the bottle occurred after it left the bottler's possession, and it can accordingly be said that he was in constructive control. Escola v. Coca Cola Bottling Co., . . . 150 P.2d 436. . . .

In the face of these examples of liberalization of the tests for res ipsa loquitur, there can be no justification for the rejection of the doctrine in the instant case. As pointed out above, if we accept the contention of defendants herein, there will rarely be any compensation for patients injured while unconscious. A hospital today conducts a highly integrated system of activities, with many persons contributing their efforts. There may be, e.g., preparation for surgery by nurses and interns who are employees of the hospital; administering of an anesthetic by a doctor who may be an employee of the hospital, an employee of the operating surgeon, or an independent contractor; performance of an operation by a surgeon and assistants who may be his employees, employees of the hospital, or independent contractors; and post-surgical care by the surgeon, a hospital physician, and nurses. The number of those in whose care the patient is placed is not a good reason for denying him all reasonable opportunity to recover for negligent harm. It is rather a good reason for re-examination of the statement of legal theories which supposedly compel such a shocking result.

We do not at this time undertake to state the extent to which the reasoning of this case may be applied to other situations in which the doctrine of res ipsa loquitur is invoked. We merely hold that where a plaintiff receives unusual injuries while unconscious and in the course of medical treatment, all those defendants who had any control over his body or the instrumentalities which might have caused the injuries may properly be called upon to meet the inference of negligence by giving an explanation of their conduct.

The judgment is reversed.

FALLOUT FROM YBARRA

Ybarra has been a controversial decision. Some like it. *See, e.g.,* Beaudoin v. Watertown Memorial Hospital, 145 N.W.2d 166 (Wis. 1966). But most don't. *See, e.g.,* Talbot v. Dr. W. H. Groves' Latter-Day Saints Hospital, Inc., 440 P.2d 872 (Utah 1968); Sanchez v. Tucson Orthopedic Inst. P.C., 202 P.3d 502 (Ariz. Ct. App. 2009); McGiff v. Gramercy Captial Corp., 2013 WL 1856233 (W.D. Va.). If you think that *Ybarra* stretched the res ipsa doctrine about as far as it could go, consider Anderson v. Somberg, 338 A.2d 1 (N.J. 1975). Plaintiff underwent a laminectomy (a back operation) performed by Dr. Somberg. During the surgery, the metal tip of a surgical instrument, a rongeur, broke off while the tool was being manipulated in the plaintiff's spinal canal. Dr. Somberg was unsuccessful in attempting to retrieve the metal tip and had to terminate the surgery. The metal tip continued to cause problems and several subsequent surgical interventions followed. Plaintiff sued: (1) Dr. Somberg for medical malpractice; (2) St. James Hospital on the grounds that it negligently furnished Dr. Somberg with a defective surgical tool; (3) Rheinhold, the medical supply distributor that sold the rongeur to the hospital; and (4) Lawton Instrument Co., the manufacturer of the rongeur. Both the hospital's and Dr. Somberg's defense was that they were not negligent. The manufacturer and seller of the rongeur defended on the ground that the tool was nondefective when sold, but that either the hospital or Dr. Somberg misused and thus broke the tool. The jury found in favor of all defendants. On appeal, the New Jersey Supreme Court held that since all the defendants were before the court, a jury should be instructed that they must find against at least one of the defendants. An instruction that the defendant must carry the burden of proof on nonliability is not sufficient. Even if each defendant were to convince a jury that it was not liable, that would not be sufficient. Since at least one of the defendants was responsible, the jury must find against the defendant most likely to be culpable. *Anderson* was more recently applied in another medical malpractice-products liability setting. *See* Estate of Chin v. St. Barnabas Medical Center, 734 A.2d 778 (N.J. 1999).

The *Ybarra-Anderson* line of cases are, for the most part, limited to plaintiffs who suffer their injuries in a hospital setting where the plaintiff is unconscious and the defendants have a common duty of care to a patient. There are a few cases that have shifted the burden of proof against multiple defendants in nonmedical cases. *See, e.g.*, Nichols v. Nold, 258 P.2d 317 (Kan. 1953); Snider v. Bob Thibodeau Ford, Inc., 202 N.W.2d 727 (Mich. Ct. App. 1972); Prutch v. Ford Motor Co., 618 P.2d 657 (Colo. 1980). But they are in a small minority. Most courts place the burden of proving liability against each defendant squarely on the plaintiff. *See, e.g.*, Giant Food, Inc. v. Washington Coca-Cola Bottling Co., 332 A.2d 1 (Md. 1975).

SULLIVAN v. CRABTREE
258 S.W.2d 782 (Tenn. Ct. App. 1953)

FELTS, Justice.

Plaintiffs sued for damages for the death of their adult son, Robert Sullivan, who was killed while a guest in a motor truck which swerved off the highway and overturned down a steep embankment. Suit was brought against both the owner and the driver of the truck, but a nonsuit was taken as to the owner, and the case went to trial against the driver alone. There was a verdict and judgment in his favor, and plaintiffs appealed in error.

The truck was a large trailer-tractor truck owned by Hoover Motor Express Company, Inc., and used by it in its business as a carrier of freight. Its driver, Crabtree, was driving the truck with a load of freight from Nashville to Atlanta, and he permitted Sullivan to ride with him as a guest in the cab of the truck. He drove from Nashville to Monteagle, arriving there in the afternoon. He then decided to drive back some ten miles to his home at Pelham, eat supper there, and go on to Atlanta that night. It was on his way back to Pelham that the accident happened.

The road on which he was driving was a paved first-class Federal-state highway (U.S. 41, Tenn. 2), but coming down the mountain from Monteagle to Pelham it had a number of moderate grades and pretty sharp curves. It was midafternoon, and the weather was dry and clear. As Crabtree was approaching a curve another truck overtook and passed him, and just after it did so, Crabtree's truck suddenly swerved from his right side over to his left, ran off the left shoulder, overturned down a steep embankment, and crushed Sullivan to death.

Defendant testified that there was some loose gravel on the road, which had perhaps been spilled there by trucks hauling gravel, and the pavement was broken a little on the right-hand side; and that when he "hit the edge of the curve on the right-hand side" he "lost control of the truck," and it turned from his right side across to the left, and ran off the left shoulder of the highway. On cross-examination he further said:

> Q. Can you tell the Jury now what caused you to lose control of the truck and permit it to run off the road down the embankment?
> A. No. The brakes could have gave way, or the brakes could have grabbed or it could have been a particular wheel grabbed, because on a tractor, if the brakes happen to grab on it, the load is so much heavier than the tractor, it whips either way and takes control of the tractor and you have nothing to do with it.
> Q. Did that happen in this case?
> A. It is possible.
> . . .
> Q. You can't tell us just what did cause the accident or cause you to lose control of the truck?
> A. Probably hitting the edge of the pavement or it could have been several different things. Like one going off the mountain, if it is pulled out with the wrecker, you don't know whether a hose got connected up in there and when you turned the curve break a hose, cut it or break it loose. The brakes are cut on and off with a catch there like that, and it is easy for a hose to get loose.

Such being the undisputed facts, plaintiffs contend that defendant was guilty, as a matter of law, of negligence causing the death sued for, and that there was no evidence to support a verdict for defendant. They show a duty of care owing by defendant to the deceased under our rule that a driver must use ordinary care for the safety of his guest, . . . and to make out a breach of that duty, or proximate negligence, they invoke the rule of *res ipsa loquitur*.

They insist that the facts of this case brought it within the rule of *res ipsa loquitur* requiring a finding of negligence, in the absence of an explanation disproving negligence; that since there was no such explanation, since defendant did not know why he lost control of the truck or what caused the accident, the jury were bound to find that it was caused by his negligence and could not reasonably render a verdict in his favor, . . .

The maxim *res ipsa loquitur* means that the facts of the occurrence evidence negligence; the circumstances unexplained justify an inference of negligence. In the principle of proof employed, a case of *res ipsa loquitur* does not differ from an ordinary case of circumstantial evidence. *Res ipsa loquitur* is not an arbitrary rule but rather "a common sense appraisal of the probative value of circumstantial evidence." Boykin v. Chase Bottling Works, 222 S.W.2d 889, 896.

This maxim does not generally apply to motor vehicle accidents, but it may apply to such an accident where the circumstances causing it were within the driver's control and the accident was such as does not usually occur without negligence. So where a motor vehicle, without apparent cause, runs off the road and causes harm, the normal inference is that the driver was negligent, and *res ipsa loquitur* is usually held to apply. . . .

[W]e agree with learned counsel for plaintiffs that the facts of this case brought it within the maxim *res ipsa loquitur*. The accident was such as does not usually occur without negligence, and the cause of it was in control of the driver, or rather it resulted from his loss of control of the truck, which he could not explain.

While we agree that these facts made a case of *res ipsa loquitur*, we do not agree that they, though unexplained, required an inference or finding of negligence, or that the jury could not reasonably refuse to find negligence and return a verdict for defendant, or that there was no evidence to support their verdict for him.

It is true there has been confusion in the cases as to the procedural effect of *res ipsa loquitur*, some cases giving it one and some another of these three different effects:

(1) It warrants an inference of negligence which the jury may draw or not, as their judgment dictates. . . .

(2) It raises a presumption of negligence which requires the jury to find negligence if defendant does not produce evidence sufficient to rebut the presumption. . . .

(3) It not only raises such a presumption but also shifts the ultimate burden of proof to defendant and requires him to prove by a preponderance of all the evidence that the injury was not caused by his negligence. . . .

For a review of the numerous cases and a clear and helpful discussion of the subject, see: Prosser, The Procedural Effect of Res Ipsa Loquitur (1936), 20 Minn. L. Rev. 241-271; Prosser, Res Ipsa Loquitur in California (1949), 37 Cal. L. Rev. 183-234; Prosser on Torts (1941), 291-310.

The effect of a case of *res ipsa loquitur*, like that of any other case of circumstantial evidence, varies from case to case, depending on the particular facts of each case; and therefore such effect can no more be fitted into a fixed formula or reduced to a rigid rule than can the effect of other cases of circumstantial evidence. The only generalization that can be safely made is that, in the words of the definition of *res ipsa loquitur*, it affords "reasonable evidence," in the absence of an explanation by defendant, that the accident arose from his negligence.

The weight or strength of such "reasonable evidence" will necessarily depend on the particular facts of each case, and the cogency of the inference of negligence from such facts may of course vary in degree all the way from practical certainty in one case to reasonable probability in another.

In exceptional cases the inference may be so strong as to require a directed verdict for plaintiff, as in cases of objects falling from defendant's premises on persons in the highway, such as Byrne v. Boadle (1863), 2 H. & C. 720, 159 Eng. Reprint 299 (a barrel of flour fell from a window of defendant's warehouse); McHarge v. M. M. Newcomer & Co., . . . 100 S.W. 700, . . . (an awning roller fell from defendant's building); and Turnpike Co. v. Yates, . . . 67 S.W. 69 (a toll gate or pole fell on a traveler). . . .

In the ordinary case, however, *res ipsa loquitur* merely makes a case for the jury — merely permits the jury to choose the inference of defendant's negligence in preference to other permissible or reasonable inferences. . . .

We think this is true in the case before us. The cause of the death sued for was defendant's loss of control of the truck. This may have been due to his own negligence, or it may have been due to no fault of his — an unavoidable accident resulting from the brakes giving way or the breaking of some part of the control mechanism of the truck. Since such conflicting inferences might be reasonably drawn from the evidence, it was for the jury to choose the inference they thought most probable; and we cannot say that there was no evidence to support their verdict for defendant. . . .

All the assignments of error are overruled and the judgment of the Circuit Court is affirmed. . . .

FOOD FOR THOUGHT

If the Tennessee court had followed the view that res ipsa creates a presumption of negligence, would the court have reversed the jury verdict for defendant? In Morejon v. Rais Construction Co., 851 N.E.2d 1143 (N.Y. 2006), the court considered the procedural effects of res ipsa loquitur. The court concluded that in the vast majority of instances, res ipsa is a permissible inference that goes to the jury under proper instruction informing them that they may conclude that the defendant was negligent. If the evidence is so weak that the elements of res ipsa are simply not made out, then a judge must direct a verdict for the defendant. In rare instances where the inference of negligence is so compelling that reasonable persons could not differ, the court may grant a plaintiff summary judgment. *Morejon* is basically in accord with *Sullivan*. A court ought to look at the strength of the inference and decide whether the issue is for the court to decide as a matter of law or is a jury issue and ought not to paste labels such as "mandatory inference" or "presumption" on a res ipsa case. In short, keep it simple.

chapter 4

Actual Causation

A. BUT-FOR CAUSATION: DID THE DEFENDANT'S NEGLIGENT CONDUCT CAUSE THE PLAINTIFF'S HARM?

PERKINS v. TEXAS & NEW ORLEANS R.R. CO.
147 So. 2d 646 (La. 1962)

This is a tort action. Plaintiff, the 67-year-old widow of Tanner Perkins, seeks damages for the death of her husband in the collision of an automobile, in which he was riding, with a train of the defendant railroad. The district court awarded damages. The Court of Appeal affirmed. We granted certiorari to review the judgment of the Court of Appeal.

The tragic accident which gave rise to this litigation occurred at the intersection of Eddy Street and The Texas and New Orleans Railroad Company track in the town of Vinton, Louisiana, at approximately 6:02 a.m., after daylight, on September 28, 1959. At this crossing Eddy Street runs north and south, and the railroad track, east and west. Involved was a 113-car freight train pulled by four diesel engines traveling east and a Dodge automobile driven by Joe Foreman in a southerly direction on Eddy Street. Tanner Perkins, a guest passenger, was riding in the front seat of the automobile with the driver.

Located in the northwest quadrant of the intersection of the railroad track and Eddy Street was a warehouse five hundred feet long. A "house track" paralleled the main track on the north to serve the warehouse. This warehouse obstructed the view to the west of an automobile driver approaching the railroad crossing from the north on Eddy Street. It likewise obstructed the view to the north of trainmen approaching the crossing from the west. Having previously served on this route, the engineer and brakeman were aware of this obstruction.

To warn the public of the approach of trains, the defendant railroad had installed at the crossing an automatic signal device consisting of a swinging red light and a bell. At the time of the accident, this signal was operating. A standard Louisiana railroad stop sign and an intersection stop sign were also located at the crossing.

Proceeding east, the train approached the intersection with its headlight burning, its bell ringing, and its whistle blowing.

The engineer, brakeman, and fireman were stationed in the forward engine of the train. The engineer was seated on the right or south side, where he was unable to observe an automobile approaching from the left of the engine. The brakeman and fireman, who were seated on the left or north side of the engine, were looking forward as the train approached the intersection. These two crewmen saw the automobile emerge from behind the warehouse. At that time the front wheels of the automobile were on or across the north rail of the house track. The fireman estimated that the train was approximately 60 feet from the crossing when the automobile emerged from behind the warehouse. The brakeman, however, estimated that the train was 30 to 40 feet from the crossing at the time the automobile came into view. Both crewmen immediately shouted a warning to the engineer, who applied the emergency brakes. The train struck the right side of the automobile and carried it approximately 1250 feet. The two occupants were inside the automobile when it came to rest. Both were killed.

The speed of the automobile in which Tanner Perkins was riding was variously estimated from 3-4 miles per hour to 20-25 miles per hour.

The plaintiff and defendant railroad concede in their pleadings that Joe Foreman, the driver of the automobile, was negligent in driving upon the track in front of the train and that his negligence was a proximate cause of the death of Tanner Perkins.

It is conceded that the railroad's safety regulations imposed a speed limit of 25 miles per hour on trains in the town of Vinton. The plaintiff has conceded in this Court that this self-imposed speed limit was a safe speed at the crossing. The train was in fact traveling at a speed of 37 miles per hour.

Applicable here is the rule that the violation by trainmen of the railroad's own speed regulations adopted in the interest of safety is evidence of negligence. The rule has special force in the instant case because of the unusually hazardous nature of the crossing. We find, as did the Court of Appeal, that the trainmen were negligent in operating the train 12 miles per hour in excess of the speed limit.

As one of several defenses, the defendant railroad strenuously contends that the excessive speed of the train was not a proximate cause of the collision for the reason that the accident would not have been averted even had the train been traveling at the prescribed speed of 25 miles per hour. Contrariwise, the plaintiff contends that the speed of the train constituted a "proximate, direct and contributing cause" of the accident. Thus presented, the prime issue in this case is whether the excessive speed of the train was a cause in fact of the fatal collision.

It is fundamental that negligence is not actionable unless it is a cause in fact of the harm for which recovery is sought. It need not, of course, be the sole cause. Negligence is a cause in fact of the harm to another if it was a substantial factor in bringing about that harm. Under the circumstances of the instant case, the excessive speed was undoubtedly a substantial factor in bringing about the collision if the collision would not have occurred without it. On the other hand, if the collision would have occurred irrespective of such negligence, then it was not a substantial factor.

The burden of proving this causal link is upon the plaintiff. Recognizing that the fact of causation is not susceptible of proof to a mathematical certainty, the law requires only that the evidence show that it is more probable than not that the harm was caused by the tortious conduct of the defendant. Stated differently, it must appear that it is more likely than not that the harm would have been averted but for the negligence of the defendant.

In the instant case the train engineer testified that at a speed of 25 miles per hour he would have been unable to stop the train in time to avoid the accident. Other facts of record support his testimony in this regard. With efficient brakes, the mile-long train required 1250 feet to stop at a speed of 37 miles per hour. It is clear, then, that even at the concededly safe speed of 25 miles per hour, the momentum of the train would have, under the circumstances, carried it well beyond the crossing. This finding, of course, does not fully determine whether the collision would have been averted at the slower speed. The automobile was also in motion during the crucial period. This necessitates the further inquiry of whether the automobile would have cleared the track and evaded the impact had the train been moving at a proper speed at the time the trainmen observed the automobile emerge from behind the warehouse. Basic to this inquiry are the speed of the automobile and the driving distance between it and a position of safety.

The testimony of the witnesses is in hopeless conflict as to the speed of the automobile at the time of the collision. The estimates range from a low of 3 miles per hour to a high of 25 miles per hour. Both the district court and Court of Appeal concluded that the speed of the automobile had not been definitely established. Each of these courts found only that the automobile was proceeding at "a slow speed." In her brief the plaintiff states: "The speed of the automobile cannot be determined, at least by the testimony." We conclude that the evidence fails to establish the speed of the automobile with reasonable certainty. Although the record discloses that the train struck the automobile broadside, it does not reflect the driving distance required to propel the vehicle from the danger zone. . . .

Despite these deficiencies in the evidence, the plaintiff argues that had the train been traveling at a proper speed the driver of the automobile would "conceivably" have had some additional time to take measures to avert disaster and the deceased would have had some additional time to extricate himself from danger. Hence, the plaintiff reasons, the collision and loss of life "might not" have occurred.

On the facts of this case, we must reject the escape theory advanced in this argument. Because of the deficiencies in the evidence which we have already noted, it is devoid of evidentiary support. The record contains no probative facts from which the Court can draw a reasonable inference of causation under this theory. In essence, the argument is pure conjecture. Based upon the evidence of record, it appears almost certain that the fatal accident would have occurred irrespective of the excessive speed of the train. It follows that this speed was not a substantial factor in bringing about the accident.

We conclude that the plaintiff has failed to discharge the burden of proving that the negligence of the defendant was a cause in fact of the tragic death. The judgment in favor of plaintiff is manifestly erroneous. For the reasons assigned, the judgment of the Court of Appeal is reversed, and the plaintiff's suit is dismissed at her cost.

HAMLIN, Justice (dissenting).

I am compelled to agree with the Court of Appeal that in view of the blind crossing the overspeeding by the employees of the Railroad Company was negligence, which was a proximate cause of the accident.

It is my opinion that this train (approximately one mile long, made up of one hundred and thirteen cars and four diesels) should not have entered the Town of Vinton at thirty-seven miles per hour, its speed at the time of the accident. Notwithstanding the rules of the Railroad Company that its speed in Vinton should not have exceeded twenty-five miles per hour, even this speed, under the circumstances found by the Court of Appeal, would be excessive. I respectfully dissent.

FOOD FOR THOUGHT

The legal principle applied in *Perkins* is universally recognized in American tort law. When the plaintiff's harm would have occurred even if the defendant had not acted negligently, then the defendant's negligence did not actually cause the plaintiff's harm. It is often said that the defendant's negligent conduct must be a "but-for" cause of the plaintiff's harm. Restatement, Third, of Torts § 26. Observe that in *Perkins* the but-for principle required judgment for the defendant as a matter of law, rather than being for the jury to decide. What factual elements in *Perkins* justified that treatment?

In Collins v. Thomas, 938 A.2d 1208 (Vt. 2007), the plaintiff's decedent fell off the defendant's pickup truck, which the plaintiff claimed was negligently maintained and in disrepair. The high court affirmed judgment as a matter of law for defendant because the plaintiff failed to demonstrate any but-for connection between the dangerous condition of the truck and the death of the decedent. What if a state statute had made it illegal to operate a vehicle in such disrepair? Would the court have held the violation of that statute to have been the cause of the death?

FORD v. TRIDENT FISHERIES CO.
122 N.E. 389 (Mass. 1919)

Tort by the administratrix of the estate of Jerome Ford . . . against the Trident Fisheries Company . . . for negligently causing the death by drowning of the plaintiff's intestate on December 21, 1916, when he was employed as the mate of the defendant's steam trawler. . . . At the close of the plaintiff's evidence, which is described in the opinion, the judge, upon motion of the defendant, ordered a verdict for the defendant; and the plaintiff alleged exceptions.

CARROLL, J.

The plaintiff's intestate was drowned while employed as mate of the defendant's steam trawler, the Long Island. This action is to recover damages for his death.

On December 21, 1916, about 5 o'clock in the afternoon, the vessel left T wharf, Boston, bound for the "Georges," which are fishing banks in Massachusetts waters. About 6 o'clock, shortly after passing Boston Light, the plaintiff's intestate, Jerome Ford, came on deck to take charge of his watch as mate of the vessel. He came from the galley in the forecastle and walked aft on the starboard side. As he was ascending a flight of four steps leading from the deck to the pilot house, the vessel rolled and he was thrown overboard. At the time of the accident there was a fresh northwest breeze and the vessel was going before the wind; no cry was heard, no clothing was seen floating in the water, and Ford was not seen by any one from the time he fell overboard . . . .

The plaintiff . . . contends that the boat which was lowered to pick up the intestate was lashed to the deck instead of being suspended from davits and in order to launch it the lashings had to be cut; that McCue, who manned it, had only one oar and was obliged to scull, instead of rowing as he might have done if he had had two oars. Even if it be assumed that upon these facts it could have been found the defendant was negligent, there is nothing to show they in any way contributed to Ford's death. He disappeared when he fell from the trawler and it does not appear that if the boat had been suspended from davits and a different method of propelling it had been used he could have been rescued . . . .

Exceptions overruled.

FOOD FOR THOUGHT

How much proof that decedent might have been saved would have sufficed to send the case to the jury? A case parallel to *Ford* on its facts reached the same outcome in Henderson v. Sargent, 677 S.E.2d 709 (Ga. Ct. App. 2009). Instead of falling off the defendant's boat, the plaintiff fell out of defendant's tree, and the plaintiff claimed negligence in defendant's failure properly to obtain necessary emergency medical assistance for the injured, helpless plaintiff. The court of appeals affirmed the trial court's granting of summary judgment for defendant, indicating that the plaintiff failed to prove that defendant's actions after the fall caused his injuries. What might such proof have looked like? What if the plaintiff's qualified expert in *Henderson* had testified that, with proper treatment that defendant's negligence denied him, the plaintiff would have had a 30 percent chance of avoiding the permanent impairments from which he suffered as a result of his fall?

authors' dialogue 15

JIM: The court may have gotten it wrong in *Ford v. Trident Fisheries*, the case where the guy fell off the fishing trawler and drowned. Shouldn't the plaintiff have reached the jury against the company that owned the trawler?

AARON: No. The plaintiff didn't prove that the company's negligence caused decedent's death — he would have drowned no matter how good their lifesaving equipment was.

JIM: But the defendant's fishing trawler was the instrument of the decedent's untimely death, Aaron. Without the boat, he wouldn't have drowned. And the boat was negligently maintained.

AARON: But the negligent maintenance didn't have anything to do with his death, Jim.

JIM: Help me understand why that should matter. We impose tort liability in order to force defendants to take reasonable care, right? Well, imposing liability in *Ford* would have helped force the defendant to install proper lifesaving equipment. Letting the defendant off on a directed verdict helps keep things as they are.

AARON: But your logic would support holding the trawler company liable for the death of a crew member's wife, back home, while the badly equipped boat was out to sea.

JIM: No, it wouldn't. In that case, the boat would not have caused the wife's death. But in *Ford*, the boat did cause decedent's death by drowning.

AARON: Touché. Even your approach admits to causation-based limits on holding the defendant liable in the name of forcing the company to fix the boat. Let me change my hypo. What if the boat with bad lifesaving equipment ran into the "perfect storm" and went down in the North Atlantic with all eight hands on board? Even though the bad equipment didn't contribute one whit to the tragedy, your suggested approach would hold the defendant liable for all eight deaths?

JIM: Hmm. I guess it would. Without the boat, they wouldn't have got caught in the storm. But "perfect storms" don't arise very often. And if they had waited to leave while they fixed the lifesaving equipment, they would've missed the storm.

BRAD: But then you've got a classic "mere fortuity," like *Berry v. Sugar Notch*, 43 A. 240 (Pa. 1899), the case where the speeding trolley got hit by a tree branch. But for the trolley's excessive speed, it wouldn't have gotten hit by the branch. That doesn't mean the accident was caused by the speeding, though — at least not in one sense of causation. In the perfect storm variation, the lack of lifesaving equipment didn't cause the harm in the right way. I suppose we should defer this until the discussion of proximate cause, in the next chapter.

AARON: Disasters at sea of one sort or another aren't uncommon. Commercial fishing in the North Atlantic is a dangerous activity. In effect, you would hold the company liable for everything bad that happens on board whenever a boat leaves the harbor with anything wrong with it. That's overkill. As my grandfather used to say, "The punishment should fit the crime."

JIM: Speaking of grandfathers, I'm taking two of my grandchildren, Jacob and Rhiannon, out for lunch today. You do that with your grandkids, don't you?

AARON: Sure. But if we did it all at one time, we'd have to rent a large restaurant.

REYNOLDS v. TEXAS & PACIFIC RY.
37 La. Ann. 694 (1885), 1885 WL 6364 (La.)

The opinion of the Court was delivered by FENNER, J.

The plaintiff and his wife claim damages of the defendant company for injuries suffered by the wife and caused by the alleged negligence of the company.

[To get from the depot sitting room to her train, plaintiff's wife had to go down an unlighted, outdoor stairway that lacked any handrail.]

It is obvious that, while such a [stairway] passage might fulfill all customary and reasonable requirements of safety in the daytime, or when well lighted, yet at night, and when not sufficiently lighted up, it undoubtedly exposed passengers unfamiliar with it to danger of fall and injury . . . .

The train was behind time. Several witnesses testify that passengers were warned to "hurry up." Mrs. Reynolds, a corpulent woman, weighing two hundred and fifty pounds, emerging from the bright light of the sitting-room, which naturally exaggerated the outside darkness, and hastening down these unlighted steps, made a misstep in some way and was precipitated beyond the narrow platform in front and down the slope beyond, incurring the serious injuries complained of. [The trial court, sitting without a jury, found the defendant negligent in failing to provide an adequate stairway and entered judgment for plaintiff in the amount of $2,000. The appellate court's treatment of the negligence issue is omitted.]

[The defendant] contends that, even conceding the negligence of the company in the above respect, it does not follow that the accident to plaintiff was necessarily caused thereby, but that she might well have made the misstep and fallen even had it been broad daylight. We concede that this is possible, and recognize the distinction between post hoc and propter hoc. But where the negligence of the defendant greatly multiplies the chances of accident to the plaintiff, and is of a character naturally leading to its occurrence, the mere possibility that it might have happened without the negligence is not sufficient to break the chain of cause and effect between the negligence and the injury. Courts, in such matters, consider the natural and ordinary course of events, and do not indulge in fanciful suppositions. The whole tendency of the evidence connects the accident with the negligence. . . .

Judgment affirmed.

hypo 40

A, a 75-year-old woman, is taking a shower in a bathtub in her son *B*'s house when she falls and breaks her hip. *B* hears her fall and runs into the bathroom to find *A* unconscious in the tub. One of five No-Slip strips, manufactured by *M*, that were attached with adhesive to the bottom of the tub, was partially unstuck and folded back on itself. A defect in the adhesive caused this to happen. *A* cannot remember why she fell. She might have fainted or she might have slipped because of the defect in the No-Slip strip. Will *A* reach the jury in an action against *M*?

SUBSTANTIAL FACTOR VS. BUT-FOR CAUSATION

You may encounter the terminology of "substantial factor" causation in a way that appears to lower the plaintiff's burden of proving factual causation. Lest you think this is simply mistaken, consider two cases decided by Judge Guido Calabresi, who literally wrote the book on torts. (His 1970 book, *The Costs of Accidents*, was highly influential on the economic analysis of tort law.) The first case, Zuchowicz v. United States, 140 F.3d 381 (2d Cir. 1998), involved a medical malpractice action against doctors at a Naval hospital who prescribed an excessive dose of a drug called Danocrine to the plaintiff. The plaintiff subsequently developed a serious and fatal condition called primary pulmonary hypertension (PPH). On appeal from an award of damages after a bench trial, the defendant argued that the plaintiff had failed to show causation. The showing is particularly difficult because the plaintiff must establish both that Danocrine caused the PPH and that *an overdose* of Danocrine (that is, the negligent act of the doctors) caused the PPH. Judge Calabresi wrote:

> The problem of linking defendant's negligence to the harm that occurred is one that many courts have addressed in the past. A car is speeding and an accident occurs. That the car was involved and was a cause of the crash is readily shown. The accident, moreover, is of the sort that rules prohibiting speeding are designed to prevent. But is this enough to support a finding of fact, in the individual case, that *speeding* was, in fact, more probably than not, the cause of the accident? The same question can be asked when a car that was driving in violation of a minimum speed requirement on a super-highway is rear-ended. Again, it is clear that the car and its driver were causes of the accident. And the accident is of the sort that minimum speeding rules are designed to prevent. But can a fact finder conclude, without more, that the driver's negligence in *driving too slowly* led to the crash? To put it more precisely — the defendant's negligence was strongly causally linked to the accident, and the defendant was undoubtedly a *but for* cause of the harm, but does this suffice to allow a fact finder to say that the defendant's *negligence* was a *but for* cause? At one time, courts were reluctant to say in such circumstances that the wrong could be deemed to be the cause. They emphasized the logical fallacy of *post hoc, ergo propter hoc,* and demanded some direct evidence connecting the defendant's wrongdoing to the harm.

140 F.3d at 390. Here is where a dangerous and slippery sense of the term substantial factor comes in. As Judge Calabresi explained, a trier of fact may be permitted to infer causation from the risk-causing aspects of the defendant's conduct, or at least the burden may shift to the defendant to disprove causation:

> [I]f (a) a negligent act was deemed wrongful because that act increased the chances that a particular type of accident would occur, and (b) a mishap of that very sort did happen, this was enough to support a finding by the trier of fact that the negligent behavior caused the harm. Where such a strong causal link exists, it is up to the negligent party to bring in evidence denying but for cause and suggesting that in the actual case the wrongful conduct had not been a substantial factor.

Id. at 390-391. Returning to *Zuchowicz*, the reasoning goes like this: One of the risks of prescribing an overdose of Danocrine is PPH. The doctors prescribed an overdose of Danocrine and the plaintiff contracted PPH. Thus, the plaintiff established causation in fact. But isn't that exactly the fallacy of *post hoc, propter hoc*, i.e. the inference that because one event followed another, the second event must have been caused by the first?

In the second case, Williams v. Utica College, 453 F.3d 112 (2d Cir. 2006), college employees failed to provide adequate security for a dormitory. A student was assaulted in her room by a masked intruder who was never caught. It was unclear whether a security officer was not present at an unlocked door, or whether a door had been left unlocked or propped open by students. The Second Circuit, with Judge Calabresi writing, affirmed the district court's entry of summary judgment for the college. Judge Calabresi distinguished *Zuchowicz*, the holding of which he restated as follows: "[W]here the causal link between the negligence and the harm that occurs is strong, a jury can decide that, more probably than not, the injury occurred *because of the negligence* and not in some other, inevitably unusual, way." *Id.* at 120-121. In other words, substantial-factor causation is similar to *res ipsa loquitur* in the proof of breach; it permits the trier of fact to infer causation from circumstantial evidence. In *Zuchowicz* there was strong circumstantial evidence of causation. There was no likely alternative explanation for the plaintiff in *Zuchowicz* developing PPH. In *Williams*, by contrast, there were other plausible explanations for the intruder's presence, including that he was also a student living in the same dormitory, or that a student had left a security door propped open. Thus, it was inappropriate to permit a trier of fact to infer causation from circumstantial evidence.

The court in the *Reynolds* case, set forth above, is appealing to the idea of substantial factor causation as a lowering of the plaintiff's burden, as compared with the ordinary but-for causation standard. The court says, "where the negligence of the defendant greatly multiplies the chances of accident to the plaintiff, and is of a character naturally leading to its occurrence, the mere possibility that it might have happened without the negligence is not sufficient to break the chain of cause and effect between the negligence and the injury." In other words, as long as the defendant has done something negligent—that is, something that greatly multiples the chance of an accident—then the element of actual causation should not be a barrier to a plaintiff recovering if the accident is the type of event that naturally follows from the creation of a particular type of risk by the defendant. As we'll see in the next chapter, consideration of the type of risk created by the defendant, and whether the resulting harm to the plaintiff is within the scope of the risk, is ordinarily part of the analysis of proximate causation, not actual cause.

Hypo 40, above, can be understood as asking whether the plaintiff has sufficient circumstantial evidence to warrant an inference that her fall was caused by the defective glue on the back of the No-Slip strips. On the version of substantial factor causation used by Judge Calabresi in *Zuchowicz*, the plaintiff should be able to get to the jury with her claim. See also Yount v. Deibert, 147 P.3d 1065 (Kan. 2006) (sufficient circumstantial evidence of but-for cause of house fire when children "engaged in various pyromaniacal activities" a few hours before the fire began). But the Judge Calabresi of *Williams* seems less willing to permit an inference of causation from the fact that the defendant did something risky.

FAILURE TO WARN AND ACTUAL CAUSATION

Many of these "What would have happened if?" questions arise in the context of a defendant who allegedly failed to warn of the risks that caused the plaintiff's injury. If the risks of harm are generally obvious to reasonable people, no duty to warn of those risks arises. Of course, the defendant may owe a duty to warn of ways that the plaintiff might avoid the obvious risks. In any event, when the risks of harm are not generally obvious, but the defendant proves that the particular plaintiff knew of the danger from other sources, courts have ruled as a matter of law that the defendant's failure to warn did not cause the accident. *See, e.g.,* Thomas v. Baltimore & Ohio R., 310 A.2d 186 (Md. Ct. Spec. App. 1973) (holding that the cause of the train-truck accident was not the failure of the railroad company to erect a warning sign, but rather the failure of the deceased to stop, look, and listen before entering upon the railroad track, which he had repeatedly crossed previously). Even when the plaintiff does not know of the relevant risk, the negligent defendant will escape liability by proving that the plaintiff would not have read and heeded a warning, had one been given. *See, e.g.,* Nelson v. Ford Motor Co., 150 F.3d 905 (8th Cir. 1998) (plaintiff admitted that he did not read the instructions to a car jack because he felt he knew how to use the jack properly; plaintiff could not recover against the manufacturer for failure to warn after the jack collapsed under the weight of plaintiff's Ford vehicle, causing injuries, because plaintiff could not prove that he would have read and heeded a warning). *But see* Haft v. Lone Palm Hotel, 478 P.2d 465 (Cal. 1970), where the plaintiff's husband and son were both found drowned at the bottom of the swimming pool at the hotel where the family stayed during a visit to Palm Springs. The hotel had no lifeguard present at the pool and, in violation of a state statute, did not post a sign advising guests of that fact. Witnesses had observed the father and son floating on rubber rafts near the deep end, laughing and playing by themselves, but no one saw how or why they drowned a short while later. The defendant argued that the plaintiff had not proven that a "No Lifeguard" sign — or even a flesh-and-blood lifeguard — would have made any difference. The jury found for the defendants. However, according to the California high court, the defendants bore the burden of showing that their statutory violation was not a cause of the deaths. The court reversed and remanded the case because the parties' respective burdens were not clearly defined by the trial court.

Many of these failure-to-warn cases involve manufacturers of products. Some courts have held that when a manufacturer distributes a product without an adequate warning, a rebuttable presumption arises that the purchaser/user would have read any warning provided and would have acted to minimize the risks of injury. *See, e.g.,* Arnold v. Ingersoll-Rand Co., 834 S.W.2d 192 (Mo. 1992). If the defendant does not rebut this so-called "heeding presumption" by proving that the particular purchaser/user would not have read and heeded the warning, the defendant is liable for the harm that a presumably effective warning would have

authors' dialogue 16

BRAD: There's something I don't get about these cases. Actual cause is supposed to be an issue of fact. Either the defendant's negligence caused the plaintiff's harm or it didn't. There can be doubt and ambiguity, of course, and the evidence may be insufficient to say whether there's more likely than not a causal connection. If that happens, though, the plaintiff hasn't met her burden of production and she loses on summary judgment. Where does the judge in *Reynolds*, or for that matter Judge Calabresi in *Zuchowicz*, get off lowering the plaintiff's burden because the defendant's conduct seems egregiously risky?

JIM: Do you know the classic article, Wex S. Malone, *Ruminations on Cause-in-Fact*, 9 Stan. L. Rev. 60 (1956)? Malone would disagree with your contention that actual cause as expressed in the but-for rule is simply a factual question as to what would have happened if the defendant had not been negligent. Important policy concerns have a profound effect on whether the evidence on causation is sufficient. It's partly a matter of the degree of the defendant's fault, as you say, but courts also take into account whether the defendant breached a duty that was designed to protect against the very type of risk to which the plaintiff was exposed,

BRAD: I have to confess to not having read that article in my torts class way back when, but forget about Wex Malone — shouldn't the right division of labor between actual and proximate cause be that policy questions are addressed under the element of proximate cause?

AARON: You're assuming that evidentiary-sufficiency rules are administered by lifeless computers, not flesh-and-blood judges. It's true that the formal incantation provides that plaintiff must establish that "more probably than not" the defendant's negligence was the but-for cause of the harm. But judges have enormous discretion in deciding whether to direct a verdict or send the case to the jury.

BRAD: I can live with judicial discretion; I just want to see it applied honestly. If the reconciliation of *Perkins* with *Reynolds* is that the real culprit in *Perkins* was the knucklehead driver whose conduct was reckless, while we want to hold the railroad liable in *Reynolds* so they have an incentive to fix the light in the stairwell, that's fine, but let's not pretend that the issue in the cases is the sufficiency of the evidence.

AARON: One final point. I don't want students to think that you bleeding hearts reflect the governing law. The but-for test is deeply entrenched in American tort law. The Third Restatement has formally adopted it in Section 26 (and thus rejected substantial factor). With all due deference to Judge Calabressi, he was probably wrong in *Zuchowitz*. The drug Danocrine clearly caused PPH. But the question was whether the overdose caused the plaintiff's injuries. There simply was no evidence that the overdose was the culprit.

prevented. In Technical Chemical Co. v. Jacobs, 480 S.W.2d 602, 606 (Tex. 1972), the Texas high court observed:

> The presumption [that the plaintiff would have heeded a proper warning may] be rebutted if the manufacturer comes forward with contrary evidence that the presumed fact did not exist . . . . Depending upon the individual facts, this may by accomplished by the manufacturer's producing evidence that the user was blind, illiterate, intoxicated at the time of the use, irresponsible or lax in judgment or by some other circumstance tending to show that the improper use [of the product] was or would have been made regardless of the warning.

But see Rivera v. Philip Morris, Inc., 209 P.3d 271 (Nev. 2009) (in answer to certified question from federal district court, Nevada law does not recognize a heeding presumption because people often don't read warnings or they ignore them altogether). Is something like a "heeding presumption" at work in *Reynolds* and *Haft, supra*? Would something like a heeding presumption be helpful to the plaintiff, *A*, in Hypo 40, *supra*? Some commentators believe that recognizing a presumption of causation in these failure-to-warn cases leads to undesirable results, arguing instead that the causation issue should be a question of fact that is determined on a case-by-case basis. *See, e.g.*, James A. Henderson, Jr. & Aaron D. Twerski, *Doctrinal Collapse in Products Liability: The Empty Shell of Failure to Warn*, 65 N.Y.U. L. Rev. 265 (1990).

B. SPECIAL PROBLEMS OF PROOF: WAS THE DEFENDANT'S CONDUCT CAPABLE OF CAUSING THE PLAINTIFF'S HARM?

All of the causation cases in the preceding section involve "problems of proof" in the sense that courts are asking whether one side or the other has produced a sufficient quantity of proof of actual causation. The court in *Perkins*, for example, justified its ruling for the defendant railroad by concluding that "the plaintiff has failed to discharge the burden of proving that the negligence of the defendant was a cause in fact of the tragic death." By contrast, the cases in this section focus not on the quantity of proof regarding the factual circumstances surrounding the accident, but on the quality of plaintiff's technical proof that the defendant's conduct actually caused the harm in question. The issue in these cases is not whether the negligent aspect of the defendant's conduct — in *Reynolds* the failure to provide adequate stairwell lighting — contributed to causing plaintiff's harm, but whether the defendant's conduct itself had anything at all to do with causing that harm. In *Reynolds*, the defendant conceded that the railroad's stairs were the ones that the plaintiff fell down and that the fall caused her injuries. Indeed, in slip-and-fall cases like *Reynolds*, the issue of whether the fall on the stairs caused the injuries almost never arises. But when the causal connection between such a fall and the defendant's injuries is controverted, technical evidence is almost always required to establish the necessary connection. Thus, most of the cases in this section involve the technical reliability of plaintiffs' expert testimony on actual causation.

KRAMER SERVICE, INC. v. WILKINS
186 So. 625 (Miss. 1939)

GRIFFITH, Justice.

[Plaintiff-appellee visited a business acquaintance at defendant-appellant's hotel. After the business meeting concluded, when appellee was leaving the room, a broken piece of the glass transom over the door fell, striking appellee on the head and imparting a jagged abrasion on his temple. The trial court entered judgment on a jury verdict for plaintiff-appellee, and defendant appeals.]

The foregoing statement of the facts is supported by competent evidence which in the light of the verdict of the jury must be accepted as true. There is further competent evidence to the effect that the condition of unrepair which resulted in the fall of the broken transom glass had existed for a sufficient length of time to charge appellant with responsible notice thereof, and that the condition was such that a reasonably prudent and careful operator should have foreseen the fall of the broken glass and an injury thereby as a likelihood of appreciable weight and moment. There is no reversible error in the record on the issue of liability, and as to that issue the judgment will be affirmed.

But there is plain and serious error in the matter of the amount of the damages. The wound on the temple did not heal, and some months after the injury appellee was advised by his local physician to visit a specialist in skin diseases, which he did in January, 1937, about two years after the injury, and it was then found that at the point where the injury occurred to appellee's temple, a skin cancer had developed, of which a cure had not been fully effected at the time of the trial, some three years after the injury first mentioned.

Appellee sued for a large sum in damages, averring and contending that the cancer resulted from the stated injury; and the jury evidently accepted that contention, since there was an award by the verdict in the sum of twenty thousand dollars. Appellant requested an instruction to the effect that the cancer or any prolongation of the trouble on account thereof should not be taken into consideration by the jury, but this instruction was refused.

Two physicians or medical experts, and only two, were introduced as witnesses, and both were specialists in skin diseases and dermal traumatisms. One testified that it was possible that a trauma such as appellee suffered upon his temple, could or would cause a skin cancer at the point of injury, but that the chances that such a result would ensue from such a cause would be only one out of one hundred cases. The other testified that there is no causal connection whatever between trauma and cancer, and went on to illustrate that if there were such a connection nearly every person of mature age would be suffering with cancer . . . .

It seems therefore hardly to be debatable but that appellant was entitled to the requested instruction as regards the cancer; and since, except as to that element, the verdict could not have been large, the verdict and judgment must be reversed on the issue of the amount of the damages.

There is one heresy in the judicial forum which appears to be Hydra-headed, and although cut off again and again, has the characteristic of an endless renewal. That heresy is that proof that a past event possibly happened, or that a certain result was possibly caused by a past event, is sufficient in probative force to take the question to a jury. Such was never the law in this state, and we are in accord with almost all of the other common-law states. Nearly a half century ago, when our Court stood forth in point of ability never excelled, and when the principles of the jurisprudence of this state were being put into a more definite form than ever before, Chief Justice Campbell said in Railroad v. Cathey, 12 So. at 253 [Miss. 1893]: "It is not enough that negligence of the employer and injury to the employee coexisted, but the injury must have been caused by the negligence . . . . 'Post hoc ergo propter hoc' is not sound as evidence or argument. Nor is it sufficient for a plaintiff seeking recovery for alleged negligence by an employer towards an employee to show a possibility that the injury complained of was caused by negligence. Possibilities will not sustain a verdict. It must have a better foundation." . . .

Taking the medical testimony in this case in the strongest light in which it could be reasonably interpreted in behalf of the plaintiff, this testimony is that as a possibility a skin cancer could be caused by an injury such as here happened, but as a probability the physicians were in agreement that there was or is no such a probability.

And the medical testimony is conclusive on both judge and jury in this case. That testimony is undisputed that after long and anxious years of research the exact cause of cancer remains unknown — there is no dependably known origin to which it can be definitely traced or ascribed. If, then, the cause be unknown to all those who have devoted their lives to a study of the subject, it is wholly beyond the range of the common experience and observation of judges and jurors, and in such a case medical testimony when undisputed, as here, must be accepted and acted upon in the same manner as is other undisputed evidence; otherwise the jury would be allowed to resort to and act upon nothing else than the proposition post hoc ergo propter hoc, which, as already mentioned, this Court has long ago rejected as unsound, whether as evidence or as argument.

In all other than the exceptional cases now to be mentioned, the testimony of medical experts, or other experts, is advisory only; but we repeat that where the issue is one which lies wholly beyond the range of the experience or observation of laymen and of which they can have no appreciable knowledge, courts and juries must of necessity depend upon and accept the undisputed testimony of reputable specialists, else there would be no substantial foundation upon which to rest a conclusion.

Affirmed as to liability; reversed and remanded on the issue of the amount of the damages.

IMPROBABLE CONSEQUENCES

Cases like *Kramer Service* arise with some frequency. In Whiteman v. Worley, 688 So. 2d 207 (La. Ct. App.), *cert. denied*, 694 So. 2d 246 (La. 1997), the defendant's 11-month-old baby jabbed the plaintiff in the eye with a ballpoint pen. Although the plaintiff's corneal abrasion healed within seven days of the incident, three days after it healed she developed a much more serious eye infection. This infection was subsequently diagnosed as chlamydia, a sexually transmitted disease. While it was particularly doubtful that the pen was responsible for transmitting the disease, it was nevertheless possible that the abrasion elevated her risk of infection. Ms. Whiteman argued that she was entitled to a unique presumption stemming from Housley v. Cerise, 579 So. 2d 973, 980 (La. 1991), which provided that "a claimant's disability is presumed to have resulted from an accident, if before the accident the injured person was in good health, but commencing with the accident the symptoms of the disabling condition appear and continuously manifest themselves afterwards, providing that the medical evidence shows there to be a reasonable possibility of causal connection between the accident and the disabling condition" (quoting Lucas v. Insurance Co. of North America, 342 So. 2d 591 (La. 1977)). Ms. Whiteman contended that, because she had no symptoms of a chlamydia eye infection before the jab in the eye with the ballpoint pen, and because she developed such a condition after the jab, the jab should be presumed to have caused the chlamydia eye infection. Based on the facts of the case, the court held that the presumption did not apply, since the medical testimony did not show a "reasonable probability" of causation, which was needed to meet the second prong of the test.

THE PROBLEM WITH PROBABILITIES

A well-known decision in Massachusetts raises the issue of whether and to what extent the plaintiff may rely on probabilities, standing alone, to prove that the defendant's negligent conduct caused the plaintiff's harm. In Smith v. Rapid Transit, Inc., 58 N.E.2d 754 (Mass. 1945), the plaintiff claimed that a negligently operated "great big, long, wide affair" ran her off the road at 1:00 a.m. The plaintiff's lawyer discovered that the only company authorized to operate public transit buses at that place and time was the defendant transit company, and argued that the bus-like vehicle that ran his client off the road must have been a transit company bus. No eyewitness or other direct proof was introduced. The Supreme Court of Massachusetts affirmed a directed verdict for defendant, concluding (*id.* at 755):

> The direction of a verdict for the defendant was right. The ownership of the bus was a matter of conjecture. While the defendant had the sole franchise for operating a bus line on Main Street, Winthrop, this did not preclude private or chartered buses from using this street; the bus in question could very well have been one operated by someone other than the defendant. It was said in Sargent v. Massachusetts Accident Co., 729 N.E.2d 825, 827, that it is "not enough that mathematically the chances somewhat favor a proposition to be proved; for example, the fact that colored automobiles made in the current year outnumber black ones would not warrant a finding that an undescribed automobile of the current year is colored and not black, nor would the fact that only a minority of men die of cancer warrant a finding that a particular man did not die of cancer." The most that can be said of the evidence in the instant case is that perhaps the

mathematical chances somewhat favor the proposition that a bus of the defendant caused the accident. This was not enough. A "proposition is proved by a preponderance of the evidence if it is made to appear more likely or probable in the sense that actual belief in its truth, derived from the evidence, exists in the mind or minds of the tribunal notwithstanding any doubts that may still linger there." Sargent v. Massachusetts Accident Co., 729 N.E.2d at 827 . . . .

See also Kennedy v. S. Cal. Edison Co., 268 F.3d 763 (9th Cir. 2001), *cert. denied,* 535 U.S. 1079 (2002) (1 in 30,000 chance that "fuel fleas"—small particles of radiation—caused plaintiff to suffer from leukemia is not sufficient to prove actual causation). Given that statistical probabilities, standing alone, were not sufficient to reach the jury in *Smith,* what would have been sufficient in that case? In connection with judicial reliance on scientifically derived probabilities, consider the following material.

DAUBERT *AND ITS PROGENY: THE CUTTING EDGE OF EXPERT TESTIMONY*

In confronting the issue as to whether the defendant's conduct was capable of causing the plaintiff's harm, courts come head to head with serious and almost intractable proof problems. For the most part the question of whether "general" or "generic" causation has been established arises in toxic tort cases such as drug and toxic chemicals. Defendants in these cases argue that, even before asking whether their negligent conduct was the cause of the harm, a plaintiff must establish that the product was generically capable of causing the harm. That a plaintiff, for example, contracted cancer after taking a drug or being exposed to a toxic chemical does not mean that the drug or chemical was capable of causing the cancer. A background risk of contracting cancer exists in society separate and apart from the drug or chemical. How does one go about proving the generic causal connection between the toxic agent and the type of cancer the plaintiff suffered? The only way to make a case is through the use of expert testimony. In many instances experts are called to testify on issues that lie at the fringes of scientific knowledge and are questionable from the standpoint of scientific methodology. Defendants frequently challenge the admissibility of such expert testimony as well as its sufficiency.

To understand how these issues get resolved it will be necessary to trace a bit of history. In 1923, in Frye v. United States, 293 F. 1013, 1014 (D.C. Cir. 1923), the District of Columbia Court of Appeals was asked whether evidence derived from a lie-detector test was admissible against a defendant in a murder trial. The court devised a standard for admissibility of scientific evidence that would become the rule for most, if not all, American courts for the next 70 years (*id.* at 1014):

> Just when a scientific principle or discovery crosses the line between the experimental and demonstrable stages is difficult to define. Somewhere in this twilight zone the evidential force of the principle must be recognized, and while courts will go a long way in admitting expert testimony deduced from a well-known scientific principle or discovery, the thing from which the deduction is made must be sufficiently established to have gained general acceptance in the particular field in which it belongs.

Thus, when faced with an objection to a party's scientific evidence, the court applying the *Frye* test must determine whether or not the method by which that evidence was obtained was generally accepted by experts "in the particular field in which it belongs." If the judge determines that the methodology is not generally accepted by the relevant field, the judge will disallow the evidence. If the plaintiff's cause of action depends on the disallowed evidence, this often marks the end of the case. In this way, the court tries to ensure that the scientific evidence admitted deserves the weight that jurors are likely to give it.

No other area of tort law in recent years reflects more vividly the problems just described than cases involving the widely used prescription drug Bendectin. Approved in 1956 by the Food and Drug Administration (FDA) as a safe treatment for morning sickness during pregnancy, Bendectin was used by over 30 million women between 1957 and 1983. Richardson-Merrell, Inc., the manufacturer, withdrew the drug from the market in 1983 due to widespread fears that it caused severe birth defects in the children of women who ingested the drug while pregnant. Whether these fears were grounded in fact is still disputed; but the fears were real enough. A large number of tort claims had been filed based on scientific studies, including epidemiological studies, allegedly revealing the drug to be a teratogen, or birth defect-causing agent.

While the Bendectin cases were pending in the courts, the established scientific community concluded in a number of major research projects that the link between the drug and the birth defects had not been established at an adequate level of statistical significance — that is, observed correlations between ingestion and injury could, for all the data showed, have been the product of random chance. Courts began issuing summary judgments for the defendant, Merrell, with increasing frequency. Not all federal courts agreed with this trend, however, and a fair amount of confusion reigned. All of these developments culminated in a Supreme Court decision that has literally revolutionized the way expert testimony is evaluated prior to admission into evidence in a tort case.

In Daubert v. Merrell Dow Pharmaceuticals, Inc., 509 U.S. 579 (1993), the Supreme Court vacated the judgment of the court of appeals in favor of the defendant in a Bendectin case. The court of appeals had ruled for defendant after excluding plaintiff's expert's testimony based on *Frye*. The Supreme Court reversed and remanded, holding that "general acceptance" is not a necessary precondition to the admissibility of scientific evidence under the Federal Rules of Evidence:

> Faced with a proffer of expert scientific testimony . . . the trial judge must make a preliminary assessment of whether the testimony's underlying reasoning or methodology is scientifically valid and properly can be applied to the facts at issue. Many considerations will bear on the inquiry, including whether the theory or technique in question can be (had has been) tested, whether it has been subjected to peer review and publication, its known or potential error rate, the existence and maintenance of standards controlling its operation, and whether it has attracted widespread acceptance within a relevant scientific community. The inquiry is a flexible one, and its focus must be solely on principles and methodology, not on the conclusions that they generate. Throughout, the judge should also be mindful of other applicable Rules . . . . [C]ross examination, presentation, presentation of

contrary evidence, and careful instruction on the burden of proof, rather than wholesale exclusion under an uncompromising "general acceptance" standard, is the appropriate means by which evidence based on valid principles may be challenged. Excerpted from official Syllabus, 509 U.S. at 580.

On remand from the Supreme Court, the court of appeals wrestled with the new test set forth in *Daubert*. In Daubert v. Merrell Dow Pharmaceuticals, Inc., 43 F.3d 1311 (9th Cir. 1995), the court affirmed the district court's grant of summary judgment. Perhaps the most important consideration in the court's analysis of the record below was the undisputed fact that none of the plaintiffs' experts based his testimony on preexisting or independent research (*id.* at 1317):

> One very significant fact to be considered is whether the experts are proposing to testify about matters growing naturally and directly out of research they have conducted independent of the litigation, or whether they have developed their opinions expressly for purposes of testifying. That an expert testifies for money does not necessarily cause doubt on the reliability of his testimony, as few experts appear in court merely as an eleemosynary gesture. But in determining whether proposed expert testimony amounts to good science, we may not ignore the fact that a scientist's normal workplace is the lab or the field, not the courtroom or the lawyer's office . . . .
>
> We have examined carefully the affidavits proffered by plaintiffs' experts, as well as the testimony from prior trials that plaintiffs have introduced in support of that testimony, and find that none of the experts based his testimony on preexisting or independent research. While plaintiffs' scientists are all experts in their respective fields, none claims to have studied the effect of Bendectin on limb reduction defects before being hired to testify in this or related cases.

The court next asked whether the testimony would assist the trier of fact in resolving the factual issue to which it purported to relate. In this case, the court observed, the crucial issue is specific causation. The court continued (*id.* at 1320):

> California tort law requires plaintiffs to show not merely that Bendectin increased the likelihood of injury, but that it more likely than not caused their injuries. In terms of statistical proof, this means that plaintiffs must establish not just that their mothers' ingestion of Bendectin increased somewhat the likelihood of birth defects, but that it more than doubled it — only then can it be said that Bendectin is more likely than not the source of their injury. Because the background rate of limb reduction defects is one per thousand births, plaintiffs must show that among children of mothers who took Bendectin the incidence of such defects was more than two per thousand.[1]

---

1. No doubt, there will be unjust results under this substantive standard. If a drug increases the likelihood of birth defects, but doesn't more than double it, some plaintiffs whose injuries are attributable to the drug will be unable to recover. There is a converse unfairness under a regime that allows recovery to everyone that may have been affected by the drug. Under this regime, all potential plaintiffs are entitled to recover, even though most will not have suffered an injury that can be attributed to the drug. One can conclude from this that unfairness is inevitable when our tools for detecting causation are imperfect and we must rely on probabilities rather than more direct proof. In any event, this is a matter to be sorted out by the states, whose legal standards we are bound to apply. *Id.*

The court of appeals concludes that the plaintiffs' experts' testimony that Bendectin caused the birth defects in this case, even if it were admissible under the first prong, does not satisfy the requirement imposed by the second prong of *Daubert.* If Bendectin was easily resolved, the tough cases were yet to come. Read on.

RIDER v. SANDOZ PHARMACEUTICAL CORP.
295 F.3d 1194 (11th Cir. 2002)

Before ANDERSON, HULL and RONEY, Circuit Judges.

RONEY, Circuit Judge:

This case involves an issue that has repeatedly come before federal courts: whether expert testimony purporting to link the drug Parlodel with hemorrhagic stroke is admissible to prove causation. Bridget Siharath and Bonnie Rider (plaintiffs) brought this action, alleging that their postpartum hemorrhagic strokes were caused by ingestion of Parlodel. Defendant Sandoz Pharmaceuticals Company (Sandoz), maker of Parlodel, moved to suppress the testimony of the plaintiffs' expert witnesses and for summary judgment. The district court [for the Northern District of Georgia] held that the plaintiffs' expert testimony was not sufficiently reliable to meet the standards established by Daubert v. Merrell Dow Pharm., 509 U.S. 579, 113 S. Ct. 2786, 125 L. Ed. 2d 469 (1993), and granted summary judgment in favor of Sandoz. Plaintiffs appeal. We affirm . . . .

I. Background

Bridget Siharath and Bonnie Rider both took the drug Parlodel to suppress lactation after childbirth. The active ingredient in Parlodel is bromocriptine, an ergot alkaloid compound. Both women subsequently suffered hemorrhagic strokes.

Siharath and Rider filed suit against Sandoz, alleging that Parlodel caused their hemorrhagic strokes. After discovery, Sandoz moved, in limine, to exclude the opinions and testimony of the plaintiffs' experts on causation, and for summary judgment. Because the motions, documentary evidence, experts, and issues were the same in both cases, the district court addressed the motions together. The district court held a *Daubert* hearing to determine whether the evidence was admissible.

The district court, in a three-day hearing, examined the evidence presented in great detail and found that the plaintiffs' claims were based on speculation and conjecture rather than the scientific method. The court drew a careful distinction between clinical process, in which conclusions must be extrapolated from incomplete data, and the scientific method, in which conclusions must be drawn from an accepted process, and concluded that the plaintiffs' experts were relying on the former. Accordingly, the district court excluded the evidence and granted summary judgment in favor of Sandoz . . . . This appeal followed.

II. The Legal Standard

Toxic tort cases, such as this one, are won or lost on the strength of the scientific evidence presented to prove causation. For many years the standard for admissibility of such evidence was the "general acceptance" test set forth in Frye v. United States, 293 F.1013 (D.C. Cir. 1923). When the Federal Rules of Evidence were enacted in 1975, a question arose as to whether the "general acceptance" test had been supplanted by the reliability test articulated in Rule 702. The question was resolved in three cases decided by the Supreme Court. Daubert v. Merrell Dow Pharm., 509 U.S. 579, 113 S. Ct. 2786, 125 L. Ed. 2d 469 (1993); Gen. Elec. Co. v. Joiner, 522 U.S. 136, 118 S. Ct. 512, 139 L. Ed. 2d 508 (1997); Kumho Tire Co., Ltd. v. Carmichael, 526 U.S. 137, 119 S. Ct. 1167, 143 L. Ed. 2d 238 (1999). These cases are commonly referred to as the *Daubert* trilogy.

Since *Daubert*, courts are charged with determining whether scientific evidence is sufficiently reliable to be presented to a jury. The *Daubert* court made it clear that the requirement of reliability found in Rule 702 was the centerpiece of any determination of admissibility. The Supreme Court identified four factors used to determine the reliability of scientific evidence: 1) whether the theory can and has been tested; 2) whether it has been subjected to peer review; 3) the known or expected rate of error; and 4) whether the theory or methodology employed is generally accepted in the relevant scientific community.

In *Joiner*, the Supreme Court established the standard for reviewing trial court rulings of admissibility, and held that such rulings would be made under an abuse of discretion standard. The *Joiner* court also established the important test of analytical "fit" between the methodology used and the conclusions drawn. The court reasoned that just because a methodology is acceptable for some purposes, it may not be acceptable for others, and a court may not admit evidence where there is "simply too great an analytical gap between the data and the opinion proffered."

In *Kumho Tire*, the Supreme Court made it clear that testimony based solely on the experience of an expert would not be admissible. The expert's conclusions must be based on sound scientific principles and the discipline itself must be a reliable one. The key consideration is whether the expert "employs in the courtroom the same level of intellectual rigor that characterizes the practice of an expert in the relevant field." The court emphasized that judges have considerable leeway in both how to test the reliability of evidence and determining whether such evidence is reliable . . . .

III. The Plaintiffs' Theory of Causation

Plaintiffs sought to introduce the testimony of five experts. All five possessed impressive credentials and were found to be well qualified by the district court, three over the defendants' objection . . . . Two of the experts, Doctors Kulig and Dukes, testified at the *Daubert* hearing. The experts presented a detailed argument for the cause of the plaintiffs' hemorrhagic strokes that may be summarized as follows:

1) The active ingredient in Parlodel is bromocriptine, a member of the class of drugs known as ergot alkaloids.

2) Other ergot alkaloids can cause vasoconstriction, which suggests that bromocriptine causes vasoconstriction.
3) Animal studies also suggest that bromocriptine causes vasoconstriction.
4) Vasoconstriction can cause high blood pressure and ischemic stroke (stroke caused by decreased blood flow to the brain).
5) If vasoconstriction and high blood pressure can cause ischemic stroke, it can also cause hemorrhagic stroke (stroke caused by a rupturing of a blood vessel).
6) Thus, Parlodell caused the plaintiffs' hemorrhagic strokes.

IV. The Evidence Presented

The scientific evidence presented by plaintiffs in support of their theory of causation may be grouped into six categories: 1) epidemiological studies that, on the whole, may point weakly toward causation; 2) case reports in which injuries were reported subsequent to the ingestion of Parlodel; 3) dechallenge/rechallenge tests that implied a relationship between Parlodel and stroke; 4) evidence that ergot alkaloids (a class of drug that includes bromocriptine) may cause ischemic stroke; 5) animal studies indicating that under some circumstances, bromocriptine may cause vasoconstriction in dogs and other animals; and, 6) the FDA statement withdrawing approval of Parlodel's indication for the prevention of lactation.

A. Epidemiology

Epidemiology, a field that concerns itself with finding the causal nexus between external factors and disease, is generally considered to be the best evidence of causation in toxic tort actions. Plaintiffs presented four epidemiological studies. Three of the four appear to have found no relationship or a negative relationship between Parlodel and stroke. Another may suggest a positive relationship. Nonetheless, both parties agree that none of the studies present statistically significant results and that the epidemiological evidence in this case is inconclusive . . . .

It is well-settled that while epidemiological studies may be powerful evidence of causation, the lack thereof is not fatal to a plaintiff's case . . . . This Court has long held that epidemiology is not required to prove causation in a toxic tort case. Accordingly, this case presents the difficult question of whether the evidence submitted to prove causation, in the absence of epidemiology, was sufficient to meet the requirements of *Daubert.*

B. Case Reports

Much of the plaintiffs' expert testimony relied on case reports in which patients suffered injuries subsequent to the ingestion of Parlodel. Although a court may rely on anecdotal evidence such as case reports, courts must consider that case reports are merely accounts of medical events. They reflect only reported data, not scientific methodology. Some case reports are a very basic form report of symptoms with little or no patient history, description of course of treatment, or reasoning to exclude other possible causes. The contents of these case reports were inadequate, even under the plaintiffs' expert's standards, to demonstrate a relationship between a drug and a potential side effect.

Some case reports do contain details of the treatment and differential diagnosis. Even these more detailed case reports, however, are not reliable enough, by themselves, to demonstrate the causal link the plaintiffs assert that they do because they report symptoms observed in a single patient in an uncontrolled context. They may rule out other potential causes of the effect, but they do not rule out the possibility that the effect manifested in the reported patient's case is simply idiosyncratic or the result of unknown confounding factors. As such, while they may support other proof of causation, case reports alone ordinarily cannot prove causation. The record demonstrates that the district court carefully considered the case reports and properly concluded that the case reports did not by themselves provide reliable proof of causation.

C. Dechallenge/Rechallenge Data

Plaintiffs' experts provided dechallenge/rechallenge data that they argue suggests a link between Parlodel and stroke. A test is a "dechallenge" test when a drug that is suspected of causing a certain reaction is withheld to see if the reaction dissipates. The drug may then be reintroduced in a "rechallenge" to see if the reaction reoccurs. These reports, which may be analogized to controlled studies with one subject, can be particularly useful in determining whether a causal relationship exists. Nonetheless, because none of the studies involved a patient with the particular injury suffered by the plaintiffs, they do not provide data useful in determining whether Parlodel caused the plaintiffs' injuries . . . .

[T]hese dechallenge/rechallenge reports suggest at most a possibility that Parlodel may cause localized vasoconstriction, and may suggest that it causes hypotension. They cannot be considered reliable evidence of a relationship between Parlodel and stroke because neither of them involve stroke. Moreover, dechallenge/rechallenge tests are still case reports and do not purport to offer definitive conclusions as to causation . . . .

D. Chemical Analogies

Bromocriptine is one of many drugs in a class known as ergot alkaloids. Plaintiffs sought to introduce evidence that because other ergot alkaloids cause vasoconstriction, then it is proper to conclude bromocriptine must do so as well. There is an insufficient basis in the record for this Court to hold that the district court abused its discretion by not drawing such a conclusion. Ergot alkaloids encompass a broad class of drugs with great chemical diversity, and "[e]ven minor deviations in chemical structure can radically change a particular substance's properties and propensities." The district court, after a detailed review of the properties of ergot alkaloids, concluded that plaintiffs failed to come forward with even a theory as to why the mechanism that causes some ergot alkaloids to act as vasoconstrictors would more probably than not be the same mechanism by which bromocriptine acts to cause vasoconstriction. The district court did not abuse its discretion in doing so.

E. Animal Studies

Plaintiffs offered evidence of animal studies in which bromocriptine demonstrated vasoconstrictive properties in dogs and certain other animals. Plaintiffs did not offer any animal studies that suggest that bromocriptine causes stroke, or even high blood pressure. The district court discussed each of these studies and was within its discretion in concluding that plaintiffs offered insufficient evidence on which that court could base a conclusion that the effect of bromocriptine would be the same on humans as it is on animals.

F. FDA Findings

Plaintiffs presented evidence that the FDA issued a statement withdrawing approval of Parlodel's indication for the prevention of lactation. The district court concluded that the language in the FDA statement itself undermined its reliability as proof of causation. In the statement, the FDA did not purport to have drawn a conclusion about causation. Instead, the statement merely states that possible risks outweigh the limited benefits of the drug. This risk-utility analysis involves a much lower standard than that which is demanded by a court of law. A regulatory agency such as the FDA may choose to err on the side of caution. Courts, however, are required by the *Daubert* trilogy to engage in objective review of evidence to determine whether it has sufficient scientific basis to be considered reliable. The district court did not abuse its discretion in concluding that the FDA actions do not, in this case, provide scientific proof of causation.

V. Applying the Evidence to the Plaintiffs' Theory of Causation

The deficiencies in the evidence reveal three gaps in the causal argument advanced by the plaintiffs. First, plaintiffs suggest that because bromocriptine is an ergot alkaloid, it causes vasoconstriction. Although some other ergot alkaloids do cause vasoconstriction, plaintiffs offered insufficient evidence for the district court to find that bromocriptine does so as well. This is not a case where the Court finds the evidence offered to be unreliable. In this case the record contains no evidence at all of this hypothesis. Instead, it contains principally speculation and conjecture . . . .

Second, the plaintiffs urge the Court to extrapolate the results of animal studies to humans. As with the plaintiffs' evidence of chemical properties, the district court did not err in finding no basis for doing so. Plaintiffs' experts admitted that with respect to animal studies generally, what happens in an animal would not necessarily happen in a human being. Accordingly, it is necessary for plaintiffs to offer some rationale for the suggestion that the vascular structures of humans and animals are sufficiently similar in this context to conclude that bromocriptine's effects on animals may be extrapolated to humans. Plaintiffs have not done so . . . .

Third, plaintiffs argue that because there is some evidence that bromocriptine causes ischemic stroke, it also causes hemorrhagic stroke. This is the most untenable link in the causal chain. Strokes are broadly classified into two categories: ischemic and hemorrhagic. Ischemic strokes occur as a result of lack of blood flow to the brain. Thus, although the two conditions share a name, they involve a wholly different biological mechanism. The evidence that suggests that Parlodel may cause ischemic stroke does not apply to situations involving hemorrhagic stroke. This is a "leap of faith" supported by little more than the fact that both conditions are commonly called strokes. Plaintiffs argue that as a result of the vasoconstriction caused by Parlodel, blood pressure may increase to the point that blood vessels in the brain rupture. Plaintiffs have offered no reliable evidence that Parlodel increases blood pressure to such dangerous levels. Even if they had, they failed to offer proof of how such an increase in blood pressure can precipitate a hemorrhagic stroke.

Since the shortcomings in the evidence render the theory unreliable, the district court did not abuse its discretion in excluding the plaintiffs' evidence of causation.

VI. Conclusion

In the absence of epidemiology, plaintiffs may still prove medical causation by other evidence. In the instant case, however, plaintiffs simply have not provided reliable evidence to support their conclusions. To admit the plaintiffs' evidence, the Court would have to make several scientifically unsupported "leaps of faith" in the causal chain. The *Daubert* rule requires more. Given time, information, and resources, courts may only admit the state of science as it is. Courts are cautioned not to admit speculation, conjecture, or inference that cannot be supported by sound scientific principles. "The courtroom is not the place for scientific guesswork, even of the inspired sort. Law lags science; it does not lead it." Rosen v. Ciba-Geigy Corp., 78 F.3d 316, 319 (7th Cir. 1996) . . . .

We hold that the district court did not abuse its discretion in concluding that the Plaintiffs' scientific proof of causation is legally unreliable and inadmissible under the standards set by the *Daubert* trilogy.

Affirmed.

FOOD FOR THOUGHT

Not all courts agree with the *Rider* court's analysis. *See, e.g.*, Hyman & Armstrong v. Gunderson, 279 S.W.3d 93 (Ky. 2008), in which the Supreme Court of Kentucky acknowledged that, while an epidemiological study would be the best evidence of a link between Parlodel and strokes and heart attacks, evidence of the sort introduced in *Rider* is sufficient to reach the jury. For an excellent treatment of the proper use of epidemiological evidence in proving causation, *see* King v. Burlington Northern Santa Fe Ry. Co., 762 N.W.2d 24 (Neb. 2009). More generally, courts continue to struggle with sufficiency-of-proof issues of the sort raised in *Rider*. *See, e.g.*, Wells v. SmithKline Beacham Corp., 601 F.3d 375 (5th Cir. 2010), in which the plaintiff claimed that defendant's prescription drug caused him to succumb to urges to gamble and that in the absence of warnings from the defendant, he had lost $10 million as a direct consequence. The Court of appeals affirmed summary judgment for defendant, concluding (601 F.3d at 381): "Perhaps [defendants' drug] is a cause of problem gambling, but the scientific knowledge is not yet there. [Plaintiff] urges the law to lead science—a sequence not countenanced by *Daubert*. And while the possibilities of their relationship properly spark concerns sufficient to warrant caution, the courts must await its result."

DOES DAUBERT *MASK SUBSTANTIVE ISSUES?*

Plaintiffs have found it increasingly difficult to meet the stringent requirements of *Daubert*. As a result plaintiffs cannot get their expert testimony on causation admitted into evidence. Though plaintiffs cannot establish causation, it is also often clear that the manufacturer of a drug or toxic chemical was aware of a cognizable risk associated with use of the drug or chemical that was not warned against. Professors Margaret Berger and Aaron Twerski argue that, even if causation cannot be established with the degree of clarity demanded by *Daubert*, plaintiffs have been deprived of the right to choose whether they wish to encounter an uncertain risk. Thus, for example, in the *Rider* case, given the fact that Parlodel presents a risk of stroke, the plaintiff was entitled to that information before taking a drug that was of marginal utility. When the plaintiff later suffers a stroke and the court denies her cause of action because causation evidence did not meet *Daubert* standards, the plaintiff's right to informed choice is totally negated. The Berger-Twerski thesis, entitled *Uncertainty and Informed Choice: Unmasking* Daubert, 104 Mich. L. Rev. 257 (2005), called forth a sharp rebuttal from Professor David Bernstein, *Learning the Wrong Lessons from "An American Tragedy": A Critique of the Berger-Twerski Informed Choice Proposal*, 104 Mich. L. Rev. 1961 (2006). Bernstein argues that the Berger-Twerski proposal, by eliminating the requirement that plaintiff prove causation between the toxic agent and the harm suffered, would deliver a new cause of action to an irresponsible plaintiff's bar based on a vague standard as to what qualifies to be a "material risk": deserving of an informed choice warning. Not to be outdone, Berger and Twerski respond to Bernstein in *From the Wrong End of the Telescope: A Response to Professor David Bernstein*, 104 Mich. L. Rev. 1983 (2006). They contend that the cause of action for informed choice is not open-ended and vague, and chastise Bernstein for not responding to the contention that the failure of drug and chemical companies to provide relevant risk information deprives plaintiffs of the right to informed choice as to whether they wish to play Russian roulette with their own lives. Fairness demands disclosure that the views of one of the authors of this casebook (Twerski) as set forth in the article noted above is not shared by the other coauthor (Henderson), who remains very skeptical about recognizing a causation-free informed-choice cause of action.

HAVE STATE COURTS BEEN DAUBERT*IZED?*

At last count 29 states have adopted *Daubert* and 17 have rejected *Daubert* and have declared their allegiance to the *Frye* standard. See Alice B. Lustre, *Post–Daubert*

Standards for Admissibility of Scientific and Other Expert Evidence in State Courts, 90 A.L.R.5th 453 (2001 & Supp.). It is difficult to make an exact count because some courts have not made a clear choice though their opinions appear to adopt the view that strict scrutiny will be given to expert opinions before they will be allowed into evidence. *See, e.g.*, Hallmark v. Eldridge, 189 P.3d 646, 650 (Nev. 2008) (although *Daubert* rests on an interpretation of the Federal Rules of Evidence, which do not apply directly in state courts, it provides "persuasive authority" regarding the admissibility of expert testimony). *See also* Ranes v. Adams Lab., Inc., 778 N.W.2d 677 (Iowa 2010) (implying that *Daubert* applies only in toxic-tort cases). For articles surveying the various states, *see* David E. Bernstein & Jeffrey D. Jackson, *The* Daubert *Trilogy in the States*, 44 Jurimetrics J. 351 (2004); Edward K. Cheng & Albert H. Yoon, *Does* Frye *or* Daubert *Matter? A Study of Scientific Admissibility Standard*s, 91 Va. L. Rev. 471, 473 (2005). It is interesting that Cheng and Yoon conclude that little rides on whether a state has formally adopted *Daubert*. They support their thesis by a study of the removal rates between state and federal courts. One would expect that defendants, when faced with litigating in a state that follows *Frye*, would remove to federal court in order to get the more demanding *Daubert* test. That has not happened. The reason why is not hard to discern. *Daubert* has sensitized both federal and state courts to the need to reject "junk science." Thus, as a practical matter, courts are applying heightened scrutiny to expert testimony. An interesting example of this phenomenon is Parker v. Mobil Oil Corp., 857 N.E.2d 1114 (N.Y. 2006). Plaintiff, a gas station attendant for 17 years, alleged that he contracted leukemia due to his exposure to gasoline that contains benzene and the defendant was negligent for failing to warn gas station attendants of the increased risk of contracting leukemia. The defendant challenged the admissibility of the plaintiff's expert's testimony on causation since it did not address the level of exposure necessary to draw the causal connection between benzene and leukemia. Though New York is formally a *Frye* state, the court relied on the methodology employed in *Daubert* jurisdictions and found that the expert's testimony on causation was inadmissible.

POST-DAUBERT *DEVELOPMENTS IN THE SUPREME COURT*

The U.S. Supreme Court has revisited the *Daubert* principle in several recent decisions. *See, e.g.*, General Electric Co. v. Joiner, 522 U.S. 136 (1997) (holding that a court of appeals should utilize the less demanding "abuse of discretion" standard in reviewing a trial court's decision to exclude expert testimony under *Daubert*). In Kumho Tire Co. v. Carmichael, 526 U.S. 137 (1999), the Court held that a district court correctly applied the *Daubert* standard when excluding the testimony of a witness who, based on years of experience in the tire industry, purported to be an expert in tire defects; *Daubert* applies to technical, as well as scientific, expert testimony. Because these cases do not involve the issue of actual causation, further discussion is beyond the scope of this chapter. Even with the Supreme Court's clarification and expansion of *Daubert* in *Joiner* and *Kumho Tire*, much debate and uncertainty still surrounds the issue of expert scientific and technical testimony. Literally hundreds of law review articles have been written on the subject. We note only a few of them: Jean Macchiaroli Eggen, *Clinical Medical Evidence of Causation in Toxic Tort Cases: Into the Crucible of* Daubert, 38 Hous. L. Rev. 369 (2001); Margaret A. Berger, *Upsetting the Balance Between Adverse Interests: The Impact of the Supreme Court's Trilogy on Expert Testimony in Toxic Tort Litigation*, 64 Law & Contemp. Probs. 289 (2001); *Expert Admissibility Symposium*, 34 Seton Hall L. Rev. 1 (2003).

The Restatement, Third, of Torts § 28 Comment *c* (4) (2010) has weighed in on the issue of expert scientific and technical testimony. The lengthy discussion in the comment and the accompanying Reporters' Note are well worth reading. The comment takes a position on one important issue. Some courts have held that for a plaintiff to prevail in a toxic tort case, she must establish "general causation" with proof that the toxic agent has doubled the risk. Often epidemiological studies will demonstrate an increased risk but not that the risk was doubled by exposure to the toxic agent. The Restatement position is that as long as evidence of increased risk exists, a court may utilize other evidence to prove that the plaintiff before the court suffered from exposure to the risk. For example, evidence of a differential diagnosis, such as offered by the plaintiff in *Rider*, may help a court to determine that the plaintiff in question, more probably than not, was harmed by the toxic agent.

HERSKOVITS v. GROUP HEALTH COOPERATIVE OF PUGET SOUND
664 P.2d 474 (Wash. 1983)

DORE, J.

This appeal raises the issue of whether an estate can maintain an action for professional negligence as a result of failure to timely diagnose lung cancer, where the estate can show probable reduction in statistical chance for survival but cannot show and/or prove that with timely diagnosis and treatment, decedent probably would have lived to normal life expectancy.

Both counsel advised that for the purpose of this appeal we are to assume that the respondent Group Health Cooperative of Puget Sound and its personnel negligently failed to diagnose Herskovits' cancer on his first visit to the hospital and proximately caused a 14 percent reduction in his chances of survival. It is undisputed that Herskovits had less than a 50 percent chance of survival at all times herein . . . .

The complaint alleged that Herskovits came to Group Health Hospital in 1974 with complaints of pain and coughing. In early 1974, chest X-rays revealed infiltrate in the left lung. Rales and coughing were present. In mid-1974, there were chest pains and coughing, which became persistent and chronic by fall of 1974. A December 5, 1974, entry in the medical records confirms the cough problem. Plaintiff contends that Herskovits was treated thereafter only with cough medicine. No further effort or inquiry was made by Group Health concerning his symptoms, other than an occasional chest X-ray. In the early spring of 1975, Mr. and Mrs. Herskovits went south in the hope that the warm weather would

authors' dialogue 17

AARON: Just when I'm about ready to give up on the idea that our tort system is built on a solid core of common sense, along comes a case like *Daubert* that restores my faith. The idea that scientific and technical expert testimony should meet minimum standards of integrity seem to be self-evident.

JIM: Are you jerking my chain, or what? Why should we care that much whether expert testimony rigorously comports with such standards? These aren't criminal cases, where we have a "beyond a reasonable doubt" burden of persuasion. Tort courts properly allow claims on a mere preponderance. So what if the plaintiff's expert has cooked something up for purposes of the trial? The defendant's experts will make such weaknesses clear to the jury, who will bring common sense to bear and decide the case fairly. Why should judges who have no technical training get into the business of trying to screen the purity of technical opinion evidence? I think Judge Kozinski, who wrote for the court of appeals on remand from the Supreme Court in *Daubert* (*see* p. 256, *supra*), would agree with me on this aspect. Moreover, *Daubert* puts the trial judge in a position to exclude plaintiff's only proof of causation and thus decide the case on the merits for the defendant. That doesn't seem right.

AARON: You are wrong on a couple of counts. Juries can't really make sense of conflicting expert testimony the way they can make sense in a garden-variety slip-and-fall case involving conflicting views of the reasonableness of human behavior. The flesh-and-blood reasonable person construct doesn't work so well in high-tech situations. If we let plaintiffs rely on what the Supreme Court in *Daubert* referred to as "junk science," snake oil experts-for-hire may do the jury's thinking for them. Judges are not technical experts, but they stand a better chance than jurors at separating the wheat from the chaff.

JIM: As always, there's some truth in what you say. But our civil justice system has a strong tradition of trial by jury. The *Daubert* doctrine allows judges, in effect, to throw cases out on the basis of the inadmissibility of evidence without those cases ever reaching the jury. And, according to the Supreme Court's decision in *G.E. v. Joiner* (p. 264, *supra*), these dispositive rulings are virtually unreviewable on appeal. No wonder the plaintiff's bar is up in arms over *Daubert* and its progeny.

BRAD: Here's a radical suggestion: Why don't we go back to *Frye*? If there's anyone who knows what is actually science and what is junk, it would be *scientists*. If I were a judge I'd throw up my hands after hearing the testimony of well-credentialed experts on both sides. How in the world is a judge supposed to decide when Dr. *X* says the association between a drug and some adverse reaction is scientifically well-founded while Dr. *Y* says it's all baloney?

JIM: But isn't the point that both *X* and *Y* must provide a rationale, which will be different, and triers of fact can rationally choose between them? It's not just credentials.

help. Upon his return to the Seattle area with no improvement in his health, Herskovits visited Dr. Jonathan Ostrow on a private basis for another medical opinion. Within 3 weeks, Dr. Ostrow's evaluation and direction to Group Health led to the diagnosis of cancer. In July of 1975, Herskovits' lung was removed, but no radiation or chemotherapy treatments were instituted. Herskovits died 20 months later, on March 22, 1977, at the age of 60.

At hearing on the motion for summary judgment, plaintiff was unable to produce expert testimony that the delay in diagnosis "probably" or "more likely than not" caused her husband's death. The affidavit and deposition of plaintiff's expert witness, Dr. Jonathan Ostrow, construed in the most favorable light possible to plaintiff, indicated that had the diagnosis of lung cancer been made in December 1974, the patient's possibility of 5-year survival was 39 percent. At the time of initial diagnosis of cancer 6 months later, the possibility of a 5-year survival was reduced to 25 percent. Dr. Ostrow testified he felt a diagnosis perhaps could have been made as early as December 1974, or January 1975, about 6 months before the surgery to remove Mr. Herskovits' lung in June 1975.

Dr. Ostrow testified that if the tumor was a "stage 1" tumor in December 1974, Herskovits' chance of a 5-year survival would have been 39 percent. In June 1975, his chances of survival were 25 percent assuming the tumor had progressed to "stage 2." Thus, the delay in diagnosis may have reduced the chance of a 5-year survival by 14 percent . . . .

The ultimate question raised here is whether the relationship between the increased risk of harm and Herskovits' death is sufficient to hold Group Health responsible. Is a 36 percent (from 39 percent to 25 percent) reduction in the decedent's chance for survival sufficient evidence of causation to allow the jury to consider the possibility that the physician's failure to timely diagnose the illness was the proximate cause of his death? We answer in the affirmative. To decide otherwise would be a blanket release from liability for doctors and hospitals any time there was less than a 50 percent chance of survival, regardless of how flagrant the negligence.

We are persuaded by the reasoning of the Pennsylvania Supreme Court in Hamil v. Bashline, 392 A.2d at 1280 [Pa. 1978]. While *Hamil* involved an original survival chance of greater than 50 percent, we find the rationale used by the *Hamil* court to apply equally to cases such as the present one, where the original survival chance is less than 50 percent. The plaintiff's decedent was suffering from severe chest pains. His wife transported him to the hospital where he was negligently treated in the emergency unit. The wife, because of the lack of help, took her husband to a private physician's office, where he died. In an action brought under the wrongful death and survivorship statutes, the main medical witness testified that if the hospital had employed proper treatment, the decedent would have had a substantial chance of surviving the attack. The medical expert expressed his opinion in terms of a 75 percent chance of survival. It was also the doctor's opinion that the substantial loss of a chance of recovery was the result of the defendant hospital's failure to provide prompt treatment. The defendant's expert witness testified that the patient would have died regardless of any treatment provided by the defendant hospital . . . .

The *Hamil* court held that once a plaintiff has demonstrated that the defendant's acts or omissions have increased the risk of harm to another, such evidence furnishes a basis for the jury to make a determination as to whether such increased risk was in turn a substantial factor in bringing about the resultant harm . . . .

Where percentage probabilities and decreased probabilities are submitted into evidence, there is simply no danger of speculation on the part of the jury. More speculation is involved in requiring the medical expert to testify as to what would have happened had the defendant not been negligent . . . .

Causing reduction of the opportunity to recover (loss of chance) by one's negligence, however, does not necessitate a total recovery against the negligent party for all damages caused by the victim's death. Damages should be awarded to the injured party or his family based only on damages caused directly by premature death, such as lost earnings and additional medical expenses, etc.

We reverse the trial court and reinstate the cause of action.

ROSELLINI, J., concurs.

PEARSON, J. (concurring)

I agree with the majority that the trial court erred in granting defendant's motion for summary judgment. I cannot, however, agree with the majority's reasoning in reaching this decision . . . .

[A]lthough the issue before us is primarily one of causation, resolution of that issue requires us to identify the nature of the injury to the decedent. Our conception of the injury will substantially affect our analysis. If the injury is determined to be the death of Mr. Herskovits, then under the established principles of proximate cause plaintiff has failed to make a prima facie case. Dr. Ostrow was unable to state that probably, or more likely than not, Mr. Herskovits' death was caused by defendant's negligence. On the contrary, it is clear from Dr. Ostrow's testimony that Mr. Herskovits would have probably died from cancer even with the exercise of reasonable care by defendant. Accordingly, if we perceive the death of Mr. Herskovits as the injury in this case, we must affirm the trial court, unless we determine that it is proper to depart substantially from the traditional requirements of establishing proximate cause in this type of case.

If, on the other hand, we view the injury to be the reduction of Mr. Herskovits' chance of survival, our analysis might well be different. Dr. Ostrow testified that the failure to diagnose cancer in December 1974 probably caused a substantial reduction in Mr. Herskovits' chance of survival . . . .

I am persuaded . . . by the thoughtful discussion of a recent commentator. King, *Causation, Valuation, and Chance in Personal Injury Torts Involving Preexisting Conditions and Future Consequences*, 90 Yale L.J. 1353 (1981).

King's basic thesis is explained in the following passage, which is particularly pertinent to the case before us:

> Causation has for the most part been treated as an all-or-nothing proposition. Either a loss was caused by the defendant or it was not . . . . A plaintiff ordinarily should be required to prove by the applicable standard of proof that the defendant caused the loss in question. What caused a loss, however, should be a separate

question from what the nature and extent of the loss are. This distinction seems to have eluded the courts, with the result that lost chances in many respects are compensated either as certainties or not at all.

To illustrate, consider the case in which a doctor negligently fails to diagnose a patient's cancerous condition until it has become inoperable. Assume further that even with a timely diagnosis the patient would have had only a 30% chance of recovering from the disease and surviving over the long term. There are two ways of handling such a case. Under the traditional approach, this loss of a not-better-than-even chance of recovering from the cancer would not be compensable because it did not appear more likely [than] not that the patient would have survived with proper care. Recoverable damages, if any, would depend on the extent to which it appeared that cancer killed the patient sooner than it would have with timely diagnosis and treatment, and on the extent to which the delay in diagnosis aggravated the patient's condition, such as by causing additional pain. A more rational approach, however, would allow recovery for the loss of the chance of cure even though the chance was not better than even. The probability of long-term survival would be reflected in the amount of damages awarded for the loss of the chance. While the plaintiff here could not prove by a preponderance of the evidence that he was denied a cure by the defendant's negligence, he could show by a preponderance that he was deprived of a 30% chance of a cure. 90 Yale L.J. at 1363-64.

. . . These reasons persuade me that the best resolution of the issue before us is to recognize the loss of a less than even chance as an actionable injury. Therefore, I would hold that plaintiff has established a prima facie issue of proximate cause by producing testimony that defendant probably caused a substantial reduction in Mr. Herskovits' chance of survival . . . .

Finally, it is necessary to consider the amount of damages recoverable in the event that a loss of a chance of recovery is established. Once again, King's discussion provides a useful illustration of the principles which should be applied.

To illustrate, consider a patient who suffers a heart attack and dies as a result. Assume that the defendant physician negligently misdiagnosed the patient's condition, but that the patient would have had only a 40 percent chance of survival even with a timely diagnosis and proper care. Regardless of whether it could be said that the defendant caused the decedent's death, he caused the loss of a chance, and that chance-interest should be completely redressed in its own right. Under the proposed rule, the plaintiff's compensation for the loss of the victim's chance of surviving the heart attack would be 40 percent of the compensable value of the victim's life had he survived (including what his earning capacity would otherwise have been in the years following death) . . . . 90 Yale L.J. at 1382.

I would remand to the trial court for proceedings consistent with this opinion.

WILLIAMS, C.J., and STAFFORD and UTTER, JJ., concur with PEARSON, J.

THE AFTERMATH OF HERSKOVITS

Since *Herskovits*, many jurisdictions have considered cases dealing with loss-of-chance or increased risk of harm. *See, e.g.*, Matsuyama v. Birnbaum, 890 N.E.2d

819, 829 n.23 (Mass. 2008) (cites "at least twenty States and District of Columbia" that have adopted the loss of chance doctrine). For a discussion of *Matsuyama* and other recent case law, *see* Tory A. Weigand, *Lost Chances, Felt Necessities, and the Tale of Two Cities*, 43 Suffolk U. L. Rev. 327 (2010). As the opinions in *Herskovits* suggest, the decisions have generally fallen into two main categories. The minority of courts refuse to allow recovery for loss-of-chance unless the plaintiff can establish causation under the traditional negligence standard. In these cases, the plaintiff must show that the defendant's failure to diagnose or treat the plaintiff did, more likely than not, cause the plaintiff's harm. *See, e.g.*, Estate of Sanders v. U.S., 736 F.3d 430, 436-437 (5th Cir. 2013) (applying Mississippi law in Federal Tort Claims Act case) (plaintiff must present evidence that proper treatment would lead to "a greater than fifty (50) percent chance of a better result than was in fact obtained"); United States v. Cumberbatch, 647 A.2d 1098 (Del. 1994) (refusing to recognize loss-of-chance recovery in a wrongful death action); Manning v. Twin Falls Clinic & Hospital, Inc., 830 P.2d 1185 (Idaho 1992) (rejecting explicitly the doctrines of lost chance and increased risk of harm); Fennell v. Southern Maryland Hospital Center Inc., 580 A.2d 206, 214 (Md. 1990) (declining to recognize either a pure loss-of-chance doctrine or a loss-of-chance approach to damages); Fabio v. Bellomo, 504 N.W.2d 758 (Minn. 1993) (declining to recognize a loss-of-chance cause of action in a medical malpractice case); Jones v. Owings, 456 S.E.2d 371 (S.C. 1995) (refusing to allow recovery for loss-of-chance); Volz v. Ledes, 895 S.W.2d 677 (Tenn. 1995) (unwilling to recognize a new cause of action for loss-of-chance); Kramer v. Lewisville Memorial Hospital, 858 S.W.2d 397, 400 (Tex. 1993) (holding that "where preexisting illnesses or injuries have made a patient's chance of avoiding the ultimate harm improbable" — 50 percent or less — recovery is totally barred).

A majority of jurisdictions allow loss-of-chance claims to reach the jury even when the plaintiff cannot prove that the defendant was, more likely than not, the cause of plaintiff's harm. For example, in McKellips v. St. Francis Hospital Inc., 741 P.2d 467 (Okla. 1987), the Supreme Court of Oklahoma lowered the standard for proof of causation to less than 50 percent. In that case, plaintiff's expert testified that if the plaintiff's decedent had received proper care, his chances of survival would have significantly improved, even though he may well have died regardless of the treatment given. The court held that it would be for a jury to decide whether the increase in risk due to the defendant's negligent failure to provide reasonable care was a "substantial factor" in causing the harm.

Similarly, in Gardner v. Pawliw, 696 A.2d 599 (N.J. 1997), the Supreme Court of New Jersey held that the plaintiff need only show on credible medical testimony that the defendant's conduct increased the risk of harm in order to reach the jury. When her nearly full-term fetus died in utero, Gardner and her husband alleged that her doctor, Pawliw, had negligently failed to perform certain diagnostic tests, and that his failure resulted in the death of her fetus from a preexisting condition. She claimed the increased risk from failing to perform the tests was a substantial factor in her fetus's death. The plaintiff's expert testified that, while he could not say with certainty what the outcome of the tests would have been, he believed that, if the tests had been performed, the abnormalities that resulted in the death of the fetus would have been discovered and the baby could have been delivered safely. At the close of the evidence, the trial court granted the defendant's motion for judgment as a matter of law on the grounds that the plaintiffs failed to prove the necessary causal relationship between the failure to perform the tests and the fetus's death. The Appellate Division affirmed, agreeing that causation had not been shown. In overturning the courts below, the Supreme Court of New Jersey, while admitting that "it is often a pretty speculative matter whether the precaution would in fact have saved the victim," held that as long as medical evidence shows that "the failure to test increased the risk of harm, the significance of that increased risk should be determined by the jury." *Id.* at 612, 614. In remanding the case for trial, the jury was to determine "whether the deviation [by the doctor], in the context of the preexistent condition, was sufficiently significant in relation to the eventual harm" to meet the causal requirement. *Id.* at 615. The court further noted that a plaintiff could show an increased risk of harm "even if such tests are helpful in a small proportion of cases." *Id.*

Legislatures in some states have eliminated or restricted the availability of loss-of-chance recovery. *See, e.g.,* S.D.C.L. § 20-9-1.1 (2002) (abrogating state high court decision adopting loss-of-chance rule); W. Va. Code § 55-7B-3 (2003) (plaintiff must prove, to a reasonable degree of medical probability, that following the accepted standard of care would have resulted in a greater than 25 percent chance that the patient would have had an improved recovery or would have survived).

SUBSTANTIALITY OF THE PLAINTIFF'S LOST OPPORTUNITY

Some courts, like *McKellips* and *Gardner*, that allow loss-of-chance cases to go to the jury on less than the traditional "more likely than not" standard, restrict recovery to cases where the lost opportunity is "substantial." *See, e.g., McKellips, supra; Gardner, supra;* Delaney v. Cade, 873 P.2d 175 (Kan. 1994); Perez v. Las Vegas Medical Center, 805 P.2d 589 (Nev. 1991); Falcon v. Memorial Hospital, 462 N.W.2d 44 (Mich. 1990) (Michigan subsequently enacted legislation that prohibits recovery unless the lost opportunity is greater than 50 percent). Other courts forgo such a requirement. *See, e.g.,* Thompson v. Sun City Community Hospital, Inc., 688 P.2d 605 (Ariz. 1984); Hastings v. Baton Rouge General Hospital, 498 So. 2d 713 (La. 1986); Aasheim v. Humberger, 695 P.2d 824 (Mont. 1985); Ehlinger v. Sipes, 454 N.W.2d 754 (Wis. 1990). Some commentators suggest that a possible explanation for the difference is that the courts imposing the requirement "are concerned that small reductions of chance are not reliable enough to impose liability for damages." Aaron D. Twerski & Neil B. Cohen, *The Second Revolution in Informed Consent: Comparing Physicians to Each Other,* 94 Nw. U. L. Rev. 1, 21 (1999).

WHAT HARM DID THE PLAINTIFF SUFFER?

Another difference among the courts is the way they conceptualize the harm for which the plaintiffs seek to recover. Some view the harm as the resulting disability or death, while others, like Justice Pearson's concurrence in *Herskovits*, view the chance itself as a valuable interest and allow recovery for its loss. One article that has been instrumental in guiding courts on this topic is Joseph H. King, Jr., *Causation, Valuation, and Chance in Personal Injury Torts Involving Preexisting Conditions and Future Consequences*, 90 Yale L.J. 1353 (1981), cited by Justice Pearson in *Herskovits*. If causation is proved, courts that follow the traditional conception of the death or injury as the harm typically leave the jury free to determine the recovery amount, allowing either full compensation or a lesser amount to be awarded at their discretion. Other courts that recognize the chance itself as the loss provide a percentage-based formula for the jury to use in calculating damages. *See, e.g.*, Mays v. United States, 608 F. Supp. 1476 (D. Colo. 1985); DeBurkarte v. Louvar, 393 N.W.2d 131 (Iowa 1986); Delaney v. Cade, 873 P.2d 175 (Kan. 1994); Wollen v. DePaul Health Center, 828 S.W.2d 681 (Mo. 1992); Perez v. Las Vegas Medical Center, 805 P.2d 589 (Nev. 1991); Scafidi v. Seiler, 574 A.2d 398 (N.J. 1990); Roberts v. Ohio Permanente Medical Group, Inc., 668 N.E.2d 480 (Ohio 1996); McMackin v. Johnson Country Healthcare Center, 73 P.3d 1094 (Wyo. 2003). *See also* Joseph H. King, *"Reduction of Likelihood" Reformulation and Other Retrofitting of the Loss-of-a-Chance Doctrine*, 28 U. Mem. L. Rev. 492 (1998).

A common method for assessing loss-of-chance damages is to multiply the full damages that the plaintiff suffered by the percentage of the patient's chance of survival that was lost. For example, if a patient would have had a 70 percent chance of survival but dies as a result of the negligence of his physician, and the full recovery for the death would have been $100,000, the physician is responsible for 70 percent of the total, or $70,000. For a probing analysis of the errors courts have made in deciding the percentage reduction based on loss of chance, *see* Lars Noah, *An Inventory of Mathematical Blunders in Applying the Loss-of-a-Chance Doctrine*, 24 Rev. Litig. 369 (2005). Professor Noah concludes that "[i]f courts routinely misapply the mathematical concepts that arise in loss-of-a-chance claims, then we may have to question the theory's practical utility." *Id.* at 403. *Also see* Martin J. McMahon, *Medical Malpractice: Measure and Elements of Damages in Actions Based on Loss of Chance*, 81 A.L.R. 4th 485 (2007).

For all the hoopla about lost-chance recovery, it has not been expanded beyond medical malpractice. Restatement, Third, of Torts § 26, Comment *n* explains:

> . . . The lost-opportunity development has been halting, as courts have sought to find appropriate limits for this reconceptualization of legally cognizable harm. Without limits, this reform is of potentially enormous scope, implicating a large swath of tortious conduct in which there is uncertainty about factual cause, including failures to warn, provide rescue or safety equipment, and otherwise take precautions to protect a person from a risk of harm that exists. To date, the courts that have accepted lost opportunity as cognizable harm have almost universally limited its recognition to medical-malpractice cases. Three features of that context are significant: 1) a contractual relationship exists between patient and physician (or physician's employer), in which the raison d'être of the contract is that the physician will take every reasonable measure to obtain an optimal outcome for the patient; 2) reasonably good empirical evidence is often available about the general statistical probability of the lost opportunity; and 3) frequently

the consequences of the physician's negligence will deprive that patient of a less-than-50-percent chance for recovery. Whether there are appropriate areas beyond the medical-malpractice area to which lost opportunity might appropriately be extended is a matter that the Institute leaves to future development . . . .

C. WHEN TWO (OR MORE) NEGLIGENT ACTORS CONCURRENTLY (OR SUCCESSIVELY) CAUSE THE PLAINTIFF'S HARM

HILL v. EDMONDS
270 N.Y.S.2d 1020 (N.Y. App. Div. 1966)

CHRIST, Acting P.J., BRENNAN, HILL, RABIN and HOPKINS, JJ., concur.

In a negligence action to recover damages for personal injury, plaintiff appeals from a judgment of the Supreme Court, Queens County, entered June 21, 1965, which dismissed the complaint as against defendant Bragoli upon the court's decision at the close of plaintiff's case upon a jury trial.

Judgment reversed, on the law, and new trial granted, with costs to appellant to abide the event. No questions of fact have been considered. At the close of plaintiff's case the court dismissed the complaint against the owner of a tractor truck who on a stormy night left it parked without lights in the middle of a road where the car in which plaintiff was a passenger collided with it from the rear. From the testimony of the driver of the car the court concluded that she was guilty of negligence and was solely responsible for the collision. That testimony was that she saw the truck when it was four car lengths ahead of her and that she saw it in enough time to turn. At other points, however, she indicated that she did not know just what happened, that she swerved to avoid the truck, "and the next thing I knew I woke up. I was unconscious." Assuming, arguendo, that she was negligent, the accident could not have happened had not the truck owner allowed his unlighted vehicle to stand in the middle of the highway. Where separate acts of negligence combine to produce directly a single injury each tort-feasor is responsible for the entire result, even though his act alone might not have caused it. Accordingly, the complaint against the truck owner must be reinstated and a new trial had.

INDIVISIBLE HARM

Hill presents the phenomenon of indivisible harm. In *Hill*, the indivisibility arose from the circumstance that the negligent conduct of either defendant would not, without the other, have caused the accident in which plaintiff suffered harm. Another example will help clarify the concept. Suppose that two hunters acting independently of one another (not in concert) negligently fire their shotguns in the direction of the plaintiff. A pellet identified as coming from the first hunter's gun destroys the plaintiff's left eye; and a pellet from the second hunter's gun destroys plaintiff's right eye. Each shooter is individually liable for the harm to the eye he happened to hit. (Their liabilities might be different in magnitude — the medical expenses in connection with the left eye might be much greater than with the right eye.) But the two hunters will be jointly and severally liable for the plaintiff's total blindness, which is an indivisible consequence of their independent negligent acts. Neither hunter's act would have sufficed to cause the total blindness; but together, they totally blinded the plaintiff.

Observe that in *Hill* and the two-hunter hypothetical the negligent acts of the two defendants occurred more or less simultaneously. (In *Hill*, the truck driver's negligence began earlier but continued — he owed a continuing duty to remove the truck — until the time of the accident.) What if the negligence of two defendants is separated in time, with both being necessary conditions for the plaintiff's ultimate injury? For example, what if one doctor administers a dangerous dose of sodium to the plaintiff before she enters the hospital, and a second doctor administers another dangerous dose after hospitalization, and the two doses combine to cause permanent neurologic injury? *See* Robinson v. Oklahoma Nephrology Associates, Inc., 154 P.3d 1250 (Okla. 2007).

The classic version of the case of separate actions of multiple defendants occurring at different points in time, leading to indivisible harm, is an accident caused by the negligence of Defendant #1, with the plaintiff then being further injured by negligent medical treatment provided by Defendant #2. It is well settled that Defendant #1 will be liable for all of the consequences of his or her initial negligent act, including Defendant #2's subsequent medical malpractice. *See, e.g.,* Dacosta v. Gibbs, 33 N.Y.S.3d 160 (App. Div. 2016); Thompson v. Cooper, 290 P.3d 393 (Alaska 2012); Infectious Disease of Indianapolis, P.S.C. v. Toney, 813 N.E.2d 1223 (Ind. Ct. App. 2004). The two defendants, though acting separately, are jointly liable for the full extent of the plaintiff's injuries. *See* Restatement (Third) of Torts: Liability for Physical and Emotional Harm § 35 (2012). The Third Restatement includes this principle in its section on proximate causation, which will be considered in the next chapter. To foreshadow that analysis, the idea is that subsequent medical negligence is foreseeable from Defendant #1's point of view; thus, Defendant #1 is liable for the foreseeable consequences of his or her negligence, including Defendant #2's negligence.

If however, the defendant can establish the amount of the damages caused by his malpractice he is only liable for that amount. Defendant #1 is liable for all foreseeable harm for which he is the but-for harm (including the malpractice). Defendant #2 is only liable for his add-on if he can establish the amount of his add-on. If he can't, the harm is indivisible and both defendants are liable for the entire amount.

Palay v. United States, 349 F.3d 418 (7th Cir. 2003), presents an interesting application of the successive-tortfeasor rule. A prisoner filed an action under the Federal Tort Claims Act (FTCA), 28 U.S.C. § 1346(b)(1), alleging that officials at a federal prison had negligently assigned him to a unit housing known members of rival gangs. The plaintiff was injured in a gang fight, and the Bureau allegedly provided negligent medical treatment. A prerequisite for bringing suit against the United States under the FTCA is exhaustion of administrative remedies — the plaintiff must first present his claim to the appropriate federal agency. 28 U.S.C. § 2675(a). The plaintiff had presented his negligent-assignment claim to the Bureau of Prisons, but he did not present his medical malpractice claim. Relying on the principle that "the original tortfeasor is responsible not only for the injury directly resulting from the tort but also for aggravation of that injury caused by negligence in the medical treatment occasioned by the injury," the court permitted the prisoner to seek relief from the Bureau of Prisons for the full amount of his harm, including those caused by medical malpractice. 349 F.3d at 427.

Although the Bureau of Prisons is formally one entity, the court did not require the plaintiff to allege that somehow the Bureau officials in charge of assignment, who should have known about the presence of rival gang members, had somehow colluded with the medical personnel employed by the Bureau who provided substandard treatment. The indivisible-injury rule is thus distinct from a different principle of joint and several liability, that of concerted action.

CONCERTED ACTION

HERMAN v. WESGATE
464 N.Y.S.2d 315 (N.Y. App. Div. 1983)

Plaintiff was injured while a guest at a stag party to celebrate the impending marriage of defendant Thomas Hauck. The party was held onboard a barge owned by defendants Donald Wesgate and Thomas Rouse. Following a three-hour cruise, the barge was anchored near the shoreline of Irondequoit Bay. The depth of the water off the bow of the barge was approximately two feet. Several guests began "skinny dipping" and, within a brief period of time, some in the party began to throw others still clothed off the bow into the water. Two or more individuals escorted plaintiff to the bow of the barge where, unwillingly, he went overboard. Trauma to his head or neck resulted in injury to his spinal cord. . . .

It was improper to grant the motions of defendants John Hauck and James Hauck. Plaintiff's complaint alleges concerted action by all of the defendants.

"Concerted action liability rests upon the principle that '[a]ll those who, in pursuance of a common plan or design to commit a tortious act, actively take part in it, or further it by cooperation or request, or who lend aid or encouragement to the wrongdoer, or ratify and adopt his acts done for their benefit, are equally liable with him'" (Prosser, Torts [4th ed], § 46, at p. 292; see, also, Restatement, Torts 2d, § 876). An injured plaintiff may pursue any one joint tort-feasor or a concerted action theory (see, Graphic Arts Mut. Ins. Co. v. Bakers Mut. Ins. Co. of N.Y., 382 N.E.2d 1347). . . .

Here, the conduct of the defendants alleged to be dangerous and tortious is the pushing or throwing of guests, against their will, from the barge into the water. Liability of an individual defendant will not depend upon whether he actually propelled plaintiff into the water; participation in the concerted activity is equivalent to participation in the accident resulting in the injury. . . .

Whether codefendants acted in concert is generally a question for the jury (DeCarvalho v. Brunner, . . . 119 N.E. 563). The complaint states a cause of action against each of the defendants and the record presents questions of fact as to whether defendants John Hauck and James Hauck acted in concert with the other defendants. Thus summary judgment should not have been granted . . .).

FOOD FOR THOUGHT

Restatement (Third) of Torts: Apportionment of Liability § 15, sets out the rule regarding joint and several liability for persona acting in concert:

> When persons are liable because they acted in concert, all persons are jointly and severally liable for the share of comparative responsibility assigned to each person engaged in concerted activity.

Naturally this summary prompts the question, "when will persons be liable because they acted in concert?" The Third Restatement actually has relatively little to say about this issue, so let's look at the comments to Section 876 of the Second Restatement:

> *a.* Parties are acting in concert when they act in accordance with an agreement to cooperate in a particular line of conduct or to accomplish a particular result. The agreement need not be expressed in words and may be implied and understood to exist from the conduct itself. Whenever two or more persons commit tortious acts in concert, each becomes subject to liability for the acts of the others, as well as for his own acts. The theory of the early common law was that there was a mutual agency of each to act for the others, which made all liable for the tortious acts of any one.
> Illustration. . . .
> 2. A and B are driving automobiles on the public highway. A attempts to pass B. B speeds up his car to prevent A from passing. A continues in his attempt and the result is a race for a mile down the highway, with the two cars abreast and both traveling at dangerous speed. At the end of the mile, A's car collides with a car driven by C and C suffers harm. Both A and B are subject to liability to C. . . .
> *d.* Advice or encouragement to act operates as a moral support to a tortfeasor and if the act encouraged is known to be tortious it has the same effect upon the liability of the adviser as participation or physical assistance. If the encouragement or assistance is a substantial factor in causing the resulting tort, the one giving it is himself a tortfeasor and is responsible for the consequences of the other's act. This is true both when the act done is an intended trespass . . . and when it is merely a negligent act. . . . The rule applies whether or not the other knows his act is tortious. . . . It likewise applies to a person who knowingly gives substantial aid to another who, as he knows, intends to do a tortious act.
> The assistance of or participation by the defendant may be so slight that he is not liable for the act of the other. In determining this, the nature of the

act encouraged, the amount of assistance given by the defendant, his presence or absence at the time of the tort, his relation to the other and his state of mind are all considered. . . .

Illustrations: . . .

9. A is employed by B to carry messages to B's workmen. B directs A to tell B's workmen to tear down a fence that B believes to be on his own land but that in fact, as A knows, is on the land of C. A delivers the message and the workmen tear down the fence. Since A was a servant used merely as a means of communication, his assistance is so slight that he is not liable to C. . . .

11. A supplies B with wire cutters to enable B to enter the land of C to recapture chattels belonging to B, who, as A knows, is not privileged to do this. In the course of the trespass upon C's land, B intentionally sets fire to C's house. A is not liable for the destruction of the house. . . .

Utilizing the criteria set forth in the Second Restatement, consider whether the defendant in *Herman, supra,* would be held to be a co-conspirator under the following circumstances:

1) The defendant is the owner of the barge and while sitting in his quarters is told of the wild activity on the deck and says nothing.
2) Same case, but he remarks, "Well, let them have a good time."
3) Same case, but he sends a message to those on deck: "Let them have a good time, but don't throw Herman (the plaintiff) overboard, he's a frightened chicken."

Who decides — judge or jury?

In *Podias v. Mairs,* 926 A.2d 859 (N.J. Super. Ct. App. Div. 2007), the court struggled with the issue of whether the assistance of a defendant in a tortious act was substantial. Michael Mairs, driving while intoxicated, struck a motorcycle driven by Antonios Podias. Andrew Swanson, Jr., and Kyle Newell were passengers in Mairs' car. Mairs, Swanson, and Newell decided to leave the scene of the accident, and none of them called for assistance to come to the aid of Podias, who was lying on the road seriously injured. After they left the scene of the accident, another car ran over Podias, who later died as a result of the two accidents. The court held that, even though the passengers did not cause the accident, they had an affirmative duty to come to the assistance of Podias. *See* Chapter 6. The court then held that, even absent a duty to come to the aid of Podias, under the theory of concerted action a jury could conclude that the defendants, Swanson and Newell, assisted Mairs (the driver) in his breach of a direct duty to Podias. The court reasoned that even if they had no independent duty to take affirmative action to rescue Podias, they should not have prevented Mairs from exercising his duty of care to come to the aid of Podias:

Vicarious liability does not have to be based on *acts* of assistance but may rest on inaction . . . or on words of encouragement. . . . "Advice or encouragement to act operates as a moral support to a tortfeasor and if the act encouraged is known to be tortious, it has the same effect upon the liability of the adviser as participation or physical assistance." 1979 *Restatement, supra,* §876(b), comment *d.* Thus, suggestive words that plant the seeds of or fuel negligent action may be enough to create joint liability. In *Rael v. Cadena*, . . . 604 P.2d 822 (N.M. App. 1979), the defendant had given verbal encouragement ("Kill him!" and "Hit him more!") to an assailant. The defendant had not physically assisted in the battery. The court explained that liability did not require a finding of action in concert, nor even that the injury had directly resulted from the encouragement. Instead, it found, citing 1979 *Restatement* § 876(b), that the fact of encouragement was enough to create joint liability for the battery. Mere presence at the scene, it noted, would not be sufficient for liability.

As to the case at hand, the court held:

> [A] jury may reasonably find defendants' assistance was "substantial." Whether the principle wrongdoer was either impaired or entirely coherent, it is reasonable to infer that at the very least, defendants collaborated in, verbally supported, or approved his decision to leave the scene, and at most, actively convinced Mairs to flee as a means of not getting caught. . . . The entire aftermath of the incident betrays an orchestrated scheme among the three to avoid detection not only by taking no action to prevent further harm to the victim, but by affirmatively abandoning the scene, particularly guaranteeing his death. . . . [A] jury could reasonably find on the evidence defendants' assistance substantial enough to justify civil liability vicariously, on an aiding and abetting theory.

JOINT AND SEVERAL LIABILITY

In *Hill* and *Herman*, the focus was on the responsibility of another party — the negligent truck owner in *Hill* and guests at the party in *Herman* who provided encouragement — for harm to the plaintiff that was caused by someone else — the negligent driver of the car in *Hill* and the guests who actually threw the plaintiff into the water in *Herman*. Might the plaintiff have joined both parties in a single action? The short answer is "Yes — they are jointly and severally liable to the plaintiff." However, one cannot fully appreciate the material in this section and the next without first understanding the legal concepts of joint and several liability and their legal consequences. The consequences that flow from joint and several liability are easily described. Defendants who are jointly liable can be joined in a single action, although a plaintiff is not required to join them. Defendants who are severally liable are each liable in full for the plaintiff's damages, although the plaintiff is entitled to only one total recovery.

When does joint and several liability arise? At common law, two circumstances in which two or more actors acted tortiously toward their victim gave rise to what is now referred to as joint and several liability. The first is the scenario from *Hill*, where they acted independently but caused indivisible harm; the second is, as in *Herman*, where they acted in concert. Liability for concerted action is vicarious liability, in which all the negligent actors will be responsible for the harm actually caused by only one of them. The Second Restatement gives the standard example of concerted action as the case of two persons engaging in an automobile race on a public street and one of them negligently runs over the plaintiff. The one who did not run over the plaintiff will be just as liable as the one who did, although the former did not actually hit the plaintiff. Joint and several liability will also be imposed if two negligent actors act independently, each causing harm to the plaintiff, but where it is impossible to allocate the harm to either defendant's conduct. Thus, as in *Hill*, if the plaintiff was a passenger in one person's automobile, which collided with another driver's automobile due to the fault of both drivers, both would be jointly and severally liable for the harm to the plaintiff. This is, of course, the "indivisible harm" situation presented in *Hill v. Edmonds* and the text immediately following that case.

At common law, if the plaintiff sued just one of the joint tortfeasors and recovered, that defendant could not compel other tortfeasors to share the burden of liability. The harshness of this earlier rule has been substantially ameliorated since most states now provide for contribution among joint tortfeasors, either by statute or judicial decision.

The next case differs from the first two categories in which multiple defendants may be held jointly and severally liable. See if you can see why.

KINGSTON v. CHICAGO & N.W. RY.
211 N.W. 913 (Wis. 1927)

Owen, J.

... We ... have this situation: [A] fire [to the northeast of the plaintiff's property] was set by sparks emitted from defendant's locomotive. This fire, according to the finding of the jury, constituted a proximate cause of the destruction of plaintiff's property. This finding we find to be well supported by the evidence. We have the northwest fire, of unknown origin. This fire, according to the finding of the jury, also constituted a proximate cause of the destruction of the plaintiff's property. This finding we also find to be well supported by the evidence. We have a union of these two fires 940 feet north of plaintiff's property, from which point the united fire bore down upon and destroyed the property. We, therefore, have two separate, independent, and distinct agencies, each of which constituted the proximate cause of plaintiff's damage, and either of which, in the absence of the other, would have accomplished such result. [Judgment for plaintiff was entered on the jury's findings.]

It is settled in the law of negligence that any one of two or more joint tortfeasors, or one of two or more wrongdoers whose concurring acts of negligence result in injury, are each individually responsible for the entire damage resulting from their joint or concurrent acts of negligence. ...

From our present consideration of the subject, we are not disposed to criticize the doctrine which exempts from liability a wrongdoer who sets a fire which unites with a fire originating from natural causes, such as lightning, not attributable to any human agency, resulting in damage. It is also conceivable that a fire so set might unite with a fire of so much greater proportions, such as a raging forest fire, so as to be enveloped or swallowed up by the greater holocaust and its identity destroyed, so that the greater fire could be said to be an intervening or superseding cause. But we have no such situation here. These fires were of comparatively equal rank. If there was any difference in their magnitude or threatening aspect the record indicates that the northeast fire was the larger fire and was really regarded as the menacing agency. At any rate, there is no intimation or suggestion that the northeast fire was enveloped and swallowed up by the northwest fire. We will err on the side of the defendant if we regard the two fires as of equal rank.

According to well-settled principles of negligence, it is undoubted that, if the proof disclosed the origin of the northwest fire, even though its origin be attributed to a third person, the railroad company, as the originator of the northwest fire, would be liable for the entire damage. There is no reason to believe that the northwest fire originated from any other than human agency. It was a small fire. It had traveled over a limited area. It had been in existence but for a day. For a time it was thought to have been extinguished. It was not in the nature of a raging forest fire. The record discloses nothing of natural phenomena which could have given rise to the fire. It is morally certain that it was set by some human agency.

Now the question is whether the railroad company, which is found to have been responsible for the origin of the northeast fire, escapes liability, because the origin of the northwest fire is not identified, although there is no reason to believe that it had any other than human origin. An affirmative answer to that question would certainly make a wrongdoer a favorite of the law at the expense of an innocent sufferer. The injustice of such a doctrine sufficiently impeaches the logic upon which it is founded. Where one who has suffered damage by fire proves the origin of a fire and the course of that fire up to the point of the destruction of his property, one has certainly established liability on the part of the originator of the fire. Granting that the union of that fire with another of natural origin, or with another of much greater proportions, is available as a defense the burden is on the defendant to show that, by reason of such union with a fire of such character, the fire set by him was not the proximate cause of the damage. No principle of justice requires that the plaintiff be placed under the burden of specifically identifying the origin of both fires in order to recover the damages for which either or both fires are responsible . . . .

There being no attempt on the part of the defendant to prove that the northwest fire was due to an irresponsible origin — that is, an origin not attributable to a human being — and the evidence in the case affording no reason to believe that it had an origin not attributable to a human being, and it appearing that the northeast fire, for the origin of which the defendant is responsible, was a proximate cause of plaintiff's loss the defendant is responsible for the entire amount of that loss. While under some circumstances a wrongdoer is not responsible for damage which would have occurred in the absence of his wrongful act, even though such wrongful act was a proximate cause of the accident, that doctrine does not obtain "where two causes, each attributable to the negligence of a responsible person, concur in producing an injury to another, either of which causes would produce it regardless of the other." This is because "it is impossible to apportion the damages or to say that either perpetrated any distinct injury that can be separated from the whole," and to permit each of two wrongdoers to plead the wrong of the other as a defense to his own wrongdoing, would permit both wrongdoers to escape and penalize the innocent party who has been damaged by their wrongful acts.

The fact that the northeast fire was set by the railroad company, which fire was a proximate cause of plaintiff's damage, is sufficient to affirm the judgment [for the plaintiff]. This conclusion renders it unnecessary to consider other grounds of liability stressed in respondent's brief.

Judgment affirmed.

INDIVISIBLE HARM REVISITED: GOOD-BYE TO SUBSTANTIAL FACTOR

The Restatement, Second, of Torts § 431 (1965) took the position that an "actor's negligent conduct is a legal cause of harm to another if . . . his conduct is a substantial factor in bringing about the harm." The Restatement used the term "substantial factor" to allow for recovery in the two-fire cases. If the court strictly adhered to the "but-for" test in the case of two potential tortfeasors who negligently started fires, each of sufficient strength to burn the plaintiff's property, both would be absolved from liability. As noted earlier, the Restatement, Third, of Torts in § 26 has adopted the but-for test as the governing rule for factual cause. To account for the two-fire cases, the Third Restatement provides:

> **§ 27. Multiple Sufficient Causes**
> If multiple acts occur, each of which under § 26 alone would have been a factual cause of the physical harm at the same time in the absence of the other act(s), each act is regarded as a factual cause of the harm.

Multiple *sufficient* causes is a different category from multiple *necessary* causes, which is another way of describing the cases in which separate actions combined to cause an indivisible injury.

Furthermore, the Third Restatement in § 27, comment *d*, holds that liability attaches even if one fire is innocent and the other negligent in origin. The Restatement has wisely rid itself of the substantial factor test. Except for the case where two tortfeasors were independently capable of causing the plaintiff's harm, the substantial factor test caused confusion. If a defendant's conduct was not the but-for cause of the harm, it could not be a substantial factor since it was not a factor at all.

By clearly articulating that the but-for test governs factual cause and providing for an exception in the case of multiple sufficient causes, the Third Restatement has simplified the rules for factual causation. This is not the confusing and dangerous sense of substantial-factor causation discussed above, after the cases in which the plaintiff had insufficient evidence to prove but-for cause. Few will mourn the passing of the "substantial factor" test. Several courts have indicated their displeasure with the "substantial factor" test. *See, e.g.,* June v. Union Carbide Corp., 577 F.3d 1234 (10th Cir. 2009) (under Colorado law, consistent with § 27 of the

---

authors' dialogue 18

JIM: You know, Aaron, my first reaction to the "natural origin fire" issue in *Kingston* was to agree, without really thinking about it, with the court's premise that if lightning had started the northwest fire, the railroad would be off the hook. To the extent that *Anderson* and §§ 431-433 of the Second Restatement and § 27 of the Third Restatement go the other way, they make no sense to me. And then I began to think more carefully about the holding in *Kingston.* If we assume that most fires that are not shown to have been caused by the defendant (or some other railroad) will be of unknown origin, and if *Kingston* assigns responsibility for all such fires to the defendant railroad, then *Kingston* accomplishes the same result of holding the railroad liable for natural-origin fires as does *Anderson* and the Restatement. And at least these last-named sources are candid about what they are doing.

AARON: It's even worse than you think, Jim. *Kingston* says that the defendant railroad will be liable whenever the northwest fire is of "responsible" origin. And then the court equates "responsible" with "human." I assume that if the northwest fire had been shown to have been started by a couple of non-negligent, judgment-proof eight-year-olds, the court would have said that they constituted a "responsible origin" and would have held the defendant railroad liable even though the eight-year-olds are the functional equivalent of natural lightning. Even tort law, itself, thinks young children are too irresponsible to be negligent, does it not?

JIM: Holy Rosenkrantz, Aaron, you're right. Why are you smiling?

AARON: I love watching a nit-picker squirm.

Restatement, Third, defendant's conduct is a substantial factor only if it is a but-for cause of plaintiff's harm); Wilkins v. Lamoille County Mental Health Service, Inc., 889 A.2d 245 (Vt. 2005); John Crane, Inc. v. Jones, 604 S.E.2d 822 (Ga. 2004). *But see* O.C.G.A. § 51-14-2 (15) (reinstating "substantial contributory factor" for asbestos cases).

It is interesting to note that the *Kingston* court was ready to accept the but-for argument if the railroad had been able to prove that lightning caused the second fire. But when two responsible human agencies negligently cause plaintiff's harm, the actors are jointly and severally liable. Returning to our example involving the two hunters, the same outcome would be reached if two pellets — one from each of the hunters' shotguns — had hit the plaintiff's left eye, either one being sufficient by itself to destroy the eye. The two hunters would be jointly and severally liable for the loss of the eye. What if a pellet from one hunter's gun also destroyed the plaintiff's right eye — who would be liable for the plaintiff's total blindness? Some courts on the facts of *Kingston* would agree with the Restatement view and hold the negligent railroad liable for the plaintiff's property damage even if it were clear that the northwest fire had been caused by lightning and would have caused plaintiff's harm independently of the railroad's negligently caused fire.

Thus, in Anderson v. Minneapolis, St. Paul R.R., 179 N.W. 45, 49 (Minn. 1920), a case decided for the plaintiff on facts similar to *Kingston*'s, the court seems to dispute *Kingston*'s underlying premise regarding nonliability if the other fire was of natural origin. Referring to an ambiguous holding in an earlier case, the *Anderson* court asserts that "if [the earlier case] decides that if [the railroad's] fire combines with another of no responsible origin, and after the union of the two fires they destroy the property, and either fire independently of the other would have destroyed it, then . . . there is no liability, we are not prepared to adopt the doctrine [from that earlier case] as the law of this state."

hypo 41

A walks on the sidewalk in front of a construction site when *B*, a crane operator, negligently drops a steel beam that kills *A* instantly. At the time of the accident, *A* was suffering from a terminal illness and had only a few months to live. In the negligence action brought on *A*'s behalf against *B*, will *A*'s preexisting illness limit, in any way, *B*'s liability?

D. WHEN ONE OF SEVERAL NEGLIGENT ACTORS CLEARLY HARMED THE PLAINTIFF, BUT WE CAN'T TELL WHICH ONE

SUMMERS v. TICE
199 P.2d 1 (Cal. 1948)

CARTER, Justice.

Each of the two defendants appeals from a judgment against them in an action for personal injuries. Pursuant to stipulation the appeals have been consolidated. Plaintiff's action was against both defendants for an injury to his right eye and face as the result of bring struck by bird shot discharged from a shotgun. The case was tried by the court without a jury and the court found that on November 20, 1945, plaintiff and the two defendants were hunting quail on the open range. Each of the defendants was armed with a 12 gauge shotgun loaded with shells containing 7½ size shot. Prior to going hunting plaintiff discussed the hunting procedure with defendants, indicating that they were to exercise care when shooting and to "keep in line." In the course of hunting plaintiff proceeded up a hill, thus placing the hunters at the points of a triangle. The view of defendants with reference to plaintiff was unobstructed and they knew his location. Defendant Tice flushed a quail which rose in flight to a ten foot elevation and flew between plaintiff and defendants. Both defendants shot at the quail, shooting in plaintiff's direction. At that time defendants were 75 yards from plaintiff. One shot struck plaintiff in his eye and another in his upper lip. Finally it was found by the court that as the direct result of the shooting by defendants the shots struck plaintiff as above mentioned and that defendants were negligent in so shooting and plaintiff was not contributorily negligent . . . .

The problem presented in this case is whether the judgment against both defendants may stand. It is argued by defendants that they are not joint tort feasors, and thus jointly and severally liable, as they were not acting in concert, and that there is not sufficient evidence to show which defendant was guilty of the negligence which caused the injuries . . . .

Considering the last argument first, we believe it is clear that the court sufficiently found on the issue that defendants were jointly liable and that thus the negligence of both was the cause of the injury or to that legal effect. It found that both defendants were negligent and "That as a direct and proximate result of the shots fired by defendants, and each of them, a birdshot pellet was caused to and did lodge in plaintiff's right eye and that another birdshot pellet was caused to and did lodge in plaintiff's upper lip." . . . Implicit in such finding is the assumption that the court was unable to ascertain whether the shots were from the gun of one defendant or the other or one shot from each of them. The one shot that entered plaintiff's eye was the major factor in assessing damages and that shot could not have come from the gun of both defendants. It was from one or the other only.

. . . Dean Wigmore has this to say: "When two or more persons by their acts are possibly the sole cause of a harm, or when two or more acts of the same person are possibly the sole cause, and the plaintiff has introduced evidence that the one of the two persons, or the one of the same person's two acts, is culpable, then the defendant has the burden of proving that the other person, or his other act, was the sole cause of the harm. (b) . . . The real reason for the rule that each joint tort feasor is responsible for the whole damage is the practical unfairness of denying the injured person redress simply because he cannot prove how much damage each did, when it is certain that between them they did all; let them be the ones to apportion it among themselves. Since, then, the difficulty of proof is the reason, the rule should apply whenever the harm has plural causes, and not merely when they acted in conscious concert . . . ." (Wigmore, Select Cases on the Law of Torts, sec. 153.) . . .

When we consider the relative position of the parties and the results that would flow if plaintiff was required to pin the injury on one of the defendants only, a requirement that the burden of proof on that subject be shifted to defendants becomes manifest. They are both wrongdoers both negligent toward plaintiff. They brought about a situation where the negligence of one of them injured the plaintiff, hence it should rest with them each to absolve himself if he can. The injured party has been placed by defendants in the unfair position of pointing to which defendant caused the harm. If one can escape the other may also and plaintiff is remediless. Ordinarily defendants are in a far better position to offer evidence to determine which one caused the injury . . . .

Cases are cited for the proposition that where two or more tort feasors acting independently of each other cause an injury to plaintiff, they are not joint tort feasors and plaintiff must establish the portion of the damage caused by each, even though it is impossible to prove the portion of the injury caused by each. In view of the foregoing discussion it is apparent that defendants in cases like the present one may be treated as liable on the same basis as joint tort feasors, and hence the last cited cases are distinguishable inasmuch as they involve independent tort feasors.

In addition to that, however, it should be pointed out that the same reasons of policy and justice shift the burden to each of defendants to absolve himself if he can relieving the wronged person of the duty of apportioning the injury to a particular defendant, apply here where we are concerned with whether plaintiff is required to supply evidence for the apportionment of damages. If defendants are independent tort feasors and thus each liable for the damage caused by him alone, and, at least, where the matter of apportionment is incapable of proof, the innocent wronged party should not be deprived of his right to redress. The wrongdoers should be left to work out between themselves any apportionment. Some of the cited cases refer to the difficulty of apportioning the burden of damages between the independent tort feasors, and say that where factually a correct division cannot be made, the trier of fact may make it the best it can, which would be more or less a guess, stressing the factor that the wrongdoers are not in a position to complain of uncertainty . . . .

The judgment is affirmed.

SUMMERS *IS A CLASSIC*

As you may have surmised, *Summers* is the factual inspiration for the "shotgun pellet" hypotheticals in the notes following *Hill* and *Kingston* in the preceding section. It is also directly relevant to the decision of the Supreme Court of California in *Ybarra v. Spangard*, p. 230, *supra*, decided four years earlier than *Summers* in that jurisdiction. And it is also featured prominently in the *Sindell* decision, immediately *infra*. In short, *Summers v. Tice* is a classic in the history of American tort law. Perhaps its most remarkable aspect is that it condones imposing liability on actors who we know did not actually cause the plaintiff's harm. We hold both hunters liable in *Summers*, even though we know one of them did not do it, because otherwise we would let the one who did it off the hook. Where is the justice in that?

Like it or not, *Summers* is firmly ensconced in the law. Restatement, Second, of Torts § 433(B) (3) (1965) and Restatement, Third, of Torts § 28(b) and case law throughout the country support the decision. *But see* Spencer v. McClure, 618 S.E.2d 451 (W. Va. 2005). Plaintiff was involved in a chain collision when her car was successively hit by several negligently driven cars and she suffered serious injury to her shoulder. She could not establish whether all the damage was done by the cars that first rear-ended her or whether the last car in the chain of rear-ending cars also contributed to her injury. Upholding the grant of summary judgment in favor of the driver of the last car in the chain, the court refused to impose liability because there was no adequate proof that the last car contributed to her shoulder injury. The dissent citing to *Summers* said that the burden of proof in this kind of case should shift to the defendant.

hypo 42

P was quail hunting with a half dozen friends. Suddenly, a covey of quail flushed in the midst of the hunters and everyone started shooting at once, in *P*'s direction. When the smoke cleared, *P* wound up with three or four pellets in each eye, resulting in total blindness. It is impossible to tell which pellets came from which hunter's gun. The plaintiff joins all the other hunters as defendants and shows them all to have been negligent. No concert of action is involved. Will the court hold the defendants jointly and severally liable to *P*?

SINDELL v. ABBOTT LABORATORIES
607 P.2d 924 (Cal. 1980)

[The plaintiff sued several manufacturers of diethylstilbesterol (DES), alleging that her mother took the drug to prevent miscarriage. The plaintiff alleged that as a result, she, the plaintiff, had developed a bladder tumor, which had been surgically removed, and that she might in the future develop a further malignancy. She alleged that DES was ineffective to prevent miscarriage, and that the defendants were negligent in marketing the drug without adequate testing as to its efficacy and as to its cancer-causing properties, and in failing to give adequate warnings. The plaintiff conceded that she would be unable to present proof as to which of the defendants produced the DES used by her mother, or even that the manufacturer that produced her mother's DES was a defendant in this action. The trial judge dismissed the complaint, and the plaintiff appealed.]

Mosk, Justice . . . . We begin with the proposition that, as a general rule, the imposition of liability depends upon a showing by the plaintiff that his or her injuries were caused by the act of the defendant or by an instrumentality under the defendant's control. The rule applies whether the injury resulted from an accidental event or from the use of a defective product.

There are, however, exceptions to this rule . . . .

I

Plaintiff places primary reliance upon cases which hold that if a party cannot identify which of two or more defendants caused an injury, the burden of proof may shift to the defendants to show that they were not responsible for the harm. This principle is sometimes referred to as the "alternative liability" theory.

The celebrated case of Summers v. Tice, *supra*, . . . 199 P.2d 1 (Cal. 1948), a unanimous opinion of this court, best exemplifies the rule . . . .

. . . There is an important difference between the situation involved in *Summers* and the present case. There, all the parties who were or could have been responsible for the harm to the plaintiff were joined as defendants. Here, by contrast, there are approximately 200 drug companies which made DES, any of which might have manufactured the injury-producing drug.

Defendants maintain that, while in *Summers* there was a 50 percent chance that one of the two defendants was responsible for the plaintiff's injuries, here since any one of 200 companies which manufactured DES might have made the product which harmed plaintiff, there is no rational basis upon which to infer that any defendant in this action caused plaintiff's injuries, nor even a reasonable possibility that they were responsible.

These arguments are persuasive if we measure the chance that any one of the defendants supplied the injury-causing drug by the number of possible tort feasors. In such a context, the possibility that any of the five defendants supplied the DES to plaintiff's mother is so remote that it would be unfair to require each defendant to exonerate itself. There may be a substantial likelihood that none of the five defendants joined in the action made the DES which caused the injury, and that the offending producer not named would escape liability altogether. While we propose, *infra*, an adaptation of the rule in *Summers* which will substantially overcome these difficulties, defendants appear to be correct that the rule, as previously applied, cannot relieve plaintiff of the burden of proving the identity of the manufacturer which made the drug causing her injuries.

II

The second principle upon which plaintiff relies is the so-called "concert of action" theory . . . . The gravamen of the charge of concert is that defendants failed to adequately test the drug or to give sufficient warning of its dangers and that they relied upon the tests performed by one another and took advantage of each others' promotional and marketing techniques. These allegations do not amount to a charge that there was a tacit understanding or a common plan among defendants to fail to conduct adequate tests or give sufficient warnings, and that they substantially aided and encouraged one another in these omissions.

The complaint charges also that defendants produced DES from a "common and mutually agreed upon formula," allowing pharmacists to treat the drug as a "fungible commodity" and to fill prescriptions from whatever brand of DES they had on hand at the time. It is difficult to understand how these allegations can form the basis of a cause of action for wrongful conduct by defendants, acting in concert. The formula for DES is a scientific constant. It is set forth in the United States Pharmacopoeia, and any manufacturer producing that drug must, with exceptions not relevant here, utilize the formula set forth in that compendium. (21 U.S.C.A. § 351, subd. (b).)

What the complaint appears to charge is defendants' parallel or imitative conduct in that they relied upon each others' testing and promotion methods. But such conduct describes a common practice in industry: a producer avails himself of the experience and methods of others making the same or similar products. Application of the concept of concert of action to this situation would expand the doctrine far beyond its intended scope and would render virtually any manufacturer liable for the defective products of an entire industry, even if it could be demonstrated that the product which caused the injury was not made by the defendant . . . .

. . . There is no allegation here that each defendant knew the other defendants' conduct was tortious toward plaintiff, and that they assisted and encouraged one another to inadequately test DES and to provide inadequate warnings. Indeed, it seems dubious whether liability on the concert of action theory can be predicated upon substantial assistance and encouragement given by one alleged tortfeasor to another pursuant to a tacit understanding to fail to perform an act. Thus, there was no concert of action among defendants within the meaning of that doctrine.

III

A third theory upon which plaintiff relies is the concept of industry-wide liability, or according to the terminology of the parties, "enterprise liability." This theory was suggested in Hall v. E.I. Du Pont de Nemours & Co., Inc. (E.D.N.Y. 1972) 345 F. Supp. 353. In that case, plaintiffs were 13 children injured by the explosion of blasting caps in 12 separate incidents which occurred in 10 different states between 1955 and 1959. The defendants were six blasting cap manufacturers, comprising virtually the entire blasting cap industry in the United States, and their trade association. There were, however, a number of Canadian blasting cap manufacturers which could have supplied the caps. The gravamen of the complaint was that the practice of the industry of omitting a warning on individual blasting caps and of failing to take other safety measures created an unreasonable risk of harm, resulting in the plaintiffs' injuries. The complaint did not identify a particular manufacturer of a cap which caused a particular injury.

The court reasoned as follows: there was evidence that defendants, acting independently, had adhered to an industry-wide standard with regard to the safety features of blasting caps, that they had in effect delegated some functions of safety investigation and design, such as labeling, to their trade association, and that there was industry-wide cooperation in the manufacture and design of blasting caps. In these circumstances, the evidence supported a conclusion that all the defendants jointly controlled the risk. Thus, if plaintiffs could establish by a preponderance of the evidence that the caps were manufactured by one of the defendants, the burden of proof as to causation would shift to all the defendants, The court noted that this theory of liability applied to industries composed of a small number of units, and that what would be fair and reasonable with regard to an industry of five or ten producers might be manifestly unreasonable if applied to a decentralized industry composed of countless small producers.

Plaintiff attempts to state a cause of action under the rationale of *Hall.* She alleges joint enterprise and collaboration among defendants in the production, marketing, promotion and testing of DES, and "concerted promulgation and adherence to industry-wide testing, safety, warning and efficacy standards" for the drug. We have concluded above that allegations that defendants relied upon one another's testing and promotion methods do not state a cause of action for concerted conduct to commit a tortious act. Under the theory of industry-wide liability, however, each manufacturer could be liable for all injuries caused by DES by virtue of adherence to an industry-wide standard of safety. . . . We decline to apply this theory in the present case. At least 200 manufacturers produced DES;

Hall, which involved 6 manufacturers representing the entire blasting cap industry in the United States, cautioned against application of the doctrine espoused therein to a large number of producers. (345 F. Supp. at p. 378.) Moreover, in *Hall*, the conclusion that the defendants jointly controlled the risk was based upon allegations that they had delegated some functions relating to safety to a trade association. There are no such allegations here, and we have concluded above that plaintiff has failed to allege liability on a concert of action theory.

Equally important, the drug industry is closely regulated by the Food and Drug Administration, which actively controls the testing and manufacture of drugs and the method by which they are marketed, including the contents of warning labels. To a considerable degree, therefore, the standards followed by drug manufacturers are suggested or compelled by the government. Adherence to those standards cannot, of course, absolve a manufacturer of liability to which it would otherwise be subject. But since the government plays such a pervasive role in formulating the criteria for the testing and marketing of drugs, it would be unfair to impose upon a manufacturer liability for injuries resulting from the use of a drug which it did not supply simply because it followed the standards of the industry.

IV

If we were confined to the theories of *Summers* and *Hall*, we would be constrained to hold that the judgment must be sustained. Should we require that plaintiff identify the manufacturer which supplied the DES used by her mother or that all DES manufacturers be joined in the action, she would effectively be precluded from any recovery. As defendants candidly admit, there is little likelihood that all the manufacturers who made DES at the time in question are still in business or that they are subject to the jurisdiction of the California courts. There are, however, forceful arguments in favor of holding that plaintiff has a cause of action.

In our contemporary complex industrialized society, advances in science and technology create fungible goods which may harm consumers and which cannot be traced to any specific producer. The response of the courts can be either to adhere rigidly to prior doctrine, denying recovery to those injured by such products, or to fashion remedies to meet these changing needs . . . .

The most persuasive reason for finding plaintiff states a cause of action is that advanced in *Summers*: as between an innocent plaintiff and negligent defendants, the latter should bear the cost of the injury. Here, as in *Summers*, plaintiff is not at fault in failing to provide evidence of causation, and although the absence of such evidence is not attributable to the defendants either, their conduct in marketing a drug the effects of which are delayed for many years played a significant role in creating the unavailability of proof.

From a broader policy standpoint, defendants are better able to bear the cost of injury resulting from the manufacture of a defective product. . . . The manufacturer is in the best position to discover and guard against defects in its products and to warn of harmful effects; thus, holding it liable for defects and failure to warn of harmful effects will provide an incentive to product safety. These considerations are particularly significant where medication is involved, for the consumer is virtually helpless to protect himself from serious, sometimes permanent, sometimes fatal, injuries caused by deleterious drugs.

Where, as here, all defendants produced a drug from an identical formula and the manufacturer of the DES which caused plaintiff's injuries cannot be identified through no fault of plaintiff, a modification of the rule of *Summers* is warranted. As we have seen, an undiluted *Summers* rationale is inappropriate to shift the burden of proof of causation to defendants because if we measure the chance that any particular manufacturer supplied the injury-causing product by the number of producers of DES, there is a possibility that none of the five defendants in this case produced the offending substance and that the responsible manufacturer, not named in the action, will escape liability.

But we approach the issue of causation from a different perspective: we hold it to be reasonable in the present context to measure the likelihood that any of the defendants supplied the product which allegedly injured plaintiff by the percentage which the DES sold by each of them for the purpose of preventing miscarriage bears to the entire production of the drug sold by all for that purpose. Plaintiff asserts in her briefs that Eli Lilly and Company and 5 or 6 other companies produced 90 percent of the DES marketed. If at trial this is established to be the fact, then there is a corresponding likelihood that this comparative handful of producers manufactured the DES which caused plaintiff's injuries, and only a 10 percent likelihood that the offending producer would escape liability.

If plaintiff joins in the action the manufacturers of a substantial share of the DES which her mother might have taken, the injustice of shifting the burden of proof to defendants to demonstrate that they could not have made the substance which injured plaintiff is significantly diminished . . . .

The presence in the action of a substantial share of the appropriate market also provides a ready means to apportion damages among the defendants. Each defendant will be held liable for the proportion of the judgment represented by its share of that market unless it demonstrates that it could not have made the product which caused plaintiff's injuries. In the present case, . . . one DES manufacturer was dismissed from the action upon filing a declaration that it had not manufactured DES until after plaintiff was born. Once plaintiff has met her burden of joining the required defendants, they in turn may cross-complaint against other DES manufacturers, not joined in the action, which they can allege might have supplied the injury-causing product.

Under this approach, each manufacturer's liability would approximate its responsibility for the injuries caused by its own products. Some minor discrepancy in the correlation between market share and liability is inevitable; therefore, a defendant may be held liable for a somewhat different percentage of the damage than its share of the appropriate market would justify. It is probably impossible, with the passage of time, to determine market share with mathematical exactitude. But . . . the difficulty of apportioning damages among the defendant producers in exact relation to their market share does not seriously militate against the rule we adopt. As we said in *Summers* with regard to the liability of independent tortfeasors, where a correct division of liability cannot be made "the trier of fact may make it the best it can." (... 199 P.2d at p. 5.)

We are not unmindful of the practical problems involved in defining the market and determining market share,[5] but these are largely matters of proof which properly cannot be determined at the pleading stage of these proceedings. Defendants urge that it would be both unfair and contrary to public policy to hold them liable for plaintiff's injuries in the absence of proof that one of them supplied the drug responsible for the damage. Most of their arguments, however, are based upon the assumption that one manufacturer would be held responsible for the products of another or for those of all other manufacturers if plaintiff ultimately prevails. But under the rule we adopt, each manufacturer's liability for an injury would be approximately equivalent to the damages caused by the DES it manufactured.

The judgments are reversed.

BIRD, C.J., and NEWMAN and WHITE, JJ., concur.

RICHARDSON, Justice, dissenting.

I respectfully dissent. In these consolidated cases the majority adopts a wholly new theory which contains these ingredients: The plaintiffs were not alive at the time of the commission of the tortious acts. They sue a generation later. They are permitted to receive substantial damages from multiple defendants without any proof that any defendant caused or even probably caused plaintiffs' injuries.

Although the majority purports to change only the required burden of proof by shifting it from plaintiffs to defendants, the effect of its holding is to guarantee that plaintiffs will prevail on the causation issue because defendants are no more capable of disproving factual causation than plaintiffs are of proving it. "Market share" liability thus represents a new high water mark in tort law. The ramifications seem almost limitless . . . . In my view, the majority's departure from traditional tort doctrine is unwise . . . .

The fact that plaintiffs cannot tie defendants to the injury-producing drug does not trouble the majority for it declares that the *Summers* requirement of proof of actual causation by a named defendant is satisfied by a joinder of those defendants who have *together* manufactured "a substantial percentage" of the DES which has been marketed. Notably lacking from the majority's expression of its new rule, unfortunately, is any definition or guidance as to what should constitute a "substantial" share of the relevant market. The issue is entirely open-ended and the answer, presumably, is anyone's guess.

Much more significant, however, is the consequence of this unprecedented extension of liability. Recovery is permitted from a handful of defendants *each* of whom *individually* may account for a comparatively small share of the relevant market, so long as the aggregate business of those who have been sued is deemed

---

5. Defendants assert that there are no figures available to determine market share, that DES was provided for a number of uses other than to prevent miscarriage and it would be difficult to ascertain what proportion of the drug was used as a miscarriage preventative, and that the establishment of a time frame and area for market share would pose problems.

"substantial." In other words, a particular defendant may be held proportionately liable *even though mathematically it is much more likely than not that it played no role whatever in causing plaintiffs' injuries*. . . . Furthermore, in bestowing on plaintiffs this new largess the majority sprinkles the rain of liability upon all the joined defendants alike — those who may be tortfeasors and those who may have had nothing at all to do with plaintiffs' injury — and an added bonus is conferred. Plaintiffs are free to pick and choose their targets . . . .

The foregoing result is directly contrary to long established tort principles. Once again, in the words of Dean Prosser, the applicable rule is: "[Plaintiff] must introduce evidence which affords a reasonable basis for the conclusion that it is more likely than not that the conduct of the defendant was a substantial factor in bringing about the result. *A mere possibility of such causation is not enough*; and when the matter remains one of pure speculation or conjecture, or the probabilities are at best evenly balanced, it becomes the duty of the court to direct a verdict for the defendant." (*Prosser, supra,* § 41, at p. 241, italics added, fns. omitted.) Under the majority's new reasoning, however, a defendant is fair game if it happens to be engaged in a similar business and causation is *possible,* even though remote . . . .

[I]t is readily apparent that "market share" liability will fall unevenly and disproportionately upon those manufacturers who are amenable to suit in California. On the assumption that no other state will adopt so radical a departure from traditional tort principles, it may be concluded that under the majority's reasoning those defendants who are brought to trial in this state will bear effective joint responsibility for 100 percent of plaintiffs' injuries despite the fact that their "substantial" aggregate market share may be considerably less. This undeniable fact forces the majority to concede that, "a defendant may be held liable for a somewhat different percentage of the damage than its share of the appropriate market would justify." (*Ante,* . . . p. 937 of 607 P.2d.) With due deference, I suggest that the complete unfairness of such a result in a case involving only five of two hundred manufacturers is readily manifest.

Furthermore, several other important policy considerations persuade me that the majority holding is both inequitable and improper. The injustice inherent in the majority's new theory of liability is compounded by the fact that plaintiffs who use it are treated far more favorably than are the plaintiffs in routine tort actions. In most tort cases plaintiff knows the identity of the person who has caused his injuries. In such a case, plaintiff, of course, has no option to seek recovery from an entire industry or a "substantial" segment thereof, but in the usual instance can recover, if at all, only from the particular defendant causing injury. Such a defendant may or may not be either solvent or amenable to process. Plaintiff in the ordinary tort case must take a chance that defendant can be reached and can respond financially. On what principle should those plaintiffs who wholly fail to prove any causation, an essential element of the traditional tort cause of action, be rewarded by being offered both a wider selection of potential defendants and a greater opportunity for recovery?

The majority attempts to justify its new liability on the ground that defendants herein are "better able to bear the cost of injury resulting from the manufacture of a defective product." (*Ante,* . . . p. 936 of 607 P.2d.) This "deep pocket" theory of liability, fastening liability on defendants presumably because they are rich, has understandable popular appeal and might be tolerable in a case disclosing substantially stronger evidence of causation than herein appears. But as a general proposition, a defendant's wealth is an unreliable indicator of fault, and should play no part, at least consciously, in the legal analysis of the problem. In the absence of proof that a particular defendant caused or at least probably caused plaintiff's injuries, a defendant's ability to bear the cost thereof is no more pertinent to the underlying issue of liability than its "substantial" share of the relevant market. A system priding itself on "*equal* justice under law" does not flower when the liability as well as the damage aspect of a tort action is determined by a defendant's wealth. The inevitable consequence of such a result is to create and perpetuate two rules of law—one applicable to wealthy defendants, and another standard pertaining to defendants who are poor or who have modest means. Moreover, considerable doubts have been expressed regarding the ability of the drug industry, and especially its smaller members, to bear the substantial economic costs (from both damage awards and high insurance premiums) inherent in imposing an industry-wide liability . . . .

Given the grave and sweeping economic, social, and medical effects of "market share" liability, the policy decision to introduce and define it should rest not with us, but with the Legislature which is currently considering not only major statutory reform of California product liability law in general, but the DES problem in particular. (See Sen. Bill No. 1392 (1979-1980 Reg. Sess.), which would establish and appropriate funds for the education, identification, and screening of persons exposed to DES, and would prohibit health care and hospital service plans from excluding or limiting coverage to persons exposed to DES.) . . .

I would affirm the judgments of dismissal.

CLARK and MANUEL, JJ., concur.

THE AFTERMATH OF SINDELL

Several jurisdictions have adopted the *Sindell* market share approach or some variation thereof in cases involving DES. *See, e.g.,* Smith v. Cutter Biological, Inc., 823 P.2d 717 (Haw. 1991); Collins v. Eli Lilly Co., 342 N.W.2d 37 (Wis. 1984). The New York high court also adopted market share, but based on a national market. *See* Hymowitz v. Eli Lilly & Co., 539 N.E.2d 1069 (N.Y. 1989). Other courts have rejected the market share approach in DES cases. *See, e.g.,* Smith v. Eli Lilly Co., 560 N.E.2d 324 (Ill. 1990); Gorman v. Abbott Labs., 599 A.2d 1364 (R.I. 1991); Sutowski v. Eli Lilly & Co., 696 N.E.2d 187 (Ohio 1998); Bortell v. Eli Lilly & Co., 406 F. Supp. 2d 1 (D.D.C. 2005) (applying Pennsylvania law).

Even in jurisdictions adopting the market share approach in DES cases, its application may be limited to cases where the percentage of the market held by the defendant is substantial. In Murphy v. E.R. Squibb & Sons, Inc., 710 P.2d 247 (Cal. 1985), the plaintiff brought suit against a manufacturer of DES who held only 10 percent of the market. Without stating what, exactly, the required threshold should be, the California Supreme Court refused to apply market share liability,

authors' dialogue **19**

JIM: Students have been asking me about my take on market share. It seems to me that it was an interesting idea but that it will have little lasting impact on the law of torts.

AARON: It sure had a powerful impact in the DES cases. Without market share the plaintiffs were dead in the water.

JIM: Look, Aaron, DES presented a law professor's dream case. We were dealing with a generic drug with the same dosage utilized by women for a short period of time during their pregnancy. The types of injuries that resulted in their daughters were unique. Young women rarely contract cancer of their reproductive system. They were signature injuries. The attempts to apply market share outside of DES have pretty much failed. Most courts have refused to apply market share to lead paint and will probably refuse to do so in the automotive asbestos cases. Auto manufacturers are being sued by auto mechanics who were exposed to asbestos in brake linings and who many years later have come down with mesothelioma and other cancers. I can't see how market share can be applied to cases where the asbestos content and the nature of plaintiffs' exposures to it differ so radically from one type of brake lining to another. Some forms of asbestos gave off toxic matter, and some did not. The time span of the exposures varied from plaintiff to plaintiff over decades. Many plaintiffs were exposed to nonautomotive asbestos because they worked in other environments where they may have been exposed to asbestos. The only reason that auto manufacturers are being sued is that the asbestos manufacturers have gone bankrupt and can't pay judgments. How can courts plausibly calculate a market share in these circumstances against the auto manufacturer?

AARON: You know, Jim, I'm reminded of the question that the late Chief Justice Warren used to ask lawyers who argued before the Supreme Court. When they made a technical argument of one sort or another he would ask, "Yes, but is that fair?" Assume that the auto manufacturers were negligent in utilizing asbestos (in that the brake linings containing asbestos were defective). Is it fair to deny workers who developed cancer a recovery against auto manufacturers as a group because we can't figure out the percentage to be allocated to any given manufacturer? The auto mechanics who inhaled these toxics did nothing wrong. They were entirely passive.

JIM: I feel your pain, Aaron, but you're wrong. We simply don't know whether any given manufacturer was responsible for any asbestos-related injury. And even if we did, the range of possible percentage responsibility may be anywhere from 0.01 percent to 50 percent. The law can't condone liability by guesswork. It's not right to take money out of Peter's pocket to pay Paul unless you have some standard for imposing liability. Robin Hood may be a sympathetic figure but no responsible jurist would set that outlaw's conduct as within the boundaries of the law.

AARON: I guess you're right. But. . . .

stating that "[s]ince [the defendant] had only a 10 percent share of the DES market, there is only a 10 percent chance that it produced the drug causing plaintiff's injuries, and a 90 percent chance that another manufacturer was the producer. In this circumstance, it must be concluded that [plaintiff] failed to meet the threshold requirement for the application of the market share doctrine." *Id.* at 255.

Attempts have been made to extend market share liability to other areas of tort litigation, including asbestos-containing products, lead-based paint, and firearms. These attempts have been overwhelmingly rejected on various grounds. The federal district court in Marshall v. Celotex Corp., 691 F. Supp. 1045 (E.D. Mich. 1988), refused to apply the market share approach in a case where the plaintiff's decedent had died due to exposure to asbestos-containing products at a naval base. Plaintiff could not prove that at least one of the named defendants was in fact responsible for supplying products that contained asbestos to the base. In Gaulding v. Celotex Corp., 772 S.W.2d 66 (Tex. 1989), the court rejected market share liability due to the plaintiff's inability to prove when the fiberboard containing the injury-causing asbestos was produced. Because different companies held different proportions of the market for asbestos-containing boards at different times, it was impossible to ascertain which companies were more likely to have produced the board that harmed the plaintiff, or if the defendant companies were even producing asbestos-containing boards at the time the harm-causing board was produced.

These same problems have also plagued plaintiffs who have tried to apply market share liability to manufacturers of lead-based paint. In Santiago v. Sherwin Williams Co., 3 F.3d 546 (1st Cir. 1993), a plaintiff had been exposed to lead-based paint as a child but was unable to establish when the paint had been applied during a 53-year period. In rejecting application of market share liability, the court noted that (*id.* at 551):

> [S]everal of the defendants were not in the white lead pigment market at all for significant portions of the period between 1917 and 1970, and therefore may well not have been market suppliers at the time the injury-causing paint was applied to the walls of plaintiff's home. This, of course, raises a substantial possibility that these defendants not only could be held liable for more harm than they actually caused, but also could be held liable when they did not, in fact, cause any harm to plaintiff at all.

Also see City of St. Louis v. Benjamin Moore & Co., 226 S.W.3d 110 (Mo. 2007) (bringing the case against lead pigment manufacturers under public nuisance theory does not relieve the plaintiff's burden of proving the identity of the manufacturer; Missouri has rejected market share liability and will not apply it to a public nuisance claim).

More recently, plaintiffs have tried to apply market share liability to gun manufacturers. In Hamilton v. Beretta U.S.A. Corp., 750 N.E.2d 1055 (N.Y. 2001), the relatives of people killed by handguns brought an action against the companies that manufactured the handguns. The New York Court of Appeals rejected the market share theory, stating that "[u]nlike DES, guns are not identical, fungible products." *Id.* at 1067. The court also distinguished DES cases by saying that "the distribution and sale of every gun is not equally negligent, nor does it involve a defective product." *Id.* Finally, the court observed, "[A] manufacturer's share of the national handgun market does not necessarily correspond to the amount of risk created by its alleged tortious conduct." *Id.* Some recent developments indicate that a few courts may be willing to extend market share to non-DES cases. In a lengthy opinion, a sharply divided Wisconsin Supreme Court expressed its willingness to apply market share to the manufacturers of lead pigment used in lead paint. Thomas v. Mallet, 701 N.W.2d 523 (Wis. 2005). The case drew a biting dissent that attacked the majority on both common law and constitutional grounds. The federal district court in Gibson v. American Cyanamid Co., 719 F. Supp. 2d 1031 (E.D. Wis. 2010), held that the Wisconsin market share rule violated the defendant's due process rights under the Fourteenth Amendment. The court concluded (*id.* at 1052): "[I]t violates due process when there is no nexus or provable connection between a damages award and the harmful conduct of the defendant." *Also see* In Re: Methyl Tertiary Butyl Ether ("MTBE") Products Liability Litigation, 475 F. Supp. 2d 286 (S.D.N.Y. 2006) (contamination of groundwater from MTBE from countless sources; the market share theory is available, however, only when claims against identifiable defendants will not make the plaintiffs whole); In re MTBE Products Liability Litigation, 739 F. Supp. 2d 576 (S.D.N.Y. 2010) (opinion on post-trial motions after jury award of $104 million in damages).

For a scholarly treatment of what the future may hold for market share liability, *see generally* Frank J. Giliberti, *Emerging Trends for Products Liability: Market Share Liability, Its History and Future,* 15 Touro L. Rev. 719 (1999); Allen Rostron, *Beyond Market Share Liability: A Theory of Proportional Share Liability for Non-fungible Products,* 52 UCLA L. Rev. 151 (2004).

chapter 5

Proximate Causation

In normal discourse, the word "proximate" means "next; nearest; . . . close; very near . . ." (*Random House Dictionary of the English Language Unabridged*, 2d ed. 1987). In tort law, the phrase "proximate causation" has little, if anything, to do with the dictionary definitions of the words used. Instead, it is a code phrase used to convey the idea that liability for negligent conduct is not unbounded. For reasons that we will explore in this chapter, courts have always imposed limits on the scope of liability for negligence. Scholars and two successive Restatements have sought to exorcize the term "proximate cause" with little success. The term is deeply ingrained in our legal jargon and will not come out, as hard as we may try. It has meaning only as it contrasts with the phrase "actual causation" explored in Chapter 4. Actual causation is concerned with the but-for connection, if any, between a defendant's negligent conduct and a victim's harm. When the victim's harm would have happened even if the defendant had not acted at all, or had not acted negligently, actual causation is missing and the chain of causation linking defendant's fault and plaintiff's harm is broken. But even when defendant's negligence was clearly a but-for cause of plaintiff's harm, defendant's negligence may not be the proximate cause of that harm. Thus, proximate causation is the second necessary link in the chain of causation. Without it, the causal chain is broken and the negligent defendant is not liable to the plaintiff even for harm the defendant has actually caused.

AN ILLUSTRATIVE EXAMPLE

A concrete example will help to clarify the substance of the proximate causation concept. Suppose that Daniel is driving home after work in his automobile when he negligently loses control of his car, drives into the curb, and damages his front right tire. While Daniel changes the tire, partially obstructing the road, Patrick approaches in his own automobile. Patrick slows his rate of travel because of the traffic caused by Daniel's breakdown, and is delayed five minutes in his trip home. Once past the traffic slowdown, Patrick resumes normal speed when, two minutes later, Susan negligently drives through a stop sign on a side road and collides with Patrick's automobile, harming Patrick. It is safe to assume that Susan is liable to Patrick. But what about Daniel? Suppose that it is clear that, if Daniel's negligent driving had not caused the traffic slowdown, Patrick would have been past the intersection where Susan ran the stop sign, and thus would not have been struck by Susan. Thus, Daniel's negligence is a but-for, actual cause of Patrick's harm. But should Daniel be liable to Patrick? That is the type of question that proximate causation addresses. If we are inclined to reject Patrick's claim against Daniel, we may do so by concluding that, although Daniel actually helped to cause Patrick's harm, Daniel did not proximately, or legally, cause Patrick's harm.

A. LIABILITY LIMITED TO REASONABLY FORESEEABLE CONSEQUENCES

MARSHALL v. NUGENT
222 F.2d 604 (1st Cir. 1955)

[Harriman was driving his automobile in northern New Hampshire during the winter with Marshall as a front-seat passenger. The road on which they traveled was covered with hard-packed snow. An oil truck owned by Socony-Vacuum and driven by Prince approached from the opposite direction and intruded into Harriman's lane as it rounded the curve. Harriman turned to the right, went into a skid, and came to a stop at right angles to the road. No one was injured. Prince stopped his truck on the road, blocking his lane of traffic. He suggested that someone go back up the hill to warn oncoming traffic about the danger. Plaintiff started walking up the hill. After he had walked about 75 feet, an automobile driven by Nugent came around the curve and down the hill. Nugent turned to his left to avoid the truck, skidded, and hit plaintiff.]

MAGRUDER, Chief Judge.
. . . Marshall filed his complaint in the court below against both Socony-Vacuum Oil Co., Inc., and Nugent, charging them as joint tortfeasors, each legally responsible for the plaintiff's personal injuries. There was complete diversity of citizenship, since Marshall was a citizen of New Hampshire, Nugent a citizen of Vermont, and Socony a New York corporation. After a rather lengthy trial, the jury reported a verdict in favor of Marshall as against Socony in the sum of $25,000, and a verdict in favor of the defendant Nugent. The district court entered judgments against Socony and in favor of Nugent in accordance with the verdict. . . .

This is an appeal by Socony from the judgment against it in favor of Marshall. Appellant has presented a great number of points, most of which do not merit extended discussion.

The most seriously pressed contentions are that the district court was in error in refusing Socony's motion for a directed verdict in its favor, made at the close of all the evidence. The motion was based on several grounds, chief of which were . . . (2) that if Socony's servant Prince were found to have been negligent in "cutting the corner" on the wrong side of the road, and thus forcing Harriman's car off the highway, Marshall suffered no hurt from this, and such negligent conduct, as a matter of law, was not the proximate cause of Marshall's subsequent injuries when he was run into by Nugent's car. . . .

Coming then to contention (2) above mentioned, this has to do with the doctrine of proximate causation, a doctrine which appellant's arguments tend to make out to be more complex and esoteric than it really is. To say that the situation created by the defendant's culpable acts constituted "merely a condition," not a cause of plaintiff's harm, is to indulge in mere verbiage, which does not solve the question at issue, but is simply a way of stating the conclusion, arrived at from other considerations, that the causal relation between the defendant's act and the plaintiff's injury is not strong enough to warrant holding the defendant legally responsible for the injury.

The adjective "proximate," as commonly used in this connection, is perhaps misleading, since to establish liability it is not necessarily true that the defendant's culpable act must be shown to have been the next or immediate cause of the plaintiff's injury. In many familiar instances, the defendant's act may be more remote in the chain of events; and the plaintiff's injury may more immediately have been caused by an intervening force of nature, or an intervening act of a third person whether culpable or not, or even an act by the plaintiff bringing himself in contact with the dangerous situation resulting from the defendant's negligence. . . .

Back of the requirement that the defendant's culpable act must have been a proximate cause of the plaintiff's harm is no doubt the widespread conviction that it would be disproportionately burdensome to hold a culpable actor potentially liable for all the injurious consequences that may flow from his act, i.e., that would not have been inflicted "but for" the occurrence of the act. This is especially so where the injurious consequence was the result of negligence merely. And so, speaking in general terms, the effort of the courts has been, in the development of this doctrine of proximate causation, to confine the liability of a negligent actor to those harmful consequences which result from the operation of the risk, or of a risk, the foreseeability of which rendered the defendant's conduct negligent.

Of course, putting the inquiry in these terms does not furnish a formula which automatically decides each of an infinite variety of cases. Flexibility is still preserved by the further need of defining the risk, or risks, either narrowly, or more broadly, as seems appropriate and just in the special type of case.

Regarding motor vehicle accidents in particular, one should contemplate a variety of risks which are created by negligent driving. There may be injuries resulting from a direct collision between the carelessly driven car and another vehicle. But such direct collision may be avoided, yet the plaintiff may fall and injure himself in frantically racing out of the way of the errant car. Or the plaintiff may be knocked down and injured by a human stampede as the car rushes toward a crowded safety zone. Or the plaintiff may faint from intense excitement stimulated by the near collision, and in falling sustain a fractured skull. Or the plaintiff may suffer a miscarriage or other physical illness as a result of intense nervous shock incident to a hair-raising escape. This bundle of risks could be enlarged indefinitely with a little imagination. In a traffic mix-up due to negligence, before the disturbed waters have become placid and normal again, the unfolding of events between the culpable act and the plaintiff's eventual injury may be bizarre indeed; yet the defendant may be liable for the result. In such a situation, it would be impossible for a person in the defendant's position to predict in advance just how his negligent act would work out to another's injury. Yet this in itself is no bar to recovery.

When an issue of proximate cause arises in a borderline case, as not infrequently happens, we leave it to the jury with appropriate instructions. We do this because it is deemed wise to obtain the judgment of the jury, reflecting as it does the earthy viewpoint of the common man — the prevalent sense of the community — as to whether the causal relation between the negligent act and the plaintiff's harm which in fact was a consequence of the tortious act is sufficiently close to make it just and expedient to hold the defendant answerable in damages. That is what the courts have in mind when they say the question of proximate causation is one of fact for the jury. It is similar to the issue of negligence, which is left to the jury as an issue of fact. Even where on the evidence the facts are undisputed, if fair-minded men might honestly and reasonably draw contrary inferences as to whether the facts do or do not establish negligence, the court leaves such issue to the determination of the jury, who are required to decide, as a matter of common-sense judgment, whether the defendant's course of conduct subjected others to a reasonable or unreasonable risk, i.e., whether under all the circumstances the defendant ought to be recognized as privileged to do the act in question or to pursue his course of conduct with immunity from liability for harm to others which might result.

In dealing with these issues of negligence and proximate causation, the trial judge has to make a preliminary decision whether the issues are such that reasonable men might differ on the inferences to be drawn. This preliminary decision is said to be a question of law, for it is one which the court has to decide, but it is nevertheless necessarily the exercise of a judgment on the facts, just as an appellate court may have to exercise a judgment on the facts, in reviewing whether the trial judge should or should not have left the issue to the jury.

Exercising that judgment on the facts in the case at bar, we have to conclude that the district court committed no error in refusing to direct a verdict for the defendant Socony on the issue of proximate cause. . . .

. . . Plaintiff Marshall was a passenger in the oncoming Chevrolet car, and thus was one of the persons whose bodily safety was primarily endangered by the negligence of Prince, as might have been found by the jury, in "cutting the corner" with the Socony truck in the circumstances above related. In that view, Prince's negligence constituted an irretrievable breach of duty to the plaintiff. Though this particular act of negligence was over and done with when the truck pulled up alongside of the stalled Chevrolet without having actually collided with it, still the consequences of such past negligence were in the bosom of time, as yet unrevealed.

If the Chevrolet had been pulled back onto the highway, and Harriman and Marshall, having got in it again, had resumed their journey and had had a collision with another car five miles down the road, in which Marshall suffered bodily injuries, it could truly be said that such subsequent injury to Marshall was a consequence in fact of the earlier delay caused by the defendant's negligence, in the sense that but for such delay the Chevrolet car would not have been at the fatal intersection at the moment the other car ran into it. But on such assumed state of facts, the courts would no doubt conclude, "as a matter of law," that Prince's earlier negligence in cutting the corner was not the "proximate cause" of this later injury received by the plaintiff. That would be because the extra risks to which such negligence by Prince had subjected the passengers in the Chevrolet car were obviously entirely over; the situation had been stabilized and become normal, and, so far as one could foresee, whatever subsequent risks the Chevrolet might have to encounter in its resumed journey were simply the inseparable risks, no more and no less, that were incident to the Chevrolet's being out on the highway at all. But in the case at bar, the circumstances under which Marshall received the personal injuries complained of presented no such clear-cut situation.

As we have indicated, the extra risks created by Prince's negligence were not all over at the moment the primary risk of collision between the truck and the Chevrolet was successfully surmounted. Many cases have held a defendant, whose negligence caused a traffic tie-up, legally liable for subsequent property damage or personal injuries more immediately caused by an oncoming motorist. This would particularly be so where, as in the present case, the negligent traffic tie-up and delay occurred in a dangerous blind spot, and where the occupants of the stalled Chevrolet, having got out onto the highway to assist in the operation of getting the Chevrolet going again, were necessarily subject to risks of injury from cars in the stream of northbound traffic coming over the crest of the hill. It is true, the Chevrolet car was not owned by the plaintiff Marshall, and no doubt, without violating any legal duty to Harriman, Marshall could have crawled up onto the snowbank at the side of the road out of harm's way and waited there, passive and inert, until his journey was resumed. But the plaintiff, who as a passenger in the Chevrolet car had already been subjected to a collision risk by the negligent operation of the Socony truck, could reasonably be expected to get out onto the highway and lend a hand to his host in getting the Chevrolet started again, especially as Marshall himself had an interest in facilitating the resumption of the journey in order to keep his business appointment in North Stratford. Marshall was therefore certainly not an "officious intermeddler," and whether or not he was barred by contributory negligence in what he did was a question for the jury, as we have already held. The injury Marshall received by being struck by the Nugent car was not remote, either in time or place, from the negligent conduct of defendant Socony's servant, and it occurred while the traffic mix-up occasioned by defendant's negligence was still persisting, not after the traffic flow had become normal again. In the circumstances presented we conclude that the district court committed no error in leaving the issue of proximate cause to the jury for determination.

Of course, the essential notion of what is meant by "proximate cause" may be expressed to the jury in a variety of ways. We are satisfied in the present case that the charge to the jury accurately enough acquainted them with the nature of the factual judgment they were called upon to exercise in their determination of the issue of proximate cause. . . .

In Socony-Vacuum Oil Co., Inc., v. Marshall, . . . the judgment of the District Court is affirmed.

IS MY LAWYER PLAYING STRAIGHT WITH ME?

The excerpt from the court's opinion in *Marshall* begins, "Marshall filed his complaint . . . against both Socony-Vacuum Oil Co., Inc., and Nugent. . . ." Did you notice any party missing from that list? Why didn't Marshall also sue Harriman, the driver of the car in which Marshall had been riding? Prince may have negligently crossed the centerline of the road, but maybe Harriman did something wrong, too. Maybe he was driving too fast, or maybe he overreacted to the truck intruding into his lane and threw the car into a skid. Marshall could have sued Harriman as another joint tortfeasor and possibly recovered from him (more likely from his insurance policy) as well as from the other two drivers.

Could the answer to the question be that the same lawyer was representing both Harriman and Marshall, and thus would not have wanted to sue one client on behalf of another? Let's hope not. Lawyers are not permitted to represent multiple clients when the representation of one client will be materially limited by responsibility to another client. *See* ABA Model Rules of Professional Conduct, Rule 1.7(a)(2). A complex and sometimes subtle body of law has grown up around the question of when two representations "materially limit" another, but the basic issue can be stated fairly simply: Given the duties that lawyers owe to their clients, is there a significant risk that what a lawyer is obligated to do on behalf of one client makes it difficult to fully carry out the obligations owed to the other client? Here it is helpful to think of the core professional duties that lawyers owe to their clients. Lawyers must be competent and diligent representatives, keep confidences, communicate information that a client needs to know, and exercise independent judgment, taking into account only the best interests of the particular client. A client need not suffer actual harm for there to be a conflict of interest. Rather, there need only be a significant risk of harm.

In this case, what is the risk? Suppose one lawyer represented both Harriman and Marshall. A truly impartial, independent lawyer might advise Marshall to sue Harriman, as long as there was a good-faith basis in law and fact to believe that Marshall might have a cause of action for negligence against Harriman. If the same lawyer were representing Harriman, however, he or she might be tempted to advise Marshall not to file the cross-claim. But that would be unethical, you say. Yes, and that is why the *possibility* of that interference with professional judgment creates a conflict of interest. The interference of another client's interests with professional judgment might be unconscious. The lawyer might be convinced that it is not in Marshall's best interests to sue Harriman, maybe because it would complicate the lawsuits against the other two defendants, or because the negligence claim against Harriman is fairly weak. It is difficult to know, however, whether that conclusion is based on the lawyer's impartial assessment of the claim, or whether it is unconsciously shaded by the lawyer's loyalty to Harriman.

DEMERS v. ROSA
925 A.2d 1165 (Conn. App. Ct. 2007)

HARPER, J.

This appeal arises out of an action by the plaintiff, Edward C. Demers, Jr., to recover damages from the defendant, Steven C. Rosa, for injuries sustained in an incident involving the defendant's roaming dog. The trial court [sitting without a jury] found the defendant liable under a theory of common-law negligence and awarded the plaintiff $48,381.76 in damages, plus costs. On appeal, the defendant argues that the judgment should be reversed because . . . his negligence did not proximately cause the plaintiff's injuries . . . .

The facts underlying the defendant's appeal are not in dispute. At approximately 5:55 p.m. on January 7, 2002, Donna Bannon called the Middlebury police department and requested assistance with a roaming dog on her property. At the time, the weather was a wintry mix of snow and sleet. Two police officers, Alton L. Cronin and the plaintiff, drove separately to Bannon's residence and parked their patrol cars in the driveway. They subsequently approached the home and spoke with Bannon. Bannon told the officers that her call was prompted by concern for the safety of the dog in light of the inclement weather . . . .

According to his testimony, Cronin recognized the dog, a yellow Labrador retriever, because the dog had been found roaming once before. Because of this prior incident, Cronin knew the identity and address of the dog's owner. Cronin took the dog from Bannon and, while holding it by its collar, led it down the driveway to his patrol car. He put the dog in the backseat and then got into the car himself.

The plaintiff followed Cronin down the driveway and, once Cronin had gotten into his car, stopped to talk with him. It was while the plaintiff was standing next to Cronin's car that he lost his footing and slipped on the ice and snow, falling on his back. Cronin exited the car and, upon learning that the plaintiff could not move, called headquarters. Shortly thereafter, an ambulance and Middlebury police Chief Patrick J. Bona arrived at the scene. Bona later testified that he took the dog and brought it to the defendant's house, situated approximately one-half mile from Bannon's residence. Bona walked the dog to the front door of the house where, according to Bona, the defendant answered the door, took possession of the dog and thanked him for bringing it home.

In August, 2002, the plaintiff filed a complaint against the defendant, [alleging] that the defendant negligently permitted the dog to roam on the day in question, thereby causing the plaintiff's fall and resulting injuries. It further alleged that the defendant frequently permitted his dogs to roam, prompting residents to file complaints with the Middlebury police department. On the basis of these facts, the plaintiff requested an award of damages, interest, costs and "such other relief as may be fair and equitable."

The parties tried the action to the court on March 1, 2006. [T]he court found that the plaintiff had established all of the elements of his negligence claim. In addressing the causation issue specifically, the court found that it was reasonably foreseeable that negligently allowing a dog to roam could precipitate complaints from local residents. The court further determined that it was reasonably foreseeable that a police officer could be injured during the course of responding to such a complaint because police officers had responded previously when the defendant's dogs were found roaming. Finally, the court found that the defendant's negligence in allowing his dogs to roam was a substantial factor in causing the plaintiff's injuries. On the basis of those conclusions, the court found the defendant liable in negligence and awarded the plaintiff $48,381.76. This appeal followed.

The defendant argues that proximate cause is absent in this case because the dog was in the backseat of Cronin's patrol car at the time of the plaintiff's fall, and the plaintiff fell because of the ice and snow, not because of barking or some other distracting behavior by the dog. On the basis of these facts, the defendant contends that the causal nexus between the plaintiff's fall and the defendant's negligence is too attenuated to justify the imposition of liability. The defendant also alleges that it was not reasonably foreseeable that a person responding to a complaint involving a roaming dog would slip and fall on the ice and snow after the dog already had been secured.

In response, the plaintiff focuses on the fact that the defendant would not have been standing on Bannon's driveway were it not for the defendant's negligence in allowing his dog to roam. He further emphasizes that the defendant's dog had been found roaming on at least one prior occasion, necessitating police intervention. By virtue of these facts, the plaintiff maintains that it is reasonably foreseeable that a person attempting to secure a roaming dog in the snow and ice would slip and fall in the process.

At the outset, it is helpful to review some of the basic principles regarding proximate cause and causation generally. "[L]egal cause is a hybrid construct, the result of balancing philosophic, pragmatic and moral approaches to causation. The first component of legal cause is causation in fact. Causation in fact is the purest legal application of . . . legal cause. The test for cause in fact is, simply, would the injury have occurred were it not for the actor's conduct. . . .

"Because actual causation, in theory, is virtually limitless, the legal construct of proximate cause serves to establish how far down the causal continuum tortfeasors will be held liable for the consequences of their actions . . . . The fundamental inquiry of proximate cause is whether the harm that occurred was within the scope of foreseeable risk created by the defendant's negligent conduct." . . .

In accordance with these legal principles, we turn to an examination of the scope of foreseeable risk created by allowing a dog to roam on a snowy and icy day. The parties seemingly agree that the involvement of police officers to secure the dog is properly within the scope of the risk created by such action. The parties disagree, however, about whether the officer's fall after the dog had been placed in the patrol car is beyond the scope of the reasonably foreseeable risk . . . .

[W]e are persuaded that the harm that befell the plaintiff was not reasonably foreseeable as a matter of law. When examining the scope of risk created by the defendant's negligence, one could easily foresee the possibility that a police officer could slip while in the midst of catching a roaming dog and returning it to its owner. Such a foreseeable mishap could occur, for instance, as a result of chasing after the dog, restraining the dog or trying to contain it in a particular area. Equally imaginable are so-called "dog fright" cases, in which the dog startles the police officer and thereby causes him or her to slip and fall. All of these situations could be considered properly within the scope of the risk because the harm suffered is of the same general type as that which makes the defendant's conduct negligent in the first instance. . . . Here, however, we agree with the defendant that the plaintiff fell because of the ice and snow on the driveway and not by virtue of the dog's roaming free or even the dog's presence at the scene of the accident. The plaintiff did not allege, and the evidence does not suggest, that the dog's behavior in the backseat of Cronin's car contributed to his fall in some fashion. By prompting the plaintiff to come to the Bannon residence, the dog's roaming became an indirect cause of the plaintiff's fall, at best. . . .

Admittedly, as the plaintiff argues, it is reasonably foreseeable that a police officer responding to a call on a snowy and icy day may become injured through a weather related accident. The general foreseeability of a weather related accident, however, does not, by itself, make *this particular accident* foreseeable. Furthermore, if we accepted this argument, the lens of foreseeability could be expanded to encompass generally any type of harm sustained in the midst of responding to a call during inclement weather. Our Supreme Court has never sanctioned such a broad view of the legal concept of foreseeability. On the contrary, the court has stated that the general foreseeability of the harm that occurred cannot justify the imposition of liability if the direct cause of the accident was not reasonably foreseeable. . . . Furthermore, the court has admonished that the proximate cause requirement must be used to temper the expansive view of causation in fact so as to exclude "[r]emote or trivial [actual] causes" of a harm. (Internal quotation marks omitted.) . . . Here, although the dog's roaming was the impetus for the plaintiff's trip to the Bannon residence, it can be viewed only as a "remote or trivial" cause of his fall and subsequent injury. As such, we reject the suggestion that by allowing the dog to roam on a snowy and icy day, the plaintiff should have been able to foresee that a police officer would slip and fall, not while catching the dog, but while standing beside a vehicle containing the dog.

. . . Furthermore, we reject the plaintiff's suggestion that recourse to the tort system is necessary to encourage the defendant to comply with General Statutes § 22-364, the "dogs roaming at large statute." The statutory penalties for violating § 22-364, as well as the threat of liability for any *foreseeable* damage caused by a roaming dog, already create a substantial incentive for dog owners to take appropriate precautions.

Although the plaintiff probably would not have been present on Bannon's driveway but for the dog's roaming, "[our Supreme Court] ha[s] declined to hold that [a] defendant's conduct in contributing to the harm, principally caused 'in fact' by another person or force, was a 'proximate cause' of the harm." . . . Here, the necessary relationship between the defendant's negligence in allowing his dog to roam, and the direct cause, i.e. the slippery driveway, is lacking. Furthermore, imposing liability on the defendant in this situation would have little effect on the prevention of the type of unforeseeable mishap suffered by the plaintiff and would contribute only modestly, if at all, to the statutory scheme already in place to prevent dogs from roaming. In light of these facts, we conclude that the defendant cannot be held legally responsible for the unforeseen consequences of his negligence in allowing his dog to roam free on the day in question. . . .

The judgment is reversed and the case is remanded to the trial court with direction to render judgment for the defendant on the plaintiff's complaint.

Do you agree with the court? What if a police car on the way to investigate an auto accident skidded on ice and a police officer was injured. Is the negligent driver of the car who caused the accident liable to the police officer? Or is this the problem to be attributed to "generally inclement weather"?

THE THIRD RESTATEMENT AND PROXIMATE CAUSE

The Restatement, Third, of Torts attempts to provide a unifying theme for proximate cause. Chapter 6 of the new Restatement, entitled "Scope of Liability" (Proximate Cause), bemoans the continued use of the term "proximate cause" to describe the analytical tool that courts utilize to limit the scope of liability of negligent tortfeasors whose conduct was the but-for cause of the plaintiff's harm. Proximate cause is inaccurate because the limitation on liability has little or nothing to do with "proximity" or "cause." Before reaching the issue of limiting the scope of liability, "actual cause" or "cause-in-fact" has already been established. And whether liability should be limited has precious little to do with the proximity of the negligent act in space or time to the plaintiff's injury. The new Restatement sets forth the following governing rule:

§ 29. Limitations on Liability for Tortious Conduct

An actor's liability is limited to those harms that result from the risks that made the actor's conduct tortious.

Comment:

d. Harm different from the harms risked by the tortious conduct. Central to the limitation on liability of this Section is the idea that an actor should be held liable only for harm that was among the potential harms — the risks — that made the actor's conduct tortious. The term "scope of liability" is employed to distinguish those harms that fall within this standard and, thus, for which the defendant is subject to liability and, on the other hand, those harms for which the defendant is not liable. This limit on liability serves the purpose of avoiding what might be unjustified or enormous liability by confining liability's scope to the reasons for holding the actor liable in the first place. To apply this rule requires consideration, at an appropriate level of generality, . . . of: a) the risks that made the actor's conduct tortious, and b) whether the harm for which recovery is sought was a result of any of those risks. . . . The magnitude of the risk is the foreseeable severity of the harm discounted by the foreseeable probability that it will occur. For purposes of negligence, which requires foreseeablity, risk is evaluated by reference to the foreseeable (if indefinite) probability of harm of a foreseeable severity. . . .

Thus, the jury should be told that, in deciding whether plaintiff's harm is within the scope of liability, it should go back to the reasons for finding the defendant engaged in negligent or other tortious conduct. If the harms risked by that tortious conduct include the general sort of harm suffered by the plaintiff, the defendant is subject to liability for the plaintiff's harm. When defendants move for a determination that plaintiff's harm is beyond the scope of liability as a matter of law, courts must initially consider all of the range of harms risked by the defendant's conduct that the jury *could* find as the basis for determining that conduct tortious. Then, the court can compare the plaintiff's harm with the range of harms risked by the defendant to determine whether a reasonable jury might find the former among the latter.

The standard imposed by this Section is often referred to as the requirement that the harm be "within the scope of the risk," or some similar phrase, for liability to be imposed. For the sake of convenience, this limitation on liability is referred to [in] the remainder of this Chapter as the "risk standard."

Aren't we asking the same question twice?

ARBITRARY LIMITS ON FORESEEABILITY

Notwithstanding the flexibility of the foreseeability-based approach set forth in *Marshall*, some courts impose arbitrary limits on what is, and is not, "reasonably foreseeable." Some of these constitute sufficiently elaborate adjustments of the underlying duties of care that they warrant separate treatment, as discussed in Chapter 8. Others are sufficiently narrow to be treated as footnote exceptions to the general rule of proximate causation. Thus, some jurisdictions (notably New York) hold that, as a matter of law, liability for a negligently caused fire on the defendant's premises extends to property destroyed on the first-adjoining property, but no further. *See* Webb v. Rome, W. & O.R., 49 N.Y. 420 (1872) (modifying Ryan v. New York Central R.R., 35 N.Y. 210 (1866)). Subsequently, the Court of Appeals modified the *Webb* rule so that negligent actors are liable for damage to the next property burned, whether or not it is adjoining. Homac v. Sun Oil Co., 258 N.Y. 462 (N.Y. 1932). This New York "fire rule" is distinctly a minority position, and has been rejected in most other jurisdictions. *See, e.g.,* Hoyt v. Jeffers, 30 Mich. 181 (1874). Most of these jurisdictions hold negligent actors liable for fires even when they spread much greater distances, depending on the circumstances. *See, e.g.,* Willner v. Wallinder Sash & Door Co., 28 N.W.2d 682 (Minn. 1947).

DON'T GET BOGGED DOWN IN THE DETAILS: THE EXACT MANNER OF THE HARM RARELY MATTERS

As the *Marshall* opinion makes clear, courts do not require that the details of how the defendant's negligence "works out to another's injury" be foreseeable to establish proximate cause. For example, when the plaintiff's automobile skidded into the snowbank in that case, suppose that the right front wheel had broken loose and hurtled into a nearby tree, only to bounce straight back and kill the plaintiff. Even if the wheel could not be made to duplicate its deadly path in repeated attempts thereafter, no one doubts that the defendant's negligent driving of the truck proximately caused the plaintiff's harm. Thus, in Bunting v. Hogsett, 21 A. 31 (Pa. 1891), a negligently operated, small locomotive, used to haul supplies short distances, collided with a train in which the plaintiff was a passenger. The engineer jumped off moments before the collision. The collision caused the small locomotive to accelerate in reverse on a circular track and come back around, striking the same train a second time, minutes later, from the opposite direction. The plaintiff was injured in the second collision. The manner in which the second collision occurred was highly unusual, and the defendant argued lack of proximate cause. The Pennsylvania high court affirmed judgment for the plaintiff against the operator of the small locomotive. The court concluded (*id.* at 32):

> [I]t was the engineer's negligence that caused the first collision, and what occurred in consequence of this collision was not broken by the intervention of any independent agent, whatever. The first collision . . . turned loose the destructive agency which inflicted the injuries complained of. The negligence of the defendant's engineer was the natural, primary, and proximate cause of the entire occurrence.

In United Novelty Co. v. Daniels, 42 So. 2d 395 (Miss. 1949), defendant negligently required plaintiff's decedent to work in an unsafe environment. Decedent, age 19, used gasoline to clean a machine in a small, poorly ventilated room containing a gas heater with an open flame. A fatal explosion occurred when a gasoline-soaked rat unexpectedly darted from under the machine, ran under the heater, caught fire, and scurried back in flames to the machine, where it ignited the gasoline vapors from the cleaning process. Defendant argued that such a freakish sequence of events was completely unforeseeable and therefore defendant's negligence in supplying a dangerous, vapor-filled workplace had not proximately caused the decedent's fatal burns. Affirming judgment for the plaintiff, the Supreme Court of Mississippi concluded (*id.* at 396) that "the particular detonating agency . . . was incidental. . . ."

Sixty years later the Mississippi Supreme Court, in Glover v. Jackson State University, 968 So. 2d 1267 (Miss. 2007), denied defendant's motion for summary judgment when a bus driver mistakenly dropped off two 15-year-old boys and a 14-year-old girl who were participants in a youth program at an unsupervised place on the grounds of the university. The two boys had a long record of violent behavior. Being left unsupervised they forcibly raped the young girl. The court held that "although the specific harm of forcible rape may not have been contemplated by JSU, rape is nonetheless both a violent and sexual act; and our law requires only that a defendant foresee that some violent act . . . might occur, not the particular violent . . . act."

The flaming rat case and the later Mississippi case raise one of the central issues in proximate cause analysis. Whether a court talks in terms of whether a risk is foreseeable, or adopts the Third Restatement approach of asking whether the harm to the plaintiff was within the risk that made the defendant's conduct wrongful, it must settle on the *level of generality* at which to define the relevant risk. Consider how the Third Restatement would handle the flaming rat case: What makes it wrongful for an employer to require an employee to use volatile solvents to clean machine parts in a small, unventilated room in which there is a heater with an open flame? If you described the employer's conduct to someone who

---

authors' dialogue 20

AARON: Something's really bugging me.

JIM: Calm down, Aaron. Get down off the chair. What is it now?

AARON: The cases discussed in the text following *Marshall — Bunting* and *Daniels —* suggest that in some cases unforeseeability of outcome is no problem under proximate cause, right? Even one-in-a-million events are included within the proximate cause umbrella?

JIM: Yes, at least regarding the details of what happens to the plaintiff.

AARON: Well, what counts as a detail?

JIM: Anything that doesn't seriously affect the type or magnitude of the plaintiff's harm. Details concern not *what* happens, but *how* it happens. In *Daniels*, the risk was that an explosion would occur — the flaming rat was just a detail.

AARON: Let's say I'm driving negligently on Joralemon Street in Brooklyn and I run over a pedestrian, who just happens to be Shaquille O'Neal, an NBA superstar. He's out for the season. Am I liable for millions of dollars for wrecking his career?

JIM: I guess so. Yes, of course you are liable.

AARON: So Shaq is a detail? A seven-foot, 350-pound detail? Give me a break!

JIM: Get down off the chair before you wreck *your* season.

---

said, "Oh my, that's dangerous!" what risk would they be thinking about? Surely not the risk that a rat would wander in, get soaked with gasoline, catch fire, and ignite the vapors. That is a risk stated at too low a level of generality. But it also will not do to say the employer's conduct risked "an accident" or "an injury." That is stated at too high a level of generality. The art in proximate cause analysis is hitting the sweet spot — finding a middle level of generality that appropriately describes the risks an actor should take into account when deciding what precautions to take. Imagine the employer thinking, "Hmm, this setup seems dangerous . . . maybe I should fix something." What should the employer do? Ventilate the workspace, use less volatile solvents to clean the machine, provide a heater that does not have an open flame, and so on. Why should the employer take those precautions? To reduce the risk of _____. Whatever you fill in the blank with, that is the "harm within the risk" in Third Restatement terms, or the risk that must be foreseen by a reasonable person, in more traditional terms.

RENDEZVOUS WITH DISASTER

Observe that *Marshall* squarely addresses the illustrative example raised at the outset of this chapter concerning the liability of an actor (Daniel) whose negligence caused a traveler (Patrick) to be delayed so that the traveler was involved in a later accident after he resumed normal travel on the road. Without the actor's initial negligence, the traveler would have made it safely home. The general rule is, as *Marshall* indicates, that the original tortfeasor is not liable for bringing about the subsequent and disastrous rendezvous. Is that the appropriate outcome? Why, exactly? Can you think of special circumstances where negligently causing delay *should* lead to liability?

TELLING TALES TO THE JURY

Marshall and the Third Restatement take the position that the proximate cause inquiry is whether the result was within the risks presented by the original negligence. One would expect that jury instructions would reflect that perspective. The truth is that when one looks at jury instructions on causation throughout the country they rarely, if ever, tell the jury what the real issues are. Here are some examples: (1) Florida instructs juries that "[n]egligence is a legal cause of . . . injury . . . if it directly and in natural and continuous sequence produces or contributes substantially to producing such . . . injury . . . so that it can reasonably be said that, but for the negligence, the . . . injury would not have occurred"; (2) The Hawaii instruction is that "[a]n act or omission is a legal cause of injury/damage if it was a substantial factor in bringing about the injury/damage"; (3) The New York instruction on proximate cause reads, "An act or omission is regarded as a cause of an injury, if it was a substantial factor in bringing about the injury, that is, if it had such an effect in producing the injury that reasonable people would regard it as the cause of the injury." In many states a jury is told only that the negligence must be the "proximate cause" of the injury, without any embellishment. Many have criticized the lack of candor of jury instructions on proximate cause. *See, e.g.*, Patrick Kelley, *Restricting Duty, Breach and Proximate Cause in Negligence Law: Descriptive Theory and the Rule of Law*, 54 Vand. L. Rev. 1039, 1042 (2001) ("ordinary jury instructions . . . [on] proximate cause . . . give little guidance on how [the] question is to be resolved"); Jane Stapleton, *Legal Cause: Cause-in-Fact and the Scope of Liability for Consequences*, 54 Vand. L. Rev. 941, 987 (2001) ("the inadequacy and vagueness of jury instructions on 'proximate cause' is notorious").

The Reporters of the Third Restatement believe that juries should be told what is going on. In the Reporters' Notes, they suggest four slightly different jury instructions for adoption by the courts. The instruction chosen by a given court would be given after the instruction on negligence and cause-in-fact. Consider the following suggested instruction:

> You must decide whether the harm to the plaintiff is within the scope of defendant's liability. To do that, you must first consider why you found the defendant negligent [or some other basis for tort liability]. You should consider all of the dangers that the defendant should have taken reasonable steps [or other tort obligation] to avoid. The defendant is liable for the plaintiff's harm if you find that the plaintiff's harm arose from the same general type of danger that was one of those that the defendants should have taken reasonable steps [or other tort obligation] to avoid. If the plaintiff's harm, however, did not arise from the same general dangers that the defendant failed to take reasonable steps [or other tort obligation] to avoid, then you must find that the defendant is not liable for the plaintiff's harm. Restatement, Third, of Torts § 29 Reporters' Notes p. 517 (2010).

Why do you think that courts have avoided giving an instruction like the one suggested by the Reporters? Are the judges not bright enough, or might there be method to their madness?

McCAHILL v. NEW YORK TRANSPORTATION CO.
94 N.E. 616 (N.Y. 1911)

Hiscock, J.

One of the appellant's taxicabs struck respondent's intestate on Broadway, in the city of New York, in the nighttime under circumstances which, as detailed by the most favorable evidence, permitted the jury to find that the former was guilty of negligence and the latter free from contributory negligence. As a result of the accident the intestate was thrown about 20 feet, his thigh broken and his knee injured. He immediately became unconscious, and was shortly removed to a hospital, where he died on the second day thereafter of delirium tremens. A physician testified that the patient when brought to the hospital "was unconscious or irrational rather than unconscious . . . . He rapidly developed delirium tremens . . . . I should say with reasonable certainty the injury precipitated his attack of delirium tremens, and understand I mean precipitated, not induced." And, again, that in his opinion "the injury to the leg and the knee hurried up the delirium tremens." He also stated: "He might have had it (delirium tremens) anyway. Nobody can tell that." Of course, it is undisputed that the injuries could not have led to delirium tremens except for the pre-existing alcoholic condition of the intestate, and under these circumstances the debatable question in the case has been whether appellant's negligence was, legally speaking, the proximate cause of intestate's death. It seems to me that it was, and that the judgment should be affirmed.

In determining this question, it will be unnecessary to quote definitions of proximate cause which might be useful in testing an obscure, involved, or apparently distant relationship between an act and its alleged results, for the relationship here is perfectly simple and obvious. The appellant's automobile struck and injured the traveler. The injuries precipitated, hastened, and developed delirium tremens, and these caused death. There can be no doubt that the negligent act directly set in motion the sequence of events which caused death at the time it occurred. Closer analysis shows that the real proposition urged by the appellant is that it should not be held liable for the results which followed its negligence, either, first, because those results would not have occurred if intestate had been in a normal condition; or, secondly, because his alcoholism might have caused delirium tremens and death at a later date even though appellant had not injured him. This proposition cannot be maintained in either of its branches which are somewhat akin.

This principle has become familiar in many phases that a negligent person is responsible for the direct effects of his acts, even if more serious, in cases of the sick and infirm as well as in those of healthy and robust people, and its application to the present case is not made less certain because the facts are somewhat unusual and the intestate's prior disorder of a discreditable character. The principle is also true, although less familiar, that one who has negligently forwarded a diseased condition, and thereby hastened and prematurely caused death, cannot escape responsibility, even though the disease probably would have resulted in death at a later time without his agency. It is easily seen that the probability of later death from existing causes for which a defendant was not responsible would probably be an important element in fixing damages, but it is not a defense.

Turner v. Nassau Electric R.R. Co., . . . 58 N.Y. Supp. 490 (N.Y. App. Div.), was a case singularly similar to this one, except that there the physician ventured the opinion that delirium tremens would not have ensued except for the accident resulting from defendant's negligence, whereas in the present case there is no opinion on this point. I think, however, that no presumption can be indulged in for the benefit of the present appellant that delirium tremens would have occurred without its agency. In that case a judgment in favor of the intestate's representative was sustained on the ground that the accident precipitated the delirium tremens which resulted in the death . . .

In Jeffersonville, etc., R.R. Co. v. Riley, 39 Ind. 568, it was said with reference to a request to charge made by the defendant and denied: "If it was intended to have the court say to the jury that when a person has a tendency to insanity or disease, and receives an injury which produces death, but which would not have produced death in a well person (the plaintiff cannot recover), the charge was rightly refused. If death was the result of the pre-existing circumstances, and the injury had nothing to do with producing or accelerating the result, then the injury would not be the cause of death." . . .

I think the judgment should be affirmed, with costs . . . .

Judgment affirmed.

THIN SKULLS AND FRAGILE PSYCHES

McCahill applies what is commonly referred to as the "thin skull" rule — a tortfeasor must "take his plaintiff as he finds him." (Where do you suppose the phrase "thin skull" came from? Think about it. Free up your imagination.) American courts unanimously recognize the thin skull rule when the unexpected consequence occurs systemically, within the plaintiff's body, as the result of a physical injury to the plaintiff's person. That is what happened in *McCahill*, and the result is the same regardless of whether the tort victim's preexisting physical condition takes the form of advanced alcoholism, a thin skull, or a fragile shin bone. *See, e.g.,* Bushong v. Park, 837 A.2d 49 (D.C. 2003) (plaintiff paralyzed as a result of collision; that plaintiff suffered from spinal stenosis — a narrowing of the back or neck spinal canal, which causes compression of the nerve roots prior to accident — does not relieve defendant from liability); Kroger v. Adcock, 25 So. 3d 1105 (Miss. Ct. App. 2010) (plaintiff suffered from a preexisting degenerative disc disease that was aggravated in an auto accident caused by defendant's negligence; plaintiff is entitled to recovery for the aggravation of the preexisting disease). Of course, it goes without saying that the thin skull rule does not bear on the question of whether the defendant was negligent in the first place. A defendant need not take into account the idiosyncrasies of possible plaintiffs when acting. She is entitled to assume that the people her actions may harm are of ordinary capacity to resist injury.

Should the thin skull rule apply when the initial, negligently caused physical invasion triggers an unusual and debilitating psychological response? Most courts allow recovery for injury to the victim's fragile psyche in such cases. In Steinhauser v. Hertz Corp., 421 F.2d 1169 (2d Cir. 1970), the 14-year-old plaintiff's involvement in an automobile accident (she was shaken, but suffered no physical injury) triggered the onset of chronic schizophrenia. The appellate court held that the jury should be instructed that the plaintiff could recover even though a predisposition caused her mental disorder if it had been "precipitated" by the accident.

In Bartolone v. Jeckovich, 481 N.Y.S.2d 545 (N.Y. App. Div. 1984), an adult plaintiff was involved in a four-car collision caused by defendants' negligence. After receiving relatively minor physical injuries, plaintiff thereafter suffered an "acute psychotic breakdown" that totally and permanently disabled him. The court described the facts as follows (*id.* at 546):

> Three psychiatrists and one neurosurgeon testified on behalf of plaintiff. From their testimony a strange and sad profile emerged: Plaintiff's mother had died of cancer when he was a very young boy. His sister had also died of cancer. Probably as a consequence, plaintiff had developed a fear and dislike of doctors and engaged in body building in order to avoid doctors and ward off illness. His bodily fitness was extremely important to him because it provided him with a sense of control over his life so that he was able to function in a relatively normal way. He had adopted a life-style in which he was something of a "loner," but he was self-supporting, had no complaints and lived a rather placid existence. After the accident, although his physical injuries were minor, he perceived that his bodily integrity was impaired and that he was physically deteriorating. Because he had such an intense emotional investment in his body, his perception of this impairment made him incapable of his former physical feats and he was thus deprived of the mechanism by which he coped with his emotional problems. As a consequence, he deteriorated psychologically and socially as well. He increasingly isolated himself and felt himself to be a victim of powerful forces over which he had no control. It was the consensus of plaintiff's medical experts that he had suffered from a preexisting schizophrenic illness which had been exacerbated by the accident and that he was now in a chronic paranoid schizophrenic state which is irreversible.

At trial, the jury returned a verdict of $500,000, which the trial court reduced to $30,000 on remittitur. Reversing the reduction in recovery, the appellate court concluded (*id.* at 547):

> The circumstances of . . . the case before us illustrate the truth of the old axiom that a defendant must take a plaintiff as he finds him and hence may be held liable in damages for aggravation of a preexisting illness. Nor may defendants avail themselves of the argument that plaintiff should be denied recovery because his condition might have occurred even without the accident.
>
> The record presents ample evidence that plaintiff, although apparently suffering from a quiescent psychotic illness, was able to function in a relatively normal manner but that this minor accident aggravated his schizophrenic condition leaving him totally and permanently disabled.

While the thin skull rule encompasses most injuries flowing directly from the defendant's negligent conduct, plaintiffs who suffer special injuries as a result of religious beliefs or past mental trauma may not take advantage of the rule. For example, in Williams v. Bright, 658 N.Y.S.2d 910, 913 n.4 (N.Y. App. Div. 1997), discussed in Chapter 3, p. 187, the court held that the thin skull rule did not apply to a plaintiff who was confined to a wheelchair as a result of injuries she suffered when the car she rode in flipped over after running off the highway. She refused corrective surgery that would have substantially normalized her life because her religion forbade the required blood transfusion. Similarly, the court of appeals in Ragin v. Macklowe Real Estate Co., 6 F.3d 898 (2d Cir. 1993) held that plaintiff could not recover for unusual emotional distress suffered, in part stemming from past trauma from racial discrimination.

DOES THE THIN SKULL RULE APPLY TO PROPERTY INTERESTS?

Thus far, in assessing applications of the thin skull rule we have considered systemic effects, both physical and mental, on the plaintiff's person. Should the rule apply when the plaintiff's harm takes the form of property damage rather than personal injury? The best-known decision on point is English. Thus, in In re Polemis & Furness, Withy & Co., [1921] 3 K.B. 560 (C.A.), the defendants unloaded plaintiffs' ship. While unloading, one of the defendants' servants dropped a plank into a hold of the ship containing cans of highly volatile petroleum-based liquids. Some of the cans had been broken, and were leaking vapors. When the plank hit the floor of the hold, it apparently caused a spark that ignited the vapor. The resulting fire destroyed the ship. Plaintiffs' claim was submitted to arbitration and the arbitrators found defendants' servants negligent in dropping the plank into the hold and that some damage to the ship could have been foreseen. However, the arbitrators also found that defendants could not have anticipated that the plank would cause an explosion. In ruling that the plaintiffs were entitled to judgment, Scrutton L.J. said in part (*id.* at 577):

> To determine whether an act is negligent, it is relevant to determine whether any reasonable person would foresee that the act would cause damage; if he would not, the act is not negligent. But if the act would or might probably cause damage, the fact that the damage it in fact causes is not the exact kind of damage one would expect is immaterial, so long as the damage is in fact directly traceable to the negligent act, and not due to the operation of independent causes having no connection with the negligent act, except that they could not avoid its results. Once the act is negligent, the fact that its exact operation was not foreseen is immaterial.

Nowhere in his opinion does Lord Justice Scrutton explicitly invoke the thin skull rule; but his analysis is consistent with treating the ship as one would treat the plaintiff's person under that rule, is it not? In any event, under the *Polemis* rule, the defendants' liability appears to depend on whether the consequences to the plaintiff could be characterized as "direct." Presumably, the consequences would not be direct if a significant new cause intervened between the defendant's negligence and the plaintiff's harm.

In 1961 *Polemis* was effectively overruled in Overseas Tankship (U.K.) Ltd. v. Morts Dock & Engineering Co. Ltd. (Wagon Mound No. 1), *Privy Council* [1961] A.C. 388. An oil-burning vessel, the Wagon Mound, spilled oil into the harbor in Sydney, Australia, on October 30, 1951. At the time of the spill, workers were using acetylene torches in repairing a nearby wharf. Those in charge of the Wagon Mound did not try to disperse the oil, which drifted in under the wharf on the surface of the water. The wharf owners asked whether the oil would ignite due to the acetylene torch work, and were assured that it would not. Shortly thereafter, on November 1, the oil ignited and the wharf area was destroyed by fire. The wharf owners sued the operators of the Wagon Mound, alleging that the spillage of oil was negligent because it was foreseeable that the oil would foul bilge pumps and other equipment in the harbor area. The defendants argued that because the oil catching fire was unforeseeable, they should not be held liable. The trial court, sitting without a jury in admiralty, found that the fire was unforeseeable, but awarded recovery to the plaintiffs, presumably on the authority of the *Polemis* decision. The defendants appealed to the Privy Council, the English high court that hears final appeals from all Commonwealth countries. In reversing the trial court the Privy Council said:

> It is, no doubt, proper when considering tortious liability for negligence to analyze its elements and to say that the plaintiff must prove a duty owed to him by the defendant, a breach of that duty by the defendant, and consequent damage. But there can be no liability until the damage has been done. It is not the act but the consequences on which tortious liability is founded. Just as (as it has been said) there is no such thing as negligence in the air, so there is no such thing as liability in the air. Suppose an action brought by A for damage caused by the carelessness (a neutral word) of B, for example, a fire caused by the careless spillage of oil. It may, of course, become relevant to know what duty B owed to A, but the only liability that is in question is the liability for damage by fire. It is vain to isolate the liability from its context and to say that B is or is not liable, and then to ask for what damage he is liable. For his liability is in respect of that damage and no other. If, as admittedly it is, B's liability (culpability) depends on the reasonable foreseeability of the consequent damage, how is that to be determined except by the foreseeability of the damage which in fact happened — the damage in suit? And, if that damage is unforeseeable so as to displace liability at large, how can the liability be restored so as to make compensation payable?

FOOD FOR THOUGHT

In rejecting the *Polemis* rule in favor of a proximate cause approach based on reasonable foreseeability, the Privy Council appears to be returning to the approach set forth in *Marshall, supra.* In a subsequent case arising out of the same events, owners of ships in the harbor that were destroyed by fire sued the defendants for their damages. In this case the plaintiffs recovered. The decision in Overseas Tankship (U.K.) Ltd. v. The Miller Steamship Co. (Wagon Mound No. 2) [Privy Council [1967] 1 A.C. 617] has confounded the authors of this casebook and other scholarly commentators. We spare you the agony of reading the case.

IT'S CRYSTAL BALL TIME: MAKING CLOSE FORESEEABILITY CALLS

In cases where the unexpected (and typically more severe) harm to the plaintiff's person or property does not flow systemically from the first tortious invasion of the plaintiff's interest, American courts generally employ the *Marshall/Wagon Mound* foreseeability approach in working out proximate cause. Thus, in Wallace v. Owens-Illinois, Inc., 389 S.E.2d 155 (S.C. Ct. App. 1989), the plaintiff escaped injury when a glass bottle of soft drink exploded in his kitchen. He left the kitchen unharmed and returned five minutes later to clean up. While doing so, he got liquid on the soles of his bedroom slippers, causing him to slip and fall, sustaining injuries. The trial court invoked proximate causation and granted summary judgment for the producers and distributors of the defective bottle of soft drink. The court of appeals reversed, concluding (*id.* at 156):

> The circuit court held Wallace's injury was not foreseeable, because he was not hurt by the explosion itself. In doing so, the court applied the wrong legal test. It is certainly surprising that Wallace was not injured by the explosion. However, it is not an expected harm which fails to occur, but the foreseeable harm which does occur that is the touchstone of proximate cause.

A different result occurred in Crankshaw v. Piedmont Driving Club, 156 S.E.2d 208 (Ga. Ct. App. 1967), where a customer in a restaurant became ill after eating negligently prepared food and vomited in the restroom. Plaintiff followed the customer into the bathroom to render assistance, slipped on the vomit, and sustained injury. The court denied plaintiff recovery as a matter of law on the ground that, while injury to the customer was reasonably foreseeable, injury to the plaintiff was not.

In Arnold v. F.J. Hab, Inc., 745 N.E.2d 912 (Ind. Ct. App. 2001), the plaintiff was a patron at defendant's nightclub. Plaintiff's sister attempted to leave the club. When the plaintiff's sister reached her car, which was parked in the club-owned parking lot across the street, she found that another patron's car, occupied only by a passenger, blocked the exit to the lot. At this time the club's security guard, normally stationed in the parking lot, had gone inside for a moment. The passenger moved to the driver's seat and attempted to move the car. In attempting to move the car out of the way, she lost control and swerved across the street toward the club. At just that moment, the plaintiff exited the club building across the street, and was struck by the out-of-control vehicle, causing severe injury. Plaintiff brought an action against the nightclub, claiming that by maintaining security officers in the lot it had assumed a duty to control the traffic flow in the parking lot, and that its failure to do so proximately caused the plaintiff's injuries. In upholding summary judgment for the defendant, the court stated (*id.* at 918):

[W]hile we acknowledge that the exact manner in which an injury occurs is not dispositive of whether the injury was foreseeable, we cannot agree with [plaintiff's] contention that it was foreseeable that the injuries, which she sustained while present on a sidewalk located across a two-lane street from the parking lot, could occur "as a result of traffic within the parking area."

In Heatherly v. Alexander, 421 F.3d 638 (8th Cir. 2005), the defendant (Gilbertson), a professional truck driver, parked his tractor-trailer unit at 1:15 a.m. on the shoulder (or emergency lane) of the deceleration portion of the exit ramp of a divided highway and went to sleep in the tractor's sleep bunk. Around 2:30 a.m. the Heatherlys' motor home approached the area towing a Ford Escort. Another tractor-trailer rig, stolen and being driven by Alexander, started to exit the highway and came up behind the motor home at a speed of nearly 90 mph. A series of four collisions occurred. Alexander's truck struck the back of the Ford Escort. This propelled the Escort forward, striking the back of the motor home. The next impact involved Alexander's truck striking the back of the motor home forcing the motor home traveling at 60 to 70 mph into the back of Gilbertson's parked tractor-trailer. The motor home and Gilbertson's rig went up in flames. One of the Heatherlys' children suffered a leg injury that required amputation below the knee. Carol Heatherly was killed in the collision. Gilbertson's parking on the exit ramp was negligent and a but-for cause of the injuries to the Heatherly family. The trial judge directed a verdict for the defendant, Gilbertson, on the grounds that his conduct in parking his truck on the exit ramp was not a proximate cause of plaintiffs' injuries as a matter of law. On appeal, the Eighth Circuit reversed, saying the "jury was not allowed to perform its duty of calibrating the limits of liability flowing from an established duty and breach thereof with regard to the collision between the motor home and the negligently parked . . . truck" (421 F.3d at 644).

In any event, courts treat as "foreseeable" any misfortunes that befall victims as a direct result of seeking medical care for the injuries suffered in the accident caused by the defendant's negligence. Thus, in Anaya v. Superior Court, 93 Cal. Rptr. 2d 228 (Cal. Ct. App. 2000), the plaintiffs' intestate was injured in an auto accident allegedly caused by the defendant's negligence. She survived the accident, but died when the helicopter taking her to the hospital crashed. The court of appeals held that (*id.* at 231) "it is foreseeable that, after a traffic collision, the . . . injuries suffered in the collision would require the victim to be transported for medical care to a medical facility. [As a result, t]he tortfeasors liable for the original accident . . . are liable for any injuries (or death) suffered by the victim on the way to the hospital." Do you suppose the court in *Anaya* would have reached the same result if the helicopter crash was clearly due to negligent maintenance (an engine failure, for example)? What if the helicopter pilot were intoxicated? What if a freak thunderstorm caused the helicopter crash? Would the court have entertained an action by the helicopter crew against the persons responsible for the auto accident? *See* Maltman v. Sauer, 530 P.2d 254 (Wash. 1975) (in a case with the same facts as *Anaya*, affirming summary judgment for defendant against families of helicopter crew because no proximate cause). The Restatement, Third, of Torts § 35 states that "[a]n actor whose tortious conduct is a factual cause of physical harm to another is subject to liability for any enhanced harm the other suffers due to the efforts of third persons to render aid reasonably required by the other's injury. . . ."

hypo 43

A seriously injured both of his legs in an auto accident caused by the negligence of *B*. Dr. *C*, a surgeon, decided that the injury to *A*'s right leg was so serious that he had to amputate the leg to save *A*'s life. When operating, Dr. *C* made a mistake and amputated the left leg instead. Is *B* liable for Dr. *C*'s malpractice in amputating the wrong leg?

hypo 44

A paid premiums for a cancer insurance policy. She received notice that if she didn't pay her premiums by December 21, 2011, her cancer insurance would lapse. In November 2011 *A* discovered a lump on her neck and underwent a CT scan. In early December Dr. *T* informed her that though the CT scan showed some abnormalities she had no cause for concern. *A* allowed her premiums to lapse. In January 2012 Dr. *X* told her that Dr. *T* had negligently misread the CT scan. *A* sues Dr. *T* for malpractice alleging that his misdiagnosis caused her to cancel her cancer policy. What result?

NEGLIGENCE PER SE AND PROXIMATE CAUSE

You will recall from Chapter 3 that dangerous conduct that violates safety statutes constitutes negligence per se, as a matter of law. As you might have expected, courts recognize a proximate causation requirement in negligence cases involving such statutory violations. Thus, in Gorris v. Scott [1874] 9 L.R. (Exch.) 125, the English court considered claims that certain sheep owned by the plaintiff had washed overboard in a storm while being transported at sea by ship. The ship in question did not have pens required by an Act of Parliament, which allegedly would have prevented the loss of the sheep. Nonetheless, the court refused to hold the defendant liable based on safety regulations under the statute. The court observed (*id.* at 127):

> The Act was passed merely for sanitary purposes, in order to prevent animals in a state of infectious disease from communicating it to other animals with which they might come in contact. . . . [I]f by reason of the default in question the plaintiffs' sheep . . . had arrived in this country in a state of disease, I do not say that they might not have maintained this action. But the damage complained of here is something totally apart from the object of the Act of Parliament, and it is in accordance with all the authorities to say that the action is not maintainable.

American courts impose a similar proximate causation requirement in the context of violations of safety statutes. *See, e.g.*, Morales v. City of New York,

---

authors' dialogue 21

BRAD: Does *Gorris v. Scott* make sense to you?

AARON: Sure. The plaintiff's harm must be of the sort we (or in *Gorris*, the English Parliament) had in mind when the defendant's conduct was judged to be negligent. It's textbook stuff.

BRAD: But can't we (or Parliament) have more than one purpose in mind in any given instance? What if the primary purpose of requiring pens was disease control, but another purpose of pens was helping to reduce the risk of livestock being lost in storms at sea?

AARON: But the court in *Gorris* said that the Act was passed "merely for sanitary purposes." Are you disagreeing with them?

BRAD: It's not so much that I'm disagreeing with them. It's just that I don't see how the statute makes any difference. Since the court has no way of knowing that every member of Parliament who voted for the Act thought about its purposes, the court ends up making an assumption about why a reasonable vessel owner would contain sheep in pens for an overseas journey. I'm okay with doing that, but are we then really talking about legislative intent?

---

521 N.E.2d 425 (N.Y. 1988) (holding that violation of a statute prohibiting dispensing gasoline in unapproved containers was not the proximate cause of later arson using the gasoline). One classic example of a court bringing proximate cause limits to bear in the context of a statutory violation is Larrimore v. American National Insurance Co., 89 P.2d 340 (Okla. 1939). In this case, a statute prohibited "lay[ing] out" poison except "in a safe place on [one's] own premises." 89 P.2d at 343. The defendant provided rat poison to its coffee-shop tenant. The poison was left lying on a counter top, negligently creating a risk of harm or death by poisoning. It was also near a coffee burner. When the plaintiff waitress lit the coffee burner, the poison exploded because of its chemical composition, severely burning her hand. The court held that the risk of explosion was not the sort of risk that the statute was intended to protect against, and thus the proximate cause link between the negligent conduct and the plaintiff's harm was missing.

PALSGRAF v. LONG ISLAND R.R.
162 N.E. 99 (N.Y. 1928)

Appeal from a judgment of the Appellate Division of the Supreme Court in the second judicial department . . . affirming a judgment in favor of plaintiff entered upon a verdict.

CARDOZO, C.J. Plaintiff was standing on a platform of defendant's railroad after buying a ticket to go to Rockaway Beach. A train stopped at the station, bound for another place. Two men ran forward to catch it. One of the men reached the platform of the car without mishap, though the train was already moving. The other man, carrying a package, jumped aboard the car, but seemed unsteady as if about to fall. A guard on the car, who had held the door open, reached forward to help him in, and another guard on the platform pushed him from behind. In this act, the package was dislodged, and fell upon the rails. It was a package of small size, about fifteen inches long, and was covered by a newspaper. In fact it contained fireworks, but there was nothing in its appearance to give notice of its contents. The fireworks when they fell exploded. The shock of the explosion threw down some scales at the other end of the platform, many feet away. The scales struck the plaintiff, causing injuries for which she sues.

The conduct of the defendant's guard, if a wrong in its relation to the holder of the package, was not a wrong in its relation to the plaintiff, standing far away. Relatively to her it was not negligence at all. Nothing in the situation gave notice that the falling package had in it the potency of peril to persons thus removed. Negligence is not actionable unless it involves the invasion of a legally protected interest, the violation of a right. "Proof of negligence in the air, so to speak, will not do" (Pollock, Torts [11th ed.], p. 455 . . .). The plaintiff as she stood upon the platform of the station might claim to be protected against intentional invasion of her bodily security. Such invasion is not charged. She might claim to be protected against unintentional invasion by conduct involving in the thought of reasonable men an unreasonable hazard that such invasion would ensue. These, from the point of view of the law, were the bounds of her immunity, with perhaps some rare exceptions, survivals for the most part of ancient forms of liability, where conduct is held to be at the peril of the actor.

If no hazard was apparent to the eye of ordinary vigilance, an act innocent and harmless, at least to outward seeming, with reference to her, did not take to itself the quality of a tort because it happened to be a wrong, though apparently not one involving the risk of bodily insecurity, with reference to some one else. . . . The plaintiff sues in her own right for a wrong personal to her, and not as the vicarious beneficiary of a breach of duty to another.

A different conclusion will involve us, and swiftly too, in a maze of contradictions. A guard stumbles over a package which has been left upon a platform. It seems to be a bundle of newspapers. It turns out to be a can of dynamite. To the eye of ordinary vigilance, the bundle is abandoned waste, which may be kicked or trod on with impunity. Is a passenger at the other end of the platform protected by the law against the unsuspected hazard concealed beneath the waste? If not, is the result to be any different, so far as the distant passenger is concerned, when the guard stumbles over a valise which a truckman or a porter has left upon the walk? The passenger far away, if the victim of a wrong at all, has a cause of action, not derivative, but original and primary. His claim to be protected against invasion of his bodily security is neither greater nor less because the act resulting in the invasion is a wrong to another far removed. In this case, the rights that are said to have been violated, the interests said to have been invaded, are not even of the same order. The man was not injured in his person nor even put in danger. The purpose of the act, as well as its effect, was to make his person safe. If there was a wrong to him at all, which may very well be doubted, it was a wrong to a property interest only, the safety of his package. Out of this wrong to property, which threatened injury to nothing else, there has passed, we are told, to the plaintiff by derivation or succession a right of action for the invasion of an interest of another order, the right to bodily security. The diversity of interests emphasizes the futility of the effort to build the plaintiff's right upon the basis of a wrong to some one else. The gain is one of emphasis, for a like result would follow if the interests were the same. Even then, the orbit of the danger as disclosed to the eye of reasonable vigilance would be the orbit of the duty. One who jostles one's neighbor in a crowd does not invade the rights of others standing at the outer fringe when the unintended contact casts a bomb upon the ground. The wrongdoer as to them is the man who carries the bomb, not the one who explodes it without suspicion of the danger. Life will have to be made over, and human nature transformed, before prevision so extravagant can be accepted as the norm of conduct, the customary standard to which behavior must conform.

The argument for the plaintiff is built upon the shifting meanings of such words as "wrong" and "wrongful," and shares their instability. What the plaintiff must show is "a wrong" to herself, i.e., a violation of her own right, and not merely a wrong to some one else, nor conduct "wrongful" because unsocial, but not "a wrong" to any one. We are told that one who drives at reckless speed through a crowded city street is guilty of a negligent act and, therefore, of a wrongful one irrespective of the consequences. Negligent the act is, and wrongful in the sense that it is unsocial, but wrongful and unsocial in relation to other travelers, only because the eye of vigilance perceives the risk of damage. If the same act were to be committed on a speedway or a race course, it would lose its wrongful quality. The risk reasonably to be perceived defines the duty to be obeyed, and risk imports relation; it is risk to another or to others within the range of apprehension. . . . The range of reasonable apprehension is at times a question for the court, and at times, if varying inferences are possible, a question for the jury. Here, by concession, there was nothing in the situation to suggest to the most cautious mind that the parcel wrapped in newspaper would spread wreckage through the station. If the guard had thrown it down knowingly and willfully, he would not have threatened the plaintiff's safety, so far as appearances could warn him. His conduct would not have involved, even then, an unreasonable probability of invasion of her bodily security. Liability can be no greater where the act is inadvertent.

Negligence, like risk, is thus a term of relation. Negligence in the abstract, apart from things related, is surely not a tort, if indeed it is understandable at all. . . .

The law of causation, remote or proximate, is thus foreign to the case before us. The question of liability is always anterior to the question of the measure of the consequences that go with liability. If there is no tort to be redressed, there is no occasion to consider what damage might be recovered if there were a finding of a tort. We may assume, without deciding, that negligence, not at large or in the abstract, but in relation to the plaintiff, would entail liability for any and all consequences, however novel or extraordinary. There is room for argument that a distinction is to be drawn according to the diversity of interests invaded by the act, as where conduct negligent in that it threatens an insignificant invasion of an interest in property results in an unforeseeable invasion of an interest of another order, as, e.g., one of bodily security. Perhaps other distinctions may be necessary. We do not go into the question now. The consequences to be followed must first be rooted in a wrong.

The judgment of the Appellate Division and that of the Trial Term should be reversed, and the complaint dismissed, with costs in all courts.

ANDREWS, J. (dissenting). . . .

. . . The result we shall reach depends upon our theory as to the nature of negligence. Is it a relative concept — the breach of some duty owing to a particular person or to particular persons? Or where there is an act which unreasonably threatens the safety of others, is the doer liable for all its proximate consequences, even where they result in injury to one who would generally be thought to be outside the radius of danger? This is not a mere dispute as to words. We might not believe that to the average mind the dropping of the bundle would seem to involve the probability of harm to the plaintiff standing many feet away whatever might be the case as to the owner or to one so near as to be likely to be struck by its fall. If, however, we adopt the second hypothesis we have to inquire only as to the relation between cause and effect. We deal in terms of proximate cause, not of negligence. . . .

But we are told that "there is no negligence unless there is in the particular case a legal duty to take care, and this duty must be one which is owed to the plaintiff himself and not merely to others." (Salmond, Torts [6th ed.], 24.) This, I think too narrow a conception. Where there is the unreasonable act, and some right that may be affected, there is negligence whether damage does or does not result. That is immaterial. Should we drive down Broadway at a reckless speed, we are negligent whether we strike an approaching car or miss it by an inch. The act itself is wrongful. It is a wrong not only to those who happen to be within the radius of danger but to all who might have been there — a wrong to the public at large. Such is the language of the street. . . . Due care is a duty imposed on each one of us to protect society from unnecessary danger, not to protect A, B or C alone.

It may well be that there is no such thing as negligence in the abstract. "Proof of negligence in the air, so to speak, will not do." In an empty world negligence would not exist. It does involve a relationship between man and his fellows. But not merely a relationship between man and those whom he might reasonably expect his act would injure. Rather, a relationship between him and those whom he does in fact injure. If his act has a tendency to harm some one, it harms him a mile away as surely as it does those on the scene. . . .

In the well-known *Polemis* case (1921, 3 K.B. 560), Scrutton, L.J., said that the dropping of a plank was negligent for it might injure "workman or cargo or ship." Because of either possibility the owner of the vessel was to be made good for his loss. The act being wrongful, the doer was liable for its proximate results. Criticized and explained as this statement may have been, I think it states the law as it should be and as it is.

The proposition is this. Every one owes to the world at large the duty of refraining from those acts that may unreasonably threaten the safety of others. Such an act occurs. Not only is he wronged to whom harm might reasonably be expected to result, but he also who is in fact injured, even if he be outside what would generally be thought the danger zone. There needs be duty due the one complaining but this is not a duty to a particular individual because as to him harm might be expected. Harm to some one being the natural result of the act, not only that one alone, but all those in fact injured may complain. We have never, I think, held otherwise. Indeed in the *Di Caprio* case we said that a breach of a general ordinance defining the degree of care to be exercised in one's calling is evidence of negligence as to every one. We did not limit this statement to those who might be expected to be exposed to danger. Unreasonable risk being taken, its consequences are not confined to those who might probably be hurt.

If this be so, we do not have a plaintiff suing by "derivation or succession." Her action is original and primary. Her claim is for a breach of duty to herself — not that she is subrogated to any right of action of the owner of the parcel or of a passenger standing at the scene of the explosion.

The right to recover damages rests on additional considerations. The plaintiff's rights must be injured, and this injury must be caused by the negligence. We build a dam, but are negligent as to its foundations. Breaking, it injures property downstream. We are not liable if all this happened because of some reason other than the insecure foundation. But when injuries do result from our unlawful act we are liable for the consequences. It does not matter that they are unusual, unexpected, unforeseen and unforeseeable. But there is one limitation. The damages must be so connected with the negligence that the latter may be said to be the proximate cause of the former.

These two words have never been given an inclusive definition. What is a cause in a legal sense, still more what is a proximate cause, depends in each case upon many considerations, as does the existence of negligence itself. Any philosophical doctrine of causation does not help us. A boy throws a stone into a pond. The ripples spread. The water level rises. The history of that pond is altered to all eternity. It will be altered by other causes also. Yet it will be forever the resultant of all causes combined. Each one will have an influence. How great only omniscience can say. You may speak of a chain, or if you please, a net. An analogy is of little aid. Each cause brings about future events. Without each the future would not be the same. Each is proximate in the sense it is essential. But that is not what we mean by the word. Nor on the other hand do we mean sole cause. There is no such thing. . . .

. . . What we do mean by the word "proximate" is, that because of convenience, of public policy, of a rough sense of justice, the law arbitrarily declines to trace a series of events beyond a certain point. This is not logic. It is practical politics. Take our rule as to fires. Sparks from my burning haystack set on fire my house and my neighbor's. I may recover from a negligent railroad. He may not. Yet the wrongful act as directly harmed the one as the other. We may regret that the line was drawn just where it was, but drawn somewhere it had to be. We said the act of the railroad was not the proximate cause of our neighbor's fire. Cause it surely was. The words we used were simply indicative of our notions of public policy. Other courts think differently. But somewhere they reach the point where they cannot say the stream comes from any one source.

Take the illustration given in an unpublished manuscript by a distinguished and helpful writer on the law of torts. A chauffeur negligently collides with another car which is filled with dynamite, although he could not know it. An explosion follows. A, walking on the sidewalk nearby, is killed. B, sitting in a window of a building opposite, is cut by flying glass. C, likewise sitting in a window a block away, is similarly injured. And a further illustration. A nursemaid, ten blocks away, startled by the noise, involuntarily drops a baby from her arms to the walk. We are told that C may not recover while A may. As to B it is a question for court or jury. We will all agree that the baby might not. Because, we are again told, the chauffeur had no reason to believe his conduct involved any risk of injuring either C or the baby. As to them he was not negligent.

But the chauffeur, being negligent in risking the collision, his belief that the scope of the harm he might do would be limited is immaterial. His act unreasonably jeopardized the safety of any one who might be affected by it. C's injury and that of the baby were directly traceable to the collision. Without that, the injury would not have happened. C had the right to sit in his office, secure from such dangers. The baby was entitled to use the sidewalk with reasonable safety.

The true theory is, it seems to me, that the injury to C, if in truth he is to be denied recovery, and the injury to the baby is that their several injuries were not the proximate result of the negligence. And here not what the chauffeur had reason to believe would be the result of his conduct, but what the prudent would foresee, may have a bearing — may have some bearing, for the problem of proximate cause is not to be solved by any one consideration.

It is all a question of expediency. There are no fixed rules to govern our judgment. There are simply matters of which we may take account. . . . There is in truth little to guide us other than common sense.

There are some hints that may help us. The proximate cause, involved as it may be with many other causes, must be, at the least, something without which the event would not happen. The court must ask itself whether there was a natural and continuous sequence between cause and effect. Was the one a substantial factor in producing the other? Was there a direct connection between them, without too many intervening causes? Is the effect of cause on result not too attenuated? Is the cause likely, in the usual judgment of mankind, to produce the result? Or by the exercise of prudent foresight could the result be foreseen? Is the result too remote from the cause, and here we consider remoteness in time and space. . . . Clearly we must so consider, for the greater the distance either in time or space, the more surely do other causes intervene to affect the result. . . .

Here another question must be answered. In the case supposed it is said, and said correctly, that the chauffeur is liable for the direct effect of the explosion although he had no reason to suppose it would follow a collision. "The fact that the injury occurred in a different manner than that which might have been expected does not prevent the chauffeur's negligence from being in law the cause of the injury." But the natural results of a negligent act — the results which a prudent man would or should foresee — do have a bearing upon the decision as to proximate cause. We have said so repeatedly. What should be foreseen? No human foresight would suggest that a collision itself might injure one a block away. On the contrary, given an explosion, such a possibility might be reasonably expected. I think the direct connection, the foresight of which the courts speak, assumes prevision of the explosion, for the immediate results of which, at least, the chauffeur is responsible.

It may be said this is unjust. Why? In fairness he should make good every injury flowing from his negligence. Not because of tenderness toward him we say he need not answer for all that follows his wrong. We look back to the catastrophe, the fire kindled by the spark, or the explosion. We trace the consequences — not indefinitely, but to a certain point. And to aid us in fixing that point we ask what might ordinarily be expected to follow the fire or the explosion.

This last suggestion is the factor which must determine the case before us. The act upon which defendant's liability rests is knocking an apparently harmless package onto the platform. The act was negligent. For its proximate consequences the defendant is liable. If its contents were broken, to the owner; if it fell upon and crushed a passenger's foot, then to him. If it exploded and injured one in the immediate vicinity, to him also as to A in the illustration. Mrs. Palsgraf was standing some distance away. How far cannot be told from the record — apparently twenty-five or thirty feet. Perhaps less. Except for the explosion, she would not have been injured. We are told by the appellant in his brief "it cannot be denied that the explosion was the direct cause of the plaintiff's injuries." So it was a substantial factor in producing the result — there was here a natural and continuous sequence — direct connection. The only intervening cause was that instead of blowing her to the ground the concussion smashed the weighing machine which in turn fell upon her. There was no remoteness in time, little in space. And surely, given such an explosion as here it needed no great foresight to predict that the natural result would be to injure one on the platform at no greater distance from its scene than was the plaintiff. Just how no one might be able to predict. Whether by flying fragments, by broken glass, by wreckage of machines or structures no one could say. But injury in some form was most probable.

Under these circumstances I cannot say as a matter of law that the plaintiff's injuries were not the proximate result of the negligence. That is all we have before us. The court refused to so charge. No request was made to submit the matter to the jury as a question of fact, even would that have been proper upon the record before us.

The judgment appealed from should be affirmed, with costs.

Pound, Lehman and Kellogg, JJ., concur with Cardozo, Ch. J.; Andrews, J., dissents in opinion in which Crane and O'Brien, JJ., concur.

Judgment reversed.

OUTSIDE THE COURTROOM: THE POOP ON PALSGRAF

Palsgraf has generated enormous historical and legal commentary. *See, e.g.,* William L. Prosser, Palsgraf *Revisited*, 52 Mich. L. Rev. 1 (1953); John T. Noonan, Jr., *Persons and Masks of the Law*, ch. 4 (1976); and Robert E. Keeton, *A* Palsgraf *Anecdote*, 56 Tex. L. Rev. 513 (1978). As a result, the facts have been discussed, rehashed, and argued over by generations of law students and commentators. Several factual controversies remain unresolved. For example, it is not clear whether the falling scales caused Mrs. Palsgraf's injuries. The original complaint alleges that the plaintiff was "violently jostled, shoved, crowded, or pushed by the force of [the] explosion or by the crowd of other passengers . . . so that [she] was knocked down or against certain of the platform stairs . . ." and contains no mention whatsoever of any scales.[1] In fact, the *New York Times*'s description of the incident (on the front page of the next day's edition, August 25, 1924) includes a list of the injured and their injuries, in which it names "Helen Polsgraf [sic]" and states her only injury as "shock." The story of the falling scales doesn't appear to come up until trial. Even then, it is hard to piece together a coherent picture of Mrs. Palsgraf's factual contentions. For example, at one point in the trial, Mrs. Palsgraf's attorney appears to assert, in questioning an expert witness, that after the scales hit her, she fell into the stairway. But Mrs. Palsgraf's own testimony leaves out the part about falling into the stairway and focuses exclusively on the falling scales. Would it matter which of these scenarios was the case under Cardozo's reasoning in the majority opinion? What about under the reasoning of Andrews in dissent?

Assuming that the falling scales caused Mrs. Palsgraf's injuries, what caused the scales to fall? One reason for this question is the content of the plaintiff's complaint recited above: it makes no mention of the scales, but does mention the pushing and shoving of the crowd. Does this mean that the scales were knocked over by the crowd's sudden dash to escape the platform? Or, as Mrs. Palsgraf's brief to the Court of Appeals states, was the fall caused by "the concussion resulting from the explosion"? Could the "concussion resulting from the explosion" of mere fireworks have knocked over such a large object? In this connection, the newspaper report of the accident stated that the explosion sent a "penny-weighing machine" situated "over ten feet away" flying, "ripped away some of the platform," and "smashed" some of the windows of the train as it left. If this account is true, then these were certainly no ordinary fireworks, and the explosion was probably powerful enough to have overturned the scales. But did it? Many years later, Mrs. Palsgraf's daughter Lillian, who was at the scene of the accident and who testified at the trial, told a newspaper reporter that the scales clearly fell because of the explosion and not from the movement of the crowd. *See* Jorie Roberts, *Palsgraf Kin Tell Human Side of Famed Case*, Harv. L. Record, April 14, 1978, at 1. Would this matter in determining the railroad's liability? Is it negligence to have a large, dangerous object like the scales sitting on a crowded platform without securing it so that it cannot easily fall?

Also, the majority opinion may mislead readers about how far Mrs. Palsgraf stood from the explosion. The opinion is framed as though the distance was quite large. For example, the phrase "at the other end of the platform, many feet away" in Cardozo's opinion might suggest that one would have to walk parallel to the railroad tracks for a long distance to reach the place where Mrs. Palsgraf stood.

---

1. Plaintiff's Complaint at 7, in 2 *Records and Briefs of Landmark Benjamin Cardozo Opinions* (William H. Manz ed., 1999).

In fact, while "the other end of the platform" is perhaps technically accurate, the plaintiff actually stood at what most people would call the "back" of the platform: one would walk perpendicular to the tracks to reach her position. Thus the accident occurred right in front of her; the distance from Mrs. Palsgraf to the exploding package was only between 12 and 15 feet. She was easily close enough to have been in danger from the explosion, even without any falling scales, as shown by the falling "penny-weighing machine" discussed *supra*. In light of this discrepancy, Mrs. Palsgraf made a motion for reargument. In denying her motion, the Court of Appeals stated that even assuming that she was nearer to the scene, "she was not so near that injury from a falling package, not known to contain explosives, would be within the range of reasonable prevision." Palsgraf v. Long Island R.R., 164 N.E. 564 (N.Y. 1928).

WHAT'S IN A NAME: DUTY OR PROXIMATE CAUSE?

In recent years, tort scholars have engaged in vigorous debate concerning whether Cardozo's reliance on "duty" has a significant role to play in the conceptual framework of negligence. The debate centers on whether judges should retain the power to use the duty rubric to rule for defendants as a matter of law on the ground that no negligence has been proved in the first instance, rather than on the issue of which particular plaintiffs may recover for harm caused by conduct that was clearly negligent toward someone. On the latter issue, most courts use Andrews's "proximate causation" terminology even when they rely on Cardozo's foreseeability analysis to determine outcomes. For an argument that Cardozo retained his duty perspective in later decisions on the New York Court of Appeals, *see* John C.P. Goldberg & Benjamin C. Zipursky, *The Moral of* MacPherson, 146 U. Pa. L. Rev. 1733 (1998). For a broader argument in favor of retaining the duty concept as a general analytical tool in negligence law, *see* John C.P. Goldberg & Benjamin C. Zipursky, *The Restatement (Third) and the Place of Duty in Negligence Law*, 54 Vand. L. Rev. 657 (2001).

THOMPSON v. KACZINSKI
774 N.W.2d 829 (Iowa 2009)

HECHT, Justice.

A motorist lost control of his car on a rural gravel road and crashed upon encountering a trampoline that had been displaced by the wind from an adjoining yard to the surface of the road. He and his spouse sued the owners of the trampoline. The district court granted summary judgment, concluding the defendants owed no duty to the motorist under the circumstances and the personal injuries resulting from the crash were not proximately caused by the defendants' alleged negligence. As we conclude the district court erred in granting summary judgment, we reverse and remand this case for trial.

I. Factual and Procedural Background.

James Kaczinski and Michelle Lockwood resided in rural Madison County, near Earlham, on property abutting a gravel road. During the late summer of 2006, they disassembled a trampoline and placed its component parts on their yard approximately thirty-eight feet from the road. Intending to dispose of them at a later time, Kaczinski and Lockwood did not secure the parts in place. A few weeks later, on the night of September 16 and morning of September 17, 2006, a severe thunderstorm moved through the Earlham area. Wind gusts from the storm displaced the top of the trampoline from the yard to the surface of the road.

Later that morning, while driving from one church to another where he served as a pastor, Charles Thompson approached the defendants' property. When he swerved to avoid the obstruction on the road, Thompson lost control of his vehicle. His car entered the ditch and rolled several times. Kaczinski and Lockwood were awakened by Thompson's screams at about 9:40 a.m., shortly after the accident. When they went outside to investigate, they discovered the top of their trampoline lying on the roadway. Lockwood dragged the object back into the yard while Kaczinski assisted Thompson.

Thompson and his wife filed suit, alleging Kaczinski and Lockwood breached . . . common law duties by negligently allowing the trampoline to obstruct the roadway. Kaczinski and Lockwood moved for summary judgment, contending they owed no duty under the circumstances because the risk of the trampoline's displacement from their yard to the surface of the road was not foreseeable. The district court granted the motion, concluding Kaczinski and Lockwood breached no duty and the damages claimed by the plaintiffs were not proximately caused by the defendants' negligence. The Thompsons appealed. We transferred the case to the court of appeals, which affirmed the district court's ruling. We granted the Thompsons' application for further review. . . .

An actionable claim of negligence requires "'the existence of a duty to conform to a standard of conduct to protect others, a failure to conform to that standard, proximate cause, and damages.'" *Stotts v. Eveleth*, 688 N.W.2d 803, 807 (Iowa 2004) (quoting *Van Essen v. McCormick Enters. Co.*, 599 N.W.2d 716, 718 (Iowa 1999)). Plaintiffs contend Kaczinski and Lockwood owed a common law duty to exercise reasonable care to prevent their personal property from obstructing the roadway and to remove their property from the roadway within a reasonable time after it became an obstruction. Whether a duty arises out of a given relationship is a matter of law for the court's determination. *Shaw v. Soo Line R.R.*, 463 N.W.2d 51, 53 (Iowa 1990).

Our cases have suggested three factors should be considered in determining whether a duty to exercise reasonable care exists: "'(1) the relationship between the parties, (2) reasonable foreseeability of harm to the person who is injured, and (3) public policy considerations.'" *Stotts*, 688 N.W.2d at 810 (quoting *J.A.H. ex rel. R.M.H. v. Wadle & Assocs., P.C.*, 589 N.W.2d 256, 258 (Iowa 1999)); *accord Leonard v. State*, 491 N.W.2d 508, 510-12 (Iowa 1992) (discussing relationship between the parties, foreseeability of harm to the plaintiff, and public policy considerations when determining if a psychiatrist owed a duty to protect members of the public from the violent behavior of a patient). Our previous decisions have characterized the proposition that the relationship giving rise to a duty of care must be premised on the foreseeability of harm to the injured person as "a fundamental rule of negligence law." *Sankey v. Richenberger,* 456 N.W.2d 206, 209-10 (Iowa 1990). The factors have not been viewed as three distinct and necessary elements, but rather as considerations employed in a balancing process. *Stotts,* 688 N.W.2d at 810. "In the end, whether a duty exists is a policy decision based upon all relevant considerations that guide us to conclude a particular person is entitled to be protected from a particular type of harm." *J.A.H.,* 589 N.W.2d at 258.

The role of foreseeability of risk in the assessment of duty in negligence actions has recently been revisited by drafters of the Restatement (Third) of Torts. "An actor ordinarily has a duty to exercise reasonable care when the actor's conduct creates a risk of physical harm." Restatement (Third) of Torts: Liab. for Physical Harm § 7(a), at 90 (Proposed Final Draft No. 1, 2005) [hereinafter Restatement (Third)]. Thus, in most cases involving physical harm, courts "need not concern themselves with the existence or content of this ordinary duty," but instead may proceed directly to the elements of liability set forth in section 6. *Id.* § 6 cmt. *f,* at 81. The general duty of reasonable care will apply in most cases, and thus courts "can rely directly on § 6 and need not refer to duty on a case-by-case basis." *Id.* § 7 cmt. *a,* at 90.

However, in exceptional cases, the general duty to exercise reasonable care can be displaced or modified. *Id.* § 6 cmt. *f,* at 81-82. An exceptional case is one in which "an articulated countervailing principle or policy warrants denying or limiting liability in a particular class of cases." *Id.* § 7(b), at 90. In such an exceptional case, when the court rules as a matter of law that no duty is owed by actors in a category of cases, the ruling "should be explained and justified based on articulated policies or principles that justify exempting [such] actors from liability or modifying the ordinary duty of reasonable care." *Id.* § 7 cmt. *j,* at 98. Reasons of policy and principle justifying a departure from the general duty to exercise reasonable care do not depend on the foreseeability of harm based on the specific facts of a case. *Id.* "A lack of foreseeable risk in a specific case may be a basis for a no-breach determination, but such a ruling is not a no-duty determination." *Id.*

The assessment of the foreseeability of a risk is allocated by the Restatement (Third) to the fact finder, to be considered when the jury decides if the defendant failed to exercise reasonable care.

> Foreseeable risk is an element in the determination of negligence. In order to determine whether appropriate care was exercised, the factfinder must assess the foreseeable risk at the time of the defendant's alleged negligence. The extent of foreseeable risk depends on the specific facts of the case and cannot be usefully assessed for a category of cases; small changes in the facts may make a dramatic change in how much risk is foreseeable. . . . [C]ourts should leave such determinations to juries unless no reasonable person could differ on the matter.

Id. at 97-98. The drafters acknowledge that courts have frequently used foreseeability in no-duty determinations, but have now explicitly disapproved the practice in the Restatement (Third) and limited no-duty rulings to "articulated policy or principle in order to facilitate more transparent explanations of the reasons for a no-duty ruling and to protect the traditional function of the jury as factfinder." *Id.* at 98-99. We find the drafters' clarification of the duty analysis in the Restatement (Third) compelling, and we now, therefore, adopt it.

The district court clearly considered foreseeability in concluding the defendants owed no duty in this case. When the consideration of foreseeability is removed from the determination of duty, as we now hold it should be, there remains the question of whether a principle or strong policy consideration justifies the exemption of Kaczinski and Lockwood — as part of a class of defendants — from the duty to exercise reasonable care. We conclude no such principle or policy consideration exempts property owners from a duty to exercise reasonable care to avoid the placement of obstructions on a roadway. In fact, we have previously noted the public's interest in ensuring roadways are safe and clear of dangerous obstructions for travelers:

> While an abutting landowner is not liable with respect to highway hazards over which he has no control, he is under an obligation to use reasonable care to keep his premises in such condition as not to create hazards in the adjoining highway. He must conduct operations on his land in such a manner as not to injure the highway traveler.

Weber v. Madison, 251 N.W.2d 523, 527 (Iowa 1977) (citation omitted); *see also Fritz v. Parkison,* 397 N.W.2d 714, 715 (Iowa 1986) (noting public policy to keep highways free from obstructions and hazards is well-developed and clearly recognized); *Stewart v. Wild,* 196 Iowa 678, 683, 195 N.W. 266, 269 (1923) ("It is the fundamental law of the highway that it is subject to the use of the traveling public, and that it must be kept free from such obstructions as are not incident to its use for travel."). Accordingly, we conclude the district court erred in determining Kaczinski and Lockwood owed no common law duty under the circumstances presented here.

Although the memorandum filed by Kaczinski and Lockwood in support of their motion for summary judgment raised only the questions of whether a duty was owed and whether a duty was breached, the district court concluded the plaintiffs' claims must fail for the further reason that they did not establish a causal connection between their claimed injuries and damages and the acts and omissions of Kaczinski and Lockwood. Again relying on its determination that the risk of the trampoline's displacement from the yard to the roadway was not foreseeable, the court resolved the causation issue against the Thompsons as a matter of law.

We have held causation has two components: cause in fact and legal cause. *Faber v. Herman,* 731 N.W.2d 1, 7 (Iowa 2007). The decisions of this court have established it is the plaintiff's burden to prove both cause in fact and legal (proximate) cause. *See City of Cedar Falls v. Cedar Falls Cmty. Sch. Dist.,* 617 N.W.2d 11, 17 (Iowa 2000). The latter component requires a policy determination of whether "the policy of the law must require the defendant to be *legally responsible* for the injury." *Gerst v. Marshall,* 549 N.W.2d 810, 815 (Iowa 1996). Causation is a question for the jury, "'*save in very exceptional cases* where the facts are so clear and undisputed, and the relation of cause and effect so apparent to every candid mind, that but one conclusion may be fairly drawn therefrom.'" *Lindquist v. Des Moines Union Ry.,* 239 Iowa 356, 362, 30 N.W.2d 120, 123 (1947) (quoting *Fitter v. Iowa Tel. Co.,* 143 Iowa 689, 693-94, 121 N.W. 48, 50 (1909)).

We have previously applied the test articulated in the Restatement (Second) of Torts when determining if a defendant's conduct is a legal or proximate cause of the plaintiff's damages. This test holds "[t]he actor's negligent conduct is a legal cause of harm to another if (a) his conduct is a substantial factor in bringing about the harm, and (b) there is no rule of law relieving the actor from liability." Restatement (Second) of Torts § 431, at 428 (1965); *accord Kelly v. Sinclair Oil Corp.,* 476 N.W.2d 341, 349 (Iowa 1991). In deciding whether conduct is a substantial factor in bringing about the harm, we have considered the "proximity between the breach and the injury based largely on the concept of foreseeability." *Estate of Long ex rel. Smith v. Broadlawns Med. Ctr.,* 656 N.W.2d 71, 83 (Iowa 2002). The word "substantial" has been used to express "the notion that the defendant's conduct has such an effect in producing the harm as to lead reasonable minds to regard it as a cause." *Sumpter v. City of Moulton,* 519 N.W.2d 427, 434 (Iowa Ct. App. 1994).

The formulation of legal or proximate cause outlined above has been the source of significant uncertainty and confusion. This court's adherence to the formulation has been less than consistent. *See Gerst,* 549 N.W.2d at 816-17 (chronicling inconsistencies in our approach to questions of proximate causation). Even had it been applied consistently, the concept of legal or proximate cause itself has been criticized for confusing factual determinations (substantial factor in bringing about harm) with policy judgments (no rule of law precluding liability). *Id.* at 816. Although we have previously noted our uneven approach to proximate cause questions and acknowledged the criticism of the doctrine, we have not yet had the opportunity to clarify this area of law. *Id.* at 817. We do now.

"Tort law does not impose liability on an actor for all harm factually caused by the actor's tortious conduct." Restatement (Third) ch. 6 Special Note on Proximate Cause, at 574. This concept has traditionally been designated "proximate cause." While this term is used extensively and appropriately by courts, practitioners, and scholars, it causes considerable confusion for juries because it does not clearly express the idea it is meant to represent. *See id.* § 29 cmt. *b,* at 576-77. The confusion arises when jurors understand "proximate cause" as implying "there is but one cause — the cause nearest in time or geography to the plaintiff's harm — and that factual causation bears on the issue of scope of liability." *Id.* § 29 cmt. *b,* at 577. Thus, in an attempt to eliminate unnecessary confusion caused by the traditional vernacular, the drafters of the third Restatement refer to the concept of proximate cause as "scope of liability."

The drafters of the Restatement (Third) explain that the "legal cause" test articulated in the second Restatement included both the "substantial factor" prong and the "rule of law" prong because it was intended to address both factual and proximate cause. *Id.* ch. 6 Special Note on Proximate Cause, at 574. Although the "substantial factor" requirement has frequently been understood to apply to proximate cause determinations, *see Gerst,* 549 N.W.2d at 815-16, the drafters contend it was never intended to do so. Restatement (Third) § 29 cmt. *a*, at 576.[3] Accordingly, to eliminate the resulting confusion of factual and policy determinations resulting from the Restatement (Second) formulation of legal cause, the drafters have opted to address factual cause and scope of liability (proximate cause) separately. Restatement (Third) ch. 6 Special Note on Proximate Cause, at 575. The assessment of scope of liability under the Restatement (Third) no longer includes a determination of whether the actor's conduct was a substantial factor in causing the harm at issue, a question properly addressed under the factual cause rubric. *See id.* § 27 cmt. *j*, at 427-29.

Most importantly, the drafters of the Restatement (Third) have clarified the essential role of policy considerations in the determination of the scope of liability. "An actor's liability is limited to those physical harms that result from the risks that made the actor's conduct tortious." *Id.* § 29, at 575. This principle, referred to as the "risk standard," is intended to prevent the unjustified imposition of liability by "confining liability's scope to the reasons for holding the actor liable in the first place." *Id.* § 29 cmt. *d*, at 579-80. As an example of the standard's application, the drafters provide an illustration of a hunter returning from the field and handing his loaded shotgun to a child as he enters the house. *Id.* cmt. *d*, illus. 3, at 581. The child drops the gun (an object assumed for the purposes of the illustration to be neither too heavy nor unwieldy for a child of that age and size to handle) which lands on her foot and breaks her toe. *Id.* Applying the risk standard described above, the hunter would not be liable for the broken toe because the risk that made his action negligent was the risk that the child would shoot someone, not that she would drop the gun and sustain an injury to her foot. *Id.*

The scope-of-liability issue is fact-intensive as it requires consideration of the risks that made the actor's conduct tortious and a determination of whether the harm at issue is a result of any of those risks. *Id.* § 29 cmt. *d*, at 580, 584. When, as in this case, the court considers in advance of trial whether the plaintiff's harm is beyond the scope of liability as a matter of law, courts must initially consider all of the range of harms risked by the defendant's conduct that the jury *could* find as the basis for determining [the defendant's] conduct tortious. Then, the court can compare the plaintiff's harm with the range of harms risked by the defendant to determine whether a reasonable jury might find the former among the latter. *Id.* at 580.

---

3. Our opinion in *Gerst* suggested the substantial factor test was developed to address a situation, in which there were two or more causes of the harm to plaintiff and either of the causes alone would have been sufficient to bring about the harm. In this situation, because a strict application of the cause-in-fact "but-for" test "would allow both tortfeasors to avoid liability, courts made the policy decision to nevertheless impose liability 'if [the defendant's conduct] was a material element and a *substantial factor* in bringing [the event] about.'" *Gerst*, 549 N.W.2d at 815 (quoting W. Page Keeton et al., *Prosser and Keeton on the Law of Torts* § 41, at 267 (5th ed. 1984)). Citing *Prosser*, we suggested in *Gerst* that "the substantial factor test was originally intended to address a legal causation issue, not one of causation in fact." *Id.* at 815-16. Having reexamined the question, we concur with the drafters of the Restatement (Third) on this point. The Restatement (Third) addresses the problem of multiple sufficient causes as part of the factual cause determination. *See* Restatement (Third) § 27, at 452.

The drafters advance several advantages of limiting liability in this way. First, the application of the risk standard is comparatively simple. *Id.* cmt. *e*, at 585. The standard "appeals to intuitive notions of fairness and proportionality by limiting liability to harms that result from risks created by the actor's wrongful conduct, but for no others." *Id.* It also is flexible enough to "accommodate fairness concerns raised by the specific facts of a case." *Id.*

Foreseeability has previously played an important role in our proximate cause determinations. *See Virden*, 656 N.W.2d at 808. For example,

> An injury that is the natural and probable consequence of an act of negligence is actionable, and such an act is the proximate cause of the injury. But an injury which could not have been foreseen or reasonably anticipated as the probable result of an act of negligence is not actionable and such an act is either the remote cause, or no cause whatever, of the injury. . . .

The drafters of the Restatement (Third) explain that foreseeability is still relevant in scope-of-liability determinations. "In a negligence action, prior incidents or other facts evidencing risks may make certain risks foreseeable that otherwise were not, thereby changing the scope-of-liability analysis." Restatement (Third) § 29 cmt. *d*, at 584-85. In fact, they acknowledge the similarity between the risk standard they articulate and the foreseeability tests applied by most jurisdictions in making causation determinations in negligence cases.

> Properly understood, both the risk standard and a foreseeability test exclude liability for harms that were sufficiently unforeseeable at the time of the actor's tortious conduct that they were not among the risks — potential harms — that made the actor negligent. . . . [W]hen scope of liability arises in a negligence case, the risks that make an actor negligent are limited to foreseeable ones, and the factfinder must determine whether the type of harm that occurred is among those reasonably foreseeable potential harms that made the actor's conduct negligent.

Id. § 29 cmt. *j*, at 594. Although the risk standard and the foreseeability test are comparable in negligence actions, the drafters favor the risk standard because it "provides greater clarity, facilitates clearer analysis in a given case, and better reveals the reason for its existence." *Id.* They explain that a foreseeability test "risks being misunderstood because of uncertainty about what must be foreseen, by whom, and at what time." *Id.* at 595.

We find the drafters' clarification of scope of liability sound and are persuaded by their explanation of the advantages of applying the risk standard as articulated in the Restatement (Third), and, accordingly, adopt it.

Our next task, then, is to consider whether the district court erred in concluding the harm suffered by the Thompsons was, a matter of law, outside the scope of the risk of Kaczinski and Lockwood's conduct. We conclude the question of whether a serious injury to a motorist was within the range of harms risked by disassembling the trampoline and leaving it untethered for a few weeks on the yard less than forty feet from the road is not so clear in this case as to justify the district court's resolution of the issue as a matter of law at the summary judgment stage. A reasonable fact finder could determine Kaczinski and Lockwood should have known high winds occasionally occur in Iowa in September and a strong gust of wind could displace the unsecured trampoline parts the short distance from the yard to the roadway and endanger motorists. Although they were in their home for several hours after the storm passed and approximately two-and-a-half hours after daybreak, Kaczinski and Lockwood did not discover their property on the nearby roadway, remove it, or warn approaching motorists of it. On this record, viewed in the light most favorable to the Thompsons, we conclude a reasonable fact finder could find the harm suffered by the Thompsons resulted from the risks that made the defendants' conduct negligent. Accordingly, the district court erred in deciding the scope-of-liability question as a matter of law in this case. . . .

Court of Appeals decision vacated; district court judgment affirmed in part, reversed in part, and case remanded.

Several courts have recently signed on to the Restatement, Third, position on duty. *See, e.g.*, Behrendt v. Gulf Underwriters Ins. Co., 768 N.W.2d 568 (Wis. 2009); A.W. v. Lancaster County School District 0001, 784 N.W.2d 907 (Neb. 2010); Gipson v. Kasey, 150 P.3d 228 (Ariz. 2007). For a critical view of the Restatement position, *see* Aaron D. Twerski, *The Cleaver, The Violin, and the Scalpel: Duty and the Restatement (Third) of Torts*, 60 Hastings L.J. 1 (2008); John C. P. Goldberg & Benjamin C. Zipursky, *The Restatement (Third) and the Place of Duty in Negligence Law*, 54 Vand. L. Rev. 657 (2001).

Behrendt, above, involved a lawsuit against a company that manufactures tanks to be used under pressure, such as those holding compressed air. It has a policy allowing its employees to use company tools and scrap materials to fabricate items for personal use. An employee of the company built a storage tank for a friend who had opened an oil-change business, expecting that the tank would never be pressurized. One day, however, the friend used the tank under pressure and it exploded, injuring the plaintiff. The trial court concluded, and the court of appeals affirmed, that "as a matter of law, it was not foreseeable that under [the company's] policy of allowing employees to do side projects, a non-pressurized tank built as a side job would later be modified and pressurized and, years later, explode and cause injury." 768 N.W.2d at 571. Assume the premise of that argument is correct — i.e., a reasonable person would not have foreseen that a tank built by company employees might one day be used under pressure. Does that lack of foreseeability go to a conclusion that:

1. The company had no duty to the plaintiff;
2. The company had a duty, but it was not breached by allowing employees to fabricate products as "side jobs"; or
3. The company was negligent in allowing employees to use its tools and materials to build things, but this negligence was not the proximate cause of the plaintiff's injury?

The Wisconsin Supreme Court said courts in that state have always followed the position of Judge Andrew in *Palsgraf*, i.e. that "[e]veryone owes to the world at large the duty of refraining from those acts that may unreasonably threaten the safety of others." *Id.* at 574. On the Andrews view, the company had a duty to ensure that its policy of permitting side jobs did not create an unreasonable risk of injury to people in the plaintiff's position. *Id.* at 576. Lack of foreseeability is one of six public-policy factors that Wisconsin state courts use to limit liability — courts consider whether:

> (1) the injury is too remote from the negligence; (2) the recovery is wholly out of proportion to the culpability of the negligent tort-feasor; (3) the harm caused is highly extraordinary given the negligent act; (4) recovery would place too unreasonable a burden on the negligent tort-feasor; (5) recovery would be too likely to open the way to fraudulent claims; and (6) recovery would enter into a field that has no sensible or just stopping point.

Id. at 577 (quotations and citations omitted). In this case, the court concluded that the remoteness of the harm from the original alleged act of negligence, and the attenuated chain of causation, should properly be considered under the element of breach, not duty or proximate cause.

Other courts have stuck with the Second Restatement approach of using open-ended tests for the existence of a legal duty as a way of handling questions related to the *scope* of duty. In this way they follow the approach sketched out by Judge Cardozo in *Palsgraf.* Consider the example of Westin Operator, LLC v. Groh, 347 P.3d 606 (Colo. 2015). A number of hotel guests had a party in their room, became drunk and belligerent, and were evicted from the hotel. Although there were taxis waiting nearby, the group decided to get rides home with one of their number who was legally intoxicated. The plaintiff, one of the group, suffered traumatic brain injuries in a traffic accident that occurred fifteen miles away. Is the hotel liable for the plaintiff's injuries? One could see this as a proximate cause case: The hotel, having allegedly been negligent by kicking out the guests, who were drunk and had access to an automobile, into a freezing cold night, would be liable for harms that were within the risks that made it negligent to evict the partygoers without taking some precaution, such as calling a cab, or summoning the police to deal with the rowdy guests. Instead, the Colorado Supreme Court handled the question under the rubric of duty. It used language you will encounter again in Chapter 6:

> Duty is "'an expression of the sum total of those considerations of policy which lead the law to say that the plaintiff is [or is not] entitled to protection.'" Univ. of Denver v. Whitlock, 744 P.2d 54, 57 (Colo. 1987) (quoting W. Page Keeton, Prosser and Keeton on Torts § 53, at 358 (5th ed. 1984)); *see also* Observatory Corp. v. Daly, 780 P.2d 462, 466 (Colo. 1989) (characterizing the determination of duty as the exercise of a court's "prudential judgment"). The guiding principle is "fairness under contemporary standards." We ask: "[W]ould reasonable persons recognize and agree that a duty of care exists"? In deciding whether a duty exists, we have traditionally examined (1) the nature of the relationship between the parties and (2) a particular set of public policy factors.

347 P.3d at 612 (some citations omitted). By relying on "public policy factors," the principle of fairness, and characterizing the issue as one for the court's prudential judgment, doesn't the court sound more like Andrews in *Palsgraf* than Cardozo? The court also referred to the common law rule that innkeepers have a "special

---

authors' dialogue 22

BRAD: I feel sorry for my students. *Thompson v. Kaczinksi* and the Third Restatement approach seem bang-on to me. You start with a general duty of reasonable care and then leave these scope-of-liability questions to juries to deal with either in determining whether the duty was breached or as a matter of proximate cause. But all these courts, like the Colorado Supreme Court in *Westin v. Groh*, keep analyzing scope of liability under the banner of duty. No wonder students can never figure out whether a set of facts presents a duty, breach, or proximate cause issue.

JIM: I agree as a general matter, but I don't think the Colorado case you added to the notes gets it wrong. The court just says that innkeepers owe a general duty not to be careless when kicking guests out in the middle of the night. It's winter in Colorado — they might have frozen to death. Surely the hotel has to use some care in dealing with their guests, even if they are drunk and obnoxious. Once the duty is established, it's for the jury to decide how far out in space and time the hotel's liability extends.

AARON: Maybe we're getting ahead of ourselves a bit, but the hotel case involves an affirmative duty. The plaintiff is asking the hotel to make sure she doesn't do something careless, like agree to ride home with a drunk driver. In a case like that you do need the open-ended duty factors to decide whether the hotel's liability extends to the later traffic accident.

BRAD: Well, maybe Chapter 6 will clear things up, but I still think all that stuff about foreseeability, magnitude of the burden, and social utility of the defendant's activity should be relevant to proximate cause, not duty. The innkeeper-guest relationship establishes a duty, and that's all a court has to consider. Then it's for the jury to decide how far out the scope of liability extends.

---

relationship" with their guests that confers a duty to use reasonable care. But that does not answer the question of whether the duty to use reasonable care extends to protecting the guests against the specific risk of getting into a drunk-driving accident at some distance from the hotel premises. To determine whether the hotel had a duty with respect to that risk, the court used a multi-factor *duty* test:

> To determine whether a defendant owes a plaintiff a duty to act to avoid injury, we assess: (1) the risk involved in the defendant's conduct; (2) the foreseeability and likelihood of injury weighed against the social utility of the defendant's conduct; (3) the magnitude of the burden of guarding against the injury; and (4) the consequences of placing that burden on the defendant.

Id. at 613-614. It concluded that the risk of drunk driving was high, that it was foreseeable that intoxicated people "do not always make well-reasoned decisions about transportation home," and that relatively low-cost protective options were available, such as "requesting police assistance, allowing intoxicated guests to wait in the lobby after they call a taxi, or procuring a taxi for an intoxicated guest." *Id.* at

614. The Colorado Supreme Court held only that there was a general duty in this case, and that a jury would still be empowered to limit liability on proximate causation principles:

> In recognizing this duty, we are not implicitly holding that hotels must provide safe transportation off premises during eviction, or even that hotels must ensure that evicted guests actually take advantage of available safe transportation after the eviction occurs. To attempt to fashion liability by imposing a bright-line, inflexible rule that purportedly governs all circumstances would result in "a kind of 'blinking light' of duty that is arbitrary in practice and not helpful to the future development of the law." In a highly fact-specific case like this one, the appropriate means of addressing limits on liability lie not in the articulation of the duty that exists, but in the application of causation principles: The causation element in a tort action functions as a natural limitation of liability . . . . "[D]uty is a preferable means for addressing limits on liability when those limitations are clear, are based on relatively bright lines, are of general application, do not usually require resort to disputed facts in a case, implicate policy concerns that apply to a class of cases that may not be fully appreciated by a jury deciding a specific case, and are employed in cases in which early resolution of liability is particularly desirable . . . . On the other hand, when the limits imposed require careful attention to the specific facts of a case, and difficult, often amorphous evaluative judgments for which modest differences in the factual circumstances may change the outcome, scope of liability [or proximate cause] is a more flexible and preferable device for placing limits on liability."

Id. at 615.

IT'S CRYSTAL BALL TIME (AGAIN)

The range of different circumstances under which courts have been called upon to decide whether injured plaintiffs were within the scope of the risks foreseeably created by defendants' conduct is very wide. In Engle v. Salisbury Township, 2004 WL 869362 (Ohio App.), plaintiff's decedent sued the township for its negligence in not repairing a road in front of her house. Several years before the accident the township, which had maintained the road, stopped doing so. Plaintiff's decedent undertook to maintain the road. The day before the accident that led to his death, there had been heavy rains that created a rut in the road running between the plaintiff's house and the house down the road belonging to the decedent's mother. Plaintiff's decedent sought to fix the road but found that his tractor was out of gas. He called his son to bring him gas to operate the tractor. Due to heavy rains, access to the main road was flooded, necessitating that the decedent use his boat to get to the main road to meet his son. As decedent approached the shoreline where his son was waiting, the boat capsized and decedent, who was not wearing his life jacket, fell into the water and drowned. In upholding the trial court's grant of summary judgment in favor of the township because proximate cause had not been made out, the court said, "It is reasonably foreseeable that one's failure to keep a portion of a road in repair would result in someone being injured while using that portion

---

authors' dialogue 23

JIM: Why was Andrews compelled to say, in the middle of his dissenting opinion in *Palsgraf*, "It is all a matter of expediency"?

AARON: It's true, isn't it?

JIM: I hope it isn't. "Expediency" implies to me that judges are free to reach any outcome that suits them. But they're not. They have taken an oath to uphold the law.

AARON: But doesn't the law of proximate cause allow judges to reach either outcome most of the time? Couldn't they write a reasonable opinion to support a decision for the plaintiff or the defendant in most cases? Didn't Cardozo and Andrews do just that in *Palsgraf*?

JIM: By "allow them to reach either outcome," you are clearly correct if you mean that they won't be impeached or disciplined in either event. But you are wrong if you mean they should feel free to reach either outcome. Cardozo may have been wrong to take victory away from Mrs. Palsgraf, but he would feel insulted if you suggested that he did so because of ethnic or sexist bias. Whenever a judge signs an opinion, or an order, he or she should sincerely believe it is required by the applicable law.

AARON: But what about subconscious factors — isn't it possible that a judge is subconsciously influenced by biases that he or she doesn't even think about? And the law is usually flexible enough to allow those biases room to play out.

JIM: Of course. This is true of all the tort law we've been talking about, almost by definition. But judges must never become cynical about such matters. They should consciously try to do the *right* thing, not the *expedient* thing. And they should try to be aware of their own biases, and keep them in check.

AARON: Your last point is a bit naïve, I think. Most people, including judges, equate what you call "biases" with what they believe is "right." They don't even think of them as "biases" in any pejorative sense. But judges are only human. I guess that's why appellate courts have more judges. The higher up you go in the appellate ladder, the more judges you need to decide the high-profile issues of law. Sort of like juries on issues of fact.

---

of the road. Perhaps it is even foreseeable that one's failure to keep a road in repair would result in someone being injured while performing the neglected repair work. However, no reasonable prudent person could foresee that his failure to keep one portion of a road in repair would result in someone drowning near an adjacent portion of that road." The court conceded that the decedent would not have been in the boat if the township had maintained the road, but held that the negligence was not the proximate cause of the harm.

Similarly, in Hebert v. Enos, 806 N.E.2d 453 (Mass. App. Ct. 2004), plaintiff suffered a severe electric shock while on defendant's property to water defendant's flowers. Plaintiff alleged that the defendant's negligent repairs of a second-floor toilet caused the toilet to overflow. The flooding water reacted with the home's electrical system, creating an electrical current that shocked the plaintiff when he touched the outside water faucet. The plaintiff suffered serious injuries, including burns and exit wounds on his body and damage to his mouth. Citing *Palsgraf,* the court said: "Although we can envision a variety of foreseeable injuries arising out of a defective toilet, the electrical shock to a neighbor when he touches a faucet outside the house is well beyond the 'range of reasonable apprehension' and therefore not foreseeable." *Id.* at 457. In contrast, in Geyer v. City of Logansport, 370 N.E.2d 333 (Ind. 1977), the Indiana Supreme Court reversed a dismissal by the trial court of a claim for damages arising out of the plaintiff being shot accidentally by a police officer. A bull had been negligently allowed to escape, and the police officer shot his revolver at the bull to prevent it from injuring others. The plaintiff, who was not within the line of fire, was struck and injured when the bullet ricocheted off one of the bull's horns. The court of appeals held that the issue of the foreseeability of harm to the plaintiff should have been given to the jury.

B. SUPERSEDING CAUSES

DERDIARIAN v. FELIX CONTRACTING CORP.
414 N.E.2d 666 (N.Y. 1980)

Chief Judge COOKE.

The operator of a motor vehicle, who failed timely to ingest a dosage of medication, suffered an epileptic seizure and his vehicle careened into an excavation site where a gas main was being installed beneath the street surface. The automobile crashed through a single wooden horse-type barricade put in place by the contractor and struck an employee of a subcontractor, who was propelled into the air. Upon landing the employee was splattered by boiling liquid enamel from a kettle also struck by the vehicle. Principally at issue on this appeal is whether plaintiffs, the employee and his wife, failed to establish as a matter of law that the contractor's inadequate safety precautions on the work site were the proximate cause of the accident.

Supreme Court, Queens County, rendered an order, upon a jury verdict, in favor of plaintiffs on the issue of liability. The Appellate Division, with one dissent, affirmed, and granted defendant Felix Contracting Corporation leave to appeal to this court upon a certified question.

The order of the Appellate Division should be affirmed. As a general rule, the question of proximate cause is to be decided by the finder of fact, aided by appropriate instructions. There is no basis on this record for concluding, as a matter of law, that a superseding cause or other factor intervened to break the nexus between defendant's negligence and plaintiff's injury.

During the fall of 1973 defendant Felix Contracting Corporation was performing a contract to install an underground gas main in the City of Mount Vernon for defendant Con Edison. Bayside Pipe Coaters, plaintiff Harold Derdiarian's employer, was engaged as a subcontractor to seal the gas main.

On the afternoon of November 21, 1973, defendant James Dickens suffered an epileptic seizure and lost consciousness, allowing his vehicle to careen into the work site and strike plaintiff with such force as to throw him into the air. When plaintiff landed, he was splattered over his face, head and body with 400 degree boiling hot liquid enamel from a kettle struck by the automobile. The enamel was used in connection with sealing the gas main. Although plaintiff's body ignited into a fire ball, he miraculously survived the incident.

At trial, plaintiff's theory was that defendant Felix had negligently failed to take adequate measures to insure the safety of workers on the excavation site. Plaintiff's evidence indicates that the accident occurred on Oak Street, a two-lane, east-west roadway. The excavation was located in the east-bound lane, and ran from approximately one foot south of the center line to within 2 or 3 feet of the curb. When plaintiff arrived on the site, he was instructed by Felix's foreman to park his truck on the west side of the excavation, parallel to the curb. As a result, there was a gap of some 7 1/2 feet between the side of the truck and the curb line. Derdiarian testified that he made a request to park his truck on the east side of the hole, so he could set up the kettle away from the oncoming eastbound traffic. The Felix foreman instructed him to leave his truck where it was, and plaintiff then put the kettle near the curb, on the west side of the excavation.

James Dickens was driving eastbound on Oak Street when he suffered a seizure and lost consciousness. Dickens was under treatment for epilepsy and had neglected to take his medication at the proper time. His car crashed through a single wooden horse-type barricade that was set up on the west side of the excavation site. As it passed through the site, the vehicle struck the kettle containing the enamel, as well as the plaintiff, resulting in plaintiff's injuries.

To support his claim of an unsafe work site, plaintiff called as a witness Lawrence Lawton, an expert in traffic safety. According to Lawton, the usual and accepted method of safeguarding the workers is to erect a barrier around the excavation. Such a barrier, consisting of a truck, a piece of heavy equipment or a pile of dirt, would keep a car out of the excavation and protect workers from oncoming traffic. The expert testified that the barrier should cover the entire width of the excavation. He also stated that there should have been two flagmen present, rather than one, and that warning signs should have been posted advising motorists that there was only one lane of traffic and that there was a flagman ahead.

Following receipt of the evidence, the trial court charged the jury, among other things, that it could consider, as some evidence of negligence, the violation of a Mount Vernon ordinance. The ordinance imposed upon a construction "permittee" certain safety duties.[2] The court charged that Con Ed was the permittee "and

---

2. The pertinent portions of the ordinance provide:

> "The permittee shall erect and maintain suitable barricades and fences around all of his work while excavation or other work is in progress and shall arrange his work in such a manner as to cause a minimum of inconvenience and delay to vehicular and pedestrian traffic.
>
> "Where free flow of traffic is interfered with, the permittee shall designate competent persons to direct and expedite traffic by means of lights or flags.
>
> "Unless otherwise authorized by the Commissioner, vehicular traffic shall be maintained at all times during the progress of the work being performed under the permit.
>
> "Safety shall be provided with suitable barricades and lights throughout project, and security supplied where necessary."

by contract Felix assumed any obligations under this ordinance that Con Ed had." Felix objected to "the Court charging that by contract Felix assumed any obligation under the ordinance that Consolidated Edison had." The jury found for plaintiff, apportioning liability at 55% for Felix, 35% for Dickens and 10% for Con Ed. Defendant Felix now argues that plaintiff was injured in a freakish accident, brought about solely by defendant Dickens' negligence, and therefore there was no causal link, as a matter of law, between Felix' breach of duty and plaintiff's injuries.

The concept of proximate cause, or more appropriately legal cause, has proven to be an elusive one, incapable of being precisely defined to cover all situations. This is, in part, because the concept stems from policy considerations that serve to place manageable limits upon the liability that flows from negligent conduct. Depending upon the nature of the case, a variety of factors may be relevant in assessing legal cause. Given the unique nature of the inquiry in each case, it is for the finder of fact to determine legal cause, once the court has been satisfied that a prima facie case has been established. To carry the burden of proving a prima facie case, the plaintiff must generally show that the defendant's negligence was a substantial cause of the events which produced the injury. Plaintiff need not demonstrate, however, that the precise manner in which the accident happened, or the extent of injuries, was foreseeable.

Where the acts of a third person intervene between the defendant's conduct and the plaintiff's injury, the causal connection is not automatically severed. In such a case, liability turns upon whether the intervening act is a normal or foreseeable consequence of the situation created by the defendant's negligence. If the intervening act is extraordinary under the circumstances, not foreseeable in the normal course of events, or independent of or far removed from the defendant's conduct, it may well be a superseding act which breaks the causal nexus. Because questions concerning what is foreseeable and what is normal may be the subject of varying inferences, as is the question of negligence itself, these issues generally are for the fact finder to resolve.

There are certain instances, to be sure, where only one conclusion may be drawn from the established facts and where the question of legal cause may be decided as a matter of law. Those cases generally involve independent intervening acts which operate upon but do not flow from the original negligence. Thus, for instance, we have held that where an automobile lessor negligently supplies a car with a defective trunk lid, it is not liable to the lessee who, while stopped to repair the trunk, was injured by the negligent driving of a third party. Although the renter's negligence undoubtedly served to place the injured party at the site of the accident, the intervening act was divorced from and not the foreseeable risk associated with the original negligence. And the injuries were different in kind than those which would have normally been expected from a defective trunk. In short, the negligence of the renter merely furnished the occasion for an unrelated act to cause injuries not ordinarily anticipated.

By contrast, in the present case, we cannot say as a matter of law that defendant Dickens' negligence was a superseding cause which interrupted the link between Felix' negligence and plaintiff's injuries. From the evidence in the record, the jury could have found that Felix negligently failed to safeguard the excavation site. A prime hazard associated with such dereliction is the possibility that a driver will negligently enter the work site and cause injury to a worker. That the driver was negligent, or even reckless, does not insulate Felix from liability. Nor is it decisive that the driver lost control of the vehicle through a negligent failure to take medication, rather than a driving mistake. The precise manner of the event need not be anticipated. The finder of fact could have concluded that the foreseeable, normal, and natural result of the risk created by Felix was the injury of a worker by a car entering the improperly protected work area. An intervening act may not serve as a superseding cause, and relieve an actor of responsibility, where the risk of the intervening act occurring is the very same risk that renders the actor negligent.

In a similar vein, plaintiff's act of placing the kettle on the west side of the excavation does not, as a matter of law, absolve defendant Felix of responsibility. Serious injury, or even death, was a foreseeable consequence of a vehicle crashing through the work area. The injury could have occurred in numerous ways, ranging from a worker being directly struck by the car to the car hitting an object that injures the worker. Placement of the kettle, or any object in the work area, could affect how the accident occurs and the extent of injuries. That defendant could not anticipate the precise manner of the accident or the exact extent of injuries, however, does not preclude liability as a matter of law where the general risk and character of injuries are foreseeable. . . .

For the foregoing reasons, the order of the Appellate Division should be affirmed, with costs. The certified question is answered in the affirmative.

Order affirmed.

OUT DAMNED SPOT: BANISHING SUPERSEDING CAUSE FROM THE TORT LEXICON

The phrases "intervening act" and "superseding cause," employed in *Derdiarian*, appear frequently in appellate decisions throughout the country. The Restatement, Second, of Torts attempts to treat the subject more or less formally, in §§ 440-453. A "superseding cause" is an act of a third person or other force that cuts off a negligent actor's liability for his own antecedent negligence. *See* § 440. Whether "intervening forces" constitute superseding causes is dealt with in §§ 442-453. Section 442 sets forth the general rule:

§ 442. Considerations Important in Determining Whether an Intervening Force Is a Superseding Cause

The following considerations are of importance in determining whether an intervening force is a superseding cause of harm to another:

(a) the fact that its intervening brings about harm different in kind from that which would otherwise have resulted from the actor's negligence;

(b) the fact that its operation or the consequences thereof appear after the event to be extraordinary rather than normal in view of the circumstances existing at the time of its operation;

(c) the fact that the intervening force is operating independently of any situation created by the actor's negligence, or, on the other hand, is or is not a normal result of such a situation;

(d) the fact that the operation of the intervening force is due to a third person's act or to his failure to act;

(e) the fact that the intervening force is due to an act of a third person which is wrongful toward the other and as such subjects the third person to liability to him;

(f) the degree of culpability of a wrongful act of a third person which sets the intervening force in motion.

Each of the subsections in § 442 is elaborated on in one of several subsequent Restatement sections. Taken together, these provisions represent an effort to bring structure to this area.

The Restatement, Third, of Torts takes dead aim at the attempt of the Restatement, Second, to formulate rules for "intervening superseding cause." It provides:

§ 34. Intervening Acts and Superseding Causes

When a force of nature or an independent act is also a factual cause of physical harm, an actor's liability is limited to those harms that result from the risks that made the actor's conduct tortious.

Very simply, the Third Restatement subjects intervening causes to the "results within the risk" rule of § 29. In doing so the Reporters relied on a body of recent case law recognizing that shifting full liability to an intervening party or event is rarely justified.

Some courts have cleansed themselves from use of the terms "intervening" and/or "superseding" cause. *See, e.g.,* Barry v. Quality Steel Products Inc., 820 A.2d 258 (Conn. 2003); Torres v, El Paso Elec. Co., 987 P.2d 386 (N.M. 1999). They take the position that after the adoption of comparative fault there is no need for the all-or-nothing doctrine of intervening/superseding cause.

In Sullivan v. Metro-North Commuter R.R. Co., 971 A.2d 676 (Conn. 2009), the Court held that in a case in which the plaintiff alleged inadequate security at defendant's railroad station, it was proper to instruct a jury that the murder of the decedent by a third party could be an intervening superseding act that absolved the defendant from liability.

Several courts acknowledge that the impact of comparative fault on the law of proximate cause has been to reduce the occasions when an intervening cause instruction will be appropriate. Nonetheless, they disagree with *Barry* and find that intervening cause has survived the adoption of comparative fault. *See, e.g.,* Puckett v. Mt. Carmel Regional Medical Center, 228 P.3d 1048 (Kan. 2010); Godbee v. Dimick, 213 S.W.3d 865 (Tenn. Ct. App. 2006). For a critique of the Restatement, Third, view doing away with intervening cause as a distinct defense, *see* John C.P. Golberg & Benjamin C. Zipursky, *Intervening Wrongdoing in Tort: The Restatement (Third)'s Unfortunate Embrace of Negligent Enabling,* 44 Wake Forest L. Rev. 1211 (2009).

ACTS OF G-D

A recurring problem is how to treat so-called acts of G-d — overwhelming forces of nature that occur now and then, harming victims who may have causes of action against actors whose negligent conduct "set up" the circumstances under which the "act of G-d" occurred. We encountered one version of this problem in Chapter 4 in *Kingston*, the case involving two fires (p. 279). According to the court in that case, if a fire caused by lightning combines with a negligently caused fire to destroy the plaintiff's property, and the fire of natural origin would have sufficed to burn the property on its own, the negligent actor is not liable to the plaintiff. And in *Marshall*, p. 298, *supra*, the hypothetical posed by the court, in which defendant's negligence causes the plaintiff to be delayed in his travel so that he is in a position 30 minutes later to be injured in another accident down the road, can be turned into an "act of G-d" situation if the subsequent accident involves lightning, or an avalanche. In that circumstance, it will be recalled, the *Marshall* court would let the defendant off the hook because proximate cause is not made out. But consider this example: the defendant's negligent driving forces the plaintiff, driving in his car, off the road and onto the bank of a river. Plaintiff's damaged car is close to the water's edge and likely to be swept away eventually as the river rises with spring flooding. As the plaintiff sits dazed behind the wheel, an unexpected thunderstorm breaks upon the scene, quickly raising the water level and sweeping plaintiff to his death by drowning. Is defendant's negligent driving a proximate cause of plaintiff's death? Is the thunderstorm a mere "detail," like the flaming rat in *Daniels*, earlier? Or is the sudden thunderstorm an intervening "act of G-d" sufficient to cut off proximate cause?

hypo 45

The *A* Coal Company negligently deposits mine refuse on the banks of a mountain stream, so close to the water that it is likely to be carried down the stream and deposited upon lower riparian lands by the normal spring and autumn rains. An extraordinary rainstorm causes an unprecedented flood, which carries the refuse with very great speed and in unusual volume upon *B*'s lower riparian land, where it causes harm. Is *A*'s negligent piling of the mine refuse the proximate cause of the entire harm done to *B*'s land?

WATSON v. KENTUCKY & INDIANA BRIDGE & R. CO.
126 S.W. 146 (Ky. Ct. App. 1910)

[Plaintiff alleged that he was harmed by the explosion of gasoline that defendants' negligence had allowed to escape from a railroad tank car. The gasoline flowed into a street, filling gutters and standing in pools. A bystander named Duerr threw a match into a pool of the spilled gasoline, causing the explosion. Duerr claimed that he lit a cigar and threw the match away, unaware of the presence of the gasoline. Other evidence suggested that he deliberately threw the match into the gasoline to ignite it. The plaintiff claimed that the several defendants who spilled the gasoline were liable for the plaintiff's harm, notwithstanding the act of Duerr. The trial judge granted the defendants' motion for a directed verdict at the close of the evidence, and plaintiff appeals from the judgment for defendants.]

SETTLE, J. . . . The lighting of the match by Duerr having resulted in the explosion, the question is, was that act merely a contributing cause, or the efficient and, therefore, proximate cause of appellant's injuries? The question of proximate cause is a question for the jury. In holding that Duerr in lighting or throwing the match acted maliciously or with intent to cause the explosion, the trial court invaded the province of the jury. There was, it is true, evidence tending to prove that the act was wanton or malicious, but also evidence conducing to prove that it was inadvertently or negligently done by Duerr. It was therefore for the jury and not the court to determine from all the evidence whether the lighting of the match was done by Duerr inadvertently or negligently, or whether it was a wanton and malicious act. . . . No better statement of the law of proximate cause can be given than is found in 21 Am. & Eng. Ency. of Law (2d ed.) 490, quoted with approval in Louisville Home Telephone Company v. Gasper, . . . 93 S.W. 1057, . . . "It is well settled that the mere fact that there have been intervening causes between the defendant's negligence and the plaintiff's injuries is not sufficient in law to relieve the former from liability; that is to say, the plaintiff's injuries may yet be natural and proximate in law, although between the defendant's negligence and the injuries other causes or conditions, or agencies, may have operated, and, when this is the case, the defendant is liable. So the defendant is clearly responsible where the intervening causes, acts, or conditions were set in motion by his earlier negligence, or naturally induced by such wrongful act or omission, or even, it is generally held, if the intervening acts or conditions were of a nature the happening of which was reasonably to have been anticipated, though they may have been acts of the plaintiff himself. An act or omission may yet be negligent and of a nature to charge a defendant with liability, although no injuries would have been sustained but for some intervening cause, if the occurrence of the latter might have been anticipated. . . . A proximate cause is that cause which naturally led to and which might have been expected to produce the result. . . . The connection of cause and effect must be established. It is also a principle well settled that when an injury is caused by two causes concurring to produce the result, for one of which the defendant is responsible, and not for the other, the defendant cannot escape responsibility. One is liable for an injury caused by the concurring negligence of himself and another to the same extent as for one caused entirely by his own negligence."

If the presence on Madison street in the city of Louisville of the great volume of loose gas that arose from the escaping gasoline was caused by the negligence of the appellee Bridge & Railroad Company, it seems to us that the probable consequences of its coming in contact with fire and causing an explosion was too plain a proposition to admit of doubt. Indeed, it was most probable that someone would strike a match to light a cigar or for other purposes in the midst of the gas. In our opinion, therefore, the act of one lighting and throwing a match under such circumstances cannot be said to be the efficient cause of the explosion. It did not of

authors' dialogue 24

JIM: I've taught *Watson* for 30 years, and I still think that the court got it wrong. Whether Duerr threw the match into the gasoline deliberately, carelessly, or indirectly shouldn't matter in deciding whether the railroad who spilled the gas should be liable.

AARON: I'm not so sure. Why do you say that?

JIM: Duerr's state of mind is a detail, like when the person my negligence ends up harming turns out to be Shaquille O'Neal. (*See* Authors' Dialogue 20, p. 309, *supra.*)

AARON: Wait a minute. In the earlier example, no human agency came between your negligence and Shaq's harm. But Duerr's willful act of arson comes in between, big time. The two cases are different, I think.

JIM: Well, let's agree on something. Let's suppose that the defendant spills gasoline, as in *Watson.* Then let's suppose that a sparrow visits the town dump and picks up a bit of mattress stuffing for a new nest nearby.

AARON: What the heck . . .

JIM: Let me finish. So the sparrow doesn't notice that the mattress stuffing is smoldering. The sparrow flies over the spilled gasoline and, startled by the gas fumes, drops the stuffing. An explosion follows. Don't you agree that the guys who spilled the gasoline are liable?

AARON: Yes. The sparrow and the smoldering stuffing are clearly "details" as we used the term earlier. But Duerr is different. He takes charge of the situation — it becomes his fire.

JIM: Just saying it doesn't make it so. I could just as easily say that when Duerr intervened it became both his and the defendant's fire. They both should be liable together, jointly and severally.

AARON: I would agree, assuming that the judge gives that issue to the jury on a "was Duerr's deliberate act reasonably foreseeable?" instruction.

JIM: I can agree with that. But I read *Watson* to be saying that the jury should be instructed that if they find that Duerr acted deliberately they should find for the defendant. That is what I object to.

AARON: Then you've moved away from your original position. You started off saying Duerr's deliberateness should be completely irrelevant. Now you're saying it's relevant, but shouldn't be controlling. There's a difference, you know.

JIM: You're right, Aaron. Relating it to other discussions we've had on this topic, what I'm saying is that while "details" may be relevant under the general "foreseeability" rubric, they should never control the outcome.

BRAD: My take on this case is that Duerr's state of mind isn't a detail, in the following sense. The jury should be instructed to make findings regarding his state of mind, because if Duerr were a dangerous pyromaniac and not just an ordinarily careless person, he would be much more culpable, in a moral sense, than the railroad. There seems to be something unfair about holding a negligent tortfeasor liable where the "real" cause of the injury is a deliberate criminal act.

itself produce the explosion, nor could it have done so without the assistance and contribution resulting from the primary negligence, if there was such negligence, on the part of the appellee Bridge & Railroad Company in furnishing the presence of the gas in the street. This conclusion, however, rests upon the theory that Duerr inadvertently or negligently lighted and threw the match in the gas. . . .

If, however, the act of Duerr in lighting the match and throwing it into the vapor or gas arising from the gasoline was malicious, and done for the purpose of causing the explosion, we do not think appellees would be responsible, for while the appellee Bridge & Railroad Company's negligence may have been the efficient cause of the presence of the gas in the street, and it should have understood enough of the consequences thereof to have foreseen that an explosion was likely to result from the inadvert or negligent lighting of a match by some person who was ignorant of the presence of the gas or of the effect of lighting or throwing a match in it, it could not have foreseen or deemed it probable that one would maliciously or wantonly do such an act for the evil purpose of producing the explosion. Therefore, if the act of Duerr was malicious, we quite agree with the trial court that it was one which the appellees could not reasonably have anticipated or guarded against, and in such case the act of Duerr, and not the primary negligence of the appellee Bridge & Railroad Company, in any of the particulars charged, was the efficient or proximate cause of appellant's injuries. The mere fact that the concurrent cause or intervening act was unforeseen will not relieve the defendant guilty of the primary negligence from liability, but if the intervening agency is something so unexpected or extraordinary as that he could not or ought not to have anticipated it, he will not be liable, and certainly he is not bound to anticipate the criminal acts of others by which damage is inflicted and hence is not liable therefor. . . .

If Throwing of match intentional, no liability

For the reasons indicated, the judgment is affirmed as to the Union Tank Line Company, but reversed as to the Bridge & Railroad Company, and cause remanded for a new trial consistent with the opinion.

Kentucky no longer follows the automatic rule applied in *Watson.* See Britton v. Wooten, 817 S.W.2d 443 (Ky. 1991), in which trash, negligently allowed to accumulate next to a building, ignited from an unknown source. The court concluded (*id.* at 451):

> In the present case whether the spark ignited in the trash accumulated next to the building was ignited negligently, intentionally, or even criminally, or if it was truly accidental, is not the critical issue. The issue is whether the movant can prove that the respondent caused or permitted trash to accumulate next to its building in a negligent manner which caused or contributed to the spread of the fire and the destruction of the lessor's building. If so, the source of the spark that ignited the fire is not a superseding cause under any reasonable application of modern tort law.

FOOD FOR THOUGHT

In Hollenbeck v. Selectone Corp., 476 N.E.2d 746 (Ill. App. Ct. 1985), a police officer was attacked and injured while attempting to arrest several suspects after the pager issued by his department failed to send a warning message to the precinct. The trial court dismissed the plaintiff's complaint against defendant pager manufacturer because the criminal acts perpetrated by the criminal suspects were not probable or foreseeable, thereby breaking the causal connection between the product's failure and the plaintiff's injury. The court of appeals reversed, holding (*id.* at 747-748):

> The intervening criminal acts were not so improbable and unforeseeable as to break the causal connection. . . . The plaintiff has alleged that the defendant represented that its product was suitable for use by police agencies and that it marketed its product specifically for use by such agencies. . . . It was objectively reasonable to expect that the pager would be utilized in a situation involving a criminal offense.

Some observers have explained cases like *Hollenbeck* on the ground that the defendant owed a contractual duty to safeguard the plaintiff from the intentional, criminal acts of others. Is the outcome in *Hollenbeck* based on explicit promises by defendant that the product would protect users from the intentional acts of others? Implicit promises? Or is the defendant's duty based on the general circumstance that it was foreseeable that such acts might occur and that the pager could have prevented plaintiff's harm? If the latter, then could not it be said of *Watson* that arson was foreseeable and that more careful handling of the gasoline could have prevented plaintiff's harm?

In Medcalf v. Washington Heights Condominium Assn. Inc., 747 A.2d 532 (Conn. App. Ct. 2000), the plaintiff stood at the door to the lobby of a condo building, waiting for a friend to buzz her in from an upstairs unit. The electronic buzzer mechanism malfunctioned and, while the friend was on her way down to let the plaintiff in, an assailant attacked and injured the plaintiff. Plaintiff brought an action against the defendant association, alleging negligent failure to maintain the door buzzer mechanism. The trial court denied the defendant's motion for directed verdict and entered judgment on a jury verdict for the plaintiff. The appellate court reversed and entered judgment for defendant as a matter of law. The court explained (*id.* at 535-536):

> Proximate cause is a question of fact to be decided by the trier of fact, but it becomes a question of law when the mind of a fair and reasonable person could reach only one conclusion. . . .

The defendants could not have reasonably foreseen that a malfunctioning intercom system might provide a substantial incentive or inducement for the commission of a violent criminal assault on their property by one stranger upon another. . . .

On the subject of a gasoline handler's duty to prevent arson, consider Morales v. City of New York, 521 N.E.2d 425 (N.Y. 1988), in which a gasoline station attendant sold gasoline in plastic milk containers to a person who used the gasoline to burn a building. Actions for personal injury and wrongful death were brought against the station for negligence based on its violation of a statute that made illegal the sale of gasoline in unapproved containers; plastic milk containers were not of a type approved by the statute. In upholding the summary judgment for the station, the court stated (*id.* at 426):

> In the case now before us the requirement that gasoline be sold or delivered only in approved containers bears no relationship to arson. It may be, as the plaintiffs contend, that the harm might not have occurred had the . . . attendant refused to sell the gasoline in an unapproved container because the arsonists may have been unable to obtain one at that hour of the night. However, that fact does not establish the requisite legal connection between the statutory violation and the injuries. The statute was obviously designed to make transport and storage of gas safe by preventing accidental leakage or explosion, not to make it more difficult to buy untanked gasoline at night. Thus, assuming there was a violation by these defendants, it was a mere technical one bearing no practical or reasonable causal connection to the injury sustained.

Does *Morales* suggest that these cases involving intentionally tortious or criminal acts by third persons should be decided on the basic foreseeability grounds developed earlier in this chapter? Is *Gorris v. Scott, supra* p. 318, relevant?

Morales and *Gorris* both involve negligence *per se* claims and thus require an analysis of the purpose of a statute. Other cases can raise the *Palsgraf*-ian question of whether the issue of liability should be handled as a matter of duty or proximate cause. Consider, for example, the tragic events in Johnson v. Jacobs, 970 N.E.2d 666 (Ind. App. 2011). The father and mother of an eight-year-old girl were in the middle of an acrimonious divorce. The father had been taking flying lessons at a local airport, but his instructor had not yet signed him off for unsupervised solo flights. He showed up at the airport, obtained the key to a plane, and took his daughter up on a flight. An hour and a half later, after an angry and profane cell phone conversation with the mother, the father intentionally crashed the plane into his mother-in-law's house, killing himself and the daughter. Well-run flight schools have security procedures, such as requiring student pilots to obtain keys from an instructor before taking a solo flight. One purpose of these procedures is to ensure that the student's level of preparation is adequate for the prevailing weather conditions and intended flight. Assume the airport (the operator of the flight school) in this case was negligent in having inadequate security procedures, and this negligence allowed the father to gain access to an airplane. If the father had merely been negligent, the daughter might have had a cause of action against the airport. In this case, however, the Indiana Court of Appeals affirmed summary judgment for the airport because "nothing in the record suggests that the appellees should have foreseen that Eric [the father] would use the rented airplane to commit murder and suicide. Put another way, the designated evidence fails to establish that Eric's murder of Emily [the daughter] by intentionally crashing the airplane was a natural, probable, and foreseeable consequence of the appellees' purported violation of a duty to properly secure the airplane." *Id.* at 673. In terms of Authors' Dialogue #20, why isn't the suicide just a detail? It is entirely foreseeable that an inexperienced student pilot might crash and kill himself, along with any passengers he is foolish enough to bring along. That is why reasonable care requires limiting access to the school's airplanes. To foreshadow some of the analysis in Chapter 6, a better way to think about this case might be that a flight school owes a duty to foolish student pilots and their passengers to limit access to airplanes, but only to protect against the ordinary harms attributable to inexperience, not to safeguard against intentional criminal acts.

FULLER v. PREIS
322 N.E.2d 263 (N.Y. 1974)

BREITEL, Chief Judge.

Plaintiff executor, in a wrongful death action, recovered a jury verdict for $200,000. The Appellate Division set aside the verdict and judgment in favor of plaintiff executor and dismissed the complaint. In doing so, that court noted that even if it were not to dismiss the complaint, it would set the verdict aside as contrary to the weight of the credible evidence. Plaintiff executor appeals.

Decedent, Dr. Lewis, committed suicide some seven months after an automobile accident from which he had walked away believing he was uninjured. In fact he had suffered head injuries with consequences to be detailed later. The theory of the case was that defendants, owner and operator of the vehicle which struck decedent's automobile, were responsible in tort for the suicide as a matter of proximate cause and effect. The issue is whether plaintiff's evidence of cause of the suicide was sufficient to withstand dismissal of the complaint.

There should be a reversal of the order of the Appellate Division and a new trial ordered. Regardless of how the evidence might be viewed by those entitled to weigh it for its probative effect, there was enough to establish plaintiff's right to have his evidence assessed by a trial jury, and it was unwarranted to dismiss the complaint. In so concluding, it is emphasized that reasonable men might, would, and do differ on how the jury as fact-finders, should have resolved the issue of fact. Indeed, the Appellate Division made it clear that, in any event, it viewed the verdict in favor of plaintiff as against the weight of the credible evidence. On dismissal of the complaint, however, the question is purely one of law and that is another matter (*see, e.g.*, Sagorsky v. Malyon, . . . 123 N.E.2d 79, 80).

Prefatorily, the court is unanimously of the view, as was the Appellate Division, that negligent tortfeasors may be liable for the wrongful death, by suicide, of a person injured by their negligence. Issues arise only on the sufficiency of the evidence to permit a jury to conclude as did the jury in this case.

On December 2, 1966, decedent Dr. Lewis, a 43-year-old surgeon, was involved in an intersection collision. Upon impact, the left side of his head struck the frame and window of his automobile. Suffering no evident injuries, he declined aid and drove himself home. Early the next day he experienced an episode of vomiting. An examination later that day at his hospital was inconclusive.

Two days after the accident, Dr. Lewis had a seizure followed by others. After a four- or five-day stay in the hospital as a patient he was diagnosed as having had a subdural contusion and cerebral concussion. Medication was prescribed.

He sustained recurring seizures, was hospitalized again, was further tested, and after five days, was discharged with diagnosis of "post traumatic focal seizures."

Then ensued a period of deterioration and gradual contraction of his professional and private activities. Meanwhile, his wife, partially paralyzed as a result of an old poliomyelitis, suffered "nervous exhaustion" and his mother became ill with cancer.

On July 7, 1967, the day he learned of his mother's illness, decedent executed his will. On July 9, after experiencing three seizures that day, he went to the bathroom of his home, closed the door and shot himself in the head. He died the following day. Just before the gunshot, his wife heard him say to himself, "I must do it, I must do it," or words to that effect.

Two suicide notes, both dated July 9, 1967, were found next to the body. One, addressed to his wife, professed his love. The other, addressed to the family, contained information about a bank account and the location of his will and requested discreet disposition of certain personal property. He warned that the note "must never be seen by anyone except the three of you as it would alter the outcome of the 'case' — i.e., it's worth a million dollars to you all." And he went on to say that "I am perfectly sane in mind" and "I know exactly what I am doing." Alluding to the accident, the loss of his office and practice, his mother's and his wife's illnesses, the imposition caused thereby to his children, and his mounting responsibilities, he professed inability to continue.

Precedent of long standing establishes that public policy permits negligent tortfeasors to be held liable for the suicide of persons who, as the result of their negligence, suffer mental disturbance destroying the will to survive. In workmen's compensation law, where, to be sure, proximate cause is considerably less circumscribed than the standard in negligence law, courts have generally sustained awards based upon findings that an insured's suicide resulted from mental illness caused by a work-related injury.

So, too, in criminal law, where proof of cause must meet a more rigorous standard than in negligence law, defendants have been held responsible for the suicides of their victims.

Hence, the act of suicide, as a matter of law, is not a superseding cause in negligence law precluding liability. An initial tortfeasor may be liable for the wrongful acts of a third party if foreseeable. Thus a tortfeasor may be liable for the ensuing malpractice of a physician treating the victim for the tortiously caused injuries. No different rule applies when death results from an "involuntary" suicidal act of the victim as a direct consequence of the wrongful conduct.

That suicide may be encouraged by allowing recovery for suicide, a highly doubtful proposition in occidental society, is unpersuasive to preclude recovery for the suicide of a mentally deranged person. The remote possibility of fraudulent claims connecting a suicide with mental derangement affords no basis for barring recovery. The obvious difficulty in proving or disproving causal relation should not bar recovery.

Thus, there is neither public policy nor precedent barring recovery for suicide of a tortiously injured person driven "insane" by the consequence of the tortious act. Indeed, recovery for negligence leading to the victim's death by suicide should perhaps, in some circumstances, be had, even absent proof of a specific mental disease or even an irresistible impulse, provided there is significant causal connection.

In any event, this case was tried for all purposes in accordance with the prevailing law. Indeed, the jury was instructed, primarily, upon the theory of liability for a suicide by an accident victim suffering from ensuing mental disease, who was unable to control the "irresistible impulse" to destroy himself. The theory of the trial, therefore, determines the rule to be applied on the appeal.

E.T.

Dr. Lewis was physically and mentally healthy immediately prior to the automobile accident in which he struck his head against the interior of his own vehicle. After the accident he suffered several epileptic seizures, often with unconsciousness. Before the accident he had never suffered a seizure. For seven months between the accident and his death, Dr. Lewis experienced no fewer than 38 separate seizures. The neurologist who treated him testified that as the result of the blow on the head he sustained a cerebral contusion which caused seizures and underlying hemorrhaging in the brain covering, destroying part of the brain. According to the neurologist, brain hemorrhage causes scarring which distorts impulses, producing further seizures, further scarring, cell atrophy, and wasting, in a deadly cycle. On the day of his death Dr. Lewis had three seizures.

The truncated description of the testimony demonstrates, and it is not seriously disputed, that there was sufficient evidence from which a reasonable person might conclude that the accident caused traumatic organic brain damage.

The only authentic issue is whether the suicide was an "irresistible impulse" caused by traumatic organic brain damage. The issue is limited on this appeal because of the theory of the case based on the traditional but not entirely satisfactory concept of the "irresistible impulse." Medical and legal lore have developed an incisive critique of that concept but its evolution or clarification must await another day and another case. It has been cogently argued that it ought to be sufficient to accept mental illness, traumatic in origin, as a substantial cause of particular behavior, including suicide. . . .

The treating neurologist testified as an expert that after the three seizures decedent was disoriented, lacked awareness, was irrational, and in postconvulsive psychosis which placed his conduct beyond his control. . . .

It is contended that the testimony of the treating neurologist was incredible as a matter of law. That the neurologist did not practice the closely related specialty of psychiatry was no bar to his testifying as a medical expert. His failure before the suicide to diagnose Dr. Lewis as mentally ill affects the weight but not the admissibility of his testimony. Of course, the issue was Dr. Lewis' sanity at the time of the suicide. The expert's opinion was based on the symptoms shown before the suicide, the three seizures on the day of the suicide, Dr. Lewis' confused state after the last of the seizures, and his muttering. Upon such facts it is logically, medically, and legally impermissible to reject his opinion as incredible as a matter of law. . . .

A suicide is a strange act and no rationalistic approach can fit the act into neat categories of rationality or irrationality. When the suicide is preceded by a history of trauma, brain damage, epileptic seizures, aberrational conduct, depression and despair, it is at the very least a fair issue of fact whether the suicide was the rational act of a sound mind or the irrational act or irresistible impulse of a deranged mind evidenced by a physically damaged brain. It would be illogical to conclude otherwise. Consequently, although the Appellate Division in exercise of its supervisory power to review the facts could set the jury verdict aside, it was impermissible for it to dismiss the complaint.

Since the Appellate Division, in reversing, stated that in any event it would have set the verdict aside as contrary to the weight of the evidence, the verdict in favor of plaintiff may not be reinstated and a new trial is required.

Accordingly, the order of the Appellate Division should be reversed, with costs, and a new trial directed.

Order reversed.

FOOD FOR THOUGHT

How much, if at all, does the outcome in *Fuller* rest on the thin skull rule considered earlier in this chapter? You will recall *Bartolone v. Jeckovich*, discussed p. 313, *supra*. The court in *Bartolone* held that the plaintiff could recover for an acute psychotic breakdown directly resulting from a four-car collision caused by defendant's negligence whether or not such a reaction was foreseeable ahead of time. Accepting as a premise that negligent actors can almost never foresee that a particular victim will commit suicide, something like the thin skull rule must be operating, must it not? But if that is true, then suicide will always be recoverable so long as the negligently caused accident triggers it, will it not?

Consider Zygmaniak v. Kawasaki Motors Corp., 330 A.2d 56 (N.J. Super. Ct. Law Div. 1974), *appeal dismissed*, 343 A.2d 97 (N.J. 1975), in which a defect in a motorcycle caused an accident that injured the plaintiff's decedent. Upon learning that he was severely and permanently disabled, decedent begged his brother to kill him. In response, the brother shot decedent to death with a sawed-off shotgun. Statutory actions for survivorship and wrongful death were brought against the motorcycle manufacturer for negligently designing the cycle so as to cause it to crash. The defendant moved for partial summary judgment of the wrongful death action on the ground that the brother's act constituted an intervening cause that eliminated proximate causation. In denying defendant's motion, the trial court concluded (*id.* at 61):

> The court is aware that elsewhere the analogous problem of suicide following an accident is resolvable by reference to whether the defendant's conduct was negligent or was intentionally wrongful and whether the suicide was the result of an irresistible impulse. Such an approach might lead to a different result on this motion. Further, it is difficult to understand why in this action seeking compensatory damages such . . . special rules should be adopted. The approach of the court reflects an emphasis on the reality of the cause and effect of the death rather than on a label characterizing conduct and embodies a realization that on this motion the court should consider the death as having limited rather than expanded the otherwise appropriate inter vivos damages. On a summary judgment motion this is not a case in which the damages must be considered expanded rather than contracted by a voluntary suicide.

Observe that in *Zygmaniak*, allowing the wrongful death action did not increase defendant's exposure to liability as much as might at first appear. Even if the court had dismissed the wrongful death action, the survivorship action would have proceeded to trial to recover for the decedent's injuries other than death. To be sure, the beneficiaries would be different under the two different statutes — decedent's estate recovers under survivorship, while close family members dependent on decedent are designated as beneficiaries under the wrongful death statute. And the measures of recovery under the two statutes are different. But the decision did not have "all or nothing" consequences. Moreover, as the excerpt from *Zygmaniak* suggests, the decedent's death probably reduced, rather than increased, the total recovery, because the decedent faced a lifetime of expensive medical care. What do you suppose the trial court would have done if the original injuries from the motorcycle accident had not caused permanent disability but only minor injuries, and imposing liability for the suicide would have greatly increased the amount of recovery?

There are, however, limits to the imposition of liability for suicides. In Kleen v. Homak Mfg. Co. Inc., 749 N.E.2d 26 (Ill. App. 2001), the plaintiff, Kleen, brought a wrongful death and survival action against Homak, the manufacturer of a gun safe. Kleen's adult son, David, broke into the locked gun safe, removed the gun that his father had put there, and committed suicide. The plaintiff's contention was that the gun safe was defective in that it contained a weak lock that could easily be broken. The appellate court, answering a certified question from the trial court, held that plaintiff's complaint should be dismissed since the defective lock was not the proximate cause of the suicide. What would be the result if plaintiff had purchased the safe because his son suffered from depression and had made several suicide threats? That may still not be enough. In Johnstone v. City of Albuquerque, 145 P.3d 76 (N.M. Ct. App. 2006), the defendant, a police officer, left his holster belt with his service pistol lying around his house. His stepdaughter used the pistol to commit suicide. A year and a half prior to this event, the stepdaughter had been hospitalized after a suicide attempt. Despite this knowledge and the family relationship, the court held that defendant had no duty to safeguard his firearm to protect his stepdaughter from suicide.

CLINKSCALES v. NELSON SECURITIES, INC.
697 N.W.2d 836 (Iowa 2005)

PER CURIAM

"Danger invites rescue."[1] A marine out for a drink at a Davenport bar rushed to the scene of a gas leak at a grill on the premises. While attempting to turn off two propane gas tanks, a grease fire reignited and he was badly burned. The district court dismissed the marine's negligence claim against the bar. The court held as a matter of law the marine was solely to blame for his injuries. The court of appeals affirmed. Because a jury could find the bar's negligence proximately caused the

1. Wagner v. Int'l Ry., 232 N.Y. 176, 133 N.E. 437, 437 (1921) (Cardozo, J.).

marine's rescue attempt and injuries, we reverse the district court, vacate the court of appeals, and remand for a trial on the merits.

I. Facts

Late one Friday afternoon in the summer of 2002, James Clinkscales went to The Gallery Lounge, a Davenport pub. Approximately fifty people were there. Clinkscales, an active-duty marine in town as a recruiter, stationed himself at the bar next to a blonde woman known only as "Dimples." The two began to share a pitcher of beer together.

On Fridays in the summer, The Gallery regularly grilled hamburgers outside and served them to its customers. The grill stood directly outside of the bar on a patio ten feet away from where Clinkscales and Dimples sat. Two tanks of propane gas placed underneath the grill fueled it. The grill was custom-made and large enough to grill twenty burgers at a time.

The Gallery employed Joe Moser to grill the burgers. The first batch of burgers Moser placed on the grill that evening were particularly greasy. When Moser flipped them over, a fire flared up on the grill. Moser did not consider this to be a problem. All of a sudden, however, Moser heard something abnormal — "a pop and a hiss." A ball of fire erupted underneath the grill and engulfed the propane tanks.

Caroline Nelson co-owns The Gallery with her husband and regularly works there. When the fire started Nelson was standing at the patio door. Moser told Nelson to get a fire extinguisher. Nelson and Moser testified Nelson and other Gallery employees made general announcements to the patrons to leave and then one employee called the fire department. Clinkscales testified he was alerted to the fire when he saw Nelson come into the bar looking for a fire extinguisher, but did not believe Nelson said anything to him or anybody else about what was happening.

Nelson came back outside with a fire extinguisher and gave it to a patron. The patron extinguished the flame, and Moser managed to turn the knobs on the grill to the "off" position. Moser could still smell gas escaping from the tanks, however, and Moser said aloud that he wanted to shut the tanks off. Moser pulled the grill away from a wall to access the tanks, but he found the valves were too hot to touch. There were customers in the patio and adjacent bar. Clinkscales came out to the patio and asked a man holding a fire extinguisher if anyone had turned the gas off. The man told Clinkscales the handle was too hot.

Clinkscales, who had received extensive training in fire suppression in the military, recognized the situation was "very dangerous." Clinkscales took off his shirt, wrapped it around one of hands, and turned the gas off. No one asked Clinkscales to do so. He reacted instinctively: "[I]t's like running after a kid when he runs into the street, you don't think about it, that there's a car coming, you just try to grab the child, and, you know, hope for the best. You could get killed doing it, but you just do it."

As Clinkscales was turning off the gas, the fire flared up. Clinkscales was burned on his face, neck, chest, arms, and legs.

Skin hanging from his arms, Clinkscales continued his rescue efforts by helping a frightened young woman in the patio over a fence. A frequent patron of the bar, a man named Norm, took Clinkscales to the hospital just as the fire department arrived.

II. Prior Proceedings

Clinkscales sued The Gallery for negligence. He claimed The Gallery owed him a duty of care as a business invitee. Clinkscales alleged The Gallery was specifically negligent because it (1) failed to properly design, manufacture, maintain, and operate the grill; (2) did not adequately train its employees in the use and maintenance of the grill; (3) did not have enough fire-suppression equipment and did not properly use the fire extinguishers it did have; and (4) did not have emergency procedures in place necessary to protect its customers. In the alternative, Clinkscales also pled res ipsa loquitur to show general negligence. Clinkscales contended that even if he could not prove the precise cause of the mishap, the defendants had exclusive control over the instrumentalities involved in the fire.

The defendants filed a motion for summary judgment, which the district court granted. As a matter of law the district court found employees of The Gallery told Clinkscales to evacuate the premises; there was no evidence there was imminent risk to life when he turned off the gas; and "a reasonable person would not determine that the benefits of approaching a fire outweigh the risk of being seriously burned or injured." The district court ruled the defendants were not liable because (1) Clinkscales's injuries were caused by a known and obvious danger and (2) the defendants' alleged negligence was not the proximate cause of Clinkscales's injuries. The court also concluded res ipsa loquitur was not applicable because grease fires can occur without negligence. The court of appeals affirmed. It declined to apply the rescue doctrine and held, as a matter of law, Clinkscales "suffers from a self-inflicted wound." . . .

A. The Rescue Doctrine

The rescue doctrine was forged at common law. It involves heroic people doing heroic things. The late Justice Cardozo aptly summarized the commonsense observations about human nature that led to the doctrine's widespread recognition across this nation when he wrote:

> Danger invites rescue. The cry of distress is the summons to relief. The law does not ignore these reactions of the mind in tracing conduct to its consequences. It recognizes them as normal. It places their effects within the range of the natural and probable. The wrong that imperils life is a wrong to the imperiled victim; it is a wrong also to his rescuer. The state that leaves an opening in a bridge is liable to the child that falls into the stream, but liable also to the parent who plunges to its aid. The railroad company whose train approaches without signal is a wrongdoer toward the traveler surprised between the rails, but a wrongdoer also to the bystander who drags him from the path . . . The risk of rescue, if only it be not

wanton, is born of the occasion. The emergency begets the man. The wrongdoer may not have foreseen the coming of a deliverer. He is accountable as if he had. Wagner v. Int'l Ry., 232 N.Y. 176, 133 N.E. 437, 437–38 (1921) (citations omitted). That is, those who negligently imperil life or property may not only be liable to their victims, but also to the rescuers.

We have consistently and liberally applied the rescue doctrine in this state for over one hundred years. Historically the doctrine arose in questions of proximate cause and contributory negligence. "In other words, did the act of the injured [rescuer] so intervene as to break the chain of causation from [the] defendant's negligence, or constitute such contributory negligence as to bar recovery?" Clayton v. Blair, 117 N.W.2d 879, 881 (Iowa 1962). The general rule was a rescuer would not be deemed to have broken the chain of causation or charged with contributory negligence for reasonable attempts to save the life or property of another. Since the advent of comparative negligence, the doctrine has only arisen on appeal in questions of proximate cause, i.e., when, as here, the defendant claims the rescuer's actions were a superseding cause of the rescuer's injuries.[2]

B. Proximate Cause

The Gallery contends its alleged negligence was not the proximate cause of Clinkscales's injuries. The Gallery asserts the facts show its employees ordered patrons to leave the premises, it had called the fire department, and at the time of the rescue attempt Moser was retrieving a rag to turn off the propane valves. The court of appeals held as a matter of law that the rescue doctrine did not apply in this case because "no one was in any danger until the plaintiff placed himself there."

It is well settled that questions of proximate cause are, absent extraordinary circumstances, for the jury to decide.

The line between what is sufficiently proximate and what is too remote is a thin one:

> If upon looking back from the injury, the connection between the negligence and the injury appears unnatural, unreasonable, and improbable in the light of common experience, such negligence would be a remote rather than a proximate cause. If, however, by a fair consideration of the facts based upon common human experience and logic, there is nothing particularly unnatural or unreasonable in connecting the injury with the negligence, a jury question would be created.

Hollingsworth v. Schminkey, 553 N.W.2d 591, 597 (Iowa 1996). Here we are concerned with Clinkscales's rescue attempt, which The Gallery characterizes as a "superseding cause" of his injuries. A superseding cause is an intervening force that "prevent[s] the defendant from being liable for harm to the plaintiff that the defendant's antecedent negligence is a substantial factor in bringing about." *Id.* (citing Restatement (Second) of Torts § 440 (1965).

---

2. Whether the risks of rescue are counted against the rescuer under the comparative fault doctrine in Iowa is unsettled and not at issue in this appeal.

When a rescue attempt is involved, matters are particularly thorny and a court should be especially wary to grant a defendant's motion for summary judgment. The rescue doctrine recognizes not all intervening forces are superseding causes:

> If the actor's negligent conduct threatens harm to another's person, land, or chattels, the normal efforts of the other or a third person to avert the threatened harm are not a superseding cause of harm resulting from such efforts.

Restatement § 445 (quoted in *Hollingsworth*, 553 N.W.2d at 598). That is, so long as the rescuer's response is "normal," the negligent actor will not escape liability for the rescuer's injuries.

What are "normal" rescue efforts? Although in *Hollingsworth* we loosely characterized the question of "normal efforts" as one solely of foreseeability, *see* 553 N.W.2d at 598, in truth the term "normal" is *not* used "in the sense of what is usual, customary, foreseeable, or to be expected." Restatement § 443 cmt. *b; see also id.* § 445 cmt. *b.* Rather, "normal" (referred to in our pre-Restatement cases as "natural") is used as "the antithesis of abnormal, of extraordinary." Restatement § 443 cmt. *b.*

> [T]he only inquiry should be whether the conduct of the plaintiff was "natural" under the circumstances, which is to be ascertained by a counter-chronological examination of the facts. Here the term "natural" must be taken to embrace those qualities of human nature leading to risk-taking in an effort to preserve property, to rescue other persons, or to save oneself. It necessarily includes actions which these well recognized and familiar human feelings bring about. Thus "natural" conduct includes not only cool and well-reasoned action but also the frantic, excited and apparently illogical movements which are too commonly exhibited by a large percentage of human beings in moments of stress.
>
> In these situations, the defendant may negligently have exposed the person or property of another to unreasonable risk of loss or destruction. "Natural" instincts will move some persons to make efforts at rescue. The movements of the rescuer may not be well judged and may result in harm either to the goods, to the person endangered by the defendant, or to the rescuer himself. In any such case the defendant will be held liable, for the "natural" conduct of the rescuer leaves no break or gap in the chain of causation.

Clayton, 117 N.W.2d at 882 (quoting Clarence M. Updegraff, *A Technique for Determining Legal Liability Based On Negligence*, 27 Iowa L. Rev. 2, 28 (1941) . . . .

We think the facts are sufficiently in conflict on the issue of proximate cause to warrant a jury determination. The dangers of fire and gas leaks are well known to all. There is evidence the danger was imminent in this case, or at least apparently so. This summary-judgment record shows customers, employees, and property of The Gallery were in the vicinity of the fire and subsequent gas leak. While it is undisputed employees of The Gallery called the fire department and asked some patrons to evacuate, a jury could find Clinkscales's rescue efforts were a normal or natural reaction under the circumstances. He may have reasonably thought danger was imminent and, given his extensive training, his help was needed.

Exhortations to leave do not, as a matter of law, preclude liability in all cases. If a defendant sets into course a series of events that induces a rescue attempt, the defendant does not necessarily insulate itself from liability when it tells the rescuer to leave. In any event, in this case there is evidence no one effectively ordered Clinkscales to leave, and some evidence The Gallery enlisted the help of other customers to fight the fire. There is nothing inconsistent with an express general call to evacuate and an implicit individual invitation to help. Even if we were to assume Clinkscales was told to leave, however, this would be but one fact for the jury to consider in evaluating his rescue attempt.

We cannot say as a matter of law that the rescue doctrine does not apply to this case. A reasonable jury could find Clinkscales's rescue of Gallery employees, customers, and property was an act done in normal or natural response to the fear or emotional disturbance caused by The Gallery's negligence. Summary judgment on the issue of proximate cause was not proper.

FOOD FOR THOUGHT

"Rescue doctrine" is a bit of a misnomer in a case like *Clinkscales*. It is not a basis for a separate cause of action, but rather an application of the usual rule of proximate causation. Just as Restatement (Third) § 34 (see p. 343) asks whether an intervening act is a result within the original risk created by the defendant's conduct, the rescue doctrine focuses on whether one result that can be expected from an initial act of negligence is an attempt by another person to save life or property. Here, if the bar was negligent in the construction or maintenance of the grill, training of employees, or failure to have a fire extinguisher nearby, then if a fire were to occur, a further expected result is that a customer or passerby might attempt to put out the fire. The rescue doctrine may expand the scope of liability, however, in cases in which a person negligently places herself in need of assistance and a rescuer is injured. *See, e.g.,* Rasmussen v. State Farm Mutual Automobile Ins. Co., 770 N.W.2d 619 (Neb. 2009) (plaintiff injured while attempting to pull plaintiff's car out of a ditch; plaintiff's negligent driving had caused her to slide off the road).

In McCoy v. American Suzuki Motor Corp., 961 P.2d 952 (Wash. 1998), the plaintiff stopped to assist the driver of a Suzuki automobile that had flipped over. The state trooper who arrived at the scene sent him back to place flares in the road to direct traffic away from the lane in which the car was located. Plaintiff also stayed and helped direct traffic away from the scene of the accident. It took two hours for the car and passenger to be cleared from the highway, after which the plaintiff began walking along the shoulder of the road toward his car. While he was doing so, warning flare in hand, a hit-and-run vehicle struck him from behind. He brought an action against Suzuki, the manufacturer of the car that had overturned in the first place, alleging that a design defect caused the accident. The manufacturer denied liability on the ground that the alleged defect had not proximately caused plaintiff's injury. Plaintiff argued that once it is determined that the defendant proximately caused the original accident, injuries incurred in any reasonable rescue efforts are recoverable as a matter of law, without regard to further considerations of proximate causation. The appellate court held that the injuries incurred in rescue must be proximately caused by defendant's original wrong, but found on the facts of the case that the causal connection between the defendant's allegedly defective manufacture and plaintiff's injuries was sufficiently close to warrant sending the issue of proximate cause to the jury.

To make sense of decisions involving liability of negligent actors to rescuers and would-be rescuers, one must bear in mind that we are here talking about proximate cause (or, as Cardozo would put it, the duty owed to rescuers). An emergency such as a raging grease fire is not an occasion for calm deliberation. It is foreseeable that someone may jump in and try to help. A reasonable rescue is therefore not one that, on balance, was a good idea. That does not mean, however, that a rescuer can be utterly reckless. As the second footnote in the *Clinkscales* opinion notes, the issue of the plaintiff-rescuer's own contributory fault is separate and distinct from that of causation. Judge Cardozo in the *Wagner* says that the defendant's responsibility includes all rescue attempts "if only [they] be not wanton." That leads to the question, what if the decision to rescue is reasonable but the would-be rescuer is negligent in how she goes about it? In that circumstance, causation is made out and plaintiff's comparative fault is for the jury. In Kimble v. Carey, 691 S.E.2d 790 (Va. 2010), a motorist traveling on an interstate highway saw a car on fire with the occupant trapped inside. The car was on the other side of the highway. Although according to the state trooper's report the night was so dark "you could not see your hand in front of your face," the plaintiff dashed across the highway and was hit by another motorist traveling at 65 miles per hour. In an action against the first driver trapped in the burning car, the jury was permitted to decide whether the would-be rescuer was contributorily negligent and, if so, whether the negligence rose to the level of "rash or reckless disregard for her own safety."

THANKS, BUT NO THANKS

What should a court do when the would-be rescuer mistakenly believes that victims require rescue when, in fact, they do not? American courts generally apply the rescue doctrine in such cases. *See, e.g.*, Gifford v. Haller, 710 N.Y.S. 2d 187 (N.Y. App. Div. 2000). Plaintiff and defendant, residents in a trailer park, were both driving their vehicles through the grounds of the park when the defendant stopped to inform residents of impending road construction within the park. Defendant had her five-year-old child in the car. Plaintiff parked his car near his trailer. When he got out he saw that defendant had left her car running and that the vehicle was rolling slowly backward. Plaintiff, believing that the little girl was still in the car, attempted to jump into the driver's seat of the moving vehicle to apply the brake. He opened the driver's side door and grabbed the steering wheel, causing the vehicle to push him into his parked vehicle. Plaintiff suffered serious injuries to his leg and hip. Plaintiff had seen the little girl in the defendant's car but he did not see her exit the vehicle. Defendant moved for summary judgment on the grounds that since the little girl was not in the car, there was no need to rescue her. The trial court denied defendant's motion for summary judgment. Defendant took an interlocutory appeal. Concluding that a jury could find that the plaintiff reasonably believed that the child was in peril and in need of rescue, the appellate court upheld the trial court's denial of summary judgment for the defendant, and remanded the case for trial.

In Harris v. Oaks Shopping Center, 82 Cal. Rptr. 2d 523 (Cal. Ct. App. 1999), the plaintiff was working at a customer service booth in a mall. Nearby, a 30-foot-high sand sculpture was being constructed. The plaintiff and several others heard the sound of construction boards snapping, and saw sand and water coming out of the sculpture. Afraid that the sculpture would crush a woman a pushing a stroller, he leaped out of the booth and attempted to aid her. In doing so, he severely injured his back and eventually required surgery. The sculpture never fell. He sued the shopping center for negligence, claiming his actions were reasonable. The trial court refused to give an "imminent peril" instruction and the jury found for defendant. Reversed and remanded.

hypo **46**

Mrs. *A*, concerned that her husband Mr. *A* was about to commit suicide, called her brother *B* to come quickly because Mr. *A*'s car was in the garage and the motor was running. She feared carbon monoxide poisoning. *B* climbed over a fence to get to *B*'s yard and fell, seriously injuring himself. *B* sues Mr. *A*. What result?

THEY ALSO SUE THOSE WHO ONLY STAND AND GAWK

The rescue doctrine is not available to those who come to the scene for purposes other than rescue. In Lambert v. Parrish, 492 N.E.2d 289 (Ind. 1986), the plaintiff was told that his wife had been involved in an accident at the end of the alley behind his office. He rushed out to go to the scene of the accident and slipped on a patch of ice, falling and injuring his back. The plaintiff brought an action against the alleged cause of his wife's accident. The court granted summary judgment for the defendant, saying (*id.* at 291):

> We hold [that] a rescuer must in fact attempt to rescue someone. A rescuer is one who actually undertakes physical activity in a reasonable and prudent attempt to rescue. . . . [Plaintiff's] only attempt was to reach the scene of the accident. He exerted no physical activity to facilitate the rescue of his wife from the consequences of the allegedly tortious acts of [the defendant].

Elsewhere, the court in *Lambert* suggests that the rescuer must hear or see the danger requiring assistance. Is this a sensible place to draw the line? Would the normal rules of proximate cause necessarily cut off recovery at this point? The plaintiff in McNair v. Boyette, 192 S.E.2d 457 (N.C. 1972), stopped at the scene of a traffic accident to see if anyone was hurt. After determining that there were no injuries, he crossed the highway and returned to his car to get a flashlight. As he attempted to return across the highway, an oncoming car hit and severely injured him. The Supreme Court of North Carolina held that as a rescuer he could not recover against the driver who caused the accident (*id.* at 240): "[p]laintiff's deposition shows . . . that neither [driver] needed rescuing. . . . Plaintiff crossed the highway to get a flashlight, not for the purpose of rescuing . . . but apparently for the purpose of directing traffic. . . ."

In Barnes v. Geiger, 446 N.E.2d 78 (Mass. App. Ct. 1983) the plaintiff's children were ice skating near the family's home. Plaintiff's wife saw a car strike a pedestrian and throw him 60 feet in the air near the place where her children were ice skating. Thinking that her son was hit, she ran to the scene. The next day she died from a cerebral vascular hemorrhage allegedly triggered by her elevated blood pressure resulting from witnessing the accident. The plaintiff brought an action against the driver of the car on the theory that his wife was a rescuer. In affirming a grant of summary judgment for the defendant, the court said (*id.* at 82):

> In the case at bar there is no suggestion that [plaintiff's wife] intervened in any fashion, attempted to do so, or that there would have been any purpose in her doing so. Danger invites rescue; accidents invite onlookers. To achieve the status of rescuer, a claimant's purpose must be more than merely investigatory. There must be some specific mission of assistance by which the plight of the imperilled could reasonably be thought to be ameliorated.

C. PLAYING THE "DUTY" CARD

HAMILTON v. BERETTA U.S.A. CORP.
750 N.E.2d 1055 (N.Y. 2001)

WESLEY, J.

In January 1995 plaintiffs — relatives of people killed by handguns — sued 49 handgun manufacturers in Federal court alleging negligent marketing, design defect, ultra-hazardous activity and fraud. A number of defendants jointly moved for summary judgment. The United States District Court for the Eastern District of New York (Weinstein, J.), dismissed the product liability and fraud causes of action, but retained plaintiffs' negligent marketing claim (*see*, Hamilton v. Accu-Tek, 935 F. Supp. 1307, 1315). Other parties intervened, including plaintiff Stephen Fox, who was shot by a friend and permanently disabled. The gun was never found; the shooter had no recollection of how he obtained it. Other evidence, however, indicated that he had purchased the gun out of the trunk of a car from a seller who said it came from the "south." Eventually, seven plaintiffs went to trial against 25 of the manufacturers.

Plaintiffs asserted that defendants distributed their products negligently so as to create and bolster an illegal, underground market in handguns, one that furnished weapons to minors and criminals involved in the shootings that precipitated this lawsuit. Because only one of the guns was recovered, plaintiffs were permitted over defense objections to proceed on a market share theory of liability against all the manufacturers, asserting that they were severally liable for failing to implement safe marketing and distribution procedures, and that this failure sent a high volume of guns into the underground market.

After a four-week trial, the jury returned a special verdict finding 15 of the 25 defendants failed to use reasonable care in the distribution of their guns. Of those 15, nine were found to have proximately caused the deaths of the decedents of two plaintiffs, but no damages were awarded. The jury awarded damages against three defendants — American Arms, Beretta U.S.A. and Taurus International Manufacturing — upon a finding that they proximately caused the injuries suffered by Fox and his mother (in the amounts of $3.95 million and $50,000, respectively). Liability was apportioned among each of the three defendants according to their share of the national handgun market: for American Arms, 0.23% ($9,000); for Beretta, 6.03% ($241,000); and for Taurus, 6.80% ($272,000).

Defendants unsuccessfully moved for judgment as a matter of law pursuant to Federal Rules of Civil Procedure rule 50(b). The District Court articulated several theories for imposing a duty on defendants "to take reasonable steps available at the point of . . . sale to primary distributors to reduce the possibility that these instruments will fall into the hands of those likely to misuse them" (Hamilton v. Accu-Tek, 62 F. Supp. 2d 802, 825). The court noted that defendants, as with all manufacturers, had the unique ability to detect and guard against any foreseeable risks associated with their products, and that ability created a special "protective relationship" between the manufacturers and potential victims of gun violence (*id.*, at 821). It further pointed out that the relationship of handgun manufacturers with their downstream distributors and retailers gave them the authority and ability to control the latter's conduct for the protection of prospective crime victims. Relying on Hymowitz v. Eli Lilly & Co. (73 N.Y.2d 487, *cert. denied,* 493 U.S. 944), the District Court held that apportionment of liability among defendants on a market share basis was appropriate and that plaintiffs need not connect Fox's shooting to the negligence of a particular manufacturer.

On appeal, the Second Circuit certified the following questions to us:

(1) Whether the defendants owed plaintiffs a duty to exercise reasonable care in the marketing and distribution of the handguns they manufacture?

(2) Whether liability in this case may be apportioned on a market share basis, and if so, how?

We accepted certification and now answer both questions in the negative.

Parties' Arguments

Plaintiffs argue that defendant-manufacturers have a duty to exercise reasonable care in the marketing and distribution of their guns based upon four factors: (1) defendants' ability to exercise control over the marketing and distribution of their guns, (2) defendants' general knowledge that large numbers of their guns enter the illegal market and are used in crime, (3) New York's policy of strict regulation of firearms and (4) the uniquely lethal nature of defendants' products.

According to plaintiffs, handguns move into the underground market in New York through several well-known and documented means including straw purchases (a friend, relative or accomplice acts as purchaser of the weapon for another), sales at gun shows, misuse of Federal firearms licenses and sales by non-stocking dealers (i.e., those operating informal businesses without a retail storefront). Plaintiffs further assert that gun manufacturers have oversaturated markets in states with weak gun control laws (primarily in the Southeast), knowing those "excess guns" will make their way into the hands of criminals in states with stricter laws such as New York, thus "profiting" from indiscriminate sales in weak gun states. Plaintiffs contend that defendants control their distributors' conduct with respect to pricing, advertising and display, yet refuse to institute practices such as requiring distribution contracts that limit sales to stocking gun dealers, training salespeople in safe sales practices (including how to recognize straw purchasers), establishing electronic monitoring of their products, limiting the number of distributors, limiting multiple purchases and franchising their retail outlets.

Defendants counter that they do not owe a duty to members of the public to protect them from the criminal acquisition and misuse of their handguns. Defendants assert that such a duty—potentially exposing them to limitless liability—should not be imposed on them for acts and omissions of numerous and remote third parties over which they have no control. Further, they contend that, in light of the comprehensive statutory and regulatory scheme governing the distribution and sale of firearms, any fundamental changes in the industry should be left to the appropriate legislative and regulatory bodies.

The Duty Equation

The threshold question in any negligence action is: does defendant owe a legally recognized duty of care to plaintiff? Courts traditionally "fix the duty point by balancing factors, including the reasonable expectations of parties and society generally, the proliferation of claims, the likelihood of unlimited or insurer-like liability, disproportionate risk and reparation allocation, and public policies affecting the expansion or limitation of new channels of liability" (Palka v. Servicemaster Mgt. Servs. Corp., 83 N.Y.2d 579, 586). Thus, in determining whether a duty exists, "courts must be mindful of the precedential, and consequential, future effects of their rulings, and 'limit the legal consequences of wrongs to a controllable degree'" (Lauer v. City of New York, 95 N.Y.2d 95, 100 [quoting Tobin v. Grossman, 24 N.Y.2d 609, 619]).

Foreseeability alone does not define duty—it merely determines the scope of the duty once it is determined to exist (see, Eiseman v. State of New York, 70 N.Y.2d 175, 187). The injured party must show that a defendant owed not merely a general duty to society but a specific duty to him or her, for "[w]ithout a duty running directly to the injured person there can be no liability in damages, however careless the conduct or foreseeable the harm" (Lauer, supra, at 100). That is required in order to avoid subjecting an actor "to limitless liability to an indeterminate class of persons conceivably injured by any negligence in that act" (Eiseman, supra, at 188). Moreover, any extension of the scope of duty must be tailored to reflect accurately the extent that its social benefits outweigh its costs.

The District Court imposed a duty on gun manufacturers "to take reasonable steps available at the point of . . . sale to primary distributors to reduce the possibility that these instruments will fall into the hands of those likely to misuse them" (Hamilton v. Accu-Tek, *supra*, 62 F. Supp. 2d, at 825). We have been cautious, however, in extending liability to defendants for their failure to control the conduct of others. "A defendant generally has no duty to control the conduct of third persons so as to prevent them from harming others, even where as a practical matter defendant can exercise such control" (D'Amico v. Christie, 71 N.Y.2d 76, 88). This judicial resistance to the expansion of duty grows out of practical concerns both about potentially limitless liability and about the unfairness of imposing liability for the acts of another.

A duty may arise, however, where there is a relationship either between defendant and a third-person tortfeasor that encompasses defendant's actual control of the third person's actions, or between defendant and plaintiff that requires defendant to protect plaintiff from the conduct of others. Examples of these relationships include master and servant, parent and child, and common carriers and their passengers.

The key in each is that the defendant's relationship with either the tortfeasor or the plaintiff places the defendant in the best position to protect against the risk of harm. In addition, the specter of limitless liability is not present because the class of potential plaintiffs to whom the duty is owed is circumscribed by the relationship. We have, for instance, recognized that landowners have a duty to protect tenants, patrons or invitees from foreseeable harm caused by the criminal conduct of others while they are on the premises. However, this duty does not extend beyond that limited class of plaintiffs to members of the community at large (*see*, Waters v. New York City Hous. Auth., 69 N.Y.2d, 225, 228-231). In *Waters*, for example, we held that the owner of a housing project who failed to keep the building's door locks in good repair did not owe a duty to a passerby to protect her from being dragged off the street into the building and assaulted. The Court concluded that imposing such a duty on landowners would do little to minimize crime, and the social benefits to be gained did "not warrant the extension of the landowner's duty to maintain secure premises to the millions of individuals who use the sidewalks of New York City each day and are thereby exposed to the dangers of street crime" (*id.*, at 230).

Similar rationale is relevant here. The pool of possible plaintiffs is very large — potentially, any of the thousands of victims of gun violence. Further, the connection between defendants, the criminal wrongdoers and plaintiffs is remote, running through several links in a chain consisting of at least the manufacturer, the federally licensed distributor or wholesaler, and the first retailer. The chain most often includes numerous subsequent legal purchasers or even a thief. Such broad liability, potentially encompassing all gunshot crime victims, should not be imposed without a more tangible showing that defendants were a direct link in the causal chain that resulted in plaintiffs' injuries, and that defendants were realistically in a position to prevent the wrongs. Giving plaintiffs' evidence the benefit of every favorable inference, they have not shown that the gun used to harm plaintiff Fox came from a source amenable to the exercise of any duty of care that plaintiffs would impose upon defendant manufacturers. . . .

In sum, analysis of this State's longstanding precedents demonstrates that defendants — given the evidence presented here — did not owe plaintiffs the duty they claim; we therefore answer the first certified question in the negative.

Market Share Liability

The Second Circuit has asked us also to determine if our market share liability jurisprudence is applicable to this case. Having concluded that these defendant-manufacturers did not owe the claimed duty to these plaintiffs, we arguably need not reach the market share issue. However, because of its particularly significant role in this case, it seems prudent to answer the second question.

Market share liability provides an exception to the general rule that in common-law negligence actions, a plaintiff must prove that the defendant's conduct was a cause-in-fact of the injury. This Court first examined and adopted the market share theory of liability in Hymowitz v. Eli Lilly & Co. (73 N.Y.2d 487, *supra*). In *Hymowitz*, we held that plaintiffs injured by the drug DES were not required to prove which defendant manufactured the drug that injured them but instead, every manufacturer would be held responsible for every plaintiff's injury based on its share of the DES market. Market share liability was necessary in *Hymowitz* because DES was a fungible product and identification of the actual manufacturer that caused the injury to a particular plaintiff was impossible. The Court carefully noted that the DES situation was unique. Key to our decision were the facts that (1) the manufacturers acted in a parallel manner to produce an identical, generically marketed product; (2) the manifestations of injury were far removed from the time of ingestion of the product; and (3) the Legislature made a clear policy decision to revive these time-barred DES claims.

Circumstances here are markedly different. Unlike DES, guns are not identical, fungible products. Significantly, it is often possible to identify the caliber and manufacturer of the handgun that caused injury to a particular plaintiff. Even more importantly — given the negligent marketing theory on which plaintiffs tried this case — plaintiffs have never asserted that the manufacturers' marketing techniques were uniform. Each manufacturer engaged in different marketing activities that allegedly contributed to the illegal handgun market in different ways and to different extents. Plaintiffs made no attempt to establish the relative fault of each manufacturer, but instead sought to hold them all liable based simply on market share.

In *Hymowitz*, each manufacturer engaged in tortious conduct parallel to that of all other manufacturers, creating the same risk to the public at large by manufacturing the same defective product. Market share was an accurate reflection of the risk they posed. Here, the distribution and sale of every gun is not equally negligent, nor does it involve a defective product. Defendants engaged in widely-varied conduct creating varied risks. Thus, a manufacturer's share of the national handgun market does not necessarily correspond to the amount of risk created by its alleged tortious conduct. No case has applied the market share theory of liability to such varied conduct and wisely so. . . .

This case challenges us to rethink traditional notions of duty, liability and causation. Tort law is ever changing; it is a reflection of the complexity and vitality of daily life. Although plaintiffs have presented us with a novel theory — negligent marketing of a potentially lethal yet legal product, based upon the acts not of one manufacturer, but of an industry — we are unconvinced that, on the record before us, the duty plaintiffs wish to impose is either reasonable or circumscribed. Nor does the market share theory of liability accurately measure defendants' conduct. Whether, in a different case, a duty may arise remains a question for the future.

Accordingly, both certified questions should be answered in the negative.

FOOD (AND DRINK) FOR THOUGHT

As *Hamilton* illustrates, in deciding whether a defendant's conduct could be found to be negligent or whether negligent conduct has proximately caused the plaintiff's injuries, courts help to define the obligations that persons generally owe to one another in society. Decisions involving the question of the extent to which a social host must protect innocent third parties from the criminally wrongful conduct of intoxicated guests within his control are particularly interesting. In Edgar v. Kajet, . . . 375 N.Y.S.2d 548 (Sup. Ct. 1975), *aff'd*, 389 N.Y.S.2d 631 (N.Y. App. Div. 1976), an action was brought against a social host whose inebriated guest had negligently caused the plaintiff's injuries while the guest drove home from the defendant's party. New York had a statutory scheme that imposed civil and criminal liability upon persons who procured alcoholic beverages for intoxicated persons for the harm caused by the latter's negligent conduct. While the statutes did not on their face distinguish between commercial dispensers and social hosts, the court refused to apply the statutes to a social host, explaining (*id.* at 552):

> The implications of imposing civil liability on [the defendant] herein are vast and far-reaching. Extending liability to non-sellers would open a virtual Pandora's box to a wide range of numerous potential defendants when the court does not believe that the Legislature ever intended to enact a law that makes social drinking of alcoholic beverages and the giving of drinks of intoxicating liquors at social events actionable. Just a recitation of a few of the considerations involved herein impels this court to conclude that any extension of liability should be a legislative act. For example, how is a host at a social gathering to know when the tolerance of one of his guests has been reached? To what extent should a host refuse to serve drinks to those nearing the point of intoxication? Further, how is a host to supervise his guests' social activities? The implications are almost limitless as to situations that might arise when liquor is dispensed at a social gathering, holiday parties, family celebrations, outdoor barbecues and picnics, to cite a few examples. If civil liability were imposed on [the defendant] herein, it could be similarly imposed on every host who, in spirit of friendship, serves liquor.

In Kelly v. Gwinnell, 476 A.2d 1219 (N.J. 1984), social hosts served their guest sufficient liquor to cause him to become visibly intoxicated and later walked the guest to his car, chatted with him, and watched him drive away. The victim of a head-on collision with the guest's car joined the hosts as defendants in a negligence action. The trial court granted the defendant social hosts' motion for summary judgment. The New Jersey high court reversed (with one justice dissenting along the lines of the *Edgar v. Kajet* opinion above). The majority opinion explains (*id.* at 1222):

> A reasonable person in [the hosts'] position could foresee quite clearly that this continued provision of alcohol to [the guest] was making it more and more likely that the guest would not be able to operate his car carefully. The host could foresee that unless he stopped providing drinks to [the guest, he] was likely to injure someone as a result of the negligent operation of his car. The usual elements of a cause of action for negligence are clearly present: an action by defendant creating an unreasonable risk of harm to plaintiff, a risk that was clearly foreseeable, and a risk that resulted in an injury equally foreseeable. Under those circumstances the only question remaining is whether a duty exists to prevent such risk or, realistically, whether this Court should impose such a duty.
>
> When the court determines that a duty exists and liability will be extended, it draws judicial lines based on fairness and policy. In a society where thousands of deaths are caused each year by drunken drivers, where the damage caused by such deaths is regarded increasingly as intolerable, where liquor licensees are prohibited from serving intoxicated adults, and where long-standing criminal sanctions against drunken driving have recently been significantly strengthened to the point where the Governor notes that they are regarded as the toughest in the nation . . . the imposition of such a duty by the judiciary seems both fair and fully in accord with the State's policy. Unlike those cases in which the definition of desirable policy is the subject of intense controversy, here the imposition of a duty is both consistent with and supportive of a social goal — the reduction of drunken driving — that is practically unanimously accepted by society.

Kelly is a minority view. The overwhelming majority of jurisdictions impose no liability on social hosts. *See, e.g.,* Bell v. Hutsell, 955 N.E.2d 1099 (Ill. 2011) (affirming dismissal of action against parents who allegedly permitted underage drinking at their house); Archer v. Sigma Tau Gamma Alpha Epsilon, 362 S.W.3d 303 (Ark. 2010) (fraternity that charged admission fee for a party was still a social host and entitled to statutory immunity from liability). Some jurisdictions impose liability that is limited in some way; in Massachusetts, for example, a social host would be liable only where the host had served the alcohol or made it available. See Juliano v. Simpson, 962 N.E.2d 175 (Mass. 2012) (after extensive review of state caselaw, affirming dismissal of action against host who provided place to drink, but not the alcohol). A similar result was reached in Nichols v. Progressive Northern Insurance Co., 746 N.W.2d 220 (Wis. 2008), where the court reversed an intermediate appellate court and reinstated the trial court's dismissal of a complaint in favor of the owner of property who knew that minors were drinking on its premises. Since the defendant-property owner did not supply the alcohol, the owner had no duty to persons injured when an underaged guest caused an alcohol-related car accident. *But see* Ah Mook Sang v. Clark, 308 P.3d 911 (Haw. 2013) (reinstating claim against social hosts who provided alcohol to 15 year-old guest and then failed to come to guest's aid when she fell ill and became unconscious).

A case that unites the discussion of intervening criminal acts and liability for providing alcohol is Auto-Owners Insurance Co. v. Seils, 871 N.W.2d 530 (Mich. App. 2015), *appeal denied,* 872 N.W.2d 454 (Mich. 2015). The defendant was a

authors' dialogue **25**

JIM: Many of the cases in this last section on "playing the duty card" share a common element: plaintiffs want the courts to require the defendants to act as watchdogs to protect society from the violent or antisocial behavior of criminal actors. And I could not agree more with the courts' response to such requests: "YOU MUST BE KIDDING!"

AARON: Don't be so quick to dismiss the possibility that the defendants in these cases should bear some of the responsibility for what happens to the victims. In some ways, a case like *Hamilton* (p. 362, *supra*) resembles the bartender who keeps serving liquor to an obviously intoxicated patron after the patron has put his car keys on the bar in front of him, in plain sight. When the drunk guy finally leaves, drives while intoxicated, and negligently injures somebody, American courts hold the bartender and his boss responsible to the victim. You don't disagree with the bartender cases, do you?

JIM: I agree with those cases. But what about the defendant who serves liquor to friends at a supper party in her home? Does the social host have to watch over her guests and cut them off at some point? I don't think so, Aaron. The scope of potential responsibility is too broad and too fuzzy. And cases like *Hamilton* strike me the same way. We can't ask gun manufacturers to act as watchdogs, tracking who is buying handguns and what they may be up to.

AARON: But don't you agree that it depends on the circumstances in each case? Couldn't you think of a situation in which a weapons manufacturer acted egregiously enough to be treated like the bartender serving the drink? How about the manufacturer of armor-piercing bullets, openly sold as "cop-killers"?

JIM: Even there, I don't like imposing liability, so long as there is any legitimate purpose served by having such ammunition available to the general public. This "watchdog" idea gives me the creeps.

AARON: Two thoughts: "Watchdog" was your word, not mine. And I seem to recall that you didn't like the *Watson* case, in which arsonist behavior cut off liability as a matter of law in an action against the railroad that negligently spilled gasoline. Why should the railroad in *Watson* have to pay for an arson while the gun maker in *Hamilton* escapes liability for a shooting? Aren't you being just a little inconsistent?

BRAD: Aaron's got a good point if the right way to read *Watson* is that the arsonist, not the railroad, is somehow the "real" bad guy. As you know, I tend to see tort liability as connected with ordinary notions of moral responsibility. We have a long tradition in this country of claiming that guns don't kill people, people do. A case like *Hamilton* must be understood as expressing moral outrage at senseless murders but withholding moral blame from an actor who does nothing more than provide the instrument of harm.

charitable organization, the Fraternal Order of Police, which sponsored a three-day fundraising event called the Detroit Hoedown, at which alcohol was served. Todd Pink, his girlfriend Carrie Seils, and Seils's roommate attended the Hoedown. Pink bought and consumed several beers and became belligerent. Seils and her roommate urged Pink to leave. The three left together and Pink dropped Seils and her roommate at their house. He then retrieved a gun, went back to the house, kicked in the door, and killed Seils and her roommate. The court agreed with the plaintiff, Seils's representative, that, in general terms, it is foreseeable that heavy drinking may be linked with violent behavior. However, the court believed there is a difference between a barroom brawl and deliberate, premeditated murder. Pink's intervening criminal act broke the causal chain connecting the provision of alcohol and the Seils's death.

WHAT ABOUT DRUGS OTHER THAN ALCOHOL?

Another example of the way courts define our obligations to one another is McKenzie v. Haw. Permanente Medical Group, 47 P.3d 1209 (Haw. 2002). The plaintiff, a pedestrian, was seriously injured when she was struck by an automobile. The driver had suffered a fainting episode. The episode was allegedly caused by the negligent prescription of a certain medication by the driver's doctor. The plaintiff brought a malpractice action against the doctor, alleging that the doctor was negligent in prescribing the rarely used medication, in failing to warn the patient of the possible side effects, and in prescribing the dosage. On certification from the U.S. District Court for the District of Hawaii, the Hawaii Supreme Court held that the doctor owed a duty to third parties that his actions in treating his patient might harm if he negligently failed to warn patients of the possible side effects of drugs, but not if he was negligent in deciding whether to prescribe a drug, what drug to prescribe, or what dosage to prescribe. The court listed policy factors that it considered in deciding whether to impose liability for the doctor's alleged negligent failure to warn of the drug's side effects (*id.* at 1220-1221):

> To summarize, we balance the considerations in favor of imposing a duty to warn for the benefit of third parties against the considerations militating against imposition of a duty. The primary considerations favoring a duty are that: (1) it is evident that a patient who is unaware of the risk of driving while under the influence of a particular prescription medication will probably do so; (2) warning against such activity could prevent substantial harm; (3) imposing a duty would create little additional burden upon physicians because physicians already owe their own patients the same duty; and (4) the majority of jurisdictions appear to recognize a duty under some circumstances. The primary consideration militating against the imposition of a duty is that it may not be worth the marginal benefit, in some circumstances, where the effectiveness of the warning is minimal or where the reasonable patient should be aware of the risk. Such circumstances may include, e.g., situations where patients have previously taken a particular medication and where patients are prescribed medications commonly known to

affect driving ability. "The relative knowledge of the risk as between a patient and a physician is [a] factor to consider in deciding the threshold question of whether a physician owes a duty to third parties to warn a patient." [citation omitted] Balancing these considerations, we believe that a logical reason exists to impose upon physicians, for the benefit of third parties, a duty to advise their patients that a medication may affect the patient's driving ability when such a duty would otherwise be owed to the patient.

Why do you suppose the court refrained from imposing a duty of care on doctors to third parties in cases where the negligence was in deciding whether to prescribe medication, what medication to prescribe, or what dosage? *Also see* Burroughs v. Magee, 118 S.W.3d 323 (Tenn. 2003) (physician owed duty of care to warn patient, a truck driver, of effects of prescribed medications on his ability to safely drive his truck; but did not owe duty of care to third persons for prescribing the medications even though the doctor prescribed addictive medication without checking the patient's chart, which noted that another doctor had refused to prescribe the addictive drug because the patient was a substance abuser). *Accord* Coombes v. Florio, 877 N.E.2d 567 (Mass. 2007) (physician had a duty to warn elderly patient that drugs he was taking could cause drowsiness).

Courts are, however, reluctant to impose liability against pharmacies who negligently dispense narcotics. In Sanchez v. Wal-Mart Stores Inc. et al., 221 P.3d 1276 (Nev. 2009), pharmacies were notified by the Prescription Controlled Substance Task Force that Patricia Copening had obtained 4,500 hydrocodone pills at 13 different pharmacies. Copening, while driving under the influence of the narcotics, killed plaintiff's decedent. The complaint alleged that the pharmacies had sold the hydrocodone to Copening after they received the Task Force letter. The Nevada Supreme Court refused to find a special relationship between a pharmacy and a third party to justify imposing a duty of care and affirmed the trial court's dismissal of the complaint.

JUST GIVE HIM THE MONEY, STUPID!

Another decision of interest here involved the liability of a bank for its employees' allegedly negligent refusal of a bank robber's demands. In Bence v. Crawford Savings & Loan Assn., 400 N.E.2d 39 (Ill. App. Ct. 1980), a wrongful death action, the plaintiff's decedent was shot to death by a bank robber who panicked when bank personnel refused to activate an electronic door buzzer system to allow the robber to leave the bank premises. In refusing to recognize a duty on the part of the bank personnel to accede to the robber's demands, the Illinois appellate court explained (*id.* at 42, quoting Goldberg v. Housing Authority of City of Newark, 186 A.2d 291, 293 (1962)):

> The question whether a private party must provide protection for another is not solved merely by recourse to "foreseeability." Everyone can foresee the commission of crime virtually anywhere and at any time. If foreseeability itself gave rise to a duty to provide "police" protection for others, every residential curtilage, every

shop, every store, every manufacturing plant would have to be patrolled by the private arms of the owner. . . .

The question is not simply whether a criminal event is foreseeable, but whether a *duty* exists to take measures to guard against it. Whether a *duty* exists is ultimately a question of fairness. The inquiry involves a weighing of the relationship of the parties, the nature of the risk, and the public interest in the proposed solution.

All of the preceding cases state the issue to have been whether the defendant owed a duty to the plaintiff. In what sense do the courts appear to be using "duty"?

SO YOU WANT TO KILL YOUR NEIGHBOR? TEN COMMON MISTAKES TO AVOID

In Rice v. Paladin Enterprises, 128 F.3d 233 (4th Cir. 1997), the court of appeals reversed a grant of summary judgment for the defendant, publisher of a how-to book entitled *Hit Man: A Technical Manual for Independent Contractors.* The plaintiff's intestate had been murdered by a man who, having been paid to kill the victim, followed the book's detailed instructions on how to plan and commit murder for hire. The publisher rested its entire defense on its freedom under the First Amendment, even stipulating for purposes of the motion that it intended to aid criminals in the commission of their crimes. In denying the motion and allowing the plaintiff's case to proceed, the court said (*id.* at 266-267):

> [Defendant] in this case has stipulated that it specifically targeted the market of murderers, would-be murderers, and other criminals for sale of its murder manual. [Defendant] has stipulated both that it had knowledge and that it intended that *Hit Man* would immediately be used by criminals and would-be criminals in the solicitation, planning, and commission of murder and murder for hire. . . . [These] astonishing stipulations, coupled with the extraordinary comprehensiveness, detail, and clarity of *Hit Man*'s instructions for criminal activity and murder in particular, the boldness of its palpable exhortation to murder, . . . the notable absence from its text of the kind of ideas for the protection of which the First Amendment exists, and the book's evident lack of any even arguably legitimate purpose beyond the promotion and teaching of murder, render this case unique in the law. In at least these circumstances, we are confident that the First Amendment does not erect [an] absolute bar to the imposition of civil liability. . . . [The Constitution] reserves to the people the ultimate and necessary authority to adjudge some conduct—and even some speech—fundamentally incompatible with the liberties they have secured unto themselves.

In Wilson v. Paladin Enterprises, 186 F. Supp. 2d 1140 (D. Or. 2001), another action was brought against the same defendant, again in connection with *Hit Man,* on nearly identical facts. The defendant publisher once again moved for summary judgment, but it did not rest its entire defense on its First Amendment freedom, as above. The district court denied defendant's motion on the ground that in addition to inference of intent to assist in commission of crime that could be gleaned from the book itself, the publisher was aware (because of the *Rice* case) that people were using its book to help them become contract killers (*id.* at 1143):

> Notwithstanding the . . . homicide that was the subject of the *Rice* litigation and their knowledge that the manual had been used to plan and carry out those murders, defendants continued to publish and market *Hit Man*. Thus, [the killer] was able to utilize the instructions provided by the book in his attempt to murder plaintiff. . . .

Note that imposition of liability in each of the above cases will rest upon whether the trier of fact finds that the defendant intentionally or knowingly aided in the commission of a crime. Would the analysis be substantially different under a pure negligence claim?

VIOLENT VIDEOS MADE THEM DO IT

In Sanders v. Acclaim Entertainment, Inc., 188 F. Supp. 2d 1264 (D. Colo. 2002), the family of a teacher who was killed during the 1999 shooting and bombing spree of Dylan Klebold and Eric Harris at Columbine High School in Colorado brought an action against the producers and distributors of some of the violent video games, movies, and music that the shooters allegedly imitated in carrying out their plan. Plaintiffs alleged that the defendants knew or should have known that their products might cause copycat violence and that, by marketing their products to minors who would foreseeably be influenced by them, the defendants created an unreasonable risk of harm to the plaintiffs' decedent. The district court granted defendants' motion to dismiss for failure to state a claim upon which relief could be granted, stating (*id.* at 1275-1276):

> Plaintiffs do not allege that the [d]efendants illegally produced or distributed the movie and video games Harris and Klebold allegedly viewed or played. . . . [M]akers of works of imagination including video games and movies may not be held liable in tort based merely on the content or ideas expressed in their creative works. Placing a duty of care on [d]efendants in the circumstances alleged would chill their rights of free expression. . . . Consequently, I hold that the [d]efendants owed no duty to [p]laintiffs as a matter of law. . . .
>
> Harris' and Klebold's intentional violent acts were the superseding cause of [plaintiffs'] death[s]. Moreover . . . their acts were not foreseeable. . . . [Therefore] their criminal acts . . . were not within the scope of any risk purportedly created by [d]efendants.

SCHOLARLY TREATMENTS OF PROXIMATE CAUSE

Proximate causation has attracted the attention of many commentators over the years. Some classic scholarly treatments include Francis H. Bohlen, *The Probable or Natural Consequences as a Test of Liability in Negligence*, 49 U. Pa. L. Rev. 79, 148 (1901); Jeremiah Smith, *Legal Cause in Actions of Tort*, 25 Harv. L. Rev. 103, 223,

303 (1911); Leon Green, *Are There Dependable Rules of Causation?*, 77 U. Pa. L. Rev. 601 (1929); Arthur L. Goodhart, *The Unforeseeable Consequences of a Negligent Act*, 39 Yale L.J. 449 (1930); and Charles O. Gregory, *Proximate Cause in Negligence — A Retreat from Rationalization*, 6 U. Chi. L. Rev. 36 (1938-1939).

The issue of proximate causation has also been explored in more comprehensive, book-length treatments, such as Leon Green, *Rationale of Proximate Cause* (1927); Robert E. Keeton, *Legal Cause in the Law of Torts* (1963); and H.L.A. Hart & M. Honoré, *Causation in the Law* (2d ed. 1985) (perhaps the most cited work on the subject). The late Professor Robert Keeton, in his work, gives this pithy summary of proximate cause (*Legal Cause in the Law of Torts, supra* at 10): "A negligent actor is legally responsible for the harm, and only the harm, that not only (1) is caused in fact by his [negligent] conduct but also (2) is a result within the scope of the risks by reason of which the actor is found to be negligent."

More recent scholarly works have also addressed the issue of proximate cause. Some of these include Mark F. Grady, *Proximate Cause and the Law of Negligence*, 69 Iowa L. Rev. 363 (1983-1984); Jim Gash, *At the Intersection of Proximate Cause and Terrorism: A Contextual Analysis of the Proposed Restatement, Third, of Torts: Approach to Intervening and Superseding Causes*, 91 Kent L.J. 523 (2002-2003); John C. P. Goldberg, *Rethinking Injury and Proximate Cause*, 40 San Diego L. Rev. 1315 (2003); Patrick J. Kelley, *Restating Duty, Breach and Proximate Cause: Descriptive Theory and the Rule of Law*, 53 Vand. L. Rev. 1039 (2001).

Scholars have also offered economic analyses of proximate cause. In addition to Grady, *supra*, representative titles include William M. Landes & Richard A. Posner, *Causation in Tort Law: An Economic Approach*, 12 J. Leg. Stud. 109 (1983); and Steven Shavell, *Analysis of Causation and the Scope of Liability in the Law of Torts*, 9 J. Legal Stud. 463 (1980).

chapter **6**

Nonliability for Foreseeable Consequences (Limited Duty Rules)

In all of the cases in this chapter, the defendants acted badly and the plaintiff's harm was reasonably foreseeable. Thus, if a court is inclined to deny recovery as a matter of law, it is awkward to rely on the absence of fault or lack of proximate cause as grounds for doing so. And yet in most of the cases in this chapter the courts deny plaintiffs recovery as a matter of law. Clearly, something is going on besides business as usual, and part of the fun in each instance will be figuring out what that "something else" is.

A. LIMITATIONS ON THE DUTY TO RESCUE

Every so often we read in newspapers, or see reported on television, stories about bystanders who stood and gawked, and did nothing, while assailants (or the forces of nature) attacked and injured innocent victims in full view. More often, thank goodness, we hear of heroic rescue efforts, often undertaken at great risk to the rescuers themselves. In any event, you may be surprised to learn that onlookers who do nothing but gawk when they could, easily, help save a victim from serious harm breach no general legal duty to rescue because no such duty exists. Whatever moral obligation onlookers may have, under American common law they are not obligated to act in any way to assist strangers who need their help. The absence of a general duty to rescue is described in Buch v. Amory Manufacturing Co., 44 A. 809, 811 (N.H. 1898):

> There is a wide difference — a broad gulf — both in reason and in law, between causing and preventing an injury; between doing by negligence or otherwise a wrong to one's neighbor; and preventing him from injuring himself; between protecting him against injury by another and guarding him from injury that may accrue to him from the condition of the premises which he has unlawfully invaded. The duty to do no wrong is a legal duty. The duty to protect against wrong is, generally speaking and excepting certain intimate relations in the nature

of a trust, a moral obligation only, not recognized or enforced by law. Is a spectator liable if he sees an intelligent man or an unintelligent infant running into danger and does not warn or forcibly restrain him? . . . I see my neighbor's two-year-old babe in dangerous proximity to the machinery of his windmill in his yard, and easily might, but do not, rescue him. I am not liable in damages to the child for his injuries, nor, if the child is killed, punishable for manslaughter by the common law or under the statute, because the child and I are strangers, and I am under no legal duty to protect him.

Commentators have criticized this general "no-duty-to-rescue" rule, especially in situations where a defendant could rescue with little or no risk to herself. Professor Ernest Weinrib, in *The Case for a Duty to Rescue*, 90 Yale L.J. 247 (1980), argues that courts should recognize an "easy rescue" doctrine whereby tort law would hold liable those defendants who could have saved a person from an emergency situation at little or no inconvenience to themselves. Liam Murphy, in *Beneficence, Law, and Liberty: The Case of Required Rescue*, 89 Geo. L.J. 605 (2001), argues that, instead of tort sanctions, criminal sanctions should be imposed on those who fail to make easy rescues. Another commentator combines insights from interdisciplinary studies (physics, ecology, anthropology, and sociology) to argue that a duty to rescue is better for society because it promotes cooperation, empathy, and altruism. *See* Nancy Levit, *The Kindness of Strangers: Interdisciplinary Foundations of a Duty to Act*, 40 Washburn L.J. 463 (2001). Many, but not all, feminist theorists criticize the traditional no-duty rule as an example of tort doctrine continuing to perpetuate male-dominated values, and insist that women would generally agree to impose a duty to act to assist others. For example, Leslie Bender, *An Overview of Feminist Torts Scholarship*, 78 Cornell L. Rev. 575, 580 (1993), argues that "caring about and for others' safety and interests . . . is a part of reasoning about tort law that has been subordinated because of its gendered identification with women." *See also* Assaf Jacob, *Tort Law: Feminist Approaches to Tort Law Revisited*, 2 Theoretical Inq. L. 211 (2001).

For a defense of the no-duty-to-rescue rule on the ground that courts could not manage a rule imposing a general duty to respond reasonably to the needs of others to be rescued, *see* James A. Henderson, Jr., *Process Constraints in Tort*, 67 Cornell L. Rev. 901 (1982). For a defense of the no-duty rule on substantive grounds, *see* Marin R. Scordato, *Understanding the Absence of a Duty to Reasonably Rescue in American Tort Law*, 82 Tul. L. Rev. 1447 (2008).

Although courts have not yet responded to this criticism by imposing a general duty to rescue, they have recognized a number of exceptional situations in which such a duty may arise. The most common of these situations occur when a preexisting relationship between the party in peril and the potential rescuer justifies recognition of a duty to act. These relations have included special relationships running between a common carrier and its passengers, a school and its students, and an employer and its injured employee. These category-based exceptions are discussed in Section 2, below. Sometimes courts prefer to dispense with the categorization exercise and reason on the basis of underlying factual or policy considerations. Frequently the foreseeability of the harm to the plaintiff is invoked as a ground for imposing affirmative duties. This approach is the subject of Section 3.

1. No Duty Where Defendant Did Not Negligently Create the Risk

YANIA v. BIGAN
155 A.2d 343 (Pa. 1959)

BENJAMIN R. JONES, Justice. A bizarre and most unusual circumstance provides the background of this appeal.

On September 25, 1957 John E. Bigan was engaged in a coal strip-mining operation in Shade Township, Somerset County. On the property being stripped were large cuts or trenches created by Bigan when he removed the earthen over-burden for the purpose of removing the coal underneath. One cut contained water 8 to 10 feet in depth with side walls or embankments 16 to 18 feet in height; at this cut Bigan had installed a pump to remove the water.

At approximately 4 p.m. on that date, Joseph F. Yania, the operator of another coal strip-mining operation, and one Boyd M. Ross went upon Bigan's property for the purpose of discussing a business matter with Bigan, and, while there, were asked by Bigan to aid him in starting the pump. Ross and Bigan entered the cut and stood at the point where the pump was located. Yania stood at the top of one of the cut's side walls and then jumped from the side wall — a height of 16 to 18 feet — into the water and was drowned.

Yania's widow, in her own right and on behalf of her three children, instituted wrongful death and survival actions against Bigan contending Bigan was respon-sible for Yania's death. Preliminary objections, in the nature of demurrers, to the complaint were filed on behalf of Bigan. The court below sustained the preliminary objections; from the entry of that order this appeal was taken.

Since Bigan has chosen to file preliminary objections, in the nature of demur-rers, every material and relevant fact well pleaded in the complaint and every inference fairly deducible therefrom are to be taken as true.

The complaint avers negligence in the following manner: (1) "The death by drowning of . . . [Yania] was caused entirely by the acts of [Bigan] . . . in *urging, enticing, taunting and inveigling* [Yania] to jump into the water, which [Bigan] knew or ought to have known was of a depth of 8 to 10 feet and dangerous to the life of anyone who would jump therein" (emphasis supplied); (2) ". . . [Bigan] violated his obligations to a business invitee in not having his premises reasonably safe, and not warning his business invitee of a dangerous condition and to the contrary urged, induced and inveigled [Yania] into a dangerous position and a dangerous act, whereby [Yania] came to his death"; (3) "After [Yania] was in the water, a highly dangerous position, having been induced and inveigled therein by [Bigan], [Bigan] failed and neglected to take reasonable steps and action to protect or assist [Yania], or extradite [Yania] from the dangerous position in which [Bigan] had placed him." Summarized, Bigan stands charged with three-fold neg-ligence: (1) by urging, enticing, taunting and inveigling Yania to jump into the water; (2) by failing to warn Yania of a dangerous condition on the land, i.e. the cut wherein lay 8 to 10 feet of water; (3) by failing to go to Yania's rescue after he had jumped into the water. . . .

Appellant initially contends that Yania's descent from the high embankment into the water and the resulting death were caused "entirely" by the spoken words and blandishments of Bigan delivered at a distance from Yania. The complaint does not allege that Yania slipped or that he was pushed or that Bigan made any *physical* impact upon Yania. On the contrary, the only inference deducible from the facts alleged in the complaint is that Bigan, by the employment of cajolery and inveiglement, caused such a *mental* impact on Yania that the latter was deprived of his volition and freedom of choice and placed under a compulsion to jump into the water. Had Yania been a child of tender years or a person mentally deficient then it is conceivable that taunting and enticement could constitute actionable negligence if it resulted in harm. However, to contend that such conduct directed to an adult in full possession of all his mental faculties constitutes actionable negligence is not only without precedent but completely without merit.

[The court next concludes that Bigan, as the possessor of the land on which Yania died, breached no duty to warn Yania of the risk presented by the water-filled trench.]

Lastly, it is urged that Bigan failed to take the necessary steps to rescue Yania from the water. The mere fact that Bigan saw Yania in a position of peril in the water imposed upon him no legal, although a moral, obligation or duty to go to his rescue unless Bigan was legally responsible, in whole or in part, for placing Yania in the perilous position. The language of this Court in Brown v. French, 104 Pa. 604, 607, 608, is apt:

> If it appeared that the deceased, by his own carelessness, contributed in any degree to the accident which caused the loss of his life, the defendants ought not to have been held to answer for the consequences resulting from that accident. . . . He voluntarily placed himself in the way of danger, and his death was the result of his own act. . . . That his undertaking was an exceedingly reckless and dangerous one, the event proves, but there was no one to blame for it but himself. He had the right to try the experiment, obviously dangerous as it was, but then also upon him rested the consequences of that experiment, and upon no one else; he may have been, and probably was, ignorant of the risk which he was taking upon himself, or knowing it, and trusting to his own skill, he may have regarded it as easily superable. But in either case, the result of his ignorance, or of his mistake, must rest with himself — and cannot be charged to the defendants.

The complaint does not aver any facts which impose upon Bigan legal responsibility for placing Yania in the dangerous position in the water and, absent such legal responsibility, the law imposes on Bigan no duty of rescue.

Recognizing that the deceased Yania is entitled to the benefit of the presumption that he was exercising due care and extending to appellant the benefit of every well pleaded fact in this complaint and the fair inferences arising therefrom, yet we can reach but one conclusion: that Yania, a reasonable and prudent adult in full possession of all his mental faculties, undertook to perform an act which he knew or should have known was attended with more or less peril and it was the performance of that act and not any conduct upon Bigan's part which caused his unfortunate death.

FOOD FOR THOUGHT

Yania reflects the general principle that an actor owes no duty to rescue when he does not create the risk. This black letter rule is set forth in Restatement, Third, of Torts § 37. Lawyers and torts scholars tend to describe these no-duty cases as involving a "rescue" but you should understand that these cases encompass more than the ordinary meaning of that word. These cases are about whether an actor should be liable for another's injuries, even though the actor had no role in bringing about the danger, but could have done something that arguably would have prevented the harm. For example, in the *Posecai* case below, the defendant (a retail store) had no role in bringing about crime in the neighborhood. The plaintiff, however, argued that the store could have done something — such as installing better lighting or security cameras, or instituting regular patrols by security guards — that would have prevented a robbery. In ordinary language one probably would not say that the plaintiff was asking the store to "rescue" her, but the case is nevertheless a core example of what may be called affirmative duty claims. Similarly, judges sometimes talk about affirmative duties to *control* the conduct of another, but that is not exactly right. It would be odd to say the retail store has a duty to control the conduct of criminals. It is better to understand cases like this as imposing a duty to create conditions that better protect customers against the risk of harm caused by crime in the surroundings. *See* Restatement, Third § 37, cmt. *b.*

When the defendant places the plaintiff in a position of peril, the defendant's conduct need not have been negligent for the defendant to owe a duty to rescue. In Tubbs v. Argus, 225 N.E.2d 841 (Ind. Ct. App. 1967), the plaintiff alleged that she suffered aggravated injuries when the defendant failed to render assistance after driving an automobile in which plaintiff was a passenger into a tree. The court quotes § 322 of the Restatement, Second, of Torts that "[i]f the actor knows or has reason to know that by his conduct, whether tortious or innocent, he has caused such bodily harm to another as to make him helpless and in danger of future harm, the actor is under a duty to exercise reasonable care to prevent such future harm." *Accord* Restatement, Third, of Torts § 39.

In Podias v. Mairs, 926 A.2d 859 (N.J. Super. Ct. App. Div. 2007), an intermediate appellate court extended the duty to rescue to passengers in a car that injured a third party. In this grisly story, two 18-year-olds got into a car being driven by a friend who had been drinking prior to the trip. Some time later the driver struck a motorcycle driven by Antonios Podias. All three got out of the car, saw Podias lying in the roadway, and assumed that he was dead. All three had cell phones and could have called for help but they did not. After five or ten minutes they all left the scene of the accident. The two passengers told the driver that if he were apprehended he should not say anything about them being in the car. Subsequent to their leaving Podias in the road, a car driven by Patricia Uribe ran over Podias. Podias died, either as a result of one individual accident (which was sufficient on its own to kill him) or from the combined effect of the injuries sustained in both accidents. The decedent's estate sued the passengers in the first car to hit Podias, but the trial court granted summary judgment in their favor on the ground that they had no duty to provide emergency assistance because they had not caused the accident that first injured the decedent. In a thoughtful opinion, the court held that under the unusual facts of this case the passengers owed a duty to call for help. The court held that the risk to the decedent was highly foreseeable and the ability to implement the rescue came at virtually no cost.

Not all courts are so sympathetic to claims that an actor must take steps to help someone whose initial injury the actor has played a role in triggering. Thus, in Cilley v. Lane, 985 A.2d 481 (Me. 2009), the defendant told her boyfriend that she wanted to take time off from their relationship. The boyfriend became upset and refused to leave the defendant's house. He then grabbed a gun, and when she left the house, she heard a gunshot and saw him fall to the floor. The defendant saw that he was injured but did nothing to help or even to call for help. Others discovered her wounded boyfriend some time thereafter and took him to the hospital, where he died of his gunshot wound. An expert testified that if the boyfriend had reached the hospital five or ten minutes earlier he would have survived. Invoking the no-duty-to-rescue rule, the Supreme Court of Maine affirmed a summary judgment for the defendant.

LEGISLATIVE ACTIVITY ON THE RESCUE FRONT

Legislatures, like courts, have been reluctant to impose a duty to rescue. However, due to extreme political pressure, some legislatures have imposed duties in a limited number of situations. Other states, perhaps responding to commentators who have asked for a duty to provide "easy rescue," have enacted criminal statutes requiring all citizens to provide reasonable assistance to strangers who are in emergency situations, when the onlooker can provide assistance without "danger or peril" to herself. *See, e.g.,* Minn. Stat. Ann. § 604A.01(1) (2001). These statutes establish general duties to rescue. More common are state statutes that impose a duty on those involved in an automobile accident to render or seek medical aid for others injured in the accident. *See, e.g.,* Ky. Rev. Stat. § 189.580(1) (2001). These statutes require some causal connection with the accident victim before a duty to rescue arises. However, both of these types of statutes are rare; most states have refused to impose a duty to rescue by statute.

One incident that brought the duty-to-rescue debate to the forefront occurred in a Nevada casino in 1997. A teenager witnessed his friend take a seven-year-old girl into a bathroom, rape the victim, and then murder her. The teenager did not report the incident to authorities. In response to questions after the incident, the teenager remarked: "I'm not going to get upset over someone else's life. I just worry about myself first. I'm not going to lose sleep over somebody else's problems." Hugo Martin, *Victim's Mother Begins Campaign,* L.A. Times, Aug. 1, 1998, at B-1. Commentators seized the opportunity to once again call for a general duty to rescue. *See, e.g., Symposium,* 40 S. Clara L. Rev. 957-1103 (2000). It also generated some legislative activity. *See, e.g.,* Sherrice Iverson Act, H.R. 4531, 105th Cong. (1998) (a proposed, but ultimately rejected, amendment to the federal Child Abuse Prevention and Treatment Act that would have required third-party witnesses of sexual crimes against children to report those crimes to law enforcement agencies).

However, as with most historical debates about the no-duty-to-rescue, this debate bore very little fruit.

2. Categorical Exceptions to No-Duty Rule

The general no-duty rule is subject to a host of exceptions spelled out in the Third Restatement §§ 38-44. These are examples of affirmative duty rules in which a court must first find that the plaintiff and defendant belong to general categories from which legal responsibilities follow. We shall attempt, in the ensuing discussion and cases, to give you a good feel for the situations in which an actor may be held liable even if the actor did not create the risk. Many of the cases will cite to sections from the Second Restatement of Torts. In the main, the Third Restatement is in accord with the Second Restatement, though there are subtle differences. One major exception to the no-duty-to-rescue rule comes under the heading of "Duty Based on Undertaking." Restatement, Third, § 42 provides as follows:

> ### § 42. Duty Based on Undertaking
> An actor who undertakes to render services to another that the actor knows or should know reduce the risk of physical harm to the other has a duty of reasonable care to the other in conducting the undertaking if:
>> (a) the failure to exercise such care increases the risk of harm beyond that which existed without the undertaking, or
>> (b) the person to whom the services are rendered or another relies on the actor's exercising reasonable care in the undertaking.

Cases struggling with the "voluntary undertaking" exception are legion. In Lacey v. United States, 98 F. Supp. 219 (D. Mass. 1951), the families of occupants in a plane that crashed at sea claimed, in an action under the Federal Tort Claims Act, that the Coast Guard had begun a rescue effort but had negligently failed to follow through, resulting in the deaths of the occupants. The district court granted the defendant's motion for judgment on the pleadings. The court acknowledged (*id.* at 220) that "[i]t is true that, while the common law imposes no duty to rescue, it does impose on the Good Samaritan the duty to act with due care *once he has undertaken rescue operations*. The rationale is that other would-be rescuers will rest on their oars in the expectation that effective aid is being rendered." Although the plaintiffs alleged that the defendant had undertaken rescue operations, the court dismissed the complaint because the plaintiffs failed to allege that other potential rescuers were deterred from acting. Similarly, in Morgan v. Scott, 291 S.W.3d 622 (Ky. 2009), the Supreme Court of Kentucky ruled for the defendant car dealership as a matter of law on a claim that the dealership had violated its own internal rule and allowed a customer to take a test drive unaccompanied by a salesman. In effect, the plaintiff argued that the defendant had undertaken to rescue and had not carried through. The customer collided with the plaintiff's car while on the test drive; the trial court entered a judgment for plaintiff against both the customer and the dealership. The Supreme Court affirmed the court of appeals' reversal of the judgment against the dealership, concluding that it was undisputed that neither the customer nor the plaintiff victim knew about the internal rule (hence no reliance on the rule), and that violation of the rule did not increase the risk of the customer's negligent driving (the customer had a valid operator's license and appeared fit to drive, and a salesman could not have prevented the accident).

Others have had better luck than the plaintiffs in *Lacey* and *Morgan* with claims of reliance-based duties to rescue. Thus, in Crowley v. Spivey, 329 S.E.2d 774 (S.C. Ct. App. 1985), the defendants assured their son-in-law that they would look after the son-in-law's children (their grandchildren) when they took the children to visit the children's mother (their daughter). They left the children alone with the mother, who they knew was seriously mentally ill, and the mother killed the children. The trial court found for the father and entered judgment against the grandparents. The Supreme Court of South Carolina affirmed on appeal, reasoning that the plaintiff father's reliance on the defendant grandparents' assurances gave rise to a duty to protect the children. And in Mixon v. Dobbs Houses, Inc., 254 S.E.2d 864 (Ga. App. 1979), the court ruled that the plaintiff stated a cause of action by alleging that her husband's employer, the defendant, had promised to relay to her husband her messages that she had begun labor, but the employer failed to do so, leaving her to give birth alone at home, unaided.

In Wakulich v. Mraz, 785 N.E.2d 843 (Ill. 2003), two defendants, 18 and 21 years old, respectively, allegedly induced a 16-year-old to drink one quart of hard liquor by offering her a prize and exerting social pressure. The young woman passed out and subsequently died the next morning when defendants provided no aid, other than removing a vomit-saturated shirt and propping her head with a pillow to avoid aspiration of the vomit. Defendants also allegedly prevented other guests from aiding the victim. The young woman's family sued under a number of theories of recovery including negligence. Applying the general no-duty rule, the trial court dismissed the complaint for failure to state a claim. The Illinois appellate court upheld in part and reversed in part the lower court's dismissal. While the appellate court admitted that the defendants did not become obligated to act merely by exerting social pressure and offering a prize for plaintiffs' decedent to drink, the court held that a jury could find the defendants negligent for failing to rescue after they began helping the young woman by removing her shirt and propping her head with a pillow. By not calling an ambulance, taking the victim to the hospital, or allowing others to aid the plaintiffs' decedent, the defendants could be found to have "increased the risk of harm" to her. The Illinois Supreme Court affirmed the intermediate appellate court and remanded the case for trial. Does the court's reasoning in *Wakulich* suggest that defendant would have been better off doing nothing at all? If so, does that make sense?

hypo **47**

Plaintiff took her car to Quik-E-Lube for an oil change. Quik-E-Lube advertises a "12-point inspection" along with oil changes. As its advertising clearly states, the inspection includes belts, hoses, wiper blades, and fluid levels. The technician performing the work failed to notice that the tires on Plaintiff's car were worn to the point that it would be extremely dangerous to drive on them. Tires are not part of the advertised 12-point inspection. The next day, Plaintiff was seriously injured when she lost control of her car and hit a tree. The state trooper who investigated the accident concluded that it was caused by the worn tires on Plaintiff's car. Is Quik-E-Lube liable for negligence?

hypo 48

A and *B* have been climbing mountains for several years. Having decided to try to break the record for the fastest wintertime climb to the top of Mount Everest, they set out together to accomplish that objective. Near the summit of the mountain, *A* slips and breaks his ankle. *B*, determined to break the record, leaves *A* on the mountain alone, covered with a blanket. *A* pleads for help, but *B* promises to help *A* down the mountain only after *B* finishes the climb. *B* carries through with his promise, but on the way back he is too late to save *A* from harm. *A* suffers frostbite and has most of his toes amputated due to the extended time he was left on the mountain. *A* brings a negligence action against *B*, claiming that *B* should have helped him down the mountain immediately, in which event *A* would have suffered only a broken ankle. Will *A*'s claim survive *B*'s motion for summary judgment?

hypo 49

Pleasantville is a small city with many attractive natural features. Among them is Ten Mile Creek, which runs through scenic gorges and waterfalls on its meandering course to Big Lake. One of the gorges on Ten Mile Creek is a perfect summertime swimming hole, with clear, cold water and fifty-foot cliffs off of which adventurous souls jump or dive. Many of these cliff dives are filmed and posted on social media sites, which has led to considerable local fame for the swimming hole on Ten Mile Creek. Unfortunately, every summer one or two intrepid cliff-divers are killed. Because the City of Pleasantville owns Ten Mile Creek and the surrounding land, the City Council has debated hiring safety officers to patrol the area to prevent cliff-diving. When this proposal was debated during a recent meeting, a local lawyer who is a member of the City Council suggested that this was not a good idea. "If we do nothing, we're not liable — it's a simple matter of the rule that there's no duty to rescue. But if we institute safety patrols, we may be considered to have voluntarily undertaken a duty to protect swimmers. Then, if the patrol doesn't stop some nitwit who kills himself cliff-diving, the City will be liable. As heartless as it sounds, we should leave the swimmers alone." Do you agree with this advice?

BAKER v. FENNEMAN & BROWN PROPERTIES, L.L.C.
793 N.E.2d 1203 (Ind. Ct. App. 2003)

Opinion by: MAY, Judge.

Aaron Baker appeals the trial court's grant of summary judgment to Fenneman & Brown Properties, L.L.C. and Southern Bells of Indiana, Inc., all d/b/a Taco Bell (hereinafter collectively "Taco Bell"). Baker raises one issue, which we restate as whether Taco Bell has a duty to assist a customer who falls to the floor and loses consciousness when the customer's fall was not due to any fault of Taco Bell.

We reverse and remand.

On August 26, 1999, Baker entered the Taco Bell store in Newburgh, Indiana, to purchase a soft drink. Upon entering the store, Baker felt nauseous, but he continued to the counter, where he ordered a drink. Baker handed the cashier money for the drink and suddenly fell backward. Baker's head hit the floor, and he was knocked unconscious and began having convulsions.

Baker and Taco Bell disagree regarding whether Taco Bell rendered assistance to Baker. Baker claims that when he regained consciousness, he was staring at the ceiling, he had no idea what was going on, and he did not know where he was. He claims that no Taco Bell employee called for medical assistance or helped him in any way. Taco Bell claims that the cashier walked around the counter to Baker, where she waited for his convulsions to stop, and then she asked Baker if he was okay and if he needed an ambulance. The employee claims Baker said he was fine and he did not need an ambulance, so she walked back around the counter.

What happened next is undisputed. Moments after Baker stood up, he fell again. This time, Baker fell forward and was knocked unconscious. The fall lacerated his chin, knocked out his four front teeth, and cracked the seventh vertebra of his neck. When Baker regained consciousness, he was choking on the blood and teeth in his mouth. Baker stumbled out of the store to a friend, who contacted Baker's fiancé to take him to the hospital.

Baker filed a complaint against Taco Bell, in which he alleged: 1) Taco Bell breached its duty to render assistance to him until he could be cared for by others when Taco Bell employees knew or should have known that he was ill or injured, and 2) Taco Bell's "conduct constituted gross negligence, wanton disregard and wanton recklessness" toward Baker. . . . Baker sought damages for medical bills, lost wages, pain and suffering, and mental anguish.

Taco Bell moved for summary judgment, claiming it owed Baker no duty. Baker responded by arguing Taco Bell had a duty to help him, and even if it did not, a Taco Bell employee testified in her deposition that she offered assistance to Baker; Taco Bell, therefore, assumed a duty to provide reasonable assistance to Baker. The trial court granted Taco Bell's motion. . . .

Baker claims Taco Bell had a duty to assist him and that it breached that duty by failing to provide assistance to him. Taco Bell argues it had no duty to assist Baker because it was not responsible for the instrumentality that caused Baker's initial injury. We believe Baker is correct.

To effectively assert a negligence claim, Baker must establish: (1) that Taco Bell had a duty "to conform [its] conduct to a standard of care arising from [its] relationship with [Baker]," (2) that Taco Bell failed to conform its conduct to that standard of care, and (3) that Baker incurred injuries as a proximate result of Taco Bell's breach of its duty. . . . The existence of a duty is a question of law for the court to decide. . . . To determine whether a duty exists, we must balance three factors: "(1) the relationship between the parties; (2) the reasonable foreseeability of harm to the person injured; and (3) public policy concerns." . . .

As a general rule, an individual does not have a duty to aid or protect another person, even if he knows that person needs assistance. L.S. Ayres v. Hicks, . . . *See also* Restatement (Second) of Torts § 314 ("The fact that the actor realizes or should realize that action on his part is necessary for another's aid or protection does not of itself impose upon him a duty to take such action.") (hereinafter, "Restatement"). However, both common law and statutory exceptions to that general rule exist. *See, e.g.,* Restatement § 314B (employer has a duty to protect or aid an injured employee); Ind. Code § 35-46-1-4 (neglect of a dependent is a felony). *See also L.S. Ayres,* 220 Ind. at 94, 40 N.E.2d at 337 ("under some circumstances, moral and humanitarian considerations may require one to render assistance to another who has been injured, even though the injury was not due to negligence on his part and may have been caused by the negligence of the injured person").

Baker claims Taco Bell had the duty to assist him described under Section 314A of the Restatement, which provides the following exception to the general rule that one person need not assist another:

§ 314A. Special Relations Giving Rise to Duty to Aid or Protect

(1) A common carrier is under a duty to its passengers to take reasonable action:

(a) to protect them against unreasonable risk of physical harm, and

(b) to give them first aid after it knows or has reason to know that they are ill or injured, and to care for them until they can be cared for by others.

(2) An innkeeper is under a similar duty to his guests.

(3) A possessor of land who holds it open to the public is under a similar duty to members of the public who enter in response to his invitation.

(4) One who is required by law to take or who voluntarily takes the custody of another under circumstances such as to deprive the other of his normal opportunities for protection is under a similar duty to the other.

The duty that arises under Section 314A exists because of the special relationship between the parties. Restatement § 314A, cmt. b. The relationships listed in the rule are not intended to be exclusive, *id.*; nevertheless, some courts have restricted the application of § 314A to business invitees. . . .

In *L.S. Ayres,* our supreme court considered whether a department store, which was not in any way liable for a boy's initial injury by an escalator, nevertheless could be held liable for aggravation of the injuries caused by its employees' failure to stop the escalator. The court determined there may be a legal obligation to take positive or affirmative steps to effect the rescue of a person who is helpless and in a situation of peril, when the one proceeded against is a master or an invitor or when the injury resulted from use of an instrumentality under the control of the defendant. Such an obligation may exist although the accident or original injury was caused by the negligence of the plaintiff or through that of a third person and without any fault on the part of the defendant. Other relationships may impose a like obligation, but it is not necessary to pursue that inquiry further at this time. . . . 40 N.E.2d at 337. The court noted that the boy "was an invitee and he received his initial injury in using an instrumentality provided by" L.S. Ayres and then held L.S. Ayres could be liable for the aggravation of the boy's injury caused by its failure to assist him. *Id.*; 40 N.E.2d at 337-38.

Taco Bell claims it had no duty to assist Baker because it was not responsible for Baker's initial illness or injury. It argues that, under *L.S. Ayres*, an Indiana business has a duty to assist a customer only if "the injury resulted from the use of an instrumentality under the control of the defendant." *Id.*; 40 N.E.2d at 337. In essence, Taco Bell argues that Indiana law recognizes only a limited duty under § 314A of the Restatement. Taco Bell's argument fails for a number of reasons.

First, the cases cited by the supreme court in *L.S. Ayres* suggest the court did not intend to limit the application of § 314A to situations where the plaintiff was an invitee *and* the instrumentality causing the injury belonged to the defendant. For example, the court discussed Depue v. Flateau, . . . 111 N.W. 1 (1907), in which a home owner was held liable for aggravation of injuries to a severely ill, fainting, and helpless businessman that the home owner sent away unattended on a cold winter night. . . . There, as here, the initial illness was not the responsibility of the defendant. Nevertheless, our supreme court relied on that case when determining whether L.S. Ayres had a duty to assist the injured boy.

Second, when the supreme court had reason later that same year to mention *L.S. Ayres* in another of its opinions, it summarized the holding as follows: "this court recognized a duty to one in peril on the defendant's premises as an invitee even though the peril was created without negligence on the part of the defendant." Jones v. State, . . . 43 N.E.2d 1017, 1018 (1942). That summarization suggests the supreme court did not intend, as Taco Bell insists, to limit its holding to situations where a plaintiff could prove both that he was an invitee and that the defendant's instrumentality caused the initial injury.

Third, the Restatement explains:

> The duty to give aid to one who is ill or injured extends to cases where the illness or injury is due to natural causes, to pure accident, to the acts of third person, or to the negligence of the plaintiff himself, as where a passenger has injured himself by clumsily bumping his head against a door.

Restatement § 314A, cmt d. A number of the illustrations provided in the Restatement parallel the fact pattern here and suggest Taco Bell had a duty to assist Baker. For example, Illustration 2 provides:

> A, a passenger riding on the train of B Railroad, suffers an apoplectic stroke, and becomes unconscious. The train crew unreasonably assumes that A is drunk, and does nothing to obtain medical assistance for him, or to turn him over at a station to those who will do so. A continues to ride on the train in an unconscious condition for five hours during which time his illness is aggravated in a manner which proper medical attention would have avoided. B Railroad is subject to liability to A for the aggravation of his illness.

Id. § 314A. Illustration 7 provides:

> A is a small child sent by his parents for the day to B's kindergarten. In the course of the day A becomes ill with scarlet fever. Although recognizing that A is seriously ill, B does nothing to obtain medical assistance, or to take the child home or

remove him to a place where help can be obtained. As a result, A's illness is aggravated in a manner which proper medical attention would have avoided. B is subject to liability to A for the aggravation of his injuries.

Id.

Review of decisions from a number of other jurisdictions suggests we should interpret Indiana law to impose a duty in this situation. *See, e.g.,* Gingeleskie v. Westin Hotel, et al., 1998 U.S. App. LEXIS 10535, 1998 WL 279393 at **2 (9th Cir. 1998) (holding question of fact existed regarding whether hotel took reasonable steps under § 314A to get a sick man to a hospital when the employee called a cab rather than an ambulance); Estate of Starling v. Fisherman's Pier, Inc., 401 So. 2d 1136, 1138 (Fla. Dist. Ct. App. 1981) (holding business has an affirmative duty to take steps to protect a drunk man passed out on business's pier, such that he would not roll into the ocean and drown), *rev. denied* 411 So. 2d 381 (Fla. 1981); . . . Lloyd v. S.S. Kresge Co., d/b/a K-MART, 85 Wis. 2d 296, 270 N.W.2d 423, 426-27 (Wis. Ct. App. 1978) (holding question of fact existed regarding whether K-Mart failed to give reasonable assistance to customer who was ill when it forced her to wait for her ride outside the store on a cold winter night).

Finally, public policy suggests Taco Bell had a duty to provide reasonable care in this situation. When a storeowner opens his property to the public, he does so because he hopes to gain some economic benefit from the public. "Social policy dictates that the storeowner, who is deriving this economic benefit from the presence of the customer, should assume the affirmative duty [to help customers who become ill as] a cost of doing business." *Id.*

Taco Bell argues placing this duty on businesses is unreasonable because then, in essence, a business would be required to hire employees who were trained to diagnose and provide medical services. . . . We disagree.

As comment f to Section 314A of the Restatement explains:

[The business] is not required to take any action beyond that which is reasonable under the circumstances. In the case of an ill or injured person, [the business] will seldom be required to do more than give such first aid as [it] reasonably can, and take reasonable steps to turn the sick man over to a physician, or to those who will look after him and see that medical assistance is obtained. [A business] is not required to give any aid to one who is in the hands of apparently competent persons who have taken charge of him, or whose friends are present and apparently in a position to give him all necessary assistance.

Accordingly, the duty that arises is a duty to "exercise reasonable care under the circumstances." *Id.* cmt. e. A high school student employed at Taco Bell would not be expected to provide the type of first aid an emergency room doctor would provide, as such an expectation would not be "reasonable." . . .

Moreover, as a practical matter, we fail to see the logic in Taco Bell's position that it should have no duty to aid in these types of situations. First, we find it unlikely customers would patronize a business that left another customer who was ill or injured lying on the floor of the business simply because the business was not responsible for the customer's illness or injury.

Second, imposing on a business a duty to provide reasonable care even when the business is not responsible for an illness or injury will rarely force a business to act in circumstances in which it should not already have been acting. For example, if, as Taco Bell asserts, a business has no duty to assist if it is not responsible for the instrumentality, then: 1) if a customer falls to the ground, an employee should determine before offering assistance whether the customer slipped on ice, in which case the business has a duty to act, or whether the customer merely passed out from syncope, in which case the business has no duty; or 2) if a customer's face is turning blue, an employee should determine before providing assistance whether the person is choking on a food item from the business, in which case the employee must offer assistance, or whether the person is having a heart attack or choking on a food item purchased from a third party, in which case the employee need not offer assistance. By implementing policies and procedures that allow their employees to assist injured persons only when the business causes the illness or injury, a business might risk liability claims caused by an employee's failure to act, or failure to act promptly, when an illness or injury *was* in fact caused by an instrumentality of the business. Consequently, we are not placing a duty on businesses that they should not have already assumed.

In sum, Indiana case law, the Restatement (Second) of Torts, authority from other jurisdictions, and public policy all suggest Taco Bell had a duty, as a business that invited members of the public to enter its facility, to provide reasonable assistance to Baker even though Taco Bell was not responsible for Baker's illness. Consequently, we hold Taco Bell had a duty to "take reasonable action . . . to give . . . aid" to Baker after he fell and "to care for [him] until [he could] be cared for by others." Restatement § 314A.

Baker asserts Taco Bell provided no assistance. Taco Bell's employee claims she offered Baker assistance, but he refused to accept it. Thus, there is a question of material fact that precludes summary judgment on this issue, and we must reverse and remand for trial.

Reversed and remanded.

BUNGLED RESCUES

Thus far, the cases and discussion in this chapter have focused on whether a person has a duty to render aid to a victim. What happens when a person renders aid, but, in doing so, enhances the plaintiff's injuries? Many may be surprised to learn that the common law would impose negligence liability on these "Good Samaritans." However, many state legislatures have seized the opportunity to intervene in this type of a situation. All states now have "Good Samaritan" statutes that provide immunity to those rendering gratuitous assistance in an emergency. Some of these statutes are limited to interveners who are medical practitioners, firefighters, rescue squad members, or police officers. Many protect all citizens who act as "Good Samaritans" from negligence actions arising out of the gratuitous actions. *See, e.g.,* Cal. Health & Safety § 1799.102 ("No person who in good faith, and not for compensation, renders emergency care at the scene of an emergency shall be liable for any civil damages resulting from any act or omission"). *See* Van Horn v. Watson, 197 P.3d 164 (Cal. 2008) (California statute limited to "emergency *medical* care"). For a complete listing of the statutes, see 3 David W. Louisell & Harold Williams, *Medical Malpractice* §§ 21.01-21.05 (2002).

hypo 50

A and *B*, along with several others, are involved in a friendly game of touch football. During the game, *A* throws the ball to *B,* who collides head-on with another player. *B* is knocked unconscious and, unknown to *A* or the others, suffers serious neck and back injuries. Fearing that *B* has suffered serious injury, *A* rushes to *B*'s aid, picks him up, puts him in a car, and drives him to the hospital. By picking *B* up, *A* aggravates *B*'s injuries, causing permanent and irreversible paralysis. Will *B*'s negligence action against *A* survive *A*'s motion for summary judgment?

IS OUR RELATIONSHIP "SPECIAL"?

Like Section 314A of the Second Restatement, discussed in *Baker*, the Third Restatement recognizes special relationships as a ground for affirmative duties in what might be called second-party and third-party cases:

> An actor in a special relationship with another owes the other a duty of reasonable care with regard to risks that arise within the scope of the relationship.

Restatement (Third) of Torts § 40(a).

> An actor in a special relationship with another owes a duty of reasonable care to third persons with regard to the risks posed by the other that arise within the scope of the relationship.

Restatement (Third) of Torts § 41(a). Both sections set out non-exhaustive categories of special relationships based on patterns that have developed in decided cases over time. Common second-party special relationships under Section 40 include a common carrier and its passengers, an innkeeper and its guests, and an employer with respect to employees who are in imminent danger or are helpless. As an example of the latter category, see Martensen v. Rejda Bros., Inc., 808 N.W.2d 855 (Neb. 2012). In that case the plaintiff was working as a hired hand on a ranch owned by the defendant. (Under state law agricultural employees were not covered by workers' compensation, so the defendant was not immune from a negligence lawsuit.) The plaintiff was riding an all-terrain vehicle as he went around the ranch repairing fences. Late in the afternoon, the plaintiff fell and was pinned beneath his vehicle. No one searched for him and he remained trapped under the ATV until the next day. As a result of the delay in rescue, the plaintiff lost one leg above the knee. The Nebraska Supreme Court adopted Section 40(a) of the Third Restatement, holding that the employer had a duty, that reasonable care may have required a search to have begun that evening when the plaintiff did not return from repairing fences, and that the delay in finding the plaintiff may have caused the loss of his leg.

Common third-party special relationships include a parent and child, employer and employee with respect to harm within the scope of the employment relationship, and a mental health professional with patients (see the *Tarasoff* case, below). As you might guess, a great deal of litigation focuses on what risks are within the scope of an employment relationship. In Barclay v. Briscoe, 47 A.3d 560 (Md. 2012), Richardson was driving home after working a 22-hour shift as a longshoreman at the Port of Baltimore. He fell asleep, drifted across the centerline, and crashed into the plaintiff, causing catastrophic injuries. Under the collective bargaining agreement the Port had with the longshoremen's union, employees could voluntarily agree to work as many shifts as they desired in order to maximize their earnings. The Maryland Court of Appeals first held that the Port was not vicariously liable for Richardson's negligence, because commuting to and from work is not within the scope of employment. 47 A.3d at 568-569. Second, it held that the Port was not independently or primarily liable to the plaintiff. While it is surely foreseeable that an exhausted employee driving home may pose a risk to other drivers, foreseeability alone is not enough to create a duty running from the employer to other motorists. Instead, there must be a special relationship with the employee. *Id.* at 575. This suggests, plainly enough, that a special relationship must go beyond the relationship of employer and employee. The court reviewed numerous cases from other jurisdictions involving accidents caused by fatigued or intoxicated employees and concluded that, in order for there to be a duty running to other motorists, the employer must exercise affirmative control over the employee's decision to drive home in a fatigued state. *Id.* at 582. Does this rule create an incentive for employers to require their employees to work long hours and then look the other way when the employees drive home at the end of a shift?

What constitutes a "special relationship" beyond traditional categories like common carriers and employers continues to challenge the courts. In Meyer v. Lindala, 675 N.W.2d 635 (Minn. Ct. App. 2004), plaintiff brought an action against the religious congregation in which both plaintiffs and an active sexual abuser were members. Under the rules of the congregation, the members were to associate only with other members of the congregation and to avoid association with nonmembers. Furthermore, all indiscretions were to be reported to the congregation elders and failure to adhere to the decision of the elders would result in excommunication. According to the allegations of the complaint, the elders received information that Lindala (the alleged sexual abuser) had, at the age of 17, repeatedly sexually abused his six-year-old sister. Lindala had also abused two other youngsters (10-12 years old), and this information had been reported to the elders. The plaintiffs argued that, given the structure of the community, the elders affirmed that Lindala was an appropriate person with whom to associate. The appellate court found no special relationship that would support a duty to the victims' parents to inform them about the conduct of the sexual abuser. The congregation did not have custody or control over the plaintiffs at the time of the alleged conduct. The sexual encounters took place outside the confines of the church. The fact that all information of sexual misconduct had to be brought to the elders of the church under threat of excommunication did not create a "special relationship" since they were acting purely in a religious capacity and within their constitutional rights to "independently decide matters of faith and doctrine" and "to believe and speak what it will." *Id.* at 641.

A LITTLE LOGICAL INTERLUDE

When you are working with the idea of special relationships, please be careful not to beg the question. People sometimes loosely consider "begs the question" synonymous with "raises the question" or "should be asked." Technically, question-begging is a logical fallacy equivalent to loading up the premises of an argument to support the conclusion, or assuming from the outset that the conclusion is true. Molière has a quack physician explain that opium induces sleep because it contains a dormitive principle, which is nothing but a way of restating the conclusion that opium induces sleep. For a more complex version, consider this example from a nineteenth century logic text: "To allow every man an unbounded freedom of speech must always be, on the whole, advantageous to the State, for it is highly conducive to the interests of the community that each individual should enjoy a liberty perfectly unlimited of expressing his sentiments." Here the conclusion (it is to the advantage of society to allow free speech) does follow from the premise (it is to the advantage of society to allow free speech), but the argument is spectacularly uninformative. More information is needed to establish the truth of the premise that it is conducive to the interests of the community as a whole to recognize the right of individuals to speak freely. The premise may very well be true, but more work needs to go into showing that. This is why begging the question is also known as making a circular argument — the reasoning goes round and round in a circle without making any progress.

Being careful with logical form matters to legal reasoning in general, but there seems to be a particular tendency to engage in question-begging when it comes to the idea of special relationships. A fallacious argument may go like this, using the *Meyer* case above:

(1) A church has a special relationship with the members of its congregation.
(2) A duty to protect others from harm may exist if there is a special relationship between the defendant and the actor who caused the harm.
(3) Therefore, the church has a duty to protect others from harm caused by the members of its congregation.

Do you see the problem? More work is required before we have sufficient confidence in the truth of (1). *Why* should a church be deemed to have a special relationship with its members? In the *Meyer* case, the answer is presumably because it has access to information about the dangerousness of members. With that information it could do something to protect others, such as disclosing it to law-enforcement authorities or potential victims. Special relationships at common law generally involve the capacity of A to do something to protect C from the risk created by B. It must be established what, exactly that "something" is, how well-positioned *A* is to safeguard against the risks created by *B*, and whether there are other policies that disfavor imposing a responsibility on *A* to act to protect *C*. All of that argumentative work has to go into establishing that there is a special relationship. Because it is the same argumentative work that goes into establishing that *A* should have a duty to protect *C*, the concepts of "duty" and "special relationship" are equivalent. That is why it is circular to use the idea of a special relationship in the premise of an argument, the conclusion of which is meant to be a duty rule, without going through the hard work of showing that it makes sense to impose responsibilities on actors in *A*'s position with respect to these types of harms.

Law teachers can frequently be heard muttering about "conclusory" arguments in student exam answers. Make sure to take the time to explain why a proposition such as "*A* has a special relationship with *B*" is true and you will not be the occasion of this grumbling.

3. Open-Ended Standards for Recognizing Affirmative Duties

One of the most famous, or notorious, summaries of a tort doctrine was written by William Prosser, a leading torts scholar and the Reporter to the Second Restatement of Torts. Here is what Prosser had to say about duty:

> The statement that there is or is not a duty begs the essential question — whether the plaintiff's interests are entitled to legal protection against the defendant's conduct. . . . It is a shorthand statement of a conclusion, rather than an aid to analysis in itself. . . . It should be recognized that "duty" is not sacrosanct in itself, but is only an expression of the sum total of those considerations of policy which lead the law to say that the particular plaintiff is entitled to protection.

W. Page Keeton, ed., *Prosser and Keeton on the Law of Torts*, 357-358 (5th ed. 1984). Did you spit out your coffee when you read that passage? Your teacher has probably been admonishing you not to rely on a "shorthand statement of a conclusion" rather than providing analysis. And is Prosser serious that duty does not function like a legal rule — i.e., one that is relatively general and capable of being grasped in advance of a particular set of facts and applied fairly by a judge? In some contexts a decision-maker may be called upon to determine what is the best option, all things considered. *Legal* decisions, on the other hand, are generally understood as the product of *adjudication*, which is different from an all-things-considered judgment about what should be done. One of the hallmarks of adjudication is the consistent application of relatively determinate rules settled in advance of the decision to be made, and subject to principled limitation. That is not to say that judges are robots or, as Chief Justice Roberts stated in his Senate confirmation hearings, like umpires calling balls and strikes. Judging can involve creativity and discretion in the application of pre-existing rules, and sometimes involves the creation of new law. But it is surprising to see an eminent tort scholar telling judges that they should not think "duty" is a legal doctrine but instead is merely a shorthand for "in this case, the defendant owes the plaintiff protection from a risk of harm."

The following classic case starts out employing the idea of special relationships, but then shifts into a style of analysis associated with the California Supreme Court in the heady days of judicially expanded liability doctrines. One way to expand liability is to tell judges that they should approach duty questions as all-things-considered policy decisions. As you read this case, see if you can discern a principled limitation in its holding. That is, does it announce a legal rule that can be applied to a novel set of facts in a consistent way, or does it represent nothing more than the determination by this group of judges that the psychologist in this case should have done more than he did to protect the plaintiff?

TARASOFF v. REGENTS OF UNIVERSITY OF CALIFORNIA
551 P.2d 334 (Cal. 1976)

TOBRINER, Justice.

On October 27, 1969, Prosenjit Poddar killed Tatiana Tarasoff. Plaintiffs, Tatiana's parents, allege that two months earlier Poddar confided his intention to kill Tatiana to Dr. Lawrence Moore, a psychologist employed by the Cowell Memorial Hospital at the University of California at Berkeley. They allege that on Moore's request, the campus police briefly detained Poddar, but released him when he appeared rational. They further claim that Dr. Harvey Powelson, Moore's superior, then directed that no further action be taken to detain Poddar. No one warned plaintiffs of Tatiana's peril.

Concluding that these facts set forth causes of action against neither therapists and policemen involved, nor against the Regents of the University of California as their employer, the superior court sustained defendants' demurrers to plaintiffs' second amended complaints without leave to amend. This appeal ensued.

[Plaintiffs' second amended complaints set forth four causes of action: (1) a claim that defendants negligently failed to detain a dangerous patient; (2) a claim that defendants negligently failed to warn Tatiana's parents; (3) a claim for punitive damages on the ground that defendants acted "maliciously and oppressively"; and (4) a claim that defendants breached their duty to their patient and the public. The court concludes that governmental immunity bars the plaintiffs' first and fourth causes of action and that a rule precluding exemplary damages in a wrongful death action bars plaintiffs' third cause of action. Therefore, the court addresses the question of whether plaintiffs' second cause of action can be amended to state a basis for recovery.]

The second cause of action can be amended to allege that Tatiana's death proximately resulted from defendants' negligent failure to warn Tatiana or others likely to apprise her of her danger. Plaintiffs contend that as amended, such allegations of negligence and proximate causation, with resulting damages, establish a cause of action. Defendants, however, contend that in the circumstances of the present case they owed no duty of care to Tatiana or her parents and that, in the absence of such duty, they were free to act in careless disregard of Tatiana's life and safety.

In analyzing this issue, we bear in mind that legal duties are not discoverable facts of nature, but merely conclusory expressions that, in cases of a particular type, liability should be imposed for damage done. As stated in Dillon v. Legg (Cal. 1968) . . . 441 P.2d 912, 916: "The assertion that liability must . . . be denied because defendant bears no 'duty' to plaintiff 'begs the essential question — whether the plaintiff's interests are entitled to legal protection against the defendant's conduct . . . (Duty) is not sacrosanct in itself, but only an expression of the sum total of those considerations of policy which lead the law to say that the particular plaintiff is entitled to protection.' (Prosser, Law of Torts (3d ed. 1964) at pp. 332-333.)"

In the landmark case of Rowland v. Christian (Cal. 1968) . . . 443 P.2d 561, Justice Peters recognized that liability should be imposed "for an injury occasioned to another by his want of ordinary care or skill" as expressed in section 1714 of the Civil Code. Thus, Justice Peters, quoting from Heaven v. Pender (1883) 11 Q.B.D. 503, 509 stated: "whenever one person is by circumstances placed in such a position with regard to another . . . that if he did not use ordinary care and skill in his own conduct . . . he would cause danger of injury to the person or property of the other, a duty arises to use ordinary care and skill to avoid such danger."

We depart from "this fundamental principle" only upon the "balancing of a number of considerations"; major ones "are the foreseeability of harm to the plaintiff, the degree of certainty that the plaintiff suffered injury, the closeness of the connection between the defendant's conduct and the injury suffered, the moral blame attached to the defendant's conduct, the policy of preventing future harm, the extent of the burden to the defendant and consequences to the community of imposing a duty to exercise care with resulting liability for breach, and the availability, cost and prevalence of insurance for the risk involved."

The most important of these considerations in establishing duty is foreseeability. As a general principle, a "defendant owes a duty of care to all persons who are foreseeably endangered by his conduct, with respect to all risks which make the conduct unreasonably dangerous." As we shall explain, however, when the avoidance of foreseeable harm requires a defendant to control the conduct of another person, or to warn of such conduct, the common law has traditionally imposed liability only if the defendant bears some special relationship to the dangerous person or to the potential victim. Since the relationship between a therapist and his patient satisfies this requirement, we need not here decide whether foreseeability alone is sufficient to create a duty to exercise reasonable care to protect a potential victim of another's conduct.

Although, as we have stated above, under the common law, as a general rule, one person owed no duty to control the conduct of another, nor to warn those endangered by such conduct, the courts have carved out an exception to this rule in cases in which the defendant stands in some special relationship to either the person whose conduct needs to be controlled or in a relationship to the foreseeable victim of that conduct. Applying this exception to the present case, we note that a relationship of defendant therapists to either Tatiana or Poddar will suffice to establish a duty of care; as explained in section 315 of the Restatement Second of Torts, a duty of care may arise from either "(a) a special relation . . . between the actor and the third person which imposes a duty upon the actor to control the third person's conduct, or (b) a special relation . . . between the actor and the other which gives to the other a right of protection."

Although plaintiffs' pleadings assert no special relation between Tatiana and defendant therapists, they establish as between Poddar and defendant therapists the special relation that arises between a patient and his doctor or psychotherapist. Such a relationship may support affirmative duties for the benefit of third persons. Thus, for example, a hospital must exercise reasonable care to control the behavior of a patient which may endanger other persons. A doctor must also warn a patient if the patient's condition or medication renders certain conduct, such as driving a car, dangerous to others.

Although the California decisions that recognize this duty have involved cases in which the defendant stood in a special relationship both to the victim and to the person whose conduct created the danger, we do not think that the duty should logically be constricted to such situations. Decisions of other jurisdictions hold that the single relationship of a doctor to his patient is sufficient to support the duty to exercise reasonable care to protect others against dangers emanating from the patient's illness. The courts hold that a doctor is liable to persons infected by his patient if he negligently fails to diagnose a contagious disease or, having diagnosed the illness, fails to warn members of the patient's family. . . .

Defendants contend, however, that imposition of a duty to exercise reasonable care to protect third persons is unworkable because therapists cannot accurately predict whether or not a patient will resort to violence. In support of this argument amicus representing the American Psychiatric Association and other professional societies cites numerous articles which indicate that therapists, in the present state of the art, are unable reliably to predict violent acts; their forecasts, amicus claims, tend consistently to overpredict violence, and indeed are more often wrong than right. Since predictions of violence are often erroneous, amicus concludes, the courts should not render rulings that predicate the liability of therapists upon the validity of such predictions.

The role of the psychiatrist, who is indeed a practitioner of medicine, and that of the psychologist who performs an allied function, are like that of the physician who must conform to the standards of the profession and who must often make diagnoses and predictions based upon such evaluations. Thus the judgment of the therapist in diagnosing emotional disorders and in predicting whether a patient presents a serious danger of violence is comparable to the judgment which doctors and professionals must regularly render under accepted rules of responsibility.

We recognize the difficulty that a therapist encounters in attempting to forecast whether a patient presents a serious danger of violence. Obviously we do not require that the therapist, in making that determination, render a perfect performance; the therapist need only exercise "that reasonable degree of skill, knowledge, and care ordinarily possessed and exercised by members of (that professional specialty) under similar circumstances." Within the broad range of reasonable practice and treatment in which professional opinion and judgment may differ, the therapist is free to exercise his or her own best judgment without liability; proof, aided by hindsight, that he or she judged wrongly is insufficient to establish negligence.

In the instant case, however, the pleadings do not raise any question as to failure of defendant therapists to predict that Poddar presented a serious danger of violence. On the contrary, the present complaints allege that defendant therapists did in fact predict that Poddar would kill, but were negligent in failing to warn.

Amicus contends, however, that even when a therapist does in fact predict that a patient poses a serious danger of violence to others, the therapist should be absolved of any responsibility for failing to act to protect the potential victim. In our view, however, once a therapist does in fact determine, or under applicable professional standards reasonably should have determined, that a patient poses a serious danger of violence to others, he bears a duty to exercise reasonable care to protect the foreseeable victim of that danger. While the discharge of this duty of due care will necessarily vary with the facts of each case, in each instance the adequacy of the therapist's conduct must be measured against the traditional negligence standard of the rendition of reasonable care under the circumstances. . . .

Contrary to the assertion of amicus, this conclusion is not inconsistent with our recent decision in People v. Burnick, *supra*, . . . 535 P.2d at 352. Taking note of the uncertain character of therapeutic prediction, we held in *Burnick* that a person cannot be committed as a mentally disordered sex offender unless found to be such by proof beyond a reasonable doubt. The issue in the present context, however, is not whether the patient should be incarcerated, but whether the therapist should take any steps at all to protect the threatened victim; some of the alternatives open to the therapist, such as warning the victim, will not result in the drastic consequences of depriving the patient of his liberty. Weighing the uncertain and conjectural character of the alleged damage done the patient by such a warning against the peril to the victim's life, we conclude that professional inaccuracy in predicting violence cannot negate the therapist's duty to protect the threatened victim.

The risk that unnecessary warnings may be given is a reasonable price to pay for the lives of possible victims that may be saved. We would hesitate to hold that the therapist who is aware that his patient expects to attempt to assassinate the President of the United States would not be obligated to warn the authorities because the therapist cannot predict with accuracy that his patient will commit the crime.

Defendants further argue that free and open communication is essential to psychotherapy; that "Unless a patient . . . is assured that . . . information (revealed by him) can and will be held in utmost confidence, he will be reluctant to make the full disclosure upon which diagnosis and treatment . . . depends." (Sen. Com. on Judiciary, comment on Evid. Code, § 1014.) The giving of a warning, defendants contend, constitutes a breach of trust which entails the revelation of confidential communications. . . .

We realize that the open and confidential character of psychotherapeutic dialogue encourages patients to express threats of violence, few of which are ever executed. Certainly a therapist should not be encouraged routinely to reveal such threats; such disclosures could seriously disrupt the patient's relationship with his therapist and with the persons threatened. To the contrary, the therapist's obligations to his patient require that he not disclose a confidence unless such disclosure is necessary to avert danger to others, and even then that he do so discreetly, and in a fashion that would preserve the privacy of his patient to the fullest extent compatible with the prevention of the threatened danger.

The revelation of a communication under the above circumstances is not a breach of trust or a violation of professional ethics; as stated in the Principles of Medical Ethics of the American Medical Association (1957), section 9: "A physician may not reveal the confidence entrusted to him in the course of medical attendance . . . *unless he is required to do so by law or unless it becomes necessary in order to protect the welfare of the individual or of the community.*" (Emphasis added.) We conclude that the public policy favoring protection of the confidential character of patient-psychotherapist communications must yield to the extent to which disclosure is essential to avert danger to others. The protective privilege ends where the public peril begins.

Our current crowded and computerized society compels the interdependence of its members. In this risk-infested society we can hardly tolerate the further exposure to danger that would result from a concealed knowledge of the therapist that his patient was lethal. If the exercise of reasonable care to protect the threatened victim requires the therapist to warn the endangered party or those who can reasonably be expected to notify him, we see no sufficient societal interest that would protect and justify concealment. The containment of such risks lies in the public interest. For the foregoing reasons, we find that plaintiffs' complaints can be amended to state a cause of action against defendants Moore, Powelson, Gold, and Yandell and against the Regents as their employer, for breach of a duty to exercise reasonable care to protect Tatiana.

[The majority concludes that the police defendants did not have a special relationship to either Tatiana or Poddar to impose upon them a duty to warn. The court also concludes that the defendant therapists are not protected by governmental immunity in connection with their failure to warn Tatiana's parents because their decisions were not "basic policy decisions" within the meaning of earlier precedent.]

For the reasons stated, we conclude that plaintiffs can amend their complaints to state a cause of action against defendant therapists by asserting that the therapists in fact determined that Poddar presented a serious danger of violence to Tatiana, or pursuant to the standards of their profession should have so determined, but nevertheless failed to exercise reasonable care to protect her from that danger. To the extent, however, that plaintiffs base their claim that defendant therapists breached that duty because they failed to procure Poddar's confinement, the therapists find immunity in Government Code section 856. Further, as to the police defendants we conclude that plaintiffs have failed to show that the trial court erred in sustaining their demurrer without leave to amend.

The judgment of the superior court in favor of defendants Atkinson, Beall, Brownrigg, Hallernan, and Teel is affirmed. The judgment of the superior court in favor of defendants Gold, Moore, Powelson, Yandell, and the Regents of the University of California is reversed, and the cause remanded for further proceedings consistent with the views expressed herein.

Wright, C.J., and Sullivan and Richardson, JJ., concur.

Mosk, Justice (concurring and dissenting).

I concur in the result in this instance only because the complaints allege that defendant therapists did in fact predict that Poddar would kill and were therefore negligent in failing to warn of that danger. Thus the issue here is very narrow: we are not concerned with whether the therapists, pursuant to the standards of their profession, "should have" predicted potential violence; they allegedly did so in actuality. Under these limited circumstances I agree that a cause of action can be stated.

Whether plaintiffs can ultimately prevail is problematical at best. As the complaints admit, the therapists did notify the police that Poddar was planning to kill a girl identifiable as Tatiana. While I doubt that more should be required, this issue may be raised in defense and its determination is a question of fact.

I cannot concur, however, in the majority's rule that a therapist may be held liable for failing to predict his patient's tendency to violence if other practitioners, pursuant to the "standards of the profession," would have done so. The question is, what standards? Defendants and a responsible amicus curiae, supported by an impressive body of literature demonstrate that psychiatric predictions of violence are inherently unreliable. . . .

I would restructure the rule designed by the majority to eliminate all reference to conformity to standards of the profession in predicting violence. If a psychiatrist does in fact predict violence, then a duty to warn arises. The majority's expansion of that rule will take us from the world of reality into the wonderland of clairvoyance.

Clark, Justice (dissenting).

Until today's majority opinion, both legal and medical authorities have agreed that confidentiality is essential to effectively treat the mentally ill, and that imposing a duty on doctors to disclose patient threats to potential victims would greatly impair treatment. . . . Moreover, . . . imposing the majority's new duty is certain to result in a net increase in violence.

Overwhelming policy considerations weigh against imposing a duty on psychotherapists to warn a potential victim against harm. While offering virtually no benefit to society, such a duty will frustrate psychiatric treatment, invade fundamental patient rights and increase violence.

The importance of psychiatric treatment and its need for confidentiality have been recognized by this court. . . .

Assurance of confidentiality is important for three reasons.

Deterrence from Treatment

First, without substantial assurance of confidentiality, those requiring treatment will be deterred from seeking assistance. It remains an unfortunate fact in our society that people seeking psychiatric guidance tend to become stigmatized. Apprehension of such stigma — apparently increased by the propensity of people considering treatment to see themselves in the worst possible light — creates a well-recognized reluctance to seek aid. This reluctance is alleviated by the psychiatrist's assurance of confidentiality.

Full Disclosure

Second, the guarantee of confidentiality is essential in eliciting the full disclosure necessary for effective treatment. The psychiatric patient approaches treatment with conscious and unconscious inhibitions against revealing his innermost thoughts. "Every person, however well-motivated, has to overcome resistances to therapeutic exploration. These resistances seek support from every possible source and the possibility of disclosure would easily be employed in the service of resistance." (Goldstein & Katz, *supra*, 36 Conn. Bar J. 175, 179; *see also*, 118 Am. J. Psych. 734, 735.) Until a patient can trust his psychiatrist not to violate their confidential relationship, "the unconscious psychological control mechanism of repression will prevent the recall of past experiences." (Butler, *Psychotherapy and Griswold: Is Confidentiality a Privilege or a Right?*, (1971) 3 Conn. L. Rev. 599, 604.)

Successful Treatment

Third, even if the patient fully discloses his thoughts, assurance that the confidential relationship will not be breached is necessary to maintain his trust in his psychiatrist — the very means by which treatment is effected. "[T]he essence of much psychotherapy is the contribution of trust in the external world and ultimately in the self, modeled upon the trusting relationship established during therapy." (Davidoff, *The Malpractice of Psychiatrists*, 1966 Duke L.J. 696, 704.) Patients will be helped only if they can form a trusting relationship with the psychiatrist. All authorities appear to agree that if the trust relationship cannot be developed because of collusive communication between the psychiatrist and others, treatment will be frustrated.

Given the importance of confidentiality to the practice of psychiatry, it becomes clear the duty to warn imposed by the majority will cripple the use and effectiveness of psychiatry. Many people, potentially violent — yet susceptible to treatment — will be deterred from seeking it; those seeking it will be inhibited from making revelations necessary to effective treatment; and, forcing the psychiatrist to violate the patient's trust will destroy the interpersonal relationship by which treatment is effected.

Violence and Civil Commitment

By imposing a duty to warn, the majority contributes to the danger to society of violence by the mentally ill and greatly increases the risk of civil commitment — the total deprivation of liberty — of those who should not be confined. The impairment of treatment and risk of improper commitment resulting from the new duty to warn will not be limited to a few patients but will extend to a large number of the mentally ill. Although under existing psychiatric procedures only a relatively few receiving treatment will ever present a risk of violence, the number making threats is huge, and it is the latter group — not just the former — whose treatment will be impaired and whose risk of commitment will be increased. . . .

Neither alternative open to the psychiatrist seeking to protect himself is in the public interest. The warning itself is an impairment of the psychiatrist's ability to

authors' dialogue 26

AARON: This "no-duty-to-rescue" material bothers me. Do the courts really mean it when they say, as the New Hampshire Supreme Court said in *Buch v. Amory Manufacturing Co.* (p. 375, *supra*), that I am not liable if I watch my neighbor's two-year-old get mangled in a windmill when I could very easily have saved the child at no cost to myself? That's not the way I was raised, I can tell you.

JIM: I think they really mean it, Aaron. And I think they are correct in denying liability when such a horrible case comes up.

AARON: Why should a court condone such horrific behavior?

JIM: Well, this is one of those times when long-run considerations of fairness and workability must take precedence over short-run considerations. In your argument, you assert as a premise that rescue would have been "easy," and could have been accomplished at "no cost" to the actor. What if the defendant argues that he has a pathological fear of windmill machinery and was frozen in his tracks?

AARON: Well, that's awfully subjective. The traditional negligence standard is objective — what a normal, reasonable person would have done.

JIM: But that's when an actor actively interferes with the plaintiff's well-being. Shouldn't the standard be more subjective when we are deciding whether to blame the defendant for what he *didn't* do — for *not* actively interfering? The neighbor who is frozen with fear is not morally to blame, is he?

AARON: Well, I suppose not.

JIM: Once we move to a subjective standard, a general duty to rescue will be very difficult to apply fairly and consistently across cases. And there is more to it than subjective psychology. What if the defendant explains that he did not intervene because the appearances were ambiguous — running over to the neighbor's yard and yelling at (or worse, grabbing) a two-year-old could be extremely embarrassing if the parents are nearby. Also, for every case that you show me where interfering made matters better I'll bet I could find one where interfering made matters worse. This is what the dissent in *Tarasoff* was getting at, I think.

AARON: But couldn't juries sort all of that out?

JIM: Should we be asking them to? Isn't a general "no-duty" rule better? The bastards who let babies die aren't going to do any different if we impose a vague threat of liability. The odds of a bad guy getting caught are very remote.

BRAD: I would just add that not all non-rescuers are bastards. Do you guys remember that plane crash off Washington National Airport into the Potomac River in the middle of winter? Some passengers had survived the crash but were in the middle of the freezing river. I mean, literally freezing — there were huge chunks of ice floating everywhere. Out of the dozens of people standing on the riverbank, a few jumped in and tried to rescue the passengers. I'm very comfortable calling those people heroes, but not condemning the others who didn't jump in. *Ex ante* it looked like a sure thing that those who jumped in would end up dead, too.

AARON: I agree that the duty to rescue shouldn't require heroism, but surely courts could craft a rule that requires people to take reasonable action in cases in which there is virtually no risk of harm to the rescuer. Even if there were a duty rule, a jury would never find that not jumping into an icy river was a breach of the standard of care.

treat, depriving many patients of adequate treatment. It is to be expected that after disclosing their threats, a significant number of patients, who would not become violent if treated according to existing practices, will engage in violent conduct as a result of unsuccessful treatment. In short, the majority's duty to warn will not only impair treatment of many who would never become violent but worse, will result in a net increase in violence.

The second alternative open to the psychiatrist is to commit his patient rather than to warn. Even in the absence of threat of civil liability, the doubts of psychiatrists as to the seriousness of patient threats have led psychiatrists to overcommit to mental institutions. This overcommitment has been authoritatively documented in both legal and psychiatric studies. . . .

Given the incentive to commit created by the majority's duty, this already serious situation will be worsened, contrary to Chief Justice Wright's admonition "that liberty is no less precious because forfeited in a civil proceeding than when taken as a consequence of a criminal conviction." (In re W. (Cal. 1971) . . . 486 P.2d 1201, 1209.) . . .

[T]he majority impedes medical treatment, resulting in increased violence from — and deprivation of liberty to — the mentally ill.

We should accept . . . medical judgment, relying upon effective treatment rather than on indiscriminate warning.

The judgment should be affirmed.

McCOMB, J., concurs.

AFTERMATH OF TARASOFF

Of the courts that have addressed the issue presented in *Tarasoff*, a clear majority have followed that decision. *See, e.g.*, Schuster v. Altenberg, 424 N.W.2d 159 (Wis. 1988). *See generally* Peter F. Lake, *Revisiting* Tarasoff, 58 Alb. L. Rev. 97 (1994). Legislatures have codified the rule in *Tarasoff. See, e.g.*, N.J. Stat. Ann § 2A: 62A-16b (West 1996); Utah Code Ann. § 78B-3-502 (2008). Some courts have rejected *Tarasoff. See, e.g.*, Nasser v. Parker, 455 S.E.2d 502 (Va. 1995). The California Legislature enacted a statute that attempts to provide some protection to therapists in *Tarasoff*-type situations. *See* Cal. Civ. Code § 43.92 (no duty arises unless the patient has communicated to the psychotherapist "a serious threat of physical violence against a reasonably identifiable victim," and duty is discharged by making "reasonable efforts to communicate the threat to the victim and to a law enforcement agency"); *see also* Shea v. Caritas County Hospital, 947 N.E.2d 99 (Mass. App. Ct. 2011) (applying statute under which there is no duty unless "the patient has a history of physical violence which is known to the licensed mental health professional and the licensed mental health professional has a reasonable basis to believe that there is a clear and present danger that the patient will attempt to kill or inflict serious bodily injury against a reasonably identified victim or victims"); Fredericks v. Jonsson, 609 F.3d 1096 (10th Cir. 2010) (similar limitation under Colorado statute). The Restatement, Third, of Torts § 41(b)(4), embraces the rule in *Tarasoff.* The Reporters' Note to Comment g to that section provides an extensive discussion of the practical impact of *Tarasoff* on mental health professionals. For an article taking the position that the "*Tarasoff* warning" may actually be a valuable clinical tool, *see* Brian Ginsberg, *Tarasoff at Thirty: Victim's Knowledge Shrinks the Psychotherapist's Duty to Warn and Protect*, 21 J. Contemp. Health L. & Policy 1 (2004).

Courts continue to struggle with the problem of how far to extend the duty to protect third persons from the malevolent conduct of evildoers. *See, e.g.,* Santana v. Rainbow Cleaners, 969 A.2d 653 (R.I. 2009) (under fact-sensitive, *ad hoc* approach, community mental health center owed no duty to victim to confine outpatient attacker based on general indications of antisocial behavior); Robinson v. Mount Logan Clinic, LLC, 182 P.3d 333 (Utah 2008) (under Utah statute cited, *supra*, no duty to act to protect victim in absence of threat to a clearly identifiable individual). In a malpractice action against a psychiatrist who abruptly discontinued a patient's medication, the patient's brutal murder of his mother was not an intervening act that relieved the psychiatrist of liability to his patient. O'Brien v. Bruscato, 715 S.E.2d 120 (Ga. 2011).

HOW FAR MUST A RESCUER GO?

Determining whether a duty to rescue exists is not the court's only task in the cases we have considered thus far. Whenever a court determines that a defendant owes such a duty, the court must determine how far the defendant must go in fulfilling that duty. For example, in *Tarasoff*, does a psychologist satisfy his duty by notifying the police? Could the wife in *J.S. and M.S.* have fulfilled her duty by simply confronting her husband? Calling the police? Physically intervening to protect the children? As the court in *Tarasoff* suggests, and other courts have followed, this question is often one of fact for the jury. Recall *Wakulich v. Mraz, supra* p. 382, where defendants induced a 16-year-old female to drink a quart of hard liquor and then, as she lay unconscious, removed her vomit-saturated shirt and propped her head up. According to the court, by propping her head up, the defendants created a duty to follow through on helping the young woman. Had the defendants called an ambulance, would that have fulfilled their duty? Should they have remained on the scene to make sure that the ambulance arrived? That the ambulance driver was sober?

Even when courts impose a duty to rescue on a particular person, that person may avoid liability if another person rushes to the aid of the injured party. For example, in McCammon v. Gifford, 2002 WL 732272 (Tenn. Ct. App.), the plaintiff was injured after his clothes caught fire from a spilled can of paint thinner at a campsite. Both the trial court and the appellate court held that the defendant campsite owner, as a possessor of land who holds it open to the public, owed a duty to rescue the plaintiff, as a member of the public who entered in response to the invitation. However, both courts also ruled that the duty did not require defendant's employees to seek medical aid after they learned that plaintiff's brother had rendered aid and rushed the plaintiff to their mother's home.

hypo 51

A and *B* are both 16 years old and close friends. *A* is over at *B*'s house for dinner and, after lengthy conversations, tells *B* and *B*'s parents that he wants to kill himself. Based on *A*'s appearance and behavior, *B* and *B*'s parents believe that *A* is telling the truth. However, in response to *A*'s pleas and promises to seek help, they promise not to tell *A*'s parents or the authorities. Two days later, *A* kills himself. *A*'s parents bring a negligence action against *B* and *B*'s parents for *A*'s death. Will *A*'s parents' claims survive a motion for summary judgment?

HAS LAWYER CONFIDENTIALITY RUN AMOK?

Imagine that Poddar had stated his intention to kill Tatiana Tarasoff not to his therapist but to his lawyer. Arguably the threat to Tatiana's life was not imminent, so a lawyer would not be permitted to disclose the threat. An appellate court in Washington State declined to impose a duty on a lawyer to disclose information that the client was mentally ill and dangerous. When the client was subsequently released on bail, assaulted his mother, and attempted suicide by jumping off a bridge, the court distinguished *Tarasoff* by noting that the client did not make a specific threat against his mother, and in any event the mother knew of the client's dangerousness, unlike Tatiana Tarasoff, who was ignorant of the threat to her life. Hawkins v. King County, 602 P.2d 361 (Wash. Ct. App. 1979).

Hypo 51 involves a promise to keep a secret, potentially in conflict with the duty to warn the foreseeable victim of threatened violence. What if the obligation to keep a secret comes not from a promise between friends but from a strict, legally enforceable duty of confidentiality? The legal profession has grappled with this problem for a long time, because lawyers have traditionally been subject to an almost absolute duty of confidentiality.

Rule 1.6(a) of the Model Rules of Professional Conduct prohibits a lawyer from disclosing any "information relating to the representation," unless the client gives informed consent to the disclosure. The scope of protected confidences is much broader than the evidentiary attorney-client privilege, which prevents adversaries in litigation from discovering confidential communications made between lawyer and client for the purpose of providing legal assistance for the client. *See* Restatement, Third, of the Law Governing Lawyers § 68. Until recently, the duty of confidentiality had very few exceptions. Relevant here is the exception permitting disclosure to prevent personal injury to others. The 1983 version of the ABA Model Rules allowed lawyers to breach confidentiality only when it was necessary "to prevent the client from committing a criminal act that the lawyer believes is likely to result in imminent death or substantial bodily harm."

Plenty of cases fail to satisfy this standard. One of the classic legal ethics cases, Spaulding v. Zimmerman, 116 N.W.2d 704 (Minn. 1962), presents a wrenching dilemma for lawyers subject to such a stringent a duty of confidentiality.[1] A lawyer — let's call her Jones — does insurance defense work. She gets a case involving an intersection collision in which both drivers were injured. From a review of the police report, it appears that Zimmerman, the insured defendant who is Jones' client, was likely at fault in the accident. The parties conduct discovery, and as part of the process, Jones requests that the plaintiff, Spaulding, submit to an independent medical examination (IME). An IME is a discovery procedure, familiar to personal injury lawyers, which permits a defendant to have its own doctor examine the plaintiff and prepare a report on the extent of the plaintiff's injuries. Spaulding goes to see Dr. Hewitt, a physician to whom Jones often refers plaintiffs for an IME. Because Spaulding had suffered a couple of cracked ribs, Dr. Hewitt takes a chest x-ray and is astonished to discover from the x-ray that Spaulding has an aortic aneurysm, a weakening of a major artery leading from the heart. Left untreated, the aneurysm may burst and kill Spaulding instantly. Dr. Hewitt writes about the aneurysm in the IME report and sends it to Jones. For good measure Dr. Hewitt calls Jones, points out the aneurysm in the report, and explains its significance.

Under the discovery rules in the state, Spaulding's lawyer is entitled to receive a copy of the IME report upon request. There is no need to file a motion or make out a showing of necessity; a simple letter, e-mail, or even phone call to Jones would obligate Jones to share a copy of the report. Unfortunately, Spaulding's lawyer is a recent law school graduate and has not handled many personal injury cases. His civil procedure class did not spend much time on discovery and he did not learn that he is entitled to receive a copy of the IME report. Adding to the problem, Spaulding's own treating physician failed to diagnose the aneurysm. Jones does some legal research and learns that she has no obligation to disclose the IME report without a request from Spaulding's lawyer. She also researches verdicts and settlements in the state and learns that if the full extent of Spaulding's injuries were known, the average range of recoveries is approximately $500,000. Without the additional information provided in the IME report, however, Spaulding's lawyer would probably value the case at $50,000 or less.

Jones calls Zimmerman and explains the situation. Zimmerman has mostly recovered from his injuries, but is facing significant future medical expenses for physical therapy and rehabilitation, which are not covered by his health insurance. Zimmerman's liability insurance policy has a limit of $100,000 per person. He directs Jones not to disclose the full extent of Spaulding's injuries.

Under the lawyer's duty of confidentiality, as stated in the 1983 version of Model Rule 1.6(a), Jones is not permitted to disclose the aneurysm. For one thing, Spaulding's death, while likely, is not imminent. In addition, if Spaulding does die, it will not be the result of a criminal act by Zimmerman. Does Jones have a duty under *Tarasoff* to disclose the aneurysm? The majority in *Tarasoff* notes that psychotherapists are required by their own rules of professional ethics to keep

---

1. The facts of the case have been modified slightly to turn it into a more interesting hypothetical, but this narrative is pretty faithful to the actual case. For a fascinating historical reexamination of *Spaulding, see* Roger C. Cramton & Lori P. Knowles, *Professional Secrecy and Its Exceptions: Spaulding v. Zimmerman Revisited,* 83 Minn. L. Rev. 63 (1998).

secrets, but that the medical ethics rule permits disclosure "in order to protect the welfare of the individual or the community." No such exception exists to the lawyer's duty of confidentiality. How much of a difference would that make to the analysis under *Tarasoff*? Does it matter that Spaulding's own lawyer could have discovered the information by making a simple request for the IME report? One of the justifications for the lawyer's duty of confidentiality is that it underpins the division of labor between opposing counsel in the adversary system. Each client bears the risk that his or her lawyer will make mistakes. It is often said that lawyers do not have duties to opposing parties in litigation, but it is surely an exceptional situation when a lawyer can prevent a threat to the life of the other party by giving a timely warning.

The dilemma presented by *Spaulding v. Zimmerman* would be lessened today, at least for lawyers practicing in jurisdictions that adopted the 2003 amendments to the confidentiality rule. Model Rule 1.6(b)(1) now permits a lawyer to disclose information relating to the representation to the extent the lawyer reasonably believes necessary "to prevent reasonably certain death or substantial bodily harm." The removal of the criminal act requirement and the element of imminent death or bodily harm means our hypothetical lawyer Jones is permitted to disclose Spaulding's aneurysm. Does that change the analysis under *Tarasoff*?

What about psychologists who assist lawyers by examining a client and providing expert testimony? A criminal defense lawyer was representing a 10-year-old boy accused of arson, and was concerned that the client may have had a developmental disability that rendered him incapable of understanding the proceedings and cooperating in his defense. The psychologist, whom the lawyer requested to be appointed as an expert, accepted the appointment on the condition that any required statutory or common-law *Tarasoff* warnings be given only to defense counsel — not to law enforcement or child-welfare authorities. The California Court of Appeals considered the attorney-client and psychotherapist-patient privilege, the Sixth Amendment right to counsel in criminal proceedings, and the statutory and common-law duties to warn and concluded that a psychologist examining a patient as part of a defense team, rather than in a therapeutic setting, may not have a duty to report a serious threat to a known victim; even if there were such a duty, notifying defense counsel would constitute reasonable care under the circumstances. Elijah W. v. Superior Court, 216 Cal. App. 4th 140, 156 Cal. Rptr. 3d 592 (2013).

4. Bringing It All Together: A Reprise of *Palsgraf* on Duty and Causation

BEUL v. ASSE INTERNATIONAL, INC.
233 F.3d 441 (7th Cir. 2000)

Posner, Circuit Judge.

In this diversity suit for negligence, governed (so far as the substantive issues are concerned) by Wisconsin law, the jury returned a verdict finding that plaintiff

Kristin Beul's damages were $1,100,000 and that she was 41 percent responsible for them; in accordance with the verdict, judgment was entered against defendant ASSE International for $649,000 (59 percent of $1.1 million). The other parties can be ignored. The appeal raises issues of both tort law and civil procedure.

The defendant is a nonprofit corporation that operates international student exchange programs. For a fee of $2,000 it placed Kristin, a 16-year-old German girl who wanted to spend a year in the United States, with the Bruce family of Fort Atkinson, Wisconsin. The family, which consisted of Richard Bruce, age 40, his wife, and their 13-year-old daughter, had been selected by Marianne Breber, the defendant's Area Representative in the part of the state that includes Fort Atkinson. Breber is described in the briefs as a "volunteer," not an employee; the only payment she receives from ASSE is reimbursement of her expenses. Nothing in the appeal, however, turns either on her "volunteer" status or on ASSE's nonprofit status. Charities are not immune from tort liability in Wisconsin, *Kojis v. Doctors Hosp.*, 107 N.W.2d 131 (Wis.1961), and ASSE does not deny that if Breber was negligent it is liable for her negligence under the doctrine of respondeat superior, even though she was not an employee of ASSE. The doctrine is nowadays usually described as making an employer liable for the torts of his employees committed within the scope of their employment, but strictly speaking the liability is that of a "master" for the torts of his "servant" and it extends to situations in which the servant is not an employee, provided that he is acting in a similar role, albeit as a volunteer. *E.g., Heims v. Hanke*, 93 N.W.2d 455, 457-58 (Wis.1958), overruled on other grounds by *Butzow v. Wausau Memorial Hospital*, 187 N.W.2d 349, 353–54 (Wis.1971); *Morgan v. Veterans of Foreign Wars*, 565 N.E.2d 73, 77 (Ill. App. 1990); *Restatement (Second) of Agency* § 225 (1958). In *Morgan*, as in this case, the defendant was a charity.

There is also no argument that the contract between ASSE and Kristin's parents is the exclusive source of ASSE's legal duties to Kristin. Negligence in the performance of a contract that foreseeably results in personal injury, including as here emotional distress, is actionable under tort law. See, e.g., *Kuehn v. Childrens Hospital*, 119 F.3d 1296 (7th Cir. 1997). As we pointed out in *Rardin v. T & D Machine Handling, Inc.*, 890 F.2d 24, 29 (7th Cir.1989), "tort law is a field largely shaped by the special considerations involved in personal-injury cases, as contract law is not. Tort doctrines are, therefore, prima facie more suitable for the governance of such cases than contract doctrines are" even when victim and injurer are linked by contract. . . .

As the sponsor of a foreign exchange student, ASSE was subject to regulations of the United States Information Agency that require sponsors to train their agents, "monitor the progress and welfare of the exchange visit," and require a "regular schedule of personal contact with the student and host family." 22 C.F.R. §§ 514.10(e)(2), 514.25(d)(1), (4) (now §§ 62.10(e)(2), 62.25(d)(1), (4)). These regulations are intended for the protection of the visitor, see "Exchange Visitor Program," 58 Fed. Reg. 15,180, 15,190 (1993) (statement of USIA accompanying promulgation of 26 C.F.R. § 514.25), and the jury was therefore properly instructed, under standard tort principles not challenged by ASSE, that it could consider the violation of them as evidence of negligence. There is no argument that the regulations create a private federal right of suit that would allow the plaintiffs to sue ASSE under the federal-question jurisdiction of the federal courts (and we have found no case suggesting there is such a right), or that Wisconsin is legally obligated to use the regulations to define the duty of care of a sponsor sued under state tort law. In other words, there is no argument that the federal regulations have preemptive force in state tort litigation. But the district court was entitled to conclude that a state court would look to the regulations for evidence of the sponsor's duty of care. Courts in tort cases commonly take their cues from statutes or regulations intended to protect the safety of the class to which the tort plaintiff belongs. See, e.g., *Bennett v. Larsen Co.*, 348 N.W.2d 540, 548–49 (Wis.1984).

ASSE is also a member of a private association of sponsors of foreign exchange students, the Council on Standards for International Educational Travel, which requires members to "maintain thorough, accurate, and continual communication with host families and school authorities." A jury could reasonably consider the Council's statement as additional evidence of the standard of care applicable to sponsors and it could also accept the plaintiff's argument that due care required Breber to try to develop rapport with Kristin so that Kristin would trust and confide in her and so that Breber could pick up any signals of something amiss that Kristin might be embarrassed to mention unless pressed.

Kristin Beul arrived in Wisconsin from Germany on September 7, 1995, and was met at the airport by Richard Bruce and his daughter. Marianne Breber did not go to the airport to meet Kristin. In fact, apart from a brief orientation meeting at a shopping mall in September with Kristin and one other foreign exchange student, at which Breber gave Kristin her phone number, she didn't meet with Kristin until January 21 of the following year — under unusual circumstances, as we'll see. She did call the Bruce home a few times during this period and spoke briefly with Kristin once or twice, but she made no effort to make sure that Kristin was alone when they spoke. She would ask in these calls how Kristin was doing and Kristin would reply that everything was fine. Breber did not talk to Mrs. Bruce, who would have told her that she was concerned that her husband seemed to be developing an inappropriate relationship with Kristin.

Kristin had led a sheltered life in Germany. She had had no sexual experiences at all and in fact had had only two dates in her life. On November 17, 1995, Richard Bruce, who weighed almost 300 pounds and who was alone at home at the time except for Kristin, came into the loft area in which she slept and raped her.

This was the start of a protracted sexual relationship. In the months that followed, Bruce frequently would call the high school that Kristin was attending and report her ill. Then, with Mrs. Bruce off at work and the Bruce's daughter at school, Bruce would have sex with Kristin. By February 22, Kristin had been absent 27 days from school. Bruce brandished a gun and told Kristin that he would kill himself if she told anyone what they were doing together.

Curiously, in January Bruce and Kristin called Marianne Breber and told her that Mrs. Bruce appeared to be jealous of the time that her husband was spending with Kristin. Bruce invited Breber to dinner on January 21. Breber did not meet privately with either Kristin or Mrs. Bruce on that occasion, and she observed nothing untoward. In February, however, Mrs. Bruce told Breber that she and her husband were getting divorced, and Breber forthwith found another host family to take in Kristin. Kristin didn't want to leave the Bruce home, but on February 22 Breber came with a sheriff's deputy to remove Kristin. The deputy asked Kristin in the presence of Richard Bruce and his daughter whether there was any inappropriate sexual activity between Richard and Kristin, and Kristin answered "no." The same day Breber, upon calling Kristin's school to tell them that Kristin would be out for a few days in connection with her change of residence, learned for the first time of Kristin's many absences.

Kristin lived with Breber for a few days between host families, but Breber didn't use the occasion to inquire about any possible sexual relationship between Kristin and Bruce. Breber told the new host family that Kristin was not to contact Bruce for a month, but she did not tell Bruce not to have any contact with Kristin. They continued to correspond and talk on the phone. Kristin had decided that she was in love with Bruce and considered herself engaged to him.

In April, Mrs. Bruce discovered some of Kristin's love letters and alerted the authorities. A sheriff's deputy interviewed Bruce. The next day Bruce, who had committed a misdemeanor by having sex with a 16 year old, Wis. Stat. § 948.09, killed himself, leaving a note expressing fear of jail. It is undisputed that the events culminating in Bruce's suicide inflicted serious psychological harm on Kristin; the jury's assessment of her damages is not claimed to be excessive.

The defendant argues that it was entitled to judgment as a matter of law, or alternatively to a new trial because of trial error. The first argument divides into three: there was insufficient proof of a causal relationship between the defendant's negligence in failing to keep closer tabs on Kristin Beul and her sexual involvement with Bruce culminating in his suicide; Bruce's criminal activity was the sole, or superseding, cause of her harm; and the harm was too "remote" in a legal sense from the defendant's lack of due care to support liability.

Since Kristin was determined to conceal her relationship with Bruce, the defendant argues, no amount of care by Breber would have warded off the harm that befell Kristin; she would have stonewalled, however pertinacious Breber had been in her questioning. This is conceivable, and if true would let ASSE off the hook; if there was no causal relation between the defendant's negligence and the plaintiff's harm, there was no tort. . . .

But it is improbable, and the jury was certainly not required to buy the argument. Suppose Breber had inquired from the school how Kristin was doing — a natural question to ask about a foreigner plunged into an American high school. She would have learned of the numerous absences, would (if minimally alert) have inquired about them from Kristin, and would have learned that Kristin had been "ill" and that Richard Bruce had been home and taken care of her. At that point the secret would have started to unravel.

As for the argument that Bruce's misconduct was so egregious as to let ASSE off the hook, it is true that the doctrine of "superseding cause" can excuse a negligent defendant. Suicide by a sane person, unless clearly foreseeable by the tortfeasor, for example a psychiatrist treating a depressed person, is a tradition al example of the operation of the doctrine. E.g., *McMahon v. St. Croix Falls School District*, 596 N.W.2d 875, 879 (Wis. App. 1999); *Wyke v. Polk County School Board*, 129

F.3d 560, 574–75 (11th Cir.1997); *Bruzga v. PMR Architects, P.C.*, 693 A.2d 401 (N.H. 1997); *Edwards v. Tardif*, 692 A.2d 1266, 1269 (Conn.1997); W. Page Keeton et al., *Prosser and Keeton on the Law of Torts* § 44, p. 311 (5th ed.1984). So if Bruce's boss had refused him a raise and Bruce had responded by killing himself, the boss even if somehow negligent in failing to give him the raise would not be considered the legal cause of the death. Or if through the carelessness of the driver a truck spilled a toxic substance and a passerby scraped it up and poisoned his mother-in-law with it, the driver would not be liable to the mother-in-law's estate; the son-in-law's criminal act would be deemed a superseding cause. . . .

Animating the doctrine is the idea that it is unreasonable to make a person liable for such improbable consequences of negligent activity as could hardly figure in his deciding how careful he should be. . . . The doctrine is not applied, therefore, when the duty of care claimed to have been violated is precisely a duty to protect against ordinarily unforeseeable conduct, as in our earlier example of a psychiatrist treating depression. The existence of the duty presupposes a probable, therefore a foreseeable, consequence of its breach. (All that "foreseeable" means in tort law is probable ex ante, that is, before the injury that is the basis of the tort suit.) Thus a hospital that fails to maintain a careful watch over patients known to be suicidal is not excused by the doctrine of superseding cause from liability for a suicide, e.g., *DeMontiney v. Desert Manor Convalescent Center*, 695 P.2d 255, 259–60 (Ariz.1985), any more than a zoo can escape liability for allowing a tiger to escape and maul people on the ground that the tiger is the superseding cause of the mauling. *City of Mangum v. Brownlee*, 75 P.2d 174 (Okla.1938); see also *Scorza v. Martinez*, 683 So. 2d 1115, 1117 (Fla. App. 1996); *Behrens v. Bertram Mills Circus, Ltd.*, [1957] 2 Q.B. 1, 1 All E.R. 583 (1957).

So Kristin's high school would not have been liable for the consequences of Bruce's sexual activity with Kristin even if the school should have reported her frequent absences to Breber; the criminal activities with their bizarre suicide sequel were not foreseeable by the school. But part of ASSE's duty and Breber's function was to protect foreign girls and boys from sexual hanky-panky initiated by members of host families. Especially when a teenage girl is brought to live with strangers in a foreign country, the risk of inappropriate sexual activity is not so slight that the organization charged by the girl's parents with the safety of their daughter can be excused as a matter of law from making a responsible effort to minimize the risk. See, e.g., *Niece v. Elmview Group Home*, 929 P.2d 420, 427 (Wash. 1997); *R.E. v. Alaska*, 878 P.2d 1341, 1346–48 (Alaska 1994); *Juarez v. Boy Scouts of America, Inc.*, 97 Cal. Rptr. 2d 12, 31 (Cal. App. 2000); *Phillips v. Deihm*, 541 N.W.2d 566, 573 (Mich. App. 1995). Sexual abuse by stepfathers is not uncommon, see, e.g., Diana E.H. Russell, "The Prevalance and Seriousness of Incestuous Abuse: Stepfathers vs. Biological Fathers," 8 Child Abuse & Neglect 15 (1984), and the husband in a host family has an analogous relationship to a teenage visitor living with the family.

It is true (we turn now to the issue of remoteness) that when through the negligence of an alarm company, to which ASSE in its role as protector of foreign students from the sexual attentions of members of host families might perhaps be analogized, a fire or burglary is not averted or controlled in time, the company is generally not liable for the consequences; the consequences are deemed too remote. E.g., *Edwards v. Honeywell, Inc.*, 50 F.3d 484, 491 (7th Cir. 1995); *Fireman's Fund American Ins. Cos. v. Burns Electronic Security Services, Inc., supra*, 417 N.E.2d at 132–33; cf. *Fireman's Fund Ins. Co. v. Morse Signal Devices*, 198 Cal. Rptr. 756, 760 (Cal. App. 1984); see also *Heitsch v. Hampton*, 423 N.W.2d 297, 299 (Mich. App. 1988). There are two related considerations. One is that so many factors outside the alarm company's control determine the likelihood and consequences (whether in property loss or personal injury) of a failure of its alarm to summon prompt aid on a particular occasion that the company is bound to lack the information that it needs to determine what level of care to take to prevent a failure of its system. See, e.g., *Guthrie v. American Protection Industries, supra*, 206 Cal. Rptr. at 836. This basis of the doctrine is the same as that of the doctrine of superseding cause. A harm is not foreseeable in the contemplation of the law if the injurer lacked the information he needed to determine whether he must use special care to avert the harm. See, e.g., *Lodge v. Arett Sales Corp.*, 717 A.2d 215, 223 (Conn. 1998). The second point is that the alarm company is not the primary accident avoider but merely a backup, and the principal responsibility for avoiding disaster lies with the victim. See, e.g., *Rardin v. T & D Machine Handling, Inc., supra*, 890 F.2d at 27; *Evra Corp. v. Swiss Bank Corp.*, 673 F.2d 951, 957–58 (7th Cir. 1982). The points are related because both involve the difficulty a backup or secondary protector against disaster has in figuring out the consequence of a lapse on its part. Neither point supports ASSE, which was standing in the shoes of the parents of a young girl living in a stranger's home far from her homeland and could reasonably be expected to exercise the kind of care that the parents themselves would exercise if they could to protect their 16-year-old daughter from the sexual pitfalls that lie about a girl of that age in those circumstances. ASSE assumed a primary role in the protection of the girl.

So the plaintiff was entitled to get to the jury, and we turn to the two alleged errors in the procedure at trial. . . .

The defendant also complains about the following instruction to the jury: "You're instructed that the law of Wisconsin does not allow a child under the age of 18 to consent to an act of intercourse." This was a reference to the state's statutory rape law, but it was not elaborated further. The jury was instructed to consider the instructions as a whole and another instruction was that it was to consider Kristin's comparative fault. The jury assessed that fault at 41 percent, so obviously it did not think the age-of-consent instruction prevented it from considering Kristin's responsibility for the harm that befell her as a consequence of her sexual relationship with Bruce.

But should the jury have been told what the age of consent is in Wisconsin and, if so, was the information conveyed to the jury in the right way? The answer to the first question is yes. The age of consent fixed by a state represents a legislative judgment about the maturity of girls in matters of sex. Eighteen is a pretty high age of consent by today's standards and of course the law was not fixed by reference to German girls; but it is nonetheless a reminder that teenage children are not considered fully responsible in sexual matters, and this was something relevant to the jury's consideration of Kristin's share of responsibility for the disaster. The criminal law is frequently used to set a standard of care for civil tort cases . . . and that was essentially the use made of it here. It would have been error to instruct the jury that because Kristin was below the age of consent her comparative fault must be reckoned at zero. That would have given too much force to the criminal statute in this civil case, for the statute cannot be considered a legislative judgment that minors are utterly incapable of avoiding becoming ensnared in sexual relationships. A comparative-fault rule, moreover, requires gradations of victim responsibility that are alien to the normal criminal prohibition. Victim fault is not a defense, either partial or complete, to criminal liability. It is not a defense to a charge of rape that, for example, the victim was dressed provocatively, or drunk, or otherwise careless in the circumstances in which the rape occurred.

It would have been better, though, if the jury had been told *how* it should take the age of consent into account in their deliberations. It should have been told that in deciding how much responsibility to assign to Kristin for the events that gave rise to the harm for which she was suing, it could consider that the state had made a judgment that girls below the age of 18 should be protected by the criminal law from sexual activity even if they agree to it. As it was, the jury was left to tease out the relation between the age-of-consent instruction and the comparative-fault instruction for itself. But we cannot think that it was other than a harmless error. Indeed, we are surprised that the jury assigned so large a responsibility to this young foreign girl virtually abandoned by the agency that was standing in for her parents. The jury verdict was rather favorable to the defendant than otherwise.

AFFIRMED.

FOOD FOR THOUGHT

The court considered numerous issues along the way toward holding the foreign-exchange program sponsor liable for the emotional distress the plaintiff suffered as a result of the coercive relationship with Richard Bruce. The first was whether a duty could be implied from regulations issued by a federal agency regarding foreign-exchange programs, which required sponsors to keep a regular schedule of contacts with students and their host families. Recall from Chapter 3 that courts sometimes imply a private right of action based on a statute that prescribes conduct by the defendant. Bootstrapping a duty off a statute or regulation is related to the use of such an enactment to specify the standard of care, but note an important difference: negligence *per se* — that is, particularizing the standard of care with reference to statutorily-mandated conduct — assumes the existence of a duty. The classic *Martin v. Herzog* case, for example, takes for granted that drivers have a duty to use reasonable care to avoid harm from an activity already undertaken. The statute in *Martin* did not, strictly speaking, require the use of lights; rather, it prohibited driving after dark without lights. In a case in which the actor is not responsible for creating the risk, however, the first issue to be resolved is whether the actor has a duty to protect potential victims from harm. Unless there is a duty, there is no standard of care to particularize; thus, the statute or regulation is not being used to establish negligence *per se*. The Third Restatement clarifies this distinction:

> Negligence per se relies on a specific statutory standard to pretermit reference to the more general reasonable-care standard for adjudicating the question of breach of duty. But even without reliance on the statute, the actor is subject to a duty of reasonable care and to potential tort liability. On the other hand, employing a statute to provide a tort duty where none previously existed creates a new basis for liability not previously recognized by tort law.

Restatement (Third) of Torts § 38, cmt. *d.* In *Beul*, Judge Posner found no evidence of intent by Congress or the agency that promulgated the regulations to create a right to sue sponsors of exchange programs who fail to monitor students' visits, and thus no implied duty to the plaintiff. Nevertheless, he said the district judge was allowed to "take a cue" from statute and regulations designed to protect a class of potential victims, including the plaintiff, from this type of harm.

Similarly, the New Jersey Supreme Court considered a state statute requiring reporting by anyone having reasonable cause to believe that a child has been sexually abused. J.S. and M.S. v. R.T.H., 714 A.2d 924 (N.J. 1998). The statute was not dispositive of the duty, as it would be in a true private right of action analysis, but it influenced the court's balancing of the factors it considered in determining that the wife of a sexual abuser could be liable for negligence for not detecting her husband's abuse of two young girls. On the other hand, in the absence of a sexual abuse reporting statute, in D.W. v. Bliss, 112 P.3d 232 (Kan. 2005), the court held that a wife was not liable for failing to warn a 15-year-old boy of the likelihood that he would be sexually abused by her husband. Although there was reason to believe the wife knew or should have known her husband had sexual relations with other men in her home, the court found the wife had no special relationship with the minor plaintiff so as to trigger a duty to be in charge or control of her husband. *See also* Newsom v. B.B., B.C., 306 S.W.3d 910 (Tex. App. 2010) (defendant father owed no duty to warn would-be victims that his adult son might sexually assault boys). Do you think the presence or absence of a statute requiring the reporting of child abuse accounts for the different result in these cases? Even if there is a reporting statute, a court may find that it has nothing to do with the defendant's duty to prevent sexual abuse. *See, e.g.,* Perry v. S.N., 973 S.W.2d 301 (Tex. 1998) (discussed in Ch. 3) (failure to report not negligence per se where the statute was vague and did not set a standard of conduct and, in any event, the statute did not particularize an already-existing duty).

The second issue dealt with by the court in *Beul* harkens back to *Palsgraf*. The chain of events that resulted in the injury — Kristin's initial rape by Richard Bruce, the subsequent clandestine sexual relationship and its discovery, and Bruce's eventual suicide — appear quite remote from any carelessness or inattention by Marianne Breber, the exchange-program employee charged with taking care of Kristin. It is difficult to see what, exactly, Breber should have done that would have prevented this harm. As the court recognizes, this argument could appeal to considerations of actual or proximate cause. But it is also relevant to whether there should be a duty in the first place for exchange programs to keep up regular communications with students and their host families in the hopes that they may learn of problems like this in time to prevent harm. Breber did have several conversations with Kristin, but Kristin denied any improper relationship with Bruce. The court concedes that Kristin's high school, which had knowledge of her frequent absences, would not be liable for the consequences of the relationship and Bruce's suicide because they were not foreseeable by the school. But somehow they were foreseeable by Breber and the exchange program? Apparently this is a peculiar sense of the word "foreseeable." Judge Posner says "foreseeable" in tort law simply means "probable ex ante, that is, before the injury that is the basis of the tort suit." Yet a fire or burglar alarm company is not liable for the consequences of negligence in maintaining the alarm because the defendant lacks the information it needs to determine whether special care is required. Wouldn't the exchange program similarly need a great deal of information about factors beyond its control to determine whether it had to take extra care to protect Kristin?

B. LIMITATIONS ON RECOVERY FOR PURE ECONOMIC LOSS

STATE OF LOUISIANA, EX REL. GUSTE v. M/V TESTBANK
752 F.2d 1019 (5th Cir.) (en banc), cert. denied, 477 U.S. 903 (1985)

HIGGINBOTHAM, Circuit Judge: We are asked to abandon physical damage to a proprietary interest as a prerequisite to recovery for economic loss in cases of unintentional maritime tort. We decline the invitation.

In the early evening of July 22, 1980, the M/V Sea Daniel, an inbound bulk carrier, and the M/V Testbank, an outbound container ship, collided at approximately mile forty-one of the Mississippi River Gulf outlet. At impact, a white haze enveloped the ships until carried away by prevailing winds, and containers aboard Testbank were damaged and lost overboard. The white haze proved to be hydrobromic acid and the contents of the containers which went overboard proved to be approximately twelve tons of pentachlorophenol, PCP, assertedly the largest such spill in United States history. The United States Coast Guard closed the outlet to navigation until August 10, 1980 and all fishing, shrimping, and related activity was temporarily suspended in the outlet and four hundred square miles of surrounding marsh and waterways.

Forty-one lawsuits were filed and consolidated before the same judge in the Eastern District of Louisiana. These suits presented claims of shipping interests, marina and boat rental operators, wholesale and retail seafood enterprises not actually engaged in fishing, seafood restaurants, tackle and bait shops, and recreational fishermen. . . .

Defendants moved for summary judgment as to all claims for economic loss unaccompanied by physical damage to property. The district court granted the requested summary judgment as to all such claims except those asserted by commercial oystermen, shrimpers, crabbers and fishermen who had been making a commercial use of the embargoed waters. . . .

On appeal a panel of this court affirmed, concluding that claims for economic loss unaccompanied by physical damage to a proprietary interest were not recoverable in maritime tort. The panel, as did the district court, pointed to the doctrine of Robins Dry Dock & Repair Co. v. Flint, 275 U.S. 303 (1927), and its development in this circuit. Judge Wisdom specially concurred, agreeing that the denial of these claims was required by precedent, but urging reexamination en banc. We then took the case en banc for that purpose. After extensive additional briefs and oral argument, we are unpersuaded that we ought to drop physical damage to a proprietary interest as a prerequisite to recovery for economic loss. To the contrary, our reexamination of the history and central purpose of this pragmatic restriction on the doctrine of foreseeability heightens our commitment to it. Ultimately we conclude that without this limitation foreseeability loses much of its ability to function as a rule of law. . . .

In *Robins*, the time charterer of a steamship sued for profits lost when the defendant dry dock negligently damaged the vessel's propeller. [The plaintiff charterer did not own the vessel nor did it have a possessory interest in her. The charterer had contracted with the owner to use the vessel when it left dry dock, but had no rights under the contract against the owner stemming from the owner's delay in delivering her to the charterer.] The propeller had to be replaced, thus extending by two weeks the time the vessel was laid up in dry dock, and it was for the loss of use of the vessel for that period that the charterer sued. The Supreme Court denied recovery to the charterer, noting: ". . . no authority need be cited to show that, as a general rule, at least, a tort to the person or property of one man does not make the tort-feasor liable to another merely because the injured person was under a contract with that other unknown to the doer of the wrong (citation omitted). The law does not spread its protection so far." 275 U.S. at 309. . . .

The principle that there could be no recovery for economic loss absent physical injury to a proprietary interest was not only well established when *Robins Dry Dock* was decided, but was remarkably resilient as well. . . . Indeed this limit on liability stood against a sea of change in the tort law. Retention of this conspicuous bright-line rule in the face of the reforms brought by the increased influence of the school of legal realism is strong testament both to the rule's utility and to the absence of a more "conceptually pure" substitute. The push to delete the restrictions on recovery for economic loss lost its support and by the early 1940's had failed. In sum, it is an old sword that plaintiffs have here picked up. . . .

Plaintiffs urge that the requirement of physical injury to a proprietary interest is arbitrary, unfair, and illogical, as it denies recovery for foreseeable injury caused by negligent acts. At its bottom the argument is that questions of remoteness ought to be left to the trier of fact. Ultimately the question becomes who ought to decide—judge or jury—and whether there will be a rule beyond the jacket of a given case. The plaintiffs contend that the "problem" need not be separately addressed, but instead should be handled by "traditional" principles of tort law. Putting the problem of which doctrine is the traditional one aside, their rhetorical questions are flawed in several respects.

Those who would delete the requirement of physical damage have no rule or principle to substitute. Their approach fails to recognize limits upon the adjudicating ability of courts. We do not mean just the ability to supply a judgment; prerequisite to this adjudicatory function are preexisting rules, whether the creature of courts or legislatures. Courts can decide cases without preexisting normative guidance but the result becomes less judicial and more the product of a managerial, legislative or negotiated function.[11]

Review of the foreseeable consequences of the collision of the Sea Daniel and Testbank demonstrates the wave upon wave of successive economic consequences and the managerial role plaintiffs would have us assume. The vessel delayed in St. Louis may be unable to fulfill its obligation to haul from Memphis, to the injury of the shipper, to the injury of the buyers, to the injury of their customers. Plaintiffs concede, as do all who attack the requirement of physical damage, that a line would need to be drawn — somewhere on the other side, each plaintiff would say in turn, of its recovery. Plaintiffs advocate not only that the lines be drawn elsewhere but also that they be drawn on an ad hoc and discrete basis. The result would be that no determinable measure of the limit of foreseeability would precede the decision on liability. We are told that when the claim is too remote, or too tenuous, recovery will be denied. Presumably then, as among all plaintiffs suffering foreseeable economic loss, recovery will turn on a judge or jury's decision. There will be no rationale for the differing results save the "judgment" of the trier of fact. Concededly, it can "decide" all the claims presented, and with comparative if not absolute ease. The point is not that such a process cannot be administered but rather that its judgments would be much less the products of a determinable rule of law. In this important sense, the resulting decisions would be judicial products only in their draw upon judicial resources.

The bright line rule of damage to a proprietary interest, as most, has the virtue of predictability with the vice of creating results in cases at its edge that are said to be "unjust" or "unfair." Plaintiffs point to seemingly perverse results, where claims the rule allows and those it disallows are juxtaposed — such as vessels striking a dock, causing minor but recoverable damage, then lurching athwart a channel causing great but unrecoverable economic loss. The answer is that when lines are drawn sufficiently sharp in their definitional edges to be reasonable and predictable, such differing results are the inevitable result — indeed, decisions are the desired product. But there is more. The line drawing sought by plaintiffs is no less arbitrary because the line drawing appears only in the outcome — as one claimant is found too remote and another is allowed to recover. The true difference is that plaintiffs' approach would mask the results. The present rule would be more candid, and in addition, by making results more predictable, serves a normative

---

11. As Professor Henderson put it: When asked, cajoled, and finally forced to try to solve unadjudicable problems, courts will inevitably respond in the only manner possible — they will begin exercising managerial authority and the discretion that goes with it. Attempts will be made to disguise the substitution, to preserve appearances, but the process which evolves should (and no doubt eventually will) be recognized for what it is — not adjudication, but an elaborate, expansive masquerade. Henderson, *Expanding the Negligence Concept: Retreat from the Rule of Law*, 51 Ind. L.J. 467, 476-77 (1976).

function. It operates as a rule of law and allows a court to adjudicate rather than manage.[12]

That the rule is identifiable and will predict outcomes in advance of the ultimate decision about recovery enables it to play additional roles. Here we agree with plaintiffs that economic analysis, even at the rudimentary level of jurists, is helpful both in the identification of such roles and the essaying of how the roles play. Thus it is suggested that placing all the consequence of its error on the maritime industry will enhance its incentive for safety. While correct, as far as such analysis goes, such *in terrorem* benefits have an optimal level. Presumably, when the cost of an unsafe condition exceeds its utility there is an incentive to change. As the costs of an accident become increasing multiples of its utility, however, there is a point at which greater accident costs lose meaning, and the incentive curve flattens. When the accident costs are added in large but unknowable amounts the value of the exercise is diminished.

With a disaster inflicting large and reverberating injuries through the economy, as here, we believe the more important economic inquiry is that of relative cost of administration, and in maritime matters administration quickly involves insurance. Those economic losses not recoverable under the present rule for lack of physical damage to a proprietary interest are the subject of first party or loss insurance. The rule change would work a shift to the more costly liability system of third party insurance. For the same reasons that courts have imposed limits on the concept of foreseeability, liability insurance might not be readily obtainable for the types of losses asserted here. As Professor James has noted, "[s]erious practical problems face insurers in handling insurance against potentially wide, open-ended liability. From an insurer's point of view it is not practical to cover, without limit, a liability that may reach catastrophic proportions, or to fix a reasonable premium on a risk that does not lend itself to actuarial measurement." James, *supra*, at 53. By contrast, first party insurance is feasible for many of the economic losses claimed here. Each businessman who might be affected by a disruption of river traffic or by a halt in fishing activities can protect against that eventuality at a relatively low cost since his own potential losses are finite and readily discernible. Thus, to the extent that economic analysis informs our decision here, we think that it favors retention of the present rule. . . .

In conclusion, having reexamined the history and central purpose of the doctrine of *Robins Dry Dock* as developed in this circuit, we remain committed to its teaching. Denying recovery for pure economic losses is a pragmatic limitation on the doctrine of foreseeability, a limitation we find to be both workable and useful. Nor do we find persuasive plaintiffs' arguments that their economic losses are recoverable under a public nuisance theory, as damages for violation of federal statutes, or under state law.

---

12. Fuller, *The Forms and Limits of Adjudication*, 92 Harv. L. Rev. 353, 396 (1978). This case illustrates how our technocratic tradition masks a deep difference in attitudes toward the roles of a judiciary. The difference between the majority and dissenting opinions is far more than a choice between competing maritime rules. The majority is driven by the principle of self ordering and modesty for the judicial role; the dissent accepts a role of management which can strain the limits of adjudication.

Accordingly, the decision of the district court granting summary judgment to defendants on all claims for economic losses unaccompanied by physical damage to property is affirmed.

GEE, Circuit Judge, with whom CLARK, Chief Judge, joins, concurring: . . .

Both the majority opinion and the dissent do our Court proud, joining a few others on that relatively short list of truly distinguished and thoughtful legal writings of which it or any court can boast. Neither opinion, however, confronts explicitly what is for me the overarching issue in the appeal. That issue, a legal one only in the broadest sense and only implicitly presented, is perhaps best addressed in a brief collateral writing such as this will be.

The issue to which I refer is, *who* should deal with questions of such magnitude as the rule for which the dissent contends would, again and again, draw before the courts? An oil spill damages hundreds, perhaps thousands, of miles of coastal area. A cloud of noxious industrial gas leaks out, kills thousands, and injures thousands more. A commonly-used building material is discovered, years after the fact, to possess unforeseen lethal qualities affecting thousands who have worked with it. The long-term effects of inhaling coal dust are found to be disabling to a significant proportion of veteran miners. None of these illustrations is fanciful; each has arisen in recent times and presented itself for resolution to our body politic. Congress has dealt effectively with Black Lung; it has signally failed to deal with the ravages of asbestosis — a scourge, I suspect, far more general and widespread — and a swelling wave of individual asbestosis claims, to be resolved on a case by case basis, pushes slowly through our court system, threatening to inundate it and to consume in punitive damage awards to early claimants the relatively meager assets available to compensate the general class affected, many of whom have not yet suffered the onset of symptoms. It is my thesis that the dispute-resolution systems of courts are poorly equipped to manage disasters of such magnitude and that we should be wary of adopting rules of decision which, as would that contended for by the dissent, encourage the drawing of their broader aspects before us. . . .

If the rule which Judge Wisdom espouses [in dissent] were one written in stone, I would be the first to enforce it by whatever means and procedures, inadequate or no, were available. That is not the question. The question is whether we should *ourselves adopt* such a rule and then proceed to apply it. My answer is that since I do not believe we are capable of administering such a procedure justly, we should not set ourselves the task. Nor am I so clear as my dissenting brethren seem to be about where the high ground lies in these premises. Extending theories of liability may not always be the more moral course, especially in such a case as this, where the extension, in the course of awarding damages to unnumbered claimants for injuries that are unavoidably speculative, may well visit destruction on enterprise after enterprise, with the consequent loss of employment and productive capacity which that entails.

[The separate concurring opinions of Williams and Garwood, JJ., are omitted.]

WISDOM, Circuit Judge, with whom ALVIN B. RUBIN, POLITZ, TATE, and JOHNSON, Circuit Judges, join, dissenting.

This Court's application of *Robins* is out of step with contemporary tort doctrine, works substantial injustice on innocent victims, and is unsupported by the considerations that justified the Supreme Court's 1927 decision. . . .

The resulting bar for claims of economic loss unaccompanied by any physical damage conflicts with conventional tort principles of foreseeability and proximate cause. I would analyze the plaintiffs' claims under these principles, using the "particular damage" requirement of public nuisance law as an additional means of limiting claims. Although this approach requires a case-by-case analysis, it comports with the fundamental idea of fairness that innocent plaintiffs should receive compensation and negligent defendants should bear the cost of their tortious acts. Such a result is worth the additional costs of adjudicating these claims, and this rule of liability appears to be more economically efficient. Finally, this result would relieve courts of the necessity of manufacturing exceptions totally inconsistent with the expanded *Robins* rule of requiring physical injury as a prerequisite to recovery. . . .

One cannot deny that *Robins*'s policy of limiting the set of plaintiffs who can recover for a person's negligence and damage to physical property provides a "bright line" for demarcating the boundary between recovery and nonrecovery. Physical harm suggests a proximate relation between the act and the interference. At bottom, however, the requirement of a tangible injury is artificial because it does not comport with accepted principles of tort law. Mrs. Palsgraf, although physically injured, could not recover. Many other plaintiffs, although physically uninjured, can recover. . . .

With deference to the majority, I suggest, notwithstanding their well reasoned opinion, that the utility derived from having a "bright line" boundary does not outweigh the disutility caused by the limitation on recovery imposed by the physical-damage requirement. *Robins* and its progeny represent a wide departure from the usual tort doctrines of foreseeability and proximate cause. Those doctrines, as refined in the law of public nuisance, provide a rule of recovery that compensates innocent plaintiffs and holds the defendants liable for much of the harm proximately caused by their negligence.

Rather than limiting recovery under an automatic application of a physical damage requirement, I would analyze the plaintiffs' claims under the conventional tort principles of negligence, foreseeability, and proximate causation. I would confine *Robins* to the "factual contours" of that case: A plaintiff's claim may be barred only if the claim is derived solely through contract with an injured party. The majority's primary criticism of this approach to a determination of liability is that it is potentially open ended. Yet, there are well-established tort principles to limit liability for a widely-suffered harm. Under the contemporary law of public nuisance, courts compensate "particularly" damaged plaintiffs for harms suffered from a wide-ranging tort, but deny recovery to more generally damaged parties. Those parties who are foreseeably and proximately injured by an oil spill or closure of a navigable river, for example, and who can also prove damages that are beyond the general economic dislocation that attends such disasters should recover whether or not they had contractual dealings with others who were also damaged by the tortious act. The limitation imposed by "particular" damages, together with refined notions of proximate cause and forseeability [sic], provides a workable scheme of liability that is in step with the rest of tort law, compensates innocent plaintiffs, and imposes the costs of harm on those who caused it. . . .

The advantages of this alternate rule of recovery are that it compensates damaged plaintiffs, imposes the cost of damages upon those who have caused the harm, is consistent with economic principles of modern tort law, and frees courts from the necessity of creating a piecemeal quilt of exceptions to avoid the harsh effects of the *Robins* rule. . . .

If tort law fails to compensate plaintiffs or to impose the cost of damages on those who caused the harm, it should be under a warrant clear of necessity. When a rule of law, once extended, leads to inequitable results and creates principles of recovery that are at odds with the great weight of tort jurisprudence, then that rule of law merits scrutiny. A strict application of the extension denies recovery to many plaintiffs who should be awarded damages.[37] Conventional tort principles of foreseeability, proximate causation, and "particular" damages would avoid such unfairness.

It is true that application of foreseeability and proximate causation would necessitate case-by-case adjudication. But I have a more optimistic assessment of courts' ability to undertake such adjudication than the majority. Certainly such an inquiry would be no different from our daily task of weighing such claims in other tort cases.

The majority opinion also states that the *Robins* rule, being free from the vagaries of factual findings in a case-by-case determination, serves an important normative function because it is more predictable and more "candid." Normative values would also be served, however, by eliminating a broad categorical rule that is insensitive to equitable and social policy concerns that would support allowing the plaintiffs' claims in many individual cases. In assessing "normative concerns," the courts' compass should be a sense of fairness and equity, both of which are better served by allowing plaintiffs to present their claims under usual tort standards. It is not clear, moreover, that a jury's finding of negligence in a case-by-case determination is "less the product of a determinable rule of law" when the finder of fact is guided in its determination by rules of law. The jury's finding of liability in this case would be no more "lawless" than a finding of proximate cause, foreseeability, and particular damages in a physical damage case. . . .

The economic arguments regarding allocation of loss that purportedly favor the *Robins* rule of nonliability are not as clear to me as they appear to be to the majority. It is true that denial of recovery may effectively spread the loss over the victims. It is not certain, however, that victims are generally better insurors against the risk of loss caused by tortious acts having widespread consequences. Although the victims do possess greater knowledge of their circumstances and their potential damages, we do not know whether insurance against these types of losses is readily available to the businesses that may be affected. We do know that insurance against this kind of loss is already available for shippers. Imposition of liability upon the

---

37. A "fishermen's exception" blunts some of the sharpest aspects of this harshness, but it is theoretically difficult to justify that recovery while denying the claims of others similarly situated.

shippers helps ensure that the potential tortfeasor faces incentives to take the proper care. The majority's point is well taken that the incentives to avoid accidents do not increase once potential losses pass a certain measure of enormity. But in truth we have no idea what this measure is: Absent hard data, I would rather err on the side of receiving little additional benefit from imposing additional quanta of liability than err by adhering to *Robins'* inequitable rule and bar victims' recovery on the mistaken belief that a "marginal incentive curve" was flat, or nearly so. If a loss must be borne, it is no worse if a "merely" negligent defendant bears the loss than an innocent plaintiff absorb the damages. . . .

The *Robins* approach restricts liability more severely than the policies behind limitations on liability require and imposes the cost of the accident on the victim, who is usually not in a superior position to obtain insurance to cover this loss. I would apply a rule of recovery based on conventional tort principles of proximate cause and foreseeability and limit eligibility only by the requirement that a claimant prove "particular" damages.

ALVIN B. RUBIN, Circuit Judge, with whom WISDOM, POLITZ and TATE, Circuit Judges, join, dissenting. . . .

Robins should not be applied in cases like this, for the result is a denial of recompense to innocent persons who have suffered a real injury as a result of someone else's fault. We should not flinch from redressing injury because Congress has been indifferent to the problem.

FOOD FOR THOUGHT

Judge Higginbotham's opinion states the majority position in this country: plaintiffs may not recover pure economic losses in tort. It should be noted that the trial court in *Testbank* did not grant summary judgment against the plaintiffs who were commercial oystermen, shrimpers, crabbers, and fishermen, so the validity of their tort claims was not involved in the appeal to the Fifth Circuit. Presumably, these plaintiffs will be allowed to recover in tort if they can prove that they had what amount to "quasi-property interests" in the oysters, shrimp, crabs, and fish destroyed by the chemical spill. These types of tort plaintiffs have come to occupy a special place in litigation involving the negligent destruction of natural resources. In Union Oil Co. v. Oppen, 501 F.2d 558 (9th Cir. 1974), discussed in deleted portions of the opinions in *Testbank*, the claims arose out of the escape of oil from one of the defendant's offshore drilling platforms in the infamous Santa Barbara oil spill in Southern California. The plaintiffs, commercial fishermen, sought to recover for the resulting reduction of the fishing potential in the waters affected by the spill. In ruling that the trial court properly entered judgment for the fisherman on a jury verdict, the California Court of Appeals stated (*id.* at 570-571):

> Finally, it must be understood that our holding in this case does not open the door to claims that may be asserted by those, other than commercial fishermen, whose economic or personal affairs were discommoded by the oil spill of January

28, 1969. The general rule urged upon us by defendants has a legitimate sphere within which to operate. Nothing said in this opinion is intended to suggest, for example, that every decline in the general commercial activity of every business in the Santa Barbara area following the occurrences of 1969 constitutes a legally cognizable injury for which the defendants may be responsible. The plaintiffs in the present action lawfully and directly make use of a resource of the sea, viz. its fish, in the ordinary course of their business. This type of use is entitled to protection from negligent conduct by the defendants in their drilling operations. Both the plaintiffs and defendants conduct their business operations away from land and in, on and under the sea. Both must carry on their commercial enterprises in a reasonably prudent manner. Neither should be permitted negligently to inflict commercial injury on the other. We decide no more than this.

In 532 Madison Avenue Gourmet Foods, Inc. v. Finlandia Center, Inc., 750 N.E.2d 1098 (N.Y. 2001), the New York Court of Appeals considered the issue of recovery in tort for pure economic loss. This decision involved consolidated cases. One case stemmed from the collapse of an office building's 39-story wall, and the other from the collapse of a construction elevator tower. Merchants who did not suffer physical damage but whose businesses were adversely affected economically by the repercussions of the catastrophe brought suit in negligence against the owners, lessees, and managing agents of the collapsed structures. The plaintiffs suffered economic losses when the adjoining streets were closed following the collapse. Before reasserting the traditional rule and denying recovery as a matter of law, the court wrestled with the problems of unlimited liability, and where to draw the line in instances in which the plaintiffs suffered no property damage.

What if the defendant's negligence consists in designing structures owned by the plaintiff? In Indianapolis-Marion County Public Library v. Charlier Clark & Linard, P.C., 929 N.E.2d 722 (2010), the plaintiff public library hired a contractor who hired a firm of architectural engineers to design an underground garage as part of a renovation and expansion project. Negligence on the part of the defendant engineers threatened the structural integrity of the entire project, causing tens of millions in additional costs to remedy. The Supreme Court of Indiana held that the plaintiff sought recovery for pure economic losses and affirmed summary judgment for the design engineers in plaintiff's tort actions. Recovery would have to come, if at all, based on the network of contracts between and among the parties, not from tort law.

DON'T BREAK THE BANK

In Pavlovich v. National City Bank, 435 F.3d 560 (6th Cir. 2006) (applying Ohio law), plaintiff, who lost a large amount of money as a result of the advice of an unscrupulous investment advisor, sought to sue the bank from which dubious transfers were made for negligence in permitting wire transfers from a custodial account to be made based on checks that had been delivered to the bank but had not yet been deposited. Throughout, the bank followed the instructions of its customer giving authority to the investment advisor to deposit and withdraw funds. The court held that the economic-loss rule prevented recovery since the bank was following the directions of its customer set forth in the establishment of the custodial account. The bank had no independent tort duty to question what might seem to be a questionable pattern of deposits and withdrawals.

IF NOT TORT, THEN CONTRACT?

Before you proceed any further into the question of recovery for pure economic loss, you must understand that here we are only talking recovery *in tort*. Little has been said so far regarding whether, in theory, one may recover *in contract* for pure economic loss. (*See Indianapolis-Marion County Public Library*, summarized earlier.) Assuming that the rule in *Testbank, supra*, represents a high-profile, categorical rule against recovery in tort (we will get to exceptions in a moment), is there a parallel rule with respect to recovery in contract? The answer is straightforwardly and unequivocally "No." Indeed, contract law is all about recovering for pure economic losses. Of course, in a case like *Testbank*, it is extremely unlikely that the plaintiffs would have contracted, ahead of time, with the companies that operate ships and barges in the Mississippi River. Marinas, seafood restaurants, and bait shops don't enter such contracts as a general rule. But if, by chance, such contracts had existed, courts would give effect to them. Such a case might arise if the collision in *Testbank* had happened near a specific docking facility at which the container ship was going to dock, and a contract between the ship owner and the dock owner contained a clause allocating to the ship owner all economic losses "caused by mismanagement of the [named] ship while approaching or docking at the [named] facility." The nice question under contract law, of course, would be what meaning to give to the contract language just quoted. But no categorical rule would prohibit the dock owners from recovering in contract from the ship owner, if a contract existed.

hypo 52

T, a commercial cargo transporter, negligently caused an explosion that nearly destroyed *R*'s restaurant, forcing it to close for a month for extensive repairs. *R* brings a tort action against *T* to recover for the costs of repair and the lost profits for the month the restaurant was closed. Will *R*'s claims survive *T*'s motion for summary judgment?

hypo 53

T, a commercial cargo transporter, negligently caused an explosion that resulted in the release of toxic fumes over a wide area of the city. *R*, a restaurant owner, suffered minor property damage to his restaurant as a result of the explosion and was forced to close for a week when, due to the toxic fumes,

could be found to constitute impact. It is interesting that, once impact is established, Georgia allows recovery for mental distress suffered from witnessing injury to a family member. In Lee v. State Farm Mutual Insurance Co., 533 S.E.2d 82 (Ga. 2000), plaintiff and her daughter sustained significant injuries in an auto collision that resulted in the daughter's death an hour later. The plaintiff sued for the emotional distress she suffered from witnessing her daughter's suffering and death. The court reaffirmed its commitment to the impact rule but held that because the plaintiff had suffered physical impact, she could recover for mental distress arising from witnessing injury to her daughter. *See also* Jarrett v. Jones, 258 S.W.3d 442 (Mo. 2008) (plaintiff suffered minor injuries in auto accident; was allowed to recover for emotional upset caused by discovering dead child in other car).

The Supreme Court of Florida formally recognized an exception to the impact rule in Florida Dept. of Corrections v. Abril, 969 So. 2d 201 (Fla. 2007). A Florida statute imposed a duty of confidentiality on testing facilities regarding the results of HIV test information. The plaintiff sought to recover for mental and emotional upset resulting from the defendant's breach of the statute. The trial court dismissed because no impact had occurred. The court of appeals certified the question to the high court, which held that an exception to the impact rule was warranted when the only harm likely to result from the statute's breach is emotional distress without impact.

THE ZONE-OF-DANGER RULE AND EXCEPTIONS

Under the zone-of-danger rule, a plaintiff who (1) is in danger of physical impact, (2) reasonably fears for her own safety, and (3) suffers serious emotional distress because of that fear can recover damages. It is not necessary that she actually suffer an impact, only that she be aware that the defendant has placed her in peril of physical impact. The Restatement, Third, of Torts sets out the following rule:

> ### § 46. Negligent Conduct Directly Inflicting Emotional Disturbance on Another
>
> An actor whose negligent conduct causes serious emotional disturbance to another is subject to liability to the other if the conduct:
>
> (a) places the other in immediate danger of bodily harm and the emotional disturbance results from the danger; or
>
> (b) occurs in the course of specified categories of activities, undertakings, or relationships in which negligent conduct is especially likely to cause serious emotional disturbance.

Note that unless one falls into the exception set forth in (b) (the category of special relationships, to be explained shortly, but which should be familiar from earlier reading) there is no cause of action for negligent infliction of emotional distress when the defendant does not place the plaintiff in immediate danger of *physical harm*. Thus, in Crutcher v. Williams, 12 So. 3d 631 (Ala. 2008), the plaintiff alleged that the defendant physician negligently failed to arrange for immediate medical care, resulting in the plaintiff being driven by a friend on a long, terrifying search for an appropriate care facility, during which the plaintiff feared for her life. The high court ruled against plaintiff as a matter of law, concluding that the plaintiff had shown, at most, fear of future injury. Especially in the absence of any physical detriment flowing from the delay in treatment, the plaintiff did not qualify for the zone-of-danger exception to the impact rule.

The courts draw a sharp distinction between *intentional* and *negligent* infliction of mental distress. In the prior, the plaintiff can make out a cause of action by proving that she suffered severe emotional distress. There need be no threat to the plaintiff's bodily integrity. In the case of negligence absent threat of bodily harm, there is no cause of action even for severe emotional distress.

What kinds of cases qualify for the exception in § 46(b) allowing for recovery for negligent infliction of mental distress absent danger of immediate bodily harm? Consider the following.

Negligent Mishandling of Corpses

One recurring situation in which courts generally impose liability for negligent infliction of emotional distress is when defendants mishandle the remains of the plaintiff's deceased loved ones. In Guth v. Freeland, 28 P.3d 982 (Haw. 2001), the defendant morgue negligently failed to refrigerate the body of the decedent properly, resulting in extreme decay and disfiguration. The plaintiff family members brought actions against the morgue for the emotional harms they allegedly suffered from being deprived of the opportunity of holding an open casket funeral and having observed her remains in their grotesquely deteriorated condition. The trial court granted summary judgment for the defendant, relying on a statute that precluded the recovery of emotional distress damages when damage to "property or material objects" causes the emotional harm. In reversing the ruling below, the Supreme Court of Hawaii held that the policies underlying the statute's goal of limiting recovery for emotional harm did not apply under the facts of the case. The court explained (*id.* at 988):

> [T]he perceived unfairness of holding defendants financially responsible for emotional distress caused by their negligent conduct is ameliorated in cases involving mishandling of a corpse. Due in part to the vulnerability of grieving loved ones . . . and the importance of the opportunity for them to pay their final respects . . . their [emotional] suffering does not seem too remote from defendant's negligence in mishandling the body.

Courts in other jurisdictions have allowed recovery for emotional distress arising out of the negligent handling of corpses. *See, e.g.*, Blackwell v. Dykes Funeral Homes, Inc., 771 N.E.2d 692 (Ind. Ct. App. 2002); Contreraz v. Michelotti-Sawyers, 896 P.2d 1118, 1121 (Mont. 1995); Brown v. Matthews Mortuary, Inc., 801 P.2d 37 (Idaho 1990); Morton v. Maricopa County, 865 P.2d 808 (Ariz. Ct. App. 1993); Carney v. Knollwood Cemetery Ass'n, 514 N.E.2d 430, 435 & n.9 (Ohio Ct. App. 1986); Chesher v. Neyer, 392 F. Supp. 2d 939 (S.D. Ohio 2005) (applying Ohio law).

Some states impose limitations on recovery for emotional distress based on the handling of corpses. For example, in Massaro v. O'Shea Funeral Home, Inc., 738 N.Y.S.2d 384 (N.Y. App. Div. 2002), the deceased's casket was discovered to have been improperly sealed after the deceased's granddaughter noticed an noxious odor coming from the mausoleum where the body was stored. The son and grandson of the deceased were present when the casket was disinterred. All three brought action against the owner of the mausoleum. The court held that, although the grandchildren could not recover because they were not the decedent's next-of-kin, the deceased's son could recover. *See also* Jaynes v. Strong-Thorne Mortuary, 954 P.2d 45 (N.M. 1997) (allowing recovery only when there is a "contemporary sensory perception" of harm to the remains); Gonzalez v. Metropolitan Dade County, 651 So. 2d 673 (Fla. 1995) (recovery only upon a showing of resulting physical injury to plaintiffs, or willful and wanton nature of defendants' conduct).

Negligent Mishandling of Genetic Material

What about recovery for emotional distress caused by negligent handling of plaintiff's genetic material? *See* Frisina v. Women & Infants Hospital of R.I., 2002 R.I. Super. LEXIS 73 (denying recovery for emotional distress due to loss of pre-embryonic genetic material). In Perry-Rogers v. Obasaju, 723 N.Y.S.2d 28 (N.Y. App. Div. 2001), doctors and a fertility clinic negligently implanted an embryo consisting of the plaintiff couple's genetic material into another woman. The clinic informed the plaintiffs that their material had been mistakenly implanted in another woman who was now pregnant, but would not give plaintiffs any information about this other woman, including information about when she had conceived, or when her baby was due to be born. After the woman gave birth to children of two different races, DNA tests were performed, which confirmed that one of the children was the genetic offspring of the plaintiffs. Plaintiffs brought separate actions against the woman and her husband to recover custody of their biological child and to control visitation rights. Plaintiffs also brought an action against the defendant medical providers for medical malpractice, seeking to recover for the emotional distress the plaintiffs had suffered as a result of the mix-up, including loss of the experiences of prenatal bonding, birth, and four months of raising the child. In ruling that this emotional distress was recoverable, the court stated (*id.* at 29-30):

> Damages for emotional harm can be recovered even in the absence of physical injury "when there is a duty owed by defendant to plaintiff, [and a] breach of that duty result[s] directly in emotional harm" (Kennedy v. McKesson Co., 58 N.Y.2d 500, 504). There is no requirement that the plaintiff must be in fear of his or her own physical safety (*see* Johnson v. State of New York, 37 N.Y.2d 378; Topor v. State of New York, 176 Misc. 2d 177, 180). However, "a plaintiff must produce evidence sufficient to guarantee the genuineness of the claim" (Kaufman v. Physical Measurements, 207 A.D.2d 595, 596), such as "contemporaneous or consequential physical harm," which is "thought to provide an index of reliability otherwise absent in a claim for psychological trauma with only psychological

consequences" (Johnson v. State of New York, *supra,* at 381). Here, it was foreseeable that the information that defendants had mistakenly implanted plaintiffs' embryos in a person whom they would not identify, which information was not conveyed until after such person had become pregnant, would cause plaintiffs emotional distress over the possibility that the child that they wanted so desperately, as evidenced by their undertaking the rigors of in vitro fertilization, might be born to someone else and that they might never know his or her fate. These circumstances, together with plaintiffs' medical affidavits attesting to objective manifestations of their emotional trauma, create a "guarantee of genuineness" that makes plaintiffs' claim for emotional distress viable.

In Andrews v. Keltz, 838 N.Y.S.2d 363 (N.Y. Sup. Ct. 2007), the court extended the right to recover even further. In that case, a husband and wife who had provided sperm and eggs for IVF gave birth to a child they suspected came from the sperm of a stranger donor. DNA testing confirmed that, in fact, the sperm was not that of the husband. The trial judge dismissed a cause of action for the emotional distress arising from giving birth to a child that was not of their genetic origin. However, she did allow a cause of action for mental distress because of the "continuing uncertainty and distrust as to whether the genetic material of either or both of them has been inappropriately used for others and that they may have natural children or half children that they are unaware of and they fear that [their child's] natural father may someday claim rights to [their child] thereby interfering with their rights and relationship as [the child's] parents."

Special Relationships

Where the parties have a direct relationship with each other or there has been an undertaking such that there are clear expectations as to appropriate conduct, courts will allow a cause of action for emotional distress even when the plaintiff has not been put in immediate danger of bodily harm. Thus, for example, in Johnson v. State, 334 N.E.2d 590 (N.Y. 1975), a state hospital notified the sister of a patient, Emma Johnson, that the patient had died. The sister notified the patient's daughter, the plaintiff. At Emma's wake, the sister and daughter discovered that the body was not that of their Emma Johnson. It turned out to be another patient at the hospital who also happened to be named Emma Johnson. Both the sister and daughter sued the hospital for emotional distress. At the trial, the court awarded the daughter damages, but not the sister. The Appellate Division reversed the daughter's recovery for emotional harm. The daughter, but not the sister, appealed, and the Court of Appeals held that the daughter was entitled to recover (*id.* at 593):

> In this case, . . . the injury was inflicted by the hospital directly on claimant by its negligent sending of a false message announcing her mother's death. Claimant was not indirectly harmed by injury caused to another; she was not a mere eyewitness of or bystander to injury caused to another. Instead, she was the one to whom a duty was directly owed by the hospital, and the one who was directly injured by the hospital's breach of that duty.

See also S. Alaska Carpenters' Health and Security Trust Fund v. Jones, 177 P.3d 844 (Alaska 2008) (employer misrepresented to plaintiffs that they were covered by health insurance; preexisting employment relationship supported claim for mental upset when the plaintiffs discovered the truth after birth of Down syndrome child). The doctor-patient relationship has been held to be sufficient to sustain a claim for emotional distress absent threat of immediate bodily harm. *See, e.g.,* Keim v. Potter, 783 N.E.2d 731 (Ind. Ct. App. 2003) (physician negligently gave the wrong test and diagnosed the patient with hepatitis C, thus causing the patient to suffer serious emotional distress); Acosta v. Byrum, 638 S.E.2d 246 (N.C. Ct. App. 2006) (psychiatrist gave access code to patient's medical records to a person who held personal animus toward the plaintiff, causing emotional distress); Broadnax v. Gonzalez, 809 N.E.2d 645 (N.Y. 2004) (negligence of obstetrician brought about stillbirth of twins; court recognized a cause of action for mental distress on behalf of the mother even absent physical harm to her). Similarly the lawyer-client relationship was sufficient to support a claim for negligent infliction of emotional distress in Rowell v. Holt, 850 So. 2d 474 (Fla. 2003). Plaintiff was arrested for being a felon in possession of a gun. Although he had been convicted of a felony some 30 years earlier, he had his civil rights restored to him some 20 years before the arrest. Plaintiff gave the paper showing the restoration of his civil rights that absolved him of the crime for which he was arrested, but the public defender did not act on it. As a result, plaintiff spent ten needless days in jail. In allowing the claim for emotional distress, the court noted the special professional duty created by the lawyer-client relationship.

Some courts have viewed a contractual relationship as sufficient to trigger a cause of action for negligent infliction of emotional distress. In Carrol v. Allstate Insurance Co., 815 A.2d 119 (Conn. 2003), the court upheld an award of $500,000 for emotional distress on behalf of an insured who was refused payment on a fire loss based on their belief that the fire was started by arson. The court held that there was sufficient evidence to conclude that the investigation was hasty and incompetent, and that the investigator was motivated to find arson in order to ensure his future employment and because he harbored racial prejudice against the insured.

hypo 55

A, a neighbor of *B*, was out shopping when he saw a serious accident with a car identical to that owned by *B*'s wife. When the emergency ambulance arrived, he thought he heard the paramedic say that the woman driver would not make it alive to the hospital. *A* ran over to *B*'s house and saw *B* just coming home from work. *A* told *B* that his wife was in a serious accident and that she "probably is dead by now." *A* was mistaken. It was not the paramedic who made the statement but rather a bystander who thought the injury was very serious. As it turned out, *B*'s wife was not seriously injured. *B* suffered severe emotional distress. He has had constant recurring nightmares. The trauma of the event also triggered a bout with depression. *B* is now taking antidepressants and is under psychiatric care. Does *B* have a cause of action against *A*?

Emotional Distress or Physical Manifestations

Restatement, Third, of Torts allows recovery for negligently inflicted emotional distress even if plaintiff has no evidence of physical manifestations. Although many courts agree with the Restatement position, others do not. *See, e.g.,* Frogley v. Meridian Joint Sch. Dist. No. 2, 314 P.3d 613, 624 (Idaho 2013); O'Donnell v. HCA Health Services of N.H. Inc., 883 A.2d 319 (N.H. 2005) (physical symptoms are necessary to ensure that emotional injury is sufficiently serious); Cole v. D. J. Quirk, Inc., 2001 WL 705730 (Mass. App. Div. 2001) (physical harm is necessary to guard against frivolous claims of emotional distress). For courts agreeing with the Restatement view and allowing recovery for serious emotional distress without physical manifestations, *see, e.g.,* Camper v. Minor, 915 S.W.2d 437 (Tenn. 1996); Taylor v. Baptist Medical Center, Inc., 400 So. 2d 369 (Ala. 1981); Molien v. Kaiser Foundation Hospitals, 616 P.2d 813 (Cal. 1980); Corgan v. Muehling, 574 N.E.2d 602 (Ill. 1991). In the following case, do you suppose the plaintiff is faking her distress? Should it make a difference whether she testified to experiencing sleeplessness, headaches, nausea, and other physical manifestations of her emotional distress? Note the difference in the standards allowing recovery for intentional and negligent infliction of emotional distress. Why are courts concerned to draw the boundaries as they do between cases in which recovery is permitted and those in which someone who suffered serious emotional distress is left to "lump it" without compensation from the wrongdoer?

TELLO v. ROYAL CARIBBEAN CRUISES, LTD.
939 F.Supp.2d 1269 (S.D. Fla. 2013)

JOAN A. LENARD, District Judge.

THIS CAUSE is before the Court on Defendant Royal Caribbean Cruises, Ltd.'s Motion to Dismiss Plaintiff's Amended Complaint

I. Background

Plaintiff's Amended Complaint alleges the following.

In January 2011, Plaintiff Margarita Tello and son Jose Miguel Pietri Tello were passengers aboard Defendant's cruise ship, "The Liberty of the Seas." Jose had recently turned twenty-one. On the night of January 4, 2011, Jose and his friends went to the cruise ship's bar/dance club. Bartenders served Jose multiple alcoholic beverages, and Jose became intoxicated.

Jose said goodnight to his friends and left the club at around 3 a.m. He proceeded to walk around the cruise ship in an inebriated and disoriented state. At around 3:30 a.m., Jose encountered a crewmember who was cleaning the game room at one of the ship's ocean decks. Jose appeared intoxicated to the crewmember, and the crewmember could sense that "something was wrong." Nonetheless, the crewmember did nothing to assist Jose. Jose exited the game room and proceeded to walk around the ocean deck. He attempted to reenter the interior of the ship twice, but the doors that he tried to open were locked. Jose then approached a service ladder and began climbing the outside railing, apparently hoping to get down to a lower deck and find access to reenter the ship. He fell overboard and presumably drowned.

When Jose fell overboard, the ship was approaching Belize City, Belize. Belize Coast Guard officers were not notified until 11 a.m. that a passenger from ship had fallen overboard. The ship allegedly maintained 800 closed circuit television cameras on board. At the time of Jose's fall, however, no one was manning the surveillance room.

At some point Margarita discovered that Jose had not returned to their cabin. She went walking around the ship to look for him and notified cruise employees that she was looking for her son. At around 7 a.m., an unidentified crewmember told Margarita that her son was likely sleeping in someone else's cabin. Margarita insisted that Jose would not act that way and requested that a search be conducted.

Following review of video footage showing Jose's fall, the ship's captain or someone in similar uniform told Margarita that her son had committed suicide. Margarita is a devout Catholic, and in the theology of the Catholic Church, death by suicide is allegedly a "grave or serious sin, preventing the sinner's soul from eternal life." Margarita thus concluded that Jose's "soul [was] not at rest," that she would "not meet [Jose] again in the afterlife," and that Jose had "gone to hell."

Margarita filed this action against Royal Caribbean raising [claims under the Death on the High Seas Act (DOHSA) as well as negligence claims under Florida law] . . .

Royal Caribbean moves, pursuant to Federal Rule of Civil Procedure 12(b)(6), to dismiss the Amended Complaint in its entirety. Royal Caribbean argues in relevant part that . . . the Amended Complaint fails to adequately allege negligent, hiring, retention, training, or supervision, negligent infliction of emotional distress, intentional infliction of emotional distress, or *respondeat superior*/agency liability . . .

IV. Discussion

c. Negligent Infliction of Emotional Distress (Count III)

Under Florida law, the so-called "impact rule" generally requires that "'before a plaintiff can recover damages for emotional distress caused by the negligence of another, the emotional distress suffered must flow from physical injuries the plaintiff sustained in an impact.'" *Fla. Dep't of Corr. v. Abril,* 969 So. 2d 201, 206 (Fla. 2007) (quoting *R.J. v. Humana of Fla., Inc.,* 652 So. 2d 360, 362 (Fla. 1995)).

To maintain a negligent-infliction-of-emotional-distress claim in the absence of a direct impact, "the complained-of mental distress must be 'manifested by physical injury,' the plaintiff must be 'involved' in the incident by seeing, hearing, or arriving on the scene as the traumatizing event occurs, ***and*** the plaintiff must suffer the complained-of mental distress and accompanying physical impairment 'within a short time' of the incident." *Willis v. Gami Golden Glades, LLC,* 967 So. 2d 846, 849 (Fla. 2007) (quoting *Eagle-Picher Indus., Inc. v. Cox,* 481 So. 2d 517, 526 (Fla. Dist. Ct. App. 1985)).

In short, a plaintiff claiming negligent infliction of emotional distress must show "either impact upon one's person or, in certain situations, at a minimum the manifestation of emotional distress in the form of a discernible physical injury or illness." *Gracey v. Eaker,* 837 So.2d 348, 355 (Fla.2002).

Based on the foregoing, the Court finds Margarita's allegations insufficient to state a claim for negligent infliction of emotional distress. The allegedly tortious conduct in this case — *i.e.,* a captain's communication to Margarita that her son had committed suicide — involved no physical impact to Margarita.[1] To sustain her claim, therefore, Margarita must allege some manifestation of physical injury beyond mere mental distress. Margarita's Amended Complaint avers only that she "has suffered severe and debilitating mental anguish, and has suffered other severe and debilitating effects such as emotional distress proximately caused by said conduct, which has irreparably, severely and permanently harmed" her. As Margarita suffered no impact and alleges no physical injury resulting from the conduct at issue, the Court finds that Margarita has pled insufficient factual matter to sustain her negligent-infliction-of-emotional-distress claim.

d. Intentional Infliction of Emotional Distress (Count IV)

To prove intentional infliction of emotional distress under Florida law, the plaintiff must establish: (1) deliberate or reckless infliction of mental suffering; (2) by outrageous conduct; (3) which conduct must have caused the suffering; and (4) the suffering must have been severe. *Metro. Life Ins. Co. v. McCarson,* 467 So. 2d 277, 278 (Fla. 1985). Behavior claimed to constitute the intentional infliction of emotional distress must be so outrageous in character, and so extreme in degree, as to go beyond all possible bounds of decency. *Ponton v. Scarfone,* 468 So. 2d 1009, 1011 (Fla. Dist. Ct. App. 1985). The court must evaluate the conduct as objectively as possible to determine whether it is atrocious and utterly intolerable in a civilized community.

Here the Court finds Plaintiff's allegations insufficient to state a claim for intentional infliction of emotional distress. One cannot say that the captain's allegedly tortious conduct — *i.e.,* informing Margarita that Jose had committed suicide — was "so outrageous in character, and so extreme in degree, as to go beyond all possible bounds of decency." The reality is that Jose had in fact climbed a railing and fallen overboard. This is not a situation in which, with no justification or factual predicate, the captain decided to play a joke on Margarita by falsely informing her of her son's death. *Cf.* Restatement (Second) of Torts § 46 cmt. d, illus. 1 (1965) ("As a practical joke, A falsely tells B that her husband has been badly injured in an accident, and is in the hospital with both legs broken. B suffers severe emotional distress. A is subject to liability to B for her emotional distress"). There is also no indication, nor any reasonable inference, that the ship's captain knew of

---

1. [Isn't the relevant conduct for a *negligent* infliction of emotional distress claim not the statement by the captain but other acts by the cruise line's employees, such as serving Jose too much to drink, not coming to his assistance when he was staggering around intoxicated, not monitoring the cameras set up for purposes including detecting passengers going overboard, not initiating search-and-rescue operations immediately when he was discovered missing, and the like? — Eds.]

Margarita's religious faith and characterized Jose's death as a "suicide" with the intention of causing Margarita extra emotional suffering. For these reasons, the Court finds Plaintiff's claim unsustainable. *See also Wallis v. Princess Cruises, Inc.,* 306 F.3d 827, 842 (9th Cir. 2002) (although ship's master stated that plaintiff's husband was "probably dead and that his body would be sucked under the ship, chopped up by the propellers, and probably not be recovered," such conduct was not "extreme and outrageous," and "there [was] nothing in the record to support a finding that anybody from Princess went out of their way to torment or mistreat the Plaintiff in a manner that our society could view as utterly deplorable").

FOOD FOR THOUGHT

If you were confused reading this case, you are not alone. Florida follows the impact rule, with limited exceptions. Those exceptions are stated in a 1985 case:

> If, however, the plaintiff has not suffered an impact, the complained-of mental distress must be "manifested by physical injury," the plaintiff must be "involved" in the incident by seeing, hearing, or arriving on the scene as the traumatizing event occurs, ***and*** the plaintiff must suffer the complained-of mental distress and accompanying physical impairment "within a short time" of the incident.

Eagle-Picher Indus., Inc. v. Cox, 481 So. 2d 517, 526 (Fla. Dist. Ct. App. 1985) (emphasis added). This case was quoted in Willis v. Gami Golden Glades, LLC, 967 So. 2d 846, 849 (Fla. 2007), and cited by the district court in the *Tello* case. But right down below that quote the court cites Gracey v. Eaker, 837 So. 2d 348, 355 (Fla.2002), for the proposition that a plaintiff must show "***either*** impact upon one's person **or**, in certain situations, at a minimum the manifestation of emotional distress in the form of a discernible physical injury or illness" (emphasis added). Which is it, "and" or "or"? *Gracey*, the case cited for the "or" version of the rule, relies on a so-called wrongful birth case, which we'll take up in Section D. That case, Kush v. Lloyd, 616 So. 2d 415, 422 (Fla. 1992), stated that the impact rule should not apply to "recognized torts in which damages often are predominately emotional, such as defamation or invasion of privacy." And, as noted above, Florida Dept. of Corrections v. Abril, 969 So. 2d 201, 207 (Fla. 2007), held that the impact rule does not apply to the negligent disclosure of the results of the plaintiff's HIV test, because "the emotional damages resulting from the dissemination of confidential HIV test results are foreseeable and grave." *Abril* relied on *Gracey, supra,* in which a psychotherapist was held liable for emotional distress damages after disclosing confidential information conveyed separately by a husband and wife during marital counseling.

Isn't the injury suffered by the plaintiff in *Tello* "predominantly emotional"? Is the problem that Margarita is too remote from the cruise line's negligence with respect to Jose to be entitled to protection from emotional harm? If so, why doesn't the court just say that? Recall the Third Restatement's treatment of emotional harm. Section 46(b) permits recovery of emotional distress damages from "[a]n actor whose negligent conduct causes serious emotional disturbance to another . . . if the conduct . . . occurs in the course of specified categories of activities, undertakings, or relationships in which negligent conduct is especially likely to cause serious emotional disturbance." In other words, if there is a special relationship between the plaintiff and the defendant, emotional distress damages may be recoverable. As we stressed earlier, however, you should beware of the tendency to use the term "special relationship" in a question-begging way. Used properly, the existence of a special relationship is the conclusion of an argument, not a premise in it.

As the next section shows, courts have struggled to articulate standards for determining which plaintiffs are close enough — literally and metaphorically — to the victims of accidents to be entitled to recover emotional distress damages. Inability to determine the genuineness of the plaintiff's distress is often cited as a reason for limiting recovery, but can there be any doubt about the anguish experienced by a mother whose son died on a celebratory cruise? What might be other reasons for precluding the plaintiff from recovering in this case? As you read the summary of *Dillon* and the *Thing* case, think about whether you believe a plaintiff like Margarita ought to be able to recover emotional distress damages from a negligent actor who caused the death of a loved one.

THE BYSTANDER DILEMMA

We turn now to a thorny problem that has no good solution. Should the law recognize a derivative cause of action for emotional distress arising from witnessing injury or death to a third person brought about by the negligence of the defendant? In Waube v. Warrington, 258 N.W. 497 (Wis. 1935), the plaintiff's decedent was looking out the window of her house, watching her child cross the highway, when she witnessed the defendant negligently run over and kill her child. She died from the result of her shock. Relying on the *Palsgraf* decision set forth in Chapter 5, the court denied plaintiff's recovery as a matter of law, concluding (*id.* at 500):

> It is one thing to say that as to those who are put in peril of physical impact, impact is immaterial if physical injury is caused by shock arising from the peril. It is the foundation of cases holding to this liberal ruling, that the person affrighted or sustaining shock was actually put in peril of physical impact, and under these conditions it was considered immaterial that the physical impact did not materialize. It is quite another thing to say that those who are out of the field of physical danger through impact shall have a legally protected right to be free from emotional distress occasioned by the peril of others, when that distress results in physical impairment. The answer to this question cannot be reached solely by logic, nor is it clear that it can be entirely disposed of by a consideration of what the defendant ought reasonably to have anticipated as a consequence of his wrong. The answer must be reached by balancing the social interests involved in order to ascertain how far the defendant's duty and plaintiff's right may justly and expediently be extended. It is our conclusion that they can neither justly nor expediently be extended to any recovery for physical injuries sustained by one out of the range of ordinary physical peril as a result of the shock of witnessing another's danger. Such consequences are so unusual and extraordinary, viewed after the event, that a user of the highway may be said not to subject others to an

unreasonable risk of them by the careless management of his vehicle. Further-more, the liability imposed by such a doctrine is wholly out of proportion to the culpability of the negligent tortfeasor, would put an unreasonable burden upon users of the highway, open the way to fraudulent claims, and enter a field that has no sensible or just stopping point.

Note that in these bystander-recovery cases there is plenty of "impact." Someone is physically injured or killed. The question now is should we borrow the "zone-of-danger" concept to limit liability and deny recovery unless the plaintiff suffering the emotional distress was personally threatened. The first case to break the "zone-of-danger" blockade in bystander cases arose in California. The fact pattern in the *Waube* decision in Wisconsin was presented to a famously pro-plaintiff court in Dillon v. Legg, 441 P.2d 912 (Cal. 1968). Although California had adopted the zone-of-danger rule several years earlier, the facts in *Dillon* did not satisfy the *Waube* criteria. A mother and her two daughters were crossing the street when a car hit and killed one of the children. The mother and surviving child both brought action against the defendant driver for emotional harm they suffered as a result of observing the death of the other daughter. Applying the zone-of-danger rule, the trial court entered summary judgment against the mother because she was still on the curb at the time of the accident, but denied the defendant's motion against the surviving daughter because the evidence indicated that she may have stepped into the road by that time. Referring to "the hopeless artificiality of the zone-of-danger rule," the Supreme Court of California struggled to formulate a new test that would avoid both the arbitrariness of the zone-of-danger rule and the open-ended liability that would flow from a pure foreseeability-based test. In reinstating the mother's complaint in *Dillon*, the court stated (*id.* at 919-921):

> We note, first, that we deal here with a case in which plaintiff suffered a shock which resulted in physical injury and we confine our ruling to that case. In determining, in such a case, whether defendant should reasonably foresee the injury to plaintiff, or, in other terminology, whether defendant owes plaintiff a duty of due care, the courts will take into account such factors as the following: (1) Whether plaintiff was located near the scene of the accident as contrasted with one who was a distance away from it. (2) Whether the shock resulted from a direct emotional impact upon plaintiff from the sensory and contemporaneous obser-vance of the accident, as contrasted with the learning of the accident from others after its occurrence. (3) Whether plaintiff and the victim were closely related, as contrasted with an absence of any relationship or the presence of only a distant relationship. . . .
>
> In light of these factors the court will determine whether the accident and harm was *reasonably* foreseeable. Such reasonable foreseeability does not turn on whether the particular [defendant] as an individual would have in actuality fore-seen the exact accident and loss; it contemplates that courts, on a case-to-case basis, analyzing all the circumstances, will decide what the ordinary man under such circumstances should reasonably have foreseen. The courts thus mark out the areas of liability, excluding the remote and unexpected. . . .

Many courts, faced with the bystander problem after *Dillon*, have followed that case in permitting recovery by persons outside the zone of danger who feared for the safety of others. Adhering to the zone-of-danger rule is Consolidated Rail Corp. v. Gottshall, 512 U.S. 532 (1994). Among the state courts more or less following *Dillon*, no consistent decisional pattern has emerged with respect to just what plaintiff must prove to recover. Even the lower California courts have had difficulty in parsing *Dillon*. For example, in Parsons v. Superior Court, 146 Cal. Rptr. 495 (Cal. Ct. App. 1978), the court held that the plaintiff's arrival at the scene of an accident involving his two daughters "before the dust had settled" was not enough to support recovery. But in Nevels v. Yeager, 199 Cal. Rptr. 300 (Cal. Ct. App. 1984), the primary victim's mother, who arrived at the scene ten minutes after the accident while the victim was still there, stated a cause of action.

The turmoil among the courts, both inside and outside California, led the Supreme Court of California to revisit the issue in the following case.

THING v. LA CHUSA
771 P.2d 814 (Cal. 1989)

[Plaintiff was near the scene where her young son was injured in an automobile accident, but the plaintiff did not witness the accident. She came upon the scene moments later and saw her son in a badly injured condition. She brought suit against the defendants for her resulting emotional harm. The trial judge granted the defendants' motion for summary judgment; the Court of Appeal reversed. The defendant appealed to the Supreme Court of California.]

EAGLESON, Justice.

The narrow issue presented by the parties in this case is whether the Court of Appeal correctly held that a mother who did not witness an accident in which an automobile struck and injured her child may recover damages from the negligent driver for the emotional distress she suffered when she arrived at the accident scene. The more important question this issue poses for the court, however, is whether the "guidelines" enunciated by this court in Dillon v. Legg (Cal. 1968) . . . 441 P.2d 912, are adequate, or if they should be refined to create greater certainty in this area of the law.

. . . [W]e shall conclude that the societal benefits of certainty in the law, as well as traditional concepts of tort law, dictate limitation of bystander recovery of damages for emotional distress. In the absence of physical injury or impact to the plaintiff himself, damages for emotional distress should be recoverable only if the plaintiff: (1) is closely related to the injury victim; (2) is present at the scene of the injury-producing event at the time it occurs and is then aware that it is causing injury to the victim; and (3) as a result suffers emotional distress beyond that which would be anticipated in a disinterested witness. . . .

[The court surveyed the law leading up to Dillon v. Legg.]. . . . In the ensuing 20 years, like the pebble cast into the pond, *Dillon*'s progeny have created ever widening circles of liability. Post-*Dillon* decisions have now permitted plaintiffs who suffer emotional distress, but no resultant physical injury, and who were not at the scene of and thus did not witness the event that injured another, to recover damages on grounds that a duty was owed to them solely because it was foreseeable that they would suffer that distress on learning of injury to a close relative. . . .

[W]hile the court [in *Dillon*] indicated that foreseeability of the injury was to be the primary consideration in finding duty, it simultaneously recognized that policy considerations mandated that infinite liability be avoided by restrictions that would somehow narrow the class of potential plaintiffs. But the test limiting liability was itself amorphous. . . .

The *Dillon* court anticipated and accepted uncertainty in the short term in application of its holding, but was confident that the boundaries of this NIED [Negligent Infliction of Emotional Distress] action could be drawn in future cases. In sum, as former Justice Potter Stewart once suggested with reference to that undefinable category of materials that are obscene, the *Dillon* court was satisfied that trial and appellate courts would be able to determine the existence of a duty because the court would know it when it saw it. (*See* Jacobellis v. Ohio (1964) 378 U.S. 184, 197, 84 S. Ct. 1676, 1683, 12 L. Ed. 2d 793 (conc. opn. of Stewart, J.).) Underscoring the questionable validity of that assumption, however, was the obvious and unaddressed problem that the injured party, the negligent tortfeasor, their insurers, and their attorneys had no means short of suit by which to determine if a duty such as to impose liability for damages would be found in cases other than those that were "on all fours" with *Dillon*. Thus, the only thing that was foreseeable from the *Dillon* decision was the uncertainty that continues to this time as to the parameters of the third-party NIED action. . . .

The expectation of the *Dillon* majority that the parameters of the tort would be further defined in future cases has not been fulfilled. Instead, subsequent decisions of the Courts of Appeal and this court, have created more uncertainty. And, just as the "zone of danger" limitation was abandoned in *Dillon* as an arbitrary restriction on recovery, the *Dillon* guidelines have been relaxed on grounds that they, too, created arbitrary limitations on recovery. Little consideration has been given in post-*Dillon* decisions to the importance of avoiding the limitless exposure to liability that the pure foreseeability test of "duty" would create and towards which these decisions have moved.

[The court's discussion of the post-*Dillon* California cases is omitted.]

. . . Not surprisingly, this "case-to-case" or ad hoc approach to development of the law that misled the Court of Appeal in this case has not only produced inconsistent rulings in the lower courts, but has provoked considerable critical comment by scholars who attempt to reconcile the cases. . . .

Our own prior decisions identify factors that will appropriately circumscribe the right to damages, but do not deny recovery to plaintiffs whose emotional injury is real even if not accompanied by out-of-pocket expense. Notwithstanding the broad language in some of those decisions, it is clear that foreseeability of the injury alone is not a useful "guideline" or a meaningful restriction on the scope of the NIED action. . . . It is apparent that reliance on foreseeability of injury alone in finding a duty, and thus a right to recover, is not adequate when the damages sought are for an intangible injury. In order to avoid limitless liability out of all proportion to the degree of a defendant's negligence, and against which it is impossible to insure without imposing unacceptable costs on those among whom the risk is spread, the right to recover for negligently caused emotional distress must be limited.

[The court's discussion of the *Dillon* factors involving the relationship of the plaintiff to the primary victim is omitted. The court discussed a variety of contexts in which that issue can arise, including claims for loss of consortium.]

Similar reasoning justifies limiting recovery to persons closely related by blood or marriage since, in common experience, it is more likely that they will suffer a greater degree of emotional distress than a disinterested witness to negligently caused pain and suffering or death. Such limitations are indisputably arbitrary since it is foreseeable that in some cases unrelated persons have a relationship to the victim or are so affected by the traumatic event that they suffer equivalent emotional distress. As we have observed, however, drawing arbitrary lines is unavoidable if we are to limit liability and establish meaningful rules for application by litigants and lower courts.

No policy supports extension of the right to recover for NIED to a larger class of plaintiffs. Emotional distress is an intangible condition experienced by most persons, even absent negligence, at some time during their lives. Close relatives suffer serious, even debilitating, emotional reactions to the injury, death, serious illness, and evident suffering of loved ones. These reactions occur regardless of the cause of the loved one's illness, injury, or death. That relatives will have severe emotional distress is an unavoidable aspect of the "human condition." The emotional distress for which monetary damages may be recovered, however, ought not to be that form of acute emotional distress or the transient emotional reaction to the occasional gruesome or horrible incident to which every person may potentially be exposed in an industrial and sometimes violent society. Regardless of the depth of feeling or the resultant physical or mental illness that results from witnessing violent events, persons unrelated to those injured or killed may not now recover for such emotional upheaval even if negligently caused. Close relatives who witness the accidental injury or death of a loved one and suffer emotional trauma may not recover when the loved one's conduct was the cause of that emotional trauma. The overwhelming majority of "emotional distress" which we endure, therefore, is not compensable.

Unlike an award of damages for intentionally caused emotional distress which is punitive, the award for NIED simply reflects society's belief that a negligent actor bears some responsibility for the effect of his conduct on persons other than those who suffer physical injury. In identifying those persons and the circumstances in which the defendant will be held to redress the injury, it is appropriate to restrict recovery to those persons who will suffer an emotional impact beyond the impact that can be anticipated whenever one learns that a relative is injured, or dies, or the emotion felt by a "disinterested" witness. The class of potential plaintiffs should be limited to those who because of their relationship suffer the greatest emotional distress. When the right to recover is limited in this manner, the liability bears a reasonable relationship to the culpability of the negligent defendant.

The elements which justify and simultaneously limit an award of damages for emotional distress caused by awareness of the negligent infliction of injury to a close relative are . . . the traumatic emotional effect on the plaintiff who contemporaneously observes both the event or conduct that causes serious injury to a close relative and the injury itself. Even if it is "foreseeable" that persons other than closely related percipient witnesses may suffer emotional distress, this fact does not justify the imposition of what threatens to become unlimited liability for emotional distress on a defendant whose conduct is simply negligent. Nor does such abstract "foreseeability" warrant continued reliance on the assumption that the limits of liability will become any clearer if lower courts are permitted to continue approaching the issue on a "case-to-case" basis some 20 years after *Dillon*.

We conclude, therefore, that a plaintiff may recover damages for emotional distress caused by observing the negligently inflicted injury of a third person if, but only if, said plaintiff: (1) is closely related to the injury victim; (2) is present at the scene of the injury producing event at the time it occurs and is then aware that it is causing injury to the victim; and (3) as a result suffers serious emotional distress — a reaction beyond that which would be anticipated in a disinterested witness and which is not an abnormal response to the circumstances. These factors were present in . . . each of this court's prior decisions upholding recovery for NIED.

The undisputed facts establish that plaintiff was not present at the scene of the accident in which her son was injured. She did not observe defendant's conduct and was not aware that her son was being injured. She could not, therefore, establish a right to recover for the emotional distress she suffered when she subsequently learned of the accident and observed its consequences. The order granting summary judgment was proper.

The judgment of the Court of Appeal is reversed.

KAUFMAN, Justice, concurring.

We granted review in this case because of the obvious and continuing difficulties that have plagued trial courts and litigants in the area of negligent infliction of emotional distress. Of course, any meaningful review of the issue necessarily entails reappraising, in the light of 20 years of experience, our landmark holding in Dillon v. Legg (Cal. 1968) . . . 441 P.2d at 912, that a plaintiff may recover for the emotional distress induced by the apprehension of negligently caused injury to a third person. Two such "reappraisals" have now been suggested.

The majority opinion by Justice Eagleson proposes to convert *Dillon*'s flexible "guidelines" for determining whether the risk of emotional injury was foreseeable or within the defendant's duty of care, into strict "elements" necessary to recovery. While conceding that such a doctrinaire approach will necessarily lead to "arbitrary" results, Justice Eagleson nevertheless concludes that "[g]reater certainty and a more reasonable limit on the exposure to liability for negligent conduct" require strict limitations. (Maj. opn., . . . p. 828 of 771 P.2d.)

Justice Broussard, in dissent, opposes the effort to rigidify the *Dillon* guidelines. He urges, instead, that the court remain faithful to the guidelines as originally conceived — as specific but "flexible" limitations on liability — and adhere to *Dillon*'s original reliance on "foreseeability as a general limit on tort liability." (Dis. opn. of Broussard, J., . . . p. 817 of 771 P.2d.) Justice Broussard denies that *Dillon* has failed to afford adequate guidance to the lower courts or to confine liability within reasonable limits. On the contrary, the *Dillon* approach, in the dissent's view, has provided — and continues to provide — a workable and "*principled* basis for determining liability. . . ." (*Id.*, . . . at p. 844 of 771 P.2d, italics added.)

✍ With all due respect, I do not believe that either the majority opinion or the dissent has articulated a genuinely "principled" rule of law. On the one hand, experience has shown that rigid doctrinal limitations on bystander liability, such as that suggested by Justice Eagleson, result inevitably in disparate treatment of plaintiffs in substantially the same position. To be sure, the majority freely — one might say almost cheerfully — acknowledges that its position is arbitrary; yet nowhere does it consider the *cost* of such institutionalized caprice, not only to the individuals involved, but to the integrity of the judiciary as a whole. ✍

On the other hand, two decades of adjudication under the inexact guidelines created by *Dillon* and touted by the dissent, has, if anything, created a body of case law marked by even greater confusion and inconsistency of result.

The situation, therefore, calls for a wholesale reappraisal of the wisdom of permitting recovery for emotional distress resulting from injury to others. . . .

While the courts rejecting bystander liability have cited a number of reasons, one argument in particular has been considered dispositive: *Dillon*'s confident prediction that future courts would be able to fix just and sensible boundaries on bystander liability has been found to be wholly illusory — both in theory and in practice. . . .

Twenty-five years ago, this court posed a series of rhetorical questions concerning the guidelines later adopted in *Dillon*: "[H]ow soon is 'fairly contemporaneous'? What is the magic in the plaintiff's being 'present'? Is the shock any less immediate if the mother does not know of the accident until the injured child is brought home? And what if the plaintiff is present at the scene but is nevertheless unaware of the danger or injury to the third person until shortly after the accident has occurred? . . ." (Amaya v. Home Ice, Fuel & Supply Co, *supra*, . . . 379 P.2d 513 (Cal. 1963).) As the foregoing sampling of *Dillon*'s progeny vividly demonstrates, we are no closer to answers today than we were then. The questions, however, are no longer hypothetical — they are real: Is there any rational basis to infer that Mrs. Arauz was any less traumatized than Mrs. Dillon because she saw her bloody infant five minutes after it was struck by defendant's car? Was the Hathaways' suffering mitigated by the fact that they witnessed their child literally in death's throes, but failed to witness the precipitating event? Could it be argued that the emotional distress is even more traumatic, more foreseeable, for parents such as the Hathaways who fail to witness the accident and later blame themselves for allowing it to occur?

Clearly, to apply the *Dillon* guidelines strictly and deny recovery for emotional distress because the plaintiff was not a contemporaneous eyewitness of the accident but viewed the immediate consequences, ill serves the policy of compensating foreseeable victims of emotional trauma. Yet once it is admitted that temporal and spatial limitations bear no rational relationship to the likelihood of psychic injury, it becomes impossible to define, as the *Amaya* court well understood, any "sensible or just stopping point." (. . . 379 P. 2d at 513.) By what humane and principled standard might a court decide, as a matter of law, that witnessing the bloody and chaotic aftermath of an accident involving a loved one is compensable if viewed within 1 minute of impact but noncompensable after 15? or 30? Is the shock of standing by while others undertake frantic efforts to save the life of one's child any less real or foreseeable when it occurs in an ambulance or emergency room rather than at the "scene"?

Obviously, a "flexible" construction of the *Dillon* guidelines cannot, ultimately, avoid drawing arbitrary and irrational distinctions any more than a strict construction. Justice Burke was right when he observed of the *Dillon* guidelines, "Upon analysis, their seeming certainty evaporates into arbitrariness, and inexplicable distinctions appear." (Dillon v. Legg, *supra*, . . . 441 P.2d at 912, dis. opn. of Burke, J.) . . .

Of course, it could be argued that recovery — not rationality — is the essential thing; that ultimately justice is better served by arbitrarily denying recovery to some, than by absolutely denying recovery to all. I find this argument to be unpersuasive, however, for two reasons.

First, the cost of the institutionalized caprice which *Dillon* has wrought should not be underestimated. The foremost duty of the courts in a free society is the *principled* declaration of public norms. The legitimacy, prestige and effectiveness of the judiciary — the "least dangerous branch" — ultimately depend on public confidence in our unwavering commitment to this ideal. Any breakdown in principled decisionmaking, any rule for which no principled basis can be found and clearly articulated, subverts and discredits the institution as a whole.

It is not always easy, of course, to accommodate the desire for individual justice with the need for reasoned, well-grounded, general principles. We sacrifice the latter for the sake of the former, however, only at our peril. For the "power-base" of the courts, as noted above, is rather fragile; it consists of the perception of our role in the structure of American government as the voice of reason, and the faith that the laws we make today, we *ourselves* will be bound by tomorrow. Any "rule" — such as *Dillon*'s — which permits and even encourages judgments based not on universal standards but individual expediency, erodes the public trust which we serve, and on which we ultimately depend.

There is a second reason, apart from the inherently corrosive effect of arbitrary rules, that points to the conclusion that "bystander" liability should not be retained. The interest in freedom from emotional distress caused by negligent injury to a third party is simply not, in my view, an interest which the law can or should protect. It is not that the interest is less than compelling. The suffering of a parent from the death or injury of a child is terribly poignant, and has always been so. It is the very universality of such injury, however, which renders it inherently unsuitable to legal protection. . . .

A final argument against overruling *Dillon* is, of course, the simple fact that it has been the law for 20 years. Stare decisis should not be lightly dismissed in any thoughtful reconsideration of the law. History and experience, however, are the final judge of whether a decision was right or wrong, whether it should be retained, modified or abandoned.

Adherence to precedent cannot justify the perpetuation of a policy ill-conceived in theory and unfair in practice. . . .

For the foregoing reasons, therefore, I would overrule Dillon v. Legg, *supra*, 68 Cal. 2d 728, 69 Cal. Rptr. 72, 441 P.2d 912, and reinstate [the zone-of-danger rule] as the law of this state. Since the plaintiff was indisputably not within the zone of

authors' dialogue 28

AARON: Knowing how you feel about courts denying recovery for pure economic harm (*see* Author's Dialogue #27, *supra*), I'll bet you're going to tell me that courts deny these claims because stand-alone emotional distress doesn't represent loss in a broader societal sense. Am I right?

JIM: Well, sort of. Any time courts deny recovery for what seem on their face to be valid claims, I suspect that something basic is at work.

AARON: Then you don't buy the traditional explanation that courts are fearful that emotional distress is so easily faked?

JIM: Sure I do, to some extent. But a lot of these emotional upset claims clearly are not faked. When so many courts rule against these claims, something must be going on more than suspicion that plaintiffs are faking.

AARON: Like what? Like emotional distress isn't real loss? Or it isn't important?

JIM: I concede that it's real enough. And it's important, certainly to the plaintiffs involved. But maybe courts intuit, deep down, that each plaintiff is better able to deal with it than tort courts are. Try this idea: stand-alone emotional distress comes into everyone's life, sooner or later. It simply cannot be avoided. Most of the causes of such distress don't involve anyone's tortious conduct. Even in a world where everybody behaved reasonably, emotional distress would abound. So when a parent learns that her child has been hurt, or even killed, through a defendant's tortious behavior, the defendant has accelerated the experience of emotional pain, but has not proximately caused it. The pain is real, but the parent would have experienced it in any event at some point, or points, in her life. Maybe not with regard to that particular child, certainly not at that particular moment. But emotional pain is always out there, waiting to happen. In the cruise line case at the beginning of this section, if the plaintiff's son committed suicide, he might have done it someplace else. Or if he drank too much and fell overboard, who's to say he wouldn't have gotten drunk on dry land and crashed his car? Maybe I'm talking about "background risk" in the sense that the court in *Marshall v. Nugent* (Chapter 5) used it. The cruise line didn't do anything to elevate the risk of what happened to the plaintiff's son.

AARON: And when the parent is an eyewitness to the event, we make an exception?

JIM: Yes. That particular load of grief and anguish is sufficiently unusual not to be treated as "background risk."

AARON: Yet, we don't make an exception when the parent comes onto the scene, after the event, and sees her child unconscious or bleeding profusely. If that's "background risk," I'm an astronaut. No, Jim. I don't think that deep jurisprudential values are at work. The courts, in my opinion, have to deal with the pragmatic management of mental distress claims. I'm unhappy with their nuts and bolts solution but I'm skeptical that your theory has much explanatory power.

danger and could not assert a claim for emotional distress as the result of fear for her *own* safety, she could not establish a right to recover. Accordingly, I concur in the majority's conclusion that the order granting summary judgment in this case was proper.

[The dissenting opinion of Mosk, J., is omitted.]

BROUSSARD, Justice, dissenting.

I dissent. . . .

The majority grope for a "bright line" rule for negligent infliction of emotional distress actions, only to grasp an admittedly arbitrary line which will deny recovery to victims whose injuries from the negligent acts of others are very real. In so doing, the majority reveal a myopic reading of Dillon v. Legg, *supra*, . . . 441 P.2d 912. They impose a strict requirement that plaintiff be present at the scene of the injury-producing event at the time it occurs and is aware that it is causing injury to the victim. This strict requirement rigidifies what *Dillon* forcefully told us should be a flexible rule, and will lead to arbitrary results. I would follow the mandate of *Dillon* and maintain that foreseeability and duty determine liability, with a view toward a policy favoring reasonable limitations on liability. There is no reason why these general rules of tort law should not apply to negligent infliction of emotional distress actions. . . .

SUMMING UP

The Restatement, Third, of Torts § 47, adopts the rule set forth in *Dillon*. It leaves open how narrowly one should read the "contemporaneous perception" requirement and is unclear as to how close the relationship of a family member must be in order to be entitled to recover. On the issue of contemporaneity, the Supreme Court of Iowa took a hard line in Moore v. Eckman, 762 N.W.2d 459 (Iowa 2009), in which the plaintiff-mother witnessed her son lying in the street with fatal head injuries moments after falling off the trunk of an automobile. Citing *Thing*, the high court denied plaintiff's claim as a matter of law, explaining that a bright line in such cases is essential. Not relying on a bright-line rule, but reaching the same result was Colbert v. Moomba Sports, Inc., 176 P.3d 497 (Wash. 2008), which held that a father who arrived at the scene of a boating accident after emergency personnel were conducting a search for his daughter's body was an unforeseeable plaintiff as a matter of law. By contrast, the Supreme Court of Tennessee allowed a claim for upset on behalf of a mother and brother who arrived moments later and witnessed a child victim of a car accident lying in a pool of blood. *See* Eskin v. Bartee, 262 S.W.3d 727 (Tenn. 2008).

The Restatement reflects the strong majority rule. Twenty-nine jurisdictions now follow *Dillon* or some variant thereof, but vary quite a bit in how strictly they read the requirements of *Dillon* for contemporaneous perception and closeness of relationship to the victim. *See, e.g.*, Kaho'ohanohano v. Department of Human Services, 178 P.3d 538, 584 (Haw. 2008) (father can recover emotional distress damages resulting from injuries to child while in custody of the mother); Jarrett v. Jones, 258 S.W.3d 442 (Mo. 2008) (professional truck driver who viewed body of two-year-old child killed in the car of negligent driver); Doe v. Greenville County Sch. Dist., 651 S.E.2d 305 (S.C. 2007) (permitting bystander recovery, but closer to *Thing* than *Dillon* in requiring a showing of all elements of a bystander claim);

Gabaldon v. Jay-Bi Property Management, Inc., 925 P.2d 510 (N.M. 1996) (contemporaneous perception of accident or its near-aftermath required); Bowen v. Lumbermens Mutual Casualty Co., 517 N.W.2d 432 (Wis. 1994); Barnhill v. Davis, 300 N.W.2d 104 (Iowa 1981). Eleven jurisdictions reject *Dillon* and follow the zone-of-danger rule. *See, e.g.,* Bovsun v. Sanperi, 461 N.E.2d 843 (N.Y. 1984); Rickey v. Chicago Transit Authority, 457 N.E.2d 1 (Ill. 1983); Engler v. Illinois Farmers Insurance Co., 706 N.W.2d 764 (Minn. 2005).

SCHOLARLY TREATMENT OF RECOVERY FOR EMOTIONAL DISTRESS

Commentators have explored the issues surrounding recovery for emotional distress. In particular, academic writers have addressed the problem of how courts should respond when the plaintiff has been exposed to a toxic substance that has not yet produced physical injury. Typically, plaintiffs seek to recover for their understandable anxieties over the prospect of contracting cancer in the future. For distinctive viewpoints, *see* James A. Henderson, Jr. & Aaron D. Twerski, *Asbestos Litigation Gone Mad: Exposure-Based Recovery for Increased Risk, Mental Distress, and Medical Monitoring*, 53 S.C. L. Rev. 815 (2002) (arguing against recovery); Kenneth W. Miller, *Toxic Torts and Emotional Distress: The Case for an Independent Cause of Action for Fear of Future Harm*, 40 Ariz. L. Rev. 681 (1998) (arguing for recovery).

More general commentary on the problem of emotional distress includes Dan B. Dobbs, *Undertakings and Special Relationships in Claims for Negligent Infliction of Emotional Distress*, 50 Ariz. L. Rev. 49 (2008); Meredith E. Green, Comment, *Who Knows Where the Love Grows?: Unmarried Cohabitants and Bystander Recovery for Negligent Infliction of Emotional Distress*, 44 Wake Forest L. Rev. 1093 (2009); Martha Chamallas, *Removing Emotional Harm from the Core of Tort Law*, 54 Vand. L. Rev. 751 (2001) (feminist criticism of the omission of emotional distress from the Restatement, Third, of Torts: Basic Principles); Robert J. Rhee, *A Principled Solution for Negligent Infliction of Emotional Distress Claims*, 36 Ariz. St. L.J. 805 (2004).

D. HARM TO UNBORN CHILDREN

However courts may react to the issue in other legal contexts, such as the validity of state regulation of abortion, unborn children are persons capable of being physically harmed for purposes of bringing an action to recover civil damages later on, after the child is born with physical injuries caused prenatally by a wrongdoer's conduct. *See generally* William L. Prosser & W. Page Keeton, *The Law of Torts* 367-370 (5th ed. 1984). Moreover, the parents of an unborn fetus may themselves be injured by the same tortious conduct that harms the fetus. The issues in this area of tort are diverse, and some are quite controversial.

Werling v. Sandy, 476 N.E.2d 1053 (Ohio 1985), is a fairly typical case involving a wrongful death action against providers of medical care, alleging that their negligence caused a child to be stillborn. Separate from the parents' claim for emotional distress, the issue is whether the parents, as the statutory beneficiaries of the child, could assert the rights of the unborn child. The state wrongful death statute provided for liability "[w]hen the death of a person is caused by wrongful act, neglect, or default which would have entitled the party injured to maintain an action and recover damages if death had not ensued." R.C. 2125.01. The Ohio Supreme Court, observing that it would be anomalous to "deny an action where the child is stillborn, and yet permit the action where the child survives birth but only for a short period of time," held that the child was a "person" for the purposes of the wrongful death statute. The court did require that the unborn child have reached the stage of viability at the time of the injury. It observed that defining personhood under the wrongful death statute at viability would avoid any constitutional issues under Roe v. Wade, 410 U.S. 113 (1973), which recognized a state interest in protecting fetal life after viability.

A clear majority of American jurisdictions agree with the position adopted in *Werling* allowing the wrongful death cause of action for the death of a fetus in utero or a stillborn infant so long as the injury occurred when the fetus was viable. *See, e.g.,* Volk v. Baldazo, 651 P.2d 11 (Idaho 1982); Shaw v. Jendzejec, 717 A.2d 367 (Me. 1998); Pino v. United States, 183 P.3d 1001 (Okla. 2008); Cavazos v. Franklin, 867 P.2d 674 (Wash. Ct. App. 1994). In Williams v. Manchester, 888 N.E.2d 1 (Ill. 2008), a pregnant woman suffered injury due to the negligence of the defendant. The fetus suffered no injury from the accident, but one week later the mother agreed to an abortion because of potential complications that might flow from her own accident-related injuries. The Supreme Court of Illinois denied as a matter of law recovery for wrongful death of the fetus, concluding that the accident had not caused injury to the fetus such that a tort action could have been brought had the fetus been born alive. *See generally* Sheldon R. Shapiro, Annotation, *Right to Maintain Action or to Recover Damages for Death of Unborn Child*, 84 A.L.R. 3d 411 (1978).

Wrongful death statutes vary considerably from state to state, leaving courts plenty of room to react differently in these cases depending partly on statutory language and partly on notions of public policy. A few courts take the position that recovery is proper even when the injury occurs before the fetus is viable. *See* Wiersma v. Maple Leaf Farms, 543 N.W.2d 787 (S.D. 1996); Farley v. Sartin, 466 S.E.2d 522 (W. Va. 1995). *But see* Jason Cuomo, *Life Begins at the Moment of Conception for the Purposes of W. Va. Code § 55-7-5: The Supreme Court "Rewrites" Our Wrongful Death Statute*, 99 W. Va. L. Rev. 237 (1996) (arguing that the court went too far in allowing recovery in the *Farley* case and that the matter is better dealt with by statute).

Some courts occupy the other end of the spectrum, requiring live birth of the fetus, even if only for one breath, before allowing recovery for the death of the newborn caused by injuries suffered in utero. The New York Court of Appeals denied wrongful death recovery in Endresz v. Friedberg, 248 N.E.2d 901 (N.Y. 1969). *Endresz* involved an automobile accident resulting, two days later, in the stillbirth of twins who were viable when the accident occurred. Chief Judge Fuld, writing for the majority, observed (*id.* at 903-904):

> . . . The considerations of justice which mandate the recovery of damages by an infant, injured in his mother's womb and born deformed through the wrong of a third party, are absent where the foetus, deprived of life while yet unborn, is never faced with the prospect of impaired mental or physical health.
>
> In the latter case, moreover, proof of pecuniary injury and causation is immeasurably more vague than in suits for prenatal injuries. . . .
>
> Beyond that, since the mother may sue for any injury which she sustained in her own person, including her suffering as a result of the stillbirth, and the father for the loss of her services and consortium, an additional award to the "distributees" of the foetus would give its parents an unmerited bounty and would constitute not compensation to the injured but punishment to the wrongdoer.

Fuld's majority opinion acknowledges that the requirement of live birth is somewhat arbitrary, but observes that the requirement of viability at the time of injury is also arbitrary and more difficult to determine factually. (Is this difficulty pervasive today, with the modern advances in medicine?) *See also* Peters v. Hospital Authority of Elbert County, 458 S.E.2d 628 (Ga. 1995) (live birth required).

Allowing recovery for other elements of loss, such as the mental upset of the mother or father, or loss of consortium, to some extent makes up for the harshness of the requirement of live birth in those jurisdictions that still require it. *See* Sosebee v. Hillcrest Baptist Medical Center, 8 S.W.3d 427 (Tex. App. 1999); Kammer v. Hurley, 765 So. 2d 975 (Fla. Dist. Ct. App. 2000); Willis v. Ashby, 801 A.2d 442 (N.J. Super. Ct. App. Div. 2002).

It should be noted that all of these cases considered thus far involved the deaths of unborn children. That is, the defendant's tortious conduct killed the fetus. What if the child injured in utero is later born alive suffering a disability caused by the defendant's negligence? Every American jurisdiction allows recovery in such a case whether or not the fetus was viable at the time of injury in utero. What if the fetus is harmed in utero and, from other unrelated causes, dies in the womb prior to birth? What if, for example, the fetus is injured in utero and two months later the mother slips and falls, suffering a miscarriage unrelated to the earlier fetal injuries? Recovery for the earlier injuries to the fetus that did not cause the death is not allowed.

In addition to these wrongful death cases, courts have recognized so-called wrongful birth or wrongful pregnancy actions brought by the parents alleging that, but for the defendant's negligence, the parents would have terminated the pregnancy or that the mother would never have become pregnant at all. These actions are usually brought against doctors and other health care personnel to recover the cost of the pregnancy, including lost wages, medical expenses, corrective surgery if needed, and loss of consortium. Additionally, many plaintiffs seek recovery for physical pain and suffering and emotional distress, as well as for the costs associated with raising the child. One such wrongful pregnancy case is Fassoulas v. Ramey, 450 So. 2d 822 (Fla. 1984). In *Fassoulas*, the defendant physician performed a vasectomy on the husband to prevent him and his wife from having any more children with severe congenital abnormalities (they already had two). The defendant performed the procedure negligently and the couple conceived two more children. One child had many congenital deformities, but the other had only a slight problem that was corrected at birth and was an otherwise healthy child. The husband and wife brought a negligence action against the defendant to recover for the wife's own injuries, both physical and emotional, and for the expense of raising each of the two children until the age of 21. The Florida court allowed recovery for the "special up-bringing expenses associated with a deformed child," but denied recovery for any of the "ordinary, everyday expenses associated with the care and upbringing" of either a healthy or a mentally or physically impaired child. According to the majority, the benefits to the parents of any child presumptively outweigh the ordinary costs of upbringing. Three justices dissented, arguing that the economic burdens of raising children who would not have been born if the defendant had not been negligent should be borne by the defendant. The dissent concludes that "Dr. Ramey did not do Edith and John a favor." *Id.* at 830.

For other courts allowing recovery for the costs of bringing up a child as a result of negligent performance of a sterilization procedure, *see, e.g.,* Lovelace Medical Center v. Mendez, 805 P.2d 603 (N.M. 1991); University of Arizona Health Sciences Center v. Superior Court, 667 P.2d 1294 (Ariz. 1983) (cost of rearing child recoverable, but must be offset by the benefits of the parent-child relationship); Sherlock v. Stillwater Clinic, 260 N.W.2d 169 (Minn. 1977). Some states do not allow recovery of child-rearing expenses. *See, e.g,,* Chaffee v. Seslar, 786 N.E.2d 705 (Ind. 2003); C.S. v. Nielson, 767 P.2d 504 (Utah 1988) (though permitting recovery of damages for medical expenses associated with pregnancy and delivery); Morris v. Sanchez, 746 P.2d 184 (Okla. 1987); Byrd v. Wesley Medical Center, 699 P.2d 459 (Kan. 1985).

PROCANIK BY PROCANIK v. CILLO
478 A.2d 755 (N.J. 1984)

POLLOCK, J.

The primary issue on this appeal is the propriety of a grant of a partial summary judgment dismissing a "wrongful life" claim brought by an infant plaintiff through his mother and guardian *ad litem*. That judgment, which was granted on the pleadings, dismissed the claim because it failed to state a cause of action upon which relief may be granted.

The infant plaintiff, Peter Procanik, alleges that the defendant doctors, Joseph Cillo [and others], negligently failed to diagnose that his mother, Rosemary Procanik, had contracted German measles in the first trimester of her pregnancy. As a result, Peter was born with congenital rubella syndrome. Alleging that the doctors negligently deprived his parents of the choice of terminating the pregnancy, he seeks general damages for his pain and suffering and for "his parents' impaired capacity to cope with his problems." He also seeks special damages attributable to the extraordinary expenses he will incur for medical, nursing, and other health care. The Law Division granted defendants' motion to dismiss, and the Appellate Division affirmed in an unreported opinion.

We granted certification. We now conclude that an infant plaintiff may recover as special damages the extraordinary medical expenses attributable to his affliction, but that he may not recover general damages for emotional distress or for an impaired childhood. Consequently, we affirm in part and reverse in part the judgment of the Appellate Division, and remand the matter to the Law Division.

Because this matter comes before us on the grant of a motion to dismiss, we focus on the complaint.... Accepting as true the allegations ..., the complaint discloses the following facts....

On June 9, 1977, during the first trimester of her pregnancy with Peter, Mrs. Procanik consulted the defendant doctors and informed Dr. Cillo "that she had recently been diagnosed as having measles but did not know if it was German measles." Dr. Cillo examined Mrs. Procanik and ordered "tests for German Measles, known as Rubella Titer Test." The results "were 'indicative of past infection of Rubella.'" Instead of ordering further tests, Dr. Cillo negligently interpreted the results and told Mrs. Procanik that she "had nothing to worry about because she had become immune to German Measles as a child." In fact, the "past infection" disclosed by the tests was the German measles that had prompted Mrs. Procanik to consult the defendant doctors.

Ignorant of what an accurate diagnosis would have disclosed, Mrs. Procanik allowed her pregnancy to continue, and Peter was born on December 26, 1977. Shortly thereafter, on January 16, 1978, he was diagnosed as suffering from congenital rubella syndrome. As a result of the doctors' negligence, Mr. and Mrs. Procanik were deprived of the choice of terminating the pregnancy, and Peter was "born with multiple birth defects," including eye lesions, heart disease, and auditory defects. The infant plaintiff states further that "he has suffered because of his parents' impaired capacity to cope with his problems," and seeks damages for his pain and suffering and for his "impaired childhood."

In April 1983, while this matter was pending in the Appellate Division, Peter moved to amend the first count to assert a claim to recover, as special damages, the expenses he will incur as an adult for medical, nursing, and related health care services. In its opinion, the Appellate Division denied without prejudice leave to amend....

In this case we survey again the changing landscape of family torts. Originally that landscape presented a bleak prospect both to children born with birth defects and to their parents. If a doctor negligently diagnosed or treated a pregnant woman who was suffering from a condition that might cause her to give birth to a defective child, neither the parents nor the child could maintain a cause of action against the negligent doctor. Gleitman v. Cosgrove, ... 227 A.2d 689 (N.J. 1967).

Like the present case, *Gleitman* involved a doctor who negligently treated a pregnant woman who had contracted German measles in the first trimester of her pregnancy. Reasoning from the premise that the doctor did not cause the infant plaintiff's birth defects, the *Gleitman* Court found it impossible to compare the infant's condition if the defendant doctor had not been negligent with the infant's impaired condition as a result of the negligence. Measurement of "the value of life with impairments against the nonexistence of life itself" was, the Court declared, a logical impossibility. Consequently, the Court rejected the infant's claim.

The Court denied the parents' claim for emotional distress and the costs of caring for the infant, because of the impossibility of weighing the intangible benefits of parenthood against the emotional and monetary injuries sustained by them. Prevailing policy considerations, which included a reluctance to acknowledge the availability of abortions and the mother's right to choose to terminate her pregnancy, prevented the Court from awarding damages to a woman for not having an abortion. Another consideration was the Court's belief that "[i]t is basic to the human condition to seek life and hold on to it however heavily burdened."

In the seventeen years that have elapsed since the *Gleitman* decision, both this Court and the United States Supreme Court have reappraised, albeit in different contexts, the rights of pregnant women and their children. The United States Supreme Court has recognized that women have a constitutional right to choose to terminate a pregnancy. Roe v. Wade, 410 U.S. 113, 93 S. Ct. 705, 35 L. Ed. 2d 147 (1973). Recognition of that right by the high court subsequently influenced this Court in Berman v. Allan, *supra*, . . . 404 A.2d at 8.

In *Berman*, the parents sought to recover for their emotional distress and for the expenses of raising a child born with Down's Syndrome. Relying on Roe v. Wade, the Court found that public policy now supports the right of a woman to choose to terminate a pregnancy. That finding eliminated one of the supports for the *Gleitman* decision — i.e., that public policy prohibited an award for depriving a woman of the right to choose whether to have an abortion. Finding that a trier of fact could place a dollar value on the parents' emotional suffering, the *Berman* Court concluded "that the monetary equivalent of this distress is an appropriate measure of the harm suffered by the parents."

Nonetheless, the Court rejected the parents' claim for "medical and other expenses that will be incurred in order to properly raise, educate and supervise the child." The Court reasoned that the parents wanted to retain "all the benefits inhering in the birth of the child — i.e., the love and joy they will experience as parents — while saddling defendants with enormous expenses attendant upon her rearing." Such an award would be disproportionate to the negligence of the defendants and constitute a windfall to the parents.

The *Berman* Court also declined to recognize a cause of action in an infant born with birth defects. Writing for the Court, Justice Pashman reasoned that even a life with serious defects is more valuable than non-existence, the alternative for the infant plaintiff if his mother chose to have an abortion.

More recently we advanced the parents' right to compensation by permitting recovery of the extraordinary expenses of raising a child born with cystic fibrosis, including medical, hospital, and pharmaceutical expenses. No claim on behalf of the infant was raised in that case, and we elected to defer consideration of such a claim until another day. That day is now upon us, and we must reconsider the right of an infant in a "wrongful life" claim to recover general damages for diminished childhood and pain and suffering, as well as special damages for medical care and the like.

The terms "wrongful birth" and "wrongful life" are but shorthand phrases that describe the causes of action of parents and children when negligent medical treatment deprives parents of the option to terminate a pregnancy to avoid the birth of a defective child. In the present context, "wrongful life" refers to a cause of action brought by or on behalf of a defective child who claims that but for the defendant doctor's negligent advice to or treatment of its parents, the child would not have been born. "Wrongful birth" applies to the cause of action of parents who claim that the negligent advice or treatment deprived them of the choice of avoiding conception or, as here, of terminating the pregnancy.

Both causes of action are distinguishable from the situation where negligent injury to a fetus causes an otherwise normal child to be born in an impaired condition. In the present case, the plaintiffs do not allege that the negligence of the defendant doctors caused the congenital rubella syndrome from which the infant plaintiff suffers. Neither do plaintiffs claim that the infant ever had a chance to be a normal child. The essence of the infant's claim is that the defendant doctors wrongfully deprived his mother of information that would have prevented his birth.

Analysis of the infant's cause of action begins with the determination whether the defendant doctors owed a duty to him. The defendant doctors do not deny they owed a duty to the infant plaintiff, and we find such a duty exists. In evaluating the infant's cause of action, we assume, furthermore, that the defendant doctors were negligent in treating the mother. Moreover, we assume that their negligence deprived the parents of the choice of terminating the pregnancy and of preventing the birth of the infant plaintiff.

Notwithstanding recognition of the existence of a duty and its breach, policy considerations have led this Court in the past to decline to recognize any cause of action in an infant for his wrongful life. The threshold problem has been the assertion by infant plaintiffs not that they should not have been born without defects, but that they should not have been born at all. The essence of the infant's cause of action is that its very life is wrongful. Berman v. Allan, *supra*, . . . 404 A.2d at 8. Resting on the belief that life, no matter how burdened, is preferable to nonexistence, the *Berman* Court stated that the infant "has not suffered any damage cognizable at law by being brought into existence." Although the premise for this part of the *Berman* decision was the absence of cognizable damages, the Court continued to be troubled, as it was in *Gleitman*, by the problem of ascertaining the measure of damages.

The courts of other jurisdictions have also struggled with the issues of injury and damages when faced with suits for wrongful life. Although two intermediate appellate courts in New York and California recognized an infant's claim for general damages, those decisions were rejected by the courts of last resort in both jurisdictions. . . .

Even when this Court declined to recognize a cause of action for wrongful life in *Gleitman* and *Berman*, dissenting members urged recognition of that claim. . . . Extending through these [dissenting] opinions is an awareness that damages would be appropriate if they were measurable by acceptable standards.

Recently we recognized that extraordinary medical expenses incurred by parents on behalf of a birth-defective child were predictable, certain, and recoverable. In reaching that conclusion, we discussed the interdependence of the interests of parents and children in a family tort. . . .

When a child requires extraordinary medical care, the financial impact is felt not just by the parents, but also by the injured child. As a practical matter, the impact may extend beyond the injured child to his brothers or sisters. Money that is spent for the health care of one child is not available for the clothes, food, or college education of another child.

Recovery of the cost of extraordinary medical expenses by either the parents or the infant, but not both, is consistent with the principle that the doctor's negligence vitally affects the entire family. . . .

Law is more than an exercise in logic, and logical analysis, although essential to a system of ordered justice, should not become an instrument of injustice. Whatever logic inheres in permitting parents to recover for the cost of extraordinary medical care incurred by a birth-defective child, but in denying the child's own right to recover those expenses, must yield to the inherent injustice of that result. The right to recover the often crushing burden of extraordinary expenses visited by an act of medical malpractice should not depend on the "wholly fortuitous circumstance of whether the parents are available to sue."

The present case proves the point. Here, the parents' claim is barred by the statute of limitations. Does this mean that Peter must forgo medical treatment for his blindness, deafness, and retardation? We think not. His claim for the medical expenses attributable to his birth defects is reasonably certain, readily calculable, and of a kind daily determined by judges and juries. We hold that a child or his parents may recover special damages for extraordinary medical expenses incurred during infancy, and that the infant may recover those expenses during his majority.

Our decision is consistent with recent decisions of the Supreme Courts of California and Washington. The Supreme Court of California has held that special damages related to the infant's birth defects may be recovered in a wrongful life suit. Turpin v. Sortini, 643 P.2d at 154 (1982). Following *Turpin*, the Supreme Court of Washington has held that either the parents or the child may recover special damages for medical and other extraordinary expenses incurred during the infant's minority, and that the child may recover for those costs to be incurred during majority. Harbeson v. Parke-Davis, . . . 656 P.2d 483 (Wash. 1983).

In restricting the infant's claim to one for special damages, we recognize that our colleagues, Justice Schreiber and Justice Handler, disagree with us and with each other. From the premise that "man does not know whether non-life would have been preferable to an impaired life," Justice Schreiber concludes that a child does not have a cause of action for wrongful life and, therefore, that is "unfair and unjust to charge the doctors with the infant's medical expenses." Justice Handler reaches a diametrically opposite conclusion. He would allow the infant to recover not only his medical expenses, but also general damages for his pain and suffering and for his impaired childhood.

We find, however, that the infant's claim for pain and suffering and for a diminished childhood presents insurmountable problems. The philosophical problem of finding that such a defective life is worth less than no life at all has perplexed not only Justice Schreiber, but . . . other distinguished members of this Court. . . . We need not become preoccupied, however, with these metaphysical considerations. Our decision to allow the recovery of extraordinary medical expenses is not premised on the concept that non-life is preferable to an impaired life, but is predicated on the needs of the living. We seek only to respond to the call of the living for help in bearing the burden of their affliction.

Sound reasons exist not to recognize a claim for general damages. Our analysis begins with the sad but true fact that the infant plaintiff never had a chance of being born as a normal, healthy child. For him, the only options were non-existence or an impaired life. Tragically, his only choice was a life burdened with his handicaps or no life at all. The congenital rubella syndrome that plagues him was not caused by the negligence of the defendant doctors; the only proximate result of their negligence was the child's birth.

The crux of the problem is that there is no rational way to measure non-existence or to compare non-existence with the pain and suffering of his impaired existence. Whatever theoretical appeal one might find in recognizing a claim for pain and suffering is outweighed by the essentially irrational and unpredictable nature of that claim. Although damages in a personal injury action need not be calculated with mathematical precision, they require at their base some modicum of rationality.

Underlying our conclusion is an evaluation of the capability of the judicial system, often proceeding in these cases through trial by jury, to appraise such a claim. Also at work is an appraisal of the role of tort law in compensating injured parties, involving as that role does, not only reason, but also fairness, predictability, and even deterrence of future wrongful acts. In brief, the ultimate decision is a policy choice summoning the most sensitive and careful judgment.

From that perspective it is simply too speculative to permit an infant plaintiff to recover for emotional distress attendant on birth defects when that plaintiff claims he would be better off if he had not been born. Such a claim would stir the passions of jurors about the nature and value of life, the fear of non-existence, and about abortion. That mix is more than the judicial system can digest. We believe that the interests of fairness and justice are better served through more predictably measured damages — the cost of the extraordinary medical expenses necessitated by the infant plaintiff's handicaps. Damages so measured are not subject to the same wild swings as a claim for pain and suffering and will carry a sufficient sting to deter future acts of medical malpractice.

As speculative and uncertain as is a comparison of the value of an impaired life with non-existence, even more problematic is the evaluation of a claim for diminished childhood. The essential proof in such a claim is that the doctor's negligence deprives the parents of the knowledge of the condition of the fetus. The deprivation of that information precludes the choice of terminating the pregnancy by abortion and leaves the parents unprepared for the birth of a defective child, a birth that causes them emotional harm. The argument proceeds that the parents are less able to love and care for the child, who thereby suffers an impaired childhood.

Several considerations lead us to decline to recognize a cause of action for impaired childhood. At the outset, we note the flaw in such a claim in those instances in which the parents assert not that the information would have prepared them for the birth of the defective child, but that they would have used the information to prevent that birth. Furthermore, even its advocates recognize that a

---

authors' dialogue 29

BRAD: I don't get it in these "wrongful life" cases when courts say that life, no matter how miserable, is better than no life at all. I just don't agree.

AARON: I'm not sure that's what the courts are saying. But let's suppose they are. Isn't that as good a reason as any to say "No" to these claims? The plaintiffs in these cases, after all, are not suicidal. It's obvious *they* prefer to continue living. So it rings hollow when they insist, in effect, that they wish they were dead.

BRAD: But there's a big difference between wishing you had never been born and, having been born, wanting to die. A jury could certainly conclude in extreme cases that the plaintiff is so badly off that never being born at all would have been preferable. I'm not talking about being born tone deaf, or with slow foot-speed. I'm talking about a shortened, physically painful life with no hope and no future. Juries should be allowed to find that such a life has a negative value.

AARON: I see your point. But what about valuation?

BRAD: What about it? Any time the judge allows a jury award for loss of enjoyment of life, the jury has to decide how much some aspect of life is worth — whether it's playing tennis, listening to music, or enjoying one's favorite wine. Juries can handle it. And if a jury went wild, the judge could use remittitur to keep things in line.

AARON: I just don't like giving legitimacy to the notion that someone would be better off dead. It's profoundly disturbing to me, and I think to the judges who write the opinions, even to say such a thing.

---

claim for "the kind of injury suffered by the child in this context may not be readily divisible from that suffered by her wronged parents." We believe the award of the cost of the extraordinary medical care to the child or the parents, when combined with the right of the parents to assert a claim for their own emotional distress, comes closer to filling the dual objectives of a tort system: the compensation of injured parties and the deterrence of future wrongful conduct. . . .

[The judgment of the Appellate Division is affirmed in part, reversed in part, and the matter is remanded to the Law Division. The separate dissenting opinions of Handler, J., and Schreiber, J., are omitted.]

FOOD FOR THOUGHT

One of the cases cited by the *Procanik* majority in support of its holding is Turpin v. Sortini, 643 P.2d 954 (Cal. 1982). In that case the plaintiffs, husband and wife, brought suit on behalf of themselves and a child born with a birth defect against their physician and a hospital for negligence for failing to inform them that their offspring would very likely be totally deaf. Subsequent to this alleged negligence, a daughter, Joy, was conceived and was born totally deaf. Plaintiffs sought damages for Joy's being "deprived of the fundamental right of a child to be born as a whole, functional human being without total deafness," and for expenses for "specialized teaching, training and hearing equipment." One of the questions that most troubled the court was whether a child should be allowed to argue that it would have been better never to have been born at all. In this connection, the court observed (*id.* at 962-963):[1]

> In this case, in which the plaintiff's only affliction is deafness, it seems quite unlikely that a jury would ever conclude that life with such a condition is worse than not being born at all. Other wrongful life cases, however, have involved children with much more serious, debilitating and painful conditions, and the academic literature refers to still other, extremely severe hereditary diseases. Considering the short life span of many of these children and their frequently very limited ability to perceive or enjoy the benefits of life, we cannot assert with confidence that in every situation there would be a societal consensus that life is preferable to never having been born at all.
>
> While it thus seems doubtful that a child's claim for general damages should properly be denied on the rationale that the value of impaired life, as a matter of law, always exceeds the value of nonlife, we believe that out-of-state decisions are on sounder grounds in holding that — with respect to the child's claim for pain and suffering or other general damages — recovery should be denied because (1) it is simply impossible to determine in any rational or seasoned fashion whether the plaintiff has in fact suffered an injury in being born impaired rather than not being born, and (2) even if it were possible to overcome the first hurdle, it would be impossible to assess general damages in any fair, nonspeculative manner. . . .

Although the California court in *Turpin* denied the child's claim for general damages, it allowed, as did the New Jersey court in *Procanik*, the parents' claim for the "extraordinary expenses for specialized teaching, training and hearing equipment that Joy will incur during her lifetime because of her deafness" (*id.* at 965).

Some critics believe that both general and extraordinary expenses for raising the child should be recoverable, arguing that full recovery is needed to deter medical malpractice as well as to completely compensate parents whose exercise of fundamental reproductive rights has been substantially impaired by the defendant's negligence. *See* Patricia Baugher, *Fundamental Protection of a Fundamental Right: Full Recovery of Child Rearing Damages for Wrongful Pregnancy*, 75 Wash. L. Rev. 1205 (2000). Many jurisdictions reject these "wrongful life" claims entirely. *See, e.g.,* Hester v. Dwivedi, 733 N.E.2d 1161, 1165 (Ohio 2000) ("the status of being alive simply does not constitute an injury"); Ellis v. Sherman, 478 A.2d 1339 (Pa. Super. Ct. 1984) (wrongful life not a cause of action); Williams v. University of Chicago Hospitals, 688 N.E.2d 130, 133 (Ill. 1997) (Supreme Court of Illinois noted that judicial rejection of wrongful life claims brought by children was "nearly universal").

---

1. *See* Martel v. Duffy-Mott Corp., 166 N.W.2d 54 (Mich. App. 1969) (bad applesauce caused loss of young plaintiffs' enjoyment; such loss recoverable).

chapter 7

Owners and Occupiers of Land

Tort law has traditionally treated owners and occupiers of land with considerable deference. The notion that they owe duties of reasonable care to those who come on the land clashes with the idea that property ownership or possession brings with it the privilege to act as one pleases within one's own domain. If one must act with reasonable care on her own property, she loses some of the value of the property right. Her home, if you will, is no longer her castle. Think for a moment about how you act within your own home or apartment. Some days your place is sparkling clean and unlittered. Other days you may leave dishes in the sink, the carpets unvacuumed, and a host of objects scattered throughout. If you were told that you had a duty to be a reasonable housekeeper, you might well react by saying, "Who's to tell me what is reasonable in my house? If I don't want to clean up because I'm not feeling well or want to watch TV, that's my business. If you come to visit me, you take me and my house as they are. I'll be damned if anyone can dictate to me what is a reasonable way to maintain my property. If you don't like my housekeeping habits, then just stay away." In short, there are many "reasonable" ways to maintain property depending on whether you are fastidious or a slob. One of the authors recalls visiting the office of one of the greatest constitutional law scholars of a previous era at Harvard Law School, whose office always looked like it was just hit by a cyclone. He had the uncanny ability to retrieve a slip of paper, nestled between mountains of books piled to the ceiling, within seconds. Did he maintain a reasonable office? Was it safe for a student to traverse? Shouldn't such a professor have the luxury to have his mind on legal scholarship rather than a squeaky clean office?

Having made the point, the law cannot give owners and occupiers of land total freedom as to how they maintain their property. Some persons, at least, come onto the land with the right to be treated decently. At common law, possessors of land had a sort of sliding scale of responsibilities depending on whether the entrant to the property was a trespasser, licensee, or invitee.

A. DUTIES OWED TO ENTRANTS ON THE LAND

1. Duties Owed to Trespassers

Trespassers are, understandably, lowest on the totem pole. In the early part of the twentieth century, the law demanded only that the possessor of land not act in a wanton and willful manner to a known trespasser. (Remember the shotgun-trap case in Chapter 2?) However, some courts developed exceptions to the rule. For example, when the trespasser was known or discovered, courts imposed a duty of reasonable care on the possessor of land in conducting activities that exposed the trespasser to danger. However, even with regard to a discovered trespasser, the duty was merely to warn about hidden dangers. Courts rarely imposed duties on possessors to discover dangers on the land or to eradicate them. A trespasser was, at most, entitled to be put on notice of a hidden danger. Some courts went further and imposed a duty of care, owed to foreseeable trespassers who frequently intrude on a limited area of the land, to alert them to dangers of which they would otherwise be unaware. Finally, many courts adopted the position set out in § 339 of the Restatement, Second, of Torts, which imposes liability on a possessor of land to a child trespasser for physical harm resulting from artificial conditions on the land when the following conditions are met:

> (a) the place where the condition exists is one upon which the possessor knows or has reason to know that children are likely to trespass, and
> (b) the condition is one of which the possessor knows or has reason to know and which he realizes or should realize will involve an unreasonable risk of death or serious bodily harm to such children, and
> (c) the children because of their youth do not discover the condition or realize the risk involved in intermeddling with it or in coming within the area made dangerous by it, and
> (d) the utility to the possessor of maintaining the condition and the burden of eliminating the danger are slight as compared with the risk to children involved, and
> (e) the possessor fails to exercise reasonable care to eliminate the danger or otherwise to protect the children.

In Sutton v. Wheeling & Lake Erie R.R., 2005 WL 3537537 (Ohio App.), plaintiff, an 11-year-old boy, was walking to school with other children near the railroad tracks when they heard a train coming. The other children moved away from the tracks. Plaintiff continued walking along the gravel incline next to the tracks, which sloped downward from the tracks to the ground. Walking on this incline put the plaintiff between two and three feet from the train as it progressed forward. After six cars had passed, plaintiff's foot slipped on the gravel and he lost his balance. As he spun to the left to regain his balance, his right arm came in contact with the train which caused him to be dragged under the train. His legs were so seriously injured that both required amputation. Although Ohio has adopted § 339 of Restatement, Second, the court upheld the grant of summary judgment for the defendant railroad. The court held that the danger of walking near an oncoming train was one that was obvious even to children. The plaintiff could not satisfy the requisite of § 339(c) since he admitted that he knew that it was dangerous to get too close to a moving train. How does § 339 differ from the ordinary negligence analysis under the Learned Hand formula?

Does the attractive nuisance doctrine require that the injured child be attracted onto the defendant's property by the same temptation that ends up causing injury? The Supreme Court of South Carolina rejected such a restriction in Henson v. International Paper Co., 650 S.E.2d 74 (S.C. 2007).

2. Duties Owed to Licensees

Licensees are persons who are on the land with the consent of the owner but are there for their own purpose. Social guests are considered by the courts as licensees, as are other entrants who come with permission to use short cuts, to distribute advertising leaflets, or to solicit charitable contributions. The common law generally treats licensees similarly to trespassers. Since they are present with the permission of the possessor, they are certainly entitled to no less protection than known or discovered trespassers. Thus, the possessor has a duty to conduct activities on the land in a reasonable manner and to warn of hidden dangers known to him.

3. Duties Owed to Invitees

The third and highest standard of care is owed to invitees. Restatement, Second, of Torts § 332 recognizes two categories of invitees: (1) persons who are invited to come on the land for a purpose connected with the business dealings of the possessor and (2) persons who come on the land as a member of the public for a purpose for which the land is held open to the public. The duty owed to an invitee is essentially a full duty of reasonable care. Thus, a possessor may have a duty to inspect her premises for dangers that create an unreasonable risk of harm and then to take reasonable steps to protect the invitee against such dangers. Very often the duty of reasonable care can be fulfilled by warning against the dangers. But in some circumstances, the fact that a danger is obvious or warned against will not eliminate the risk of harm. In Wilk v. Georges, 514 P.2d 877 (Or. 1973), for example, a nursery selling Christmas trees warned patrons that the walkway inside the building was slippery due to flower petals that always fall on the floor. Though the plaintiff knew that the walkway was slippery and dangerous, she slipped and injured herself. The court held that the nursery owed a duty to make the walkway reasonably safe and did not fulfill its obligation merely by warning of the danger. Similarly, in Fieldhouse v. Tam Investment Co., 959 So. 2d 1214 (Fla. Dist. Ct. App. 2007), plaintiff was walking in the common area behind her apartment to get her bicycle when she tripped on a tree root that was hidden by leaves. Plaintiff had made prior complaints to the landlord about the root and was aware of the danger it presented. Citing to an earlier case, the court said, "[A]lthough the open and obvious nature of a hazard may discharge a landowner's duty to warn, it does not discharge the duty to maintain the property in a reasonably safe condition." *See also* Restatement, Second, of Torts § 343A (possessor of land is liable to invitees for harm caused by obvious dangers when possessor should anticipate that harm may befall them despite the obviousness of the danger).

Taking all of this together, determining the status of an entrant to land can be very tricky. One may be a trespasser or licensee at one moment and an invitee seconds later. Or one may be a business invitee at one moment and a licensee or a trespasser the next. *See* Byers v. Radiant Group, L.L.C., 966 So. 2d 506 (Fla. Dist. Ct. App. 2007) (patrons of defendant's store did not lose their invitee status by leaving store and entering store's parking lot, nor did they lose status by engaging in an injury-causing fracas in the parking lot). It is the function of the court, not the jury, to determine the status of the entrant. Under the system in which the standard of care varies so significantly depending on how an entrant is categorized, appellate courts face a steady diet of cases importuning them to label the entrant in one way or another.

In Gladon v. Greater Cleveland Regional Transit Authority, 662 N.E.2d 287 (Ohio 1996), the plaintiff purchased a ticket on a regional commuter rail line operated by the defendant. The plaintiff, who had been drinking at a baseball game, had only a hazy recollection of what subsequently occurred. He got off at the wrong stop where two unknown assailants attacked him. He was either pushed or jumped onto the train tracks. As he lay near the tracks with his leg draped over the rail, he was struck by one of the defendant's trains. The Ohio Supreme Court concluded that the plaintiff was an invitee when he purchased his ticket, but became either a licensee or a trespasser when he entered the defendant's land after getting off at the wrong stop. The distinction between those two categories was immaterial, since the defendant owed the same duty to either — solely to refrain from willful, wanton or reckless conduct. That conclusion would seem to have eliminated any possibility of the plaintiff recovering from the railroad. However, the court softened the harsh result by remanding for a new trial on the issue of whether the operator of the train that hit the plaintiff engaged in willful and wanton conduct.

The following case illustrates the importance to the plaintiff's case of the categorization exercise. As you read it, think about what the plaintiff alleges the landowner should have done, and ask yourself why the plaintiff's purpose in coming to the defendants' house should make all the difference.

CARTER v. KINNEY
896 S.W.2d 926 (Mo. 1995)

Robertson, Justice. . . .

I.

Ronald and Mary Kinney hosted a Bible study at their home for members of the Northwest Bible Church. Appellant Jonathan Carter, a member of the

Northwest Bible Church, attended the early morning Bible study at the Kinney's home on February 3, 1990. Mr. Kinney had shoveled snow from his driveway the previous evening, but was not aware that ice had formed overnight. Mr. Carter arrived shortly after 7:00 a.m., slipped on a patch of ice in the Kinneys' driveway, and broke his leg. The Carters filed suit against the Kinneys.

The parties agree that the Kinneys offered their home for the Bible study as part of a series sponsored by their church; that some Bible studies took place at the church and others were held at the homes of church members; that interested church members signed up for the studies on a sheet at the church, which actively encouraged enrollment but did not solicit contributions through the classes or issue an invitation to the general public to attend the studies; that the Kinneys and the Carters had not engaged in any social interaction outside of church prior to Mr. Carter's injury, and that Mr. Carter had no social relationship with the other participants in the class. Finally, the parties agree that the Kinneys received neither a financial nor other tangible benefit from Mr. Carter in connection with the Bible study class.

They disagree, however, as to Mr. Carter's status. Mr. Carter claims he was an invitee; the Kinneys say he was a licensee. And the parties dispute certain facts bearing on the purpose of his visit, specifically, whether the parties intended a future social relationship, and whether the Kinneys held the Bible study class in order to confer some intangible benefit on themselves and others.

On the basis of these facts, the Kinneys moved for summary judgment. The trial court sustained the Kinneys' summary judgment motion on the ground that Mr. Carter was a licensee and that the Kinneys did not have a duty to a licensee with respect to a dangerous condition of which they had no knowledge. This appeal followed.

II.

A. . . .

As to premises liability, "the particular standard of care that society recognizes as applicable under a given set of facts is a question of law for the courts." Harris v. Niehaus, 857 S.W.2d 222, 225 (Mo. banc 1993). Thus, whether Mr. Carter was an invitee, as he claims, or a licensee is a question of law and summary judgment is appropriate if the defendants' conduct conforms to the standard of care Mr. Carter's status imposes on them.

B.

The Kinneys' motion for summary judgment characterizes Mr. Carter as a social guest. The Kinneys' description of Mr. Carter's status as a social guest has led to some confusion in the parties' briefing of the legal issues in this case. Indeed, the Carters assign error to the trial court's decision to sustain the Kinneys' motion for summary judgment, because they believe factual issues are in dispute as to that status.

Historically, premises liability cases recognize three broad classes of plaintiffs: trespassers, licensees and invitees. All entrants to land are trespassers until the possessor of the land gives them permission to enter. All persons who enter a premises with permission are licensees until the possessor has an interest in the visit such that the visitor "has reason to believe that the premises have been made safe to receive him." 65 C.J.S. Negligence, § 63(41), 719. That makes the visitor an invitee. The possessor's intention in offering the invitation determines the status of the visitor and establishes the duty of care the possessor owes the visitor. Generally, the possessor owes a trespasser no duty of care, ... the possessor owes a licensee the duty to make safe dangers of which the possessor is aware, ... and the possessor owes invitees the duty to exercise reasonable care to protect them against both known dangers and those that would be revealed by inspection. ... The exceptions to these general rules are myriad, but not germane here.

A social guest is a person who has received a social invitation. Wolfson v. Chelist, 284 S.W.2d 447, 450 (Mo. 1955). Though the parties seem to believe otherwise, Missouri does not recognize social guests as a fourth class of entrant. ... In Missouri, social guests are but a subclass of licensees. The fact that an invitation underlies a visit does not render the visitor an invitee for purposes of premises liability law. This is because "the invitation was not tendered with any material benefit motive" ... and "the invitation was not extended to the public generally or to some undefined portion of the public from which invitation, ... entrants might reasonably expect precautions have been taken, in the exercise of ordinary care, to protect them from danger." ... Thus, this Court held that there "is no reason for concluding it is unjust to the parties ... to put a social guest in the legal category of licensee." *Id.* at 451.

It does not follow from this that a person invited for purposes not strictly social is perforce an invitee. As *Wolfson* clearly indicates, an entrant becomes an invitee when the possessor invites with the expectation of a material benefit from the visit or extends an invitation to the public generally. *See also* Restatement (Second) of Torts, § 332 (defining an invitee for business purposes) and 65 C.J.S. Negligence, § 63(41) (A person is an invitee "if the premises are thrown open to the public and [the person] enters pursuant to the purposes for which they are thrown open."). Absent the sort of invitation from the possessor that lifts a licensee to invitee status, the visitor remains a licensee as a matter of law.

The record shows beyond cavil that Mr. Carter did not enter the Kinneys' land to afford the Kinneys any material benefit. He is therefore not an invitee under the definition of invitee contained in Section 332 of the Restatement. The record also demonstrates that the Kinneys did not "throw open" their premises to the public in such a way as would imply a warranty of safety. The Kinneys took no steps to encourage general attendance by some undefined portion of the public; they invited only church members who signed up at church. They did nothing more than give permission to a limited class of persons—church members—to enter their property.

Mr. Carter's response to the Kinneys' motion for summary judgment includes Mr. Carter's affidavit in which he says that he did not intend to socialize with the Kinneys and that the Kinneys would obtain an intangible benefit, albeit mutual, from Mr. Carter's participation in the class. Mr. Carter's affidavit attempts to create an issue of fact for the purpose of defeating summary judgment. But taking Mr. Carter's statement of the facts as true in all respects, he argues a factual distinction that has no meaning under Missouri law. Human intercourse and the intangible benefits of sharing one's property with others for a mutual purpose are hallmarks of a licensee's permission to enter. Mr. Carter's factual argument makes the legal point he wishes to avoid: his invitation is not of the sort that makes an invitee. He is a licensee.

The trial court concluded as a matter of law that Mr. Carter was a licensee, that the Kinneys had no duty to protect him from unknown dangerous conditions, and that the defendants were entitled to summary judgment as a matter of law. In that conclusion, the trial court was eminently correct.

C.

The Carters next argue that this Court should abolish the distinction between licensees and invitees and hold all possessors to a standard of reasonable care under the circumstances. They argue that the current system that recognizes a lower standard of care for licensees than invitees is arbitrary and denies deserving plaintiffs compensation for their injuries. *See* Mounsey v. Ellard, . . . 297 N.E.2d 43, 52 (Mass. 1973) (Abolition of the licensee/invitee distinction in favor of a duty of reasonable care in all circumstances "prevents the plaintiff's status as licensee or invitee from being the sole determinative factor in assessing the occupier's liability.") The Carters note that twenty states have abolished the distinction since 1968 and encourage Missouri to join this "trend."

The Kinneys claim that the trend is little more than a fad. They note that twelve states[4] have expressly rejected the abolition of the distinction since the "trend" began in 1968 and that the remaining eighteen states, including Missouri, have not directly addressed the issue and maintain the common law distinctions.

We are not persuaded that the licensee/invitee distinction no longer serves. The possessor's intentions in issuing the invitation determine not only the status of the entrant but the possessor's duty of care to that entrant. The contours of the legal relationship that results from the possessor's invitation reflect a careful and patient effort by courts over time to balance the interests of persons injured by conditions of land against the interests of possessors of land to enjoy and employ their land for the purposes they wish. Moreover, and despite the exceptions courts have

---

4. McMullan v. Butler, 346 So. 2d 950, 951 (Ala. 1977); Baldwin v. Mosley, 748 S.W.2d 146, 147 (Ark. 1988); Morin v. Bell Court Condominium Ass'n, Inc., 612 A.2d 1197, 1201 (Conn. 1992); Bailey v. Pennington, 406 A.2d 44, 47-48 (Del. 1979), *appeal dismissed*, 444 U.S. 1061 (1980); Mooney v. Robinson, 471 P.2d 63, 65 (Idaho 1970); Kirschner v. Louisville Gas & Elec. Co., 743 S.W.2d 840, 844 (Ky. 1988); Astleford v. Milner Enterprises, Inc., 233 So. 2d 524, 525 (Miss. 1970); Di Gildo v. Caponi, 247 N.E.2d 732, 736 (Ohio 1969); Sutherland v. Saint Francis Hosp., Inc., 595 P.2d 780, 782 (Okla. 1979); Tjas v. Proctor, 591 P.2d 438, 441 (Utah 1979); Younce v. Ferguson, 724 P.2d 991, 995 (Wash. 1986); and Yalowizer v. Husky Oil Co., 629 P.2d 465, 469 (Wyo. 1981).

developed to the general rules, the maintenance of the distinction between licensee and invitee creates fairly predictable rules within which entrants and possessors can determine appropriate conduct and juries can assess liability. To abandon the careful work of generations for an amorphous "reasonable care under the circumstances" standard seems — to put it kindly — improvident.

Though six states have abolished the distinction between licensee and invitee since Professor Keeton penned his words, he speculates that the failure of more states to join the "trend" may reflect a more fundamental dissatisfaction with certain developments in accident law that accelerated during the 1960's — reduction of whole systems of legal principles to a single, perhaps simplistic, standard of reasonable care, the sometimes blind subordination of other legitimate social objectives to the goals of accident prevention and compensation, and the commensurate shifting of the balance of power to the jury from the judge. At least it appears that the courts are . . . acquiring a more healthy skepticism toward invitations to jettison years of developed jurisprudence in favor of beguiling legal panacea. W.P. Keeton, Prosser and Keeton on the Law of Torts § 62 (1984).

We remain among the healthy skeptics. The experience of the states that have abolished the distinction between licensee and invitee does not convince us that their idea is a better one. Indeed, we are convinced that they have chosen wrongly. . . .

The judgment of the trial court is affirmed.

hypo **56**

A is a student at *X* Law School. After class, *B* spilled a cup of coffee on the floor in the hall. An attendant, *X*'s employee, mopped the floor and placed a triangular "Wet Floor – Caution" sign on the wet floor. *A*, in a hurry to get to class, did not see the sign, slipped, and fell, seriously injuring herself. *A* sues *X* alleging negligence for failing to rope off the area on the floor that was mopped. What result?

hypo **57**

X invited friends to her home for their weekly bridge party. After playing bridge for an hour she announced that she had a special surprise. She had invited a salesperson to sell Tupperware (a high-quality brand of plastic containers). If enough orders were placed, *X* would receive free Tupperware. Just before the sales pitch *X* asked *Y* to help serve refreshments from the kitchen so that the friends could eat while listening to the sales pitch. *X* told *Y* that she waxed the floor just before the group arrived and the floor might be slippery. *Y* entered the kitchen and slipped and fell, breaking her hip. *Y* alleges that *X* was negligent in that she had waxed the floor so heavily that it was unusually slippery. Does *Y* have a viable negligence case against *X*?

4. Rejection of the Categories

One did not have to be prescient to predict that social guests would argue that they were not on the possessor's premises solely for their own benefit but also to benefit the possessor and thus should be entitled to the more favorable rules that extend to invitees rather than the limited duties owed to licensees. Furthermore, risks to social guests might be more formidable than those to business invitees and the ease with which those risks could be avoided might be less than in the case of an invitee. In 1968 the California Supreme Court became the first court to abolish the use of categories of entrants to determine the duties of possessors of land in favor of an across-the-board duty of reasonable care.

ROWLAND v. CHRISTIAN
443 P.2d 561 (Cal. 1968)

PETERS, Justice.

Plaintiff appeals from a summary judgment for defendant Nancy Christian in this personal injury action.

In his complaint plaintiff alleged that about November 1, 1963, Miss Christian told the lessors of her apartment that the knob of the cold water faucet on the bathroom basin was cracked and should be replaced; that on November 30, 1963, plaintiff entered the apartment at the invitation of Miss Christian; that he was injured while using the bathroom fixtures, suffering severed tendons and nerves of his right hand; and that he has incurred medical and hospital expenses. He further alleged that the bathroom fixtures were dangerous, that Miss Christian was aware of the dangerous condition, and that his injuries were proximately caused by the negligence of Miss Christian. Plaintiff sought recovery of his medical and hospital expenses, loss of wages, damage to his clothing, and $100,000 general damages. It does not appear from the complaint whether the crack in the faucet handle was obvious to an ordinary inspection or was concealed.

Miss Christian filed an answer containing a general denial except that she alleged that plaintiff was a social guest and admitted the allegations that she had told the lessors that the faucet was defective and that it should be replaced. Miss Christian also alleged contributory negligence and assumption of the risk. In connection with the defenses, she alleged that plaintiff had failed to use his "eyesight" and knew of the condition of the premises. Apart from these allegations, Miss Christian did not allege whether the crack in the faucet handle was obvious or concealed.

Miss Christian's affidavit in support of the motion for summary judgment alleged facts showing that plaintiff was a social guest in her apartment when, as he was using the bathroom, the porcelain handle of one of the water faucets broke in his hand causing injuries to his hand and that plaintiff had used the bathroom on a prior occasion. In opposition to the motion for summary judgment, plaintiff filed an affidavit stating that immediately prior to the accident he told Miss Christian that he was going to use the bathroom facilities, that she had known for two weeks prior to the accident that the faucet handle that caused injury was cracked, that she warned the manager of the building of the condition, that nothing was done to repair the condition of the handle, that she did not say anything to plaintiff as to the condition of the handle, and that when plaintiff turned off the faucet the handle broke in his hands severing the tendons and medial nerve in his right hand.

In the instant case, Miss Christian's affidavit and admissions made by plaintiff show that plaintiff was a social guest and that he suffered injury when the faucet handle broke; they do not show that the faucet handle crack was obvious or even nonconcealed. Without in any way contradicting her affidavit or his own admissions, plaintiff at trial could establish that she was aware of the condition and realized or should have realized that it involved an unreasonable risk of harm to him, that defendant should have expected that he would not discover the danger, that she did not exercise reasonable care to eliminate the danger or warn him of it, and that he did not know or have reason to know of the danger. Plaintiff also could establish, without contradicting Miss Christian's affidavit or his admissions, that the crack was not obvious and was concealed. Under the circumstances, a summary judgment is proper in this case only if, after proof of such facts, a judgment would be required as a matter of law for Miss Christian. The record supports no such conclusion.

Section 1714 of the Civil Code provides: "Everyone is responsible, not only for the result of his willful acts, but also for an injury occasioned to another by his want of ordinary care or skill in the management of his property or person, except so far as the latter has, willfully or by want of ordinary care, brought the injury upon himself. . . ." This code section, which has been unchanged in our law since 1872, states a civil law and not a common law principle. (Fernandez v. Consolidated Fisheries, Inc., 219 P.2d 73.)

Nevertheless, some common law judges and commentators have urged that the principle embodied in this code section serves as the foundation of our negligence law. Thus in a concurring opinion, Brett, M.R. in Heaven v. Pender (1883) 11 Q.B.D. 503, 509, states: "whenever one person is by circumstances placed in such a position with regard to another that everyone of ordinary sense who did think would at once recognize that if he did not use ordinary care and skill in his own conduct with regard to those circumstances he would cause danger of injury to the person or property of the other, a duty arises to use ordinary care and skill to avoid such danger."

California cases have occasionally stated a similar view: "All persons are required to use ordinary care to prevent others being injured as the result of their conduct." . . . Although it is true that some exceptions have been made to the general principle that a person is liable for injuries caused by his failure to exercise reasonable care in the circumstances, it is clear that in the absence of statutory provision declaring an exception to the fundamental principle enunciated by section 1714 of the Civil Code, no such exception should be made unless clearly supported by public policy. . . .

A departure from this fundamental principle involves the balancing of a number of considerations; the major ones are the foreseeability of harm to the plaintiff, the degree of certainty that the plaintiff suffered injury, the closeness of the connection between the defendant's conduct and the injury suffered, the moral blame attached to the defendant's conduct, the policy of preventing future harm, the extent of the burden to the defendant and consequences to the community of imposing a duty to exercise care with resulting liability for breach, and the availability, cost, and prevalence of insurance for the risk involved. . . .

One of the areas where this court and other courts have departed from the fundamental concept that a man is liable for injuries caused by his carelessness is with regard to the liability of a possessor of land for injuries to persons who have entered upon that land. It has been suggested that the special rules regarding liability of the possessor of land are due to historical considerations stemming from the high place which land has traditionally held in English and American thought, the dominance and prestige of the landowning class in England during the formative period of the rules governing the possessor's liability, and the heritage of feudalism. (2 Harper and James, The Law of Torts (1956) p. 1432.)

The departure from the fundamental rule of liability for negligence has been accomplished by classifying the plaintiff either as a trespasser, licensee, or invitee and then adopting special rules as to the duty owed by the possessor to each of the classifications. Generally speaking a trespasser is a person who enters or remains upon land of another without a privilege to do so; a licensee is a person like a social guest who is not an invitee and who is privileged to enter or remain upon land by virtue of the possessor's consent, and an invitee is a business visitor who is invited or permitted to enter or remain on the land for a purpose directly or indirectly connected with business dealings between them. . . .

Although the invitor owes the invitee a duty to exercise ordinary care to avoid injuring him . . . the general rule is that a trespasser and licensee or social guest are obliged to take the premises as they find them insofar as any alleged defective condition thereon may exist, and that the possessor of the land owes them only the duty of refraining from wanton or willful injury. . . . The ordinary justification for the general rule severely restricting the occupier's liability to social guests is based on the theory that the guest should not expect special precautions to be made on his account and that if the host does not inspect and maintain his property the guest should not expect this to be done on his account. . . .

An increasing regard for human safety has led to a retreat from this position, and an exception to the general rule limiting liability has been made as to active operations where an obligation to exercise reasonable care for the protection of the licensee has been imposed on the occupier of land. . . . In an apparent attempt to avoid the general rule limiting liability, courts have broadly defined active operations, sometimes giving the term a strained construction in cases involving dangers known to the occupier.

Thus in Hansen v. Richey, 46 Cal. Rptr. 909, 913, . . . an action for wrongful death of a drowned youth, the court held that liability could be predicated not upon the maintenance of a dangerous swimming pool but upon negligence "in the active conduct of a party for a large number of youthful guests in the light of knowledge of the dangerous pool." In Howard v. Howard, 9 Cal. Rptr. 311 . . . where plaintiff was injured by slipping on spilled grease, active negligence was found on the ground that the defendant requested the plaintiff to enter the kitchen by a route which he knew would be dangerous and defective and that the defendant failed to warn her of the dangerous condition. . . .

Another exception to the general rule limiting liability has been recognized for cases where the occupier is aware of the dangerous condition, the condition amounts to a concealed trap, and the guest is unaware of the trap. . . .

The cases dealing with the active negligence and the trap exceptions are indicative of the subtleties and confusion which have resulted from application of the common law principles governing the liability of the possessor of land. Similar confusion and complexity exist as to the definitions of trespasser, licensee, and invitee. . . .

There is another fundamental objection to the approach to the question of the possessor's liability on the basis of the common law distinctions based upon the status of the injured party as a trespasser, licensee, or invitee. Complexity can be borne and confusion remedied where the underlying principles governing liability are based upon proper considerations. Whatever may have been the historical justifications for the common law distinctions, it is clear that those distinctions are not justified in the light of our modern society and that the complexity and confusion which has arisen is not due to difficulty in applying the original common law rules — they are all too easy to apply in their original formulation — but is due to the attempts to apply just rules in our modern society within the ancient terminology.

Without attempting to labor all of the rules relating to the possessor's liability, it is apparent that the classifications of trespasser, licensee, and invitee, the immunities from liability predicated upon those classifications, and the exceptions to those immunities, often do not reflect the major factors which should determine whether immunity should be conferred upon the possessor of land. Some of those factors, including the closeness of the connection between the injury and the defendant's conduct, the moral blame attached to the defendant's conduct, the policy of preventing future harm, and the prevalence and availability of insurance, bear little, if any, relationship to the classifications of trespasser, licensee and invitee and the existing rules conferring immunity.

Although in general there may be a relationship between the remaining factors and the classifications of trespasser, licensee, and invitee, there are many cases in which no such relationship may exist. Thus, although the foreseeability of harm to an invitee would ordinarily seem greater than the foreseeability of harm to a trespasser, in a particular case the opposite may be true. The same may be said of the issue of certainty of injury. The burden to the defendant and consequences to the community of imposing a duty to exercise care with resulting liability for breach may often be greater with respect to trespassers than with respect to invitees, but it by no means follows that this is true in every case. In many situations, the burden will be the same, i.e., the conduct necessary upon the defendant's part to meet the burden of exercising due care as to invitees will also meet his burden with respect to licensees and trespassers. The last of the major factors, the cost of insurance, will, of course, vary depending upon the rules of liability adopted, but there is no persuasive evidence that applying ordinary principles of negligence law to the land occupier's liability will materially reduce the prevalence of insurance due to increased cost or even substantially increase the cost. . . .

A man's life or limb does not become less worthy of protection by the law nor a loss less worthy of compensation under the law because he has come upon the land of another without permission or with permission but without a business purpose. Reasonable people do not ordinarily vary their conduct depending upon such matters, and to focus upon the status of the injured party as a trespasser, licensee, or invitee in order to determine the question whether the landowner has a duty of care, is contrary to our modern social mores and humanitarian values. The common law rules obscure rather than illuminate the proper considerations which should govern determination of the question of duty. . . .

Once the ancient concepts as to the liability of the occupier of land are stripped away, the status of the plaintiff relegated to its proper place in determining such liability, and ordinary principles of negligence applied, the result in the instant case presents no substantial difficulties. As we have seen, when we view the matters presented on the motion for summary judgment as we must, we must assume defendant Miss Christian was aware that the faucet handle was defective and dangerous, that the defect was not obvious, and that plaintiff was about to come in contact with the defective condition, and under the undisputed facts she neither remedied the condition nor warned plaintiff of it. Where the occupier of land is aware of a concealed condition involving in the absence of precautions an unreasonable risk of harm to those coming in contact with it and is aware that a person on the premises is about to come in contact with it, the trier of fact can reasonably conclude that a failure to warn or to repair the condition constitutes negligence. Whether or not a guest has a right to expect that his host will remedy dangerous conditions on his account, he should reasonably be entitled to rely upon a warning of the dangerous condition so that he, like the host, will be in a position to take special precautions when he comes in contact with it.

The judgment is reversed.

FOOD FOR THOUGHT

Isn't *Rowland* a case in which the plaintiff could have prevailed even under the classical limited duty rule that governs the liability of occupiers of land to licensees? In the last paragraph of the opinion, the court notes that the defendant knew of the defective faucet; that the danger was hidden; and that the defendant did not warn the plaintiff of the hidden danger. Why does this scenario not fit neatly into the "hidden trap" exception that imposes a duty on occupiers of land to warn social guests of hidden dangers?

What if the faucet had broken several hours before the plaintiff was injured and defendant was unaware of the problem? Another guest might have used the bathroom and failed to tell the defendant that the faucet was broken. Assume that the guest left the bathroom a mess. There were towels on the floor and the sink was dirty. Would the plaintiff, under the new *Rowland* rules, have a viable case for negligence since a jury could find that a reasonable host would have cleaned the bathroom and would have discovered the defective faucet? Isn't there more than a tad of common sense to the common law categories?

SOME LEGISLATIVE CUTBACKS

Subsequent to *Rowland*, California enacted legislation carving out several statutory exceptions to the full duty of reasonable care imposed on occupiers of land:

> (1) *The Moving Train Exception:* Cal. Civil Code § 1714.7 denies recovery for persons injured while attempting to get on or off a moving train. *See* Perez v. Southern Pacific Transportation Co., 267 Cal. Rptr. 100 (Cal. Ct. App. 1990).
>
> (2) *The Felony Exception:* Cal. Civ. Code § 847 denies recovery to any person who was in the process of committing one or more of 25 enumerated felonies while on the land of another unless the possessor acted in a willful or wanton manner or willfully failed to guard against a dangerous condition on the premises. *See* Calvillo-Silva v. Home Grocery, 968 P.2d 65 (Cal. 1998).

THE SCORECARD

It first appeared that *Rowland* might sweep the country. Approximately one-fifth of the states followed *Rowland* and fully abolished the common law categories. *See, e.g.,* Pickard v. City & County of Honolulu, 452 P.2d 445, 446 (Haw. 1969); Smith v. Arbaugh's Restaurant, 469 F.2d 97 (D.C. Cir. 1972); Basso v. Miller, 352 N.E.2d 868 (N.Y. 1976).[1] See also Kermarec v. Compagnie Generale, 358 U.S. 625 (1959) (refusing to use the common law categories in maritime law). A slightly greater number abolished the distinction between licensees and invitees but retained the common law rules limiting liability to trespassers. *See, e.g.,* Wood v. Camp, 284 So. 2d 691 (Fla. 1973); Mounsey v. Ellard, 297 N.E.2d 43 (Mass. 1973); Nelson v. Freeland, 507 S.E.2d 882 (N.C. 1998); Alexander v. Medical Associates Clinic, 646 N.W.2d 74 (Iowa 2002). The rest have either retained the common law categories or have yet to address the issue. For a comprehensive review of the law in all jurisdictions, *see* Vitauts M. Gulbis, Annotation, *Modern Status of Rules Conditioning Landowner's Liability upon Status of Injured Party as Invitee, Licensee, or Trespasser,* 22 A.L.R. 4th 294 (1983 & Supp. 2006) (listing cases in which the plaintiff's status as invitee, licensee, or trespasser was determinative). *See also* Koenig v. Koenig, 766 N.W.2d 635 (Iowa 2009) (abolishing distinction between invitees and licensees after exhaustive review of post-*Rowland* authority nationwide).

Scholars remain firmly behind the movement to eliminate the distinction between licensees and invitees. *See, e.g.,* Osborne M. Reynolds, Jr., *Licensees in Landoccupiers' Liability Law—Should They Be Exterminated or Resurrected?,* 55 Okla. L. Rev. 67 (2002). *But see* Keith N. Hylton, *Tort Duties of Landowners: A Positive Theory,* 44 Wake Forest L. Rev. 1049 (2009); Robert S. Driscoll, *The Law of Premises Liability in America: Its Past, Present and Considerations for Its Future,* 82 Notre Dame L. Rev. 881 (2006) (arguing that the common law rule governing trespasses should be retained). For an amusing case illustrating the arbitrariness of

---

1. After the Colorado Supreme Court abrogated the common law categories in Mile High Fence Co. v. Radovich, 489 P.2d 308 (Colo. 1971), the legislature restored them. Colo. Rev. Stat. § 13-21-115 (2006).

the invitee/licensee distinction, see Heins v. Webster County, 552 N.W.2d 51 (Neb. 1996). Like Carter v. Kinney, above, the case involved a plaintiff who slipped on snow and ice, in this case at a hospital. Under state law, if the plaintiff had been an invitee, reasonable care would have required the hospital to clear the snow and ice; if he had been a licensee, on the other hand, the only duty would have been to warn him of known dangers that were not open and obvious, and the snow was plainly visible. At trial the parties disputed the purpose of the plaintiff's visit. The defendant contended he was at the hospital to visit his daughter, who worked there as the director of nursing. The plaintiff claimed that he was there to discuss his plans to play Santa Claus at a party for hospital staff. The court held that the hospital should be subject to a reasonable care standard with respect to all lawful entrants upon its land. The care owed to the plaintiff should not vary depending on whether he was there to visit his daughter or talk about playing Santa Claus.

The Restatement, Third, of Torts deals with the duties of land possessors. It takes the position that the tripartite division of entrants should be abolished in favor of a general reasonableness standard, thus buying into *Rowland v. Christian*. It does, however, create a notable exception to the reasonableness standard by drawing a distinction in § 52 between "ordinary" and "flagrant" trespassers. For the former the landowner owes a duty of reasonable care. For the latter the landowner's duty is limited to (a) not acting in an intentional, wanton, or willful manner to cause physical harm; (b) exercising reasonable care for a trespasser who reasonably appears to be imperiled and (1) helpless or (2) unable to protect himself or herself. Comment *a* to § 52 defines "flagrant" as egregious or atrocious. For a critique of this concept in § 52 by one of the authors, *see* James A. Henderson, Jr., *The Status of Trespassers on Land*, 44 Wake Forest L. Rev. 1071, 1074-1078 (2009).

LIFE AFTER REJECTION OF THE CATEGORIES

Even in the states that have rejected the categories, courts have had to struggle with the problem of when it is appropriate to direct a verdict in favor of the occupier of land. On the very day that the New York Court of Appeals abolished the common law categories in Basso v. Miller, 352 N.E.2d 868 (N.Y. 1976), the court in Scurti v. City of New York, 354 N.E.2d 794 (N.Y. 1976), dealt with the case of a 14-year-old boy who entered a railroad yard through the hole in a fence at the rear of a playground. He climbed onto the top of a freight car and was electrocuted when he came in contact with a high-voltage wire used to supply power to the locomotives. The court said that it would not rule in favor of the railroad yard as a matter of law. Prior to this accident several other cases of serious injuries and death had occurred when children had made their way into the railroad yard. The court went out of its way to deliver a homily to trial courts as to what weight should be given to the factors that were embodied in the now-rejected limited duty rules. The court said (*id.* at 798-799):

> Under the standard of reasonable care adopted by the court today the factors which sustained the landowner's immunity and inspired the exceptions under prior law will no longer be considered decisive. But, as indicated, most of them

authors' dialogue 30

AARON: Jim, I just reread your 1976 article in which you critique *Rowland*. In that article you predict that courts will not jump on the *Rowland* bandwagon and will likely retain the common law categories. With only ten jurisdictions opting for the abolition of all categories and with another ten abolishing only the distinction between licensees and invitees, it appears that you were a pretty good prognosticator. The revolution seems to have been only a blip.

JIM: From here on out call me Jim, the prophet.

AARON: Don't get swell-headed on me. I was just about to deliver a sharp response to your article. Your critique of *Rowland* is based on the reasoning that *Rowland* acknowledges that, while the traditional categories no longer control, they remain relevant. Many of the considerations that went into supporting the limited duties for the various categories of entrants to land are retained as matters to be considered by juries. Thus, juries must not only take into account the need of landowners to utilize their property with considerable freedom, the lack of foreseeability that a trespasser may be on the land, and the difficulty of imposing a duty to inspect the property to discover hidden risks, but they also should somehow weigh the plaintiff's status, as such. You argue that juries will be taking plaintiff's status into account in a totally unstructured way. They will be deciding matters of important social policy for occupiers of land without any guidance by the courts as to how to weigh the plaintiff's status.

JIM: I think that's right. Under the common law categories, for example, an occupier does not owe a duty to a licensee to inspect the property. The jury is given a firm rule and if the plaintiff's only argument is based on a failure to inspect, the court directs a verdict for defendant. Juries are not given the negligence balancing

have some probative value and to that extent they will continue to have some relevance in determining whether, under all the facts and circumstances, there has been a breach of duty.

The fact that the injury occurred on the defendant's property is certainly a relevant circumstance in assessing the reasonableness of the defendant's conduct. The defendant has the right to use his property and to develop it for his profit and enjoyment. That often means that he must conduct dangerous activities or permit dangerous instruments and conditions to exist on the premises. However under those circumstances he must take reasonable measures to prevent injury to those whose presence on the property can reasonably be foreseen. . . . In this connection it is important to note that the elimination of the immunity conferred by prior law should not pose an unreasonable burden on the use of the property since all that is now required is the exercise of reasonable care under the circumstances. . . . The defendant can always show that it would have been unduly burdensome to have done more. . . .

The fact that the plaintiff entered without permission is also a relevant circumstance. . . . It may well demonstrate that the plaintiff's presence was not foreseeable at the time and place of the injury. However the likelihood of one entering

formula and asked to determine whether, adding in the plaintiff's status in some undefined way, it was unreasonable for her to undertake that responsibility.

AARON: You have it wrong, Jim. What the courts in *Rowland* and *Scurti* were saying was not addressed to juries at all. They were giving instructions to trial courts as to the factors they are to consider in deciding whether to direct a verdict for the defendant-occupier of land. What they were saying to the trial judges is that they ought not to be skittish about directing a verdict in cases where they believe that the plaintiff's status that played such an important role in the common law approach was of crucial importance in a given case. If, for example, the trial court concluded that to impose a duty of inspection would be particularly onerous, they ought to find for the defendant as a matter of law.

JIM: I never said directed verdicts aren't an important part of what I call the "rule of law." But trial judges are always free to direct a verdict when they believe that reasonable persons cannot differ. In fact, I think that *Rowland* implies that courts should direct verdicts *less* often.

AARON: Look, Jim. We all know that trial judges have the power to grant a d.v. or a judgment n.o.v. We also know that they rarely do so because appellate courts don't want them taking cases from juries. What *Rowland* is signaling to the trial judges is that in the area of occupier liability they will be more receptive to trial judge intervention. I really think you missed the boat when you criticized *Rowland* for allowing juries to decide how much weight to give the plaintiff's status without formal guidance. Juries decide difficult cases all the time. The real question for me is whether trial judges will get the message to be aggressive in directing verdicts and whether appellate courts will uphold their directed verdicts for defendants.

JIM: I think you got it exactly wrong, Aaron. Status used to support directed verdicts. Now it is grist for the jury's mill.

---

without permission depends on the facts of the case including the location of the property in relation to populated areas, its accessibility and whether there have been any prior incidents of trespassing in the area where the injury occurred. . . .

This does not mean that every case involving injury on private property raises a factual question for the jury's consideration. In any negligence case the court must always determine as a threshold matter whether the facts will support an inference of negligence or lack of negligence. . . .

Do you have any confidence that trial judges will have the backbone to direct verdicts in favor of occupiers of land rather than send the cases to juries? In an article written by Professor Carl S. Hawkins a little more than a decade after *Rowland*, entitled *Premises Liability After Repudiation of the Status Categories: Allocation of Judge and Jury Functions*, 1981 Utah L. Rev. 15, Hawkins surprisingly found that a significant number of courts that had abandoned the common law categories directed verdicts for defendant occupiers of land. He also found that most cases that he had reviewed would have come out the same way had the category system been in place. One of the authors of this book (Henderson) early on argued that the position taken by *Rowland* (and later on by *Scurti*) would lead to unprincipled results. Henderson contended that if the courts rejecting the common law categories had concluded that the status of entrants was no longer worthy of consideration in deciding a negligence case, he could see the jury performing its traditional factfinding role. However, *Rowland* (and later *Scurti*) made it clear that the occupier-entrant relationship should be taken into account in deciding whether a defendant was negligent. Henceforth, juries will be deciding this issue without any formal guidance by the law. Henderson concluded that the courts that have abandoned the categories but purport "to retain the substance of the prior law" have in actuality retreated from the rule of law. James A. Henderson, Jr., *Expanding the Negligence Concept: Retreat from the Rule of Law*, 51 Ind. L.J. 467, 513 (1976).

B. SPECIAL RULES LIMITING POSSESSORS' LIABILITY

1. The Firefighter's Rule

The rules limiting the liability of possessors of land depending on whether the entrant was a trespasser, licensee, or invitee gave birth to what became known as the firefighter's rule. Firefighters or police who entered on the premises of another to perform their functions were treated as licensees. The possessor of land owed no duty to make the premises safe for a licensee nor to inspect for dangers unknown to the possessor. *See* Fordham v. Oldroyd, 171 P.3d 411 (Utah 2007) (court refuses to abandon traditional firefighter's rule); Segarra v. Electrical Wholesalers, Inc., 2007 WL 1676806 (Conn. Super. Ct.) (police officer on duty has no action for injuries suffered due to negligent maintenance of parking lot; firefighter's rule bars recovery). *Prosser and Keeton on Torts* § 61 (5th ed. 1984). Over time, limits on liability to professional rescuers expanded well beyond liability arising from dangerous conditions on the land to encompass a broad immunity for injuries to such rescuers arising within the line of duty. In Pinter v. American Family Mutual Insurance Co., 613 N.W.2d 110 (Wis. 2000), plaintiff, a firefighter who was also an emergency medical technician, suffered injuries when ministering to a passenger who was involved in an auto accident. Plaintiff sued the drivers whose negligence caused the accident claiming that his injuries were the proximate result of the drivers' negligence. The court acknowledged that the firefighter's rule had its origin in the rule limiting liability of occupiers of premises to licensees. But the court went on to say that reasons independent of limited landowner liability supported the continued vitality of the rule. The court cited to Thomas v. Pang, 811 P.2d 821, 825 (Haw. 1991), where the court said:

> The very purpose of the fire fighting profession is to confront danger. Fire fighters are hired, trained, and compensated to deal with dangerous situations that are often caused by negligent conduct or acts. "[I]t offends public policy to say that a citizen invites private liability merely because he happens to create a need for those public services."

The Wisconsin court went on to say that "[i]t would contravene public policy to permit a firefighter to recover damages from an individual who has already been taxed to provide compensation to injured firefighters." 613 N.W.2d at 117. *See also* Jamison v. Ulrich, 206 S.W.3d 419 (Tenn. Ct. App. 2006) (animal control officer bitten by Doberman pinscher has no action against owner of dog for failing to warn about the dangerous nature of the dog; plaintiff is barred by firefighter's rule). Thomas v. CNC Investments, L.L.P., 234 S.W.3d 111 (Tex. App. 2007) (deputy sheriff shot while seeking to stop the thief of a stolen vehicle has no action against the owner of apartment complex for maintaining inadequate security on the premises; claim is barred by firefighter's rule).

Despite the majority status of the firefighter's rule, the rationales offered to support it are weak. Professor Dobbs correctly points out that workers' compensation has a lien on tort awards that a plaintiff recovers and therefore the argument of dual taxation set forth in *Pinter* simply does not wash. The public employer who paid out workers' compensation benefits to the injured firefighter would recoup its outlay from the award that the tortfeasor pays to the plaintiff. Dobbs notes that "in foreclosing the firefighter's recovery, the courts have eliminated the possibility that the city would recoup any of the monies it has paid in compensation." Dan B. Dobbs, *The Law of Torts* 771 (2000). The argument that no duty is owed to the firefighter because he has already been compensated in advance for facing negligent risks is suspect as well. The courts have refused to apply the firefighter's rule in the case of a privately employed professional rescuer whose pay similarly reflects the possibility that he will be exposed to negligent risks. Neighbarger v. Irwin Industries, Inc., 882 P.2d 347 (Cal. 1994). On the other hand, courts have applied the firefighter's rule to volunteer firefighters, even though they are not monetarily compensated for their services. Flowers v. Rock Creek Terrace Limited Partnership, 520 A.2d 361 (Md. 1987).

It is no surprise that the firefighter's rule has been whittled away with a myriad of exceptions (*see* Dobbs, *supra*, §§ 286-287) and been outright rejected in a number of jurisdictions. Some have abolished the doctrine by judicial decision. *See, e.g.,* Christensen v. Murphy, 678 P.2d 1210 (Or. 1984); Hopkins v. Medeiros, 724 N.E.2d 336 (Mass. App. Ct. 2000); Ruiz v. Mero, 917 A.2d 239 (N.J. 2007) (interpreting the New Jersey statute as totally abolishing the firefighter's rule); and others by statute, Fla. Stat. § 112.182 (1990); Minn. Stat. § 604.06 (1982); N.J. Stat. Ann. 2A:62A-21 (1994); N.Y. Gen. Oblig. Law § 11-106 (1996); N.Y. Gen. Mun. Law § 205-a and 205-e (1996).

Even the courts that favor the firefighter's rule recognize that public servants do not assume the risk of every possible harm that might result from performance of their duties. In these jurisdictions, negligence other than that which causes the need for intervention by the plaintiff in the first place may be considered outside the risk assumed in accepting employment and be recoverable. Thus, in Melton v. Crane Rental Co., 742 A.2d 875 (D.C. 1999), plaintiff was allowed to recover for injuries sustained when a crane-operating company negligently smashed the ambulance he was riding in, despite the fact that he was taking a patient to the hospital and was thus in the course of his employment at the time. And in Beaupre v. Pierce County, 166 P.3d 712 (Wash. 2007), a police sergeant avoided summary judgment in a claim against an intervening party for injuries suffered while apprehending a criminal suspect. Also, in Hauboldt v. Union Carbide Corp., 467 N.W.2d 508 (Wis. 1991), the court held that a suit by a firefighter who was injured when an acetylene tank blew up as he was attempting to extinguish a fire could proceed against the manufacturer on the theory that the tank was defective. *See also* Torchik v. Boyce, 905 N.E.2d 179 (Ohio 2009) (independent contractor who built faulty deck on premises not allowed to invoke firefighter's rule).

2. Recreational-Use Statutes

When private landowners open up their property for public recreational use, traditional tort law confronts them with the specter of significant liability for accidents that occur to entrants on their premises. Courts might classify such entrants as licensees or public invitees or otherwise hold the landowner to a full duty of reasonable care. To provide incentives to landowners to allow the public to use their property for recreation (and remove demand on public parks), most states have enacted recreational-use statutes that partially immunize the owner for accidents that take place on the property. The statutes do not apply to landowners who charge money for the use of the land; but if the public has free access to the land, the statutes provide an effective shield to the host. Some laws speak of recreational activities in general terms, but New York General Obligation Law § 9-103 gives a sense of the potential range of activities covered by recreational-use acts:

> 1. Except as provided in subdivision two,
>   a. an owner, lessee or occupant of premises . . . owes no duty to keep the premises safe for entry or use by others for hunting, fishing, organized gleaning as defined in section seventy-one-y of the agriculture and markets law, canoeing, boating, trapping, hiking, cross-country skiing, tobogganing, sledding, speleological activities, horseback riding, bicycle riding, hang gliding, motorized vehicle operation for recreational purposes, snowmobile operation, cutting or gathering of wood for non-commercial purposes or training of dogs, or to give warning of any hazardous condition or use of or structure or activity on such premises to persons entering for such purposes. . . .
> 2. This section does not limit the liability which would otherwise exist
>   a. for willful or malicious failure to guard, or to warn against, a dangerous condition, use, structure or activity. . . .

As the New York statute suggests, many lawmakers balk at insulating owners from responsibility for recklessly putting people at risk. *See, e.g.,* Cal. Civ. Code § 846 (1963) ("willful or malicious failure to guard or warn"); Mich. Comp. Laws § 324.73301 (1995) ("gross negligence"). At a minimum, intentional tortfeasors do not benefit from recreational-use statutes. Many state statutes do not expressly establish liability of a landowner who knows of a hidden danger and fails to warn of its existence. In these states a public user of land covered by a recreational-use statute may be offered less protection than the common law granted to a trespasser. Recreational-use statutes sometimes supersede the special protection given by some states to child trespassers; thus, injured children may find themselves without a remedy. Recreational-use statutes may protect land unsuitable for recreation (*see, e.g.,* Ornelas v. Randolph, 847 P.2d 560 (Cal. 1993)), and sometimes even land that the owner does not intend for public use (*see, e.g.,* Larini v. Biomass Industries, Inc., 918 F.2d 1046 (2d Cir. 1990) (recreational-use statute held to apply even though owner posted "no trespassing" signs). For a treatment of one state's recreational-use statute, *see* Amy M. Caldwell, *The Hawaii Recreational Use Statute: A Practical Guide to Landowner Liability,* 22 U. Haw. L. Rev. 237 (2000).

C. DUTIES OWED TO THOSE OUTSIDE THE PREMISES

The rule of liability for owners and possessors of land for harm done to persons off the land are, in general, quite well settled. A possessor of land is liable for harm negligently done by activity on the premises or for artificial conditions created by her on the premises to persons injured off the premises. For example, in Salevan v. Wilmington Park, Inc., 72 A.2d 239 (Del. 1950), plaintiff brought an action against the operator of a baseball stadium for negligent maintenance of the premises. During the course of an average baseball game, a large number of foul balls would exit the park onto the street. Plaintiff was injured by a foul ball while walking on the street. In upholding a jury verdict for plaintiff, the court held that the operator of the stadium had a duty of reasonable care to those outside the premises and the precaution taken to avoid harm was not reasonably adequate to pedestrians walking outside the stadium. Similarly, if a possessor of land constructs the gutters on her house such that water is discharged onto the street and the water freezes and someone slips on the ice, liability will ensue if the possessor has not acted reasonably to prevent harm to pedestrians. The corollary to this rule is that the possessor is not responsible for natural conditions on the land that cause injury off the land. For example, if after a heavy snowstorm the snow melts and the water flows off the premises and onto the street and then freezes up and someone slips on the ice, the law imposes no duty on the possessor to prevent such natural drainage. The Third Restatement recognizes the artificial vs. natural distinction. For artificial conditions, the landowner has a duty of reasonable care to persons or property not on the land. For natural conditions, a commercial user of land has a duty of reasonable care; however, if the land is used for other (*e.g.,* residential) purposes, the possessor has a duty only if the risk is known or obvious. *See* Restatement (Third) of Torts: Liability for Physical and Emotional Harm § 54.

D. DUTIES OWED BY LESSORS

At common law the duties of a lessor to persons injured on land that had been leased to a tenant were virtually nil. The lessor was treated as the equivalent of a vendor of property who had sold the land. Unless the vendor knows of the dangerous condition and conceals it from the purchaser, he is not liable for injuries that occur after the vendee has taken possession. Furthermore, once the vendee discovers the dangerous condition and has had the opportunity to correct it, the vendor's obligation comes to an end.

This rigid nonforgiving rule was simply draconian. Courts developed a host of exceptions that allowed injured persons to recover. Not unlike the situation with categories of entrants upon property, where the courts created so many exceptions to the rules that, in frustration, some courts scrapped the rules and opted for a standard of reasonable care to govern all entrants in a similar fashion, many courts have opted to impose a duty of reasonable care on lessors. The story is well told in the following case.

SARGENT v. ROSS
308 A.2d 528 (N.H. 1973)

KENISON, Justice.

The question in this case is whether the defendant landlord is liable to the plaintiff in tort for the death of plaintiff's four-year-old daughter who fell to her death from an outdoor stairway at a residential building owned by the defendant in Nashua. The defendant resided in a ground floor apartment in the building, and her son and daughter-in-law occupied a second story apartment serviced by the stairway from which the child fell. . . .

Plaintiff brought suit against . . . the defendant for negligent construction and maintenance of the stairway which was added to the building by the defendant about eight years before the accident. There was no apparent cause for the fall except for evidence that the stairs were dangerously steep, and that the railing was insufficient to prevent the child from falling over the side. The jury returned a verdict . . . in favor of the plaintiff in her action against the defendant landlord. The defendant seasonably excepted to the denial of her motions for a . . . judgment n.o.v. . . .

Claiming that there was no evidence that the defendant retained control over the stairway, that it was used in common with other tenants, or that it contained a concealed defect, defendant urges that there was accordingly no duty owing to the deceased child for the defendant to breach. This contention rests upon the general rule which has long obtained in this and most other jurisdictions that a landlord is not liable, except in certain limited situations, for injuries caused by defective or dangerous conditions in the leased premises. . . . Prosser, Torts § 63 (4th ed. 1971). . . . The plaintiff does not directly attack this rule of nonliability but instead attempts to show, rather futilely under the facts, defendant's control of the stairway. She also relies upon an exception to the general rule of nonliability, to wit, that a landlord is liable for injuries resulting from his negligent repair of the premises. . . . The issue, as framed by the parties, is whether the rule of nonliability should prevail or whether the facts of this case can be squeezed into the negligent repair or some other exception to the general rule of landlord immunity.

General principles of tort law ordinarily impose liability upon persons for injuries caused by their failure to exercise reasonable care under all the circumstances. . . . But, except in certain instances, landlords are immune from these simple rules of reasonable conduct which govern other persons in their daily activities. This "quasi-sovereignty of the landowner" (2 Harper and F. James, Law of Torts 1495 (1956)) finds its source in an agrarian England of the dark ages. . . . Due to the untoward favoritism of the law for landlords, it has been justly stated that "the law in this area is a scandal." Quinn and Phillips, *The Law of Landlord-Tenant: A Critical Evaluation of the Past with Guidelines for the Future,* 38 Ford. L. Rev. 225 (1969). "For decades the courts persistently refused to pierce the hardened wax that preserved the landlord-tenant relationship in its agrarian state." Note, 59 Geo. L.J. 1153, 1163 (1971). But courts and legislatures alike are beginning to reevaluate the rigid rules of landlord-tenant law in light of current needs and principles of law from related areas. . . . "Justifiable dissatisfaction with the rule" of landlord tort immunity . . . compels its reevaluation in a case such as this where we are asked either to apply the rule, and hold the landlord harmless for a foreseeable death resulting from an act of negligence, or to broaden one of the existing exceptions and hence perpetuate an artificial and illogical rule. . . .

One court recognized at an early date that ordinary principles of tort liability ought to apply to landlords as other persons. "The ground of liability upon the part of a landlord when he demises dangerous property has nothing special to do with the relation of landlord and tenant. It is the ordinary case of liability for personal misfeasance, which runs through all the relations of individuals to each other." Wilcox v. Hines, . . . 46 S.W. 297, 299 (1898). Most courts, however, while recognizing from an early date that "the law is unusually strict in exempting the landlord from liability" . . . sought refuge from the rigors of the rule by straining other legal principles such as deceit . . . and by carving out exceptions to the general rule of nonliability. . . . Thus, a landlord is now generally conceded to be liable in tort for injuries resulting from defective and dangerous conditions in the premises if the injury is attributable to (1) a hidden danger in the premises of which the landlord but not the tenant is aware, (2) premises leased for public use, (3) premises retained under the landlord's control, such as common stairways, or (4) premises negligently repaired by the landlord. *See generally* . . . Restatement (Second) of Torts §§ 358-62 (1965).

As is to be expected where exceptions to a rule of law form the only basis of liability, the parties in this action concentrated at trial and on appeal on whether any of the exceptions applied, particularly whether the landlord or the tenant had control of the stairway. . . . The determination of the question of which party had control of the defective part of the premises causing the injury has generally been considered dispositive of the landlord's liability. . . . This was a logical modification to the rule of nonliability since ordinarily a landlord can reasonably be expected to maintain the property and guard against injuries only in common areas and other areas under his control. A landlord, for example, cannot fairly be held responsible in most instances for an injury arising out of the tenant's negligent maintenance of the leased premises. . . . But the control test is insufficient since it substitutes a facile and conclusive test for a reasoned consideration of whether due care was exercised under all the circumstances. . . .

There was evidence from which the jury could find that the landlord negligently designed or constructed a stairway which was dangerously steep or that she negligently failed to remedy or adequately warn the deceased of the danger. A proper rule of law would not preclude recovery in such a case by a person foreseeably injured by a dangerous hazard solely because the stairs serviced one apartment instead of two. But that would be the result if the control test were applied to this case, since this was not a "common stairway" or otherwise under the landlord's control. . . . While we could strain this test to the limits and find control in the landlord . . . as plaintiff suggests, we are not inclined to so expand the fiction since we agree that "it is not part of the general law of negligence to exonerate a defendant simply because the condition attributable to his negligence has passed beyond his control before it causes injury. . . ." 2 F. Harper and F. James, Law of Torts § 27.16, at 1509 (1956). . . .

The anomaly of the general rule of landlord tort immunity and the inflexibility of the standard exceptions, such as the control exception, is pointedly demonstrated by this case. A child is killed by a dangerous condition of the premises. Both husband and wife tenants testify that they could do nothing to remedy the defect because they did not own the house nor have authority to alter the defect. But the landlord claims that she should not be liable because the stairs were not under her control. Both of these contentions are premised on the theory that the other party should be responsible. So the orthodox analysis would leave us with neither landlord nor tenant responsible for dangerous conditions on the premises. This would be both illogical and intolerable, particularly since neither party then would have any legal reason to remedy or take precautionary measures with respect to dangerous conditions. In fact, the traditional "control" rule actually discourages a landlord from remedying a dangerous condition since his repairs may be evidence of his control. . . . Nor can there be serious doubt that ordinarily the landlord is best able to remedy dangerous conditions, particularly where a substantial alteration is required. . . .

Similarly, the truly pertinent questions involved in determining who should bear responsibility for the loss in this case were clouded by the question of whether the accident was caused by a hidden defect or secret danger. . . . The mere fact that a condition is open and obvious, as was the steepness of the steps in this case, does not preclude it from being unreasonably dangerous, and defendants are not infrequently "held liable for creating or maintaining a perfectly obvious danger of which plaintiffs are fully aware." 2 F. Harper and F. James, *supra* at 1493. . . . Additionally, while the dangerous quality of the steps might have been obvious to an adult, the danger and risk would very likely be imperceptible to a young child such as the deceased. . . .

Finally, plaintiff's reliance on the negligent repairs exception to the rule of nonliability . . . would require us to broaden the exception to include the negligent construction of improvements to the premises. We recognize that this would be no great leap in logic . . . but we think it more realistic instead to consider reversing the general rule of nonliability. . . . The emphasis on control and other exceptions to the rule of nonliability, both at trial and on appeal, unduly complicated the jury's task and diverted effort and attention from the central issue of the unreasonableness of the risk. . . .

In recent years, immunities from tort liability affording "special protection in some types of relationships have been steadily giving way" in this and other jurisdictions. . . . We think that now is the time for the landlord's limited tort immunity to be relegated to the history books where it more properly belongs.

This conclusion springs naturally and inexorably from our recent decision in Kline v. Burns, . . . 276 A.2d 248 (1971). *Kline* was an apartment rental claim suit in which the tenant claimed that the premises were uninhabitable. Following a small vanguard of other jurisdictions, we modernized the landlord-tenant contractual relationship by holding that there is an implied warranty of habitability in an apartment lease transaction. As a necessary predicate to our decision, we discarded from landlord-tenant law "that obnoxious legal cliche, *caveat emptor.*" Pines v. Perssion, 111 N.W.2d 409, 413 (1961). In so doing, we discarded the very legal foundation and justification for the landlord's immunity in tort for injuries to the tenant or third persons. . . .

To the extent that Kline v. Burns did not do so, we today discard the rule of "caveat lessee" and the doctrine of landlord nonliability in tort to which it gave birth. We thus bring up to date the other half of landlord-tenant law. Henceforth, landlords as other persons must exercise reasonable care not to subject others to an unreasonable risk of harm. . . . A landlord must act as a reasonable person under all of the circumstances including the likelihood of injury to others, the probable seriousness of such injuries, and the burden of reducing or avoiding the risk. . . . The questions of control, hidden defects and common or public use, which formerly had to be established as a prerequisite to even considering the negligence of a landlord, will now be relevant only inasmuch as they bear on the basic tort issues such as the foreseeability and unreasonableness of the particular risk of harm. . . .

Our decision will shift the primary focus of inquiry for judge and jury from the traditional question of "Who had control?" to a determination of whether the landlord, and the injured party, exercised due care under all the circumstances. Perhaps even more significantly, the ordinary negligence standard should help insure that a landlord will take whatever precautions are reasonably necessary under the circumstances to reduce the likelihood of injuries from defects in his property. "It is appropriate that the landlord who will retain ownership of the premises and any permanent improvements should bear the cost of repairs necessary to make the premises safe. . . ." Kline v. Burns, . . . 276 A.2d 248, 251 (1971).

Although the trial court's instructions to the jury in the instant case were cast according to the traditional exceptions of control and hidden danger, the charge clearly set forth the elements of ordinary negligence which were presented by the court as a prerequisite to a finding of liability on either issue. Thus, the jury could find that the defendant was negligent in the design or construction of the steep stairway or in failing to take adequate precautionary measures to reduce the risk of injury. We have carefully reviewed the record and conclude that there is sufficient evidence, on the basis of the principles set forth above, to support the verdict of the jury which had the benefit of a view. . . . Both plaintiff and the wife tenant testified that the stairs were too steep, and the husband tenant testified that his wife complained to him of this fact. . . . In any event, the use of these steps by young children should have been anticipated by the defendant. . . .

The verdict of the jury is sustained. . . .

THE SCORECARD

A fair number of courts agree with *Sargent. See, e.g.,* Scott v. Garfield, 912 N.E.2d 1000 (Mass. 2009); Miller v. David Grace, Inc., 212 P.3d 1223 (Okla. 2009); Pagelsdorf v. Safeco Insurance Co. of America, 284 N.W.2d 55 (Wis. 1979); Young v. Garwacki, 402 N.E.2d 1045 (Mass. 1980); Mansur v. Eubanks, 401 So. 2d 1328 (Fla. 1981); Stephens v. Stearns, 678 P.2d 41 (Idaho 1984); Favreau v. Miller, 591 A.2d 68 (Vt. 1991). But others still favor the common law rules which impose no duty on a lessor unless they come within the exceptions enumerated in *Sargent. See, e.g.,* Ortega v. Flaim, 902 P.2d 199 (Wyo. 1995); Moreno v. Balmoral Racing Club, 577 N.E.2d 179 (Ill. App. Ct. 1991); Johnson County Sheriff's Posse, Inc. v. Endsley, 926 S.W.2d 284 (Tex. 1996); Chandler v. Furrer, 823 S.W.2d 27 (Mo. Ct. App. 1991). The Third Restatement imposes a duty of reasonable care on lessors for portions of the leased premises over which they retain control. *See* Restatement (Third) of Torts: Liability for Physical and Emotional Harm § 53(a),(b).

The law of lessor liability for personal injury has been affected somewhat by statutes in most states imposing upon the lessor of residential housing a warranty of habitability. The statutes vary in the scope of the duties imposed on lessors. They range from a guarantee that the leased property contains no hidden defects to an obligation to keep the leased property in good repair during the term of the lease. Most statutes do not specifically provide that violation of the statutory warranty is grounds for the imposition of civil liability. However, courts can treat such violations as negligence per se. In Becker v. IRM, 698 P.2d 116 (Cal. 1985), the California court held that a lessor was strictly liable for defects in leased property that caused physical injury. A decade later in Peterson v. Superior Court, 899 P.2d 905, 909 (Cal. 1995), the court acknowledged that *Becker* had received a "chilly reception" both in the courts and in the law reviews and held that landlords would only be held to a standard of reasonable care. Restatement (Third) § 53(f) recognizes a duty based on statutes imposing obligations on lessors in regard to the condition of leased premises.

E. PREMISES LIABILITY: SECURING AGAINST CRIME

In Chapter 5, which deals with proximate cause, we discussed cases where the plaintiff claimed that the defendant should have acted to thwart foreseeable criminal acts of third parties. In general, courts have been less than enthusiastic in imposing a duty of reasonable care on actors to protect strangers against criminal conduct by third parties. In the case that follows, you will note that owners and occupiers of premises may have rather substantial responsibilities to customers and others to provide "reasonable security" to prevent crime.

POSECAI v. WAL-MART STORES, INC.
752 So. 2d 762 (La. 1999)

MARCUS, Justice.

Shirley Posecai brought suit against Sam's Wholesale Club ("Sam's") in Kenner after she was robbed at gunpoint in the store's parking lot. On July 20, 1995, Mrs. Posecai went to Sam's to make an exchange and to do some shopping. She exited the store and returned to her parked car at approximately 7:20 p.m. It was not dark at the time. As Mrs. Posecai was placing her purchases in the trunk, a man who was hiding under her car grabbed her ankle and pointed a gun at her. The unknown assailant instructed her to hand over her jewelry and her wallet. While begging the robber to spare her life, she gave him her purse and all her jewelry. Mrs. Posecai was wearing her most valuable jewelry at the time of the robbery because she had attended a downtown luncheon earlier in the day. She lost a two and a half carat diamond ring given to her by her husband for their twenty-fifth wedding anniversary, a diamond and ruby bracelet and a diamond and gold watch, all valued at close to $19,000. . . .

At the time of this armed robbery, a security guard was stationed inside the store to protect the cash office from 5:00 p.m. until the store closed at 8:00 p.m. He could not see outside and Sam's did not have security guards patrolling the parking lot. At trial, the security guard on duty, Kenner Police Officer Emile Sanchez, testified that he had worked security detail at Sam's since 1986 and was not aware of any similar criminal incidents occurring in Sam's parking lot during the nine years prior to the robbery of Mrs. Posecai. He further testified that he did not consider Sam's parking lot to be a high crime area, but admitted that he had not conducted a study on the issue.

The plaintiff presented the testimony of two other Kenner police officers. Officer Russell Moran testified that he had patrolled the area around Sam's from 1993 to 1995. He stated that the subdivision behind Sam's, Lincoln Manor, is generally known as a high crime area, but that the Kenner Police were rarely called out to Sam's. Officer George Ansardi, the investigating officer, similarly testified that Lincoln Manor is a high crime area but explained that Sam's is not considered a high crime location. He further stated that to his knowledge none of the other businesses in the area employed security guards at the time of this robbery.

An expert on crime risk assessment and premises security, David Kent, was qualified and testified on behalf of the plaintiff. It was his opinion that the robbery of Mrs. Posecai could have been prevented by an exterior security presence. He presented crime data from the Kenner Police Department indicating that between 1989 and June of 1995 there were three robberies or "predatory offenses" on Sam's premises, and provided details from the police reports on each of these crimes. The first offense occurred at 12:45 a.m. on March 20, 1989, when a delivery man sleeping in his truck parked in back of the store was robbed. In May of 1992, a person was mugged in the store's parking lot. Finally, on February 7, 1994, an employee of the store was the victim of a purse snatching, but she indicated to the police that the crime was related to a domestic dispute.

In order to broaden the geographic scope of his crime data analysis, Mr. Kent looked at the crime statistics at thirteen businesses on the same block as Sam's, all of which were either fast food restaurants, convenience stores or gas stations. He found a total of eighty-three predatory offenses in the six and a half years before Mrs. Posecai was robbed. Mr. Kent concluded that the area around Sam's was "heavily crime impacted," although he did not compare the crime statistics he found around Sam's to any other area in Kenner or the New Orleans metro area.

Mrs. Posecai contends that Sam's was negligent in failing to provide adequate security in the parking lot considering the high level of crime in the surrounding area. . . . After a bench trial, the trial judge held that Sam's owed a duty to provide security in the parking lot because the robbery of the plaintiff was foreseeable and could have been prevented by the use of security. A judgment was rendered in favor of Mrs. Posecai, awarding $18,968 for her lost jewelry and $10,000 in general damages for her mental anguish. . . . [W]e granted certiorari to review the correctness of that decision. . . .

A threshold issue in any negligence action is whether the defendant owed the plaintiff a duty. . . . In deciding whether to impose a duty in a particular case, the court must make a policy decision in light of the unique facts and circumstances presented. . . . The court may consider various moral, social, and economic factors, including the fairness of imposing liability; the economic impact on the defendant and on similarly situated parties; the need for an incentive to prevent future harm; the nature of defendant's activity; the potential for an unmanageable flow of litigation; the historical development of precedent; and the direction in which society and its institutions are evolving. . . .

This court has never squarely decided whether business owners owe a duty to protect their patrons from crimes perpetrated by third parties. It is therefore helpful to look to the way in which other jurisdictions have resolved this question. Most state supreme courts that have considered the issue agree that business owners do have a duty to take reasonable precautions to protect invitees from foreseeable criminal attacks.

We now join other states in adopting the rule that although business owners are not the insurers of their patrons' safety, they do have a duty to implement reasonable measures to protect their patrons from criminal acts when those acts are foreseeable. We emphasize, however, that there is generally no duty to protect others from the criminal activities of third persons. *See* Harris v. Pizza Hut of Louisiana, Inc., 455 So. 2d 1364, 1371 (La. 1984). This duty only arises under limited circumstances, when the criminal act in question was reasonably foreseeable to the owner of the business. Determining when a crime is foreseeable is therefore a critical inquiry.

Other jurisdictions have resolved the foreseeability issue in a variety of ways, but four basic approaches have emerged. . . . The first approach, although somewhat outdated, is known as the specific harm rule. . . . According to this rule, a landowner does not owe a duty to protect patrons from the violent acts of third parties unless he is aware of specific, imminent harm about to befall them. . . . Courts have generally agreed that this rule is too restrictive in limiting the duty of protection that business owners owe their invitees. . . .

More recently, some courts have adopted a prior similar incidents test. *See* Timberwalk Apartments, Partners, Inc. v. Cain, 972 S.W.2d 749, 756-57 (Tex. 1998); Sturbridge Partners, Ltd. v. Walker, 482 S.E.2d 339, 341 (Ga. 1997); Polomie v. Golub Corp., 226 A.D.2d 979, 640 N.Y.S.2d 700, 701 (N.Y. App. Div. 1996). Under this test, foreseeability is established by evidence of previous crimes on or near the premises. . . . The idea is that a past history of criminal conduct will put the landowner on notice of a future risk. Therefore, courts consider the nature and extent of the previous crimes, as well as their recency, frequency, and similarity to the crime in question. . . . This approach can lead to arbitrary results because it is applied with different standards regarding the number of previous crimes and the degree of similarity required to give rise to a duty. . . .

The third and most common approach used in other jurisdictions is known as the totality of the circumstances test. *See* Clohesy v. Food Circus Supermkts., . . . 694 A.2d 1017, 1027 (N.J. 1997); . . . Whittaker v. Saraceno, . . . 635 N.E.2d 1185, 1188 (Mass. 1994). . . . This test takes additional factors into account, such as the nature, condition, and location of the land, as well as any other relevant factual circumstances bearing on foreseeability. . . . As the Indiana Supreme Court explained, "[a] substantial factor in the determination of duty is the number, nature, and location of prior similar incidents, but the lack of prior similar incidents will not preclude a claim where the landowner knew or should have known that the criminal act was foreseeable." . . . The application of this test often focuses on the level of crime in the surrounding area and courts that apply this test are more willing to see property crimes or minor offenses as precursors to more violent crimes. See *Clohesy*, 694 A.2d at 1028. In general, the totality of the circumstances test tends to place a greater duty on business owners to foresee the risk of criminal attacks on their property and has been criticized "as being too broad a standard, effectively imposing an unqualified duty to protect customers in areas experiencing any significant level of criminal activity." . . .

The final standard that has been used to determine foreseeability is a balancing test, an approach which has been adopted in California and Tennessee. This approach was originally formulated by the California Supreme Court in Ann M. v. Pacific Plaza Shopping Center in response to the perceived unfairness of the totality test. . . . 863 P.2d 207, 214-15 (Cal. 1993). The balancing test seeks to address the interests of both business proprietors and their customers by balancing the foreseeability of harm against the burden of imposing a duty to protect against the criminal acts of third persons. . . . The Tennessee Supreme Court formulated the test as follows: "In determining the duty that exists, the foreseeability of harm and the gravity of harm must be balanced against the commensurate burden imposed on the business to protect against that harm. In cases in which there is a high degree of foreseeability of harm and the probable harm is great, the burden imposed upon defendant may be substantial. Alternatively, in cases in which a lesser degree of foreseeability is present or the potential harm is slight, less onerous burdens may be imposed." . . . McClung v. Delta Square Ltd. Partnership, 937 S.W.2d 891, 902 (Tenn. 1996). Under this test, the high degree of foreseeability necessary to impose a duty to provide security, will rarely, if ever, be proven in the absence of prior similar incidents of crime on the property. See *Ann M.,* . . . 863 P.2d at 215. . . .

We agree that a balancing test is the best method for determining when business owners owe a duty to provide security for their patrons. The economic and social impact of requiring businesses to provide security on their premises is an important factor. Security is a significant monetary expense for any business and further increases the cost of doing business in high crime areas that are already economically depressed. Moreover, businesses are generally not responsible for the endemic crime that plagues our communities, a societal problem that even our law enforcement and other government agencies have been unable to solve. At the same time, business owners are in the best position to appreciate the crime risks that are posed on their premises and to take reasonable precautions to counteract those risks.

With the foregoing considerations in mind, we adopt the following balancing test to be used in deciding whether a business owes a duty of care to protect its customers from the criminal acts of third parties. The foreseeability of the crime risk on the defendant's property and the gravity of the risk determine the existence and the extent of the defendant's duty. The greater the foreseeability and gravity of the harm, the greater the duty of care that will be imposed on the business. A very high degree of foreseeability is required to give rise to a duty to post security guards, but a lower degree of foreseeability may support a duty to implement lesser security measures such as using surveillance cameras, installing improved lighting or fencing, or trimming shrubbery. The plaintiff has the burden of establishing the duty the defendant owed under the circumstances.

The foreseeability and gravity of the harm are to be determined by the facts and circumstances of the case. The most important factor to be considered is the existence, frequency and similarity of prior incidents of crime on the premises, but the location, nature and condition of the property should also be taken into account. It is highly unlikely that a crime risk will be sufficiently foreseeable for the imposition of a duty to provide security guards if there have not been previous instances of crime on the business' premises.

In the instant case, there were only three predatory offenses on Sam's premises in the six and a half years prior to the robbery of Mrs. Posecai. The first of these offenses occurred well after store hours, at almost one o'clock in the morning, and involved the robbery of a delivery man who was caught unaware as he slept near Sam's loading dock behind the store. In 1992, a person was mugged while walking through the parking lot. Two years later, an employee of the store was attacked in the parking lot and her purse was taken, apparently by her husband. A careful consideration of the previous incidents of predatory offenses on the property reveals that there was only one other crime in Sam's parking lot, the mugging in 1992, that was perpetrated against a Sam's customer and that bears any similarity to the crime that occurred in this case. Given the large number of customers that used Sam's parking lot, the previous robbery of only one customer in all those years indicates a very low crime risk. It is also relevant that Sam's only operates during daylight hours and must provide an accessible parking lot to the multitude of customers that shop at its store each year. Although the neighborhood bordering Sam's is considered a high crime area by local law enforcement, the foreseeability and gravity of harm in Sam's parking lot remained slight.

We conclude that Sam's did not possess the requisite degree of foreseeability for the imposition of a duty to provide security patrols in its parking lot. Nor was the degree of foreseeability sufficient to support a duty to implement lesser security measures. Accordingly, Sam's owed no duty to protect Mrs. Posecai from the criminal acts of third parties under the facts and circumstances of this case. . . .

For the reasons assigned, the judgment of the court of appeal is reversed. It is ordered that judgment be rendered in favor of Wal-Mart Stores, Inc. d/b/a Sam's Wholesale Club and against Shirley Posecai, dismissing plaintiff's suit at her cost. . . .

FOOD FOR THOUGHT

The first two approaches set forth in *Posecai* are classic limited-duty rules. Under the first approach, plaintiff must establish that defendant was aware of specific imminent harm to patrons. Under the second, there must be evidence of previous crimes on or near the premises. If the plaintiff fails to establish these elements, the defendant is entitled to a directed verdict. One does not proceed further with risk-utility balancing. However, whether one looks at the "totality of the circumstances" or performs a "balancing test," it all comes down to whether, taking all the factors into account, the defendant was negligent. What's the "shootin and hollerin" all about?

The answer to this puzzle is that Louisiana, California, and Tennessee view the balancing test as a judicial function in deciding whether there is a duty in the first place. Their decisions indicate a desire to screen out cases that they believe don't meet risk-utility norms. In theory, all courts have the power to decide that a plaintiff has failed to make out a credible risk-utility case. Recall that in Washington v. Louisiana Power and Light Co., in Chapter 3, the court found that to impose a duty on the electric company to insulate its wires was simply too heavy a burden to place on the defendant given the relatively low foreseeability of the harm. But, when a court goes out of its way to announce that it is performing a "balancing test" in the area of landowner liability for failure to provide adequate security against crime, it is signaling that it will require considerable proof as to the foreseeability of harm and will be especially watchful as to the high cost of implementing security before it will let the case get past the duty stage. The courts opting for a "totality of circumstances" approach appear more willing to treat these cases as run-of-the-mill negligence cases that go to juries as a matter of course.

California courts have struggled mightily with the implementation of their "balancing of interests" test. Two cases are especially noteworthy. In the first, Wiener v. Southcoast Childcare Centers, Inc., 88 P.3d 517 (Cal. 2004), parents of two children killed when a man intentionally drove his car through a chain link fence that surrounded a playground sued the child care center and the lessor of the property for negligence. The contention was that the chain link fence provided inadequate protection against intrusion by motor vehicles into the property. The driver was convicted of first degree murder and sentenced to life without parole. In two earlier cases, the California court held that, for a landowner to be liable for crimes committed by third parties, there must be a "high degree of foreseeability." Otherwise, the burden of providing protection through the retention of security guards and other devices designed to curb crime was too high to justify the imposition of a duty. The trial court had granted summary judgment for the defendants but was reversed by the intermediate appellate court on the ground that the claim of negligence in maintaining a weak chain link fence was to protect the children from any vehicle entering the close, whether it be through negligence or intentional criminal conduct. The California Supreme Court reversed, saying that the appellate court "did not give due consideration to the *criminal* nature of the injury producing conduct [of the driver]." The court concluded that plaintiffs could not establish that this heinous act met the high standard of foreseeability that is required to trigger the duty of due care.

A year later, in Delgado v. Trax Bar & Grill, 113 P.3d 1159 (Cal. 2005), the court found it necessary to again reverse its intermediate appellate court. This time the trial court had entered judgment against the defendant bar for failing to provide adequate security to prevent an assault on the plaintiff. The intermediate court reversed, finding no duty. The Supreme Court, in a prolix opinion, sought to provide guidance as to the circumstances in which they would impose a duty on a landowner or entrepreneur to protect against crime. In this case, plaintiff and his wife were patrons in a bar and, while sitting in the bar for over an hour, were the object of hostile stares from several other patrons. When the plaintiff decided to leave the bar, his wife approached the "bouncer" and expressed concern that there was going to be a fight. The bouncer urged the plaintiff and his wife to leave the bar because he thought a fight was imminent. He did not accompany the couple to the parking lot. When they got to the parking lot they were accosted by 12-20 men who delivered a severe beating to the plaintiff causing him serious injuries. The defendant argued that this kind of massive assault on a patron did not meet the "heightened foreseeability" standard. The court reformulated its approach to "prevention of crime" cases, holding that where the burden of prevention is high (such as hiring security guards), there must be heightened foreseeability. However, where the burden is minimal, then it would recognize a duty with a lesser degree of foreseeability. Since the bouncer in this case had actual notice of an impending fight, he could have cautioned the patron who was obviously hostile to the plaintiff not to go after the plaintiff. The failure to attempt to do so was sufficiently minimal as to trigger a duty of due care.

After struggling through the California cases, we are at a loss to understand how trial courts are to divine when a duty to deter crime comes into being. By lowering the foreseeability standard the court has basically opted for nothing more than classic risk-utility balancing. Whether the California courts will now step in less frequently to deny liability on no-duty grounds is anyone's guess. The adage that hard cases make bad law might be restated. Hard cases often make for confused law.

IT ALL STARTED WITH KLINE

The leading case that articulated a duty of a lessor to protect against crime was Kline v. 1500 Massachusetts Ave. Apartment Corp., 439 F.2d 477 (D.C. Cir. 1970). In that case, criminals attacked and seriously injured plaintiff, a tenant in a combined office-apartment building, in a common hallway of the building. Plaintiff alleged that when she moved into the building a decade earlier, there was a doorman on duty 24 hours a day, attendants at the parking garage, and a firm policy of locking side entrances to the building in the evening. Ten years later these security precautions were gone. She alleged negligence on the part of the lessor of the apartment, given that there had been an increasing number of crimes in the common hallways of the building. The District Court ruled as a matter of law that a landlord had no duty to take steps to protect tenants from foreseeable criminal acts. The lower court's ruling was consistent with the generally accepted law at that time. In reversing, the D.C. Circuit held that the landlord was the only one in position to implement security measures. The court acknowledged that the landlord was not an insurer against criminal acts but was obligated to take reasonable steps to minimize the risk of criminal attacks on tenants. For an excellent discussion of how courts have developed liability for conduct that enables others to commit criminal acts, *see* Robert L. Rabin, *Enabling Torts,* 49 DePaul L. Rev. 435 (1999).

IF IT'S BROKE DON'T FIX IT

Although a majority of courts impose liability on lessors for failing to maintain reasonable security, some courts refuse to recognize such a duty. For example, in Funchess v. Cecil Newman Corp., 632 N.W.2d 666 (Minn. 2001), intruders killed a tenant after they entered the apartment building through a security door whose lock was broken. They then got access to the tenant's apartment because the intercom was broken and the tenant buzzed the intruders in without being able to identify who was seeking entry. The Minnesota court held that the landlord-tenant relationship did not impose a duty to provide adequate security. The court was also unwilling to impose liability because the landlord did not repair existing security devices (i.e., the security door and the intercom). The court said (*id.* at 675):

> Transforming a landlord's gratuitous provision of security measures into a duty to maintain those measures and subjecting the landlord to liability for all harm occasioned by a failure to maintain that security would tend to discourage landlords from instituting security measures for fear of being held liable for the actions of a criminal.

THE CAUSATION QUESTION: WOULD IT HAVE MADE ANY DIFFERENCE?

In *Kline,* the breaches in security were so blatant that the causal relationship between the lax security and the attack on the plaintiff was well established. The defendant's argument that the crime may have been committed by another resident of the building or a guest did not warrant taking the causation question away from the jury. *Id.* at 439 F.2d at 487. However, in several cases, courts have struggled with the causation issue and have found the causal link between the negligence in providing inadequate security and the criminal assault to be too speculative to send to a jury. *See, e.g.,* Lopez v. McDonald Corp., 238 Cal. Rptr. 436 (Cal. Ct. App. 1987) (failure to provide unarmed security guard was not cause-in-fact of plaintiff's injuries caused by an armed psychopath); Nola M. v. University of Southern California, 20 Cal. Rptr. 2d 97 (Cal. Ct. App. 1993) (even if campus security was negligent there were no grounds to conclude that better security would have prevented the attack on the victim; case contains an excellent discussion of the causation issue and review of authority); Saelzler v. Advanced Group 400, 23 P.3d 1143 (Cal. 2001) (accord with *Nola*); Godfrey v. Boddie-Noell Enterprises, Inc., 843 F. Supp. 114, 122-123 (E.D. Va. 1994) (same); Kolodziejak v. Melvin Simon & Assoc., 685 N.E.2d 985 (Ill. App. Ct. 1997) (same). For discussion of the difficult problem of establishing causation in cases where the negligence alleged is that the conduct of the defendant enabled the criminal in some manner to commit a crime, *see* Aaron D. Twerski & Anthony J. Sebok, *Liability Without Cause: Further Ruminations on Cause-in-Fact as Applied to Handgun Liability,* 32 Conn. L. Rev. 1379, 1384-1389 (2000) (discussion of breach of security cases); Julie Davies, *Undercutting Premises Liability: Reflections on the Use and Abuse of Causation Doctrine,* 40 San Diego L. Rev. 971 (2003); Dennis T. Yokoyama, *The Law of Causation in Actions Involving Third Party Assaults When the Landowner Negligently Fails to Hire Security Guards: A Critical Examination of Saelzler v. Advanced Group 400,* 40 Cal. W. L. Rev. 79 (2003).

In Chapter 4 (on actual causation) we discussed at length how the courts have struggled with the problem arising in cases where no direct proof of causation is available. Is there some general principle that can be utilized to get out of this morass in the "security gap" cases? Or will this issue be decided by the seat of the pants on a case-by-case basis?

SCHOLARLY COMMENTARY

The liability of lessor and business enterprises for criminal attacks on lessees or business customers continues to be a subject of great interest to the law reviews. *See, e.g.,* Matthew J. Landwehr, *"Come One, Come All, but Watch Your Back!" Missouri Sides with Business Owners in Negligent Security Action — Hudson v. Riverport Performance Arts Centre,* 67 Mo. L. Rev. 59 (2002); Sarah Stephens McNeal, *Torts — Premises Liability — Liability of Tennessee Business Owners for Third-Party Criminal Attacks: Staples v. CBL & Assocs., Inc., 15 S.W.3d 83 (Tenn. 2000),* 68 Tenn. L. Rev. 141 (2000); Steven C. Minson, *A Duty Not to Become a Victim: Assessing the Plaintiff's Fault in Negligent Security Actions,* 57 Wash. & Lee L. Rev. 611 (2000); William K. Jones, *Tort Triad: Slumbering Sentinels, Vicious Assailants, and Victims Variously Vigilant,* 30 Hofstra L. Rev. 253 (2001); Deborah J. LaFetca, *A Moving Target: Property Owner's Duty to Prevent Criminal Acts on the Premises,* 28 Whittier L. Rev. 409 (2006); Ronald Steiner, *Policy Oscillation in California's Law of Premises Liability,* 39 McGeorge L. Rev. 131 (2008).

chapter 8

Affirmative Defenses

A. DEFENSES BASED ON PLAINTIFF'S CONDUCT

Once plaintiff has established a prima facie case for recovery against the defendant, the question arises whether plaintiff's negligent conduct contributed to her injury and, if so, whether plaintiff should be barred from recovery or have her recovery reduced. Defendant has several arrows in his quiver to either defeat plaintiff's claim or at least lessen the damages assessed against him. First, defendant may claim that plaintiff failed to act reasonably. Second, he may claim that plaintiff assumed the risk of injury. Both of these defenses have deep roots in the law of torts and both underwent serious reexamination by courts and legislatures in the latter half of the twentieth century. Finally, the defendant may claim that plaintiff has failed to undertake ameliorative action that would lessen any injury that plaintiff may have incurred.

1. Contributory Negligence

BUTTERFIELD v. FORRESTER
103 Eng. Rep. 926 (K.B. 1809)

This was an action on the case for obstructing a highway, by means of which obstruction the plaintiff, who was riding along the road, was thrown down with his horse, and injured, . . . At the trial before Bayley J. at Derby, it appeared that the defendant, for the purpose of making some repairs to his house, which was close by the road side at one end of the town, had put up a pole across this part of the road, a free passage being left by another branch or street in the same direction. That the plaintiff left a public house not far distant from the place in question at 8 o'clock in the evening in August, when they were just beginning to light candles, but while there was light enough left to discern the obstruction at 100 yards distance: and the witness, who proved this, said that if the plaintiff had not been riding very hard he might have observed and avoided it: the plaintiff however, who was riding violently, did not observe it, but rode against it, and fell with his horse and was much hurt in consequence of the accident; and there was no evidence of his being intoxicated at the time. On this evidence Bayley J. directed the jury, that if a person riding with reasonable and ordinary care could have seen and avoided the obstruction; and if they were satisfied that the plaintiff was riding along the street extremely hard, and without ordinary care, they should find a verdict for the defendant: which they accordingly did. . . .

BAYLEY, J. The plaintiff was proved to be riding as fast as his horse could go, and this was through the streets of Derby. If he had used ordinary care he must have seen the obstruction; so that the accident appeared to happen entirely from his own fault.

Lord ELLENBOROUGH, C.J. A party is not to cast himself upon an obstruction which has been made by the fault of another, and avail himself of it, if he do not himself use common and ordinary caution to be in the right. In cases of persons riding upon what is considered to be the wrong side of the road, that would not authorize another purposely to ride up against them. One person being in fault will not dispense with another's using ordinary care for himself. Two things must occur to support this action, an obstruction in the road by the fault of the defendant, and no want of ordinary care to avoid it on the part of the plaintiff.

Per Curiam. Rule refused.

FOOD FOR THOUGHT

In modern terms the doctrine of contributory negligence can be explained on economic efficiency grounds (it may have been cheaper for the plaintiff than the defendant to avoid the injury). Richard Posner, *Economic Analysis of Law* § 6.4 (3d ed. 1986). It can hardly be defended on fairness grounds since, under the rule of contributory negligence, a plaintiff is totally barred from recovery even if the plaintiff's negligence is far less than the defendant's negligence. The rationales offered by the justices in *Butterfield* do not withstand scrutiny. The argument by J. Bayley that the accident "appeared to happen entirely from his [the plaintiff's] own fault," is simply not true. If the defendant was negligent in placing the pole across the road, then the accident happened as a result of the joint negligence of the defendant and the plaintiff. It is, of course, possible that the defendant, who was making repairs to his house, had a legitimate reason for temporarily placing the pole in the roadway. Furthermore, by leaving the free passage on part of the road well within the view of oncoming riders, he may not have created a significant risk of harm, and thus he may not have been negligent in the first place. If that is Bayley's reasoning, this case has nothing to do with contributory negligence.

C.J. Ellenborough's statement that the plaintiff cannot cast himself upon the obstruction placed by another and avail himself of it if he fails to use reasonable care sounds like he is saying that the plaintiff's contributory negligence is some sort of "intervening superseding cause." If that is what he is saying, it, too, is plainly wrong. Let's put the case in a more modern setting. A builder who is doing some home repairs negligently places some construction materials in the road, partially obstructing the road. A driver speeding 40 mph in a 25-mph zone is not able to stop in time and hits the obstruction. The car goes out of control, injuring both the driver and a passenger sitting in the car. Do you have any doubt that the passenger can recover against the builder? Is the driver's speeding an intervening superseding cause such that it would bar the passenger from recovering against the builder who negligently blocked the road? If you think the answer is yes, then go back and review the cases in Chapter 5.

ESCAPING THE DEADLY DOCTRINE

Whatever the rationale offered to support contributory negligence as a complete bar, the reality is that courts came to detest the doctrine. The idea that a defendant who was negligent would get away scot-free when the plaintiff was guilty of even a little bit of negligence was anathema. Almost from the start the courts sought to mitigate the harshness of the rule barring the plaintiff's recovery. They engaged in several stratagems. First, many courts would almost never direct a verdict against a plaintiff on the issue of contributory negligence even in the presence of overwhelming plaintiff fault. The hope was that a jury would refuse to find the plaintiff was negligent and thereby allow recovery. *See, e.g.,* Rossman v. La Grega, 270 N.E.2d 313 (N.Y. 1971) (holding that it was a jury issue whether standing next to the door of a car with a flat and waving traffic away was contributory negligence); Lazar v. Cleveland Electric Illuminating Co., 331 N.E.2d 424 (Ohio 1975) (holding that reasonable minds could differ as to whether person coming into contact with uninsulated electrical wire while working on roof was contributorily negligent); Paraskevaides v. Four Seasons Washington, 292 F.3d 886 (D.C. Cir. 2002) (reversing lower court ruling that hotel guests were contributorily negligent as a matter of law when their jewelry worth $1.2 million was stolen from a safe in their hotel room since they should have placed the jewelry in the hotel's safe deposit box; court on appeal held that whether their conduct was unreasonable was a fact question for jury).

Second, courts developed an elaborate doctrine that flew under the label of "last clear chance." Under this doctrine, if plaintiff was negligent but was in a position of peril unable to extricate herself from danger and the defendant discovered the plaintiff's peril, then plaintiff's contributory negligence was not a bar ("doctrine of discovered peril"). Other states treated the plaintiff even more kindly under "last clear chance" and negated contributory negligence if the defendant "should have discovered the plaintiff's peril" ("doctrine of undiscovered peril"). *See* Restatement, Second, of Torts, §§ 479, 480. The reasoning behind last clear chance was that a defendant who had the last opportunity to avoid harm was certainly more negligent than the plaintiff who was frozen in a position of peril. (Is this always necessarily so?) Or that the defendant and not the plaintiff was the proximate cause of the harm. (This can't be right, can it?) Third, contributory negligence was not a defense to either intentional torts or to conduct that was reckless or wanton. Fourth, courts were very demanding in requiring that defendant prove that the plaintiff's negligence was both the cause-in-fact and the proximate cause of her own harm. In Chapters 4 and 5 we saw how elastic and free-wheeling courts could be in finding that a defendant's negligence met these two causation requirements. When it came to plaintiff's fault, the courts seeking to negate contributory negligence played it by the book. All doubts on these issues were resolved in favor of plaintiff. Finally, there is evidence that some courts treated plaintiffs with more deference since contributory negligence is self-regarding (creating risk to oneself) and not as socially objectionable as primary negligence (creating risks to others).

All of the carping at contributory negligence took its toll. Beginning in the early 1960s, state legislatures and courts abandoned the rule that contributory negligence operated as a complete bar to recovery and replaced it with a kinder and gentler regime of comparative fault. With the adoption of comparative fault, the ameliorative doctrines like last clear chance that had softened the harsh, all-or-nothing rule of contributory negligence had less of a role to play. The Third Restatement abolishes them entirely, in favor of a general approach of apportioning liability among responsible parties. *See* Restatement (Third) of Torts: Apportionment of Liability § 3. The opening case in the next section demonstrates the complexity involved in shifting to what is widely regarded as a fairer and more flexible system for allocating damages based on fault.

2. Comparative Negligence

McINTYRE v. BALENTINE
833 S.W.2d 52 (Tenn. 1992)

DROWOTA, Justice.

In this personal injury action, we granted Plaintiff's application for permission to appeal in order to decide whether to adopt a system of comparative fault in Tennessee. . . .

In the early morning darkness of November 2, 1986, Plaintiff Harry Douglas McIntyre and Defendant Clifford Balentine were involved in a motor vehicle accident resulting in severe injuries to Plaintiff. The accident occurred in the vicinity of Smith's Truck Stop in Savannah, Tennessee. As Defendant Balentine was traveling south on Highway 69, Plaintiff entered the highway (also traveling south) from the truck stop parking lot. Shortly after Plaintiff entered the highway, his pickup truck was struck by Defendant's Peterbilt tractor. At trial, the parties disputed the exact chronology of events immediately preceding the accident.

Both men had consumed alcohol the evening of the accident. After the accident, Plaintiff's blood alcohol level was measured at .17 percent by weight. Testimony suggested that Defendant was traveling in excess of the posted speed limit.

Plaintiff brought a negligence action against Defendant Balentine and Defendant East-West Motor Freight, Inc. [the lessee of the tractor]. Defendants answered that Plaintiff was contributorially negligent, in part due to operating his vehicle while intoxicated. After trial, the jury returned a verdict stating: "We, the jury, find the plaintiff and the defendant equally at fault in this accident; therefore, we rule in favor of the defendant."

After judgment was entered for Defendants, Plaintiff brought an appeal alleging the trial court erred by . . . refusing to instruct the jury regarding the doctrine of comparative negligence. . . . The Court of Appeals affirmed, holding that . . . comparative negligence is not the law in Tennessee.

I

The common law contributory negligence doctrine has traditionally been traced to Lord Ellenborough's opinion in Butterfield v. Forrester, . . . 103 Eng. Rep. 926 (1809). There, plaintiff, "riding as fast as his horse would go," was injured after running into an obstruction defendant had placed in the road. Stating as the rule that "[o]ne person being in fault will not dispense with another's using ordinary care," plaintiff was denied recovery on the basis that he did not use ordinary care to avoid the obstruction. *See* 11 East at 61, 103 Eng. Rep. at 927.

The contributory negligence bar was soon brought to America as part of the common law, *see* Smith v. Smith, 19 Mass. 621, 624 (1924), and proceeded to spread throughout the states. . . . A number of . . . rationalizations have been advanced in the attempt to justify the harshness of the "all-or-nothing" bar. Among these: the plaintiff should be penalized for his misconduct; the plaintiff should be deterred from injuring himself; and the plaintiff's negligence supersedes the defendant's so as to render defendant's negligence no longer proximate. *See* W. Keeton, Prosser and Keeton on the Law of Torts, § 65, at 452 (5th ed. 1984). . . .

In Tennessee, the rule as initially stated was that "if a party, by his own gross negligence, brings an injury upon himself, or contributes to such injury, he cannot recover;" for, in such cases, the party "must be regarded as the author of his own misfortune." Whirley v. Whiteman, 38 Tenn. 610, 619 (1858). In subsequent decisions, we have continued to follow the general rule that a plaintiff's contributory negligence completely bars recovery. . . .

Equally entrenched in Tennessee jurisprudence are exceptions to the general all-or-nothing rule: contributory negligence does not absolutely bar recovery where defendant's conduct was intentional . . . where defendant's conduct was "grossly" negligent, . . . where defendant had the "last clear chance" with which, through the exercise of ordinary care, to avoid plaintiff's injury, . . . or where plaintiff's negligence may be classified as "remote." . . .

Between 1920 and 1969, a few states began utilizing the principles of comparative fault in all tort litigation. . . . Then, between 1969 and 1984, comparative fault replaced contributory negligence in 37 additional states. . . . In 1991, South Carolina became the 45th state to adopt comparative fault, *see* Nelson v. Concrete Supply Co., . . . 399 S.E.2d 783 (1991), leaving Alabama, Maryland, North Carolina, Virginia, and Tennessee as the only remaining common law contributory negligence jurisdictions.

Eleven states have judicially adopted comparative fault. Thirty-four states have legislatively adopted comparative fault.

II

Over 15 years ago, we stated, when asked to adopt a system of comparative fault:

> We do not deem it appropriate to consider making such a change unless and until a case reaches us wherein the pleadings and proof present an issue of contributory negligence accompanied by advocacy that the ends of justice will be served by adopting the rule of comparative negligence.

Street v. Calvert, 541 S.W.2d at 586. Such a case is now before us. After exhaustive deliberation that was facilitated by extensive briefing and argument by the parties, amicus curiae, and Tennessee's scholastic community, we conclude that it is time to abandon the outmoded and unjust common law doctrine of contributory negligence and adopt in its place a system of comparative fault. Justice simply will not permit our continued adherence to a rule that, in the face of a judicial determination that others bear primary responsibility, nevertheless completely denies injured litigants recompense for their damages.

We recognize that this action could be taken by our General Assembly. However, legislative inaction has never prevented judicial abolition of obsolete common law doctrines, especially those, such as contributory negligence, conceived in the judicial womb. *See* Hanover v. Ruch, 809 S.W.2d 893, 896 (Tenn. 1991) (citing cases). Indeed, our abstinence would sanction "a mutual state of inaction in which the court awaits action by the legislature and the legislature awaits guidance from the court," Alvis v. Ribar, . . . 421 N.E.2d 886, 896 (Ill. 1981), thereby prejudicing the equitable resolution of legal conflicts. . . .

III

Two basic forms of comparative fault are utilized by 45 of our sister jurisdictions, these variants being commonly referred to as either "pure" or "modified." In the "pure" form,[5] a plaintiff's damages are reduced in proportion to the percentage negligence attributed to him; for example, a plaintiff responsible for 90 percent of the negligence that caused his injuries nevertheless may recover 10 percent of his damages. In the "modified" form,[6] plaintiffs recover as in pure jurisdictions, but only if the plaintiff's negligence either (1) does not exceed ("50 percent"

---

5. The 13 states utilizing pure comparative fault are Alaska, Arizona, California, Florida, Kentucky, Louisiana, Mississippi, Missouri, Michigan, New Mexico, New York, Rhode Island, and Washington. . . .

6. The 21 states using the "50 percent" modified form: Connecticut, Delaware, Hawaii, Illinois, Indiana, Iowa, Massachusetts, Montana, Nevada, New Hampshire, New Jersey, Ohio, Oklahoma, Oregon, Pennsylvania, South Carolina, Texas, Vermont, Wisconsin, and Wyoming. The 9 states using the "49 percent" form: Arkansas, Colorado, Georgia, Idaho, Kansas, Maine, North Dakota, Utah, and West Virginia. Two states, Nebraska and South Dakota, use a slight-gross system of comparative fault. . . .

jurisdictions) or (2) is less than ("49 percent" jurisdictions) the defendant's negligence. . . .

Although we conclude that the all-or-nothing rule of contributory negligence must be replaced, we nevertheless decline to abandon totally our fault-based tort system. We do not agree that a party should necessarily be able to recover in tort even though he may be 80, 90, or 95 percent at fault. We therefore reject the pure form of comparative fault.

We recognize that modified comparative fault systems have been criticized as merely shifting the arbitrary contributory negligence bar to a new ground. *See, e.g.*, Li v. Yellow Cab Co., . . . 532 P.2d 1226 . . . (1975). However, we feel the "49 percent rule" ameliorates the harshness of the common law rule while remaining compatible with a fault-based tort system. *Accord* Bradley v. Appalachian Power Co., . . . 256 S.E.2d 879, 887 (W. Va. 1979). We therefore hold that so long as a plaintiff's negligence remains less than the defendant's negligence the plaintiff may recover; in such a case, plaintiff's damages are to be reduced in proportion to the percentage of the total negligence attributable to the plaintiff.

In all trials where the issue of comparative fault is before a jury, the trial court shall instruct the jury on the effect of the jury's finding as to the percentage of negligence as between the plaintiff or plaintiffs and the defendant or defendants. *Accord* Colo. Rev. Stat. § 13-21-111.5(5) (1987). The attorneys for each party shall be allowed to argue how this instruction affects a plaintiff's ability to recover.

IV

Turning to the case at bar, the jury found that "the plaintiff and defendant [were] equally at fault." Because the jury, without the benefit of proper instructions by the trial court, made a gratuitous apportionment of fault, we find that their "equal" apportionment is not sufficiently trustworthy to form the basis of a final determination between these parties. Therefore, the case is remanded for a new trial in accordance with the dictates of this opinion.

V

We recognize that today's decision affects numerous legal principles surrounding tort litigation. For the most part, harmonizing these principles with comparative fault must await another day. However, we feel compelled to provide some guidance to the trial courts charged with implementing this new system.

First, and most obviously, the new rule makes the doctrines of remote contributory negligence and last clear chance obsolete. The circumstances formerly taken into account by those two doctrines will henceforth be addressed when assessing relative degrees of fault.

Second, in cases of multiple tortfeasors, plaintiff will be entitled to recover so long as plaintiff's fault is less than the combined fault of all tortfeasors.

Third, today's holding renders the doctrine of joint and several liability obsolete. Our adoption of comparative fault is due largely to considerations of fairness: the contributory negligence doctrine unjustly allowed the entire loss to be borne by a negligent plaintiff, notwithstanding that the plaintiff's fault was minor in comparison to defendant's. Having thus adopted a rule more closely linking liability and fault, it would be inconsistent to simultaneously retain a rule, joint and several liability, which may fortuitously impose a degree of liability that is out of all proportion to fault.[7]

Further, because a particular defendant will henceforth be liable only for the percentage of a plaintiff's damages occasioned by that defendant's negligence, situations where a defendant has paid more than his "share" of a judgment will no longer arise, and therefore the Uniform Contribution Among Tort-feasors Act, T.C.A. §§ 29-11-101 to 106 (1980), will no longer determine the apportionment of liability between codefendants.

Fourth, fairness and efficiency require that defendants called upon to answer allegations in negligence be permitted to allege, as an affirmative defense, that a nonparty caused or contributed to the injury or damage for which recovery is sought. In cases where such a defense is raised, the trial court shall instruct the jury to assign this nonparty the percentage of the total negligence for which he is responsible. However, in order for a plaintiff to recover a judgment against such additional person, the plaintiff must have made a timely amendment to his complaint and caused process to be served on such additional person. Thereafter, the additional party will be required to answer the amended complaint. The procedures shall be in accordance with the Tennessee Rules of Civil Procedure. . . .

VI

The principles set forth today apply to (1) all cases tried or retried after the date of this opinion, and (2) all cases on appeal in which the comparative fault issue has been raised at an appropriate stage in the litigation. . . .

REID, C.J., and O'BRIEN, DAUGHTREY and ANDERSON, JJ., concur.

THE FALLOUT FROM McINTYRE

For an examination of the issues that Tennessee faced in the wake of *McIntyre*, especially the problems associated with the abolition of joint and several liability, *see* Brian P. Dunigan & Jerry J. Phillips, *Comparative Fault in Tennessee: Where Are We Going, and Why Are We in This Handbasket?*, 67 Tenn. L. Rev. 765 (2000).

THE SCORECARD

McIntyre adopts one of the modified forms of comparative fault. The Restatement, Third, of Torts: Apportionment of Liability § 7 (2000) and most scholars

---

7. Numerous other comparative fault jurisdictions have eliminated joint and several liability. *See, e.g.*, Alaska Stat. § 09.17.080(d) (Supp. 1991); Colo. Rev. Stat. § 13-21-111.5(1) (1987); Kan. Stat. Ann. § 60-258a(d) (Supp. 1991); N.M. Stat. Ann. § 41-3A-1 (1989); N.D. Cent. Code § 32-03.2-02 (Supp. 1991); Utah Code Ann. § 78-27-38;-40 (1992); Wyo. Stat. Ann. § 1-1-109(d) (1988).

favor the pure form of comparative negligence. *See, e.g., Prosser and Keeton on Torts* §67 (5th ed. 1984); Arthur Best, *Impediments to Reasonable Tort Reform: Lessons from the Adoption of Comparative Negligence*, 40 Ind. L. Rev. 1 (2007) (harsh critique of modified comparative fault); John W. Wade, *A Uniform Comparative Fault Act — What Should It Provide*, 10 U. Mich. J.L. Reform 220, 225 (1977); John G. Fleming, *Foreword: Comparative Negligence at Last — By Judicial Choice*, 64 Cal. L. Rev. 239, 244-247 (1976); Jerry J. Phillips, *The Case for Judicial Adoption of Comparative Negligence in South Carolina*, 32 S.C. L. Rev. 295, 296-297 (1980). Only a minority of states (13), however, follow this view. A strong majority (33), either through judicial decisions or legislative enactment, have opted for one of the modified forms of comparative fault. Under the modified forms of comparative fault, once a plaintiff's fault reaches either 50 or 51 percent (depending on which scheme of modified fault the state follows), the plaintiff is entirely barred from recovery. *See* William P. Kratzke, *A Case for a Rule of Modified Comparative Negligence*, 65 UMKC L. Rev. 15 (1996) (arguing that a modified system of comparative negligence is superior to a pure system because it provides stronger incentives to both plaintiffs and potential defendants to prevent accidents). Only four states (Alabama, Maryland, North Carolina, and Virginia) and the District of Columbia retain the rule that contributory negligence completely prevents plaintiff from recovering, and one state (South Dakota) uses a system which bars plaintiff's recovery when her fault is gross, but permits recovery when it is only slight. A bill seeking to introduce a modified form of comparative fault was before the Maryland legislature in 2007. The bill never got out of committee because it was linked to the abolishment of the joint and several liability doctrine. The Daily Record (Baltimore, Md.), Apr. 13, 2007. The Maryland Court of Appeals (the state's highest court) declined in 2013 to abrogate contributory negligence, with two judges dissenting. Coleman v. Soccer Ass'n of Columbia, 69 A.3d 1149 (Md. 2013).

WHAT COUNTS AS FAULT

The Restatement, Third, speaks not only to the various forms of comparative fault, but also to what factors should be taken into account by the factfinder in allocating fault. Consider the following section from the Apportionment Restatement:

§8. Factors for Assigning Shares of Responsibility

Factors for assigning percentages of responsibility to each person whose legal responsibility has been established include

(a) the nature of the person's risk-creating conduct, including any awareness or indifference with respect to the risks created by the conduct and any intent with respect to the harm created by the conduct; and

(b) the strength of the causal connection between the person's risk-creating conduct and the harm.

Comment: . . .

b. Causation and scope of liability. Conduct is relevant for determining percentage shares of responsibility only when it caused the harm and when the harm is within the scope of the person's liability. . . .

c. Factors in assigning shares of responsibility. The relevant factors for assigning percentages of responsibility include the nature of each person's risk-creating conduct and the comparative strength of the causal connection between each person's risk-creating conduct and the harm. The nature of each person's risk-creating conduct includes such things as how unreasonable the conduct was under the circumstances, the extent to which the conduct failed to meet the applicable legal standard, the circumstances surrounding the conduct, each person's abilities and disabilities, and each person's awareness, intent, or indifference with respect to the risks. The comparative strength of the causal connection between the conduct and the harm depends on how attenuated the causal connection is, the timing of each person's conduct in causing the harm, and a comparison of the risks created by the conduct and the actual harm suffered by the plaintiff. . . .

Comment *b* makes it clear that, to reduce her recovery, a plaintiff's fault must be the cause-in-fact and the proximate cause of her own harm. If defendant fails to establish either of these basic elements of causation, the plaintiff's negligence will never be taken into account to reduce her recovery. But what the devil are the restaters talking about in Comment *c* when they say that the "comparative strength of the causal connection between each person's risk-creating conduct and the harm" is to be taken into account?

It is hard to believe that the drafters of the Restatement are talking about cause-in-fact. Either a party's conduct is or is not the cause-in-fact of the harm. We presume that, if a semi-trailer whose driver was negligent in lookout collided with a Volkswagen Rabbit whose driver was speeding, the semi-trailer is not more causally responsible than the Volkswagen. They must be talking about comparing the relative proximate cause of the parties.

hypo 58

X, an employee of a subcontractor working on a construction site, was injured when a car driven by *Y* careened into the site and struck a kettle of boiling hot liquid enamel. The spray from the hot liquid hit *X* in his eyes causing blindness. The accident happened when *Y* suffered a sudden epileptic seizure. The general contractor, *Z*, responsible for the safety of the construction site, was negligent in failing to properly barricade the construction site to prevent invasion of the site by vehicles traveling in the area. *X* was negligent for failing to wear eye goggles. Such goggles were standard for all employees working around hot caustic liquid. In an action by *X* v. *Z*, is the relative proximate cause of the parties a consideration in apportioning fault? (This hypo is a variant of *Derdiarian v. Felix Contracting Co.*, in Chapter 5.)

LAW AND ECONOMICS: IS COMPARATIVE NEGLIGENCE EFFICIENT?

Economic efficiency theorists have traditionally defended contributory negligence as the rule which operates best to maximize wealth. *See, e.g.,* Guido Calabresi, *The Cost of Accidents: A Legal and Economic Analysis* (1970); Richard A. Posner, *A Theory of Negligence,* 1 J. Legal Stud. 29 (1972); John P. Brown, *Toward an Economic Theory of Liability,* 2 J. Legal Stud. 323 (1973). However, many commentators in the law and economics movement have come to regard comparative negligence as the more economically efficient rule. *See, e.g.,* Robert D. Cooter & Thomas S. Ulen, *An Economic Case for Comparative Negligence,* 61 N.Y.U. L. Rev. 1067 (1986); Daniel L. Rubinfeld, *The Efficiency of Comparative Negligence,* 16 J. Legal Stud. 375 (1987); Daniel Orr, *The Superiority of Comparative Negligence: Another Vote,* 20 J. Legal Stud. 119 (1991). For the proposition that either system can be made efficient if an appropriate standard for negligence is submitted to the jury, *see* Aaron S. Edlin, *Efficient Standards of Due Care: Should Courts Find More Parties Negligent Under Comparative Negligence?,* 14 Intl. Rev. L. & Econ. 21 (1994).

WORKING OUT THE NUANCES OF COMPARATIVE NEGLIGENCE

With a comparative negligence scheme in place, courts were forced to deal with a host of problems anew:

(1) Last Clear Chance. Because last clear chance was created to ameliorate the harsh effects of contributory negligence as a complete bar, most courts have held that it has no place in a regime where juries can assess the relative degree of fault and apportion damages accordingly. In addition to the principal case, *see* Spahn v. Town of Port Royal, 499 S.E.2d 205 (S.C. 1998); Miller v. Hometown Propane Gas, Inc., 167 S.W.3d 172 (Ark. Ct. App. 2004); Hale v. Beckstead, 116 P.3d 263 (Utah 2005). The fact that the defendant may have had the last clear chance to avoid injuring the plaintiff may be a factor to be considered by the jury in deciding the percentage of fault to be assessed against the defendant, but the doctrine no longer has independent status to negate plaintiff's contributory negligence. But some courts stubbornly still apply the doctrine even after adopting comparative negligence. *See, e.g.,* Juvenalis v. District of Columbia, 955 A.2d 187 (D.C. 2008); Fountain v. Thompson, 312 S.E.2d 788 (Ga. 1984).

(2) Comparative Negligence Meets Joint and Several Liability. The *McIntyre* court concluded that, with the adoption of comparative fault, it was no longer necessary to retain the doctrine of joint and several liability. Other courts disagree. *See* American Motorcycle Assn. v. Superior Court, 578 P.2d 899 (Cal. 1978) [reproduced in Chapter 9 at p. 575]. For a full treatment of the issue of joint and several liability, *see* Chapter 9.

(3) Comparative Negligence as a Defense to Intentional or Reckless Conduct. Earlier we noted that when contributory negligence was a complete bar, courts refused to apply the doctrine when a defendant had acted either intentionally or recklessly. With regard to reckless conduct, most courts applying comparative fault will allow a jury to assess the relative fault of the plaintiff and the reckless defendant. If defendant is speeding at 70 mph in a 25-mph zone and plaintiff is injured when she crosses against the light, there seems to be no good reason that a jury should not be allowed to compare the fault of the two parties. *See, e.g.,* White v. Hansen, 837 P.2d 1229 (Colo. 1992) (plaintiff's negligence in walking with his back to traffic reduced his recovery from a defendant drunk driver); Vining v. City of Detroit, 413 N.W.2d 486 (Mich. Ct. App. 1987) (defendant police officer reckless in giving chase to plaintiff causing the plaintiff's car to collide with a telephone pole; damages reduced 40 percent because of plaintiff's negligence).

When it comes to comparing a plaintiff's negligent conduct with the intentionally tortious conduct of the defendant, many courts resist reducing a plaintiff's recovery based on her comparative fault. *See, e.g.,* Winkler v. Rocky Mountain Conference of United Methodist Church, 923 P.2d 152 (Colo. Ct. App. 1995) (in suit by formal parishioner for inappropriate sexual conduct by pastor, plaintiff's comparative negligence is not a defense); Hampton Tree Farms, Inc. v. Jewett, 974 P.2d 738 (Or. Ct. App. 1999) (comparative negligence is not a defense to willful or intentional conduct); Kellerman v. Zeno, 983 S.W.2d 136 (Ark. Ct. App. 1998) (same); Specialized Commercial Lending Inc. v. Murphy-Blossman Appraisal Services L.L.C., 978 So. 2d 927 (La. Ct. App. 2007) (same).

The majority view notwithstanding, it seems that there are situations involving intentional torts where it would make good sense to reduce plaintiff's recovery based on comparative fault. Where defendant battered plaintiff after plaintiff constantly provoked her throughout the day, one court reduced plaintiff's damages based on her comparative fault. Wijngaarde v. Parents of Guy, 720 So. 2d 6 (La. Ct. App. 1998). Similarly, when defendant, a member of a rock band, assaulted the plaintiff who had been drinking and acting in a disorderly manner, a New York court allowed a 10 percent reduction in the plaintiff's damages. Comeau v. Lucas, 455 N.Y.S.2d 871 (N.Y. App. Div. 1982); Lamp v. Reynolds, 645 N.W.2d 311 (Mich. Ct. App. 2002) (comparative fault is a defense to willful or intentional conduct). Courts frequently compare the "fault," whether negligence or intentional misconduct, of two or more defendant tortfeasors under state comparative fault schemes. For example, where a hotel owner negligently fails to provide adequate security and a guest is injured by a third party, damages could be apportioned between the hotel owner, the security company, and the criminal assailant. See Couch v. Red Roof Inns, Inc., 729 S.E.2d 378 (Ga. 2012); see also Graves v. North Eastern Services, Inc., 345 P.3d 619 (Utah 2015); Santelli v. Rahmatullah, 993 N.E.2d 167 (Ind. 2013). Does this not suggest that the negligence of a plaintiff may be compared with the intentional conduct of the defendant in a multi-party case?

Recall *Ranson v. Kitner*, Chapter 1, the case where the hunter killed someone's dog reasonably believing it to be a wolf. Defendant was held liable for the intentional tort of converting another's property. Should not the owner of the wolf-like dog be charged with comparative negligence for letting his look-alike dog roam freely? Or consider a defendant who acts in self-defense, but uses excessive force and is thus held liable for a battery. Should not the plaintiff, whose conduct brought about the necessity to act in self-defense, be charged with comparative fault and have her damages reduced? For a discussion of these questions, *see* Gail D. Hollister, *Using Comparative Fault to Replace the All-or-Nothing Lottery Imposed in Intentional Torts Suits in Which Both Plaintiff and Defendant Are at Fault*, 46 Vand. L. Rev. 121 (1993).

The trend to broad use of comparative negligence is exemplified in People v. Millard, 95 Cal. Rptr. 3d 751 (Cal. Ct. App. 2009). California has enacted a statute that requires a court at the time of sentencing of a criminal to order restitution to the victim of all economic loss suffered by the victim as a result of the crime. The statute provides that the restitution shall be sufficient to "fully reimburse" the victim for every economic loss incurred. The defendant had been convicted for drunken driving and was obligated to pay for the victim's economic loss. He argued that he should be entitled to reduce his recovery based on the victim's comparative fault in contributing to the accident. The court acknowledged that it was facing a question of first impression because no court had yet applied comparative fault to a defendant obligated to pay under a criminal negligence statute. Notwithstanding the language of the statute that required the defendant to "fully reimburse" the plaintiff, the court applied comparative fault and reduced the plaintiff's verdict.

(4) Rape Cases and Comparative Fault.   The question of whether to invoke comparative fault is especially troublesome in cases involving rape. It arises with fair frequency when a rape victim brings an action against a third party for failing to provide adequate security that would have prevented the rape from taking place. The third-party defendant then alleges that the plaintiff was negligent in failing to take precautions that would have avoided the rape. *See, e.g.,* Wassell v. Adams, 865 F.2d 849 (7th Cir. 1989) (victim opened the door of her motel room and allowed the rapist to use the bathroom in the middle of the night; appellate court upheld jury verdict that assessed 97 percent of negligence to the victim and 3 percent to the motel). Raven H v. Gamette, 68 Cal. Rptr. 3d 897 (Cal. Ct. App. 2007) (claim of inadequate security due to insufficient locks and bars on windows allowing rapist to enter plaintiff's room can be partially offset by plaintiff's comparative negligence in leaving the window open). For an article arguing that a rape victim ought never to have fault assessed against her, *see* Ellen M. Bublick, *Citizen No-Duty Rules: Rape Victims and Comparative Fault*, 99 Columb. L. Rev. 1413 (1999).

(5) Allocating Fault Among Multiple Parties.   When a plaintiff joins several defendants, the question arises whether the plaintiff's fault is to be compared with the fault of each defendant separately or all the defendants in the aggregate. This problem arises only under modified comparative fault. Under pure comparative fault, a plaintiff is entitled to recover from any defendant no matter how high the plaintiff's percentage of fault. A plaintiff 90 percent at fault will recover 10 percent of her damages. Under modified comparative fault, if the plaintiff's fault is greater than that of the defendant, the plaintiff recovers nothing. What happens, for example, when the plaintiff is found to be 40 percent at fault and each defendant is 30 percent at fault? The plaintiff's fault is greater than that of each defendant considered separately but less than that of both defendants together. A small minority of states deny the plaintiff recovery. *See* Hofflander v. St. Catherine's Hospital, Inc., 664 N.W.2d 545 (Wis. 2003), and Wis. Stat. § 895.045 (2007); Minn. Stat. Ann. § 604.01 (West 2000); Idaho Code § 6-801 (Michie 1998). The vast majority allow the plaintiff to recover if the plaintiff's fault is less than the combined fault of the defendants. *See, e.g.,* Gross v. B.G. Inc., 7 P.3d 1003 (Colo. Ct. App. 1999), *aff'd,* 23 P.3d 691 (Colo. 2001); Ariz. Rev. Stat. Ann. § 12-2505 (West 1994); Conn. Gen. Stat. Ann. § 52-572h (West Supp. 2002); Mont. Code Ann. § 27-1-702 (2001). In Chapter 9 we will examine the judicial decisions and statutes abolishing or modifying joint and several liability. In states where joint and several liability has been abolished, no tortfeasor ever pays more than her own share of the fault. Thus, even those states that allow aggregation for the purpose of determining whether plaintiff is entitled to any recovery will still not allow recovery from any individual defendant that exceeds any defendant's percentage of the total damages suffered by the plaintiff.

(6) The Interplay Between Comparative Negligence and Proximate Cause. A host of scholars have taken the position that, with the adoption of comparative negligence, cases that "a plaintiff might have lost under proximate cause rules because the act of the plaintiff or third parties were regarded as 'supervening cause'" should go to a jury to apportion fault among the plaintiff, defendant, and any third party. Victor E. Schwartz, *Comparative Negligence* 95 (3d ed. 1994). *See also* John G. Phillips, *The Sole Proximate Cause "Defense": A Misfit in the World of Contribution and Comparative Negligence,* 22 S. Ill. U. L.J. 1, 15 (2000) ("the theory of sole proximate cause resurrects the former defense of contributory negligence that is incompatible with today's comparative fault system"); Michael D. Green, *The Unanticipated Ripples of Comparative Negligence: Superseding Cause in Products Liability and Beyond,* 53 S.C. L. Rev. 1103 (arguing that courts should not treat plaintiff's conduct as a superseding cause but should take the conduct into account when apportioning fault). *But see* Richard W. Laugesen, *Colorado Comparative Negligence,* Denv. L.J. 469, 486 (1972) ("considerations of proximate cause under comparative negligence should theoretically remain as they existed before the [comparative negligence] Act)"; Paul T. Hayden, Butterfield *Rides Again: Plaintiff's Negligence as Superseding or Sole Proximate Cause in Systems of Pure Comparative Responsibility,* 33 Loy. L.A. L. Rev. 887 (2000) (arguing that pure comparative fault must be tempered by superseding cause or some other subsidiary doctrine as a "safety valve" to allow courts to bar plaintiff's recovery in hard cases where it would be unfair to hold defendant responsible).

(7) Rescue and Comparative Fault. Assume that one undertakes a rescue and suffers injury in the process. You will recall from Chapter 5 that the rescuer has a cause of action against the tortfeasor who brought about the dangerous condition that led the rescuer to act to save the rescuee from injury. What should be the law if the rescuer herself was negligent in effecting the rescue, thus contributing to her own injury? Should her recovery be reduced by the percentage of her fault? Many courts hold that it shouldn't unless the conduct of the rescuer is either grossly negligent or amounts to willful or wanton conduct. *See* Yasamine J. Christopherson, *The Rescue Doctrine Following the Advent of Comparative Negligence in South Carolina*, 58 S.C. L. Rev. 641 (2007).

(8) With Regard to Comparative Fault, Crime Does Not Pay—at Least Sometimes. Although comparative fault has carried the day, situations arise when courts cannot bring themselves to allow plaintiff any recovery. The following case struggles with the question of when a plaintiff's criminal conduct should serve as a total bar to recovery.

ALAMI v. VOLKSWAGEN OF AMERICA, INC.
766 N.E.2d 574 (N.Y. 2002)

WESLEY, J.

In the early morning hours of May 10, 1995 Silhadi Alami was driving home alone in his Volkswagen Jetta on the Saw Mill River Parkway in Yonkers. Traveling at approximately 35 miles per hour, the Jetta left an exit ramp and collided with a steel utility pole. Alami died as a result of his injuries—fractures of the ribs, rupture of the liver and massive internal hemorrhaging. At the time of the collision, his blood alcohol content exceeded the limits set forth in Vehicle and Traffic Law § 1192(2).

Alami's widow commenced this action against Volkswagen of America, Inc. seeking to recover damages on the theory that a defect in the vehicle's design enhanced decedent's injuries. Volkswagen moved for summary judgment.... In light of Alami's intoxication at the time of the accident, Volkswagen ... asserted that plaintiff's claim was precluded on public policy grounds....

[Plaintiff opposed the motion of summary judgment, contending that had the Volkswagen Jetta been reasonably designed, the decedent would have survived the crash with minimal injury.]

Supreme Court granted Volkswagen's motion. The court applied our holdings in Barker v. Kallash, ... 468 N.E.2d 39 and Manning v. Brown, ... 689 N.E.2d 1382 to preclude plaintiff's claim based on its finding that decedent's drunk driving constituted a serious violation of the law and that his injuries were the direct result of that violation. The Appellate Division affirmed. ... We now reverse.

Volkswagen and amici argue that plaintiff's claim should be precluded on public policy grounds because the decedent was intoxicated at the time of the accident. They point to *Barker* and *Manning*, in which we held "that where a plaintiff has engaged in unlawful conduct, the courts will not entertain suit if the plaintiff's conduct constitutes a *serious* violation of the law and the injuries for which the plaintiff seeks recovery are the *direct* result of that violation" ... When this test is met, recovery is precluded "at the very threshold of the plaintiff's application for judicial relief" (*Barker*, ... 468 N.E.2d 39).

Operating a motor vehicle while in an intoxicated condition is indisputably a serious violation of the law. "The importance of the governmental interest [in deterring drunk drivers] is beyond question." ... But plaintiff contends that her husband's intoxication was not the direct cause of the injuries for which recovery is sought. . . .

She . . . argues that her husband's injuries were caused by design defects in the vehicle that rendered it unsafe. Thus, plaintiff asserts that under these circumstances, her claim is not precluded on public policy grounds because the injuries upon which the claim is based do not have the necessary causal link to the decedent's serious violation of the law. . . .

We first applied [the] public policy imperative in a tort context in Reno v. D'Javid, . . . 369 N.E.2d 766, where we denied a claim against a doctor for negligence in performing an illegal abortion. In *Barker*, we precluded the plaintiff's claim against those who had facilitated his construction of a pipe-bomb. More recently, in *Manning* we . . . preclud[ed] a joyrider from bringing a claim against her fellow miscreant for injuries received during their illicit ride.

The *Barker/Manning* rule is based on the sound premise that a plaintiff cannot rely upon an *illegal act* or *relationship* to define the defendant's duty (*see*, W. Page Keeton, et al., Prosser & Keeton on the Law of Torts, § 36 at 232 [5th ed. 1984]). We refuse to extend its application beyond claims where the parties to the suit were involved in the underlying criminal conduct, or where the criminal plaintiff seeks to impose a duty arising out of an illegal act.

If Volkswagen did defectively design the Jetta as asserted by plaintiff's expert, it breached a duty to any driver of a Jetta involved in a crash regardless of the initial cause. . . . Plaintiff does not seek to "profit" from her husband's intoxication — she asks only that Volkswagen honor its well-recognized duty to produce a product that does not unreasonably enhance or aggravate a user's injuries. . . . The duty she seeks to impose on Volkswagen originates not from her husband's act, but from Volkswagen's obligation to design, manufacture and market a safe vehicle.

That same reasoning, however, would deny a burglar injured on a defective staircase from asserting a claim against his victim. . . . Although landowners do have a general duty to the public to maintain their premises in a reasonably safe condition (*see*, Basso v. Miller, . . . N.E.2d 868), this duty does not exist in the abstract. It takes form when someone enters the premises and is injured. Thus, the injured burglar is not entitled to benefit from his burglary because he cannot invoke a duty triggered by his unlawful entry.

The *Barker/Manning* rule embodies a narrow application of public policy imperatives under limited circumstances. Extension of the rule here would abrogate legislatively mandated comparative fault analysis in a wide range of tort claims. In essence, the dissent would have this court extend the *Barker/Manning* rule to relieve Volkswagen in this case of its duty to manufacture a safe vehicle. This we will not do. . . .

Accordingly, the order of the Appellate Division should be reversed, with costs, and defendant's motion for summary judgment dismissing the complaint should be denied.

Rosenblatt, J. (dissenting).

I would apply the doctrine of Barker v. Kallash . . . and Manning v. Brown . . . and preclude plaintiff's suit.

The majority now limits the *Barker-Manning* doctrine to cases that fall within either of two narrow categories: (1) those in which the parties to the suit were involved in the underlying criminal conduct, or (2) those in which the criminal plaintiff seeks to impose a duty "arising out of" an illegal act. . . . This latter categorization imposes a vexing limitation on the preclusion doctrine and is inconsistent with *Barker* and *Manning*. Indeed, it undermines the thrust of those cases.

In *Barker*, we stated that preclusion must bar suit against a homeowner by a burglar "who breaks his leg while descending the cellar stairs, due to the failure of the owner to replace a missing step." . . . I agree with my colleagues that the hypothetical *Barker* burglar should be barred, but their analysis, if applied, would not preclude that suit.

In Basso v. Miller, . . . 352 N.E.2d 868 (1976), we held that landowners owe *everyone* on the property (whether lawfully or not) a duty of care to maintain the premises in a reasonably safe condition. That duty has nothing to do with the reason a particular person comes onto the property. Thus, the duty owed to the *Barker* burglar does not "arise out of" the burglar's illegal act, but exists independent of it. Despite *Basso*'s express recognition of a landowner's duty to a lawbreaker, the Court went out of its way in *Barker* (eight years after *Basso*) to emphasize that any breach of the property owner's duty to maintain the premises could never justify a suit by a burglar injured on the landowner's defective staircase.

Under the majority's unwarranted contraction of the preclusion doctrine, suits prosecuted by plaintiffs injured as a result of their own serious violations of law may now more easily avoid dismissal. A plaintiff who commits a serious violation of law and sues for damages need only invoke a duty on the part of the defendant that does not "arise out of" the illegality (for example, the landowner's duty to keep the premises safe for *everyone*). That duty is thus converted into a defense against preclusion. As a result, despite the express prohibition of *Barker* and the majority's reaffirmation that the hypothetical burglar cannot sue, today's opinion validates a contrary result. . . .

The majority's rationale therefore invites people injured as a result of their own seriously unlawful acts to blame others and recover damages previously prohibited under *Barker* and *Manning*. That invitation confounds this Court's preclusion jurisprudence, which courts had readily understood and followed. Under today's analysis, unless a defendant was complicit in a plaintiff's criminal act, a court cannot preclude suit without first concluding that the alleged duty arose out of that illegal act. However, the majority offers no theory explaining when a duty "arises out of" illegal conduct — an inquiry that is, in any event, fundamentally inconsistent with the policy of preclusion. In short, the majority obliges lower courts to apply an internally inconsistent theory and answer arcane questions with no effective guidance. . . .

FOOD FOR THOUGHT

When a drunk driver brings an action against the auto manufacturer for design defects that caused enhanced injury in a one-car accident, courts may not need the

Barker doctrine to prevent recovery. In a state with modified comparative fault a plaintiff who was tipsy behind the wheel will generally get nothing from the manufacturer for add-on injuries, since a jury will almost always find that a person driving under the influence is more than 51 percent at fault. On the other hand, some courts have allowed drunk drivers complete recovery for enhanced injuries resulting from the defective design, holding that a crashworthiness claim has nothing to do with how the accident came about. Thus, even if the driver seeking to recover from the car's manufacturer was the sole cause of the accident because of his alcohol consumption, he still recovers his enhancement damages. *See, e.g.,* D'Amario v. Ford Motor Company, 806 So. 2d 424 (Fla. 2001) (evidence that driver was intoxicated was irrelevant to determination of whether a defective relay switch in a car contributed to injuries sustained when car burst into flames after colliding with tree); [overruled by statute Fla. Stat. Ann. § 768.81(3)(b) (West 2011)]; Foreman v. Jeep Corp., 1984 WL 2751 (D. Mont.) (intoxication of driver irrelevant to determination of whether unreasonably dangerous design of Jeep, causing it to roll over, enhanced driver's injuries). *Also see* Ryan P. Harkins, *Holding Tortfeasors Accountable: Apportionment of Enhanced Injuries Under Washington's Comparative Fault Scheme,* 76 Wash. L. Rev. 1185 (2001) (arguing that primary fault should not reduce plaintiff's recovery for enhanced injuries and comparative negligence should only operate with respect to enhanced injury fault). Some courts agree with *Alami* that driving drunk does not automatically bar plaintiff's suit against a manufacturer of a defectively designed car for enhanced injury, but weigh plaintiff's intoxication against him in assessing comparative fault. *See, e.g.,* Doupnik v. General Motors Corp., 275 Cal. Rptr. 715 (Cal. Ct. App. 1990) (intoxicated driver 80 percent at fault and auto manufacturer 20 percent at fault for injuries sustained when defect in car roof enhanced injury to driver, rendering him quadriplegic). *Also see* Green v. Ford Motor Co., 942 N.E.2d 791 (Ind. 2011). The United States District Court (S.D. Ind.) certified the following question to the Indiana Supreme Court: "Whether, in a crashworthiness case alleging enhanced injuries under the Indiana Products Liability Act, the finder of fact shall apportion fault to the person suffering physical harm when that alleged fault relates to the cause of the underlying accident." The court answered the question in the affirmative so long as the conduct of the plaintiff was a proximate cause in bringing about the harm for which the damages are sought. *Accord* Jahn v. Hyundai Motor Co., 773 N.W.2d 550 (Iowa 2009).

States have applied the *Barker* doctrine in a variety of contexts. For example, the parents of a boy who was crushed by a vending machine could not recover for the negligence of the vending machine company in failing to install certain safety devices because the boy was tilting the machine to steal drinks from it when it fell on him. Oden v. Pepsi Cola Bottling Co. of Decatur, Inc., 621 So. 2d 953 (Ala. 1993). Similarly, after a man died of a cocaine overdose his wife could not bring a malpractice action against: (1) a psychiatrist for failing to diagnose or treat her husband's drug addiction; (2) a pharmacist who discovered her husband's attempts to illegally procure drugs for failing to alert other pharmacies; (3) the other pharmacies for themselves not adequately screening her husband's requests for prescriptions. Pappas v. Clark, 494 N.W.2d 245 (Iowa Ct. App. 1992). Citing

Barker, the court dismissed the wife's claim, holding that the husband's illegal conduct did not merely constitute contributory negligence but barred recovery altogether. These decisions effectively preserve contributory negligence as a total bar for cases where plaintiff's moral turpitude displeases the court. That plaintiff drove his motorcycle without a valid license, without formal training, and the motorcycle was not registered or insured not only does not call for the application of the Barker/Manning doctrine but is also not relevant to apportionment of damages based on the driver's comparative fault. Firmes v. Chase Manhattan Automotive Finance Corp., 852 N.Y.S.2d 148 (N.Y. App. Div. 2008). When is criminal conduct so serious that it should foreclose the possibility of recovery even though defendant's fault is extreme? For an historical review of the doctrine barring recovery by plaintiffs who have engaged in criminal conduct and an argument against the doctrine, *see* Joseph H. King, Jr., *Outlaws and Outlier Doctrines: The Serious Misconduct Bar in Tort Law*, 43 Wm. & Mary L. Rev. 1011 (2002).

A final word to the wise. The permutations on comparative fault vary significantly from state to state. This casebook can only paint with a very broad brush. Two excellent treatises provide comprehensive analyses of all the fine points of comparative fault. Victor E. Schwartz, *Comparative Negligence* (3d ed. 1994); Henry Woods & Beth Deere, *Comparative Fault* (3d ed. 1996 & Pocket Part 2007).

3. Assumption of Risk

Side by side with contributory negligence that operated as a complete bar, courts recognized another defense that similarly barred a plaintiff's claim. When it could be said that plaintiff voluntarily assumed a known risk, courts refused him a right to recover. Whether the law of torts should recognize an independent defense of assumption of risk has been a matter of intense debate among courts and scholars for half a century. With the advent of comparative fault, the movement to abolish assumption of risk as an independent defense that totally bars plaintiff's recovery has taken on tidal wave proportions. However, like an Australian boomerang, the harder one throws it, the harder it seems to come back. We shall do our very best to set forth the controversy that swirls around assumption of risk and to dispel much of the confusion.

a. Express Assumption of Risk

We begin by examining cases where the defendant agreed to allow the plaintiff to be exposed to her conduct only if the plaintiff agreed to exculpate the defendant from liability for negligence. Two factors militate in favor of giving effect to such contracts. First, because the exculpatory agreement is made in advance of the relationship between the parties, the defendant acts in reliance on the plaintiff's agreement not to hold her liable. The analogy to consent that operates as a defense to intentional torts is very close. Second, agreements made in advance of entering a relationship can specify the scope of the conduct covered by the contractual exculpation. Defendants who deal in risky business can, if they wish, set out the kind of negligent conduct to be exculpated from liability for negligence. What happens, however, when the agreements are embodied in contracts of adhesion?

STELLUTI v. CASAPENN ENTERPRISES, L.L.C.
1 A.3d 678 (N.J. 2010)

Justice LA VECCHIA delivered the opinion of the Court.

On January 13, 2004, while participating in a spinning class at a private fitness center, the handlebars on plaintiff Gina Stelluti's spin bike dislodged from the bike, causing her to fall and suffer injuries. In this appeal we must determine whether plaintiff should be bound to a pre-injury waiver of liability that she executed in connection with her membership application and agreement. We conclude, for the reasons expressed herein, that the exculpatory agreement between the fitness center and Stelluti is enforceable as to the injury Stelluti sustained when riding the spin bike.

I.

Stelluti entered into an agreement with defendant Powerhouse Gym for membership at its Brick, New Jersey facility. To do so, she filled out [several forms].

[Among the forms she signed was a Waiver & Release form which read in part:]

This waiver and release of liability includes, without limitation, all injuries which may occur as a result of, (a) your use of all amenities and equipment in the facility and your participation in any activity, class, program, personal training or instruction, (b) the sudden and unforeseen malfunctioning of any equipment, (c) our instruction, training, supervision, or dietary recommendations, and (d) your slipping and/or falling while in the club, or on the club premises, including adjacent sidewalks and parking areas.

You acknowledge that you have carefully read this "waiver and release" and fully understand that it is a release of liability. You expressly agree to release and discharge the health club, and all affiliates, employees, agents, representatives, successors, or assigns, from any and all claims or causes of action and you agree to voluntarily give up or waive any right that you may otherwise have to bring a legal action against the club for personal injury or property damage.

To the extent that statute or case law does not prohibit releases for negligence, this release is also for negligence on the part of the Club, its agents, and employees.

If any portion of this release from liability shall be deemed by a Court of competent jurisdiction to be invalid, then the remainder of this release from liability shall remain in full force and effect and the offending provision or provisions severed here from.

By signing this release, I acknowledge that I understand its content and that this release cannot be modified orally.

Signed: /s/ Gina Stelluti Names of family members (if applicable):

Any patron who declined to sign the waiver was not permitted to use the Powerhouse Gym.

Stelluti's injury occurred at the gym the day that she joined. After signing the requisite paperwork to become a member, she went to participate in a spinning class. She advised the instructor of her inexperience and the instructor helped her to adjust the bike seat for height and showed her how to strap her feet to the pedals. The instructor then told Stelluti to watch and imitate her during the class.

As the class began, the participants started out pedaling in a seated position. Shortly afterward, the instructor told the participants to change from a seated to a standing position on their bikes. When Stelluti rose to a standing position, the handlebars dislodged from the bike. As a result, Stelluti fell forward while her feet remained strapped to the pedals. With assistance, she succeeded in detaching herself from the bike. When she tried to resume participation after resting for fifteen minutes, she soon had to quit, finding herself in too much pain to continue.

Stelluti's injuries included pain in her neck and shoulders, soreness in her thighs and back, a cracked tooth, and bruises on her legs. After a hospital visit, she was diagnosed with back and neck strain, prescribed medication, and discharged with a recommendation for a follow-up appointment with a doctor. She claims also to experience persistent pain as a result of the incident. Her medical expert has stated that three years after her accident Stelluti suffers from chronic pain associated with myofascial pain syndrome.

Stelluti filed a timely complaint for damages in the Law Division against Powerhouse; Star Trac, the manufacturer of the spin bikes used at Powerhouse; and ABI Property Partnership, the premises owner. The complaint alleged the following negligence claims against Powerhouse and ABI: 1) "fail[ing] to properly maintain and set up the stationary bike"; 2) "fail[ing] to properly instruct the plaintiff as to how to use the bike [or] exercise proper care"; 3) "caus[ing] a dangerous and hazardous condition to exist"; 4) "allow[ing] a nuisance to exist"; 5) "fail[ing] to provide proper safeguards or warnings on the bike"; 6) "fail[ing] to provide proper and safe equipment"; 7) "maintain[ing] the bike in an unsafe, hazardous and/or defective manner"; and 8) acting in "a negligent, careless and reckless manner so as to cause an unsafe hazardous and/or defective condition to exist . . . [and failing] to provide proper safeguards and/or warnings." Plaintiff also asserted a products liability claim against Star Trac Fitness.[1]

This appeal comes to us from a summary judgment record. That record reveals the following contrasting views about the spin bike that was involved in Stelluti's fall and resultant injuries. . . .

Stelluti's liability expert, a college professor with an advanced degree in physical education and certifications in specialized fitness activities including spinning instruction, issued a report that opined that Powerhouse was "negligent in providing a safe environment" and, specifically that the spinning instructor "failed to provide effective specific supervision, instruction and assistance" to Stelluti. He

---

1. Defendants Star Trac and ABI are no longer parties to the case. ABI was not represented at oral argument on Powerhouse's motion for summary judgment, nor was ABI a party to the case before the Appellate Division. *See Stelluti v. Casapenn Enters.*, 408 N.J. Super. 435, 443 n.3, 975 A.2d 494 (App. Div. 2009). Further, we were informed at oral argument that plaintiff's claims against Star Trac have been resolved.

also stated that Stelluti sustained her injuries as a result of the handlebar stem becoming dislodged from the locked position and explained how the handlebars may be raised or lowered, and locked into place, consistent with defendant's liability expert. Plaintiff's expert also agreed with those statements by defendant's representatives, the spinning instructor, and plaintiff, that the only way the handlebars could have become dislodged would be if the lock pin had not been engaged and, instead, the stem had been resting on the lock pin. He explained that, when in that position, the stem would recede only one inch into the vertical support member, thus creating an unstable position for the handlebars. Therefore, when plaintiff raised herself from a seated position, and leaned forward and downward on the handlebars, the handlebars and post would separate from the frame. . . .

II.

The issue of general public importance in this appeal, *see* R. 2:12-4, concerns the enforceability of an exculpatory agreement executed in a commercial setting involving membership in an exercise facility, where the exculpation brought about by the agreement does not implicate the violation of any statutory or regulatory legal duty owed by the facility. It is not the circumstances of the forming of this take-it-or-leave-it waiver agreement that drew our attention, although that is among Stelluti's points of error in seeking certification. We reject that claim of error in her petition.

A contract of adhesion is defined as one "presented on a take-it-or-leave-it basis, commonly in a standardized printed form, without opportunity for the 'adhering' party to negotiate." *Rudbart, supra*, 127 N.J. at 353, 605 A.2d 681 (citations omitted). Although a contract of adhesion may require one party to choose either to accept or reject the contract as is, the agreement nevertheless may be enforced. *See id.* at 353, 356-61, 605 A.2d 681 (noting such considerations as "the subject matter of the contract, the parties' relative bargaining positions, the degree of economic compulsion motivating the 'adhering' party, and the public interests affected by the contract"). Plainly, courts can, and do, refuse to enforce an unconscionable contract of adhesion. *See Muhammad v. County Bank of Rehoboth Beach, Del.*, 189 N.J. 1, 15, 912 A.2d 88 (2006). When making the determination that a contract of adhesion is unconscionable and unenforceable, we consider, using a sliding scale analysis, the way in which the contract was formed and, further, whether enforcement of the contract implicates matters of public interest. *Delta Funding Corp. v. Harris*, 189 N.J. 28, 39-40, 912 A.2d 104 (2006).

Here, Powerhouse's agreement was a standard pre-printed form presented to Stelluti and other prospective members on a typical "take-it-or-leave-it basis." No doubt, this agreement was one of adhesion. As for the relative bargaining positions of the parties, . . . we assume that Stelluti was a layperson without any specialized knowledge about contracts generally or exculpatory ones specifically. Giving her the benefit of all inferences from the record, including that Powerhouse may not have explained to Stelluti the legal effect of the contract that released Powerhouse from liability, we nevertheless do not regard her in a classic "position of unequal bargaining power" such that the contract must be voided. As the Appellate Division decision noted, Stelluti could have taken her business to another fitness club, could have found another means of exercise aside from joining a private gym, or could have thought about it and even sought advice before signing up and using the facility's equipment. No time limitation was imposed on her ability to review and consider whether to sign the agreement. In sum, although the terms of the agreement were presented "as is" to Stelluti, rendering this a fairly typical adhesion contract in its procedural aspects, we hold that the agreement was not void based on any notion of procedural unconscionability. . . .

III.

As a general and long-standing matter, contracting parties are afforded the liberty to bind themselves as they see fit. *See Twin City Pipe Line Co. v. Harding Glass Co.*, 283 *U.S.* 353, 356, 51 *S. Ct.* 476, 477, 75 *L. Ed.* 1112, 1116 (1931) ("The general rule is that competent persons shall have the utmost liberty of contracting and that their agreements voluntarily and fairly made shall be held valid and enforced in the courts."). *See generally* 11 *Williston on Contracts* § 30:9, at 96 (Lord ed., 4d ed. 1999). Out of respect for that very basic freedom, courts are hesitant to interfere with purely private agreements. *See, e.g., Twin City Pipe Line Co., supra*, 283 *U.S.* at 356-57, 51 *S. Ct.* at 477, 75 *L. Ed.* at 1116 (evaluating unenforceability with "caution"); *Allen v. Commercial Cas. Ins. Co.*, 131 *N.J.L.* 475, 478, 37 *A.2d* 37 (E. & A.1944) (finding freedom to contract "sacred," and thus not to be interfered with "lightly" (citation omitted)); *Chem. Bank v. Bailey*, 296 *N.J. Super.* 515, 526-27, 687 *A.2d* 316 (App. Div.) (noting ability of parties to apportion risk of loss through contractual limitation of liabilities), *certif. denied*, 150 *N.J.* 28, 695 *A.2d* 671 (1997).

However, certain categories of substantive contracts, including those that contain exculpatory clauses, have historically been disfavored in law and thus have been subjected to close judicial scrutiny.

In that consideration, it has been held contrary to the public interest to sanction the contracting-away of a statutorily imposed duty. *McCarthy v. NASCAR, Inc.*, 48 *N.J.* 539, 542, 226 *A.2d* 713 (1967). An agreement containing a pre-injury release from liability for intentional or reckless conduct also is plainly inconsistent with public policy. . . . Beyond those clear parameters to inviolate public policy principles, the weighing process becomes opaque. The Appellate Division identified four considerations, pertinent to the enforcement of an exculpatory agreement . . .

> will be enforced if (1) it does not adversely affect the public interest; (2) the exculpated party is not under a legal duty to perform; (3) it does not involve a public utility or common carrier; or (4) the contract does not grow out of unequal bargaining power or is otherwise unconscionable.

[368 *N.J. Super.* at 248, 845 *A.2d* 720 (citations omitted).]

The . . . test, used by the panel below, captures the essential features to be explored when considering whether enforcement of an exculpatory agreement would be contrary to public policy. Other courts in sister jurisdictions have developed similar tests. One, which originated with the Supreme Court of California in *Tunkl v. Regents of the University of California*, 60 *Cal.* 2d 92, 32 *Cal. Rptr.* 33, 383 *P.*2d 441, 445-46 (1963), uses six inquiries[2] and it also has been identified as helpful. Although slightly more nuanced, *Tunkl's* considerations . . . can provide additional guidance when applying the test that has been employed by our appellate courts and that we find acceptable also in the resolution of the instant exculpatory agreement. We thus turn to consider the specifics of the agreement.

IV.

A.

As a threshold matter, to be enforceable an exculpatory agreement must "reflect the unequivocal expression of the party giving up his or her legal rights that this decision was made voluntarily, intelligently and with the full knowledge of its legal consequences." . . . When a party enters into a signed, written contract, that party is presumed to understand and assent to its terms, unless fraudulent conduct is suspected. . . .

The agreement in question explicitly stated that it covered "the sudden and unforeseen malfunctioning of any equipment, . . . use of all amenities and equipment in the facility and . . . participation in any activity, class, program, personal training or instruction." In addition, the agreement explicitly covered negligence: "this release is also for negligence on the part of the Club, its agents, and employees." Further, terms that limited Powerhouse's liability — "entirely at your own risk," "assume all risks," and "release of liability," — were set forth prominently in the written document that Stelluti signed and from which she now seeks to be excused. Although Stelluti argues that she did not know what she was signing, she does not claim that she signed the waiver form as the result of fraud, deceit, or misrepresentation. Therefore, the trial court was well within reason to presume that she understood the terms of the agreement, *see ibid.*, and the finding to that effect is unassailable.

Furthermore, as we have already addressed and rejected Stelluti's argument in respect of unequal bargaining power, we need address that aspect of *Gershon's* inquiries no further. And, because Powerhouse is not a public utility or common carrier, that inquiry is inapplicable to our analysis. Besides not being such an entity, Powerhouse also was not providing a necessary service akin to that provided by a public utility or common carrier.

---

2. *Tunkl* references the following inquiries as pertinent when determining whether to enforce an exculpatory agreement: 1) whether the agreement involves a business generally suitable for public regulation; 2) whether the exculpated party provides a service important and necessary to the public; 3) whether the exculpated party offers services to any person of the public seeking those services; 4) whether the exculpated party possesses a stronger bargaining power relative to the member of the public seeking services; 5) whether the exculpated party presents the member of the public with a contract of adhesion; and 6) whether the member of the public is under the control of the exculpated party and thus is subject to the careless risks of the more powerful party. *Tunkl, supra,* 32 *Cal. Rptr.* 33, 383 *P.*2d at 445-46.

B.

When considering whether enforcement of the instant exculpatory agreement would adversely affect the public interest, the inquiry naturally blends into an examination of whether the exculpated party is under a legal duty to perform. Exculpatory agreements that attempt to release liability for statutorily imposed duties have been held invalid. When the subject of an exculpatory agreement is not governed by statute, we also have considered common law duties in weighing relevant public policy considerations. To a certain extent, we cannot view [the] public-interest inquiry separate from the question of whether there is a legal duty owed that is inviolate and non-waivable. In performing the weighing of public policy interests, then, we must take into account, in this private setting, both the extant common law duties and the right to freely agree to a waiver of a right to sue, which is part and parcel to the freedom to contract to which we earlier adverted. The mere existence of a common law duty does not mean that there is no room for an exculpatory agreement. In other words, our analysis begins from the starting point that public policy does not demand a per se ban against enforcement of an exculpatory agreement based on the mere existence of a duty recognized in the common law in respect of premises liability. . . .

Our Court recognized that reality associated with sports and sport activity when we held that some activities, due to their very nature, require the participant to assume some risk because injury is a common and inherent aspect of the activity. *Crawn v. Campo*, 136 N.J. 494, 500, 643 A.2d 600 (1994). In *Crawn*, we considered the duty of care owed to individuals who participate in informal recreational sports, softball in that particular instance. *Id.* at 497, 643 A.2d 600. We determined that the standard of care must exceed mere negligence because of the inherent risk of injury that cannot be eliminated through the exercise of reasonable care. *Id.* at 500, 643 A.2d 600. To determine the proper standard of care, we focused on the relationship between the participants and the nature of risk involved, specifying unique aspects of recreational activities such as the inherent and expected physical contact and high level of emotional intensity, both deemed appropriate when participating in those sports. *Id.* at 504, 643 A.2d 600. We stressed the centrality of public policy and fairness in reaching our conclusion about the appropriate standard of care. *Id.* at 503, 643 A.2d 600. Two important public policies were identified: 1) "promotion of vigorous participation in athletic activities" as evidenced by pervasive interest and participation in recreational sports, and 2) the "avoid[ance of] a flood of litigation." *Id.* at 501, 643 A.2d 600. That said, those interests do not completely immunize participants. *Id.* at 503-04, 643 A.2d 600. Participants retain a duty to participate in a reasonable manner, with regard for other players, and also in a way that fits with the common expectations of acceptable conduct for the activity. *Id.* at 501, 507, 643 A.2d 600. Thus, the *Crawn* decision held that "liability arising out of mutual, informal, recreational sports activity should not be based on a standard of ordinary negligence but on the heightened standard of recklessness or intent to harm," *id.* at 503, 643 A.2d 600, a standard that "recognizes a commonsense distinction between excessively harmful conduct and the more routine rough-and-tumble of sports that should occur freely on the playing fields." *Id.* at 508, 643 A.2d 600. Application of that standard later was extended to sports that do not involve physical contact. *See Schick v. Ferolito,* 167 *N.J.* 7, 18, 767 A.2d 962 (2001) (upholding recklessness standard to the game of golf, finding "no persuasive reasons to apply an artificial distinction between 'contact' and 'noncontact' sports").

To properly balance the public-policy interests implicated in the instant matter one must consider the nature of the activity and the inherent risks involved.[3] Engaging in physical activity, particularly in private gyms and health clubs is commonplace in today's society. The United States Bureau of Labor estimates that over the next decade jobs for physical fitness workers will increase faster than other occupations due to the increasing recognition of health benefits associated with physical activity and, consequently, increase the amount of time and money spent on fitness. U.S. Dep't of Labor, *Bureau of Labor Statistics: Occupational Outlook Handbook* 3 (2010-11), http://www.bls.gov/oco/pdf/ocos296.pdf.

By its nature, exercising entails vigorous physical exertion. Injuries from exercise are common; indeed minor injuries can be expected — for example, sore muscles following completion of a tough exercise or workout may be indicative of building or toning muscles. Those injuries and others may result from faulty equipment, improper use of equipment, inadequate instruction, inexperience or poor physical condition of the user, or excessive exertion. . . .

Although there is public interest in holding a health club to its general common law duty to business invitees — to maintain its premises in a condition safe from defects that the business is charged with knowing or discovering — it need not ensure the safety of its patrons who voluntarily assume some risk by engaging in strenuous physical activities that have a potential to result in injuries. Any requirement to so guarantee a patron's safety from *all* risk in using equipment, which understandably is passed from patron to patron, could chill the establishment of health clubs. Health clubs perform a salutary purpose by offering activities and equipment so that patrons can enjoy challenging physical exercise. There has been recognized a "positive social value" in allowing gyms to limit their liability in respect of patrons who wish to assume the risk of participation in activities that could cause an injury. And, further, it is not unreasonable to encourage patrons of a fitness center to take proper steps to prepare, such as identifying their own physical limitations and learning about the activity, before engaging in a foreign activity for the first time.

However, just as we held in *Crawn, supra,* that there remains a standard for liability even in contact recreational sports, albeit a heightened one, 136 *N.J.* at 503-04, 643 A.2d 600, there is also a limit to the protections that a private fitness center reasonably may exact from its patrons through the mechanism of an

---

3. Our focus here substantially contemplates one of *Tunkl's* inquiries, specifically whether the member of the public is under the control of the exculpated party and thus subject to the careless risks by the more powerful party. *See Tunkl, supra,* 32 *Cal. Rptr.* 33, 383 *P.2d* at 445-46. That question takes into account the patron's opportunity for self-protection, which removes the possibility that the injury could only be prevented by the operator. *See* Robert Heidt, *The Avid Sportsman and the Scope for Self-Protection: When Exculpatory Clauses Should be Enforced,* 38 *U. Rich. L. Rev.* 381, 460-73 (2004).

exculpatory agreement. Although it would be unreasonable to demand that a fitness center inspect each individual piece of equipment after every patron's use, it would be unreasonable, and contrary to the public interest, to condone willful blindness to problems that arise with the equipment provided for patrons' use. Thus, had Powerhouse's management or employees been aware of a piece of defective exercise equipment and failed to remedy the condition or to warn adequately of the dangerous condition, or if it had dangerously or improperly maintained equipment, Powerhouse could not exculpate itself from such reckless or gross negligence. That showing was not made on this record.

As previously noted, the Appellate Division specifically found that the record was barren of evidence that Powerhouse had neglected over time to maintain its equipment. *Stelluti, supra,* 408 *N.J. Super.* at 460-61, 975 *A.*2d 494 (finding absence of any "chronic or repetitive patterns of inattention to the safety of the equipment"). There simply was no evidence in this record rising to such reckless or gross negligence in respect of Powerhouse's duty to inspect and maintain its equipment. Thus, we do not share the concern voiced by the dissent. Our decision cannot reasonably be read to signal that health clubs will be free to engage in "chronic or repetitive patterns of inattention to the safety of the[ir] equipment." *Ibid.* Nor do we share the dissent's view that today's holding gives a green light to permit widespread use of exculpatory agreements in restaurants, malls, and supermarkets. That extrapolation fails to account for our careful examination into the relevant nature of the type of activity that takes place in a private health club.

In sum, the standard we apply here places in fair and proper balance the respective public-policy interests in permitting parties to freely contract in this context (i.e. private fitness center memberships) and requires private gyms and fitness centers to adhere to a standard of conduct in respect of their business. Specifically, we hold such business owners to a standard of care congruent with the nature of their business, which is to make available the specialized equipment and facility to their invitees who are there to exercise, train, and to push their physical limits. That is, we impose a duty not to engage in reckless or gross negligence. We glean such prohibition as a fair sharing of risk in this setting, which is also consistent with the analogous assumption-of-risk approach used by the Legislature to allocate risks in other recreational settings with limited retained-liability imposed on operators.

V.

For the foregoing reasons, we affirm the judgment of the Appellate Division that sustained the award of summary judgment to defendant.

Justice ALBIN, dissenting.

Today the Court has abandoned its traditional role as the steward of the common law. For the first time in its modern history, the Court upholds a contract of adhesion with an exculpatory clause that will allow a commercial, profit-making company to operate negligently — injuring, maiming, and perhaps killing one of its consumer-patrons — without consequence. Under the Court's ruling, a health club will have no obligation to maintain its equipment in a reasonably safe manner or to require its employees to act with due care toward its patrons. That is because, the Court says, a health club patron has the *right* to contract not only for unsafe conditions at a health club, but also for careless conduct by its employees. The Court's decision will ensure that these contracts of adhesion will become an industry-wide practice and that membership in health clubs will be conditioned on powerless consumers signing a waiver immunizing clubs from their own negligence. The Court's ruling undermines the common-law duty of care that every commercial operator owes to a person invited on to its premises.

Without the incentive to place safety over profits, the cost to the public will be an increase in the number of avoidable accidents in health clubs. And like the plaintiff in this case, the victims of the clubs' negligence will suffer the ultimate injustice — they will have no legal remedy.

Tens of thousands of New Jersey citizens join health clubs to stay healthy-to reduce the prospect of suffering from heart disease or a stroke, to battle obesity, and to improve the likelihood of living a longer life. The irony is that those who seek to live a better lifestyle through membership at a health club, now, will have a greater likelihood of having their well-being impaired through the careless acts of a club employee.

The ruling today is not in the public interest, not consistent with this Court's long-standing, progressive common-law jurisprudence protecting vulnerable consumers, and not in step with the enlightened approaches taken by courts of other jurisdictions that have barred the very type of exculpatory clause to which this Court gives its imprimatur.

Because in upholding the exculpatory agreement the Court wrongly dismisses the case of plaintiff, Gina Stelluti, I respectfully dissent. . . .

FOOD FOR THOUGHT

The general rule recognizing contractual limitations on tort liability as an absolute bar to plaintiff recovery (not subject to comparative fault) is recognized in the Restatement, Third, of Torts: Apportionment of Liability § 2 (2000). The comments to that section note that such contracts are strictly construed against the defendant.

THE PUBLIC POLICY EXCEPTION

Many courts have struck down clauses exculpating a defendant from gross negligence as contrary to public policy. *See, e.g.,* Gross v. Sweet, 400 N.E.2d 306 (N.Y. 1979); Walsh v. Luedtke, 704 N.W.2d 423 (Wis. Ct. App. 2005) (applying Ohio law) (under Ohio law an exculpatory contract may relieve a party for negligent acts but not for "willful or wanton conduct"; conduct of defendant in trailer-pulling contest did not meet this threshold and the waiver was upheld). And some states have enacted statutes negating exculpation clauses for certain enterprises. *See, e.g.,* N.Y. Gen. Oblig. Law § 5-326 (McKinney 2001) (owners of pools, gymnasiums, places of amusement, recreation, and similar establishments); N.Y. Gen. Oblig. Law § 5-321 (McKinney 2001) (owners of rental property).

The long and short of it is that courts look with a jaundiced eye at clauses exculpating defendants from negligence. However, by and large they are enforced. *See, e.g.*, Plant v. Wilbur, 47 S.W.3d 889 (Ark. 2001) (member of pit crew could not sue for negligence of racetrack after signing an exculpatory agreement); Winterstein v. Wilcom, 293 A.2d 821 (Md. Ct. Spec. App. 1972) (racetrack release from negligence upheld against claim that defendant employees negligently failed to warn about an obstacle on the racetrack); McGrath v. SNH Development, Inc., 969 A.2d 392 (N.H. 2009) (release pre-injury of ski resort by snowboarder who was injured by alleged negligence of employee while operating snowmobile is valid and not against public policy.); Pearce v. Utah Athletic Foundation, 179 P.3d 760 (Utah 2008) (pre-injury releases of ordinary negligence are not violative of public policy); Myers v. Lutsen Mountains Corp., 587 F.3d 891 (8th Cir. 2009) (applying Minnesota law upheld pre-injury disclaimer of ski resort of negligence); Chepkevich v. Hidden Valley Resort C.P., 2 A.3d 1174 (Pa. 2010) (pre-injury exculpatory clause relieving ski resort of negligence is not against public policy); Seigneur v. National Fitness Institute, Inc., 752 A.2d 631 (Md. Ct. Spec. App. 2000) (exculpatory clause barred recovery by plaintiff who injured shoulder on weight machine at health club). But some courts remain hostile. *See, e.g.*, Hanks v. Power Ridge Restaurant Corp., 885 A.2d 734 (Conn. 2005) (holding disclaimer of negligence to a patron of a ski resort who was injured when snowtubing was invalid as against public policy); Reardon v. Windswept Farm, L.L.C., 905 A.2d 1156 (Conn. 2006) (release by horseback-riding student to riding stable for negligence void as against public policy). Dalury v. S-K-I, Ltd., 670 A.2d 795 (Vt. 1995) (refusing to give effect to a clause exculpating the operator of a ski resort from negligence in maintenance of its ski slopes). Many courts hold waivers in which parents sign away rights of their children to violate strong public policy and have refused to enforce them. In Cooper v. Aspen Skiing, 48 P.3d 1229 (Colo. 2002), the claim of a 17-year-old seriously injured in a skiing accident was not barred by the parents' waiver of the right to sue in tort. Furthermore, the parents' obligation to indemnify defendant for personal injury claims was held unenforceable because it created an unacceptable conflict of interest between the child and parents. (Case contains exhaustive review of authority.) The Colorado legislature specifically overruled *Cooper* and now allows parents to effectively waive prospective negligence claims for minors under the age of 18. Colo. Rev. Stat. Ann. § 13-22-107 (2007).

IS IT ETHICAL TO DRAFT UNENFORCEABLE CONTRACT PROVISIONS?

As the preceding text observes, courts in some states take a rather dim view of exculpatory clauses in contracts, and in some circumstances they are unenforceable. Yet this does not seem to stop the operators of ski resorts, skydiving outfits, summer camps for children, amusement parks, health clubs, and other potential defendants from requiring customers to sign waivers of liability. Suppose a lawyer is practicing in one of the states described above, in which the courts have generally refused to enforce contractual waivers of liability. Now imagine that a longtime client of the lawyer wants to open a recreational business — say, a go-kart racing track — and asks the lawyer to draft a release of liability which customers will be required to sign. Is the lawyer permitted to do this, consistent with her ethical obligations?

If you asked a bunch of practicing lawyers the question about drafting waivers of liability that are probably not enforceable under state law, it is likely that many of them would see nothing wrong with doing it. The surprising thing is the reason they would likely give. You wouldn't have to talk to many lawyers before someone mentioned the idea of "zealous advocacy within the bounds of the law." Think about that for a minute. Lawyers tend to appeal to the ethics of advocacy to justify their conduct in any context. There is something odd about that analytical move, yet it is very common in lawyers' analysis of their ethical obligations.

The Model Rules have surprisingly little to say about a lawyer's responsibilities in transactional settings such as contract drafting. Lawyers are prohibited from making material, false statements to third parties. Model Rule 4.1(a). They also have a duty to disclose facts where necessary to avoid assisting a criminal or fraudulent act by a client, although that duty has interesting and complicated interactions with the lawyer's duty of confidentiality. Model Rule 4.1(b). Lawyers may not counsel or assist in a client's crime or fraud. Model Rule 1.2(d). More generally, lawyers may not engage in any "conduct involving dishonesty, fraud, deceit or misrepresentation." Model Rule 8.4(c). But that's about it for disciplinary rules that bear on this question.

Moreover, as you are probably already figuring out from torts and your other first-year courses, American law students learn the law through the study of litigated disputes. There are good reasons for this. For one, it is essential to understand that in common law reasoning, "the law" only acquires meaning in the context of the facts of a case. You might state a principle of law such as "contractual waivers of liability will not be enforceable where enforcement would be against public policy," and maybe even cite the *Tunkl* case in support, but this little summary leaves open the question of whether a waiver will be enforceable in a contract for the use of the facilities of a ski resort, a horseback-riding stable, a health club, a go-kart track, or whatever. To answer this question, a lawyer in a common law system would need to read a bunch of cases to figure out exactly when it would be against public policy to enforce exculpatory clauses in contracts.

This does not mean, however, that a lawyer should necessarily be reading those cases with the mindset of an advocate. A lawyer may be called upon to advise her client based on the lawyer's best reading of what the law actually provides. That is different from coming up with an argument that a lawyer could make in court with a straight face. (See the note on p. 631 on creative legal arguments.) "Is such-and-such really lawful?" is a different question from "Could I get away with doing such-and-such?" Suppose there is a case from the state's highest court invalidating a waiver of liability entered into between a customer and a horseback-riding stable, like Reardon v. Windswept Farm, L.L.C., 905 A.2d 1156 (Conn. 2006). Would a lawyer in that jurisdiction be permitted to draft a waiver to be used at her client's go-kart track? Here is where lawyers make an analytical mistake by invoking the duty of zealous advocacy. It would be one thing to argue to a court that waivers should be treated differently when they pertain to horseback-riding stables and go-kart tracks. It might not be a very good argument, but as long as it is not legally frivolous, a lawyer could make it. Lawyers are ethically permitted to make a non-frivolous legal argument because there is generally an opposing lawyer who can challenge it, a judge who can evaluate the arguments of counsel and make a ruling, and an appellate process to correct legal errors by the trial judge. The process is set up to take care of excessively creative or aggressive interpretations of the law by lawyers. When a lawyer is advising a client, however, or drafting a contract for a client, there is no comparable process for sorting out which legal positions are well supported and which are bogus. It falls to the individual lawyer to exercise judgment and differentiate between valid interpretations of law and those that are excessively creative or aggressive.

There is a long tradition in American law of lawyers subscribing to principles of ethics or professionalism that go beyond the requirements of the disciplinary rules. One distinguished legal scholar concludes, based largely on this professional tradition, that lawyers should not draft contract provisions they know are unlikely to be enforceable, including waivers of liability, forum-selection clauses, and unreasonable arbitration provisions. Paul D. Carrington, *Unconscionable Lawyers*, 19 Ga. St. L. Rev. 361 (2002). On the other hand, there is very little likelihood of professional discipline for drafting an unenforceable contract provision. Geoffrey C. Hazard, Jr. & W. William Hodes, *The Law of Lawyering* § 5.12, Illustration 5-13 (Supp. 2003). How you resolve this ethical issue turns largely on whether you think legal ethics is something more than mere compliance with the disciplinary rules and other legal obligations that are binding on lawyers.

b. Implied Assumption of Risk

Let's make a deal. Before we even begin to discuss whether or not a plaintiff should be barred from liability because she "voluntarily assumed a known risk," make sure that plaintiff has made out a prima facie case for liability. We can then face the question of whether we should or should not recognize assumption of risk as an independent defense.

Consider the following hypothetical cases:

(1) A landowner owns property in a summer resort area. Adjacent to her summer home she has an unfenced swimming pool. One summer day a social guest of the owner who came for the weekend was wandering around near the pool. He was gazing at the mountains and was so taken by the scenery that he did not notice that he had backed up ten feet and was at the lip of the pool. When he did notice where he was standing, he was unsteady and fell into the pool and drowned.

(2) A baseball fan sitting in the center-field bleachers was injured when baseball's most prolific home-run hitter hit a monster home run that traveled 500 feet and the ball landed smack in the fan's eye.

In cases closely analogous to these two hypotheticals, courts have barred plaintiffs from recovery on the ground that plaintiff voluntarily assumed a known risk. In both cases, resort to assumption of the risk is unnecessary. In Chapter 7 we encountered a host of rules dealing with the duty of landowners to people who come on their property. You will recall that in many jurisdictions a landowner has no duty to take reasonable care to make her property reasonably safe for social guests. In these jurisdictions they need only warn guests of hidden dangers. In the swimming pool hypothetical, courts have been prone to say that social guests assume the risks of the host's property. But that is not why the plaintiff loses his case. It is not because he did or did not know the risks. For all we know or care, he may have walked blindfolded around the defendant's property. The defendant is absolved from liability because she has no legal duty to make her property safe for guests. In a colloquial sense we might say, "social guests take their friends and their property as they find them." That insight may help explain why the licensee limited-duty rule allows one to not fence in one's pool. But, the actual reason for the defendant's nonliability is that defendant has not breached any duty to her social guest.

In a similar vein, in the baseball hypothetical the plaintiff loses his case for reasons having little or nothing to do with the defense of voluntary assumption of risk. The owners of baseball stadiums could put netting around all exposed seats and prevent baseballs hit into any area of the park from striking spectators. But they are not negligent for failing to screen in the center-field bleachers. To do so would obstruct the view of patrons sitting so far away from the action. Furthermore, by the time a ball travels 500 feet, most of the zip is out of the ball. Using the Learned Hand formula, the probability and gravity of potential harm is very low and the burden of precaution is very high. The defendant is simply not negligent as a matter of law. Again, courts often say that spectators assume the normal risks of the game, which include balls being hit into the center-field bleachers. But whether they do or not is irrelevant. The defendant prevails because of non-negligence — not because the conduct of the plaintiff bars him from recovery.

Now let's change the swimming pool hypothetical. This time assume the events transpire in a jurisdiction that takes the position that a landowner has a duty of reasonable care to social guests and further assume that defendant has acted negligently in not constructing a fence around the swimming pool. One of the guests, Vic, is playing a game of catch with another guest, Sheila, in the general vicinity of the pool. Sheila throws the ball over Vic's head. Vic goes back to catch the ball. He believes that he can catch the ball several feet in front of the pool. He is mistaken. He catches the ball on the lip of the pool and falls into the pool, injuring himself. Should assumption of risk be a total bar to recovery?

The late Professor Fleming James, an outstanding torts scholar and a harsh critic of assumption of risk, argued that the defense should be abolished from the law of torts. The crux of his attack is that you don't need assumption of risk because either the case is covered by a no-duty rule or by comparative fault. When you do need to resort to assumption of risk, it gives you a wrong result. If defendant's duty is only to warn about hidden dangers, then there is no liability since the pool is not a hidden danger. If, on the other hand, the duty is to make the grounds reasonably safe for social guests, then defendant, by failing to erect the fence, has breached a duty. Vic, who decided to chase the ball, may have been negligent and, if so, he should have his recovery reduced by comparative fault. But if a jury were to find that his conduct in playing ball in the general vicinity of the pool was not negligent, he should not be barred from recovery because he acted reasonably in confronting a risk that should never have been put to him. *See* Fleming James, Jr., *Assumption of Risk: Unhappy Reincarnation*, 78 Yale L.J. 185 (1968). With this background in mind, consider the following cases.

BLACKBURN v. DORTA
348 So. 2d 287 (Fla. 1977)

SUNDBERG, J., Justice.

[In 1973, the Florida Supreme Court judicially adopted comparative fault in Hoffman v. Jones, 280 So. 2d 431 (Fla. 1973).]

Since our decision in *Hoffman v. Jones, supra,* contributory negligence no longer serves as a complete bar to plaintiff's recovery but is to be considered in apportioning damages according to the principles of comparative negligence. We are now asked to determine the effect of the *Hoffman* decision on the common law doctrine of assumption of risk. If assumption of risk is equivalent to contributory negligence, then *Hoffman* mandates that it can no longer operate as a complete bar to recovery. However, if it has a distinct purpose apart from contributory negligence, its continued existence remains unaffected by *Hoffman.* This question was expressly reserved in *Hoffman* as being not ripe for decision. 280 So. 2d 431, 439.

At the outset, we note that assumption of risk is not a favored defense. There is a puissant drift toward abrogating the defense. The argument is that assumption of risk serves no purpose which is not subsumed by either the doctrine of contributory negligence or the common law concept of duty. It is said that this redundancy results in confusion and, in some cases, denies recovery unjustly. The leading case in Florida dealing with the distinction between the doctrines recognizes that "at times the line of demarcation between contributory negligence and assumption of risk is exceedingly difficult to define." Byers v. Gunn, 81 So. 2d 723, 727 (Fla. 1955). The issue is most salient in states which have enacted comparative negligence legislation. Those statutes provide that the common law defense of contributory negligence no longer necessarily acts as a complete bar to recovery. The effect of these statutes upon the doctrine of assumption of risk has proved to be controversial. Joining the intensifying assault upon the doctrine, a number of comparative negligence jurisdictions have abrogated assumption of risk. Those jurisdictions hold that assumption of risk is interchangeable with contributory negligence and should be treated equivalently. Today we are invited to join this trend of dissatisfaction with the doctrine. For the reasons herein expressed, we accept the invitation.

At the commencement of any analysis of the doctrine of assumption of risk, we must recognize that we deal with a potpourri of labels, concepts, definitions, thoughts, and doctrines. The confusion of labels does not end with the indiscriminate and interchangeable use of the terms "contributory negligence" and "assumption of risk." In the case law and among text writers, there have developed categories of assumption of risk. Distinctions exist between *express* and *implied;* between *primary* and *secondary;* and between *reasonable* and *unreasonable* or, as sometimes expressed, *strict* and *qualified.* It will be our task to analyze these various labels and to trace the historical basis of the doctrine to unravel what has been in the law an "enigma wrapped in a mystery."

It should be pointed out that we are not here concerned with express assumption of risk which is a contractual concept outside the purview of this inquiry and upon which we express no opinion herein. . . . Included within the definition of express assumption of risk are express contracts not to sue for injury or loss which may thereafter be occasioned by the covenantee's negligence as well as situations in which actual consent exists such as where one voluntarily participates in a contact sport.

The breed of assumption of risk with which we deal here is that which arises by implication or *implied* assumption of risk. Initially it may be divided into the categories of *primary* and *secondary.* The term primary assumption of risk is simply another means of stating that the defendant was not negligent, either because he owed no duty to the plaintiff in the first instance, or because he did not breach the duty owed. Secondary assumption of risk is an affirmative defense to an established breach of a duty owed by the defendant to the plaintiff. . . .

It is apparent that no useful purpose is served by retaining terminology which expresses the thought embodied in primary assumption of risk. This branch (or trunk) of the tree of assumption of risk is subsumed in the principle of negligence itself. Under our Florida jury instructions, the jury is directed first to determine whether the defendant has been negligent, i.e., did he owe a duty to the plaintiff and, if so, did he breach that duty? To sprinkle the term assumption of risk into the equation can only lead to confusion of a jury. . . . An example of this concept is presented in the operation of a passenger train. It can be said that a passenger assumes the risk of lurches and jerks which are ordinary and usual to the proper operation of the train, but that he does not assume the risk of extraordinary or unusual lurches and jerks resulting from substandard operation of the train. The same issue can be characterized in terms of the standard of care of the railroad. Thus, it can be said that the railroad owes a duty to operate its train with the degree of care of an ordinary prudent person under similar circumstances which includes some lurching and jerking while a train is in motion or commencing to move under ideal circumstances. So long as the lurching or jerking is not extraordinary due to substandard conduct of the railroad, there is no breach of duty and, hence, no negligence on the part of the railroad. The latter characterization of the issue clearly seems preferable and is consistent with the manner in which the jury is instructed under our standard jury instructions.

Having dispensed with *express* and *primary-implied* assumption of risk, we recur to *secondary-implied* assumption of risk which is the affirmative defense variety that has been such a thorn in the judicial side. The affirmative defense brand of assumption of risk can be subdivided into the type of conduct which is reasonable but nonetheless bars recovery (sometimes called *pure* or *strict* assumption of risk), and the type of conduct which is unreasonable and bars recovery (sometimes referred to as *qualified* assumption of risk). . . . Application of pure or strict assumption of risk is exemplified by the hypothetical situation in which a landlord has negligently permitted his tenant's premises to become highly flammable and a fire ensues. The tenant returns from work to find the premises a blazing inferno with his infant child trapped within. He rushes in to retrieve the child and is injured in so doing. Under the pure doctrine of assumption of risk, the tenant is barred from recovery because it can be said he voluntarily exposed himself to a known risk. Under this view of assumption of risk, the tenant is precluded from recovery notwithstanding the fact that his conduct could be said to be entirely reasonable under the circumstances. Morrison & Conklin Construction Co. v. Cooper, 256 S.W.2d 505 (Ky. 1953); Restatement (Second) of Torts, § 496C, Comments *d-g* (1965). There is little to commend this doctrine of implied-pure or strict assumption of risk, and our research discloses no Florida case in which it has been applied. Certainly, in light of *Hoffman v. Jones, supra,* there is no reason supported by law or justice in this state to give credence to such a principle of law.

There remains, then, for analysis only the principle of implied-qualified assumption of risk, and it can be demonstrated in the hypothetical recited above with the minor alteration that the tenant rushes into the blazing premises to retrieve his favorite fedora. Such conduct on the tenant's part clearly would be unreasonable. Consequently, his conduct can just as readily be characterized as contributory negligence. It is the failure to exercise the care of a reasonably prudent man under similar circumstances. It is this last category of assumption of risk which has caused persistent confusion in the law of torts because of the lack of analytic difference between it and contributory negligence. If the only significant form of assumption of risk (implied-qualified) is so readily characterized, conceptualized, and verbalized as contributory negligence, can there be any sound rationale for retaining it as a separate affirmative defense to negligent conduct which bars recovery altogether? In the absence of any historical imperative, the answer must be no. We are persuaded that there is no historical significance to the doctrine of implied-secondary assumption of risk.

We find no discernible basis analytically or historically to maintain a distinction between the affirmative defense of contributory negligence and assumption of risk. The latter appears to be a viable, rational doctrine only in the sense described herein as implied-qualified assumption of risk which connotes unreasonable conduct on the part of the plaintiff. This result comports with the definition of contributory negligence appearing in Restatement (Second) of Torts, § 466 (1965). Furthermore, were we not otherwise persuaded to elimination of assumption of risk as a separate affirmative defense in the context herein described, the decision of this Court in *Hoffman v. Jones, supra,* would dictate such a result. As stated therein:

> . . . A primary function of a court is to see that legal conflicts are equitably resolved. In the field of tort law, the most equitable result that can ever be reached by a court is the equation of liability with fault. Comparative negligence does this more completely than contributory negligence, and we would be shirking our duty if we did not adopt the better doctrine. 280 So. 2d 431, 438.

authors' dialogue 31

From: aaron.twerski@brooklaw.edu

To: henderson@postoffice.law.cornell.edu

I just got off the phone with you and you tell me that you agree with *Blackburn* that assumption of risk as an independent doctrine should be laid to rest. Well, try out this hypothetical: Jack and Jill get into a car with a driver named Giant. Jill falls asleep in the back seat. Giant has a flask of Kentucky bourbon in his back pocket and imbibes half a flask. Jack, who is awake, asks him to stop drinking. Giant refuses and consumes the entire flask. By this time Giant is drunk. They stop in town. Jack could easily get out and take the bus home. Instead he decides to continue on as a passenger in Giant's car. Ten minutes later, Giant loses control of his car and hits a tree, seriously injuring Jack. Are you inclined to allow Jack to recover some part of his damages on the basis of comparative fault? If not, how do you defeat his claim without resorting to assumption of risk?

Henderson's reply:

What's the problem? I wouldn't give Jack a nickel. Giant has no duty to Jack since Jack agreed to ride with Giant in his drunken state. Giant has no obligation to Jack to drive soberly.

Twerski's reply:

That seems an awkward way to talk about duty. Giant has breached a duty to act reasonably — certainly to Jill. If he has no duty to Jack, it is not because of some unspoken contract between Giant and Jack, it is because Jack voluntarily decided to encounter a risk. If Jack's decision to continue on was less than voluntary, he would be entitled to recover. Thus, for example, if Jack was given the choice to get out of the car on a lonely country road in the middle of the night, assumption of risk would not be a defense.

Is liability equated with fault under a doctrine which would totally bar recovery by one who voluntarily, but reasonably, assumes a known risk while one whose conduct is unreasonable but denominated "contributory negligence" is permitted to recover a proportionate amount of his damages for injury? Certainly not. Therefore, we hold that the affirmative defense of implied assumption of risk is merged into the defense of contributory negligence and the principles of comparative negligence enunciated in *Hoffman v. Jones, supra,* shall apply in all cases where such defense is asserted.

It is so ordered.

OVERTON, C.J., ADKINS, BOYD, ENGLAND and HATCHETT, JJ., concur.

Henderson's reply:

No, Aaron. You have it wrong. Giant gets off on no-duty grounds based on their tacit agreement. I'll prove it to you. Let's say that Giant is dead drunk and is driving on a country road and spots Jack. It's freezing cold and Jack's car broke down and the poor guy is freezing to death. Giant stops and offers Jack a ride. He tells Jack that he is drunk. Jack accepts the ride and is subsequently injured when Giant loses control of his car. If you use the duty analysis, Giant gets off. If you resort to assumption of risk, can you honestly say that Jack acted voluntarily?

Twerski's reply:

Nice point. But, Jack did act voluntarily vis-à-vis Giant. It is only when the defendant acts in a way to deprive a plaintiff of a voluntary choice by narrowing his options, that there is a problem with voluntariness. Giant did not put Jack in his dilemma. Jack's lousy car did. Assumption of risk works just fine. And for whatever it's worth, didn't Giant's drinking spree narrow choices for anyone that might need a ride? So even under your no-duty analysis, you face the same problem.

Wendel says:

I know I'm late to this party, but I wanted to add my two cents. I very much agree that tort law would be better off without an independent doctrine of *implied* assumption of risk. But I'm also with Aaron that it feels strained to talk in no-duty terms here, since Giant clearly did something wrong. Maybe the best way to handle a case like this hypo is not to try to assimilate it to no-duty cases or comparative fault cases, but to treat a tacit agreement like an express waiver. Although you could talk about it as a no-duty case because of the waiver, it seems more natural to say there would ordinarily be a duty, but the plaintiff has made his or her own private cost-benefit analysis and agreed to bear the costs of any resulting accident. So Giant breached a duty, but Jack has forgone the right to sue for negligence. Does that work better?

TURCOTTE v. FELL
502 N.E.2d 964 (N.Y. 1986)

SIMONS, Justice.

The issue raised in this appeal is the scope of the duty of care owed to a professional athlete injured during a sporting event. The defendants are a coparticipant and his employer and the owner and operator of the sports facility in which the event took place.

Plaintiff Ronald J. Turcotte is a former jockey. Before his injury he had ridden over 22,000 races in his 17-year career and achieved international fame as the jockey aboard "Secretariat" when that horse won the "Triple Crown" races in

1973. On July 13, 1978 plaintiff was injured while riding in the eighth race at Belmont Park, a racetrack owned and operated by defendant New York Racing Association (NYRA). Plaintiff had been assigned the third pole position for the race on a horse named "Flag of Leyte Gulf." Defendant jockey Jeffrey Fell was in the second pole position riding "Small Raja," a horse owned by defendant David P. Reynolds. On the other side of plaintiff, in the fourth position, was the horse "Walter Malone." Seconds after the race began, Turcotte's horse clipped the heels of "Walter Malone" and then tripped and fell, propelling plaintiff to the ground and causing him severe personal injuries which left him a paraplegic.

Plaintiffs, husband and wife, commenced this action against Jeffrey Fell, David P. Reynolds, [and] NYRA. . . . In their supplemental complaint, they charge that Fell is liable to them because [he's] guilty of common-law negligence and of violating the rules of the New York Racing and Wagering Board regulating "foul riding," that Reynolds is liable for Fell's negligence under the doctrine of respondent superior, and that defendant NYRA is liable because it "negligently" failed to water and groom that portion of the racetrack near the starting gate or watered and groomed the same in an "improper and careless manner" causing it to be unsafe.

Special Term granted the motions of Fell and Reynolds for summary judgment, holding that Turcotte, by engaging in the sport of horseracing, relieved other participants of any duty of reasonable care with respect to known dangers or risks which inhere in that activity. Finding no allegations of Fell's wanton, reckless, or intentional conduct, it dismissed the complaint as to Fell and Reynolds. . . . NYRA subsequently moved for summary judgment and Special Term denied its motion because it found there were questions of fact concerning NYRA's negligent maintenance of the track. On separate appeals, the Appellate Division affirmed . . . denying NYRA's motion for summary judgment, and the matters are before us as cross appeals by its leave. The order should be affirmed as to defendants Fell and Reynolds and reversed as to defendant NYRA, and NYRA's motion for summary judgment should be granted. The complaint should be dismissed as to all defendants because by participating in the race, plaintiff consented that the duty of care owed him by defendants was no more than a duty to avoid reckless or intentionally harmful conduct. Although a sport's safety rules are an important consideration in determining the scope of plaintiff's consent, the alleged violation of the rule in this case did not constitute reckless or intentional conduct and the complaint against defendants Fell and Reynolds was properly dismissed. NYRA's duty is similarly measured by plaintiff's consent to accept the risk of injuries that are known, apparent or reasonably foreseeable consequences of his participation in the race. Inasmuch as there are no factual issues concerning its liability, its motion for summary judgment should have been granted also.

I.

It is fundamental that to recover in a negligence action a plaintiff must establish that the defendant owed him a duty to use reasonable care, and that it breached that duty. . . . The statement that there is or is not a duty, however, "begs the essential question — whether the plaintiff's interests are entitled to legal protection against the defendant's conduct" (Prosser and Keeton, Torts § 53, at 357 [5th ed.]. . . . Thus, while the determination of the existence of a duty and the concomitant scope of that duty involve a consideration not only of the wrongfulness of the defendant's action or inaction, they also necessitate an examination of plaintiff's reasonable expectations of the care owed him by others. This is particularly true in professional sporting contests, which by their nature involve an elevated degree of danger. If a participant makes an informed estimate of the risks involved in the activity and willingly undertakes them, then there can be no liability if he is injured as a result of those risks.

Traditionally, the participant's conduct was conveniently analyzed in terms of the defensive doctrine of assumption of risk. With the enactment of the comparative negligence statute, however, assumption of risk is no longer an absolute defense (*see,* CPLR 1411, eff Sept. 1, 1975). Thus, it has become necessary, and quite proper, when measuring a defendant's duty to a plaintiff to consider the risks assumed by the plaintiff. . . . The shift in analysis is proper because the "doctrine [of assumption of risk] deserves no separate existence (except for *express* assumption of risk) and is simply a confusing way of stating certain no-duty rules" (James, *Assumption of Risk: Unhappy Reincarnation,* 78 Yale L.J. 185, 187-188). Accordingly, the analysis of care owed to plaintiff in the professional sporting event by a coparticipant and by the proprietor of the facility in which it takes place must be evaluated by considering the risks plaintiff assumed when he elected to participate in the event and how those assumed risks qualified defendants' duty to him.

The risk assumed has been defined a number of ways but in its most basic sense it "means that the plaintiff, in advance, has given his . . . consent to relieve the defendant of an obligation of conduct toward him, and to take his chances of injury from a known risk arising from what the defendant is to do or leave undone. The situation is then the same as where the plaintiff consents to the infliction of what would otherwise be an intentional tort, except that the consent is to run the risk of unintended injury. . . . The result is that the defendant is relieved of legal duty to the plaintiff; and being under no duty, he cannot be charged with negligence" (Prosser and Keeton, Torts § 68, at 480-481 [5th ed.] . . . Restatement [Second] of Torts § 496A comments *b, c.* . . .

The doctrine has been divided into several categories but as the term applies to sporting events it involves what commentators call "primary" assumption of risk. Risks in this category are incidental to a relationship of free association between the defendant and the plaintiff in the sense that either party is perfectly free to engage in the activity or not as he wishes. Defendant's duty under such circumstances is a duty to exercise care to make the conditions as safe as they appear to be. If the risks of the activity are fully comprehended or perfectly obvious, plaintiff has consented to them and defendant has performed its duty (Prosser and Keeton, Torts § 68 [5th ed.]; 4 Harper, James & Gray, Torts § 21.1 [2d ed.]). Plaintiff's "consent" is not constructive consent; it is actual consent implied from the act of the electing to participate in the activity *(see,* Restatement [Second] of Torts § 892 [2]). When thus analyzed and applied, assumption of risk is not an absolute defense but a measure of the defendant's duty of care and thus survives the enactment of the comparative fault statute. . . .

authors' dialogue 32

JIM: See, Aaron, the *Turcotte* case proves my point. New York has a statute abolishing assumption of risk as a complete bar to recovery and merging the doctrine into comparative fault. Under the facts of *Turcotte*, the New York Court of Appeals concluded that the voluntary nature of the relationship between jockeys and the owner of the racetrack was such that the racetrack owner had no duty to protect jockeys from ordinary conditions that exist on racetracks. The court thus did not allow the plaintiff-jockey to recover anything and deftly bypassed the comparative fault statute.

AARON: I agree that in many situations a court can use the no-duty approach to bar recovery entirely and thus bypass comparative fault. But try this hypothetical. It's a variation of a hypothetical that I raised earlier. The case takes place in a jurisdiction that imposes a full duty of reasonable care on landowners toward social guests. Vic and Sheila are social guests of the landowner. On the premises is a swimming pool. Assume that reasonable care would require the landowner to place a fence around the perimeter of the pool. The landowner did not put up such a fence. Vic and Sheila decide to play a game of catch in the vicinity of the pool. Before they get started, Sheila asks Vic, "Do you think that you should be playing catch while standing so near to the pool?" To which Vic answers, "Sheila, I'm a super athlete and a great swimmer. Even if I fall into the pool, I'll be just fine. In fact, have your camera ready. If I fall in, take a picture; it will be a great memento of this weekend." Sheila throws the ball over Vic's head. He runs back in the direction of the pool and falls backward into the water. Vic hits his head on the side of the pool and drowns. Now, Jim, what are you going to say? Does the landowner owe a duty to have a fence around the swimming pool to protect guests from inadvertently falling in, but owes no duty to Vic? The fence should have been there. If Vic does not recover, it's because he voluntarily assumed a known risk. He actually relished the risk.

JIM: I agree that Vic doesn't recover. But it's not because he assumed the risk. It's because the fence was required as a protection against trespassing children, not

II.

We turn then to an analysis of these two requirements — the nature and scope of plaintiff's consent. It would be a rare thing, indeed, if the election of a professional athlete to participate in a sport at which he makes his living could be said to be involuntary. Plaintiff's participation certainly was not involuntary in this case and thus we are concerned only with the scope of his consent.

As a general rule, participants properly may be held to have consented, by their participation, to those injury-causing events which are known, apparent or reasonably foreseeable consequences of the participation. . . .

Whether a professional athlete should be held under this standard to have consented to the act or omission of a coparticipant which caused his injury involves

as a protection against frolicking adults. For me, it's like *Palsgraf* and the land-owner's duty to fence doesn't extend to Vic. It's a "no duty to Vic" situation. I don't think that assumption of risk even comes into play.

AARON: You aren't playing by my rules — I asked you to *assume* it was negligence toward Vic not to have a fence.

JIM: OK, then it's a harder case. I admit that using the no-duty analysis in your hypo is awkward. But, you know, Aaron, sometimes you have to make hard choices. If you keep assumption of risk around as an independent defense, it will be used by defendants in any case where you can conceivably argue that plaintiff knew about a risk and voluntarily chose it. In most cases the plaintiffs will not be like Vic, the guy who is looking for a thrill and chooses to take a risk. The simple fact is that if you keep the doctrine around, it will be misused and abused by the courts and plaintiffs will be barred when they should only have their recovery reduced. The worst that's going to happen is that a jury, in your hypothetical case where Vic takes the risk, will assess comparative fault. Think about it. Most juries would assess the lion's share of the fault against Vic. In a state that has modified comparative fault, plaintiff would likely recover nothing. And even in a pure comparative fault state, recovery will be minimal. I'll stick with my position that the world would be a better place if we relegated assumption of risk to the junk heap.

BRAD: Not to belabor my point, but this is a perfect example of a type of implied assumption of risk that should function like an express waiver. On Aaron's stipulation, Sheila was negligent, so we can't treat this as implied primary assumption of risk in the no-duty sense. But it does feel like Vic ought to be zeroed out here. We all agree that if Sheila had been a lawyer and had drafted a written express waiver that Vic signed, he couldn't recover, right? Then why not treat Vic's words and conduct as amounting to the same thing? I take Jim's point that we don't want implied assumption of risk being misused by defendants, but there will probably be very few cases in which the plaintiff's words and actions function as an agreement to waive liability, as opposed to merely a voluntary decision to encounter a known risk, which would get cranked into the state's comparative fault scheme.

---

consideration of a variety of factors including but not limited to: the ultimate purpose of the game and the method or methods of winning it; the relationship of defendant's conduct to the game's ultimate purpose, especially his conduct with respect to rules and customs whose purpose is to enhance the safety of the participants; and the equipment or animals involved in the playing of the game. The question of whether the consent was an informed one includes consideration of the participant's knowledge and experience in the activity generally. Manifestly a professional athlete is more aware of the dangers of the activity, and presumably more willing to accept them in exchange for a salary, than is an amateur.

In this case plaintiff testified before trial to facts establishing that horse racing is a dangerous activity. . . . Plaintiff testified that every professional jockey had experiences when he was not able to keep a horse running on a straight line, or a horse would veer, or jump up on its hind legs, or go faster or slower than the jockey indicated. . . . Turcotte conceded that there is a fine line between what is lawful and unlawful in the movement of a horse on the track during a race and that when and where a horse can lawfully change its position is a matter of judgment. Such dangers are inherent in the sport. Because they are recognized as such by plaintiff, the courts below properly held that he consented to relieve defendant Jeffrey Fell of the legal duty to use reasonable care to avoid crossing into his lane of travel. . . .

IV.

The complaint against NYRA should also be dismissed. . . .

NYRA's duty to plaintiff is similarly measured by his position and purpose for being on the track on July 13 and the risks he accepted by being there. In deciding whether plaintiff consented to the conditions which existed at the time, the court should consider the nature of professional horseracing and the facilities used for it, the playing conditions under which horseracing is carried out, the frequency of the track's use and the correlative ability of the owner to repair or refurbish the track, and the standards maintained by other similarly used facilities.

Plaintiffs charge that NYRA was negligent in failing to water the "chute," which leads to the main track, and "over-watering" the main track. Thus, they claim the horses had to run from the dry surface of the chute onto the overly watered, unsafe "cuppy" surface of the main track. Plaintiff testified, however, that "cupping" conditions are common on racetracks and that he had experienced them before at Belmont Park and also at many other tracks. Indeed, he testified that he had never ridden on a track where he had not observed a cupping condition at one time or another. Thus, Turcotte's participation in three prior races at this same track on the day of his injury, his ability to observe the condition of the track before the eighth race and his general knowledge and experience with cupping conditions and their prevalence establish that he was well aware of these conditions and the possible dangers from them and that he accepted the risk. . . .

Accordingly, on appeal by plaintiffs, the order of the Appellate Division should be affirmed. . . . On appeal by defendant NYRA, the order should be reversed . . . (and) defendant's motion for summary judgment granted. . . .

WHAT'S LEFT OF ASSUMPTION OF RISK?

With comparative fault solidly entrenched in the law, some states have abolished assumption of risk as an independent defense. *See, e.g.,* Mass. Gen. Laws Ann. ch. 231, § 85 (West 2000) (statute abolishes assumption of risk; thus, if the plaintiff's assumption of risk is reasonable, he will be entitled to full recovery; if it is unreasonable, it will constitute contributory negligence and will be governed by the comparative negligence statute). A good number of states treat assumption of risk as a form of fault to be compared with that of the defendant. *See, e.g.*, Alaska Stat. § 09.17.900 (Michie 2000); Colo. Rev. Stat. § 13-21-111.7 (2001); N.Y. C.P.L.R. 1411 (McKinney 1997); Knight v. Jewett, 834 P.2d 696 (Cal. 1992); Meistrich v. Casino Arena Attractions, Inc., 155 A.2d 90 (N.J. 1959); Moore v. Phi Delta Theta Co., 976 S.W.2d 738 (Tex. App. 1998). However, as *Turcotte* teaches us, when the relationship between the parties is such that the defendant owes no duty to the plaintiff (otherwise known as primary assumption of risk), the plaintiff has no viable claim. *See, e.g.*, Herrle v. Estate of Marshall, 53 Cal. Rptr. 2d 713 (Cal. Ct. App. 1996) (nurse hired to care for combative Alzheimer patient has no cause of action against the patient who struck her since, given the nature of the relationship between patient and nurse, there is no duty on the patient's part to act reasonably); Mastro v. Petrick, 112 Cal. Rptr. 2d 185 (Cal. Ct. App. 2001) (snowboarder who collided with skier on ski resort slope had no duty of care to skier who chose to ski where he knew others would be snowboarding); American Golf Corp. v. Superior Court, 93 Cal. Rptr. 2d 683 (Cal. Ct. App. 2000) (under primary assumption of risk doctrine, golf course had no duty to golfer to prevent injury incurred from ball ricocheting off of yardage marker and hitting golfer's eye).

At bottom, whether we recognize an independent defense of assumption of risk as a complete bar or whether we say that in cases of primary assumption of risk the defendant has no duty to a plaintiff, we will be faced with the question of just when to invoke the no-duty/assumption of risk rule and when to relegate the plaintiff's conduct to comparative fault. Ultimately, we have to identify those situations in which the relationship between the parties is sufficiently free and noncoercive, and the information about the risks to be confronted well enough defined, that we deem it just to bar the plaintiff from all recovery. In Trupia v. Lake George Central School Dist., 927 N.E.2d 547 (N.Y. 2010), Chief Judge Lippman held that the no-duty formulation in *Turcotte* was limited to athletic and recreational activities but that otherwise comparative fault would be utilized to reduce but not bar recovery. How would Judge Lippman deal with a passenger who got into a car with a drunk driver fully aware that the driver was inebriated? In Shin v. Ahn, 165 P.3d 581 (Cal. 2007), the court affirmed that the inherent risks attendant to golf bar recovery under primary assumption of risk. *Accord* Sanchez v. Candia Woods Golf Links, 13 A.3d 268 (N.H. 2010). For a critical analysis of Shin, *see* Brian P. Harlan, *The California Supreme Court Should Take a Mulligan: How the Court Shanked by Applying the Primary Assumption of Risk Doctrine to Golf*, 29 Loy. L.A. Ent. L. Rev. 91 (2008-2009).

SCHOLARLY TREATMENT OF ASSUMPTION OF RISK

Assumption of risk has been the subject of intense scholarly debate. Professor Kenneth W. Simons, in one of the most thoughtful articles on the subject, *Reflections on Assumption of Risk*, 50 UCLA L. Rev. 481 (2002), argues that implied assumption of risk should operate as a total bar even under a comparative negligence regime when the plaintiff's conduct expresses a true and full preference for the risky alternatives that he chose, or if plaintiff requests the defendant to confront a tortious risk where the defendant could decline any further relationship with him. *See also* John L. Diamond, *Assumption of Risk After Comparative Negligence: Integrating Contract Theory into Tort Doctrine*, 52 Ohio St. L.J. 717 (1991); Stephen D. Sugarman, *Assumption of Risk*, 31 Val. U. L. Rev. 833 (1997); William Powers, Jr., *Sports, Assumption of Risk, and the New Restatement*, 38 Washburn L.J. 771 (1999); Daniel E. Wanat, *Torts and Sporting Events: Spectator and Participant Injuries — Using Defendant's Duty to Limit Liability as an Alternative to the Defense of Primary Implied Assumption of the Risk*, 31 U. Mem. L. Rev. 237 (2001); Alexander J. Drago, *Assumption of Risk: An Age-Old Defense Still Viable in Sports and Recreation Cases*, 12 Fordham Intell. Prop. Media & Ent. L.J. 583 (2002); David Horton, *Extreme Sports and Assumption of Risk: A Blueprint*, 38 U.S.F. L. Rev. 599 (2004); Eric A. Feldman & Alison Stein, *Assuming the Risk: Tort Law, Policy and Politics on the Slippery Slopes*, 59 DePaul L. Rev. 259 (2010).

4. Avoidable Consequences

The role of plaintiff fault as a factor in reducing damages does not come to an end with the events leading up to the injury. Even after a plaintiff is injured, she may fail to take reasonable steps to avoid aggravation of her injury and mitigate her damages. Assume that a plaintiff suffered a broken elbow in an auto accident as a result of the defendant's negligence. Her doctor informs her that if she wishes to regain mobility in her arm, she must undergo surgery to correctly position the bones. She unreasonably refuses the surgery and ultimately suffers permanent damage to her elbow. The defendant is responsible for the injury that he caused to the plaintiff's arm, but the plaintiff is responsible for the permanent damage that could have been avoided had she taken the reasonable step to undergo surgery. *See* Dobbs, Hayden and Bublick, *The Law of Torts*, Sec.16.9 (2016). In the pre–comparative fault era it was clear that plaintiff's recovery would be reduced by the dollar amount that could be attributed to the plaintiff's failure to undergo the surgery. The issue was dealt with as one of causation. The plaintiff, having failed to undergo surgery, caused additional injury to herself (or failed to mitigate damages) and she is thus solely responsible for the permanent loss of mobility to her arm.

NOVKO v. STATE OF NEW YORK
728 N.Y.S.2d 259 (N.Y. App. Div. 2001)

Spain, J. . . .

In July 1996, claimant Paul J. Novko (hereinafter claimant), a self-employed dairy farmer, sustained injuries when, stopped at a red light on State Route 23 in the Town of Oneonta, Otsego County, the vehicle he was driving was struck in the rear by a State Trooper's patrol vehicle. Claimant and his spouse, derivatively, commenced this action against the State seeking damages for past and future pain and suffering and loss of earning capacity alleging that claimant sustained a serious injury within the meaning of Insurance Law § 5102 (d). Following a nonjury trial, the Court of Claims rendered judgment finding the State 100% liable for the collision and concluded that claimant sustained a significant limitation of the use of his thoracic spine due to a degenerative disc condition in the area of T7-T8 that was aggravated and became symptomatic as the result of the accident. The court awarded claimant significantly limited damages for past and future pain and suffering in the amount of $40,000 but made no award for his loss of earning capacity. Claimant's wife was awarded $6,000 on her derivative claim. The court temporally limited its award of damages to both claimants to the period between the July 1996 accident and the spring of 1997, concluding that the pain and suffering experienced by claimant thereafter was the result of his failure to mitigate his damages. Claimants appeal from these damage awards.

Initially, we find merit to claimants' contention that the Court of Claims erred in applying the doctrine of mitigation of damages to preclude recovery for pain and suffering after the spring of 1997. In invoking the doctrine, the court essentially concluded that claimant's pain could have been avoided or reduced had he made a timely decision — i.e., by the spring of 1997 — to change his lifestyle by giving up dairy farming and becoming a farming equipment salesperson, and that his failure to do so constituted a breach of his duty to mitigate his damages. The court apparently rationalized that had claimant left the farming profession, his thoracic pain would have ceased or become tolerable.

We are guided by the principle that "mitigation of damages is usually thought of in the context of steps that a reasonable plaintiff could have taken subsequent to the incident giving rise to injuries, in order to reduce the amount of damages" (Giannetti v. Darling, . . . 666 N.Y.S.2d 372). As a general rule, "a party who claims to have suffered damage by the tort of another is bound 'to use reasonable and proper efforts to make the damage as small as practicable' . . . and if an injured party allows the damages to be unnecessarily enhanced, the incurred loss justly falls upon him" (Williams v. Bright, . . . 658 N.Y.S.2d 910, *appeal dismissed* 90 N.Y.2d 935. . . .

Here, claimant testified that he is a self-employed dairy farmer which requires, *inter alia*, milking cows, baling hay and tending to crops. While of necessity he continued working the farm following the accident, he testified that he made numerous and substantial adjustments to reduce the stress on his back. Specifically, claimant often assumed the role of manager instead of physical laborer and, in an effort to reduce his physical labor, he changed the way he stored crops, used a tractor, remodeled a building on the farm, changed his baling system and hired a full-time employee. Additionally, claimant's wife left her full-time employment for a period of time to assist claimant on the farm. In August 1998, claimant began selling farm equipment on a part-time basis which entailed demonstrating the equipment while performing his farm work. In our view, the record demonstrates that having made significant adjustments to reduce the stress on his spine, it was not unreasonable for claimant to continue his livelihood of farming and, indeed, it was unreasonable for the Court of Claims to require that he completely change his occupation. In fact, this Court is unaware of any case law requiring changes in lifestyle and occupation to the extent effectively required by the Court of Claims. We find that the court's presumptions that other jobs and, in particular, selling farm equipment, were available to claimant on a full-time basis and would not have aggravated the stress on claimant's thoracic spine are speculative and not supported by medical testimony or any other part of the record. As such, there was no basis to invoke the doctrine and correspondingly limit the award of damages.

Turning to the derivative claim, while the Court of Claims found that claimant's wife assumed many of the functions that claimant had performed around the house prior to the accident, it stated that "her damages must be limited the same way the [c]laimant's are limited, that is to a reasonable period of time subsequent to this accident, during which arrangements could have been made for [c]laimant to end his career as a dairy farmer and begin a far more lucrative career as a farm equipment salesman." The application of mitigation of damages doctrine to her derivative claim was also erroneous.

However, we find no reason to disturb the Court of Claims' decision not to award damages on the loss of earning capacity claim. It is axiomatic that loss of earning capacity must be established with reasonable certainty. . . . Here, the opinion of the vocational economic analyst who testified on behalf of claimant was only based upon general information — i.e., the preaccident earning capacity of a nondisabled male with a four-year college degree. Notably, the analyst failed to rely upon claimant's income tax statements or to take into consideration the earning capacity of a farmer in claimant's situation. Consequently, we are constrained to agree that claimant failed to establish with reasonable certainty his loss of earning capacity.

Finally, while claimants do not challenge the Court of Claims' finding that claimant did not sustain a "permanent consequential limitation of use" (Insurance Law § 5102 [d]), they do contend that the court improperly concluded that claimant's restricted range of motion caused by his thoracic back pain was not permanent. Specifically, the court concluded that there was no basis to find that claimant's injury to his back was permanent because "it [was] likely that the condition would have resolved and the pain ended, or at least resolved to a mild level, had [c]laimant followed a sensible regimen of rest and medical treatment for a reasonable period of time following the accident, instead of immediately continuing to lift heavy objects." A review of the medical evidence does not support the court's broad conclusion. Additionally, we agree with claimants that the court's analysis is flawed in the same respect as the analysis leading the court to curtail the damages award.

Ordered that the judgment is modified . . . by reversing the award of damages; matter remitted to the Court of Claims for a new trial on the issue of damages for claimant Paul J. Novko's past and future pain and suffering and claimant Michelle J. Novko's derivative claim; and, as so modified, affirmed.

FOOD FOR THOUGHT

Who bears the burden of proving mitigation of damages and how rigorous must the proof be to sustain mitigation? In Willis v. Westerfield, 839 N.E.2d 1179 (Ind. 2006), the court said that the defendant has the burden of proof that plaintiff's post-injury conduct increased the plaintiff's harm and, if so, by how much. The court held that in many cases expert testimony is necessary to establish that the failure to take ameliorative action caused the plaintiff additional damages but there may be cases where a lay juror could reasonably decide the mitigation issue without expert testimony. The mere testimony by the plaintiff's expert on cross-examination that the plaintiff did not "help herself" when she failed to listen to her doctor's advice and go for physical therapy, was not sufficient for the defendant to meet his burden of proof or mitigation. The defendant failed to show "how [the plaintiff's] failure to follow the doctor's recommendation increased her harm, and if so, by any quantifiable amount. . . ."

AVOIDABLE CONSEQUENCES: BUCKLE UP IN CASE OF ACCIDENT

Now if you are not sufficiently confused, consider the problem of pre-injury avoidable consequences. If you fail to buckle your seat belt and are involved in an accident due to the negligence of another driver, should your damages be reduced by the fact that you failed to mitigate your damages by taking reasonable precautions before the accident? Most jurisdictions will not allow a defendant to introduce evidence that the plaintiff failed to buckle up. *See, e.g.,* Barron v. Ford Motor Co., 965 F.2d 195 (7th Cir. 1992) (N.C. law.); Vogel v. Wells, 566 N.E.2d 154 (Ohio 1991); Clarkson v. Wright, 483 N.E.2d 268 (Ill. 1985). They outright refuse to reduce a plaintiff's damages for the failure to undertake pre-accident preventive steps to lessen injury. But other states apply the avoidable consequences doctrine to the failure to use a seat belt. *See, e.g.,* Hutchins v. Schwartz, 724 P.2d 1194 (Alaska 1986); Law v. Superior Court, 755 P.2d 1135 (Ariz. 1988); Cal. Veh. § 27315(j) (2000); N.Y. Veh. & Traf. Law § 1229-c(8) (McKinney 1996); Waterson v. General Motors Corp., 544 A.2d 357 (N.J. 1988). Some states allow a reduction of damages for failure to wear a seat belt but cap the percentage of reduction. *See, e.g.,* Iowa Code § 321.445(4)(b) (1997) (5 percent); Wis. Stat. § 347.48(7)(g) (1999) (15 percent). Some states apply an analogous "helmet defense" to reduce damages where a motorcyclist or other driver of a dangerous vehicle fails to wear a helmet before the accident. *See, e.g.,* Rodgers v. Am. Honda Motor Co., 46 F.3d 1 (1st Cir. 1995) (all-terrain vehicle); Stehlik v. Rhoads, 645 N.W.2d 889 (Wis. 2002) (all-terrain vehicle). As with the seat-belt defense, there is a split of authority over whether failure to wear a helmet constitutes contributory negligence or failure to mitigate damages. *See, e.g.,* Dare v. Sobule, 674 P.2d 960 (Colo 1984) (not contributory negligence to fail to wear helmet); Hukill v. Di Gregorio, 484 N.E.2d 795 (Ill. Ct. App. 1985) (same, citing Clarkson v. Wright, *supra,* on seat-belt defense).

B. NON-CONDUCT-BASED DEFENSES

1. Immunities

a. Intrafamily Immunities

At one time the law protected spouses from tort actions against each other and parents from suits by their children. For the most part these immunities have passed from the American scene. Interspousal immunity had its origin in the common law doctrine in which wives had no separate legal identity, since after marriage the couple was viewed as "one" and the husband — being in charge of the marriage — was "the one." With the passage of the Married Women's Property Acts allowing women to own property in their own right and thus giving married women independent legal standing, a major obstacle to interspousal suits fell by the wayside.

Courts offered other reasons to support intrafamily immunity from suit. These reasons were articulated to bar both interspousal litigation and suits between children and parents. The two major arguments were that intrafamily suits (1) would bring about family discord and (2) would result in collusive actions between the family members who would cook up a story to defraud the insurance company who was the true defendant in the case. These two stated goals are at war with each other. One argues that a lawsuit will destroy family harmony and the other that they will be too harmonious and be in cahoots together.

In the run-of-the-mill action when one family member sues another for negligence in driving a car and causing injury, the fear of family discord arising from the lawsuit is remote. The concern of possible fraudulent collusion, however, is less far-fetched. It is possible that a parent may confess negligence where there was none, since either the spouse or a child will be the beneficiary. Nonetheless, if opportunity for fraud were to be a total bar to a plaintiff's recovery against a parent or spouse, actions between relatives and friends should be similarly barred.

(1) Interspousal Immunity

There is very little left of the doctrine of interspousal immunity. In most states negligence actions proceed no differently than if they involved strangers. We have already made reference in Chapter 1 to the special problems that arise out of domestic violence. Courts have been willing to recognize a cause of action for battery and other forms of physical abuse. Claims for emotional abuse must pass muster under the rules set forth for intentional infliction of emotional distress. But courts have not been willing to treat the pain accompanying marital infidelity and other forms of emotional distress within the marriage as sufficiently outrageous to support a mental distress claim. On the other hand, even within the marriage some conduct can be so abusive that liability may attach. *See* Chapter 1, section E; Brandi Monger, *Family Law — Wyoming's Adoption of Intentional Infliction of Emotional Distress in the Marital Context: McCulloh v. Drake, 24*

P.3d 1162 (Wyo. 2001), 2 Wyo. L. Rev. 563 (2002); Douglas Scherer, *Tort Remedies for Victims of Domestic Abuse*, 43 S.C. L. Rev. 543 (1992).

(2) Parental Immunity

For many of the same reasons that courts discarded interspousal immunity, they found parental immunity to be unsound. Beginning in the early 1960s, courts began dismantling the child/parent immunity doctrine. Goller v. White, 122 N.W.2d 193 (Wis. 1963), led the way. Noting the widespread availability of insurance for vehicular accidents, the court found little merit in the concern that family harmony would be compromised if children were able to bring an action against their parents. The court did recognize two situations in which parental immunity from tort actions should remain intact: (1) where the negligence involved parental discipline over the child; and (2) where the negligence involved exercise of normal parental discretion over such matters as providing food, housing, and medical services. Other courts have expressed similar concern. *See, e.g.*, Holodook v. Spencer, 324 N.E.2d 338 (N.Y. 1974). But, on the whole, most states have abandoned parental immunity. *See, e.g.*, Glaskox v. Glaskox, 614 So. 2d 906 (Miss. 1992) (holding doctrine of parental immunity did not apply when children sue parents for negligent operation of a motor vehicle); Broadbent v. Broadbent, 907 P.2d 43 (Ariz. 1995) (abolishing doctrine of parental immunity when mother was sued on behalf of infant who sustained brain damage from nearly drowning when mother was supervising); Gibson v. Gibson, 479 P.2d 648, 648 (Cal. 1971) ("parental immunity has become a legal anachronism"). A minority remain convinced that the immunity is well founded. *See* Renko v. McLean, 697 A.2d 468 (Md. 1997) (good review of authority). In 2001, the legislature enacted a special statutory exception for automobile accidents. *See also* Greenwood v. Anderson, 324 S.W.3d 324 (Ark. 2009); Zellmer v. Zellmer, 188 P.3d 497 (Wash. 2008) (doctrine of parental immunity precludes liability for negligent parental supervision). A patchwork of exceptions can be found in various jurisdictions. *See, e.g.*, Rodebaugh v. Grand Trunk W. R.R., 145 N.W.2d 401 (Mich. Ct. App. 1966) (liability for intentional or willful torts); Conn. Gen. Stat Ann. § 52-572c (automobile accidents); Eagan v. Calhoun, 698 A.2d 1097 (Md. 1997) (wrongful death action by children against father for killing mother).

b. Charitable Immunity

For almost a century, charitable organizations were immune from actions based on a charity's negligence. The charitable immunity doctrine was first recognized in a nineteenth-century English case. Even though English courts repudiated the doctrine, it was widely adopted in the United States and applied to a broad range of charitable organizations including hospitals, churches, little league baseball, and the Boy Scouts. A host of reasons have been offered in support of the immunity: (1) tort recoveries would invade "trust funds" dedicated to the charity; (2) beneficiaries of the charity impliedly waived any claims by assuming the risk of any negligence; and (3) tort liability would put charities in financial jeopardy and thus threaten their continued existence.

Beginning with President and Directors of Georgetown College v. Hughes, 130 F.2d 810 (D.C. Cir. 1942), the courts began a broadside attack on the charitable immunity doctrine. The two most important reasons for abrogating the immunity were that many charities had become big business and were no longer in need of special protection. Furthermore, the widespread availability of insurance simply abrogated the threat that responsible charities would disappear from the face of the earth without immunity from tort liability. Though many of the leading opinions doing away with the immunity involved hospitals, *see, e.g.*, Hungerford v. Portland Sanitarium & Benevolent Assn., 384 P.2d 1009 (Or. 1963); Bing v. Thunig, 143 N.E.2d 3 (N.Y. 1957), once the assault on charitable immunity took hold, all charitable organizations saw their immunity abrogated. *See* Janet Fairchild, Annotation, *Tort Immunity of Non-Governmental Charities*, 25 A.L.R. 4th 517 (1981).

It appeared for a while that charitable immunities would go the way of intrafamily immunities and would become an historical relic. However, in many states the doctrine retains considerable vigor. *See, e.g.*, Gain, Inc. v. Martin, 485 S.W.3d 729 (Ark. App. 2016) (retaining charitable immunity in personal-injury action against organization serving adults with debilitating mental illnesses); Ola v. YMCA of South Hampton Roads, Inc., 621 S.E.2d 70 (Va. 2005) (child abducted and sexually abused in the bathroom of YMCA alleged negligence in allowing the nonmember assailant to enter the building, failing to provide adequate staffing, and failing to repair a broken lock on the bathroom, could not recover; charitable immunity "is firmly embedded in the law of this Commonwealth and has become part of the general public policy of the state."). The overall insurance crisis over the last two decades has made the argument that, without immunity, charities may, in fact, be endangered, a more plausible argument. Some states passed legislation reinstating the immunity and others have capped the liability of charitable organizations. In an unusual case, Schultz v. Boy Scouts of America, 480 N.E.2d 679 (N.Y. 1985), a priest who was a New Jersey scoutmaster accompanied some young boys to a scout summer camp in upstate New York. While in camp, he sexually assaulted two boys. As a result, one of the boys committed suicide. In an action against the New Jersey Boy Scouts for negligence in hiring the priest, the New York Court of Appeals applied the New Jersey charitable immunity rule negating liability, since New Jersey was the state in which the relationship between the parties was centered. It did not apply the law of New York, which had abolished charitable immunity, reasoning that the deterrence role of tort law in New York did not take precedence over the law of New Jersey that sought to foster charitable organizations by granting them immunity. For states that still retain charitable immunity, the number of permutations on the scope and nature of the immunity are so significant that one must carefully examine state law before deciding whether a given charity is subject to liability.

The sexual abuse cases brought against the Catholic church have raised anew the issue of charitable immunity. In Picher v. Roman Catholic Bishop of Portland, 974 A.2d 286 (Me. 2009), the court reviewed the charitable immunity doctrine throughout the country and decided that it would recognize the immunity for negligent but not intentional torts.

c. Governmental Immunity

The saga of governmental immunity begins with the medieval view that the sovereign could do no wrong. This doctrine was imported into the United States and — though the original rationale for immunity was clearly inappropriate to federal, state, and municipal governments — the notion that the government was immune from liability for its tortious conduct remained unquestioned for many years. Once Congress, state legislatures, and courts began to examine the immunity, it became clear that blanket immunity from tort liability was unjustified. On the other hand, sound policy concerns justified limited immunity. What follows is a bird's-eye view of how the various governmental entities worked out the appropriate balance between responsibility for tort and the need to allow government to function without the heavy hand of tort law looking over its shoulder.

(1) Federal Government: The Federal Tort Claims Act

(a) Discretionary Immunity

In 1946, Congress enacted the Federal Tort Claims Act (FTCA) abolishing tort immunity against the federal government subject to very important limitations. Although the FTCA is binding only on the federal government, the basic philosophy of the act has influenced state legislatures and courts in developing the proper scope of governmental immunity. Clearly the most important area in which the FTCA retained governmental immunity from tort liability was in prohibiting tort actions "based upon the exercise or performance or the failure to exercise or perform a discretionary function of duty on the part of a federal agency or an employee of the Government, whether or not the discretion involved be abused." 28 U.S.C.A. § 2680(a). What constitutes an exercise of discretion has been the subject of unremitting litigation for over a half century. The United States Supreme Court has stepped in on several occasions to try to clarify the issue. *See, e.g.,* Dalehite v. United States, 346 U.S. 15 (1953); Berkovitz v. United States, 486 U.S. 531 (1988); and United States v. Gaubert, 499 U.S. 315 (1991). But as the following case demonstrates, courts remain at loggerheads as to how broadly to read the discretionary exemption.

TIPPETT v. UNITED STATES
108 F.3d 1194 (10th Cir. 1997)

Briscoe, Justice. . . .

Plaintiff Frank Tippett and his wife Judy Rand were members of a guided snowmobile tour exploring parts of Yellowstone National Park in February 1993. Plaintiffs' group entered the park through the south gate and, as they began up the road toward Old Faithful, they encountered a moose standing in the road. When a group of snowmobilers ahead of plaintiffs' group attempted to pass the moose, the moose charged one of the snowmobiles and knocked two passengers to the ground. The moose then proceeded south past plaintiffs' vehicles, and plaintiffs' group proceeded into the interior of the park.

Mr. Dave Phillips, a Yellowstone park ranger, learned of the moose's presence and monitored its activities during the day. At the end of the day, he observed several groups of snowmobilers going southbound who successfully passed the moose on their way out of the park. When plaintiffs' group approached the moose in the course of their departure, Ranger Phillips directed them to pass the moose on the right, staying in line with other snowmobilers. As Mr. Tippett attempted to go around the moose, the animal charged his vehicle and kicked in his windscreen striking him in the helmet and knocking him off the snowmobile. Mr. Tippett suffered a broken neck from which he has since recovered; the moose broke one of its legs as a result of the encounter and had to be destroyed.

Plaintiffs filed negligence and loss of consortium claims against the United States under the FTCA. . . . [T]he district court dismissed plaintiffs' claims finding them barred by the discretionary function exception to the Act. . . .

Under the FTCA, the United States waives its sovereign immunity with respect to certain injuries caused by government employees acting within the scope of their employment. 28 U.S.C. § 1346(b). The FTCA contains an exception to this broad waiver of immunity, however, for claims "based upon the exercise or performance or the failure to exercise or perform a discretionary function or duty on the part of a federal agency or an employee of the Government, whether or not the discretion involved be abused." *Id.* § 2680(a). Section 2680(a) is commonly referred to as the "discretionary function exception" to the FTCA. . . . "The discretionary function exception . . . marks the boundary between Congress' willingness to impose tort liability upon the United States and its desire to protect certain governmental activities from exposure to suit by private individuals." United States v. S.A. Empresa de Viacao Aerea Rio Grandense (Varig Airlines), 467 U.S. 797, 808 (1984). If the discretionary function exception applies to the challenged governmental conduct, the United States retains its sovereign immunity, and the district court lacks subject matter jurisdiction to hear the suit. . . .

In order to determine whether the discretionary function exception applies in cases brought under the FTCA, we utilize the two-prong analysis of Berkovitz ex rel. Berkovitz v. United States, 486 U.S. 531 (1988). Under that scheme, we determine (1) whether the action at issue was one of choice for the government employee; and (2) if the conduct involved such an element of judgment, "whether that judgment is of the kind that the discretionary function exception was designed to shield." *Id.* at 536. . . .

Citing Aslakson v. United States, 790 F.2d 688, 693 (8th Cir. 1986), plaintiffs argue that because there was an existing park safety policy in place, Ranger Phillips had no discretion in the situation he encountered. In *Aslakson*, the plaintiff was injured when the aluminum mast of his sailboat made contact with electrical power lines owned and operated by an agent of the United States. In rejecting the government's claim of immunity, the court reasoned that the government's decision was one involving "safety considerations under an established policy rather than the balancing of competing policy considerations," and that the exception could not apply. *See id.* at 693.

Plaintiffs point to Chapter 8:5 of the Management Policies, U.S. Department of the Interior National Park Service, 1988, which provides that "[t]he saving of human life will take precedence over all other management actions." Appellants' App. at 56. Plaintiffs contend that this is the type of specific mandatory directive which Ranger Phillips failed to observe, and which renders the action at issue here nondiscretionary. We disagree because we find the cited directive too general to remove the discretion from Ranger Phillips' conduct.

In *Varig Airlines*, 467 U.S. 797, . . . the Supreme Court considered an action asserting claims against the FAA for negligence in the spot checking of airplanes. Despite the fact that the FAA had a statutory duty to promote the safety of American air transportation, decisions surrounding the implementation of that policy, including the spot checking program, were protected by the discretionary function exception. *See id.* at 820-21. . . .

Similarly, here, the general goal of protecting human life in the nation's national parks is not the kind of specific mandatory directive that operated to divest Ranger Phillips of discretion in the situation he faced. *See Berkovitz,* 486 U.S. at 536 (stating that "the discretionary function exception will not apply when a federal statute, regulation, or policy *specifically prescribes* a course of action for an employee to follow") (emphasis added). The district court was correct to conclude that the actions of Ranger Phillips were discretionary.

Turning to the second prong of the *Berkovitz* analysis, plaintiffs argue that this case does not implicate public policy and thus their claims against the United States should have survived the motion to dismiss. Because we have held above that the conduct here involved discretionary judgment, we must now determine "whether that judgment is of the kind that the discretionary function exception was designed to shield." *Id.* at 536. . . . The "exception insulates the Government from liability if the action challenged in the case involves the permissible exercise of policy judgment." *Id.* at 537. . . . The focus of our analysis, therefore, is on the nature of the action taken and whether it is subject to policy analysis. United States v. Gaubert, U.S. 315, 324-25. . . .

It is clear that balancing the interest of conserving wildlife in the national parks with the opportunity for public access has been a cornerstone of park management since the creation of the national park system. This overarching policy concern in national park management is expressed in 16 U.S.C. § 1, enacted in 1916 at the creation of the National Park Service, which provides in relevant part that the purpose of the National Park Service is to

> promote and regulate the use of . . . national parks . . . by such means and measures as conform to the fundamental purpose of the said parks . . . which purpose is to conserve the scenery and the natural and historic objects and the wild life therein and to provide for the enjoyment of the same in such manner and by such means as will leave them unimpaired for the enjoyment of future generations. . . .

In determining whether the discretion exercised here is of the type the discretionary function exception was designed to shield, we are aided in our analysis by the existence of regulations which allow park employees discretion in situations similar to that faced by Ranger Phillips. The existence of these regulations creates a strong presumption that "a discretionary act authorized by the regulations involves consideration of the same policies which led to the promulgation of the regulations." *Gaubert*, 499 U.S. at 324. . . .

There are no specific regulations dealing with confrontations between wildlife and snowmobiles or other motorized vehicles. *See* Affidavit of Yellowstone Chief Ranger, Appellee's Supp. App. at 54. However, among the regulations guiding Ranger Phillips' conduct is the Ranger Operating Procedure dealing with the occasional need to temporarily close or restrict an area. That regulation provides:

> Decision/Action
>
> Any . . . road . . . should be temporarily closed by any NPS employee when imminent life threatening or potential serious injury situations exist . . . or there is an immediate serious threat to natural or cultural resources. . . .
>
> . . .
>
> Resolution
>
> The District Ranger is responsible for resolving the cause of the restriction as soon as possible. Resolution alternatives may include actions to prevent or remove the threats to humans and/or resources, if possible, or allow natural activities to occur.
>
> Yellowstone National Park Ranger Operating Procedure, *id.* at 91.

While we realize that this directive indicates that a road "should" be closed under certain circumstances, possibly implying at least a limitation on discretion, the determination of when circumstances constitute an imminent life threatening situation or pose the risk of potential serious injury is clearly a discretionary one to be made on the basis of judgment, observation, and experience. Further, the regulation governing the resolution of any such situation expressly gives the ranger a choice among an unlimited number of actions, thus inarguably allowing employee discretion.

The second directive cited by the parties deals with stranded animals. While it is not clear whether this animal was "stranded," we do note that the directive provides in relevant part that

> In some cases the destruction of injured, dead, or stranded animals may be necessary. The destruction of a native animal is acceptable only when relocation is not a feasible alternative; the animal was injured or deceased through human-induced impacts (e.g. hunting, automobile collision); or human safety is a concern and the numbers/location of people cannot be effectively managed. . . .

This directive fairly reflects the policy concerns underlying it: balancing the conservation of wild animals with the interests of those who want to see them. The directive itself requires an exercise of discretion in its implementation. Thus, the existence of these two regulations allowing discretion to park employees creates the "strong presumption" described in *Gaubert* that Ranger Phillips' actions here were driven by the same policy concerns which led to the promulgation of the regulations in the first place. . . . Because plaintiffs have not alleged any facts which would "support a finding that the challenged actions are not the kind of conduct that can be said to be grounded in the policy of the regulatory regime," . . . *Id.* at 324-25 . . . , we affirm the conclusion of the district court that the government has met the second prong of the *Berkovitz* test and is entitled to the protection of the discretionary function exception.

Plaintiffs rely heavily on our decision in Boyd v. United States ex rel. United States Army, Corps of Engineers, 881 F.2d 895 (10th Cir. 1989), in which we refused to extend the shield of the discretionary function exception where an agency of the United States failed to warn swimmers of a dangerous area in Tenkiller Lake in Oklahoma. In *Boyd*, however, the government's failure to warn swimmers of dangerous conditions was not connected to the policy which created the hazard, thus making the exception inapplicable. . . . The fact that Ranger Phillips' failure to somehow remove the moose to avoid its further contact with snowmobilers was connected to the policy of balancing the conservation of wildlife with the interest of public access distinguishes this case from *Boyd*. Here, the conduct at issue was clearly an attempt by Ranger Phillips to balance the preservation of wildlife with the desire of the citizenry to access the park, and the analysis of *Boyd* is inapposite. . . .

The judgment of the district court is affirmed.

FOOD FOR THOUGHT

Tippett might be viewed as a negligence case where the ranger exercised terrible judgment. The court's contention that the ranger was making a policy decision of some moment rings hollow. Less exotic activity has been found not to trigger the "discretionary function" immunity of the FTCA. Thus, failure to warn about a hazardous roadway condition on a navy base does not constitute policy making of any kind. Hughes v. United States, 116 F. Supp. 2d 1145 (N.D. Cal. 2000); *see also* Collazo v. United States, 850 F.2d 1 (1st Cir. 1988) (medical malpractice by a physician working for the Veterans Administration does not involve policy making); Andrulonis v. United States, 952 F.2d 652 (2d Cir. 1991) (*Gaubert* did not affect decision that claim against federal official was not barred when official failed to warn about hazards of rabies vaccine). *But see* Mitchell v. United States, 225 F.3d 361 (3d Cir. 2000) (failure of National Park Service to redesign concrete wall that abutted paved road was discretionary function since Park Service had to make priority decision as to which roads were more dangerous and likely to be the source of an accident); Hinsley v. Standing Rock Child Protective Services, 516 F.3d 668 (8th Cir. 2008) (negligent failure of Bureau of Indian Affairs to warn plaintiff that her half-brother was a sexual abuser before placing him in plaintiff's home was a discretionary function since agency had to balance confidentiality of the brother's past actions against the safety concerns of the children in the placement home). How to draw the boundaries for the discretionary function exception from the general rule of liability under the FTCA has been the subject of considerable scholarly debate. *See, e.g.,* John W. Bagby & Gary L. Gittings, *The Elusive Discretionary Function Exception from Government Tort Liability: The Narrowing Scope of Federal Liability,* 30 Am. Bus. L.J. 223 (1992) (containing an extensive listing of articles on this subject); Peter H. Schuck & James J. Park, *The Discretionary Function Exception in the Second Circuit,* 20 Quinnipiac L. Rev. 55 (2000) (arguing that a challenged action must be actually grounded in policy and not merely involve a small degree of choice on the part of a low-level official in order to trigger immunity). For a statistical survey of the discretionary function exception, *see* Stephen P. Nelson, *The King's Wrongs and the Federal District Courts: Understanding the Discretionary Function Exception to the Federal Tort Claims Act,* 51 S. Tex. L. Rev. 259 (2009).

(b) Immunity for Torts in the Military Setting

A vast amount of litigation has been spawned by military personnel bringing actions against the government for torts committed by the military and nonmilitary arms of government. In Feres v. United States, 340 U.S. 135 (1950), the United States Supreme Court provided the United States sweeping immunity against such suits. In short, tort actions against the United States that are "incident to service" in the military are barred. What constitutes "incident to service" has been the subject of contentious litigation. Some of the cases are simply astounding. In Kitwoski v. United States, 931 F.2d 1526 (11th Cir. 1991), plaintiff had been enrolled in a Naval Rescue Swimmer School. Part of the program required that he take part in a difficult training maneuver in which students, using only swim fins and no safety equipment, swim in a circle with their hands behind their backs. Instructors grab the students in either a front or rear head hold to simulate panicking victims in need of rescue. Plaintiff had a fear acquired in childhood of being held under water and was thus not able to successfully complete the maneuver. He dropped out of the program but was pressured back into it by several instructors. On the day of his death, plaintiff was undergoing this difficult swimming maneuver. The court described the facts as follows:

> According to the plaintiff, at least two of the instructors on duty that day were aware of Mirecki's earlier problem with the drill. Once again, Mirecki had extreme difficulty with the drill and requested that he be dropped from the course and not be forced to re-enter the pool. Instead of honoring his request, the instructors seized him and forced him back into the water, and began "smurfing" him — holding him under the water until he was unconscious and had turned blue. At this time, other recruits were commanded to line up, turn their backs and sing the national anthem. After being held under the water for a considerable length of time, Mirecki died from heart arrhythmia, ventricular fibrillation and decreased oxygen.

Id. at 1528. Though uncomfortable with the conclusion, the court held that the plaintiff's death resulted from negligence in persisting in the exercise and not from an intention to kill him. The *Feres* doctrine insulated the government from liability.

In United States v. Stanley, 483 U.S. 669 (1987), a serviceman suffered serious injuries arising from his having volunteered to undergo an experiment with LSD. The serviceman was not informed of the risks. Though he argued that the military's negligence had nothing to do with military discipline and was thus not "incident to service," the Supreme Court held that he was barred from recovery under the broad sweep of *Feres. Also see* Costo v. United States, 248 F.3d 863 (9th Cir. 2001) (sailor who drowned in Navy-led recreational rafting trip and alleged negligence in planning and supervising the trip was barred from recovering under *Feres*; the plaintiff was on active duty, the rafts were rented, and the trip was planned by the military and provided as a benefit of military service).

An extensive discussion of the scope of the military immunity defense is beyond the scope of this book. For good scholarly treatment of the subject, *see* Dan B. Dobbs, The Law of Torts §§ 263-266; Michael L. Richmond, *Protecting the Power Brokers: Of* Feres, *Immunity, and Privilege*, 22 Suffolk U. L. Rev. 623 (1988) (contending that the *Feres* doctrine fits comfortably with other traditional immunities in tort law such as the fireman's rule and workers' compensation); Gregory T. Higgins, *Persian Gulf War Genetic Birth Defects and Inherited Injustice in* Minns v. United States, 34 Wake Forest L. Rev. 935 (1999) (arguing that the *Feres* doctrine is routinely misapplied and leads to unjust results).

(2) State Immunity

State immunity from suit has its origins in sovereign immunity. Like the federal government, state governments were totally immune from all tort liability. The overwhelming majority of states have legislatively provided for significant abrogation of their immunity from tort liability. Many have followed the model of the Federal Tort Claims Act. In almost all states, significant pockets of immunity remain in place. The differences among the states as to which suits are permitted and which are prohibited does not allow for broad generalizations.

(3) Municipal Immunity

Unlike the federal and state governments, municipalities are corporate entities created by the state. Historically their immunity derives from a 1798 English opinion. But this immunity was never as broad as that of the federal and state governments. For example, courts drew a distinction between governmental and proprietary functions. When acting in the latter capacity, they had no immunity. Thus, the municipality would not be held liable for negligence of police officers for failure to provide adequate services, but could be held liable for negligence in maintaining public housing. Municipal immunity from tort was abrogated in some states by state legislation and in others by judicial opinion. No matter which route is taken, the end result is that municipalities are subject to liability for some torts. The scope of the immunities has been worked out in some states by very detailed legislation and in others by judicial opinion. Once again, the state-by-state differences do not allow for broad generalizations. The following case is a classic, in which the majority and dissent disagree bitterly as to whether the municipality should be held liable for negligent police conduct in failing to protect a citizen from highly foreseeable harm.

RISS v. CITY OF NEW YORK
240 N.E.2d 860 (N.Y. 1968)

BREITEL, Justice.

[The author of the majority opinion, Judge Breitel, did not set forth the facts but referred the reader to Judge Keating's dissenting opinion for the facts in the case. The bracketed description is taken from the dissent.]

[Linda Riss, an attractive young woman, was for more than six months terrorized by a rejected suitor well known to the courts of this State, one Burton Pugach. This miscreant, masquerading as a respectable attorney, repeatedly threatened to have Linda killed or maimed if she did not yield to him: "If I can't have you, no one else will have you, and when I get through with you, no one else will want you." In fear for her life, she went to those charged by law with the duty of preserving and safeguarding the lives of the citizens and residents of this State. Linda's repeated and almost pathetic pleas for aid were received with little more than indifference. Whatever help she was given was not commensurate with the identifiable danger. On June 14, 1959, Linda became engaged to another man. At a party held to celebrate the event, she received a phone call warning her that it was her "last chance." Completely distraught, she called the police, begging for help, but was refused. The next day Pugach carried out his dire threats in the very manner he had foretold by having a hired thug throw lye in Linda's face. Linda was blinded in one eye, lost a good portion of her vision in the other, and her face was permanently scarred. After the assault the authorities concluded that there was some basis for Linda's fears, and for the next three and one-half years, she was given around-the-clock protection.]

This appeal presents, in a very sympathetic framework, the issue of the liability of a municipality for failure to provide special protection to a member of the public who was repeatedly threatened with personal harm and eventually suffered dire personal injuries for lack of such protection. . . . The issue arises upon the affirmance by a divided Appellate Division of a dismissal of the complaint, after both sides had rested but before submission to the jury.

It is necessary immediately to distinguish those liabilities attendant upon governmental activities which have displaced or supplemented traditionally private enterprises, such as are involved in the operation of rapid transit systems, hospitals, and places of public assembly. Once sovereign immunity was abolished by statute the extension of liability on ordinary principles of tort law logically followed. To be equally distinguished are certain activities of government which provide services and facilities for the use of the public, such as highways, public buildings and the like, in the performance of which the municipality or the State may be liable under ordinary principles of tort law. The ground for liability is the provision of the services or facilities for the direct use by members of the public.

In contrast, this case involves the provision of a governmental service to protect the public generally from external hazards and particularly to control the activities of criminal wrongdoers. . . . The amount of protection that may be provided is limited by the resources of the community and by a considered legislative-executive decision as to how those resources may be deployed. For the courts to proclaim a new and general duty of protection in the law of tort, even to those who may be the particular seekers of protection based on specific hazards, could and would inevitably determine how the limited police resources of the community should be allocated and without predictable limits. This is quite different from the predictable allocation of resources and liabilities when public hospitals, rapid transit systems, or even highways are provided.

Before such extension of responsibilities should be dictated by the indirect imposition of tort liabilities, there should be a legislative determination that that should be the scope of public responsibility (Van Alystyne, *Governmental Tort Liability*, 10 U.C.L.A. L. Rev. 463, 467; Note, 60 Mich. L. Rev. 379, 382). . . .

When one considers the greatly increased amount of crime committed throughout the cities, but especially in certain portions of them, with a repetitive and predictable pattern, it is easy to see the consequences of fixing municipal liability upon a showing of probable need for and request for protection. To be sure these are grave problems at the present time, exciting high priority activity on the part of the national, State and local governments, to which the answers are neither simple, known, or presently within reasonable controls. To foist a presumed cure for these problems by judicial innovation of a new kind of liability in tort would be foolhardy indeed and an assumption of judicial wisdom and power not possessed by the courts.

Nor is the analysis progressed by the analogy to compensation for losses sustained. It is instructive that the Crime Victims Compensation and "Good Samaritan" statutes, compensating limited classes of victims of crime, were enacted only after the most careful study of conditions and the impact of such a scheme upon governmental operations and the public fisc. . . . And then the limitations were particular and narrow.

For all of these reasons, there is no warrant in judicial tradition or in the proper allocation of the powers of government for the courts, in the absence of legislation, to carve out an area of tort liability for police protection to members of the public. Quite distinguishable, of course, is the situation where the police authorities undertake responsibilities to particular members of the public and expose them, without adequate protection, to the risks which then materialize into actual losses (Schuster v. City of New York, 154 N.E.2d 534).

Accordingly, the order of the Appellate Division affirming the judgment of dismissal should be affirmed.

KEATING, Judge (dissenting).

Certainly, the record in this case, sound legal analysis, relevant policy considerations and even precedent cannot account for or sustain the result which the majority have here reached. For the result is premised upon a legal rule which long ago should have been abandoned, having lost any justification it might once have had. Despite almost universal condemnation by legal scholars, the rule survives, finding its continuing strength, not in its power to persuade, but in its ability to arouse unwarranted judicial fears of the consequences of overturning it. . . .

It is not a distortion to summarize the essence of the city's case here in the following language: "Because we owe a duty to everybody, we owe it to nobody." Were it not for the fact that this position has been hallowed by much ancient and revered precedent, we would surely dismiss it as preposterous. To say that there is no duty is, of course, to start with the conclusion. The question is whether or not there should be liability for the negligent failure to provide adequate police protection.

The foremost justification repeatedly urged for the existing rule is the claim that the State and the municipalities will be exposed to limitless liability. The city invokes the specter of a "crushing burden" . . . if we should depart from the existing rule and enunciate even the limited proposition that the State and its municipalities can be held liable for the negligent acts of their police employees in executing whatever police services they do in fact provide. . . .

The fear of financial disaster is a myth. The same argument was made a generation ago in opposition to proposals that the State waive its defense of "sovereign immunity." The prophecy proved false then, and it would now. The supposed astronomical financial burden does not and would not exist. No municipality has gone bankrupt because it has had to respond in damages when a policeman causes injury through carelessly driving a police car or in the thousands of other situations where, by judicial fiat or legislative enactment, the State and its subdivisions have been held liable for the tortious conduct of their employees. Thus, in the past four or five years, New York City has been presented with an average of some 10,000 claims each year. The figure would sound ominous except for the fact the city has been paying out less than $8,000,000 on tort claims each year and this amount includes all those sidewalk defect and snow and ice cases about which the courts fret so often. . . . Court delay has reduced the figure paid somewhat, but not substantially. Certainly this is a slight burden in a budget of more than six billion dollars (less than two tenths of 1%) and of no importance as compared to the injustice of permitting unredressed wrongs to continue to go unrepaired. That Linda Riss should be asked to bear the loss, which should properly fall on the city if we assume, as we must, in the present posture of the case, that her injuries resulted from the city's failure to provide sufficient police to protect Linda is contrary to the most elementary notions of justice. . . .

It is also contended that liability for inadequate police protection will make the courts the arbiters of decisions taken by the Police Commissioner in allocating his manpower and his resources. We are not dealing here with a situation where the injury or loss occurred as a result of a conscious choice of policy made by those exercising high administrative responsibility after a complete and thorough deliberation of various alternatives. There was no major policy decision taken by the Police Commissioner to disregard Linda Riss' appeal for help because there was absolutely no manpower available to deal with Pugach. This "garden variety" negligence case arose in the course of "day-by-day operations of government" . . . Linda Riss' tragedy resulted not from high policy or inadequate manpower, but plain negligence on the part of persons with whom Linda dealt.

(*See* . . . Prosser, Torts [3d ed.], pp. 999-1001; Peck, *Federal Tort Claims — Discretionary Function,* 31 Wash. L. Rev. 207.)

More significant, however, is the fundamental flaw in the reasoning behind the argument alleging judicial interference. It is a complete oversimplification of the problem of municipal tort liability. What it ignores is the fact that indirectly courts are reviewing administrative practices in almost every tort case against the State or a municipality, including even decisions of the Police Commissioner. Every time a municipal hospital is held liable for malpractice resulting from inadequate record-keeping, the courts are in effect making a determination that the municipality should have hired or assigned more clerical help or more competent help to [sic] medical records or should have done something to improve its record-keeping procedures so that the particular injury would not have occurred. Every time a municipality is held liable for a defective sidewalk, it is as if the courts are saying that more money and resources should have been allocated to sidewalk repair, instead of to other public services. . . .

Perhaps, on a fuller record after a true trial on the merits, the city's position will not appear so damaging as it does now. But with actual notice of danger and ample opportunity to confirm and take reasonable remedial steps, a jury could find that the persons involved acted unreasonably and negligently. Linda Riss is entitled to have a jury determine the issue of the city's liability. This right should not be terminated by the adoption of a question-begging conclusion that there is no duty owed to her. The order of the Appellate Division should be reversed and a new trial granted.

FULD, C.J., and BURKE, SCILEPPI, BERGAN and JASEN, JJ., concur with BREITEL, JJ. KEATING, J., dissents and votes to reverse in a separate opinion.

Order affirmed, without costs.

In 1974, Linda Riss married Burton Pugach, after Pugach served a 14-year prison sentence for ordering the attack. They remained married until her death in 2013. *See* Margalit Fox, "Linda Riss Pugach, Whose Life Was Ripped From Headlines, Dies at 75," N.Y. Times (Jan. 23, 2013). The couple was the subject of a 2007 documentary, *Crazy Love,* directed by Dan Klores.

FOOD FOR THOUGHT

Assume that a physician employed by a city hospital decides that a patient's condition does not warrant taking a CT scan and is satisfied with an old-fashioned x-ray. It turns out that a CT scan would have revealed the beginning of a tumor on the patient's lung. When asked why he did not order a CT scan, the doctor replies that the x-ray did not give him grounds for suspicion. Furthermore, he says, "I don't give everyone a CT scan. It's too darned expensive. Besides, we would have a line from here to tomorrow for our CT scan machine." Do you have any doubt that the failure to take the CT scan would be treated as garden variety malpractice and would not implicate municipal immunity? Why, then, is Judge Keating not correct that many negligence actions against the city involve judgments regarding the proper allocation of resources? Where does one draw the line?

One case that clearly falls on the nonimmunity side of the line is DeLong v. Erie County, 455 N.Y.S.2d 887 (N.Y. App. Div. 1982). In that case Amelia DeLong called 911 and reported that a burglar was in the process of breaking into her home. She reported her address as 319 Victoria and pleaded with the operator for the police to "come right away." The complaint writer recorded the address on the complaint as 219 Victoria. Because the police were sent to a wrong address, they never arrived on the scene. The burglar viciously attacked Ms. DeLong and she died as a result of her wounds. The court cited to the majority opinion in *Riss* in which Judge Breitel distinguished *Riss* from the "situation where the police authorities undertake responsibilities to members of the public and expose them without adequate protection, to the risks which then materialize into actual losses." Similarly *see* Reis v. Delaware River Port Authority, 2008 WL 425522 (N.J. Super. Ct. App. Div.) (the failure of a 911 operator to enter the call of an abduction into the dispatch system was purely a failure to perform a ministerial duty for which liability may ensue).

DeLong remains the exception. Police are not held liable for discretionary activities unless the plaintiff establishes a "special relationship" with the municipality. In Kovit v. Estate of Hallums, 829 N.E.2d 1188 (N.Y. 2005), the court said that to establish a special relationship requires (1) an assumption by a municipality, through promises or actions, of an affirmative duty to act on behalf of the injured party; (2) knowledge on the part of a municipality's agents that inaction could lead to harm; (3) some form of direct contact between the municipality's agents and the injured party; and (4) that party's justifiable reliance on the municipality's affirmative undertaking. In *Kovit*, a woman, while driving her car, collided with another vehicle. The accident left her shaken and hysterical. When New York City police came on the scene, an officer told the woman to move her car forward out of the intersection. Plaintiff was standing behind the woman's car. Instead of moving the car forward, she put it in reverse, crushing plaintiff's legs. Plaintiff claimed that the city was negligent in that the officer told the woman to move her car when she was unfit to drive. A jury found for the plaintiff and the award was upheld by the Appellate Division. Applying the four-part standard, the Court of Appeals reversed on the ground that there was no direct contact between the municipality and the injured party.

In a companion case, *Lazan v. County of Suffolk, id.*, the plaintiff pulled over to the shoulder of the Long Island Expressway. A Suffolk County police officer came up behind him. Plaintiff told the officer that he had pulled over because he had chest pains and was not feeling well. The officer ordered him to move his car off the shoulder and drive it to the nearest service station. Plaintiff drove off, but lost control of his car and suffered serious injuries when he hit a telephone pole. The trial court denied the county's motion for summary judgment. The Appellate Division affirmed and certified the question of municipal immunity to the Court of Appeals. The court held that the plaintiff could not establish the second prong of the test for liability, i.e., "[k]nowledge on the part of the municipality's agents that inaction could lead to harm." The plaintiff had not told the officer that he was too sick to drive the short distance to the service station. "Under these circumstances, we cannot expect the police to make a refined, expert medical diagnosis of the motorist's latent condition. Requiring them to do so would improperly burden police in carrying out their duties." *Id.* at 1192.

Notwithstanding the general rule immunizing municipalities from the negligent failure of police to protect citizens from the criminal acts of third parties, special circumstances may trigger liability. In Brandon v. County of Richardson, 624 N.W.2d 604 (Neb. 2001), the Nebraska Supreme Court held that a county was subject to liability for the sheriff's negligent failure to protect a victim of a crime from future harm by the same criminals in retaliation for reporting the crime. Teena Brandon, a biological female diagnosed with "gender identity disorder," was living as a male in Falls City, Nebraska. When two of her male acquaintances discovered that Brandon was a female, they beat and sexually assaulted her. The county sheriff interviewed Brandon hours after she was raped, and the sheriff knew that her assailants had prior criminal histories and that Brandon feared that the men would kill her if she reported the rape. The sheriff did not take Brandon into protective custody or arrest the men who attacked her, and a few days later the men, in fact, murdered Brandon and two other people with her. The Nebraska Supreme Court held that, though the "general rule [was] that law enforcement officials may not be held liable for failure to protect individual citizens from criminal acts," an exception existed when a "special relationship" was created between a victim and the law enforcement officials because the victim "agreed to aid law enforcement officials in the performance of their duties." *Id.* at 627. Because Brandon reported the assault and agreed to testify against the men who attacked her, the court found that the county had negligently breached a duty to protect Brandon.

Is the rule then "See no evil, hear no evil . . ." and the city won't be liable? Is this any way to run a police department or a system of justice?

hypo 59

X, the driver of a city ambulance, speeds at 30 mph over the limit while transporting a heart attack patient to the hospital. *X* loses control of the ambulance and collides with *Y*'s car, seriously injuring *Y*. *X* contends that the medic warned him that the patient was experiencing heart failure and that time was of the essence. "Get there fast or we're going to lose this guy." Is the city immune from a negligence action by *Y*?

2. Statutes of Limitations

Statutes of limitations fix the time within which a plaintiff may commence an action. If the statute of limitations has passed, the most meritorious case will die an ignoble death. Lawyers are admonished to keep time bars firmly in mind. Failure to do so can be disastrous not only for the client but for the lawyer as well. Every year countless legal malpractice claims are filed because lawyers have not filed claims in a timely fashion.

Why is it necessary to set arbitrary cut-off dates for bringing a tort action? Perhaps the most compelling argument in favor of statutes of limitations is that as time passes memories fade, witnesses die, and evidence is lost or destroyed. Not only is the defendant hard put to defend a case when she learns of the necessity to defend so many years after the alleged tort has taken place, but the quality of justice meted out by the courts is compromised. *See, e.g.,* Order of Railroad Telegraphers v. Railway Express Agency, 321 U.S. 342, 348-349 (1944). A second reason to cut off claims after a given time period is to allow a defendant to have some peace of mind. At some point, the defendant can put the threat of a lawsuit behind her and know that she need no longer worry about suit being brought. *See Development in the Law—Statutes of Limitation,* 63 Harv. L. Rev. 1177, 1185 (1950).

Statutes of limitations vary from state to state. Most jurisdictions cut off negligence actions after two to three years from injury to the plaintiff. For many defendants, a statute of limitations that is triggered by injury to the plaintiff provides little assurance against stale claims or any sense of repose. Manufacturers of products can be sued for defects in their products that cause injury decades after the products were sold. Builders whose negligence causes a building to collapse many years after original construction are similarly disadvantaged.

WHEN DOES INJURY TO THE PLAINTIFF OCCUR?

In the run-of-the-mill negligence case there is no mystery as to when plaintiff is injured. If plaintiff is hit by a car, or loses a limb because a defective punch press suddenly descends on her arm, there is no difficulty in establishing when the injury occurred. But in a world where toxic substances or negligent medical treatment may cause latent injury that remains undiscovered for many years, the "injury to plaintiff" rule requires rethinking. A plaintiff may, in fact, have been injured many years before, and by the time the injury becomes manifest, the statute of limitations may have already run. Most states have responded to this problem by either legislatively enacting a "discovery" rule or by judicially interpreting "injury to plaintiff" to mean that plaintiff must have discovered the injury. When, under a discovery rule, does the statute of limitations begin to run? Is it when the plaintiff knows or should know that she has suffered injury? What if she knows about the injury but does not know until many years later who or what was the cause of the injury?

The overwhelming majority of states do not trigger the statute of limitations unless the plaintiff knows or reasonably should know that she has suffered injury. But, this standard is not self-defining. Not only does the "reasonably should have known" standard raise factual questions about when was it reasonable for the plaintiff to conclude that she has suffered injury, it raises legal questions as well. What if plaintiff was exposed to a toxic substance and years later an x-ray reveals some abnormality? *See* Wyatt v. A-Best Co., Inc., 910 S.W.2d 851, 853 (Tenn. 1995) (x-ray result revealing the possibility of an asbestos-related disease does not trigger the statute of limitations but obligates plaintiff to exercise due diligence to discover if plaintiff, in fact, was suffering from such a disease). And what if a plaintiff who was exposed to asbestos suffers from asbestosis (a nonfatal lung disease) and many years later contracts mesothelioma (a fatal form of lung cancer). Does the discovery of the asbestosis trigger the statute of limitations? If it does, when the plaintiff contracts mesothelioma, the statute of limitations has already run. Most states now hold that the discovery of the nonfatal disease does not bar a new action many years later when the plaintiff contracts the fatal disease. *See* James A. Henderson, Jr. & Aaron D. Twerski, *Asbestos Litigation Gone Mad: Exposure-Based Recovery for Increased Risk, Mental Distress and Medical Monitoring,* 53 S.C. L. Rev. 815, 821 (2002) (review of authority). However, in non-asbestos cases, the courts are less charitable to plaintiffs and routinely hold that the onset of symptoms for a less serious disease triggers the statute of limitations and plaintiff cannot bring an action after the statute has run when a more serious disease develops. *See, e.g.,* Gnazzo v. G.D. Searle & Co., 973 F.2d 136 (2d Cir. 1992) (applying Connecticut law) (suit against IUD manufacturer barred when plaintiff developed infertility problems as a result of using the IUD, because years earlier plaintiff had developed a pelvic inflammatory disease caused by the IUD).

The discovery rule can rear its head in legal malpractice cases as well. In Estate of Spry v. Batey, 804 N.E.2d 250 (Ind. Ct. App. 2004), a law firm was sued for malpractice for giving a general release to all parties, thereby negating the right of the decedent's estate to sue a joint tortfeasor. The estate sought to convince the Indiana courts to find that the general release did not cut off its right to sue the joint tortfeasor. The trial court decided against the estate. The statute of limitations for legal malpractice cases is two years. More than two years had elapsed from the time that the estate was aware that the defendant attorneys had given one tortfeasor a general release. The estate, however, claimed that, until the trial court ruled that the general release cut off liability to the joint tortfeasor, there was no certainty of injury and the two-year statute of limitations did not begin to run. The court held that the estate knew that malpractice had been committed well before the court's decision upholding the general release and thus barred the malpractice claim against the attorneys.

When the plaintiff discovers the injury, but does not know the cause of the injury, most courts will not trigger the statute until the plaintiff should reasonably have made the causal connection between the defendant's conduct or product and the injury. *See, e.g.,* Moll v. Abbott Laboratories, 506 N.W.2d 816 (Mich. 1993) (trigger depends on whether a reasonable person would have concluded that she had suffered an injury as a result of ingestion of a drug). However, the statute begins running when the plaintiff discovers the causal connection to the defendant's conduct or product. That plaintiff did not know that the product was defective or the defendant's conduct negligent will not stop the statute of limitations from running. Kimble v. Tennis, 2007 WL 2022078 (U.S. M.D. Pa.) (plaintiff, who contracted a highly contagious staph infection in prison, is barred by two-year tort statute of limitations from bringing suit; that he did not know of defendant prison's deliberate indifference to the spread of the disease does not toll the statute as long as he had sufficient notice "to place him on alert of the need to begin investigating"). A few isolated cases have held that the statute of limitations does not begin to run until the plaintiff should reasonably have discovered that the defendant's conduct was wrongful or the product defective. Anthony v. Abbott Laboratories, 490 A.2d 43 (R.I. 1985). Some courts will not begin the running of the statute of limitations unless the plaintiff knew or reasonably should have known the identity of the defendant. Orear v. International Paint Co., 796 P.2d 759 (Wash. Ct. App. 1990) (action against manufacturer of defective epoxy paint was not time-barred until the plaintiff knew or reasonably should have known of the defendant's identity). Finally, even if plaintiff discovers the injury and the cause of the injury within the limitation period, in some instances the statute will not begin running until the plaintiff fully appreciates the magnitude of his injury. Fine v. Checcio, 870 A.2d 850 (Pa. 2005) (dentist assured patient that numbness following wisdom tooth extraction was normal and would subside; statute is tolled until patient knew that his numbness was due to permanent nerve damage and not temporary discomfort).

A fascinating new issue that has arisen in sexual abuse cases has engendered substantial controversy in the courts. Plaintiffs who suffer sexual abuse as youngsters and repress the horrific experience until many years later contend that they should not be barred by statutes of limitation since they have come to "discover" the abuse at a later time. Most states toll the statute of limitations for minors until they reach the age of majority. They then have a period of time to bring suit. The contention of plaintiffs in these sexual abuse cases is that when they reach majority, the sexual abuse had been so repressed that they are not able to recollect the events and bring suit for the tortious conduct. In Doe v. Maskell, 679 A.2d 1087 (Md. 1996), the court refused to apply the "discovery" rule to resurrect such a claim. The court said (*id.* at 1091):

> We find that the critical question to the determination of the applicability of the discovery rule to lost memory cases is whether there is a difference between forgetting and repression. It is crystal clear that in a suit in which a plaintiff "forgot" and later "remembered" the existence of a cause of action beyond the 3-year limitations period, that suit would be time-barred. Dismissal of such a case reflects our judgment that the potential plaintiff had "slumbered on his rights," should have known of his cause of action, and was blameworthy. To permit a forgetful plaintiff to maintain an action would vitiate the statute of limitations and deny repose for all defendants.
>
> Plaintiffs in this case, however, claim that in order to avoid the pain associated with recalling the abuse they suffered, their memories were "repressed," not merely "forgotten," and later "recovered," rather than "remembered." They argue that this difference renders them "blamelessly ignorant" and excuses their failure to file suit in a timely manner. To aid in an understanding of plaintiffs' argument, we have extracted two implicit assumptions:
>
> 1. That there is a qualitative and quantitative difference between "repression" and mere "forgetting;" and
> 2. That this difference is of a sufficient quality to compel us to find that plaintiff is excused by operation of the discovery rule and had no reason to have known about the existence of her cause of action. . . .

After reviewing the arguments on both sides of the issue, we are unconvinced that repression exists as a phenomenon separate and apart from the normal process of forgetting. Because we find these two processes to be indistinguishable scientifically, it follows that they should be treated the same legally. Therefore we hold that the mental process of repression of memories of past sexual abuse does not activate the discovery rule.

In Pratte v. Stewart, 929 N.E.2d 415 (Ohio 2010), the court held that the limitations period was not tolled during the time the alleged victim had repressed memories of sexual abuse. *See* also John Doe 1 v. Archdiocese of Milwaukee, 734 N.W.2d 827 (Wis. 2007).

Other courts have been more friendly to the argument that psychological repression is different than forgetting and that the discovery rule should trigger the statute of limitations when the plaintiff recollects the events. *See, e.g.,* Turner v. Roman Catholic Diocese of Burlington, Vermont, 987 A.2d 960 (Vt. 2009); Doe v. Roe, 955 P.2d 951 (Ariz. 1998). Several states have enacted statutes allowing for claims to be brought after the "discovery" by sexually abused plaintiffs of the abuse. *See, e.g.,* Conn. Gen. Stat. Ann. § 52-577d (West 1991) (actions based upon sexual acts toward minors may be commenced at any time); Me. Rev. Stat. Ann. tit. 14, § 752-C (2001) (statute of limitations for actions for damages for injury to a minor as a result of sexual abuse allows victims to bring actions until 17 years after they reach the age of majority).

In Zumpano v. Quinn, 849 N.E.2d 926 (N.Y. 2006), plaintiffs argued that the statute of limitations should not bar them from suing the Syracuse Catholic diocese for the conduct of priests who sexually abused them because the diocese should be equitably estopped from asserting the statute of limitations as a defense. They alleged that the diocese did not report abuse by priests to law enforcement officials; reassigned offending priests without disclosure of their offenses; and, when other victims complained, made private payments to them so that the charges would not be publicized. The court held that the alleged conduct, though morally reprehensible, did not amount to fraudulent concealment necessary to support a claim of equitable estoppel.

3. Statutes of Repose

Earlier we noted that tort statutes of limitation give little in the way of closure to defendants. No defendant can sleep peacefully and be assured that he will not be sued at some later time when his prior negligence is discovered to have caused injury. In several areas legislatures have been successfully lobbied to enact statutes of repose to protect defendants from long-tailed liability. Some states, for example, limit the liability of architects and engineers to a given number of years after a building has been completed. *See, e.g.,* Cal. Civ. Proc. Code § 337.15 (ten years after substantial completion of the development or improvement of structure). Others limit the liability of manufacturers to a number of years after the first purchase by a consumer. *See, e.g.,* Or. Rev. Stat. § 30.905 (1995) (eight years after first sale);

General Aviation Revitalization Act, 49 U.S.C. § 40101 note (1994) (18-year statute of repose for lawsuits against manufacturers of general aviation aircraft or component parts). Repose statutes have received a mixed reception by the courts. Some have declared them unconstitutional under various provisions of state constitutions. *See, e.g.,* De Young v. Providence Medical Center, 960 P.2d 919 (Wash. 1998) (eight-year statute of repose for medical malpractice action violates the state constitution's privileges and immunities clause). Other courts have upheld them from federal or state constitutional attack. *See, e.g.,* Lyon v. Agusta S.P.A., 252 F.3d 1078, 1086 (9th Cir. 2001) (General Aviation Revitalization Act does not violate due process or equal protection rights of plaintiffs; "when we focus, as Congress did, on the need to revitalize a flagging industry, it is difficult to see any real unfairness in the decision to cut the infinite-liability tail"); Love v. Whirlpool Corp., 449 S.E.2d 602 (Ga. 1994) (bars product liability actions ten years after first sale). Several writers have been sharply critical of decisions overriding "tort reform" statutes on state constitutional grounds. *See, e.g.,* Jonathan M. Hoffman, *By the Court of the Law: The Origins of the Open Courts Clause of State Constitutions,* 74 Or. L. Rev. 1279 (1995); Victor E. Schwartz & Leah Lorber, *Judicial Nullification of Civil Justice Reform Violates the Fundamental Federal Constitutional Principle of Separation of Powers: How to Restore the Right Balance,* 32 Rutgers L.J. 907 (2001).

For a comprehensive treatment of the nuances of statutes of limitation and repose, *see* Dan B. Dobbs, The Law of Torts §§ 216-223 (2000). *See also* Prosser and Keeton on Torts § 30 (5th ed. 1984).

chapter 9

Joint Tortfeasors

In Chapter 4 we briefly introduced the concept of joint tortfeasor liability. In this chapter we more fully explore the subject. In three situations a tortfeasor can be held responsible to pay all of the plaintiff's damages even though other tortfeasors are also responsible for the harm: (1) where defendants act in concert to cause the harm; (2) where defendants are held liable by operation of law; and (3) where defendants cause a single indivisible injury.

A. JOINT AND SEVERAL LIABILITY AT COMMON LAW

In Chapter 4 (on actual causation) we introduced the idea that two or more actors may be jointly and severally responsible for the plaintiff's injury. At common law centuries ago, before the liberalization of joinder rules, only certain categories of actors could be joined in the same action (but need not be joined — joinder was permissive, not compulsory). Joint liability in this sense was limited to tortfeasors who acted in concert. W. Page Keeton, *Prosser and Keeton on Torts* § 47 (5th ed. 1984). Under modern joinder rules, however, the plaintiff may join all persons potentially liable for a claim that arises out of the same transaction or occurrence and presenting a common question of law or fact. See Wright & Miller, *Federal Practice and Procedure* § 1652. For example, a plaintiff injured by a forceful airbag deployment may join both the manufacturer of the car and the retail dealer in a products liability action, where the common issue of law and fact is failure to warn of the danger posed by airbags to drivers of small stature. Juliano v. Toyota Motor Sales, U.S.A., Inc., 20 F. Supp. 2d 573 (S.D.N.Y. 1998). Permissive joinder today does not require that an event fall into one of the categories in which joint and several liability was recognized at common law. The continuing significance of those categories is related to *several* liability — that is, the principle that any defendant may be required to pay the full amount of the plaintiff's damages, even if the defendant's act combined with the act of another to produce the injury. It is important not to confuse permissive or compulsory joinder rules, which are questions of civil procedure, with substantive tort principles establishing what might be called "entire liability" of individual tortfeasors for the full extent of the plaintiff's losses. Prosser & Keeton, above, pp. 328-329.

The three most frequently encountered categories of common law joint and several liability are:

(1) **Acting in concert** pursuant to an express or implied agreement to cooperate in a particular line of conduct or to accomplish a particular result. See Restatement (Second) of Torts §876 and comment *a*. The classic example is a drag race between Driver *A* and Driver *B*. If Driver *B*, who has no assets or liability insurance, runs over *P* causing serious harm, *P* can recover damages from Driver *A*, a wealthy individual, for the full amount of his losses. The agreement to participate in the concerted action may be implied from circumstances. Suppose Driver *A* is sitting at a stoplight when Driver *B* arrives, begins honking his horn, revving his engine, making obscene gestures, and shouting that Driver *A* is a loser. Both drivers go roaring off down the road when the light turns green. A trier of fact could find that the drivers had a tacit plan to engage in a race.

(2) **Jointly necessary causes** — sometimes called independent acts — combining to form an indivisible harm. The classic example here is an injury to *P*, the passenger in a car driven by Driver *C*, which was involved in a collision with a car driven by Driver *D*. Driver *C* was speeding, while Driver *D* ran a stop sign. The result was that *P* sustained a broken leg. The combined negligence of Driver *C* and Driver *D* brought about the accident. *P*'s leg would not have been broken if either driver had been acting as a reasonable person. Remember from Chapter 4 that the two independent actions need not occur at the same time. If Driver *E* causes an accident injuring *P*, and *P*'s injury is aggravated by the negligent medical treatment of Doctor *F*, as long as it is impossible to differentiate between the original and aggravated portions of the injury, *P* can recover full damages from either Driver *E* or Doctor *F*, or split between them.

(3) **Jointly sufficient causes.** See the two-fires cases, such as Kingston v. Chicago & N.W. Railway, 211 N.W. 913 (Wis. 1927), excerpted in Chapter 4. In those cases, either fire (assuming they are both of human origin) would have been sufficient to destroy the plaintiff's house. The plaintiff can recover the full amount of damages from either defendant.

Cases like *Summers v. Tice* in Chapter 4 extend the principles of joint and several liability to situations not fitting exactly within one of these categories. In all of these cases, one defendant may be *vicariously* liable for the acts of another. That is, liability will be imposed even though the plaintiff's injury was caused, in whole or in part, by the acts of another.

Recall from Chapter 1 that a very common form of vicarious liability involves an employer answering in damages for a tort committed by an employee, acting within the scope and course of employment. There are literally thousands of cases nationwide raising one of the following issues:

WAS THE TORTFEASOR AN EMPLOYEE OR AN INDEPENDENT CONTRACTOR?

The vicarious liability of an employer generally requires an employment relationship, and this in turn requires control by the would-be employer over the performance of the job. In Lazo v. Mak's Trading Co., Inc., 605 N.Y.S.2d 272 (App. Div. 1993), three men beat up the plaintiff. The men had been hired by a grocery store to unload a truck. The manager of the store testified that the three men, known only as "Tony," "Tony's father," and "Willie," would show up in the morning and ask if there was a truck to unload. If there was, they would be told to return at a certain time. The manager then paid $80 to Tony's father to distribute among the three workers. The plaintiff testified at his deposition that he had seen the three men unloading trucks at other stores in the area. Further,

> there was no evidence that anyone from the defendant company actively directed or controlled the work done by the three men apart from telling them where to place the sacks inside the store. The defendant did not supply the three with equipment or direct the manner in which the sacks were unloaded from the truck and transported into the store. Plaintiff stated only that when "Tony" cursed at him sometime before the assault occurred, he reported the incident to an unidentified agent of the defendant, who in turn told "Tony" not to disrupt plaintiff's work.

605 N.Y.S.2d at 273. Based on this record, the Appellate Division held that the three men were independent contractors, as a matter of law. Thus, the store was not vicariously liable for the torts of Tony, Tony's father, and Willie.

The employee ("servant" in traditional terminology) vs. independent contractor relationship issue arises frequently where businesses employ off-duty police officers as security guards. In Page v. CFJ Properties, 578 S.E.2d 522 (Ga. Ct. App. 2003), an off-duty sheriff's deputy was providing security at a truck stop. He detained a customer for shoplifting, and the customer sued the truck stop owner for false imprisonment. The security guard testified that the truck stop "did not give him a job description or list of duties and responsibilities at the time he began work for them," that it "provided him with neither orientation nor training," and indeed said nothing at all about what was expected of him. Under those circumstances, where the would-be employer did not control the time, manner, and method of executing the work, an employer-employee relationship does not exist and vicarious liability does not attach. The Restatement (Third) of Agency § 7.07 also looks to the extent of control exercised by the would-be employer to determine whether the tortfeasor was an employee or independent contractor. Comment f says a court should consider a number of factors, including:

> the extent of control that the agent [employee] and the principal [employer] have agreed the principal may exercise over details of the work; whether the agent is

engaged in a distinct occupation or business; whether the type of work done by the agent is customarily done under a principal's direction or without supervision; the skill required in the agent's occupation; whether the agent or the principal supplies the tools and other instrumentalities required for the work and the place in which to perform it; the length of time during which the agent is engaged by a principal; whether the agent is paid by the job or by the time worked; whether the agent's work is part of the principal's regular business; whether the principal and the agent believe that they are creating an employment relationship; and whether the principal is or is not in business. Also relevant is the extent of control that the principal has exercised in practice over the details of the agent's work.

Vicarious liability of the employer follows control because the party with the power to control how work is performed also has the capacity to insist that precautions be taken to avoid harm to others.

In *Lazo v. Mak's*, above, the grocery store owner did not direct or control the activities of Tony, Tony's father, and Willie; thus, there was little he could do to prevent them from doing dangerous things. Does this result create incentives to look the other way and not supervise the conduct of independent contractors? Presumably the store manager could have done *something* to prevent the three guys he hired from beating up bystanders. But if he had, he would have risked exercising sufficient control to make the three hired hands into employees, and thus exposed the store to vicarious liability.

In a few cases involving activities that carry a high degree of danger and special risks of harm, or where an actor has traditionally been responsible for a particular type of activity, the actor may be said to have a non-delegable duty of care. *See, e.g.,* Brandenburg v. Briarwood Forestry Services, LLC, 847 N.W.2d 395 (Wis. 2014) (landowner liable to neighbors for damage caused by herbicide sprayed by independent contractor); Maloney v. Rath, 445 P.2d 513 (Cal. 1968). Where a duty is non-delegable, the employer will be liable even if the activity is conducted using independent contractors. *See* Restatement (Third) of Torts — Physical and Emotional Harm § 57. For example, where a municipality hires a paving contractor to perform road work, and the contractor is negligent, the municipality remains liable even though the contractor is not an employee. The state traditionally owes a duty to keep roads in good repair, and so while it may hire an independent contractor to perform road work, a city remains liable if the work is negligently performed. Machado v. City of Hartford, 972 A.2d 724 (Conn. 2009); *see also* Springer v. City and County of Denver, 13 P.3d 794 (Colo. 2000). It is hard to generalize about what duties will be deemed non-delegable, although courts sometimes say that where "the responsibility is so important to the community that the employer should not be permitted to transfer it to another," the employer will remain liable for work performed by an independent contractor. Kleeman v. Rheingold, 614 N.E.2d 712, 598 N.Y.S.2d 149 (N.Y. 1993) (attorney remains liable for negligence of independent process server who failed to properly serve summons and complaint on opposing party). The non-delegable duty exception should not be understood so broadly that it swallows up the rule that actors are not liable for the negligence of independent contractors. *See, e.g.,* Eastlick v. Lueder Constr. Co., 741 N.W.2d 628 (Neb. 2007) (general contractor does not have non-delegable duty to employee of subcontractor injured when scaffolding erected by subcontractor collapsed).

WAS THE ACTION WITHIN THE SCOPE OF EMPLOYMENT OR WAS THE EMPLOYEE ON A "FROLIC OF HIS OWN"?

Recall the 1933 Alabama case of *Western Union v. Hill,* from Chapter 1. The defendant's employee, Sapp, sexually harassed the plaintiff, who had asked Sapp to fix her clock. The court held that "the assault in this case, if committed, was clearly from a motive or purpose solely and alone to satisfy the sensuous desires of Sapp, and not in furtherance of the business of defendant." The court apparently believed that because the defendant company was in the business of, among other things, fixing clocks, not of making unwanted advances on customers, the tortious acts of Sapp could never be within the scope of his employment. This traditional analysis has come in for criticism in intervening years. Some courts today may follow the approach of Judge Henry Friendly in the classic case of Ira S. Bushey & Sons, Inc. v. United States, 398 F.2d 167 (2d Cir. 1968). In that case, an employee of the U.S. Coast Guard was returning from shore leave "in the condition for which seamen are famed." He drunkenly opened some valves on a drydock, causing it to sink. The United States argued that the sailor's actions were not within the scope of his employment. Judge Friendly's opinion reframed the question away from the tasks the sailor was hired to perform — presumably not including excessive drinking and vandalism — to a consideration of the risks "which may fairly be said to be characteristic" of the activities of an enterprise. 398 F.2d at 171. The test for scope of employment thus boils down to the foreseeability of a risk, and "the proclivity of seamen to find solace for solitude by copious resort to the bottle while ashore has been noted in opinions too numerous to warrant citation." *Id.* at 172. Allowing sailors to go ashore and drink increases the risk of certain types of accidents, including the damage to the plaintiff's drydock. It is not unfair to require the United States to assume liability for those risks that are fairly characteristic of employing sailors. This decision is therefore a kind of proximate cause test for the scope of employment.

Not all courts will impose *respondeat superior* liability merely upon a showing that the employer's activities increased the risk of a certain type of harm. For example, in Tall v. Board of School Com'rs of Baltimore City, 706 A.2d 659 (Md. Ct. Spec. App. 1998), a public school teacher beat a nine-year-old special education student for urinating in his pants. The plaintiff argued that the teacher's conduct was foreseeable and incidental to the activity of educating special-needs children. The court conceded that conduct may be within the scope of employment even if not expressly authorized by the employer, but if it is purely personal in nature, vicarious liability is not appropriate. 706 A.2d at 668. Where there was no conceivable educational purpose in beating a student, and where the district had expressly prohibited corporal punishment, the conduct was not within the scope of the teacher's employment. *Id.* at 670-672.

If the employer furnishes a vehicle to the employee and exercises control over the employee's travels to and from work—for example, if it is important to the employer that the employee be "on call" and available to respond quickly to the employer's needs—travel to and from work may be within the scope of employment. Restatement (Third) of Agency § 7.07, comment *e*. However, an employee traveling on the employer's business may be deemed to be off on a "frolic of his own" and not acting within the scope of employment when taking a detour from the assigned route.

> P, who owns a nursery, employs A. A's assigned duties include caring for the nursery's lawn and keeping the nursery's lawn mower filled with gas. En route to the nursery from home, A stops at a drugstore to pick up medicine for A's spouse, then stops at a gas station across the street to buy a can of gas for the nursery's lawn mower. A next returns home to drop off the medicine, then stops at another gas station to buy gas for A's truck. Leaving this second gas station, A drives negligently and collides with T. P is subject to liability to T. A was transporting gas to fill the nursery's lawnmower, necessary for A to perform A's assigned work. A's stop for gas was an incidental deviation from A's performance of assigned work.

Id., Illustration 14.

What is the rationale for holding employers vicariously liable for the torts of their employees? Judge Friendly's opinion in *Ira S. Bushey* offers a fairness rationale: one of the costs of an enterprise's activities is the foreseeable negligence, and even intentional misconduct, of employees. If that is the rationale, then the plaintiff need not show that the employee's tortious conduct somehow benefitted the employer. That is why the reasoning in *Western Union v. Hill* is no longer representative of modern *respondeat superior* cases. The lecherous Sapp did not benefit his employer by harassing the customer, but if that sort of misconduct can fairly be considered a cost of the defendant's enterprise (perhaps because it is foreseeable that customers will be alone in the store with an employee, at night in a rural area), then the employer should have to answer in damages for its employee's torts. The older "purpose of the employer" test would tend to exclude liability for intentional torts, but the fairness-based approach from *Ira S. Bushey* would not. The Restatement (Third) of Agency continues to recognize, however, that if the employee's conduct is independent of any purpose of the employer, vicarious liability would not be appropriate:

> an employee's tortious conduct is outside the scope of employment when the employee is engaged in an independent course of conduct not intended to further any purpose of the employer. An independent course of conduct represents a departure from, not an escalation of, conduct involved in performing assigned work or other conduct that an employer permits or controls. When an employee commits a tort with the sole intention of furthering the employee's own purposes, and not any purpose of the employer, it is neither fair nor true-to-life to characterize the employee's action as that of a representative of the employer.

§ 7.07, comment *b*. The comment goes on to argue that foreseeability tests, like the one used by Judge Friendly in *Ira S. Bushey*, are "potentially confusing and may generate outcomes that are less predictable than intent-based formulations."

---

authors' dialogue 33

BRAD: I can't figure out these vicarious liability cases. I've always liked the *Ira S. Bushey* case and think Judge Friendly got it right. If you employ a bunch of sailors, you have to know that when they get shore leave, they're going to get drunk and cause mayhem. You can't turn around and claim that was totally unrelated to your enterprise

JIM: But that just collapses the test for scope of employment into general considerations of foreseeability, and if you take that too far, you're essentially creating strict liability for employers. Go back to that old Alabama case with the creepy store clerk. Even if the company had policies on how to treat customers, and mandated sensitivity training for all its independent agents, it's foreseeable that somewhere in its far-flung operations there will be a jerk like this Sapp character who does something purely for his own purposes. What sense would there be in holding the employer liable for that? Monitoring all these independent agents in small towns is way too expensive for a big company like Western Union.

BRAD: It's fairness, as Judge Friendly says. It's just a cost of doing business that sometimes an employee will depart from the well-intentioned policies and procedures of the employer. Better the loss should fall on the employer than on the customer who did nothing more than come in to the store to get her clock fixed.

JIM: If there's nothing more the employer could have done, how is it fair? I think you're actually appealing to a kind of loss-spreading rationale. You sound like the California Supreme Court in *Rowland* and *Tarasoff.*

BRAD: Ooh, you really know how to hurt a guy!

Whether a court will consider the purposes of the employer (as in *Hill* or *Tall*) or broader considerations such as foreseeable risks may depend on what the court takes the purpose of the *respondeat superior* doctrine to be. Restatement (Third) of Agency § 7.07, comment *b*, argues for a test focusing on the employee's intention to serve a purpose of the employer. It relies on a best cost-avoider rationale, arguing that when the employer has the ability to control the employee's conduct, it may take measures to reduce the extent of tortious conduct. There would be no point in imposing liability for conduct by employees that is foreseeable but beyond the ability of employers to control. Can you think of a rationale for the foreseeability test from *Ira S. Bushey* that responds to the Restatement drafters' concern?

It is important to keep in mind that vicarious liability is not the only way an employer can be held liable. It also may have independent liability for its own torts. For example, the employer may have a duty to use reasonable care in selecting or training employees or independent contractors. The following case illustrates how an organization that might have an employment relationship with a tortfeasor may also have its own direct liability to the plaintiff with whom it has a special relationship.

LINDEMAN V. CORPORATION OF THE PRESIDENT OF THE CHURCH OF JESUS CHRIST OF LATTER-DAY SAINTS
43 F. Supp. 3d 1197 (D. Colo. 2014)

RAYMOND P. MOORE, United States District Judge

THIS MATTER is before the Court on the following motions: (1) Defendant the Corporation of the President of the Church of Jesus Christ of Latter–Day Saints' ("Defendant Church" or "the Church") Motion for Summary Judgment; (2) Plaintiff Ashley Lindeman's ("Plaintiff") Motion for Summary Judgment on Plaintiff's Claims of Negligent Hiring and Supervision against Defendant Church; (3) Plaintiff's Motion for Summary Judgment on Plaintiff's Claim of Battery against Defendant David Scott Frank ("Defendant Frank" or "Frank"); and (4) Frank's Motion for Summary Judgment on Plaintiff's First, Second, Fifth, and Sixth Claims for Relief. . . .

II. OVERVIEW

Plaintiff met Frank through his son, one of Plaintiff's classmates. Plaintiff began attending the Franks' church, Defendant Church, including the Sunday School class which Frank taught. Over time, and after many communications, Frank and Plaintiff had sexual intercourse twice. At the time, Frank was 40 and Plaintiff was 15. Frank subsequently pled guilty to sexual assault with a 10–year age difference. The issue before the Court is whether either Defendant is liable to Plaintiff civilly for the sexual encounters. Defendants unequivocally admit that what occurred should not have, and Frank's actions cannot be condoned, but argue, independently, each is not liable in whole or in part. The Court agrees, in part.

III. FACTUAL BACKGROUND

The Church's "Calling" of Frank to be a Sunday School teacher. The Church "calls" on virtually all adult members who attend church regularly to perform unpaid, volunteer service within their local "ward" (congregation). The ecclesiastical leader of a local church ward is the bishop and he has two counselors with whom he consults regarding most decisions, including which members to call to volunteer positions in the ward. A name may be suggested to the bishop as to whom to call. The bishop prays for inspiration and, after deciding whom to call, he conducts an ecclesiastical interview to determine that person's moral worthiness and willingness to serve. If the member affirms his/her worthiness and accepts the calling, the bishop or one of the counselors announces the assignment to the congregation in an open meeting and asks if there are any objections. If there is an objection, the bishop meets with the objector to determine the reason for his/her objection. A single objection may thwart the calling. The Church seeks to mitigate the risk of abuse and other misconduct by drawing upon the collective knowledge of the congregation. . . .

The calling of a Sunday School teacher is limited to teaching a class on religious doctrine for about 40 minutes each Sunday in a group setting. The Church has a "two-deep" policy for certain settings where two adults must be present, including Sunday classrooms with "children" age 11 or under. The Church does not apply the two-deep policy to teenage Sunday School classes because there are several teenagers in the classroom, the doors are not locked, the church is full of people, other adults are frequently in and out of the classroom, and the class is short. Across all of its churches, The Church holds thousands of Sunday School classes each Sunday and is aware of only one instance of sexual misconduct on church property involving a Sunday School teacher and a member of his class. That incident involved a brief grope in the hallway outside the classroom. . . .

As a Sunday School teacher, Frank's duties were limited to preparing for and teaching Sunday School class. At the time of his calling, Frank's membership record bore no annotation for abuse. Bishop Miller had no knowledge of any criminal history involving Frank but was aware that around the time of the end of Frank's first marriage, he had taken his children across state lines. Bishop Miller viewed this as a dispute between husband and wife; a misunderstanding. The Church does not conduct background checks, and none was conducted of Frank. If a criminal background check had been conducted of Frank it would have revealed the following:

(1) March 26, 2002: Frank was arrested for misdemeanor violation of a restraining order;

(2) April 25, 2002: In a domestic relations matter, a permanent protective order was entered by consent with no admission of the allegations;

(3) January 13, 2003: After initially being arrested on March 19, 2002, Frank was found guilty of four counts of violation of custody (class 5 felony), fined, and sentenced to 60 days work release and three years' probation. On January 6, 2006, Frank was discharged from supervision and his sentence terminated after satisfying all court orders and probation terms and conditions. This is the matter to which the parties refer to as "kidnapping," which arose from Frank moving with his children to Tennessee;

(4) June 5, 2003: Frank pled guilty to violating a restraining order, resulting in a fine, suspended jail sentence, and probation. On April 15, 2005, he was discharged from further supervision and his probation sentence terminated after satisfying all court orders and conditions of probation;

(5) August 11, 2005: Frank was arrested for violating a restraining order for calling his ex-wife 38 minutes after the time permitted by the order. The arrest was made pursuant to a domestic violence complaint;

(6) August 24, 2005: Frank was arrested for violating a restraining order for calling his ex-wife eight minutes prior to the time permitted by the order. The arrest was made pursuant to a domestic violence complaint; and

(7) December 12, 2008: Frank was arrested for misdemeanor violation of a restraining order. He had called his daughter on her birthday.

If Bishop Miller had knowledge of the information stated in the Colorado Database concerning Frank, he probably would not have extended a calling. The information shown to Bishop Miller and eliciting the negative response was, however, a summary which contained no explanation.

Plaintiff's Interactions with Frank. [The court described the facts leading up to the sexual contact between Frank and Plaintiff. Plaintiff attended numerous Sunday School classes taught by Frank. Nothing inappropriate happened at those classes. However, at some point Plaintiff and Frank began communicating outside of class by text message. Over a six-month period they exchanged hundreds of texts and thousands of phone calls. Eventually the parties met in Frank's car outside Plaintiff's house, where they had sexual intercourse on two occasions.]

In October 2010, after criminal charges were filed against Frank, Bishop Miller became aware of the relationship and removed Frank as a Sunday School teacher. On April 18, 2011, Frank pled guilty to sexual assault with a 10–year age difference, a class 1 misdemeanor. Frank had no prior arrests or convictions for sexual misconduct.

Plaintiff's suit seeks to recover damages for physical and psychological injury, "impairment," and medical, psychological treatment and therapy bills and related expenses for treatment.

IV. ANALYSIS

[Regarding plaintiff's battery claim against Frank, the court held that consent, which would ordinarily be an affirmative defense to a battery claim, is not available as a defense where a criminal statute does not recognize consent as a defense. A state statutes makes it a misdemeanor to have sexual relations with another, at least 15 years of age but less than 17 years of age, and at least ten years younger than the actor. Thus, consent did not bar the plaintiff's battery claim. Frank also argued that the claim was barred by the state heart balm statute, which abolishes "[a]ll civil causes of actions for breach of promise to marry, alienation of affections, criminal conversation, and seduction." Frank argued that the plaintiff's claim was in effect one for seduction—i.e. "the act of a man in enticing a woman to have unlawful intercourse with him by means of persuasion, solicitation, promise, bribes, or other means without the employment of force." The court did not resolve that argument on summary judgment because it was unclear whether the plaintiff was seeking damages for emotional distress "occasioned by discovering that Frank allegedly lied to her about wanting to marry her in order to induce her into having sexual intercourse." The court similarly declined to determine on summary judgment whether the plaintiff's negligent infliction of emotional distress claims were disguised heart balm claims.]

D. Plaintiff's Third Claim for Negligent Hiring and Fourth Claim for
Negligent Supervision against Defendant Church.

. . .

ii. Negligent Hiring.

Negligent hiring involves an "employer's responsibility for the dangerous propensities of the employee, which were known or should have been known by the
employer at the time of hiring, gauged in relation to the employee's job duties."
Raleigh v. Performance Plumbing & Heating, 130 P.3d 1011, 1016 (Colo. 2006). "An
employer has a duty to exercise reasonable care in making his decision to hire."
Moses v. Diocese of Colo., 863 P.2d 310, 327 (Colo. 1993). "The requisite degree of
care increases, and may require expanded inquiry into the employee's background,
when the employer expects the employee to have frequent contact with the public
or when the nature of the employment fosters close contact and a special relationship between particular persons and the employee." *Moses,* 863 P.2d at 328.

In this case, Plaintiff argues Defendant Church was negligent in appointing
Frank as a Sunday School teacher. In essence, she asserts the Church owed her a
duty to protect her from the sexual assault which occurred off church premises,
and at times other than when Sunday School class was held. Neither the facts nor
the law, however, support such a legal duty.

Plaintiff argues this duty existed because the Church was aware of Frank's
history of domestic violence and crimes involving his own children, but failed
to discover his character to cause harm to women and children. The undisputed
facts, however, are to the contrary. Instead, the evidence establishes that, at the time
of his calling, Frank had been a church member for several years; the Church's
membership record bore no annotation for abuse; and Bishop Miller was only
aware that around the time of the end of Frank's first marriage he had taken his
children across state lines, which Bishop Miller viewed as domestic issues between a
husband and wife. Such facts show no propensity or characteristic that put the
Church on notice that Frank posed a risk of harm to minors as implicated in this
case.

Plaintiff also contends the Church had a heightened duty to investigate due to
Frank's regular contact with the public. In a church setting, the Colorado Supreme
Courts has recognized that a church's duty is increased when placing a clergy with
duties that not only required frequent contact with others (close association with
parishioners) but also included counseling which induced reliance and trust by the
parishioner. *Moses,* 863 P.2d at 328. But, no such facts exist here. Nonetheless, even
assuming, *arguendo,* teaching a weekly 40–minute Sunday School class to a limited
number of students in a group setting constitutes sufficient "regular contact"
requiring an independent inquiry, that inquiry would have shown the "domestic
violence" and other violations Plaintiff relies on arose from domestic disputes with
Frank's ex-wife, such as calling her eight minutes earlier than allowed under a court
order. Such facts would not have put the Church on notice of any character or
propensity on the part of Frank to engage in sexual misconduct involving a minor
at church or, for that matter, anywhere else.

Plaintiff also relies on Bishop Miller's testimony that if he had knowledge of the information in the Colorado Database concerning Frank, Bishop Miller probably would not have extended the calling to Frank. The reliance, however, is misplaced because the information which the Church would have received would not have been so limited. As discussed, a background check would have disclosed the bases for the various domestic related charges. Such violations would not have been sufficient to put the Church on notice of any predisposition that would subject Plaintiff to a serious risk of harm. In other words, the harm complained of was not foreseeable. As such, the Church owed no legal duty to protect Plaintiff as claimed.

iii. Negligent Supervision.

"[I]n a claim for negligent supervision against an employer the plaintiff must prove that the defendant knew his employee posed a risk of harm to the plaintiff and that the harm that occurred was a foreseeable manifestation of that risk." *Keller v. Koca*, 111 P.3d 445, 446 (Colo. 2005). In other words, "the plaintiff must prove that the employer has a duty to prevent an unreasonable risk of harm to third persons to whom the employer knows or should have known that the employee would cause harm." *Keller*, 111 P.3d at 448; *Moses*, 863 F.2d at 329; *Destefano v. Grabrian*, 763 P.2d 275, 288 (Colo. 1988). "While the tort of negligent supervision applies to instances where the employee is acting outside his scope of employment, it does not extend to *all* acts undertaken by an employee that are actionable in tort." *Keller*, 111 P.3d at 448 (emphasis in original). As with negligent hiring, liability is "predicated on the employer's *antecedent ability* to recognize a potential employee's attributes of character or prior conduct which would create an undue risk of harm to those with whom the employee came in contact in executing his employment responsibilities." *Keller*, 111 P.3d at 448 (quotation and brackets omitted; emphasis added). Accordingly:

> the question of whether the employer owes a duty of care to the injured third party boils down to issues of *knowledge* and *causation*—whether the employee's acts are so connected with the employment in time and place such that the employer knows that harm may result from the employee's conduct and that the employer is given the opportunity to control such conduct.

Keller, 111 P.3d at 448–449 (emphasis added).

In this case, Plaintiff argues Bishop Miller's knowledge of Frank's "history of domestic violence and taking his children across state lines" created a special duty to supervise Frank's performance as a Sunday School teacher. As previously discussed, Bishop Miller had no such knowledge. Moreover, even if the Church had conducted a criminal background check, it would have shown the "domestic violence" consisted of, for example, Frank calling his ex-wife earlier or later than otherwise allowed by court order. The "known risk" of "harm" disclosed, if any, would be toward Frank's family. Such knowledge would not have disclosed a known risk of "grooming" or sexual assault on an unrelated minor—or on any member of the public in general—by Frank, at church or anywhere else. *Cf. Keller*, 111 P.3d at 450 (employer's knowledge of employee's proclivities to engage in lewd and sexual behavior with female employees on premises during business hours imposed duty on employer "to take reasonable steps to prevent *that* harm from occurring" (emphasis in original)).

There is an obvious and significant disconnect between the conduct causing or constituting harm — the sexual intercourse — and the duty to supervise which Plaintiff seeks to recognize in this case. The conduct occurred off of church property at a time and place wholly disconnected from the church and, more importantly, from the Sunday School class which Plaintiff alleges was negligently supervised. In the language of *Keller,* what is lacking is an "opportunity to control such conduct" by the Church. *Keller,* 111 P.3d at 449. In an effort to bridge the gap between the conduct and the Church's ability to supervise, Plaintiff focuses on two matters — first, a lack of training and other physical attributes of the Sunday School class and, second, "grooming" of Plaintiff by Frank.

Plaintiff relies on the "lack" of the following: training of Frank before assigning him the role as a Sunday School teacher; a co-teacher in the Sunday School class; a window in the closed Sunday School classroom door; and supervision in general. Before a duty of care may exist, however, "there must be a connection between the employer's knowledge of the employee's dangerous propensities and the harm caused." *Keller,* 111 P.3d at 450. In this case, there is insufficient evidence that any alleged supervision deficiencies caused the harm.

Here, there is no evidence that Frank's lack of training on religious education was the cause of the sexual intercourse, and it should go without saying that an employer need not have to "train" a 40–year old adult male that he is prohibited from engaging in sexual intercourse with a 15–year old. There is also no evidence that the lack of a co-teacher or a window in the classroom door caused the harm — the sexual interactions occurred at night, outside of Plaintiff's house.

Undoubtedly aware of this difficulty, Plaintiff turns to her argument of "grooming." Here, Plaintiff alleges that Frank "groomed" Plaintiff during Sunday School class, that the grooming occurred due to a lack of supervision and that the intercourse would not have occurred without the grooming. In constructing the argument, however, Plaintiff consistently fails to identify specific conduct constituting grooming; to tie that conduct to the Sunday School class; and to explain how that conduct would have been deterred by some specific form of supervision. The only conduct directed toward Plaintiff during Sunday School class was the sending of text messages from Frank while he was teaching, but there is no evidence this had any sexual content or was "grooming." In short, Plaintiff constructs a series of precarious lily pads and invites the Court to hop from one to another to connect harmful conduct on one shore with a supervision deficiency on the other. The law does not allow the Court to do so.

Moreover, even assuming, *arguendo,* that the referenced conduct could be deemed grooming, it would be dwarfed by the non-controllable instances of identical conduct. Plaintiff testified that she and Frank exchanged hundreds of text messages and thousands of calls outside of church — all between about 9:00 p.m. to 2:00 a.m. or 3:00 a.m. — when Frank got off of work from Chili's. If any grooming occurred, it was far from a time and place connected with Defendant Frank's "employment" at the Church.

In summary, there is simply no evidence the conduct complained was reasonably foreseeable by the Church thus triggering a duty to impose specific forms of supervision to prevent it. Under Plaintiff's theory, due to Frank's violation of court orders in disputes with his ex-wife, the Church owed Plaintiff a duty to supervise Frank to prevent sexual intercourse with minors, something the law does not require. Moreover, even if the operative conduct is the grooming, as opposed to the sexual intercourse, there is simply no conduct constituting grooming supported by, or which may be inferred from, the evidence which would or could have been prevented by a window, co-teacher or other forms of supervision of the Sunday School class. On this record, Plaintiff's claim for negligent supervision cannot be sustained.

V. CONCLUSION

For the reasons stated, (1) Defendant Church's motion for summary judgment on all claims is granted and it is dismissed from this case entirely; (2) Plaintiff's motion for summary judgment on the claims for negligent hiring and supervision is denied; (3) Plaintiff's motion for summary judgment on the claim for battery is denied . . .

FOOD FOR THOUGHT

Why wasn't the Church vicariously liable for the tortious acts of Frank? Frank was engaged in the Church's business by teaching Sunday school classes. Using Judge Friendly's analysis in the drunken-sailor case, *Ira S. Bushey*, isn't it foreseeable that some adult leaders of youth activities may engage in unlawful sexual activity with minors under their supervision? Litigation against the Roman Catholic Church, the Boy Scouts, and other organizations has surely established the existence and seriousness of this risk. (Many of those cases rely not on *respondeat superior* but on independently tortious acts by the institutional defendant, such as failing to remove clergy accused of sexual abuse.) Note that the court in *Lindeman* talks about the "non-controllable conduct" of Frank, calling to mind the reasoning given in the Third Restatement § 7.07, comment *b* for imposing vicarious liability.

Note, however, that the scope-of-employment analysis assumes an employment relationship. Frank was a volunteer. Should it matter that he wasn't being compensated for his services? The Restatement (Third) of Agency § 7.07, comment *f*, states that "The fact that an agent performs work gratuitously does not relieve a principal of vicarious liability when the principal controls or has the right to control the manner and means of the agent's performance of work." For example, where a church member volunteered to deliver cookies to infirm members of the congregation around Christmastime and on his way to deliver the cookies was involved in a collision with a motorcyclist, there was sufficient evidence for a jury to find the church vicariously liable:

> The [Ladies'] Guild [of the Church] picked the delivery date, provided the cookies, organized the list of shut-in members who were to receive cookies, and chose

the people to whom Goodman was to deliver cookies. Goodman testified the Guild told him where to go, his only purpose in driving was to deliver the cookies, he would have gone to any address which the Guild directed, and he would not have delivered the cookies if he had been so instructed. The test for determining a master servant relationship is whether one has the right to direct and control the conduct of the alleged servant at the time of the incident. The jury could have easily found from the evidence that the Guild had the right to direct and control Goodman at the time of the accident.

The facts establish that Goodman was acting within the scope of his employment when the accident occurred. The parties stipulated the cookie bake and delivery are the work of the Guild. Goodman testified his only purpose in driving was to deliver cookies. He was clearly within the scope of the Guild's activity when he struck Miller's motorcycle.

Trinity Lutheran Church, Inc. of Evansville, Ind. v. Miller, 451 N.E.2d 1099, 1102-03 (Ind. Ct. App. 1983). Is control really the reason for imposing liability on the church? Isn't this case more like *Ira S. Bushey*, in that traffic accidents on the way to deliver cookies to infirm members of the congregation are fairly regarded as an incident of the activities of the church?

The plaintiff in *Lindeman* had a potentially strong fallback argument that the Church *itself* was negligent. In a direct-liability claim, the plaintiff relies not on the bad acts of the would-be employee, but on the employer itself. By failing to conduct a background check, the Church failed to learn of Frank's history of resisting domestic violence restraining orders. Why, then, does the plaintiff's negligent hiring claim fail? As for negligent supervision, what does the plaintiff say the Church should have done that would have prevented the harm in this case? Does this claim go off on duty, breach, or causation?

B. IMPACT OF COMPARATIVE FAULT ON JOINT AND SEVERAL LIABILITY

AMERICAN MOTORCYCLE ASS'N v. SUPERIOR COURT OF LOS ANGELES COUNTY
578 P.2d 899 (Cal. 1978)

TOBRINER, Justice.

Three years ago, in Li v. Yellow Cab Co. (1975) . . . 532 P.2d 1226, we concluded that the harsh and much criticized contributory negligence doctrine, which totally barred an injured person from recovering damages whenever his own negligence had contributed in any degree to the injury, should be replaced in this state by a rule of comparative negligence, under which an injured individual's recovery is simply proportionately diminished, rather than completely eliminated, when he is partially responsible for the injury. In reaching the conclusion to adopt comparative negligence in *Li,* we explicitly recognized that our innovation inevitably raised numerous collateral issues, "[t]he most serious [of which] are those attendant upon the administration of a rule of comparative negligence in cases involving multiple parties." . . . Because the *Li* litigation itself involved only a single plaintiff and a single defendant, however, we concluded that it was "neither necessary nor wise" . . . to address such multiple party questions at that juncture, and we accordingly postponed consideration of such questions until a case directly presenting such issues came before our court. The present mandamus proceeding presents such a case, and requires us to resolve a number of the thorny multiple party problems to which *Li* adverted.

For the reasons explained below, we have reached the following conclusions with respect to the multiple party issues presented by this case. [W]e conclude that our adoption of comparative negligence to ameliorate the inequitable consequences of the contributory negligence rule does not warrant the abolition or contraction of the established "joint and several liability" doctrine; each tortfeasor whose negligence is a proximate cause of an indivisible injury remains individually liable for all compensable damages attributable to that injury. Contrary to petitioner's contention, we conclude that joint and several liability does not logically conflict with a comparative negligence regime. Indeed, as we point out, the great majority of jurisdictions which have adopted comparative negligence have retained the joint and several liability rule; we are aware of no judicial decision which intimates that the adoption of comparative negligence compels the abandonment of this long-standing common law rule. The joint and several liability doctrine continues, after *Li,* to play an important and legitimate role in protecting the ability of a negligently injured person to obtain adequate compensation for his injuries from those tortfeasors who have negligently inflicted the harm. . . .

1. The facts

In the underlying action in this case, plaintiff Glen Gregos, a teenage boy, seeks to recover damages for serious injuries which he incurred while participating in a cross-country motorcycle race for novices. Glen's second amended complaint alleges, in relevant part, that defendants American Motorcycle Association (AMA) and the Viking Motorcycle Club (Viking) — the organizations that sponsored and collected the entry fee for the race — negligently designed, managed, supervised and administered the race, and negligently solicited the entrants for the race. The . . . complaint . . . alleges that as a direct and proximate cause of such negligence, Glen suffered a crushing of his spine, resulting in the permanent loss of the use of his legs and his permanent inability to perform sexual functions. Although the negligence count of the complaint does not identify the specific acts or omissions of which plaintiff complains, additional allegations in the complaint assert, inter alia, that defendants failed to give the novice participants reasonable instructions that were necessary for their safety, failed to segregate the entrants into reasonable classes of equivalently skilled participants, and failed to limit the entry of participants to prevent the racecourse from becoming overcrowded and hazardous.

AMA filed an answer to the complaint, denying the charging allegations and asserting a number of affirmative defenses. . . .

In the second cause of action of its proposed cross-complaint, AMA seeks declaratory relief. It reasserts Glen's parents' negligence, declares that Glen has failed to join his parents in the action, and asks for a declaration of the "allocable negligence" of Glen's parents so that "the damages awarded [against AMA], if any, [may] be reduced by the percentage of damages allocable to cross-defendants' negligence." As more fully explained in the accompanying points and authorities, this second cause of action is based on an implicit assumption that the *Li* decision abrogates the rule of joint and several liability of concurrent tortfeasors and establishes in its stead a new rule of "proportionate liability," under which each concurrent tortfeasor who has proximately caused an indivisible harm may be held liable only for a *portion* of plaintiff's recovery, determined on a comparative fault basis. . . .

2. The adoption of comparative negligence in Li does not warrant the abolition of joint and several liability of concurrent tortfeasors. . . .

Under well-established common law principles, a negligent tortfeasor is generally liable for all damage of which his negligence is a proximate cause; stated another way, in order to recover damages sustained as a result of an indivisible injury, a plaintiff is not required to prove that a tortfeasor's conduct was *the sole* proximate cause of the injury, but only that such negligence was a proximate cause. . . .

In cases involving multiple tortfeasors, the principle that each tortfeasor is personally liable for any indivisible injury of which his negligence is a proximate cause has commonly been expressed in terms of "joint and several liability." As many commentators have noted, the "joint and several liability" concept has sometimes caused confusion because the terminology has been used with reference to a number of distinct situations. . . . The terminology originated with respect to tortfeasors who acted in concert to commit a tort, and in that context it reflected the principle, applied in both the criminal and civil realm, that all members of a "conspiracy" or partnership are equally responsible for the acts of each member in furtherance of such conspiracy.

Subsequently, the courts applied the "joint and several liability" terminology to other contexts in which a preexisting relationship between two individuals made it appropriate to hold one individual liable for the act of the other; common examples are instances of vicarious liability between employer and employee or principal and agent, or situations in which joint owners of property owe a common duty to some third party. In these situations, the joint and several liability concept reflects the legal conclusion that one individual may be held liable for the consequences of the negligent act of another.

In the concurrent tortfeasor context, however, the "joint and several liability" label does not express the imposition of any form of vicarious liability, but instead simply embodies the general common law principle, noted above, that a tortfeasor is liable for any injury of which his negligence is a proximate cause. Liability attaches to a concurrent tortfeasor in this situation not because he is responsible for the acts of other independent tortfeasors who may also have caused the injury, but because he is responsible for all damage of which his own negligence was a proximate cause. When independent negligent actions of a number of tortfeasors are each a proximate cause of a single injury, each tortfeasor is thus personally liable for the damage sustained, and the injured person may sue one or all of the tortfeasors to obtain a recovery for his injuries; the fact that one of the tortfeasors is impecunious or otherwise immune from suit does not relieve another tortfeasor of his liability for damage which he himself has proximately caused. . . .

In the instant case AMA argues that the *Li* decision, by repudiating the all-or-nothing contributory negligence rule and replacing it by a rule which simply diminishes an injured party's recovery on the basis of his comparative fault, in effect undermined the fundamental rationale of the entire joint and several liability doctrine as applied to concurrent tortfeasors. . . .

First, the simple feasibility of apportioning fault on a comparative negligence basis does not render an indivisible injury "divisible" for purposes of the joint and several liability rule. As we have already explained, a concurrent tortfeasor is liable for the whole of an indivisible injury whenever his negligence is a proximate cause of that injury. In many instances, the negligence of each of several concurrent tortfeasors may be sufficient, in itself, to cause the entire injury; in other instances, it is simply impossible to determine whether or not a particular concurrent tortfeasor's negligence, acting alone, would have caused the same injury. Under such circumstances, a defendant has no equitable claim vis-à-vis an injured plaintiff to be relieved of liability for damage which he has proximately caused simply because some other tortfeasor's negligence may also have caused the same harm. In other words, the mere fact that it may be possible to assign some percentage figure to the relative culpability of one negligent defendant as compared to another does not in any way suggest that each defendant's negligence is not a proximate cause of the entire indivisible injury.

Second, abandonment of the joint and several liability rule is not warranted by AMA's claim that, after *Li*, a plaintiff is no longer "innocent." Initially, of course, it is by no means invariably true that after *Li* injured plaintiffs will be guilty of negligence. In many instances a plaintiff will be completely free of all responsibility for the accident, and yet, under the proposed abolition of joint and several liability, such a completely faultless plaintiff, rather than a wrongdoing defendant, would be forced to bear a portion of the loss if any one of the concurrent tortfeasors should prove financially unable to satisfy his proportioned share of the damages.

Moreover, even when a plaintiff is partially at fault for his own injury, a plaintiff's culpability is not equivalent to that of a defendant. In this setting, a plaintiff's negligence relates only to a failure to use due care for his own protection, while a defendant's negligence relates to a lack of due care for the safety of others. Although we recognized in *Li* that a plaintiff's self-directed negligence would justify reducing his recovery in proportion to his degree of fault for the accident, the fact remains that insofar as the plaintiff's conduct creates only a risk of self-injury, such conduct, unlike that of a negligent defendant, is not tortious. . . .

Finally, from a realistic standpoint, we think that AMA's suggested abandonment of the joint and several liability rule would work a serious and unwarranted deleterious effect on the practical ability of negligently injured persons to receive adequate compensation for their injuries. One of the principal by-products of the joint and several liability rule is that it frequently permits an injured person to obtain full recovery for his injuries even when one or more of the responsible parties do not have the financial resources to cover their liability. In such a case the rule recognizes that fairness dictates that the "wronged party should not be deprived of his right to redress," but that "[the] wrongdoers should be left to work out between themselves any apportionment." (Summers v. Tice (1948) . . . 199 P.2d 1 . . . .) The *Li* decision does not detract in the slightest from this pragmatic policy determination.

For all of the foregoing reasons, we reject AMA's suggestion that our adoption of comparative negligence logically compels the abolition of joint and several liability of concurrent tortfeasors. Indeed, although AMA fervently asserts that the joint and several liability concept is totally incompatible with a comparative negligence regime, the simple truth is that the overwhelming majority of jurisdictions which have adopted comparative negligence have retained the joint and several liability doctrine. As Professor Schwartz notes in his treatise on comparative negligence: "The concept of joint and several liability of tortfeasors has been retained under comparative negligence, unless the statute specifically abolishes it, in all states that have been called upon to decide the question." (Schwartz, Comparative Negligence (1974) § 16.4, p. 253 . . . . AMA has not cited a single judicial authority to support its contention that the advent of comparative negligence rationally compels the demise of the joint and several liability rule. Under the circumstances, we hold that after *Li,* a concurrent tortfeasor whose negligence is a proximate cause of an indivisible injury remains liable for the total amount of damages, diminished only "in proportion to the amount of negligence attributable to the person recovering." (13 Cal. 3d at p. 829.) . . .

THE SCORECARD

In 1978 the California court was correct in its observation that jurisdictions that had adopted comparative negligence still retained the common law joint and several liability doctrine. In the quarter century since then, a sea change in the law has occurred. Today, a majority of jurisdictions do not impose joint and several liability across the board. Legislatures in most states have either abolished or modified the common law joint tortfeasor doctrine. Here is the lay of the land:

(1) *States Adhering to the Common Law Doctrine:* Ten jurisdictions still follow the traditional joint and several liability rule — Alabama, Delaware, the District of Columbia, Maine, Maryland, Massachusetts, North Carolina, Pennsylvania, Rhode Island, and Virginia.

(2) *States Abolishing Joint and Several Liability*: Eighteen states have abolished the joint and several doctrine — Alaska, Arizona, Arkansas, Colorado, Georgia, Idaho, Indiana, Kansas, Kentucky, Louisiana, Mississippi, Nevada, New Mexico, North Dakota, Tennessee, Utah, Vermont, and Wyoming. A number of these states make some exception to the several liability rule, however. (See discussion of exceptions, *infra.*)

(3) *States Applying Joint and Several Liability for Economic Harm Only*: Six states — California, Hawaii, Florida, Nebraska, New York, and Ohio — have abolished joint and several liability for noneconomic damages (e.g., pain and suffering) only and have retained the doctrine for economic loss (i.e., lost wages, medical expenses, etc.).

(4) *States Applying Joint and Several Liability After a Threshold Has Been Met*: A common feature of joint and several reform measures is application of a percentage threshold that triggers a reversion to joint liability. Fifteen states — Hawaii, Illinois, Iowa, Minnesota, Missouri, Montana, New Hampshire, New Jersey, New York, Ohio, Oklahoma, South Carolina, South Dakota, Texas, and Wisconsin — apply joint and several liability only to a defendant whose share of fault is greater than some percentage threshold. If the defendant is determined to be more than, say, 50 percent at fault, then liability is joint and several rather than several only. For example, in Wisconsin, if a defendant is 51 percent or more at fault, he is jointly and severally liable; otherwise several liability applies. Wis. Stat. Ann. § 895.045 (West 1997). New Jersey's threshold is 60 percent. N.J. Stat. Ann. § 2A:15-5.3 (West 2000). South Carolina's is 50 percent. S.C. Code Ann. § 15-38-15(A) (Supp. 2005). Minnesota's is 50 percent as well. Minn. Stat. § 604.02 (2006). West Virginia's threshold is 30 percent. W. Va. Code Ann. § 55-7-24 (West 2005). South Dakota limits the liability of defendants less than 50 percent at fault to two times their share. S.D. Codified Laws § 15-8-15.1 (Supp. 2000).

(5) *States Applying Joint Tortfeasor Liability Only When Plaintiff Is Not at Fault*: Two states — Oklahoma and Washington — tie several recovery to plaintiff's fault (i.e., only a faultless plaintiff will be entitled to a joint and several award).

(6) *States Reallocating the Share of Insolvent Tortfeasor to All Parties*: Several states (Connecticut, Michigan, Minnesota, Montana, New Hampshire, and Oregon) pattern their joint tortfeasor doctrine after the Uniform Comparative Fault Act. According to this model, an insolvent tortfeasor's share is reallocated among the remaining parties, including the plaintiff if the plaintiff was negligent.

(7) *States Retaining Joint and Several Liability for Certain Activities*: Many of the states include exceptions for certain types of torts. Some states retain joint and several liability for intentional tortfeasors and persons acting in concert. *See, e.g.*, Idaho Code Ann. § 6-803(5) (2004); S.C. Code Ann. § 15-38-15(F) (Supp. 2005); Reilly v. Anderson, 727 N.W.2d 102 (Iowa 2006) (joint and several liability attaches to concerted action of defendants despite Iowa statute that sets threshold of 50 percent for joint and several liability); Richards v. Badger Mutual Insurance Co., 749 N.W.2d 581 (Wis. 2008) (joint and several liability retained for concerted action); Restatement, Third, of Torts: Apportionment of Liability §§ 12, 15 (1999) (same). Furthermore, many states retain joint and several liability for claims of vicarious liability. *See, e.g.*, Wash. Rev. Code Ann. § 4.22.070 (West 2005); Restatement, Third, of Torts: Apportionment of Liability § 13 (1999). An

interesting example is New Mexico's law, N.M. Stat. Ann. §41-3A-1 (Michie 2007), which retains joint and several liability for intentional tort claims, claims of vicarious liability, strict products liability claims, and claims that the courts find implicate a "sound basis in public policy" that demands application of the joint and several rule. Michigan retains joint and several liability in medical malpractice cases only when plaintiff is free from fault. Mich. Comp. Laws Ann. §600.6304(6)(a) (West 2000). A handful of jurisdictions apply joint and several liability only when defendants act in concert. And a few states (e.g., Hawaii, Minnesota, and Nevada) make exceptions for toxic torts, environmental torts, or cases involving solid waste disposal sites.

The alternative approaches listed above do not fully describe all the legislative schemes. Some states abolish joint and several liability when the defendant has met a threshold (e.g., 51 percent of fault) and then only for noneconomic loss (i.e., pain and suffering). *See, e.g.,* Iowa Code Ann. §668.4 (West 1998) (50 percent threshold). You can't tell a player without a scorecard. If you want to know the status of joint and several liability in any jurisdiction, you must not only master the governing statute, but also decisions that have interpreted the statute. For a discussion on the current status of joint and several liability, *see* F. Patrick Hubbard, *The Nature and Impact of the* "Tort Reform" *Movement,* 35 Hofstra L. Rev. 437, 490-492 (2006); Nancy C. Marcus, *Phantom Parties and Other Practical Problems with the Attempted Abolition of Joint and Several Liability,* 60 Ark. L. Rev. 437 (2007).

ALLOCATING LIABILITY WHEN A TORTFEASOR FAILS TO PROTECT THE PLAINTIFF FROM THE SPECIFIC RISK OF AN INTENTIONAL TORT

One issue that comes up in discussions about joint and several liability is what courts should do when a party who clearly caused intentional injury to a plaintiff is unidentified or insolvent, but a party who is accused of breaching a duty to protect the plaintiff from such intentional conduct is available. The Restatement, Third, of Torts: Apportionment of Liability §14 (2000), takes a strong position imposing joint and several liability in these situations:

> A person who is liable to another based on a failure to protect the other from the specific risk of an intentional tort is jointly and severally liable for the share of comparative responsibility assigned to the intentional tortfeasor in addition to the share of comparative responsibility assigned to the person.

Many states that have abolished or modified joint-tortfeasor liability agree with the Restatement and will not limit plaintiff's recovery to the available negligent tortfeasor's percentage of fault. *See, e.g.,* Burns International Security Services Inc. v. Philadelphia Indemnity Insurance Co., 899 So. 2d 361 (Fla. Dist. Ct. App. 2005) (security service liable for breaching its duty to protect a warehouse from theft by unknown perpetrators; apportionment was among the negligent

---

authors' dialogue 34

AARON: Jim, I have a riddle for you. When is two less than one?

JIM: On a Bernie Madoff financial statement? Just kidding. OK, I give up.

AARON: When you have joint tortfeasors. If you were hit by a truck owned by Walmart you can recover all your damages. But if you are hit by two trucks, one owned by Walmart and one owned by Joe Shmoe who can't rub two nickels together, you may be worse off. You only recover part of your damages from Walmart. At least that's the law in jurisdictions that have either wholly or partially done away with joint and several liability.

JIM: Well, I'm better off in your second hypo than if I were hit by Joe Shmoe by himself. Then I wouldn't be likely to recover anything. At least this way I can recover from Walmart its proportional liability.

AARON: I guess you're right. The glass is either half-full or half-empty depending on your perspective. But putting riddles aside, where do you come down on the joint and several liability debate?

JIM: This is one of the issues in modern tort law for which there is no good solution. Plaintiffs have a right to feel cheated when solvent defendants walk away paying only a small percentage of the damages they cause, leaving the plaintiff holding the bag for the uncompensated loss. Corporate defendants, on the other hand, are terribly put out when they are forced to pay out, even though their negligent conduct is minuscule compared to that of the insolvent or immune co-defendant.

AARON: Maybe the legislatures that compromised by creating thresholds before imposing joint and several liability, or by keeping joint and several liability intact

---

tortfeasors, not the negligent and intentional tortfeasors); Merrill Crossings Associates v. McDonald, 705 So. 2d 560 (Fla. 1997) (joint and several liability applies against firm in charge of security in parking lot when unknown assailant shot a shopper); Veazey v. Elmwood Plantation Associates, 650 So. 2d 712 (La. 1994) (when tenant was raped in the parking lot of her apartment building, the trial court was permitted to allocate 100 percent of damages to negligent management company); Shin v. Sunriver Preparatory School, Inc., 111 P.3d 762 (Or. Ct. App. 2005) (in negligence action against school for failure to protect student from sexual abuse, apportionment between the negligent and intentional tortfeasors was not allowed). But other states limit plaintiff's recovery to the negligent defendant's share of the fault. Since the intentional tortfeasor bears the lion's share of the fault, when one tortfeasor's conduct was intentional, plaintiff will recover only a small percentage of her total damages from the negligent party. *See, e.g.,* McIntosh v. McElveen, 893 So. 2d 986 (La. Ct. App. 2005) (the sheriff's office negligent in failing to warn its deputy of gunshots being fired in deputy's vicinity was responsible for only a percentage of fault represented by its negligence); Martin v. United States, 984 F.2d 1033 (9th Cir. 1993) (applying California law) (government employee negligent in supervising children was not held liable for the fault of a

for economic harm but doing away with the joint and several doctrine for pain and suffering, were on to something.

JIM: I think if I had my druthers I would opt for a threshold rather than abolishing joint and several for noneconomic loss. The threshold addresses a real problem. Defendants with a small percentage of fault may, in fact, not be liable at all. Juries may feel free to assign some small percentage of fault to a corporate defendant even when evidence on negligence or causation is weak. Trial judges are not inclined to direct verdicts when a jury finds for plaintiff. Doing away with joint and several liability for noneconomic loss serves as little more than a cap on liability.

AARON: Not so fast. There may be something to be said for limiting liability to proportional fault for noneconomic loss. Maybe, if I had some confidence that we had some reliable standards for evaluating pain and suffering, I would feel differently. But the variations among pain and suffering awards in different parts of even the same state, let alone different states, are so great that what plaintiffs receive in compensation has an arbitrary quality to it. At least fault apportionment is not arbitrary.

JIM: Even if you are right, limiting liability based on fault apportionment only aggravates a bad situation. A plaintiff who recovers only the proportional fault of each defendant will now be doubly cursed if it turns out that the case is tried in a locale that provides modest or inadequate pain and suffering awards. I stick to my view that if there is to be a compromise, it should be based on some significant threshold that assures that the defendant did, in fact, truly cause harm to the plaintiff.

---

rapist who had abducted a child and was held responsible for only the percentage of fault represented by his negligent supervision); Paragon Family Restaurant v. Bartolini, 799 N.E.2d 1048 (Ind. 2003) (restaurant was liable only for its own percentage of fault in failing to prevent criminal assault on its property); Siler v. 146 Montague Associates, 652 N.Y.S.2d 315 (N.Y. App. Div. 1997) (in action against landlord for negligent hiring of an employee who viciously assaulted a tenant in her apartment, landlord was held liable only for the percentage of fault represented by his negligence). Scholars generally agree that several liability is not appropriate when one of the tortfeasors intentionally causes an indivisible injury for which another's negligence is a causal factor. *See, e.g.,* Ellen M. Bublick, *The End Game of Tort Reform: Comparative Apportionment and Intentional Torts,* 78 Notre Dame L. Rev. 355, 363 (2003) (discussing the implications of the recent trend to allow comparative fault between intentional and negligent tortfeasors and noting that with the abandonment of joint and several liability, deserving plaintiffs will be deprived of just recovery because the lion's share of fault will be assessed against the rapist); Christopher M. Brown & Kirk A. Morgan, *Consideration of Intentional Torts in Fault Allocation: Disarming the Duty to Protect Against Intentional Conduct,* 2 Wyo. L. Rev. 483, 486 (2002) ("defendants who have failed to protect against the intentional harm it was their specific duty to prevent should be held responsible for the entire amount of harm suffered when the intentional tortfeasor is unknown or insolvent"); William K. Jones, *Tort Triad: Slumbering Sentinels, Vicious Assailants, and Victims Variously Vigilant*, 30 Hofstra L. Rev. 253 (2001) (deplores the case law in many states that allows victims to recover only the proportion of fault allocated to their negligent "sentinels").

Professor Ellen Bublick, in *Citizen No-Duty Rules: Rape Victims and Comparative Fault*, 99 Colum. L. Rev. 1413 (1999), asserts that many jurisdictions allow negligent third parties, such as hotels and landlords, to raise defenses of rape victim fault. *See id.* at 1415. Bublick argues that "a citizen should be entitled to shape her life around the assumption that others will not intentionally rape her." *Id.* at 1416. As a result, Bublick contends that courts should not allow defendants, either rapists or third parties, to raise defenses of rape victim fault. *See id.* Along the same lines, in Bublick's *Tort Suits Filed by Rape and Sexual Assault Victims in Civil Courts: Lessons for Courts, Classrooms and Constituencies*, 59 S.M.U. L. Rev. 55, 83 (2006), she contends that "permitting comparative fault to serve as a defense to an intentional tort raises the alarming prospect that an intentional tortfeasor, like a rapist, can diminish his legal responsibility to the victim by blaming her for the rape."

TORT REFORM AND THE FALL OF JOINT AND SEVERAL LIABILITY

This much is certain. The joint and several liability doctrine that once prevailed almost unanimously throughout the country is now a distinctly minority view. What brought about such a drastic change? The court in *American Motorcycle* made a compelling case as to why the change to comparative fault should not affect the vitality of the joint and several doctrine. The reality is that, whether the doctrine is abolished in whole or in part, whenever plaintiffs obtain a judgment against joint tortfeasors and one is insolvent, the plaintiff will end up eating the loss attributable to the insolvent tortfeasor.

During the last two decades, corporations began bombarding state legislatures with the argument that the tort system was unfair and imposed huge costs on their ability to engage in business. They sought a whole host of legislative reforms that would grant them some relief from what they believed to be an oppressive system of liability. They were most successful in convincing legislatures that a defendant who, for example, was 10 or 20 percent at fault should not be liable for the entire judgment merely because another tortfeasor was insolvent and could not pay his fair share. Some commentators contend that the legislatures were hoodwinked by defense advocates who misled them concerning the role of cause and fault in a tort action. Even a defendant who is only 10 or 20 percent at fault is not liable unless his fault was both the cause-in-fact and the proximate cause of the plaintiff's harm. There is nothing unfair in requiring a defendant who caused the plaintiff's harm to be responsible for the entirety of the damages that would not have taken place but for his fault. *See* Richard W. Wright, *Allocating Liability Among Multiple Responsible Causes: A Principled Defense of Joint and Several Liability for Actual Harm and*

Risk Exposure, 21 U. Cal. Davis L. Rev. 1141 (1988). Some writers argue against tort reform on the grounds that it works an injustice against plaintiffs. *See, e.g.,* Richard A. Michael, *Joint Liability: Should It Be Reformed or Abolished? — The Illinois Experience,* 27 Loy. U. Chi. L.J. 867, 920-921 (1996) ("[abolishing joint and several liability is] a mistake because it places the burden of an insolvent, underinsured, or immune defendant on the plaintiff").

One of the authors of this casebook wrote a spirited defense of the legislative movement to limit joint and several tort liability. *See* Aaron D. Twerski, *The Joint Tortfeasor Legislative Revolt: A Rational Response to the Critics,* 22 U.C. Davis L. Rev. 1125 (1989). Consider the following hypotheticals:

1. Plaintiff was injured when a speeding drunken driver (*D1*) rear-ended the plaintiff's car. Upon examination of *D1*'s automobile after the collision, the brakes were found in damaged condition. There is conflicting evidence as to whether the seal that permitted brake fluid to leak out broke before or after the collision. Suit is thus also brought against the manufacturer of the car (*D2*). *D1* carries 10/20 liability insurance.

   The jury returns a verdict of $1 million and apportions fault as follows:
   $$D1 — 95\%$$
   $$D2 — 5\%$$

   Since *D1* is judgment-proof and carries only 10/20 liability insurance, the plaintiff recovers only $10,000 from him. *D2*, who was assessed 5 percent of the fault, will pay $990,000.

2. Plaintiff, an employee at *XYZ* Plastics, Inc., was injured when a safety guard failed to operate properly. *XYZ* Plastics (*D1*) was on notice that the punch press was not working correctly but continued to use the machine rather than effect repairs over a six-month period. *ABC* Machines Co. (*D2*) had manufactured the machine that misfired due to a defective weld. *D1* is only liable to plaintiff for his workers' compensation recovery but is otherwise immune from tort recovery.

   The jury returns a verdict assessing fault in the following percentages:
   $$\text{Plaintiff} — 10\%$$
   $$D1 — 75\%$$
   $$D2 — 15\%$$

   Assuming that plaintiff's injuries are $1 million, *D2* (15 percent at fault) could be liable for as much as $900,000. The defendant with the greater percentage of fault is immune (in most jurisdictions) from both a direct action by plaintiff or a contribution action by defendant.

Note that in both of the examples, the insolvent defendant is not just someone who happens not to have money to pay the judgment. In the case of the drunken driver, one reason that the defendant cannot pay the judgment is that state legislatures allow insolvent people to drive with inadequate insurance coverage. Similarly, the defendant employer, who was 75 percent at fault, pays only workers' compensation and has no tort liability. Legislatures believed that it was unfair to make solvent defendants pay for the immunities handed out to defendants, who were thereby granted a license to injure without having to own up to the full implications of their conduct. *See id.* at 1144.

One notorious case provides a real-life illustration of the defendant's nightmare discussed above. In Walt Disney World Co. v. Wood, 515 So. 2d 198 (Fla. 1987), the plaintiff and her fiancé were driving bumper cars at Disney's grand prix attraction when the fiancé rear-ended the plaintiff's car. The plaintiff sustained injuries and brought an action against Disney, whereupon Disney sought contribution from her former fiancé — now her husband. The jury awarded $75,000 damages to the plaintiff and found plaintiff 14 percent at fault, her husband 85 percent at fault, and Disney only 1 percent at fault. Nevertheless, the court entered judgment against Disney for 86 percent of the damages because the plaintiff's husband was immune from judgment. The court "[could not] say with certainty that joint and several liability is an unjust doctrine or that it should necessarily be eliminated upon the adoption of comparative negligence. . . . The viability of the doctrine is a matter which should best be decided by the legislature." Id. at 202. The Florida legislature swiftly took up the challenge and enacted a measure that abolished joint and several liability when a defendant was less than 10 percent at fault. Fla. Stat. Ann. § 768.81 (West Supp. 2002).

This issue is politically charged. For example, the *American Motorcycle* case was radically altered by tort reformers who were successful in getting a proposition on the ballot in California that limited joint and several liability to economic harm only. The initiative won. Liability in California for noneconomic harm (i.e., pain and suffering) is limited to each defendant's percentage of fault. Cal. Civ. Code §§ 1431 and 1431.2 (West Supp. 2002). Legislatures in the states that still maintain common law joint and several liability continue to be importuned to adopt one of the alternative systems set forth above.

THE RESTATEMENT AND THE DIFFICULTY OF TRYING TO BE NEUTRAL

The Restatement, Third, of Torts: Apportionment of Liability § 17 comment *a* (2000) takes no position on which system of apportionment for joint tortfeasors should be adopted by the states. Because apportionment of liability is such a contentious area, even with a disclaimer the Restatement's position has been challenged. One commentator questioned the Restatement's neutrality, saying "though the ALI takes no official position against joint and several liability, it registers disapproval repeatedly." Mark M. Hager, *What's (Not!) in a Restatement? ALI Issue-Dodging on Liability Apportionment*, 33 Conn. L. Rev. 77, 96 (2000). The writer challenges the ALI to look at the "dizzying array of statutory and common law apportionment rules" with more "theoretical penetration." *Id.* at 95. Another scholar accuses the restatement of giving too much "prospective content" and failing to "restate the common law." Frank J. Vandall, *A Critique of the Restatement (Third), Apportionment as It Affects Joint and Several Liability*, 49 Emory L.J. 565, 619 (2000). Escaping an appearance of pro-defendant or pro-plaintiff bias on this issue seems nigh unto impossible. Is it any wonder that the *American Motorcycle* court, and many others, have deferred to their legislatures on the issue of joint tortfeasor liability?

C. SATISFACTION OF A JUDGMENT AND THE AFTERMATH: CONTRIBUTION AND INDEMNITY

Where the joint and several liability rule governs either in whole or in part (e.g., for noneconomic loss), a plaintiff may take a judgment against several tortfeasors and is free to collect all of her damages from any of the tortfeasors. Thus, a plaintiff may get a judgment of $100,000 against *D1* (20 percent at fault) and *D2* (80 percent at fault). She may recover the full $100,000 from either of the defendants. However, once her judgment is satisfied, she cannot turn to collect again from the other defendant. Only one satisfaction per customer is allowed. Any amount paid by one defendant is deducted when the plaintiff seeks to recover from the second defendant. A defendant who has paid more than his fair share may then seek contribution from the second defendant. Prior to the adoption of comparative fault, a defendant who sought contribution would recover pro rata depending on the number of defendants. If there were two defendants, they would split the damages; if there were three defendants, the defendant who paid the entire damages could collect one-third of the damages from each of the two remaining defendants. *See, e.g.,* Uniform Contribution Among Tortfeasors Act §§ 1 and 2 (1955) and National Health Labs, Inc. v. Ahmadi, 596 A.2d 555 (D.C. 1991). With the adoption of comparative fault, most jurisdictions that impose joint and several liability allocate contribution damages on the basis of each defendant's fault. Thus, in the hypothetical case set forth above, if *D2* paid the plaintiff $100,000 damages in satisfaction of her judgment, he would be entitled to recover 20 percent of the $100,000 from *D1*. *See* Restatement of Torts, Third, Apportionment of Liability § 33 (2000).

What happens if one of the tortfeasors is immune from suit from the plaintiff? Assume that in the hypothetical, *D2* is an employer who sits under the protection of workers' compensation and is not liable for tort damages. *D1*, who is a joint tortfeasor, pays the plaintiff $100,000 in damages in satisfaction of her judgment. Can *D1*, who is 20 percent at fault, turn around and sue *D2* for $80,000 in contribution? In most jurisdictions, a party's immunity from liability against a plaintiff protects him from a contribution action as well. *See* Arthur Larson, Larson's Workers' Compensation Law § 121.02 (2000). Some jurisdictions allow contribution up to the amount of liability that the workers' compensation would normally pay. *See, e.g.,* Kotecki v. Cyclops Welding Corp., 585 N.E.2d 1023 (Ill. 1991).

In jurisdictions that have done away with joint and several liability, no tortfeasor pays more than his proportional share of the total damages awarded at judgment. There is thus no occasion to seek contribution from another defendant.

On occasion, a defendant who either settled a case or paid a judgment may be entitled to full reimbursement from a joint tortfeasor. The rule is set forth in Restatement, Third, of Torts: Apportionment of Liability (2000).

§ 22. Indemnity

(a) When two or more persons are or may be liable for the same harm and one of them discharges the liability of another in whole or in part by settlement or discharge of judgment, the person discharging the liability is entitled to recover indemnity in the amount paid to the plaintiff, plus reasonable legal expenses, if:

>   (1) the indemnitor has agreed by contract to indemnify the indemnitee, or
>
>   (2) the indemnitee
>
>   (i) was not liable except vicariously for the tort of the indemnitor, or
>
>   (ii) was not liable except as a seller of a product supplied to the indemnitee by the indemnitor and the indemnitee was not independently culpable.
>
>   (b) A person who is otherwise entitled to recover indemnity pursuant to contract may do so even if the party against whom indemnity is sought would not be liable to the plaintiff.

Consider the following examples:

(1) An employer is held liable for the negligent driving of an employee who causes injury. The liability of the employer is not based on his own fault but rather on the doctrine of respondeat superior that holds an employer liable for the torts of his employees performed in the scope of employment. The employer is entitled to total indemnity from the employee for the full amount of the judgment rendered against her.

(2) The owner of a car is held liable for the negligent driving of a friend to whom he lent his car. The owner is not held liable under the doctrine of respondeat superior since the lender is not his employee. Liability is based on a statute which holds the owner of a car liable for the negligence of anyone who drove his car with the owner's permission. If the owner pays a judgment based on the negligence of the lendee, he is entitled to total indemnity from the lendee whose negligent conduct caused the plaintiff's harm.

(3) A retailer is held liable for selling a defective electric tea kettle. The wiring in the tea kettle was defective and caused a fire that destroyed the plaintiff's home. Under the rule of strict liability, the seller of a defective product is liable for harm caused by the defect even though he could not discover the defect. If the retailer pays a judgment to the plaintiff for the loss of her home, the retailer may recover total indemnity from the manufacturer who was responsible for the defective wiring.

D. SETTLEMENT AND RELEASE

The overwhelming majority of tort cases are never litigated; they are settled by the parties before trial. Even with high settlement rates, the judicial backlog for a typical tort case is huge. It is common to wait four or five years to get to trial. When joint tortfeasors are involved, the problem of settlement can grow very complex.

At common law, settlement with one tortfeasor released all joint tortfeasors from liability. This rule discouraged settlements, since plaintiffs were unwilling to settle when the consequence of settlement was to surrender their rights against other joint tortfeasors. Courts utilized a range of techniques to bypass the rule that a release of one joint tortfeasor effected a release of all. Some allowed a suit against a nonsettling tortfeasor when the plaintiff executed a covenant not to sue with the settling tortfeasor. *See* Cox v. Pearl Investment Co., 450 P.2d 60 (Colo. 1969). Such a contract was treated as a separate agreement with the settler and not a release of the joint tortfeasor. Other states would allow suit against the nonsettler when the plaintiff expressly reserved his right to sue in the release with the settling tortfeasor. Most recently, legislatures have provided that a release of one tortfeasor does not release other joint tortfeasors unless the release specifically so provides. *See, e.g.,* N.Y. Gen. Oblig. Law § 15-108(a) (2001). *See also* Restatement, Third, of Torts: Apportionment of Liability § 24(b) (2000).

SETTLING TORTFEASORS AND CONTRIBUTION

One intractable problem continues to haunt the settlement process when joint tortfeasors are involved. One defendant settles with the plaintiff and the plaintiff reserves his right to sue the remaining tortfeasor. The nonsettling tortfeasor goes to trial and suffers a substantial judgment. May the litigating defendant who loses the lawsuit turn to the settling defendant and seek contribution for the damages he has paid out as a result of the judgment?

If contribution against the settling defendant is permitted, defendants will be discouraged from entering into settlements; under such a rule, settlement may not buy the settler peace but may only delay the lawsuit for a later day. On the other hand, if contribution against the settling defendant is not allowed and the judgment is reduced only by the dollar amount of the settlement, a "sweetheart settlement" between friendly parties may leave the nonsettling tortfeasor holding the bag. A succession of Uniform Contribution Among Tortfeasor Acts have dealt with this problem in different ways. The 1939 Act left the settling tortfeasor liable for contribution (thus discouraging settlement) and the 1955 Act adjusted the rule slightly by releasing the settling tortfeasor from contribution if, but only if, the settlement had been made in good faith. Section 23 of the Restatement, Third, of Torts: Allocation of Liability (2000) bars contribution against the settling party who obtains a release from the plaintiff.

The Uniform Comparative Fault Act, promulgated in 1979, takes a markedly different approach to resolving this problem. The act provides for allocation of fault for each party in the action. Section 6 of the Act provides:

> A release, covenant not to sue, or similar agreement entered into by a claimant and a person liable discharges that person from all liability for contribution, but it does not discharge any other persons liable upon the same claim unless it so provides. However, the claim of the releasing person against other persons is reduced by the amount of the released person's equitable share of the obligation, determined in accordance with the provisions of [another] Section. . . .

A simple hypothetical demonstrates how this works. Consider the following example propounded in a leading treatise:[1]

> Assume plaintiff (P) has suffered $100,000 in damages because of the combined negligence of two defendants (D1 and D2). Plaintiff settles with D1 for $10,000 and proceeds to trial against D2. In a jurisdiction following the Uniform Act, the jury finds P 10% at fault, D1 60% at fault, and D2 30% at fault. Had P not settled with D1, P would have received a judgment against both defendants for 90% of P's damages (D1's 60% plus D2's 30%) or $90,000. Under the Uniform Act's principle of joint-and-several liability, P could have recovered $90,000 from either joined defendant. But because P has settled with D1, P's judgment under the Uniform Act is reduced by D1's share of the fault; thus P receives a judgment not for 90% of the damages, but only for 90% less 60% (D1's share), or 30%. This amounts to a $30,000 judgment against D2; when added to the $10,000 received in settlement from D1, P has received a total of $40,000 — as opposed to the $90,000 P would have received had P not settled. Settling with D1 has cost plaintiff $50,000.

Comparative Negligence: Law and Practice § 19.10[6] (1995). In short, plaintiff settled out not only the dollar amount of the claim with the settling tortfeasor, but also the percentage of fault that will ultimately be attributed to him. Under this approach, plaintiff can no longer profitably enter into a sweetheart settlement with the settling tortfeasor. If the defendant's fault percentage is higher than plaintiff has estimated, the difference comes out of the plaintiff's pocket.

Although reduction of the plaintiff's claim against the nonsettling tortfeasor by the percentage of fault a court ultimately attributes to him is certain to prevent collusive settlements, it may discourage plaintiffs from settling. Settlement turns into a high-stakes guessing game. If the settler's fault turns out to be higher than plaintiff contemplated, the plaintiff bears the loss of the miscalculation.

Another problem requiring resolution concerns a tortfeasor who settles out and receives a full release from the plaintiff, extinguishing the liability of all parties. The tortfeasor then seeks contribution from the nonsettlers. Most states allow contribution. *See, e.g.,* Ariz. Rev. Stat. Ann. § 12-2501(D) (West 1994); Iowa Code Ann. § 668.5(2) (West 1998); Mass. Gen. Laws Ann. Ch. 231B, § 1(c) (West 2000); Or. Rev. Stat. § 31.800 (2001); 42 Pa. Cons. Stat. Ann. § 8324(c) (1998); Tenn. Code Ann. § 29-11-103 (2000); Va. Code. Ann. § 8.01-35.1 (2011). *Also see* Sullivan v. Robertson Drug Co., Inc., 639 S.E.2d 250 (2007). A few states take the position that a settling tortfeasor waives all contribution rights. *See, e.g.,* N.Y. Gen. Oblig. Law § 15-108(c) (McKinney 2001). Why should a settling tortfeasor not be entitled to contribution if, in fact, his or her payment exceeds his or her proportional share of fault? But, note that in Murphy v. Florida Keys Electric Co-op. Assn., 329 F.3d 1311 (11th Cir. 2003), the court held "that a settling defendant cannot bring a suit for contribution against a nonsettling defendant who was not released from liability to the plaintiff by the settlement agreement." *Id.* at 1313. The court reasoned that such a settling defendant settles only its proportionate share of the total damages, and the

---

1. Copyright © 1995 by Mathew Bender & Co., Inc. Reprinted with permission from *Comparative Negligence: Law and Practice.* All rights reserved.

amount that remains is determined at trial. *Id.* at 1314. The nonsettling tortfeasor is liable only to the plaintiff, not to the settling defendant.

An interesting issue arose in Ready v. United/Goedecke Services, Inc., 905 N.E.2d 725 (Ill. 2009). Plaintiff sued several defendants and settled with all but one. In the trial against the remaining defendant it argued that since under Illinois law, if any defendant's fault was below 25 percent, liability is several only, the court should have permitted the defendant to introduce the fault of the settling defendants. The court disagreed and held that the settling defendants were not within the interpretation of the statute that abolished the common law rule of joint and several liability and that the statute "was never intended to include settling tortfeasors in the apportionment of fault." *Id.* at 733.

For treatments of the problems attendant to settlement, *see* Lewis A. Kornhauser & Richard L. Revesz, *Settlements Under Joint and Several Liability*, 68 N.Y.U. L. Rev. 427 (1993); Jean Macchiaroli Eggen, *Understanding State Contribution Laws and Their Effect on the Settlement of Mass Torts Actions*, 73 Tex. L. Rev. 1701 (1995); Daniel Klerman, *Settling Multidefendant Lawsuits: The Advantage of Conditional Setoff Rules*, 25 J. Legal Stud. 445 (1996).

E. WHERE THE ISSUE OF DIVISIBILITY OF DAMAGES IS UNCLEAR

In general, a defendant should be held liable only for the damages that she causes. If damages can be reasonably apportioned between two tortfeasors, then the issue of apportionment should be left to the trier of fact. Thus, if *D1*'s car collides with plaintiff and causes damage to her right arm, and ten seconds later *D2*'s car hits plaintiff and causes damage to her left arm, the jury should be asked to apportion damages as best they can. It may be that the injury to both arms caused the plaintiff to suffer general pain and suffering. Nonetheless, in this imperfect world, some reasonable attempt at apportionment is better than holding both defendants jointly and severally liable. *See* Restatement, Second, of Torts § 433A, comment *b*. However, some cases present great difficulties in apportionment.

MICHIE v. GREAT LAKES STEEL DIVISION, NATIONAL STEEL CORP.
495 F.2d 213 (6th Cir. 1974)

EDWARDS, Circuit Judge.

This is an interlocutory appeal from a District Judge's denial of a motion to dismiss filed by three corporations which are defendants-appellants herein. . . .

Appellants' motion to dismiss was based upon the contention that each plaintiff individually had failed to meet the requirement of a $10,000 amount in controversy for diversity jurisdiction set forth in 28 U.S.C. § 1332 (1970).

The facts in this matter, as alleged in the pleadings, are somewhat unique. Thirty-seven persons, members of thirteen families residing near LaSalle, Ontario,

Canada, have filed a complaint against three corporations which operate seven plants in the United States immediately across the Detroit River from Canada. Plaintiffs claim that pollutants emitted by plants of defendants are noxious in character and that their discharge in the ambient air violates various municipal and state ordinances and laws. They assert that the discharges represent a nuisance and that the pollutants are carried by air currents onto their premises in Canada, thereby damaging their persons and property. Each plaintiff individually claims damages ranging from $11,000 to $35,000 from all three corporate defendants jointly and severally. There is, however, no assertion of joint action or conspiracy on the part of defendants. . . .

We believe the principal question presented by this appeal may be phrased thus: Under the law of the State of Michigan, may multiple defendants, whose independent actions of allegedly discharging pollutants into the ambient air thereby allegedly create a nuisance, be jointly and severally liable to multiple plaintiffs for numerous individual injuries which plaintiffs claim to have sustained as a result of said actions, where said pollutants mix in the air so that their separate effects in creating the individual injuries are impossible to analyze.

Appellants argue that the law applicable is that of the State of Michigan and that Michigan law does not allow for joint and several liability on the part of persons charged with maintaining a nuisance. They cite and rely on an old Michigan case. Robinson v. Baugh, 31 Mich. 290 (1875). They also quote and rely upon Restatement of Torts (First) § 881:

> Where two or more persons, each acting independently, create or maintain a situation which is a tortious invasion of a landowner's interest in the use and enjoyment of land by interfering with his quiet, light, air or flowing water, each is liable only for such proportion of the harm caused to the land or of the loss of enjoyment of it by the owner as his contribution to the harm bears to the total harm. . . .

This court is of the view that this is not the state of the law in Michigan with respect to air pollution. In the absence of any Michigan cases on point, analogous Michigan cases in the automobile negligence area involving questions of joint liability after the simultaneous impact of vehicles and resultant injuries, are instructive. . . .

In Maddux v. Donaldson, 362 Mich. 425, [108 N.W.2d 33] the Michigan Supreme Court cites Landers v. East Texas Salt Water Disposal Company, 151 Tex. 251, 248 S.W.2d 731, a pollution case, in support of the above stated proposition. The court indicated that

> . . . it is clear that there is a manifest unfairness in putting on the injured party the impossible burden of proving the specific shares of harm done by each. . . . Such results are simply the law's callous dullness to innocent sufferers. One would think that the obvious meanness [sic] of letting wrongdoers go scot free in such cases would cause the courts to think twice and to suspect some fallacy in their rule of law.

Plaintiffs contend that the *Maddux*, . . . language applies here since there is no possibility of dividing the injuries herein alleged to have occurred and that it is impossible to judge which of the alleged tortfeasors caused what harm.

It is the opinion of this court that the rule of *Maddux, supra,* and *Landers, supra,* cited therein is the better, and applicable rule in this air pollution case.

On this point we affirm the decision of the District Judge. This complaint appears to have been filed under the diversity jurisdiction of the federal courts. All parties have agreed that Michigan law alone controls.

Like most jurisdictions, Michigan has had great difficulty with the problems posed in tort cases by multiple causes for single or indivisible injuries. . . .

We believe that the issue was decided in the lengthy consideration given by the Michigan court in the *Maddux* case. There Justice Talbot Smith (now Senior Judge, United States District Court for the Eastern District of Michigan, Southern Division) in an opinion for the court majority (joined by the writer of this opinion) held:

> It is our conclusion that if there is competent testimony, adduced either by plaintiff or defendant, that the injuries are factually and medically separable, and that the liability for all such injuries and damages, or parts thereof, may be allocated with reasonable certainty to the impacts in turn, the jury will be instructed accordingly and mere difficulty in so doing will not relieve the triers of the facts of this responsibility. This merely follows the general rule that "where the independent concurring acts have caused distinct and separate injuries to the plaintiff, or where some reasonable means of apportioning the damages is evident, the courts generally will not hold the tort-feasors jointly and severally liable."
>
> But if, on the other hand, the triers of the facts conclude that they cannot reasonably make the division of liability between the tort-feasors, this is the point where the road of authority divides. Much ancient authority, not in truth precedent, would say that the case is now over, and that plaintiff shall take nothing. . . . Such precedents are not apt. When the triers of the facts decide that they cannot make a division of injuries we have, by their own finding, nothing more or less than an indivisible injury, and the precedents as to indivisible injuries will control. They were well summarized in Cooley on Torts in these words: "Where the negligence of two or more persons concur in producing a single, indivisible injury, then such persons are jointly and severally liable, although there was no common duty, common design, or concert action." Maddux v. Donaldson, 362 Mich. 425, 432-33, 108 N.W.2d 33, 36 (1961). . . .

We recognize, of course, that the *Maddux* . . . [case] involve[s] multiple collisions causing allegedly indivisible injuries. Hence, appellants are free to argue that the rule stated does not necessarily apply to the nuisance category of torts with which we deal here. Indeed, appellants call our attention to what appears to be a contrary rule applicable to nuisance cases referred to in the *Maddux* opinion. Restatement of Torts (First) § 881.

In the latest Restatement, however, both the old and the newer rule are recognized and as the Michigan court held in *Maddux,* the question of whether liability of alleged polluters is joint or several is left to the trier of the facts. Where the injury itself is indivisible, the judge or jury must determine whether or not it is practicable to apportion the harm among the tortfeasors. If not, the entire liability may be imposed upon one (or several) tortfeasors subject, of course, to subsequent right of contribution among the joint offenders.

Perhaps the best summary of the rationale for such a rule is found in Harper and James:

> In the earlier discussion of the substantive liability of joint tort-feasors and independent concurring wrongdoers who have produced indivisible harm it was indicated that there were four categories into which these parties may be placed: situations in which (1) the actors knowingly join in the performance of the tortious act or acts; (2) the actors fail to perform a common duty owed to the plaintiff; (3) there is a special relationship between the parties (e.g., master and servant or joint entrepreneurs); (4) although there is no concerted action nevertheless the independent acts of several actors concur to produce indivisible harmful consequences. . . .

While the Restatement of Torts contains a short and apparently simple statement of the rule in category four, this type of situation has caused a great deal of disagreement in the courts. Here joint and several liability is sometimes imposed for the harm caused by the independent concurring acts of a number of persons. In all the situations in which such recovery is permitted the court must find first that the harm for which the plaintiff seeks damages is "indivisible." This can mean that the harm is not even theoretically divisible (as death or total destruction of a building) or that the harm, while theoretically divisible, is single in a practical sense so far as the plaintiff's ability to apportion it among the wrongdoers is concerned (as where a stream is polluted as a result of refuse from several factories). In the first type of case almost uniformly courts will permit entire recovery from any or all defendants. There is conflict, however, in the second situation, with some well-reasoned recent cases recognizing that the plaintiff's right to recover for his harm should not depend on his ability to apportion the damage but that this is a problem which is properly left with the defendants themselves. 1 F. Harper & F. James, The Law of Torts § 10.1 at 697-98, 701-02 (1956) (Footnotes omitted.) . . .

Assuming plaintiffs in this case prove injury and liability as to several tortfeasors, the net effect of Michigan's new rule is to shift the burden of proof as to which one was responsible and to what degree from the injured party to the wrongdoers. The injustice of the old rule is vividly illustrated in an early Michigan case, Frye v. City of Detroit, . . . 239 N.W. 886 (Mich. 1932). There a pedestrian was struck by an automobile, thrown in the path of a street car and struck again. Since his widow could not establish which impact killed him, a verdict was directed against her case.

Since our instant case has not been tried, we do not speculate about what the facts may show, either as to injury or liability. But it is obvious from the briefs that appellant corporations intend to make the defense that if there was injury, other corporations, persons and instrumentalities contributed to the pollution of the ambient air so as to make it impossible to prove whose emissions did what damage to plaintiffs' persons or homes. Like the District Judge, we see a close analogy between this situation and the *Maddux* case. We believe the Michigan Supreme Court would do so likewise. . . .

Like the District Judge, we believe that the Michigan courts would apply the *Maddux* principles to the case at bar. Under *Maddux,* each plaintiff's complaint should be read as alleging $11,000 or more in damages against each defendant.

Therefore, the principle of Zahn v. International Paper Co., . . . (1973), which would disallow aggregation of plaintiffs' claims for the purpose of establishing diversity jurisdiction, does not apply to this case. . . .

As modified, [on another issue not included in this opinion] the judgment of the District Court is affirmed.

FOOD FOR THOUGHT

Why should plaintiffs not be required to undertake discovery to determine what percentage of pollution came from each defendant? Why is this not a case where the contribution of each defendant can be determined? Even if the burden of proof on apportionment is shifted to the defendant, shouldn't each defendant be allowed to show how much pollutant it added to the air and then pay its fair share? If this case were to take place today and the litigation were to take place in a state that has abolished joint and several liability, would not each defendant be held liable only for its percentage of fault that contributed to the total harm? Once a court has held that the harm is indivisible and that the defendants are joint tortfeasors, then they would be subject to the rules governing joint tortfeasors. Instead of being held liable for the percentage of the harm that they caused, they would now he held liable for their percentage of fault. If cause cannot be apportioned, that is not true of fault. In doing such a fault apportionment, would we not take into consideration the causal contribution to the harm? Is there now to be a doctrine of comparative cause-fault?

In Burlington Northern and Santa Fe Railway Co. v. United States, 129 S. Ct. 1870 (2009), the Supreme Court reversed the Ninth Circuit and found that the defendant had produced sufficient evidence that its contaminants were only responsible for 10 percent of the total site contamination and was thus not jointly and severally liable for all the environmental damages on the site. The Court also held that a manufacturer of a toxic chemical is not liable under the Comprehensive Environmental Response, Compensation and Liability Act (CERCLA) merely because it has knowledge that spills and leaks will take place; the manufacturer must have entered into the sale of the toxic chemical with the intention that "at least a portion of the product" would be disposed of during the transfer process. Evidence of minor or accidental spills does not support liability.

See also United States v. Capital Tax Corp., 545 F.3d 525 (7th Cir. 2008) (defendant was jointly and severally liable for contamination on properties it did not own because contaminants migrated to those parcels of land); United States v. Manzo, 279 F. Supp. 2d 558 (D.N.J. 2003) (defendants were unable to prove divisibility and, as a result, they were jointly and severally liable for cleanup costs associated with the release of hazardous substances at a superfund site). *Also see* In re Methyl Tertiary Butyl Ether Products Liability Litigation, 447 F. Supp. 2d 289 (S.D.N.Y. 2006) (given that there were almost 50 defendants, court found that it would be fundamentally unfair to hold the defendants jointly and severally liable when there are a large number of defendants). Typically, the joint and several doctrine is applied when only a few defendants are involved. When a large number of defendants are sued, the possibility exists that a defendant who bears only a small portion of responsibility will be held liable for all the damages.

Although the above cases agree with *Michie* that there must be reasonable grounds to apportion damages, we repeat our observation that with a comparative fault scheme in place, in most jurisdictions the defendants will be liable only for their percentage of fault if joint and several liability has been abolished.

DILLON v. TWIN STATE GAS & ELECTRIC CO.
163 A. 111 (N.H. 1932)

[In a negligence action arising from a minor's death by electrocution after falling from a bridge and grabbing defendant utility company's live wires, defendant appealed New Hampshire trial court's entry of judgment for plaintiff administrator of decedent's estate.]

ALLEN, Justice.

The bridge was in the compact part of the city. It was in evidence that at one time the defendant's construction foreman had complained to the city marshal about its use by boys as a playground and in his complaint had referred to the defendant's wires. The only wires were those over the bridge superstructure. From this evidence and that relating to the extent of the practice for boys to climb up to and upon the horizontal girders, an inference that the defendant had notice of the practice was reasonable. The occasion for the complaint might be found due to apprehension of danger from proximity to the wires. This only came about from climbing upon the upper framework of the bridge. There was no suggestion of danger in any use of the bridge confined to the floor level.

The use of the girders brought the wires leading to the lamp close to those making the use, and as to them it was in effect the same as though the wires were near the floor of the bridge. While the current in the wires over the bridge was mechanically shut off during the day-time, other wires carried a commercial current, and there was a risk from many causes of the energizing of the bridge wires at any time. It is claimed that these causes could not be overcome or prevented. If they could not, their consequences might be. Having notice of the use made of the girders and knowing the chance of the wires becoming charged at any time, the defendant may not say that it was not called upon to take action until the chance happened. Due care demanded reasonable measures to forestall the consequences of a chance current if the chance was too likely to occur to be ignored.

The evidence tended to show that changes in the construction and arrangement of the lamp and its wires were practical. So that the wires running from the post to the lamp would be out of the way of one on the girders, a bracket carrying the wires inside it and specially insulated wires running down from a post to be set up on the outer side of the girder were testified to as suitable measures and devices which would avoid or lessen the danger of contact. The evidence to the contrary is not conclusive.

The defendant, however, makes the contention that it owed no duty of care to those not using the bridge in a rightful manner to make their wrongful use safe. If a duty might arise towards such a person as a workman painting the girders, yet it says there was none towards a boy in the decedent's position of climbing and mounting the girders without right.

The present state of the law here in force does not support the claim. The duty not to carelessly intervene against known trespassers is not doubtful, and known trespassers include those whose presence should in reason be anticipated. . . . Knowledge or notice of actual presence may be necessary to give notice of probable later presence, but when the latter notice is once acquired, the duty of care may not be avoided by ignorance of actual presence thereafter. . . .

In passing upon the issue of reasonableness, relative and comparative considerations are made. In general, when the danger is great and the wrongful conduct of the injured person is not serious, it is reasonable for the law to find a relationship and to impose a duty of protection. A defendant in his own interest causing dangerous forces to operate or dangerous conditions to exist should reasonably protect those likely to be exposed to them and not reasonably in fault for the exposure. . . .

The circumstances of the decedent's death give rise to an unusual issue of its cause. In leaning over from the girder and losing his balance he was entitled to no protection from the defendant to keep from falling. Its only liability was in exposing him to the danger of charged wires. If but for the current in the wires he would have fallen down on the floor of the bridge or into the river, he would without doubt have been either killed or seriously injured. Although he died from electrocution, yet if by reason of his preceding loss of balance he was bound to fall except for the intervention of the current, he either did not have long to live or was to be maimed. In such an outcome of his loss of balance the defendant deprived him, not of a life of normal expectancy, but of one too short to be given pecuniary allowance, in one alternative, and not of normal, but of limited, earning capacity, in the other.

If it were found that he would have thus fallen with death probably resulting, the defendant would not be liable unless for conscious suffering found to have been sustained from the shock. In that situation his life or earning capacity had no value. To constitute actionable negligence there must be damage, and damage is limited to those elements the statute prescribes.

If it should be found that but for the current he would have fallen with serious injury, then the loss of life or earning capacity resulting from the electrocution would be measured by its value in such injured condition. Evidence that he would be crippled would be taken into account in the same manner as though he had already been crippled.

His probable future but for the current thus bears on liability as well as damages. Whether the shock from the current threw him back on the girder or whether he would have recovered his balance, with or without the aid of the wire he took hold of if it had not been charged, are issues of fact, as to which the evidence as it stands may lead to different conclusions.

Exception overruled.

All concurred.

FOOD FOR THOUGHT

Is this a correct statement of the holding? If plaintiff would have been rendered a quadriplegic by the fall in any event, he is to be treated as a quadriplegic when he hit the electrified wire. Thus, damages should reflect the expected life span of a quadriplegic with diminished capacities and not that of a healthy youngster who can enjoy the full range of pleasures and opportunities that are normal to a person of such young age.

chapter 10

Strict Liability

All of the liability rules we have considered up to now are based on wrongful conduct, which includes both intentional torts and negligence. This chapter introduces liability without fault — strict liability based merely on the defendant's lawful conduct having caused harm to the plaintiff. Under strict liability, the defendant actor who causes harm is liable even if the actor exercises reasonable care and does not intend to interfere in any way with the plaintiff. It is not useful to equate strict liability with absolute liability. The phrase "absolute liability" suggests that the defendant's liability has no limits. In that sense, absolute liability does not exist in American tort law. As you will discover, strict liability is subject to important limitations in the form of limits on the activities that trigger liability, proximate cause, plaintiff's fault, and the like.

Contrasting strict liability with negligence is useful. Under negligence, when an actor exercises reasonable care the accident victim bears the residual accident costs caused by the actor's conduct — those accident costs that are cheaper to incur than to make costly efforts to avoid — and the actor escapes negligence-based tort liability. Thus, when actors take adequate care under negligence, you might say that the accident victims are "strictly liable" for the residual accident costs. In contrast, holding actors liable strictly, rather than merely for their negligence, shifts responsibility for the residual accident costs from the victims to the actors. Thus, one explanation for why strict liability is appropriate is that it is only fair, as between the innocent victims who suffer harm and the innocent (non-negligent) actors who cause harm, that the actors should bear the accident costs. This is especially true when the actors are the ones primarily benefiting from the activities in which, after all, they choose to engage. Is there an efficiency-based reason why moving from negligence to strict liability is justified? Will making the move cause actors to be more careful? If not, are there *any* gains in efficiency to be had from moving to strict liability?

Recall that the duty of reasonable care applies to all activities — the negligence rule says that *any actor* who acts negligently in connection with *any activity* is liable for the harm the actor's negligence proximately causes. In effect, the negligence concept itself identifies the actors and activities to be held liable. When we eliminate negligence as a linchpin liability concept, we must identify ahead of time which actors and which activities will be strictly liable for which harms. These definitions might be said to identify the boundaries of strict liability. As you work through the materials in this chapter, you should keep an eye open for how the courts handle the boundary problems. For example, if the courts adopted an approach that held all actors who engage in grossly antisocial activities strictly liable, do you suppose that the "grossly antisocial" question would be determined by juries on a case-by-case basis, or categorically by judges, over time, as a matter of law?

A. POSSESSION OF ANIMALS

One of the earliest forms of strict liability at common law involved those who possess, confine, and manage animals that are capable of causing harm both to persons and property when they escape confinement. Most of the reported cases involve animals falling into three basic categories: (1) livestock, including cattle, horses, sheep, goats, and the like; (2) wild animals confined for a variety of reasons, both personal and commercial; and (3) dogs, cats, and other domesticated animals other than livestock. In general, courts impose strict liability on possessors of livestock and wild animals, but they hold possessors of domestic animals in the third category — dogs, cats, and the like — liable only if the plaintiff proves that the defendant pet owner knew ahead of time that the animal was prone to violence. Regarding livestock, the overwhelming majority of cases involve damage caused to land, crops, and other property interests by the escaping animals. *See* Restatement, Third, of Torts § 21 (strict liability for physical harm caused by intrusion of livestock onto land of another). American jurisdictions differ on the issue of whether plaintiffs must show that they took reasonable steps, such as fencing, to protect their property interests.

Are owners of livestock strictly liable for harm their straying animals cause other than damage to the lands of others? In Hastings v. Sauve, 21 N.Y.3d 122 (N.Y. 2013), the plaintiff suffered injury when she drove her car into a cow in the road. The cow allegedly strayed from the defendant's property. Instead of imposing strict liability, the court held that an owner of livestock "may be liable under ordinary tort-law principles when a farm animal . . . is negligently allowed to stray from property on which the animal is kept." *Id.* At 125-26. See also Wrinkle v. Norman, 44 Kan. App. 2d 950, 957 (Kan. Ct. App. 2010) overruled on other grounds Wrinkle v. Norman, 297 Kan. 420 (Kan. 2013) (holding that "strict liability . . . do[es] not apply in livestock escape cases. In order to recover for damages, the injured party must prove negligence"). However, Restatement, Third, of Torts § 23 indicates that if an animal owner knows of her animal's dangerous tendencies, which may include a tendency to stray, the owner will no longer merely face a negligence standard, but will also face strict liability for the harm caused by her animal.

In Andersen v. Two Dot Ranch, 49 P.3d 1011 (Wyo. 2002), the Supreme Court of Wyoming faced a case of first impression when motorists collided with defendant's livestock that had entered a public highway in a posted "open range" zone. Western states often permit, sometimes by statute, livestock owners to graze their cows in open areas — without fences. An "open range" policy immunizes owners from liability when their livestock enter another's land. Before this case, Wyoming had not faced a personal injury case that resulted from livestock entering a public highway. In affirming the trial court's grant of summary judgment in favor of the defendant, the Wyoming high court refused to impose strict liability. Instead, both motorists and livestock owners simply owe a reciprocal and general duty of care to each other in posted "open range" zones. *See also* Moreland v. Adams, 152 P.3d 558 (Idaho 2007) (court rejected plaintiff's attempt to narrow the open range immunity afforded by Idaho statute).

The cases involving wild animals are, as you might have guessed, among the most interesting. The leading English decision is Filburn v. People's Palace & Aquarium, Ltd., 25 Q.B. Div. 258 (1890). Defendants were publicly exhibiting an elephant when the huge beast went on a rampage, harming the plaintiff. The jury found specially that defendants did not know beforehand that the elephant might go crazy, but the trial court entered judgment for plaintiff on a general verdict. The Court of Appeal affirmed, explaining (25 Q.B. Div. at 260): "It cannot possibly be said that an elephant comes within the class of animals known to be harmless by nature . . . and consequently it falls within the class of animals that a man keeps at his peril. . . ." In Zinter v. Oswskey, 633 N.W.2d 278 (Wis. Ct. App. 2001), the appellate court reversed a lower court's grant of summary judgment, holding that a jury could find defendant's rabbit that injured the plaintiff's finger to be either a wild species of rabbit, and thus a wild animal, or a domesticated species. What about a wild animal that someone domesticates and keeps as a pet? In Gallick v. Barto, 828 F. Supp. 1168 (M.D. Pa. 1993), the court held that a pet ferret that unexpectedly bit a child was a "wild animal with domestic propensities," and imposed strict liability on the owner/possessor. David L. Herman, *California Law and Ferrets: Are They Truly "Wild Weasels"?*, 23 Environs Envtl. L. & Pol'y 37 (2000), argues that ferrets are not wild animals and that the *Gallick* decision was wrongly decided. An exception to the general rule imposing strict liability for wild animals concerns public zookeepers, who are liable only if shown to have been negligent. Why do you suppose the court in *Gallick* determined that the ferret was a wild animal, while the court in *Zinter* gave the issue of whether a rabbit was domestic or wild to the jury?

Even if a plaintiff can prove that the animal that injured him was a wild animal, he still has to establish that the defendant in fact owned or controlled the animal. While discussions regarding ownership are typically reserved for a course in property, Woods-Leber v. Hyatt Hotels of Puerto Rico, Inc., 124 F.3d 47 (1st Cir. 1997), provides a straightforward example of ownership and possession issues. In *Leber*, a hotel guest sunbathed near the hotel pool when a mongoose attacked and bit her. The mongoose came from a swamp area that bordered the hotel. The guest sued the hotel for her injuries, claiming, inter alia, that the court should hold the hotel strictly liable for the harm caused by wild animals on its property. The appellate court affirmed a grant of summary judgment for the defendant, holding that, since the hotel did not own the swamp area behind the hotel in which the mongoose lived it did not control the animal and thus could not be strictly liable for damages that the animal caused.

What about dogs and cats? The general rule is that the owner/possessor of a domestic animal other than livestock is liable to an injured plaintiff only if the owner/possessor knows of her particular animal's dangerous propensities. *See* Restatement, Third, of Torts § 23. The most obvious way to establish prior knowledge is for the plaintiff to prove that the dog or cat in question had, to the defendant's knowledge, attacked someone else before. This has led to the common observation that "every dog is entitled to one bite," implying that the first time a dog bites someone comes as a surprise to its owner. This is, of course, an overstatement. Even if the plaintiff is a dog's first victim, the defendant owner/possessor will be liable if the plaintiff can prove prior knowledge from some other source. Are owners of breeds of dogs generally known to be violent assumed to have knowledge of their own pet's dangerous propensities? Probably not. See Nutt v. Florio, 75 Mass. App. Ct. 482 (Ma. App. 2009) (noting that "the decision to create a species-specific standard of care is likely one for the Legislature"); *see also* Ferrara ex re. Com. Of Massachusetts Dept. of Social Services v. Marra, 823 A.2d 1134 (R.I. 2003).

Often, the issue of the owner's knowledge of a domesticated animal's dangerous propensities is difficult to prove. Therefore, many state legislatures have intervened to protect dog bite victims by eliminating the common law requirement of knowledge. Some of these statutes are broad and seem to impose almost absolute liability. *See, e.g.,* Wis. Stat. § 174.02(1)(a) (2001) ("the owner of a dog is liable for the full amount of damages caused by the dog injuring or causing injury to a person, domestic animal, or property"). In fact, many of these statutes increase the damages in those cases where the defendant owner knows of the dangerous propensities. *See, e.g.,* Wis. Stat. § 174.02(1)(b) (2001) ("the owner of a dog is liable for 2 times the full amount of damages caused by the dog injuring or causing injury to a person, domestic animal or property if the owner was notified or knew that the dog previously injured or caused injury to a person, domestic animal or property").

The breadth of these statutes causes problems in some situations. Some courts have interpreted the Wisconsin statute to hold owners liable for any injury of which the dog is a but-for cause. *See* Helmeid v. American Mutual Insurance Co., 640 N.W.2d 565 (Wis. Ct. App. 2002) (a neighbor could recover against a dog owner after the neighbor went into the street to rescue the owner's escaped dog and was injured when she was bitten by the dog and hit by a car). However, this same court recognized that some limits must be placed on liability. In Alwin v. State Farm Fire and Casualty Co., 610 N.W.2d 218 (Wis. Ct. App. 2000), the appellate court refused to hold a dog owner liable for injuries caused to plaintiff after the plaintiff tripped over the defendant's dog. The court noted that while the literal language of the statute would permit application to this case, public policy compels the court to refuse to apply it.

While many states have addressed the liability of pet owners by statute, not all states have statutes that protect victims. In those states, courts are reluctant to abrogate the common law rule of prior knowledge. In Gehrts v. Batteen, 620 N.W.2d 775 (S.D. 2001), the plaintiff, who was bitten by defendant's eight-month-old German shepherd, argued that the knowledge requirement was outdated and that South Dakota should abrogate it in favor of strict liability. However, the Supreme Court of South Dakota refused to change the common law requirement. After analyzing many other states' statutes, the high court held that "the legislature is the proper place to decide such public policy questions." *Id.* at 779.

BARD v. JAHNKE
848 N.E.2d 463 (N.Y. 2006)

READ, J.

The accident underlying this litigation occurred on September 27, 2001 at Hemlock Valley Farms in Otsego County, a dairy farm owned and operated by defendant Reinhardt Jahnke and his wife in partnership with their two sons. At roughly 8:00 a.m., plaintiff Larry Bard, a self-employed carpenter, arrived at the farm to meet defendant John Timer, another self-employed carpenter. One of Jahnke's sons had asked Timer to repair ripped cow mattresses in a certain section — called the "low cow district" — of the farm's free-stall dairy barn. This large barn, which was divided into several sections, housed approximately 400 cows at the time, 130 of them in the low cow district. The repair work involved chiseling off the bolts fastening the damaged mattresses to the concrete base of a stall, stretching the mattresses and then refastening the bolts. Timer had asked Bard the day before if he would be interested in helping him carry out this task, and Bard had replied that he would.

Bard retrieved some tools from his truck and started to work at about 8:30 a.m. He testified that a number of cows wandered into the area as he was working. Further, he was "familiar with working in and around cows," which would "come up, drool on you, lick on you and everything else," and that he didn't "usually pay much attention to them." At about 9:00 a.m., as Bard was down on his knees removing bolts, he first noticed a bull "[w]hen he stepped in behind him" and "bellered" within a distance of two to three feet. Bard testified that he "slowly kind of looked around, and didn't know what to do at that point." As he "went to stand up," the bull "took [him] in the chest. [The bull] charged [him] then [and] proceeded to start slamming [him] into the pipes" in the stall. No one else was present in the low cow district at the time. Neither Jahnke nor anyone else associated with the farm knew ahead of time that Timer planned to repair the mattresses that day, or that Bard would be working for Timer to carry out this task.

Bard pulled himself outdoors through an opening at the bottom of the barn, and crawled over to his truck, where he lay for "quite awhile to get some wind and establish what was going on." He caught the attention of someone working in the field, whom he asked to call an ambulance. Bard's injuries included fractured ribs, a lacerated liver and exacerbation of a preexisting cervical spine condition.

The hornless dairy bull who injured Bard was named Fred. He was about 1½ years old, and had been the resident "cleanup" bull at the farm for at least six months prior to September 27, 2001. The cows and heifers on the farm are bred by artificial insemination. Fred was housed and roamed freely in the low cow district of the dairy barn so that he might impregnate cows stabled there who had failed to conceive by artificial insemination. Before this accident, Fred had concededly never threatened or injured any other farm animal or human being. As was the case with all the dairy bulls ever owned by Jahnke, a longtime dairy farmer, Fred was never chained, caged or barricaded within the barn. Prior to September 27, 2001, none of the bulls on any of the farms worked on or owned by Jahnke had ever acted aggressively toward, or injured, another farm animal or human being. . . .

Bard . . . commenced an action against both Jahnke and Timer to recover damages for his personal injuries, alleging causes of action sounding in strict liability and negligence. . . . [D]efendants cross-moved for summary judgment dismissing the complaint. Ruling on defendant's cross motion, Supreme Court first observed that New York's appellate courts had been "markedly consistent in applying the common-law vicious propensity rule to decide whether owners of dogs and cats were liable for injuries caused by their animals. . . . [H]owever, the court concluded that a different rule applied to owners of domestic animals other than dogs and cats. According to Supreme Court, these owners are subject to "some duty of enhanced care" to restrain or confine the animal or to warn a human being who might come into contact with it. Applying this rule to the facts, Supreme Court granted defendants' motions for summary judgment because Jahnke did not know that Bard would be at his farm or working in the dairy barn, and Timer was unaware of the cleanup bull's presence in the barn.

The Appellate Division affirmed, but on a different basis. . . . Noting that a bull is a domestic animal . . . the Court concluded that Jahnke was not liable for Bard's injuries unless he knew or should have known of the bull's vicious or violent propensities. The Court noted that the record contained no evince of this, and "[t]o the contrary, it contains competent evidence establishing that, prior to [Bard's] accident, the subject bull had never injured another person or animal or behaved in a hostile or threatening manner."

[Bard had submitted the affidavit of a professor of animal science, who opined that "bulls, in particular breeding bulls, are generally dangerous and vicious animals," and that therefore Jahnke should have restrained the bull or warned Bard of its presence. . . .]

Only two years ago, in [Collier v. Zambito, 807 N.E.2d 254 (2004)] we restated our long-standing rule

> that the owner of a domestic animal who either knows or should have known of that animal's vicious propensities will be held liable for the harm the animal causes as a result of those propensities. Vicious propensities include the propensity to do any act that might endanger the safety of the persons and property of others in a given situation. . . .

Once this knowledge is established, the owner faces strict liability.[1] We made two additional points in *Collier*, which bear repeating.

First, while knowledge of vicious propensities "may of course be established by proof of prior acts of a similar kind of which the owner had notice," a triable issue of fact as to whether the owner knew or should have known that its animal harbored vicious propensities may be raised by proof of something less. . . . In *Collier*, a case in which a dog bit a child, we gave the example of evidence that a dog had, for example, "been known to growl, snap or bare its teeth," or that "the owner chose to restrain the dog, and the manner in which the dog was restrained". . . . "In addition, an animal that behaves in a manner that would not necessarily be considered dangerous or ferocious, but nevertheless reflects a proclivity to act in a way that puts others at risk of harm, can be found to have vicious propensities — albeit only when such proclivity results in the injury giving rise to the lawsuit" (*id.*).

Here, Fred had never attacked any farm animal or human being before September 27, 2001. He had always moved unrestrained within the limits of the barn's low cow district, regularly coming into contact with other farm animals, farm workers and members of the Jahnke family without incident or hint of hostility. He had never acted in a way that put others at risk of harm. As a result, Bard cannot recover under our traditional rule.

Bard therefore argues alternatively that he can recover under a common-law cause of action for negligence, as expressed in Restatement (Second) of Torts § 518, Comments *g* and *h*. This common-law cause of action is, he claims, separate and apart from and in addition to our traditional rule.

Section 518 provides generally that the owner of a domestic animal, which the owner does not know or have reason to know to be abnormally dangerous, is nonetheless liable if he intentionally causes the animal to do harm, or is negligent in failing to prevent harm. Comment *g*, "*Knowledge of normal characteristics*" provides that

> [i]n determining the care that the keeper of a not abnormally dangerous domestic animal is required to exercise to keep it under control, the characteristics that are normal to its class are decisive, and one who keeps the animal is required to know the characteristics. Thus the keeper of a bull or stallion is required to take greater precautions to confine it to the land on which it is kept and to keep it under effective control when it is taken from the land than would be required of the keeper of a cow or gelding.

Comment *h*, "*Animals dangerous under particular circumstances*" states that

> [o]ne who keeps a domestic animal that possesses only those dangerous propensities that are normal to its class is required to know its normal habits and tendencies. He is therefore required to realize that even ordinarily gentle animals are likely to be dangerous under particular circumstances and to exercise reasonable

---

1. Our rule is virtually identical to Restatement (Second) of Torts § 509(1) (1977):

> A possessor of a domestic animal that he knows or has reason to know has dangerous propensities abnormal to its class, is subject to liability for harm done by the animal to another, although he has exercised the utmost care to prevent it from doing the harm.

care to prevent foreseeable harm. Thus the keeper of even a gentle bull must take into account the tendencies of bulls as a class to attack moving objects and must exercise greater precautions to keep his bull under complete control if he drives it upon a public highway. So, too, the keeper of an ordinarily gentle bitch or cat is required to know that while caring for her puppies or kittens she is likely to attack other animals and human beings.

Building on these provisions and their specific references to bulls, Bard contends that because Fred was not only a bull, but a breeding bull housed with the herd over whom he exercised dominance, Jahnke was negligent in failing to restrain Fred, or to warn non-farm personnel of his presence. But this is no different from arguing that Jahnke was negligent in that he *should have known* of Fred's vicious propensities because — as plaintiffs' expert put it — "bulls, in particular breeding bulls, are generally dangerous and vicious animals. . . ."

As already noted, an animal's propensity to cause injury may be proven by something other than prior comparably vicious acts. As a result, a common shorthand name for our traditional rule — the "one-bite rule" — is a misnomer. We have never, however, held that particular breeds or kinds of domestic animals are dangerous, and therefore when an individual animal of the breed or kind causes harm, its owner is charged with knowledge of vicious propensities. Similarly, we have never held that male domestic animals kept for breeding or female domestic animals caring for their young are dangerous as a class. We decline to do so now, or otherwise to dilute our traditional rule under the guise of a companion common-law cause of action for negligence. In sum, when harm is caused by a domestic animal, its owner's liability is determined solely by application of the rule articulated in *Collier*.

Accordingly, the order of Appellate Division should be affirmed, with costs.

R.S. SMITH, J. (dissenting).

Under the Restatement (Second) of Torts, the owner of a domestic animal who does not know or have reason to know that the animal is more dangerous than others of its class may still be liable for negligently failing to prevent the animal from inflicting an injury. This Court today becomes the first state court of last resort to reject the Restatement rule. I think that is a mistake. It leaves New York with an archaic, rigid rule, contrary to fairness and common sense, that will probably be eroded by ad hoc exceptions.

In this case, as the majority seems to recognize, a jury could have found Jahnke to be negligent, though he had no reason to think that Fred was any more dangerous than any other breeding bull. An expert's affidavit provides the unsurprising information that all breeding bulls are dangerous, because they "have high libido," and "will challenge or attack . . . unknown individuals, in order to establish dominance over the herd." . . .

Thus, if ordinary negligence principles apply here, this case should not have been dismissed. The Restatement says that ordinary negligence principles do apply: With exceptions not relevant here, "one who possesses or harbors a domestic animal that he does not know or have reason to know to be abnormally dangerous, is subject to liability for harm done by the animal if, but only if . . . he is negligent in failing to prevent the harm" (Restatement [Second] of Torts § 518[b][1977]). The Comments to this Restatement section, quoted in the majority opinion . . . point out the application of this rule specifically to bulls: "the keeper of a bull or stallion is required to take greater precautions . . . than . . . the keeper of a cow or gelding" (Restatement [Second] of Torts § 518, Comment *g*); "the keeper of even a gentle bull must take into account the tendencies of bulls as a class to attack moving objects" (§ 518, Comment *h*). . . .

For all the faults of modern tort law, and they are many, I do not think that this attempt to cling to the certainties of a distant era will work out well. The rule the majority adopts is contrary to simple fairness. Why should a person who is negligent in managing an automobile or a child be subject to liability, and not one who is negligent in managing a horse or bull? Why should a person hit by a subway train be able to recover and one hit by a breeding bull be left without a remedy? I think there are no good answers to these questions, and it is possible to imagine future cases that will put the rule adopted by the majority under strain. Suppose, for example, a variation on the facts of *Collier:* What if defendant there had encouraged a child to play not with a grown dog, but with a litter of puppies, thus predictably provoking an otherwise gentle mother dog to rage? Or suppose facts like those in Duren v. Kunkel, 814 S.W.2d 935 [Mo. 1991] [Holstein, J.], where a bull was stirred to attack because his owner negligently caused him to be driven through an area where fresh blood was on the ground? In such a case, we would either deny recovery to a deserving plaintiff, despite negligence more blatant than what Jahnke is accused of here, or we could invent a "mother dog" exception or a "fresh blood" exception to the rule adopted in this case. I think it would be wiser to follow the Restatement rule, as has almost every other state that has considered the question.

FOOD FOR THOUGHT

Some states have eliminated distinctions between livestock and domestic animals. In Young v. Shelby, 566 S.E.2d 426 (Ga. Ct. App. 2002), two bulls, owned by the defendant, injured the plaintiff while the plaintiff manned the gates to a pen. Both the plaintiff and the defendant were experienced cattlemen who planned to display the bulls during a beef exposition. The plaintiff sustained injury when one of the bulls, after being released from the trailer, bolted toward the gate and collided with a panel on the gate. The panel pierced through the plaintiff's thigh, knocking him down. The bulls then trampled over the plaintiff, causing more serious injuries. The appellate court sustained the trial court's grant of summary judgment for the defendant, holding that a bull is a domestic animal and thus an owner must have prior knowledge of the dangerous propensities. In this case, since no evidence of aggressive past behavior was presented, the plaintiff had not made out a case. The defendant also claimed that the plaintiff was an experienced cattleman and should have known how to protect himself from bulls. The court responded that a plaintiff must prove not only that the owner knew of the dangerous propensities, but also that the owner had knowledge superior to that of the plaintiff. The court seems to say that if the plaintiff, as an experienced cattleman, had the same knowledge of the dangerous propensities that the owner had, then the owner would not be held liable. Is the court correct in comparing the plaintiff's and defendant's knowledge? Is something else going on here?

The New York Court of Appeals reaffirmed its holding in *Bard* in Petrone v. Fernandez, 910 N.E.2d 993 (N.Y. 2009) (defendant's violation of a leash law was irrelevant in an action for harm caused by an unleashed animal; such a violation would be relevant in a negligence action, but strict liability based on defendant's knowledge of dangerous propensity is the only theory available to someone harmed by defendant's domesticated animal). Courts tend to be tough on plaintiffs who suffer injury arising from the inherent risks attendant to interaction with animals. For instance, in Levinson v. Owens, 176 Cal. App. 4th 1534 (Ca. App. 2009), the plaintiff attended a barbeque at the defendants' ranch. At the barbeque, the plaintiff was riding one of the defendants' horses in a field, when the horse suddenly began galloping, causing the plaintiff to fall and suffer injury. The appellate court affirmed the trial court's grant of summary judgment, holding that defendants were not liable because (1) horseback riding is an inherently dangerous activity, (2) the defendants did nothing to increase the risk inherent to horseback riding, and (3) it was reasonable for the defendants to rely upon the plaintiff's claims that she had prior experience in riding horses. See also Fenty v. Seven Meadows Farms, Inc. 108 A.D.3d 588 (N.Y. App. 2013).

In all of the cases considered thus far, the owners and possessors of domestic animals are sought to be held liable for having been instrumental in bringing the animal into contact with the plaintiff. In Bushnell v. Mott, 254 S.W.3d 451 (Tex. 2008), the defendant's dogs attacked and injured the plaintiff. Although the defendant did not know of any dangerous propensity, the plaintiff claimed that the defendant was negligent in failing to stop the attack once it began. The Texas high court reversed summary judgment for defendant, recognizing a cause of action for negligent handling independent of strict liability based on prior knowledge of dangerous propensity. Even though New York State does not recognize a negligence cause of action for an animal owner/possessor's conduct leading up to an attack, might New York courts allow a negligence claim on the facts in *Bushnell*— i.e., for failing to take reasonable steps to stop an attack once it has started?

hypo **60**

A owns a pot-bellied pig that he keeps as a house pet. *A* often walks the pig on the city sidewalks, controlled by a collar and leash. One day, however, *A* cannot find the collar and leash so he decides to take the pig out without a leash. Although the pig responds to commands like "sit" and "stay," it enjoys running free in open space. After walking for ten minutes without the collar and leash, the pig becomes excited and darts into the street. *B*, driving an automobile, swerves to miss the pig and collides with a parked car, suffering serious injury. *B* brings an action against *A* in a state that follows the common law strict liability standard. Will *B*'s strict liability claim survive a summary judgment motion by *A*?

B. ABNORMALLY DANGEROUS ACTIVITIES

FLETCHER v. RYLANDS
L.R. 1 Exch. 265 (1866)

[This action was originally tried at the Liverpool Summer Assizes in 1862, and resulted in a verdict for the plaintiff. An arbitrator, appointed to assess damages, was later empowered by court order to state a special case in the Exchequer for the purpose of obtaining that court's opinion on the novel question of law presented. In the Exchequer, two judges voted for the defendants and one for the plaintiff, and judgment was entered for the defendants. The plaintiff appealed to the next higher court, the Exchequer Chamber, the decision of which follows.]

BLACKBURN, J. This was a special case stated by an arbitrator, under an order of nisi prius, in which the question for the Court is stated to be, whether the plaintiff is entitled to recover any, and, if any, what damages from the defendants, by reason of the matters thereinbefore stated.

In the Court of Exchequer, the Chief Baron and Martin, B., were of opinion that the plaintiff was not entitled to recover at all, Bramwell, B., being of a different opinion. The judgment in the Exchequer was consequently given for the defendants, in conformity with the opinion of the majority of the court. The only question argued before us was, whether this judgment was right, nothing being said about the measure of damages in case the plaintiff should be held entitled to recover. We have come to the conclusion that the opinion of Bramwell, B., was right, and that the answer to the question should be that the plaintiff was entitled to recover damages from the defendants, by reason of the matters stated in the case, and consequently, that the judgment below should be reversed, but we cannot at present say to what damages the plaintiff is entitled.

It appears from the statement in the case, that the plaintiff was damaged by his property being flooded by water, which, without any fault on his part, broke out of a reservoir constructed on the defendants' land by the defendants' orders, and maintained by the defendants.

It appears from the statement in the case that the coal under the defendants' land had, at some remote period, been worked out; but this was unknown at the time when the defendants gave directions to erect the reservoir, and the water in the reservoir would not have escaped from the defendants' land, and no mischief would have been done to the plaintiff, but for this latent defect in the defendants' subsoil. And it further appears, that the defendants selected competent engineers and contractors to make their reservoir, and themselves personally continued in total ignorance of what we have called the latent defect in the subsoil; but that these persons employed by them in the course of the work became aware of the existence of the ancient shafts filled up with soil, though they did not know or suspect that they were shafts communicating with old workings.

It is found that the defendants, personally, were free from all blame, but that in fact proper care and skill was not used by the persons employed by them, to provide for the sufficiency of the reservoir with reference to these shafts. The consequence was, that the reservoir when filled with water burst into the shafts, the water flowed down through them into the old workings, and thence into the plaintiff's mine, and there did the mischief.

The plaintiff, though free from all blame on his part, must bear the loss, unless he can establish that it was the consequence of some default for which the defendants are responsible. The question of law therefore arises, what is the obligation which the law casts on a person who, like the defendants, lawfully brings on his land something which, though harmless whilst it remains there, will naturally do mischief if it escape[s] out of his land. It is agreed on all hands that he must take care to keep in that which he has brought on the land and keeps there, in order that it may not escape and damage his neighbours, but the question arises whether the duty which the law casts upon him, under such circumstances, is an absolute duty to keep it in at his peril, or is, as the majority of the Court of Exchequer have thought, merely a duty to take all reasonable and prudent precautions, in order to keep it in, but no more. If the first be the law, the person who has brought on his land and kept there something dangerous, and failed to keep it in, is responsible for all the natural consequences of its escape. If the second be the limit of his duty, he would not be answerable except on proof of negligence, and consequently would not be answerable for escape arising from any latent defect which ordinary prudence and skill could not detect.

Supposing the second to be the correct view of the law, a further question arises subsidiary to the first, viz., whether the defendants are not so far identified with the contractors whom they employed, as to be responsible for the consequences of their want of care and skill in making the reservoir in fact insufficient with reference to the old shafts, or the existence of which they were aware, though they had not ascertained where the shafts went to.

We think that the true rule of law is, that the person who for his own purposes brings on his lands and collects and keeps there anything likely to do mischief if it escapes, must keep it in at his peril, and, if he does not do so, is prima facie answerable for all the damages which is the natural consequence of its escape. He can excuse himself by shewing that the escape was owing to the plaintiff's default; or perhaps that the escape was the consequences of vis major, or the act of God; but as nothing of this sort exists here, it is unnecessary to inquire what excuse would be sufficient. The general rule, as above stated, seems on principle just. The person whose grass or corn is eaten down by the escaping cattle of his neighbour, or whose mine is flooded by the water from his neighbour's reservoir, or whose cellar is invaded by the filth of his neighbour's privy, or whose habitation is made unhealthy by the fumes and noisome vapours of his neighbour's alkali works, is damnified without any fault of his own; and it seems but reasonable and just that the neighbour, who has brought something on his own property which was not naturally there, harmless to others so long as it is confined to his own property, but which he knows to be mischievous if it gets on his neighbour's, should be obliged to make good the damage which ensues if he does not succeed in confining it to his own property. But for his act that he should at his peril keep it there so that no mischief may accrue, or answer for the natural and anticipated consequences. And upon authority, this we think is established to be the law whether the things so brought be beasts, or water, or filth, or stenches.

The case that has most commonly occurred, and which is most frequently to be found in the books, is as to the obligation of the owner of cattle which he has brought on his land, to prevent their escaping and doing mischief. The law as to them seems to be perfectly settled from early times; the owner must keep them in at his peril, or he will be answerable for the natural consequences of their escape; that is with regard to tame beasts, for the grass they eat and trample upon, though not for any injury to the person of others, for our ancestors have settled that it is not the general nature of horses to kick, or bulls to gore; but if the owner knows that the beast has a vicious propensity to attack man, he will be answerable for that too. . . .

. . . But it was further said by Martin, B., [a majority judge in the Court of Exchequer] that when damage is done to personal property, or even to the person, by collision, either upon land or at sea, there must be negligence in the party doing the damage to render him legally responsible; and this is no doubt true, and as was pointed out by Mr. Mellich during his argument before us, this is not confined to cases of collision, for there are many cases in which proof of negligence is essential, as for instance, where an unruly horse gets on the footpath of a public street and kills a passenger, or where a person in a dock is struck by the falling of a bale of cotton which the defendant's servants are lowering; and many other similar cases may be found. But we think these cases distinguishable from the present. Traffic on the highways, whether by land or sea, cannot be conducted without exposing those whose persons or property are near it to some inevitable risk; and that being so, those who go on the highway, or have their property adjacent to it, may well be held to do so subject to their taking upon themselves the risk of injury from that inevitable danger; and persons who by the license of the owner pass near to warehouses where goods are being raised or lowered, certainly do so subject to the inevitable risk of accident. In neither case, therefore, can they recover without proof of want of care or skill occasioning the accident; and it is believed that all the cases in which inevitable accident has been held an excuse for what prima facie was a trespass, can be explained on the same principle, viz., that the circumstances were such as to shew that the plaintiff had taken that risk upon himself. But there is no ground for saying that the plaintiff here took upon himself any risk arising from the uses to which the defendants should choose to apply their land. He neither knew what these might be, nor could he in any way control the defendants, or hinder their building what reservoirs they liked, and storing up in them what water they pleased, so long as the defendants succeeded in preventing the water which they there brought from interfering with the plaintiff's property.

The view which we take of the first point renders it unnecessary to consider whether the defendants would or would not be responsible for the want of care and skill in the persons employed by them, under the circumstances stated in the case.

We are of the opinion that the plaintiff is entitled to recover, but as we have not heard any argument as to the amount, we are not able to give judgment for what damages. The parties probably will empower their counsel to agree on the amount of damages; should they differ on the principle, the case may be mentioned again.

Judgment for the plaintiff.

RYLANDS v. FLETCHER
L.R. 3 H.L. 330 (1868)

THE LORD CHANCELLOR (Lord Cairns): . . . My Lords, the principles on which this case must be determined appear to me to be extremely simple. The Defendants, treating them as the owners or occupiers of the close on which the reservoir was constructed, might lawfully have used that close for any purpose for which it might in the ordinary course of the enjoyment of land be used; and if, in what I may term the natural user of that land, there had been any accumulation of water, either on the surface or underground, and if, by the operation of the laws of nature, that accumulation of water had passed off into the close occupied by the Plaintiff, the Plaintiff could not have complained. . . .

On the other hand if the Defendants, not stopping at the natural use of their close, had desired to use it for any purpose which I may term a non-natural use, for the purpose of introducing into the close that which in its natural condition was not in or upon it, for the purpose of introducing water either above or below ground in quantities and in a manner not the result of any work or operation on or under the land,—and if in consequence of their doing so, or in consequence of any imperfection in the mode of their doing so, the water came to escape and to pass off into the close of the Plaintiff, then it appears to me that that which the Defendants were doing they were doing at their own peril; and, if in the course of their doing it, the evil arose to which I have referred, the evil, namely, of the escape of the water and its passing away to the close of the Plaintiff and injuring the Plaintiff, then for the consequence of that, in my opinion, the Defendants would be liable. . . .

My Lords, these simple principles, if they are well founded, as it appears to me they are, really dispose of this case. . . .

Judgment of the Court of Exchequer Chamber affirmed.

NO FLOODGATES AFTER FLETCHER, NO REVOLUTION AFTER RYLANDS

Rylands is one of the most discussed cases in American jurisprudence, despite the fact that it is not an American decision and only a handful of cases after *Rylands* have involved water that caused damage after escaping from a reservoir. Professor A.W.B. Simpson, in *Legal Liability for Bursting Reservoirs: The Historical Context of* Rylands v. Fletcher, 13 J. Legal Stud. 209, 263-264 (1984), writes:

> Since 1930 there have been no serious reservoir disasters in Britain, though there exist many ancient dams, some very ill maintained, and in the whole long curious story the only individual in Britain who ever seems actually to have employed the rule in Rylands v. Fletcher to recover damages for a burst reservoir is Thomas Fletcher himself. Where this leaves the great cases of common law, I leave to the reader. But insofar as the whole story is relevant to the general and much-discussed question of the relationship between the state of the law and economic development, there is perhaps one general moral. To an extent generally underestimated, the mechanism used to regulate enterprises and cope with the

problems of rapid industrial and agricultural change was not the common law but the private act of Parliament, and the judges played only a peripheral role in interpreting such legislation. Those who, like S.F.C. Milsom,[1] incline to think that in the common law nobody ever knows where he is going, may find some support in this story; but another way of looking at the matter is that the concept of strict liability, having acquired an assured status in the law in the special context of bursting reservoirs, survived to flourish in other fields of twentieth-century law.

TURNER v. BIG LAKE OIL CO.
96 S.W.2d 221 (Tex. 1936)

Mr. Chief Justice CURETON delivered the opinion of the court.

The primary question for determination here is whether or not the defendants in error, without negligence on their part, may be held liable in damages for the destruction or injury to property occasioned by the escape of salt water from ponds constructed and used by them in the operation of their oil wells. . . .

The defendants in error in the operation of certain oil wells in Reagan County constructed large artificial earthen ponds or pools into which they ran the polluted waters from the wells. On the occasion complained of, water escaped from one or more of these ponds, and, passing over the grass lands of the plaintiffs in error, injured the turf, and after entering Garrison draw flowed down the same into Centralia draw. In Garrison draw there were natural water holes, which supplied water for the livestock of plaintiffs in error. The pond, or ponds, of water from which the salt water escaped were, we judge from the map, some six miles from the stock water holes to which we refer. The plaintiffs in error brought suit, basing their action on alleged neglect on the part of the defendants in error in permitting the levees and dams, etc., of their artificial ponds to break and overflow the land of plaintiffs in error, and thereby pollute the waters to which we have above refered [sic] and injure the turf in the pasture of plaintiffs in error. The question was submitted to a jury on special issues, and the jury answered that the defendants in error did permit salt water to overflow from their salt ponds and lakes down Garrison draw and on to the land of the plaintiffs in error. *However, the jury acquitted the defendants in error of negligence in the premises.* . . .

[T]he immediate question presented is whether or not defendants in error are to be held liable as insurers, or whether the cause of action against them must be predicated upon negligence. We believe the question is one of first impression in this court, and so we shall endeavor to discuss it in a manner in keeping with its importance.

Upon both reason and authority, we believe that the conclusion of the Court of Civil Appeals that negligence is a prerequisite to recovery in a case of this character is a correct one. There is some difference of opinion on the subject in American jurisprudence brought about by differing views as to the correctness or applicability of the decision of the English courts in Rylands v. Fletcher, L.R. 3 H.L. 330. . . .

---

1. S.F.C. Milsom, *Reason in the Development of the Common Law*, 81 Law Q. Rev. 496 (1965).

In Rylands v. Fletcher the court predicated the absolute liability of the defendants on the proposition that the use of land for the artificial storage of water was not a natural use, and that, therefore, the landowner was bound at his peril to keep the waters on his own land. This basis of the English rule is to be found in the meteorological conditions which obtain there. England is a pluvial country, where constant streams and abundant rains make the storage of water unnecessary for ordinary or general purposes. When the court said in Rylands v. Fletcher that the use of land for storage of water was an unnatural use, it meant such use was not a general or an ordinary one; not one within the contemplation of the parties to the original grant of the land involved, nor of the grantor and grantees of adjacent lands, but was a special or extraordinary use, and for that reason applied the rule of absolute liability. This conclusion is supported by the fact that those jurisdictions which adhere to the rule in Rylands v. Fletcher do not apply that rule to dams or reservoirs constructed in rivers and streams, which they say is a natural use, but apply the principle of negligence. In other words, the impounding of water in stream-ways, being an obvious and natural use, was necessarily within the contemplation of the parties to the original and adjacent grants, and damages must be predicated upon negligent use of a granted right and power; while things not within the contemplation of the parties to the original grants, such as unnatural uses of the land, the landowner may do only at his peril. As to what use of land is or may be a natural use, one within the contemplation of the parties to the original grant of land, necessarily depends upon the attendant circumstances and conditions which obtain land, necessarily depends upon the attendant or the initial terms of those grants.

In Texas we have conditions very different from those which obtain in England. A large portion of Texas is an arid or semiarid region. West of the 98th meridian of longitude, where the rainfall is approximately 30 inches, the rainfall decreases until finally, in the extreme western part of the state, it is only about 10 inches. This land of decreasing rainfall is the great ranch or livestock region of the state, water for which is stored in thousands of ponds, tanks, and lakes on the surface of the ground. The country is almost without streams; and without the storage of water from rainfall in basins constructed for the purpose, or to hold waters pumped from the earth, the great livestock industry of West Texas must perish. No such condition obtains in England. With us the storage of water is a natural or necessary and common use of the land, necessarily within the contemplation of the state and its grantees when grants were made, and obviously the rule announced in Rylands v. Fletcher, predicated upon different conditions, can have no application here.

Again, in England there are no oil wells, no necessity for using surface storage facilities for impounding and evaporating salt waters therefrom. In Texas the situation is different. Texas has many great oil fields, tens of thousands of wells in almost every part of the state. Producing oil is one of our major industries. One of the by-products of oil production is salt water, which must be disposed of without injury to property or the pollution of streams. The construction of basins or ponds to hold this salt water is a necessary part of the oil business. In Texas much of our land was granted without mineral reservation to the state, and where minerals were reserved, provision has usually been made for leasing and operating. It follows, therefore, that as to these grants and leases the right to mine in the usual and appropriate way, as, for example, by the construction and maintenance of salt water pools such as here involved, incident to the production of oil, was contemplated by the state and all its grantees and mineral lessees, that being a use of the surface incident and necessary to the right to produce oil. . . .

The judgments of the Court of Civil Appeals and of the district court are affirmed.

FOOD FOR THOUGHT

In Atlas Chemical Industries, Inc. v. Anderson, 514 S.W.2d 309 (Tex. Civ. App. 1974), the plaintiff won a verdict and judgment against the defendant for deliberately dumping industrial waste on 60 acres of the plaintiff's land. The defendant claimed that while he intentionally dumped the waste, he did not intentionally harm the plaintiff. The Texas Court of Appeals affirmed the judgment of the trial court, concluding that strict liability attaches whenever pollutants are intentionally discharged. The court noted (*id.* at 315-316):

> We recognize that the rule of law hereinabove set out by this court may be a departure from the rules heretofore established by our courts and may be in conflict with some of decisions. However, we believe that the common law rules of tort liability in pollution cases arising out of the intentional discharge of pollutants should be in conformity with the public policy of this state as declared by the Legislature in the Texas Water Code, (1971). . . . Basically, the public policy is that the quality of water in this State shall be maintained free of pollution. . . . Texas Water Code § 21.003(11) states that "'Pollution' means the alteration of the physical, thermal, chemical, or biological quality of, or the contamination of, any water in the state that renders the water harmful, detrimental, or injurious to humans, animal life, vegetation, or property, or to public health, safety, or welfare, or impairs the usefulness or the public enjoyment of the water for any lawful or reasonable purpose." . . .
>
> We further believe the public policy of this State to be that however laudable an industry may be, its owners or managers are still subject to the rule that its industry or its property cannot be so used as to inflict injury to the property of its neighbors. To allow industry to inflict injury to the property of its neighbors without just compensation amounts to inverse condemnation which is not permitted under our law. We know of no acceptable rule of jurisprudence which permits those engaged in important and desirable enterprises to injure with impunity those who are engaged in enterprises of lesser economic significance. The costs of injuries resulting from pollution must be internalized by industry as a cost of production and borne by consumers or shareholders, or both, and not by the injured individual.

Is the Texas Court of Appeals correct when it says that "no acceptable rule of jurisprudence" allows actors to impose accident costs on others? What about the rule of negligence, in which reasonably careful actors may impose residual costs on victims harmed by the actors' activities?

hypo **61**

A attends a citywide Fourth of July celebration knowing that part of the celebration includes a fireworks display that *B* will conduct. [D]uring the display, one of the rockets malfunctions and shoots horizontally into a crowd of onlookers. *A* and several others are injured by the errant rocket. *A* brings an action against *B*, claiming that strict liability applies. Will *A*'s claim survive a summary judgment motion by *B*?

INDIANA HARBOR BELT R.R. v. AMERICAN CYANAMID CO.
916 F.2d 1174 (7th Cir. 1990)

Posner, Circuit Judge.

American Cyanamid Company, the defendant in this diversity tort suit governed by Illinois law, is a major manufacturer of chemicals, including acrylonitrile, a chemical used in large quantities in making acrylic fibers, plastics, dyes, pharmaceutical chemicals, and other intermediate and final goods. On January 2, 1979, at its manufacturing plant in Louisiana, Cyanamid loaded 20,000 gallons of liquid acrylonitrile into a railroad tank car that it had leased from the North American Car Corporation. The next day, a train of the Missouri Pacific Railroad picked up the car at Cyanamid's siding. The car's ultimate destination was a Cyanamid plant in New Jersey served by Conrail rather than by Missouri Pacific. The Missouri Pacific train carried the car north to the Blue Island railroad yard of Indiana Harbor Belt Railroad, the plaintiff in this case, a small switching line that has a contract with Conrail to switch cars from other lines to Conrail, in this case for travel east. The Blue Island yard is in the Village of Riverdale, which is just south of Chicago and part of the Chicago metropolitan area.

The car arrived in the Blue Island yard on the morning of January 9, 1979. Several hours after it arrived, employees of the switching line noticed fluid gushing from the bottom outlet of the car. The lid on the outlet was broken. After two hours, the line's supervisor of equipment was able to stop the leak by closing a shut-off valve controlled from the top of the car. No one was sure at the time just how much of the contents of the car had leaked, but it was feared that all 20,000 gallons had, and since acrylonitrile is flammable at a temperature of 30 degrees Fahrenheit or above, highly toxic, and possibly carcinogenic, the local authorities ordered the homes near the yard evacuated. The evacuation lasted only a few hours, until the car was moved to a remote part of the yard and it was discovered that only about a quarter of the acrylonitrile had leaked. Concerned nevertheless that there had been some contamination of soil and water, the Illinois Department of Environmental Protection ordered the switching line to take decontamination measures that cost the line $981,022.75, which it sought to recover by this suit.

One count of the two-count complaint charges Cyanamid with having maintained the leased tank car negligently. The other count asserts that the transportation of acrylonitrile in bulk through the Chicago metropolitan area is an abnormally dangerous activity, for the consequences of which the shipper (Cyanamid) is strictly liable to the switching line, which bore the financial brunt of those consequences because of the decontamination measures that it was forced to take. After the district judge denied Cyanamid's motion to dismiss the strict liability count, the switching line moved for summary judgment on that count — and won. The judge directed the entry of judgment for $981,022.75 under Fed. R. Civ. P. 54(b) to permit Cyanamid to take an immediate appeal even though the negligence count remained pending. [Rule 54(b) asserts that when more than one claim for relief is presented in an action, the trial court may enter final, appealable judgment as to one or more but fewer than all such separate claims only upon an express determination that there is no just reason for delay in seeking appellate review.] We threw out the appeal on the ground that the negligence and strict liability counts were not separate claims but merely separate theories involving the same facts, making Rule 54(b) inapplicable. The district judge then, over the switching line's objection, dismissed the negligence claim with prejudice, thus terminating proceedings in the district court and clearing the way for Cyanamid to file an appeal of which we would have jurisdiction. There is no doubt about our appellate jurisdiction this time. Whether or not the judge was correct to dismiss the negligence claim merely to terminate the lawsuit so that Cyanamid could appeal (the only ground he gave for the dismissal), he did it, and by doing so produced an incontestably final judgment. The switching line has cross-appealed, challenging the dismissal of the negligence count.

The question whether the shipper of a hazardous chemical by rail should be strictly liable for the consequences of a spill or other accident to the shipment en route is a novel one in Illinois. . . .

The parties agree that the question whether placing acrylonitrile in a rail shipment that will pass through a metropolitan area subjects the shipper to strict liability is, as recommended in Restatement, (Second), of Torts § 520, comment *l* (1977), a question of law, so that we owe no particular deference to the conclusion of the district court. They also agree . . . that the Supreme Court of Illinois would treat as authoritative the provisions of the Restatement governing abnormally dangerous activities. The key provision is section 520, which sets forth six factors to be considered in deciding whether an activity is abnormally dangerous and the actor therefore strictly liable.

The roots of section 520 are in nineteenth-century cases. The most famous one is Rylands v. Fletcher, 1 Ex. 265, *aff'd*, L.R. 3 H.L. 300 (1868), but a more illuminating one in the present context is Guille v. Swan, 19 Johns. (N.Y.) 381 (1822). A man took off in a hot-air balloon and landed, without intending to, in a vegetable garden in New York City. A crowd that had been anxiously watching his involuntary descent trampled the vegetables in their endeavor to rescue him when he landed. The owner of the garden sued the balloonist for the resulting damage, and won. Yet the balloonist had not been careless. In the then state of ballooning it was impossible to make a pinpoint landing.

Guille is a paradigmatic case for strict liability. (a) The risk (probability) of harm was great, and (b) the harm that would ensue if the risk materialized could be, although luckily was not, great (the balloonist could have crashed into the crowd rather than into the vegetables). The confluence of these two factors established the urgency of seeking to prevent such accidents. (c) Yet such accidents could not be prevented by the exercise of due care; the technology of care in ballooning was insufficiently developed. (d) The activity was not a matter of common usage, so there was no presumption that it was a highly valuable activity despite its unavoidable riskiness. (e) The activity was inappropriate to the place in which it took place — densely populated New York City. The risk of serious harm to others (other than the balloonist himself, that is) could have been reduced by shifting the activity to the sparsely inhabited areas that surrounded the city in those days. (f) Reinforcing (d), the value to the community of the activity of recreational ballooning did not appear to be great enough to offset its unavoidable risks.

These are, of course, the six factors in section 520. They are related to each other in that each is a different facet of a common quest for a proper legal regime to govern accidents that negligence liability cannot adequately control. The interrelations might be more perspicuous if the six factors were reordered. One might for example start with (c), inability to eliminate the risk of accident by the exercise of due care. The baseline common law regime of tort liability is negligence. When it is a workable regime, because the hazards of an activity can be avoided by being careful (which is to say, nonnegligent), there is no need to switch to strict liability. Sometimes, however, a particular type of accident cannot be prevented by taking care but can be avoided, or its consequences minimized, by shifting the activity in which the accident occurs to another locale, where the risk or harm of an accident will be less ((e)), or by reducing the scale of the activity in order to minimize the number of accidents caused by it ((f)). The greater the risk of an accident ((a)) and the costs of an accident if one occurs ((b)), the more we want the actor to consider the possibility of making accident-reducing activity changes; the stronger, therefore, is the case for strict liability. Finally, if an activity is extremely common ((d)), like driving an automobile, it is unlikely either that its hazards are perceived as great or that there is no technology of care available to minimize them; so the case for strict liability is weakened.

The largest class of cases in which strict liability has been imposed under the standard codified in the Second Restatement of Torts involves the use of dynamite and other explosives for demolition in residential or urban areas. Explosives are dangerous even when handled carefully, and we therefore want blasters to choose the location of the activity with care and also to explore the feasibility of using safer substitutes (such as a wrecking ball), as well as to be careful in the blasting itself. Blasting is not a commonplace activity like driving a car, or so superior to substitute methods of demolition that the imposition of liability is unlikely to have any effect except to raise the activity's costs.

Against this background we turn to the particulars of acrylonitrile. Acrylonitrile is one of a large number of chemicals that are hazardous in the sense of being flammable, toxic, or both; acrylonitrile is both, as are many others. A table in the record . . . contains a list of the 125 hazardous materials that are shipped in highest volume on the nation's railroads. Acrylonitrile is the fifty-third most hazardous on the list. . . . The plaintiff's lawyer acknowledged at argument that the logic of the district court's opinion dictated strict liability for all 52 materials that rank higher than acrylonitrile on the list, and quite possibly for the 72 that rank lower as well, since all are hazardous if spilled in quantity while being shipped by rail. Every shipper of any of these materials would therefore be strictly liable for the consequences of a spill or other accident that occurred while the material was being shipped through a metropolitan area. The plaintiff's lawyer further acknowledged the irrelevance, on her view of the case, of the fact that Cyanamid had leased and filled the car that spilled the acrylonitrile; all she thought important is that Cyanamid introduced the product into the stream of commerce that happened to pass through the Chicago metropolitan area. Her concession may have been incautious. One might want to distinguish between the shipper who merely places his goods on his loading dock to be picked up by the carrier and the shipper who, as in this case, participates actively in the transportation. But the concession is illustrative of the potential scope of the district court's decision.

No cases recognize so sweeping a liability. Several reject it, though none has facts much like those of the present case. [The court's discussion of the case law is omitted.]

Siegler v. Kuhlman, . . . 502 P.2d 1181 (Wash. 1972), also imposed strict liability on a transporter of hazardous materials, but the circumstances were again rather special. A gasoline truck blew up, obliterating the plaintiff's decedent and her car. The court emphasized that the explosion had destroyed the evidence necessary to establish whether the accident had been due to negligence; so, unless liability was strict, there would be no liability — and this as the very consequence of the defendant's hazardous activity. . . . We shall see that a . . . distinction of great importance between the present case and *Siegler* is that the defendant there was the transporter, and here it is the shipper.

Cases . . . that impose strict liability for the storage of a dangerous chemical provide a potentially helpful analogy to our case. But they can be distinguished on the ground that the storer (like the transporter, as in *Siegler*) has more control than the shipper.

So we can get little help from precedent, and might as well apply section 520 to the acrylonitrile problem from the ground up. To begin with, we have been given no reason . . . for believing that a negligence regime is not perfectly adequate to remedy and deter, at reasonable cost, the accidental spillage of acrylonitrile from rail cars. Acrylonitrile could explode and destroy evidence, but of course did not here, making imposition of strict liability on the theory of the *Siegler* decision premature. More important, although acrylonitrile is flammable even at relatively low temperatures, and toxic, it is not so corrosive or otherwise destructive that it will eat through or otherwise damage or weaken a tank car's valves although they are maintained with due (which essentially means, with average) care. No one suggests, therefore, that the leak in this case was caused by the *inherent* properties of acrylonitrile. It was caused by carelessness — whether that of the North American Car Corporation in failing to maintain or inspect the car properly, or that of Cyanamid in failing to maintain or inspect it, or that of the Missouri Pacific when it had custody of the car, or that of the switching line itself in failing to notice the ruptured lid, or some combination of these possible failures of care. Accidents that are due to a lack of care can be prevented by taking care; and when a lack of care can (unlike *Siegler*) be shown in court, such accidents are adequately deterred by the threat of liability for negligence.

It is true that the district court purported to find as a fact that there is an inevitable risk of derailment or other calamity in transporting "large quantities of anything." This is not a finding of fact, but a truism: anything can happen. The question is, how likely is this type of accident if the actor uses due care? For all that appears from the record of the case or any other sources of information that we have found, if a tank car is carefully maintained the danger of a spill of acrylonitrile is negligible. If this is right, there is no compelling reason to move to a regime of strict liability, especially one that might embrace all other hazardous materials shipped by rail as well. This also means, however, that the amici curiae who have filed briefs in support of Cyanamid cry wolf in predicting "devastating" effects on the chemical industry if the district court's decision is affirmed. If the vast majority of chemical spills by railroads are preventable by due care, the imposition of strict liability should cause only a slight, not as they argue a substantial, rise in liability insurance rates, because the incremental liability should be slight. The amici have momentarily lost sight of the fact that the feasibility of avoiding accidents simply by being careful is an argument *against* strict liability.

This discussion helps to show why *Siegler* is indeed distinguishable. . . . There are so many highway hazards that the transportation of gasoline by truck is, or at least might plausibly be thought, inherently dangerous in the sense that a serious danger of accident would remain even if the truck driver used all due care. . . . Which in turn means, contrary to our earlier suggestion, that the plaintiff really might have difficulty invoking res ipsa loquitur, because a gasoline truck might well blow up without negligence on the part of the driver. The plaintiff in this case has not shown that the danger of a comparable disaster to a tank car filled with acrylonitrile is as great and might have similar consequences for proof of negligence. And to repeat a previous point, if the reason for strict liability is fear that an accident might destroy the critical evidence of negligence we should wait to impose such liability until such a case appears. . . .

The difference between shipper and carrier points to a deep flaw in the plaintiff's case. Unlike *Guille*, and unlike *Siegler*, and unlike the storage cases, beginning with *Rylands* itself, here it is not the actors—that is, the transporters of acrylonitrile and other chemicals—but the manufacturers, who are sought to be held strictly liable. A shipper can in the bill of lading designate the route of his shipment if he likes, but is it realistic to suppose that shippers will become students of railroading in order to lay out the safest route by which to ship their goods? Anyway, rerouting is no panacea. Often it will increase the length of the journey, or compel the use of poorer track, or both. When this happens, the probability of an accident is increased, even if the consequences of an accident if one occurs are reduced; so the expected accident cost, being the product of the probability of an accident and the harm if the accident occurs, may rise. It is easy to see how the accident in this case might have been prevented at reasonable cost by greater care on the part of those who handled the tank car of acrylonitrile. It is difficult to see how it might have been prevented at reasonable cost by a change in the activity of transporting the chemical. This is therefore not an apt case for strict liability. . . .

In emphasizing the flammability and toxicity of acrylonitrile rather than the hazards of transporting it, . . . the plaintiff overlooks the fact that ultrahazardousness or abnormal dangerousness is, in the contemplation of the law at least, a property not of substances, but of activities: not of acrylonitrile, but of the transportation of acrylonitrile by rail through populated areas. Natural gas is both flammable and poisonous, but the operation of a natural gas well is not an ultrahazardous activity. Whatever the situation under products liability law (section 402A of the Restatement), the manufacturer of a product is not considered to be engaged in an abnormally dangerous activity merely because the product becomes dangerous when it is handled or used in some way after it leaves his premises, even if the danger is foreseeable. The plaintiff does not suggest that Cyanamid should switch to making some less hazardous chemical that would substitute for acrylonitrile in the textiles and other goods in which acrylonitrile is used. Were this a feasible method of accident avoidance, there would be an argument for making manufacturers strictly liable for accidents that occur during the shipment of their products (how strong an argument we need not decide). Apparently it is not a feasible method.

The relevant activity is transportation, not manufacturing and shipping. This essential distinction the plaintiff ignores. But even if the plaintiff is treated as a transporter and not merely a shipper, it has not shown that the transportation of acrylonitrile in bulk by rail through populated areas is so hazardous an activity, even when due care is exercised, that the law should seek to create — perhaps quixotically — incentives to relocate the activity to nonpopulated areas, or to reduce the scale of the activity, or to switch to transporting acrylonitrile by road rather than by rail, perhaps to set the stage for a replay of Siegler v. Kuhlman. It is no more realistic to propose to reroute the shipment of all hazardous materials around Chicago than it is to propose the relocation of homes adjacent to the Blue Island switching yard to more distant suburbs. It may be less realistic. Brutal though it may seem to say it, the inappropriate use to which land is being put in the Blue Island yard and neighborhood may be, not the transportation of hazardous chemicals, but residential living. The analogy is to building your home between the runways at O'Hare.

The briefs hew closely to the Restatement, whose approach to the issue of strict liability is mainly *allocative* rather than *distributive*. By this we mean that the emphasis is on picking a liability regime (negligence or strict liability) that will control the particular class of accidents in question most effectively, rather than on finding the deepest pocket and placing liability there. At argument, however, the plaintiff's lawyer invoked distributive considerations by pointing out that Cyanamid is a huge firm and the Indiana Harbor Belt Railroad a fifty-mile-long switching line that almost went broke in the winter of 1979, when the accident occurred. Well, so what? A corporation is not a living person but a set of contracts the terms of which determine who will bear the brunt of liability. Tracing the incidence of a cost is a complex undertaking which the plaintiff sensibly has made no effort to assume, since its legal relevance would be dubious. We add only that however small the plaintiff may be, it has mighty parents: it is a jointly owned subsidiary of Conrail and the Soo line.

The case for strict liability has not been made. Not in this suit in any event. . . .

The defendant concedes that if the strict liability count is thrown out, the negligence count must be reinstated, as requested by the cross-appeal. We therefore need not consider the plaintiff's argument that the district judge was wrong to throw out the negligence count merely to create an appealable order. . . . [W]ith damages having been fixed at a relatively modest level by the district court and not challenged by the plaintiff, and a voluminous record having been compiled in the summary judgment proceedings, we trust the parties will find it possible now to settle the case. Even the Trojan War lasted only ten years.

The judgment is reversed (with no award of costs in this court) and the case remanded for further proceedings, consistent with this opinion, on the plaintiff's claim for negligence.

Reversed and Remanded, with Directions.

FOOD FOR THOUGHT

In the middle of his opinion for the court, in the paragraph that begins "These are, of course, the six factors in section 520," Judge Posner suggests that the main reason for moving from negligence to strict liability is not to increase levels of care — negligence does that just as well as strict liability — but to affect the levels, and locales, of the activities in question:

> By making the actor strictly liable — by denying him in other words an excuse based on his inability to avoid accidents by being more careful — we give him an incentive, missing in a negligence regime, to experiment with methods of preventing accidents that involve not greater exertions of care, assumed to be futile, but instead relocating, changing, or reducing (perhaps to the vanishing point) the activity giving rise to the accident.

How does strict liability affect "activity levels" in this way? Some efficiency theorists argue that by holding actors liable for the residual accident costs that are cheaper to incur than to avoid, strict liability makes the activity — e.g., hauling large quantities of gasoline by truck — more costly to engage in. If the activity is commercial, the price of the activity to consumers will go up, reducing demand for it in the market. The trucking company involved may decide to shift its routes to less populous areas, even if the new routes are longer than before. (How will the company make the decision whether it is "worth it" to shift to a new, longer-but-less-crowded truck route?)

Of course, one might ask why the negligence system cannot simply decide to call "shipping in populated areas" negligent, and achieve the same route shifts without moving to strict liability. One answer is that courts are ill-equipped to decide on a case-by-case basis whether driving gasoline trucks on one route or the other is, or is not, negligent. Moving to strict liability takes the onus off the courts to make "which route is best?" decisions and places it on the trucking companies themselves. Moreover, one strategy for reducing accident costs would be for trucking companies to reduce the overall amount — the relative frequency — of their gasoline hauling activities. As with the question of which route is safest, strict liability is probably the only plausible way for tort law to address the "how much gasoline hauling is appropriate?" question.

Who decides whether a particular activity is abnormally dangerous and thus qualifies for strict liability treatment? As Judge Posner indicates in *Indiana Harbor*, comment *l* to § 520 of the Restatement, Second, of Torts says it is an issue of law for the court to decide. American courts overwhelmingly agree. *See, e.g.,* Great American Ins. Co. of New York v. Heneghan Wrecking and Excavating Co., Inc., 46 N.E.3d 859 (Ill. App. 2015).

Restatement, Third, of Torts § 20 has simplified the factors set forth in Restatement, Second, § 520.

§ 20. Abnormally Dangerous Activities

(a) An actor who carries on an abnormally dangerous activity is subject to strict liability for physical harm resulting from the activity.

(b) An activity is abnormally dangerous if:

(1) the activity creates a foreseeable and highly significant risk of physical harm even when reasonable care is exercised by all actors; and

(2) the activity is not one of common usage.

Courts continue to struggle regarding which activities should come within the rubric of strict liability, and which should remain under the aegis of negligence. *See, e.g.,* In re Hanford Nuclear Reservation Litigation, 534 F.3d 986 (9th Cir. 2008) (plutonium facility that emitted radioactive elements into the atmosphere was abnormally dangerous activity; risks need not have been knowable at the time of operation); Patterson Enterprises, Inc. v. Johnson, 272 P.3d 93 (Mont. 2012) (blasting is an abnormally dangerous activity); Gallagher v. H.V. Pierhomes, 957 A.2d 628 (Md. App. 2008) (pile driving is not an abnormally dangerous activity); GCM Air Group, LLC v. Chevron, 286 Fed. Appx. 717 (9th Cir. 2010) (storing gasoline in underground tanks is not an abnormally dangerous activity because it can be accomplished safely with reasonable care, is commonplace, and is of significant utility to the community).

Attempts to hold manufacturers of inherently dangerous products liable for those dangers under the rubric of "abnormally dangerous activity" have been soundly rejected by most courts. *See, e.g.,* Akee v. Dow Chemical Co., 293 F. Supp. 2d 1140 (D. Haw. 2002) (manufacturer of a highly toxic fumigant is not liable for contamination of air, soil, and water; "generally the manufacture of a product will not be considered . . . an ultra-hazardous activity"); Copier v. Smith & Wesson Corp., 138 F.3d 833 (10th Cir. 1998) (sale of firearms is not abnormally dangerous activity). *See also* James A. Henderson, Jr. & Aaron D. Twerski, *Closing the American Products Liability Frontier: The Rejection of Liability Without Defect,* 66 N.Y.U. L. Rev. 1263 (1991). *But see* Carl T. Bogus, *War on the Common Law: The Struggle at the Center of Products Liability,* 60 Mo. L. Rev. 1 (1995).

FOSTER v. PRESTON MILL CO.
268 P.2d 645 (Wash. 1954)

HAMLEY, Justice. Blasting operations conducted by Preston Mill Company frightened mother mink owned by B.W. Foster, and caused the mink to kill their kittens. Foster brought this action against the company to recover damages.

---

authors' dialogue 35

JIM: Aaron, *Indiana Harbor* is right on. Posner is something else, isn't he?

AARON: You'll get no argument from me about Posner's intellect. The man is awesome. But he missed the boat in *Indiana Harbor.* Excuse the pun.

JIM: I don't think so. It's a well-reasoned decision.

AARON: Listen up, Jim. I think he's wrong on several of his arguments. The claim that it is unrealistic for the manufacturer/shipper to lay out the safest route to transport the acrylonitrile misses the point. Think about the role of the carrier in this case. They provide the tanker that Cyanamid fills with gook. They haven't the foggiest notion what's in the tanker. It could be chocolate milk for all they know or care. If they had to learn the content and danger level of what goes into every tanker in order to decide how to route the toxic chemicals, they would have to develop the expertise of DuPont. The only party with the knowledge to decide the risk of transport is Cyanamid, not the rinky-dink switching line.

JIM: I think you're wrong on your underlying assumptions. The carriers know or should know when a potentially deadly chemical is being shipped. I'll bet they even file forms with regulators on some of the stuff. Posner is right. The ones who control the risks of spillage are the carriers. They can charge the shippers more to carry dangerous chemicals than to carry chocolate milk.

AARON: Well, Posner's argument that the negligence regime is perfectly capable of managing the risks is clearly wrong. He says that the risk of derailment is not inevitable. I'll bet my bottom dollar that there are hundreds, if not thousands, of freight cars that get derailed every year. Most of the time you don't hear about derailments because they are of little consequence. But if you think of the hundreds of thousands of freight cars all over the country, the risk of derailment is not de minimis. And even if a freight tanker carrying toxics derails, most of the

---

His second amended complaint, upon which the case was tried, sets forth a cause of action on the theory of absolute liability, and, in the alternative, a cause of action on the theory of nuisance.

After a trial to the court without a jury, judgment was rendered for plaintiff in the sum of $1,953.68. The theory adopted by the court was that, after defendant received notice of the effect which its blasting operations were having upon the mink, it was absolutely liable for all damages of that nature thereafter sustained. The trial court concluded that defendant's blasting did not constitute a public nuisance, but did not expressly rule on the question of private nuisance. Plaintiff concedes, however, that, in effect, the trial court decided in defendant's favor on the question of nuisance. Defendant appeals.

[The court describes the operation of the plaintiff's mink ranch, explaining that during the whelping season, which lasts several weeks, female mink are very excitable. The defendant had been engaged in a logging operation adjacent to the plaintiff's land for more than fifty years. They began the blasting in order to clear a path for a road, approximately two and one-quarter miles away from the ranch.

time nothing happens. But when the derailment causes leakage — in those rare cases — all hell breaks loose.

JIM: I think you're making the case for holding the carrier strictly liable. They can't avoid all derailments, but they can avoid sending toxics through big cities, or they can insure against losses if they do. Besides, this is not a derailment. The acrylonitrile leaked due to something wrong with the tanker.

AARON: Your last point is wrong. Strict liability depends on defining the category of activity that you identify as justifying the special liability rule. Whether the particular accident took place because of a problem with the tanker or because of derailment makes no difference. Besides, what happens if the plaintiff can't establish negligence against Cyanamid? Posner assumes that negligence can be made out. But, that's not a sure thing. Having ruled against the switching line on the strict liability count, if they lose on negligence the plaintiffs can't reopen the case and come hat in hand on appeal again, asking Posner to give them another shot at strict. They will have a little problem with res judicata.

JIM: I still think Posner is right. This is a case where the evidence is intact and plaintiff has every opportunity to prove negligence. We should not pull out the elephant gun of strict liability for no good reason.

AARON: Jim, you of all people should not fall for this argument. You, the self-styled champion of rules and process, are now ready to decide on a case-by-case basis whether strict liability should apply? Either shipping of toxics is or is not subject to strict liability. You can't decide if the activity fits the category depending on whether the toxic chemical blows up and destroys the tanker.

JIM: You're right on that, Aaron. But in a more general sense it's relevant to consider whether proof will be available in these cases. I think in the typical spillage case, as here, direct proof or a res ipsa inference on the negligence issue will be available.

The vibrations at the ranch excited the mother mink, who began killing their young. After the plaintiff told the defendant about the loss of mink kittens, the defendant reduced the strength of the dynamite charges, but continued blasting throughout the remainder of the whelping season. Defendant's experts testified that unless the road had been cleared, the logging operation would have been delayed and the company's log production disrupted, with attendant costs to the defendant company.]

In this action, respondent sought and recovered judgment only for such damages as were claimed to have been sustained as a result of blasting operations conducted after appellant received notice that its activity was causing loss of mink kittens.

The primary question presented by appellant's assignments of error is whether, on these facts, the judgment against appellant is sustainable on the theory of absolute liability.

The modern doctrine of strict liability for dangerous substances and activities stems from Justice Blackburn's decision in Rylands v. Fletcher, 1 Exch. 265, decided in 1866 and affirmed two years later in Fletcher v. Rylands, L.R. 3 H.L. 330. Prosser on Torts, 449, § 59. As applied to blasting operations, the doctrine has quite uniformly been held to establish liability, irrespective of negligence, for property damage sustained as a result of casting rocks or other debris on adjoining or neighboring premises.

There is a division of judicial opinion as to whether the doctrine of absolute liability should apply where the damage from blasting is caused, not by the casting of rocks and debris, but by concussion, vibration, or jarring. This court has adopted the view that the doctrine applies in such cases. . . .

However, the authorities may be divided on the point just discussed, they appear to be agreed that strict liability should be confined to consequences which lie within the extraordinary risk whose existence calls for such responsibility. Prosser on Torts, 458, § 60; Harper, *Liability Without Fault and Proximate Cause*, 30 Mich. L. Rev. 1001, 1006; 3 Restatement of Torts, 41, § 519. This limitation on the doctrine is indicated in the italicized portion of the rule as set forth in Restatement of Torts, *supra:*

> Except as stated in §§ 521-4, one who carries on an ultrahazardous activity is liable to another whose person, land or chattels the actor should recognize as likely to be harmed by the unpreventable miscarringe [sic] of the activity for harm resulting thereto *from that which makes the activity ultrahazardous,* although the utmost care is exercised to prevent the harm. (italics ours.)

This restriction which has been placed upon the application of the doctrine of absolute liability is based upon considerations of policy. As Professor Prosser has said:

> It is one thing to say that a dangerous enterprise must pay its way within reasonable limits, and quite another to say that it must bear responsibility for every extreme of harm that it may cause. The same practical necessity for the restriction of liability within some reasonable bounds, which arises in connection with problems of "proximate cause" in negligence cases, demands here that some limit be set. . . . This limitation has been expressed by saying that the defendant's duty to insure safety extends only to certain consequences. More commonly, it is said that the defendant's conduct is not the "proximate cause" of the damage. But ordinarily in such cases no question of causation is involved, and the limitation is one of the policy underlying liability. Prosser on Torts, 457, § 60.

Applying this principle to the case before us, the question comes down to this: Is the risk that any unusual vibration or noise may cause wild animals, which are being raised for commercial purposes, to kill their young, one of the things which make the activity of blasting ultrahazardous?

We have found nothing in the decisional law which would support an affirmative answer to this question. The decided cases. [sic] as well as common experience, indicate that the thing which makes blasting ultrahazardous is the risk that property or persons may be damaged or injured by coming into direct contact with flying debris, or by being directly affected by vibrations of the earth or concussions of the air. . . .

The relatively moderate vibration and noise which appellant's blasting produced at a distance of two and a quarter miles was no more than a usual incident of the ordinary life of the community. *See* 3 Restatement of Torts, 48, § 522, comment *a.* The trial court specifically found that the blasting did not unreasonably interfere with the enjoyment of their property by nearby landowners, except in the case of respondent's mink ranch.

It is the exceedingly nervous disposition of mink, rather than the normal risks inherent in blasting operations, which therefore must, as a matter of sound policy, bear the responsibility for the loss here sustained. We subscribe to the view . . . that the policy of the law does not impose the rule of strict liability to protect against harms incident to the plaintiff's extraordinary and unusual use of land. This is perhaps but an application of the principle that the extent to which one man in the lawful conduct of his business is liable for injuries to another involves an adjustment of conflicting interests. . . .

It is our conclusion that the risk of causing harm of the kind here experienced, as a result of the relatively minor vibration, concussion, and noise from distant blasting, is not the kind of risk which makes the activity of blasting ultrahazardous. The doctrine of absolute liability is therefore inapplicable under the facts of this case, and respondent is not entitled to recover damages.

The judgment is reversed.

GRADY, C.J., and MALLERY, FINLEY and OLSON, JJ., concur.

FOOD FOR THOUGHT

Foster is an example of causation issues limiting the applicability of strict liability. The Restatement, Second, of Torts § 524 supports *Foster* by limiting the application of strict liability to those harms that "would not have resulted but for the abnormally sensitive character of the plaintiff's activity." The Restatement also recognizes various other defenses that a defendant can raise. Section 523 permits a defendant to raise an assumption of the risk defense. Interestingly, § 524(2) states that a plaintiff's contributory negligence is not a defense unless the plaintiff "knowingly and unreasonably subject[ed] himself to the risk of harm. . . ." What would happen if the plaintiff knowingly, but reasonably, subjected himself to the risk of harm?

THE SURPRISING RESILIENCE OF THE NEGLIGENCE PRINCIPLE

Not long after American courts began applying strict liability in certain carefully selected areas, commentators began calling for broader applications of strict liability. The perceived benefits of compensating greater numbers of injured victims attracted scholars and judges alike. However, over the years strict liability has not yet fulfilled its much anticipated promise. Gerald W. Boston, in *Strict Liability for Abnormally Dangerous Activity: The Negligence Barrier*, 36 San Diego L. Rev. 597

(1999), concludes that courts continue to rely primarily on negligence, not strict liability, when they decide abnormally dangerous activity cases. Professor James A. Henderson, Jr., in *Why Negligence Dominates Tort*, 50 UCLA L. Rev. 377 (2002), reaches the same conclusion about the tort system generally. One explanation he offers for strict liability's relatively limited application is that, as a broad principle, strict liability calls for a system of social insurance that is not workable. In contrast, negligence leaves the question of insurance largely to the victims of dangerous activities, and thus does not confront these problems of uninsurability. For an argument that strict liability is alive and well and that scholars overstate the prominence of negligence-based liability, *see* Gregory C. Keating, *The Theory of Enterprise Liability and Common Law Strict Liability*, 54 Vand. L. Rev. 1285 (2001).

chapter 11

Products Liability

If one had to choose the area of tort law that has demonstrated the most growth in the past half century, products liability would win hands down. From a trickle of cases in the 1950s and a virtual explosion in the mid-1960s, the field has finally begun to mature in the first decades of this century. Today litigation for injury caused by defective and dangerous products is daily headline news. Whether it be litigation against manufacturers of automobiles, drugs, asbestos, cigarettes, industrial machinery, or sports equipment, products liability is a vibrant and developing field of law. A host of legal theories have been brought to bear to support plaintiffs' claims for liability: (1) Negligence, (2) Strict Tort Liability, (3) Express Warranty, (4) Misrepresentation, (5) Implied Warranty of Merchantability, and (6) Implied Warranty of Fitness for Particular Purpose. Sorting out all these theories is no easy task. Depending on the claim and depending on the jurisdiction, these theories may be duplicative or they may allow plaintiffs different avenues of recovery.

A. IN THE BEGINNING THERE WAS PRIVITY: THE NEGLIGENCE ACTION

You will recall that in Chapter 6, the chapter dealing with "limited duty rules," we identified several areas of negligence law in which the courts established special rules of limited liability or nonliability for conduct that could otherwise lead to foreseeable harm through the negligent conduct of the defendant. Each such limit was premised on policy considerations that supported a conclusion that to allow the negligence action to proceed would likely lead to an expansion of liability that would either be beyond the capability of courts to fairly adjudicate or would impose crushing liability on defendants.

The oldest and most dramatic no-duty rule in products liability limited the right of an injured person to recover against a negligent supplier of a defective product to the product supplier with whom the plaintiff had directly contracted. If the plaintiff was not in "contractual privity" with the seller, she had no cause of action. The English case first enunciating this rule, Winterbottom v. Wright, 10 M & W 109 (Exch. 1842), involved a plaintiff who sought to recover in negligence for injuries suffered when a horse-drawn mail coach collapsed while plaintiff was driving it. The defendant had sold the coach to the Postmaster General and contractually agreed to keep the coach in good repair. The plaintiff's claim was that the defendant was negligent in his duty to repair the coach and thus caused the plaintiff's injuries. The court rejected the plaintiff's claim, saying (*id.* at 114):

> There is no privity of contract between [the plaintiff and the defendant]; and if the plaintiff can sue, every passenger, or even any person passing along the road, who was injured by the upsetting of the coach, might bring a similar action. Unless we confine the operation of such contracts as this to the parties who entered into them, the most absurd and outrageous consequences, as to which I can see no limit, would ensue.

Although the privity doctrine crossed the ocean and became a staple of American products liability law, it did not take long before the courts began engrafting exceptions to it. In Thomas v. Winchester, 6 N.Y. 397 (1852), a seller of vegetable extracts mislabeled a poison and sold it to a pharmacist who in turn sold it to a customer. Though the customer was not in privity with the seller who was guilty of mislabeling, the court bypassed the privity rule since the defendant's negligence "put human life in imminent danger." *Id.* at 409. What did or did not constitute an "imminent danger" was the subject of considerable litigation over the years by plaintiffs who sought to bypass the privity barrier.

The true beginning of the modern products liability era came when Justice Cardozo slew the "privity dragon" in MacPherson v. Buick Motor Co., 111 N.E. 1050 (N.Y. 1916). Buick had sold a new car to a dealer who resold it to plaintiff. While plaintiff was driving, one of the wooden spokes of a wheel made of defective wood broke, crumbling into fragments. As a result, plaintiff was thrown from the car and suffered injuries. Since the injured plaintiff was not in privity with Buick, he could not sue the manufacturer for negligence. Cardozo, writing in his majestic style, had this to say (*id.* at 1053):

> We hold, then, that the principle of Thomas v. Winchester is not limited to poisons, explosives, and things of like nature, to things which in their normal operation are implements of destruction. If the nature of a thing is such that it is reasonably certain to place life and limb in peril when negligently made, it is then a thing of danger. Its nature gives warning of the consequences to be expected. If to the element of danger there is added knowledge that the thing will be used by persons other than the purchaser, and used without new tests, then, irrespective of contract, the manufacturer of this thing of danger is under a duty to make it carefully. . . . There must be knowledge of a danger, not merely possible, but probable. It is possible to use almost anything in a way that will make it dangerous if defective. That is not enough to charge the manufacturer with a duty independent of his contract. Whether a given thing is dangerous may be sometimes a question for the court and sometimes a question for the jury. There must also be

knowledge that in the usual course of events the danger will be shared by others than the buyer. Such knowledge may often be inferred from the nature of the transaction. . . . We have put aside the notion that the duty to safeguard life and limb, when the consequences of negligence may be foreseen, grows out of contract and nothing else. We have put the source of the obligation where it ought to be. We have put its source in the law.

Today the privity doctrine does not bar a plaintiff's personal injury claim for negligence in any American jurisdiction. Restatement, Second, of Torts § 395, comment *a* (1965). Nor, for that matter, does lack of privity bar recovery based on strict liability in tort. *Id.* at § 402A. Lack of privity does, however, remain an obstacle to recovery when a plaintiff seeks to recover for economic loss. Claims for economic loss are based in contract law and the lack of direct contractual relationship may be fatal for recovery. *See* Restatement, Third, of Torts: Products Liability § 21 (1998).

MAY A LAWYER THINK OUT OF THE BOX?

Roscoe Pound famously observed that the law must be stable, but it must not stand still. A lawyer has an obligation to advocate for an interpretation of the law that would be to the advantage of her client, but at the same time is subject to significant constraints on permissible legal arguments. In extreme cases, lawyers may be sanctioned for making false statements of law to a court, under Model Rule 3.3(a)(1). Consider the following example, taken from a real case. *See* Precision Specialty Metals, Inc. v. United States, 315 F.3d 1346 (Fed. Cir. 2003).

L is a lawyer representing a state agency in a dispute over a government contract. The opponent filed a motion for summary judgment, and according to the court's pretrial schedule, the state agency's response to the motion for summary judgment was to be filed by May 5, 2000. Because *L* could not comply with that deadline, she filed a motion seeking a 30-day extension of time. It was denied and the court ordered her to file a response "forthwith." Twelve days later, *L* filed the response. The opponent moved to strike it as untimely, and in response to the motion to strike, *L* quoted the following language from a decision of that state's supreme court:

> "Forthwith" means immediately, without delay, or as soon as the object may be accomplished by reasonable exertion. [Citing the case of *X v. Y.*]

She did not, however, quote the following sentence from the same decision:

> The Supreme Court has said of the word ["forthwith"] that "in matters of practice and pleading it is usually construed, and sometimes defined by rule of court, as within twenty-four hours."

Is *L*'s argument in the response to the motion to strike an honest one?

In the actual case, the federal court considered the lawyer's conduct a deliberate attempt to mislead it into thinking that a 12-day delay could still be considered filing "forthwith." In the example, *L* made a false statement to the court by omitting the sentence. There is a great deal of difference in meaning between these two statements:

"Forthwith" means as soon as possible.

"Forthwith" means as soon as possible, and courts generally have defined that to mean within 24 hours.

By stating that the *X v. Y* case stood for the former proposition but not the latter, *L* misrepresented the state of the law to the court in violation of Model Rule 3.3(a)(1). In the actual case, the lawyer was punished rather severely for mischaracterizing the law in this way.

In less extreme cases, lawyers are prohibited from bringing or defending a proceeding, or making any legal claim within a proceeding, without a basis in law and fact that is not frivolous, including a good-faith argument for the extension, modification, or reversal of existing law. *See* Model Rule 3.1. The word "frivolous" is meant to invoke the lawyer's "laugh test" — if the only argument you could offer to a court is one that makes you burst out laughing, it is frivolous. That is not much of a constraint, because there is usually some argument that a lawyer could make without cracking up. However, similar limitations exist in the civil procedure rules of most jurisdictions, including Rule 11 of the Federal Rules of Civil Procedure, and courts have sometimes been more aggressive in sanctioning lawyers who make inadequately supported legal arguments.

The reason we are talking about this issue now is that the *MacPherson* case is rightly considered one of the great turning points in the law. Critics of Rule 11 and other limitations on lawyers' legal advocacy sometimes suggest that a lawyer would be subject to sanctions for arguing, prior to *MacPherson*, that the privity rule should be abolished. If lawyers were not permitted to make that argument, how could we ever get to *MacPherson*? How can the law be stable without standing still? The answer is that lawyers are permitted to make a good-faith argument for the extension, modification, or reversal of existing law. At some point in time, prior to *MacPherson*, a lawyer was not able to say, "A plaintiff can maintain a claim against the manufacturer of a defective product, regardless of the lack of privity of contract." That would have been a false statement about the law. A lawyer, however, could make an argument that was more explicitly one for modification of existing law — for example: "The privity rule is anachronistic and inconsistent with negligence cases in other contexts, and should be abolished." There's nothing at all wrong with that argument. In order to be a good-faith argument, there must be some reason that the law should be modified or reversed. Inconsistency with the foreseeability rule, developing elsewhere in negligence law, would be enough of a reason to support a good-faith argument for the modification of the privity rule.

At some point, the law arguably evolved to the point that a lawyer might make a somewhat different argument — for example: "The principle of Thomas v. Winchester has now been applied to so many different products that it can no longer be said to be a special rule for inherently dangerous things like poisons, but has come to stand for liability whenever there is a defect in the product that puts a foreseeable user in danger." That's essentially what Cardozo said in MacPherson.

Debate has raged ever since over whether Cardozo engaged in some legal sleight of hand or whether he was fairly synthesizing the cases that had followed *Thomas*. (The first chapter of Edward Levi's 1949 book, *An Introduction to Legal Reasoning*, is a careful analysis of all of these cases.) One of the fascinating things about the common law is that lawyers can disagree reasonably about what the law provides. For the purposes of legal ethics, therefore, the question is whether a lawyer is permitted to argue that the law, properly understood, no longer included the privity limitation on actions against product manufacturers. Within a zone of reasonable disagreement, a lawyer is permitted to argue for an interpretation of the law that supports her client's position. Thus, the plaintiff's lawyer in *MacPherson* did not do anything wrong by suing the manufacturer and maintaining that the law permitted the plaintiff to recover. Cardozo's opinion recognized this change in law, but the lawyer's arguments anticipated it. Without the significant erosion of the principle of *Winterbottom v. Wright*, however, the lawyer would not have been permitted to file the lawsuit.

B. THE IMPLIED WARRANTY OF MERCHANTABILITY: THE CONTRACT ACTION

Negligence was not the only viable theory for an injured plaintiff to bring a cause of action for a product-related injury. Under the Uniform Sales Act, and later under the Uniform Commercial Code, a plaintiff who was injured by a defective product could bring an action for breach of the implied warranty of merchantability. U.C.C. § 2-314(2)(c). Accompanying the sale of every product came a warranty from the seller to the buyer that the product is "reasonably fit for the ordinary purposes for which such goods are used." A plaintiff proceeding under this U.C.C. provision did not have to prove that the defendant was negligent in producing or marketing the product. Plaintiff needed only to establish that the product that injured him was defective at the time of sale. As inviting as this theory was, it came with considerable baggage. First, since the action was in contract, plaintiff had to be in contractual privity with the seller. Typically, this limited the plaintiff to seeking recovery against the retailer, who was often judgment-proof. Second, under U.C.C. § 2-316, a seller was able to disclaim liability. Third, the U.C.C. statute of limitations requires that an action be brought within four years from tender of delivery (sale). U.C.C. § 2-725. Fourth, under U.C.C. § 2-607, a buyer had to give notice of breach within a reasonable time after discovery of the breach. These four horsemen rendered the U.C.C. practically useless for a plaintiff seeking to recover for her injuries.

C. STRICT TORT LIABILITY: COMBINING CONTRACT AND TORT

By the early 1960s, it became clear that serious change was in the works. The negligence cause of action was privity free, allowing a plaintiff to sue the manufacturer — but the plaintiff was saddled with the difficult task of proving fault. Admittedly, in cases where the plaintiff alleged that the product had a manufacturing defect because a bad apple slipped past quality control, the plaintiff could very often get the case to the jury under the doctrine of res ipsa loquitur. However, defendants in these cases sought to prove that they were not, in fact, negligent and that they had used the best quality control extant. If defendants were victorious, plaintiffs were resentful that they had suffered an injury as a result of a defective product and would not be compensated. If the plaintiffs were victorious despite evidence that the defendant had not been negligent, it was clear that although the courts were talking negligence they were, in actuality, imposing strict liability. As early as 1944, Judge Roger Traynor in Escola v. Coca Cola Bottling Co., 150 P.2d 436 (Cal. 1944), wrote a concurring opinion in a case where the California court had let a jury verdict against the defendant stand in spite of evidence that the defendant had exercised reasonable quality control in the manufacture of the Coke. Traynor argued that it was disingenuous to allow a plaintiff to recover for negligence when defendant had done nothing wrong. It was time to recognize that a plaintiff could recover in tort for the sale of a defective product without any fault on the part of the manufacturer.

If the desideratum was to get to a privity-free strict liability action against any seller of a defective product, the question remained what legal theory would optimally accomplish that result. Two options were available. Either courts could find some way around the U.C.C. barriers to recovery and impose strict liability under the implied warranty of merchantability, or they could flat out recognize strict liability in tort for the sale of defective products. The first case to allow for privity-free no-fault recovery was Henningsen v. Bloomfield Motors, Inc., 161 A.2d 69 (N.J. 1960). In that case, plaintiff brought suit for injuries sustained when a new Plymouth that her husband had purchased two weeks earlier went out of control. Mrs. Henningsen was driving when she heard a loud noise "from the bottom, by the hood." It "felt as if something cracked." The steering wheel spun in her hands; the car veered sharply to the right and crashed into a highway sign and a brick wall. The trial judge dismissed negligence counts against Chrysler, the manufacturer of the car. The judge submitted the issue of breach of implied warranty of merchantability to the jury, which found against both the retailer and the manufacturer.

The auto manufacturer, Chrysler, appealed the verdict against it on the grounds that it was not in privity with the injured plaintiff. In striking down the privity defense the court said (*id.* at 83-84):

> Under modern conditions the ordinary layman, on responding to the importuning of colorful advertising, has neither the opportunity nor the capacity to inspect or to determine the fitness of an automobile for use; he must rely on the manufacturer who has control of its construction, and to some degree on the dealer who, to the limited extent called for by the manufacturer's instructions, inspects and services it before delivery. In such a marketing milieu his remedies and those of persons who properly claim through him should not depend "upon the intricacies of the law of sales. The obligation of the manufacturer should not be based alone on privity of contract. It should rest, as was once said, upon 'the demands of social justice.'" ...

Accordingly, we hold that under modern marketing conditions, when a manufacturer puts a new automobile in the stream of trade and promotes its purchase by the public, an implied warranty that it is reasonably suitable for use as such accompanies it into the hands of the ultimate purchaser. Absence of agency between the manufacturer and the dealer who makes the ultimate sale is immaterial.

The *Henningsen* decision, as important as it was, sought to impose strict liability against manufacturers within the framework of the Uniform Commercial Code. Three years later, Judge Traynor, who had urged the adoption of strict liability almost two decades earlier, authored an opinion that rejected the U.C.C. contract-based approach to strict liability in favor of a straightforward tort-based theory. In Greenman v. Yuba Power Products, Inc., 377 P.2d 897 (Cal. 1963), plaintiff was injured by a defective power tool that his wife bought for him as a Christmas present. The court, in affirming a jury verdict against the manufacturer, made it clear that "the liability is not one governed by the law of contract warranties but by the law of strict liability in tort." *Id.* at 901.

In the early 1960s, the legendary Dean William Prosser served as the Reporter for the Restatement, Second, of Torts. He was well on the way to convincing the American Law Institute to adopt strict liability for the sale of defective products. If he needed any help to make his case, *Greenman* now gave him solid authority backed with the imprimatur of the country's most prestigious state appellate court judge. The American Law Institute approved the adoption of § 402A for inclusion in the Restatement, Second, of Torts. Its influence on the courts cannot be overstated. It reads:

§ 402A. Special Liability of Seller of Product for Physical Harm to User or Consumer

(1) One who sells any product in a defective condition unreasonably dangerous to the user or consumer or to his property is subject to liability for physical harm thereby caused to the ultimate user or consumer, or to his property, if

(a) the seller is engaged in the business of selling such a product, and

(b) it is expected to and does reach the user or consumer without substantial change in the condition in which it is sold.

(2) The rule stated in Subsection (1) applies although

(a) the seller has exercised all possible care in the preparation and sale of his product, and

(b) the user or consumer has not bought the product from or entered into any contractual relation with the seller.

Comment:

i. Unreasonably dangerous. The rule stated in this Section applies only where the defective condition of the product makes it unreasonably dangerous to the user or consumer. Many products cannot possibly be made entirely safe for all consumption, and any food or drug necessarily involves some risk of harm, if only from over-consumption. Ordinary sugar is a deadly poison to diabetics, and castor oil found use under Mussolini as an instrument of torture. That is not what is meant by "unreasonably dangerous" in this Section. The article sold must be dangerous to an extent beyond that which would be contemplated by the ordinary consumer who purchases it, with the ordinary knowledge common to the community as to its characteristics. Good whiskey is not unreasonably dangerous merely because it will make some people drunk, and is especially dangerous to alcoholics; but bad whiskey, containing a dangerous amount of fusel oil, is unreasonably dangerous. Good tobacco is not unreasonably dangerous merely because the effects of smoking may be harmful; but tobacco containing something like marijuana may be unreasonably dangerous. Good butter is not unreasonably dangerous merely because, if such be the case, it deposits cholesterol in the arteries and leads to heart attacks; but bad butter, contaminated with poisonous fish oil, is unreasonably dangerous.

D. THE HARD WORK: DEFINING AND PROVING DEFECT

The euphoria among plaintiff's lawyers that accompanied the adoption of § 402A's adoption in 1965, dispensing with the detested privity defense, masked problems that were to come to the fore over the next several decades. The most serious problem that was to emerge over time was the definition of defect. When Dean Prosser drafted § 402A imposing strict liability for the sale of defective products, he clearly had manufacturing defects in mind. There could be little argument that a bottle of Coca-Cola that came off the assembly line with a weakness in the glass structure that broke when the user handled the bottle was defective. The imposition of privity-free strict liability did not signal a significant expansion of liability. As Judge Traynor had concluded decades earlier in *Escola*, courts had been imposing strict liability under the guise of negligence in any event.

Over the years, as the case law developed, attention shifted from claims alleging manufacturing defects to those claiming that a product was defectively designed, or marketed with inadequate instructions or warnings. A huge body of appellate decisions sought to work out the rules that would govern design and warning cases. Since § 402A provided very little guidance as to what strict liability meant for design and warning cases, courts were at sea. In the case of a manufacturing defect, strict liability meant that if a product unit came off the assembly line and did not meet the manufacturer's own standard, the product was defective. The manufacturer, so to speak, set its own design standard — the design to which all units were intended to conform. If the product departed from that standard and the defect was the cause of the harm, the manufacturer would be subject to liability even if the manufacturer exercised reasonable care in its quality control. But, in a case alleging defective design or warning, by what standard would the defendant's product be measured to decide whether or not it was defective? And what did it mean to say the defendant was strictly liable? In the ensuing material, we shall examine the three categories of defect. We shall find that there is almost no controversy about the law governing manufacturing defects, some controversy about failure to warn, and great controversy about what it takes to establish a claim of defective design.

In 1992, the American Law Institute undertook a project to restate the law of products liability. Professors Twerski and Henderson were appointed as Reporters charged with the responsibility of drafting the Restatement, Third, of Torts: Products Liability (hereinafter Products Liability Restatement). In 1998 the American Law Institute approved the Products Liability Restatement. How this new Restatement has fared in the courts will be discussed in the ensuing materials. Perhaps the most significant departure of the Products Liability Restatement from § 402A is that it abandons the single definition of "defect" in favor of separate definitions for each category of defect depending on the nature of the defect. The Products Liability Restatement provides as follows:

§ 1. Liability of Commercial Seller or Distributor for Harm Caused by Defective Products

One engaged in the business of selling or otherwise distributing products who sells or distributes a defective product is subject to liability for harm to persons or property caused by the defect.

§ 2. Categories of Product Defect

A product is defective when, at the time of sale or distribution, it contains a manufacturing defect, is defective in design, or is defective because of inadequate instructions or warnings. A product:

(a) contains a manufacturing defect when the product departs from its intended design even though all possible care was exercised in the preparation and marketing of the product;

(b) is defective in design when the foreseeable risks of harm posed by the product could have been reduced or avoided by the adoption of a reasonable alternative design by the seller or other distributor, or a predecessor in the commercial chain of distribution, and the omission of the alternative design renders the product not reasonably safe;

(c) is defective because of inadequate instructions or warnings when the foreseeable risks of harm posed by the product could have been reduced or avoided by the provision of reasonable instructions or warnings by the seller or other distributor, or a predecessor in the commercial chain of distribution, and the omission of the instructions or warnings renders the product not reasonably safe.

1. Manufacturing Defects

As noted earlier, few disagree with the definition of defect set forth in § 2(a). A product unit that departs from its intended design is defective. Most of the litigation dealing with manufacturing defects concerns how to prove that the product was defective at the time of sale. A product that has left the hands of the manufacturer may have been compromised over time. Often expert testimony is available to prove that the defect was present in the product when it was first manufactured. When such testimony is not available or is, at best, equivocal, plaintiffs may face problems establishing defect. The following case illustrates one way that defect may be made out.

WELGE v. PLANTERS LIFESAVERS CO.
17 F.3d 209 (7th Cir. 1994)

POSNER, Chief Judge.

Richard Welge, forty-something but young in spirit, loves to sprinkle peanuts on his ice cream sundaes. On January 18, 1991, Karen Godfrey, with whom Welge boards, bought a 24-ounce vacuum-sealed plastic-capped jar of Planters peanuts for him at a K-Mart store in Chicago. To obtain a $2 rebate that the maker of Alka-Seltzer was offering to anyone who bought a "party" item, such as peanuts, Godfrey needed proof of her purchase of the jar of peanuts; so, using an Exacto knife (basically a razor blade with a handle), she removed the part of the label that contained the bar code. She then placed the jar on top of the refrigerator, where Welge could get at it without rooting about in her cupboards. About a week later, Welge removed the plastic seal from the jar, uncapped it, took some peanuts, replaced the cap, and returned the jar to the top of the refrigerator, all without incident. A week after that, on February 3, the accident occurred. Welge took down the jar, removed the plastic cap, spilled some peanuts into his left hand to put on his sundae, and replaced the cap with his right hand — but as he pushed the cap down on the open jar the jar shattered. His hand, continuing in its downward motion, was severely cut, and is now, he claims, permanently impaired.

Welge brought this products liability suit in federal district court under the diversity jurisdiction; Illinois law governs the substantive issues. Welge named three defendants. . . . They are K-Mart, which sold the jar of peanuts to Karen Godfrey; Planters, which manufactured the product — that is to say, filled the glass jar with peanuts and sealed and capped it; and Brockway, which manufactured the glass jar itself and sold it to Planters. After pretrial discovery was complete, the defendants moved for summary judgment. The district judge granted the motion on the ground that the plaintiff had failed to exclude possible causes of the accident other than a defect introduced during the manufacturing process.

No doubt there are men strong enough to shatter a thick glass jar with one blow. But Welge's testimony stands uncontradicted that he used no more than the normal force that one exerts in snapping a plastic lid onto a jar. So the jar must have been defective. No expert testimony and no fancy doctrine are required for such a conclusion. A nondefective jar does not shatter when normal force is used to clamp its plastic lid on. The question is when the defect was introduced. . . . [T]estimony by Welge and Karen Godfrey, if believed — and at this stage in the proceedings we are required to believe it — excludes all reasonable possibility that the defect was introduced into the jar after Godfrey plucked it from a shelf in the K-Mart store. From the shelf she put it in her shopping cart. The checker at the check-out counter scanned the bar code without banging the jar. She then placed the jar in a plastic bag. Godfrey carried the bag to her car and put it on the floor. She drove directly home, without incident. After the bar-code portion of the label was removed, the jar sat on top of the refrigerator except for the two times Welge removed it to take peanuts out of it. Throughout this process it was not, so far as anyone knows, jostled, dropped, bumped, or otherwise subjected to stress beyond what is to be expected in the ordinary use of the product. Chicago is not Los Angeles; there were no earthquakes. Chicago is not Amityville either; no supernatural interventions are alleged. So the defect must have been introduced earlier, when the jar was in the hands of the defendants.

But, they argue, this overlooks two things. One is that Karen Godfrey took a knife to the jar. And no doubt one can weaken a glass jar with a knife. But nothing is more common or, we should have thought, more harmless than to use a knife or a razor blade to remove a label from a jar or bottle. . . . The Alka-Seltzer promotion to which Karen Godfrey was responding when she removed a portion of the label of the jar of Planters peanuts was in the K-Mart store. . . . If one just wants to efface a label one can usually do that by scraping it off with a fingernail, but to remove the label intact requires the use of a knife or a razor blade. . . .

Even so, the defendants point out, it is always *possible* that the jar was damaged while it was sitting unattended on the top of the refrigerator, in which event they are not responsible. Only if it had been securely under lock and key when not being used could the plaintiff and Karen Godfrey be *certain* that nothing happened to damage it after she brought it home. That is true — there are no meta-physical certainties — but it leads nowhere. Elves may have played ninepins with the jar of peanuts while Welge and Godfrey were sleeping; but elves could remove a jar of peanuts from a locked cupboard. The plaintiff in a products liability suit is not required to exclude every possibility, however fantastic or remote, that the defect which led to the accident was caused by someone other than one of the defendants. The doctrine of res ipsa loquitur teaches that an accident that is unlikely to occur unless the defendant *was* negligent is itself circumstantial evidence that the defendant was negligent. The doctrine is not strictly applicable to a products liability case because unlike an ordinary accident case the defendant in a products case has parted with possession and control of the harmful object before the accident occurs. . . . But the doctrine merely instantiates the broader principle, which is as applicable to a products case as to any other tort case, that an accident can itself be evidence of liability. . . . If it is the kind of accident that would not have occurred but for a defect in the product, and if it is reasonably plain that the defect was not introduced after the product was sold. The accident is evidence that the product was defective when sold. The second condition (as well as the first) has been established here, at least to a probability sufficient to defeat a motion for summary judgment. . . .

Of course, unlikely as it may seem that the defect was introduced into the jar after Karen Godfrey bought it, if the plaintiffs' testimony is believed, other evidence might make their testimony unworthy of belief — might even show, contrary to all the probabilities, that the knife or some mysterious night visitor caused the defect after all. The fragments of glass into which the jar shattered were preserved and were examined by experts for both sides. The experts agreed that the jar must have contained a defect but they could not find the fracture that had precipitated the shattering of the jar and they could not figure out when the defect that caused the fracture that caused the collapse of the jar had come into being. The defendants' experts could neither rule out, nor rule in, the possibility that the defect had been introduced at some stage of the manufacturing process. The plaintiff's expert noticed what he thought was a preexisting crack in one of the fragments, and he speculated that a similar crack might have caused the fracture that shattered the jar. This, the district judge ruled, was not enough. . . .

In reaching the result she did the district judge relied heavily on Erzrumly v. Dominick's Finer Foods, Inc., 365 N.E.2d 684 (Ill. App. 1977). A six-year-old was injured by a Coke bottle that she was carrying up a flight of stairs to her family's apartment shortly after its purchase. The court held that the plaintiff had failed to eliminate the possibility that the Coke bottle had failed because of something that had happened after it left the store. If, as the defendants in our case represent, the bottle in *Erzrumly* "exploded," that case would be very close to this one. A non-defective Coke bottle is unlikely to explode without very rough handling. The contents are under pressure, it is true, but the glass is strengthened accordingly. But it was unclear in *Erzrumly* what had happened to the bottle. There was testimony that the accident had been preceded by the sound of a bottle exploding but there was other evidence that the bottle may simply have been dropped and have broken — the latter being the sort of accident that happens commonly after purchase. Although the opinion contains some broad language helpful to the defendants in the present case, the holding was simply that murky facts required the plaintiff to make a greater effort to determine whether the product was defective when it left the store. Here we know to a virtual certainty (always assuming that the plaintiff's evidence is believed, which is a matter for the jury) that the accident was not due to mishandling after purchase but to a defect that had been introduced earlier. . . .

Reversed and Remanded.

THE RESTATEMENT AND CASE LAW ON INFERENCE OF DEFECT

The Products Liability Restatement provides:

§ 3. Circumstantial Evidence Supporting Inference of Product Defect

It may be inferred that the harm sustained by the plaintiff was caused by a product defect existing at the time of sale or distribution, without proof of a specific defect, when the incident that harmed the plaintiff:

(a) was of a kind that ordinarily occurs as a result of product defect; and

(b) was not, in the particular case, solely the result of causes other than product defect existing at the time of sale or distribution.

Case law, both before and after the adoption of the Restatement, is in agreement that a res ipsa-like inference may be drawn when the requisite conditions set forth in § 3 are met. *See, e.g.,* Martin v. Apex Tool Group, 961 F. Supp. 2d 954 (N.D. Iowa 2013) (denying defendant's motion for summary judgment, in case where a pry bar snapped while in use, causing injuries to plaintiff's arm, on ground that the plaintiff could use circumstantial evidence to establish that a pry bar was defective under Iowa law); Varner v. MHS, Ltd., 2 F. Supp. 3d 584 (M.D. Pa. 2014) (denying defendant's motion for summary judgment, where the plaintiff used a remote-control crane to lift heavy equipment, and the strap connecting the crane to the equipment broke, causing the equipment to fall and land on the plaintiff's arm, because the circumstantial evidence created a question of fact as to whether a boothopper strap broke because it was manufactured defectively, or because it was not used correctly); General Dynamics Armament and Tech. Prod., Inc., 696 F. Supp. 2d 1163 (D. Haw. 2010) (res ipsa applies to a strict liability claim where plaintiff was killed due to a premature explosion of a mortar cartridge even though the cause of the explosion was not conclusively determined because the cartridge was destroyed); Ellis v. Beemiller, 910 F. Supp. 2d 768 (W.D. Pa. 2012) (granting summary judgment to defendant on ground that the plaintiff did not put forth enough circumstantial evidence to support their theory that the plaintiff's gun malfunctioned and exploded without the trigger being pulled).

For an exhaustive list of authority supporting the general principle set forth in § 3, *see* Products Liability Restatement § 3, Reporters Notes. *See also* Matthew P. Johnson, *Rolling the "Barrel" a Little Further: Allowing Res Ipsa Loquitur to Assist in Proving Strict Liability in Tort Manufacturing Defects,* 38 Wm. & Mary L. Rev. 1197 (1997).

2. Design Defects

When a plaintiff alleges that a product is defectively designed, the question of what standard courts should apply in determining whether the design is defective has no easy resolution. One cannot simply say that strict liability applies and the plaintiff is entitled to recover for any injury suffered caused by the product's design. Every product has a design. If an automobile runs over a plaintiff because the driver was speeding 30 mph over the limit, the plaintiff was injured by the product's design. Unless the law is ready to impose liability for all product-related injuries without regard to defect, courts must find some way to define what constitutes a defective design.

a. Risk-Utility Balancing: Reasonable Alternative Design

The simplest and most straightforward solution to the problem of defining sign defects would be to utilize Learned Hand's risk-utility balancing test to decide whether a product design is reasonably safe. This approach is adopted in the Products Liability Restatement § 2(b). In requiring that a plaintiff establish that "the foreseeable risks of harm could have been reduced or avoided by the adoption of a reasonable alternative design," the Restatement advocates that courts examine the risk-utility trade-offs in determining whether a product is defective. Section 2(b), comment *f* sets out some of the major factors to be considered in making the determination:

> *f. Design defects: factors relevant in determining whether the omission of a reasonable alternative design renders a product not reasonably safe.* Subsection (b) states that a product is defective in design if the omission of a reasonable alternative

design renders the product not reasonably safe. A broad range of factors may be considered in determining whether an alternative design is reasonable and whether its omission renders a product not reasonably safe. The factors include, among others, the magnitude and probability of the foreseeable risks of harm, the instructions and warnings accompanying the product, and the nature and strength of consumer expectations regarding the product, including expectations arising from product portrayal and marketing. . . . The relative advantages and disadvantages of the product as designed and as it alternatively could have been designed may also be considered. Thus, the likely effects of the alternative design on production costs; the effects of the alternative design on product longevity, maintenance, repair, and esthetics; and the range of consumer choice among products are factors that may be taken into account. A plaintiff is not necessarily required to introduce proof on all of these factors; their relevance, and the relevance of other factors, will vary from case to case. Moreover, the factors interact with one another. For example, evidence of the magnitude and probability of foreseeable harm may be offset by evidence that the proposed alternative design would reduce the efficiency and the utility of the product. On the other hand, evidence that a proposed alternative design would increase production costs may be offset by evidence that product portrayal and marketing created substantial expectations of performance or safety, thus increasing the probability of foreseeable harm. Depending on the mix of these factors, a number of variations in the design of a given product may meet the test in Subsection (b). On the other hand, it is not a factor under Subsection (b) that the imposition of liability would have a negative effect on corporate earnings or would reduce employment in a given industry.

When evaluating the reasonableness of a design alternative, the overall safety of the product must be considered. It is not sufficient that the alternative design would have reduced or prevented the harm suffered by the plaintiff if it would also have introduced into the product other dangers of equal or greater magnitude.

For our money, one of the best-reasoned decisions on the subject of design defect emanated from the Michigan Supreme Court in 1984. It deserves a careful reading.

PRENTIS v. YALE MANUFACTURING CO.
365 N.W.2d 176 (Mich. 1984)

BOYLE, J.

This products liability action arose out of injuries sustained in an accident involving the operation of a hand-operated forklift manufactured by defendant. . . . Plaintiffs John Prentis and his wife, Helen, brought suit alleging both negligence and breach of implied warranty, predicating defendant manufacturer's liability upon the alleged defective design of the forklift. Although the trial judge included both negligence and breach of warranty in his statement of plaintiffs' theory of the case to the jury, he refused to give plaintiffs' requested instructions on breach of implied warranty. A judgment for the defendant, upon a jury verdict of no cause of action, was reversed by the Court of Appeals, which held that the trial court's failure to charge the jury as requested was reversible error, mandating a new trial. . . .

I

Facts

The facts of this case are not seriously in dispute. In April of 1970, plaintiff John Prentis, who was employed as foreman of the parts department at an automobile dealership, sustained a hip injury in an accident involving the use of a forklift manufactured by defendant Yale Manufacturing Company and sold to plaintiff's employer in 1952. The forklift was a stand-up or walking type, termed by defendant a "walkie hi-lo" model, rather than a riding or sit down variety. It was operated by lifting its handle up, much like the handle of a wagon. The forklift was estimated by plaintiff to weigh about two thousand pounds and was powered by a large battery, which had to be recharged every night. The machine was equipped with a hand controlled "dead-man" switch which normally prevented it from moving if the operator let go of the handle or controls.

Mr. Prentis, who was sixty-three years old at the time of the accident, had been working at the automobile dealership for two years prior to his injury, and testified that he had occasionally operated the forklift during that period, although he had never been formally instructed as to its operation by his employer. He testified that he was aware of and had previously experienced problems with the machine. After use for five or six hours, the battery charge would run down and the machine would operate erratically. When the battery was low, Mr. Prentis said he would play the handle back and forth to get the machine to start and when he did this the machine was subject to power surges which he said could throw a person off balance if care was not taken. He testified that prior to his accident, the machine had broken through the garage door of the dealership five or six times due to such power surges.

The accident in which Mr. Prentis was injured occurred late in the day, and he testified that he was aware at the time that the battery charge on the forklift was running low. After using the machine to assist him in placing an engine inside the cargo area of a delivery van, while the forklift was in tow behind him on a slightly inclined ramp leading from the delivery bay, Mr. Prentis attempted to start the machine by working the handle up and down. When the machine experienced a power surge, he lost his footing and fell to the ground. It appears that plaintiff's injuries were a result of the fall only, as the machine did not hit or run over him, but continued past him and stopped when it ran into a parked car. Mr. Prentis received extensive treatment for multiple fractures of his left hip. . . .

II

Analysis of the Current Status of the Law Regarding Manufacturers' Liability for Defective Design

The development of the law of tort liability for physical injury caused by products is perhaps the most striking and dramatic of all the numerous stories in the portfolio of modern tort scenarios. When the societal goal of holding manufacturers accountable for the safety of their products has been threatened by the interposition of technical rules of law, it has been the rules that have gradually given way.

However, this has never meant that courts have been willing to impose absolute liability in this context and from their earliest application, theories of products liability have been viewed as tort doctrines which should not be confused with the imposition of absolute liability. As this Court noted in Piercefield v. Remington Arms Co., Inc., . . . 133 N.W.2d 129 (1965):

> Some quibbler may allege that this is liability without fault. It is not. . . . [A] plaintiff relying upon the rule must prove a defect attributable to the manufacturer and causal connection between that defect and the injury or damage of which he complains. When able to do that, then and only then may he recover against the manufacturer of the defective product. . . .

Like the courts in every other state, whether a suit is based upon negligence or implied warranty, we require the plaintiff to prove that the product itself is actionable — that something is wrong with it that makes it dangerous. This idea of "something wrong" is usually expressed by the adjective "defective" and the plaintiff must, in every case, in every jurisdiction, show that the product was defective. . . .

As a term of art, "defective" gives little difficulty when something goes wrong in the manufacturing process and the product is not in its intended condition. In the case of a "manufacturing defect," the product may be evaluated against the manufacturer's own production standards, as manifested by that manufacturer's other like products.

However, injuries caused by the condition of a product may also be actionable if the product's design, which is the result of intentional design decisions of the manufacturer, is not sufficiently safe. Conscious design defect cases provide no such simple test. The very question whether a defect in fact exists is central to a court's inquiry. It is only in design defect cases that a court is called upon to supply the standard for defectiveness. Thus, the term "defect" in design cases is "an epithet — an expression for the legal conclusion rather than a test for reaching that conclusion." See Wade, *On Product "Design Defects" and Their Actionability*, 33 Vand. L.R. 551, 552 (1980). . . .

The approaches for determination of the meaning of "defect" in design cases fall into four general categories. The first, usually associated with Dean Wade, employs a negligence risk-utility analysis, but focuses upon whether the manufacturer would be judged negligent if it had known of the product's dangerous condition at the time it was marketed. The second, associated with Dean Keeton, compares the risk and utility of the product at the time of trial. The third focuses on consumer expectations about the product. The fourth combines the risk-utility and consumer-expectation tests. While courts have included many other individual variations in their formulations, the overwhelming consensus among courts deciding defective design cases is in the use of some form of risk-utility analysis, either as an exclusive or alternative ground of liability. Risk-utility analysis in this context always involves assessment of the decisions made by manufacturers with respect to the design of their products.

"The law purports to stand as a watchdog to ensure that product design decisions made by manufacturers do not expose product users to unreasonable risks of injury. Thus, in a design defect case, the issue is whether the manufacturer properly weighed the alternatives and evaluated the trade-offs and thereby developed a reasonably safe product; the focus is unmistakably on the *quality* of the decision and whether the decision conforms to socially acceptable standards." [Twerski, et al., *Shifting Perspectives in Products Liability: From Quality to Process Standards,* 55 N.Y.U. L. Rev. 259 (1980).]

The risk-utility balancing test is merely a detailed version of Judge Learned Hand's negligence calculus. *See* United States v. Carroll Towing Co., 159 F.2d 169, 173 (CA 2, 1947). As Dean Prosser has pointed out, the liability of the manufacturer rests "upon a departure from proper standards of care, so that the tort is essentially a matter of negligence."[25]

Although many courts have insisted that the risk-utility tests they are applying are not negligence tests because their focus is on the *product* rather than the manufacturer's *conduct,* see, e.g., Barker v. Lull Engineering Co., Inc., 573 P.2d 443 (1978), the distinction on closer examination appears to be nothing more than semantic. As a common-sense matter, the jury weighs competing factors presented in evidence and reaches a conclusion about the judgment or decision (i.e., *conduct*) of the manufacturer. The underlying negligence calculus is inescapable. As noted by Professor Birnbaum:

> When a jury decides that the risk of harm outweighs the utility of a particular design (that the product is not as safe as it *should* be) it is saying that in choosing the particular design and cost trade-offs, the manufacturer exposed the consumer to greater risk of danger than he should have. Conceptually and analytically, this approach bespeaks negligence. Birnbaum, *Unmasking the Test for Design Defect: From Negligence [to Warranty] to Strict Liability to Negligence*, 33 Van. L.R. 593, 610 (1980). . . .

The competing factors to be weighed under a risk-utility balancing test invite the trier of fact to consider the alternatives and risks faced by the manufacturer and to determine whether in light of these the manufacturer exercised reasonable care in making the design choices it made. Instructing a jury that weighing factors concerning conduct and judgment must yield a conclusion that does not describe conduct is confusing at best.

The Model Uniform Product Liability Act was published in 1979 by the Department of Commerce for voluntary use by the states. The act adopts a negligence or fault system with respect to design defects. It is important to examine the rationale underlying the UPLA's adoption of negligence as the criteria for liability

---

25. Prosser, Torts (4th ed), § 96, p. 644. This discussion took place in the context of strict liability in tort, which, contrary to the assertions of Justice Levin in his dissent, this Court has never adopted. See post, p. 697 (Levin, J., dissenting,) see also fn 9. However, as Prosser emphasized in the quoted passage, even in jurisdictions that have adopted the strict liability doctrine, the proper test for determining a manufacturer's liability for defective design is negligence.

in design defect cases. The drafters rejected, as a reason for application of strict liability to design defect cases, the theory of risk distribution wherein the product seller distributes the costs of all product-related risks through liability insurance. They believe that a "firmer liability foundation" than strict liability is needed in a design defect case because the whole product line is at risk. Furthermore, the drafters believed that a fault system would provide greater incentives for loss prevention. . . .

The approach of the UPLA has been approved by several commentators, whose analysis is also instructive. First, unlike manufacturing defects, design defects result from deliberate and documentable decisions on the part of manufacturers, and plaintiffs should be able to learn the facts surrounding these decisions through liberalized modern discovery rules. Access to expert witnesses and technical data are available to aid plaintiffs in proving the manufacturer's design decision was ill considered.

Second, to the extent that a primary purpose of products liability law is to encourage the design of safer products and thereby reduce the incidence of injuries, a negligence standard that would reward the careful manufacturer and penalize the careless is more likely to achieve that purpose. A greater incentive to design safer products will result from a fault system where resources devoted to careful and safe design will pay dividends in the form of fewer claims and lower insurance premiums for the manufacturer with a good design safety record. The incentive will result from the knowledge that a distinction is made between those who are careful and those who are not.

Third, a verdict for the plaintiff in a design defect case is the equivalent of a determination that an entire product line is defective. It usually will involve a significant portion of the manufacturer's assets and the public may be deprived of a product. Thus, the plaintiff should be required to pass the higher threshold of a fault test in order to threaten an entire product line. The traditional tort law of negligence better serves this purpose.

Fourth, a fault system incorporates greater intrinsic fairness in that the careful safety-oriented manufacturer will not bear the burden of paying for losses caused by the negligent product seller. It will also follow that the customers of the careful manufacturer will not through its prices pay for the negligence of the careless. As a final bonus, the careful manufacturer with fewer claims and lower insurance premiums may, through lower prices as well as safer products, attract the customers of less careful competitors.

We find the formula adopted by the UPLA on the question of defective design to have the merit of being clear and understandable. We recognize that in products liability cases against manufacturers based upon alleged defects in the design of a product, the courts of this state have attempted to avoid both the notion of fault implicit in negligence and the harshness of no-fault implicit in absolute liability. Thus, on the basis of the heritage of contract and sales law underlying concepts of implied warranty, we have in the past approved instructions that attempted to focus a jury's attention on the condition of a product rather than on the reasonableness of the manufacturer's conduct or decision. We are persuaded that in so doing in the context of cases against the manufacturers of products *based upon allegations of defective design,* we have engaged in a process that may have served to confuse, rather than enlighten, jurors, who must ultimately apply understandable guidelines if they are to justly adjudicate the rights and duties of all parties. Imposing a negligence standard for design defect litigation is only to define in a coherent fashion what our litigants in this case are in fact arguing and what our jurors are in essence analyzing. Thus we adopt, forthrightly, a pure negligence, risk-utility test in products liability actions against manufacturers of products, where liability is predicated upon defective design.

III

Application to the Facts of This Case

Applying these principles to the facts of this case, although plaintiffs alleged that their injuries were proximately caused by defendant's negligence and breach of an implied warranty, their evidence and proofs at trial focused on the single claim that the defendant *defectively designed* the "walkie hi-lo" forklift, because it failed to provide a seat or platform for the operator. Thus, recovery under either theory required the jury to determine that the forklift was defectively designed by defendant. . . . The factual inquiry was: whether the design of defendant's forklift was "unreasonably dangerous" because it did not contain a seat or platform for the operator. . . .

The trial court properly recognized that the standards of liability under the theories of implied warranty and negligence were indistinguishable and that instructions on both would only confuse the jury. Accordingly, the trial judge's instructions regarding the standard of care and theories of liability properly informed the jury of defendant's legal duties as the manufacturer of the forklift. The court set forth the necessary elements for determining whether defendant defectively designed the forklift when it stated:

> A manufacturer of a product made under a plan or design which makes it dangerous for uses for which it is manufactured is[, however,] subject to liability to others whom he should expect to use the product or to be endangered by its probable use from physical harm caused by his failure to exercise reasonable care in the adoption of a safe plan or design.
>
> A manufacturer has a duty to use reasonable care in designing his product and guard it against a foreseeable and unreasonable risk of injury and this may even include misuse which might reasonably be anticipated.

In essence, the jury was instructed to consider whether the manufacturer took reasonable care in light of any reasonably foreseeable use of the product which might cause harm or injury. Caldwell v. Fox, *supra.*

Therefore we hold that in a products liability action against a manufacturer, based upon defective design, the jury need only be instructed on a single unified theory of negligent design.

The judgment of the Court of Appeals is reversed, and the judgment of the trial court is reinstated.

WILLIAMS, C.J., and BRICKLEY and RYAN, JJ., concur. CAVANAGH, J., concurring in result.

[Dissenting opinion omitted.]

DOES RISK-UTILITY BALANCING REQUIRE PROOF OF A REASONABLE ALTERNATIVE DESIGN?

When applying the risk-utility test to the facts in *Prentis*, the court said that the plaintiff's claim boiled down to whether the forklift manufacturer should have provided a seat or platform for the operator. In short, should the manufacturer have adopted a "reasonable alternative design" (RAD). Later Michigan cases have been explicit in requiring plaintiff to prove a RAD in order to make out a prima facie case for design defect. For example, in Reeves v. Cincinnati, Inc., 439 N.W.2d 326, 329 (Mich. Ct. App. 1989) the court said:

> A prima facie case of a design defect premised upon the omission of a safety device requires first a showing of the magnitude of foreseeable risks, including the likelihood of occurrence of the type of accident precipitating the need for the safety device, and the severity of the injuries sustainable from such an accident. It *secondly requires a showing of alternative safety devices and whether those devices would have been effective as a reasonable means of minimizing the foreseeable risk of danger.* This latter showing may entail an evaluation of the alternative design in terms of its additional utility as a safety measure and its trade-offs against the costs and effective use of the product. (Emphasis added.)

See also Wingard v. Nutro Corp., 2007 Mich. App. LEXIS 633 (requiring alternative design to impose liability); Miller v. Ingersoll-Rand Co., 148 Fed. Appx. 420 (6th Cir. 2005) (applying Michigan law) (summary judgment for defendant manufacturer affirmed on ground that plaintiff had not proved that any of plaintiff's alternative designs would have been feasible or would have prevented plaintiff's injuries).

New Jersey and Iowa have also explicitly held that plaintiff has the burden of proving a RAD. Lewis v. American Cyanamid Co., 715 A.2d 967, 983 (N.J. 1998); Cavanaugh v. Skil Corp., 751 A.2d 518, 521 (N.J. 2000); Wright v. Brooke Group Ltd., 652 N.W.2d 159 (Iowa 2002) (court adopts § 2(b)). *See also* Morales v. E.D. Etnyre & Co., 382 F. Supp. 2d 1278 (D.N.M. 2005) (*Erie* guess that New Mexico would adopt § 2(b) of the Restatement of Products Liability); Beech v. Outboard Marine Corp., 584 So. 2d 447 (Ala. 1991) (plaintiff must prove practical alternative design was available to the manufacturer); Branham v. Ford Motor Co., 701 S.E.2d 5 (S.C. 2010) (the exclusive test in a products liability design case is the risk-utility test with its requirement of showing a feasible alternative design; court adopts § 2(b) of the Products Liability Restatement).

In an effort to survey the case law since the publication of the Restatement, the authors undertook a state-by-state analysis of relevant law. *See* Aaron D. Twerski & James A. Henderson, Jr., *Manufacturers' Liability for Defective Product Designs: The Triumph of Risk-Utility,* 74 Brook. L. Rev. 1061 (2009). They found that 25 jurisdictions have wholly adopted § 2(b)'s RAD requirement; 20 by case law and five by statute. Eleven jurisdictions combine risk-utility balancing and consumer expectations into a two-prong test; however, these jurisdictions have limited the use of consumer expectations to res ipsa-like cases that would appropriately fall under Restatement § 3. Four states do not require a RAD. Five jurisdictions follow the consumer expectations test alone, and six have not yet determined their approach. *See e.g.*, Branham v. Ford Motor Co., 701 S.E.2d 5 (S.C. 2010) (court adopts § 2(b) of the Products Liability Restatement, requiring a RAD; Quincy Mut. Fire Ins. Co. v. Scripto USA, 573 F. Supp. 2d 875 (D.N.J. 2008) (granting summary judgment to defendant on grounds that the plaintiff had not put forth a RAD); Rock v. Smith, 985 F. Supp. 2d 1066 (S.D. Iowa 2013) (granting defendant summary judgment on grounds that the plaintiff was unable to put forth a RAD that would have prevented his injury); Garrie v. Summit Treestands, LLC, 50 So. 3d 458 (Ala. Civ. App. 2010) (affirming summary judgment as to plaintiff's strict liability claim against manufacturer on grounds that the plaintiff put forth no evidence that the utility of his alternative design was greater than the utility of the design that the manufacturer used).

VAUTOUR v. BODY MASTERS SPORTS INDUSTRIES, INC.
784 A.2d 1178 (N.H. 2001)

Duggan, J.

The plaintiffs in this products liability action, David S. Vautour and Susan Vautour, appeal an order of the Superior Court (Fitzgerald, J.) granting a motion for directed verdict to the defendant, Body Masters Sports Industries, Inc. We reverse and remand.

Mr. Vautour was injured while using a leg press machine manufactured by the defendant. The leg press is designed to strengthen a weightlifter's leg muscles by allowing him or her to raise and lower a metal sled, which may be loaded with weights, along fixed carriage tracks. A manually engaged safety system allows weightlifters to adjust safety stops and to operate the machine while sitting in a fixed, inclined position. In this position, a weightlifter may perform either deep leg presses or calf raise exercises. With legs extended along the carriage track and the balls of the weightlifter's feet on the sled, a weightlifter performs calf raise exercises by rotating the ankles up and down so that the sled and weights move up and down.

The leg press has two sets of safety stops, the upper and the lower stops. The upper stops provide a place for the weightlifter to rest the weight after extending his or her legs and pushing up the sled. The lower stops prevent the sled and weights from landing in the weightlifter's lap if he or she loses control of the machine. When the upper stops of the machine are disengaged the lower stops are engaged. The warning label on the machine states, "Caution. Handles must be in locked position when doing calf exercises," thereby instructing weightlifters to engage the upper stops when performing calf raises.

Mr. Vautour's injury occurred while moving his feet down to do calf raises. Although he was aware of the machine's warning label, Mr. Vautour did not have the upper stops engaged at the time of his accident. As a result, the sled and his knees fell rapidly toward his chest, injuring his feet. Mr. Vautour brought suit against the defendant under the theories of strict liability, negligence, and breach of warranty. Mr. Vautour contends that the location of the safety stops "exposed users to an unreasonable risk of harm and that this design defect" caused his injuries.

At trial, Barry Bates, the plaintiffs' biomechanics expert, testified that the machine, as designed, is hazardous because it does not adapt well to a wide range of body sizes and weightlifters may perform calf raise exercises without the upper stops engaged. He testified that in his opinion the leg press was defective and dangerous to weightlifters "because of the location of the lower stops and the possibility that the weight carriage can drop onto the person, putting them beyond their normal performance range of motion." Bates proposed that the leg press should be designed with adjustable, rather than fixed stops. He testified that he had not designed a machine with adjustable stops and did not know of any manufacturer in the industry who made a machine using adjustable stops. He testified, however, that by using adjustable stops "anything that was used would be better" than the fixed stops to prevent injuries. Under cross-examination, Bates admitted that the adjustable stops would not reduce the risk of injury to a user if he or she failed to manually set the stops before operating the machine.

After the close of the plaintiffs' case in chief, the defendant moved for a directed verdict, or, in the alternative, for dismissal, on the ground that the plaintiffs had failed to introduce evidence sufficient to make out a prima facie case. After the plaintiffs withdrew their claim for breach of warranty, the superior court granted the defendant's motion for directed verdict on the strict liability and negligence claims, concluding that:

> The point at which safety stops could be placed along the sled carriage without interfering with the muscle-strengthening function of the machine, the point at which stops must be placed to ensure that users are reasonably safe from physical injury, and the degree of risk to which users might reasonably be exposed when engaging in such leg strengthening exercises are each factual questions which appear, by their nature, to require specialized knowledge in the areas of design engineering, physiognomy, bio-mechanics, and safety standards in the field of athletic training.

Because the average juror could not be expected to know about these topics and because the plaintiffs' expert failed to offer any testimony regarding the acceptable risk of injury, where the safety stops should be located, or how his proposed alternative design would prevent the type of injuries suffered by Mr. Vautour, the superior court concluded that the plaintiffs failed to introduce evidence sufficient to support their strict liability and negligence claims.

On appeal, the plaintiffs assert that they proved all of the essential elements of their strict liability claim and the superior court erred by requiring them to prove an alternative design as an additional element in the case. . . .

A product is defectively designed when it "is manufactured in conformity with the intended design but the design itself poses unreasonable dangers to consumers." Thibault v. Sears, Roebuck & Co., . . . 395 A.2d 843 (1978). To prevail on a defective design products liability claim, a plaintiff must prove the following four elements: (1) the design of the product created a defective condition unreasonably dangerous to the user; (2) the condition existed when the product was sold by a seller in the business of selling such products; (3) the use of the product was reasonably foreseeable by the manufacturer; and (4) the condition caused injury to the user or the user's property. Chellman v. Saab-Scania AB, . . . 637 A.2d 148 (1993).

To determine whether a product is unreasonably dangerous, we explained in Bellotte v. Zayre Corp., . . . 352 A.2d 723 (1976), that a product "must be dangerous to an extent beyond that which would be contemplated by the ordinary consumer who purchases it, with the ordinary knowledge common to the community as to its characteristics." *Id.* In Price v. BIC Corp., . . . 702 A.2d 330 (1997), we further explained that whether a product is unreasonably dangerous to an extent beyond that which would be contemplated by the ordinary consumer is determined by the jury using a risk-utility balancing test.

Under a risk-utility approach, a product is defective as designed "if the magnitude of the danger outweighs the utility of the product." W. Keeton et al., Prosser and Keeton on the Law of Torts § 99, at 699 (5th ed. 1984). We have articulated the risk-utility test as requiring a "multifaceted balancing process involving evaluation of many conflicting factors." *Thibault,* . . . 395 A.2d 843. In order to determine whether the risks outweigh the benefits of the product design, a jury must evaluate many possible factors including the usefulness and desirability of the product to the public as a whole, whether the risk of danger could have been reduced without significantly affecting either the product's effectiveness or manufacturing cost, and the presence and efficacy of a warning to avoid an unreasonable risk of harm from hidden dangers or from foreseeable uses. *See Price,* . . . 702 A.2d 330. "Reasonableness, forseeability, utility, and similar factors are questions of fact for the jury." *Thibault,* . . . 395 A.2d 843.

The defendant contends that the risk-utility test, as articulated in *Thibault,* implicitly requires a plaintiff to offer evidence of a reasonable alternative design. Because the jury is instructed to consider whether the risk of danger could have been reduced without significantly affecting the effectiveness of the product and the cost of manufacturing, the defendant contends that evidence of a reasonable alternative design is required. The defendant urges us to adopt the Restatement (Third) of Torts § 2(b)(1998), which requires a plaintiff in a design defect case to prove that the risks of harm posed by the product could have been reduced or avoided by a reasonable alternative design. Restatement (Third) of Torts § 2(b) provides that:

> [A product] . . . is defective in design when the foreseeable risks of harm posed by the product could have been reduced or avoided by the adoption of a reasonable alternative design by the seller or other distributor, or a predecessor in the commercial chain of distribution, and the omission of the alternative design renders the product not reasonably safe.

By requiring a plaintiff to present evidence of a safer alternative design, section 2(b) of the Restatement thus elevates the availability of a reasonable alternative design from merely "a factor to be considered in the risk-utility analysis to a requisite element of a cause of action for defective design." Hernandez v. Tokai Corp., 2 S.W.3d 251, 256 (Tex. 1999).

There has been considerable controversy surrounding the adoption of Restatement (Third) of Torts § 2(b). *See, e.g.,* Note, *Just What You'd Expect: Professor Henderson's Redesign of Products Liability,* 111 Harv. L. Rev. 2366 (1998); Lavelle, *Crashing Into Proof of a Reasonable Alternative Design: The Fallacy of The Restatement (Third) of Torts: Products Liability,* 38 Duq. L. Rev. 1059 (2000); Schwartz, *The Restatement, Third, Tort: Products Liability: A Model of Fairness and Balance,* 10 Kan. J.L. & Pub. Pol'y 41 (2000); Vandall, *The Restatement (Third) of Torts: Products Liability Section 2(B): The Reasonable Alternative Design Requirement,* 61 Tenn. L. Rev. 1407 (1994). Most of the controversy stems from the concern that a reasonable alternative design requirement would impose an undue burden on plaintiffs because it places a "potentially insurmountable stumbling block in the way of those injured by badly designed products." *Just What You'd Expect: Professor Henderson's Redesign of Products Liability, supra* at 2373 (quotation omitted). Commentators have noted that for suits against manufacturers who produce highly complex products, the reasonable alternative design requirement will deter the complainant from filing suit because of the enormous costs involved in obtaining expert testimony. *See id.* Thus, because of the increased costs to plaintiffs of bringing actions based on defective product design, commentators fear that an alternative design requirement presents the possibility that substantial litigation expenses may effectively eliminate recourse, especially in cases in which the plaintiff has suffered little damage. *See id.; see also* Vandall, *supra* at 1425-26.

On a practical level, the Restatement's requirement of proof of an alternative design may be difficult for courts and juries to apply. To determine whether the manufacturer is liable for a design defect, the jury must currently decide whether the plaintiff has proven the four essential elements of a design defect case. *See* LeBlanc v. American Honda Motor Co., . . . 688 A.2d 556 (1997). As part of this analysis, the jury must determine whether the design of the product created a defective condition unreasonably dangerous to the user. In order to prove this element under the Restatement, a plaintiff must meet the requirement of proving the "availability of a technologically feasible and practical alternative design that would have reduced or prevented the plaintiff's harm." Restatement (Third) of Torts § 2 comment *f* at 24 (1998). The Restatement, however, contains far-reaching exceptions. According to the Restatement, the reasonable alternative design requirement does not apply when the product design is "manifestly unreasonable." *Id.* comment *e* at 21-22. Plaintiffs are additionally not required to produce expert testimony in cases in which the feasibility of a reasonable alternative design is obvious and understandable to laypersons. *See id.* comment *f* at 23. . . . Consequently, a requirement of proving a reasonable alternative design coupled with these broad exceptions will introduce even more complex issues for judges and juries to unravel.

A more important consideration is that while proof of an alternative design is relevant in a design defect case, it should be neither a controlling factor nor an essential element that must be proved in every case. As articulated in *Thibault,* the risk-utility test requires a jury to consider a number of factors when deciding whether a product is unreasonably dangerous. *See Thibault,* . . . 395 A.2d 843. This list is not meant to be exclusive, but merely illustrative. "Depending on the circumstances of each case, flexibility is necessary to decide which factors" may be relevant. Armentrout v. FMC Corp., 842 P.2d 175, 184 (Colo. 1992) (explaining in dictum that relevant factors cannot be confined to a single list which must always be applied regardless of circumstances). Thus, the rigid prerequisite of a reasonable alternative design places too much emphasis on one of many possible factors that could potentially affect the risk-utility analysis. *See* Bodymasters v. Wimberley, . . . 501 S.E.2d 556, 559 (Ga. Ct. App. 1998) (explaining that a risk-utility test requires the balancing of several factors, and no one factor alone is a prerequisite for bringing a claim). We are therefore satisfied that the risk-utility test as currently applied protects the interests of both consumers and manufacturers in design defect cases, and we decline to adopt section 2(b) of the Restatement. . . .

Here, the plaintiffs presented sufficient evidence that the leg press machine was unreasonably dangerous pursuant to the risk-utility balancing test. The plaintiffs' expert testified that the defendant's design was "dangerous to the user, from an injury perspective," and his proposed design was safer than the defendant's current design. Although he did not specify exactly where the safety stops should have been placed to prevent Mr. Vautour's injuries, he did testify that his design was mechanically feasible and, under similar circumstances, machines with such a design would be, overall, less dangerous. It was up to the jury to assess the weight to be given this testimony. . . . "Weighing of substantive evidence is the very essence of the jury's function. Consequently the trial judge has been granted little discretion to withdraw questions of substantive fact from a jury's consideration." . . . While certainly a reasonable jury could have found this evidence insufficient to establish that the leg press design was unreasonably dangerous, we cannot say that no reasonable jury could have found otherwise. Nor can we say, when viewing the evidence in the light most favorable to the plaintiffs, that the sole reasonable inference from this testimony is so overwhelmingly in favor of the defendant that no contrary verdict could stand. . . . Thus, we hold that the trial court erroneously granted the defendant's motion for directed verdict upon the plaintiffs' strict liability, design defect claim. Under New Hampshire law, the plaintiffs' evidence was sufficient to establish a prima facie case.

Reversed and remanded.

BROCK, C.J., and BRODERICK, J., sat for oral argument but did not take part in the final vote; NADEAU and DALIANIS, JJ., concurred.

FOOD FOR THOUGHT

We are genuinely puzzled. If the court is utilizing risk-utility balancing, how can it conclude that a RAD is only a factor in deciding whether a product design is defective? Assume that there was no better place to locate the safety stops to avoid the risk of the weight carriage dropping and further assume that the defendant had adequately warned about the necessity of locking the upper stops. Would the court still have found this leg press machine to be unreasonably dangerous? Except in very rare instances (which will be discussed *infra*), courts have been loath to find that products for which there are no alternative designs should be declared unreasonably dangerous per se. Furthermore, after trashing the RAD requirement, the court goes on to say that plaintiff had presented evidence of a RAD, in that he had suggested a better location for the stops, and it was the function of the jury, not the judge, to decide whether the plaintiff's suggested alternative design would have made the leg press machine safer. The authors have responded to much of the criticism aimed at the RAD requirement in James A. Henderson, Jr., & Aaron D. Twerski, *Achieving Consensus on Defective Product Design,* 83 Cornell L. Rev. 867 (1998) (article cites the scholarly articles that support and are critical of the RAD requirement).

b. The Consumer Expectations Test

Some scholars and courts reject risk-utility balancing as the standard for defining design defect and substitute a consumer expectations test in its stead. Having perceived that a risk-utility test does not really impose strict liability on a manufacturer, they argue that one way to move toward strict liability is not to ask whether there was a better way to design the product, but to impose liability if the product disappoints consumer expectations. If it does, then even if there was no reasonable alternative design, the plaintiff prevails.

IZZARELLI v. R.J. REYNOLDS TOB. CO.
321 Conn. 172 (Conn. 2016)

McDONALD, J.

We have been asked by the United States Court of Appeals for the Second Circuit to consider whether the "[g]ood tobacco" exception to strict products liability contained in comment (i) to § 402A of the Restatement (Second) of Torts[26] precludes an action in this state against a cigarette manufacturer for including additives and manipulating the nicotine in its cigarettes in a manner that ultimately increases the user's risk of cancer. The defendant, R.J. Reynolds Tobacco Company, appealed to that court from the judgment of the United States District Court for the District of Connecticut in favor of the plaintiff, Barbara A. Izzarelli, a former smoker and cancer survivor, on an action brought pursuant to Connecticut's Product Liability Act (liability act), General Statutes § 52-572m et seq. Pursuant to General Statutes § 51-199b (d), we accepted certification with respect to

---

26. Comment (i) to § 402A of the Restatement (Second) of Torts provides in relevant part: "The rule stated in this [s]ection applies only where the defective condition of the product makes it unreasonably dangerous to the user or consumer. . . . Good tobacco is not unreasonably dangerous merely because the effects of smoking may be harmful; but tobacco containing something like marijuana may be unreasonably dangerous. . . ."

the following question from the Second Circuit: "Does [comment (i) to § 402A] preclude a suit premised on strict products liability against a cigarette manufacturer based on evidence that the defendant purposefully manufactured cigarettes to increase daily consumption without regard to the resultant increase in exposure to carcinogens, but in the absence of evidence of adulteration or contamination?" See Izzarelli v. R.J. Reynolds Tobacco Co., 731 F.3d 164, 169 (2d Cir. 2013).

This case requires us to revisit our seminal strict product liability precedent, Potter v. Chicago Pneumatic Tool Co., 241 Conn. 199, 694 A.2d 1319 (1997), and to clarify the proper purview of the two strict liability tests recognized in that case: the ordinary consumer expectation test and the modified consumer expectation test. We conclude that the modified consumer expectation test is our primary strict product liability test, and the sole test applicable to the present case. Because the obvious danger exceptions to strict liability in comment (i) to § 402A of the Restatement (Second), including "[g]ood tobacco," are not dispositive under the multifactor modified consumer expectation test, we answer the certified question in the negative.

The District Court's ruling on the defendant's motion for a new trial and its renewed motion for judgment as a matter of law sets forth the following facts that the jury reasonably could have found, which we supplement with relevant procedural history. The relevant time frame in this case spans from the early 1970s, when the plaintiff first began to smoke, until the late 1990s, when she was diagnosed with, and treated for, cancer. The defendant has manufactured Salem King (Salem) cigarettes, the menthol cigarette brand smoked by the plaintiff, since 1956. In the early 1970s, the defendant identified certain weaknesses in its brand. One of the concerns identified was that almost one half of Salem users were light smokers, meaning that they smoked one to fifteen cigarettes per day. In an effort to capture a larger share of its desired market, the defendant modified Salem's design.

The defendant's internal research had disclosed two important factors concerning nicotine, a naturally occurring but addictive component of tobacco. First, the form of the nicotine affects the rate at which it is absorbed and delivers its "'kick'" to the smoker. Of nicotine's two principal forms, bound and free, free nicotine (also known as freebase nicotine) moves through the body's blood/brain barrier faster and provides the smoker with a higher and more immediate kick. Addiction liability increases in relation to the amount and speed of the delivery of free nicotine. Second, there is an effective dose range of nicotine necessary to maintain addiction. Id. The lowest nicotine yield (nicotine actually delivered to the smoker) that would maintain addiction requires the smoker to receive between five and eight milligrams of nicotine daily.

The defendant modified its Salem cigarettes in a manner that took both of these factors into account. The defendant had identified seven methods for manipulating the nicotine kick of its cigarettes, which it incorporated into its product. Among those methods was adding ammonia compounds to turn the nicotine into its more potent freebase form. Adding acetaldehyde, one of scores of chemicals added to Salem cigarettes, would cut the harshness of the nicotine while reinforcing its effects. Lowering nicotine levels below those naturally occurring could be achieved through various processes whereby the nicotine is extracted from the tobacco leaf and added back at the desired level. The defendant understood that increasing the free nicotine would enhance the addictive properties of Salem cigarettes, while decreasing the nicotine yield of the cigarettes would increase the number of cigarettes needed to meet the smoker's addiction demand.

The fact that the smoker would need to smoke more cigarettes to satisfy his or her addiction had two obvious consequences. First, the smoker would purchase more cigarettes. Second, the smoker would be exposed to more carcinogens, specifically, "tar." "Tar" is the tobacco industry term for all byproducts of smoking other than water and nicotine. Tar yield is affected by numerous factors, including the type of filter, the type of paper, how the paper is ventilated, the length and composition of the cigarette, and the blend of the tobacco.

By the early 1970s, the defendant had lowered the nicotine yield in Salem cigarettes from its 1956 level of 3.1 milligrams to 1.3 milligrams — a level determined to be optimal to maintain addiction. At that time, Salem cigarettes contained fifteen to nineteen milligrams of tar, an amount that exceeded the level in its main competitor for menthol cigarettes, Kool. The defendant had the capability of reducing the level of tar in its cigarettes to one milligram or less; in fact, two of its brands had two milligrams of tar in 1973. Thus, the defendant manipulated the natural effect of nicotine through the use of additives, tobacco formulation, and other methods. In so doing, the defendant enhanced the addictive nature of the product, increased the number of cigarettes smoked by its consumer, and ultimately delivered a higher level of carcinogens to the consumer as compared to other cigarettes. Because the causal relationship between smoking and cancer is dose related, increasing the Salem smoker's exposure to carcinogens increased the likelihood of cancer.

The plaintiff began smoking in the early 1970s, when she was approximately twelve years old. She quickly became severely addicted, eventually smoking two to three packs of Salem cigarettes daily. Throughout the period when the plaintiff smoked, a warning from the Surgeon General of the United States that smoking is dangerous to one's health appeared on the packaging of Salem cigarettes.

In 1996, at age thirty-six and after smoking for twenty-five years, the plaintiff was diagnosed with cancer of the larynx. A person with the plaintiff's smoking history has between a 6.9 and 20 times greater chance of developing laryngeal cancer than a nonsmoker. To treat her cancer, the plaintiff's larynx was removed and she received radiation. In 1997, the plaintiff quit smoking. She is cancer free, but continues to have various disabilities and problems related to her laryngectomy.

After the plaintiff's cancer diagnosis and treatment, she commenced the present product liability action in federal court under theories of strict liability and negligent design. At trial, the crux of the factual dispute was whether the defendant had designed and manufactured a tobacco product with heightened addictive properties that delivered more carcinogens than necessary. In addition to denying that allegation, the defendant also argued that the product "defect" identified by the plaintiff was merely the inherent risk common to all tobacco products insofar as all cigarettes contain nicotine and carcinogens. As such, the defendant characterized the plaintiff's action as impermissibly claiming that cigarettes generally are unreasonably dangerous, in contravention to the proviso in comment (i) to § 402A that "[g]ood tobacco" (i.e., an ordinary, unadulterated cigarette) is not unreasonably dangerous. The defendant made a related claim that the determination whether Salem cigarettes are unreasonably dangerous is exclusively governed by the ordinary consumer expectation test, as defined by comment (i) to § 402A, not the modified consumer expectation test that the plaintiff sought to apply. The defendant argued that application of the modified consumer expectation test would be improper because that test (a) only applies to products based on complex designs, which it claimed cigarettes are not

The District Court rejected these claims in prejudgment and postjudgment motions. With respect to the plaintiff's theory of the case, the court concluded that the plaintiff's claim alleged, and the evidence demonstrated, that Salem cigarettes are uniquely designed and manufactured in such a way to make that product different from other cigarettes. With respect to the governing law, the court concluded that, although Connecticut derives an essential definition for product liability actions from comment (i) to § 402A, there is no evidence that Connecticut has adopted the limitations in comment (i), including "[g]ood tobacco." The court further concluded that the jury properly could be instructed on the modified consumer expectation test. The court reasoned that this test was appropriate because the evidence demonstrated the complex design of cigarettes and the potential inability of the ordinary consumer (a beginner smoker, often a youth or minor) to form proper safety expectations. . . .

Ultimately, the court decided to instruct the jury on both the ordinary and modified consumer expectation tests as alternative bases for liability. In its instructions applicable to both tests, the District Court cautioned: "For [the] plaintiff to meet her burden of proving . . . that Salem . . . cigarettes are defective, she must show that the Salem . . . cigarettes were 'unreasonably dangerous' to her, the user. . . . With respect to cigarettes in general, I instruct you that cigarettes are not defective merely because nicotine and/or carcinogenic substances may be inherent in the tobacco from which such cigarettes are manufactured." The jury returned a verdict in favor of the plaintiff, finding the defendant liable for both strict liability and negligent design. The verdict form did not indicate whether the jury's strict liability verdict was premised on the ordinary consumer expectation test or the modified consumer expectation test.

In accordance with the defendant's request, the jury assessed comparative responsibility for the plaintiff's injuries, attributing 42 percent to the plaintiff and 58 percent to the defendant. After reducing the damages in accordance with the verdict, the District Court rendered judgment in the plaintiff's favor in the amount of $7,982,250 in compensatory damages, as well as $3,970,289.87 in punitive damages and offer of judgment interest.

The defendant appealed to the Second Circuit, renewing, inter alia, its claim that the plaintiff's product liability cause of action is foreclosed by comment (i) to § 402A because comment (i) precludes liability of a seller of good tobacco. Because the Second Circuit deemed Connecticut law to be unsettled regarding this matter, it certified a question of law to this court regarding the preclusive effect of comment (i) on a strict product liability claim.

Before this court, the plaintiff argues: (1) the ordinary consumer expectation test, on which both comment (i) to § 402A and its good tobacco example are predicated, has been superseded as a matter of Connecticut law in favor of the modified consumer expectation test, under which consumer expectations are but one factor in assessing liability; (2) even under the ordinary consumer expectation test, the good tobacco exception in comment (i) to § 402A is limited to raw tobacco and does not require proof of "adulteration" or "contamination" of the cigarettes; and (3) public policy considerations militate against applying comment (i) to § 402A in a manner that would immunize cigarette manufacturers from strict liability for design defects. In response, the defendant contends that, because the only question before this court is whether comment (i) to § 402A precludes an action against a cigarette manufacturer premised on an unadulterated cigarette, a question that arises in connection with the ordinary consumer expectation test, the plaintiff's argument relating to the modified consumer expectation test is outside the scope of the certified question and should not be addressed. Moreover, it contends that the modified test is an improper test for unadulterated, generic cigarettes. As to the ordinary consumer expectation test that it claims should govern, the defendant contends that, because the addictive and cancer causing properties of cigarettes have been well-known since at least the 1960s, jurisdictions espousing the standard in comment (i) to § 402A have routinely dismissed claims predicted on such alleged defects and this court should conclude likewise.

I

To resolve these competing contentions, it is necessary to provide some background on the development of Connecticut's strict product liability law. In 1965, Connecticut became one of the first jurisdictions to adopt, as a matter of state common law, § 402A of the Restatement (Second) of Torts, which had been adopted the previous year by the American Law Institute. See Potter v. Chicago Pneumatic Tool Co., 241 Conn. 214. Section 402A recognized an action for strict product liability in tort without the requirement of privity between the seller and the consumer or proof of manufacturer fault. The elements of a strict liability action that this court derived from § 402A required the plaintiff to prove: "(1) the defendant was engaged in the business of selling the product; (2) the product was in a defective condition unreasonably dangerous to the consumer or user; (3) the defect caused the injury for which compensation was sought; (4) the defect existed at the time of the sale; and (5) the product was expected to and did reach the consumer without substantial change in condition." (Emphasis added.)

This court derived our definition of unreasonably dangerous, the second element of our strict liability test, from comment (i) to § 402A: "To be considered unreasonably dangerous, the article sold must be dangerous to an extent beyond that which would be contemplated by the ordinary consumer who purchases it, with the ordinary knowledge common to the community as to its characteristics." This definition eventually came to be known under our law as the ordinary consumer expectation test. . . .

To place comment (i) in its proper context, it is important to recognize that § 402A was adopted at a time when products liability historically had focused on manufacturing defects, particularly with respect to food safety issues, before design defects and inadequate safety warnings had become well established theories of strict product liability. . . .

In 1979, our legislature adopted our product liability act. See Public Acts 1979, No. 79-483. That liability act required all common-law theories of product liability to be brought as a statutory cause of action. See General Statutes § 52-572n. However, the liability act neither expressly codified our common-law definition of defective product under § 402A and comment (i) nor supplanted it with its own definition. . . .

As product liability jurisprudence began to develop beyond its historical focus to include design defects and failure to warn defects, many jurisdictions found the ordinary consumer expectation test to be an inadequate tool. See Restatement (Third), § 1, comment (a), pp. 6-7 ("it soon became evident that § 402A, created to deal with liability for manufacturing defects, could not appropriately be applied to cases of design defects or defects based on inadequate instructions or warnings"). Most obviously, one could not simply compare the defective product to others in the product line to make an objective assessment of the consumer's expectations of the product.

For this and other reasons principally related to problems of proof, many jurisdictions adopted a multifactor "risk-utility" balancing test for design defect cases in lieu of, or in addition, to the consumer expectation test. . . . Under the Restatement (Third) of Torts and the various jurisdictions' risk-utility tests, consumer expectations were a relevant, but not necessarily dispositive, consideration in determining whether there was a design defect.

In 1997, in *Potter*, this court considered the viability of our ordinary consumer expectation test for design defect cases. The defendants in that case had requested that the court abandon that test for such cases in favor of the risk-utility test in the second tentative draft of the Restatement (Third) of Torts. Link to the text of the note Id., 215. The court declined to adopt the test in the draft Restatement (Third). The court viewed an absolute requirement of proof of a feasible alternative design to impose an undue burden on plaintiffs and to preclude claims that should be valid even in the absence of such proof.

Although the court in *Potter* maintained its allegiance to § 402A, it acknowledged criticisms of the ordinary consumer expectation test and decided that some change in our law was necessary because that test also could preclude relief for valid claims. In particular, the court pointed to the problem of complex products for which a consumer might not have informed safety expectations. The court was concerned, however, with shifting the focus to the conduct of the manufacturer and in turn abandoning strict liability. Accordingly, the court decided to adopt a test that would incorporate risk-utility factors into the ordinary consumer framework. Under the "modified" consumer expectation test, the jury would weigh the product's risks and utility and then inquire, in light of those factors, whether a "reasonable consumer would consider the product design unreasonably dangerous." The court's sample jury instruction incorporated the definition of unreasonably dangerous from comment (i) to § 402A and then provided a non-exclusive list of factors that could be used to determine what an ordinary consumer would expect. "The availability of a feasible alternative design is a factor that a plaintiff may, rather than must, prove in order to establish that a product's risks outweigh its utility."

The court in *Potter* emphasized that it would "not require a plaintiff to present evidence relating to the product's risks and utility in every case. . . . There are certain kinds of accidents — even where fairly complex machinery is involved — [that] are so bizarre that the average juror, upon hearing the particulars, might reasonably think: Whatever the user may have expected from that contraption, it certainly wasn't that. . . . Accordingly, the ordinary consumer expectation test [would be] appropriate when the everyday experience of the particular product's users permits the inference that the product did not meet minimum safety expectations." . . .

Potter was decided at a point in time when Connecticut design defect jurisprudence was not well developed. Indeed, as the present case illustrates, because actions under our liability act often have been brought in federal court, this court has had limited opportunities to do so. Subsequent case law and commentary has indicated that *Potter* was not clear as to when resort to each test would be appropriate and under what circumstances both tests properly could be submitted to a jury. The present case is a paradigmatic example of the confusion left in *Potter*'s wake. The defendant contends that, under *Potter*, only the ordinary consumer expectation test applies to the present case because the modified test is limited to complex designs for which consumers lack safety expectations. The plaintiff contends that, under *Potter*, the modified consumer expectation test is the default test with the ordinary test limited to res ipsa type cases, in which the consumer's minimum expectations of the product have not been met. We have not been presented with an opportunity since Potter to address squarely our design defect standards. We therefore take this opportunity to revisit Potter and dispel the ambiguity created by it, with the advantage of hindsight informed by almost two decades of subsequent developments in product liability law.

II

. . .

For the reasons set forth subsequently, we reach the following conclusions regarding the standards for a strict product liability action based on defective design generally and in the present case. Under *Potter*, the modified consumer expectation test is our primary test. The ordinary consumer expectation test is reserved for cases in which the product failed to meet the ordinary consumer's minimum safety expectations, such as res ipsa type cases. A jury could not reasonably conclude that cigarettes that cause cancer fail to meet the consumer's minimum safety expectations. Therefore, the plaintiff was required to proceed under the modified consumer expectation test. Comment (i) to § 402A does not present a per se bar to recovery under the modified consumer expectation test. Accordingly, the answer to the certified question is "no."

To begin, we acknowledge that there is language in *Potter*, as well as in subsequent Connecticut case law, that could support the ordinary consumer expectation test [as] the primary test, with the modified consumer expectation test reserved exclusively for complex product designs for which an ordinary consumer could not form safety expectations (simple/complex divide); . . .

We are not persuaded that *Potter* intended to draw a simple/complex divide. The court in *Potter* pointed to the problem in proving consumers' safety expectations for complex products because that concern was implicated in the case before the court and was the most obvious misfit for the ordinary consumer expectation test. *Potter* involved pneumatic hand tools alleged to be defective because they exposed users to excessive vibration, which in turn caused permanent vascular and neurological damage to the users' hands. The plaintiffs relied on expert testimony from various engineers and industry standards to prove their case. Notably, although concerns about proof for complex products was foremost in the court's mind when adopting the modified test, the court stated no limitations on the circumstances in which that test could be applied. . . .

Moreover, a simple/complex divide would not be ideal because the line between these categories is not always clear. Indeed, one could readily categorize the defendant's Salem cigarettes as a complex product because of the hundreds of ingredients incorporated into Salem cigarettes, as well as the myriad physical, chemical and biochemical variables that were considered in designing that product. Alternatively, one could view the defendant's cigarettes as a simple product if characterized as nothing more than a nicotine delivery system that carries a known risk of causing cancer. . . .

Although some of the shortcomings of the ordinary consumer expectation test have been best illustrated in relation to complex designs, the concerns with this test have never been limited to such designs. . . . One significant concern has been that the ordinary consumer expectation test, which deems unreasonable only those dangers that would not be anticipated by an ordinary consumer, could preclude recovery whenever a product's dangers were open and obvious. A. Weinstein et al., Products Liability and the Reasonably Safe Product (1978) pp. 45-46 ("The difficulty with [the ordinary consumer expectation] test is that it suggests that a manufacturer has fulfilled all his duties to the consumer if the product's dangers are open and obvious. In many instances manufacturers have been absolved from liability when an obvious danger caused serious injury, even though that injury could have been averted by a design modification that would not have added significantly to the cost of the product or impaired its usefulness.").

The court in *Potter* had no occasion to address this concern. Nonetheless, it is evident that limiting the modified test to complex products for which the consumer could not form safety expectations would be antithetical to the public policies informing our product liability law. . . .

Making the modified consumer expectation test our default test for design defect claims, and reserving the ordinary consumer expectation test for those products that fail to meet legitimate, commonly accepted minimum safety expectations, provides a safety incentive that is consonant with our state's public policies. Moreover, such a framework is the only one that can be reconciled with this court's direction in Potter that the jury could be instructed on both tests if supported by the evidence. Allowing the jury to consider both tests is only logical if the standard, and not merely the nature of proof, differs under each test. If the two tests were merely alternative methods of proving the same standard — the product failed to meet the ordinary consumer's expectations — then a jury's verdict that this standard was not met under one test could not logically be reconciled with a verdict that this standard was met under the other test. Either the product met the ordinary consumer's expectations, or it did not. If, however, one test sets the floor for recovery — a product that meets minimum safety expectations — then a verdict for the defendant on that test logically could be reconciled with a plaintiff's verdict on a test that sets a higher standard. In other words, a product might meet the consumer's minimum safety expectations because the product's dangers are known or obvious but nonetheless be defective because it could have been designed to be less dangerous without unreasonably compromising cost or utility (*e.g.*, a table saw lacking a safety guard).

Accordingly, we hold that, under our product liability law, the ordinary consumer expectation test is reserved for those limited cases in which a product fails to meet a consumer's legitimate, commonly accepted minimum safety expectations. Expert testimony on product design is not needed to prove the product's defect, nor is the utility of the product's design an excuse for the undisclosed defect. See A. Twerski & J. Henderson, "Manufacturers' Liability for Defective Product Designs: The Triumph of Risk-Utility," 74 Brook. L. Rev. 1061, 1108 (2009) ("overwhelming majority of cases that rely on consumer expectations as the theory for imposing liability do so only in res ipsa-like situations in which an inference of defect can be drawn from the happening of a product-related accident"). All other cases should be determined under the modified consumer expectation test.

With this clarification of our law, it is evident that the plaintiff in the present case properly could proceed only under the modified consumer expectation test. A cigarette that exposes the user to carcinogens and the attendant risk of cancer cannot be said to fail to meet an ordinary consumer's legitimate, commonly accepted minimum safety expectations. To establish the defect, the plaintiff's case required expert testimony on cigarette design and manufacture, as well as the feasibility of an alternative design. The defendant contends, however, that applying the modified consumer expectation test to cigarettes would be improper because it would effectively result in a de facto ban on cigarettes, in violation of our legislature's "ratifi[cation]" of this court's adoption of comment (i) to § 402A in our product liability act and Congress' declaration that cigarettes are a legal product. We are not persuaded.

Our legislature did not ratify this court's previous adoption of comment (i) to § 402A when it enacted the liability act. Neither § 402A nor comment (i) is expressly or implicitly referenced in the liability act. . . . *Potter* plainly reflects this court's understanding . . .

Finally, we note that other jurisdictions applying some form of risk-utility test to design defect claims against cigarette manufacturers have found no impediment to the application of that test if the plaintiff identifies some defect specific to the cigarette brand(s) at issue and/or a reasonably safer alternative. . . . [citations omitted.]

We answer the certified question "no."

In this opinion Eveleigh, Robinson and Vertefeuille, Js., concurred.

Zarella, J., with whom Espinosa, J., joins, concurring. I agree with the majority's answer to the certified question but not its analysis because I believe we should replace the dual design defect standards announced in Potter v. Chicago Pneumatic Tool Co. with the more modern standard for design defect claims set forth in the Restatement (Third) of Torts, Products Liability.

This case presents our first occasion to directly consider our design defect standards since *Potter* was decided nearly twenty years ago. *Potter* formulated our standards at a time when design defect law was in transition. Courts had acknowledged that the ordinary consumer expectations test, derived from comment (i) to § 402A was ill-suited for judging product design cases because it did not provide sufficient guidance to juries and was often used to deny recovery to plaintiffs for product related injuries. In its place, courts overwhelmingly turned to the risk-utility test, an alternative to the ordinary consumer expectations test, which allows a jury to assess a product design by weighing factors relating to its risks and benefits against those of possible design alternatives.

Sensitive to criticisms of the ordinary test, *Potter* created the "modified" consumer expectations test by incorporating risk-utility factors into the existing consumer expectations test. In formulating its standards, however, *Potter* rejected the approach of a draft form of the Restatement (Third) of Torts, Products Liability, which required, as an essential part of its risk-utility test, that a plaintiff present evidence of a reasonable alternative design. Such evidence allows for a jury to assess the manufacturer's chosen design by comparing it against the costs and benefits of adopting a safer alternative. In *Potter*, the court expressed concern that requiring this proof might harm a plaintiff by placing too many evidentiary hurdles along the path to recovery by, for example, forcing the plaintiff to present expert testimony in every case.

Both of *Potter*'s tests were ill-conceived, however, and they remain problematic today, even with the majority's clarification of when each test should be applied. The problems with *Potter*'s standards are not limited to their lack of clarity. More fundamentally, its rejection of a reasonable alternative design requirement leaves a jury applying its standards without any objective basis against which to assess the product design at issue.

Since *Potter* was decided, a consensus has emerged among courts and commentators that, in design defect cases, proof of some safer and reasonable alternative design is generally necessary to provide the jury with an objective basis for assessing whether a manufacturer's chosen design is defective. Proof of a reasonable alternative design allows the jury to compare the manufacturer's design against safer alternatives to decide whether the manufacturer could reasonably have made a safer product.

Reflecting this consensus, the Restatement (Third) requires proof of a reasonable alternative design. See Restatement (Third), Torts, Products Liability § 2 (b). Notably, however, the Restatement (Third), which was adopted shortly after *Potter* was decided, resolves *Potter*'s stated concerns by incorporating appropriate exceptions to the reasonable alternative design requirement and by making clear that expert testimony is not required in all cases to satisfy this obligation. *See id.,* § 2, comment (e) id., § 3; § 4 (a).

In light of these developments favoring the use of a pure risk-utility balancing standard based on proof of a reasonable alternative design, I believe that we should take this rare opportunity to reconsider our design defect standards rather than simply clarifying and reaffirming them, as the majority does today.

On the basis of my review of the Restatement (Third), I am persuaded that we should now adopt the approach set forth therein as an accurate statement of our law controlling design defect claims. The Restatement (Third) has resolved the concerns identified in *Potter* and provides a clearer and fairer method for resolving design claims. Because the Restatement (Third) does not rely on the standards contained in § 402A of the Restatement (Second) of Torts, and does not provide an absolute bar to an action against a cigarette manufacturer for defective design, I join in the majority's answer to the certified question, although not its analysis. . . .

III

[Thus,] I would accept the invitation of the reporters of the Restatement (Third) to reconsider the standard that this court employs in design defect cases and to adopt the approach for resolving design defect claims described in §§ 1, 2 and 4 of the Restatement (Third). Doing so will bring our design defect law in line with current product liability jurisprudence and eliminate our reliance on the now outdated consumer expectations standard from the Restatement (Second), which has proven ill-suited for design defect claims. . . .

Consequently, I agree with the majority that we should answer the certified question in the negative. Because I cannot join the majority's analysis in support of this conclusion, however, I respectfully concur in the result only.

FOOD FOR THOUGHT

Assume that the Chicago Pneumatic Tool Company (the defendant in *Potter*) warned about the dangers attendant to using pneumatic tools and further assume that there were no reasonable alternative designs that could practically be adopted to make them reasonably safer. Would the court still impose liability on the manufacturer of such tools because they disappoint consumer expectations? If one asks whether products with adequate warnings can still disappoint consumer expectations, we would venture to say that consumers could still argue they were disappointed when they suffered physical injury over years of use. Many consumers don't read even the best of warnings and if they do, they often push them out of their mind because they don't want to think about the possible bad results that may come to haunt them. Are we then ready to declare well-designed products accompanied by adequate warnings to be defective?

In any event, the plaintiff in *Potter* produced a wide array of reasonable alternative designs that would have rendered the pneumatic tools safer and would have reduced the risks of the very harms suffered by him. Can you imagine a plaintiff trying to convince a jury that pneumatic tools should be declared defective without suggesting how they can be made safer?

The court in *Potter*, as did the court in *Vautour*, said that they were adopting a consumer expectations-based risk-utility test. Isn't this just plain gobbledygook? To say that consumers have a right to expect a reasonably designed product that meets risk-utility standards ultimately requires the finder of fact to decide the risk-utility question. If so, then why not call it risk-utility rather than consumer expectations?

THE CONSUMER EXPECTATIONS TEST: NOT ALWAYS GOOD FOR PLAINTIFFS

Those who have argued in favor of the consumer expectations test believe that it is a more hospitable test for plaintiffs. But such is not always the case. Thus, in Halliday v. Sturm, Ruger & Co., 792 A.2d 1145 (Md. 2002), a defendant manufacturer successfully utilized the consumer expectations test. In that case, a three-year-old child was killed while playing with his father's handgun. The instruction manual for the gun came with multiple warnings about safe storage of the gun and the need to store the gun so that children could not gain access to it. It further warned that firearms should be unloaded when not in use. The child's father disregarded virtually every warning. The court noted that "he did not store either the gun or the magazine in the lock box but rather placed the gun under his mattress and kept the loaded magazine on a bookshelf in the same room" so that it was visible to the child. From watching television, the child figured out how to load the magazine into the gun and did so. While playing with the loaded handgun, the child shot and killed himself. Plaintiff alleged that the gun was defective because the design failed to incorporate such reasonable devices as (1) a grip safety, (2) a heavy trigger pull, (3) a child-resistant manual safety, (4) a built-in lock, (5) a trigger lock, or (6) a personalized gun code that would prevent the child from using the weapon. The Maryland court that had heretofore written numerous decisions supporting risk-utility balancing and the need to prove a reasonable alternative design to make out a case for design defect held that the plaintiff could not recover because the handgun met the consumer expectations test. The gun worked exactly as any reasonable consumer would have expected it to work. Note that in *Halliday*, it was the plaintiff who was urging the court to consider a host of RADs and the defendant who argued the consumer expectations test. The Maryland court in *Halliday* adopted the consumer expectation test in the case of handgun liability. More recently a Maryland intermediate appellate court stated, "When the product does not operate as it was designed, the risk-utility test, not the consumer-expectation test, is to be utilized." Hoon v. Lightolier, 857 A.2d 1184, 1195 (Md. Ct. Spec. App. 2004), *rev'd on other grounds*, Lightolier v. Hoon, 876 A.2d 100 (Md. 2005) (misuse of light bulb, not defect, was the sole proximate cause of plaintiff's harm).

Although a fair reading of *Halliday* may restrict application of that holding to handguns and other products that are inherently very dangerous, a leading products liability treatise notes more generally that "courts have used the consumer expectations test most frequently to *deny* recovery to plaintiffs in cases involving obvious design hazards." D. Owens, M. Madden & M. Davis, *Madden & Owens on Products Liability* § 8.3 (3d ed. 2000). In McSwain v. Sunrise Medical, Inc., 689 F. Supp. 2d 835 (S.D. Miss. 2010), the court held that pursuant to a Mississippi statute a product that met consumer expectations was not defective even though plaintiff was able to prove the availability of a reasonable alternative design that would have avoided plaintiff's injury. Legislation in several states negates liability for dangers that are commonly known and are inherent in the product. *See, e.g.,* N.J. Stat. Ann. § 2A:58C-3 (West 2000):

> In any product liability action against a manufacturer or seller for harm allegedly caused by a product that was designed in a defective manner, the manufacturer or seller shall not be liable if: . . .
>
> > (2) the characteristics of the product are known to the ordinary consumer or user, and the harm was caused by an unsafe aspect of the product that is an inherent characteristic of the product and that would be recognized by the ordinary person who uses or consumes the product with the ordinary knowledge common to the class of persons for whom the product is intended, except that this paragraph shall not apply to industrial machinery or other equipment used in the workplace and it is not intended to apply to dangers posed by products such as machinery or equipment that can feasibly be eliminated without impairing the usefulness of the product; . . .

See also Ohio Rev. Code Ann. § 2307.75(E) (LexisNexis 2005).

hypo 62

A, an 80-year-old man, took an aisle seat in a public bus. The bus driver executed a left turn at 30 mph, causing *A* to fall off his seat and break his hip. *A* sues *B Motor Co.,* the manufacturer of the bus, claiming that the bus should have had a metal pole in the aisle adjacent to his seat, so that he could have grabbed on to it and prevented his fall. *A* claims that reasonable consumers would have expected to have a pole available to prevent sudden falls by passengers. *B* introduces uncontradicted evidence that to install such poles would make it more difficult for passengers to exit the bus and would cause injuries when passengers push and shove to get off at their stop. Is *A* likely to reach the jury under a consumer expectations test? Under a risk-utility test?

c. The Two-Pronged Test for Defect

SOULE v. GENERAL MOTORS CORP.
882 P.2d 298 (Cal. 1994)

BAXTER, Justice.

Plaintiff's ankles were badly injured when her General Motors (GM) car collided with another vehicle. She sued GM, asserting that defects in her automobile allowed its left front wheel to break free, collapse rearward, and smash the floorboard into her feet. GM denied any defect and claimed that the force of the collision itself was the sole cause of the injuries. Expert witnesses debated the issues at length. Plaintiff prevailed at trial, and the Court of Appeal affirmed the judgment.

We granted review to resolve . . . [whether] a product's design [may] be found defective on grounds that the product's performance fell below the safety expectations of the ordinary consumer . . . if the question of how safely the product should have performed cannot be answered by the common experience of its users. . . .

On the early afternoon of January 16, 1984, plaintiff was driving her 1982 Camaro in the southbound center lane of Bolsa Chica Road, an arterial street in Westminster. There was a slight drizzle, the roadway was damp, and apparently plaintiff was not wearing her seat belt. A 1972 Datsun, approaching northbound, suddenly skidded into the path of plaintiff's car. The Datsun's left rear quarter struck plaintiff's Camaro in an area near the left front wheel. Estimates of the vehicles' combined closing speeds on impact vary from 30 to 70 miles per hour.

The collision bent the Camaro's frame adjacent to the wheel and tore loose the bracket that attached the wheel assembly (specifically, the lower control arm) to the frame. As a result, the wheel collapsed rearward and inward. The wheel hit the underside of the "toe pan" — the slanted floorboard area beneath the pedals — causing the toe pan to crumple, or "deform," upward into the passenger compartment.

Plaintiff received a fractured rib and relatively minor scalp and knee injuries. Her most severe injuries were fractures of both ankles, and the more serious of these was the compound compression fracture of her left ankle. This injury never healed properly. In order to relieve plaintiff's pain, an orthopedic surgeon fused the joint. As a permanent result, plaintiff cannot flex her left ankle. She walks with considerable difficulty, and her condition is expected to deteriorate. . . .

Plaintiff sued GM for her ankle injuries, asserting a theory of strict tort liability for a defective product. She claimed the severe trauma to her ankles was not a natural consequence of the accident, but occurred when the collapse of the Camaro's wheel caused the toe pan to crush violently upward against her feet. Plaintiff attributed the wheel collapse to a manufacturing defect, the substandard quality of the weld attaching the lower control arm bracket to the frame. She also claimed that the placement of the bracket, and the configuration of the frame, were defective designs because they did not limit the wheel's rearward travel in the event the bracket should fail. . . .

---

authors' dialogue 36

AARON: Jim, why is it that some courts cling to the consumer expectations test? It truly is a vacuous idea.

JIM: It was part of comment *i* to §402 of the Second Restatement. It's a way that courts can avoid admitting that design liability is based on fault and continue to talk "strict liability." And it sounds pro-consumer. Language has a powerful influence on the law. "Protecting consumer expectations" sounds so good. It's like being in favor of apple pie, motherhood, and the American flag.

AARON: There must be more to it. Courts have been talking risk-utility balancing for decades. They must know that without risk-utility balancing there is no intelligent way to decide whether a product is defectively designed.

JIM: They may know it, but they don't want to say it. Look at the courts that say they utilize a consumer expectation-based risk-utility test. As we point out in the text, that is plain and simple gobbledygook. To say that consumers have a right to expect product designs that meet risk-utility norms makes sense substantively, but you don't really need the "expectations" part. Don't underestimate the power of words that have been used for almost half a century.

AARON: Maybe it's more than language. Maybe risk-utility balancing was acceptable to the courts when it was used in the standard negligence context. They talked about balancing risk and utility, but everyone knew that it was all intuitive. It did not have to be taken seriously by anyone other than Richard Posner and his cohorts. But when you do risk-utility balancing with regard to product design, it's not intuitive at all. It's dead serious. Experts testify on the stand as to all the trade-offs. Now courts are forced to behave like economists and they don't like it one bit. So to loosen things up, they put a consumer expectations slant on design defect. Are we doing risk-utility balancing? Yes, but we won't say it. And even if we do say it, we'll disguise it with the sugar coating of consumer expectations.

JIM: Maybe you're right. But I still think that the imagery that consumer expectations conjures up is appealing. Never mind that it is a test that has little meaning of its own. It's warm and fuzzy.

AARON: It's distressing. Apparently there is widespread agreement that risk-utility balancing is what is really at work. But some courts still can't tell it straight.

The court instructed the jury that a manufacturer is liable for "enhanced" injuries caused by a manufacturing or design defect in its product while the product is being used in a foreseeable way. Over GM's objection, the court gave the standard design defect instruction without modification. . . . This instruction advised that a product is defective in design "if it fails to perform as safely as an ordinary consumer would expect when used in an intended or reasonably foreseeable manner *or* if there is a risk of danger inherent in the design which outweighs the benefit of the design." (Italics added.)

The jury was also told that in order to establish liability for a design defect under the "ordinary consumer expectations" standard, plaintiff must show (1) the manufacturer's product failed to perform as safely as an ordinary consumer would expect, (2) the defect existed when the product left the manufacturer's possession, (3) the defect was a "legal cause" of plaintiff's "enhanced injury," and (4) the product was used in a reasonably foreseeable manner. . . .

In a series of special findings, the jury determined that the Camaro contained a defect (of unspecified nature) which was a "legal cause" of plaintiff's "enhanced injury." . . . Plaintiff received an award of $1.65 million.

GM appealed. Among other things, it argued that the trial court erred by instructing on ordinary consumer expectations in a complex design-defect case, and by failing to give GM's special instruction on causation.

Following one line of authority, the Court of Appeal concluded that a jury may rely on expert assistance to determine what level of safe performance an ordinary consumer would expect under particular circumstances. Hence, the Court of Appeal ruled, there was no error in use of the ordinary consumer expectations standard for design defect in this case. . . .

Discussion

1. Test for Design Defect

A manufacturer, distributor, or retailer is liable in tort if a defect in the manufacture or design of its product causes injury while the product is being used in a reasonably foreseeable way. (Cronin v. J.B.E. Olson Corp. (1972) 8 Cal. 3d 121, 126-130, 104 Cal. Rptr. 433, 501 P.2d 1153 [*Cronin*]; Greenman v. Yuba Power Products, Inc. (1963) 59 Cal. 2d 57, 62, 27 Cal. Rptr. 697, 377 P.2d 897 [*Greenman*].) Because traffic accidents are foreseeable, vehicle manufacturers must consider collision safety when they design and build their products. Thus, whatever the cause of an accident, a vehicle's producer is liable for specific collision injuries that would not have occurred but for a manufacturing or design defect in the vehicle. . . .

In *Cronin, supra,* a bread van driver was hurt when the hasp retaining the bread trays broke during a collision, causing the trays to shift forward and propel him through the windshield. He sued the van's producer, alleging that the hasp had failed because of the defective metal used in its manufacture. The court instructed that the driver could recover if he proved a defect, unknown to him, which caused injury while the van was being used as intended or designed. The manufacturer appealed the subsequent damage award. It urged the court should have instructed that liability could not be imposed unless the defect rendered the product "unreasonably dangerous."

We rejected this contention, holding that the "unreasonably dangerous" test derived from the Restatement (see Rest. 2d Torts, § 402A) is inapplicable in California. As we observed, the Restatement defines "unreasonably dangerous" as "dangerous to an extent beyond that which would be contemplated by the ordinary consumer who purchases it, *with the ordinary knowledge common to the community as to its characteristics.*" (*Id.,* com. *i,* p. 352, italics added.) The original purpose of this formula, we explained, was to make clear that common products such as sugar, butter, and liquor are not defective simply because they pose inherent health risks well known to the general public. However, *Cronin* indicated, the formula had been applied so as to force injured persons to prove *both* an actual defect *and* "unreasonable" danger. . . .

This "double burden," *Cronin* reasoned, ran contrary to the purpose of *Greenman, supra,* to relieve persons injured by defective products from proof of elements that ring of negligence. Instead, *Cronin* concluded, an injured plaintiff should recover so long as he proves that the product was defective, and that the defect caused injury in reasonably foreseeable use. . . .

In Barker v. Lull Engineering Co., *supra,* 20 Cal. 3d 413, 143 Cal. Rptr. 225, 573 P.2d 443 (*Barker*), the operator of a high-lift loader sued its manufacturer for injuries he received when the loader toppled during a lift on sloping ground. The operator alleged various *design* defects which made the loader unsafe to use on a slope. In a pre-*Cronin* trial, the court instructed that the operator could recover only if a defect in the loader's design made the machine "'unreasonably dangerous for its intended use.'" (*Id.,* at p. [449].) The operator appealed the defense verdict, citing the "unreasonably dangerous" instruction as prejudicial error.

The manufacturer responded that even if the "unreasonably dangerous" test was inappropriate for manufacturing defects, such as the substandard fastener material in *Cronin,* it should be retained for design defects. This rule would not produce the undue double burden that concerned us in *Cronin,* the manufacturer insisted, because unreasonable danger is part of the *definition* of design defect, not an additional element of strict product liability. Without this limitation, the manufacturer contended, juries would lack guidance when determining if a defect had sprung not from a mistake in supply or assembly, but from a flaw in the product's specifications.

The *Barker* court disagreed. It reasoned as follows: Our concerns in *Cronin* extended beyond double-burden problems. There we also sought to avoid the danger that a jury would *deny* recovery, as the Restatement had intended, "so long as the product did not fall below the ordinary consumer's expectations as to [its] safety. . . ." (*Barker, supra,* . . . fn. omitted.) This danger was particularly acute in design defect cases, where a manufacturer might argue that because the item which caused injury was identical to others of the same product line, it must necessarily have satisfied ordinary consumer expectations. . . .

Despite these difficulties, *Barker* explained, it is possible to define a design defect, and the expectations of the ordinary consumer are relevant to that issue. At a minimum, said *Barker,* a product is defective in design if it does fail to perform as safely as an ordinary consumer would expect. This principle, *Barker* asserted, acknowledges the relationship between strict tort liability for a defective product and the common law doctrine of warranty, which holds that a product's presence on the market includes an implied representation "'that it [will] safely do the jobs for which it was built.'" . . . "Under this [minimum] standard," *Barker* observed, "an injured plaintiff will frequently be able to demonstrate the defectiveness of the product *by resort to circumstantial evidence, even when the accident itself precludes identification of the specific defect at fault.* [Citations.]" [Citations.] (italics added.)

However, *Barker* asserted, the Restatement had erred in proposing that a violation of ordinary consumer expectations was necessary for recovery on this ground. "As Professor Wade has pointed out, . . . the expectations of the ordinary consumer cannot be viewed as the exclusive yardstick for evaluating design defectiveness because '[i]n many situations . . . *the consumer would not know what to expect,* because he would have *no idea* how safe the product could be made.'" (20 Cal. 3d at p. 430, 143 Cal. Rptr. 225, 573 P.2d 443, quoting Wade, *On the Nature of Strict Tort Liability for Products* (1973) 44 Miss. L.J. 825, 829, italics added.)

Thus, *Barker* concluded, "a product may be found defective in design, even if it satisfies ordinary consumer expectations, if through hindsight the jury determines that the product's design embodies 'excessive preventable danger,' or, in other words, if the jury finds that the risk of danger inherent in the challenged design outweighs the benefits of such design. [Citations.]" . . . *Barker* held that under this latter standard, "a jury may consider, among other relevant factors, the gravity of the danger posed by the challenged design, the likelihood that such danger would occur, the mechanical feasibility of a safer alternative design, the financial cost of an improved design, and the adverse consequences to the product and to the consumer that would result from an alternative design. [Citations.]" (*Id.,* at p. [455].)

Barker also made clear that when the ultimate issue of design defect calls for a careful assessment of feasibility, practicality, risk, and benefit, the case should not be resolved simply on the basis of ordinary consumer expectations. As *Barker* observed, "past design defect decisions demonstrate that, as a practical matter, in many instances it is simply impossible to eliminate the balancing or weighing of competing considerations in determining whether a product is defectively designed or not. . . ." . . .

An example, *Barker* noted, was the "crashworthiness" issue presented in Self v. General Motors Corp., *supra.* . . . The debate there was whether the explosion of a vehicle's fuel tank in an accident was due to a defect in design. This, in turn, entailed concerns about whether placement of the tank in a position less vulnerable to rear end collisions, even if technically feasible, "would have created a greater risk of injury in other, more common situations." (*Barker, supra.* . . .) Because this complex weighing of risks, benefits, and practical alternatives is "implicit" in so many design-defect determinations, *Barker* concluded, "an instruction which appears to preclude such a weighing process under all circumstances may mislead the jury." (*Id.* . . .) . . .

In *Barker,* we offered two alternative ways to prove a design defect, each appropriate to its own circumstances. The purposes, behaviors, and dangers of certain products are commonly understood by those who ordinarily use them. By the same token, the ordinary users or consumers of a product may have reasonable, widely accepted minimum expectations about the circumstances under which it should perform safely. Consumers govern their own conduct by these expectations, and products on the market should conform to them.

In some cases, therefore, "ordinary knowledge . . . as to . . . [the product's] characteristics" (Rest. 2d Torts, *supra,* §402A, com. *i.,* p. 352) may permit an inference that the product did not perform as safely as it should. *If* the facts permit such a conclusion, and *if* the failure resulted from the product's design, a finding of defect is warranted without any further proof. The manufacturer may not defend a claim that a product's design failed to perform as safely as its ordinary consumers would expect by presenting expert evidence of the design's relative risks and benefits.[3]

However, as we noted in *Barker,* a complex product, even when it is being used as intended, may often cause injury in a way that does not engage its ordinary consumers' reasonable minimum assumptions about safe performance. For example, the ordinary consumer of an automobile simply has "no idea" how it should perform in all foreseeable situations, or how safe it should be made against all foreseeable hazards. (*Barker, supra.* . . .)

An injured person is not foreclosed from proving a defect in the product's design simply because he cannot show that the reasonable minimum safety expectations of its ordinary consumers were violated. Under *Barker*'s alternative test, a product is still defective if its design embodies "excessive preventable danger" . . . that is, unless "the benefits of the . . . design outweigh the risk of danger inherent in such design" (*id.* . . .). But this determination involves technical issues of feasibility, cost, practicality, risk, and benefit (*id.,* at p. 431, 143 Cal. Rptr. 225, 573 P.2d 443) which are "impossible" to avoid. . . . In such cases, the jury *must* consider the manufacturer's evidence of competing design considerations . . . and the issue of design defect cannot fairly be resolved by standardless reference to the "expectations" of an "ordinary consumer."

As we have seen, the consumer expectations test is reserved for cases in which the *everyday experience* of the product's users permits a conclusion that the product's design violated *minimum* safety assumptions, and is thus defective *regardless of expert opinion about the merits of the design.* It follows that where the minimum safety of a product is within the common knowledge of lay jurors, expert witnesses may not be used to demonstrate what an ordinary consumer would or should expect. Use of expert testimony for that purpose would invade the jury's function (see Evid. Code, § 801, subd. (a)), and would invite circumvention of the rule that the risks and benefits of a challenged design must be carefully balanced whenever the issue of design defect goes beyond the common experience of the product's users.

By the same token, the jury may not be left free to find a violation of ordinary consumer expectations whenever it chooses. Unless the facts actually permit an inference that the product's performance did not meet the minimum safety expectations of its ordinary users, the jury must engage in the balancing of risks and benefits required by the second prong of *Barker.*

Accordingly, as *Barker* indicated, instructions are misleading and incorrect if they allow a jury to avoid this risk-benefit analysis in a case where it is required. (20 Cal. 3d at p. 434, 143 Cal. Rptr. 225, 573 P.2d 443.) Instructions based on the

---

3. For example, the ordinary consumers of modern automobiles may and do expect that such vehicles will be designed so as not to explode while idling at stoplights, experience sudden steering or brake failure as they leave the dealership, or roll over and catch fire in two-mile-per-hour collisions. If the plaintiff in a product liability action proved that a vehicle's design produced such a result, the jury could find forthwith that the car failed to perform as safely as its ordinary consumers would expect, and was therefore defective.

ordinary consumer expectations prong of *Barker* are not appropriate where, as a matter of law, the evidence would not support a jury verdict on that theory. Whenever that is so, the jury must be instructed solely on the alternative risk-benefit theory of design defect announced in *Barker*.

GM suggests that the consumer expectations test is improper whenever "crash-worthiness," a complex product, or technical questions of causation are at issue. Because the variety of potential product injuries is infinite, the line cannot be drawn as clearly as GM proposes. But the fundamental distinction is not impossible to define. The crucial question in each individual case is whether the circumstances of the product's failure permit an inference that the product's design performed below the legitimate, commonly accepted minimum safety assumptions of its ordinary consumers.

GM argues at length that the consumer expectations test is an "unworkable, amorphic, fleeting standard" which should be entirely abolished as a basis for design defect. In GM's view, the test is deficient and unfair in several respects: First, it defies definition. Second, it focuses not on the objective condition of products, but on the subjective, unstable, and often unreasonable opinions of consumers. Third, it ignores the reality that ordinary consumers know little about how safe the complex products they use can or should be made. Fourth, it invites the jury to isolate the particular consumer, component, accident, and injury before it instead of considering whether the whole product fairly accommodates the competing expectations of all consumers in all situations (see Daly v. General Motors Corp., *supra* . . .). Fifth, it eliminates the careful balancing of risks and benefits which is essential to any design issue. . . .

We fully understand the dangers of improper use of the consumer expectations test. However, we cannot accept GM's insinuation that ordinary consumers lack any legitimate expectations about the minimum safety of the products they use. In particular circumstances, a product's design may perform so unsafely that the defect is apparent to the common reason, experience, and understanding of its ordinary consumers. In such cases, a lay jury is competent to make that determination. . . .

Applying our conclusions to the facts of this case, however, we agree that the instant jury should not have been instructed on ordinary consumer expectations. Plaintiff's theory of design defect was one of technical and mechanical detail. It sought to examine the precise behavior of several obscure components of her car under the complex circumstances of a particular accident. The collision's exact speed, angle, and point of impact were disputed. It seems settled, however, that plaintiff's Camaro received a substantial oblique blow near the left front wheel, and that the adjacent frame members and bracket assembly absorbed considerable inertial force.

An ordinary consumer of automobiles cannot reasonably expect that a car's frame, suspension, or interior will be designed to remain intact in any and all accidents. Nor would ordinary experience and understanding inform such a consumer how safely an automobile's design should perform under the esoteric circumstances of the collision at issue here. Indeed, both parties assumed that quite complicated design considerations were at issue, and that expert testimony was necessary to illuminate these matters. Therefore, injection of ordinary consumer expectations into the design defect equation was improper.

We are equally persuaded, however, that the error was harmless, because it is not reasonably probable defendant would have obtained a more favorable result in its absence. . . .

Here there were no instructions which specifically remedied the erroneous placement of the consumer expectations alternative before the jury. Moreover, plaintiff's counsel briefly reminded the jury that the instructions allowed it to find a design defect under either the consumer expectations or risk-benefit tests. However, the consumer expectations theory was never emphasized at any point. As previously noted, the case was tried on the assumption that the alleged design defect was a matter of technical debate. Virtually all the evidence and argument on design defect focused on expert evaluation of the strengths, shortcomings, risks, and benefits of the challenged design, as compared with a competitor's approach. . . .

Under these circumstances, we find it highly unlikely that a reasonable jury took that path. We see no reasonable probability that the jury disregarded the voluminous evidence on the risks and benefits of the Camaro's design, and instead rested its verdict on its independent assessment of what an ordinary consumer would expect. Accordingly, we conclude, the error in presenting that theory to the jury provides no basis for disturbing the trial judgment.

[Discussion of other issues omitted.]

Soule clearly cut back on the consumer expectations test. By limiting its application to cases that are very much res ipsa–like (see footnote 3 on page 642), *Soule* comes very close to the position adopted in the Products Liability Restatement. It will be recalled that under § 3, a plaintiff may make out a prima facie case of defect without proving a reasonable alternative design.

Some decisions suggest that California will read the consumer expectations test narrowly. *See, e.g.,* Bispo v. GSW, Inc., 361 Fed. Appx 834, 836 (9th Cir. 2010) (affirming summary judgment against plaintiff's consumer expectations-theory because "ordinary consumers have no firm expectations regarding the gas pressure that safety valves should withstand"); Kim v. Toyota Motor Corp., 243 Cal. App. 4th 1366, 1394 (Cal. Ct. App. 2016) (affirming trial court's holding that consumer expectations test was inapplicable to plaintiff's claim that his pickup truck, which went off the road after plaintiff swerved to avoid another car, was defective because it lacked an electronic stability control system (ESC), because an ESC is "an obscure and complex electronic component"); Mansur v. Ford Motor Co., 197 Cal. App. 4th 1365 (Cal. Ct. App. 2011) (affirming district court's refusal to give consumer expectations jury instruction on ground that plaintiff failed to put forth evidence regarding how the objective features of the SUV would influence consumer expectations as to how the vehicle would perform if it rolled-over); *But see* Romine v. Johnson Controls, Inc., 224 Cal. App. 4th 990 (Cal. Ct. App. 2014) (applying consumer expectations test to how a seat in a car ought to function when a car is struck from behind while stopped at a red light).

More recent intermediate appellate decisions suggest that California will apply the consumer expectations test narrowly. *See, e.g.,* Snyder v. Ortho-McNeil Pharmaceuticals, 2002 WL 1161208 (Cal. Ct. App.) (consumer expectations test unsuitable for medical devices); Stephen v. Ford Motor Co., 37 Cal. Rptr. 3d 9 (Cal. Ct. App. 2005) (consumer expectations test unsuitable to decide defect claims regarding a well-used tire's tread separation and an SUV's directional stability); Morson v. Superior Court, 109 Cal. Rptr. 2d 343 (Cal. Ct. App. 2001) (consumer expectations test not appropriate to decide whether design of latex gloves is defective); *but see* Arnold v. Dow Chemical Co., 110 Cal. Rptr. 2d 722, 745 (Cal. Ct. App. 2001) (insecticide "within the ordinary experience and understanding of the consumer").

Illinois has adopted a strange version of the two-pronged test for defect. In Mikolajczyk v. Ford Motor Co., 901 N.E.2d 329 (Ill. 2008), the driver of a 1996 Ford Escort suffered severe, irreversible brain trauma when the defendant, a drunk driver, rear-ended his car at high speed. His widow brought an action in strict liability against Ford Motor Co. claiming that the driver's seat was defectively designed in that it propelled her husband rearward, causing him to hit his head on the back seat.

Defendants introduced evidence that the seat in the Ford Escort met risk-utility standards and provided greater overall safety than an alternative design. Plaintiff insisted that the jury be allowed to conclude that the seat design was defective if it failed to meet consumer expectations. Defendants urged the court to adopt §2(b) of the Products Liability Restatement. The court denied defendants' request on the ground that doing so would require a plaintiff "to plead and prove the existence of a feasible alternative design in every case." Then, in an interesting turnaround, the court said:

> Although we have declined to adopt section 2 of the Products Liability Restatement as a statement of substantive law, we do find its formulation of the risk-utility test to be instructive. Under section 2(b) the risk-utility balance is to be determined based on consideration of a "broad range of factors," including . . . the *nature and strength of consumer expectations regarding the product, including expectations arising from product portrayal and marketing.* . . .
>
> We adopt this formulation of the risk-utility test and hold that when the evidence presented by either or both parties supports the application of this integrated test, an appropriate instruction is to be given at the request of either party. *If, however, both parties' theories of the case are framed entirely in terms of consumer expectations, including those based on advertising and marketing messages, and/or whether the product was being put to a reasonably foreseeable use at the time of the injury, the jury should be instructed only on the consumer-expectation test.*
>
> Adoption of this integrated test resolves the question of whether the answer to the risk-utility test "trumps" the answer to the consumer-expectation test because the latter is incorporated into the former and is but one factor among many for the jury to consider.

In an article the authors set forth their belief that there is not much (if anything) left to the Illinois version of the consumer expectation test:

Rhetoric aside, what is the bottom line of *Mikolajczyk*? From a functional standpoint, it would appear that the consumer expectations test is a dead letter in Illinois. In any case in which a plaintiff seeks to proceed solely under the consumer expectations test, a defendant need only counter with risk-utility evidence to cause the court to apply the factors set forth in section 2, comment *f*. Under that test, consumer expectations are but one factor among other risk-utility factors to be considered in deciding whether a product is unreasonably dangerous. Conversely, when a defendant defends on the ground that a product meets consumer expectations, perhaps because the risks are obvious, a plaintiff need only introduce risk-utility evidence for the court to apply risk-utility balancing.

Aaron D. Twerski & James A. Henderson, Jr., *Manufacturers' Liability for Defective Product Designs: The Triumph of Risk-Utility*, 74 Brook. L. Rev. 1061, 1075 (2009).

d. Should Product Categories Be Declared Defective?

O'BRIEN v. MUSKIN CORP.
463 A.2d 298 (N.J. 1983)

Pollock, J.

Plaintiff, Gary O'Brien, seeks to recover in strict liability for personal injuries sustained because defendant, Muskin Corporation, allegedly marketed a product, an above-ground swimming pool, that was defectively designed and bore an inadequate warning. In an unreported decision, the Appellate Division reversed the judgment for defendants and remanded the matter for trial. We granted certification, 91 N.J. 548, 453 A.2d 866 (1982), and now modify and affirm the judgment of the Appellate Division. . . .

O'Brien sued to recover damages for serious personal injuries sustained when he dove into a swimming pool at the home of Jean Henry, widow of Arthur Henry, now Jean Glass. . . . At the close of the plaintiff's case, the trial court determined that he had failed to prove a design defect in the pool. Accordingly, at the close of the entire case, the court refused to charge the jury on design defect. Instead, the court submitted the case to the jury solely on the adequacy of the warning.

In response to special interrogatories, . . . the jury found that O'Brien was guilty of contributory negligence, and allocated fault for the injury as 15% attributable to Muskin and 85% attributable to O'Brien. Thus, under New Jersey's comparative negligence statute, O'Brien was barred from recovery. *See* N.J.S.A. 2A:15-5.1. The trial occurred before our decision in Roman v. Mitchell, 82 N.J. 336, 413 A.2d 322 (1980), and the court did not give an "ultimate outcome" instruction; that is, the court failed to instruct the jury on the effect on plaintiff's recovery of its allocation of fault.

On appeal, the Appellate Division found that the trial court erred in removing from the jury the issue of design defect. Consequently, that court reversed the judgment against Muskin and remanded the matter for a new trial. . . .

I

Muskin, a swimming pool manufacturer, made and distributed a line of above-ground pools. Typically, the pools consisted of a corrugated metal wall, which the purchaser placed into an oval frame assembled over a shallow bed of sand. This outer structure was then fitted with an embossed vinyl liner and filled with water.

In 1971, Arthur Henry bought a Muskin pool and assembled it in his backyard. The pool was a twenty-foot by twenty-four-foot model, with four-foot walls. An embossed vinyl liner fit within the outer structure and was filled with water to a depth of approximately three and one-half feet. At one point, the outer wall of the pool bore the logo of the manufacturer, and below it a decal that warned "DO NOT DIVE" in letters roughly one-half inch high.

On May 17, 1974, O'Brien, then twenty-three years old, arrived uninvited at the Henry home and dove into the pool. A fact issue exists whether O'Brien dove from the platform by the pool or from the roof of the adjacent eight-foot high garage. As his outstretched hands hit the vinyl-lined pool bottom, they slid apart, and O'Brien struck his head on the bottom of the pool, thereby sustaining his injuries.

In his complaint, O'Brien alleged that Muskin was strictly liable for his injuries because it had manufactured and marketed a defectively designed pool. In support of this contention, O'Brien cited the slippery quality of the pool liner and the lack of adequate warnings.

At trial, both parties produced experts who testified about the use of vinyl as a pool liner. One of the plaintiff's witnesses, an expert in the characteristics of vinyl, testified that wet vinyl was more than twice as slippery as rubber latex, which is used to line in-ground pools. The trial court, however, sustained an objection to the expert's opinion about alternative kinds of pool bottoms, specifically whether rubber latex was a feasible liner for above-ground pools. The expert admitted that he knew of no above-ground pool lined with a material other than vinyl, but plaintiff contended that vinyl should not be used in above-ground pools, even though no alternative material was available. A second expert testified that the slippery vinyl bottom and lack of adequate warnings rendered the pool unfit and unsafe for its foreseeable uses.

Muskin's expert testified that vinyl was not only an appropriate material to line an above-ground pool, but was the best material because it permitted the out-stretched arms of the diver to glide when they hit the liner, thereby preventing the diver's head from striking the bottom of the pool. Thus, he concluded that in some situations, specifically those in which a diver executes a shallow dive, slipperiness operates as a safety feature. Another witness, Muskin's customer service manager, who was indirectly in charge of quality control, testified that the vinyl bottom could have been thicker and the embossing deeper. A fair inference could be drawn that deeper embossing would have rendered the pool bottom less slippery.

At the close of the entire case, the trial court instructed the jury on the elements of strict liability, both with respect to design defects and the failure to warn adequately. The court, however, then limited the jury's consideration to the adequacy of the warning. That is, the court took from the jury the issue whether manufacturing a pool with a vinyl liner constituted either a design or manufacturing defect.

[The court reviews the history of products liability law, observing that in design and warning cases, the critical question is the legal standard by which one measures defectiveness.]

Although the appropriate standard might be variously defined, one definition, based on a comparison of the utility of the product with the risk of injury that it poses to the public, has gained prominence. To the extent that "risk-utility analysis," as it is known, implicates the reasonableness of the manufacturer's conduct, strict liability law continues to manifest that part of its heritage attributable to the law of negligence. . . . Risk-utility analysis is appropriate when the product may function satisfactorily under one set of circumstances, yet because of its design present undue risk of injury to the user in another situation. . . .

Although state-of-the-art evidence may be dispositive on the facts of a particular case, it does not constitute an absolute defense apart from risk-utility analysis. *See* Beshada v. Johns-Manville Products Corp., 90 N.J. 191, 202-05 & n.6, 447 A.2d 539 (1982). The ultimate burden of proving a defect is on the plaintiff, but the burden is on the defendant to prove that compliance with state-of-the-art, in conjunction with other relevant evidence, justifies placing a product on the market. Compliance with proof of state-of-the-art need not, as a matter of law, compel a judgment for a defendant. State-of-the-art evidence, together with other evidence relevant to risk-utility analysis, however, may support a judgment for a defendant. In brief, state-of-the-art evidence is relevant to, but not necessarily dispositive of, risk-utility analysis. That is, a product may embody the state-of-the-art and still fail to satisfy the risk-utility equation.

The assessment of the utility of a design involves the consideration of available alternatives. If no alternatives are available, recourse to a unique design is more defensible. The existence of a safer and equally efficacious design, however, diminishes the justification for using a challenged design.

The evaluation of the utility of a product also involves the relative need for that product; some products are essentials, while others are luxuries. A product that fills a critical need and can be designed in only one way should be viewed differently from a luxury item. Still other products, including some for which no alternative exists, are so dangerous and of such little use that under the risk-utility analysis, a manufacturer would bear the cost of liability of harm to others. That cost might dissuade a manufacturer from placing the product on the market, even if the product has been made as safely as possible. Indeed, plaintiff contends that above-ground pools with vinyl liners are such products and that manufacturers who market those pools should bear the cost of injuries they cause to foreseeable users.

A critical issue at trial was whether the design of the pool, calling for a vinyl bottom in a pool four feet deep, was defective. The trial court should have permitted the jury to consider whether, because of the dimensions of the pool and slipperiness of the bottom, the risks of injury so outweighed the utility of the product as to constitute a defect. In removing that issue from consideration by the jury, the trial court erred. To establish sufficient proof to compel submission of the issue to the jury for appropriate fact-finding under risk-utility analysis, it was not necessary for plaintiff to prove the existence of alternative, safer designs. Viewing the evidence in the light most favorable to plaintiff, even if there are no alternative methods of making bottoms for above-ground pools, the jury might have found that the risk posed by the pool outweighed its utility.

In a design-defect case, the plaintiff bears the burden of both going forward with the evidence and of persuasion that the product contained a defect. To establish a prima facie case, the plaintiff should adduce sufficient evidence on the risk-utility factors to establish a defect. With respect to above-ground swimming pools, for example, the plaintiff might seek to establish that pools are marketed primarily for recreational, not therapeutic purposes; that because of their design, including their configuration, inadequate warnings, and the use of vinyl liners, injury is likely; that, without impairing the usefulness of the pool or pricing it out of the market, warnings against diving could be made more prominent and a liner less dangerous. It may not be necessary for the plaintiff to introduce evidence on all those alternatives. Conversely, the plaintiff may wish to offer proof on other matters relevant to the risk-utility analysis. It is not a foregone conclusion that plaintiff ultimately will prevail on a risk-utility analysis, but he should have an opportunity to prove his case. . . .

In concluding, we find that, although the jury allocated fault between the parties, the allocation was based upon the consideration of the fault of Muskin without reference to the design defect. Perhaps the jury would have made a different allocation if, in addition to the inadequacy of the warning, it had considered also the alleged defect in the design of the pool.

All parties consented at trial to a dismissal of all claims against Kiddie City, on the assumption that it did not manufacture the vinyl liner and that it was merely a conduit between the manufacturer and the purchaser. That assumption was based on Muskin's acknowledgment throughout the pre-trial proceedings that it made the vinyl liner. In the course of the trial, the purchaser testified that all parts of the pool, including the liner, arrived in Muskin boxes, but a Muskin witness testified, to everyone's surprise, that the liner was not a Muskin product. To avoid possible prejudice to Muskin and plaintiff, the Appellate Division vacated the dismissal of the claims as to Kiddie City. We believe the appropriate disposition is to reinstate the dismissal as to Kiddie City and to preclude Muskin from denying that it made the vinyl liner.

We modify and affirm the judgment of the Appellate Division reversing and remanding the matter for a new trial. . . .

SCHREIBER, J., concurring and dissenting.

Until today, the existence of a defect was an essential element in strict product liability. This no longer is so. Indeed, the majority has transformed strict product liability into absolute liability and delegated the function of making that determination to a jury. I must dissent from that conclusion because the jury will not be cognizant of all the elements that should be considered in formulating a policy supporting absolute liability, because it is not satisfactory to have a jury make a value judgment with respect to a type or class of product, and because its judgment will not have precedential effect. . . .

My research has disclosed no case where liability was imposed, utilizing the risk-utility analysis, as a matter of law for an accident ascribable to a product in the absence of a defect (manufacturing flaw, available alternative, or inadequate warning) other than in the absolute liability context. . . .

There are occasions where the court has determined as a matter of law because of policy reasons that liability should be imposed even though there is no defect in the product. This is the absolute liability model. The typical example is fixing absolute liability when an ultrahazardous activity causes injury or damage. Liability is imposed irrespective of any wrongdoing by the defendant. . . . In this situation the ultimate determination is that the industry should bear such costs, provided the jury has made the requisite findings on causation and damages.

Factors similar to those used in the risk-utility analysis for products liability are applied in the ultrahazardous activity case. The Restatement (Second) of Torts lists these elements:

§ 520. Abnormally Dangerous Activities

In determining whether an activity is abnormally dangerous, the following factors are to be considered:

(a) existence of a high degree of risk of some harm to the person, land or chattels of others;

(b) likelihood that the harm that results from it will be great;

(c) inability to eliminate the risk by the exercise of reasonable care;

(d) extent to which the activity is not a matter of common usage;

(e) inappropriateness of the activity to the place where it is carried on; and

(f) extent to which its value to the community is outweighed by its dangerous attributes.

It is conceivable that a court could decide that a manufacturer should have absolute liability for a defect-free product where as a matter of policy liability should be imposed. Suppose a manufacturer produced toy guns for children that emitted hard rubber pellets — an obviously dangerous situation. A court could reasonably conclude that the risks (despite warnings) outweighed the recreational value of the toy, that the manufacturer should bear the costs and that there should be absolute liability to a child injured by the toy.

The Restatement also cautions that whether an activity is an abnormally dangerous one so that it should be placed in the ultrahazardous category is to be settled by the court, not the jury. In its comment it states:

The imposition of [absolute] liability, on the other hand, involves a characterization of the defendant's activity or enterprise itself, and a decision as to whether he is free to conduct it at all without becoming subject to liability for the harm that ensues even though he has used all reasonable care. This calls for a decision of the court; and it is no part of the province of the jury to decide whether an industrial enterprise upon which the community's prosperity might depend is located in the wrong place or whether such an activity as blasting is to be permitted without liability in the center of a large city. [3 Restatement (Second) of Torts § 520 comment *l*, at 43 (1965).]

It is important to note that the risk-utility analysis is not submitted to the jury for the purpose of determining absolute liability for a class or type of product. Dean Wade has explained that when a whole group or class or type of a product may be unsafe, "the policy issues become very important and the factors [the seven listed in the risk-utility analysis] must be collected and carefully weighed. It is here that the court—whether trial or appellate—does consider these issues in deciding whether to submit the case to the jury." [Wade, *On the Nature of Strict Tort Liability for Products*, 44 Miss. L.J. 825, 838 (1973).]

When the case is submitted to the jury in strict liability, the jury must decide whether the product is defective and reasonably safe, not whether as a matter of policy the manufacturer should be absolutely liable. In determining questions of defectiveness and safety, some of the same risk-utility factors may be pertinent. However, reference to any one of the factors is to be made only when it is relevant and may be of assistance in deciding whether the product is defective and whether it is not reasonably safe. . . .

The majority holds that the jury should have been permitted to decide whether the risks of above-ground swimming pools with vinyl bottoms exceed their usefulness despite adequate warnings and despite unavailability of any other design. The plaintiff had the burden of proving this proposition. Yet he adduced no evidence on many of the factors bearing on the risk-utility analysis. There was no evidence on the extent that these pools are used and enjoyed throughout the country; how many families obtain the recreational benefits of swimming and play during a summer; how many accidents occur in the same period of time; the nature of the injuries and how many result from diving. There was no evidence of the feasibility of risk spreading or of the availability of liability insurance or its cost. There was no evidence introduced to enable one to gauge the effect on the price of the product, with or without insurance. The liability exposures, particularly if today's decision is given retroactive effect, could be financially devastating.

These factors should be given some consideration when deciding the policy question of whether pool manufacturers and, in the final analysis, consumers should bear the costs of accidents arising out of the use of pools when no fault can be attributed to the manufacturer because of a flaw in the pool, unavailability of a better design, or inadequate warning. If this Court wishes to make absolute liability available in product cases and not leave such decisions to the Legislature, it should require that trial courts determine in the first instance as a matter of law what products should be subject to absolute liability. In that event the court would consider all relevant factors including those utilized in the risk-utility analysis. . . .

I join in the result, however. There was proof that the pool liner was slippery and that the vinyl bottom could have been thicker and the embossing deeper. As the majority states, a "fair inference could be drawn that deeper embossing would have rendered the pool bottom less slippery." . . . The plaintiff's theory was that the dangerous condition was the extreme slipperiness of the bottom. Viewing the facts favorably from the plaintiff's frame of reference, I would agree that he had some proof that the pool was incorrectly designed and therefore was defective. This issue, together with causation, should have been submitted to the jury.

Other than as stated herein, I join in the majority's opinion and concur in the judgment reversing and remanding the matter for a new trial.

CLIFFORD, J., concurring in the result.

For affirmance as modified — Chief Justice WILENTZ, and Justices CLIFFORD, HANDLER, POLLOCK and O'HERN — 5.

Concurring and dissenting — Justice SCHREIBER — 1.

FOOD FOR THOUGHT

O'Brien was effectively overruled by a statute in New Jersey that states that a product cannot be found defective in design if "there was not a practical and technically feasible alternative design that would have prevented the harm without substantially impairing the reasonably anticipated or intended function of the product." N.J. Stat. Ann. § 2A:58C-3(a)(1).

Other attempts to declare entire categories of products to be defectively designed have been rejected by courts. *See e.g.,* Graham v. R.J. Reynolds Tobacco Co., 2015 WL 1546522 (11th Cir. 2015) (the State of Florida "may not enforce a duty . . . premised on the theory that all cigarettes are inherently defective and that every cigarette sale is an inherently negligent act . . . these specific, sweeping bases for state tort liability . . . frustrate the full purposes and objectives of Congress"); S.F. v. Archer Daniels Midland Co., 594 Fed. App'x 11 (2nd Cir. 2014) (affirming dismissal of suit against manufacturer of high fructose corn syrup for allegedly causing diabetes because, under New York law, "a design-defect claim will not stand if the only alternative is an outright ban"); Fabiano v. Philip Morris Inc., 909 N.Y.S.2d 314, 320 (Sup. Ct. N.Y. County 2010) (observing "the vast majority of courts have been markedly unreceptive to the call that they displace markets, legislatures, and governmental agencies by decreeing whole categories of products to be outlaws"); Junk v. Terminix Intern. Co. Ltd. Partnership, 2008 WL 5191865 (S.D. Iowa 2008) (refusing to hold that the insecticide manufactured by the defendants was a manifestly unreasonable product as defined in Restatement, Third, of Products Liability § 2, comment *e*, given that only .07 percent of users suffered injury and the product was a very useful insecticide).

If products are to be declared defective based on the theory that they do not measure up to risk-utility norms, even though there was no better design available, which products might qualify to be declared defective on these grounds? (1) motorcycles? (2) switchblades? (3) alcoholic spirits? (4) all-terrain vehicles? (5) skateboards?

The Products Liability Restatement § 2(b), comment *e*, suggests that there may be some "manifestly unreasonable" products that have such great risk and so little social utility that a court might declare such a product defectively designed even though no reasonable alternative design was available. The comment and illustrations suggest that a toy gun that shoots hard rubber pellets or an exploding cigar that can cause serious facial burns might qualify. In Parish v. Jumpking, Inc., 719

N.W.2d 540 (Iowa 2006), the plaintiff was jumping on defendant manufacturer's backyard trampoline when he landed on his head attempting a back somersault and was rendered a quadriplegic. The plaintiff claimed, inter alia, that trampolines fall within the "manifestly unreasonable" exception in comment *e* to § 2(b). Observing that trampolines provide valuable exercise and entertainment, and are statistically less dangerous than such common recreational activities as basketball, bicycle riding, football, soccer, and skating, the court rejected plaintiff's category liability claim as a matter of law. Do you foresee product category liability becoming a big ticket item for plaintiffs in American courts? How about cigarettes?

ADAMO v. BROWN & WILLIAMSON TOBACCO CORP.
900 N.E.2d 966 (N.Y. 2008)

SMITH, J.

Plaintiffs claim that two cigarette companies were negligent in designing their product, in that they should have used lower levels of tar and nicotine. We agree with the Appellate Division that plaintiffs failed to prove an essential element of their case: that regular cigarettes and "light" cigarettes have the same "utility." The only "utility" of a cigarette is to gratify smokers' desires for a certain experience, and plaintiffs did not prove, or try to prove, that light cigarettes perform this function as well as regular cigarettes.

Norma Rose, who died during the pendency of this appeal, smoked for more than 40 years, consuming more than a pack a day of regular cigarettes. Beginning in the late 1960s, the products she smoked were manufactured by the American Tobacco Company and Philip Morris USA Inc. Ms. Rose quit smoking in 1993, and was diagnosed two years later with lung cancer and another condition allegedly caused by smoking. She and her husband brought a number of claims against American Tobacco's successor (Brown & Williamson Tobacco Corporation), Philip Morris and a third company. All their claims except one for negligent product design were dismissed at the trial level and are not now before us.

A jury found that American Tobacco and Philip Morris negligently designed the cigarettes Ms. Rose smoked and, in later phases of the trial, awarded compensatory and punitive damages. The Appellate Division reversed the resulting judgment, with two Justices dissenting, and granted judgment in defendants' favor (855 N.Y.S.2d 119 (2008). . . .

In *Voss v. Black & Decker Mfg. Co.,* 59 N.Y.2d 102, 108, 463 N.Y.S.2d 398, 450 N.E.2d 204 [1983], speaking of a claim of strict product liability, we said: "The plaintiff . . . is under an obligation to present evidence that the product, as designed, was not reasonably safe because there was a substantial likelihood of harm and it was feasible to design the product in a safer manner." While this is a negligence, not a strict liability, case, similar requirements apply—specifically, plaintiffs here had to prove that "it was feasible to design the product in a safer manner." This means, to use again the language of *Voss,* the plaintiffs must show "the potential for designing . . . the product so that it is safer but remains functional" (*id.* at 109, 463 N.Y.S.2d 398, 450 N.E.2d 204).

Here, plaintiffs presented evidence from which a jury could find that light cigarettes — cigarettes containing significantly lower levels of tar and nicotine — are "safer" than regular cigarettes, but they did not show that cigarettes from which much of the tar and nicotine has been removed remain "functional." The function of a cigarette is to give pleasure to a smoker; plaintiffs have identified no other function. Plaintiffs made no attempt to prove that smokers find light cigarettes as satisfying as regular cigarettes — indeed, it is virtually uncontested that they do not. Both regular and light cigarettes are available on the market, and the enhanced dangers that come from smoking regular cigarettes are well known, but large numbers of consumers continue to prefer regular cigarettes.

It is not necessary in every product liability case that the plaintiff show the safer product is as acceptable to consumers as the one the defendant sold; but such a showing is necessary where, as here, satisfying the consumer is the only function the product has. A cigarette is a different kind of product from the circular saw in *Voss,* whose function was to cut wood, or the molding machine in *Robinson v. Reed-Prentice Div. of Package Mach. Co.,* 403 N.E.2d 440 (1980), whose function was to melt and form plastic. . . .

Of course we are conscious, as everyone must be, of the irony in speaking of cigarettes' "utility." A strong argument can be made that, when the pleasure they give smokers is balanced against the harm they do, regular cigarettes are worse than useless. But it is still lawful for people to buy and smoke regular cigarettes, and for cigarette companies to sell them. To hold, as plaintiffs ask, that every sale of regular cigarettes exposes the manufacturer to tort liability would amount to a judicial ban on the product. If regular cigarettes are to be banned, that should be done by legislative bodies, not by courts.

Accordingly, the order of the Appellate Division should be affirmed, with costs.

[Dissenting opinion omitted.]

3. Failure to Warn

ANDERSON v. OWENS-CORNING FIBERGLAS CORP.
810 P.2d 549 (Cal. 1991)

PANELLI, Associate Justice. . . .

Defendants are or were manufacturers of products containing asbestos. Plaintiff Carl Anderson filed suit in 1984, alleging that he contracted asbestosis and other lung ailments through exposure to asbestos and asbestos products (i.e., preformed blocks, cloth and cloth tape, cement, and floor tiles) while working as an electrician at the Long Beach Naval Shipyard from 1941 to 1976. Plaintiff allegedly encountered asbestos while working in the vicinity of others who were removing and installing insulation products aboard ships. . . .

Plaintiff's amended complaint alleged a cause of action in strict liability for the manufacture and distribution of "asbestos, and other products containing said substance [...]" which caused injury to users and consumers, including plaintiff.... Plaintiff alleged that defendants marketed their products with specific prior knowledge, from scientific studies and medical data, that there was a high risk of injury and death from exposure to asbestos or asbestos-containing products; that defendants knew consumers and members of the general public had no knowledge of the potentially injurious nature of asbestos; and that defendants failed to warn users of the risk of danger. Defendants' pleadings raised the state-of-the-art defense, i.e., that even those at the vanguard of scientific knowledge at the time the products were sold could not have known that asbestos was dangerous to users in the concentrations associated with defendants' products.

Plaintiff moved before trial to prevent defendants from presenting state-of-the-art evidence. . . . The trial court granted the motion. . . . The defendants then moved to prevent plaintiff from proceeding on the failure-to-warn theory. . . . In response to the court's request for an offer of proof on the alleged failure to warn, plaintiff referred to catalogs and other literature depicting workers without respirators or protective devices and offered to prove that, until the mid-1960's, defendants had given no warnings of the dangers associated with asbestos, that various warnings given by some of the defendants after 1965 were inadequate, and, finally, that defendants removed the products from the market entirely in the early 1970's. Defendants argued in turn that the state of the art, i.e., what was scientifically knowable in the period 1943-1974, was their obvious and only defense to any cause of action for failure to warn, and that, in view of the court's decision to exclude state-of-the-art evidence, fairness dictated that plaintiff be precluded from proceeding on that theory. With no statement of reasons, the trial court granted defendants' motion. . . . After a four-week trial, the jury returned a verdict for defendants. . . .

Plaintiff moved for a new trial, asserting that the court erred in precluding proof of liability on a failure-to-warn theory. . . . The court granted the motion. . . . Plaintiff . . . urged that knowledge or knowability, and thus state-of-the-art evidence, was irrelevant in strict liability for failure to warn. . . . The trial court agreed.

The Court of Appeal, in a two-to-one decision, upheld the order granting a new trial on both grounds. The appellate court added that, "in strict liability asbestos cases, including those prosecuted on a failure to warn theory, state of the art evidence is not admissible since it focuses on the reasonableness of the defendant's conduct, which is irrelevant in strict liability." The dissenting justice urged that the majority had imposed "absolute liability," contrary to the tenets of the strict liability doctrine, and that the manufacturers' right to a fair trial included the right to litigate all relevant issues, including the state of the art of scientific knowledge at the relevant time. We granted review.

Failure to Warn Theory of Strict Liability . . .

In Cavers v. Cushman Motor Sales, Inc. (1979) 95 Cal. App. 3d 338, 157 Cal. Rptr. 142, the first case in which failure to warn was the sole theory of liability, the appellate court approved the instruction that a golf cart, otherwise properly manufactured, could be defective if no warning was given of the cart's propensity to tip over when turning and if the absence of the warning rendered the product substantially dangerous to the user. Cavers was principally concerned with the propriety of the term "substantially dangerous" and concluded that it is necessary to weigh the degree of danger involved when determining whether a warning defect exists. . . .

[Early] cases did not address the specific factual question whether or not the manufacturer or distributor knew or should have known of the risks involved in the products, either because the nature of the product or the risk involved made such a discussion unnecessary or because the plaintiff limited the action to risks about which the manufacturer/distributor obviously knew or should have known. Moreover, the appellate courts in these same cases did not discuss knowledge or knowability as a component of the failure to warn theory of strict liability. However, a knowledge or knowability component clearly was included as an implicit condition of strict liability. In that regard, California was in accord with authorities in a majority of other states.

Only when the danger to be warned against was "unknowable" did the knowledge component of the failure-to-warn theory come into focus. Such cases made it apparent that eliminating the knowledge component had the effect of turning strict liability into absolute liability. . . .

[The court reviews other California Court of Appeals decisions.]

In sum, the foregoing review of the decisions of the Courts of Appeal persuade us that California is well settled into the majority view that knowledge, actual or constructive, is a requisite for strict liability for failure to warn and that [our earlier decision] if not directly, at least by implication, reaffirms that position.

However, even if we are implying too much from the language in [our earlier decision], the fact remains that we are now squarely faced with the issue of knowledge and knowability in strict liability for failure to warn in other than the drug context. Whatever the ambiguity of [our earlier decision], we hereby adopt the requirement, as propounded by the Restatement Second of Torts and acknowledged by the lower courts of this state and the majority of jurisdictions, that knowledge or knowability is a component of strict liability for failure to warn.

One of the guiding principles of the strict liability doctrine was to relieve a plaintiff of the evidentiary burdens inherent in a negligence cause of action. . . . Indeed, it was the limitations of negligence theories that prompted the development and expansion of the doctrine. The proponents of the minority rule, including the Court of Appeal in this case, argue that the knowability requirement, and admission of state-of-the-art evidence, improperly infuse negligence concepts into strict liability cases by directing the trier of fact's attention to the conduct of the manufacturer or distributor rather than to the condition of the product. Similar claims have been made as to other aspects of strict liability, sometimes resulting in limitations on the doctrine and sometimes not. . . .

[The court discusses earlier decisions not involving failure to warn.]

As these cases illustrate, the strict liability doctrine has incorporated some well-settled rules from the law of negligence and has survived judicial challenges asserting that such incorporation violates the fundamental principles of the doctrine. It may also be true that the "warning defect" theory is "rooted in negligence" to a greater extent than are the manufacturing- or design-defect theories. The "warning defect" relates to a failure extraneous to the product itself. Thus, while a manufacturing or

design defect can be evaluated without reference to the conduct of the manufacturer . . . the giving of a warning cannot. The latter necessarily requires the communicating of something to someone. How can one warn of something that is
unknowable? If every product that has no warning were defective per se and for
that reason subject to strict liability, the mere fact of injury by an unlabelled product
would automatically permit recovery. That is not, and has never been, the purpose
and goal of the failure-to-warn theory of strict liability. Further, if a warning automatically precluded liability in every case, a manufacturer or distributor could easily
escape liability with overly broad, and thus practically useless, warnings. . . .

We therefore reject the contention that every reference to a feature shared with
theories of negligence can serve to defeat limitations on the doctrine of strict
liability. Furthermore, despite its roots in negligence, failure to warn in strict
liability differs markedly from failure to warn in the negligence context. Negligence
law in a failure-to-warn case requires a plaintiff to prove that a manufacturer or
distributor did not warn of a particular risk for reasons which fell below the
acceptable standard of care, i.e., what a reasonably prudent manufacturer would
have known and warned about. Strict liability is not concerned with the standard of
due care or the reasonableness of a manufacturer's conduct. The rules of strict
liability require a plaintiff to prove only that the defendant did not adequately warn
of a particular risk that was known or knowable in light of the generally recognized
and prevailing best scientific and medical knowledge available at the time of manufacture and distribution. Thus, in strict liability, as opposed to negligence, the
reasonableness of the defendant's failure to warn is immaterial.

Stated another way, a reasonably prudent manufacturer might reasonably
decide that the risk of harm was such as not to require a warning as, for example,
if the manufacturer's own testing showed a result contrary to that of others in the
scientific community. Such a manufacturer might escape liability under negligence
principles. In contrast, under strict liability principles the manufacturer has no
such leeway; the manufacturer is liable if it failed to give warning of dangers that
were known to the scientific community at the time it manufactured or distributed
the product. Whatever may be reasonable from the point of view of the manufacturer, the user of the product must be given the option either to refrain from
using the product at all or to use it in such a way as to minimize the degree of
danger. Davis v. Wyeth Laboratories, Inc. (9th Cir. 1968) 399 F.2d 121, 129-130,
described the need to warn in order to provide "true choice": "When, in a particular case, the risk qualitatively (e.g., of death or major disability) as well as
quantitatively, on balance with the end sought to be achieved, is such as to call
for a true choice judgment, medical or personal, the warning must be given. [Fn.
omitted.]" . . . Thus, the fact that a manufacturer acted as a reasonably prudent
manufacturer in deciding not to warn, while perhaps absolving the manufacturer
of liability under the negligence theory, will not preclude liability under strict
liability principles if the trier of fact concludes that, based on the information
scientifically available to the manufacturer, the manufacturer's failure to warn
rendered the product unsafe to its users.

The foregoing examination of the failure-to-warn theory of strict liability in
California compels the conclusion that knowability is relevant to imposition of

liability under that theory. Our conclusion not only accords with precedent but also with the considerations of policy that underlie the doctrine of strict liability.

We recognize that an important goal of strict liability is to spread the risks and costs of injury to those most able to bear them. However, it was never the intention of the drafters of the doctrine to make the manufacturer or distributor the insurer of the safety of their products. It was never their intention to impose absolute liability.

Conclusion

Therefore, in answer to the question raised in our order granting review, a defendant in a strict products liability action based upon an alleged failure to warn of a risk of harm may present evidence of the state of the art, i.e., evidence that the particular risk was neither known nor knowable by the application of scientific knowledge available at the time of manufacture and/or distribution. The judgment of the Court of Appeal is affirmed with directions that the matter be remanded to the trial court for proceedings in accord with our decision herein.

Lucas, C.J., and Kennard, Arabian and Baxter, JJ., concur. . . .

Mosk, Associate Justice, concurring and dissenting.

In my view the trial court properly granted a new trial and the Court of Appeal, in a thoughtful analysis of the law, correctly affirmed the order. I thus concur in the result.

I must express my apprehension, however, that we are once again retreating from "[t]he pure concepts of products liability so pridefully fashioned and nurtured by this court." (Daly v. General Motors Corp. (1978) 20 Cal. 3d 725, 757, 144 Cal. Rptr. 380, 575 P.2d 1162 (dis. opn. by Mosk, J.).) . . .

The majority distinguish failure-to-warn strict liability claims from negligence claims on the ground that strict liability is not concerned with a standard of due care or the reasonableness of a manufacturer's conduct. This is generally accurate. However in practice this is often a distinction without a substantial difference. Under either theory, imposition of liability is conditioned on the defendant's actual or constructive knowledge of the risk. Recovery will be allowed only if the defendant has such knowledge yet fails to warn. . . .

We should consider the possibility of holding that failure-to-warn actions lie solely on a negligence theory. "[A]lthough mixing negligence and strict liability concepts is often a game of semantics, the game has more than semantic impact — it breeds confusion and inevitably, bad law." (Henderson & Twerski, *Doctrinal Collapse in Products Liability: The Empty Shell of Failure to Warn, supra*, 65 N.Y.U. L. Rev. at p. 278.) If, however, the majority are not ready to take that step, I would still use this opportunity to enunciate a bright-line rule to apply in failure-to-warn strict liability actions.

Here plaintiff alleged, among other claims, that defendants marketed their products "with specific prior knowledge" of the high risks of injury and death from their use. If plaintiff can establish at the new trial that defendants had actual knowledge, then state of the art evidence — or what everyone else was doing at the time — would be irrelevant and the trial court could properly exclude it. Actual knowledge may often be difficult to prove, but it is not impossible with adequately probing discovery. Defendants, of course, can produce evidence that they had no such prior actual knowledge.

On the other hand, if plaintiff is only able to show, by medical and scientific data or other means, that defendants should have known of the risks inherent in their products, then contrary medical and scientific data and state of the art evidence would be admissible if offered by defendants.

Thus I would draw a clear distinction in failure-to-warn cases between evidence that the defendants had actual knowledge of the dangers and evidence that the defendants should have known of the dangers.

With the foregoing rule in mind, the parties should proceed to the new trial ordered by the trial court and upheld by the Court of Appeal. Thus I would affirm the judgment of the Court of Appeal.

FOOD FOR THOUGHT

Complete the following sentence in 25 words or less: Although foreseeability of risk is a requisite element of a strict liability failure to warn case, plaintiff is advantaged by bringing his case under strict liability because _____. Several courts have said that they can discern no difference between the two theories. *See, e.g.,* May v. Air & Liquid Systems Corp., 446 Md. 1, 10 (Md. App. 2015) ("We analyze the negligent and strict liability failure to warn issues in turn, even though the analytical basis for each overlaps with the other."); Authement v. Ingram Barge Co., 977 F. Supp. 2d 606 (E.D. La. 2013) (noting that little difference exists between negligence and strict liability failure to warn cases for the purposes of federal maritime law).

In Chapter 4, we alluded to the difficult but-for causation problem that attends failure to warn cases. Even if a product is found to be defective because of failure to warn, how can we have any confidence that the plaintiff would have read and heeded the warning? A significant number of courts have eased the plaintiff's burden by creating a "heeding presumption." When a defendant fails to warn, the court presumes that the plaintiff would have read the warning and would have avoided the warned-against risk. It is then the task of the defendant to rebut the presumption. *See, e.g.,* Moore v. Ford Motor Company, 332 S.W.3d 749 (Mo. 2011) (reversing the trial court's directed verdict for the defendant on ground that the question of whether the defendant had rebutted the heeding presumption was for the jury); Kirkbride v. Terex USA, LLC, 798 F.3d 1343 (10th Cir. 2015) (reversing a jury verdict in favor of the plaintiff on ground that, under Utah law, the defendant had successfully rebutted the heeding presumption, where the plaintiff admitted that he did not read the safety manual, and questioned why one would read such a manual). Some courts still insist that the plaintiff meet the traditional burden of proving that the failure to warn was the cause of the harm. *See, e.g.,* Rivera v. Philip Morris, Inc., 125 Nev. 185 (Nev. 2009) (rejecting plaintiff's request that Nevada adopt a heeding presumption in failure to warn cases); Merck & Co., Inc. v. Garza, 277 S.W.3d 430, 437 (Tex. App. 2008) *overruled on other grounds* Merck & Co., Inc. v. Garza, 347 S.W.3d 256 (Tex. 2011)

authors' dialogue 37

AARON: Jim, how to deal with the causation problem in failure to warn cases presents a genuine dilemma. How the devil is anyone to know how a plaintiff would have reacted to a warning that was not given? In design defect cases a plaintiff posits a reasonable alternative design. Experts can testify as to whether, had the design been present at the time the plaintiff was hurt, the plaintiff could have avoided injury or at least have his injury reduced. But in warning cases we hypothesize a warning and then ask, if the warning had been there, would it have made a difference? The only one who knows the answer to that question is G-d.

JIM: Look, Aaron, the hypothetical but-for is an integral part of the law of causation. We faced the identical problem in a set of causation cases in Chapter 4. We found that courts will take the cases from juries when it is clear that but-for causation has not been made out. In most cases where the evidence is fuzzy, they let the juries pass on whether the evidence convinces them more probably than not that the negligence was the cause of the harm. I see no palpable difference.

AARON: In principle you are right. I guess what makes me so uncomfortable in the products liability setting is that I have little confidence that we are making a sound decision on the basic issue of failure to warn. What standards govern whether a warning should be given or not? I know the stock answer is that a manufacturer has a duty to provide reasonable warnings. But the reasonableness question is often so hokey. In every case plaintiff will want a warning about the very risk that caused her injury. After the fact, with 20-20 hindsight, it's easy to point to that specific risk and claim that it should have been warned against. But before the fact it's very difficult to prognosticate all forms of plaintiff misbehavior. And if we did, we would need the New York telephone book to list all the crazy things that plaintiffs may do with a product. So what I see is a fuzzy standard for what risks need to be warned against and a fuzzy standard on causation. All this fuzziness gives me an itch.

JIM: You may be right. But if plaintiff has jumped through the hoops of both defect and causation, there is little that can be done to deny her a recovery. What probably is unnecessary is the "heeding presumption" that shifts the burden to defendant to come forward with evidence. Since courts are already so liberal in letting causation cases go to the jury on minimal evidence of causation, plaintiffs do not need and should not get a formal presumption in their favor. A plaintiff will always testify that, if she had only been given a warning, she would have read and heeded it. So why give her a presumption?

AARON: What if plaintiff is truthful and says that she really does not know if she would have read or heeded the warning?

JIM: I hate to be a cynic. But when you come across such a case, send me the plaintiff's name. I will send it on to Ripley's "Believe It or Not."

AARON: What if the plaintiff is dead?

JIM: You know, that might be the rare instance when a presumption could be justified.

(in a failure to warn case involving prescription drugs, a plaintiff must establish not only that the warnings were inadequate, but "must show that a proper warning would have changed the decision of the intermediary to prescribe the product").

One of the authors (Twerski) believes that a radical change is necessary to deal with the hypothetical but-for question in failure-to-warn cases. In Aaron D. Twerski & Neil B. Cohen, *Resolving the Dilemma of Nonjusticiable Causation in Failure to Warn Litigation*, 84 S. Cal. L. Rev. 126 (2010), the authors argue that a substantial body of social science literature demonstrates that in all but extreme cases, it is impossible for an injured party to demonstrate that he/she would have acted differently had a warning been given. The authors propose eliminating causation as an independent requirement in failure-to-warn cases and instead allow a plaintiff proportional recovery taking into account the severity of the manufacturer's fault in failing to warn of the dangers and the likelihood that the plaintiff's injuries would have been prevented by a warning. Henderson believes that the Twerski-Cohen thesis is not only radical but unrealistic.

I WOULDN'T HAVE BOUGHT THE PRODUCT IF I HAD KNOWN: INFORMED CHOICE WARNINGS

Most often warnings serve to alert a consumer to a risk that she can avoid by using the product more carefully. For example, a warning on an electric blow dryer that the dryer is not to be immersed in water because it can cause the wire to short out and create a fire hazard serves to reduce risk. If the consumer heeds the warning, the risk of fire can be avoided. For some products, warnings may not serve to help the consumer avoid the risk while using the product. Some risks associated with drugs cannot be avoided by more judicious use of the drug. Instead, there is a slight risk that the user may suffer some reaction to the drug. It is up to the consumer whether she wishes to take the drug and incur the risk or avoid the risk and also give up on the benefits of the drug. When a manufacturer fails to provide such an "informed choice" warning, many courts have held that liability may attach. The Products Liability Restatement, §2, comment *i* agrees with this basis of liability:

> In addition to alerting users and consumers to the existence and nature of product risks so that they can, by appropriate conduct during use or consumption, reduce the risk of harm, warning also may be needed to inform users and consumers of nonobvious and not generally known risks that unavoidably inhere in using or consuming the product. Such warnings allow the user or consumer to avoid the risk warned against by making an informed decision not to purchase or use the product at all and hence not to encounter the risk. In this context, warnings must be provided for inherent risks that reasonably foreseeable product users and consumers would reasonably deem material or significant in deciding whether to use or consume the product. Whether or not many persons would, when warned, nonetheless decide to use or consume the product, warnings are required to protect the interests of those reasonably foreseeable users or consumers who would, based on their own reasonable assessments of the risks and benefits, decline product use or consumption. When such warnings are necessary, their

omission renders the product not reasonably safe at time of sale. Notwithstanding the defective condition of the product in the absence of adequate warnings, if a particular user or consumer would have decided to use or consume even if warned, the lack of warnings is not a legal cause of that plaintiff's harm. Judicial decisions supporting the duty to provide warnings for informed decisionmaking have arisen almost exclusively with regard to those toxic agents and pharmaceutical products with respect to which courts have recognized a distinctive need to provide risk information so that recipients of the information can decide whether they wish to purchase or utilize the product.

The informed choice theory has long been recognized in cases involving prescription drugs and toxic substances. (*See, e.g.,* Davis v. Wyeth Laboratories, 399 F.2d 121 (9th Cir. 1968) (failure to warn about the risk of developing polio from taking the polio vaccine); Borel v. Fibreboard Paper Products Corp., 493 F.2d 1076 (5th Cir. 1973) (failure to warn about the dangers of asbestos).)

One of the authors of this book co-authored an article that argues that proving causation in informed-choice prescription drug cases is too difficult, prohibiting even deserving plaintiffs from recovering. *See* Margaret A. Berger & Aaron D. Twerski, *Uncertainty and Informed Choice: Unmasking* Daubert, 104 Mich. L. Rev. 257 (2005). They propose "a cause of action for negligent infliction of emotional distress when [a] plaintiff is deprived of an informed choice about [a] material risk even if causation of the actual physical injury cannot be established with the certainty demanded by traditional causation norms." *Id.* at 285. They argue that some consumers would refrain from using nontherapeutic drugs if they knew there was even a minor risk of detrimental side effects, and when drug manufacturers delay warning, despite studies indicating possible negative side effects, the drug manufacturers have taken from the consumers the right to make an informed choice. A challenging response from Professor David Bernstein asserts that the Berger-Twerski proposal would have numerous negative consequences, including increasing the amount of litigation, inviting unreliable testimony, demanding too much expertise from juries, and eliminating the effectiveness of warnings by causing a proliferation of warnings about conceivable — but highly unlikely — side effects. *See* David E. Bernstein, *Learning the Wrong Lessons from* "*An American Tragedy*"*: A Critique of the Berger-Twerski Informed Choice Proposal,* 104 Mich. L. Rev. 1961, 1978 (2006). *See also* Margaret A. Berger & Aaron D. Twerski, *From the Wrong End of the Telescope: A Response to Professor David Bernstein,* 104 Mich. L. Rev. 1983 (2006).

Informed choice theory has been extended to other products as well. *See, e.g.,* Watkins v. Ford Motor Co., 190 F.3d 1213 (11th Cir. 1999), in which the driver and occupants of a Ford Bronco II sued for injuries suffered when the Bronco rolled over after the driver lost control of the vehicle. Plaintiff alleged that Ford failed to warn about the rollover propensity of the Ford Bronco II. Ford responded that even had they provided a warning, it would not have avoided the accident. Once the user had made a decision to drive a Bronco, the warning would not have protected against the danger of a rollover. There was no way a driver could respond to the warning to reduce the risk of rollover. The court rejected Ford's argument, concluding that though a warning might not serve to reduce the risk, it could serve to allow the user to make an informed decision as to "whether to take the risk warned of." *Id.* at 1219. *See also* Santos v. Ford Motor Co., 69 A.D.3d 502 (N.Y. App. 2010) (affirming trial court's refusal to send a failure to warn instruction to the jury on ground that the plaintiffs failed to put forth evidence that they would have bought a different car if the manufacturer had provided different warnings); Liriano v. Hobart Corp., 170 F.3d 264 (2d Cir. 1999) (court determined that jury could find that if warnings of the need for a shield on a meat grinder without one had been given, employee would have chosen not to use machine).

hypo **63**

A purchased a new Pugo. The Pugo is a very light, compact car. Several weeks after buying the car, while driving his Pugo, *A* collided head on with a Cadillac. The driver of the Cadillac suffered minor injuries. *A* suffered severe injuries as a result of the collision. *A* is suing Pugo on the ground that Pugo did not inform *A* that the risk of injury arising from a collision while a passenger in a Pugo is three times greater than that of a mid-size car and ten times greater than a full-size car. *A* alleges that he would never have purchased the Pugo had he been aware that the difference in risks was that great. Does *A* have an action against Pugo?

E. PROXIMATE CAUSE

UNION PUMP CO. v. ALLBRITTON
898 S.W.2d 773 (Tex. 1995)

OWEN, Justice.

The issue in this case is whether the condition, act, or omission of which a personal injury plaintiff complains was, as a matter of law, too remote to constitute legal causation. Plaintiff brought suit alleging negligence, gross negligence, and strict liability, and the trial court granted summary judgment for the defendant. The court of appeals reversed and remanded, holding that the plaintiff raised issues of fact concerning proximate and producing cause. 888 S.W.2d 833. Because we conclude that there was no legal causation as a matter of law, we reverse the judgment of the court of appeals and render judgment that plaintiff take nothing.

On the night of September 4, 1989, a fire occurred at Texaco Chemical Company's facility in Port Arthur, Texas. A pump manufactured by Union Pump Company caught fire and ignited the surrounding area. This particular pump had caught on fire twice before. Sue Allbritton, a trainee employee of Texaco Chemical, had just finished her shift and was about to leave the plant when the fire erupted. She and her supervisor Felipe Subia, Jr., were directed to and did assist in abating the fire.

Approximately two hours later, the fire was extinguished. However, there appeared to be a problem with a nitrogen purge valve, and Subia was instructed to block in the valve. Viewing the facts in a light most favorable to Allbritton, there was some evidence that an emergency situation existed at that point in time. Allbritton asked if she could accompany Subia and was allowed to do so. To get to the nitrogen purge valve, Allbritton followed Subia over an aboveground pipe rack, which was approximately two and one-half feet high, rather than going around it. It is undisputed that this was not the safer route, but it was the shorter one. Upon reaching the valve, Subia and Allbritton were notified that it was not necessary to block it off. Instead of returning by the route around the pipe rack, Subia chose to walk across it, and Allbritton followed. Allbritton was injured when she hopped or slipped off the pipe rack. There is evidence that the pipe rack was wet because of the fire and that Allbritton and Subia were still wearing fireman's hip boots and other firefighting gear when the injury occurred. Subia admitted that he chose to walk over the pipe rack rather than taking a safer alternative route because he had a "bad habit" of doing so.

Allbritton sued Union Pump, alleging negligence, gross negligence, and strict liability theories of recovery, and accordingly, that the defective pump was a proximate or producing cause of her injuries. But for the pump fire, she asserts, she would never have walked over the pipe rack, which was wet with water or firefighting foam.

Following discovery, Union Pump moved for summary judgment. To be entitled to summary judgment, the movant has the burden of establishing that there is no genuine issue of material fact and that it is entitled to judgment as a matter of law. Nixon v. Mr. Property Management Co., 690 S.W.2d 546, 548 (Tex. 1985). A defendant who moves for summary judgment must conclusively disprove one of the elements of each of the plaintiff's causes of action. Lear Siegler, Inc. v. Perez, 819 S.W.2d 470, 471 (Tex. 1991). All doubts must be resolved against Union Pump and all evidence must be viewed in the light most favorable to Allbritton. *Id.* The question before this Court is whether Union Pump established as a matter of law that neither its conduct nor its product was a legal cause of Allbritton's injuries. Stated another way, was Union Pump correct in contending that there was no causative link between the defective pump and Allbritton's injuries as a matter of law?

Negligence requires a showing of proximate cause, while producing cause is the test in strict liability. General Motors Corp. v. Saenz, 873 S.W.2d 353, 357 (Tex. 1993). Proximate and producing cause differ in that foreseeability is an element of proximate cause, but not of producing cause. *Id.* Proximate cause consists of both cause in fact and foreseeability. Travis v. City of Mesquite, 830 S.W.2d 94, 98 (Tex. 1992); Missouri Pac. R.R. Co. v. American Statesman, 552 S.W.2d 99, 103 (Tex. 1977); *Nixon,* 690 S.W.2d at 549. Cause in fact means that the defendant's act or omission was a substantial factor in bringing about the injury which would not otherwise have occurred. Prudential Ins. Co. v. Jefferson Assocs., 896 S.W.2d 156 (Tex. 1995); *Nixon,* 690 S.W.2d at 549; Havner v. E-Z Mart Stores, Inc., 825 S.W.2d 456, 458-59 (Tex. 1992). A producing cause is "an efficient, exciting, or contributing cause, which in a natural sequence, produced injuries or damages complained of, if any." Haynes & Boone v. Bowser Bouldin, Ltd., 896 S.W.2d 179 (Tex. 1995); Rourke v. Garza, 530 S.W.2d 794, 801 (Tex. 1975). Common to both proximate and producing cause is causation in fact, including the requirement that the defendant's conduct or product be a substantial factor in bringing about the plaintiff's injuries. *Prudential*, 896 S.W.2d at 161; *Lear Siegler*, 819 S.W.2d at 472 n.1 (quoting Restatement (Second) of Torts § 431 cmt. *e* (1965)).

At some point in the causal chain, the defendant's conduct or product may be too remotely connected with the plaintiff's injury to constitute legal causation. As this Court noted in City of Gladewater v. Pike, 727 S.W.2d 514, 518 (Tex. 1987), defining the limits of legal causation "eventually mandates weighing of policy considerations." See also Springall v. Fredericksburg Hospital and Clinic, 225 S.W.2d 232, 235 (Tex. Civ. App. — San Antonio 1949, no writ), in which the court of appeals observed:

> [T]he law does not hold one legally responsible for the remote results of his wrongful acts and therefore a line must be drawn between immediate and remote causes. The doctrine of "proximate cause" is employed to determine and fix this line and "is the result of an effort by the courts to avoid, as far as possible the metaphysical and philosophical niceties in the age-old discussion of causation, and to lay down a rule of general application which will, as nearly as may be done by a general rule, apply a practical test, the test of common experience, to human conduct when determining legal rights and legal liability."

Id. at 235 (quoting City of Dallas v. Maxwell, 248 S.W. 667, 670 (Tex. Comm'n App. 1923, holding approved)).

Drawing the line between where legal causation may exist and where, as a matter of law, it cannot, has generated a considerable body of law.[1] Our Court has considered where the limits of legal causation should lie in the factually analogous case of Lear Siegler, Inc. v. Perez, *supra*. The threshold issue was whether causation was negated as a matter of law in an action where negligence and product liability theories were asserted. Perez, an employee of the Texas Highway Department, was driving a truck pulling a flashing arrow sign behind a highway sweeping operation to warn traffic of the highway maintenance. *Id.* at 471. The sign malfunctioned when wires connecting it to the generator became loose, as they had the previous day. *Id.* Perez got out of the truck to push the wire connections back together, and an oncoming vehicle, whose driver was asleep, struck the sign, which in turn struck Perez. *Id.* Perez's survivors brought suit against the manufacturer of the sign. In holding that any defect in the sign was not the legal cause of Perez's injuries, we found a comment to the Restatement (Second) of Torts, section 431, instructive on the issue of legal causation:

---

1. In the seminal decision in Palsgraf v. Long Island Railroad Co., 248 N.Y. 339, 162 N.E. 99 (1928), for example, a railway guard knocked explosives from under the arm of a passenger who was hurrying to board a train. The resulting explosion caused scales some distance away to fall on Palsgraf. The majority in *Palsgraf* held that as a matter of law, the defendant owed no duty to Palsgraf because "[t]he risk reasonably to be perceived defines the duty to be obeyed; . . . it is risk to another or to others within the range of apprehension." *Id.* 162 N.E. at 100. In his dissent in *Palsgraf*, Judge Andrews opined that the decision should turn not on duty but on proximate cause. In analyzing proximate cause, he recognized: What we do mean by the word "proximate" is that, because of convenience, of public policy, of a rough sense of justice, the law arbitrarily declines to trace a series of events beyond a certain point. *Id.* at 103 (Andrews, J., dissenting).

> In order to be a legal cause of another's harm, it is not enough that the harm would not have occurred had the actor not been negligent. . . . The negligence must also be a substantial factor in bringing about the plaintiff's harm. The word "substantial" is used to denote the fact that the defendant's conduct has such an effect in producing the harm as to lead reasonable men to regard it as a cause, using that word in the popular sense, in which there always lurks the idea of responsibility, rather than in the so-called "philosophic sense," which includes every one of the great number of events without which any happening would not have occurred.

Lear Siegler, 819 S.W.2d at 472 (quoting Restatement (Second) of Torts § 431 cmt. *a* (1965)).

As this Court explained in *Lear Siegler,* the connection between the defendant and the plaintiff's injuries simply may be too attenuated to constitute legal cause. 819 S.W.2d at 472. Legal cause is not established if the defendant's conduct or product does no more than furnish the condition that makes the plaintiff's injury possible. *Id.* This principle applies with equal force to proximate cause and producing cause. *Id.* at 472 n.1.

This Court similarly considered the parameters of legal causation in Bell v. Campbell, 434 S.W.2d 117, 122 (Tex. 1968). In *Bell,* two cars collided, and a trailer attached to one of them disengaged and overturned into the opposite lane. A number of people gathered, and three of them were attempting to move the trailer when they were struck by another vehicle. *Id.* at 119. This Court held that the parties to the first accident were not a proximate cause of the plaintiffs' injuries, reasoning:

> All acts and omissions charged against respondents had run their course and were complete. Their negligence did not actively contribute in any way to the injuries involved in this suit. It simply created a condition which attracted [the plaintiffs] to the scene, where they were injured by a third party.

Id. at 122.

In *Bell,* this Court examined at some length decisions dealing with intervening causes and decisions dealing with concurring causes. The principles underlying the various legal theories of causation overlap in many respects, but they are not coextensive. While in *Bell,* this Court held "the injuries involved in this suit were not proximately caused by any negligence of [defendants] but by an independent and intervening agency," *id.,* we also held "[a]ll forces involved in or generated by the first collision had come to rest, and no one was in any real or apparent danger therefrom[,]" *id.* at 120, and accordingly, that the "[defendants'] negligence was not a concurring cause of [the plaintiffs'] injuries." *Id.* at 122. This reasoning applies with equal force to Allbritton's claims.

Even if the pump fire were in some sense a "philosophic" or "but for" cause of Allbritton's injuries, the forces generated by the fire had come to rest when she fell off the pipe rack. The fire had been extinguished, and Allbritton was walking away from the scene. Viewing the evidence in the light most favorable to Allbritton, the pump fire did no more than create the condition that made Allbritton's injuries possible. We conclude that the circumstances surrounding her injuries are too remotely connected with Union Pump's conduct or pump to constitute a legal cause of her injuries. *See Lear Siegler,* 819 S.W.2d at 472.

Accordingly, we reverse the judgment of the court of appeals and render judgment that plaintiff take nothing.

FOOD FOR THOUGHT

Union Pump demonstrates that proximate cause considerations are alive and well in products liability actions. All of the considerations that were germane to deciding whether a defendant's negligence was the proximate cause of the harm are applicable to whether the defect in the defendant's product was the proximate cause of the harm.

Remember *Marshall v. Nugent* in Chapter 5? In that case, the defendant negligently drove his truck around a curve on an icy mountain road and forced a car in which the plaintiff was a passenger off the road and into a snowbank. The truck driver stopped to help extricate the car from the snowbank and sent the plaintiff up the hill to warn oncoming traffic. While discharging this task up the hill, the plaintiff was struck by another car. You will recall that in *Marshall* the court let the plaintiff's case against the truck driver go to the jury to decide the proximate cause question. How broadly to read the risk created by a defendant's negligence or product defect is a tough call. It is likely that Judge Magruder, the author of the *Marshall* opinion, would have let the plaintiff get to the jury in *Union Pump.* No one ever has been, and no one ever will be, able to predict when judges will decide that proximate cause has not been established as a matter of law and take the case from the jury.

The court in *Union Pump* makes a big deal about the difference between proximate cause and producing cause. In Ford Motor Co. v. Ledesma, 242 S.W.3d 32 (Tex. 2007) the Texas court finally rid itself of the term "producing cause" and utilized a proximate cause analysis for products liability cases. No one will mourn the disappearance of "producing cause" from tort case law. It was a meaningless term understood by nobody.

F. COMPARATIVE FAULT

WEBB v. NAVISTAR INTERNATIONAL TRANSPORTATION CORP.
692 A.2d 343 (Vt. 1996)

DOOLEY, J. . . .

I

On November 13, 1985, at approximately 9:30 p.m., Bruce Webb learned that some of his cows might be out of the pasture. He and his father got out their tractor, a 1978 Model 464 farm tractor manufactured by Navistar, and they proceeded down Route 207 with Bruce Webb standing on the draw bar and his father driving. En route, the tractor was struck in the rear by a car driven by an allegedly intoxicated operator. As a result of the accident, Bruce Webb suffered serious injuries to his legs.

Plaintiffs filed suit against Navistar, the driver of the car, and others. The complaint alleged negligence, breach of warranty, and strict products liability. Claims against all defendants other than Navistar were ultimately dismissed, and the case proceeded to trial against Navistar solely on the products liability claim. Plaintiffs argued that the tractor was defectively designed because (1) it allowed operation of a white field light at highway speeds without provision for separate red tail lights, and (2) it failed to provide a safe passenger location so that Bruce Webb could have ridden on the tractor without exposure to injury. They contended further that defendant failed to provide adequate warnings of these dangers.

The case was tried, and the trial court directed a verdict in defendant's favor on both claims. On appeal, we affirmed the directed verdict regarding defendant's failure to provide a safe passenger location, but reversed as to whether the design of the field light was defective and whether the manufacturer's warning on its use was inadequate. . . .

The second trial focused on the lighting system of the tractor. The Model 464 tractor has a red taillight, two amber lights with road flashers, two red rear reflectors, a reflective slow-moving-vehicle triangle and a white field light mounted on the left rear bumper. A cautionary decal on the left front fender directs operators to use the flashing amber lights at all times when on public roads. The light system is designed so that when the flashing amber lights are in use, the red taillight activates and the white field light does not work. At the time of the accident, the flashing amber lights and the taillight did not work, and the reflectors were missing. In addition, by riding on the draw bar, Webb blocked the view of the reflective triangle. The cautionary decal also warned against riding the tractor unless a seat or platform is provided and instructed the operator to "[k]eep others off."

The owner's manual for the tractor also provides warnings and instructions. On pages 3 and 4, the manual sets forth rules for safe operation of the tractor. Here, the manual warns: "No riders allowed." It also contains an instruction not to use the white field light on the highway on page 55, under the heading CAUTION!

Webb testified that while travelling on the highway he employed both the headlights and the rear field light on the rationale that more light was better than less light. He indicated that it had not occurred to him that operating the tractor on the highway at night with the rear field light on was a hazard. The operator of the automobile that collided with the tractor testified that he believed the white field light mounted on the left rear bumper was the headlight of an approaching "one-eyed" car.

Plaintiffs tried the case on two theories: (1) that the lighting system was defective because it allowed the tractor to be operated on highways with the field light illuminated, and (2) that defendant failed to adequately warn consumers of the known risk of using the field light while operating the tractor on the highway. The jury returned a verdict in favor of plaintiffs on liability, and the parties stipulated to damages. Defendant appeals, arguing that the evidence was insufficient to support the verdict and that the court erred by failing to instruct the jury that it may apportion liability between the parties. We have the benefit of briefs of amicus parties on both sides of the comparative liability issue.

II

Defendant argues that the evidence was insufficient for the jury to find that its tractor was defective, that its warnings were inadequate, and that either the defective tractor or the inadequate warnings proximately caused Webb's injuries. . . .

The jury could reasonably conclude that the danger of operating the tractor on a highway at night with the field light illuminated was not a danger obvious to the ordinary consumer, and plaintiffs presented evidence of a safety device that could have been installed by defendant to prevent such use. . . . Moreover, the question of whether a manufacturer provided adequate warnings about foreseeable dangers is a question of fact properly left to the jury. . . .

III

I do not believe, however, that the judgment in this case can be affirmed. I agree with defendant that comparative liability principles are applicable in strict products liability actions and should have been charged to the jury in this case. Because the split in the Court reserves the details of implementing comparative principles for another day, I state only the reasons we adopt a comparative causation rule. . . .

The overwhelming majority of states have rejected the "all or nothing" rule, either by rejecting the limits of § 402A or by supplementing its provisions, and have applied principles of comparative liability in strict products liability actions [citing authority].[3] The United States District Court for the District of Vermont has endorsed this approach and predicted we will do so also. See Smith v. Goodyear Tire & Rubber Co., 600 F. Supp. 1561, 1568 (D. Vt. 1985).

In addition, the tentative draft of the Restatement (Third) of Torts provides for apportioning liability between the plaintiff and the manufacturer or seller. See Restatement (Third) of Torts: Products Liability § 7 (Tentative Draft No. 1, 1994). Similarly, the Uniform Comparative Fault Act § 1 provides that a claimant's contributory fault proportionately reduces compensatory damages in strict products liability actions. 12 U.L.A. 127 (1996). Many commentators maintain that adopting comparative liability principles in strict products liability actions is the fairest approach. See, e.g., . . . D. Noel, Defective Products: Abnormal Use, Contributory Negligence, and Assumption of Risk, 25 Vand. L. Rev. 93, 117-18 (1972) (contributory negligence should diminish plaintiff's damages); V. Schwartz, Strict

---

3. In addition, some states have adopted comparative principles in strict products liability actions by statute. See, e.g., Ark. Code Ann. § 16-64-122 (Michie 1987 & Supp. 1995); Colo. Rev. Stat. § 13-21-406 (1987); Minn. Stat. Ann. § 604.01 (West 1988 & Supp. 1997); Miss. Code Ann. § 11-7-15 (1972); Mo. Ann. Stat. § 537.765 (Vernon 1988); N.Y. Civ. Prac. L. & R. § 1411 (McKinney 1976); Utah Code Ann. §§ 78-27-37, -38 (1996); Wash. Rev. Code Ann. §§ 4.22.005.015 (West 1988).

Liability and Comparative Negligence, 42 Tenn. L. Rev. 171, 179-81 (1974) (comparative principles should apply in strict products liability); J. Wade, On the Nature of Strict Tort Liability for Products, 44 Miss. L.J. 825, 850 (1973) (same).

The primary reason that courts adopt comparative liability principles in strict products liability actions is "because it is fair to do so." . . . Adopting comparative liability principles "will accomplish a fairer and more equitable result" because the plaintiff's award is reduced by an amount equal to the degree to which the plaintiff is responsible for the accident. . . . Most courts reject the framework that places the burden of loss on one party where two parties contributed to causing the injury. . . . Comparative liability principles also further fairness by preventing a negligent plaintiff from recovering as much as a plaintiff who has taken all reasonable precautions. . . .

Moreover, there is no reason to impose the cost of a plaintiff's negligence upon the manufacturer to spread among other consumers of the product . . . see also Restatement (Third) of Torts: Products Liability § 7 cmt. *a* (Tentative Draft No. 1, 1994) (unfair to impose costs of substandard plaintiff conduct on manufacturers, who will be impelled to pass on costs to all consumers, including those who use and consume product safely). The instant case is illustrative. Here, plaintiff stood on the draw bar of the tractor while it traveled down a public road. Although he understood the importance of the warning against such action, he chose to disregard the warning. As a result, he blocked the view of the reflective triangle and the single amber flashing light that may have been operable. Moreover, he failed to maintain the reflectors and the other flashing light. If the jury may reduce plaintiff's recovery to the extent that his injuries were caused by his negligence, defendant is not held liable for the cost of injuries attributed to plaintiff's negligence and does not pass this cost on to those farmers who heed the warnings posted on their tractors. Strict products liability was intended to spread the cost of injuries resulting from defective products; it was never intended to spread the cost of injuries resulting from user negligence. . . .

Apportioning liability more effectively spreads recoveries from manufacturers for selling defective products than the "all or nothing" framework. Under the "all or nothing" framework, some plaintiffs receive windfalls because they collect damages for injuries caused by their own negligence in addition to damages for injuries caused by the product defect. On the other hand, some plaintiffs receive nothing because the court or jury has determined that their negligence constitutes misuse, assumption of risk or an intervening cause, concepts often difficult to distinguish. . . . Applying principles of comparative liability will reduce the total damages awarded to some plaintiffs but will also extend recoveries to some plaintiffs formerly barred from any recovery; thus, recoveries will be more equitably distributed among plaintiffs.

A minority of courts have rejected comparative liability principles in the context of strict products liability actions and continue to impose the "all or nothing" framework set forth in the Restatement (Second) of Torts § 402A. See, e.g., Bowling v. Heil Co., . . . 511 N.E.2d 373, 380 [Ohio 1987] (finding no rationale to persuade it that comparative fault principles should apply to products liability actions);

Kimco Dev. Corp., 637 A.2d at 606 [Pa. 1993] (declining to extend negligence concepts to strict products liability area). . . .

We draw two reasons from those decisions for retaining the "all or nothing" rule. First, several courts have suggested that it is too confusing to inject negligence concepts into strict liability actions, see, e.g., *Kimco Dev. Corp.*, 637 A.2d at 606 (conceptual confusion would ensue should negligence and strict liability concepts be commingled), and that juries will be unable to compare a defective product with a plaintiff's negligent conduct to apportion liability. . . .

Most courts have rejected this concern as semantic and theoretical. "We are convinced that in merging the two principles what may be lost in symmetry is more than gained in fundamental fairness," *Daly*, . . . 575 P.2d at 1172 [Cal. 1978], and "fairness and equity are more important than conceptual and semantic consistency." *Kaneko,* 654 P.2d at 352 [Haw. 1982]. Further, apportioning liability will be less difficult for juries than the current framework, which requires juries to distinguish between defenses that courts and scholars are often unable to differentiate. As the Supreme Court of Texas noted, assumed risk and unforeseeable misuse are nothing more than extreme variants of contributory negligence. See *Duncan*, 665 S.W.2d at 423 [Tex. 1984]. And the line between contributory negligence — resulting in total recovery — and assumed risk or misuse — resulting in no recovery — is difficult to draw. . . . There is no need to draw shadowy lines between misuse, assumption of risk and contributory negligence, however, if all defenses may constitute a basis for apportioning liability. . . .

Second, the "all or nothing" courts maintain that comparative principles would undermine the purposes of imposing strict liability on manufacturers because this approach reduces the incentive to produce safe products and fails to allocate the risk for loss from injury to manufacturers who are in a better position to absorb it. See *Kimco Dev. Corp.*, 637 A.2d at 606-07. On the contrary, applying principles of comparative liability in strict products liability actions is completely consistent with the purposes of imposing strict liability on manufacturers. Indeed, it will have no effect on the principal purpose of adopting this doctrine; the plaintiff is still relieved from proving negligence of the manufacturer or privity of contract with it. . . .

Nor is it clear that adopting comparative principles will significantly reduce the incentive to produce safe products. . . . Recoveries may be reduced in some cases, but more plaintiffs will recover if assumption of the risk and product misuse are no longer total bars to recovery. Overall, the cost of a defect may be the same under either approach.

Courts rejecting comparative liability assume that the primary purpose in strict products liability actions is to spread the cost of injury. Because manufacturers are in a better position than plaintiffs to spread this cost, they reason that it is inconsistent with strict products liability to reduce recoveries in proportion to plaintiff negligence. . . . If spreading the cost of all injuries were the goal, then apportioning liability between the parties would be adverse to the goal. We note, however, that the purpose has been to spread the cost of injuries resulting from *defective products.* The issue here is whether to spread the cost of injuries resulting from *user negligence* in addition to that resulting from a defect. No rationale to support such risk allocation has been presented. Strict liability is not absolute liability; manufacturers are not insurers of user safety. . . .

On balance the reasons to adopt comparative principles greatly outweigh the reasons to reject this approach. The comparative approach is fairer to all parties, and properly implemented, will not reduce the incentive to produce safe products.

IV

. . . I reach this conclusion as part of the development of the common law of products liability in this state and not because of the Vermont comparative negligence statute, 12 V.S.A. § 1036. The statute applies only to "an action . . . to recover damages for *negligence.*" (Emphasis added.) We must presume that the Legislature intended the plain meaning of the statutory language. . . . The wording covers actions based on negligence, but not on strict liability. The majority of courts confronting this question have reached the same conclusion. . . .

Even though the comparative negligence statute does not apply, we could construct a comparable causation rule that would mirror its terms. In this case, the main significance of such a rule is that plaintiffs could not recover if the causal effect of the negligence of Bruce Webb was greater than the causal effect of the liability of defendant. Using this test, Justice Morse would hold that, as a matter of law, a majority of plaintiffs' damages were caused by the negligence of Bruce Webb so that plaintiffs cannot recover at all.

I do not subscribe to the "half-or-nothing" framework of [the comparative negligence statute] for products liability cases. The rule is inconsistent with the policy of ensuring that manufacturers bear the cost of casting defective products into the market. The manufacturer must remain responsible for damages resulting from the defect, regardless of the extent to which other factors contributed to the injuries. . . .

The dissent characterizes the adoption of comparative causation as a major step toward abolishing the doctrine of strict products liability. I find this conclusion to be greatly exaggerated. I doubt that a balanced and properly designed rule on comparative causation will significantly reduce the incentive for manufacturers to produce safe products; indeed, it may increase the incentive. . . .

If comparative principles ever apply in a strict liability case, they should apply here. The jury could find that a number of Bruce Webb's actions or omissions reflected lack of due care for his safety. Some of these actions or omissions do not involve the condition of the tractor and are not related to plaintiffs' liability theory. For example, irrespective of what lighting was available or in use, the jury could find that Bruce Webb was negligent in riding on the draw bar and covering up a reflector and an amber light while the tractor was being operated on a highway. On remand, I would allow at least that determination.

Reversed and remanded.

[The concurring opinion of Justice Morse is omitted.]

JOHNSON, Justice, dissenting. . . .

I

Justice Dooley and Justice Morse would hold, under varying circumstances, that when a plaintiff alleges injury caused by a defective product, the defendant that produced or distributed the product can reduce or eliminate its liability for damages by showing that the plaintiff's negligent conduct was a contributing cause of the injury. I believe that such a holding would take a major step toward abolition of the doctrine of strict products liability by undermining the principal purpose of the doctrine — to promote the manufacture and distribution of safe products. I see no justification in law, policy, or the facts of this case to extend the doctrine of comparative fault to strict products liability actions.

Notwithstanding assertions to the contrary in Justice Dooley's opinion, my position is followed by a significant number of jurisdiction. 1 A. Best, Comparative Negligence: Law and Practice § 9.20[6], at 41-42 (1996) (significant number of jurisdictions continue to reject or limit application of comparative negligence in strict products liability actions); Annotation, Applicability of Comparative Negligence Doctrine to Actions Based on Strict Liability in Tort, 9 A.L.R. 4th 633, 638-41 (1981) (reviewing cases in which courts have refused to compare fault); see, e.g., Kinard v. Coats Co., . . . 553 P.2d 835, 837 (Colo. Ct. App. 1976) (better-reasoned position is that comparative negligence has no application to products liability actions); Lippard v. Houdaille Indus., Inc., 715 S.W.2d 491, 493 (Mo. 1986) (en banc) (refusing to apply comparative fault principles to products liability actions); Bowling v. Heil Co., . . . 511 N.E.2d 373, 380 (Ohio 1987) (better-reasoned decisions are those that have declined to inject plaintiff's negligence into law of products liability); Kimco Dev. Corp. v. Michael D's Carpet Outlets, . . . 637 A.2d 603, 605-06 (Pa. 1993) (agreeing with cited jurisdictions refusing to extend negligence concepts to products liability actions).

Further, although a majority of jurisdictions compare fault in products liability actions, that majority is hopelessly divided on when and what to compare and how to implement the comparison. See M. Roszkowski & R. Prentice, Reconciling Comparative Negligence and Strict Liability: A Public Policy Analysis, 33 St. Louis U. L.J. 19, 40-47 (1988) (discussing various approaches taken by jurisdictions that compare fault in products liability actions). Some courts compare any and every type of contributory negligence, other courts compare only contributory negligence that rises to the level of assumption of risk or unforeseeable misuse, and still others compare all types of contributory negligence except when the negligence can be labeled as a failure to discover or guard against the risk posed by the defective product. . . .

III

The principal argument for comparing plaintiffs' negligence in products liability actions is couched in terms of fairness. It is fairer to compare, so the argument goes, because the comparison avoids imposing upon manufacturers and careful consumers the costs caused by negligent consumers. But the real issue is whether a higher value should be placed on the deterrence of product defects than is placed on laying the correct amount of blame on the particular actors involved in an accident that was statistically predictable. . . .

Some courts have reasoned that comparing negligence does not greatly affect the incentive to produce safe products because a manufacturer's liability is reduced only to the extent that the trier of fact finds that the user's conduct contributed to the injury, and manufacturers are not able to predict in any given case whether contributory negligence will reduce the plaintiff's judgment. . . . This reasoning does not hold up under scrutiny.

Although manufacturers may not be able to anticipate careless behavior in any given case, they know with virtual certainty that a product will cause a calculable number of accidents, and they will often be able to predict the extent of plaintiffs' negligence by evaluating accidents on a statistical basis. H. Latin, The Preliminary Draft of a Proposed Restatement (Third) of Torts: Products Liability — Letter, 15 J. Prod. & Tox. Liab. 169, 179 (1993); D. Sobelsohn, Comparing Fault, 60 Ind. L.J. 413, 438 (1985). From their calculations, manufacturers can approximate the total liability exposure that those accidents will create, and will then incur increased production costs for safety features only when it makes economic sense to do so. In this way, "the effect of reductions in liability costs as a result of comparative apportionment can make a major difference on the manufacturer's marginal investments in safety." Latin, supra, at 179.

To the extent that product liability would be reduced by comparing plaintiffs' negligence, the incentive to produce safe products would also be reduced. . . . M. Davis, Individual and Institutional Responsibility: A Vision for Comparative Fault in Products Liability, 39 Vill. L. Rev. 281, 344 (1994) (if manufacturers need only compensate those injured during careful use, losses resulting from defective product will never be fully considered in evaluating needed investment in safety). For example, if a particular feature of a product results in accidents costing $1 million, and redesign of the product to eliminate the dangerous feature would cost $900,000, the manufacturer would not have any incentive to redesign the product if the manufacturer could predict that a certain percentage of consumers would negligently contribute to their injuries while using the product, thereby making it cheaper for the manufacturer to pay tort claims rather than redesign the defective product. . . .

We can be certain that, based on statistical accident data and marketing analyses, manufacturers make conscious, calculated choices regarding the safety of their products, choices that are affected by legal principles. If the law provides an economic incentive for a manufacturer to add safety features to a particular product, thousands of people may be spared injury. If, on the other hand, reduced tort damages from comparing plaintiffs' negligence convinces a manufacturer that it would not make economic sense to add safety features to its product, many consumers, including careful ones, may later be injured by the defective product. Assuming that they are able to fend off a defendant's claims of comparative negligence, those careful consumers may obtain full monetary damages, but at the expense of their health or even their lives. This is *not* a fair result. . . .

But there is another important reason why I am persuaded that it is unfair to use comparative principles in strict liability cases. The victim's negligence may be the result of a moment's inattention to some detail, carelessness in a time of crisis, or miscalculation as to the danger involved in using a product a certain way. These types of ordinary negligence, to which all of us fall prey at times, cannot be regarded as equivalent to the manufacturer's responsibility to design safe products and warn the public of dangers that accompany use of their products. . . .

This is where the superficial appeal to fairness falls apart. As a general proposition, we can all agree that each person should bear responsibility for his or her own conduct. It is for this reason that comparative negligence has been accepted as fair in other contexts. But the doctrine of comparative negligence arose in cases where the fault of the parties was of a similar order — carelessness versus carelessness. In strict products liability cases, however, we have fault of very different kinds. The garden-variety carelessness that may contribute to an injury in the use of a product is simply not of the same magnitude as the design, manufacture and release into commerce of a dangerously defective product or a product whose dangers are hidden by inadequate warnings. It is *not* fair, therefore, to treat the two as equivalent. . . .

Plaintiffs who voluntarily assume a known risk should, in my judgment, be barred from recovery. Limiting the assumption-of-risk defense tends to penalize legitimate commercial interests unfairly rather than promote fairness to consumers. Justice Dooley's opinion proclaims that comparing conduct amounting to a voluntary assumption of a known risk benefits consumers, but it undermines the doctrine of strict liability, which provides a powerful incentive for manufacturers and vendors to create and purvey only those products that are safe for everyone. In short, the majority imagines a problem negatively affecting consumers and then creates a cure far worse than the "problem" it seeks to rectify.

Second, while it may not always be easy to distinguish assumption of risk from ordinary contributory negligence, the subjective component of assumption of risk makes the defense qualitatively distinct from other forms of contributory negligence . . . (plaintiff must voluntarily encounter risk despite being subjectively aware of existence of risk and appreciating extent of danger; many courts distinguish assumption of risk from contributory negligence on point that only assumption of risk involves application of subjective standard to plaintiff's conduct); see also Zahrte v. Sturm, Ruger & Co., . . . 661 P.2d 17, 18 (Mont. 1983) (subjective element of assumption of risk makes it distinct from contributory negligence). . . .

In sum, (1) manufacturers have the opportunity to make calculated, informed choices concerning product safety; (2) economic factors and legal principles drive their decisions; (3) those decisions can affect the health and safety of thousands or even millions of people; and (4) enterprises can more easily absorb and equitably pass on to the public the costs of defective products as part of doing business. On the other hand, (1) consumers lack the expertise and information about products possessed by manufacturers; (2) liability law provides no incentive for them to be more careful; (3) their contributory negligence is foreseeable, such that its costs can be equitably spread among all product users; and (4) most importantly, their negligence is simply not equivalent in kind to the act of designing and manufacturing a defective product. For these reasons, there is nothing unfair about imposing full liability on a manufacturer who places in the stream of commerce a defective product that is a proximate cause of the plaintiff's injuries, even if the plaintiff's negligence contributed to those injuries. Products should be designed to protect not only ideal consumers, but also careless, illiterate, ignorant, and inattentive ones as well. . . .

I would affirm the judgment below. I am authorized to say that Justice Gibson joins in my opinion.

THE SCORECARD

An overwhelming majority of jurisdictions allow for the reduction of plaintiff's recovery based on comparative fault. Some state statutes specifically provide that comparative fault applies to products liability cases. Others states do so by judicial decision. The Products Liability Restatement § 17 agrees with the national trend. For cases and statutes supporting the view that comparative fault applies to products liability cases, *see* Reporters' Notes to § 17. A few courts resist any reduction of plaintiff's damages based on comparative fault on the ground that it is the manufacturer's responsibility to avoid the introduction of defective products into the stream of commerce. *See, e.g.,* Reott v. Asia Trend Inc., 7 A.3d 830 (Pa. Super. Ct. 2010).

G. EXPRESS WARRANTY AND MISREPRESENTATION

In addition to theories predicated on product defect, plaintiff may recover damages even when the product was not defective but defendant represented characteristics of the product or its ability to perform in a certain manner. When the product fails to live up to its advance billing and injury ensues, an action for breach of express warranty or misrepresentation may be brought.

BAXTER v. FORD MOTOR CO.
12 P.2d 409 (Wash. 1932)

HERMAN, J.

During the month of May, 1930, plaintiff purchased a model A Ford town sedan from defendant St. John Motors, a Ford dealer, who had acquired the automobile in question by purchase from defendant Ford Motor Company. Plaintiff claims that representations were made to him by both defendants that the windshield of the automobile was made of nonshatterable glass which would not break, fly, or shatter. October 12, 1930, while plaintiff was driving the automobile through Snoqualmie pass, a pebble from a passing car struck the windshield of the car in question, causing small pieces of glass to fly into plaintiff's left eye, resulting in the loss thereof. Plaintiff brought this action for damages for the loss of his left eye and for injuries to the sight of his right eye. The case came on for trial,

authors' dialogue **38**

JIM: The problem of how to compare the negligence of the plaintiff with a product defect is overblown. The contention that strict liability and negligence cannot be compared is not true in most products liability cases.

AARON: It seems to me that the problem is quite real.

JIM: The only place I see the problem is when the plaintiff brings an action alleging a manufacturing defect. In that case the liability against the defendant manufacturer is truly strict. If the plaintiff is negligent in misusing the product, then I can see that there might be difficulty in comparing the negligence of the plaintiff with the non-fault defect of the defendant manufacturer. But most of the litigation today involves defects based on design and failure to warn. In both of these cases the heart of the claim is that the manufacturer has failed to meet risk-utility norms — in short, that the manufacturer was negligent. I see no problem in comparing the fault of the defendant and the fault of the plaintiff.

AARON: You have a point. But in those jurisdictions that have adopted the consumer expectations test there will be a problem in comparing fault. The manufacturer is liable even if the product was reasonably safe and met risk-utility norms. If the manufacturer has provided adequate warnings and has designed the product safely, it is still held liable. The consumer expectation test imposes true strict liability and we would face the problem of comparing the no-fault liability of the manufacturer with the fault of the plaintiff.

JIM: If there weren't enough reasons for rejecting the consumer expectations test, you have come up with another one. In design and failure to warn litigation, plaintiffs are often substantially at fault and under consumer expectations we have no sensible mechanism for comparing the fault. In manufacturing defect cases it is rare that plaintiff fault plays a significant role since plaintiff has no knowledge of the hidden defect in the product.

AARON: What about the argument that in design defect cases the plaintiff's fault should play no role whatsoever since the manufacturers should have foreseen that some plaintiff would be stupid enough to misuse the product? Now when the plaintiffs perform up to expectations, why should the defendant not pay the plaintiff's loss in its entirety? The purpose of an alternative design was to protect against the very harm that took place.

JIM: I'm not impressed with the argument. Negligence of defendants in design very often takes into account the possibility that plaintiffs may also act negligently. Nonetheless, the law seeks to have all parties act reasonably. And there are some forms of plaintiff fault that can't, and shouldn't, be foreseen by defendants. Furthermore, liability costs are spread throughout the populace in the higher cost of products. Why should I pay, in the price that I pay for a product, the share of the cost of accidents that could have been prevented by a plaintiff's reasonable care? I do use products with reasonable care. It's unfair for me to have to pay for the negligence of plaintiffs who don't have their heads screwed on right.

and, at the conclusion of plaintiff's testimony, the court took the case from the jury and entered judgment for both defendants. From that judgment, plaintiff appeals. . . .

The principal question in this case is whether the trial court erred in refusing to admit in evidence, as against respondent Ford Motor Company, the catalogues and printed matter furnished by that respondent to respondent St. John Motors to be distributed for sales assistance. Contained in such printed matter were statements which appellant maintains constituted representations or warranties with reference to the nature of the glass used in the windshield of the car purchased by appellant. A typical statement, as it appears in appellant's exhibit for identification No. 1, is here set forth:

> Triplex Shatter-Proof Glass Windshield. All of the new Ford cars have a Triplex shatter-proof glass windshield — so made that it will not fly or shatter under the hardest impact. This is an important safety factor because it eliminates the dangers of flying glass — the cause of most of the injuries in automobile accidents. In these days of crowded, heavy traffic, the use of this Triplex glass is an absolute necessity. Its extra margin of safety is something that every motorist should look for in the purchase of a car — especially where there are women and children.

Respondent Ford Motor Company contends that there can be no implied or express warranty without privity of contract, and warranties as to personal property do not attach themselves to, and run with, the article sold. . . .

Since the rule of caveat emptor was first formulated, vast changes have taken place in the economic structures of the English speaking peoples. Methods of doing business have undergone a great transition. Radio, billboards, and the products of the printing press have become the means of creating a large part of the demand that causes goods to depart from factories to the ultimate consumer. It would be unjust to recognize a rule that would permit manufacturers of goods to create a demand for their products by representing that they possess qualities which they, in fact, do not possess, and then, because there is no privity of contract existing between the consumer and the manufacturer, deny the consumer the right to recover if damages result from the absence of those qualities, when such absence is not readily noticeable. . . .

We hold that the catalogues and printed matter furnished by respondent Ford Motor Company for distribution and assistance in sales . . . were improperly excluded from evidence, because they set forth representations by the manufacturer that the windshield of the car which appellant bought contained Triplex nonshatterable glass which would not fly or shatter. The nature of nonshatterable glass is such that the falsity of the representations with reference to the glass would not be readily detected by a person of ordinary experience and reasonable prudence. Appellant, under the circumstances shown in this case, had the right to rely upon the representations made by respondent Ford Motor Company relative to qualities possessed by its products, even though there was no privity of contract between appellant and respondent Ford Motor Company. . . .

With the exception of so much of the offer as related to the representations of Mr. St. John and Johnnie Delaney (a salesman for respondent St. John Motors), the testimony contemplated by the offer to prove was relevant and should have been received. While it is a matter of common knowledge that the difference between glass which will not fly or shatter and ordinary glass is not readily noticeable to a person of ordinary experience, nevertheless appellant was entitled to show an absence of familiarity with nonshatterable glass. His testimony would have tended to show that he had no experience which should have enabled him to recognize the glass in the windshield as other than what it was represented to be.

The trial court erred in taking the case from the jury and entering judgment for respondent Ford Motor Company. It was for the jury to determine, under proper instructions, whether the failure of respondent Ford Motor Company to equip the windshield with glass which did not fly or shatter was the proximate cause of appellant's injury. . . .

Reversed, with directions to grant a new trial with reference to respondent Ford Motor Company; affirmed as to respondent St. John Motors.

FOOD FOR THOUGHT

On remand, Ford sought to introduce evidence that no better windshield was available. The trial court refused to admit expert testimony to support Ford's claim. Plaintiff won and the defendant raised the exclusion of its expert testimony as grounds for reversal. The court affirmed the jury verdict, saying that it was irrelevant that the windshield was the best extant at the time. It still wasn't shatter-proof and didn't match up to the defendant's representations. Baxter v. Ford Motor Co., 35 P.2d 1090 (Wash. 1934).

Now for a mind twister. How was the breach of the warranty the proximate cause of plaintiff's injury? If, in fact, no better windshield was available, any car that plaintiff would have driven would have had a windshield no better than that of Ford. Plaintiff is entitled to get the difference between the product as represented (shatterproof) and as it was (not totally shatterproof), but why is plaintiff entitled to personal injury damages? Did the defendant's misrepresentations or breach of express warranty cause his harm? Unless plaintiff were to argue that he would have given up driving and ridden a bicycle instead, he would have suffered the very same injury in any other car. Why don't courts take these arguments seriously?

Two aspects of express warranty law deserve mention, even in a brief summary of the subject. First, courts do not recognize sales-talk "puffery" as express warranties, even if the plaintiff argues convincingly that she was influenced by the ads to buy the goods that ended up causing her harm. Thus, if in *Baxter* the defendant's advertising had referred to the car as "premium quality," and "perfect in every way," the plaintiff injured by the shattered windshield would not have had a claim for breach of express warranty. *See, e.g.,* Elias v. Hewlett-Packard Co., 903 F. Supp. 2d 843 (N.D. Cal. 2012) (granting defendant's motion to dismiss on grounds that defendant's claims that a computer would provide "ultra-reliable performance," "full power and performance," and "versatile, reliable system" were mere puffery, and did not create an express warranty). Second, express warranty is a form of strict liability ("put your money where your mouth is"); the plaintiff need not prove any fault on the defendant's part. *See, e.g.,* Morgan v. Cabela's Inc., 788 F. Supp. 2d 552 (E.D. Ky. 2011) (denying summary judgment to a retailer that sold a tree stand that collapsed while being used by a hunter, on grounds that a genuine issue of material fact existed as to whether the retailer had given an express warranty, despite the fact that the retailer did not manufacture the product).

WAS ANYONE PAYING ATTENTION? THE RELIANCE ISSUE

Contract actions for breach of express warranty and tort actions for misrepresentation are nonidentical twins. Although for the most part what satisfies one will satisfy the other, there are differences that count. The action for breach of express warranty is today a creature of the Uniform Commercial Code § 2-313. It provides:

§ 2-313. Express Warranties by Affirmation, Promise, Description, Sample

(1) Express warranties by the seller are created as follows:

(a) Any affirmation of fact or promise made by the seller to the buyer which relates to the goods and becomes part of the basis of the bargain creates an express warranty that the goods shall conform to the affirmation or promise.

(b) Any description of the goods which is made part of the basis of the bargain creates an express warranty that the goods shall conform to the description.

(c) Any sample or model which is made part of the basis of the bargain creates an express warranty that the whole of the goods shall conform to the sample or model.

(2) It is not necessary to the creation of an express warranty that the seller use formal words such as "warrant" or "guarantee" or that he have a specific intention to make a warranty, but an affirmation merely of the value of the goods or a statement purporting to be merely the seller's opinion or commendation of the goods does not create a warranty.

Official Comment . . .

3. The present section deals with affirmations of fact by the seller, descriptions of the goods or exhibitions of samples, exactly as any other part of a negotiation which ends in a contract is dealt with. No specific intention to make a warranty is necessary if any of these factors is made part of the basis of the bargain. In actual practice affirmations of fact made by the seller about the goods during a bargain are regarded as part of the description of those goods; hence no particular reliance on such statements need be shown in order to weave them into the fabric of the agreement. Rather, any fact which is to take such affirmations, once made, out of the agreement requires clear affirmative proof. The issue normally is one of fact. . . .

An interesting question that has haunted the courts is whether a plaintiff must establish reliance on the express warranty. If the written affirmations of fact or promises are contained in the sales materials accompanying the product upon delivery, the warranty is part of the basis of the bargain, whether or not the purchaser reads the material prior to the sale. *See, e.g.,* Appalachian Leasing, Inc. v. Mack Trucks, Inc., 234 W. Va. 334 (W. Va. 2014). But what if the warranty was made in an advertisement — must plaintiff prove that she read the ad? And if she read the ad, must she prove that she relied on it? This became a hot issue in the tobacco cases, where plaintiffs alleged that the tobacco companies made fraudulent statements about the safety of cigarettes. In many instances, plaintiffs could not remember whether they saw the ads. And even if they saw them, did they believe the statements of the tobacco companies? In many cases, family and physicians told plaintiffs that cigarette smoking would kill them.

In Cipollone v. Liggett Group, Inc., 893 F.2d 541 (3d Cir. 1990), the court tackled the question of whether a plaintiff must establish reliance under U.C.C. §2-313. The language of comment 3, set forth above, is ambiguous. In the end, the court held that plaintiff must prove that she at least had seen the tobacco advertisement. But once she proved that she had read the ad, the burden shifted to the defendant tobacco companies to prove that she did not believe the warranty. For an extensive discussion of the reliance issue, *see* Steven Z. Hodaszy, *Express Warranties Under the Uniform Commercial Code: Is There a Reliance Requirement?*, 66 N.Y.U. L. Rev. 468 (1991).

Misrepresentation is the tort analogue to express warranty. Because the case is styled in tort, it is not subject to the four-year statute of repose that runs from the time of sale under the U.C.C. §2-725. As with all tort actions, the statute of limitations begins to run at the time of injury. Three sections of the Restatement, Second, are relevant to products liability claims:

§310. Conscious Misrepresentation Involving Risk of Physical Harm

An actor who makes a misrepresentation is subject to liability to another for physical harm which results from an act done by the other or a third person in reliance upon the truth of the representation, if the actor

(a) intends his statement to induce or should realize that it is likely to induce action by the other, or a third person, which involves an unreasonable risk of physical harm to the other, and

(b) knows

(i) that the statement is false, or

(ii) that he has not the knowledge which he professes.

§311. Negligent Misrepresentation Involving Risk of Physical Harm

(1) One who negligently gives false information to another is subject to liability for physical harm caused by action taken by the other in reasonable reliance upon such information, where such harm results

(a) to the other, or

(b) to such third persons as the actor should expect to be put in peril by the action taken.

(2) Such negligence may consist of failure to exercise reasonable care
  (a) in ascertaining the accuracy of the information, or
  (b) in the manner in which it is communicated.

§ 402B. Misrepresentation by Seller of Chattels to Consumer

One engaged in the business of selling chattels who, by advertising, labels, or otherwise, makes to the public a misrepresentation of a material fact concerning the character or quality of a chattel sold by him is subject to liability for physical harm to a consumer of the chattel caused by justifiable reliance upon the misrepresentation, even though

  (a) it is not made fraudulently or negligently, and

  (b) the consumer has not bought the chattel from or entered into any contractual relation with the seller.

Note that justifiable reliance on the misrepresentation is an element of the tort under all these sections. A plaintiff deciding whether to bring suit under misrepresentation or under express warranty must reckon with the heavier burden to prove reliance when bringing the tort action. Nonetheless, plaintiff may prefer the misrepresentation action to escape the strictures imposed by the Uniform Commercial Code on such issues as the statute of limitations and contractual limitations on liability. Furthermore, the malevolence that often attends misrepresentation may serve as a predicate for punitive damages.

chapter **12**

Trespass to Land and Nuisance

A. AN INTRODUCTION TO THE BASICS

In Chapter 1 we briefly discussed trespass to land. It is a simple and quite inflexible tort. If one intentionally enters upon land in the possession of another or intentionally causes a thing or a third person to do so, one is subject to liability for trespass. The possessor need not establish that she suffered any harm as a result of the entry. The right to exclusive possession of the land is protected even if the entrant acted reasonably, believing that the land actually belonged to him. Thus if *A* enters upon *B*'s property because, based on an erroneous survey, *A* believes the property to be his own, he is liable for trespass even if *B* suffered no harm whatsoever. *B* is entitled to nominal damages in an action against *A* to establish *B*'s right to exclusive possession.

Trespass to land is an intentional tort in the sense that when the entrant intends to be physically present on land that is legally in the possession of another, he is liable even when acting on a mistaken belief as to rights to possession. But, if he has no such intent, liability will attach only on the basis of another recognized action in tort. Thus, for example, if *A* is driving and loses control of his car and ends up on *B*'s property with no intent to be there, he will be liable only if he is negligent. Or if *A* is using reasonable care in dynamiting a building and rocks are unexpectedly hurtled onto *B*'s property, *A* will be liable only under the rules that govern negligence or strict liability for ultrahazardous activities.

The remedies for trespass include nominal damages, rental value for use of the land, recovery for damage caused by the defendant's conduct while trespassing, and injunctions against continuing trespass. Courts can be unforgiving in enjoining a continuing trespass. In Peters v. Archambault, 278 N.E.2d 729 (Mass. 1972), plaintiff sought to compel the defendants to remove a significant part of their home that encroached on the plaintiff's property. The encroachment had existed for some 22 years. During that period, neither the plaintiff's predecessor in title nor the plaintiff complained about the encroachment. The encroachment was discovered when the plaintiff had the property surveyed in order to construct a retaining wall. Notwithstanding that enjoining the encroachment meant removing a substantial portion of the defendants' home thereby causing significant financial loss to the defendants, the court granted the plaintiff an injunction rather than damages reflecting the value of the property. The fact that the defendants had acted innocently and that both parties had assumed for many years that the defendant was rightfully in possession of the land did not stop the court from granting the injunction. See also Rose Nulman Park Foundation ex rel. Nulman v. Four Twenty Corp., 93 A.3d 25 (R.I. 2014) (affirming trial court's injunction requiring defendants to either tear down or move a house they had mistakenly built on plaintiff's land, despite the facts that defendants had built the house in good faith reliance upon a land survey, and the cost to move the house would be approximately 50 percent of what it had cost to build; the defendant's house was on the plaintiff's property, and the remedy for a continued trespass is an injunction); City of Rincon v. Sean and Ashleigh, Inc., 667 S.E.2d 354 (Ga. 2008) (when conduct constitutes continuing trespass, injunction is proper remedy).

When an encroaching trespasser faces the prospect of removing his property or ceasing an otherwise valuable activity, he may approach the injured plaintiff and offer to purchase the right to continue to encroach. And yet, in the cases cited in the preceding paragraph, such a deal may not have been struck. For more extensive consideration of these possibilities in the context of nuisance see pp. 734-742, *infra*.

The tort of nuisance protects one's right to the use and enjoyment of property. Unlike trespass, which protects against tangible intrusion, the tort of nuisance protects against intangible invasions of one's land. Thus, a landowner who is inconvenienced by noise, smoke, or other pollutants coming from industrial plants operating in the vicinity may be able successfully to assert a claim for private nuisance. Nuisance, unlike trespass, is fairly flexible. The right to the use and enjoyment of property cannot be totally unfettered, since to do so would limit the rights of adjacent landowners to the use and enjoyment of their property. If you desire total quiet on your property after 8:00 p.m., that may mean that adjoining property owners cannot listen to the ball game on the radio with the windows open on a warm summer night. Some balancing of the conflicting rights must be undertaken. The nature of the balancing will be discussed later in this chapter, but suffice it to say that nuisance does not have the black-white quality of trespass. Traditional trespass had no gray areas. One either was or was not a trespasser. Nuisance is a more nuanced tort that by necessity must accommodate multiple interests. The essence of nuisance is differentiating between various shades of gray.

B. TRESPASS IN SHADES OF GRAY

For the most part, trespass to land cases are easy and straightforward. However, in the second half of the twentieth century, plaintiffs sought to utilize the trespass to land theory in cases where the interference with the right to possession was not so clear cut. For example, possessors of land located near airports argued that flights over their property should be considered violations of their right to exclusive possession of the air space over their land. Similarly, cases were brought against industrial polluters for intentionally causing dust and toxic fumes to enter onto land in the vicinity of their plants. If indeed these defendants were to be treated as trespassers, then even insignificant invasions of the exclusive right to possession would be subject to actions for damages and for injunctive relief to prevent future trespasses. Something had to give.

BRADLEY v. AMERICAN SMELTING AND REFINING CO.
709 P.2d 782 (Wash. 1985)

CALLOW, J.

This comes before us on a certification from the United States District Court for the Western District of Washington. Plaintiffs, landowners on Vashon Island, had sued for damages in trespass and nuisance from the deposit on their property of microscopic, airborne particles of heavy metals which came from the American Smelting and Refining Company (ASARCO) copper smelter at Ruston, Washington. . . .

Plaintiffs . . . purchased their property in 1978. . . . Plaintiffs' property is located some 4 miles north of defendant's smelter. Defendant's primary copper smelter (also referred to as the Tacoma smelter) has operated in its present location since 1890. It has operated as a copper smelter since 1902, and in 1905 it was purchased and operated by a corporate entity which is now ASARCO. As a part of the industrial process of smelting copper at the Tacoma smelter, various gases such as sulfur dioxide and particulate matter, including arsenic, cadmium and other metals, are emitted. Particulate matter is composed of distinct particles of matter other than water, which cannot be detected by the human senses.

The emissions from the Tacoma smelter are subject to regulation under the Federal Clean Air Act, the Washington Clean Air Act (RCW 70.94) and the Puget Sound Air Pollution Control Agency (PSAPCA). Currently, the Tacoma smelter meets the National Ambient Air Quality Standards, both primary and secondary, for both sulfur dioxide and particulate matter. As a result of the variance granted by PSAPCA, the Tacoma smelter is also in compliance with PSAPCA Regulation I concerning particulate emissions. . . .

This case was initiated in King County Superior Court and later removed to the United States District Court. Upon the plaintiffs moving for summary judgment on the issue of liability for the claimed trespass, the stated issues were certified to this court. The issues present the conflict in an industrial society between the need of all for the production of goods and the desire of the landowner near the manufacturing plant producing those goods that his use and enjoyment of his land not be diminished by the unpleasant side effects of the manufacturing process. . . .

1. Did the Defendant Have the Requisite Intent to Commit Intentional Trespass as a Matter of Law?

The parties stipulated that as a part of the smelting process, particulate matter including arsenic and cadmium was emitted, that some of the emissions had been deposited on the plaintiffs' land and that the defendant has been aware since 1905 that the wind, on occasion, caused these emissions to be blown over the plaintiffs' land. The defendant cannot and does not deny that whenever the smelter was in operation the whim of the winds could bring these deleterious substances to the plaintiffs' premises. We are asked if the defendant, knowing what it had to know from the facts it admits, had the legal intent to commit trespass. . . .

Addressing the definition, scope and meaning of "intent," section 8A of the Restatement (Second) of Torts says:

> The word "intent" is used . . . to denote that the actor desires to cause consequences of his act, or that he believes that the consequences are substantially certain to result from it.

and we find in comment *b*, at 15:

> Intent is not, however, limited to consequences which are desired. If the actor knows that the consequences are certain, or substantially certain, to result from his act, and still goes ahead, he is treated by the law as if he had in fact desired to produce the result. . . .

It is patent that the defendant acted on its own volition and had to appreciate with substantial certainty that the law of gravity would visit the effluence upon someone, somewhere. . . .

We find that the defendant had the requisite intent to commit intentional trespass as a matter of law.

2. Does an Intentional Deposit of Microscopic Particulates, Undetectable by the Human Senses, Upon a Person's Property Give Rise to a Cause of Action for Trespassory Invasion of the Person's Right to Exclusive Possession of Property as Well as a Claim of Nuisance?

The courts have been groping for a reconciliation of the doctrines of trespass and nuisance over a long period of time and, to a great extent, have concluded that little of substance remains to any distinction between the two when air pollution is involved. . . .

We agree with the observations on the inconsequential nature of the efforts to reconcile the trappings of the concepts of trespass and nuisance in the face of industrial airborne pollution when Professor Rodgers states: . . .

> The first and most important proposition about trespass and nuisance principles is that they are largely coextensive. Both concepts are often discussed in the same cases without differentiation between the elements of recovery. . . .
>
> It is also true that in the environmental arena both nuisance and trespass cases typically involve intentional conduct by the defendant who knows that his activities are substantially certain to result in an invasion of plaintiff's interests. The

principal difference in theories is that the tort of trespass is complete upon a tangible invasion of plaintiff's property, however slight, whereas a nuisance requires proof that the interference with use and enjoyment is "substantial and unreasonable." This burden of proof advantage in a trespass case is accompanied by a slight remedial advantage as well. Upon proof of a technical trespass plaintiff always is entitled to nominal damages. It is possible also that a plaintiff could get injunctive relief against a technical trespass — for example, the deposit of particles of air pollutant on his property causing no known adverse effects. The protection of the integrity of his possessory interests might justify the injunction even without proof of the substantial injury necessary to establish a nuisance. Of course absent proof of injury, or at least a reasonable suspicion of it, courts are unlikely to invoke their equitable powers to require expensive control efforts. . . .

The insistence that a trespass involve an invasion by a "thing" or "object" was repudiated in the well known (but not particularly influential) case of Martin v. Reynolds Metals Co., [342 P.2d 790 (1959)], which held that gaseous and particulate fluorides from an aluminum smelter constituted a trespass for purposes of the statute of limitations:

> [L]iability on the theory of trespass has been recognized where the harm was produced by the vibration of the soil or by the concussion of the air which, of course, is nothing more than the movement of molecules one against the other.

> . . . The view recognizing a trespassory invasion where there is no "thing" which can be seen with the naked eye undoubtedly runs counter to the definition of trespass expressed in some quarters. [Citing the Restatement (First) of Torts and Prosser.] It is quite possible that in an earlier day when science had not yet peered into the molecular and atomic world of small particles, the courts could not fit an invasion through unseen physical instrumentalities into the requirement that a trespass can result only from a *direct* invasion. But in this atomic age even the uneducated know the great and awful force contained in the atom and what it can do to a man's property if it is released. In fact, the now famous equation $E = MC^2$ has taught us that mass and energy are equivalents and that our concept of "things" must be reframed. If these observations on science in relation to the law of trespass should appear theoretical and unreal in the abstract, they become very practical and real to the possessor of land when the unseen force cracks the foundation of his house. The force is just as real if it is chemical in nature and must be awakened by the intervention of another agency before it does harm. . . .

W. Rodgers, *Environmental Law* § 2.13 at 154-57 (1977). . . .

Having held that there was an intentional trespass, we adopt, in part, the rationale of Borland v. Sanders Lead Co., 369 So. 2d 523, 529 (Ala. 1979), which stated in part:

> Although we view this decision as an application, and not an extension, of our present law of trespass, we feel that a brief restatement and summary of the principles involved in this area would be appropriate. Whether an invasion of a property interest is a trespass or a nuisance does not depend upon whether the intruding agent is "tangible" or "intangible." Instead, an analysis must be made to determine the interest interfered with. If the intrusion interferes with the right to exclusive possession of property, the law of trespass applies. . . .

. . . Under the modern theory of trespass, the law presently allows an action to be maintained in trespass for invasions that, at one time, were considered indirect and, hence, only a nuisance. In order to recover in trespass for this type of invasion . . . a plaintiff must show 1) an invasion affecting an interest in the exclusive possession of his property; 2) an intentional doing of the act which results in the invasion; 3) reasonable foreseeability that the act done could result in an invasion of plaintiff's possessory interest; and 4) substantial damages to the *res*. . . .

3. Does the Cause of Action for Trespassory Invasion Require Proof of Actual Damages? . . .

While at common law any trespass entitled a landowner to recover nominal or punitive damages for the invasion of his property, such a rule is not appropriate under the circumstances before us. No useful purpose would be served by sanctioning actions in trespass by every landowner within a hundred miles of a manufacturing plant. Manufacturers would be harassed and the litigious few would cause the escalation of costs to the detriment of the many. The elements that we have adopted for an action in trespass from *Borland* require that a plaintiff has suffered actual and substantial damages. Since this is an element of the action, the plaintiff who cannot show that actual and substantial damages have been suffered should be subject to dismissal of his cause upon a motion for summary judgment. . . .

The United States District Court for the Western District of Washington shall be notified for such further action as it deems appropriate. . . .

FOOD FOR THOUGHT

It would seem that courts following the *Bradley* line of reasoning recognize two kinds of trespass: (1) direct trespass, which is subject to the traditional rule that any interference with exclusive possession constitutes a trespass and (2) indirect trespasses arising from some form of pollutions which requires proof of actual harm. When a plaintiff establishes a direct trespass, she is entitled to nominal damages and an almost automatic right to enjoin further trespassory invasions. When alleging trespass via pollution, a plaintiff must prove actual and substantial damages, and the right to enjoin the activity causing the pollution is anything but automatic.

If, in fact, environmental trespasses are subject to the doctrine that governs the law of nuisance, why should anyone care what label is pasted on the cause of action? The answer is that plaintiff is seeking some procedural advantage. In *Bradley,* plaintiff sought to take advantage of the three-year statute of limitations for trespass, rather than the shorter statute of limitations that governed a nuisance action. But, if the legislature mandated a shorter statute of limitations for nuisance actions, where the gravamen of the harm is interference with use and enjoyment of property, why should a court feel free to subvert the shorter statute of limitations by labeling the action as one in trespass and then investing the trespass action with the same proof requirements that apply to nuisance?

In Parry v. Murphy, 913 N.Y.S.2d 285 (N.Y. App. Div. 2010), a hydroelectric facility installed an underground pipeline that encroached upon the plaintiff's land. The trial court granted permanent injunctive relief. The intermediate court of appeals reversed and remanded for the determination of an appropriate award of damages, describing the injunction as an excessively drastic remedy. *See also* Carter v. Done, 276 P.3d 1127 (Utah 2012) (defendants wanted to raise the level of the lot that their house was on, so they filled the lot with additional dirt, which resulted in said dirt flowing onto the plaintiffs' land; Utah Supreme Court affirmed trial court's decision to award plaintiff damages rather than an injunction, where it may have cost the defendant "hundreds of thousands of dollars" to dig up the driveway and RV pad in order to prevent dirt from spilling over onto the plaintiff's property, and the loss of property value to the plaintiff was just $319).

In Tally Bissell Neighbors, Inc. v. Eyrie Shotgun Ranch, L.L.C., 228 P.3d 1134 (Mont. 2010), the plaintiffs claimed that a shooting range made so much noise that it constituted an enjoinable trespass onto their adjoining properties. In reversing the trial court's dismissal, the Montana high court held that an intangible invasion may constitute an enjoinable trespass if it causes actual damage to plaintiff's land. Otherwise, the invasion must be tangible to constitute trespass. *See also* John Larkin, Inc. v. Marceau, 959 A.2d 551 (Vt. 2008) (to constitute enjoinable trespass, airborne particles must cause some physical impact on plaintiff's property). *But see* Barnes v. Morris Oil Co., 263 S.W.3d 697 (Mo. App. 2008) (holding that a plaintiff can establish trespass for an oil leak on the plaintiff's property, despite a lack of harm, if the plaintiff can establish that the invasion was so significant as to interfere with the plaintiff's possession of their land).

WE CAN LIVE WITH DRONES AND HAVE THEM TOO

The growing use of drones in recent years presents new challenges for the law of trespass. Congress signed into law the FAA Modernization and Reform Act of 2012, which required the FAA to "issue guidance regarding the operation of public unmanned aircraft systems to . . . allow for an incremental expansion of access to the national airspace system as technology matures and the necessary safety analysis and data become available." The FAA complied in June of 2016, promulgating a rule that allows for small drones to be flown during the day, provided that they are used within the line of sight of the operator. The regulation also created a waiver process, allowing operators to apply for a waiver from the requirements outlined above, provided that they can use drones safely. Operation and Certification of Small Unmanned Aircraft Systems, 81 FR 42063 (June 28, 2016). These new regulations by the FAA are expected to lead to a significant rise in the use of private drones.

While case law dealing with drones is still very sparse, conflicts regarding their use are beginning to occur on a regular basis. See Troy Rule, Airspace in an Age of Drones, 95 B.U. L. Rev. 155, 164 (2015) (outlining various incidents involving drones, including: a drone flying over a baseball stadium in Pittsburgh during a game; in Seattle, a woman getting dressed in an apartment building saw a drone with a camera outside her window; in Nashville, a drone with a camera on it flew very close to a 4th of July fireworks display; and in Los Angeles, a group of hockey fans knocked a drone out of the sky near the entrance of an arena before a game). In a case in Texas, a landowner who shot down a drone was held liable in an action by the drone owner. See Eric Joe v. Brett McBay, Stanilaus County Superior Court, Small Claims Division, Case No. 2101429 (filed Dec. 22, 2014).

One issue to be resolved is whether flying a drone over an individual's private property constitutes trespass. In Causby v. United States, 328 U.S. 256, 264 (1946), the Supreme Court held that a property owner does not own all of the sky above their property; rather they own the space that they can "occupy or use in connection with the land." Before the advent of drones, it was unnecessary to define this more precisely, as planes were the only things that regularly flew over a landowner's property and they fly at altitudes well above that which landowners can use.

Whether a drone flying over an individual's property is considered trespass will also have a significant impact on how law enforcement officers can use drones. The Fourth Amendment requires law enforcement officers to obtain a warrant before executing searches. If the use of a drone over one's property is considered trespassing, then using a drone for surveillance will be considered a search for the purposes of the Fourth Amendment. See United States v. Jones, 132 S. Ct. 945 (2012). If that is the case, then law enforcement will be required to get a warrant before using drones for surveillance. If not, the possibility exists that law enforcement agencies across the country will have the power to fly a drone over homes for search purposes without a warrant.

C. PRIVATE NUISANCE

To make out a case for interference with the use and enjoyment of property, a plaintiff must establish (1) a basis for liability, (2) significant harm, and (3) an unreasonable invasion of the plaintiff's land.

Tort liability can be predicated on intent, negligence, or strict liability. In order to find a defendant liable for nuisance, the defendant's conduct must fit into one of the traditional categories that support tort liability. If a defendant's conduct that brought about the interference with a plaintiff's use and enjoyment of her property is neither intentional nor negligent, liability would have to be based on the rules governing abnormally dangerous activity. In short, the mere fact that a plaintiff has suffered a significant and unreasonable invasion of her property will not make out a cause of action for nuisance absent conduct that is tortious. See Restatement, Second, of Torts § 822 (1979). Also see Morrissey v. New England Deaconess Assn., 940 N.E.2d 391 (Mass. 2010).

The second requirement, that the harm be significant, is easily understood. It would be sheer folly to protect a landowner's right to use and enjoyment of her property from trivial harm or annoyance. Restatement, Second, of Torts § 821F

(1965). Common noise from a neighbor's air conditioner, or smoke emanating from a chimney, or smoke drifting onto plaintiffs' land from neighbors smoking outdoors, are the price we pay for living in a urban setting. Similarly, the ringing of a church bell during daytime hours, or the noise of children playing in a schoolyard, will not support a nuisance action. *See* Langan v. Bellinger, 611 N.Y.S.2d 59 (N.Y. App. Div. 1994) (church bells); Beckman v. Marshall, 85 So. 2d 552 (Fla. 1956) (noise from nursery school); Boffoli v. Orton, 2010 WL 1533397 (Wash. Ct. Att. 2010) (outdoor smoking); Balunas v. Town of Owego, 56 A.D.3d 1097 (N.Y. App. Div. 2008) (affirming trial court's dismissal of plaintiffs' injunction, which would have stopped town from installing a water tower that would have been visible from the plaintiffs' home, on ground that simply being able to see the water tank was insufficient to create a private nuisance; the court concluded that the interference was not significant and that the case for nuisance had not been made out). *See also* Capitol Properties Group, L.L.C. v. 1247 Center St., L.L.C., 770 N.W.2d 105 (Mich. Ct. App. 2009) (noisy nightclub not a nuisance in area zoned for such use); Rankin v. FPL Energy, L.L.C., 226 S.W.3d 506 (Tex. App. 2008) (wind turbine farm not a nuisance merely because it interfered with plaintiffs' view); Bansbach v. Harbin, 229 W. Va. 287, 292 (W.V. 2012) (defendant's development of a second junkyard on their property was not a private nuisance as "unsightliness alone is an insufficient basis upon which to seek abatement under nuisance law").

HUGHES v. EMERALD MINES CORP.
450 A.2d 1 (Pa. Super. Ct. 1982)

Montemuro, J.

The instant action concerns the complaint of landowners that a coal company operating on adjacent property caused the failure of one water-well and the pollution of a second well located on plaintiff-appellees' own land.

A jury found for the plaintiffs in the amount of $32,500, basing their measure of damages on the testimony of a local real estate dealer that the property had been worth $42,500 while served by two wells of pure water and that without a source of potable water the salvage value of the land together with a mobile home located thereon would be $10,000. . . .

The plaintiffs bought this property by a deed dated 1953, pursuant to a mining rights clause set forth in an earlier deed conveying to a predecessor in title in 1921. Thereafter they erected a dwelling and drilled a well to supply water. There was a continuous, ample, potable water supply from this well (hereinafter well #1) for some twenty-five years until late May or early June of 1978.

In 1977 the plaintiffs purchased a mobile home and installed it on the property for their son's use. At that time a second well (hereinafter well #2), was drilled, and from its installation until the same period in late May or early June of 1978 the supply was plentiful and potable. . . .

. . . Defendant owns surface rights in addition to subsurface rights to a portion of the tract contiguous to plaintiffs' property.

In 1975 defendant began to expand its operations into that contiguous portion of the tract. Several airshaft holes were prepared in the same general area. The airshaft which is the focus of this action is located 540 and 600 feet from defendant's two wells, and is known as "grout hole #4." It was begun on May 9, 1978 and was completed May 29, 1978.

On May 31, 1978, well #1 went dry. Two or three days later, well #2 became polluted. During this same period of time, neighboring properties also experienced similar problems with their wells.

On June 8, 1978 plaintiffs notified an agent of defendant of their problems. Since early June of 1978 the plaintiffs have had a tank installed at their residence and their son-in-law hauls water from his own home to theirs in 55 gallon lots daily. The plaintiffs travel two miles to the home of their son-in-law and daughter to shower, and must now take their laundry to the Laundromat twice weekly instead of using the washer in their basement. Water at well #2 can be used to flush the commode in the trailer, but cannot be used for cooking, cleaning, bathing, or drinking. The court below permitted these damages to be explored, stating that "they have the right to use their land and if the liability deprived them the use of their property, it is their damage." (N.T. 108). Cost of hauling water, attempted well repair, and laundry amounted to some $7,000 worth of out-of-pocket expenses in consequence of the well failures. . . .

This action was tried on the basis of non-trespassory invasion of another's land as set forth in Restatement of Torts, 2d at § 822, and as adopted by the Supreme Court of Pennsylvania in the 1954 case of Waschak v. Moffat, 109 A.2d 310 (1954). That section provides as follows:

> One is subject to liability for a private nuisance if, but only if, his conduct is a legal cause of an invasion of another's interest in the private use and enjoyment of land, and the invasion is either:
> (a) intentional and unreasonable, or
> (b) unintentional and otherwise actionable under the rules controlling liability for negligent or reckless conduct, or for abnormally dangerous conditions or activities.

The instant action was tried on the first of the two theories outlined above: that the act of the coal company was intentional and unreasonable. The Restatement at § 825 further defines intentional invasion as follows:

> An invasion of another's interest in the use and enjoyment of land or an interference with the public right is intentional if the actor
> (a) acts for the purpose of causing it, or
> (b) knows that it is resulting or is substantially certain to result from his conduct.

An intentional invasion becomes unreasonable, according to § 826 if:

> (a) the gravity of the harm outweighs the utility of the actor's conduct, or
> (b) the harm caused by the conduct is serious and the financial burden of compensating for this and similar harm to others would not make the continuation of the conduct not feasible.

Section 829(a) contributes this analysis of "unreasonableness":

> An intentional invasion of another's interest in the use and enjoyment of land is unreasonable if the harm resulting from the invasion is severe and greater than the other should be required to bear without compensation.

Comments following the section immediately *supra* supply further explanation in pertinent part:

> . . . certain types of harm may be so severe as to require a holding of unreasonableness as a matter of law, regardless of the utility of the conduct. This is particularly true if the harm resulting from the invasion is physical in character. . . . Aside from the normal requirement that the harm be significant . . . , it is apparent that the more serious the harm is found to be, the more likely it is that the trier of fact will hold that the invasion is unreasonable.

There is no doubt that plaintiffs have suffered a significant harm to use and enjoyment of their property which occurred on or about May 31, 1978. . . .

The defendant's view that the injury, . . . is without remedy, presents a . . . difficult task of analysis. As noted above, analysis is proper under § 822 of the Restatement of Torts, 2d. . . .

As to "intent," plaintiffs clearly are not contending that the activities of defendant amount to a deliberate plot to ruin their wells. They contend, however, and the jury obviously agreed, that defendant's acts came under the language of § 825(b) as set forth *supra,* and that defendant knew that the grouting injected was substantially certain to injure nearby wells, but nevertheless dug the airshaft and pumped in the grout. . . .

As to the finding that the invasion of plaintiffs' right to their enjoyment of their well-water was "unreasonable," we again turn to the wording of the Restatement of Torts 2d at § 829(a), as set forth *supra,* and the comment following it.

No one is contending that the mining of coal is not a useful activity, and airshafts are a necessary part of that activity as safeguards to the health of miners. "Unreasonable," however, is a term of art, a legal definition rather than a moral judgment on the good sense of a party. Utility of an act must be balanced against the bad effects resulting from that act in determining its reasonableness.

The harm to plaintiffs in the loss of both their wells was undeniably "severe," and we are inclined to agree with the finder of fact that the loss is "greater than they should be required to bear without compensation," "*regardless of the utility of the conduct.*" See § 829(a) and comment following, *supra.*

Case law further recognizes this principle, and has done so from an early date:

> . . . the defendant's right to injure another's land at all, to any extent, is an exception, and *the burden is always upon him to bring himself within it.* . . .
>
> Where conflict is irreconcilable, the right to use one's own land [sic] must prevail, but it can do so without compensation where the resulting damage is *not avoidable at all, or only at such expense as would be practically prohibitory,* Pfeiffer v. Brown, 30 A.844 (1895). . . .

Defendant made no effort on the record to show that the damage inflicted was "not avoidable at all" or that it was avoidable "only at such expense as would be practically prohibitory." In fact, the whole thrust of its arguments was that its operations had not harmed plaintiffs' property, and that the legitimacy of its lawful use of its own property was unquestioned.

No testimony was offered to show that this location was the only possible place for an effective airshaft; no discussion of a lack of less destructive methods of waterflow prevention was placed on record; no claim of prohibitive expense in use of other methods or other locations was made.

In short, defendant made no attempt to fulfill its burden to prove that its acts were not avoidable at all or only avoidable at prohibitory expense. Once the plaintiff had met its burden of proof of causation by a preponderance of the evidence, Section 829A and case law agree that the burden shifts to the actor to defend its conduct as "reasonable." Defendant here did not meet its burden, and we affirm the jury's finding of intentional and unreasonable damage to plaintiffs, for which compensation is due. . . .

One . . . problem remains to be discussed. The lower court correctly stated the measure of damages in the charge to the jury:

> The measure of damages . . . is the cost of the remedy unless it exceeds the value of the property, in which case the value of the property is the measure of damages. Where the damage is permanent, the measure of damages is the difference between the value of the land before the loss or damage, and the value of it afterwards.

The lower court's opinion, reflecting upon the jury decision, also came to a conclusion on the verdict rendered:

> What the jury did, we must infer, was to find the damage permanent and the cost of restoration greater than the difference in value, and accepted the before and after values submitted in the testimony of Mr. Arnold. [Plaintiffs' real estate agent witness.]

We absolutely agree with the lower court's inference as to the workings of the jury's mind on that decision. Unlike the lower court, we cannot find foundation in the testimony to support such a conjunction of facts. True, Mr. Arnold opined that the lost value would be to the amount of $32,500 if there were no water on the property.

As far as we can determine, not a single witness for either party ever stated that restoration of the wells to working order was impossible or even unlikely. The testimony of plaintiffs' own witnesses guaranteed a good supply of water at well #2 for $1,000 to $2,000, plus modest maintenance costs. Neighbors had also shortened and/or deepened wells to reestablish supplies of water, at, presumably, the local estimated costs of $1,200 to $1,500; therefore, an assumption that plaintiffs would not be able to restore or replace well #1 has only slightly more credible testimony to support it than the assumption that well #2 could not be made potable. As to the necessary assumption that the entire property would remain without water and that damages should be based on a salvage value, we find that assumption incredible. The evidence simply does not support the verdict. The jury's findings on that measure of damages should not have been permitted to stand.

Conclusion

We therefore affirm the holding of the court below insofar as it held the defendants liable for damage sustained by these plaintiffs to their wells; however, as the evidence does not support a finding of total, permanent loss of water, the award of $32,500 is excessive. The correct measure of damages is remedial, and the case is remanded solely for determination of a reasonable sum for consequential damages and costs of restoration.

Affirmed as to liability, reversed and remanded as to damages. . . .

CARPENTER v. DOUBLE R CATTLE CO., INC.
701 P.2d 222 (Idaho 1985)

BAKES, J.

Plaintiffs appealed a district court judgment based upon a court and jury finding that defendant's feedlot did not constitute a nuisance. The Court of Appeals . . . reversed and remanded for a new trial. On petition for review, we vacate the decision of the Court of Appeals and affirm the judgment of the district court.

Plaintiff appellants are homeowners who live near a cattle feedlot owned and operated by respondents. Appellants filed a complaint in March, 1978, alleging that the feedlot had been expanded in 1977 to accommodate the feeding of approximately 9,000 cattle. Appellants further alleged that "the spread and accumulation of manure, pollution of river and ground water, odor, insect infestation, increased concentration of birds, . . . dust and noise" allegedly caused by the feedlot constituted a nuisance. After a trial on the merits a jury found that the feedlot did not constitute a nuisance. The trial court then also made findings and conclusions that the feedlot did not constitute a nuisance.

Appellants assigned as error the jury instructions which instructed the jury that in the determination of whether a nuisance exists consideration should be given to such factors as community interest, utility of conduct, business standards and practices, gravity of harm caused, and the circumstances surrounding the parties' movement to their locations. On appeal, appellants chose not to provide an evidentiary record, but merely claimed that the instructions misstated the law in Idaho.

The case was assigned to the Court of Appeals which reversed and remanded for a new trial. The basis for this reversal was that the trial court did not give a jury instruction based upon subsection (b) of Section 826 of the Restatement (Second) of Torts. That subsection allows for a finding of a nuisance even though the gravity of harm is outweighed by the utility of the conduct if the harm is "serious" and the payment of damages is "feasible" without forcing the business to discontinue.

This Court granted defendant's petition for review. We hold that the instructions which the trial court gave were not erroneous, being consistent with our prior case law and other persuasive authority. We further hold that the trial court did not err in not giving an instruction based on subsection (b) of Section 826 of the

Second Restatement, which does not represent the law in the State of Idaho. . . . Accordingly, the decision of the Court of Appeals is vacated, and the judgment of the district court is affirmed. . . .

III.

The Court of Appeals adopted subsection (b) of Section 826 of the Restatement Second, that a defendant can be held liable for a nuisance regardless of the utility of the conduct if the harm is "serious" and the payment of damages is "feasible" without jeopardizing the continuance of the conduct. We disagree that this is the law in Idaho. . . .

The State of Idaho is sparsely populated and its economy depends largely upon the benefits of agriculture, lumber, mining and industrial development. To eliminate the utility of conduct and other factors listed by the trial court from the criteria to be considered in determining whether a nuisance exists, as the appellant has argued throughout this appeal, would place an unreasonable burden upon these industries. We see no policy reasons which should compel this Court to accept appellant's argument and depart from our present law. Accordingly, the judgment of the district court is affirmed and the Court of Appeals decision is set aside.

Costs to respondents. No attorney fees.

DONALDSON, C.J., and SHEPARD, J., concur.

BISPLINE, J., dissenting. . . .

The majority today continues to adhere to ideas on the law of nuisance that should have gone out with the use of buffalo chips as fuel. We have before us today homeowners complaining of a nearby feedlot — not a small operation, but rather a feedlot which accommodates 9,000 cattle. The homeowners advanced the theory that after the expansion of the feedlot in 1977, the odor, manure, dust, insect infestation and increased concentration of birds which accompanied all of the foregoing, constituted a nuisance. If the odoriferous quagmire created by 9,000 head of cattle is *not* a nuisance, it is difficult for me to imagine what is. However, the real question for us today is the legal basis on which a finding of nuisance can be made.

The Court of Appeals adopted subsection (b) of §826 of the Restatement (Second) of Torts. . . . The majority holds that the 1953 case of McNichols v. J.R. Simplot Co., 262 P.2d 1012 (1953) espoused the correct rule of law for Idaho: in a nuisance action seeking damages, the interests of the community, which includes the utility of the conduct, should be considered in determining the existence of a nuisance. I find nothing immediately wrong with this statement of the law and agree wholeheartedly that the interests of the community should be considered in determining the existence of a nuisance. However, where this primitive rule of law fails is in recognizing that in our society, while it may be desirable to have a serious nuisance continue because the utility of the operation causing the nuisance is great, at the same time, those directly impacted by the serious nuisance deserve some compensation for the invasion they suffer as a result of the continuation of the nuisance. This is exactly what the more progressive provisions of

§ 826(b) of the Restatement (Second) of Torts addresses. Clearly, § 826(b) recognizes that the continuation of the serious harm must remain feasible. See especially comment on clause (b), subpart f of § 826 of the Restatement. What § 826(b) adds is a method of compensating those who must suffer the invasion without putting out of business the source or cause of the invasion. This does not strike me as a particularly adventuresome or far-reaching rule of law. In fact, the fairness of it is overwhelming.

The majority's rule today overlooks the option of compensating those who suffer a nuisance because the interests of the community outweigh the interests of those afflicted by the nuisance. This unsophisticated balancing overlooks the possibility that it is not necessary that one interest be ignored when the community interest is strong. We should not be adopting a rule of preference which suggests that if the community interest is preferred any other interest must be disregarded. Instead, § 826(b) accommodates adverse interests by contemplating continuation of the facility which creates the nuisance while compensating those who suffer the direct impact of the nuisance — in the instant case the homeowners who live in the vicinity of the feedlot.

The majority's rule today suggests that part of the cost of industry, agriculture or development must be borne by those unfortunate few who have the fortuitous luck to live in the immediate vicinity of a nuisance producing facility. Frankly, I think this naive economic view is ridiculous in both its simplicity and its outdated view of modern economic society. The "cost" of a product includes not only the amount it takes to produce such a product but also includes the external costs: the damage done to the environment through pollution of air or water is an example of an external cost. In the instant case, the nuisance suffered by the homeowners should be considered an external cost of operating a feedlot and producing beef for public consumption. I do not believe that a few should be required to pay this extra cost of doing business by going uncompensated for a nuisance of this sort. If a feedlot wants to continue, I say fine, providing compensation is paid for the serious invasion (the odors, flies, dust, etc.) of the homeowner's interest. My only qualification is that the financial burden of compensating for this harm should not be such as to force the feedlot (or any other industry) out of business. The true cost can then be shifted to the consumer who rightfully should pay for the *entire* cost of producing the product he desires to obtain.

The majority today blithely suggests that because the State of Idaho is sparsely populated and because our economy is largely dependent on agriculture, lumber, mining and industrial development, we should forego compensating those who suffer a serious invasion. If humans are such a rare item in this state, maybe there is all the more reason to protect them from the discharge of industry. At a minimum, we should compensate those who suffer a nuisance at the hands of industry and agriculture. What the majority overlooks is that the cost of development should not be absorbed by few, but rather should be spread out and paid by all. I am not convinced that agriculture or industry will be put out of business by requiring compensation for the nuisance they generate. Let us look at the case before us. The owners of the feedlot will not find themselves looking for new jobs if they are required to compensate the homeowners for the stench and dust and flies attendant with 9,000 head of cattle. Rather, meat prices at the grocery store will undoubtedly go up. But, in my view it is far better that the cost of the nuisance be carried by the consumer of a product than by the unfortunate homeowners currently suffering under adverse conditions. Some compensation should be paid the homeowners for suffering the burden from which we all benefit.

The decision of the Court of Appeals is an outstanding example of a judicial opinion which comes from a truly exhaustive and analytical review. *See* 669 P.2d 643 (Idaho Ct. App. 1983). I see no need to reiterate the authority cited therein. The Court of Appeals clarified the standard for determining the existence of a nuisance. Because the jury instructions were inconsistent with this Idaho law, the Court of Appeals properly vacated the lower court judgment. . . .

FOOD FOR THOUGHT

Up to this point in the course, whenever you confronted the word "unreasonable" it referred to the conduct of either the defendant or the plaintiff. Risk-utility balancing of some sort determined whether one's conduct was reasonable *vel non*. *Carpenter* appears to hold that standard risk-utility balancing will determine whether a defendant's conduct (even if intentional) constitutes a nuisance. *Hughes* generally buys into the position of Restatement, Second, of Torts § 829A, which holds an invasion of another's interest in the use and enjoyment of land to be unreasonable "if the harm resulting from the invasion is severe and greater than the other should be required to bear without compensation." The focus is not on the conduct of the defendant but rather on the unreasonable nature of the harm to the landowner. Where the harm to the plaintiff is unreasonable, nuisance can be established regardless of the utility of the defendant's conduct.

Though *Hughes* appears to embrace the Restatement position that the utility of the actor's conduct is not relevant when the plaintiff suffers severe harm, a close look at the opinion indicates that it recognizes a loophole that is not found in the Restatement. After setting forth Restatement § 829A, the court says that if defendant had been able to establish that the damage inflicted "was not avoidable at all" or "only at such expense as would be practically prohibitory," then the defendant would not be held liable for nuisance. The Restatement does not recognize the exception, set forth in *Hughes,* where plaintiff suffers severe harm. Under the *Hughes* exception it would seem that a court would take into account the utility of the actor's conduct. Even if the harm is not avoidable or avoidable only at a prohibitory cost, the activity still should be found to constitute a nuisance, unless the utility of the activity is significant. Rhetoric notwithstanding, risk-utility balancing of some sort will be at work in nuisance litigation. It may very well be weighted in favor of plaintiffs but it is unlikely to be banished. *See, e.g.,* Traetto v. Palazzo, 436 N.J. Super. 6 (N.J. App. 2014) (the appellate court reversed the trial court's grant of summary judgment for the defendant, whom plaintiff alleged played a set of drums in a neighboring house, on ground that how frequently the defendant played the drums was in dispute, and the trier of fact needed to weigh the utility of the drum-playing against the harm that it caused the plaintiff).

I WAS HERE FIRST

One factor to be considered in deciding whether the invasion of plaintiff's use and enjoyment of her land was unreasonable is whether the defendant's activity existed before the plaintiff came into possession of the land or put the land to the use that is incompatible with that of the defendant. If you move to an area that is commercial, you have little ground to complain that noise attending commerce is disturbing your peace. Although courts may take into account who got there first, it will not necessarily be determinative. In a much-cited case, Spur Industries, Inc. v. Del E. Webb Development Co., 494 P.2d 700 (Ariz. 1972), defendant, Spur, had been operating a feedlot for 8,000 head of cattle on 35 acres of land located some 15 miles from Phoenix, Arizona. Cattle feedlots had existed in the general area since 1956. Spur expanded on the existing use, and by 1962 had acquired 114 acres. In 1959, plaintiff, Webb, began to plan a large housing project on a 20,000-acre plot. In 1960, it had already completed construction of 500 to 600 new homes. The construction of the homes dovetailed with the expansion by Spur of its new feedlot facilities. The clash between the new development and the feedlot was inevitable. The flies and odor emanating from 1,000,000 pounds of wet manure per day, from some 30,000 head of cattle dwelling on Spur's expanded facilities, made life a nightmare for those living in the new development, and made the houses built by the developer impossible to sell. In a Solomon-like decision, the court held that the impact on those who had purchased homes in the new development was so great that it would enjoin the nuisance. But, given the fact that the developer had purchased and built homes near the feedlots, it would have to pay damages to Spur for the costs associated with ceasing to operate its feedlots.

In Mark v. State of Oregon, 84 P.3d 155 (Or. Ct. App. 2004), plaintiff purchased a home and waterfront property adjacent to state-owned beaches. Plaintiff was unaware that these beaches were used by hundreds of nude sunbathers. In addition, explicit sexual conduct took place on the beaches in full view of anyone on the plaintiff's property. Plaintiff sought an injunction against the state of Oregon for creating a private nuisance. The state argued that the plaintiff had moved to the nuisance. The court, in granting the injunction, rejected the state's argument for two reasons. First, "coming to the nuisance" is not an absolute defense; rather, it is one of a number of considerations that a court may take into account in deciding whether a nuisance claim can be established. Second, the plaintiff, who had come to look at the property in the winter, had neither actual nor constructive knowledge of the nude sunbathing when he purchased the property.

THE NOISE IS GIVING US EXCEDRIN HEADACHES

A particularly vexing set of cases has pitted homeowners living in the vicinity of airports against either airlines or the various city and state entities that own and operate the airports. The homeowners complain bitterly that takeoffs and landings at airports cause deafening noise and make their lives miserable. Even though the airports attempt to vary flight patterns so as to spread the misery, the simple fact is that there is no quiet way to land a 747. When the flight pattern hits a given neighborhood several times a week, the inhabitants have looked to the courts for relief from the intolerable noise.

For the most part, the homeowners come out on the short end of the stick. Any attempt to enjoin the airports to reduce the number of flights or to vary flight patterns is doomed to failure. The Noise Control Act of 1972 (42 U.S.C. §§ 4901-4918) establishes an administrative scheme to control noise. In City of Burbank v. Lockheed Air Terminal, Inc., 411 U.S. 624 (1973), the Supreme Court held that the Noise Control Act barred the enforcement of a city ordinance that sought to control airport noise. As long as an airport conforms to the federal standards, it cannot be enjoined from continuing its operations.

A more promising approach is for the homeowner to claim that the airport operations constitute an unjust taking of property without due process of law. This class of claims flies under the banner of "inverse condemnation." Normally when a state or municipality seeks to condemn property for public use, the governmental entity acts affirmatively to acquire the property under eminent domain. In the case of homeowners who suffer as a result of the noise levels caused by air traffic, the claim is that the governmental agency that operates the airport has, in fact, decreased the value of the property by its conduct and has taken private property without payment. Plaintiffs who allege a taking of property after the fact seek reimbursement based on inverse condemnation. Two cases decided by the United States Supreme Court, United States v. Causby, 328 U.S. 256 (1946), and Griggs v. Allegheny County, 369 U.S. 84 (1962), established the basic principle that when a governmental entity operates an airport such that flight over a plaintiff's land significantly diminishes the value of the property, the government must pay for the diminution in value. Several courts have expanded the inverse condemnation theory and have held that it is not necessary to allege direct overflight to establish a claim for inverse condemnation. They have found an unconstitutional taking when the noise from repeated flights in the general area causes a substantial diminution in property value. *See, e.g.,* Interstate Companies, Inc. v. City of Bloomington, 790 N.W.2d 409 (Minn. App. 2010) (reversing summary judgment for the defendants on ground that the question of whether or not the noise caused by an airport reduced the plaintiff's property value, was a question for the jury); Alevizos v. Metropolitan Airports Commission of Minneapolis & St. Paul, 216 N.W.2d 651 (Minn. 1974); Martin v. Port of Seattle, 391 P.2d 540 (Wash. 1964).

Of course, not all plaintiffs have been successful. *See, e.g.,* Alewine v. Houston, 309 S.W.3d 771 (Tex. App. 2010) (plaintiff homeowners failed to show that over-flight effects were so severe as to render their property no longer usable for its intended purpose); Powell v. County of Humboldt, 222 Cal. App. 4th 1424 (Cal. App. 2014) (holding that requiring plaintiff to grant defendants an easement to fly planes over plaintiffs' property did not constitute a taking, on ground that plaintiffs failed to put forth evidence that the easement would either render the plaintiffs unable to use their property, or would cause the plaintiffs' property value to decline).

There remains the possibility that a plaintiff may seek relief under a nuisance theory. See, e.g., Aviation Cadet Museum, Inc., v. Hammer, 373 Ark. 202 (Ark.

2008) (affirming injunction that required the defendant to stop operating a small airport, because the planes departed at extremely low and dangerous altitudes). However, the nuisance cause of action is not without its difficulties. Many homeowners moved to the nuisance, in that they purchased homes with full knowledge of airport noise. Their claims are not compelling. Recall also that some courts engage in classic risk-utility balancing. In those jurisdictions, the inconvenience to the plaintiffs must be balanced against the important benefit to the public of having a well-functioning air transportation system. Furthermore, some governmental entities may be immune from suit. For a review of the case law in this area, *see* Jay M. Zilter, *Airport Operations of Flight of Aircraft as Constituted Taking or Damaging of Property,* 22 A.L.R. 4th 863 (1983); Jack L. Litwin, *Aircraft Operations or Flight of Aircraft as Nuisance,* 79 A.L.R. 3d 253 (1977); Luis G. Zambrano, *Balancing the Rights of Landowners with the Needs of Airports,* 66 J. Air L. & Com. 445, 484-490 (2000) (discusses the limitations of nuisance and trespass suits against airports, citing Provident Mutual Life Insurance Co. v. City of Atlanta, 938 F. Supp. 829 (N.D. Ga. 1995), in which the court determined that an entity that benefits the public could not be enjoined from continuing its operations). However, landowners may prevail in a suit for damages. *See* Scott P. Keifer, *Note: Aircraft Overflights as a Fifth Amendment Taking: The Extension of Damages for the Loss of Potential Future Uses to Aviation Easements* — Brown v. United States, 4 Mo. Envtl. L. & Pol'y Rev. 88 (1996) (focuses on Brown v. United States, 73 F.3d 1100 (Fed. Cir. 1996), in which the court expanded the concept of aviation easement by allowing a landowner without any current damages to seek restitution for losses for potential future uses of the land which have been precluded by the aircraft overflights); David Casanova, *Comment: The Possibility and Consequences of the Recognition of Prescriptive Aviation Easements by State Courts,* 28 B.C. Envtl. Aff. L. Rev. 399 (2001) (examines the ability, state by state, of airports to acquire prescriptive aviation easements, noting that the trend toward the recognition may be influential to the large majority of states that have not yet addressed this issue); Carlos A. Ball, *The Curious Intersection of Nuisance and Takings Law,* 86 B.U. L. Rev. 819 (2006) (arguing that courts need to steer a middle ground between being overly deferential to adjacent landowners who allege little more than classic nuisance and being overly deferential to government who seek to avoid liability for all but the most serious invasions).

D. PUBLIC NUISANCE

The Restatement, Second, of Torts § 821B defines public nuisance as "an unreasonable interference with a right common to the general public." To make out a public nuisance, a plaintiff must establish that the defendant's conduct involves a significant interference with public health, public safety, or public convenience. Frequently, the conduct is proscribed by statute and is of a continuing nature. For an individual to recover damages for a public nuisance, the plaintiff must have suffered harm of a kind different from that suffered by the general public. In § 821C, the Restatement sets forth two examples that illustrate this point:

1. *A* digs a trench across the public street, which not only prevents travel on the street but also blocks the entrance to *B*'s private driveway, so that *B* cannot get his car out of his garage. *B* can recover for the public nuisance.
2. *A* travels daily from his home to his office over a public highway that is the most convenient route. Ten miles from *A*'s home *B* obstructs the highway, compelling all those traveling on it to detour two miles. *A* cannot recover for the nuisance.

Thus, the most significant difference between private and public nuisance is who has standing to sue. Under private nuisance, one who has an interest in land has standing to bring an action. Where the nuisance involves a right common to the general public, a plaintiff has no standing to sue unless she has suffered harm "different in kind" from that suffered by the general public.

Where the plaintiff seeks to enjoin the activity allegedly causing a public nuisance, rather than to recover money damages, the standing requirement is somewhat relaxed. *See* Restatement, Second, of Torts § 821C, comment *j*. For example, in Armory Park Neighborhood Assn. v. Episcopal Community Services in Arizona, 712 P.2d 914 (Ariz. 1985), a neighborhood association successfully enjoined the Episcopal Church from operating a center whose sole purpose was to provide one free meal per day for indigent persons. The center attracted large numbers of people to an area that had been primarily residential with only a few small businesses. Long lines of people queued up on the street before the designated hour to distribute meals and many lingered on well after the closing time of the center. Transients frequently trespassed on residents' yards, sometimes urinating, drinking, or littering on their properties. Although it is unlikely that any individual could sustain a private nuisance action, the activity constituted a public nuisance. The neighborhood association was an appropriate party to seek an injunction on behalf of all the residents. It is interesting to note that the court enjoined the church from operating the center even though the center did not violate any zoning law. The court held that compliance with zoning requirements was a factor to be considered as to whether the activity constituted an unreasonable invasion of the neighborhood's rights, but it was not dispositive.

The most interesting debate about public nuisance surrounds the attempts by municipalities to seek relief from the ills created by lead paint and handguns under the rubric of public nuisance. Several courts have turned thumbs down on attempts to use public nuisance as an end-run around products liability doctrine that rejects these claims.

The recent New Jersey decision, In Re Lead Paint Litigation, 924 A.2d 484 (N.J. 2007), is illustrative. Plaintiffs brought suit against lead paint manufacturers for the costs of inspecting for and abating lead paint in thousands of dwellings in New Jersey. Lead paint and lead additive was banned for use in the United States in 1978. However, thousands of home and apartment buildings still have layers of lead paint on their walls. Through deterioration and chipping, the lead paint comes off the walls and is imbibed by children, who suffer a host of serious ills from the ingestion including blood, kidney, and nervous system diseases. The effect on the nervous system can cause learning disabilities, decreased hearing, and mental retardation. New Jersey and the federal government have passed legislation requiring owners of dwellings that have lead paint to abate the condition. This litigation sought to shift the costs of abatement and other damages to the manufacturers who supplied the lead paint and additives in the first instance. After undertaking a lengthy analysis of the New Jersey lead paint statute, the court confronted the question of whether under the statute an action for public nuisance could be pursued. In rejecting the plaintiff's claim for public nuisance the court said:

> First, . . . , the conduct that has given rise to the public health crisis is, in point of fact, poor maintenance of premises where lead paint may be found by the owners of those premises. That conduct creates the flaking, peeling, and dust that gives rise to the ingestion hazard and thus creates the public nuisance. The Lead Paint Act's focus on owners maintains the traditional public nuisance theory's link to the conduct of an actor, generally in a particular location. Unlike the Legislature's careful adherence to these long-established notions, plaintiffs ignore the fact that the conduct that created the health crisis is the conduct of the premises owner. Plaintiffs therefore would separate conduct and location and thus eliminate entirely the concept of control of the nuisance.
>
> Second, however, the very meaning of conduct in the public nuisance realm is separate, and entirely different, from the only conduct of these defendants. Fundamental to this aspect of our analysis is the fact that we here address an ordinary, unregulated consumer product that defendants sold in the ordinary course of commerce. In public nuisance terms, then, were we to conclude that plaintiffs have stated a claim, we would necessarily be concluding that the conduct of merely offering an everyday household product for sale can suffice for the purpose of interfering with a common right as we understand it. Such an interpretation would far exceed any cognizable cause of action.
>
> Although one might argue that the product, now in its deteriorated state, interferes with the public health, one cannot also argue persuasively that the conduct of defendants in distributing it, at the time when they did, bears the necessary link to the current health crisis. Absent that link, the claims of plaintiffs cannot sound in public nuisance. Indeed, the suggestion that plaintiffs can proceed against these defendants on a public nuisance theory would stretch the theory to the point of creating strict liability to be imposed on manufacturers of ordinary consumer products which, although legal when sold, and although sold no more recently than a quarter of a century ago, have become dangerous through deterioration and poor maintenance by the purchasers. *Id.* at 433-434.

The New Jersey Supreme Court thus based its denial of the nuisance cause-of-action for lead paint contamination on the ground that plaintiff had not made out the elements of the common law claim. *See also* City of Milwaukee v. NL Industries, 762 N.W.2d 757 (Wis. Ct. App. 2008) (verdict/judgment for defendant upheld; jury could find that paint manufacturer did not know of risks to children when paint distributed); City of St. Louis v. Benjamin Moore & Co., 226 S.W.3d 110 (Mo. 2007) (plaintiff cannot identify which defendant was responsible for each individual home's lead paint problem; Missouri does not recognize market-share liability); City of Chicago v. American Cyanamid Co., 823 N.E.2d 126 (Ill. App. Ct.

2005) (plaintiffs cannot establish either factual or legal causation); State of Rhode Island v. Lead Industries Assn., 951 A.2d 428 (R.I. 2008) (claims failed on several grounds; claims sound in products liability rather than public nuisance). *But see* County of Santa Clara v. Atlantic Richfield Co., 40 Cal. Rptr. 3d 313 (Cal. Ct. App. 2006) (reversing trial court's dismissal of the plaintiff's complaint and allowing a public nuisance claim for abatement of lead paint). For a comprehensive discussion of the case law, *see* Victor E. Schwartz & Phil Goldberg, *The Law of Public Nuisance: Maintaining Rational Boundaries on a Rational Tort*, 42 Washburn L.J. 541 (2006).

A similar split is found in the courts that have grappled with gun-related injuries. Some courts have found that the pervasive presence of handguns in society constitutes a public nuisance and liability should attach against gun manufacturers when criminals use these guns for nefarious purposes. *See, e.g.*, City of Cincinnati v. Beretta, 768 N.E.2d 1136 (Ohio 2002). *But see* District of Columbia v. Beretta, U.S.A. Corp., 872 A.2d 633 (D.C. 2005) (rejecting such an "unprecedented expansion of the law of public nuisance"); City of Chicago v. Beretta U.S.A. Corp., 821 N.E.2d 1099 (Ill. 2004) (rejecting public nuisance claim because of comprehensive state and federal legislation governing the subject). In response to this litigation, Congress passed the Protection of Lawful Commerce in Arms Act, Pub. L. No. 109-192, 119 Stat. 2095 (2005) (immunizing federally licensed gun manufacturers and distributors for most civil actions arising from criminal or unlawful use of firearms). *See* Ileto v. Glock, Inc., 565 F.3d 1126 (9th Cir. 2009) (claims against unlicensed foreign manufacturers may proceed under state law).

E. THE COASE THEOREM: UNDERSTANDING NUISANCE THROUGH THE PRISM OF ECONOMICS

Before examining the issue of what remedies courts should utilize to work out competing claims to use and enjoyment of property, we turn to the work of Ronald Coase. It is not our intent to turn you into instant economists. But, as you shall see, the Coase theorem can be of great significance in trying to figure out whether an injunction or damages is the appropriate remedy. In his landmark article, *The Problem of Social Cost*, 3 J.L. & Econ. 1 (1960), Coase demonstrates the economic principles underlying nuisance law. Coase postulates a situation in which two neighboring landowners use their lands in ways that are incompatible. Coase argues that in resolving problems of conflicting land use, it is not useful to label one of the uses "the cause" of harm to the other. Rather, the causation is reciprocal. For example, the desire of homeowners to enjoy a pollution-free environment does not necessarily imply that a neighboring factory, which has been there for years, "causes" harm to them any more than their presence and demand for clean air "causes" harm to the factory. The pollution, which is a *negative externality* to the homeowners, is a side effect of the factory's productive use of its property, a use that *benefits* the factory. Thus, it is not a question of who is "at fault," but rather whose use should be preferred, that presents the problem.

Coase demonstrates that under ideal negotiation conditions, which he equates with knowledgeable parties and the absence of transaction costs, the problem would be resolved by bargaining to an *efficient outcome,* meaning that whoever valued their land use more would eventually prevail, and would pay the other party for the loss or infringement of her use. Thus, if the homeowners wanted clean air badly enough, they would pay the company to stop polluting. Conversely, if the company valued its productive capacity more, it would bribe the homeowners to move somewhere else. Or, the parties might compromise and agree that homeowners would tolerate some pollution in exchange for monetary compensation. If there were no impediments to bargaining, or *transaction costs,* the parties would bargain to an efficient outcome regardless of which party was initially assigned the legal right. However, Coase recognizes that transaction costs may be substantial. For example, injured homeowners may have to get together to bargain. Furthermore, in the bargaining process, parties may take extreme positions in order to extract concessions from each other (engage in strategic behavior). For example, in *Peters v. Archambault, supra,* the court ordered the encroaching party to remove a significant part of his home. The court fully expected that the parties would strike a deal allowing the 22-year-old encroachment to continue. But the parties were stubborn. No deal was reached and the encroacher had to tear down a significant part of his home. Coase argues that when transaction costs prevent parties from negotiating successfully, the law should decide the dispute in such a way that the outcome is one that the parties would have bargained for in the absence of transaction costs.

In determining the efficient outcome, the court will need to estimate the effects that various levels of the factory's output will have on both parties. At each level of operation, the factory will be expected to earn a certain profit, and homeowners will be expected to accrue an estimated amount of damages. The efficient outcome will be the output level that maximizes the net result in efficiency; that is, the total profits of the factory less the total damages suffered by the resident. For example, if the factory stands to profit $10,000 by operating 8 hours a day, and homeowners will incur $1,000 in damages as a result, the net combined gain will be $9,000. If the factory ratchets production up to 16 hours a day, the factory will profit an additional $4,000, while the homeowners expected loss jumps an additional $6,000. At this level of output, the factory's total profits amount to $14,000 but the homeowners' damages amount to $7,000, for a net combined gain of only $7,000, compared with the $9,000 combined gain earlier. By keeping the factory running 24 hours a day, the factory can marginally increase its profits by an additional $2,000, for a total of $16,000, whereas the homeowners' damages skyrocket an additional $20,000, totaling $36,000. Thus, when the factory is operating at its maximum level of output, there is a net combined loss of $20,000. In this example, assuming that the 8-hour, 16-hour, and 24-hour levels of production are the only ones available, the efficient level of production is for the factory to operate 8 hours a day.[1] Do you see why?

1. A. Mitchell Polinsky, *An Introduction to Law and Economics* 17-19 (3d. ed. 2003). This example is based on Polinsky's application of the Coase theorem to nuisance law.

Returning to the real world, where transaction costs must be reckoned with, for those who believe that the efficient allocation of resources is a proper social objective the question becomes can the law bring about the economically efficient result? In a highly influential article by Guido Calabresi and A. Douglas Melamed, *Property Rules, Liability Rules and Inalienability: One View of the Cathedral,* 85 Harv. L. Rev. 1089 (1972), the authors note that courts may utilize property rules or liability rules in seeking to achieve an efficient result. Property rules provide the owner of the entitlement with the right to exclude others (by enjoining their conduct) or to sell the entitlement to those who wish to engage in activity that would otherwise constitute a nuisance. Very simply, the party to whom the entitlement is granted must consent beforehand to use by others of the entitlement. Liability rules allow the owner of the entitlement to obtain compensation from those who, without prior consent, take or interfere with the entitlement. The authors argue that property rules should be used when bargaining costs are low. In that setting, once the entitlements are assigned the parties will presumably bargain their way to an efficient solution. When transaction costs are high and bargaining is difficult or impossible, liability rules should be applied. The court would then impose the efficient outcome without relying on the parties to reach it on their own.

For an interesting argument supporting the position that liability rules may be superior to property rules even when transaction costs are low, *see* Louis Kaplow & Steven Shavell, *Property Rules Versus Liability Rules: An Economic Analysis,* 109 Harv. L. Rev. 713 (1996). Several scholars are sharply critical of the view that liability rules foster greater efficiency. *See, e.g.,* Lucian Arye Bebchuk, *Property Rights and Liability Rules: The Ex Ante View of the Cathedral,* 100 Mich. L. Rev. 601 (2001); Daphna Lewinsohn-Zamir, *The Choice Between Property Rules and Liability Rules Revisited: Critical Observations from Behavioral Studies,* 80 Tex. L. Rev. 219 (2001). In a fascinating article, *Do Parties to Nuisance Cases Bargain After Judgment? A Glimpse Inside the Cathedral,* 66 U. Chi. L. Rev. 373 (1999), Professor Ward Farnsworth examines the assumption by most scholars that, postjudgment, parties will bargain to an efficient result when transaction costs are low. His empirical study of 20 cases that went to judgment revealed that in none did the parties enter into bargaining to purchase or sell the adjudicated rights. The article examines the reasons why such bargaining does not occur and the implications of his finding for nuisance law.

F. REMEDIES

BOOMER v. ATLANTIC CEMENT CO., INC.
257 N.E.2d 870 (N.Y. 1970)

Bergan, J.

Defendant operates a large cement plant near Albany. These are actions for injunction and damages by neighboring land owners alleging injury to property from dirt, smoke and vibration emanating from the plant. A nuisance has been found after trial, temporary damages have been allowed; but an injunction has been denied.

The public concern with air pollution arising from many sources in industry and in transportation is currently accorded ever wider recognition accompanied by a growing sense of responsibility in State and Federal Governments to control it. Cement plants are obvious sources of air pollution in the neighborhoods where they operate.

But there is now before the court private litigation in which individual property owners have sought specific relief from a single plant operation. The threshold question raised by the division of view on this appeal is whether the court should resolve the litigation between the parties now before it as equitably as seems possible; or whether, seeking promotion of the general public welfare, it should channel private litigation into broad public objectives.

A court performs its essential function when it decides the rights of parties before it. Its decision of private controversies may sometimes greatly affect public issues. Large questions of law are often resolved by the manner in which private litigation is decided. But this is normally an incident to the court's main function to settle controversy. It is a rare exercise of judicial power to use a decision in private litigation as a purposeful mechanism to achieve direct public objectives greatly beyond the rights and interests before the court.

Effective control of air pollution is a problem presently far from solution even with the full public and financial powers of government. In large measure adequate technical procedures are yet to be developed and some that appear possible may be economically impracticable.

It seems apparent that the amelioration of air pollution will depend on technical research in great depth; on a carefully balanced consideration of the economic impact of close regulation; and of the actual effect on public health. It is likely to require massive public expenditure and to demand more than any local community can accomplish and to depend on regional and interstate controls.

A court should not try to do this on its own as a by-product of private litigation and it seems manifest that the judicial establishment is neither equipped in the limited nature of any judgment it can pronounce nor prepared to lay down and implement an effective policy for the elimination of air pollution. This is an area beyond the circumference of one private lawsuit. It is a direct responsibility for government and should not thus be undertaken as an incident to solving a dispute between property owners and a single cement plant — one of many — in the Hudson River valley.

The cement making operations of defendant have been found by the court at Special Term to have damaged the nearby properties of plaintiffs in these two actions. That court, as it has been noted, accordingly found defendant maintained a nuisance and this has been affirmed at the Appellate Division. The total damage to plaintiffs' properties is, however, relatively small in comparison with the value of defendant's operation and with the consequences of the injunction which plaintiffs seek.

The ground for the denial of injunction, notwithstanding the finding both that there is a nuisance and that plaintiffs have been damaged substantially, is the large disparity in economic consequences of the nuisance and of the injunction. This theory cannot, however, be sustained without overruling a doctrine which has been consistently reaffirmed in several leading cases in this court and which has never been disavowed here, namely that where a nuisance has been found and where there has been any substantial damage shown by the party complaining an injunction will be granted.

The rule in New York has been that such a nuisance will be enjoined although marked disparity be shown in economic consequence between the effect of the injunction and the effect of the nuisance.

The problem of disparity in economic consequence was sharply in focus in Whalen v. Union Bag & Paper Co. (208 N.Y. 1). A pulp mill entailing an investment of more than a million dollars polluted a stream in which plaintiff, who owned a farm, was "a lower riparian owner." The economic loss to plaintiff from this pollution was small. This court, reversing the Appellate Division, reinstated the injunction granted by the Special Term against the argument of the mill owner that in view of "the slight advantage to plaintiff and the great loss that will be inflicted on defendant" an injunction should not be granted. "Such a balancing of injuries cannot be justified by the circumstances of this case," Judge Werner noted. He continued: "Although the damage to the plaintiff may be slight as compared with the defendant's expense of abating the condition, that is not a good reason for refusing an injunction."

Thus the unconditional injunction granted at Special Term was reinstated. The rule laid down in that case, then, is that whenever the damage resulting from a nuisance is found not "unsubstantial," viz., $100 a year, injunction would follow. This states a rule that had been followed in this court with marked consistency. . . .

Although the court at Special Term and the Appellate Division held that injunction should be denied, it was found that plaintiffs had been damaged in various specific amounts up to the time of the trial and damages to the respective plaintiffs were awarded for those amounts. The effect of this was, injunction having been denied, plaintiffs could maintain successive actions at law for damages thereafter as further damage was incurred.

The court at Special Term also found the amount of permanent damage attributable to each plaintiff, for the guidance of the parties in the event both sides stipulated to the payment and acceptance of such permanent damage as a settlement of all the controversies among the parties. The total of permanent damages to all plaintiffs thus found was $185,000. This basis of adjustment has not resulted in any stipulation by the parties.

This result at Special Term and at the Appellate Division is a departure from a rule that has become settled; but to follow the rule literally in these cases would be to close down the plant at once. This court is fully agreed to avoid that immediately drastic remedy; the difference in view is how best to avoid it.*

One alternative is to grant the injunction but postpone its effect to a specified future date to give opportunity for technical advances to permit defendant to

---

* Respondent's investment in the plant is in excess of $45,000,000. There are over 300 people employed there.

eliminate the nuisance; another is to grant the injunction conditioned on the payment of permanent damages to plaintiffs which would compensate them for the total economic loss to their property present and future caused by defendant's operations. For reasons which will be developed the court chooses the latter alternative.

If the injunction were to be granted unless within a short period — e.g., 18 months — the nuisance be abated by improved methods, there would be no assurance that any significant technical improvement would occur.

The parties could settle this private litigation at any time if defendant paid enough money and the imminent threat of closing the plant would build up the pressure on defendant. If there were no improved techniques found, there would inevitably be applications to the court at Special Term for extensions of time to perform on showing of good faith efforts to find such techniques.

Moreover, techniques to eliminate dust and other annoying by-products of cement making are unlikely to be developed by any research the defendant can undertake within any short period, but will depend on the total resources of the cement industry nationwide and throughout the world. The problem is universal wherever cement is made.

For obvious reasons the rate of the research is beyond control of defendant. If at the end of 18 months the whole industry has not found a technical solution a court would be hard put to close down this one cement plant if due regard be given to equitable principles.

On the other hand, to grant the injunction unless defendant pays plaintiffs such permanent damages as may be fixed by the court seems to do justice between the contending parties. All of the attributions of economic loss to the properties on which plaintiffs' complaints are based will have been redressed.

The nuisance complained of by these plaintiffs may have other public or private consequences, but these particular parties are the only ones who have sought remedies and the judgment proposed will fully redress them. The limitation of relief granted is a limitation only within the four corners of these actions and does not foreclose public health or other public agencies from seeking proper relief in a proper court.

It seems reasonable to think that the risk of being required to pay permanent damages to injured property owners by cement plant owners would itself be a reasonable effective spur to research for improved techniques to minimize nuisance.

The power of the court to condition on equitable grounds the continuance of an injunction on the payment of permanent damages seems undoubted. . . .

The present cases and the remedy here proposed are in a number of other respects rather similar to Northern Indiana Public Serv. Co. v. Vesey . . . 200 N.E. 620 decided by the Supreme Court of Indiana. The gases, odors, ammonia and smoke from the Northern Indiana company's gas plant damaged the nearby Vesey greenhouse operation. An injunction and damages were sought, but an injunction was denied and the relief granted was limited to permanent damages "present, past, and future" . . . .

Denial of injunction was grounded on a public interest in the operation of the gas plant and on the court's conclusion "that less injury would be occasioned by requiring the appellant [Public Service] to pay the appellee [Vesey] all damages suffered by it . . . than by enjoining the operation of the gas plant; and that the maintenance and operation of the gas plant should not be enjoined" . . . .

Thus it seems fair to both sides to grant permanent damages to plaintiffs which will terminate this private litigation. The theory of damage is the "servitude on land" of plaintiffs imposed by defendant's nuisance. (See United States v. Causby, 328 U.S. 256, 261 . . . , where the term "servitude" addressed to the land was used by Justice Douglas relating to the effect of airplane noise on property near an airport.)

The judgment, by allowance of permanent damages imposing a servitude on land, which is the basis of the actions, would preclude future recovery by plaintiffs or their grantees. . . .

This should be placed beyond debate by a provision of the judgment that the payment by defendant and the acceptance by plaintiffs of permanent damages found by the court shall be in compensation for a servitude on the land.

Although the Trial Term has found permanent damages as a possible basis of settlement of the litigation, on remission the court should be entirely free to re-examine this subject. It may again find the permanent damage already found; or make new findings.

The orders should be reversed, without costs, and the cases remitted to Supreme Court, Albany County to grant an injunction which shall be vacated upon payment by defendant of such amounts of permanent damage to the respective plaintiffs as shall for this purpose be determined by the court.

JASEN, J. (dissenting).

I agree with the majority that a reversal is required here, but I do not subscribe to the newly enunciated doctrine of assessment of permanent damages, in lieu of an injunction, where substantial property rights have been impaired by the creation of a nuisance.

It has long been the rule in this State, as the majority acknowledges, that a nuisance which results in substantial continuing damage to neighbors must be enjoined. . . . To now change the rule to permit the cement company to continue polluting the air indefinitely upon the payment of permanent damages is, in my opinion, compounding the magnitude of a very serious problem in our State and Nation today. . . .

The specific problem faced here is known as particulate contamination because of the fine dust particles emanating from defendant's cement plant. The particular type of nuisance is not new, having appeared in many cases for at least the past 60 years. . . . It is interesting to note that cement production has recently been identified as a significant source of particulate contamination in the Hudson Valley. . . . This type of pollution, wherein very small particles escape and stay in the atmosphere, has been denominated as the type of air pollution which produces the greatest hazard to human health. We have thus a nuisance which not only is damaging to the plaintiffs, . . . but also is decidedly harmful to the general public.

I see grave dangers in overruling our long-established rule of granting an injunction where a nuisance results in substantial continuing damage. In permitting the injunction to become inoperative upon the payment of permanent damages, the majority is, in effect, licensing a continuing wrong. It is the same as saying to the cement company, you may continue to do harm to your neighbors so long as you pay a fee for it. Furthermore, once such permanent damages are assessed and paid, the incentive to alleviate the wrong would be eliminated, thereby continuing air pollution of an area without abatement.

It is true that some courts have sanctioned the remedy here proposed by the majority in a number of cases, . . . but none of the authorities relied upon by the majority are analogous to the situation before us. In those cases, the courts, in denying an injunction and awarding money damages, grounded their decision on a showing that the use to which the property was intended to be put was primarily for the public benefit. Here, on the other hand, it is clearly established that the cement company is creating a continuing air pollution nuisance primarily for its own private interest with no public benefit.

This kind of inverse condemnation . . . may not be invoked by a private person or corporation for private gain or advantage. Inverse condemnation should only be permitted when the public is primarily served in the taking or impairment of property. . . . The promotion of the interests of the polluting cement company has, in my opinion, no public use or benefit.

Nor is it constitutionally permissible to impose servitude on land, without consent of the owner, by payment of permanent damages where the continuing impairment of the land is for a private use. . . . This is made clear by the State Constitution (art. I, § 7, subd. [a]) which provides that "[private] property shall not be taken for *public use* without just compensation" (emphasis added). It is, of course, significant that the section makes no mention of taking for a *private* use.

In sum, then, by constitutional mandate as well as by judicial pronouncement, the permanent impairment of private property for private purposes is not authorized in the absence of clearly demonstrated public benefit and use.

I would enjoin the defendant cement company from continuing the discharge of dust particles upon its neighbors' properties unless, within 18 months, the cement company abated this nuisance. . . .

It is not my intention to cause the removal of the cement plant from the Albany area, but to recognize the urgency of the problem stemming from this stationary source of air pollution, and to allow the company a specified period of time to develop a means to alleviate this nuisance.

I am aware that the trial court found that the most modern dust control devices available have been installed in defendant's plant, but, I submit, this does not mean that *better* and more effective dust control devices could not be developed within the time allowed to abate the pollution.

Moreover, I believe it is incumbent upon the defendant to develop such devices, since the cement company, at the time the plant commenced production (1962), was well aware of the plaintiffs' presence in the area, as well as the probable consequences of its contemplated operation. Yet, it still chose to build and operate the plant at this site.

---

authors' dialogue 39

AARON: Jim, how influential has the Coase theorem been?

JIM: It's been very influential on scholars. Coase's article has been cited thousands of times. It won the man a Nobel prize. You can't be seriously questioning the influence of the Coase article.

AARON: Of course not, Jim. I'm not that dumb. What I am questioning is the impact Coase and the huge body of scholarly articles that followed his article have had on the courts. Do judges seriously pay attention to the extensive law and economics literature? I have my doubts. One reads the nuisance cases and one finds occasional references to the landmark articles. But, for the most part, the courts go their merry way, deciding cases intuitively with little attention to the literature. I hate to sound anti-intellectual, but most of the writing isn't easy to read. And when you do get through it, much of it, although brilliant, leaves the reader with a host of factors to consider. Even when the writers take positions, one can easily find articles that go the other way. Even schooled economists are left scratching their heads. What can you expect from an appellate court with a heavy docket? Prosser has been dead for over 30 years, yet the courts continue to cite the section in his treatise dealing with nuisance extensively. Articles dealing with the varying views as to how economic principles should affect nuisance law appear with great regularity in the law reviews but one rarely finds citations to them in the cases. The academy pays attention to this genre of scholarship, but do the courts?

JIM: I believe you are right that some of the literature has gone beyond the ability of courts to cope. Nevertheless, the impact of this literature on the courts has been substantial. For the last four decades, law students have been sensitized to the economic debates. It has become part of mainstream thinking and finds its way into briefs and oral arguments. Lawyers have been given a set of intellectual tools to utilize that they did not have before. They think about efficiency and whether the law can approximate outcomes that would be reached by bargaining.

AARON: I can buy into that. But, I wonder whether the academy does not have a greater responsibility to communicate with the courts more effectively. More often than not, the writers seem to be talking to each other. It reminds me of the conflict-of-laws literature. In the early years, the writing had a direct impact on the courts. In recent years, the squabbling among the scholars has had almost no impact on the courts. It's the profs talking to each other in a jargon that only they seem to understand.

In a day when there is a growing concern for clean air, highly developed industry should not expect acquiescence by the courts, but should, instead, plan its operations to eliminate contamination of our air and damage to its neighbors. . . .

FOOD FOR THOUGHT

Although the case law prior to *Boomer* took the position that the injured party would be granted an injunction if the injury was substantial even though the effect of granting an injunction would result in greater financial harm to the injurer, the court simply could not bring itself to allow injunctive relief and close down the cement plant. The court could not close its eyes to the $345 million investment in the plant and the fate of 300 employees who would be sent out to pasture. The utility of the injurer's conduct apparently plays a greater role when the issue is whether to grant an injunction than it does when the issue is whether to require the payment of damages.

The post-*Boomer* literature dealing with the issue of whether the appropriate remedy for a nuisance is an injunction or damages is extensive. *See, e.g.,* A. Mitchell Polinsky, *Resolving Nuisance Disputes: The Simple Economics of Injunctive and Damage Remedies,* 32 Stan. L. Rev. 1075 (1980) (arguing that whether damages or an injunction should be granted depends on a multitude of factors, including a consideration of distribution effects of either remedy); Raymond D. Hiley, *Involuntary Sale Damages in Permanent Nuisance Cases: A Bigger Bang from* Boomer, 14 B.C. Envtl. Aff. L. Rev. 61 (1986) (arguing that diminution of market value should not be the sole measure of damages but that damages should include recovery for the loss to the plaintiff of the right to dispose of the property and the subjective value of the property to the plaintiff).

REVISITING SPUR INDUSTRIES

You will recall that earlier we discussed the claim of landowners who, in defense of charges that their use of land was creating a nuisance, argued that plaintiffs moved to the area after the defendant had already been engaged in the activity of which the plaintiff complains. We noted that courts give some weight to the contention that the plaintiff "moved to the nuisance" but that the argument does not always carry the day. In that context we discussed the case of Spur Industries, Inc. v. Del E. Webb Development Co., *supra,* page 729. In that case the Arizona court granted a developer who had built a large number of homes adjacent to a cattle feedlot an injunction barring the feedlot from further operation. The stench caused by the feedlot made it impossible for those who had purchased homes to live a normal life. The fact that the developer had come to the nuisance did not stop the court from granting the injunction against the continued operation of the feedlot. Having granted the entitlement to the feedlot, one would have thought the case would come to an end. However, the court was troubled by the fact that the developer had "moved to the nuisance." The court decided to impose a liability rule on the developer to pay damages to the feedlot owner for the cost of giving up its entitlement. At least one writer believes that this novel remedy should be limited to cases very much like *Spur Industries. See* Osborne M. Reynolds, Jr., *Of Time and Feedlots: The Effect of* Spur Industries *on Nuisance Law,* 41 Wash. U. J. Urb. & Contemp. L. 75 (1992).

chapter **13**

Damages

Assuming the plaintiff has established the defendant's liability in tort for the harm the plaintiff has suffered, it remains to place a dollar amount on that harm. How is that amount to be determined? That is the question the law of damages seeks to answer. Although the issues of liability and damages are theoretically independent of one another, as a practical matter it is difficult to keep them separate. Certainly when the parties agree to settle the case, the dollar amount of the settlement is affected by both the likelihood of the defendant being held liable and the severity of the plaintiff's injuries. A strong claim on liability, when coupled with less serious injuries, may actually be worth less than a weak claim on liability that is coupled with horrific harm. Even in cases that go to trial, there is no reason to believe that juries keep the issues hermetically sealed from one another. It is widely assumed that juries reach compromise verdicts in which the wrongfulness of the defendant's conduct plays off against the severity of the plaintiff's injuries no less than in the context of claims settlement.

The law of damages explored in this chapter breaks down into two parts: compensatory damages, which seek to pay the plaintiff what it takes to make him whole; and punitive damages, which, as the name suggests, seek to teach egregious wrongdoers a lesson they won't soon forget.

A. COMPENSATORY DAMAGES

Compensatory damages are the primary instrument of recovery in tort. They are aimed at restoring the plaintiff to her pre-injury condition by paying an amount equal to the value of the interests that the defendant has diminished or destroyed. In the sections that follow we take up the subject of compensatory damages as it relates, in turn, to personal injury, harm to property, and wrongful death.

1. Damages for Personal Injury

ANDERSON v. SEARS, ROEBUCK & CO.
377 F. Supp. 136 (E.D. La. 1974)

CASSIBRY, District Judge.

[A jury found that a defective Sears heater caused the home of Mildred and Harry Britain to burn down. The fire caused burn injuries to both plaintiffs, and severe burns to their infant daughter, Helen, who suffered multiple permanent injuries. The jury awarded Mildred $250,000, Harry $23,000, and Helen $2,000,000 in compensatory damages. Defendants filed post-trial motions claiming that the damages for Helen were excessive.]

The sole issue presently before the court is whether the damages awarded to Helen Britain were excessive.

. . . Defendants ground their argument of excessiveness merely on the size of the verdict. The reasonableness of quantum, however, is not to be decided in a vacuum but rather is to be considered in light of the evidence as to the injuries and actual damages sustained and the future effects thereof. In this context, defendants have not offered any evidence at trial nor have they directed any cogent arguments in their briefs to sustain their burden of proving that the verdict was excessive.

The legal standard on which to gauge a jury verdict for remittitur purposes is the "maximum recovery rule." [Remittitur is a procedure whereby the court orders a new trial unless the plaintiff agrees to a lesser award set by the court.] This rule directs the trial judge to determine whether the verdict of the jury exceeds the maximum amount which the jury could reasonably find and if it does, the trial judge may then reduce the verdict to the highest amount that the jury could properly have awarded. Functionally, the maximum recovery rule both preserves the constitutionally protected role of the jury as finder of facts and prevents the predilections of the judge from infecting the jury's determination. Thus, the court's task is to ascertain, by scrutinizing all of the evidence as to each element of damages, what amount would be the maximum the jury could have reasonably awarded. In this case there are five cardinal elements of damages: past physical and mental pain; future physical and mental pain; future medical expenses; loss of earning capacity and permanent disability and disfigurement.

Past Physical and Mental Pain

The infant child, Helen Britain, was almost burned to death in the tragic fire that swept her home. She was burned over forty per cent of her entire body; third degree burns cover eighty per cent of her scalp and second and third degree burns of the trunk and of her extremities account for the remainder. Helen Britain's immediate post trauma treatment required hospitalization for twenty-eight days, during which time the child developed pneumonia, required numerous transfusions, suffered fever, vomiting, diarrhea, and infection, and underwent skin graft surgery, under general anesthesia, to her scalp, which was only partially successful. Keloid scarring caused webbing and ankylosis of the child's extremities and severely limited their motion. The child's fingers became adhered together; scarring bent the arm at the elbow in a burdensome, fixed position; and thick scarring on the thighs and on the side of and behind the knees impaired walking.

This child had to undergo subsequent hospitalizations for further major operations and treatment. The second major operation under general anesthesia was undertaken to graft new skin from the back and stomach to the remaining bare areas of the scalp. The third operation under general anesthesia was an attempt to relieve the deformity of her left hand caused by the webbing scars which bound down the fingers of that hand. A fourth operation under general anesthesia was performed to reduce scars which had grown back on the left hand again webbing the fingers. I cannot envisage the breadth and intensity of the pain experienced by Helen Britain throughout this ordeal.

The undisputed testimony reveals that one of the most tragic aspects of this case is that the horrible mental and emotional trauma caused to this child occurred at an age which medical experts maintain is crucial to a child's entire psyche and personality formation. Helen Britain's persistent emotional and mental disturbance is evidenced by bed wetting, nightmares, refusing to sleep alone, withdrawal, and speech impediments. Dr. Cyril Phillips, a psychiatrist, and Dr. Diamond both indicated that the child manifested to them, even at this early age, emotional illness and retarded mental growth.

The evidence reflects that an award of six hundred thousand dollars for this element of damages alone would not be unreasonable.

Future Physical and Mental Pain

There is clear evidence that the stretching, pulling, and breaking down of scars inherent in growth will continue to cause severe pain and a crippling limitation of motion in varying degrees to all of Helen Britain's upper and lower extremities. Very little can be done to improve the condition of the scalp which will never be able to breathe, sweat or grow hair. There will be risks, trauma and pain, both physical and mental, with each of the recommended twenty-seven future operations which will extend over most of the child's adult life, if she is in fact fortunate enough to be able to risk undergoing these recommended surgeries. Furthermore, Helen Britain must vigilantly guard against irritation, infection and further injury to the damaged and abnormal skin, scars and grafts because any injury, however slight, can generate cancer in these adynamic areas.

The inherent stresses and tensions of each new phase of life will severely tax this little girl's debilitated and delicate mental and emotional capacity. Throughout her future life expectancy of seventy-five years, it is reasonable to expect, that she will be deprived of a normal social life and that she will never find a husband and raise a family. On top of this, Helen Britain will always be subjected to rejection, stares and tactless inquiries from children and adults.

The court concludes that an award of seven hundred fifty thousand dollars for this element of damages alone would not be excessive.

Future Medical Expenses

A large award for future medical expenses is justified. The uncontradicted testimony was that Helen Britain would need the guidance, treatment and counseling of a team of doctors, including plastic surgeons, psychiatrists and sociologists, throughout her lifetime. Add to this the cost of the twenty-seven recommended operations and the cost of private tutoring necessitated by the child's mental and emotional needs and the jury could justifiably award a figure of two hundred and fifty thousand dollars to cover these future expenses.

Loss of Earning Capacity

The evidence of Helen Britain's disabilities both physical, mental and emotional was such that this court holds that the jury could properly find that these disabilities would prevent her from earning a living for the rest of her life. Not only do the physical impairments to her extremities disable her but her emotional limitations require avoiding stress and the combined effect is the permanent incapacity to maintain serious employment.

The jury was provided with actuarial figures which accurately calculated both the deduction of interest to be earned and the addition of an inflationary buffer, on any award made for future loss of earning capacity. In view of these incontrovertible projections at trial, it was within the province of the jury to award as much as $330,000.00 for the loss of earning capacity.

Permanent Disability and Disfigurement

The award for this element of damage must evaluate in monetary terms the compensation due this plaintiff for the permanent physical, mental and emotional disabilities and disfigurements proved by the evidence adduced at trial. A narration treating Miss Britain's permanent disabilities and disfigurements would be lengthy and redundant; therefore, I resort to listing.

1. The complete permanent loss of 80% of the scalp caused by the destruction of sweat glands, hair follicles and tissue—all of which effects a grotesque disfigurement and freakish appearance.
2. The permanent loss of the normal use of the legs.
3. The permanent impairment of the left fingers and hand caused by recurring webbing and resulting in limited motion.
4. The permanent impairment of the right hand caused by scars and webbing of the fingers.
5. The permanent injury to the left elbow and left arm with ankylosis and resulting in a crippling deformity.
6. The permanent destruction of 40% of the normal skin. As a result of this a large portion of the body is covered by "pigskin." Pigskin resembles the dry, cracked skin of an aged person and is highly susceptible to irritation from such ordinary things as temperature changes and washing.

7. Permanent scars over the majority of the body where skin donor sites were removed.
8. The permanent impairment of speech.
9. The loss of three years of formative and impressionable childhood.
10. Permanently reduced and impaired emotional capacity.
11. The permanent impairment of normal social, recreational and educational life.
12. The permanent imprint of her mother's hand on her stomach.

Considering each of the foregoing items, the court concludes that the jury had the prerogative of awarding up to one million, one hundred thousand dollars for this element of damages.

By totaling the estimated maximum recovery for each element of damages, the jury's actual award is placed in proper perspective. According to my calculations the maximum jury award supported by the evidence in this case could have been two million, nine hundred eighty thousand dollars. Obviously, the jury's two-million-dollar verdict is well within the periphery established by the maximum award test.

The defendants assert three other grounds for a remittitur. They contend that there was error in the verdict since the verdict exceeded the amount prayed for in the plaintiff's pleadings. This contention fails because the plaintiffs' pleadings were amended subsequent to the jury verdict to conform to the evidence and the verdict of the jury. This amendment was permitted by the court in accordance with law.

[Defendants] argue that the introduction of photographs of the plaintiff was inflammatory. Since a part of plaintiff's claim for damages is for disfigurement and the humiliation and embarrassment resulting therefrom, I hold that these photographs were properly admitted to show the condition of the plaintiff as she appeared to others, at the time they were taken.

The defendants suggest that the presence of the child in the courtroom and in the corridors of the courthouse in some way inflamed or prejudiced the jury. This allegation is unfounded; the defendants have not pointed out any wrongful conduct on the part of Helen Britain, her parents, or counsel for plaintiffs. Helen Britain was well behaved and quiet the entire time she was in the courtroom.

Accordingly, I hold that there was not any bias, prejudice, or any other improper influence which motivated the jury in making its award.

The defendants' motions for a remittitur are denied.

To the list of elements in *Anderson* for which a successful tort plaintiff may recover one may add, in several American jurisdictions, damages for a shortened life expectancy. *See, e.g.,* Durham v. Marberry, 156 S.W.3d 242 (Ark. 2004); Alexander v. Scheid, 726 N.E.2d 272 (Ind. 2000). Observe that this is an aspect of plaintiff's harm separate from reduced earning capacity. Here, recovery is allowed for a reduction in the noneconomic value of being alive, whether or not one is capable of earning an income.

RICHARDSON v. CHAPMAN
676 N.E.2d 621 (Ill. 1997)

Justice MILLER delivered the opinion of the court:

The plaintiffs, Keva Richardson and Ann E. McGregor, were injured when the car in which they were riding was hit from behind by a truck driven by defendant Jeffrey Chapman in Highland Park. The plaintiffs brought the present action in the circuit court of Cook County against Chapman; his employer, Tandem Transport, Inc., successor to Carrier Service Company of Wisconsin, Inc. (Tandem/Carrier); and Rollins Leasing Corp., which had leased the truck in Wisconsin to Chapman's employer. Following a jury trial, the court entered judgment on verdicts in favor of Richardson and McGregor and against Tandem/Carrier and Chapman.

[T]he jury returned verdicts against Tandem/Carrier and Chapman and in favor of Richardson and McGregor in the amounts of $22,358,814 and $102,215, respectively. [After credits for monies advanced in partial satisfaction of verdicts, the] court therefore entered judgment against Rollins and in favor of Richardson for $21,368,814, and judgment against Rollins and in favor of McGregor for $92,215, representing the unsatisfied portions of their awards from Tandem/Carrier and Chapman.

The [intermediate] appellate court affirmed the judgments. . . .

The defendants contend that the damages awarded to the plaintiffs are excessive. Before resolving this question, we will briefly summarize the evidence presented at trial regarding the two women's injuries.

Keva Richardson was 23 years old at the time of the accident. She grew up in Pampa, Texas, and received a bachelor's degree in elementary education in May 1987 from Texas Tech University. While in college, she participated in a number of athletic activities and was, by all accounts, a popular, happy person. After graduating from college, Keva obtained a position as a flight attendant with American Airlines. She planned to work in that capacity for several years before returning to school to gain a post-graduate degree in education; her ultimate goal was to teach. Keva met Ann McGregor in the flight attendant training program, and the two decided to room together upon completion of their training. At the conclusion of the program, they were assigned to the Chicago area, and they had moved there just several days before the accident occurred.

Following the accident, Keva was initially taken to Highland Park Hospital for treatment. Because of the seriousness of her injuries, however, Keva was transferred that morning to Northwestern Memorial Hospital. Dr. Giri Gereesan, an orthopedic surgeon specializing in spinal surgery, determined that Keva had incurred a fracture of the fifth cervical vertebra, which severely damaged her spinal cord and resulted in incomplete quadriplegia. Dr. Gereesan performed surgery on Keva on December 1, 1987, to stabilize her spine so that she would be able to support her head; the surgery did not repair the damage to her spinal cord, and no treatment exists that could do so.

Keva was transferred to the Rehabilitation Institute of Chicago in December 1987, where she came under the care of Dr. Gary Yarkony. Keva was initially dependent on others in all aspects of her daily life. At the Rehabilitation Institute she learned how to perform a number of basic tasks, such as sitting in a wheelchair, transferring from a bed to a wheelchair, brushing her teeth, washing her face, and putting on loose-fitting tops. Keva's initial stay at the Rehabilitation Institute lasted until April 1988, when she moved to her parents' home in Texas. Keva returned to the Rehabilitation Institute in 1988 and in 1989 for follow-up visits. Keva also required hospitalization in Texas on three subsequent occasions for treatment of conditions arising from the accident.

Testifying in Keva's behalf at trial, Dr. Gary Yarkony, who had served as her primary physician at the Rehabilitation Institute, described Keva's current condition. He explained that she cannot use her legs and that she has only limited functioning in her arms, with loss of control of her fingers and fine muscles in her hands. She suffers pain in her legs and shoulders. Her chest and abdomen are paralyzed, and she has restrictive pulmonary disease. In addition, she has no control over her bladder or bowel functions and requires assistance in emptying them. As a consequence of her physical condition, she is at risk for bladder infections, pneumonia, and pressure ulcers. Keva also suffered a number of facial injuries in the accident. Some of these scars were later repaired through plastic surgery, but others remain.

At trial, Keva's mother, Dixie Richardson, described her daughter's current activities and the level of care necessary to assist her in her daily routine. Keva requires help in taking a shower and getting dressed. She cannot put on underwear, socks, or pants by herself but is able to put on pullover shirts and sweaters. With assistance, she can brush her teeth, apply makeup, and put in her contact lenses. She is unable to cut food or button a sweater. She can push her wheelchair on a smooth, level surface but otherwise needs assistance. In her own testimony, Keva said that she is self-conscious about her appearance now and the impression she makes on others. She said that the thing she misses most is just being able to get up in the morning and begin her day; now she requires the assistance of others, throughout the day.

The jury awarded Richardson a total of $22,358,814 in damages, divided among the following six elements: $258,814 for past medical care; $11,000,000 for future medical care; $900,000 for past and future lost earnings; $3,500,000 for disability; $2,100,000 for disfigurement; and $4,600,000 for pain and suffering. In challenging Richardson's award of damages, the defendants first argue that the sum of the future medical costs found by the jury — $11,000,000 — is not supported by the evidence, for it exceeds even the larger of the two figures supplied by [Richardson's expert], $9,570,034. The defendants contend that the decision to award Richardson nearly $1.5 million more illustrates the jury's failure to properly determine damages in this case.

In response, Richardson argues that the larger award may simply be attributable to the jury's decision to make an award of expenses that she is likely to incur in the future but that were not specifically included in the calculations performed by [her expert]. Richardson thus argues that the jury's decision to award an amount for future medical costs greater than Professor Linke's higher estimate might simply reflect the jury's desire to compensate her for those unspecified but likely expenses. We agree with Richardson that the trier of fact enjoys a certain degree of leeway in awarding compensation for medical costs that, as shown by the evidence, are likely to arise in the future but are not specifically itemized in the testimony. In the present case, however, the amount awarded by the jury for future medical costs is nearly $1.5 million more than the higher of the two figures claimed at trial by Richardson. . . . Given the disparity between the trial testimony and the jury's eventual award, we will not attribute the entire difference between those sums simply to miscellaneous costs Richardson is likely to incur in the future. For these reasons, we conclude that it is appropriate, by way of remittitur, to reduce by $1 million the nearly $1.5 million differential between the award for Richardson's future medical expenses and the higher figure presented in the testimony. This adjustment allows Richardson recovery for expected future medical costs for which no specific estimates were introduced, yet is not so large that it represents a departure from the trial testimony.

We do not agree with the defendants, however, that the remainder of the award of damages to Richardson, including the sums for pain and suffering, disability, and disfigurement, is duplicative or excessive or lacks support in the record. The determination of damages is a question reserved to the trier of fact, and a reviewing court will not lightly substitute its opinion for the judgment rendered in the trial court. An award of damages will be deemed excessive if it falls outside the range of fair and reasonable compensation or results from passion or prejudice, or if it is so large that it shocks the judicial conscience. When reviewing an award of compensatory damages for a nonfatal injury, a court may consider, among other things, the permanency of the plaintiff's condition, the possibility of future deterioration, the extent of the plaintiff's medical expenses, and the restrictions imposed on the plaintiff by the injuries.

Here, it was the jury's function to consider the credibility of the witnesses and to determine an appropriate award of damages. We cannot say that the present award to Richardson is the result of passion or prejudice, "shocks the conscience," or lacks support in the evidence. The record shows that Richardson suffered devastating, disabling injuries as a consequence of the accident. The defendants urge us to compare Richardson's damages with amounts awarded in other cases. Courts in this state, however, have traditionally declined to make such comparisons in determining whether a particular award is excessive and we do not believe that such comparisons would be helpful here.

The defendants also contend that the jury's award of damages to Ann McGregor is excessive. McGregor was 22 years old at the time of the accident. She grew up in Houston, Texas, and graduated from Southern Methodist University in May 1987 with a degree in psychology. Like Keva Richardson, McGregor was accepted after graduation for a position as a flight attendant with American Airlines. As mentioned earlier, the two women met while enrolled in the flight attendant training program and were sharing an apartment in the Chicago area at the time of the accident. Following the accident, McGregor was taken to Highland Park Hospital, where she was treated and released that day; she was then off work for about two weeks. A laceration she suffered on her forehead eventually healed, with only minimal scarring. At trial McGregor testified that she continues to suffer from nightmares about the accident. The jury awarded McGregor a total of $102,215 in damages, divided among the following components: $1,615 for past medical expenses, $600 for lost earnings, and $100,000 for pain and suffering.

[W]e believe that the award of $100,000 for pain and suffering is, in these circumstances, excessive. McGregor was not seriously injured in the accident, incurring a laceration on her forehead, which left only a slight scar. The jury declined to award McGregor any compensation for disfigurement; rather, the bulk of her recovery consisted of compensation for pain and suffering. We conclude that a more appropriate figure for pain and suffering would be $50,000, which would reduce her total damages to $52,215. By way of remittitur, we accordingly reduce the judgment entered in favor of McGregor and against Tandem/Carrier and Chapman to that amount.

For the reasons stated, . . . we affirm the judgments entered in favor of plaintiffs and against Tandem/Carrier and Chapman in their reduced amounts. In the absence of consent to the entry of a remittitur by each plaintiff within 21 days of the filing of this opinion or any further period in which the mandate is stayed, her individual action will be remanded to the circuit court of Cook County for a new trial on the question of damages. . . .

Judgments affirmed in part, reversed in part, and vacated in part; cause remanded.

[Justice McMorrow's concurring/dissenting opinion is omitted.]

FOOD FOR THOUGHT

The court in *Anderson* set about determining whether the verdict was excessive by calculating the maximum value a reasonable jury could place on each element of damages claimed by the plaintiff and then totaling the elements to determine the maximum reasonable award in the case. The court in *Richardson* suggested several tests for determining the reasonableness of the jury's verdict, including whether the verdict "falls outside the range of reasonable and fair compensation," "results from passion or prejudice," or "is so large that it shocks the judicial conscience." In Shipler v. General Motors Corp., 710 N.W.2d 807 (Neb. 2006), the court affirmed a judgment of $18,583,900 for the plaintiff, who was rendered a quadriplegic as a result of a motor vehicle rollover. The court rejected the defendant's argument for a new trial on the ground that the damages were excessive. The court held that there was "no evidence that the damages were excessive or that they were awarded in the heat of passion or under any other undue influence." *Id.* at 840. The court found that the jury had properly evaluated the items it could consider in determining the amount of damages, including the reasonable monetary value of medical care and supplies, lost wages, lost earning capacity, physical pain and suffering, inconvenience, and loss of future enjoyment.

MEASURING ECONOMIC/PECUNIARY LOSSES

Together with medical expenses, the most significant components of economic harm are wage loss and reduced earning capacity. In most jurisdictions, a plaintiff may choose one or the other measure, with wage loss representing specific income lost to the plaintiff both past and future, while reduced earning capacity equals an estimate of lost present and future ability to work, regardless of specific wage losses. If a plaintiff had a steady job prior to injury, lost wages are fairly simple to calculate and not normally a matter of dispute, since the time the plaintiff has missed work in the past and is expected to do so in the future can easily be multiplied by the documented wage the plaintiff had received. Often, however, the issue of economic harm can become complicated, particularly where a plaintiff chooses to seek the remedy of reduced earning capacity. Reduced earning capacity has even been allowed where the plaintiff was unable to show actual earnings before or after the injury. *See* Conwed Corp. v. Union Carbide Corp., 443 F.3d 1032, 1043 (8th Cir. 2006) (applying Minnesota law) (plaintiff need only prove "that an impairment in his or her *power* to earn a living was reasonably certain to occur as a result of the injuries").

An example will help to clarify this concept of a reduction in the capacity to earn. Imagine an attorney who loses an arm in an accident. The attorney is likely to be able to continue earning the same amount after the injury as she did before, and it appears a reduction in earning capacity has not occurred. However, such a plaintiff may desire to have the choice of some day taking a job for which two arms would be beneficial. Indeed, a stressed-out attorney may want to move to the country to pitch hay for a living. Thus, the attorney has experienced a reduced capacity to earn a living. When a plaintiff shows a likely diminution in earnings in the future (perhaps as in our hay-pitching attorney hypothetical), he can recover for this lost earning capacity, but you can understand how such damages can be seen as speculative and hard to measure.

Measurement of economic/pecuniary losses may be further complicated if the plaintiff is not a wage earner at the time of the accident. What if the plaintiff is a full-time homemaker, for example? In such cases, courts allow the plaintiff to recover the value of the services that the injury prevented the plaintiff from providing in the home. *See, e.g.,* Delong v. Erie County, 455 N.Y.S.2d 887 (N.Y. App. Div. 1982) (expert testified that the replacement cost of future services performed by a married 28-year-old mother of three was $527,659). The plaintiff in some cases may alternatively choose recovery based on reduced earning capacity, which reflects the value of work the plaintiff could have performed in the home, or even work the plaintiff could have done outside the home. *See, e.g.,* Alaska Department of Transportation & Public Facilities v. Miller, 145 P.3d 521, 531 (Alaska 2006) ("A plaintiff whose actual lost earnings are negligible or nonexistent may still be compensated for lost earning capacity, even where the lack of actual earnings is a result of the plaintiff's own choices"); Nelson v. Patrick, 326 S.E.2d 45 (N.C. Ct. App. 1985); Richard A. Posner, *Economic Analysis of Law* 209-214 (5th ed. 1998).

In cases where the plaintiff was employed at the time of injury, she typically will use expert testimony to estimate her expected income stream over the projected period of disability. The difference between the future expected earnings with and without injury represents the sum required to place the plaintiff in her pre-injury condition. Thus, if the plaintiff's income has been reduced from $60,000 to $50,000 per year, and the disability will continue for ten years, the unadjusted total loss to the plaintiff is $100,000.

Notice the word "unadjusted" in the previous sentence. This reflects the fact that our calculations do not likely represent the final award. Because the plaintiff's recovery even for future losses is paid all at once, many courts reduce the plaintiff's damages to what is known as "present value." Reduction to present value involves adjusting the award downward to reflect the extra value received by being paid now, all at once. Returning to our example above, if the plaintiff receives the full $100,000, she can invest it. Assume that a reasonable annual rate of return for a safe investment is 5 percent. If the plaintiff does invest the $100,000 award at the assumed rate of return, in the first year she would receive $5,000 in interest without invading the principal, an amount that happens to equal one-half of the $10,000 per year by which her income has been reduced. Thus, the opportunity to invest lump-sum awards lowers the amount that must be paid in order to restore the income stream disrupted by the defendant's tortious conduct. Reducing a lump sum award to present value ensures that the plaintiff will receive over the ten-year disability period only the amount that she would have received in earnings had she not been injured. In reducing a sum to present value, courts make educated estimates of what prevailing interest rates on "safe" investments will be in the future. Once the appropriate rate of interest is established, together with the time period over which the hypothetical income will be earned, present value tables indicate the lump-sum amounts that plaintiffs are entitled to receive.

Another factor that may influence the calculation of awards for economic/pecuniary losses is future inflation. While it is true that the plaintiff's receipt of a lump sum will, unless reduced to present value, give her a financial advantage, it is also true that the money she is given now will almost certainly become less valuable as time passes, due to the general inflationary trends in the U.S. economy. To compensate for this, some courts adjust plaintiffs' awards upward to compensate for future inflation. This adjustment can also apply to awards for items other than loss of earning capacity. For example, plaintiffs who are awarded money to cover the cost of future medical care can have their awards adjusted upward for inflation, since it is reasonable to assume that the costs of medical care will rise, along with other prices, in the future.

In addition to the difficulties of adjusting economic awards for the effects of investment returns and inflation, courts must also deal with other problems of evaluating claims for lost future wages and earning capacity. For instance, it is not always easy to predict the future income of a plaintiff. What about permanently incapacitated plaintiffs who are children, such as the plaintiff in *Anderson*, who have not yet entered the workforce? Assuming that they should be compensated for future loss of earning capacity, how should we calculate their loss? When courts have good reason to believe that a young plaintiff would have pursued a particular profession or earned a particular salary, especially when the young plaintiff has already embarked on a career path at time of injury, they may allow juries to award a sum based on that profession or salary. For example, a plaintiff who had planned on becoming an attorney might be able to recover for loss of earning capacity as an attorney if she were already in law school at the time of the defendant's injury-causing behavior, but might not recover based on a future attorney's income if she were still in high school, or even college. *See, e.g.*, Kenyon v. Hyatt Hotels Corp., 693 S.W.2d 83 (Mo. 1985) (plaintiff law student who had completed two years of law school was awarded $4 million as a result of her injuries, which prevented her completion of school); Waldorf v. Shuta, 896 F.2d 723 (3d Cir. 1990) (plaintiff, recipient of high school equivalency diploma who was only partway through a two-year associate degree program, was denied recovery based on future earnings as an attorney). In one case, where the plaintiff was a professional baseball player who was injured while still in the minor leagues, the court allowed the plaintiff to recover damages based on his potential as a major league prospect. *See* Felder v. Physiotherapy Assocs., 158 P.3d 877 (Ariz. App. Div. 2007).

There have been many approaches to these problems, including reliance on intelligence tests, family background, and the minimum wage. *See* Martin v. United States, 471 F. Supp. 6 (D. Ariz. 1979); Altman v. Alpha Obstetrics and Gynecology, P.C., 679 N.Y.S.2d 642 (N.Y. App. Div. 1998); McNeill v. United States, 519 F. Supp. 283 (D.S.C. 1981). What about gender-related salary differences? Should young female plaintiffs receive less than their male counterparts because they will probably earn less on average? *See* Martha Chamallas, *Questioning the Use of Race-Specific and Gender-Specific Economic Data in Tort Litigation: A Constitutional Argument*, 63 Fordham L. Rev. 73, 75 (1994) (arguing that such distinctions tend to perpetuate discrimination). *See also* Lucinda M. Finley, *The Hidden Victims of Tort Reform: Women, Children, and the Elderly*, 53 Emory L.J. 1263, 1281 (2004) (arguing that women, minorities, and the poor receive less compensation for past or future wage loss than do white males).

Another interesting facet to the adjustment of tort awards is that compensatory damages are not taxed as income, even when they represent losses of earnings. This can make a large difference in the amount of money a plaintiff receives from a tort award versus the amount she would have received from earnings, which are taxable. However, most courts have not allowed tax-related adjustments of tort judgments, largely because future events are too uncertain for any accurate future estimate of tax liability to be made. It is nearly impossible to project, for example, the number and amount of deductions the plaintiff would have taken in future years, the tax rate that would apply to her income level, or whether she would have had any other income. In fact, in most jurisdictions, the court cannot even tell the jury that the award is tax free, for fear that the jury will try to adjust the award downward based on ad hoc guesses at the value of the tax savings. One exception to this general rule relates to tort actions based on federal law, where courts have held that juries can be informed of the tax-free nature of the award. *See* Norfolk & Western Ry. v. Liepelt, 444 U.S. 490 (1980) (juries can be informed of the tax-free nature of any award in Federal Employers' Liability Act actions); Fanetti v. Hellenic Lines Ltd., 678 F.2d 424 (2d Cir. 1982), *cert. denied*, 463 U.S. 1206 (1983) (applying the rule of *Norfolk* to all actions based on federal law). *But see* Blake v. Clein, 903 So. 2d 710 (Miss. 2005). *See generally* Joseph M. Dodge, *Taxes and Torts*, 77 Cornell L. Rev. 143 (1992).

NONECONOMIC/NONPECUNIARY LOSSES

While a number of problems plague courts as they try to assess damages for economic/pecuniary losses, the difficulties surrounding measurement of noneconomic damages are even greater. When tort law places a value on things that are continually bought and sold in the marketplace, such as labor, medical services, or care giving for the disabled, it has a comparatively easy frame of reference for its evaluation of what the plaintiff has lost. However, with respect to items that inherently cannot be bought and sold, such as pain and suffering, there is no standard price to which tort may refer. Indeed, even if such items were part of a theoretical "marketplace," evaluation might not be any easier. Imagine for a moment that someone offered you money if you would go through some very difficult emotional trauma or agree to suffer intense physical pain. What price would you agree to? Is there any such price? If there is such a price, is it a useful guide for assessing damages against tortfeasors? Would any tortfeasor be able to pay the amount such an approach might call for? Can we fairly insist that tortfeasors pay such a price?

Since we cannot value these intangible items, or at least are not willing to fully compensate victims for them, why allow tort damages for them in the first place? At one level, the answer may be simple: we believe that these harms are real, and that plaintiffs do indeed suffer as a result of them. While we realize money cannot fully alleviate such losses, we nevertheless feel compelled to make defendants at least attempt to compensate for them. In the end we leave it to the jury to say, within reasonable limits, how much the plaintiff should be compensated.

The most common element of noneconomic/nonpecuniary damages is pain and suffering. Plaintiffs can recover for both past and future pain and suffering. In the case of future pain and suffering the plaintiff must establish (normally through expert testimony) that certain elements of the pain resulting from the injury will continue into the future, or that necessary medical care in the future will entail pain and suffering. Because this type of damages award is supposed to compensate for pain the plaintiff actually experiences, she must be conscious in order to recover. This usually becomes an issue when the plaintiff's injuries are severe and the plaintiff dies a short time after the accident caused by the defendant's tortious conduct. In such cases, the consciousness or unconsciousness of the plaintiff between the time of the accident and the time of death becomes important to the determination of an appropriate damage award.

McDOUGALD v. GARBER
536 N.E.2d 372 (N.Y. 1989)

WACHTLER, Chief Judge.

This appeal raises fundamental questions about the nature and role of nonpecuniary damages in personal injury litigation. By nonpecuniary damages, we mean those damages awarded to compensate an injured person for the physical and emotional consequences of the injury, such as pain and suffering and the loss of the ability to engage in certain activities. Pecuniary damages, on the other hand, compensate the victim for the economic consequences of the injury, such as medical expenses, lost earnings and the cost of custodial care.

The specific questions raised here deal with the assessment of nonpecuniary damages and are (1) whether some degree of cognitive awareness is a prerequisite to recovery for loss of enjoyment of life and (2) whether a jury should be instructed to consider and award damages for loss of enjoyment of life separately from damages for pain and suffering. We answer the first question in the affirmative and the second question in the negative.

I.

On September 7, 1978, plaintiff Emma McDougald, then 31 years old, underwent a Caesarean section and tubal ligation at New York Infirmary. Defendant Garber performed the surgery; defendants Armengol and Kulkarni provided anesthesia. During the surgery, Mrs. McDougald suffered oxygen deprivation which resulted in severe brain damage and left her in a permanent comatose condition. This action was brought by Mrs. McDougald and her husband, suing derivatively, alleging that the injuries were caused by the defendants' acts of malpractice.

A jury found all defendants liable and awarded Emma McDougald a total of $9,650,102 in damages, including $1,000,000 for conscious pain and suffering and a separate award of $3,500,000 for loss of the pleasures and pursuits of life. The balance of the damages awarded to her were for pecuniary damages — lost earnings and the cost of custodial and nursing care. Her husband was awarded $1,500,000 on his derivative claim for the loss of his wife's services. On defendants' posttrial motions, the Trial Judge reduced the total award to Emma McDougald to $4,796,728 by striking the entire award for future nursing care ($2,353,374) and by reducing the separate awards for conscious pain and suffering and loss of the pleasures and pursuits of life to a single award of $2,000,000 (McDougald v. Garber, 132 Misc. 2d 457). Her husband's award was left intact. On cross appeals, the Appellate Division affirmed (135 A.D.2d 80) and later granted defendants leave to appeal to this court.

II.

At trial, defendants sought to show that Mrs. McDougald's injuries were so severe that she was incapable of either experiencing pain or appreciating her condition. Plaintiffs, on the other hand, introduced proof that Mrs. McDougald responded to certain stimuli to a sufficient extent to indicate that she was aware of her circumstances. Thus, the extent of Mrs. McDougald's cognitive abilities, if any, was sharply disputed. The parties and the trial court agreed that Mrs. McDougald could not recover for pain and suffering unless she were conscious of the pain. Defendants maintained that such consciousness was also required to support an award for loss of enjoyment of life. The court, however, accepted plaintiffs' view that loss of enjoyment of life was compensable without regard to whether the plaintiff was aware of the loss. Accordingly, because the level of Mrs. McDougald's cognitive abilities was in dispute, the court instructed the jury to consider loss of enjoyment of life as an element of nonpecuniary damages separate from pain and suffering. . . .

We conclude that the court erred, both in instructing the jury that Mrs. McDougald's awareness was irrelevant to their consideration of damages for loss of enjoyment of life and in directing the jury to consider that aspect of damages separately from pain and suffering.

III.

We begin with the familiar proposition that an award of damages to a person injured by the negligence of another is to compensate the victim, not to punish the wrongdoer. The goal is to restore the injured party, to the extent possible, to the position that would have been occupied had the wrong not occurred. To be sure, placing the burden of compensation on the negligent party also serves as a deterrent, but purely punitive damages — that is, those which have no compensatory purpose — are prohibited unless the harmful conduct is intentional, malicious, outrageous, or otherwise aggravated beyond mere negligence.

Damages for nonpecuniary losses are, of course, among those that can be awarded as compensation to the victim. This aspect of damages, however, stands on less certain ground than does an award for pecuniary damages. An economic loss can be compensated in kind by an economic gain; but recovery for non-economic losses such as pain and suffering and loss of enjoyment of life rests on "the legal fiction that money damages can compensate for a victim's injury" (Howard v. Lecher, 42 N.Y.2d 109, 111, 397 N.Y.S.2d 363, 366 N.E.2d 64). We accept this fiction, knowing that although money will neither ease the pain nor restore the victim's abilities, this device is as close as the law can come in its effort to right the wrong. We have no hope of evaluating what has been lost, but a monetary award may provide a measure of solace for the condition created.

Our willingness to indulge this fiction comes to an end, however, when it ceases to serve the compensatory goals of tort recovery. When that limit is met, further indulgence can only result in assessing damages that are punitive. The question posed by this case, then, is whether an award of damages for loss of enjoyment of life to a person whose injuries preclude any awareness of the loss serves a compensatory purpose. We conclude that it does not.

Simply put, an award of money damages in such circumstances has no meaning or utility to the injured person. An award for the loss of enjoyment of life "cannot provide [such a victim] with any consolation or ease any burden resting on him. . . . He cannot spend it upon necessities or pleasures. He cannot experience the pleasure of giving it away" (Flannery v. United States, 718 F.2d 108, 111, *cert. denied*, 467 US 1226, 104 S. Ct. 2679, 81 L. Ed. 2d 874).

We recognize that, as the trial court noted, requiring some cognitive awareness as a prerequisite to recovery for loss of enjoyment of life will result in some cases "in the paradoxical situation that the greater the degree of brain injury inflicted by a negligent defendant, the smaller the award the plaintiff can recover in general damages" (McDougald v. Garber, 132 Misc. 2d 457, 460, *supra*). The force of this argument, however — the temptation to achieve a balance between injury and damages — has nothing to do with meaningful compensation for the victim. Instead, the temptation is rooted in a desire to punish the defendant in proportion to the harm inflicted. However relevant such retributive symmetry may be in the criminal law, it has no place in the law of civil damages, at least in the absence of culpability beyond mere negligence.

Accordingly, we conclude that cognitive awareness is a prerequisite to recovery for loss of enjoyment of life. We do not go so far, however, as to require the fact finder to sort out varying degrees of cognition and determine at what level a particular deprivation can be fully appreciated. With respect to pain and suffering, the trial court charged simply that there must be "some level of awareness" in order for plaintiff to recover. We think that this is an appropriate standard for all aspects of nonpecuniary loss. No doubt the standard ignores analytically relevant levels of cognition, but we resist the desire for analytical purity in favor of simplicity. A more complex instruction might give the appearance of greater precision but, given the limits of our understanding of the human mind, it would in reality lead only to greater speculation. We turn next to the question whether loss of enjoyment of life should be considered a category of damages separate from pain and suffering.

IV.

There is no dispute here that the fact finder may, in assessing nonpecuniary damages, consider the effect of the injuries on the plaintiff's capacity to lead a normal life. Traditionally, in this State and elsewhere, this aspect of suffering has not been treated as a separate category of damages; instead, the plaintiff's inability to enjoy life to its fullest has been considered one type of suffering to be factored into a general award for nonpecuniary damages, commonly known as pain and suffering.

Recently, however, there has been an attempt to segregate the suffering associated with physical pain from the mental anguish that stems from the inability to engage in certain activities, and to have juries provide a separate award for each.

Some courts have resisted the effort, primarily on the ground that duplicative and therefore excessive awards would result. Other courts have allowed separate awards, noting that the types of suffering involved are analytically distinguishable. Still other courts have questioned the propriety of the practice but held that, in the particular case, separate awards did not constitute reversible error. . . .

We do not dispute that distinctions can be found or created between the concepts of pain and suffering and loss of enjoyment of life. If the term "suffering" is limited to the emotional response to the sensation of pain, then the emotional response caused by the limitation of life's activities may be considered qualitatively different. But suffering need not be so limited — it can easily encompass the frustration and anguish caused by the inability to participate in activities that once brought pleasure. Traditionally, by treating loss of enjoyment of life as a permissible factor in assessing pain and suffering, courts have given the term this broad meaning.

If we are to depart from this traditional approach and approve a separate award for loss of enjoyment of life, it must be on the basis that such an approach will yield a more accurate evaluation of the compensation due to the plaintiff. We have no doubt that, in general, the total award for nonpecuniary damages would increase if we adopted the rule. That separate awards are advocated by plaintiffs and resisted by defendants is sufficient evidence that larger awards are at stake here. But a larger award does not by itself indicate that the goal of compensation has been better served.

The advocates of separate awards contend that because pain and suffering and loss of enjoyment of life can be distinguished, they must be treated separately if the plaintiff is to be compensated fully for each distinct injury suffered. We disagree. Such an analytical approach may have its place when the subject is pecuniary damages, which can be calculated with some precision. But the estimation of nonpecuniary damages is not amenable to such analytical precision and may, in fact, suffer from its application. Translating human suffering into dollars and cents involves no mathematical formula; it rests, as we have said, on a legal fiction. The figure that emerges is unavoidably distorted by the translation. Application of this murky process to the component parts of nonpecuniary injuries (however analytically distinguishable they may be) cannot make it more accurate. If anything, the distortion will be amplified by repetition.

Thus, we are not persuaded that any salutary purpose would be served by having the jury make separate awards for pain and suffering and loss of enjoyment of life. We are confident, furthermore, that the trial advocate's art is a sufficient guarantee that none of the plaintiff's losses will be ignored by the jury.

The errors in the instructions given to the jury require a new trial on the issue of nonpecuniary damages to be awarded to plaintiff Emma McDougald. Defendants' remaining contentions are either without merit, beyond the scope of our review or are rendered academic by our disposition of the case.

Accordingly, the order of the Appellate Division, insofar as appealed from, should be modified, with costs to defendants, by granting a new trial on the issue of nonpecuniary damages of plaintiff Emma McDougald, and as so modified, affirmed.

TITONE, Judge (dissenting).

The majority's holding represents a compromise position that neither comports with the fundamental principles of tort compensation nor furnishes a satisfactory, logically consistent framework for compensating nonpecuniary loss. Because I conclude that loss of enjoyment of life is an objective damage item, conceptually distinct from conscious pain and suffering, I can find no fault with the trial court's instruction authorizing separate awards and permitting an award for "loss of enjoyment of life" even in the absence of any awareness of that loss on the part of the injured plaintiff. Accordingly, I dissent.

It is elementary that the purpose of awarding tort damages is to compensate the wronged party for the actual loss he or she has sustained. Personal injury damages are awarded "to restore the injured person to the state of health he had prior to his injuries because that is the only way the law knows how to recompense one for personal injuries suffered" (Romeo v. New York City Tr. Auth., 73 Misc. 2d 124, 126, 341 N.Y.S.2d 733; [other citations omitted]). Thus, this court has held that "[t]he person responsible for the injury must respond for all damages resulting directly from and as a natural consequence of the wrongful act" (Steitz v. Gifford, 280 N.Y. 15, 20, 19 N.E.2d 661).

The capacity to enjoy life — by watching one's children grow, participating in recreational activities, and drinking in the many other pleasures that life has to offer — is unquestionably an attribute of an ordinary healthy individual. The loss of that capacity as a result of another's negligent act is at least as serious an impairment as the permanent destruction of a physical function, which has always been treated as a compensable item under traditional tort principles. Indeed, I can imagine no physical loss that is more central to the quality of a tort victim's continuing life than the destruction of the capacity to enjoy that life to the fullest.

Unquestionably, recovery of a damage item such as "pain and suffering" requires a showing of some degree of cognitive capacity. Such a requirement exists for the simple reason that pain and suffering are wholly subjective concepts and cannot exist separate and apart from the human consciousness that experiences them. In contrast, the destruction of an individual's capacity to enjoy life as a result of a crippling injury is an objective fact that does not differ in principle from the permanent loss of an eye or limb. As in the case of a lost limb, an essential characteristic of a healthy human life has been wrongfully taken, and, consequently, the injured party is entitled to a monetary award as a substitute, if, as the majority asserts, the goal of tort compensation is "to restore the injured party, to the extent possible, to the position that would have been occupied had the wrong not occurred" (majority opn., at 254, at 939 of 538 N.Y.S.2d, at 374 of 536 N.E.2d).

Significantly, this equation does not suggest a need to establish the injured's awareness of the loss. The victim's ability to comprehend the degree to which his or her life has been impaired is irrelevant, since, unlike "conscious pain and suffering," the impairment exists independent of the victim's ability to apprehend it. Indeed, the majority reaches the conclusion that a degree of awareness must be shown only after injecting a new element into the equation. Under the majority's formulation, the victim must be aware of the loss because, in addition to being compensatory, the award must have "meaning or utility to the injured person." (Majority opn., at 254, at 940 of 538 N.Y.S.2d, at 375 of 536 N.E.2d.) This additional requirement, however, has no real foundation in law or logic. "Meaning" and "utility" are subjective value judgments that have no place in the law of tort recovery, where the primary goal is to find ways of quantifying, to the extent possible, the worth of various forms of human tragedy.

Moreover, the compensatory nature of a monetary award for loss of enjoyment of life is not altered or rendered punitive by the fact that the unaware injured plaintiff cannot experience the pleasure of having it. The fundamental distinction between punitive and compensatory damages is that the former exceed the amount necessary to replace what the plaintiff lost. As the Court of Appeals for the Second Circuit has observed, "[t]he fact that the compensation [for loss of enjoyment of life] may inure as a practical matter to third parties in a given case does not transform the nature of the damages" (Rufino v. United States, 829 F.2d 354, 362).

Ironically, the majority's expressed goal of limiting recovery for nonpecuniary loss to compensation that the injured plaintiff has the capacity to appreciate is directly undercut by the majority's ultimate holding, adopted in the interest of "simplicity," that recovery for loss of enjoyment of life may be had as long as the injured plaintiff has "some level of awareness," however slight (majority opn., at 255, at 940 of 538 N.Y.S.2d, at 375 of 536 N.E.2d). Manifestly, there are many different forms and levels of awareness, particularly in cases involving brain injury. Further, the type and degree of cognitive functioning necessary to experience "pain and suffering" is certainly of a lower order than that needed to apprehend the loss of the ability to enjoy life in all of its subtleties. Accordingly, the existence of "some level of awareness" on the part of the injured plaintiff says nothing about that plaintiff's ability to derive some comfort from the award or even to appreciate its significance. Hence, that standard does not assure that loss of enjoyment of life damages will be awarded only when they serve "a compensatory purpose," as that term is defined by the majority.

In the final analysis, the rule that the majority has chosen is an arbitrary one, in that it denies or allows recovery on the basis of a criterion that is not truly related to its stated goal. In my view, it is fundamentally unsound, as well as grossly unfair, to deny recovery to those who are completely without cognitive capacity while permitting it for those with a mere spark of awareness, regardless of the latter's ability to appreciate either the loss sustained or the benefits of the monetary award offered in compensation. In both instances, the injured plaintiff is in essentially the same position, and an award that is punitive as to one is equally punitive as to the other. Of course, since I do not subscribe to the majority's conclusion that an award to an unaware plaintiff is punitive, I would have no difficulty permitting recovery to both classes of plaintiffs.

Having concluded that the injured plaintiff's awareness should not be a necessary precondition to recovery for loss of enjoyment of life, I also have no difficulty going on to conclude that loss of enjoyment of life is a distinct damage item which is recoverable separate and apart from the award for conscious pain and suffering. The majority has rejected separate recovery, in part because it apparently perceives some overlap between the two damage categories and in part because it believes that the goal of enhancing the precision of jury awards for nonpecuniary loss would not be advanced. However, the overlap the majority perceives exists only if one assumes, as the majority evidently has (*see*, majority opn., at 256-257, at 940-942 of 538 N.Y.S.2d, at 375-377 of 536 N.E.2d), that the "loss of enjoyment" category of damages is designed to compensate only for "the emotional response caused by the limitation of life's activities" and "the frustration and anguish caused by the inability to participate in activities that once brought pleasure" (emphasis added), both of which are highly subjective concepts.

In fact, while "pain and suffering compensates the victim for the physical and mental discomfort caused by the injury; . . . loss of enjoyment of life compensates the victim for the limitations on the person's life created by the injury," a distinctly objective loss (Thompson v. National R.R. Passenger Corp., [6th Cir., 621 F.2d 814, 824, *cert. denied*, 449 U.S. 1035, 101 S. Ct. 611, 66 L. Ed. 2d 497]). In other words, while the victim's "emotional response" and "frustration and anguish" are elements of the award for pain and suffering, the "limitation of life's activities" and the "inability to participate in activities" that the majority identifies are recoverable under the "loss of enjoyment of life" rubric. Thus, there is no real overlap, and no real basis for concern about potentially duplicative awards where, as here, there is a properly instructed jury.

Finally, given the clear distinction between the two categories of nonpecuniary damages, I cannot help but assume that permitting separate awards for conscious pain and suffering and loss of enjoyment of life would contribute to accuracy and precision in thought in the jury's deliberations on the issue of damages. . . . In light of the concrete benefit to be gained by compelling the jury to differentiate between the specific objective and subjective elements of the plaintiff's nonpecuniary loss, I find unpersuasive the majority's reliance on vague concerns about potential distortion owing to the inherently difficult task of computing the value of intangible loss. My belief in the jury system, and in the collective wisdom of the deliberating jury, leads me to conclude that we may safely leave that task in the jurors' hands.

For all of these reasons, I approve of the approach that the trial court adopted in its charge to the jury. Accordingly, I would affirm the order below affirming the judgment.

FOOD FOR THOUGHT

The court in *McDougald* takes the view that, since noneconomic/nonpecuniary damages such as pain and suffering and loss of enjoyment of life can never really compensate the plaintiff, they are awarded only to "provide a measure of solace for the condition created." Do you agree with the court? If not, what do you think is the purpose of awarding noneconomic damages?

The damages that the trial court allowed the jury to award in *McDougald*, for loss of enjoyment of life, are also called "hedonic damages" (taken from the Greek word for pleasure). In courts that allow such damages to be calculated separately from pain and suffering, they compensate the plaintiff for loss of the ability to do things the plaintiff enjoys. A distinction often made between this form of damages and pain and suffering is that pain and suffering damages compensate the plaintiff for negative sensations she experiences as a result of the injury, whereas loss of enjoyment of life damages compensate the plaintiff for the inability to experience certain positive sensations. Is this distinction useful? Vacuous? In any event, the New York Court of Appeals in *McDougald* held that loss of enjoyment of life should be considered part of the general pain and suffering category of damages. What do you think? Will collapsing the two categories help or hinder the goal of fully compensating the plaintiff? Is "loss of pleasurable sensation" equivalent to "suffering"? *See* Fantozzi v. Sandusky Cement Products Co., 597 N.E.2d 474 (Ohio 1992) (holding that loss of enjoyment of life is separately compensable in some circumstances). *See also* McGee v. AC & S, Inc., 933 So. 2d 770, 775 (La. 2006), in which the court distinguished loss of enjoyment of life from other components of compensatory damages. Defining loss of enjoyment of life as "detrimental alterations of the person's life or lifestyle or the person's inability to participate in the activities or pleasures of life that were formerly enjoyed prior to the injury," the court held that loss of enjoyment of life is recoverable as an element of general damages that may be included as a separate item on the jury verdict form. *Id.* at 772-773. For a sharply critical appraisal of the separate awarding of hedonic damages, *see* Victor E. Schwartz & Cary Silverman, *Hedonic Damages: The Rapidly Bubbling Cauldron*, 69 Brook. L. Rev. 1037 (2004) (arguing that hedonic damages create a risk of redundancy, may be used to circumvent existing liability rules, promote large, arbitrary awards, and provide little basis for meaningful appellate review).

SENSORY LOSS AND DISFIGUREMENT

Other important elements of noneconomic/nonpecuniary damages, closely related to loss of enjoyment of life, are loss of sensory function and disfigurement. These elements of damages compensate the plaintiff for permanent, or temporary, loss of the ability to enjoy in pleasurable sensory perceptions and for any permanent changes in the plaintiff's appearance. In *Anderson, supra,* the court allowed the plaintiff to recover for changes to her appearance caused by the accident. Courts have allowed recovery for many different kinds of sensory disabilities and disfigurement, including impotency, Guilbeaux v. Lafayette General Hospital, 589 So. 2d 629 (La. Ct. App. 1991); incontinence, Curtiss v. YMCA, 511 P.2d 991 (Wash. 1973); loss of short-term memory and sense of smell, Braud v. Painter, 730 F. Supp. 1 (M.D. La. 1990); and loss of ability to climb stairs and drive a car, Ramos v. Kuzas, 600 N.E.2d 241 (Ohio 1992). In Ocampo v. Paper Converting Machine Co., 2005 U.S. Dist. LEXIS 17107 (N.D. Ill. 2005), the plaintiff suffered permanent disfigurement after she was "scalped" when her long hair got caught in workplace machinery. The trial court entered judgment on a jury verdict of $5,612,000, of which $2,300,000 were damages for disfigurement.

MEASURING NONECONOMIC/NONPECUNIARY LOSSES

Some courts have allowed controversial techniques to help juries measure the value of noneconomic losses to the plaintiff. One technique, known as the per diem argument, divides the plaintiff's pain and suffering into discrete units of time, such as days or hours, or even minutes or seconds, and assigns a monetary value to each unit. The jury is asked to determine the relevant value and then to multiply that value by the number of units of time the plaintiff has endured and will endure, to reach a total pain and suffering figure. Some jurisdictions do not allow counsel for the plaintiff to make this argument. In Caley v. Manicke, 182 N.E.2d 206 (Ill. 1962), the Supreme Court of Illinois explained its reasons for disallowing such arguments:

> Those courts that have allowed counsel to use a formula and figures in argument generally do so because they feel (1) that a jury's determination of reasonable compensation for pain and suffering is arrived at by "a blind guess" and (2) that the jury needs to be guided by some reasonable and practical consideration. We do not take such a dim view of the jury's reasoning processes.
>
> . . . While a jury cannot translate pain and suffering into monetary units with the precision that it would employ in converting feet into inches, we do not believe that its determination of reasonable compensation for pain and suffering can be characterized as a "blind guess." To reduce the aggregate into hours and minutes, and then multiply by the number of time units involved produces an illusion of certainty, but it is only an illusion, for there is no more precision in the one case than in the other.
>
> . . . It begs the question to say that the jury needs to be guided by some reasonable and practical consideration. A formula by definition is a "conventional rule

or method for something, especially when used, applied, or repeated without thought." (Webster's New Twentieth Century Dictionary, 2 ed. (1958).) It would appear that a formula, rather than encouraging reasonable and practical consideration, would tend to discourage such consideration.

Jurors are as familiar with pain and suffering and with money as are counsel. We are of the opinion that an impartial jury which has been properly informed by the evidence and the court's instructions will, by the exercise of its conscience and sound judgment, be better able to determine reasonable compensation than it would if it were subjected to expressions of counsels' partisan conscience and judgment on the matter.

In Beagle v. Vasold, 417 P.2d 673 (Cal. 1966), the Supreme Court of California disagreed with this assessment, noting (*Id.* at 680):

> . . . [Two common] objections made to the use of a mathematical formula are that it produces an illusion of certainty which appeals to the jury but can only mislead it [citation omitted] and that it can result in grossly magnifying the total damages by shrewd manipulation of the unit of time employed.
> . . . There are at least two answers to the foregoing objections. First, whatever manner of calculation is proposed by counsel or employed by the jury, the verdict must meet the test of reasonableness. The "per diem" argument is only a suggestion as to one method of reaching the goal of reasonableness, not a substitute for it. If the jury's award does not meet this test, the trial court has the duty to reduce it, and the appellate court has the authority to review the result. . . . [T]here is no convincing assurance that the accuracy of [the jury's] evaluation would be enhanced by prohibiting counsel from suggesting that the plaintiff's compensation for pain and suffering be measured in aggregates of short periods of time rather than by a total sum award for a longer period.
> . . . [Second, u]nder some circumstances, the concept of pain and suffering may become more meaningful when it is measured in short periods of time. . . . The "worth" of pain over a period of decades is often more difficult to grasp as a concept of reality than is the same experience limited to a day, a week or a month. It is this very consideration which underlies much of the controversy over the issue before us. The fact that the "per diem" argument provides a more explicit comprehension and humanization of the plaintiff's predicament to lay jurors makes this approach an effective tool in the hands of his attorney. This alone is not, however, a sufficient reason to condemn it.

In any event, many U.S. jurisdictions permit some form of the per diem argument. A substantial minority do not allow the argument at all.

Noneconomic/nonpecuniary damages for future suffering are generally not reduced to present value. *See, e.g.,* Purdy v. Belcher Refining Co., 781 F. Supp. 1559 (S.D. Ala. 1992); Friedman v. C & S Car Service, 527 A.2d 871 (N.J. 1987); Texas & Pac. Ry. Co. v. Buckles, 232 F.2d 257 (5th Cir.), *cert. denied,* 351 U.S. 984 (1956) (since these damages do not have a known market value, reducing them to present value is not necessary). However, a minority of courts require that awards for future pain and suffering be reduced. *See, e.g.,* Oliveri v. Delta S.S. Lines, Inc., 849 F.2d 742 (2d Cir. 1988) (since the jury does not make precise calculations as to pain and suffering as it does with future earnings, and since future pain and suffering is compensated now, a less precise discount is appropriate). *See generally* Emily Sherwin, *Compensation and Revenge*, 40 San Diego L. Rev. 1387 (2003), in which the author argues that the "practice of awarding lump sums for future pain and suffering without discounting to present value confirms that these awards are not seriously understood to conform to actual loss." *Id.* at 1393. Instead, Professor Sherwin believes that pain and suffering awards serve goals that have "a close affinity to revenge." *Id.* at 1389.

COYNE v. CAMPBELL
183 N.E.2d 891 (N.Y. 1962)

FROESSEL, J.

On July 5, 1957 plaintiff sustained a whiplash injury when his automobile was struck in the rear by a motor vehicle driven by defendant. Inasmuch as plaintiff is a practicing physician and surgeon, he received medical treatment, physiotherapy and care from his professional colleagues and his nurse, and incurred no out-of-pocket expenses therefor. Nevertheless, in his bill of particulars, he stated that his special damages for medical and nursing care and treatment amounted to $2,235. The trial court ruled that the value of these services was not a proper item of special damages, and that no recovery could be had therefore since they had been rendered gratuitously. He thus excluded evidence as to their value. The sole question here presented is the correctness of this ruling.

In the leading case of Drinkwater v. Dinsmore (80 N.Y. 390) we unanimously reversed a plaintiff's judgment entered upon a jury verdict, because defendant was precluded from showing that plaintiff had been paid his wages by his employer during the period of his incapacitation. We held such evidence admissible on the theory that plaintiff was entitled to recover only his pecuniary losses, of which wages gratuitously paid were not an item. With respect to medical expenses, we stated (p. 393) that "the plaintiff must show what he paid the doctor, and can recover only so much as he paid or was bound to pay." Although decided more than 80 years ago, the *Drinkwater* case has continuously been and still is recognized as the prevailing law of this State.

As recently as 1957, the Legislature declined to enact a proposed amendment to the Civil Practice Act, the avowed purpose of which (1957 Report of N.Y. Law Rev. Comm., p. 223) was "to abrogate the rule of Drinkwater v. Dinsmore, 80 N.Y. 390 (1880) and to conform New York law to the rule followed in most states that payments from collateral sources do not reduce the amount recoverable in a personal injury action. . . ." The Legislature and not the judiciary is the proper body to decide such a policy question involving the accommodation of various interests. We should not now seek to assume their powers and overrule their decision not to change the well-settled law of this State. No matter what may be the rule in other jurisdictions, Drinkwater is still the law in this State.

We find no merit in plaintiff's contention that the medical and nursing services for which damages are sought were supported by consideration. Plaintiff testified that he did not have to pay for the physiotherapy, and his counsel confirmed the fact that "these various items were not payable by the doctor nor were they actual obligations of his, and that he will not have to pay them."

Plaintiff's colleagues rendered the necessary medical services gratuitously as a professional courtesy. It may well be that as a result of having accepted their generosity plaintiff is under a moral obligation to act for them in a similar manner should his services ever be required; such need may never arise, however, and in any event such a moral obligation is not an injury for which tort damages, which "must be compensatory only" may be awarded. A moral obligation, without more, will not support a claim for legal damages. . . .

We are also told that the physiotherapy treatments which plaintiff received from his nurse consumed approximately two hours per week, and that they were given during the usual office hours for which she received her regular salary. Plaintiff does not claim that he was required to or in fact did pay any additional compensation to his nurse for her performance of these duties, and, therefore, this has not resulted in compensable damage to plaintiff.

Finally, we reject as unwarranted plaintiff's suggestion that our decision in Healy v. Rennert (9 N.Y.2d 202, 206) casts doubt on the continued validity of the *Drinkwater* rule in a case such as the instant one. In *Healy*, we held that it was error to permit defendants to establish on cross-examination that plaintiff was a member of a health insurance plan and that he was receiving increased disability pension benefits. In that case, however, the plaintiff had given value for the benefits he received; he paid a premium for the health insurance, and had worked for 18 years, in order to be eligible for the disability retirement benefits. We were not confronted with — and did not attempt to pass upon — a situation where the injured plaintiff received wholly gratuitous services for which he had given no consideration in return and which he was under no legal obligation to repay. In short, insurance, pension, vacation and other benefits which were contracted and paid for are not relevant here. Gratuitous services rendered by relatives, neighbors and friends are not compensable.

. . . It would hardly be fair in a negligence action, where damages are compensatory and not punitive, to change the *Drinkwater* rule of long standing in the face of the Legislature's refusal to do so, and to punish a defendant by requiring him to pay plaintiff for a friend's generosity. If we were to allow a plaintiff the reasonable value of the services of the physician who treated him gratuitously, logic would dictate that the plaintiff would then be entitled to the reasonable value of such services, despite the fact that the physician charged him but a fraction of such value. Such a rule would involve odd consequences, and in the end simply require a defendant to pay a plaintiff the value of a gift.

The judgment appealed from should be affirmed.

Chief Judge DESMOND (concurring).

The reason why this plaintiff cannot include in his damages anything for physicians' bills or nursing expense is that he has paid nothing for those services. . . .

Settled and consistent precedents provide the answer to the question posed by this appeal. Neither justice nor morality require a different answer. Diminution of damages because medical services were furnished gratuitously results in a windfall of sorts to a defendant but allowance of such items although not paid for would unjustly enrich a plaintiff.

I vote to affirm.

FULD, J. (dissenting).

It is elementary that damages in personal injury actions are awarded in order to compensate the plaintiff, but, under an established exception, the collateral source doctrine — which we recognized in Healy v. Rennert (9 N.Y.2d 202) — a wrongdoer will not be allowed to deduct benefits which the plaintiff may have received from another source. To put the matter broadly, the defendant should not be given credit for an amount of money, or its equivalent in services, received by the plaintiff from other sources. "The rationale of the collateral source doctrine in tort actions," it has been said, "is that a tort-feasor should not be allowed to escape the pecuniary consequences of his wrongful act merely because his victim has received benefit from a third party" (Note, 26 Fordham L. Rev. 372, 381).

In the *Healy* case (9 N.Y.2d 202, *supra*), this court held that, if one is negligently injured by another, the damages recoverable from the latter are diminished neither (1) by the fact that the injured party has been indemnified for his loss by insurance effected by him nor (2) by the fact that his medical expenses were paid by HIP or some other health insurance plan. In the case before us, the plaintiff suffered injuries and required medical and nursing care. He had no health insurance, but he received the necessary medical care and services from fellow doctors without being required to pay them in cash. In addition, he received physiotherapy treatments from the nurse employed by him in his office and to whom he, of course, paid a salary.

I fail to see any real difference between the situation in Healy v. Rennert and the case now before us. In neither case was the injured person burdened with any charges for the medical services rendered and, accordingly, when the defendant is required to pay as "damages" for those services or their value, such damages are no less "compensatory" in the one case than in the other. Nor do I understand why a distinction should be made depending upon whether the medical services were rendered gratuitously or for a consideration. What difference should it make, either to the plaintiff or to the defendant, whether an injured plaintiff has his medical bills taken care of by an insurer or by a wealthy uncle or by a fellow doctor? Certainly, neither the uncle, who acted out of affection, nor the doctor, impelled by so-called professional courtesy, intended to benefit the tort-feasor.

The crucial question in cases such as this is whether the tort-feasor would, in fairness and justice, be given credit for the amounts, or their equivalent in services, which the plaintiff has received from some collateral source. The collateral source doctrine is not, and should not be, limited to cases where the plaintiff had previously paid consideration (in the form of insurance premiums, for instance) for the benefits or services which he receives or where there has been a payment of cash or out-of-pocket expenses. The rationale underlying the rule is that a wrongdoer, responsible for injuring the plaintiff, should not receive a windfall. Were it not for the fortuitous circumstance that the plaintiff was a doctor, he would have been billed for the medical services and the defendant would have had to pay for them.

The medical services were supplied to help the plaintiff, not to relieve the defendant from any part of his liability or to benefit him. It should not matter, in reason, logic or justice, whether the benefit received was in return for a consideration or given gratuitously, or whether it represented money paid out or its equivalent in services.

The rule reflected by the decision in Drinkwater v. Dinsmore (80 N.Y. 390) is court made and, accordingly, since I believe . . . that it is not only "completely opposite to the majority rule" but also "unfair, illogical and unduly complex," I cannot vote for its perpetuation. Indeed, as I have already indicated, an even stronger case for its repudiation is made out by our recent decision in Healy v. Rennert (9 N.Y.2d 202, *supra*).

I would reverse the judgment appealed from and direct a new trial.

Judges DYE, VAN VOORHIS, BURKE and FOSTER concur with Judge FROESSEL; Chief Judge DESMOND concurs in a separate opinion; Judge FULD dissents in an opinion.

Judgment affirmed.

FOOD FOR THOUGHT

Coyne represents a minority position. *See, e.g.,* Schultz v. Harrison Radiator Division GMC, 683 N.E.2d 307, 311 (N.Y. 1997) (New York court continued to follow *Coyne*, noting that it ensures "compensatory damages awarded to plaintiff are truly compensatory"). Plaintiffs in most jurisdictions can recover the reasonable value of gratuitously rendered services, such as care given by family members and free medical care of the sort received by the plaintiff in *Coyne*. Plaintiffs also receive the full damage award from the defendant notwithstanding compensation they receive from sources like insurance, employee benefit programs, and most government aid programs. *See, e.g.,* Lindholm v. Hassan, 369 F. Supp. 2d 1104 (D.S.D. 2005); McKinney v. California Portland Cement Co., 117 Cal. Rptr. 2d 849 (Cal. Ct. App. 2002); Cox v. Spangler, 5 P.3d 1265 (Wash. 2000); Werner v. Lane, 393 A.2d 1329 (Me. 1978); Oddo v. Cardi, 218 A.2d 373 (R.I. 1966); Bell v. Primeau, 183 A.2d 729, 730 (N.H. 1962). Most jurisdictions that recognize the collateral source rule limit the situations in which evidence of any collateral sources may be given to the jury. The fear is that, notwithstanding instructions to the contrary, juries will adjust awards downward to reflect the collateral sources.

ANOTHER PERSPECTIVE: MONTGOMERY WARD V. ANDERSON

In Montgomery Ward & Co. v. Anderson, 976 S.W.2d 382 (Ark. 1998), the plaintiff suffered injuries when she fell while shopping in the defendant's store. The plaintiff claimed the entire amount of her medical bills as damages. The defendant sought to introduce evidence that the plaintiff had negotiated a 50 percent discount on these medical bills and sought a deduction from any damage award to reflect the discount. The trial court ruled that the discount was a collateral source, and should not reduce the plaintiff's recovery. On the defendant's appeal from a judgment against it, which included the full amount of the plaintiff's medical bills, the Supreme Court of Arkansas affirmed, stating (976 S.W.2d at 383-384):

> A trial court must "exclude evidence of payments received by an injured party from sources 'collateral' to . . . the wrongdoer, such as private insurance or government benefits . . ." [citations omitted]. Recoveries from collateral sources "do not redound to the benefit of a tortfeasor, even though double recovery for the same damage by the injured party may result." Bell v. Estate of Bell, 318 Ark. at 490, 885 S.W.2d at 880; Green Forest v. Herrington, 287 Ark. at 49, 696 S.W.2d at 718.
>
> In the *Bell* case, we recognized that commentators had criticized the rule as being "incongruous with the compensatory goal of the tort system" and that some jurisdictions had modified or abrogated the rule. *Bell*, 318 Ark. at 490, 885 S.W.2d at 880. To refute that criticism, we quoted . . . from F. Harper, et al., The Law of Torts § 25.22, at p. 651 (2d ed. 1986) as follows:
>
>> But in these cases the courts measure "compensation" by the total amount of the harm done, even though some of it has been repaired by the collateral source, not by what it would take to make the plaintiff whole. It is "compensation" in a purely Pickwickian sense that only half conceals an emphasis on what defendant should pay rather than on what plaintiff should get.
>
> . . . In a later case, East Texas Motor Freight Lines, Inc. v. Freeman, 289 Ark. 539, 713 S.W.2d 456 (1986), a defendant argued that the collateral-source rule was inequitable because it resulted in a windfall to the plaintiff. We . . . explain[ed] the policy behind the rule as follows:
>
>> Whether [the plaintiff] received the money from her employer or from an insurance policy, [the plaintiff], rather than the alleged tortfeasor, is entitled to the benefit of the collateral source, even though in one sense a double recovery occurs. Vermillion v. Peterson, 275 Ark. 367, 630 S.W.2d 30 (1982). The law rationalizes that the claimant should benefit from the collateral source recovery rather than the tortfeasor, since the claimant has usually paid an insurance premium or lost sick leave, whereas to the tortfeasor it would be a total windfall. *Id.* at 548, 713 S.W.2d at 462.
>>
>> That statement of policy and the cases cited favor including discounted and gratuitous medical services within the shelter of the collateral-source rule. There is no evidence of record showing that [the defendant] had anything to do with procuring the discount of [the plaintiff's] bill by [the hospital]. The rationale of the rule favors her, just as it would had she been compensated by insurance for which she had arranged.

What do you think of the *Montgomery Ward* court's reasons for applying the collateral source rule on those facts? Do you find the court's policy arguments persuasive?

LIMITATIONS ON THE COLLATERAL SOURCE RULE: NO DOUBLE-DIPPING, PLEASE

The major criticism of the collateral source rule is that of the court in *Coyne*: plaintiffs may be allowed a double recovery. For example, a plaintiff may be compensated for medical bills from both a medical insurance policy and the defendant. In response to this criticism, legislatures in some states have reversed or modified the traditional collateral source rule. When challenged on constitutional grounds, some of these statutes have been struck down and others upheld. *See, e.g.,* Reid v. Williams, 964 P.2d 453 (Alaska 1998); and Rudolph v. Iowa Methodist Medical Center, 293 N.W.2d 550 (Iowa 1980) (upheld); Thompson v. KFB Insurance Co., 850 P.2d 773 (Kan. 1993); and Carson v. Maurer, 424 A.2d 825 (N.H. 1980) (struck down). *Also see* Howell v. Hamilton Meats & Provisions, 257 P.3d 1130 (Cal. 2011) (court held that the insured plaintiff could not recover the undiscounted medical expenses because her insurance was liable for the billed amount, not her).

Double recovery can also be avoided when the collateral source is subrogated to the rights of the plaintiff against the defendant. Subrogation allows an insurer the right to recover, from the tort defendant, the cost of any benefits the insurer has provided to the plaintiff that were included in the original calculation of the award to the plaintiff. Ordinarily the right to subrogation is bestowed by agreement, ahead of time, between the tort plaintiff and the collateral source. Insurance policies, for example, often contain subrogation clauses. When the parties have not entered such an agreement, the collateral source may not have a right to subrogation. *See, e.g.,* Perreira v. Rediger, 778 A.2d 429 (N.J. 2001); Shumpert v. Time Insurance Co., 496 S.E.2d 653 (S.C. 1998). When courts do allow the collateral source to be subrogated to the rights of the plaintiff in the absence of an express agreement, it is because they view the insurance agreement in question as an agreement of indemnity, whereby the insurer promises to indemnify the insured as a result of losses, and the insured impliedly promises to allow the insurer to seek reimbursement if tort recovery becomes available. *See, e.g.,* Cunningham v. Metropolitan Life Insurance Co., 360 N.W.2d 33 (Wis. 1985). Not surprisingly, life insurance is never thought of in this way, and life policies never contain subrogation clauses.

THE PLAINTIFF'S DUTY TO MITIGATE

In Zimmerman v. Ausland, 513 P.2d 1167 (Or. 1973), the plaintiff won a verdict based on instructions that gave the issue of the permanency of her knee injuries to the jury to decide, notwithstanding defendant's medical expert's testimony that her knee condition was curable by low-cost, almost risk-free surgery. The Supreme Court of Oregon affirmed the judgment for the plaintiff, ruling that the decision regarding whether to believe the defendant's expert was for the jury.

Zimmerman deals with the tort doctrine of mitigation of damages, sometimes referred to as the "avoidable consequences" doctrine. It imposes a duty on the plaintiff to act affirmatively and reasonably after the accident to minimize the harm that the defendant's conduct has caused. In this sense, it is similar to the doctrines of contributory negligence and comparative fault, and especially the common law doctrine of "last clear chance." The purpose of the duty to mitigate is to ensure that the defendant is not held liable for harms that the law considers to be part of the plaintiff's responsibility. As did the court in *Zimmerman*, most courts hold that the burden is on the defendant to prove that the plaintiff failed to act reasonably to mitigate her injuries. When the plaintiff fails to submit to surgery as a reasonable person would have, the plaintiff's damages can be limited to what they would have been had she undergone the surgery. The reasonableness of the plaintiff's decision to resist treatment is often determined using a risk-utility analysis similar to the famous Hand formula from *Carroll Towing* (p. 139, Chapter 3) and is a determination ultimately for the jury. The defendant bears the burden of proving mitigation of damages. *See, e.g.,* Willis v. Westerfield, 839 N.E.2d 1179 (Ind. 2006) (defendant has the burden of proof that plaintiff's post-injury conduct increased the plaintiff's harm and, if so, by how much). In some cases, plaintiffs may have religious reasons for refusing to submit to surgery. How should juries assess the reasonableness of a decision based on religious convictions? Courts are divided over this issue, with some allowing the jury to consider evidence of the plaintiff's religious beliefs in determining reasonableness, and others prohibiting any evidence of religious reasons for refusing treatment. *See* Williams v. Bright, p. 187, Chapter 3; Braverman v. Granger, 844 N.W.2d 486 (Mich. 2014) (decedent's refusal of blood transfusion due to religious reasons caused her death and thus her estate could not receive because she failed to reasonably mitigate her damage).

2. Measuring Recovery for Harm to Property

The basic rule of recovery for harm to property is the same as for harm to plaintiff's person: the plaintiff should be restored, as nearly as possible, to the position the plaintiff occupied before the harm occurred. In general, the market value of property that has been destroyed is the proper measure of recovery, on the assumption that the plaintiff can purchase a replacement on the market. Evaluation of property loss can be difficult in cases involving one-of-a-kind items for which no market exists. A striking example is presented in Gasperini v. Center for Humanities, 66 F.3d 427 (2d Cir. 1995), *vacated,* 518 U.S. 415 (1996). In *Gasperini* the plaintiff was a journalist who had covered Central America for CBS News and the *Christian Science Monitor.* While in Central America, he took over 5,000 slide transparencies, including depictions of war zones, scenes from daily life, and portraits of political leaders. He loaned 300 of these one-of-a-kind slides to the defendant for use in a video production. When the project was finished, the defendant discovered that the slides were lost. The plaintiff brought an action in federal court alleging, inter alia, negligence and conversion. The defendant conceded liability and a trial was held to determine the appropriate damages. At trial, the plaintiff's expert testified that the average value of a lost transparency within the photographic publishing industry was $1,500 per slide, representing the average license fee produced by a commercial photograph over the life of the photographer's copyright. To this the plaintiff added testimony that he had intended to produce a book containing his best photographs from Central America. The jury awarded the plaintiff $450,000 in compensatory damages, $1,500 per slide, and the district court entered judgment on the verdict.

The defendant appealed on the ground that the verdict was excessive. The court of appeals, applying New York law, set aside the verdict and ordered a new trial. It noted that, in addition to industry standards, both the uniqueness of the subject matter and the photographer's earning level were relevant to the valuation of lost slides (66 F.3d at 429-431):

> Without question, some of the transparencies were unique: as [the plaintiff] described them, they depicted combat situations in which [the plaintiff] was the only photographer present. But [the plaintiff] also testified that on numerous occasions other able, professional photographers were present, sometimes in large numbers, when he took photographs that were among the three hundred lost. Although we accept the proposition that each photographer brings his or her own skills, judgment, and perspective to a particular scene, leading to some variation between photographs of a single event, no reasonable jury could have concluded, as the jury in this case did, that each of the lost three hundred transparencies was equally, and significantly, original.
>
> [The plaintiff's] earning record as a photographer further undercuts the jury verdict. The only evidence presented on this point was that the commercial use of [the plaintiff's] photographs yielded income of slightly more than $10,000 over the ten-year period from 1984 through 1993; in no year did he earn more than $3,720.40. For all his skills as a photographer, [the plaintiff] did not earn his living with his camera, and there was no evidence presented that he would do so in the future. [The plaintiff] did testify that he had intended to produce a book about his experiences in Central America, a project that he claims is now doomed to failure by the loss of the three hundred transparencies. But there was no evidence presented that [the plaintiff] had found, or would have been able to find, a publisher for such a work, much less that the volume would have earned him significant income. . . .
>
> Drawing all reasonable inferences in favor of Gasperini, we conclude that the jury could have awarded damages of up to $1,500 per transparency for the transparencies as to which there was plausible evidence of significant uniqueness. As to the remaining transparencies, however, in light of Gasperini's limited earnings and the lack of uniqueness, any damage award of more than $100 per transparency would be excessive. Accordingly, we conclude that any award totaling more than $100,000 would exceed reasonable compensation.

Note the wide range of values placed on commercial photographs in *Gasperini*. Suppose that the lost transparencies were old family photographs, of which there were no copies. How should they be valued? The sentimental value of such items is not easily compensable with reference to market value, since by definition no similar items or otherwise acceptable substitutes exist. In such cases, courts allow the jury to consider factors other than market value in determining the worth of the items, including the uses to which they are put and their condition.

MEASURING THE LOSS BY THE PROPERTY OWNER'S EMOTIONAL UPSET

Another indirect way these damages can be measured is reference to the emotional reactions of the owner upon their loss. However, most jurisdictions are reluctant to award emotional distress damages in actions based on loss of property, unless there is also a physical injury to the plaintiff (*see* Chapter 6, section C for materials on recovery for emotional distress in negligence actions). For example, in White

Consolidated Industries, Inc. v. Wilkerson, 737 So. 2d 447 (Ala. 1999), the plaintiffs were a family who had lost their home, including all of their family photos and heirlooms, in a fire caused by a manufacturing defect in an air conditioner manufactured by the defendants. At trial, the plaintiffs introduced evidence regarding sentimental items that had been lost in the fire, as well as testimony describing their mental and emotional state immediately afterward. The jury awarded damages for mental anguish. In overturning the verdict, the Supreme Court of Alabama stated (737 So. 2d at 449):

> We must determine whether a breach of a duty under the [applicable statute] allows a recovery of damages for mental anguish where, as here, the breach of duty has caused no physical injury.
>
> In Reinhardt Motors, Inc. v. Boston, 516 So. 2d 509 (Ala. 1986), we stated the general rule that "the law will not allow recovery of damages for mental distress where the tort results in *mere* injury to property." *Id.* at 511 (emphasis in original). However, in *Boston* we also recognized the exception that "where the injury to property is committed under circumstances of insult or contumely, [damages for] mental suffering may be recoverable." *Id.*
>
> The [plaintiffs] urge us to hold that the sale of an air conditioner that has a defect that causes damage to property supports an award of mental-anguish damages. The evidence indicates that the defect in the air conditioner caused harm only to the [plaintiff's] property. Additionally, at the time of the fire the [plaintiffs] were away from home and at their places of employment. Therefore, they were not in the "zone of danger" created by the defect — a zone in which they would have been at immediate risk of physical harm. Thus, the [plaintiffs] are not entitled to recover damages for mental anguish.

CONSIDERATIONS OF TIME AND PLACE

Generally, when the market value of an item depends on the geographical location in which it is sold, courts will use the value at the location in which the harm occurred. Similarly, the market value that forms the basis for a calculation of damages is the value of the item at the time the property was destroyed. However, the market values of some types of property fluctuate enormously over time. In some cases, the very object of owning such property is to resell it at a higher value. For example, when a plaintiff loses stock or bond certificates, their value may be very different by the time of trial than it was at the time the defendant caused the harm, and the plaintiff may have been harmed by loss of the opportunity to take advantage of the fluctuation in price as well as by being deprived of his property. In such cases, some courts have steadfastly clung to valuing the lost item based on the market value at the time of the wrong. A majority, however, make some allowance for possible upward fluctuation. One rule allows for the plaintiff to recover the highest price of the item between the time of the wrong and the time of the trial. An alternative rule, probably better reasoned, allows the plaintiff to recover the highest market value from the time the plaintiff learns of the wrong and the end of a reasonable time in which the plaintiff could have purchased a replacement.

A plaintiff whose property is damaged rather than destroyed can recover the difference in the value of the item before the harm and its value after the harm. This is often calculated using the cost of repair as a measure of damage, but occasionally that exceeds the value of the property before it was damaged. Indeed, the cost of repair may also exceed the difference between the value of the damaged property and the property before the damage. In such cases, the court will often look to other factors, including the property's fitness for its intended use in its damaged condition, in order to determine which measure to employ.

When the plaintiff has been only temporarily deprived of the use of his property, he can recover the fair rental value of the property for the time that it is unavailable to him. Further, he can recover any consequential damages of being deprived of the use of the property, subject to the limits of proximate cause. These damages would include any loss caused by temporary inability to use the property in business or other money-making endeavors as well as the cost of reasonable efforts to recover the property.

3. Wrongful Death and Survival

NORFOLK SHIPBUILDING & DRYDOCK CORP. v. GARRIS
532 U.S. 811 (2001)

Justice SCALIA delivered the opinion of the Court.

The question presented in this case is whether the negligent breach of a general maritime duty of care is actionable when it causes death, as it is when it causes injury.

I

According to the complaint that respondent filed in the United States District Court for the Eastern District of Virginia, her son, Christopher Garris, sustained injuries on April 8, 1997, that caused his death one day later. The injuries were suffered while Garris was performing sandblasting work aboard the USNS Maj. Stephen W. Pless in the employ of Tidewater Temps, Inc., a subcontractor for Mid-Atlantic Coatings, Inc., which was in turn a subcontractor for petitioner Norfolk Shipbuilding & Drydock Corporation. And the injuries were caused, the complaint continued, by the negligence of petitioner and one of its other subcontractors, since dismissed from this case. Because the vessel was berthed in the navigable waters of the United States when Garris was injured, respondent invoked federal admiralty jurisdiction, and prayed for damages under general maritime law. She also asserted claims under the Virginia wrongful death statute.

The District Court dismissed the complaint for failure to state a federal claim, for the categorical reason that "no cause of action exists, under general maritime law, for death of a nonseaman in state territorial waters resulting from negligence." The United States Court of Appeals for the Fourth Circuit reversed and remanded for further proceedings, explaining that although this Court had not yet recognized a maritime cause of action for wrongful death resulting from negligence, the principles contained in our decision in Moragne v. States Marine Lines, Inc., 398 U.S. 375, 90 S. Ct. 1772, 26 L. Ed. 2d 339 (1970), made such an action appropriate. Judge Hall concurred in the judgment because, in her view, *Moragne* had itself recognized the action. The Court of Appeals denied petitioner's suggestion for rehearing en banc, with two judges dissenting. We granted certiorari.

II

Three of four issues of general maritime law are settled, and the fourth is before us. It is settled that the general maritime law imposes duties to avoid unseaworthiness and negligence, that nonfatal injuries caused by the breach of either duty are compensable, and that death caused by breach of the duty of seaworthiness is also compensable, Moragne v. States Marine Lines, Inc., *supra*, at 409, 90 S. Ct. 1772. Before us is the question whether death caused by negligence should, or must under direction of a federal statute, be treated differently.

A

For more than 80 years, from 1886 until 1970, all four issues were considered resolved, though the third not in the manner we have just described. The governing rule then was the rule of *The Harrisburg*, 119 U.S. 199, 213, 7 S. Ct. 140, 30 L. Ed. 358 (1886): Although the general maritime law provides relief for injuries caused by the breach of maritime duties, it does not provide relief for wrongful death. *The Harrisburg* said that rule was compelled by existence of the same rule at common law, — although it acknowledged, that admiralty courts had held that damages for wrongful death were recoverable under maritime law.

In 1969, however, we granted certiorari in Moragne v. States Marine Lines, Inc., *supra*, for the express purpose of considering "whether *The Harrisburg* . . . should any longer be regarded as acceptable law." 398 U.S., at 375-376, 90 S. Ct. 1772. We inquired whether the rule of *The Harrisburg* was defensible under either the general maritime law or the policy displayed in the maritime statutes Congress had since enacted, whether those statutes pre-empted judicial action overruling *The Harrisburg*, whether stare decisis required adherence to *The Harrisburg*, and whether insuperable practical difficulties would accompany *The Harrisburg's* overruling. Answering every question no, we overruled the case and declared a new rule of maritime law: "We . . . hold that an action does lie under general maritime law for death caused by violation of maritime duties." *Id.*, at 409.

As we have noted in an earlier opinion, the wrongful-death rule of *Moragne* was not limited to any particular maritime duty, but *Moragne's* facts were limited to the duty of seaworthiness, and so the issue of wrongful death for negligence has remained technically open. We are able to find no rational basis, however, for distinguishing negligence from seaworthiness. It is no less a distinctively maritime duty than seaworthiness: The common-law duties of care have not been adopted and retained unmodified by admiralty, but have been adjusted to fit their maritime context, and a century ago the maritime law exchanged the common law's rule of contributory negligence for one of comparative negligence. Consequently the "tensions and discrepancies" in our precedent arising "from the necessity to accommodate state remedial statutes to exclusively maritime substantive concepts" — which ultimately drove this Court in *Moragne* to abandon *The Harrisburg*, — were no less pronounced with maritime negligence than with unseaworthiness. In fact, both cases cited by *Moragne* to exemplify those discrepancies involved maritime negligence. It is true, as petitioner observes, that we have held admiralty accommodation of state remedial statutes to be constitutionally permissible, but that does not resolve the issue here: whether requiring such an accommodation by refusing to recognize a federal remedy is preferable as a matter of maritime policy. We think it is not.

The choice-of-law anomaly occasioned by providing a federal remedy for injury but not death is no less strange when the duty is negligence than when it is seaworthiness. Of two victims injured at the same instant in the same location by the same negligence, only one would be covered by federal law, provided only that the other died of his injuries. And cutting off the law's remedy at the death of the injured person is no less "a striking departure from the result dictated by elementary principles in the law of remedies," Moragne v. States Marine Lines, Inc., 398 U.S., at 381, 90 S. Ct. 1772, when the duty breached is negligence than when it is seaworthiness. "Where existing law imposes a primary duty, violations of which are compensable if they cause injury, nothing in ordinary notions of justice suggests that a violation should be nonactionable simply because it was serious enough to cause death." *Ibid.* Finally, the maritime policy favoring recovery for wrongful death that *Moragne* found implicit in federal statutory law cannot be limited to unseaworthiness, for both of the federal acts on which *Moragne* relied permit recovery for negligence. In sum, a negligent breach of a maritime duty of care being assumed by the posture of this case, no rational basis within the maritime law exists for denying respondent the recovery recognized by *Moragne* for the death of her son.

The maritime cause of action that *Moragne* established for unseaworthiness is equally available for negligence.

We affirm the judgment of the Court of Appeals.

It is so ordered.

DEAD MEN FILE NO SUITS

Garris, supra, tells a part of the wrongful death story in the maritime context that has been a century and a half in the telling at common law. Originally, the common law did not recognize a cause of action when the would-be plaintiff died. There was no recovery for the death itself, even if caused by defendant's wrongdoing; and once a person injured by the defendant's tortious behavior died, any existing cause of action died with him. Under this state of affairs, defendants who killed their victims were significantly better off than those who merely caused serious injury.

This often paradoxical situation no longer exists. In every state, as well as in England, statutes provide that the death of parties or would-be parties has far less draconian legal consequences. These statutes are of two types: survival statutes, which preserve the cause of action when either the victim or the tortfeasor dies before judgment; and wrongful death statutes, which give the decedent's estate or close family members rights of action when the defendant tortiously causes someone's death. All states have survival statutes of one form or another, and most have wrongful death statutes, as well. In states where there is no separate wrongful death statute, courts have held that the survival statutes create causes of action based on deaths caused by tort defendants.

On the subject of wrongful death generally, *see* Eric A. Posner & Cass R. Sunstein, *Dollars and Death*, 72 U. Chi. L. Rev. 537 (2005); Wex S. Malone, *The Genesis of Wrongful Death*, 17 Stan. L. Rev. 1043 (1965); T.A. Smedley, *Wrongful Death — Bases of the Common Law Rules*, 13 Vand. L. Rev. 605 (1960).

SURVIVAL VS. WRONGFUL DEATH: WHAT'S THE DIFFERENCE?

The primary difference between the two types of statute is that survival statutes allow representative plaintiffs to stand in the shoes of the decedent and recover from the tortfeasor any amounts that the decedent could have recovered. Thus, the survival statutes generally do not create new causes of action so much as they allow specified persons to assume the rights of the deceased under existing causes of action. By contrast, wrongful death statutes create new causes of action in favor of family members, allowing them to recover for harms they, themselves, have suffered as a result of the tortfeasor's behavior. Thus, the measures of recovery under the two statutes differ. In an action authorized by a survival statute, the plaintiff recovers for harm to the deceased. In an action authorized by a wrongful death statute, the plaintiff, in the largest number of states, recovers based on harm the plaintiff has suffered as a result of the decedent's tortiously caused death. Alabama is the only state that measures damages for wrongful death by the degree of the defendant's fault. *See, e.g.*, Tillis Trucking Co. v. Moses, 748 So. 2d 874 (Ala. 1999); Estes Health Care Centers, Inc. v. Bannerman, 411 So. 2d 109 (Ala. 1982). A large majority of states adhere to the rule that the plaintiffs (usually close family members) can recover for their loss (usually including emotional harm) suffered as a result of the decedent's death. A relatively small number of jurisdictions measure recovery for wrongful death in terms of the monetary losses suffered by the decedent's estate as a result of his or her death. Regarding the differences between the two types of statutes, consider the following case:

MURPHY v. MARTIN OIL CO.
308 N.E.2d 583 (Ill. 1974)

Mr. Justice WARD delivered the opinion of the court.

The plaintiff, Charryl Murphy, as administratrix of her late husband, Jack Raymond Murphy, and individually, and as next friend of Debbie Ann Murphy, Jack Kenneth Murphy and Carrie Lynn Murphy, their children, filed a complaint in the circuit court of Cook County against the defendants, Martin Oil Company and James Hocker. Count I of the complaint claimed damages for wrongful death under the Illinois Wrongful Death Act and count II sought damages for conscious pain and suffering, loss of wages and property damage. The circuit court allowed the defendants' motion to strike the second count of the complaint on the ground that it failed to state a cause of action. . . . [The intermediate appellate] court affirmed the dismissal of count II of the complaint as to its allegations of pain and suffering and reversed the judgment as to its allegations of loss of wages and property damage. The cause was remanded with directions to reinstate as much of count II as related to loss of wages and property damage. We granted the plaintiff's petition for leave to appeal.

The first count set out the factual background for the complaint. It alleged that on June 11, 1968, the defendants owned and operated a gasoline station in Oak Lawn, Cook County, and that on that date the plaintiff's decedent, Jack Raymond Murphy, while having his truck filled with gasoline, was injured through the defendants' negligence in a fire on the defendants' premises. Nine days later he died from the injuries. Damages for wrongful death were claimed under the Illinois Wrongful Death Act. (Ill. Rev. Stat. 1971, ch. 70, pars. 1 and 2.) The language of section 1 of the statute is:

> Whenever the death of a person shall be caused by wrongful act, neglect or default, and the act, neglect or default is such as would, if death had not ensued, have entitled the party injured to maintain an action and recover damages in respect thereof, then and in every such case the person who or company or corporation which would have been liable if death had not ensued, shall be liable to an action for damages, notwithstanding the death of the person injured, and although the death shall have been caused under such circumstances as amount in law to felony.

The second count of the complaint asked for damages for the decedent's physical and mental suffering, for loss of wages for the nine-day period following his injury and for the loss of his clothing worn at the time of injury. These damages were claimed under the common law and under our survival statute, which provides that certain rights of action survive the death of the person with the right of action. (Ill. Rev. Stat. 1971, ch. 3, par. 339.) The statute states:

> In addition to the actions which survive by the common law, the following also survive: actions of replevin, actions to recover damages for an injury to the person (except slander and libel), actions to recover damages for an injury to real or personal property or for the detention or conversion of personal property, actions against officers for misfeasance, malfeasance, or nonfeasance of themselves or their deputies, actions for fraud or deceit, and actions provided in Section 14 of Article VI of "An Act relating to alcoholic liquors," approved January 31, 1934, as amended.

On this appeal we shall consider: (1) whether the plaintiff can recover for the loss of wages which her decedent would have earned during the interval between his injury and death; (2) whether the plaintiff can recover for the destruction of the decedent's personal property (clothing) at the time of the injury; (3) whether the plaintiff can recover damages for conscious pain and suffering of the decedent from the time of his injuries to the time of death.

This State in 1853 enacted the Wrongful Death Act and in 1872 enacted the so-called Survival Act (now section 339 of the Probate Act). This court first had occasion to consider the statutes in combination in 1882 in Holton v. Daly, 106 Ill. 131. The court declared that the effect of the Wrongful Death Act was that a cause of action for personal injuries, which would have abated under the common law upon the death of the injured party from those injuries, would continue on behalf of the spouse or the next of kin and would be "enlarged to embrace the injury resulting from the death." (106 Ill. 131, 140.) In other words, it was held that the Wrongful Death Act provided the exclusive remedy available when death came as a result of given tortious conduct. In considering the Survival Act the court stated that it was intended to allow for the survival of a cause of action only when the injured party died from a cause other than that which caused the injuries which created the cause of action. Thus, the court said, an action for personal injury would not survive death if death resulted from the tortious conduct which caused the injury.

This construction of the two statutes persisted for over 70 years. Damages, therefore, under the Wrongful Death Act were limited to pecuniary losses, as from loss of support, to the surviving spouse and next of kin as a result of the death. Under the survival statute damages recoverable in a personal injury action, as for conscious pain and suffering, loss of earnings, medical expenses and physical disability, could be had only if death resulted from a cause other than the one which gave rise to the personal injury action.

This court was asked in 1941 to depart from its decision in Holton v. Daly and to permit, in addition to a wrongful death action, an action for personal injuries to be brought, though the injuries had resulted in the death of the injured person. This court acknowledged that there had been other jurisdictions which held contrary to *Holton v. Daly* and permitted the bringing of both actions, but the court said that any change in the rule in *Holton* must come from the legislature. In 1960, however, in Saunders v. Schultz, . . . 170 N.E.2d 163, this court noted the absence of legislative action and permitted a widow to recover for funeral and medical expenses in an action which was independent of and in addition to an action brought by her for damages under the Wrongful Death Act. It was said:

> Viewing the situation realistically, this liability of the surviving spouse for such expenses constitutes very real damages. Since that liability results from defendant's tortious conduct, it is only legally sound, and in accordance with basic negligence principles, that the burden of such damages should fall, not on the innocent victim, but upon the tortfeasor. . . .
>
> The estate or the spouse, either or both as the circumstances indicate, are entitled to recover for pecuniary losses suffered by either or both which are not recoverable under the Wrongful Death Act, and all cases holding the contrary are overruled. 20 Ill. 2d 301, 310-311.

Later, in Graul v. Adrian (1965), . . . 205 N.E.2d 444, this court approved an action brought for medical and funeral expenses of a child, which had been concurrently brought with an action brought under the Wrongful Death Act.

While the specific ground of decision in *Graul* was the family-expense section of the Husband and Wife Act (Ill. Rev. Stat. 1961, ch. 68, par. 15), and though some have contended that Saunders v. Schultz was based on the liability of the widow there under the Husband and Wife Act, it has become obvious that the Wrongful Death Act is no longer regarded as the exclusive remedy available when the injuries cause death. Too, it is clear that the abatement of actions is not favored.

This disapproval of abatement was expressed in McDaniel v. Bullard (1966), ... 216 N.E.2d 140, where the parents and sister of an infant, Yvonne McDaniel, had been killed in an automobile collision. An action was begun on behalf of Yvonne under the Wrongful Death Act and shortly after the filing of the action Yvonne died from causes which were unrelated to the collision. This court rejected the defendant's contention that the pending action under the Wrongful Death Act was abated or extinguished upon Yvonne's death. In holding that an action under the Wrongful Death Act survived under the terms of the Survival Act upon the death of the victim's next of kin, this court said, at pages 493-494, 216 N.E.2d at page 144: "Today damages from most torts are recognized as compensatory rather than punitive, and there is no reason why an estate that has been injured or depleted by the wrong of another should not be compensated whether the injured party is living or not. (Citation.) The rule of abatement has its roots in archaic conceptions of remedy which have long since lost their validity. The reason having ceased the rule is out of place and ought not to be perpetuated." We concluded that under the Survival Act the action for wrongful death did not abate but might be maintained for the benefit of Yvonne's estate.

This disfavoring of abatement and enlarging of survival statutes has been general. In Prosser, Handbook of the Law of Torts (4th ed. 1971). At page 906 Prosser observes that where there have been wrongful death and survival statutes the usual holding has been that actions may be concurrently maintained under those statutes. The usual method of dealing with the two causes of action, he notes, is to allocate conscious pain and suffering, expenses and loss of earnings of the decedent up to the date of death to the survival statute, and to allocate the loss of benefits of the survivors to the action for wrongful death.

As the cited comments of Prosser indicate, the majority of jurisdictions which have considered the question allow an action for personal injuries in addition to an action under the wrongful death statute, though death is attributable to the injuries. Recovery for conscious pain and suffering is permitted in most of these jurisdictions.

Too, recovery is allowed under the Federal Employers' Liability Act for a decedent's conscious pain and suffering provided it was not substantially contemporaneous with his death.

We consider that those decisions which allow an action for fatal injuries as well as for wrongful death are to be preferred to this court's holding in *Holton v. Daly* that the Wrongful Death Act was the only remedy available when injury resulted in death.

The holding in *Holton* was not compelled, we judge, by the language or the nature of the statutes examined. The statutes were conceptually separable and different. The one related to an action arising upon wrongful death; the other related to a right of action for personal injury arising during the life of the injured person.

The remedy available under *Holton* will often be grievously incomplete. There may be a substantial loss of earnings, medical expenses, prolonged pain and suffering, as well as property damage sustained, before an injured person may succumb to his injuries. To say that there can be recovery only for his wrongful death is to provide an obviously inadequate justice. Too, the result in such a case is that the wrongdoer will have to answer for only a portion of the damages he caused. Incongruously, if the injury caused is so severe that death results, the wrongdoer's liability for the damages before death will be extinguished. It is obvious that in order to have a full liability and a full recovery there must be an action allowed for damages up to the time of death, as well as thereafter. Considering "It is more important that the court should be right upon later and more elaborate consideration of the cases than consistent with previous declarations" (Barden v. Northern Pacific R.R. Co. (1894), 154 U.S. 288, 322, 14 S. Ct. 1030, 1036, 38 L. Ed. 992, 1000), we declare *Holton* and the cases which have followed it overruled. What this court observed in Molitor v. Kaneland Community Unit Dist. No. 302 (1959), . . . 163 N.E.2d 89, 96, may appropriately be said again:

> We have repeatedly held that the doctrine of Stare decisis is not an inflexible rule requiring this court to blindly follow precedents and adhere to prior decisions, and that when it appears that public policy and social needs require a departure from prior decisions, it is our duty as a court of last resort to overrule those decisions and establish a rule consonant with out present day concepts of right and justice.

For the reasons given, the judgment of the appellate court is affirmed insofar as it held that an action may be maintained by the plaintiff for loss of property and loss of wages during the interval between injury and death, and that judgment is reversed insofar as it held that the plaintiff cannot maintain an action for her decedent's pain and suffering.

Affirmed in part; reversed in part.

FOOD FOR THOUGHT

Why did the lower courts in *Murphy* deny recovery for the decedent's conscious pain and suffering? Was it the wording of the survival and wrongful death statutes? The internal logic of the statutes? Past interpretations of the statutes by Illinois courts? Can you think of an underlying policy reason for not allowing family members to recover for the pain and suffering of the decedent?

WRONGFUL DEATH: WHO RECOVERS?

As we have already seen, the decedent's estate recovers under a survival statute, so that the proceeds of any judgment are divided among the heirs or legatees. By contrast, in actions for wrongful death, most statutes designate beneficiaries in terms of their relationship to the decedent. Typically, these beneficiaries include spouses, parents, and children of the deceased, depending on who survives the decedent. While this may seem straightforward, difficulties may arise in determining who is eligible to bring an action for wrongful death. For example, in the case of spouses, the general rule in the United States seems to be that couples living together out of wedlock cannot bring actions for wrongful death. The Supreme Court of California, in Elden v. Sheldon, 758 P.2d 582, 586-587 (Cal. 1988), explained the reasons supporting this rule:

> Our emphasis on the state's interest in promoting the marriage relationship is not based on anarchronistic notions of morality. The policy favoring marriage is "rooted in the necessity of providing an institutional basis for defining the fundamental relational rights and responsibilities of persons in organized society." (Laws v. Griep, 332 N.W.2d 339, 341 (Iowa 1983)). Formally married couples are granted significant rights and bear important responsibilities toward one another which are not shared by those who cohabit without marriage. For example, a detailed set of statutes governs the requirements for the entry into and termination of marriage and the property rights which flow from that relationship (Civ. Code, § 4000 et seq.), and the law imposes various obligations on spouses, such as the duty of support (*id.*, §§ 242, 244). Plaintiff does not suggest a convincing reason why cohabiting unmarried couples, who do not bear such legal obligations toward one another, should be permitted to recover for injuries to their partners to the same extent as those who undertake these responsibilities.
>
> . . . A second basis for our determination is that the allowance of a cause of action in the circumstances of this case would impose a difficult burden on the courts. It would require a court to inquire into the relationship of the partners to determine whether the "emotional attachments of the family relationship" existed between the parties (*Mobaldi, supra*, 55 Cal. App. 3d at p. 582), and whether the relationship was "stable and significant" (Butcher v. Superior Court (1983), 139 Cal. App. 3d 58, 70). *Butcher*, which will be discussed *infra* in connection with the cause of action for loss of consortium, suggested that the stability of a cohabitation relationship could be established by evidence of its duration, whether the parties had a contract, the degree of economic cooperation, the exclusivity of sexual relationships, and whether the couple had children. In Norman v. Unemployment Ins. Appeals Board, *supra*, 34 Cal. 3d 1, 8-10, we commented on the "difficult problems of proof" involved in determining whether a relationship is equivalent to a marriage. Authorities in this state and elsewhere have rejected the *Butcher* test as inviting "mischief and inconsistent results."

How persuasive do you find the court's reasoning in *Elden*?

Another question that can sometimes be difficult to resolve is the question of who may be considered a child for purposes of wrongful death recovery. Stepchildren of a decedent generally do not qualify, in the absence of statutory language. *See, e.g.*, Greer Tank & Welding, Inc. v. Boettger, 609 P.2d 548 (Alaska 1980) (holding that stepson was not a "child" for purposes of the statute, but that he could recover as an "other dependent"). Children born out of wedlock can often recover, however. In Levy v. Louisiana, 391 U.S. 68 (1968), the U.S. Supreme Court held that Louisiana's wrongful death statute violated the Fourteenth Amendment guarantee of equal protection of the laws when the state court refused to allow a child born out of wedlock to bring a wrongful death action upon the death of her mother. Similarly, in another case decided that term, the Court held the same statute unconstitutional insofar as it barred a mother from recovering for the wrongful death of her child born out of wedlock. *See* Glona v. American Guarantee & Liability Insurance Co., 391 U.S. 73 (1968). Most states permit a wrongful death action by a child born out of wedlock for the wrongful death of his father, upon a showing of paternity. *See, e.g.*, Millman v. County of Butler, 504 N.W.2d 820 (Neb. 1993). In some states, paternity must have been established before the decedent's death in order for the child to recover.

A parent may recover for the wrongful death of a child only if the child is not married and has no children. When the child is a minor, and the action is allowed, there is a division regarding what the parent may recover. In some jurisdictions, parents, like spouses, may recover for loss of the society and companionship (often called "loss of consortium") of a child. In others, they may recover for their grief and emotional upset. In still others, they may recover only for their pecuniary losses occasioned by the child's death. In some of the states that use the parents' pecuniary loss as the measure of recovery, money damages have been upheld on the theory that the child would eventually have provided some form of monetary assistance to her parents. A minority of states measure wrongful death recovery by the pecuniary loss to the estate of the decedent. In these states, the parents would be entitled to recover lost wages of their children from future employment. In the normal case, this would be subject to an offset for the child's living expenses.

B. PUNITIVE DAMAGES

THE BIG PICTURE

Punitive damages are exactly what the name implies. Courts award them, not to compensate for harm the plaintiff has suffered, but to punish the defendant for egregious wrongdoing. Punitive damages are supposed to provide incentives to the defendant and others in the defendant's position not to engage in the same bad behaviors. Courts award punitives in addition to any compensatory damages the plaintiff may be due, and will not award them in the absence of compensatories. Punitive damages have been the subject of a wide-ranging and, at times, heated debate that is not necessarily reflective of their practical importance in most tort litigation. *See generally* Benjamin C. Zipursky, *A Theory of Punitive Damages*, 84 Tex. L. Rev. 105 (2005) (attributing punitive damages' controversial nature and tentative constitutional status to ambivalence regarding nongovernmental plaintiffs' rights to inflict quasi-criminal punishment on defendants).

The best estimates are that punitive damages are awarded in less than 5 percent of reported cases in which plaintiffs ultimately prevail. *See, e.g.*, Robert A. Klinck, *Reforming Punitive Damages: The Punitive Damage Debate*, 38 Harv. J. on Legis. 469 (2001); David Luban, *A Flawed Case Against Punitive Damages*, 87 Geo. L.J. 359, 360 (1998). It is also true that some of the most publicized tort cases involve punitive damage awards. For example, one case that has achieved "urban legend" notoriety involved a $2.9 million punitive damages verdict against the McDonald's restaurant chain when a woman was severely burned after spilling hot coffee on her lap. *See* Liebeck v. McDonald's Restaurants P.T.S., Inc., 1995 WL 360309, at *1 (N.M. Dist. Ct. 1994). The award was reduced on appeal to $480,000, but the case stirred enormous controversy and contributed to the common public perception of punitive damage awards as unfair and out of control.

EMPIRICAL WORK ON PUNITIVES

Research by legal scholars has led to different conclusions about trends in the size of punitive damage verdicts. Commentaries criticizing the punitive damages system for being "out of control" include W. Kip Viscusi, *The Social Costs of Punitive Damages Against Corporations in Environmental and Safety Torts*, 87 Geo. L.J. 285, 333 (1998); and Michael J. Saks, *Do We Really Know Anything About the Behavior of the Tort Litigation System — And Why Not?*, 140 U. Pa. L. Rev. 1147, 1254 (1992). Commentaries concluding that trends in punitive damage awards are not causes for concern include Theodore Eisenberg, Jeffrey J. Rachlinski, & Martin T. Wells, *Reconciling Experimental Incoherence with Real World Coherence in Punitive Damages*, 54 Stan. L. Rev. 1239 (2002) (reviewing available empirical evidence on punitive damages awards and concluding that "researchers have not identified either a crazy pattern of awards or a substantial series of actual punitive damage awards that constitute a shocking pattern of incoherence or unfairness"). *See also* Theodore Eisenberg et al., *Juries, Judges, and Punitive Damages: Empirical Analysis Using the Civil Justice Survey of State Courts 1992, 1996, and 2001 Data*, 3 J. Empirical Legal Stud. 263 (2006). For a survey of empirical work on punitive damages, *see* Jennifer K. Robbennolt, *Determining Punitive Damages: Empirical Insights and Implications for Reform*, 50 Buffalo L. Rev. 103 (2002).

POLICY CONSIDERATIONS PRO AND CON

Those commentators who favor awarding punitive damages have advanced three policies justifying the practice: deterrence, retribution, and compensation. Those who argue that the deterrence objective justifies punitive damages claim that compensatory damages may often be insufficient to deter certain tortious behavior, especially when the behavior is profitable and likely to go undetected. In such cases, punitive damages should be calculated, in the few instances where the defendant is caught in the act, to approximate a hypothetical compensatory award for all the damages the tortfeasor's actions have caused in all the cases that have gone undetected. For examples of deterrence-based justifications of punitive damages, *see* Cass R. Sunstein, David Schkade, & Daniel Kahneman, *Do People Want Optimal Deterrence?*, 29 J. Legal Stud. 237, 237-238 (2000); David Crump, *Evidence, Economics, and Ethics: What Information Should Jurors Be Given to Determine the Amount of a Punitive-Damage Award?*, 57 Md. L. Rev. 174, 182 (1998); A. Mitchell Polinsky & Steven Shavell, *Punitive Damages: An Economic Analysis*, 111 Harv. L. Rev. 869, 873-874 (1998). The contention that punitive damages deter undesirable behaviors has been contested. *See, e.g.*, E. Donald Elliott, *Why Punitive Damages*

Don't Deter Corporate Misconduct Effectively, 40 Ala. L. Rev. 1053, 1057-1058 (1989).

Scholars who justify punitive damage awards on the basis of retribution focus on the wrongful character of the defendant's actions and argue that punitive damages should be awarded because bad actors deserve it — wrongful actions should be punished in the interest of justice. *See, e.g.*, Anthony J. Sebok, *Punitive Damages: From Myth to Theory*, 92 Iowa L. Rev. 957 (2007); David Luban, *A Flawed Case Against Punitive Damages*, 87 Geo. L.J. 359, 360 (1998); Marc Galanter & David Luban, *Poetic Justice: Punitive Damages and Legal Pluralism*, 42 Am. U. L. Rev. 1393, 1426-1427 (1993); Michael Rustad & Thomas Koenig, *The Historical Continuity of Punitive Damages Awards: Reforming the Tort Reformers*, 42 Am. U. L. Rev. 1269, 1320-1321 (1993).

One issue that arises frequently in connection with punitive damages is the possibility that multiple punitive awards will be granted sequentially, to different plaintiffs, based on the same conduct that happens to cause harm to a number of victims. This may result, in the aggregate, in unfair and inefficiently excessive punishment. The possibility of multiple punishments will be considered below in connection with the unconstitutionality of allegedly excessive punitive damages awards. One scholar has suggested that a national registry of punitive awards be established, by which previous awards for the same conduct would be taken into account in setting appropriate punitive damages awards in the future. *See* Jim Gash, *Solving the Multiple Punishments Problem: A Call for a National Punitive Damages Registry*, 99 Nw. L. Rev. 1613 (2004-05).

Finally, some scholars have observed that punitive damage awards help ensure that victims are fully compensated for their losses. For example, because legal rules in the United States do not allow the winner of a tort action to collect attorneys' fees, many plaintiffs who receive a compensatory damage award are not made completely whole, since the attorney takes a significant percentage of any award. Punitive damages can be used to pay attorneys' fees, leaving the plaintiff more fully compensated for any harm he suffered.

Critics of punitive damages argue that they provide an unfair windfall to the plaintiff. However desirable it may be to deter wrongful behavior, there is no reason to convert the tort system into a lottery, awarding damages to one plaintiff based on harms that the defendant's conduct may have caused to innumerable other plaintiffs. Further, it is argued, punitive damages involve a kind of double jeopardy: the defendant can often be subject to criminal sanctions after having paid a large punitive award. To the extent that both criminal penalties and punitive damages seek to deter undesirable conduct and punish those whose conduct warrants punishment, the defendant can be said to have been punished twice for the same conduct. Another criticism of punitive damage awards is that juries have very little guidance in assessing them, which, it is claimed, leads to exorbitantly high awards in some cases. *See, e.g.*, Richard W. Murphy, *Punitive Damages, Explanatory Verdicts, and the Hard Look*, 76 Wash. L. Rev. 995 (2001) (arguing that juries should be required to explain the factual bases for punitive damage awards). As a result, some commentators have urged caps (outside limits) on punitive damage awards. *See, e.g.*, Linda Babcock & Greg Pogarsky, *Damage Caps and Settlement: A*

Behavioral Approach, 28 J. Legal Stud. 341, 343-344 (1999). Many legislatures have implemented this suggestion in one form or another. *See, e.g.*, Ga. Code Ann. §768.73(1)(a) (West Supp. 2001).

Arguments about the purposes and policies behind punitive damage awards are more than merely academic. Indeed, both the concern of critics that juries have little guidance in formulating punitive damage verdicts and the arguments by proponents about the policy reasons for making punitive damage awards in the first place are implicated in the following case.

OWENS-ILLINOIS, INC. v. ZENOBIA
601 A.2d 633 (Md. 1992)

ELDRIDGE, Judge.

[The plaintiffs alleged that asbestos manufactured by the defendants caused them to suffer harm. The jury awarded punitive damages against some defendants, including Owens-Illinois. The appellate court affirmed the punitive damages award against Owens-Illinois.]

We issued a writ of certiorari in these cases to consider several important questions relating to a strict products liability cause of action based on failure to warn of the dangerousness of the products, and to reconsider some of the principles governing awards of punitive damages in tort cases. . . .

IV.

In granting the petitions for a writ of certiorari in these cases, this Court issued an order requesting that the briefs and argument encompass the following issue:

> [W]hat should be the correct standard under Maryland law for the allowance of punitive damages in negligence and products liability cases, i.e., gross negligence, actual malice, or some other standard. . . .

[I]n recent years there has been a proliferation of claims for punitive damages in tort cases, and awards of punitive damages have often been extremely high. . . .

Accompanying this increase in punitive damages claims, awards and amounts of awards, is renewed criticism of the concept of punitive damages in a tort system designed primarily to compensate injured parties for harm. In Maryland the criticism has been partly fueled and justified because juries are provided with imprecise and uncertain characterizations of the type of conduct which will expose a defendant to a potential award of punitive damages. Accordingly, we shall (1) examine these characterizations of a defendant's conduct in light of the historic objectives of punitive damages, (2) more precisely define the nature of conduct potentially subject to a punitive damages award in non-intentional tort cases, and (3) heighten the standard of proof required of a plaintiff seeking an award of punitive damages.

These cases, along with two others heard by us on the same day, directly raise the problem of what basic standard of wrongful conduct should be used for the allowance of punitive damages in negligence actions generally, and in products liability actions based on either negligence or on strict liability. The jury in these cases received the following instruction on punitive damages:

> Implied malice, which the plaintiffs have to prove in order to recover punitive damages in this case, requires a finding by you of a wanton disposition, grossly irresponsible to the rights of others, extreme recklessness and utter disregard for the rights of others. . . .

[The] court required the plaintiffs to show by a preponderance of evidence that the defendants acted with "implied" rather than "actual" malice. That is, the plaintiffs were not required to show that the defendants' conduct was characterized by evil motive, intent to injure, fraud, or actual knowledge of the defective nature of the products coupled with a deliberate disregard of the consequences. Instead, the plaintiffs were required to show only that the defendants' conduct was grossly negligent.

The standard applied by the trial court and the Court of Special Appeals results from, and consequently requires re-examination of, some of the decisions of this Court relating to punitive damages. . . .

B . . .

In 1972 this Court, for the first time in a non-intentional tort action, allowed an award of punitive damages based upon implied malice. The Court . . . allowed the plaintiff to recover punitive damages upon a showing that the defendant was guilty of "gross negligence," which was defined as a "wanton or reckless disregard for human life." . . .

The gross negligence standard has led to inconsistent results and frustration of the purposes of punitive damages in non-intentional tort cases. . . .

In the face of "a literal explosion of punitive damage law and practice," many states have acted to define more accurately the type of conduct which can form the basis for a punitive damages award. In Tuttle v. Raymond, 494 A.2d 1353 (Me. 1985), the Supreme Judicial Court of Maine reviewed its law on punitive damages. The implied malice standard applied by the lower courts in Tuttle allowed recovery of punitive damages upon a showing that the defendant's conduct was "wanton, malicious, reckless or grossly negligent." 494 A.2d at 1360. The court rejected this standard, stating (494 A.2d at 1361):

> "Gross" negligence simply covers too broad and too vague an area of behavior, resulting in an unfair and inefficient use of the doctrine of punitive damages. . . . A similar problem exists with allowing punitive damages based merely upon "reckless" conduct. "To sanction punitive damages solely upon the basis of conduct characterized as heedless disregard of the consequences would be to allow virtually limitless imposition of punitive damages."

The Maine court went on to point out that the implied malice standard "over-extends the availability of punitive damages" and consequently "dulls the potentially keen edge of the doctrine as an effective deterrent of truly reprehensible conduct." *Ibid.* . . .

As previously indicated, arbitrary and inconsistent application of the standard for awarding punitive damages frustrates the dual purposes of punishment and deterrence. Implied malice as that term has been used, with its various and imprecise formulations, fosters this uncertainty. As pointed out by Professor Ellis (D. Ellis, *Fairness and Efficiency in the Law of Punitive Damages*, 56 S. Cal. L. Rev. 1, 52-53 (1982)): "[T]he law of punitive damages is characterized by a high degree of uncertainty that stems from the use of a multiplicity of vague, overlapping terms. . . . Accordingly, there is little reason to believe that only deserving defendants are punished, or that fair notice of punishable conduct is provided." . . .

The implied malice test . . . has been overbroad in its application and has resulted in inconsistent jury verdicts involving similar facts. It provides little guidance for individuals and companies to enable them to predict behavior that will either trigger or avoid punitive damages liability, and it undermines the deterrent effect of these awards. . . . In a non-intentional tort action, the trier of facts may not award punitive damages unless the plaintiff has established that the defendant's conduct was characterized by evil motive, intent to injure, ill will, or fraud, i.e., "actual malice." . . .

E.

The defendant Owens-Illinois and some amici have argued that, in order for a jury to consider a punitive damages award, a plaintiff should be required to establish by clear and convincing evidence that the defendant's conduct was characterized by actual malice. . . .

A growing majority of states requires that a plaintiff prove the defendant's malicious conduct by clear and convincing evidence before punitive damages can be considered. Many states have adopted the clear and convincing standard by statute. Other states have adopted the standard by judicial decisions. . . .

Use of a clear and convincing standard of proof will help to insure that punitive damages are properly awarded. We hold that this heightened standard is appropriate in the assessment of punitive damages because of their penal nature and potential for debilitating harm. Consequently, in any tort case a plaintiff must establish by clear and convincing evidence the basis for an award of punitive damages. . . .

[The concurring opinion of McAuliffe, J. is omitted.]

ROBERT M. BELL, Judge, concurring and dissenting.

I part company with the majority on the question of what is the appropriate standard for determining the cases in which punitive damages are appropriate. While I have no quarrel with requiring that, in some cases, "actual malice," characterized as "evil motive," "intent to injure," "ill will," "fraud," or, in the case of products liability actions, "actual knowledge of the defective nature of the product, coupled with a deliberate disregard of the consequences," be shown, I am opposed to excising from the standard the concept . . . : "wanton or reckless disregard for human life," sometimes characterized as "gross negligence." That standard, now the old one, is a floor, not a ceiling; it sets a minimum requirement, not a maximum. Therefore, if a defendant acts with "actual malice," however, characterized, he or she will be subject to an award of punitive damages under the old standard. On the other hand, by adopting the "actual malice" standard, the majority does much more than excise a useless phrase, it places outside the scope of punitive damages eligibility numerous deserving cases, differing from cases that remain punitive damages eligible only in the subjective element. That change simply goes too far.

The perception is that more claims for punitive damages, involving conduct so diverse that predictability and, therefore, the ability to choose the proper conduct and avoid being culpable, than were justified, were being brought and allowed with the result that the purposes of punitive damages were being undermined. The changes proposed are for the purpose of making the awards more uniform and consistent with the historical bases for punitive damages awards: punishment and deterrence. The purposes of punitive damages are better served, it has been determined, by requiring a more stringent standard for assessing punitive damages and by requiring a greater burden of proof. To be sure, one of the goals of today's decision is to set a higher threshold for punitive damages eligibility. That is accomplished by changing the burden of proof, that clearly will exclude some undeserving cases, no doubt, a large number, even applying the old standard. But, by both changing the burden of proof and the standard, an even greater percentage of deserving cases, heretofore eligible for punitive damages awards, is affected. Indeed, by so doing, not only is the threshold raised, but excluded is an entire category of cases, non-intentional torts, involving, in many instances, injuries of greater severity than in cases that still qualify and, thus, not necessarily those least deserving of an award of punitive damages. And the distinction causing the exclusion is the subjective intent of the defendant. While I can agree, as I have previously indicated, to raising the threshold by raising the level of the proof required, I cannot agree that punitive damages should be awarded only in cases of "actual malice," where there is a subjective intent element. In cases where there is no actual malice, the totality of the circumstances may reveal conduct on the part of a defendant that is just as heinous as the conduct motivated by that actual malice and, so, for all intents and purposes is the same.

Although not intentional, i.e., willful, conduct, nevertheless, may be outrageousness [sic] and extreme in the context in which it occurs, and may produce injuries commensurate with those caused by intentional conduct. In other words, conduct may be so reckless and outrageous as to be the equivalent of intentional conduct. . . .

Permitting punitive damages when one acts with actual malice, but not when, given the totality of the circumstances, that same person acts in total disregard for the safety of others has no reasoned basis.

Consider the following example. A hot water pipe bursts in a crowded apartment complex quite near an open area upon which young people are playing baseball. A repair team dispatched to make repairs observes young people playing baseball nearby. It also sees that the area of the affected pipe is in easy reach of a baseball hit to the outfield. Nevertheless, they dig a hole, but, being unable to proceed due to the temperature of the water, suspend operations. Although aware of the young people playing in the area, they leave without warning them of the hole or its contents or in any way marking or obstructing the hole. One of the outfielders, having chased and caught a ball hit to the outfield, falls into the hole and is severely injured.

Under the new standard, if it could be proved that a member of the repair team harbored ill will toward the outfielder and, in the back of his mind, entertained a hope that the outfielder, or one of the other players, would fall in the unattended hole, then, in addition to compensable damages, the outfielder could recover punitive damages. On the other hand, if none of the members of the repair team knew any of the ball players and, in fact, harbored no evil motive at all, no punitive damages could be recovered, notwithstanding that they acted, given the circumstances, in total disregard of the safety of the ballplayers. I can see no reasoned difference between these scenarios. The state of mind of the individual simply is not so important a factor as to permit recovery in one case and not in the other.

I am satisfied that allowing punitive damages for "wanton and reckless conduct," . . . serves the purposes of punishment and deterrence. Gross negligence, outrageous conduct, etc. cannot be defined in a vacuum. To have meaning, the terms must be viewed in a factual context. The conduct described in the example is not only outrageous and extraordinary, it is the sine qua non of reckless conduct. Such conduct should be punished. And that scenario presents a striking example of the kind of conduct a defendant must not engage in if he or she is to avoid paying punitive damages. The example I have proffered is not the only one that can be posited. There are hundreds of such cases. The long and short of it is that changing the standard for punitive damages will eliminate numbers of cases, in which, heretofore, punitive damages would have been appropriate and those cases now are eliminated not because their facts are not egregious enough to justify such an award but because other, less serious, and perhaps, undeserving, cases may also qualify for such damages. With all due respect, that is not a sufficiently good reason to change the rules of the game.

Insulating a defendant from an award of punitive damages except when he or she acts with actual malice, meaning with an evil intent, ill will, with intent to injure, or to defraud, provides a disincentive for that defendant to act reasonably. Since, from the standpoint of a defendant's pocketbook, it makes no difference in the award of damages, whether he or she is negligent or grossly negligent, that is, his or her conduct is extreme to a point just short of being intentional, requiring that defendant to pay compensatory damages for the victims's injuries is not likely to have a deterrent effect; it is not likely to cause him or her to consider, not to mention, change, his or her conduct. . . .

WHAT SORTS OF CONDUCT JUSTIFY PUNITIVES?

The standard for punitive damages varies from jurisdiction to jurisdiction. As in *Zenobia*, some jurisdictions award punitive damages only where actual malice is present. Other tests for awarding punitive damages include "conscious disregard for the consequences" (Ford Motor Co. v. Stubblefield, 319 S.E.2d 470 (Ga. 1984)); "evil mind" (including evil acts, spiteful motive, or outrageous, oppressive, or intolerant conduct creating a substantial risk of tremendous harm) (Volz v. Coleman Co., Inc., 748 P.2d 1191 (Ariz. 1987)); and "wanton disregard for safety"

(Axen v. American Home Products Corp., 974 P.2d 224 (Or. Ct. App. 1999)). All of these tests require something more than mere negligence on the part of the defendant. Either the conduct must be intentional, or it must exhibit awareness of, and indifference toward, significant attendant risks. Conduct creating a serious risk of harm of which the actor is aware has been dubbed "negligence with an attitude." *See* James A. Henderson, Jr. & Aaron D. Twerski, *Intent and Recklessness in Tort: The Practical Craft of Restating Law*, 54 Vand. L. Rev. 1133, 1143 (2001).

Regardless of the tortfeasor's state of mind, to justify punitive damages the conduct must be tortious in the first instance; it must satisfy the requirements of some theory of tort liability. Courts commonly award punitive damages in cases of intentional torts, such as battery, false imprisonment, or assault. However, even though the defendant in such cases acts intending to cause harm, the defendant's motive or the general outrageousness of her conduct can be relevant in determining whether an award of punitive damages is justified. *See, e.g.*, Banks v. Fritsch, 39 S.W.3d 474 (Ky. Ct. App. 2001) (teacher who chained student to a tree for misbehavior was not liable for punitive damages because teacher's actions did not exhibit "conscious wrongdoing"); Budgar v. State of New York, 414 N.Y.S.2d 463 (N.Y. Ct. Cl. 1979) (state was not subject to punitive damages for false imprisonment and malicious prosecution because conduct of state trooper was "not so egregious" as to support such damages).

When the underlying tort theory is negligence, courts usually use some form of heightened standard relating to recklessness or gross negligence in order to determine whether punitive damages are appropriate. Gross negligence, by contrast to recklessness, does not require an awareness of risk. *See, e.g.*, Williams v. Wilson, 972 So. 2d 260 (Ky. 1998) (holding a statutory requirement of awareness invalid under the state constitution because it effectively eliminated the traditional right to punitive damages upon a showing of "gross negligence"). Gross negligence can thus be thought of as conduct that, while not necessarily undertaken with awareness of risk, is nevertheless either extremely likely to cause harm, extremely easy to avoid, or both. In some states, the term "gross negligence" merely means recklessness. *See, e.g.*, Fla. Stat. § 768.72(2)(b). Punitive damages can also be assessed in strict liability cases, typically upon a showing of either intentional or reckless conduct.

IS LIABILITY INSURANCE FOR PUNITIVE DAMAGES AGAINST PUBLIC POLICY?

In Price v. Hartford Accident & Indemnity Co., 502 P.2d 522 (Ariz. 1972), Hartford insured the plaintiff-insured and her 17-year-old son for "all sums" for which either might become liable to pay as damages "arising out of the ownership, maintenance or use of the plaintiffs' automobile." The son was involved in a drag race in the covered vehicle that injured a third person, the tort plaintiff, who sought both compensatory and punitive damages in a subsequent tort action against both mother and son. Hartford agreed to defend the tort action on behalf of the insureds, but disclaimed insurance coverage for punitive damages. The plaintiff-insured brought a declaratory judgment against Hartford, insisting that coverage included punitives. The trial court sided with Hartford on the ground that liability insurance coverage for punitive damages would be against public policy by undermining both the punishment and deterrence objectives justifying such awards. The intermediate appellate court affirmed the trial court's ruling.

The Supreme Court of Arizona reversed the rulings below, reasoning as follows (502 P.2d at 524):

> [The] arguments [against coverage], at first blush, seem to have merit, but a careful analysis of them reveals several weaknesses. First, even though a driver is insured for punitive damages he cannot engage in wanton conduct with impunity. In the instant case, drag racing would subject him to criminal penalties. His insurance rates would soar. Hartford argues that the assigned risk provisions of the Arizona system would prevent them from soaring. However, the assigned risk procedure would not enable him to procure more than the minimum coverage of $15,000/30,000, and in order to replace his $1,000,000.00 limits, his premium would be tremendous. Second, Hartford has voluntarily covered its insured's liability for punitive damages, and since its premiums were based on its exposure, it may be presumed that holding it liable for what it has promised to pay would not result in additional burdens on the driving public. Third, the criminal penalties include possible loss of the driver's license and compulsory attendance at the traffic school. Fourth, punitive damages are not only designed to punish the offender but are also designed to serve as a deterrent to others. Since it is common knowledge that the vast majority of drivers do not carry million dollar liability policies, the possibility that punitive damages will exceed their policy limits will exercise a deterrent effect on them. Fifth, there is no evidence that those states which deny coverage have accomplished any appreciable effect on the slaughter on their highways. Sixth, the state of Arizona has more than one public policy. Such policy appears in many fields. One such public policy is that an insurance company which admittedly took a premium for covering all liability for damages, should honor its obligation.

VICARIOUS LIABILITY FOR PUNITIVE DAMAGES

Another situation in which questions arise concerning the policies underlying punitive damages is when an employer or other entity is held vicariously liable for the actions of employees or other servants. The jurisdictions divide into three camps on the issue. Some courts do not allow vicarious liability for punitive damages at all, on the theory that the fiction upon which vicarious liability is based (that the actions of the servant are equivalent to the actions of the principal) is unsupported when the conduct of the servant is egregious enough to warrant punitive damages. Another camp treats punitive damages the same as compensatory awards: when the servant commits an act that merits a punitive damage award, the principal is vicariously liable. *See, e.g.,* Hill v. USA Truck, Inc., 2007 WL 1574545 (D.S.C. 2007) (applying South Carolina law). The majority of jurisdictions, however, take a middle ground approach, holding that the principal is vicariously liable for punitive damages when the principal explicitly or implicitly assents to the servant's actions, or when the principal is aware of a high risk of such behavior in hiring, or subsequently not firing, the servant. *See, e.g.,* Speedway SuperAmerica, LLC v. Dupont, 933 So. 2d 75 (Fla. Dist. Ct. App. 2006) (employer vicariously liable for punitive damages for employee-agent's sexual harassment of another employee because employer took no action after being notified of harassment). Punitive damages may also be assessed vicariously when the servant is a manager, director, or other person charged with overseeing the organization and acts within the scope of her employment. In some states, this is not thought of as vicarious liability, but as direct liability, because such agents' actions are considered the actions of the principal itself. *See, e.g.,* Mercury Motors Express, Inc. v. Smith, 393 So. 2d 545 (Fla. 1981); and Restatement, Second, of Torts § 909 (1979).

WHO, EXACTLY, GETS THE PUNITIVES AWARD?

A significant handful of states have enacted statutes that require a percentage of punitive damages to be contributed to a state-administered fund. *See, e.g.,* Alaska Stat. § 09.17.020(j) (LexisNexis 2002) (50 percent of punitive damage award must be paid to state fund); Ga. Code Ann. § 51-12-5.1(2) (2000) (75 percent of punitive damage award must be paid to a state fund); Ind. Code Ann. § 34-51-3-6(b) (LexisNexis 1998) (75 percent of punitive damage award must be paid to a state fund); Iowa Code Ann. § 668A.1 (West 1998) (75 percent of punitive damage award must be paid to a state fund if the conduct that harmed the plaintiff was not intentional); Mo. Ann. Stat. § 537.675(3) (West Supp. 2003) (50 percent of punitive damage award must be paid to state fund); Utah Code Ann. § 78B-8-201(3)(a) (2002) (50 percent of punitive damage awarded in excess of $20,000 must be paid to state fund). In McBride v. General Motors Corp., 737 F. Supp. 1563 (M.D. Ga. 1990), a federal district court held that fund contribution statutes violate the federal constitution on a number of grounds, including equal protection. Some state courts that have addressed the same issue have disagreed. In Dardinger v. Anthem Blue Cross & Blue Shield, 781 N.E.2d 121 (Ohio 2002), the Supreme Court of Ohio reduced a jury verdict for punitive damages from $39 million to $20 million against a health insurer who wrongfully denied coverage for chemotherapy treatment to a cancer patient. The court did not, however, award the full $20 million to the plaintiff decedent's estate. Instead it awarded $10 million plus attorneys' fees to the estate. The court earmarked the remainder for a cancer research fund in the name of the decedent and designated Ohio State University as the institution to conduct the research and administer the fund. To our knowledge, this is the first time a court has made such an allocation absent a legislative directive.

DETERMINING THE APPROPRIATE SIZE OF PUNITIVE DAMAGES AWARDS

Zenobia refers to the difficulty the jury faces in applying the legal standard for punitive damages. The jury faces another difficulty in reaching appropriate punitive damage awards: how to arrive at an appropriate dollar amount. Traditionally, the amount is largely within the discretion of the jury. *See* Cater v. Cater, 846 S.W.2d 173 (Ark. 1993). Some factors for consideration in reaching an amount include the defendant's intent or lack thereof, the degree of the defendant's culpability, the amount necessary to deter both the defendant and others similarly situated from engaging in such conduct in the future, the duration of the conduct, and the defendant's ability to pay. This last factor—the defendant's ability to pay—is unique to punitive damages. In most other contexts, ability to pay is, and should be, irrelevant when determining a defendant's liability. "Deep pockets" may lurk behind our tort system as a background principle, but it should not be relevant on a case-by-case basis. Why do you suppose courts allow juries to weigh the defendant's wealth as a factor in connection with punitive damages?

A significant minority of states have statutes that limit the dollar amount of punitive damages awards, either by imposing an absolute cap or by limiting punitives to some multiple of compensatories. *See, e.g.*, Ala. Code §§ 6-11-20, 6-11-21 (1993 & Supp. 2003) (in physical injury cases, the greater of three times compensatories or $1.5 million); Miss. Code Ann. § 11-1-65 (West Supp. 2003) (between $20 million and 4 percent of the defendant's net worth as determined by a sliding scale in the statute); N.J. Stat. Ann. § 2A: 15-5.14 (West 2000) (generally, the greater of $350,000 or five times compensatories); Va. Code Ann. § 8.01-38.1 (Michie 2000) (cap of $350,000).

STATE FARM MUTUAL AUTOMOBILE INSURANCE CO. v. CAMPBELL
538 U.S. 408 (2003)

Justice KENNEDY delivered the opinion of the Court.

We address once again the measure of punishment, by means of punitive damages, a State may impose upon a defendant in a civil case. The question is whether, in the circumstances we shall recount, an award of $145 million in punitive damages, where full compensatory damages are $1 million, is excessive and in violation of the Due Process Clause of the Fourteenth Amendment to the Constitution of the United States.

I

In 1981, Curtis Campbell (Campbell) was driving with his wife, Inez Preece Campbell, in Cache County, Utah. He decided to pass six vans traveling ahead of them on a two-lane highway. Todd Ospital was driving a small car approaching from the opposite direction. To avoid a head-on collision with Campbell, who by then was driving on the wrong side of the highway and toward oncoming traffic, Ospital swerved onto the shoulder, lost control of his automobile, and collided with a vehicle driven by Robert G. Slusher. Ospital was killed, and Slusher was rendered permanently disabled. The Campbells escaped unscathed. . . .

In the ensuing wrongful death and tort action, Campbell insisted he was not at fault. Early investigations did support differing conclusions as to who caused the accident, but "consensus was reached early on by the investigators and witnesses that Mr. Campbell's unsafe pass had indeed caused the crash." . . . Campbell's insurance company, petitioner State Farm Mutual Automobile Insurance Company (State Farm), nonetheless decided to contest liability and declined offers by Slusher and Ospital's estate (Ospital) to settle the claims for the policy limit of $50,000 ($25,000 per claimant). State Farm also ignored the advice of one of its own investigators and took the case to trial, assuring the Campbells that "their assets were safe, that they had no liability for the accident, that [State Farm] would represent their interests, and that they did not need to procure separate counsel." . . . To the contrary, a jury determined that Campbell was 100 percent at fault, and a judgment was returned for $185,849, far more than the amount offered in settlement.

At first State Farm refused to cover the $135,849 in excess liability. Its counsel made this clear to the Campbells: "'You may want to put for sale signs on your property to get things moving.'" . . . Nor was State Farm willing to post a supersedeas bond to allow Campbell to appeal the judgment against him. Campbell obtained his own counsel to appeal the verdict. During the pendency of the appeal, in late 1984, Slusher, Ospital, and the Campbells reached an agreement whereby Slusher and Ospital agreed not to seek satisfaction of their claims against the Campbells. In exchange the Campbells agreed to pursue a bad faith action against State Farm and to be represented by Slusher's and Ospital's attorneys. The Campbells also agreed that Slusher and Ospital would have a right to play a part in all major decisions concerning the bad faith action. No settlement could be concluded without Slusher's and Ospital's approval, and Slusher and Ospital would receive 90 percent of any verdict against State Farm.

In 1989, the Utah Supreme Court denied Campbell's appeal in the wrongful death and tort actions. . . . State Farm then paid the entire judgment, including the amounts in excess of the policy limits. The Campbells nonetheless filed a complaint against State Farm alleging bad faith, fraud, and intentional infliction of emotional distress. The trial court initially granted State Farm's motion for summary judgment because State Farm had paid the excess verdict, but that ruling was reversed on appeal. . . . On remand State Farm moved *in limine* to exclude evidence of alleged conduct that occurred in unrelated cases outside of Utah, but the trial court denied the motion. At State Farm's request the trial court bifurcated the trial into two phases conducted before different juries. In the first phase the jury determined that State Farm's decision not to settle was unreasonable because there was a substantial likelihood of an excess verdict.

Before the second phase of the action against State Farm we decided BMW of North America, Inc. v. Gore, 517 U.S. 559, L. Ed. 2d 809 (1996), and refused to sustain a $2 million punitive damages award which accompanied a verdict of only $4,000 in compensatory damages. Based on that decision, State Farm again moved for the exclusion of evidence of dissimilar out-of-state conduct. . . . The trial court denied State Farm's motion. . . .

The second phase addressed State Farm's liability for fraud and intentional infliction of emotional distress, as well as compensatory and punitive damages. The Utah Supreme Court aptly characterized this phase of the trial:

> State Farm argued during phase II that its decision to take the case to trial was an "honest mistake" that did not warrant punitive damages. In contrast, the

Campbells introduced evidence that State Farm's decision to take the case to trial was a result of a national scheme to meet corporate fiscal goals by capping payouts on claims company wide. This scheme was referred to as State Farm's "Performance, Planning and Review," or PP & R, policy. To prove the existence of this scheme, the trial court allowed the Campbells to introduce extensive expert testimony regarding fraudulent practices by State Farm in its nation-wide operations. Although State Farm moved prior to phase II of the trial for the exclusion of such evidence and continued to object to it at trial, the trial court ruled that such evidence was admissible to determine whether State Farm's conduct in the Campbell case was indeed intentional and sufficiently egregious to warrant punitive damages. . . .

Evidence pertaining to the PP&R policy concerned State Farm's business practices for over 20 years in numerous States. Most of these practices bore no relation to third-party automobile insurance claims, the type of claim underlying the Campbells' complaint against the company. The jury awarded the Campbells $2.6 million in compensatory damages and $145 million in punitive damages, which the trial court reduced to $1 million and $25 million respectively. Both parties appealed.

The Utah Supreme Court sought to apply the three guideposts we identified in *Gore, supra,* . . . and it reinstated the $145 million punitive damages award. Relying in large part on the extensive evidence concerning the PP&R policy, the court concluded State Farm's conduct was reprehensible. The court also relied upon State Farm's "massive wealth" and on testimony indicating that "State Farm's actions, because of their clandestine nature, will be punished at most in one out of every 50,000 cases as a matter of statistical probability," . . . and concluded that the ratio between punitive and compensatory damages was not unwarranted. Finally, the court noted that the punitive damages award was not excessive when compared to various civil and criminal penalties State Farm could have faced, including $10,000 for each act of fraud, the suspension of its license to conduct business in Utah, the disgorgement of profits, and imprisonment. . . . We granted certiorari. . . .

II

We recognized in Cooper Industries, Inc. v. Leatherman Tool Group, Inc., 532 U.S. 424, . . . that in our judicial system compensatory and punitive damages, although usually awarded at the same time by the same decisionmaker, serve different purposes. . . . Compensatory damages "are intended to redress the concrete loss that the plaintiff has suffered by reason of the defendant's wrongful conduct." . . . (citing Restatement (Second) of Torts § 903, pp. 453-454 (1979)). By contrast, punitive damages serve a broader function; they are aimed at deterrence and retribution. *Cooper Industries, supra.* . . .

While States possess discretion over the imposition of punitive damages, it is well established that there are procedural and substantive constitutional limitations on these awards. . . . The reason is that "elementary notions of fairness enshrined in our constitutional jurisprudence dictate that a person receive fair notice not only of the conduct that will subject him to punishment, but also of the severity of the penalty that a State may impose." . . . To the extent an award is grossly excessive, it furthers no legitimate purpose and constitutes an arbitrary deprivation of property. . . .

Although these awards serve the same purposes as criminal penalties, defendants subjected to punitive damages in civil cases have not been accorded the protections applicable in a criminal proceeding. This increases our concerns over the imprecise manner in which punitive damages systems are administered. We have admonished that "punitive damages pose an acute danger of arbitrary deprivation of property. Jury instructions typically leave the jury with wide discretion in choosing amounts, and the presentation of evidence of a defendant's net worth creates the potential that juries will use their verdicts to express biases against big businesses, particularly those without strong local presences." . . .

In light of these concerns, in *Gore supra*, . . . we instructed courts reviewing punitive damages to consider three guideposts: (1) the degree of reprehensibility of the defendant's misconduct; (2) the disparity between the actual or potential harm suffered by the plaintiff and the punitive damages award; and (3) the difference between the punitive damages awarded by the jury and the civil penalties authorized or imposed in comparable cases. . . . We reiterated the importance of these three guideposts in *Cooper Industries* and mandated appellate courts to conduct *de novo* review of a trial court's application of them to the jury's award. . . . Exacting appellate review ensures that an award of punitive damages is based upon an "'application of law, rather than a decisionmaker's caprice.'" . . .

III

Under the principles outlined in BMW of North America, Inc. v. Gore, this case is neither close nor difficult. It was error to reinstate the jury's $145 million punitive damages award. We address each guidepost of *Gore* in some detail.

A

"The most important indicium of the reasonableness of a punitive damages award is the degree of reprehensibility of the defendant's conduct." . . . We have instructed courts to determine the reprehensibility of a defendant by considering whether: the harm caused was physical as opposed to economic; the tortious conduct evinced an indifference to or a reckless disregard of the health or safety of others; the target of the conduct had financial vulnerability; the conduct involved repeated actions or was an isolated incident; and the harm was the result of intentional malice, trickery, or deceit, or mere accident. . . . The existence of any one of these factors weighing in favor of a plaintiff may not be sufficient to sustain a punitive damages award; and the absence of all of them renders any award suspect. It should be presumed a plaintiff has been made whole for his injuries by compensatory damages, so punitive damages should only be awarded if the defendant's culpability, after having paid compensatory damages, is so reprehensible as to warrant the imposition of further sanctions to achieve punishment or deterrence. . . .

Applying these factors in the instant case, we must acknowledge that State Farm's handling of the claims against the Campbells merits no praise. The trial court found that State Farm's employees altered the company's records to make Campbell appear less culpable. State Farm disregarded the overwhelming likelihood of liability and the near-certain probability that, by taking the case to trial, a judgment in excess of the policy limits would be awarded. State Farm amplified the harm by at first assuring the Campbells their assets would be safe from any verdict and by later telling them, postjudgment, to put a for-sale sign on their house. While we do not suggest there was error in awarding punitive damages based upon State Farm's conduct toward the Campbells, a more modest punishment for this reprehensible conduct could have satisfied the State's legitimate objectives, and the Utah courts should have gone no further.

This case, instead, was used as a platform to expose, and punish, the perceived deficiencies of State Farm's operations throughout the country. The Utah Supreme Court's opinion makes explicit that State Farm was being condemned for its nationwide policies rather than for the conduct direct toward the Campbells. 65 P.3d at 1143 ("The Campbells introduced evidence that State Farm's decision to take the case to trial was a result of a national scheme to meet corporate fiscal goals by capping payouts on claims company wide"). This was, as well, an explicit rationale of the trial court's decision in approving the award, though reduced from $145 million to $25 million. . . . ("[T]he Campbells demonstrated, through the testimony of State Farm employees who had worked outside of Utah, and through expert testimony, that this pattern of claims adjustment under the PP&R program was not a local anomaly, but was a consistent, nationwide feature of State Farm's business operations, orchestrated from the highest levels of corporate management").

The Campbells contend that State Farm has only itself to blame for the reliance upon dissimilar and out-of-state conduct evidence. The record does not support this contention. From their opening statements onward the Campbells framed this case as a chance to rebuke State Farm for its nationwide activities. . . . ("You're going to hear evidence that even the insurance commission in Utah and around the country are unwilling or inept at protecting people against abuses"); . . . ("[T]his is a very important case. . . . It transcends the Campbell file. It involves a nationwide practice. And you, here, are going to be evaluating and assessing, and hopefully requiring State Farm to stand accountable for what it's doing across the country, which is the purpose of punitive damages"). This was a position maintained throughout the litigation. In opposing State Farm's motion to exclude such evidence under *Gore*, the Campbells' counsel convinced the trial court that there was no limitation on the scope of evidence that could be considered under our precedents. . . .

A State cannot punish a defendant for conduct that may have been lawful where it occurred. . . . Nor, as a general rule, does a State have a legitimate concern in imposing punitive damages to punish a defendant for unlawful acts committed outside of the State's jurisdiction. Any proper adjudication of conduct that occurred outside Utah to other persons would require their inclusion, and, to those parties, the Utah courts, in the usual case, would need to apply the laws of their relevant jurisdiction. Phillips Petroleum Co. v. Shutts, 472 U.S. 797. . . .

Here, the Campbells do not dispute that much of the out-of-state conduct was lawful where it occurred. They argue, however, that such evidence was not the primary basis for the punitive damages award and was relevant to the extent it demonstrated, in a general sense, State Farm's motive against its insured. Brief for Respondents 46-47 ("Even if the practices described by State Farm were not malum in se or malum prohibitum, they became relevant to punitive damages to the extent they were used as tools to implement State Farm's wrongful PP&R policy"). This argument misses the mark. Lawful out-of-state conduct may be probative when it demonstrates the deliberateness and culpability of the defendant's action in the State where it is tortious, but that conduct must have a nexus to the specific harm suffered by the plaintiff. A jury must be instructed, furthermore, that it may not use evidence of out-of-state conduct to punish a defendant for action that was lawful in the jurisdiction where it occurred. . . .

For a more fundamental reason, however, the Utah courts erred in relying upon this and other evidence: The courts awarded punitive damages to punish and deter conduct that bore no relation to the Campbells' harm. A defendant's dissimilar acts, independent from the acts upon which liability was premised, may not serve as the basis for punitive damages. A defendant should be punished for the conduct that harmed the plaintiff, not for being an unsavory individual or business. Due process does not permit courts, in the calculation of punitive damages, to adjudicate the merits of other parties' hypothetical claims against a defendant under the guise of the reprehensibility analysis, but we have no doubt the Utah Supreme Court did that here. . . . Punishment on these bases creates the possibility of multiple punitive damages awards for the same conduct; for in the usual case nonparties are not bound by the judgment some other plaintiff obtains. . . .

The Campbells have identified scant evidence of repeated misconduct of the sort that injured them. Nor does our review of the Utah courts' decisions convince us that State Farm was only punished for its actions toward the Campbells. Although evidence of other acts need not be identical to have relevance in the calculation of punitive damages, the Utah court erred here because evidence pertaining to claims that had nothing to do with a third-party lawsuit was introduced at length. Other evidence concerning reprehensibility was even more tangential. For example, the Utah Supreme Court criticized State Farm's investigation into the personal life of one of its employees and, in a broader approach, the manner in which State Farm's policies corrupted its employees. . . . The Campbells attempt to justify the courts' reliance upon this unrelated testimony on the theory that each dollar of profit made by underpaying a third-party claimant is the same as a dollar made by underpaying a first-party one. . . . For the reasons already stated, this argument is unconvincing. The reprehensibility guidepost does not permit courts to expand the scope of the case so that a defendant may be punished for any malfeasance, which in this case extended for a 20-year period. In this case, because the Campbells have shown no conduct by State Farm similar to that which harmed them, the conduct that harmed them is the only conduct relevant to the reprehensibility analysis.

B

Turning to the second *Gore* guidepost, we have been reluctant to identify concrete constitutional limits on the ratio between harm, or potential harm, to the plaintiff and the punitive damages award. *Gore, supra,* at 582, 116 S. Ct. 1589 ("[W]e have consistently rejected the notion that the constitutional line is marked by a simple mathematical formula, even one that compares actual *and potential* damages to the punitive award"). . . . We decline again to impose a bright-line ratio which a punitive damages award cannot exceed. Our jurisprudence and the principles it has now established demonstrate, however, that, in practice, few awards exceeding a single-digit ratio between punitive and compensatory damages, to a significant degree, will satisfy due process. In *Haslip,* in upholding a punitive damages award, we concluded that an award of more than four times the amount of compensatory damages might be close to the line of constitutional impropriety. 499 U.S., at 23-24. . . . We cited that 4-to-1 ratio again in *Gore.* 517 U.S., at 581. . . . The Court further referenced a long legislative history, dating back over 700 years and going forward to today, providing for sanctions of double, treble, or quadruple damages to deter and punish. . . . While these ratios are not binding, they are instructive. They demonstrate what should be obvious: Single-digit multipliers are more likely to comport with due process, while still achieving the State's goals of deterrence and retribution, than awards with ratios in range of 500 to 1, . . . or, in this case, of 145 to 1.

Nonetheless, because there are no rigid benchmarks that a punitive damages award may not surpass, ratios greater than those we have previously upheld may comport with due process where "a particularly egregious act has resulted in only a small amount of economic damages." . . . The converse is also true, however. When compensatory damages are substantial, then a lesser ratio, perhaps only equal to compensatory damages, can reach the outermost limit of the due process guarantee. The precise award in any case, of course, must be based upon the facts and circumstances of the defendant's conduct and the harm to the plaintiff.

In sum, courts must ensure that the measure of punishment is both reasonable and proportionate to the amount of harm to the plaintiff and to the general damages recovered. In the context of this case, we have no doubt that there is a presumption against an award that has a 145-to-1 ratio. The compensatory award in this case was substantial; the Campbells were awarded $1 million for a year and a half of emotional distress. This was complete compensation. The harm arose from a transaction in the economic realm, not from some physical assault or trauma; there were no physical injuries; and State Farm paid the excess verdict before the complaint was filed, so the Campbells suffered only minor economic injuries for the 18-month period in which State Farm refused to resolve the claim against them. The compensatory damages for the injury suffered here, moreover, likely were based on a component which was duplicated in the punitive award. Much of the distress was caused by the outrage and humiliation the Campbells suffered at the actions of their insurer; and it is a major role of punitive damages to condemn such conduct. Compensatory damages, however, already contain this punitive element. . . .

The Utah Supreme Court sought to justify the massive award by pointing to State Farm's purported failure to report a prior $100 million punitive damages award in Texas to its corporate headquarters; the fact that State Farm's policies have affected numerous Utah consumers; the fact that State Farm will only be punished in one out of every 50,000 cases as a matter of statistical probability; and State Farm's enormous wealth. . . . Since the Supreme Court of Utah discussed the Texas award when applying the ratio guidepost, we discuss it here. The Texas award, however, should have been analyzed in the context of the reprehensibility guidepost only. The failure of the company to report the Texas award is out-of-state conduct that, if the conduct were similar, might have had some bearing on the degree of reprehensibility, subject to the limitations we have described. Here, it was dissimilar, and of such marginal relevance that it should have been accorded little or no weight. The award was rendered in a first-party lawsuit; no judgment was entered in the case; and it was later settled for a fraction of the verdict. With respect to the Utah Supreme Court's second justification, the Campbells' inability to direct us to testimony demonstrating harm to the people of Utah (other than those directly involved in this case) indicates that the adverse effect on the State's general population was in fact minor.

The remaining premises for the Utah Supreme Court's decision bear no relation to the award's reasonableness or proportionality to the harm. They are, rather, arguments that seek to defend a departure from well-established constraints on punitive damages. While States enjoy considerable discretion in deducing when punitive damages are warranted, each award must comport with the principles set forth in *Gore*. Here the argument that State Farm will be punished in only the rare case, coupled with reference to its assets (which, of course, are what other insured parties in Utah and other States must rely upon for payment of claims) had little to do with the actual harm sustained by the Campbells. The wealth of a defendant cannot justify an otherwise unconstitutional punitive damages award. . . . ("[Wealth] provides an open-ended basis for inflating awards when the defendant is wealthy. . . . That does not make its use unlawful or inappropriate; it simply means that this factor cannot make up for the failure of other factors, such as 'reprehensibility,' to constrain significantly an award that purports to punish a defendant's conduct"). The principles set forth in *Gore* must be implemented with care, to ensure both reasonableness and proportionality.

C

The third guidepost in *Gore* is the disparity between the punitive damages award and the "civil penalties authorized or imposed in comparable cases." . . . We note that, in the past, we have also looked to criminal penalties that could be imposed. . . . The existence of a criminal penalty does have bearing on the seriousness with which a State views the wrongful action. When used to determine the dollar amount of the award, however, the criminal penalty has less utility. Great care must be taken to avoid use of the civil process to assess criminal penalties that can be imposed only after the heightened protections of a criminal trial have been observed, including, of course, its higher standards of proof. Punitive damages are not a substitute for the criminal process, and the remote possibility of a criminal sanction does not automatically sustain a punitive damages award.

Here, we need not dwell long on this guidepost. The most relevant civil sanction under Utah state law for the wrong done to the Campbells appears to be a $10,000 fine for an act of fraud . . . an amount dwarfed by the $145 million punitive damages award. The Supreme Court of Utah speculated about the loss of State Farm's business license, the disgorgement of profits, and possible imprisonment, but here again its references were to the broad fraudulent scheme drawn from evidence of out-of-state and dissimilar conduct. This analysis was insufficient to justify the award.

IV

An application of the *Gore* guideposts to the facts of this case, especially in light of the substantial compensatory damages awarded (a portion of which contained a punitive element), likely would justify a punitive damages award at or near the amount of compensatory damages. The punitive award of $145 million, therefore, was neither reasonable nor proportionate to the wrong committed, and it was an irrational and arbitrary deprivation of the property of the defendant. The proper calculation of punitive damages under the principles we have discussed should be resolved, in the first instance, by the Utah courts.

The judgment of the Utah Supreme Court is reversed, and the case is remanded for proceedings not inconsistent with this opinion.

It is so ordered.

[The dissenting opinion by Justices Scalia and Thomas are omitted.]

[Justice Ginsburg (dissenting) reviews the evidence of State Farm's conduct and finds it to be outrageous.]

The Court dismisses the evidence describing and documenting State Farm's PP&R policy and practices as essentially irrelevant, bearing "no relation to the Campbells' harm." . . . It is hardly apparent why that should be so. What is infirm about the Campbells' theory that their experience with State Farm exemplifies and reflects an overarching underpayment scheme, one that caused "repeated misconduct of the sort that injured them," . . . ? The Court's silence on that score is revealing: Once one recognizes that the Campbells did show "conduct by State Farm similar to that which harmed them," . . . it becomes impossible to shrink the reprehensibility analysis to this sole case, or to maintain, at odds with the determination of the trial court, . . . that "the adverse effect on the State's general population was in fact minor," *ante,* at 1525.

Evidence of out-of-state conduct, the Court acknowledges, may be "probative [even if the conduct is lawful in the state where it occurred] when it demonstrates the deliberateness and culpability of the defendant's action in the State where it is tortious. . . ." "Other acts" evidence concerning practices both in and out of State was introduced in this case to show just such "deliberateness" and "culpability." The evidence was admissible, the trial court ruled: (1) to document State Farm's "reprehensible" PP&R program; and (2) to "rebut [State Farm's] assertion that

[its] actions toward the Campbells were inadvertent errors or mistakes in judgment." . . . Viewed in this light, there surely was "a nexus" . . . between much of the "other acts" evidence and "the specific harm suffered by [the Campbells]." . . .

When the Court first ventured to override state-court punitive damages awards, it did so moderately. The Court recalled that "in our federal system, States necessarily have considerable flexibility in determining the level of punitive damages that they will allow in different classes of cases and in any particular case." *Gore*, 517 U.S., at 568. . . . Today's decision exhibits no such respect and restraint. No longer content to accord state-court judgments "a strong presumption of validity" . . . the Court announces that "few awards exceeding a single-digit ratio between punitive and compensatory damages, to a significant degree, will satisfy due process." . . . Moreover, the Court adds, when compensatory damages are substantial, doubling those damages "can reach the outermost limit of the due process guarantee." . . . In a legislative scheme or a state high court's design to cap punitive damages, the handiwork in setting single-digit and 1-to-1 benchmarks could hardly be questioned; in a judicial decree imposed on the States by this Court under the banner of substantive due process, the numerical controls today's decision installs seem to me boldly out of order.

. . .

I remain of the view that this Court has no warrant to reform state law governing awards of punitive damages. . . . Even if I were prepared to accept the flexible guides prescribed in *Gore*, I would not join the Court's swift conversion of those guides into instructions that begin to resemble marching orders. For the reasons stated, I would leave the judgment of the Utah Supreme Court undisturbed. . . .

FOOD FOR THOUGHT

How do you think state and lower federal courts will apply the *State Farm* criteria? Will punitive awards exceeding single-digit ratios pass constitutional scrutiny? *State Farm* implies that a few double-digit (or higher) awards, presumably involving reprehensible defendant conduct in the context of low compensatory damages, might do so. Although courts continue to recognize the possibility that an award might exceed a single-digit ratio, in fact they have reduced punitive awards to single-digit ratios with regularity since *State Farm. See, e.g.,* Gober v. Ralphs Grocery Co., 40 Cal. Rptr. 3d 92 (Cal. Ct. App. 2006) (reducing punitive damages to six times compensatory damages); Grassilli v. Barr, 48 Cal. Rptr. 3d 715 (Cal. Ct. App. 2006) (reducing punitives from an eight-to-one ratio to a four-to-one ratio); Romo v. Ford Motor Co., 6 Cal. Rptr. 3d 793 (Cal. Ct. App. 2003) (reducing punitive damages to a five-to-one ratio); Henley v. Philip Morris, Inc., 9 Cal. Rptr. 3d 29 (Cal. Ct. App. 2004) (reducing punitive damages to six to one); Bardis v. Oates, 14 Cal. Rptr. 3d 89 (Cal. Ct. App. 2004) (reducing punitive damages to a nine-to-one ratio); Textron Fin. Corp. v. National Union Fire Insurance Co., 13 Cal. Rptr. 3d 586 (Cal. Ct. App. 2004) (reducing punitive damages to a four-to-one ratio); Security Title Agency, Inc. v. Pope, 200 P.3d 977 (Ariz. Ct. App. 2008) ($35 million punitive damage award reduced to $6.1 million); Chasan v.

Farmer's Group, Inc., 2009 WL 3335341 (Ariz. Ct. App. 2009) (37-to-1 ratio of punitive damages to compensatory damages reduced to four-to-one ratio); McDonald's Corp. v. Ogborn, 309 S.W.3d 274 (Ky. Ct. App. 2009) ($1 million punitive damages reduced to $400,000 — four times the amount of compensatory damages); Goff v. Elmo Greer & Sons Construction Co., 297 S.W.3d 175 (Tenn. 2009) ($1 million punitive damages represented a ratio of 302 to 1 reduced to $500,000); Goddard v. Farmer's Insurance Co. of Oregon, 179 P.3d 645 (Or. 2008) (jury award of $20 million of punitive damages to compensatory damages of $863,000 was excessive — ratio of 16 to 1 reduced to four to one). *Also see* CGB Occupational Therapy, Inc. v. RHA Health Services, Inc. 499 F.3d 184 3rd Cir. 2007) (tortious interference with contract compensatory damages of $109,000 jury awarded $2 million in punitive damages; reduced to $750,000); Lompe v. Sunridge Partners, L.L.C., 818 F.3d 1041 (10th Cir. 2016) ($22.5 million in punitive damages where compensatory damages were $1.95 million for reckless monitoring of carbon monoxide; plaintiff renters' punitive damages against management company reduced to $1.9 million).

Where compensatory damages were low and defendant's conduct was egregious courts have upheld very high ratios. *See, e.g.,* Estate of Overbey v. Chad Franklin National Auto Sales North LLG, 361 S.W.3d 364 (Mo. 2012) ($500,000 punitive upheld even though compensatory damages were $4,5000; (conduct of misrepresenting terms of its agreement to customers); Howard Univ. v. Wilkins ($42,677 punitive and $1 compensatory damages upheld for retaliating against employees for filing a sexual harassment claim). In the famous Exxon Shipping Co. v. Baker case, 554 U.S. 471 (2008), the United States Supreme Court reduced the punitive damages from $2.5 billion to $507.5 million based on its interpretation of the appropriate limits of punitive damages under maritime law.

PHILIP MORRIS USA v. WILLIAMS
549 U.S. 346 (2007)

Justice BREYER delivered the opinion of the Court.

The question we address today concerns a large state-court punitive damages award. We are asked whether the Constitution's Due Process Clause permits a jury to base that award in part upon its desire to *punish* the defendant for harming persons who are not before the court (*e.g.*, victims whom the parties do not represent). We hold that such an award would amount to a taking of "property" from the defendant without due process.

I

This lawsuit arises out of the death of Jesse Williams, a heavy cigarette smoker. Respondent, Williams' widow, represents his estate in this state lawsuit for negligence and deceit against Philip Morris, the manufacturer of Marlboro, the brand that Williams favored. A jury found that Williams' death was caused by smoking; that Williams smoked in significant part because he thought it was safe to do so;

and that Philip Morris knowingly and falsely led him to believe that this was so. The jury ultimately found that Philip Morris was negligent (as was Williams) and that Philip Morris had engaged in deceit. In respect to deceit, the claim at issue here, it awarded compensatory damages of about $821,000 (about $21,000 economic and $800,000 noneconomic) along with $79.5 million in punitive damages.

The trial judge subsequently found the $79.5 million punitive damages award "excessive," and reduced it to $32 million. Both sides appealed. The Oregon Court of Appeals rejected Philip Morris' arguments and restored the $79.5 million jury award. Subsequently, Philip Morris sought review in the Oregon Supreme Court (which denied review) and then here. We remanded the case in light of State Farm Mut. Automobile Ins. Co. v. Campbell, 123 S. Ct. 1513 (2003). The Oregon Court of Appeals adhered to its original views. And Philip Morris sought, and this time obtained, review in the Oregon Supreme Court.

Philip Morris then made two arguments relevant here. First, it said that the trial court should have accepted, but did not accept, a proposed "punitive damages" instruction that specified the jury could not seek to punish Philip Morris for injury to other persons not before the court. In particular, Philip Morris pointed out that the plaintiff's attorney had told the jury to "think about how many other Jesse Williams in the last 40 years in the State of Oregon there have been. . . . In Oregon, how many people do we see outside, driving home . . . smoking cigarettes? . . . [C]igarettes . . . are going to kill ten [of every hundred]. [And] the market share of Marlboros [i.e., Philip Morris] is one-third [i.e., one of every three killed]." In light of this argument, Philip Morris asked the trial court to tell the jury that "you may consider the extent of harm suffered by others in determining what [the] reasonable relationship is" between any punitive award and "the harm caused to Jesse Williams" by Philip Morris' misconduct, "[but] you are not to punish the defendant for the impact of its alleged misconduct on other persons, who may bring lawsuits of their own in which other juries can resolve their claims. . . ." The judge rejected this proposal and instead told the jury that "[p]unitive damages are awarded against a defendant to punish misconduct and to deter misconduct," and "are not intended to compensate the plaintiff or anyone else for damages caused by the defendant's conduct." In Philip Morris' view, the result was a significant likelihood that a portion of the $79.5 million award represented punishment for its having harmed others, a punishment that the Due Process Clause would here forbid.

Second, Philip Morris pointed to the roughly 100-to-1 ratio the $79.5 million punitive damages award bears to $821,000 in compensatory damages. Philip Morris noted that this Court in BMW emphasized the constitutional need for punitive damages awards to reflect (1) the "reprehensibility" of the defendant's conduct, (2) a "reasonable relationship" to the harm the plaintiff (or related victim) suffered, and (3) the presence (or absence) of "sanctions," e.g., criminal penalties, that state law provided for comparable conduct. And in State Farm, this Court said that the longstanding historical practice of setting punitive damages at two, three, or four times the size of compensatory damages, while "not binding," is "instructive," and that "[s]ingle-digit multipliers are more likely to comport with due process." 123 S. Ct. 1513. Philip Morris claimed that, in light of this case law, the punitive award was "grossly excessive."

The Oregon Supreme Court rejected these and other Philip Morris arguments. In particular, it rejected Philip Morris' claim that the Constitution prohibits a state jury "from using punitive damages to punish a defendant for harm to nonparties." 127 P.3d 1165, 1175 (2006). And in light of Philip Morris' reprehensible conduct, it found that the $79.5 million award was not "grossly excessive."

Philip Morris then sought certiorari. It asked us to consider, among other things, (1) its claim that Oregon had unconstitutionally permitted it to be punished for harming nonparty victims; and (2) whether Oregon had in effect disregarded "the constitutional requirement that punitive damages be reasonably related to the plaintiff's harm." We granted certiorari limited to these two questions.

For reasons we shall set forth, we consider only the first of these questions. We vacate the Oregon Supreme Court's judgment, and we remand the case for further proceedings.

II

This Court has long made clear that "[p]unitive damages may properly be imposed to further a State's legitimate interests in punishing unlawful conduct and deterring its repetition." *BMW*, 116 S. Ct. 1589. At the same time, we have emphasized the need to avoid an arbitrary determination of an award's amount. Unless a State insists upon proper standards that will cabin the jury's discretionary authority, its punitive damages system may deprive a defendant of "fair notice . . . of the severity of the penalty that a State may impose," *BMW, supra*; it may threaten "arbitrary punishments," *i.e.*, punishments that reflect not an "application of law" but "a decisionmaker's caprice," *State Farm, supra*; and, where the amounts are sufficiently large, it may impose one State's (or one jury's) "policy choice," say as to the conditions under which (or even whether) certain products can be sold, upon "neighboring States" with different public policies, *BMW, supra*.

For these and similar reasons, this Court has found that the Constitution imposes certain limits, in respect both to procedures for awarding punitive damages and to amounts forbidden as "grossly excessive." *See* Honda Motor Co. v. Oberg, 114 S. Ct. 2331 (1994) (requiring judicial review of the size of punitive awards); Cooper Industries, Inc. v. Leatherman Tool Group, Inc., 121 S. Ct. 1678 (2001) (review must be *de novo*); *BMW, supra* (excessiveness decision depends upon the reprehensibility of the defendant's conduct, whether the award bears a reasonable relationship to the actual and potential harm caused by the defendant to the plaintiff, and the difference between the award and sanctions "authorized or imposed in comparable cases"); *State Farm, supra* (excessiveness more likely where ratio exceeds single digits). Because we shall not decide whether the award here at issue is "grossly excessive," we need now only consider the Constitution's procedural limitations.

III

In our view, the Constitution's Due Process Clause forbids a State to use a punitive damages award to punish a defendant for injury that it inflicts upon nonparties or those whom they directly represent, *i.e.,* injury that it inflicts upon those who are, essentially, strangers to the litigation. For one thing, the Due Process Clause prohibits a State from punishing an individual without first providing that individual with "an opportunity to present every available defense." Lindsey v. Normet, 92 S. Ct. 862 (1972). Yet a defendant threatened with punishment for injuring a nonparty victim has no opportunity to defend against the charge, by showing, for example in a case such as this, that the other victim was not entitled to damages because he or she knew that smoking was dangerous or did not rely upon the defendant's statements to the contrary.

For another, to permit punishment for injuring a nonparty victim would add a near standardless dimension to the punitive damages equation. How many such victims are there? How seriously were they injured? Under what circumstances did injury occur? The trial will not likely answer such questions as to nonparty victims. The jury will be left to speculate. And the fundamental due process concerns to which our punitive damages cases refer — risks of arbitrariness, uncertainty and lack of notice — will be magnified.

Finally, we can find no authority supporting the use of punitive damages awards for the purpose of punishing a defendant for harming others. We have said that it may be appropriate to consider the reasonableness of a punitive damages award in light of the *potential* harm the defendant's conduct could have caused. But we have made clear that the potential harm at issue was harm potentially caused *the plaintiff.* . . .

Respondent argues that she is free to show harm to other victims because it is relevant to a different part of the punitive damages constitutional equation, namely, reprehensibility. That is to say, harm to others shows more reprehensible conduct. Philip Morris, in turn, does not deny that a plaintiff may show harm to others in order to demonstrate reprehensibility. Nor do we. Evidence of actual harm to nonparties can help to show that the conduct that harmed the plaintiff also posed a substantial risk of harm to the general public, and so was particularly reprehensible — although counsel may argue in a particular case that conduct resulting in no harm to others nonetheless posed a grave risk to the public, or the converse. Yet for the reasons given above, a jury may not go further than this and use a punitive damages verdict to punish a defendant directly on account of harms it is alleged to have visited on nonparties.

Given the risks of unfairness that we have mentioned, it is constitutionally important for a court to provide assurance that the jury will ask the right question, not the wrong one. And given the risks of arbitrariness, the concern for adequate notice, and the risk that punitive damages awards can, in practice, impose one State's (or one jury's) policies (*e.g.,* banning cigarettes) upon other States — all of which accompany awards that, today, may be many times the size of such awards in the 18th and 19th centuries — it is particularly important that States avoid procedure that unnecessarily deprives juries of proper legal guidance. We therefore conclude that the Due Process Clause requires States to provide assurance that juries are not asking the wrong question, *i.e.,* seeking, not simply to determine reprehensibility, but also to punish for harm caused strangers.

IV

Respondent suggests as well that the Oregon Supreme Court, in essence, agreed with us, that it did not authorize punitive damages awards based upon punishment for harm caused to nonparties. We concede that one might read some portions of the Oregon Supreme Court's opinion as focusing only upon reprehensibility. But the Oregon court's opinion elsewhere makes clear that that court held more than these few phrases might suggest.

The instruction that Philip Morris said the trial court should have given distinguishes between using harm to others as part of the "reasonable relationship" equation (which it would allow) and using it directly as a basis for punishment. The instruction asked the trial court to tell the jury that "you *may* consider the extent of harm suffered by others *in determining what [the] reasonable relationship is*" between Philip Morris' punishable misconduct and harm caused to Jesse Williams, "*[but] you are not to punish the defendant for the impact of its alleged misconduct on other persons, who may bring lawsuits of their own* in which other juries can resolve their claims. . . ." And as the Oregon Supreme Court explicitly recognized, Philip Morris argued that the Constitution "prohibits the state, acting through a civil jury, from using punitive damages to punish a defendant for harm to nonparties." 127 P.3d, at 1175.

The court rejected that claim. In doing so, it pointed out (1) that this Court in *State Farm* had held only that a jury could not base its award upon "dissimilar" acts of a defendant. 127 P.3d, at 1175-1176. It added (2) that "[i]f a jury cannot punish for the conduct, then it is difficult to see why it may consider it at all." 127 P.3d, at 1175, n.3. And it stated (3) that "[i]t is unclear to us how a jury could 'consider' harm to others, yet withhold that consideration from the punishment calculus." *Ibid.*

The Oregon court's first statement is correct. We did not previously hold explicitly that a jury may not punish for the harm caused others. But we do so hold now. We do not agree with the Oregon court's second statement. We have explained why we believe the Due Process Clause prohibits a State's inflicting punishment for harm caused strangers to the litigation. At the same time we recognize that conduct that risks harm to many is likely more reprehensible than conduct that risks harm to only a few. And a jury consequently may take this fact into account in determining reprehensibility.

The Oregon court's third statement raises a practical problem. How can we know whether a jury, in taking account of harm caused others under the rubric of reprehensibility, also seeks to *punish* the defendant for having caused injury to others? Our answer is that state courts cannot authorize procedures that create an unreasonable and unnecessary risk of any such confusion occurring. In particular, we believe that where the risk of that misunderstanding is a significant one — because, for instance, of the sort of evidence that was introduced at trial or the kinds of argument the plaintiff made to the jury — a court, upon request, must protect against that risk. Although the States have some flexibility to determine what *kind* of procedures they will implement, federal constitutional law obligates them to provide *some* form of protection in appropriate cases.

V

As the preceding discussion makes clear, we believe that the Oregon Supreme Court applied the wrong constitutional standard when considering Philip Morris' appeal. We remand this case so that the Oregon Supreme Court can apply the standard we have set forth. Because the application of this standard may lead to the need for a new trial, or a change in the level of the punitive damages award, we shall not consider whether the award is constitutionally "grossly excessive." We vacate the Oregon Supreme Court's judgment and remand the case for further proceedings not inconsistent with this opinion.

It is so ordered.

Justice STEVENS, dissenting.

The Due Process Clause of the Fourteenth Amendment imposes both substantive and procedural constraints on the power of the States to impose punitive damages on tortfeasors. I remain firmly convinced that the cases announcing those constraints were correctly decided. In my view the Oregon Supreme Court faithfully applied the reasoning in those opinions to the egregious facts disclosed by this record. . . .

Whereas compensatory damages are measured by the harm the defendant has caused the plaintiff, punitive damages are a sanction for the public harm the defendant's conduct has caused or threatened. There is little difference between the justification for a criminal sanction, such as a fine or a term of imprisonment, and an award of punitive damages. . . . And while in neither context would the sanction typically include a pecuniary award measured by the harm that the conduct had caused to any third parties, in both contexts the harm to third parties would surely be a relevant factor to consider in evaluating the reprehensibility of the defendant's wrongdoing. We have never held otherwise.

In the case before us, evidence attesting to the possible harm the defendant's extensive deceitful conduct caused other Oregonians was properly presented to the jury. No evidence was offered to establish an appropriate measure of damages to compensate such third parties for their injuries, and no one argued that the punitive damages award would serve any such purpose. To award compensatory damages to remedy such third-party harm might well constitute a taking of property from the defendant without due process. But a punitive damages award, instead of serving a compensatory purpose, serves the entirely different purposes of retribution and deterrence that underlie every criminal sanction. . . .

While apparently recognizing the novelty of its holding, the majority relies on a distinction between taking third-party harm into account in order to assess the reprehensibility of the defendant's conduct — which is permitted — from doing so in order to punish the defendant "directly" — which is forbidden. This nuance eludes me. When a jury increases a punitive damages award because injuries to third parties enhanced the reprehensibility of the defendant's conduct, the jury is by definition punishing the defendant — directly — for third-party harm. A murderer who kills his victim by throwing a bomb that injures dozens of bystanders should be punished more severely than one who harms no one other than his intended victim. Similarly, there is no reason why the measure of the appropriate punishment for engaging in a campaign of deceit in distributing a poisonous and addictive substance to thousands of cigarette smokers statewide should not include consideration of the harm to those "bystanders" as well as the harm to the individual plaintiff. The Court endorses a contrary conclusion without providing us with any reasoned justification.

I would affirm the Supreme Court of Oregon's judgment.

Justice THOMAS, dissenting.

I join Justice GINSBURG's dissent in full. I write separately to reiterate my view that "'the Constitution does not constrain the size of punitive damages awards.'" State Farm Mut. Automobile Ins. Co. v. Campbell, (Thomas, J., dissenting). It matters not that the Court styles today's holding as "procedural" because the "procedural" rule is simply a confusing implementation of the substantive due process regime this Court has created for punitive damages. . . . Today's opinion proves once again that this Court's punitive damages jurisprudence is "insusceptible of principled application." BMW of North America, Inc. v. Gore, (Scalia, J., joined by Thomas, J., dissenting).

Justice GINSBURG, with whom Justice SCALIA and Justice THOMAS join, dissenting.

The purpose of punitive damages, it can hardly be denied, is not to compensate, but to punish. Punish for what? Not for harm actually caused "strangers to the litigation," the Court states, but for the *reprehensibility* of defendant's conduct, *ante*, at 1063-1064. "[C]onduct that risks harm to many," the Court observes, "is likely more reprehensible than conduct that risks harm to only a few." The Court thus conveys that, when punitive damages are at issue, a jury is properly instructed to consider the extent of harm suffered by others as a measure of reprehensibility, but not to mete out punishment for injuries in fact sustained by nonparties. The Oregon courts did not rule otherwise. They have endeavored to follow our decisions . . . and have "deprive[d][no jury] of proper legal guidance." Vacation of the Oregon Supreme Court's judgment, I am convinced, is unwarranted. . . .

For the reasons stated, and in light of the abundant evidence of "the potential harm [Philip Morris'] conduct could have caused," I would affirm the decision of the Oregon Supreme Court.

FOOD FOR THOUGHT

The Supreme Court never reached the issue of excessiveness-based-on-ratio in *Phillip Morris USA v. Williams*. On remand, the Oregon Supreme Court affirmed the $79.5 million punitive damage award. Surprisingly, the Oregon Court found that the plaintiff's request for instructions in the original trial was inadequate on state grounds and thus the constitutional issue dealing with the problem of punitive damages based on injury to nonparty victims was moot. *See* Williams v. Philip Morris Inc., 176 P.3d 1255 (Or. 2008). After originally granting certiorari to review the Oregon Supreme Court decision on remand, 553 U.S. 1093 (2008), the U.S. Supreme Court subsequently dismissed certiorari as improvidently granted (2009).

Whether the Supreme Court will allow trial courts to impose substantial, high-ratio punitive awards in favor of products liability plaintiffs suffering personal injury is not clear. On the one hand, the four dissenting Justices in *Williams* voted to uphold a punitive award based on nearly a 100-to-1 ratio. It would take only one more vote to establish the principle that, at least in personal injury cases involving allegedly egregious conduct, the ratio-based approach considered in *State Farm* does not apply. On the other hand, the *Williams* restrictions on the conduct for which plaintiffs may ask juries to punish defendants may dampen somewhat attempts by plaintiffs hereafter to inflame the passions of juries by arguing that defendant companies deserve to pay hugely for all the harm they have done to so many other victims. Moreover, the Supreme Court has yet to address an issue that has for decades been recognized as troublesome: the unfairness of punishing a defendant multiple times, in a succession of tort actions by different plaintiffs, for the same egregious conduct. Assuming that, when the Court finally addresses the issue of successive, redundant punishment, it will attempt to place due-process-based restrictions on multiple punishments; such restrictions will further limit the power of state courts to allow huge punitive damages awards.

In recent years there has been an outpouring of law review commentary on punitive damages. *See, e.g.,* Thomas B. Colby, *Clearing the Smoke From* Philip Morris v. Williams*: The Past, Present and Future of Punitive Damages*, 118 Yale L.J. 392 (2008) (punitive damages as punishment for public wrongs demands criminal due process protection; punishment for individual wrongs does not require similar constitutional protection); Benjamin C. Zipursky, *A Theory of Punitive Damages*, 85 Tex. L. Rev. 105 (2005) (examining the civil-criminal law interplay in punitive damages). *Also see* Dan Markel, *Retributive Damages: A Theory of Punitive Damages as Intermediate Sanction*, 94 Cornell L. Rev. 239 (2009); and Dan Markel, *How Should Punitive Damages Work?*, 157 U. Pa. L. Rev. 1383 (2009).

chapter **14**

Defamation

A. INTRODUCTION

The law of defamation is a mess. It is an amalgam of centuries-old common law and modern constitutional doctrine. Unlike old soldiers who never die but just fade away, some of the antiquated doctrine has refused to pass from the scene. Over the last four decades, the United States Supreme Court has taken huge bites out of the common law of defamation. Where common law doctrine was in conflict with the First Amendment right of free speech, the Court scuttled age-old defamation rules. The law of defamation today has significant remnants of the "something old," but is dominated by the "something new" of First Amendment jurisprudence.

Before examining both the common law and constitutional doctrine in depth, it will be helpful to get a bird's-eye view of the basic elements of a defamation action. To make out a prima facie case, plaintiff must establish that: (1) the defendant made a defamatory statement, (2) the defendant communicated ("published") the statement to a third party, and (3) the statement could reasonably be understood to refer to the plaintiff. At common law, defamation was a strict liability tort. Even the most innocent mistake of fact on the part of the defendant was actionable if the statement was defamatory. In the famous case of E. Hulton & Co. v. Jones, [1910] A.C., defendant newspaper ran an article about Artemus Jones being with a woman "who is not his wife." Plaintiff, one Artemus Jones, sued claiming that people believed the article to be about him. The author of the article claimed that he chose a fictitious name for the article and had never heard of the plaintiff. In upholding a verdict for the plaintiff, the court held that libel was a strict liability tort. "It consists in using language which others knowing the circumstances would reasonably think to be defamatory of the person complaining of and injured by it." Furthermore, plaintiff did not have to establish that the defamatory statement was false. Its falsity was presumed. Truth was an affirmative defense to be proven by the defendant. And for many forms of defamation, a jury was entitled to presume damages without proof that the plaintiff had suffered actual damages. Finally,

815

even if plaintiff established a prima facie case for defamation, defendant could seek to establish that the defamation was not actionable because the defendant had a privilege to communicate even defamatory information to a third party. Some privileges were absolute. Judges and legislators, for example, while acting in their official capacity, were immune from suit for defamation. Other privileges were conditional. If one communicated defamatory information to another for the purpose of protecting one's own interests or the interests of the other party and (depending on the jurisdiction) either believed or had reasonable grounds to believe in the truth of the statement, liability for defamation could be thwarted.

As we shall see, decisions of the United States Supreme Court have rendered obsolete a good bit of the common law of defamation. Thus, for example, defamation actions against public officials and public figures cannot be predicated on strict liability. Indeed, a plaintiff must establish that the defendant made the defamatory statement with knowledge of its falsity or in reckless disregard of the truth. Furthermore, neither the falsity of the defamation nor damages may be presumed. Plaintiff must establish both. More difficult to discern is what constitutional limitations exist for defamatory statements made by one private person about another. The cases are clear as mud. We are left to speculate regarding how much of the antiquated law of defamation is still in place. Having thoroughly confused you, we take you first through the basics of the common law of defamation and then to the constitutional law cases. We promise to be as clear as possible. We will identify those areas in which the common law doctrine has been radically affected by constitutional law and will set out the areas in which the law is unclear and why it is so. We disclaim responsibility for the lack of clarity brought about by the interface between vague (sometimes needlessly so) constitutional law cases and state defamation law.

For a general overview of the history and development of defamation, *see* David A. Elder, *Defamation: A Lawyer's Guide* (1993); David A. Elder, *Small Town Police Forces, Other Governmental Entities and the Misapplication of the First Amendment to the Small Group Defamation Theory — A Plea for Fundamental Fairness for Mayberry*, 6 U. Pa. J. Const. L. 881 (2004); Robert D. Sack, *Sack on Defamation: Libel, Slander and Related Problems* (3d ed., P.L.I. 2007); Rodney A. Smolla, *Law of Defamation* (1986).

B. WHAT IS DEFAMATORY?

SUSAN B. ANTHONY LIST v. DRIEHAUS
805 F. Supp. 2d 423 (S.D. Ohio 2011)

TIMOTHY S. BLACK, District Judge.

[Then-Congressman Steven Dreihaus filed a complaint with the Ohio Elections Commission, alleging that a pro-life advocacy group, Susan B. Anthony List, intended to run advertisements containing false or misleading statements about him. The group filed an action seeking declaratory and injunctive relief against the Commission and Dreihaus counterclaimed for defamation.]

Mr. Driehaus's counterclaim for defamation involves five allegedly defamatory statements: (1) SBA List's statement on or about August 9, 2010 that Mr. Driehaus "voted for a health care bill that includes taxpayer-funded abortion."; (2) SBA List's planned billboard, made public on September 28, 2010, which stated: "Driehaus voted FOR taxpayer-funded abortion."; (3) SBA List's statement released on October 7, 2010: "It is a fact that Steve Driehaus has voted for a bill that includes taxpayer funding of abortion."; (4) SBA List's other statement of October 7, 2010 that Mr. Driehaus "ordered Lamar Companies not to put up the billboards until the matter was settled by the Ohio Elections Commission."; and (5) SBA List's radio ad, which started running on or about October 19, 2010, stating: "Steve Driehaus voted for taxpayer funding of abortion when he cast his vote for the health care reform bill . . . Driehaus voted for taxpayer funding of abortion."

Mr. Driehaus claims that the statements defamed him by impugning his professional reputation as a pro-life Member of Congress and by falsely characterizing his performance and conduct while in office. Mr. Driehaus alleges that SBA List's statements characterizing his vote on the Patient Protection and Affordable Care Act ("PPACA") were false and were made with the intended effect of deceiving the electorate as to Mr. Driehaus's position on abortion. As a result, Mr. Driehaus maintains that he suffered reputational and other economic damage.

SBA List moves for summary judgment on the counterclaim, alleging that the statements are: (1) protected opinion; (2) not capable of defamatory meaning; and (3) not false or made with actual malice.

. . .

III. ANALYSIS

. . .

B. Capable of Defamatory Meaning

First, SBA List claims that the taxpayer funded abortion statements are "not capable of defamatory meaning" because they are not defamatory *per se,* and the ordered statement does not "reflect[] injuriously on a person's reputation, or expos[e] a person to public hatred or contempt, ridicule, shame or disgrace, or affect[] a person adversely in his or her trade, business or profession."

SBA List suggests that the only way it could have hurt Mr. Driehaus's reputation or harmed him in his professional capacity as a public official was by claiming that he "engaged in illegal conduct while in office." In support of its argument, SBA List cites *McKimm v. Ohio Elections Comm'n,* 89 Ohio St. 3d 139, 729 N.E.2d 364 (2000), which held that the "[sic] was capable of defamatory meaning because the cartoon implied the plaintiff 'committed an illegal act while in office.'" SBA List claims that its own "statement that Rep. Driehaus 'voted FOR taxpayer funded abortion'" is incapable of defamatory meaning because it "does not allege or imply that Rep. Driehaus engaged in illegal conduct, as the defendant's statement implied in *McKimm.*" *Id.* Additionally, SBA List claims that its statement [that Rep. Driehaus ordered the company not to put up the billboard] is incapable of defamatory meaning because it was an "innocuous statement" that, unlike the cartoon in *McKimm,* did not imply that the public official committed any illegal conduct, nor did it "reflect on Rep. Driehaus'[s] integrity or suggest dishonest conduct on his part." *Id.* at 23. Although the Court recognizes that committing an illegal act while in office is certainly one way to evidence that Mr. Driehaus was harmed in his official capacity, there is absolutely no authority in *McKimm* that an illegal act is the *only* way to evidence reputational harm.[1]

Second, SBA List made its statements in writing. Under Ohio law, libel "is defined generally as a false written publication, made with some degree of fact, reflecting injuriously on a person's reputation, or exposing a person to public hatred, contempt, ridicule, shame or disgrace, or affecting a person adversely in his or her trade, business or profession." There is no rule stating that a public official alleging defamation may not rely on false statements that injure his reputation, expose him to public hatred or contempt, or affect him in his profession as a public servant.

Finally, whether a false statement is capable of inflicting injury depends on the totality of the circumstances. Mr. Driehaus maintains that "accusing [him] of ordering Lamar Advertising not to put up the SBA List billboard did further damage to [his] reputation for fairness, honesty, and integrity by making it appear to [his] constituents and fellow members of the community that [he] had abused my power as a public official."

Construing the facts in the light most favorable to the non-moving party, the Court finds that the taxpayer funded statements and ordered statement are certainly capable of defamatory meaning.

FOOD FOR THOUGHT

A classic case authored by Judge Learned Hand, *Grant v. Reader's Digest Association*, 151 F.2d 733 (2d Cir. 1945), arose out of an article insinuating that the plaintiff may "have been in general sympathy" with the "objects and methods" of the Communist Party. Judge Hand said the court need not decide whether "right-thinking people" would shun, despise, or condemn a lawyer who had Communist sympathies, as long as there are some people who would feel that way. For the most part courts no longer refer to the opinions of "right-thinking people." The more commonly accepted definition is set forth in Restatement, Second, of Torts § 559:

> A communication is defamatory if it tends so to harm the reputation of another as to lower him in the estimation of the community or to deter third persons from associating with him.

1. Ohio courts have never held that imputation of a crime is the only basis for a defamation claim by a public official. If there were such a rule, it is safe to assume that decisions like *Vail v. Plain Dealer Publ'g Co.*, 72 Ohio St. 3d 279, 649 N.E.2d 182 (2005), involving public officials not accused of crimes, would have applied such a rule. Moreover, the out-of-state decisions cited by SBA List do not stand for the propositions for which they are cited. *Tatur v. Solsrud*, 174 Wis. 2d 735, 498 N.W.2d 232, 234 (1992), does not hold that a candidate may not use loss of votes to show defamation, only that he may not rely solely on loss of votes. Mr. Driehaus does not claim loss of votes, but rather that lost votes was one indicator of his reputational and professional injury, among others. Similarly, there is no rule that a public official may never predicate a defamation claim on a false attack on his voting record. *See also Fong v. Merena*, 66 Haw. 72, 655 P.2d 875, 876 (1982) (an attack on the official's voting record "was reasonably susceptible to a defamatory interpretation"). In this case, unlike the cases cited by SBA List, Defendant has evidenced that the attack on his voting record rises to the level of an injury to his reputation for character and personal integrity.

See Lyrissa Lidsky, *Defamation, Reputation, and the Myth of Community,* 71 Wash. L. Rev. 1 (1996). The statement that Rep. Dreihaus voted for taxpayer-funded abortion might not lower him in the estimation of certain communities (liberal Democrats, let's say), but the statement would have been harmful in light of Rep. Dreihaus's reputation as a pro-life member of Congress.

Take your guess as to whether the following accusations are defamatory:

1. A truck stop owner reported truckers' violations to the Interstate Commerce Commission. Plaintiff lost trucking business. Connelly v. McKay, 28 N.Y.S.2d 327 (N.Y. Sup. Ct. 1941).
2. Police chief is a dumb S.O.B. Finck v. City of Tea, 443 N.W.2d 632 (S.D. 1989).
3. *X* is a homosexual. Robinson v. Radio One, Inc., 695 F. Supp. 2d 425 (N.D. Tex. 2010); Murphy v. Millennium Radio Group LLC, 2010 WL 1372408 (D.N.J. 2010).
4. Statement that a famous lawyer who spoke at a bar association conference for no fee on the promise that his hotel expenses would be covered charged clothes that he purchased in a hotel shop to the bar association. Belli v. Orlando Daily Newspapers, Inc., 389 F.2d 579 (5th Cir. 1967).
5. Statement that a Democrat running for governor had once considered running as an Independent, made by state Democratic chairman to hurt the candidacy of the plaintiff several days prior to the election. Frinzi v. Hanson, 140 N.W.2d 259 (Wis. 1966).
6. *X* is an "Uncle Tom." Moore v. P.W. Publishing Co., 209 N.E.2d 412 (Ohio 1965).
7. The District Attorney was electioneering and he was the "David Duke of Chester County." MacElree v. Philadelphia Newspapers, Inc., 674 A.2d 1050 (Pa. 1996).
8. Husband and wife are separated and getting a divorce. Andreason v. Guard Publishing Co., 489 P.2d 944 (Or. 1971).
9. A Russian princess was raped by Rasputin. Yousssoupoff v. Metro-Gold-wyn-Mayer Pictures, Ltd., 50 T.L.R. 851 (1934).
10. *X* is suffering from terminal cancer. Ravnikar v. Bogojavlensky, 782 N.E.2d 508 (Mass. 2003); Golub v. Enquirer/Star Group, Inc., 681 N.E.2d 1282 (N.Y. 1997).
11. Attorney had been a prosecutor in South Africa. Partington v. Bugliosi, 825 F. Supp. 906, 913 (D. Haw. 1993).
12. She is a bitch and she and her husband hate Jews. Ward v. Zelikovsky, 643 A.2d 972, 978 (N.J. 1994).
13. Landlord's statement that another landlord had a reputation for not closing deals. Bertsch v. Duemeland, 639 N.W.2d 455, 461, 462 (N.D. 2002).
14. The City Chief Medical Examiner issued false and misleading reports about deaths in order to protect police. Gross v. New York Times Co., 623 N.E.2d 1163 (N.Y. 1993).
15. He is an evil man. Afftrex, Ltd. v. General Electric Co., 555 N.Y.S.2d 903 (N.Y. App. Div. 1990).
16. Newspaper article regarding Olympic security guard suspected of bombing, using terms such as "Rambo," "home-grown failure," "disgraced," and

"disaster" regarding his prior employment, describing him as a "fat, failed former" sheriff's deputy, and referring to his having "over-investigated everything," being a "straight arrow who overdid everything," having turned minor incidents "into federal cases," and being "desperate to stand out as a hero." Jewell v. NYP Holdings, Inc., 23 F. Supp. 2d 348 (S.D.N.Y. 1998).

17. A statement to a customer that a subcontractor's product is inferior and not engineered properly. Re: Engineered Framing Sys., Inc. v. Vescom Structures, Inc., 2005 U.S. Dist. Lexis 26295, *6 (D.N.J. 2005).

The answers to the above statements are: (1) no; (2) no; (3) yes or no depending on the jurisdiction; (4) yes; (5) no; (6) no; (7) yes; (8) no; (9) yes; (10) yes or no depending on whether the defendant actually asserted that the plaintiff was dying; (11) yes; (12) no; (13) yes; (14) yes; (15) yes; (16) no; (17) yes.

Can you make sense out of the decisions? Assume that a happily married couple live in a rural community where divorce is frowned upon. Why is a statement that the couple is divorced not defamatory? Some people tend to shun terminally ill cancer patients and refuse to associate with them. They are certainly wrong in doing so, but human nature is what it is. Shouldn't a statement that one is suffering from terminal cancer be defamatory? Answering these questions is more difficult today. At one time a statement about the plaintiff might be printed in a local newspaper, so a court could more readily ascertain the local norms (such as divorce being frowned upon) that made a statement defamatory or not. But what about a statement that is published in the online edition of a newspaper, picked up on blogs or Twitter, and transmitted all around the world? Which norms should govern the determination of whether the statement is defamatory? Courts have only begun the task of defining the relevant community against the background of instantaneous electronic communication. *See* Amy Kristin Sanders, *Defining Community in the Age of the Internet*, 15 Comm. L. & Pol'y 21 (2010).

For an in-depth treatment of what constitutes a defamatory statement, *see* Robert C. Post, *The Social Foundations of Defamation Law: Reputation and the Constitution*, 74 Cal. L. Rev. 691 (1986) (analyzes three distinct concepts of reputation that the common law has protected at various times, and the correspondence between these concepts and the kinds of social relationships that defamation law is designed to uphold). *See also* Joseph H. King, Jr., *Defining the Internal Context for Communications Containing Allegedly Defamatory Headline Language*, 71 U. Cin. L. Rev. 863 (2003).

C. THE FORM OF COMMUNICATION — LIBEL AND SLANDER

Historically, the common law drew a sharp distinction between libel and slander. When a defamation was reduced to writing or was embodied in some permanent form such as a book or a painting, it fell into the category of libel. Slander, on the other hand, was the term used for defamations transmitted by the spoken word. A lot depended on the distinction. If the defamation was libelous, a plaintiff could recover presumed damages, i.e., a jury could assess damages even though plaintiff could not prove that she suffered pecuniary loss. To be successful in an action for slander, a plaintiff had to establish actual pecuniary loss. Since very often plaintiffs in defamation actions did not suffer pecuniary loss but only had their reputations sullied, the libel/slander distinction was of considerable importance.

But the story is more complex. Some categories of slander were considered to be so egregious that presumed damages could be awarded even if pecuniary loss was not established. If the defamatory statement accused the plaintiff of (1) a major (not a minor) crime; (2) suffering from a loathsome disease, e.g., leprosy or venereal disease; (3) conduct that would affect the plaintiff in her business, trade, profession, or office; or (4) serious sexual misconduct, then slander would be treated as the equivalent of libel. And if all this were not sufficiently confusing, common law courts drew a distinction between statements that were defamatory on their face and those which required extrinsic evidence to prove the defamation. For example, to write of a woman that she had given birth to her first child is not defamatory on its face. If, however, the woman is unmarried, the statement is defamatory. Since to make out the defamation it is necessary to resort to extrinsic facts, the common law treated such written libels as if they were slander. Once they were treated as slander, a plaintiff could not recover presumed damages unless she were able to establish that she fit into one of the four categories which allowed presumed damages for slander.

Whether any given form of communication constituted libel rather than slander became a question of considerable moment. What about a defamation made on radio or television? Is it libel or slander? Does it make a difference whether the speaker was reading from a script? (We kid you not.) *See* Hartmann v. Winchell, 73 N.E.2d 30, 31 (N.Y. 1947). What about a speech made in Madison Square Garden in front of 15,000 people? *See* Restatement, Second, of Torts § 568 (1964).

In the ensuing materials, we shall see that the distinctions between libel and slander are of lesser importance today as a result of decisions by the United States Supreme Court that sharply cut back on the ability of courts to award presumed damages. But, we caution you that the distinctions set forth above are not dead. One can find cases to this very day that resort to much of the common law nonsense. The district court in *Dreihaus*, above, referred to the libel/slander distinction in concluding that the statements made by the interest group were capable of a defamatory meaning, but did not explain what difference it made to the analysis that the statements were in writing.

D. FACT OR OPINION

GREEN v. COSBY
138 F. Supp. 3d 114 (D. Mass. 2015)

Mastroianni, J.

I. INTRODUCTION

On December 10, 2014, Tamara Green filed a complaint alleging that William H. Cosby, Jr. ("Defendant") publicly defamed her in statements made by individuals operating at his direction and/or within the scope of their employment. . . .

IV. FACTS AS ALLEGED BY PLAINTIFFS

During the 1970s, Defendant, "an internationally known actor and comedian," met each Plaintiff and subsequently sexually assaulted her. With respect to Plaintiff Green, "[o]n a certain date in the early 1970s," Defendant offered her two pills, telling her they were over-the-counter cold medicine. She took the pills and became weak and dizzy. Defendant then drove Plaintiff Green to her apartment, where he subjected her to sexual contact against her will and despite her repeated demands to stop. Plaintiff Green was unable to defend herself during the sexual assault because she remained weak and vulnerable. . . .

Many years later, in February of 2005, the *Philadelphia Daily News* published an interview with Plaintiff Green in which she publicly disclosed the sexual assault that had occurred in the 1970s. Plaintiff Green also disclosed the allegations during appearances on television shows around the same time. Nine years later, on or about February 7, 2014, *Newsweek* published an interview with Plaintiff Green in which she repeated her description of being sexually assaulted by Defendant in the 1970s. . . .

Plaintiffs allege that Defendant, acting through his agents, issued statements to the media in response to the public disclosures made by Plaintiffs. Defendant knew each statement was false at the time it was made. Despite knowing the statements were false, Defendant directed the statements be made. Each of the statements was widely read by many people, including Plaintiffs' families, friends, and neighbors, and Plaintiffs suffered damages, including to their reputations, as a result of the publication of the statements. The statements were made as follows:

A. Newsweek Statement — February 7, 2014

Prior to the publication of *Newsweek's* interview with Plaintiff Green in February of 2014, Defendant, acting through a publicist, believed by Plaintiffs to be David Brokaw ("Brokaw"), made a statement to *Newsweek*. The publicist provided the statement to *Newsweek* while acting as Defendant's authorized agent, employee, or authorized representative and he knew or should have known the statement was false when it was made. The statement was appended to the end of the story and read, in its entirety:

This is a 10-year-old, discredited accusation that proved to be nothing at the time, and is still nothing.

. . .

V. DISCUSSION

. . .

C. Adequacy of Plaintiffs' Defamation Allegations

Having determined the laws of California and Florida are applicable . . . the court next considers the substance of Plaintiffs' defamation claims. Both California and Florida recognize the following essential elements of defamation: (1) a publication; (2) that is false; (3) defamatory, meaning damaging to the good reputation of the person who is the subject of the statement; (4) made by an actor with the requisite degree of fault; (5) is not protected by any privilege; and (6) causes injury to the subject. *See, e.g., Jews For Jesus, Inc. v. Rapp*, 997 So.2d 1098, 1106 (Fla.2008); *Taus v. Loftus*, 40 Cal.4th 683, 54 Cal.Rptr.3d 775, 151 P.3d 1185, 1209 (2007), *abrogated on other grounds by Oasis West Realty, LLC v. Goldman*, 51 Cal.4th 811, 124 Cal.Rptr.3d 256, 250 P.3d 1115 (2011); *Blatty v. N.Y. Times Co.*, 42 Cal.3d 1033, 232 Cal.Rptr. 542, 728 P.2d 1177, 1182–83, 1186 (1986)....

1. The Statements: Factual, True, Defamatory, Of and Concerning

In order for a defamation claim to survive a motion to dismiss, the allegedly defamatory statement must contain at least one false factual assertion which is also defamatory. *See, e.g., Jews For Jesus, Inc.*, 997 So.2d at 1106; *Taus*, 54 Cal.Rptr.3d 775, 151 P.3d at 1209. Depending on the nature of the statement and the context in which it was made, courts will place different emphasis on these two components. In this case, Defendant argues three of the four statements at issue do not contain factual assertions that are false, or even capable of being false. Defendant further asserts that even if the statements can be understood as expressing false factual assertions, they are not defamatory because they do not hold Plaintiffs " 'up to contempt, hatred, scorn, or ridicule or tend to impair [their] standing in the community.'" (Def.'s Mem. 14-15 (quoting *Yohe v. Nugent*, 321 F.3d 35, 40 (1st Cir.2003)).) The court addresses each statement individually, applying California law to the Newsweek Statement regarding Plaintiff Green ....

Before delving into the state-specific analysis, the court considers the Supreme Court case law applicable to defamation cases in which the parties dispute whether a statement contains actionable statements of fact or protected statements of opinion. In *Milkovich v. Lorain Journal Co.*, the Supreme Court reviewed the history of the tort of defamation and development of constitutional protections to ensure the tort does not interfere with "the freedom of expression guaranteed by the First Amendment." 497 U.S. 1, 21, 110 S.Ct. 2695, 111 L.Ed.2d 1 (1990). The Court reviewed existing constitutional requirements, including that plaintiffs must (a) establish the requisite level of fault on the part of a defendant and (b) allege a statement that can " 'reasonably [be] interpreted as stating actual facts' about an individual." *Id.* at 20, 110 S.Ct. 2695 (quoting *Hustler Magazine, Inc. v. Falwell*, 485 U.S. 46, 50, 108 S.Ct. 876, 99 L.Ed.2d 41 (1988)). The Court considered whether to create an additional constitutional privilege for "anything that might be labeled 'opinion.'" *Id.* at 18, 110 S.Ct. 2695. In declining to adopt such a privilege, the Court explained there is not a clear division between statements of opinion and fact. "If a speaker says, 'in my opinion John Jones is a liar,' [the speaker] implies a knowledge of facts which lead to the conclusion that Jones told an untruth" and, as a result, such a statement may imply a false assertion of fact by failing to state what it was based on or because any facts referenced are incorrect or incomplete. *Id.* The Supreme Court directs courts to determine "whether a reasonable factfinder could conclude that the [allegedly defamatory] statements ... imply an assertion [of fact]" and whether that assertion "is sufficiently factual to be susceptible of being proved true or false," rather than simply determine whether a statement expresses an opinion or asserts a fact. *Id.* at 21, 110 S.Ct. 2695. At this stage of the litigation, the court's concern is whether any fact contained in or implied by an allegedly defamatory statement is susceptible to being proved true or false; if so capable, Defendant cannot avoid application of defamation law by claiming the statement expresses only opinion. *See Ferlauto v. Hamsher,* 74 Cal. App. 4th 1394, 88 Cal. Rptr. 2d 843, 849 (1999); *Zambrano v. Devanesan,* 484 So. 2d 603, 606 (Fla. Dist. Ct. App. 1986). Ultimately, if Plaintiffs' claims survive this initial challenge, Defendant will have the opportunity, at the procedurally appropriate time, to fully develop a defense based on the truth of the facts contained in or implied by each statement.

a. The Newsweek Statement Pertaining to Plaintiff Green

. . .

ii. Opinion or Fact

In addition to asserting the Newsweek Statement is not defamatory since it is substantially true, Defendant argues it is not defamatory because it expresses an opinion rather than a fact capable of being proved false. California courts have interpreted the Supreme Court's decision in *Milkovich* as establishing that the First Amendment only prohibits defamation liability for the expression of an opinion where the factual basis for the opinion is provided, the facts provided are true, and the opinion does not imply false assertions of facts. *GetFugu, Inc. v. Patton Boggs LLP,* 220 Cal. App. 4th 141, 162 Cal. Rptr. 3d 831, 842 (2013) (citing *Milkovich,* 497 U.S. at 18–19, 110 S.Ct. 2695 and *McGarry v. Univ. of San Diego,* 154 Cal. App. 4th 97, 64 Cal. Rptr. 3d 467, 479 (2007)). Accordingly, "it is not the literal truth or falsity of each word or detail used in a statement" which determines whether it is a potentially defamatory statement of fact; "rather, the determinative question is whether the 'gist or sting' of the statement is true or false, benign or defamatory, in substance." *Ringler Assocs. Inc. v. Md. Cas. Co.,* 80 Cal. App. 4th 1165, 96 Cal. Rptr. 2d 136, 150 (2000) (emphasis omitted) (internal quotation omitted); *see also Campanelli,* 51 Cal.Rptr.2d at 897. The court can, as a matter of law, find a statement is not actionable, but when an allegedly defamatory statement can reasonably be interpreted as either stating or implying a false fact or articulating an opinion, California courts put the issue before a jury. *See Ferlauto,* 88 Cal. Rptr. 2d at 849 ("If the court concludes the statement could reasonably be construed as either fact or opinion, the issue should be resolved by a jury."). In determining whether a statement is capable of being interpreted as asserting or implying a fact, California courts use the "totality of the circumstances test." *Id.* This test has three parts: "(1) whether the general tenor of the entire work negates the impression that the defendant was asserting an objective fact, (2) whether the defendant used figurative or hyperbolic language that negates that impression, and (3) whether the statement in question is susceptible of being proved true or false." *Lieberman v. Fieger,* 338 F.3d 1076, 1080 (9th Cir. 2003) (citations omitted) (applying California law).

As to the first part — general tenor — Defendant points out the statement was made "in response to serious charges" and argues this "is a strong contextual signal that the statement is non-actionable opinion." Specifically, Defendant suggests the court should treat the response as a "predictable opinion," which an average reader would understand as a one-sided attempt to bolster his position in a dispute. Several California courts have used the phrase "predictable opinion" to describe a statement that, due to the context in which it is made, is understood to be a one-sided expression of opinion rather than fact. However, California courts have only applied the principle to cases where the statements related to pending or completed litigation. *See Dreamstone Entm't Ltd. v. Maysalward Inc.*, 2014 WL 4181026, at *6 (C.D. Cal. Aug. 18, 2014) (treating statement attributed to attorneys, and linking to recently filed complaint, as "predictable opinion" rather than statement of fact); *Amaretto Ranch Breedables, LLC v. Ozimals, Inc.*, 2013 WL 3460707, at *4 (N.D. Cal. July 9, 2013) (finding the broad context of a blog entry, describing reasons for bringing lawsuit, demonstrated that the statement was a "predictable opinion," rather than an actionable statement of fact); *GetFugu, Inc.*, 162 Cal.Rptr.3d at 842 (finding tweet by attorney identifying opposing lawsuit as frivolous was a "predictable opinion" that could not be the basis for a defamation claim); *Ferlauto*, 88 Cal.Rptr.2d at 850 (finding statements describing lawsuit as "frivolous" expressed only "predictable opinion" and could not be the basis of a defamation action, especially because context and literary tone of work where statements appeared clearly indicated to readers they were reading the subjective views of partisan participants to litigation); *Info. Control Corp. v. Genesis One Comput. Corp.*, 611 F.2d 781, 784 (9th Cir.1980) (coining phrase "predicable opinion" to describe a statement unlikely to be understood by audience as a statement of fact because of the litigation position of the maker of the statement).

The context in which Defendant's agent made the Newsweek Statement was different from the context in which California courts have identified statements as "predictable opinions"; at the time this statement was made there was no pending litigation between Defendant and Plaintiff Green. Some readers may have understood any statement from Defendant to have been predictably self-serving, but there was no litigation pending when a publicist for Defendant provided the statement to the media. Accordingly, the court cannot determine at this stage that the statement fits within the "predictable opinion" doctrine recognized in California. Nor can the court conclude that the general tenor of the statement negates the impression that Defendant was asserting an objective fact.

Turning next to the specific language of the statement, the phrase — "discredited accusation that proved to be nothing at the time, and is still nothing" — has an obvious literal meaning, specifically, that Plaintiff Green's allegations are completely without merit and have been so proven. The operative phrases are not surrounded by hyperbole or figurative language that undercuts their literal meaning. *Cf. Standing Comm. on Discipline of U.S. Dist. Court v. Yagman*, 55 F.3d 1430, 1440 (9th Cir.1995) (applying California law) (treating as rhetorical hyperbole the word "dishonest" because it was used within a "string of colorful adjectives"); *see also Knievel v. ESPN*, 393 F.3d 1068, 1077 (9th Cir.2005) (describing "slang phrases such as '[d]udes rollin' deep' and '[k]ickin' it with much flavor'" as using loose and figurative language incapable of a "literal interpretation"). The phrasing used here allows a "reasonable factfinder [to] conclude the [statement] impl[ies] an assertion of defamatory fact," specifically, that there was some unidentified investigation or hearing into the allegations which officially determined Plaintiff Green's accusation was false. *Ringler Assocs. Inc.*, 96 Cal. Rptr. 2d at 149 (emphasis omitted).

Finally, the court considers whether Defendant's response, directly or by implication, makes a statement which is susceptible of being proved true or false. To the extent Defendant's response implies an investigation into Plaintiff Green's allegations was conducted, it is provable as true or false. Additionally, the gist of the statement — that Plaintiff Green fabricated her allegations — is also provable as true or false. It may take a trial to produce such proof, but Defendant's allegations are sufficiently specific "to be susceptible to proof or disproof." *James v. San Jose Mercury News, Inc.*, 17 Cal. App. 4th 1, 20 Cal. Rptr. 2d 890, 898 (1993) (finding statements not susceptible of being proved true or false because the statements contained too many generalizations, elastic terms, and subjective elements for it to be clear what facts were stated or implied); *see also Amaretto Ranch Breedables, LLC*, 2013 WL 3460707, at *5 (finding a statement might be provable as true or false, though it would require a lengthy lawsuit, but determining other factors prevented statement from being defamatory). Based on this "totality of the circumstances" analysis, the court concludes a reasonable factfinder could determine, based on the context and content, the Newsweek Statement asserted or implied factual statements that were susceptible of being proved true or false.

iii. Defamatory Meaning

The court considers next whether the statement could be understood to have a defamatory meaning. Analogizing to *Gibney v. Fitzgibbon*, 547 Fed. Appx. 111 (3d Cir.2013) (unpublished), Defendant argues an assertion by a person that an allegation is unfounded cannot reasonably be viewed as exposing the person who made the allegation to "scorn or ridicule." The facts of this case are easily distinguished from those in *Gibney* and the differences require the court to reach a different conclusion here.

In *Gibney*, the plaintiff had contacted a company that did business with his employer to allege his employer was improperly billing the company. The company responded that the allegations had been investigated and determined to be unfounded. The Third Circuit held that the company's response, even if untrue, was not capable of a defamatory meaning because a statement that "his allegations were unfounded" would not "'lower him in the estimation of the community or . . . deter third parties from associating or dealing with him.'" *Id.* at 114 (quoting *Tucker v. Phila. Daily News*, 577 Pa. 598, 848 A.2d 113, 124 (2004)). This conclusion makes sense where the detail of business billing procedures leaves open the possibility that a person making an allegation of wrongdoing could have made an honest mistake. In this respect, it is hard to even compare an allegation regarding billing procedures to a sexual assault allegation. A neutral-toned response relative to an investigation of billing history does not impart any flavor of fabrication or moral repugnance, both of which attach to Defendant's statement and its suggestion that Plaintiff intentionally lied about being sexually assaulted. Unlike a billing dispute, Plaintiff Green's allegations detail a specific set of events that either occurred substantially as alleged or were fabricated, leaving no room for an honest mistake.

The potential for reputational damage is increased where the response lacks the neutral tone conveyed in *Gibney* by the word "unfounded," which means "lacking a sound basis in . . . fact." *Webster's Third New International Dictionary* 2496 (1971). Defendant referred to serious sexual assault allegations as "discredited" and "nothing," both words suggesting that the allegations were not made in good faith. Given the different nature of the allegations in this case and the wording of the response, the court cannot conclude here that, as a matter of law, Defendant's response is incapable of negatively impacting Plaintiff Green's reputation within the community. Ultimately, it will be up to a jury to decide whether those who read the Newsweek Statement understood it to have been defamatory. At this stage, however, the court finds Defendant has not identified sufficient grounds for dismissal of Plaintiff Green's claims based on the Newsweek Statement.

FOOD FOR THOUGHT

Why doesn't the statement by a public-relations flack to *Newsweek* that the plaintiff's allegation is 10 years old and proves nothing fall within the "predictable opinion" exception in California? That doctrine protects statements that are obviously self-serving when considered in context. Isn't this exactly the sort of thing one would expect a publicist to say in response to an allegation of misconduct against a celebrity? Even if there were no pending litigation, and the statement therefore would not be within the narrow exception for predictable opinions, why is it not on the opinion side of the fact/opinion distinction as determined by the California three-part test? In Lieberman v. Fieger, 338 F.3d 1076 (9th Cir. 2003), cited in *Green*, the court held that an attorney's references, during an interview on Court TV, to a psychiatrist as "Looney Tunes," "crazy," "nuts," and "mentally imbalanced," were protected statements of opinion. The court relied on the context of the statements, which was a bitter and public dispute between the attorney and the psychiatrist over payment for the psychiatrist's service as an expert witness. The reasonable expectations of the audience would be that the lawyer's hyperbolic language would not be understood literally, as stating facts capable of being proven false. 338 F.3d at 1080.

In the *Milkovich* case discussed in *Green*, the Supreme Court declined to create a per se rule of First Amendment protection for statements of opinion. Nonetheless, as a matter of common law, a publication will not be defamatory unless it contains statements of fact capable of being proven false. We are so accustomed to hearing "spin" in the news media that it is possible to forget that the statement of a public-relations agent that "this is a discredited allegation" can be defamatory. In cases like this, courts must continue to struggle with the common law distinction between fact and opinion. The court in *Green* used a three-part test from California law to determine whether the statement reprinted by Newsweek was one of fact or opinion. Other courts use a four-factor test first articulated in Ollman v. Evans, 750 F.2d 970 (D.C. Cir. 1984). The opinion written by then Judge Kenneth Starr (later special prosecutor investigating the alleged wrongdoings of President Bill Clinton) is scholarly and exceptionally well reasoned. The totality-of-circumstances test it articulates has been quite influential:

> First, we will analyze the common usage or meaning of the specific language of the challenged statement itself. Our analysis of the specific language under scrutiny will be aimed at determining whether the statement has a precise core of meaning for which a consensus of understanding exists or, conversely, whether the statement is indefinite and ambiguous. Readers are, in our judgment, considerably less likely to infer facts from an indefinite or ambiguous statement than one with a commonly understood meaning. Second, we will consider the statement's verifiability — is the statement capable of being objectively characterized as true or false? Insofar as a statement lacks a plausible method of verification, a reasonable reader will not believe that the statement has specific factual content. And, in the setting of litigation, the trier of fact obliged in a defamation action to assess the truth of an unverifiable statement will have considerable difficulty returning a verdict based upon anything but speculation. Third, moving from the challenged language itself, we will consider the full context of the statement — the entire article or column, for example — inasmuch as other, unchallenged language surrounding the allegedly defamatory statement will influence the average reader's readiness to infer that a particular statement has factual content. Finally, we will consider the broader context or setting in which the statement appears. Different types of writing have, as we shall more fully see, widely varying social conventions which signal to the reader the likelihood of a statement's being either fact or opinion.

750 F.2d at 979.

I WAS JUST KIDDING — GET OVER IT!

A variation on the fact/opinion distinction is presented by cases in which the defendant claims the statement was a joke, parody, or satire, and not intended to make a literally true or false statement about the plaintiff. Consider, for example, the incident which led to the case of New Times, Inc. v. Isaacks, 146 S.W.3d 144 (Tex. 2004). A 13-year-old, seventh-grade student was given an assignment for Halloween, to write a scary story. He responded by writing a story about shooting a teacher and two classmates, for which he was arrested and held in jail for five days for making terroristic threats. An alternative newspaper in Dallas subsequently published a satirical article, entitled "Stop the Madness," about the arrest and prosecution of a six-year-old for writing a book report about "cannibalism, fanaticism, and disorderly conduct" in Maurice Sendak's *Where the Wild Things Are*. The article attributed fictional quotes to the judge and district attorney who had been involved in the case of the seventh grader. The school superintendent was quoted as saying, "Frankly, these kids scare the crap out of me," and then-governor

George W. Bush is to have said he was "appalled that such material could find its way into the hands of a Texas schoolchild. This book clearly has deviant, violent sexual overtones. Parents must understand that zero tolerance means just that. We won't tolerate anything." When the district attorney and judge demanded an apology, the newspaper printed the following notice:

> Here's a clue for our cerebrally challenged readers who thought the story was real: It wasn't. It was a joke. We made it up. Not even Judge Whitten, we hope, would throw a 6-year-old girl in the slammer for writing a book report. Not yet, anyway.

The trial court and the court of appeals held that there was a fact issue, precluding summary judgment, regarding whether a reasonable reader would believe the district attorney and judge really did and said the things reported in the article. The Texas Supreme Court, after an extensive discussion of principles from both constitutional law and the common law of defamation, held that the hypothetical reasonable reader can tell the difference between satire and factual reporting.

> As the relevant cases show, the hypothetical reasonable person — the mythic Cheshire cat who darts about the pages of the tort law — is no dullard. He or she does not represent the lowest common denominator, but reasonable intelligence and learning. He or she can tell the difference between satire and sincerity.

Id. at 157 (quoting Patrick v. Superior Court, 27 Cal. Rptr. 2d 883, 887 (Cal. Ct. App. 1994). Noting that the reasonable reader might understand the article as satire even if some readers did not get the joke, the court listed all of the features of the story that should have clued in a reader that the article should not be taken literally, including the quote attributed to the six-year-old: "It's bad enough people like Salinger and Twain are dangerous, but Sendak? Give me a break, for Christ's sake. Excuse my French." As the court asked, rhetorically, "Would a six-year-old be able to comment intelligently on the works of Salinger and Twain, while using expressions like "[e]xcuse my French"? The lesson is, even in Texas,[1] an author is entitled to rely on readers to exercise a little bit of intelligence and common sense.

Hyperbolic language is generally treated as opinion, not a provably false statement of fact, in reviews of books, movies, and restaurants. In the well known case of Mr. Chow of New York v. Ste. Jour Azur S.A., 759 F.2d 219 (2d Cir. 1985), a reviewer for the *Gault/Millau* restaurant guide published a scathing review of a Chinese restaurant. It read, in part:

> While his London restaurant enjoys an honorable reputation (although it is clearly overrated) the branch which the clever Mr. Chow has just opened in New York is simply astounding from a culinary point of view. In a pinch, you might not care that you have to wait ten minutes to obtain chop-sticks instead of forks, that it is impossible to have the basic condiments (soy sauce, hot sauce, etc.) on the table, that the principal concern of the waiters (Italians) is to sell you expensive alcoholic drinks, but the last straw is that the dishes on the menu (very short) have only the slightest relationship to the essential spirit of Chinese

---

1. Wendel, who is originally from Texas and inordinately proud of that fact, figures many of you would be thinking this anyway, so we might as well preempt the joke.

cuisine. With their heavy and greasy dough, the dumplings, on our visit, resembled bad Italian ravioli, the steamed meatballs had a disturbingly gamy taste, the sweet and sour pork contained more dough (badly cooked) than meat, and the green peppers which accompanied it remained still frozen on the plate. The chicken with chili was rubbery and the rice, soaking, for some reason, in oil, totally insipid. Had we been specially punished for being so pretentious as to drink only tea? Apparently not, for the drinkers of alcohol seemed as badly off as we. At a near-by table, the Peking lacquered duck (although ordered in advance) was made up of only one dish (instead of the three traditional ones), composed of pancakes the size of a saucer and the thickness of a finger. At another table, the egg-rolls had the gauge of andouillette sausages, and the dough the thickness of large tagliatelle. No matter, since the wine kept flowing. We do not know where Mr. Chow recruits his cooks, but he would do well to send them for instruction somewhere in Chinatown. There, at least, they still know the traditions.

759 F.2d at 221-222. While some of the statements — such as "the sweet and sour pork contained more dough than meat" — might theoretically be capable of being proven false, the court, applying the factors in *Ollman v. Evans*, concluded that five of the six statements in the passage above were opinion rather than fact in context. The review was an exaggerated or hyperbolic way of making the following point, which clearly would be protected as a statement of opinion:

> "I found it difficult to get the basic seasonings on my table. The sweet and sour pork was too doughy for my tastes. The green peppers served with the pork were not hot enough. The fried rice was too oily. And the pancakes served with the Peking Duck were too thick."

Id. at 228. Only the statement that the restaurant served Peking Duck in one dish rather than the traditional three could be considered a statement of fact.

E. COMMUNICATING THE DEFAMATION TO OTHERS — PUBLICATION

In order to be held liable for defamation, the defendant must communicate the defamatory statement to a third party. The term of art for this element of the tort is publication. A defendant is responsible only for intentional or negligent communication of a defamation. *Prosser and Keeton on Torts* § 113 (5th ed. 1984) note that:

> Courts have never imposed strict liability on the defendant for accidental and non-negligent publication of defamatory matter. There is in fact no liability for publication which the defendant did not intend and could not reasonably anticipate, as in the case of words spoken with no reason to suppose that anyone but the plaintiff would overhear them, or a sealed letter sent to the plaintiff himself which is unexpectedly opened and read by another.

An interesting twist on the publication element occurs when the plaintiff is, in effect, compelled to repeat a defamatory statement about himself or herself. In Van-Go Transport Co. v. New York City Board of Education, 971 F. Supp. 90 (E.D.N.Y. 1997), a corporation with a contract to transport children for the Board of Education sued for libel after the Board sent a letter explaining its reason for denying to renew the contract. The letter stated that the Board had received allegations of criminal conduct by employees of the transportation corporation, including the payment of bribes to government officials. The defendant argued that the plaintiff had essentially consented to the publication of the defamatory statement when it entered the information about the allegations of criminal conduct into the City's computerized system for managing applications for government contracts. The court held that the plaintiff had adequately pled the "publication" element even though it had voluntarily submitted the information, because there was a high degree of compulsion associated with the process of applying for a government contract, and because the plaintiff had no power to control the subsequent dissemination of the information.

Courts are not of one mind as to whether an employee who repeats a defamatory statement about himself in a subsequent job application can lay the blame for the communication of the defamation at the doorstep of the defendant who made the accusation solely to the plaintiff. In Sullivan v. Baptist Memorial Hospital, 995 S.W.2d 569 (Tenn. 1999), plaintiff, a nurse, was fired because the hospital believed that she was stealing medical devices from the hospital's neonatal unit and giving the devices to another hospital in which she was a part-time nurse. The nurse denied the accusations. In seeking employment at other hospitals, the nurse was "compelled" by prospective employers to explain why she was terminated. In doing so, the plaintiff herself repeated the defamatory charges. Her contention was that the employer who made the defamatory charges could reasonably foresee that the defamation would have to be communicated to others and should thus bear the responsibility for the communication. The Tennessee court reviewed the authority nationally and concluded that the majority of courts refuse to hold an employer liable for defamation communicated by an employee to prospective employers. *Accord* Cweklinsky v. Mobil Chemical Co., 837 A.2d 759 (Conn. 2004) (comprehensive review of authority pro and con); White v. Blue Cross & Blue Shield, 809 N.E.2d 1034 (Mass. 2004). The Tennessee court cited an article by Louis B. Eble, *Self-Publication Defamation: Employee Right or Employee Burden?*, 47 Baylor L. Rev. 745, 779-780 (1995), in which the author argues:

> A shutdown of communication would hurt both employees and employers. Employees falsely accused of misconduct may be wrongfully terminated because they would never have a chance to rebut the false accusations. Employees who may be able to improve substandard job performances may fail to do so because needed feedback is withheld. . . . It seems that both employees and employers stand to lose if employers adopt a policy of silence. . . . Unfortunately, employees will bear the costs of such a policy without a corresponding benefit.

Even if one were to agree with the Tennessee court, might not Judge Trager still be correct in *Van-Go*? The requirement of reporting alleged crimes was mandated by the very governmental agency that was the defamer. On the other hand, there was no compulsion for the plaintiff to seek additional governmental contracts. *See Sack on Defamation*, §§ 2.5.2, 8.2 (2007); Bernard E. Jacques, *Defamation in an Employment Context: Selected Issues*, 625 PLI/Lit 829 (2000).

SECONDARY PUBLISHERS AND TRANSMITTERS

Those who publish newspapers and books are subject to the same rules that govern those who author defamatory material. They are not vicariously liable for the statements of the authors but they are held to whatever standards of care the law imposes on anyone who communicates defamatory material. A special problem arises with regard to secondary publishers such as libraries, bookstores, and news vendors. It would seem unjust and impractical to hold them liable for selling or distributing defamatory material. Restatement, Second, of Torts § 581 recognizes a limited privilege for such secondary disseminators of information. They cannot be held liable unless they know or have reason to know of the defamatory content of the material that they are distributing. Statutes in many states immunize radio or TV stations who lease time to purchasers who in turn defame over the airwaves.

An important issue in modern defamation and privacy law concerns the liability of Web sites, search engines, content hosts, Internet service providers, and other online intermediaries for republishing statements that would otherwise be potentially tortious. Section 230 of the Communications Decency Act of 1996 (CDA) creates nearly absolute immunity for online intermediaries, stating that "[n]o provider or user of an interactive computer service shall be treated as the publisher or speaker of any information provided by another information content provider." 47 U.S.C. § 230 (c)(1). This immunity is supported by several congressional findings and statements of policy concerning the value of online free speech — e.g.:

- The Internet and other interactive computer services offer a forum for a true diversity of political discourse, unique opportunities for cultural development, and myriad avenues for intellectual activity.
- The Internet and other interactive computer services have flourished, to the benefit of all Americans, with a minimum of government regulation.

47 U.S.C. § 230 (a)(3)-(4). Passage of the statute was motivated by decisions such as Stratton Oakmont, Inc. v. Prodigy Services Co., 1995 WL 323710 (N.Y. Sup. Ct. 1995), which held an electronic bulletin board service liable for republishing defamatory material.

In a sense, content hosts such as Yahoo!, Facebook, and YouTube are the electronic equivalent of newspapers, magazines, broadcasters, and the printers of pamphlets and posters. Why should they be treated differently? Proponents of § 230 respond that the decentralized structure of the Internet makes it extremely difficult for online service providers to control the content of information to which they provide access. In addition, online communications seldom involve only one intermediary. The late senator Ted Stevens famously described the Internet as "a series of tubes," and the process of accessing an online communication often involves many of these "tubes," including those belonging to an Internet service provider (such as a cable or telephone company), a search engine, a content host (such as YouTube or a blog hosting service), and backbone providers that transmit information between networks. Section 230 of the CDA was intended to clarify that these actors should not be deemed publishers for the purposes of liability. "Publication" generally involves some process of reviewing, editing, or deciding whether to make available or withdraw content. Thus, many online intermediaries are not "publishers," as that notion was developed in the common law of defamation and privacy, because they take a purely passive role with respect to the information they convey. As the following case shows, however, online republication of defamatory material can cause serious harm, so plaintiffs may try to plead a theory of recovery that is not barred by the CDA.

BARNES v. YAHOO!, INC.
570 F.3d 1096 (9th Cir. 2009)

O'SCANNLAIN, J.

We must decide whether the Communications Decency Act of 1996 protects an internet service provider from suit where it undertook to remove from its website material harmful to the plaintiff but failed to do so.

I

This case stems from a dangerous, cruel, and highly indecent use of the internet for the apparent purpose of revenge.

In late 2004, Cecilia Barnes broke off a lengthy relationship with her boyfriend. For reasons that are unclear, he responded by posting profiles of Barnes on a website run by Yahoo!, Inc. ("Yahoo"). According to Yahoo's Member Directory, "[a] public profile is a page with information about you that other Yahoo! members can view. You[r] profile allows you to publicly post information about yourself that you want to share with the world. Many people post their age, pictures, location, and hobbies on their profiles." Through Yahoo's online service, computer users all over the country and the world can view such profiles.

Barnes did not authorize her now former boyfriend to post the profiles, which is hardly surprising considering their content. The profiles contained nude photographs of Barnes and her boyfriend, taken without her knowledge, and some kind of open solicitation, whether express or implied is unclear, to engage in sexual intercourse. The ex-boyfriend then conducted discussions in Yahoo's online "chat rooms," posing as Barnes and directing male correspondents to the fraudulent profiles he had created. The profiles also included the addresses, real and electronic, and telephone number at Barnes' place of employment. Before long, men whom Barnes did not know were peppering her office with emails, phone calls, and personal visits, all in the expectation of sex.

In accordance with Yahoo policy, Barnes mailed Yahoo a copy of her photo ID and a signed statement denying her involvement with the profiles and requesting their removal. One month later, Yahoo had not responded but the undesired advances from unknown men continued; Barnes again asked Yahoo by mail to remove the profiles. Nothing happened. The following month, Barnes sent Yahoo two more mailings. During the same period, a local news program was preparing to broadcast a report on the incident. A day before the initial air date of the broadcast, Yahoo broke its silence; its Director of Communications, a Ms. Osako, called Barnes and asked her to fax directly the previous statements she had mailed. Ms. Osako told Barnes that she would "personally walk the statements over to the division responsible for stopping unauthorized profiles and they would take care of it." Barnes claims to have relied on this statement and took no further action regarding the profiles and the trouble they had caused. Approximately two months passed without word from Yahoo, at which point Barnes filed this lawsuit against Yahoo in Oregon state court. Shortly thereafter, the profiles disappeared from Yahoo's website, apparently never to return.

Barnes' complaint against Yahoo is somewhat unclear, but it appears to allege two causes of action under Oregon law. First, the complaint suggests a tort for the negligent provision or non-provision of services which Yahoo undertook to provide. As Barnes pointed out in her briefs, Oregon has adopted section 323 of the Restatement (Second) of Torts (1965), which describes the elements of this claim. For the sake of brevity, we refer to this tort, which is really a species of negligence, as a "negligent undertaking." Barnes also refers in her complaint and in her briefs to Yahoo's "promise" to remove the indecent profiles and her reliance thereon to her detriment. We construe such references to allege a cause of action under section 90 of the Restatement (Second) of Contracts (1981).

After Yahoo removed the action to federal court, it moved to dismiss the complaint under Federal Rule of Civil Procedure 12(b)(6). Yahoo contended that section 230(c)(1) of the Communications Decency Act ("the Act") renders it immune from liability in this case. *See* 47 U.S.C. § 230(c)(1). The district court granted the motion to dismiss, finding that the Act did in fact protect Yahoo from liability as a matter of law. Barnes timely appealed, claiming that, in the first place, the so-called immunity under section 230(c) did not apply to the cause of action she has brought and that, even if it did, Yahoo did not fit under the terms of such immunity.

II

The district court dismissed Barnes' claim on the ground that section 230(c)(1) makes Yahoo "immune" against any liability for the content that Barnes' former boyfriend had posted. We begin by analyzing the structure and reach of the statute itself.

A

Section 230 of the Act, also known as the Cox-Wyden Amendment ("the Amendment"), protects certain internet-based actors from certain kinds of lawsuits. The Amendment begins with a statement of findings and a statement of policy, in subsections 230(a) and (b), respectively. These are rather general, but they illustrate Congress' appreciation for the internet as a "forum for a true diversity of . . . myriad avenues for intellectual activity," which "ha[s] flourished . . . with a minimum of government regulation." § 230(a)(3)-(4). The statute's "policy" includes the promotion of interactive computer services and the "vibrant and competitive free market" for such services, as well as the encouragement of "blocking and filtering technologies that empower parents to restrict their children's access to objectionable or inappropriate online material." § 230(b)(1)-(2) & (4)-(5). We have recognized in this declaration of statutory purpose two parallel goals. The statute is designed at once "to promote the free exchange of information and ideas over the Internet and to encourage voluntary monitoring for offensive or obscene material." *Carafano v. Metrosplash.com, Inc.*, 339 F.3d 1119, 1122 (9th Cir. 2003).

Though we keep these goals, which the statutory language declares, in mind, we must closely hew to the text of the statutory bar on liability in construing its extent. The operative section of the Amendment is section 230(c), which states in full:

> (c) Protection for "good samaritan" blocking and screening of offensive material
>> (1) Treatment of publisher or speaker No provider or user of an interactive computer service shall be treated as the publisher or speaker of any information provided by another information content provider.
>> (2) Civil liability
>> No provider or user of an interactive computer service shall be held liable on account of—
>>> (A) any action voluntarily taken in good faith to restrict access to or availability of material that the provider or user considers to be obscene, lewd, lascivious, filthy, excessively violent, harassing, or otherwise objectionable, whether or not such material is constitutionally protected; or
>>> (B) any action taken to enable or make available to information content providers or others the technical means to restrict access to material described in paragraph (1).

. . .

Following this approach, one notices that subsection (c)(1), which after all is captioned "Treatment of publisher or speaker," precludes liability only by means of a definition. "No provider or user of an interactive computer service," it says, "*shall be treated* as the publisher or speaker of any information provided by another information content provider." § 230(c)(1) (emphasis added). Subsection 230(e)(3) makes explicit the relevance of this definition, for it cautions that "[n]o cause of action may be brought and no liability may be imposed under any State or local law that is inconsistent with this section." Bringing these two subsections together, it appears that subsection (c)(1) only protects from liability (1) a provider or user of an interactive computer service (2) whom a plaintiff seeks to treat, under a state law cause of action, as a publisher or speaker (3) of information provided by another information content provider.

Barnes did not contest in the district court that Yahoo is a provider of an interactive computer service, and we have no trouble concluding that it qualifies as one. Nor is there any dispute that the "information content" — such as it is — at issue in this case was provided by another "information content provider." The flashpoint in this case is the meaning of the "publisher or speaker" part of subsection (c)(1), and that is where we train our sights.

B

By its terms, then, section (c)(1) only ensures that in certain cases an internet service provider will not be "treated" as the "publisher or speaker" of third-party content for the purposes of another cause of action. The question before us is how to determine when, for purposes of this statute, a plaintiff's theory of liability would treat a defendant as a publisher or speaker of third-party content.

The cause of action most frequently associated with the cases on section 230 is defamation. This is not surprising, because, as we and some of our sister circuits have recognized, Congress enacted the Amendment in part to respond to a New York state court decision, *Stratton Oakmont, Inc. v. Prodigy Servs. Co.*, 1995 WL 323710 (N.Y. Sup. Ct. May 24, 1995) (unpublished), which held that an internet service provider could be liable for defamation.

But "a law's scope often differs from its genesis," and the language of the statute does not limit its application to defamation cases. Indeed, many causes of action might be premised on the publication or speaking of what one might call "information content." A provider of information services might get sued for violating anti-discrimination laws; for fraud, negligent misrepresentation, and ordinary negligence; for false light; or even for negligent publication of advertisements that cause harm to third parties. Thus, what matters is not the name of the cause of action-defamation versus negligence versus intentional infliction of emotional distress—what matters is whether the cause of action inherently requires the court to treat the defendant as the "publisher or speaker" of content provided by another. To put it another way, courts must ask whether the duty that the plaintiff alleges the defendant violated derives from the defendant's status or conduct as a "publisher or speaker." If it does, section 230(c)(1) precludes liability.

We have indicated that publication involves reviewing, editing, and deciding whether to publish or to withdraw from publication third-party content. We need not perform any intellectual gymnastics to arrive at this result, for it is rooted in the common sense and common definition of what a publisher does. One dictionary defines "publisher," in relevant part, as "the reproducer of a work intended for public consumption" and also as "one whose business is publication." *See* Webster's Third New International Dictionary 1837 (Philip Babcock Gove ed., 1986). Thus, a publisher reviews material submitted for publication, perhaps edits it for style or technical fluency, and then decides whether to publish it.

III

Which leads us to whether Barnes, in her negligent undertaking claim, seeks to treat Yahoo as a "publisher or speaker" of the indecent profiles in order to hold Yahoo liable.

A

The Oregon law tort that Barnes claims Yahoo committed derives from section 323 of the Restatement (Second) of Torts, which states:

One who undertakes, gratuitously or for consideration, to render services to another which he should recognize as necessary for the protection of the other's person or things, is subject to liability to the other for physical harm resulting from his failure to exercise reasonable care to perform his undertaking, if

(a) his failure to exercise such care increases the risk of such harm, or

(b) the harm is suffered because of the other's reliance upon the undertaking.

Barnes argues that this tort claim would not treat Yahoo as a publisher. She points to her complaint, which acknowledges that although Yahoo "may have had no initial responsibility to act, once [Yahoo,] through its agent, undertook to act, [it] must do so reasonably." According to Barnes, this makes the undertaking, not the publishing or failure to withdraw from publication, the source of liability. Under this theory, Barnes' cause of action would evade the reach of section 230(c) entirely because it treats Yahoo not as a publisher, but rather as one who undertook to perform a service and did it negligently.

We are not persuaded. As we implied above, a plaintiff cannot sue someone for publishing third-party content simply by changing the name of the theory from defamation to negligence. Nor can he or she escape section 230(c) by labeling as a "negligent undertaking" an action that is quintessentially that of a publisher. The word "undertaking," after all, is meaningless without the following verb. That is, one does not merely undertake; one undertakes *to do* something. And what is the undertaking that Barnes alleges Yahoo failed to perform with due care? The removal of the indecent profiles that her former boyfriend posted on Yahoo's website. But removing content is something publishers do, and to impose liability on the basis of such conduct necessarily involves treating the liable party as a publisher of the content it failed to remove. In other words, the duty that Barnes claims Yahoo violated derives from Yahoo's conduct as a publisher — the steps it allegedly took, but later supposedly abandoned, to de-publish the offensive profiles. It is because such conduct is *publishing conduct* that we have insisted that section 230 protects from liability "any activity that can be boiled down to deciding whether to exclude material that third parties seek to post online."

Although the tort of defamation is not the only form of liability for publishers to which subsection (c)(1) applies, its reach confirms our conclusion. Indeed, we note that Yahoo could be liable for defamation for precisely the conduct of which Barnes accuses it. Defamation law sometimes imposes "an affirmative duty to remove a publication made by another." Courts have applied this principle, including in a case that reads like a low-tech version of the situation before us. In *Hellar v. Bianco*, 111 Cal. App. 2d 424, 244 P.2d 757, 758 (Cal. Ct. App. 1952), a woman received a phone call from a man who sought to arrange an unconventional, but apparently amorous, liaison. After being rebuffed, the man informed the woman that her phone number appeared on the bathroom wall of a local bar along with writing indicating that she "was an unchaste woman who indulged in illicit amatory ventures." The woman's husband promptly called the bartender and demanded he remove the defamatory graffito, which the bartender said he would do when he got around to it. Shortly thereafter, the husband marched to the bar, policeman in tow, and discovered the offending scrawl still gracing the wall. He defended his wife's honor by suing the bar's owner.

The California Court of Appeal held that it was "a question for the jury whether, after knowledge of its existence, [the bar owner] negligently allowed the defamatory matter to remain for so long a time as to be chargeable with its republication." This holding suggests that Yahoo could have been sued under our facts for defamation, one of the elements of which is publication, which strongly confirms our view that section 230(c)(1) bars this lawsuit. . . .

IV

As we indicated above, Barnes' complaint could also be read to base liability on section 90 of the Restatement (Second) of Contracts, which describes a theory of recovery often known as promissory estoppel. At oral argument, counsel for Barnes acknowledged that its tort claim might be "recast" in terms of promissory estoppel. We think it might, and in analyzing it as such now we add that liability for breach of promise is different from, and not merely a rephrasing of, liability for negligent undertaking.

A

Oregon has accepted promissory estoppel as a theory of recovery. The "principal criteria" that determine "when action renders a promise enforceable" under this doctrine are: "(1) a promise[;] (2) which the promisor, as a reasonable person, could foresee would induce conduct of the kind which occurred[;] (3) actual reliance on the promise[;] (4) resulting in a substantial change in position." . . .

B

Against this background, we inquire whether Barnes' theory of recovery under promissory estoppel would treat Yahoo as a "publisher or speaker" under the Act.

As we explained above, subsection 230(c)(1) precludes liability when the duty the plaintiff alleges the defendant violated derives from the defendant's status or conduct as a publisher or speaker. In a promissory estoppel case, as in any other contract case, the duty the defendant allegedly violated springs from a contract — an enforceable promise — not from any non-contractual conduct or capacity of the defendant. Barnes does not seek to hold Yahoo liable as a publisher or speaker of third-party content, but rather as the counter-party to a contract, as a promisor who has breached.

How does this analysis differ from our discussion of liability for the tort of negligent undertaking? After all, even if Yahoo did make a promise, it promised to take down third-party content from its website, which is quintessential publisher conduct, just as what Yahoo allegedly undertook to do consisted in publishing activity. The difference is that the various torts we referred to above each derive liability from behavior that is identical to publishing or speaking: publishing defamatory material; publishing material that inflicts emotional distress; or indeed attempting to de-publish hurtful material but doing it badly. To undertake a thing, within the meaning of the tort, *is* to do it.

Promising is different because it is not synonymous with the performance of the action promised. That is, whereas one cannot undertake to do something without simultaneously doing it, one can, and often does, promise to do something without actually doing it at the same time. Contract liability here would come not from Yahoo's publishing conduct, but from Yahoo's manifest intention to be legally obligated to do something, which happens to be removal of material from publication. Contract law treats the outwardly manifested intention to create an expectation on the part of another as a legally significant event. That event generates a legal duty distinct from the conduct at hand, be it the conduct of a publisher, of a doctor, or of an overzealous uncle.

Furthermore, a court cannot simply infer a promise from an attempt to de-publish of the sort that might support tort liability under section 323 of the Restatement (Second) of Torts. For, as a matter of contract law, the promise must "be as clear and well defined as a promise that could serve as an offer, or that otherwise might be sufficient to give rise to a traditional contract supported by consideration." "The formation of a contract," indeed, "requires a meeting of the minds of the parties, a standard that is measured by the objective manifestations of intent by both parties to bind themselves to an agreement." Thus a general monitoring policy, or even an attempt to help a particular person, on the part of an interactive computer service such as Yahoo does not suffice for contract liability. This makes it easy for Yahoo to avoid liability: it need only disclaim any intention to be bound.

One might also approach this question from the perspective of waiver. The objective intention to be bound by a promise — which, again, promissory estoppel derives from a promise that induces reasonably foreseeable, detrimental reliance — also signifies the waiver of certain defenses. A putative promisor might defend on grounds that show that the contract was never formed (the lack of acceptance or a meeting of the minds, for example) or that he could not have intended as the evidence at first suggests he did (unconscionability, duress, or incapacity, for example). Such defenses go to the integrity of the promise and the intention it signifies; they usually cannot be waived by the agreement they purport to undermine. But once a court concludes a promise is legally enforceable according to contract law, it has implicitly concluded that the promisor has manifestly intended that the court enforce his promise. By so intending, he has agreed to depart from the baseline rules (usually derived from tort or statute) that govern the mine-run of relationships between strangers. Subsection 230(c)(1) creates a baseline rule: no liability for publishing or speaking the content of other information service providers. Insofar as Yahoo made a promise with the constructive intent that it be enforceable, it has implicitly agreed to an alteration in such baseline.

Therefore, we conclude that, insofar as Barnes alleges a breach of contract claim under the theory of promissory estoppel, subsection 230(c)(1) of the Act does not preclude her cause of action. Because we have only reviewed the affirmative defense that Yahoo raised in this appeal, we do not reach the question whether Barnes has a viable contract claim or whether Yahoo has an affirmative defense under subsection 230(c)(2) of the Act.

V

For the foregoing reasons, we AFFIRM IN PART, REVERSE IN PART, and REMAND for further proceedings. Each party shall bear its own costs.

FOOD FOR THOUGHT

Online intermediaries such as Yahoo! have reason to be nervous when they survey the common law of defamation. The bar owner in *Heller*, the California case cited in the preceding case, was potentially liable for permitting defamatory graffiti to remain on the bathroom wall after being asked to remove it. The Internet has sometimes been called a gigantic bathroom wall that all can see. If the owners of parts of this virtual bathroom wall could be held liable for all of the scrawled slurs left by users of their services, the costs of monitoring and responding to complaints would be enormous. On the other hand, there are very real costs that must be borne by victims of online defamation. Like the plaintiff in *Heller*, who was alleged to be "an unchaste woman who indulged in illicit amatory ventures," as the California court so delicately put it, the plaintiff in *Barnes* had to put up with men calling her, e-mailing her, and showing up at her workplace soliciting sex. Plainly her ex-boyfriend is to blame for exposing her to this harassment, but as you have seen in many cases throughout the book, a harm can have multiple causes, and tort law often provides a remedy against a party who contributes to the harm set into motion by another. Often it is for the jury to determine whether a joint tortfeasor should be held liable for playing a role in the plaintiff's injury, but in other cases courts relieve actors from liability, even where the harm was foreseeable, as it surely was in *Barnes*.

Do you buy the court's argument that Yahoo! isn't being held liable as a publisher for promising to remove the fake profile but then failing to follow through on its promise? The court says publishing, which is absolutely immune from liability, extends to any kind of decision whether to post, edit, or remove material generated by third parties. Why is that immunity lost when Yahoo! promised to remove the material (i.e., made a publication decision) but then forgot about it? The court says Yahoo! is being held liable for promising, which is not synonymous with the underlying act of publishing. Yet a promise to publish, or not, seems indistinguishable in its effect on potential victims of defamation from a decision to publish, or not, which is immunized by the CDA. The court also notes that § 230 of the CDA was intended to immunize any defendant who otherwise could be treated as a publisher for the purposes of liability. The plaintiff's promissory estoppel theory seems to treat Yahoo! as a publisher, because only a publisher could meaningfully make, and break, a promise to remove the offending material.

This case may signal a certain amount of judicial discontent with the breadth of the CDA, particularly given the prevalence of online harassment. Most readers of this book will be familiar with Web sites, chat rooms, the comments sections of blogs, or online forums that have degenerated into venues for the worst racist, misogynistic, anti-Semitic, and homophobic speech. Brian Leiter has called these cites "cyber-cesspools" and wondered whether our existing approach to regulation — taking into account both tort law and the First Amendment — is adequate to deal with the harm caused by this speech. *See* Brian Leiter, *Cleaning Cyber-Cesspools: Google and Free Speech*, in *The Offensive Internet: Speech, Privacy and Reputation* 155 (Saul Levmore & Martha Nussbaum, eds., 2010). Leiter recommends that online intermediaries set up some sort of process so that people can demonstrate that they have been harmed by speech in a cesspool maintained by that service provider. Because this speech is valueless, there is no reason not to require its removal. He recognizes that his proposal requires repeal of § 230 of the CDA, because as it stands there is no legal incentive for Yahoo!, Google, or any other online intermediary to provide the redress Leiter proposes. Repealing the CDA, however, risks interfering with the free and open marketplace of ideas online. The debate over the best balance to strike between dignity harms and freedom of speech online is likely to be an ongoing one.

F. DID THE ARROW HIT THE TARGET? OF AND CONCERNING THE PLAINTIFF

THREE AMIGOS SJL RESTAURANT, INC. v. CBS NEWS INC.
15 N.Y.S.3d 36 (N.Y. App. Div. 2015)

Tom, J.P.

This defamation action arises out of a wholly accurate news report stating that federal authorities raided The Cheetah Club (Cheetah's), a midtown Manhattan strip club, which they alleged to be "run by the [M]afia" and at the center of an underground immigration ring that brought Russian and eastern European women into the United States, forcing them to work as exotic dancers.

On November 30, 2011, federal agencies charged seven alleged members and associates of the Gambino and Bonanno crime families with, inter alia, transporting and harboring illegal aliens to work as dancers in New York area strip clubs. The indictment alleged that organized crime defendants controlled certain strip clubs and forced women who had been trafficked from eastern Europe to dance at the clubs. As the women would be placed in sham marriages for citizenship purposes, the federal operation was called "Operation Dancing Brides."

On November 30, 2011, federal authorities executed a search warrant at Cheetah's. In support of the warrant's application, a federal officer averred that organized crime conspirators had negotiated terms with strip clubs, including Cheetah's, for trafficked dancers to perform because, in Cheetah's case, other providers had not been able to meet the club's needs. According to the affidavit, the trafficked women were brought to Cheetah's, where they were video recorded reading contracts and where the women thereafter danced. Plaintiffs take the position that no one at Cheetah's was involved in the crimes underlying Operation Dancing Brides.

The relationship of the Times Square plaintiffs and their employees, the individual plaintiffs, to Cheetah's is not explained, but there is no allegation that these entities are anything more than independent contractors. According to the complaint, plaintiff Times Square Restaurant No. 1, Inc. (No. 1) provides management and promotional services for the Champagne and VIP lounge areas of Cheetah's. Plaintiff Dominica O'Neill is president of No. 1, and plaintiff Sean

Callahan is employed as a manager and consultant whose responsibilities include food and beverages, as well as vendor coordination. Plaintiff Times Square Restaurant Group (the Group) operates a booking agency for the talent (dancers) at Cheetah's, and plaintiff Philip Stein is employed by the Group as a manager. Plaintiff Three Amigos SJL Rest., Inc., doing business as The Cheetah Club, is not a party to this appeal.

After the raid at Cheetah's, defendant CBS News broadcast the event during its noon news broadcast. Reporter Kathryn Brown (in front of Cheetah's) broadcast the following:

> [S]ources tell CBS–2 News this bust is being dubbed 'Operation Dancing Brides,' and this strip club here, Cheetahs in Midtown, they say is at the center of the operation. Cheetahs advertises exotic women and the . . . federal authorities say it is run by the mafia. They have been here — feds have been here all morning. They conducted an early morning raid and they've been here for hours inside collecting evidence. They are still inside right now. Meantime, earlier this morning, agents with the immigrations and customs enforcement arrested 25 men described as ringleaders of this entire operation. Many of them they say are members of the Gambino and Bonanno crime families. They say the men were involved in an elaborate operation to recruit women from Russia and eastern Europe into the U.S. . . . [to] force the women to work as dancers in strip clubs across New York City, including Cheetahs . . . This is still a developing story and we will have much more on this tonight on CBS–2 News at 5:00.

At 5:00 p.m., defendants broadcast a news program called The Evening Report, which contained, inter alia, the following segment:

> Federal authorities carried out boxes of evidence from this Midtown strip club during an early morning raid. They say the club, Cheetahs, is one of several at the center of an underground immigration ring that stretches from Times Square to the heart of Russia. Investigators say Russian and Italian mobsters were working together in the elaborate scheme to bring Russian and eastern European women to the U.S., then funnel them to strip clubs to work as exotic dancers.

The Report then showed Kathryn Brown interviewing a federal law enforcement official, the director of the National Organization for Women, and David Carlebach, an attorney for Cheetah's. Carlebach was broadcast saying, "There is absolutely no La Cosa Nostra, as you say, connection."

At 9:25 p.m., the local CBS New York website posted a summary of the story, embedding a PDF copy of the indictment. The website included the statements that Cheetah's had been "raided," and that Cheetah's was "one of several [strip clubs] at the center of an underground immigration ring" controlled by indicted defendants who "protected their turf through intimidation and threats of physical and economic harm." The story ended, "As federal teams cast a wide net around strip clubs and their owners[,] attorney David Carlebach . . . insisted his client's hands are clean. 'There is absolutely no "La Cosa Nostra," as you say, connection,' Carlebach said."

By summons and verified complaint filed April 27, 2012, plaintiffs alleged that defendants, in broadcasting and publishing stories concerning Operation Dancing

Brides, defamed them. Plaintiffs claimed that the stories were misleading, false, and malicious, and that plaintiffs had no connection with the Mafia, Operation Dancing Brides, human trafficking, extortion, or any other human rights abuse. The complaint contains four causes of action-defamation per quod, defamation per se, injurious falsehood, and respondeat superior. Plaintiffs assert that the false allegations of Cheetah's involvement subjected plaintiffs to scorn and ridicule and adversely affected their ability to earn income from their activities on behalf of the club.

Defendants moved . . . for dismissal of the complaint. Defendants argued, inter alia, that all claims made by the Times Square plaintiffs and by the individual plaintiffs (collectively plaintiffs) must be dismissed because the challenged news reports were not "of and concerning" plaintiffs, as a matter of law.

Plaintiffs opposed defendants' motion, arguing that the alleged libel designated plaintiffs in such a way so as to let those who knew them understand that they were the persons meant and that plaintiffs were entitled to so prove that fact to a jury. Specifically, plaintiffs pointed to the reports' assertions that Cheetah's was "run by the mafia" and "at the center" of a human trafficking ring. By making such statements, plaintiffs argued, defendants were asserting that O'Neill, Stein, and Callahan were members of organized crime.

The motion court granted defendants' motion, found that all of the challenged statements related solely to Cheetah's, and dismissed the claims of the Times Square plaintiffs and the individual plaintiffs. The court further found that nothing in any of the broadcasts mentioned, or even indirectly referred to, the Times Square corporations, nor did any statement assert or even imply that the individually named plaintiffs were part of the Mafia or a global trafficking scheme. That the broadcast might have a negative impact on the business of the Times Square corporations, or that they might have caused plaintiffs' friends to shun them did not demonstrate that the statements were "of and concerning" plaintiffs. The court also noted that First Amendment concerns required plaintiffs to be clearly identifiable, which they were not.

On appeal, plaintiffs cling to their contention that they are clearly identifiable as the persons and entities that "run" Cheetah's on account of the functions they perform for the club. At the outset, plaintiffs do not explain why entities that merely supply services to an establishment should be perceived by the public to exercise such control over its operation as to be identified with illegal activities on the premises. To the contrary, plaintiffs' relationship to Cheetah's is peripheral, and the public at large would have no reason to think that they were implicated in the federal investigation. As to patrons, there is no explanation of why they would be aware of the businesses that supply food and beverages to the club (Times Square Restaurant No. 1) or book dancers to perform there (Times Square Restaurant Group). While the individual plaintiffs involved in the operation of those businesses may be present at the club "on a daily basis . . . and are highly visible to . . . customers," as the affidavit of Dominica O'Neill states, they are nevertheless mere employees. Significantly, they are not employees of Cheetah's itself, but rather, present at the club to perform the services provided to it by their own employers. They can hardly be understood to be "those who 'run' the Cheetah

Club," which implies persons in a position of ownership or control, not vendors that supply management services or their employees, whose presence is required in order to render those services.

As noted, Cheetah's is not a party to this appeal. The club's owner, nonparty Sam Zherka, is currently being held without bail, awaiting trial on an indictment charging him with fraud, income tax fraud and witness tampering. Zherka has filed numerous civil rights actions against government officials who he claims described him as a "mobster." The lawsuits assert that allegations of his organized crime connections are false and are either motivated by prejudice against his Albanian ethnicity or retaliation for his ownership of strip clubs. Each case has either been dismissed prior to adjudication or voluntarily withdrawn by Zherka. Zherka, as the owner of Cheetah's, is in a position of ownership and control, not plaintiffs. The Times Square plaintiffs are not identified in the news reports as being operated by organized crime, and their capacity as vendors to Cheetah's hardly serves to equate them with those identified by the report as "the [M]afia." . . .

As the dissent acknowledges, whether a particular publication is capable of the meaning ascribed to it is a question for the court. Similarly, whether a plaintiff in a defamation action has demonstrated that a particular statement names or so identifies him so that the statement can be said to be "of and concerning" that plaintiff may be decided as a matter of law and need not be determined by a jury. Where, as here, the statement does not name the plaintiffs at all and contains nothing that would cause a reader to think defendant was referring to them, the statement is not "of and concerning" the plaintiffs. As this Court has noted, a statement made about an organization is not understood to refer to any of its individual members unless that person is distinguished from other members of the group. Likewise, where an allegedly defamatory statement is directed at a company, it does not implicate the company's suppliers, partners, vendors or affiliated enterprises even if they sustain injury as a result.

The dissent accepts, as a matter of law and fact, that the individual plaintiffs (though not the Times Square plaintiffs) "run" Cheetah's, as the complaint alleges. While this contention is superficially plausible, it does not withstand closer inspection. The argument is specious, founded upon an attempt to conflate the meaning of the terms "manage" and "run." The fundamental flaw in the complaint is the failure to distinguish the concept of *control* over an organization from the mere provision of management services to the entity by a vendor or, more specifically, the employees of a vendor. The general understanding of a business "run by the [M]afia" is the subjugation of the entity by organized crime, typically by force and intimidation, in furtherance of illegal activities. Ultimately, the theory of recovery espoused in the complaint amounts to an exercise in semantics. While "run" may colloquially refer to management of the routine, day-to-day operation of a business, its meaning acquires a significantly more sinister connotation when used in the same sentence as "[M]afia." The public certainly appreciates this distinction, even if the dissent does not appear to grasp its import. Significantly, the dissent does not contend that the individual plaintiffs were in a position to exercise such authority over Cheetah's operation that they can be said to have been in control of its affairs (conceding that their employers, the Times Square plaintiffs, do not occupy such a position of dominance). Were the individual plaintiffs to attempt to meddle in the affairs of an entity truly "run" by organized crime, they would need to adopt yet a third, considerably more dynamic definition of the term.

A plaintiff bears the burden of pleading and proving that the asserted defamatory statement "designates the plaintiff in such a way as to let those who knew him understand that he was the person meant". While a plaintiff may use extrinsic facts to prove that the statement is "of and concerning" him, he must show the reasonableness of concluding that the extrinsic facts were known to those to whom the statement was made. Plaintiffs seek to state their case by innuendo. As this Court stated:

> The question which an innuendo raises, is [one] of logic. It is, simply, whether the explanation given is a legitimate conclusion from the premise stated.' The innuendo, therefore, may not enlarge upon the meaning of words so as to convey a meaning that is not expressed.

The suggestion that the individual plaintiffs are necessarily identified as members of organized crime because they are employees of entities that provide management services to Cheetah's — reported to be "run" by the Mafia — is simply not logical. It is based on innuendo and constitutes an attempt to enlarge the concept of managerial services to include domination and control of an organization by force, whether actual or threatened . . . .

Accordingly, the order of Supreme Court, New York County (Ellen M. Coin, J.), entered on or about April 18, 2013, which to the extent appealed from as limited by the briefs, granted defendants' motion for dismissal of the defamation claims asserted by plaintiffs Times Square Restaurant No. 1, Inc., Times Square Restaurant Group, Dominica O'Neill, Shawn Callahan, and Philip Stein . . . should be affirmed, without costs.

KAPNICK, J. (dissenting in part).

I respectfully dissent in part from the majority's opinion and find that the motion court's decision should be modified to the extent of denying the motion to dismiss as to Dominica O'Neill, Shawn Callahan and Philip Stein's claims arising out of the alleged defamatory statement "it is run by the mafia," but otherwise agree that the remainder of the alleged defamatory statements are not actionable and that the Times Square plaintiffs were properly dismissed.

It is axiomatic that "to prevail in defamation litigation, a plaintiff must establish that it was he or she who was libeled or slandered: that the allegedly defamatory communication was about ('of and concerning') him or her". It is also well settled that

> [i]t is unnecessary for an article [or statement] to name a person in order for it to be 'of and concerning' that person. If it can be shown either that the implication of the article was that the plaintiff was the person meant or that he or she was understood to be the person spoken about in light of the existence of extrinsic facts not stated in the article, then it is 'of and concerning' the plaintiff as though the plaintiff was specifically named.

Further, "[i]t is not necessary that all the world should understand the libel; it is sufficient if those who knew the plaintiff can make out that he is the person meant." . . .

While there can be no dispute that a defamation plaintiff ultimately has the heavy burden of proving the "of and concerning" prong, the question raised by this appeal is what burden does the plaintiff, who is not named directly and must rely on extrinsic evidence, have at the *pleading stage* to overcome a motion to dismiss based on the assertion that the statements were not "of and concerning" plaintiff. . . .

> When a defamation concerns a group of people, and one or more members of that group bring a libel or slander action, thorny questions are presented as to whether the communication is 'of and concerning' the plaintiff or plaintiffs". "Under some circumstances, courts have permitted an unnamed member of a group to maintain a claim for defamation where a defamatory statement has been made against the group.

Courts look to a number of factors to determine the sufficiency of group defamation allegations. First, "the size of a group is critical to the sufficiency of a claim by an unnamed member of a group" (*Algarin v. Town of Wallkill*, 421 F.3d 137, 139 (2d Cir.2005), comparing *Neiman-Marcus v. Lait*, 13 F.R.D. 311, 313, 316 (S.D.N.Y.1952) (claim by members of a group of 25 sufficient), with *Abramson v. Pataki*, 278 F.3d 93, 102 (2d Cir.2002) (claim by members of a group of more than 1,000 insufficient). . . . In *Brady v. Ottaway Newspapers*, 84 A.D.2d 226, 445 N.Y.S.2d 786 (2d Dept.1981), the Appellate Division, Second Department, rejected a definitive size limitation and allowed libel claims to proceed for a group of at least 53 police officers out of a department of more than 70.[2] . . . *Brady* adopted the " intensity of suspicion test:"

> With the intensity of suspicion test, size is a consideration and the probability of recovery diminishes with increasing size. Size, however, is not the only factor evaluated. It is balanced against the definiteness in number and composition of the group and its degree of organization. This list of balancing factors or reference elements is not meant to be exclusive.

The court went on to note that "the prominence of the group and the prominence of the individual within the group" are other proper "reference elements".

In addition to these factors, courts also consider "whether the defamatory statement refers to 'all' or only 'some' members of the group". In *Brady*, for example, the statement at issue referred to *all* members of a relatively small, identifiable group (the 53 unindicted police officers of the City of Newburgh in 1972), as opposed to a statement that only refers to "some" members of a group, making it less likely for an individual plaintiff to be linked to the statement.

2. The First Amendment dictates courts' long-standing disfavor of group defamation claims. In *Brady*, the court explained that "the larger the collectivity named in the libel, the less likely it is that a reader would understand it to refer to a particular individual". As a result, the court reasoned that

> individual harm cannot occur as the result of a group-libelous statement, because the hearer of the statement will make the rational assessment that such a statement is, by its nature, less likely to be true with respect to every member of a large group than it is to be true with respect to a particular individual.

This reasoning serves to "encourage frank discussions of matters of public concern under the First Amendment guarantees."

Here, there are sufficient facts pleaded at this early stage in the litigation to reasonably connect the individual plaintiffs with the following statement: "it [meaning Cheetah's] is run by the mafia." O'Neill provided an affidavit in which she alleged extrinsic facts that she, Callahan, and Stein were part of a "small and exclusive group of individuals" who ran and managed Cheetah's, with constant visible contact with customers, officials, dancers, and vendors. Taking these allegations as true, as we must on a motion to dismiss, the individual plaintiffs are members of a small, identifiable group that allegedly "ran" Cheetah's and are thus implicated in the allegedly defamatory statement. We note that the result might be different had the statement only implicated *some* of those running Cheetah's. While we do not know the exact size, organization, composition or prominence of the alleged defamation group at this stage in the litigation, there are enough facts alleged at this time to demonstrate the requisite connection.

Whether or not the individual plaintiffs can come forward with evidence to support these allegations and ultimately prove that they were each individually understood to be referred to in light of extrinsic facts not stated in the broadcast, is not to be decided on a pre-answer motion to dismiss.

Moreover, in reaching its result, the majority usurps the role of the trier of fact by outright deciding the meaning or the "general understanding" of the phrase "run by the mafia." The majority goes on to assert its understanding of the "colloquial[ ]" meaning of the phrase "to run a business" and states that the public can appreciate the "sinister connotation" of a reference to the "Mafia." Not only are these clearly questions for a jury, it is unclear why these questions are relevant to the inquiry of whether the statement is "of and concerning" the individual plaintiffs. The majority's parsing of whether "run" means to have control over an organization or whether it means to merely provide management services is misplaced. The majority argues that "run" must mean having ownership or control of the business and that because the individual plaintiffs do not allege that they have such ownership or control over Cheetah's, their claim must fail. This argument, which is not set forth by defendants, is unsound. On a motion to dismiss, we must accept the complaint as true, and here it sufficiently alleges that the individual plaintiffs "run" the operations at Cheetah's. No further inquiry into what that means can properly be made on a pre-answer motion to dismiss.

I agree with the majority that the remaining statements are not actionable by the individual plaintiffs as they only refer to "Cheetah's," which is too general a reference to implicate even the individual plaintiffs.

With respect to the Times Square plaintiffs, they have not met their burden of showing that any of the allegedly defamatory statements are "of and concerning" them, as there are no allegations to support a reasonable connection linking these corporate entities to the statements.

FOOD FOR THOUGHT

The preceding case is an appeal from a motion to dismiss, which means the allegations in the plaintiff's claim must be assumed true for the purposes of the motion.

The plaintiffs alleged that they were part of a small, identifiable group that ran the club. Isn't that enough to satisfy the "of and concerning" requirement? At the motion to dismiss stage, it must be taken as true that customers, officials, dancers, and vendors would have known the identity of the small group of people who managed the club and thus were implicated in criminal activity. This should be an easy case on the "of and concerning" element, unlike some of the cases cited in the dissenting opinion. In Neiman-Marcus v. Lait, 13 F.R.D. 311 (S.D.N.Y. 1952), for example, a book alleged that some employees of a department store were gay, which at the time would have been a statement capable of defamatory meaning. The issue in the case was whether the statement was of and concerning any individual or subset of all male Neiman-Marcus employees. The court held that the statement "most . . . are fairies" was sufficiently specific to satisfy the "of and concerning" element.

The dissent is surely right that the majority is conflating that element with the "defamatory meaning" element in its discussion of whether "run by the Mafia" would be understood by the average viewer of the CBS News broadcast as having sinister connotations. Would it be appropriate to decide, at the motion to dismiss stage, whether the statements in the broadcast are capable of a defamatory meaning?

If a case survives a motion to dismiss, the jury may still decide that the statement was not sufficiently specific to identify the plaintiff. For example, in Robinson v. Radio One, Inc., 695 F. Supp. 2d 425 (N.D. Tex. 2010), the plaintiff claimed that a morning radio show host who referred to "Henry the gay security guard" at Love Field in Dallas had intended to refer to him. The district court denied the radio station's motion to dismiss, but noted that the plaintiff must still establish that listeners of the show who knew the plaintiff believed that the statement referred to him. *Id.* at 430.

As the footnote in the court's opinion rightly points out, whether a defamation can be understood to refer to the plaintiff can sometimes raise serious constitutional questions. In *New York Times v. Sullivan, infra,* the court opined that criticism of government can be easily transformed into criticism of those who make governmental policy. Citing First Amendment concerns, the Court held that the references to plaintiffs were too veiled to withstand constitutional scrutiny. *See* Joseph H. King Jr., *Reference to the Plaintiff Requirement in Defamatory Statements Directed at Groups,* 35 Wake Forest L. Rev. 343, 394 (2000) (discusses the uncertainty that has plagued the requirement and proposes adoption of a bright-line rule which would protect those individuals most adversely impacted by defamatory statements aimed at small groups while providing potential defendants sufficient "breathing space" for freedom of expression). *See also* David A. Elder, *Small Town Police Forces, Other Governmental Entities and the Misapplication of the First Amendment to the Small Group Defamation Theory — A Plea for Fundamental Fairness for Mayberry,* 6 U. Pa. J. Const. L. 881 (2004); Michael J. Polelle, *Racial and Ethnic Group Defamation: A Speech-Friendly Proposal,* 23 B.C. Third World L.J. 213 (2003).

AW, SHUCKS! IT WAS JUST A STORY

The issue of whether the defamation can be understood to refer to the plaintiff arises with considerable frequency in works of fiction where the identity of the plaintiff is thinly (or not so thinly) disguised. In an oft-cited case, Bindrim v. Mitchell, 155 Cal. Rptr. 29 (Cal. Ct. App. 1979), plaintiff, a licensed psychologist, utilized "a nude marathon in group therapy as a means of helping people to shed their psychological inhibitions with the removal of their clothes." Defendant registered into the "nude therapy program" after promising not to write about it. He then proceeded to write and publish a novel that depicted the plaintiff using vulgar language and obscenities. Defendant argued that he had altered the description of the plaintiff so that readers would not recognize the identity and in any event the fact that it was a novel should insulate him from liability. The court held that, if "a reasonable person, reading the book, would understand that the fictional character therein pictured was, in actual fact, the plaintiff," liability would attach. The court found no reason to disturb the jury verdict for the plaintiff.

Similarly, in Bryson v. News America Publications, 672 N.E.2d 1207 (Ill. 1996), Lucy Logsdon, a native of Southern Illinois, wrote a fictional article entitled *Bryson* for *Seventeen Magazine*. In the article Bryson was referred to as a "slut" by the author. The defendant sought to escape liability on the grounds that the article was fictional. The court held that the fact that the plaintiff was identified by name was sufficient for third parties to reasonably interpret the reference to the actual plaintiff, who lived in the same locale as the defendant. *Accord* Geisler v. Petrocelli, 616 F.2d 636 (2d Cir. 1980).

Some courts, however, follow the innocent construction rule. Under this rule, if a defamatory statement can be reasonably construed to refer to someone other than plaintiff, the statement cannot be defamatory per se. *See, e.g.,* Madison v. Frazer, 478 F. Supp. 2d 1056 (C.D. Ill. 2007) (found that the innocent construction rule applied to the fantasy section of defendant's book, in which the characters could be interpreted as someone other than the plaintiff). In Muzikowski v. Paramount Pictures Corp., 477 F.3d 899 (7th Cir. 2007), plaintiff, a securities broker, had been active in organizing little league baseball teams. An assistant coach of one of the teams wrote a nonfiction account of his coaching experience. The book was entitled *Hardball: A Season in the Projects* and made several references to Muzikowski by name. Paramount Pictures released a film, a work of fiction, portraying a character who could be understood to be Muzikowski. The fictional character was portrayed as a gambling addict and as a violent, self-centered person who engaged in illegal activities. Although the fictional character had some similarities to Muzikowski, there were many differences. Muzikowski was not mentioned by name; the fictional character's name was O'Neill. Since the character in the film could reasonably be construed to be another person or no actual person, the court concluded that the innocent construction rule prevented the court from finding the film to be defamatory per se.

For an exhaustive treatment of this subject, *see Defamation in Fiction*, 51 Brook. L. Rev. 223 (1985) (symposium issue contains a treasure trove of articles). For the particular challenges involved in docudramas, *see* Jacqui Gold Grunfeld, *Docudramas: The Legality of Producing Fact-Based Dramas — What Every Producer's Attorney Should Know*, 14 Hastings Comm. & Ent. L.J. 483 (1992).

G. THE CONSTITUTION AND THE LAW OF DEFAMATION

In the preceding pages, we have sought to provide a bird's-eye view of the common law of defamation. A sea change took place in 1964 with the United States Supreme Court's opinion in *New York Times Co. v. Sullivan*, reproduced *infra*. The case marked the beginning point for the Court in determining the impact of the First Amendment on the common law of defamation. The Court embarked on a journey that ultimately found many of the common law rules to be inconsistent with the right of free speech embodied in the First Amendment. But as we shall see, significant pockets remain in which the common law rules may still be applied by state courts if they so desire. As the preceding cases also show, constitutional concerns influence courts in their application of the common law rules regarding defamation.

The materials that follow begin with a true landmark case. It is presented at some length because it deserves careful reading. It has been enormously influential, not only in the law of defamation, but also in the law and theory of free speech and free press in this country. Following that case we have attempted to summarize some of the ways in which the First Amendment has altered the common law of defamation. A full consideration of this topic would require a small book, however, so we can only hope to introduce the fascinating subject that is modern media law.

NEW YORK TIMES CO. v. SULLIVAN
376 U.S. 254 (1964)

BRENNAN, J.

We are required in this case to determine for the first time the extent to which the constitutional protections for speech and press limit a State's power to award damages in a libel action brought by a public official against critics of his official conduct.

Respondent L.B. Sullivan is one of the three elected Commissioners of the City of Montgomery, Alabama. He testified that he was "Commissioner of Public Affairs and the duties are supervision of the Police Department, Fire Department, Department of Cemetery and Department of Scales." He brought this civil libel action against the four individual petitioners, who are Negroes and Alabama clergymen, and against petitioner the New York Times Company, a New York corporation which publishes the *New York Times*, a daily newspaper. A jury in the Circuit Court of Montgomery County awarded him damages of $500,000, the full amount claimed, against all the petitioners, and the Supreme Court of Alabama affirmed. . . .

Respondent's complaint alleged that he had been libeled by statements in a full-page advertisement that was carried in the *New York Times* on March 29, 1960. Entitled "Heed Their Rising Voices," the advertisement began by stating that "As the whole world knows by now, thousands of Southern Negro students are engaged in widespread non-violent demonstrations in positive affirmation of the right to live in human dignity as guaranteed by the U.S. Constitution and the Bill of

Rights." It went on to charge that "in their efforts to uphold these guarantees, they are being met by an unprecedented wave of terror by those who would deny and negate that document which the whole world looks upon as setting the pattern for modern freedom. . . ." Succeeding paragraphs purported to illustrate the "wave of terror" by describing certain alleged events. The text concluded with an appeal for funds for three purposes: support of the student movement, "the struggle for the right-to-vote," and the legal defense of Dr. Martin Luther King, Jr., leader of the movement, against a perjury indictment then pending in Montgomery.

The text appeared over the names of 64 persons, many widely known for their activities in public affairs, religion, trade unions, and the performing arts. Below these names, and under a line reading "We in the south who are struggling daily for dignity and freedom warmly endorse this appeal," appeared the names of the four individual petitioners and of 16 other persons, all but two of whom were identified as clergymen in various Southern cities. The advertisement was signed at the bottom of the page by the "Committee to Defend Martin Luther King and the Struggle for Freedom in the South," and the officers of the Committee were listed.

Of the 10 paragraphs of text in the advertisement, the third and a portion of the sixth were the basis of respondent's claim of libel. They read as follows:

Third paragraph:

In Montgomery, Alabama, after students sang "My Country, 'Tis of Thee" on the State Capitol steps, their leaders were expelled from school, and truckloads of police armed with shotguns and tear-gas ringed the Alabama State College Campus. When the entire student body protested to state authorities by refusing to re-register, their dining hall was padlocked in an attempt to starve them into submission.

Sixth paragraph:

Again and again the Southern violators have answered Dr. King's peaceful protests with intimidation and violence. They have bombed his home almost killing his wife and child. They have assaulted his person. They have arrested him seven times — for "speeding," "loitering" and similar "offenses." And now they have charged him with "perjury" — a *felony* under which they could imprison him for *ten years.* . . .

Although neither of these statements mentions respondent by name, he contended that the word "police" in the third paragraph referred to him as the Montgomery Commissioner who supervised the Police Department, so that he was being accused of "ringing" the campus with police. He further claimed that the paragraph would be read as imputing to the police, and hence to him, the padlocking of the dining hall in order to starve the students into submission. As to the sixth paragraph, he contended that since arrests are ordinarily made by the police, the statement "They have arrested [Dr. King] seven times" would be read as referring to him; he further contended that the "They" who did the arresting would be equated with the "They" who committed the other described acts and with the "Southern violators." Thus, he argued, the paragraph would be read as accusing the Montgomery police, and hence him, of answering Dr. King's protests with "intimidation and violence," bombing his home, assaulting his person, and charging him with perjury. Respondent and six other Montgomery residents testified that they read some or all of the statements as referring to him in his capacity as Commissioner.

It is uncontroverted that some of the statements contained in the two paragraphs were not accurate descriptions of events which occurred in Montgomery. Although Negro students staged a demonstration on the State Capital [sic] steps, they sang the National Anthem and not "My Country, 'Tis of Thee." Although nine students were expelled by the State Board of Education, this was not for leading the demonstration at the Capitol, but for demanding service at a lunch counter in the Montgomery County Courthouse on another day. Not the entire student body, but most of it, had protested the expulsion, not by refusing to register, but by boycotting classes on a single day; virtually all the students did register for the ensuing semester. The campus dining hall was not padlocked on any occasion, and the only students who may have been barred from eating there were the few who had neither signed a preregistration application nor requested temporary meal tickets. Although the police were deployed near the campus in large numbers on three occasions, they did not at any time "ring" the campus, and they were not called to the campus in connection with the demonstration on the State Capitol steps, as the third paragraph implied. Dr. King had not been arrested seven times, but only four; and although he claimed to have been assaulted some years earlier in connection with his arrest for loitering outside a courtroom, one of the officers who made the arrest denied that there was such an assault.

On the premise that the charges in the sixth paragraph could be read as referring to him, respondent was allowed to prove that he had not participated in the events described. Although Dr. King's home had in fact been bombed twice when his wife and child were there, both of these occasions antedated respondent's tenure as Commissioner, and the police were not only not implicated in the bombings, but had made every effort to apprehend those who were. Three of Dr. King's four arrests took place before respondent became Commissioner. Although Dr. King had in fact been indicted (he was subsequently acquitted) on two counts of perjury, each of which carried a possible five-year sentence, respondent had nothing to do with procuring the indictment.

Respondent made no effort to prove that he suffered actual pecuniary loss as a result of the alleged libel. One of his witnesses, a former employer, testified that if he had believed the statements, he doubted whether he "would want to be associated with anybody who would be a party to such things that are stated in that ad," and that he would not re-employ respondent if he believed "that he allowed the Police Department to do the things that the paper say he did." But neither this witness nor any of the others testified that he had actually believed the statements in their supposed reference to respondent.

The cost of the advertisement was approximately $4800, and it was published by the *Times* upon an order from a New York advertising agency acting for the signatory Committee. The agency submitted the advertisement with a letter from A. Philip Randolph, Chairman of the Committee, certifying that the persons whose names appeared on the advertisement had given their permission. Mr. Randolph was known to the *Times*' Advertising Acceptability Department as a responsible person, and in accepting the letter as sufficient proof of authorization it followed its established practice. There was testimony that the copy of the advertisement which accompanied the letter listed only the 64 names appearing under the text, and that the statement, "We in the south . . . warmly endorse this appeal," and the list of names thereunder, which included those of the individual petitioners, were subsequently added when the first proof of the advertisement was received. Each of the individual petitioners testified that he had not authorized the use of his name, and that he had been unaware of its use until receipt of respondent's demand for a retraction. The manager of the Advertising Acceptability Department testified that he had approved the advertisement for publication because he knew nothing to cause him to believe that anything in it was false, and because it bore the endorsement of "a number of people who are well known and whose reputation" he "had no reason to question." Neither he nor anyone else at the Times made an effort to confirm the accuracy of the advertisement, either by checking it against recent Times news stories relating to some of the described events or by any other means.

Alabama law denies a public officer recovery of punitive damages in a libel action brought on account of a publication concerning his official conduct unless he first makes a written demand for a public retraction and the defendant fails or refuses to comply. Alabama Code, Tit. 7, § 914. Respondent served such a demand upon each of the petitioners. None of the individual petitioners responded to the demand, primarily because each took the position that he had not authorized the use of his name on the advertisement and therefore had not published the statements that respondent alleged had libeled him. The *Times* did not publish a retraction in response to the demand, but wrote respondent a letter stating, among other things, that "we . . . are somewhat puzzled as to how you think the statements in any way reflect on you," and "you might, if you desire, let us know in what respect you claim that the statements in the advertisement reflect on you." Respondent filed this suit a few days later without answering the letter. The *Times* did, however, subsequently publish a retraction of the advertisement upon the demand of Governor John Patterson of Alabama, who asserted that the publication charged him with "grave misconduct and . . . improper actions and omissions as Governor of Alabama and Ex-Officio Chairman of the State Board of Education of Alabama." When asked to explain why there had been a retraction for the Governor but not for respondent, the Secretary of the *Times* testified: "We did that because we didn't want anything that was published by The *Times* to be a reflection on the State of Alabama and the Governor was, as far as we could see, the embodiment of the State of Alabama and the proper representative of the State and, furthermore, we had by that time learned more of the actual facts which the ad purported to recite and, finally, the ad did refer to the action of the State authorities and the Board of Education presumably of which the Governor is the ex-officio chairman. . . ." On the other hand, he testified that he did not think that "any of the language in there referred to Mr. Sullivan."

The trial judge submitted the case to the jury under instructions that the statements in the advertisement were "libelous per se" and were not privileged, so that petitioners might be held liable if the jury found that they had published the advertisement and that the statements were made "of and concerning" respondent. The jury was instructed that, because the statements were libelous per se, "the law . . . implies legal injury from the bare fact of publication itself," "falsity and malice are presumed," "general damages need not be alleged or proved but are presumed," and "punitive damages may be awarded by the jury even though the amount of actual damages is neither found nor shown." An award of punitive damages — as distinguished from "general" damages, which are compensatory in nature — apparently requires proof of actual malice under Alabama law, and the judge charged that "mere negligence or carelessness is not evidence of actual malice or malice in fact, and does not justify an award of exemplary or punitive damages." He refused to charge, however, that the jury must be "convinced" of malice, in the sense of "actual intent" to harm or "gross negligence and recklessness," to make such an award, and he also refused to require that a verdict for respondent differentiate between compensatory and punitive damages. The judge rejected petitioners' contention that his rulings abridged the freedoms of speech and of the press that are guaranteed by the First and Fourteenth Amendments. . . .

Because of the importance of the constitutional issues involved, we granted the separate petitions for certiorari of the individual petitioners and of the *Times*. . . . We reverse the judgment. We hold that the rule of law applied by the Alabama courts is constitutionally deficient for failure to provide the safeguards for freedom of speech and of the press that are required by the First and Fourteenth Amendments in a libel action brought by a public official against critics of his official conduct. We further hold that under the proper safeguards the evidence presented in this case is constitutionally insufficient to support the judgment for respondent. . . .

Under Alabama law as applied in this case, a publication is "libelous per se" if the words "tend to injure a person . . . in his reputation" or to "bring [him] into public contempt"; the trial court stated that the standard was met if the words are such as to "injure him in his public office, or impute misconduct to him in his office, or want of official integrity, or want of fidelity to a public trust. . . ." The jury must find that the words were published "of and concerning" the plaintiff, but where the plaintiff is a public official his place in the governmental hierarchy is sufficient evidence to support a finding that his reputation has been affected by statements that reflect upon the agency of which he is in charge. Once "libel per se" has been established, the defendant has no defense as to stated facts unless he can persuade the jury that they were true in all their particulars. . . . His privilege of "fair comment" for expressions of opinion depends on the truth of the facts upon which the comment is based. . . . Unless he can discharge the burden of proving truth, general damages are presumed, and may be awarded without proof of pecuniary injury. A showing of actual malice is apparently a prerequisite to recovery of punitive damages, and the defendant may in any event forestall a punitive award by a retraction meeting the statutory requirements. Good motives and belief in truth do not negate an inference of malice, but are relevant only in mitigation of punitive damages if the jury chooses to accord them weight. . . .

The question before us is whether this rule of liability, as applied to an action brought by a public official against critics of his official conduct, abridges the freedom of speech and of the press that is guaranteed by the First and Fourteenth Amendments. . . .

The general proposition that freedom of expression upon public questions is secured by the First Amendment has long been settled by our decisions. The constitutional safeguard, we have said, "was fashioned to assure unfettered interchange of ideas for the bringing about of political and social changes desired by the people." Roth v. United States, 354 U.S. 476, . . .

Thus we consider this case against the background of a profound national commitment to the principle that debate on public issues should be uninhibited, robust, and wide-open, and that it may well include vehement, caustic, and sometimes unpleasantly sharp attacks on government and public officials. . . . The present advertisement, as an expression of grievance and protest on one of the major public issues of our time, would seem clearly to qualify for the constitutional protection. The question is whether it forfeits that protection by the falsity of some of its factual statements and by its alleged defamation of respondent.

Authoritative interpretations of the First Amendment guarantees have consistently refused to recognize an exception for any test of truth — whether administered by judges, juries, or administrative officials — and especially one that puts the burden of proving truth on the speaker. . . . The constitutional protection does not turn upon "the truth, popularity, or social utility of the ideas and beliefs which are offered." N.A.A.C.P. v. Button, 371 U.S. 415. . . . As Madison said, "Some degree of abuse is inseparable from the proper use of every thing; and in no instance is this more true than in that of the press." 4 Elliot's Debates on the Federal Constitution (1876), p. 571. In Cantwell v. Connecticut, 310 U.S. 296, 310, the Court declared:

> In the realm of religious faith, and in that of political belief, sharp differences arise. In both fields the tenets of one man may seem the rankest error to his neighbor. To persuade others to his own point of view, the pleader, as we know, at times, resorts to exaggeration, to vilification of men who have been, or are, prominent in church or state, and even to false statement. But the people of this nation have ordained in the light of history, that, in spite of the probability of excesses and abuses, these liberties are, in the long view, essential to enlightened opinion and right conduct on the part of the citizens of a democracy. . . .

Injury to official reputation error affords no more warrant for repressing speech that would otherwise be free than does factual error. Where judicial officers are involved, this Court has held that concern for the dignity and reputation of the courts does not justify the punishment as criminal contempt of criticism of the judge or his decision. . . . This is true even though the utterance contains "half-truths" and "misinformation." . . . Such repression can be justified, if at all, only by a clear and present danger of the obstruction of justice. . . . If judges are to be treated as "men of fortitude, able to thrive in a hardy climate," . . . surely the same must be true of other government officials, such as elected city commissioners. Criticism of their official conduct does not lose its constitutional protection merely because it is effective criticism and hence diminishes their official reputations. . . .

If neither factual error nor defamatory content suffices to remove the constitutional shield from criticism of official conduct, the combination of the two elements is no less inadequate. This is the lesson to be drawn from the great controversy over the Sedition Act of 1798, 1 Stat. 596, which first crystallized a national awareness of the central meaning of the First Amendment. . . . That statute made it a crime, punishable by a $5,000 fine and five years in prison, "if any person shall write, print, utter or publish . . . any false, scandalous and malicious writing or writings against the government of the United States, or either house of the Congress . . . , or the President . . . , with intent to defame . . . or to bring them, or either of them, into contempt or disrepute; or to excite against them, or either or any of them, the hatred of the good people of the United States." The Act allowed the defendant the defense of truth, and provided that the jury were to be judges both of the law and the facts. Despite these qualifications, the Act was vigorously condemned as unconstitutional in an attack joined in by Jefferson and Madison. . . .

Although the Sedition Act was never tested in this Court, the attack upon its validity has carried the day in the court of history. Fines levied in its prosecution were repaid by Act of Congress on the ground that it was unconstitutional. . . . Jefferson, as President, pardoned those who had been convicted and sentenced under the Act and remitted their fines, stating: "I discharged every person under punishment or prosecution under the sedition law, because I considered, and now consider, that law to be a nullity, as absolute and as palpable as if Congress had ordered us to fall down and worship a golden image." . . .

What a State may not constitutionally bring about by means of a criminal statute is likewise beyond the reach of its civil law of libel. The fear of damage awards under a rule such as that invoked by the Alabama courts here may be markedly more inhibiting than the fear of prosecution under a criminal statute. . . . Alabama, for example, has a criminal libel law which subjects to prosecution "any person who speaks, writes, or prints of and concerning another any accusation falsely and maliciously importing the commission by such person of a felony, or any other indictable offense involving moral turpitude," and which allows as punishment upon conviction a fine not exceeding $500 and a prison sentence of six months. Alabama Code, Tit. 14, § 350. Presumably a person charged with violation of this statute enjoys ordinary criminal-law safeguards such as the requirements of an indictment and of proof beyond a reasonable doubt. These safeguards are not available to the defendant in a civil action. The judgment awarded in this case — without the need for any proof of actual pecuniary loss — was one thousand times greater than the maximum fine provided by the Alabama criminal statute, and one hundred times greater than that provided by the Sedition Act. And since there is no double-jeopardy limitation applicable to civil lawsuits, this is not the only judgment that may be awarded against petitioners for the same publication.[18] Whether or not a newspaper can survive a succession of such judgments, the pall of fear and timidity imposed upon those who would give voice to public criticism is an

---

18. The *Times* states that four other libel suits based on the advertisement have been filed against it by others who have served as Montgomery City Commissioners and by the Governor of Alabama; that another $500,000 verdict has been awarded in the only one of these cases that has yet gone to trial; and that the damages sought in the other three total $2,000,000.

atmosphere in which the First Amendment freedoms cannot survive. Plainly the Alabama law of civil libel is "a form of regulation that creates hazards to protected freedoms markedly greater than those that attend reliance upon the criminal law." . . .

The state rule of law is not saved by its allowance of the defense of truth. . . .

A rule compelling the critic of official conduct to guarantee the truth of all his factual assertions — and to do so on pain of libel judgments virtually unlimited in amount — leads to a comparable "self-censorship." Allowance of the defense of truth, with the burden of proving it on the defendant, does not mean that only false speech will be deterred. Even courts accepting this defense as an adequate safeguard have recognized the difficulties of adducing legal proofs that the alleged libel was true in all its factual particulars. . . . Under such a rule, would-be critics of official conduct may be deterred from voicing their criticism, even though it is believed to be true and even though it is in fact true, because of doubt whether it can be proved in court or fear of the expense of having to do so. They tend to make only statements which "steer far wider of the unlawful zone." . . . The rule thus dampens the vigor and limits the variety of public debate. It is inconsistent with the First and Fourteenth Amendments.

The constitutional guarantees require, we think, a federal rule that prohibits a public official from recovering damages for a defamatory falsehood relating to his official conduct unless he proves that the statement was made with "actual malice" — that is, with knowledge that it was false or with reckless disregard of whether it was false or not. An oft-cited statement of a like rule . . . has been adopted by a number of state courts. . . .

We hold today that the Constitution delimits a State's power to award damages for libel in actions brought by public officials against critics of their official conduct. Since this is such an action, the rule requiring proof of actual malice is applicable. While Alabama law apparently requires proof of actual malice for an award of punitive damages, where general damages are concerned malice is "presumed." Such a presumption is inconsistent with the federal rule. . . . Since the trial judge did not instruct the jury to differentiate between general and punitive damages, it may be that the verdict was wholly an award of one or the other. But it is impossible to know, in view of the general verdict returned. Because of this uncertainty, the judgment must be reversed and the case remanded. . . .

Since respondent may seek a new trial, we deem that considerations of effective judicial administration require us to review the evidence in the present record to determine whether it could constitutionally support a judgment for respondent. This Court's duty is not limited to the elaboration of constitutional principles; we must also in proper cases review the evidence to make certain that those principles have been constitutionally applied. . . .

Applying these standards, we consider that the proof presented to show actual malice lacks the convincing clarity which the constitutional standard demands, and hence that it would not constitutionally sustain the judgment for respondent under the proper rule of law. The case of the individual petitioners requires little discussion. Even assuming that they could constitutionally be found to have authorized the use of their names on the advertisement, there was no evidence whatever that they were aware of any erroneous statements or were in any way reckless in that regard. The judgment against them is thus without constitutional support.

As to the *Times*, we similarly conclude that the facts do not support a finding of actual malice. The statement by the *Times*' Secretary that, apart from the padlocking allegation, he thought the advertisement was "substantially correct," affords no constitutional warrant for the Alabama Supreme Court's conclusion that it was a "cavalier ignoring of the falsity of the advertisement [from which] the jury could not have but been impressed with the bad faith of The *Times*, and its maliciousness inferable therefrom." The statement does not indicate malice at the time of the publication; even if the advertisement was not "substantially correct" — although respondent's own proofs tend to show that it was — that opinion was at least a reasonable one, and there was no evidence to impeach the witness' good faith in holding it. The *Times*' failure to retract upon respondent's demand, although it later retracted upon the demand of Governor Patterson, is likewise not adequate evidence of malice for constitutional purposes. Whether or not a failure to retract may ever constitute such evidence, there are two reasons why it does not here. *First*, the letter written by the *Times* reflected a reasonable doubt on its part as to whether the advertisement could reasonably be taken to refer to respondent at all. *Second*, it was not a final refusal, since it asked for an explanation on this point — a request that respondent chose to ignore. Nor does the retraction upon the demand of the Governor supply the necessary proof. It may be doubted that a failure to retract which is not itself evidence of malice can retroactively become such by virtue of a retraction subsequently made to another party. But in any event that did not happen here, since the explanation given by the *Times*' Secretary for the distinction drawn between respondent and the Governor was a reasonable one, the good faith of which was not impeached.

Finally, there is evidence that the *Times* published the advertisement without checking its accuracy against the news stories in the *Times*' own files. The mere presence of the stories in the files does not, of course, establish that the *Times* "knew" the advertisement was false, since the state of mind required for actual malice would have to be brought home to the persons in the *Times*' organization having responsibility for the publication of the advertisement. With respect to the failure of those persons to make the check, the record shows that they relied upon their knowledge of the good reputation of many of those whose names were listed as sponsors of the advertisement, and upon the letter from A. Philip Randolph, known to them as a responsible individual, certifying that the use of the names was authorized. There was testimony that the persons handling the advertisement saw nothing in it that would render it unacceptable under the *Times*' policy of rejecting advertisements containing "attacks of a personal character;" their failure to reject it on this ground was not unreasonable. We think the evidence against the *Times* supports at most a finding of negligence in failing to discover the misstatements, and is constitutionally insufficient to show the recklessness that is required for a finding of actual malice. . . .

We also think the evidence was constitutionally defective in another respect: it was incapable of supporting the jury's finding that the allegedly libelous statements were made "of and concerning" respondent. Respondent relies on the words of the advertisement and the testimony of six witnesses to establish a connection between it and himself. Thus, in his brief to this Court, he states:

> The reference to respondent as police commissioner is clear from the ad. In addition, the jury heard the testimony of a newspaper editor . . . ; a real estate and insurance man . . . ; the sales manager of a men's clothing store . . . ; a food equipment man . . . ; a service station operator . . . ; and the operator of a truck line for whom respondent had formerly worked. . . . Each of these witnesses stated that he associated the statements with respondent. . . . (Citations to record omitted.)

There was no reference to respondent in the advertisement, either by name or official position. A number of the allegedly libelous statements — the charges that the dining hall was padlocked and that Dr. King's home was bombed, his person assaulted, and a perjury prosecution instituted against him — did not even concern the police; despite the ingenuity of the arguments which would attach this significance to the word "They," it is plain that these statements could not reasonably be read as accusing respondent of personal involvement in the acts in question. The statements upon which respondent principally relies as referring to him are the two allegations that did concern the police or police functions: that "truckloads of police . . . ringed the Alabama State College Campus" after the demonstration on the State Capitol steps, and that Dr. King had been "arrested . . . seven times." These statements were false only in that the police had been "deployed near" the campus but had not actually "ringed" it and had not gone there in connection with the State Capitol demonstration, and in that Dr. King had been arrested only four times. The ruling that these discrepancies between what was true and what was asserted were sufficient to injure respondent's reputation may itself raise constitutional problems, but we need not consider them here. Although the statements may be taken as referring to the police, they did not on their face make even an oblique reference to respondent as an individual. Support for the asserted reference must, therefore, be sought in the testimony of respondent's witnesses. But none of them suggested any basis for the belief that respondent himself was attacked in the advertisement beyond the bare fact that he was in overall charge of the Police Department and thus bore official responsibility for police conduct; to the extent that some of the witnesses thought respondent to have been charged with ordering or approving the conduct or otherwise being personally involved in it, they based this notion not on any statements in the advertisement, and not on any evidence that he had in fact been so involved, but solely on the unsupported assumption that, because of his official position, he must have been. . . .

There is no legal alchemy by which a State may . . . create the cause of action that would otherwise be denied for a publication which, as respondent himself said of the advertisement, "reflects not only on me but on the other Commissioners and the community." Raising as it does the possibility that a good-faith critic of government will be penalized for his criticism, the proposition relied on by the Alabama courts strikes at the very center of the constitutionally protected area of free expression. We hold that such a proposition may not constitutionally be utilized to establish that an otherwise impersonal attack on governmental operations was a libel of an official responsible for those operations. Since it was relied on exclusively here, and there was no other evidence to connect the statements with respondent, the evidence was constitutionally insufficient to support a finding that the statements referred to respondent.

The judgment of the Supreme Court of Alabama is reversed and the case is remanded to that court for further proceedings not inconsistent with this opinion.

Reversed and remanded.

BLACK, J. with whom DOUGLAS, J. joins, concurring. . . .

I concur in reversing this half-million-dollar judgment against the New York Times Company and the four individual defendants. In reversing the Court holds that "the Constitution delimits a State's power to award damages for libel in actions brought by public officials against critics of their official conduct." . . . I base my vote to reverse on the belief that the First and Fourteenth Amendments not merely "delimit" a State's power to award damages to "public officials against critics of their official conduct" but completely prohibit a State from exercising such a power. The Court goes on to hold that a State can subject such critics to damages if "actual malice" can be proved against them. "Malice," even as defined by the Court, is an elusive, abstract concept, hard to prove and hard to disprove. The requirement that malice be proved provides at best an evanescent protection for the right critically to discuss public affairs and certainly does not measure up to the sturdy safeguard embodied in the First Amendment. Unlike the Court, therefore, I vote to reverse exclusively on the ground that the *Times* and the individual defendants had an absolute, unconditional constitutional right to publish in the *Times* advertisement their criticisms of the Montgomery agencies and officials. I do not base my vote to reverse on any failure to prove that these individual defendants signed the advertisement or that their criticism of the Police Department was aimed at the plaintiff Sullivan, who was then the Montgomery City Commissioner having supervision of the city's police; for present purposes I assume these things were proved. Nor is my reason for reversal the size of the half-million-dollar judgment, large as it is. If Alabama has constitutional power to use its civil libel law to impose damages on the press for criticizing the way public officials perform or fail to perform their duties, I know of no provision in the Federal Constitution which either expressly or impliedly bars the State from fixing the amount of damages.

The half-million-dollar verdict does give dramatic proof, however, that state libel laws threaten the very existence of an American press virile enough to publish unpopular views on public affairs and bold enough to criticize the conduct of public officials. The factual background of this case emphasizes the imminence and enormity of that threat. One of the acute and highly emotional issues in this country arises out of efforts of many people, even including some public officials, to continue state-commanded segregation of races in the public schools and other public places, despite our several holdings that such a state practice is forbidden by the Fourteenth Amendment. Montgomery is one of the localities in which widespread hostility to desegregation has been manifested. This hostility has sometimes extended itself to persons who favor desegregation, particularly to so-called "outside agitators," a term which can be made to fit papers like the *Times*, which is published in New York. The scarcity of testimony to show that Commissioner Sullivan suffered any actual damages at all suggests that these feelings of hostility had at least as much to do with rendition of this half-million-dollar verdict as did an appraisal of damages. Viewed realistically, this record lends support to an inference that instead of being damaged Commissioner Sullivan's political, social, and financial prestige has likely been enhanced by the *Times'* publication. Moreover, a second half-million-dollar libel verdict against the *Times* based on the same advertisement has already been awarded to another Commissioner. There a jury again gave the full amount claimed. There is no reason to believe that there are not more such huge verdicts lurking just around the corner for the *Times* or any other newspaper or broadcaster which might dare to criticize public officials. In fact, briefs before us show that in Alabama there are now pending eleven libel suits by local and state officials against the *Times* seeking $5,600,000, and five such suits against the Columbia Broadcasting System seeking $1,700,000. . . .

In my opinion the Federal Constitution has dealt with this deadly danger to the press in the only way possible without leaving the free press open to destruction — by granting the press an absolute immunity for criticism of the way public officials do their public duty. . . .

We would, I think, more faithfully interpret the First Amendment by holding that at the very least it leaves the people and the press free to criticize officials and discuss public affairs with impunity. . . . To punish the exercise of this right to discuss public affairs or to penalize it through libel judgments is to abridge or shut off discussion of the very kind most needed. This Nation, I suspect, can live in peace without libel suits based on public discussions of public affairs and public officials. But I doubt that a country can live in freedom where its people can be made to suffer physically or financially for criticizing their government, its actions, or its officials. "For a representative democracy ceases to exist the moment that the public functionaries are by any means absolved from their responsibility to their constituents; and this happens whenever the constituent can be restrained in any manner from speaking, writing, or publishing his opinions upon any public measure, or upon the conduct of those who may advise or execute it." An unconditional right to say what one pleases about public affairs is what I consider to be the minimum guarantee of the First Amendment.

I regret that the Court has stopped short of this holding indispensable to preserve our free press from destruction.

[The concurring opinion of Mr. Justice Goldberg is omitted.]

Although not a paradigm-changing case like *New York Times v. Sullivan*, a case decided ten years later established an important distinction in the constitutional law of defamation. Gertz v. Robert Welch, Inc., 418 U.S. 323 (1974), involved a defamation action against a magazine published by the John Birch Society — a far-right-wing conspiratorial group dedicated to, among other things, warning of incursions on American institutions by Communists. The plaintiff, Gertz, was a lawyer retained by the family of a young man who had been shot and killed by a Chicago police officer. The magazine accused many people, including those involved with the criminal prosecution of the police officer and the civil lawsuit against the city, of Communist affiliations. The articles in question stated that Gertz was a "Leninist," a "Communist-fronter," and had been a member of the "Marxist League for Industrial Democracy" and the "Intercollegiate Socialist Society." All of these statements were false.

The defendant sought to take shelter under the protection of the *New York Times v. Sullivan* standard, arguing that Gertz was a public figure and the article pertained to a matter of public concern. The district court concluded that Gertz was neither a public official nor a public figure, but that the defendant was still entitled to the benefit of the *Times* malice standard. The Supreme Court opinion tackled the application of the *Times* standard to non-public-figure cases, but it began its analysis with tantalizing dicta on the fact/opinion distinction:

> Under the First Amendment there is no such thing as a false idea. However pernicious an opinion may seem, we depend for its correction not on the conscience of judges and juries but on the competition of other ideas. But there is no constitutional value in false statements of fact. Neither the intentional lie nor the careless error materially advances society's interest in "uninhibited, robust, and wide-open" debate on public issues. They belong to that category of utterances which "are no essential part of any exposition of ideas, and are of such slight social value as a step to truth that any benefit that may be derived from them is clearly outweighed by the social interest in order and morality." . . .

Because the action brought by Gertz involved an allegedly defamatory false statement of fact, however, the Court's statement about the constitutional protection for opinions was irrelevant to the holding. What is essential is the following discussion of the applicability of the *Times* standard to defamation lawsuits brought by public officials, public figures, and private plaintiffs:

> The *New York Times* standard defines the level of constitutional protection appropriate to the context of defamation of a public person. Those who, by reason of the notoriety of their achievements or the vigor and success with which they seek the public's attention, are properly classed as public figures and those who hold governmental office may recover for injury to reputation only on clear and convincing proof that the defamatory falsehood was made with knowledge of its falsity or with reckless disregard for the truth. This standard administers an extremely powerful antidote to the inducement to media self-censorship of the common-law rule of strict liability for libel and slander. And it exacts a correspondingly high price from the victims of defamatory falsehood. Plainly many deserving plaintiffs, including some intentionally subjected to injury, will be unable to surmount the barrier of the *New York Times* test. Despite this substantial abridgment of the state law right to compensation for wrongful hurt to one's reputation, the Court has concluded that the protection of the *New York Times* privilege should be available to publishers and broadcasters of defamatory falsehood concerning public officials and public figures. . . . We think that these decisions are correct, but we do not find their holdings justified solely

by reference to the interest of the press and broadcast media in immunity from liability. Rather, we believe that the *New York Times* rule states an accommodation between this concern and the limited state interest present in the context of libel actions brought by public persons. For the reasons stated below, we conclude that the state interest in compensating injury to the reputation of private individuals requires that a different rule should obtain with respect to them. . . .

[W]e have no difficulty in distinguishing among defamation plaintiffs. The first remedy of any victim of defamation is self-help — using available opportunities to contradict the lie or correct the error and thereby to minimize its adverse impact on reputation. Public officials and public figures usually enjoy significantly greater access to the channels of effective communication and hence have a more realistic opportunity to counteract false statements than private individuals normally enjoy. Private individuals are therefore more vulnerable to injury, and the state interest in protecting them is correspondingly greater.

More important than the likelihood that private individuals will lack effective opportunities for rebuttal, there is a compelling normative consideration underlying the distinction between public and private defamation plaintiffs. An individual who decides to seek governmental office must accept certain necessary consequences of that involvement in public affairs. He runs the risk of closer public scrutiny than might otherwise be the case. And society's interest in the officers of government is not strictly limited to the formal discharge of official duties. As the Court pointed out in Garrison v. Louisiana, 379 U.S., at 77, the public's interest extends to "anything which might touch on an official's fitness for office. . . . Few personal attributes are more germane to fitness for office than dishonesty, malfeasance, or improper motivation, even though these characteristics may also affect the official's private character."

Those classed as public figures stand in a similar position. Hypothetically, it may be possible for someone to become a public figure through no purposeful action of his own, but the instances of truly involuntary public figures must be exceedingly rare. For the most part those who attain this status have assumed roles of special prominence in the affairs of society. Some occupy positions of such persuasive power and influence that they are deemed public figures for all purposes. More commonly, those classed as public figures have thrust themselves to the forefront of particular public controversies in order to influence the resolution of the issues involved. In either event, they invite attention and comment. . . .

For these reasons we conclude that the States should retain substantial latitude in their efforts to enforce a legal remedy for defamatory falsehood injurious to the reputation of a private individual. . . .

We hold that, so long as they do not impose liability without fault, the States may define for themselves the appropriate standard of liability for a publisher or broadcaster of defamatory falsehood injurious to a private individual. This approach provides a more equitable boundary between the competing concerns involved here. It recognizes the strength of the legitimate state interest in compensating private individuals for wrongful injury to reputation, yet shields the press and broadcast media from the rigors of strict liability for defamation. At least this conclusion obtains where, as here, the substance of the defamatory statement "makes substantial danger to reputation apparent." This phrase places in perspective the conclusion we announce today. Our inquiry would involve considerations somewhat different from those discussed above if a State purported to condition civil liability on a factual misstatement whose content did not warn a reasonably prudent editor or broadcaster of its defamatory potential. Such a case is not now before us, and we intimate no view as to its proper resolution.

Our accommodation of the competing values at stake in defamation suits by private individuals allows the States to impose liability on the publisher or broadcaster of defamatory falsehood on a less demanding showing than that required by *New York Times*. This conclusion is not based on a belief that the considerations which prompted the adoption of the *New York Times* privilege for defamation of public officials and its extension to public figures are wholly inapplicable to the context of private individuals. Rather, we endorse this approach in recognition of the strong and legitimate state interest in compensating private individuals for injury to reputation. But this countervailing state interest extends no further than compensation for actual injury. For the reasons stated below, we hold that the States may not permit recovery of presumed or punitive damages, at least when liability is not based on a showing of knowledge of falsity or reckless disregard for the truth.

The common law of defamation is an oddity of tort law, for it allows recovery of purportedly compensatory damages without evidence of actual loss. Under the traditional rules pertaining to actions for libel, the existence of injury is presumed from the fact of publication. Juries may award substantial sums as compensation for supposed damage to reputation without any proof that such harm actually occurred. The largely uncontrolled discretion of juries to award damages where there is no loss unnecessarily compounds the potential of any system of liability for defamatory falsehood to inhibit the vigorous exercise of First Amendment freedoms. Additionally, the doctrine of presumed damages invites juries to punish unpopular opinion rather than to compensate individuals for injury sustained by the publication of a false fact. More to the point, the States have no substantial interest in securing for plaintiffs such as this petitioner gratuitous awards of money damages far in excess of any actual injury.

We would not, of course, invalidate state law simply because we doubt its wisdom, but here we are attempting to reconcile state law with a competing interest grounded in the constitutional command of the First Amendment. It is therefore appropriate to require that state remedies for defamatory falsehood reach no farther than is necessary to protect the legitimate interest involved. It is necessary to restrict defamation plaintiffs who do not prove knowledge of falsity or reckless disregard for the truth to compensation for actual injury. We need not define "actual injury," as trial courts have wide experience in framing appropriate jury instructions in tort actions. Suffice it to say that actual injury is not limited to out-of-pocket loss. Indeed, the more customary types of actual harm inflicted by defamatory falsehood include impairment of reputation and standing in the community, personal humiliation, and mental anguish and suffering. Of course, juries must be limited by appropriate instructions, and all awards must be supported by competent evidence concerning the injury, although there need be no evidence which assigns an actual dollar value to the injury.

We also find no justification for allowing awards of punitive damages against publishers and broadcasters held liable under state-defined standards of liability for defamation. In most jurisdictions jury discretion over the amounts awarded is limited only by the gentle rule that they not be excessive. Consequently, juries assess punitive damages in wholly unpredictable amounts bearing no necessary relation to the actual harm caused. And they remain free to use their discretion selectively to punish expressions of unpopular views. Like the doctrine of presumed damages, jury discretion to award punitive damages unnecessarily exacerbates the danger of media self-censorship, but, unlike the former rule, punitive damages are wholly irrelevant to the state interest that justifies a negligence standard for private defamation actions. They are not compensation for injury. Instead, they are private fines levied by civil juries to punish reprehensible conduct and to deter its future occurrence. In short, the private defamation plaintiff who establishes liability under a less demanding standard than that stated by *New York Times* may recover only such damages as are sufficient to compensate him for actual injury.

The Court went on to conclude that Gertz was not a public official even though he had served at one time on housing committees appointed by the mayor of Chicago. Nor was he a public figure by reason of having achieved "general fame or notoriety in the community." Although not a general-purpose public figure, one may be a limited-purpose public figure as a result of extensive participation in a particular public controversy. In this case, however, Gertz served only as a lawyer representing the plaintiffs in a civil lawsuit against the city. He did not discuss the case in the media, nor was he quoted in the press. "He plainly did not thrust himself into the vortex of this public issue, nor did he engage the public's attention in an attempt to influence its outcome," in Justice Powell's words. Thus, the *Times v. Sullivan* standard was inapplicable to the case.

THE WORLD OF DEFAMATION AFTER TIMES AND GERTZ

After digesting *Times* and *Gertz*, one can conclude the following:

(1) Public Officials and All-Purpose Public Figures

One cannot make out a case for either of these categories of plaintiffs unless the plaintiff establishes by clear and convincing evidence that the defendant made the defamatory statement with actual malice — that is, with knowledge of its falsity or in reckless disregard of the truth. The Court has on several occasions noted that defining the words *actual malice* to mean *knowledge of falsity or reckless disregard of the truth* was unfortunate. In common parlance, actual malice denotes evil intent or motive arising from spite or ill-will. It was a mistake to use such a loaded term as a surrogate for the true test for liability, which is totally dependent on whether the defendant had knowledge of falsity or spoke with reckless disregard of the truth of the defamatory statement. *See* Masson v. New Yorker Magazine, 501 U.S. 496, 510-511 (1991). Scholars have critiqued the determinative effect that the categorization of plaintiff as a "public official" has on her chances of winning. *See* Brian Markovitz, *Note: Public School Teachers as Plaintiffs in Defamation Suits: Do They Deserve Actual Malice?*, 88 Geo. L.J. 1953 (2000) (argues that public school teachers who are plaintiffs in defamation suits are as entitled to the same protections as other private persons); Kristian D. Whitten, *The Economics of Actual Malice: A Proposal for Legislative Change to the Rule of New York Times v. Sullivan*, 32 Cumb. L. Rev. 519 (2002) (questions whether state legislatures may properly enact state libel laws that are "at least as effective" in protecting the media's free press rights as the *New York Times* standard).

(2) Limited Public Figures

The category that will almost certainly be the most difficult to pin down is the limited public figure. Under *Gertz*, this category of plaintiffs are to be judged by the unforgiving *Times* standard rather than the more gentle fault standard that governs private plaintiffs. The Court provided little in the way of guidance as to how to define this category other than to say, "more commonly, an individual injects himself or is drawn into a particular public controversy and thereby becomes a public figure for a limited range of issues." Although the plaintiff in *Gertz* was the lawyer for the victim of a police shooting in a civil action, the Court found that the mere fact that he represented a plaintiff, in what was, in effect, a police brutality action against an officer did not turn Gertz as plaintiff into a "limited public figure." These cases tend to attract significant public attention. Surely plaintiff knew that in taking on this case he might well become a lightning rod for those who believe that police officers can do no wrong. Furthermore, the defamation in this case accused the plaintiff of being a "Leninist" and a "Communist-Fronter." This is the very kind of accusation that tends to be directed at those whose views are left of center. Admittedly, the defamation was much broader and virulent (especially the claim that the police file on plaintiff was so thick that it would take an Irish cop to lift it). Nonetheless, the trial judge held that, if the *Times* standard were to govern, he would have directed a verdict for the defendant. It is not surprising that this intermediate "limited public figure" category has been elusive and hard to define. Indeed, one court said that trying to distinguish between public figures and private individuals is "much like trying to nail a jellyfish to the wall." Rosanova v. Playboy Enterprises, Inc., 411 F. Supp. 440, 443 (S.D. Ga. 1976). *See* Dan B. Dobbs, The Law of Torts § 418 (2000); W. Wat Hopkins, *The Involuntary Public Figure: Not So Dead After All*, 21 Cardozo Arts & Ent. L.J. (2003).

In OAO Afa Bank v. Center for Public Integrity, 387 F. Supp. 2d 20 (D.D.C. Cir. 2005), the court applied a three-part inquiry to determine that the plaintiffs, two powerful Russian oligarchs who played an important role in Yeltsin's move to privatize the Russian economy, were limited public figures. The court had to determine (1) whether a public controversy was at issue, (2) whether the plaintiffs achieved prominence in the debate, and (3) whether the alleged defamation was related to the plaintiffs' participation in the controversy. *Id.* at 42-44. The court in Sewell v. Trib Publications, Inc., 622 S.E.2d 919 (Ga. Ct. App. 2005), applied a similar three-part test and held that an assistant university professor who discussed America's military involvement in Iraq in his classroom was not a limited-purpose public figure because he did not "thrust himself to the forefront of the controversy in any public forum, so as to have gained access to media outlets generally unavailable to private citizens or to have assumed any risk incident to acceptance of a public role in the matter." *Id.* at 923-924. The court reversed the grant of summary judgment to defendant and remanded the case for trial to determine whether the newspaper was negligent in reporting that the plaintiff had made anti-American remarks in class.

(3) What Constitutes Reckless Disregard of the Truth?

In *New York Times*, the Court made it clear that the failure of the *Times* to check its records and its reliance on the signatories to the advertisement did not make out reckless disregard of the truth. The Court addressed this issue with greater specificity in St. Amant v. Thompson, 390 U.S. 727 (1968), in which Justice White articulated two tests that appear inconsistent. At one point in the opinion, he says that "there must be sufficient evidence to permit the conclusion that the defendant in fact entertained serious doubts as to the truth of his publication." Later in the opinion, he says that the defamer of a public official is not "likely to prevail when the publisher's allegations are so inherently improbable that only a reckless man would have put them in circulation." The former test appears to be subjective whereas the latter test has an objective ring to it. The Court revisited the question of whether a given fact pattern met the constitutional minimum for "reckless disregard of the truth" in Harte-Hanks Communications, Inc. v. Connaughton, 491 U.S. 657 (1989). It found that purposeful avoidance of the truth would suffice to meet the constitutional standard of recklessness. *See also* Moore v. Vislosky, 240 Fed. Appx. 457 (3d Cir. 2007) (held that a jury could find that the defendant acted with actual malice by making defamatory statements about the plaintiff because the defendant admitted in her statements that she had no evidence of plaintiff's wrongdoing). Both state and federal courts have had considerable difficulty in deciding when the conduct of the defamer falls on one side of the line or the other. Much has been written regarding the standard of care media defendants are held to. *See* Lackland H. Bloom, Jr., *Proof of Fault in Media Defamation Litigation*, 38 Vand. L. Rev. 247 (1985); Todd F. Simon, *Libel as Malpractice: News Media Ethics and the Standard of Care*, 53 Fordham L. Rev. 449 (1984); Robert Franklin, *What Does Negligence Mean in Defamation Cases?*, 6 Com./Ent. L.J. 259 (1984); John W. Wade, *The Tort Liability of Investigative Reporters*, 37 Vand. L. Rev. 301 (1984).

(4) What Standard Governs Private Plaintiffs?

Gertz draws a sharp distinction between public officials and public figures, on the one hand, and private plaintiffs, on the other. The demanding *Times* standard applies only to public officials and public figures. With regard to private persons, the *Gertz* Court holds that as long as state courts do not impose liability without fault, they may choose whichever standard of liability they want in a defamation action. In practical terms, this means that as long as the plaintiff establishes some form of negligence against the defamer, the finding will withstand constitutional scrutiny. A fair reading of *Gertz* would lead one to the conclusion that any defamation case brought by a private person requires some proof of fault. *See* Marc A. Franklin & Daniel J. Bussel, *The Plaintiff's Burden in Defamation: Awareness and*

Falsity, 25 Wm. & Mary L. Rev. 825 (1984). It should make no difference whether the issue that was the subject of defamation involved a matter of public concern or was a matter in which the public had no interest. The Court seemed quite clear in rejecting a test that would require judges to decide which information was or was not in the "public interest." But the *Dun & Bradstreet* case, excerpted below, complicates matters.

(5) Presumed Damages and Punitive Damages Can Be Assessed Only Under the *Times* Standard

Unless a plaintiff establishes knowledge of falsity or reckless disregard of the truth, a court may not assess presumed damages or punitive damages. That is true whether the plaintiff is a public official, a public figure, or a private person. The language in *Gertz* is about as clear as it gets. But, once again, you are in for a surprise when you read *Dun & Bradstreet, infra*.

(6) Does the First Amendment Protect the Expression of Opinion Without Qualification?

Gertz is clear. The Court said, "However pernicious an opinion may seem we depend for its correction not on the conscience of judges and juries but on the competition of other ideas." That suggests constitutional protection for expressions of opinion. Remember that under the common law of defamation, the plaintiff must show that the defendant made a defamatory, false statement of *fact*. Thus, it may not matter whether there is a specific First Amendment doctrine protecting expressions of opinion. The Supreme Court addressed this question in Milkovich v. Lorain Journal Co., 497 U.S. 1 (1990). That case involved a defamation lawsuit brought against a newspaper after an article reported that a high school wrestling coach had lied under oath in a judicial proceeding. The proceeding arose out of an altercation at a wrestling match, and the article stated:

> The teachers responsible were mainly head Maple wrestling coach, Mike Milkovich, and former superintendent of schools H. Donald Scott. . . .
> Anyone who attended the meet, whether he be from Maple Heights, Mentor, or impartial observer, knows in his heart that Milkovich and Scott lied at the hearing after each having given his solemn oath to tell the truth.

Superintendent Scott brought his own defamation action, and in it the Ohio Supreme Court used the totality-of-circumstances test from *Ollman v. Evans* (see the discussion above, following *Green v. Cosby*) to conclude that the article was opinion. Although the statement about lying under oath was verifiable, the most important factor in the court's analysis was that the statement was contained on the sports page, "a traditional haven for cajoling, invective, and hyperbole." *See* Scott v. News-Herald, 496 N.E.2d 699 (Ohio 1986). The Supreme Court granted certiorari to consider whether the Ohio court was correct in recognizing a *constitutional* "opinion" exception to the application of its defamation laws.

The Court noted the concern that "unduly burdensome defamation laws could stifle public debate," but then cited with approval the common-law privilege of fair comment:

> "The principle of 'fair comment' afforded legal immunity for the honest expression of opinion on matters of legitimate public interest when based upon a true or privileged statement of fact." 1 F. Harper & F. James, Law of Torts § 5.28, p. 456 (1956). . . . As this statement implies, comment was generally privileged when it concerned a matter of public concern, was upon true or privileged facts, represented the actual opinion of the speaker, and was not made solely for the purpose of causing harm. *See* Restatement of Torts, *supra*, § 606. "According to the majority rule, the privilege of fair comment applied only to an expression of opinion and not to a false statement of fact, whether it was expressly stated or implied from an expression of opinion." Restatement (Second) of Torts, *supra*, § 566, Comment *a*. Thus under the common law, the privilege of "fair comment" was the device employed to strike the appropriate balance between the need for vigorous public discourse and the need to redress injury to citizens wrought by invidious or irresponsible speech. . . .

The defendant sought to give this privilege constitutional significance, citing the dictum from *Gertz* that "[u]nder the First Amendment there is no such thing as a false idea." However, the Court denied that the *Gertz* dictum created a *per se* constitutional exemption from liability for any statement that might be labeled "opinion":

> If a speaker says, "In my opinion John Jones is a liar," he implies a knowledge of facts which lead to the conclusion that Jones told an untruth. Even if the speaker states the facts upon which he bases his opinion, if those facts are either incorrect or incomplete, or if his assessment of them is erroneous, the statement may still imply a false assertion of fact. Simply couching such statements in terms of opinion does not dispel these implications; and the statement, "In my opinion Jones is a liar," can cause as much damage to reputation as the statement, "Jones is a liar." As Judge Friendly aptly stated: "[It] would be destructive of the law of libel if a writer could escape liability for accusations of [defamatory conduct] simply by using, explicitly or implicitly, the words 'I think.'" . . . It is worthy of note that at common law, even the privilege of fair comment did not extend to "a false statement of fact, whether it was expressly stated or implied from an expression of opinion." Restatement (Second) of Torts, § 566, Comment *a* (1977).

Apart from their reliance on the *Gertz* dictum, respondents do not really contend that a statement such as, "In my opinion John Jones is a liar," should be protected by a separate privilege for "opinion" under the First Amendment. But they do contend that in every defamation case the First Amendment mandates an inquiry into whether a statement is "opinion" or "fact," and that only the latter statements may be actionable. They propose that a number of factors developed by the lower courts (in what we hold was a mistaken reliance on the *Gertz* dictum) be considered in deciding which is which. But we think the " 'breathing space'" which "'freedoms of expression require in order to survive,'" . . . is adequately secured by existing constitutional doctrine without the creation of an artificial dichotomy between "opinion" and fact. . . .

We are not persuaded that, in addition to these protections, an additional separate constitutional privilege for "opinion" is required to ensure the freedom of expression guaranteed by the First Amendment. The dispositive question in the present case then becomes whether a reasonable factfinder could conclude that the statements in the Diadiun column imply an assertion that petitioner Milkovich perjured himself in a judicial proceeding. We think this question must be answered in the affirmative. As the Ohio Supreme Court itself observed: "The clear impact in some nine sentences and a caption is that [Milkovich] 'lied at the hearing after . . . having given his solemn oath to tell the truth.'" . . . This is not the sort of loose, figurative, or hyperbolic language which would negate the impression that the writer was seriously maintaining that petitioner committed the crime of perjury. Nor does the general tenor of the article negate this impression.

The Court concluded with a reaffirmation of its dedication to the First Amendment's "guarantee of free and uninhibited discussion of public issues," but then added a shout-out to the "important social values which underlie the law of defamation," including the strong social interest in protecting reputation. The Court says that the fact/opinion issue can be resolved by focusing on the truth or falsity of the alleged defamatory statement. In cases where the problem is that the statement cannot be easily characterized as to whether it is subject to falsification, there is almost no alternative but to resort to a contextual analysis, as in the four-part *Ollman v. Evans* test. *See, e.g.*, Knievel v. ESPN, 393 F.3d 1068, 1078 (9th Cir. 2005). In that case, the formerly famous stuntman Evel Knievel was photographed with his right arm around his wife, Krystal, and his left arm around another young woman. ESPN published the photograph on its Web site with a caption that read, "Evel Knievel proves that you are never too old to be a pimp." The court analyzed the context in which the word "pimp" was used and determined that because the word could not be interpreted literally in the context in which it was used, "the fact that its literal interpretation could be proven true or false is immaterial" to whether it was defamatory. In context the statement was clearly an attempt at humor rather than a factual accusation.

When all the dust has settled, *Milkovich* appears to be a case that will easily be distinguished away. Courts will go on their merry way finding some statements to be opinion, either because the general tenor or surrounding context makes it more likely that the statement is not understood as fact. *See, e.g.*, Fortson v. Colangelo, 434 F. Supp. 2d 1369, 1379 (S.D. Fla. 2006) ("In determining whether an allegedly defamatory statement is an expression of fact or an expression of pure opinion and/or rhetorical hyperbole, context is paramount"). The Supreme Court's attempt to brush away the fact/opinion dichotomy as having no independent constitutional significance appears to have been a failure. It is important to remind the reader that state courts are free to allow greater freedom to speakers than that granted by the federal constitution. The fact/opinion dichotomy is so deeply ingrained that courts who believe that context renders a statement to be opinion rather than fact can refuse to find the statement to be defamatory. The *Milkovich* opinion will not stand in their way.

The two following decisions provide further refinements on the *Times* malice standard, whether actual damages may be presumed, and the recoverability of punitive damages, in cases involving private-figure plaintiffs.

DUN & BRADSTREET, INC. v. GREENMOSS BUILDERS, INC.
472 U.S. 749 (1985)

Powell, J.

In Gertz v. Robert Welch, Inc., 418 U.S. 323 (1974), we held that the First Amendment restricted the damages that a private individual could obtain from a publisher for a libel that involved a matter of public concern. More specifically, we held that in these circumstances the First Amendment prohibited awards of presumed and punitive damages for false and defamatory statements unless the plaintiff shows "actual malice," that is, knowledge of falsity or reckless disregard for the truth. The question presented in this case is whether this rule of *Gertz* applies when the false and defamatory statements do not involve matters of public concern.

I

Petitioner Dun & Bradstreet, a credit reporting agency, provides subscribers with financial and related information about businesses. All the information is confidential; under the terms of the subscription agreement the subscribers may not reveal it to anyone else. On July 26, 1976, petitioner sent a report to five subscribers indicating that respondent, a construction contractor, had filed a voluntary petition for bankruptcy. This report was false and grossly misrepresented respondent's assets and liabilities. That same day, while discussing the possibility of future financing with its bank, respondent's president was told that the bank had received the defamatory report. He immediately called petitioner's regional office, explained the error, and asked for a correction. In addition, he requested the names of the firms that had received the false report in order to assure them that the company was solvent. Petitioner promised to look into the matter but refused to divulge the names of those who had received the report.

After determining that its report was indeed false, petitioner issued a corrective notice on or about August 3, 1976, to the five subscribers who had received the initial report. The notice stated that one of respondent's former employees, not respondent itself, had filed for bankruptcy and that respondent "continued in business as usual." Respondent told petitioner that it was dissatisfied with the notice, and it again asked for a list of subscribers who had seen the initial report. Again petitioner refused to divulge their names.

Respondent then brought this defamation action in Vermont state court. It alleged that the false report had injured its reputation and sought both compensatory and punitive damages. The trial established that the error in petitioner's report had been caused when one of its employees, a 17-year-old high school student paid to review Vermont bankruptcy pleadings, had inadvertently attributed to respondent a bankruptcy petition filed by one of respondent's former employees. Although petitioner's representative testified that it was routine practice to check the accuracy of such reports with the businesses themselves, it did not try to verify the information about respondent before reporting it.

After trial, the jury returned a verdict in favor of respondent and awarded $50,000 in compensatory or presumed damages and $300,000 in punitive damages. Petitioner moved for a new trial. It argued that in Gertz v. Robert Welch, Inc., *supra*, at 349, this Court had ruled broadly that "the States may not permit recovery of presumed or punitive damages, at least when liability is not based on a showing of knowledge of falsity or reckless disregard for the truth," and it argued that the judge's instructions in this case permitted the jury to award such damages on a lesser showing. . . . The trial court indicated some doubt as to whether *Gertz* applied to "non-media cases," but granted a new trial "[because] of . . . dissatisfaction with its charge and . . . conviction that the interests of justice [required] it." . . .

The Vermont Supreme Court reversed. . . . Although recognizing that "in certain instances the distinction between media and nonmedia defendants may be difficult to draw," the court stated that "no such difficulty is presented with credit reporting agencies, which are in the business of selling financial information to a limited number of subscribers who have paid substantial fees for their services." . . . Relying on this distinguishing characteristic of credit reporting firms, the court concluded that such firms are not "the type of media worthy of First Amendment protection as contemplated by New York Times Co. v. Sullivan, 376 U.S. 254 (1964), and its progeny." . . .

In *Gertz*, we held that the fact that expression concerned a public issue did not by itself entitle the libel defendant to the constitutional protections of *New York Times*. These protections, we found, were not "justified solely by reference to the interest of the press and broadcast media in immunity from liability." 418 U.S., at 343. Rather, they represented "an accommodation between [First Amendment] concern[s] and the limited state interest present in the context of libel actions brought by public persons." *Ibid*. In libel actions brought by private persons we found the competing interests different. Largely because private persons have not voluntarily exposed themselves to increased risk of injury from defamatory statements and because they generally lack effective opportunities for rebutting such statements . . . we found that the State possessed a "strong and legitimate . . . interest in compensating private individuals for injury to reputation." . . . Balancing this stronger state interest against the same First Amendment interest at stake in *New York Times*, we held that a State could not allow recovery of presumed and punitive damages absent a showing of "actual malice." Nothing in our opinion, however, indicated that this same balance would be struck regardless of the type of speech involved.

IV

We have never considered whether the *Gertz* balance obtains when the defamatory statements involve no issue of public concern. To make this determination, we must employ the approach approved in *Gertz* and balance the State's interest in compensating private individuals for injury to their reputation against the First Amendment interest in protecting this type of expression. This state interest is identical to the one weighed in *Gertz*. There we found that it was "strong and legitimate." 418 U.S., at 348. A State should not lightly be required to abandon it. . . .

The First Amendment interest, on the other hand, is less important than the one weighed in *Gertz*. We have long recognized that not all speech is of equal First Amendment importance. It is speech on "'matters of public concern'" that is "at the heart of the First Amendment's protection." . . .

While such speech [on matters of purely private concern] is not totally unprotected by the First Amendment, . . . its protections are less stringent. In *Gertz*, we found that the state interest in awarding presumed and punitive damages was not "substantial" in view of their effect on speech at the core of First Amendment concern. . . . This interest, however, *is* "substantial" relative to the incidental effect these remedies may have on speech of significantly less constitutional interest. The rationale of the common-law rules has been the experience and judgment of history that "proof of actual damage will be impossible in a great many cases where, from the character of the defamatory words and the circumstances of publication, it is all but certain that serious harm has resulted in fact." W. Prosser, Law of Torts § 112, p. 765 (4th ed. 1971). . . . As a result, courts for centuries have allowed juries to presume that some damage occurred from many defamatory utterances and publications. Restatement of Torts § 568, Comment *b*, p. 162 (1938). . . . This rule furthers the state interest in providing remedies for defamation by ensuring that those remedies are effective. In light of the reduced constitutional value of speech involving no matters of public concern, we hold that the state interest adequately supports awards of presumed and punitive damages — even absent a showing of "actual malice." . . .

V

The only remaining issue is whether petitioner's credit report involved a matter of public concern. In a related context, we have held that "[w]hether . . . speech addresses a matter of public concern must be determined by [the expression's] content, form, and context . . . as revealed by the whole record." . . . These factors indicate that petitioner's credit report concerns no public issue. It was speech solely in the individual interest of the speaker and its specific business audience. . . . This particular interest warrants no special protection when — as in this case — the speech is wholly false and clearly damaging to the victim's business reputation. . . .

In addition, the speech here, like advertising, is hardy and unlikely to be deterred by incidental state regulation. . . . It is solely motivated by the desire for profit, which, we have noted, is a force less likely to be deterred than others. *Ibid.* Arguably, the reporting here was also more objectively verifiable than speech deserving of greater protection. . . . In any case, the market provides a powerful incentive to a credit reporting agency to be accurate, since false credit reporting is of no use to creditors. Thus, any incremental "chilling" effect of libel suits would be of decreased significance. . . .

We conclude that permitting recovery of presumed and punitive damages in defamation cases absent a showing of "actual malice" does not violate the First Amendment when the defamatory statements do not involve matters of public concern. Accordingly, we affirm the judgment of the Vermont Supreme Court.

[Chief Justice Burger and Justice White concurred. Both of these justices had dissented in *Gertz* and believed that common law, not constitutional standards should govern private plaintiffs — even when the defamatory statement involved matters of public concern. They would overrule *Gertz*. In any event, the instant case presented no constitutional problems for them.]

[Justice Brennan, joined by Justices Marshall, Blackmun, and Stevens, dissented. The dissenters first considered whether the protections set forth in *Gertz* should be applicable only where the defendant is a "media" entity. Finding nothing in the First Amendment that limits its guarantees to the institutional media, the dissenters rejected this distinction. Next the dissenting Justices questioned whether the line between matters of public and private concern can be drawn with clarity. The distinction could turn on the subject matter of the expression or on the extent and conditions of its dissemination. Either way, argued the dissenters, the credit reporting of Dun & Bradstreet should fall within the definition of "public concern."]

FOOD FOR THOUGHT

If you are surprised by the Court's decision in *Dun & Bradstreet*, you are in good company. The four dissenters, in a lengthy footnote, argue that there is no hint in *Gertz* that presumed damages and punitive damages should be allowed in cases where the defamatory statement dealt with a matter of purely private concern, when plaintiff cannot establish that the defamer acted with knowledge of falsity or reckless disregard of the truth. More importantly, they note that courts will now be required to decide whether a defamation was a matter of public rather than private concern. *Gertz* was quite clear in saying that it did not want courts to enter the thicket of deciding whether a defamatory statement fell into one category or another. What gives? Is the distinction between categories of public and private concern based on the susceptibility of certain types of speech to being "chilled" by a defamation action analytically sound? *See* Daniel A. Farber, *Free Speech Without Romance: Public Choice and the First Amendment*, 105 Harv. L. Rev. 554 (1991).

For better or worse, the Supreme Court has apparently returned defamation of private persons dealing with matters of purely private concern to the common law rules that governed the law of defamation before the *Times-Gertz* revolution. We say "apparently" because we are not absolutely sure how the Court would deal with the issues of "falsity" raised in the next case, in a purely private defamation action involving issues of private concern. So once again, read on.

PHILADELPHIA NEWSPAPERS, INC. v. HEPPS
475 U.S. 767 (1986)

O'CONNOR., J.

This case requires us once more to "struggle . . . to define the proper accommodation between the law of defamation and the freedoms of speech and press protected by the First Amendment." Gertz v. Robert Welch, Inc., 418 U.S. 323, 325 (1974). In *Gertz*, the Court held that a private figure who brings a suit for defamation cannot recover without some showing that the media defendant was at fault in publishing the statements at issue. . . . Here, we hold that, at least where a newspaper publishes speech of public concern, a private-figure plaintiff cannot recover damages without also showing that the statements at issue are false.

I

Maurice S. Hepps is the principal stockholder of General Programming, Inc. (GPI), a corporation that franchises a chain of stores — known at the relevant time as "Thrifty" stores — selling beer, soft drinks, and snacks. Mr. Hepps, GPI, and a number of its franchisees are the appellees here. Appellant Philadelphia Newspapers, Inc., owns the *Philadelphia Inquirer* (*Inquirer*). The *Inquirer* published a series of articles . . . containing the statements at issue here. The general theme of the five articles, which appeared in the *Inquirer* between May 1975 and May 1976, was that appellees had links to organized crime and used some of those links to influence the State's governmental processes, both legislative and administrative. The articles discussed a state legislator, described as "a Pittsburgh Democrat and convicted felon," . . . whose actions displayed "a clear pattern of interference in state government by [the legislator] on behalf of Hepps and Thrifty". . . . The stories reported that federal "investigators have found connections between Thrifty and underworld figures," . . . and that Thrifty had "won a series of competitive advantages through rulings by the State Liquor Control Board". . . . A grand jury was said to be investigating the "alleged relationship between the Thrifty chain and known Mafia figures," and "[whether] the chain received special treatment from the [state Governor's] administration and the Liquor Control Board." . . .

Appellees brought suit for defamation against appellants in a Pennsylvania state court. Consistent with *Gertz, supra*, Pennsylvania requires a private figure who brings a suit for defamation to bear the burden of proving negligence or malice by the defendant in publishing the statements at issue. 42 Pa. Cons. Stat. § 8344 (1982). As to falsity, Pennsylvania follows the common law's presumption that an individual's reputation is a good one. Statements defaming that person are therefore presumptively false, although a publisher who bears the burden of proving the truth of the statements has an absolute defense. . . . *See also* 42 Pa. Cons. Stat. § 8343(b)(1) (1982) (defendant has the burden of proving the truth of a defamatory statement).

The parties first raised the issue of burden of proof as to falsity before trial, but the trial court reserved its ruling on the matter. Appellee Hepps testified at length that the statements at issue were false, . . . and he extensively cross-examined the author of the stories as to the veracity of the statements at issue. After all the evidence had been presented by both sides, the trial court concluded that Pennsylvania's statute giving the defendant the burden of proving the truth of the statements violated the Federal Constitution. . . . The trial court therefore instructed the jury that the plaintiffs bore the burden of proving falsity. . . .

The jury ruled for appellants and therefore awarded no damages to appellees.

. . . [T]the appellees here brought an appeal directly to the Pennsylvania Supreme Court. That court viewed *Gertz* as simply requiring the plaintiff to show fault in actions for defamation. It concluded that a showing of fault did not require a showing of falsity, held that to place the burden of showing truth on the defendant did not unconstitutionally inhibit free debate, and remanded the case for a new trial. . . . We noted probable jurisdiction, . . . and now reverse. . . .

<h2 style="text-align:center">II</h2>

[The court reviewed its decisions in *New York Times v. Sullivan* and *Gertz v. Robert Welch, Inc.*]

One can discern in these decisions two forces that may reshape the common-law landscape to conform to the First Amendment. The first is whether the plaintiff is a public official or figure, or is instead a private figure. The second is whether the speech at issue is of public concern. When the speech is of public concern and the plaintiff is a public official or public figure, the Constitution clearly requires the plaintiff to surmount a much higher barrier before recovering damages from a media defendant than is raised by the common law. When the speech is of public concern but the plaintiff is a private figure, as in *Gertz*, the Constitution still supplants the standards of the common law, but the constitutional requirements are, in at least some of their range, less forbidding than when the plaintiff is a public figure and the speech is of public concern. When the speech is of exclusively private concern and the plaintiff is a private figure, as in *Dun & Bradstreet*, the constitutional requirements do not necessarily force any change in at least some of the features of the common-law landscape.

Our opinions to date have chiefly treated the necessary showings of fault rather than of falsity. Nonetheless, as one might expect given the language of the Court in *New York Times* . . . a public-figure plaintiff must show the falsity of the statements at issue in order to prevail in a suit for defamation. . . .

Here, as in *Gertz*, the plaintiff is a private figure and the newspaper articles are of public concern. In *Gertz*, as in *New York Times*, the common-law rule was superseded by a constitutional rule. We believe that the common law's rule on falsity — that the defendant must bear the burden of proving truth — must similarly fall here to a constitutional requirement that the plaintiff bear the burden of showing falsity, as well as fault, before recovering damages.

There will always be instances when the factfinding process will be unable to resolve conclusively whether the speech is true or false; it is in those cases that the burden of proof is dispositive. Under a rule forcing the plaintiff to bear the burden of showing falsity, there will be some cases in which plaintiffs cannot meet their burden despite the fact that the speech is in fact false. The plaintiff's suit will fail despite the fact that, in some abstract sense, the suit is meritorious. Similarly, under an alternative rule placing the burden of showing truth on defendants, there would be some cases in which defendants could not bear their burden despite the fact that the speech is in fact true. Those suits would succeed despite the fact that, in some abstract sense, those suits are unmeritorious. Under either rule, then, the outcome of the suit will sometimes be at variance with the outcome that we would desire if all speech were either demonstrably true or demonstrably false.

This dilemma stems from the fact that the allocation of the burden of proof will determine liability for some speech that is true and some that is false, but *all* of such speech is *unknowably* true or false. Because the burden of proof is the deciding factor only when the evidence is ambiguous, we cannot know how much of the speech affected by the allocation of the burden of proof is true and how much is false. In a case presenting a configuration of speech and plaintiff like the one we face here, and where the scales are in such an uncertain balance, we believe that the Constitution requires us to tip them in favor of protecting true speech. To ensure that true speech on matters of public concern is not deterred, we hold that the common-law presumption that defamatory speech is false cannot stand when a plaintiff seeks damages against a media defendant for speech of public concern. . . .

For the reasons stated above, the judgment of the Pennsylvania Supreme Court is reversed, and the case is remanded for further proceedings not inconsistent with this opinion.

It is so ordered.

[Concurring and dissenting opinions are omitted.]

FOOD FOR THOUGHT

Hepps does away with the presumption of falsity for cases involving private persons when the issue deals with a matter of public concern. The entire tone of the decision suggests that if the defamation dealt with a matter of purely private concern, the common law presumption of falsity would not raise constitutional problems. Isn't it likely that, in the purely private action, the common law rule that defamation can also be established without any proof of fault on the part of the defendant remains in place? One leading scholar, Professor Rodney Smolla, believes that this is so. *See* Smolla, *Law of Defamation* § 3.02 [5] (1996). Does it make sense to shift the burden from the media defendant to the individual? *See* Frederick Schauer, *Uncoupling Free Speech*, 92 Colum. L. Rev. 1321, 1339-1343 (1992).

Gertz, Hepps, and *Dun & Bradstreet* all seem to turn on whether the issue that is the subject of defamation is a matter of public or private concern. If the defamation involves a matter of public concern, constitutional restraints kick in. If not, the common law rules may govern. If the wrangling of the majority and dissent in *Dun & Bradstreet* are a good harbinger of the difficulties that courts will have in deciding what is or is not a matter of public or private concern, we are in for a rocky ride. *See* Joseph H. King, Jr., *Deus ex Machina and the Unfulfilled Promise of* New York

Times v. Sullivan: *Applying the Times for All Seasons*, 95 Ky. L.J. 649, 659 (2006/2007) (King proposes extending "the requirement of proof of knowledge or reckless disregard, falsity, and a provably false statement to all defamation plaintiffs in all cases without regard to either the status of the plaintiff or the nature of the content of the defendant's communication").

Summing up the rules established in the case we have just read, think about what the plaintiff must prove to make out a prima facie case, given the plaintiff's status and the nature of the speech at issue:

Plaintiff	Matter	Elements/mens rea	Damages	Case
General purpose public figure or public official; also limited purpose public figure	Public concern	Plaintiff must show knowledge of falsity or reckless disregard for truth or falsity ("actual malice")	No presumption of damages; no punitive	*NYT v. Sullivan; Gertz*
Private	Public concern	Negligence okay; just can't be strict liability. However, P must show falsity — cannot be presumed.	No presumption of damages; no punitive	*Gertz; Hepps*
	Private	Negligence okay; falsity may be presumed (i.e. truth would be affirmative defense — burden of proof on D).	Presumed okay; punitive recoverable	*Dun & Bradstreet*

Is this scheme of presumptions, burdens of proof, and recoverable damages normatively appropriate, in light of the underlying interests of the plaintiff, the defendant, and the public? In Snyder v. Phelps, 562 U.S. 443 (2011), the Supreme Court held that the First Amendment precluded the father of a service member who had been killed in Iraq from suing protesters at his son's funeral for intentional infliction of emotional distress. Crucial to this holding was the Court's determination that the protesters' speech was on a matter of public concern. "Speech on matters of public concern is at the heart of the First Amendment's protection," but "where matters of purely private significance are at issue, First Amendment protections are often less rigorous." *Id.* at 1215 (internal alterations omitted). Defendant Fred Phelps and other members of the Westboro Baptist Church believe that G-d is punishing the United States for its tolerant attitudes toward homosexuality by permitting American soldiers to be killed in combat. One could categorize Phelps' speech in at least two different ways: as a protest to draw attention to public policies regarding homosexuality in the military (a matter of public concern) or as an intrusion on the solitude of grieving family members at a funeral (a matter of private concern). The Court in this case chose to emphasize the public aspects of the speech, noting that the protesters appeared in public carrying signs, and chose a military funeral as a way of increasing the visibility of the protest. Justice Alito, the lone dissenter, characterized the protesters' speech as relating to a purely private matter and therefore entitled to less constitutional protection.

Although states remain free to continue to apply the common law rules in cases of private persons dealing with matters of private concern, they are free to revise their common law rules to be more restrictive and require plaintiff to prove the defamer was at fault and that the defamatory statement was false. They may also refuse to allow presumed damages and punitive damages unless the plaintiff establishes that the defamation was uttered with knowledge of its falsity or reckless disregard of the truth. In short, nothing we have considered thus far prevents a state from granting private persons greater rights of free speech than mandated by the United States Supreme Court decisions.

H. PRIVILEGES AFTER THE CONSTITUTIONAL TAKEOVER

We now know that, with regard to public officials and public figures, a defamation will not be actionable unless the statement is made with knowledge of its falsity or with reckless disregard of the truth. We have also established that a defamation concerning a private person that relates to a matter of public concern is not actionable unless the defamer was at fault in not ascertaining the falsity of the defamatory statement. Furthermore, a plaintiff (whether a public figure or private person) is required to prove the falsity of the defamatory statement in any case where the issue is one of public concern. These constitutional privileges give greater breathing room for one seeking to comment on matters of public concern than existed at common law. What was once known as the "fair comment" privilege has now been constitutionalized. For a critique of the constitutional limitations on libel law, propounded by *New York Times* and its progeny, as affording little protection for reputation, *see* David A. Anderson, *Is Libel Law Worth Reforming?*, 140 U. Pa. L. Rev. 487, 488 n.2 & n.3 (1991); Gerald G. Ashdown, *Journalism Police*, 89 Marq. L. Rev. 739 (2006) (arguing that a simple negligence standard should govern all defamation cases against media defendants). For discussion of the reporters' privilege, *see* David A. Elder, *The Fair Report Privilege* (1998); Mary-Rose Papandrea, *Citizen Journalism and the Reporter's Privilege*, 91 Minn. L. Rev. 515 (2007) (arguing that nontraditional journalism provided by bloggers need be

---

authors' dialogue 40

JIM: How do you view the division between those areas that are governed by constitutional First Amendment considerations and those that are left to state common law doctrine?

AARON: I'm not sure whether you are asking me how much of defamation is left to state common law or whether I am satisfied as to which aspects of defamation have been constitutionalized and which areas have been left to the states.

JIM: I know what the Court has said and which areas they have left to state common law. I'm asking if you think they got it right.

AARON: Here's my take. I think they got *Times* and *Gertz* right. Any sensible reading of *Gertz* is that defamation plaintiffs, regardless of the circumstances, must establish that defendant was at fault. If they had stuck with that position, they could have avoided the whole common law question of qualified privilege. The law would be simple: You cannot make out a prima facie case for defamation without proving that the defendant did something wrong. With *Dun & Bradstreet* and *Hepps,* the Court left open the question whether, in defamation of a private person dealing with issues that are not of public concern, it is necessary for the plaintiff to establish fault or, for that matter, to prove the falsity of the defamatory statement. Now we have a mess. Unless state courts are to adopt an across-the-board rule that requires the plaintiff to prove the fault and falsity of the defamatory statement, they will revert to the common law rules. Those rules allow for the presumption that any defamatory statement is false and also make the issue of privilege an affirmative defense to be proven by defendant. Furthermore, the privilege can be lost if plaintiff can prove that the privilege was abused. All this complicated nonsense could have been avoided if the Court had simply stuck with *Gertz.*

JIM: I agree; it would be simple. An across-the-board requirement of fault could have been substituted for the complex question of whether the occasion was

---

considered in defining the scope of the "reporter's privilege"); Kathryn Dix Sowle, *Defamation and the First Amendment: The Case for a Constitutional Privilege of Fair Report,* 54 N.Y.U. L. Rev. 469 (1979) (argues that fair report should be constitutionally protected rather than left to state law).

However, after *Dun & Bradstreet, supra,* it appears that a defamatory statement made about a private person that is not a matter of public concern is still largely (if not entirely) governed by the common law rules of defamation. It is thus important to examine the privileges that the common law recognized that protected a speaker from liability even when he had communicated a false defamatory statement. *See, e.g.,* Howell v. Enterprise Publishing Co., 920 N.E.2d 1 (Mass. 2010) (newspaper protected by fair report privilege for reporting that town official had been placed on administrative leave after pornography was found on his work computer). We shall first examine the "conditional" or "qualified" privileges and then briefly comment on those privileges that were deemed "absolute."

privileged and whether the privilege was abused. But it would come at a rather high cost in terms of federalism. For better or worse, state common law is quirky and somewhat irrational. However, it is really hard to see a significant federal interest in controlling the law of defamation when the plaintiff is a private person and the issue is not one of public concern. If the Court were to constitutionally control this cause of action, why should it not control the tort of intentional infliction of mental distress? That tort is almost always brought about by irresponsible speech. Should the Supreme Court weigh in on what the elements of that tort should be?

AARON: I'm not oblivious to the questions you raise. It seems to me, however, that having constitutionalized about 80 percent (if not more) of the cases by prescribing the standards that should govern, the Court should not have left the short tail hanging out for state courts to mess up. Certainly, after *Gertz*, the general impression was that the Court had mandated a fault standard for all defamation cases. Admittedly, Justice White was upset with the takeover, but it is also clear that the pillars of the republic were not about to fall with the imposition of a fault standard. The Court could have struck a blow for simplicity in an area of the law that so badly needed it. They left us with the need to distinguish between public figures and private persons and between matters of public concern and those that are exclusively private. Distinguishing among these categories of plaintiffs and issues is no picnic. If the task is nearly impossible to accomplish, the Court could have said that the simple across-the-board fault rule was necessary to protect true federal interests (by the way, I think that the argument is solid) and they could have struck a blow for simplicity at the same time.

JIM: Aaron, I'm not so sure. The distinctions between categories of plaintiffs and types of issues (public or private concern) are difficult at the margin. But the private defamation case really does exist. The Supreme Court has no business federalizing it.

---

1. Qualified Privileges at Common Law

Constitutional privileges aside, the common law recognized that it was necessary for people to freely communicate about matters of interest to the speaker, the recipient, or both. To insist on truth as the only defense to a defamation would place serious limitations on the right to communicate freely. To provide the necessary breathing room for communications of importance to society, the common law defined categories of communication that would be privileged. That is, if one defamed another, and the "occasion" was privileged, then liability would not attach, even if the defamatory statement was false. The privilege was subject to an additional caveat: a defamer who "abused the privilege" could be held liable. Defining the situations in which one is entitled to share defamatory information is not easy. One may defame another because (1) he seeks to defend himself against an accusation by the other person; (2) he seeks to protect the interest of the recipient; (3) he seeks to protect the interest of a family member; or (4) he shares a common interest with others in a particular subject matter. *See* Restatement, Second, of Torts §§ 594-597 (1977). What does it take to "abuse" a privilege? What conduct by the defamer will lead a court to say that, even though the occasion was privileged, the actor's conduct forfeits the privilege?

A frequent arena of defamation litigation involves references provided by employers. In Erickson v. Marsh & McLennan Co., 569 A.2d 793 (N.J. 1990), the defendant provided a lukewarm letter of reference for the plaintiff, who was seeking another job in the insurance industry. The letter stated:

> John left our operation because his level of expertise and areas of interest in insurance did not match the depth required for the proper service of [the defendant's] clients. . . . John does possess a general knowledge of commercial insurance and is well known among the insurance markets. If these are qualities you are seeking for your Account Executive position, we would recommend John Erickson to you.

The New Jersey Supreme Court recognized a qualified privilege for the evaluation of an employee given to prospective employers, who have a legitimate interest in the professional qualifications, skill, and experience of the plaintiff. Qualified privileges may be abused, however, and the protection of the privilege will be lost if the statement is made with "actual malice" — here, understood in the *Times v. Sullivan* sense of knowledge or reckless disregard with respect to truth or falsity. The court also held that the plaintiff must prove actual malice by clear and convincing evidence. Because the jury had found malice only by a preponderance of the evidence, the court reversed the intermediate appellate court's decision regarding malice.

Erickson reflects the trend that to defeat a common law privilege, the plaintiff must show that the defamation was made with knowledge of falsity or reckless disregard of the truth. Restatement, Second, of Torts § 600 (1977). *See also* Barreca v. Nickolas, 683 N.W.2d 111 (Iowa 2004). Some courts will defeat the privilege if the primary motive for making the defamation was personal ill-will, spite, or malice toward the plaintiff. *See, e.g.,* Caulde v. Thomason, 992 F. Supp. 1, 5 (D.D.C. 1997); Brehany v. Nordstrom Inc., 812 P.2d 49, 59 (Utah 1991). Keeping with the spirit of the privilege (to communicate to those who need to know the information), if the defamation is disseminated beyond those who have an interest in the communication, the privilege will be lost. Thus, for example, if one communicates to a potential spouse or her parents the bad character attributes of the boyfriend, the communication is privileged. If the information is delivered to the parents in the presence of a second cousin, the "excessive publication" destroys the privilege. *See also* Phelan v. May Department Stores Co., 806 N.E.2d 939 (Mass. App. Ct. 2004) (Plaintiff, an accountant, was wrongfully suspected of improper conduct in the performance of his job. He was called into his employer's office and kept under guard for six hours. When he needed to use the restroom, he was escorted by a guard in plain sight of other employees. A jury awarded plaintiff $1,500 for false imprisonment and $75,000 for defamation. The trial judge granted the defendant a judgment n.o.v. on the defamation claim. In reversing, the court held that the conduct of the defendant effectively communicated to other employees that plaintiff was suspected of criminal wrongdoing. "Employers are conditionally privileged to publish defamatory material that is reasonably related to the employer's legitimate business interest." However, a jury was "warranted in finding that defendants recklessly overpublished their defamatory statements about plaintiff by holding him at work under guard for more than six hours and repeatedly escorting him in front of his colleagues"). *Id.* at 946. The Massachusetts Supreme Court had the final say on this matter. In reversing the intermediate appellate court, it found that plaintiff had failed to present evidence that his fellow employees had understood that his being escorted meant that he was under suspicion for committing a crime. To validate his claim plaintiff would have to present testimony from fellow employees that they interpreted the fact that he was being escorted as tantamount to an accusation of criminal behavior. 819 N.E.2d 550, 555 (Mass. 2004).

The legal issues surrounding employment references have become a popular topic of scholarly debate. *See* Deborah A. Ballam, *Employment References — Speak No Evil, Hear No Evil: A Proposal for Meaningful Reform*, 30 Am. Bus. L.J. 445 (2002) (in order to achieve a balance between the interests of employers and employees, the author proposes a model statute that balances the two by requiring, inter alia, employers to provide certain information in writing when authorized by an employee); Markita D. Cooper, *Job Reference Immunity Statutes: Prevalent but Irrelevant*, 11 Cornell J.L. & Pub. Pol'y 1 (2001) (analyzes the ineffectiveness of current reference immunity statutes in encouraging employers to provide references and proposes that the statutes will achieve their purpose only when combined with educational campaigns aimed at changing longstanding perceptions and conduct related to the workplace); Murray Schwartz et al., *Claims for Damage to an Employee's Reputation and Future Employment*, 600 PLI/Lit 745, 758-778 (1999); Bernard E. Jacques, *Defamation in an Employment Context: Selected Issues*, 625 PLI/Lit 829 (2000).

2. Absolute Privileges at Common Law

In *Erickson*, the court made mention of absolute privileges that are granted to members of government when they speak while in the course of performing executive, legislative, or judicial functions. The blanket of judicial immunity covers all the participants in the judicial theater, be they judges, attorneys, parties, or witnesses. The immunity extends to statements in pleadings, in pre-trial discovery and post-trial motions as well as appellate proceedings.

At the federal level, absolute immunity for statements made in legislative proceedings is ensconced in the Constitution itself. Article I, § 6 provides that members of Congress "shall not be questioned in any other place for any Speech or Debate in either house." Judicial interpretation has broadened this immunity to include committee hearings and other legislative activity, be they performed by a member of Congress or her staff. Gravel v. United States, 408 U.S. 606 (1972). But, there are limits. *See, e.g.,* Doe v. McMillan, 412 U.S. 306 (1973) (Government

Printing Office violated privacy rights of children by publishing identifiable information of their substandard performance in the District of Columbia public schools. The immunity granted to congressional committees did not extend to the GPO because it was not part of the deliberative process.). Similar immunity has been granted to state legislators by state constitutions, state statutes, and judicial decisions. For an historical overview, *see* Van Vechten Veeder, *Absolute Privilege in Defamation: Judicial Proceedings*, 9 Colum. L. Rev. 463, 600 (1909); Van Vechten Veeder, *Absolute Immunity in Defamation: Legislature and Executive Proceedings*, 10 Colum. L. Rev. 131 (1919); Leon R. Yankwich, *The Immunity of Congressional Speech — Its Origin, Meaning and Scope*, 99 U. Pa. L. Rev. 960 (1951).

MONKEY BUSINESS

Although legislative immunity is very broad, it is not without boundaries. If a legislator leaves the halls of Congress and communicates to her constituents, she may be held liable for defamation. A rather humorous example found its way to the United States Supreme Court. The late senator William Proxmire of Wisconsin, a colorful and controversial member of Congress, would regularly call attention to wasteful spending of taxpayer monies by announcing the "Golden Fleece of the Month Award." In April 1975, in a speech to Congress, he made the award to the National Science Foundation for spending $500,000 to fund research on the aggressive behavior of primates. The recipient of the award, Dr. Robert Hutchinson, studied such matters as what caused primates to clench their teeth. Proxmire declared:

> The funding of this nonsense makes me almost angry enough to scream and kick and even clench my jaw. It seems to me it is outrageous. Dr. Hutchinson's studies should make the taxpayers as well as his monkeys grind their teeth. In fact, the good doctor has made a fortune from his monkeys and in the process made a monkey out of the American taxpayer.

Senator Proxmire not only made this speech to Congress, but also issued a press release and repeated his remarks in a newsletter to his constituents. Dr. Hutchinson was furious. He brought suit against Proxmire alleging that he suffered "extreme mental distress and humiliation" as a result of the Senator's tirade and that Proxmire had interfered with his contractual relationships with federal agencies, causing him financial losses since they would no longer fund his research. Although Hutchinson did not sue Proxmire for defamation, the Court's holding in Hutchinson v. Proxmire, 443 U.S. 111 (1979), is relevant to the issue of legislative immunity. The Court held that any statements Senator Proxmire made to Congress were fully protected by legislative immunity. However, his press releases and the statements he made in his newsletter were not covered by legislative immunity. It is interesting to note that a newspaper report of Proxmire's speech to Congress would not subject the newspaper to liability, since there long existed a qualified privilege that allows one to publish a fair and accurate report of public proceedings. *See* W. Prosser & P. Keeton, The Law of Torts §115 (1984). Why Proxmire's own newsletter or news release repeating what he said on the floor of Congress should not come within the common law privilege was not addressed by the Court.

The leading case granting immunity to members of the executive branch of the federal government, Barr v. Matteo, 360 U.S. 564 (1959), protects federal officials from defamation actions for statements made within the scope of their official duties. *See also* Murray v. Northrop Grumman Info. Tech., Inc., 444 F.3d 169 (2d Cir. 2006) (government contractor charged with the administration of a cultural training program has absolute immunity for transmitting defamatory information about participants to the U.S. State Department and to the Immigration and Naturalization Service). At the state level, the picture is mixed. Some states confer on state executives broad immunity from defamation and do so for both high- and low-level officials. Others protect the big wigs only. Finally, some states grant state officials only a qualified privilege that can be lost if the privilege is abused.

chapter 15

Privacy

The law of the "right to privacy" begins with a story. Dean William L. Prosser tells it well in his article, *Privacy*, 48 Cal. L. Rev. 383, 383-384 (1960). He relates that:

> In the year 1890 Mrs. Samuel D. Warren, a young matron of Boston, which is a large city in Massachusetts, held at her home a series of social entertainments on an elaborate scale. She was the daughter of Senator Bayard of Delaware, and her husband was a wealthy young paper manufacturer, who only the year before had given up the practice of law to devote himself to an inherited business. Socially Mrs. Warren was among the élite; and the newspapers of Boston, and in particular the *Saturday Evening Gazette*, which specialized in "blue blood" items, covered her parties in highly personal and embarrassing detail. It was the era of "yellow journalism," when the press had begun to resort to excesses in the way of prying that have become more or less commonplace today; and Boston was perhaps, of all the cities in the country, the one in which a lady and a gentleman kept their names and their personal affairs out of the papers. The matter came to a head when the newspapers had a field day on the occasion of the wedding of a daughter, and Mr. Warren became annoyed. It was an annoyance for which the press, the advertisers and the entertainment industry of America were to pay dearly over the next seventy years.
>
> Mr. Warren turned to his recent law partner, Louis D. Brandeis, who was destined not to be unknown to history. The result was a noted article, *The Right to Privacy*, in the Harvard Law Review [4 Harv. L. Rev. 193 (1890)], upon which the two men collaborated. It has come to be regarded as the outstanding example of the influence of legal periodicals upon the American law. In the Harvard Law School class of 1877 the two authors had stood respectively second and first, and both of them were gifted with scholarship, imagination, and ability. Internal evidences of style, and the probabilities of the situation, suggest that the writing, and perhaps most of the research, was done by Brandeis; but it was undoubtedly a joint effort, to which both men contributed their ideas.

This right to privacy that was to be protected by an action in tort was a new breed. It shared some common ground with its first cousin, the tort of defamation, but there were important differences. In defamation, the gravamen of the harm is injury to reputation in that the plaintiff is held up to shame, ridicule, or contempt. Truth is an absolute defense. Privacy seeks to protect the right to be left alone with regard to one's private life. The underlying theme is that "it is none of your business." Thus, truth is not a defense. Yet, in general, the privileges that attend the law of defamation operate to limit the "privacy" tort. And, as we shall see, constitutional privileges play a role, because the more serious forms of invasion of privacy arise from publication in the media of aspects of people's private lives that are newsworthy and are legitimate matters of public concern. Well then, what kinds of privacy rights are protected by the law of torts? We turn once again to Prosser's *Privacy* article.

(1) Intrusion upon the plaintiff's seclusion or solitude, or into his private affairs.
(2) Public disclosure of embarrassing private facts about the plaintiff.
(3) Publicity which places the plaintiff in a false light in the public eye.
(4) Appropriation, for the defendant's advantage, of the plaintiff's name or likeness.

Prosser's influence on the law of privacy cannot be overstated. Prosser was the Reporter for the Restatement, Second, of Torts. The classification set forth in his article found its way into Sections 652A-652L and has been heavily cited by the courts. For two very different views on the privacy tort, *see* Edward J. Blaustein, *Privacy as an Aspect of Human Dignity: An Answer to Dean Prosser*, 39 N.Y.U. L. Rev. 962 (1964) (arguing that the common thread that unites the four branches of the privacy tort is concern for human dignity); Diane L. Zimmerman, *Requiem for a Heavyweight: A Farewell to Warren and Brandeis's Privacy Tort*, 68 Cornell L. Rev. 291 (1983) (argues that the tort is not a usable and effective means of redress for plaintiffs).

A. APPROPRIATION OF THE PLAINTIFF'S NAME OR LIKENESS FOR THE DEFENDANT'S ADVANTAGE

It is interesting that the earliest cases recognizing a right of privacy involve less of an invasion of a privacy right and more of a taking of a "property-like" right. About a decade after the appearance of the Warren and Brandeis article, a flour company circulated some 25,000 lithographs of an attractive young woman with the legend "Franklin Mills Flour" printed in large letters above the portrait. These flyers were conspicuously posted in stores, warehouses, saloons, and other public places. Claiming that she was humiliated by this public posting of her picture on the flour advertisement, plaintiff brought suit for the violation of her privacy right. The court in Roberson v. Rochester Folding Box Co., 64 N.E. 443 (N.Y. 1902), refused to recognize a privacy right saying:

There is no precedent for such an action to be found in the decisions of this court. Indeed, the learned judge who wrote the very able and interesting opinion in the appellate division said, while upon the threshold of the discussion of the question: "It may be said, in the first place, that the theory upon which this action is predicated is new, at least in instance, if not in principle, and that few precedents can be found to sustain the claim made by the plaintiff, if, indeed, it can be said that there are any authoritative cases establishing her right to recover in this action." Nevertheless that court reached the conclusion that plaintiff had a good cause of action against defendants, in that defendants had invaded what is called a "right of privacy;" in other words, the right to be let alone. Mention of such a right is not to be found in Blackstone, Kent, or any other of the great commentators upon the law; nor, so far as the learning of counsel or the courts in this case have been able to discover, does its existence seem to have been asserted prior to about the year 1890, when it was presented with attractiveness, and no inconsiderable ability, in the Harvard Law Review (. . .) in an article entitled "Rights of a Citizen to His Reputation." The so-called "right of privacy" is, as the phrase suggests, founded upon the claim that a man has the right to pass through this world, if he wills, without having his picture published, his business enterprises discussed, his successful experiments written up for the benefit of others, or his eccentricities commented upon either in handbills, circulars, catalogues, periodicals, or newspapers; and necessarily, that the things which may not be written and published of him must not be spoken of him by his neighbors, whether the comment be favorable or otherwise. While most persons would much prefer to have a good likeness of themselves appear in a responsible periodical or leading newspaper rather than upon an advertising card or sheet, the doctrine which the courts are asked to create for this case would apply as well to the one publication as to the other, for the principle which a court of equity is asked to assert in support of a recovery in this action is that the right of privacy exists and is enforceable in equity, and that the publication of that which purports to be a portrait of another person, even if obtained upon the street by an impertinent individual with a camera, will be restrained in equity on the ground that an individual has the right to prevent his features from becoming known to those outside of his circle of friends and acquaintances. If such a principle be incorporated into the body of the law through the instrumentality of a court of equity, the attempts to logically apply the principle will necessarily result not only in a vast amount of litigation, but in litigation bordering upon the absurd, for the right of privacy, once established as a legal doctrine, cannot be confined to the restraint of the publication of a likeness, but must necessarily embrace as well the publication of a word, picture, a comment upon one's looks, conduct, domestic relations or habits.

The *Roberson* decision caused something of an uproar. The New York legislature responded by enacting a right of privacy statute in 1903. It survives to this very day in §§ 50 and 51 of the New York Civil Rights Law:

§ 50. Right of Privacy

A person, firm or corporation that uses for advertising purposes, or for the purposes of trade, the name, portrait or picture of any living person without having first obtained the written consent of such person, or if a minor of his or her parent or guardian, is guilty of a misdemeanor.

§ 51. Action for Injunction and for Damages

Any person whose name, portrait, picture or voice is used within this state for advertising purposes or for the purposes of trade without the written consent first obtained as above provided may maintain an equitable action in the supreme court of this state against the person, firm or corporation so using his name, portrait, picture or voice, to prevent and restrain the use thereof; and may also sue and recover damages for any injuries sustained by reason of such use and if the defendant shall have knowingly used such person's name, portrait, picture or voice in such manner as is forbidden or declared to be unlawful by section fifty of this article, the jury, in its discretion, may award exemplary damages.

Georgia was the first state to adopt the "appropriation" right to privacy tort. In Pavesich v. New England Life Insurance Co., 50 S.E. 68 (1905), an insurance company was held liable for utilizing the plaintiff's name and picture in a testimonial for the company. The testimonial was bogus. The court rejected *Roberson* and adopted the Warren-Brandeis view that an independent privacy tort should be recognized.

CARSON v. HERE'S JOHNNY PORTABLE TOILETS, INC.
698 F.2d 831 (6th Cir. 1983)

Brown, J.

This case involves claims of unfair competition and invasion of the right of privacy and the right of publicity arising from appellee's adoption of a phrase generally associated with a popular entertainer.

Appellant, John W. Carson (Carson), is the host and star of "The Tonight Show," a well-known television program broadcast five nights a week by the National Broadcasting Company. Carson also appears as an entertainer in night clubs and theaters around the country. From the time he began hosting "The Tonight Show" in 1962, he has been introduced on the show each night with the phrase "Here's Johnny." This method of introduction was first used for Carson in 1957 when he hosted a daily television program for the American Broadcasting Company. The phrase "Here's Johnny" is generally associated with Carson by a substantial segment of the television viewing public. In 1967, Carson first authorized use of this phrase by an outside business venture, permitting it to be used by a chain of restaurants called "Here's Johnny Restaurants." . . .

The phrase "Here's Johnny" has never been registered by appellants as a trademark or service mark.

Appellee, Here's Johnny Portable Toilets, Inc., is a Michigan corporation engaged in the business of renting and selling "Here's Johnny" portable toilets. Appellee's founder was aware at the time he formed the corporation that "Here's Johnny" was the introductory slogan for Carson on "The Tonight Show." He indicated that he coupled the phrase with a second one, "The World's Foremost Commodian," to make "a good play on a phrase."

Shortly after appellee went into business in 1976, appellants brought this action alleging unfair competition, trademark infringement under federal and state law, and invasion of privacy and publicity rights. They sought damages and an injunction prohibiting appellee's further use of the phrase "Here's Johnny" as a corporate name or in connection with the sale or rental of its portable toilets.

After a bench trial, the district court issued a memorandum opinion and order, Carson v. Here's Johnny Portable Toilets, Inc., 498 F. Supp. 71 (E.D. Mich. 1980), which served as its findings of fact and conclusions of law. The court ordered the dismissal of the appellants' complaint. On the unfair competition claim, the court concluded that the appellants had failed to satisfy the "likelihood of confusion" test. On the right of privacy and right of publicity theories, the court held that these rights extend only to a "name or likeness," and "Here's Johnny" did not qualify. . . .

II.

The appellants . . . claim that the appellee's use of the phrase "Here's Johnny" violates the common law right of privacy and right of publicity. The confusion in this area of the law requires a brief analysis of the relationship between these two rights.

In an influential article, Dean Prosser delineated four distinct types of the right of privacy: (1) intrusion upon one's seclusion or solitude, (2) public disclosure of embarrassing private facts, (3) publicity which places one in a false light, and (4) appropriation of one's name or likeness for the defendant's advantage. Prosser, *Privacy*, 48 Calif. L. Rev. 383, 389 (1960). This fourth type has become known as the "right of publicity." Factors Etc., Inc. v. Pro Arts, Inc., 579 F.2d 215, 220 (2d Cir. 1978). . . . Henceforth we will refer to Prosser's last, or fourth, category as the "right of publicity."

Dean Prosser's analysis has been a source of some confusion in the law. His first three types of the right of privacy generally protect the right "to be let alone," while the right of publicity protects the celebrity's pecuniary interest in the commercial exploitation of his identity. . . . *See generally The Right of Publicity—Protection for Public Figures and Celebrities*, 42 Brooklyn L. Rev. 527 (1976). Thus, the right of privacy and the right of publicity protect fundamentally different interests and must be analyzed separately.

We do not believe that Carson's claim that his right of privacy has been invaded is supported by the law or the facts. Apparently, the gist of this claim is that Carson is embarrassed by and considers it odious to be associated with the appellee's product. Clearly, the association does not appeal to Carson's sense of humor. But the facts here presented do not, it appears to us, amount to an invasion of any of the interests protected by the right of privacy. In any event, our disposition of the claim of an invasion of the right of publicity makes it unnecessary for us to accept or reject the claim of an invasion of the right of privacy.

The right of publicity has developed to protect the commercial interest of celebrities in their identities. The theory of the right is that a celebrity's identity can be valuable in the promotion of products, and the celebrity has an interest that may be protected from the unauthorized commercial exploitation of that identity. In Memphis Development Foundation v. Factors Etc., Inc., 616 F.2d 956 (6th Cir.), *cert. denied*, 449 U.S. 953 . . . (1980), we stated: "The famous have an exclusive legal right during life to control and profit from the commercial use of their name and personality." *Id.* at 957.

The district court dismissed appellants' claim based on the right of publicity because appellee does not use Carson's name or likeness. . . . It held that it "would not be prudent to allow recovery for a right of publicity claim which does not more specifically identify Johnny Carson." . . . We believe that, on the contrary, the district court's conception of the right of publicity is too narrow. The right of publicity, as we have stated, is that a celebrity has a protected pecuniary interest in the commercial exploitation of his identity. If the celebrity's identity is commercially exploited, there has been an invasion of his right whether or not his "name or likeness" is used. Carson's identity may be exploited even if his name, John W. Carson, or his picture is not used.

In Motschenbacher v. R.J. Reynolds Tobacco Co., 498 F.2d 821 (9th Cir. 1974), the court held that the unauthorized use of a picture of a distinctive race car of a well known professional race car driver, whose name or likeness were not used, violated his right of publicity. In this connection, the court said:

> We turn now to the question of "identifiability." Clearly, if the district court correctly determined as a matter of law that plaintiff is not identifiable in the commercial, then in no sense has plaintiff's identity been misappropriated nor his interest violated.
>
> Having viewed a film of the commercial, we agree with the district court that the "likeness" of plaintiff is itself unrecognizable; however, the court's further conclusion of law to the effect that the driver is not identifiable as plaintiff is erroneous in that it wholly fails to attribute proper significance to the distinctive decorations appearing on the car. As pointed out earlier, these markings were not only peculiar to the plaintiff's cars but they caused some persons to think the car in question was plaintiff's and to infer that the person driving the car was the plaintiff.

Id. at 826-827 (footnote omitted).

In Ali v. Playgirl, Inc., 447 F. Supp. 723 (S.D.N.Y. 1978), Muhammad Ali, former heavyweight champion, sued Playgirl magazine under the New York "right of privacy" statute and also alleged a violation of his common law right of publicity. The magazine published a drawing of a nude, black male sitting on a stool in a corner of a boxing ring with hands taped and arms outstretched on the ropes. The district court concluded that Ali's right of publicity was invaded because the drawing sufficiently identified him in spite of the fact that the drawing was captioned "Mystery Man." The district court found that the identification of Ali was made certain because of an accompanying verse that identified the figure as "The Greatest." The district court took judicial notice of the fact that "Ali has regularly claimed that appellation for himself." *Id.* at 727. . . .

In this case, Earl Braxton, president and owner of Here's Johnny Portable Toilets, Inc., admitted that he knew that the phrase "Here's Johnny" had been used for years to introduce Carson. Moreover, in the opening statement in the district court, appellee's counsel stated:

> Now, we've stipulated in this case that the public tends to associate the words "Johnny Carson," the words "Here's Johnny" with plaintiff, John Carson and, Mr. Braxton, in his deposition, admitted that he knew that and probably absent that identification, he would not have chosen it.

That the "Here's Johnny" name was selected by Braxton because of its identification with Carson was the clear inference from Braxton's testimony irrespective of such admission in the opening statement.

We therefore conclude that, applying the correct legal standards, appellants are entitled to judgment. The proof showed without question that appellee had appropriated Carson's identity in connection with its corporate name and its product. . . .

The judgment of the district court is vacated and the case remanded for further proceedings consistent with this opinion.

KENNEDY, Circuit Judge, dissenting.

I respectfully dissent from that part of the majority's opinion which holds that appellee's use of the phrase "Here's Johnny" violates appellant Johnny Carson's common law right of publicity. While I agree that an individual's identity may be impermissibly exploited, I do not believe that the common law right of publicity may be extended beyond an individual's name, likeness, achievements, identifying characteristics or actual performances, to include phrases or other things which are merely associated with the individual, as of the phrase "Here's Johnny." The majority's extension of the right of publicity to include phrases or other things which are merely associated with the individual permits a popular entertainer or public figure, by associating himself or herself with a common phrase, to remove those words from the public domain.

The phrase "Here's Johnny" is merely associated with Johnny Carson, the host and star of "The Tonight Show" broadcast by the National Broadcasting Company. Since 1962, the opening format of "The Tonight Show," after the theme music is played, is to introduce Johnny Carson with the phrase "Here's Johnny." The words are spoken by an announcer, generally Ed McMahon, in a drawn out and distinctive manner. Immediately after the phrase "Here's Johnny" is spoken, Johnny Carson appears to begin the program. This method of introduction was first used by Johnny Carson in 1957 when he hosted a daily television show for the American Broadcasting Company. This case is not transformed into a "name" case simply because the diminutive form of John W. Carson's given name and the first name of his full stage name, Johnny Carson, appears in it. The first name is so common, in light of the millions of persons named John, Johnny or Jonathan that no doubt inhabit this world, that, alone, it is meaningless or ambiguous at best in identifying Johnny Carson, the celebrity. In addition, the phrase containing Johnny Carson's first stage name was certainly selected for its value as a double entendre. Appellee manufactures portable toilets. The value of the phrase to appellee's product is in the risqué meaning of "John" as a toilet or bathroom. For this reason, too, this is not a "name" case.

Appellee has stipulated that the phrase "Here's Johnny" is associated with Johnny Carson and that absent this association, he would not have chosen to use it for his product and corporation, Here's Johnny Portable Toilets, Inc. I do not consider it relevant that appellee intentionally chose to incorporate into the name of his corporation and product a phrase that is merely associated with Johnny Carson. What is not protected by law is not taken from public use. Research reveals no case in which the right of publicity has been extended to phrases or other things which are merely associated with an individual and are not part of his name, likeness, achievements, identifying characteristics or actual performances. Both the policies behind the right of publicity and countervailing interests and considerations indicate that such an extension should not be made.

The three primary policy considerations behind the right of publicity are succinctly stated in Hoffman, *Limitations on the Right of Publicity*, 28 Bull. Copr. Soc'y, 111, 116-22 (1980). First, "the right of publicity vindicates the economic interests of celebrities, enabling those whose achievements have imbued their identities with pecuniary value to profit from their fame." . . . Second, the right of publicity fosters "the production of intellectual and creative works by providing the financial incentive for individuals to expend the time and resources necessary to produce them." . . . Third, "[t]he right of publicity serves both individual and societal interests by preventing what our legal tradition regards as wrongful conduct: unjust enrichment and deceptive trade practices." . . .

None of the above-mentioned policy arguments supports the extension of the right of publicity to phrases or other things which are merely associated with an individual. First, the majority is awarding Johnny Carson a windfall, rather than vindicating his economic interests, by protecting the phrase "Here's Johnny" which is merely associated with him. In [Zacchini v. Scripps-Howard Broadcasting Co., reproduced *infra*], the Supreme Court stated that a mechanism to vindicate an individual's economic rights is indicated where the appropriated thing is "the product of . . . [the individual's] own talents and energy, the end result of much time, effort and expense." . . . There is nothing in the record to suggest that "Here's Johnny" has any nexus to Johnny Carson other than being the introduction to his personal appearances. The phrase is not part of an identity that he created. In its content "Here's Johnny" is a very simple and common introduction. The content of the phrase neither originated with Johnny Carson nor is it confined to the world of entertainment. The phrase is not said by Johnny Carson, but said of him. Its association with him is derived, in large part, by the context in which it is said — generally by Ed McMahon in a drawn out and distinctive voice after the theme music to "The Tonight Show" is played, and immediately prior to Johnny Carson's own entrance. Appellee's use of the content "Here's Johnny," in light of its value as a double entendre, written on its product and corporate name, and therefore outside of the context in which it is associated with Johnny Carson, does little to rob Johnny Carson of something which is unique to him or a product of his own efforts.

The second policy goal of fostering the production of creative and intellectual works is not met by the majority's rule because in awarding publicity rights in a phrase neither created by him nor performed by him, economic reward and protection is divorced from personal incentive to produce on the part of the protected and benefited individual. Johnny Carson is simply reaping the rewards of the time, effort and work product of others.

Third, the majority's extension of the right of publicity to include the phrase "Here's Johnny" which is merely associated with Johnny Carson is not needed to provide alternatives to existing legal avenues for redressing wrongful conduct. The existence of a cause of action under section 42(a) of the Lanham Act, 15 U.S.C.A. § 1125(a) (1976) and Michigan common law does much to undercut the need for policing against unfair competition through an additional legal remedy such as the right of publicity. The majority has concluded, and I concur, that the District Court was warranted in finding that there was not a reasonable likelihood that members of the public would be confused by appellee's use of the "Here's Johnny" trademark on a product as dissimilar to those licensed by Johnny Carson as portable toilets. In this case, this eliminates the argument of wrongdoing. . . .

The common law right of publicity has been held to protect various aspects of an individual's identity from commercial exploitation: name, likeness, achievements, identifying characteristics, actual performances, and fictitious characters created by a performer. Research reveals no case which has extended the right of publicity to phrases and other things which are merely associated with an individual.

The . . . cases cited by the majority in reaching their conclusion that the right of privacy should be extended to encompass phrases and other things merely associated with an individual and one other case merit further comment. . . .

In *Ali*, Muhammad Ali sought protection under the right of publicity for the unauthorized use of his picture in Playgirl Magazine. *Ali* is a "likeness" case reinforced by the context in which the likeness occurs and further bolstered by a phrase, "the Greatest," commonly stated by Ali regarding himself. The essence of the case, and the unauthorized act from which Ali claims protection, is a drawing of a nude black man seated in the corner of a boxing ring with both hands taped and outstretched resting on the ropes on either side. The *Ali* court found that even a cursory inspection of the picture suggests that the facial characteristics of the man are those of Ali. The court stated: "The cheekbones, broad nose and wideset brown eyes, together with the distinctive smile and close cropped black hair are recognizable as the features of . . . [Ali]." *Ali, supra*, 726. Augmenting this likeness and reinforcing its identification with Ali was the context in which the likeness appeared — a boxing ring. The court found that identification of the individual depicted as Ali was further implied by the accompanying phrase "the Greatest." *Id.* 727. Based on these facts, the court had no difficulty concluding that the drawing was Ali's portrait or picture. *See id.* 726. To the extent the majority uses the phrase "the Greatest" to support its position that the right of publicity encompasses phrases or other things which are merely associated with an individual, they misstate the law of *Ali*. Once again, *Ali* is clearly a "likeness" case. To the extent the likeness was not a photographic one free from all ambiguity, identification with Muhammad Ali was reinforced by context and a phrase "the Greatest" stated by Ali about himself. The result in that case is so dependent on the identifying features in the drawing and the boxing context in which the man is portrayed that the phrase "the Greatest" may not be severed from this whole and the legal propositions developed by the *Ali* court in response to the whole applied to the phrase alone. To be analogous, a likeness of Johnny Carson would be required in addition to the words "Here's Johnny" suggesting the context of "The Tonight Show" or the *Ali* court would have to have enjoined all others from using the phrase "the Greatest." In short, *Ali* does not support the majority's holding.

Motschenbacher, the third case cited by the majority, is an "identifying characteristics" case. Motschenbacher, a professional driver of racing cars who is internationally known, sought protection in the right of publicity for the unauthorized use of a photograph of his racing car, slightly altered, in a televised cigarette commercial. Although he was in fact driving the car at the time it was photographed, his facial features are not visible in the commercial. *Motschenbacher, supra*, 822. The Ninth Circuit found as a matter of California law, that the right of publicity extended to protect the unauthorized use of photographs of Motschenbacher's racing car as one of his identifying characteristics. Identifying characteristics, such as Motschenbacher's racing car, are not synonymous with phrases or other things which are merely associated with an individual. In *Motschenbacher*, the Ninth Circuit determined that the car driver had "consistently 'individualized' his cars to set them apart from those of other drivers and to make them more readily identifiable as his own." *Id.* Since 1966, each car had a distinctive narrow white pinstripe appearing on no other car. This decoration has always been in the same place on the car bodies, which have uniformly been red. In addition, his racing number "11" has always been against an oval background in contrast to the circular white background used by other drivers. *Id.* In the commercial, the photo of Motschenbacher's car was altered so that the number "11" was changed to "71," a spoiler with the name "Winston" was added, and other advertisements removed. The remainder of the individualized decorations remained the same. *Id.* Despite these alterations, the Ninth Circuit determined that car possessed identifying characteristics *peculiar* to Motschenbacher. *Id.* 827. This case is factually and legally distinguishable from the case on appeal. Motschenbacher's racing car was not merely associated with him but was the vehicle, literally and figuratively, by which he achieved his fame. The identifying characteristics, in the form of several decorations peculiar to his car, were the product of his personal time, energy, effort and expense and as such are inextricably interwoven with him as his individual work product, rather than being merely associated with him. Furthermore, the number and combination of the peculiar decorations on his cars results in a set of identifying characteristics, which although inanimate, are unique enough to resist duplication other than by intentional copying. This uniqueness provides notice to the public of what is claimed as part of his publicity right, as does an individual's name, likeness or actual performance, and narrowly limits the scope of his monopoly. In contrast to *Motschenbacher*, Johnny Carson's fame as a comedian and talk show host is severable from the phrase with which he is associated, "Here's Johnny." This phrase is not Johnny Carson's "thumbprint"; it is not his work product; it is not original; it is a common, simple combination of a direct object, a contracted verb and a common first name; divorced from context, it is two dimensional and ambiguous. It can hardly be said to be a symbol or synthesis, i.e., a tangible "expression" of the "idea," of Johnny Carson the comedian and talk show host, as Motschenbacher's racing car was the tangible expression of the man. . . .

Accordingly, neither policy nor case law supports the extension of the right of publicity to encompass phrases and other things merely associated with an individual as in this case. I would affirm the judgment of the District Court on this basis as well.

PRIVACY OR PIRACY?

In the early cases, like *Roberson*, plaintiffs were ordinary people whose likeness was used in an advertisement. They were upset with the invasion of their privacy and sought damages for the mental distress and anguish that came about because of the publicity. In more recent years, the bulk of the litigation has arisen from celebrities who are seeking damages because their likenesses have real value. They barter their names and identities for all sorts of endorsements and are upset by the pirating of their identities without paying the appropriate fee. In the *Carson* case, it is likely that Johnny Carson would not have sold the "Here's Johnny" phrase, because he may not have wanted to have his name connected with toilets.

Note that the New York Civil Rights Law and the *Carson* case deal with use of a person's identity for advertisement or trade purposes. However, the common law privacy tort is considerably broader. In Hinish v. Meier & Frank Co., 113 P.2d 438 (Or. 1941), defendant operated a general mercantile establishment and had as part of its operations an optical department. The Oregon legislature had passed a bill that would have prohibited such establishments from engaging in the business of fitting and selling optical glasses. Unbeknownst to the plaintiff, the defendant signed plaintiff's name to a letter urging the governor to veto the bill. Not only was plaintiff offended by the unauthorized use of his name, but he contended that, as a postal employee, he was prohibited by law from engaging in political activities. The sending of the telegram jeopardized plaintiff's position and his right to receive a pension upon retirement. In an exhaustive decision reviewing the cases pro and con as to the wisdom of adopting a right to privacy tort, the court came down in favor of the new tort and said it would confer on the plaintiff, in the case at bar, the right to recover damages.

In a more recent case, Cox v. Hatch, 761 P.2d 556 (Utah 1988), Senator Hatch went to the office of the United States Postal Service and posed with employees for a picture. The photo was used by Senator Hatch in an eight-page political flyer entitled "Senator Orrin Hatch Labor Letter." The flyer extolled the virtues of Senator Hatch's record on labor issues. The plaintiffs who were pictured in the flyer admitted that they consented to having their pictures taken but not to their inclusion in promotional material for Senator Hatch, which implied that they were endorsing his candidacy. In rejecting the claim, the Utah court said that the photos were taken in an open place and those who posed for the picture had no reasonable expectation of privacy. The court also rejected the claim that the defendant had "appropriated their likeness." The court held that the likeness of the plaintiffs had no "intrinsic value" since they were individuals who were unknown to the general public.

The constitutionalization of defamation law, discussed in Chapter 15, has made it difficult for plaintiffs to recover if there is some public interest in facts about them. This appears to be true of intentional infliction of emotional distress as well, as demonstrated by Snyder v. Phelps, 562 U.S. 443 (2011), the case involving protests at military funerals. In the privacy context, however, a plaintiff may still be able to recover for appropriation of likeness, even if there is a public interest in the likeness. In Toffoloni v. LFP Publishing Group, 572 F.3d 1201 (11th Cir.

2009), *Hustler* magazine published nude photographs of the plaintiff, which had been taken 20 years prior to her death. The plaintiff had been murdered, along with her son, by her professional wrestler husband Christopher Benoit. The defendant asserted that there was substantial public interest in the story of the life, career, and tragic death of Benoit (who committed suicide after killing his wife and son), and in the parallel story of the plaintiff, her modest beginnings and youthful interest in modeling, and violent death. Applying Georgia law, the federal court of appeals held that the publication of the nude photographs was not incidental to the article, which was conceded to be of public interest. Rather, the article was incidental to the photographs. The story was only of tangential relevance to the magazine's desire to publish the photographs for commercial gain. "[S]omeone's notorious death [does not] constitute[] a carte blanche for the publication of any and all images of that person during his or her life . . . regardless of whether those images are of any relevance to the incident currently of public concern."

ZACCHINI v. SCRIPPS-HOWARD BROADCASTING CO.
433 U.S. 562 (1977)

White, J.

Petitioner, Hugo Zacchini, is an entertainer. He performs a "human cannonball" act in which he is shot from a cannon into a net some 200 feet away. Each performance occupies some 15 seconds. In August and September 1972, petitioner was engaged to perform his act on a regular basis at the Geauga County Fair in Burton, Ohio. He performed in a fenced area, surrounded by grandstands, at the fair grounds. Members of the public attending the fair were not charged a separate admission fee to observe his act.

On August 30, a free-lance reporter for Scripps-Howard Broadcasting Co., the operator of a television broadcasting station and respondent in this case, attended the fair. He carried a small movie camera. Petitioner noticed the reporter and asked him not to film the performance. The reporter did not do so on that day; but on the instructions of the producer of respondent's daily newscast, he returned the following day and videotaped the entire act. This film clip, approximately 15 seconds in length, was shown on the 11 o'clock news program that night, together with favorable commentary.

Petitioner then brought this action for damages, alleging that he is "engaged in the entertainment business," that the act he performs is one "invented by his father and . . . performed only by his family for the last fifty years," that respondent "showed and commercialized the film of his act without his consent," and that such conduct was an "unlawful appropriation of plaintiff's professional property." App. 4-5. Respondent answered and moved for summary judgment, which was granted by the trial court.

The Court of Appeals of Ohio reversed. The majority held that petitioner's complaint stated a cause of action for conversion and for infringement of a common-law copyright, and one judge concurred in the judgment on the ground that the complaint stated a cause of action for appropriation of petitioner's "right of publicity" in the film of his act. All three judges agreed that the First Amendment did not privilege the press to show the entire performance on a news program without compensating petitioner for any financial injury he could prove at trial.

Like the concurring judge in the Court of Appeals, the Supreme Court of Ohio rested petitioner's cause of action under state law on his "right to publicity value of his performance." . . . 351 N.E.2d 454, 455 (1976). The opinion syllabus, to which we are to look for the rule of law used to decide the case, declared first that one may not use for his own benefit the name or likeness of another, whether or not the use or benefit is a commercial one, and second that respondent would be liable for the appropriation, over petitioner's objection and in the absence of license or privilege, of petitioner's right to the publicity value of his performance. . . . The court nevertheless gave judgment for respondent because, in the words of the syllabus:

> A TV station has a privilege to report in its newscasts matters of legitimate public interest which would otherwise be protected by an individual's right of publicity, unless the actual intent of the TV station was to appropriate the benefit of the publicity for some non-privileged private use, or unless the actual intent was to injure the individual. *Ibid.*

We granted certiorari . . . to consider an issue unresolved by this Court: whether the First and Fourteenth Amendments immunized respondent from damages for its alleged infringement of petitioner's state-law "right of publicity." . . . Insofar as the Ohio Supreme Court held that the First and Fourteenth Amendments of the United States Constitution required judgment for respondent, we reverse the judgment of that court. . . .

The Ohio Supreme Court held that respondent is constitutionally privileged to include in its newscasts matters of public interest that would otherwise be protected by the right of publicity, absent an intent to injure or to appropriate for some nonprivileged purpose. If under this standard respondent had merely reported that petitioner was performing at the fair and described or commented on his act, with or without showing his picture on television, we would have a very different case. But petitioner is not contending that his appearance at the fair and his performance could not be reported by the press as newsworthy items. His complaint is that respondent filmed his entire act and displayed that film on television for the public to see and enjoy. This, he claimed, was an appropriation of his professional property. The Ohio Supreme Court agreed that petitioner had "a right of publicity" that gave him "personal control over commercial display and exploitation of his personality and the exercise of his talents." This right of "exclusive control over the publicity given to his performances" was said to be such a "valuable part of the benefit which may be attained by his talents and efforts" that it was entitled to legal protection. It was also observed, or at least expressly assumed, that petitioner had not abandoned his rights by performing under the circumstances present at the Geauga County Fair Grounds.

The Ohio Supreme Court nevertheless held that the challenged invasion was privileged, saying that the press "must be accorded broad latitude in its choice of how much it presents of each story or incident, and of the emphasis to be given to such presentation. No fixed standard which would bar the press from reporting or depicting either an entire occurrence or an entire discrete part of a public performance can be formulated which would not unduly restrict the 'breathing room' in reporting which freedom of the press requires." 235, 351 N.E.2d, at 461. Under this view, respondent was thus constitutionally free to film and display petitioner's entire act.

The Ohio Supreme Court relied heavily on *Time, Inc. v. Hill,* 385 U.S. 374 (1967), but that case does not mandate a media privilege to televise a performer's entire act without his consent. Involved in *Time, Inc. v. Hill* was a claim under the New York "Right of Privacy" statute that *Life* Magazine, in the course of reviewing a new play, had connected the play with a long-past incident involving petitioner and his family and had falsely described their experience and conduct at that time. The complaint sought damages for humiliation and suffering flowing from these nondefamatory falsehoods that allegedly invaded Hill's privacy. The Court held, however, that the opening of a new play linked to an actual incident was a matter of public interest and that Hill could not recover without showing that the *Life* report was knowingly false or was published with reckless disregard for the truth — the same rigorous standard that had been applied in New York Times Co. v. Sullivan, 376 U.S. 254 (1964).

Time, Inc. v. Hill, which was hotly contested and decided by a divided Court, involved an entirely different tort from the "right of publicity" recognized by the Ohio Supreme Court. As the opinion reveals in *Time, Inc. v. Hill,* the Court was steeped in the literature of privacy law and was aware of the developing distinctions and nuances in this branch of the law. The Court, for example, cited W. Prosser, Law of Torts 831-832 (3d ed. 1964), and the same author's well-known article, *Privacy,* 48 Calif. L. Rev. 383 (1960), both of which divided privacy into four distinct branches. The Court was aware that it was adjudicating a "false light" privacy case involving a matter of public interest, not a case involving "intrusion," 385 U.S., at 384-385, n.9, "appropriation" of a name or likeness for the purposes of trade. . . .

The differences between these two torts are important. First, the State's interests in providing a cause of action in each instance are different. "The interest protected" in permitting recovery for placing the plaintiff in a false light "is clearly that of reputation, with the same overtones of mental distress as in defamation." Prosser, *supra,* 48 Calif. L. Rev., at 400. By contrast, the State's interest in permitting a "right of publicity" is in protecting the proprietary interest of the individual in his act in part to encourage such entertainment. . . . The State's interest is closely analogous to the goals of patent and copyright law, focusing on the right of the individual to reap the reward of his endeavors and having little to do with protecting feelings or reputation. Second, the two torts differ in the degree to which they intrude on dissemination of information to the public. In "false light" cases the only way to protect the interests involved is to attempt to minimize publication of the damaging matter, while in "right of publicity" cases the only question is who gets to do the publishing. An entertainer such as petitioner usually has no objection to the widespread publication of his act as long as he gets the commercial benefit of such publication. Indeed, in the present case petitioner did not seek to enjoin the broadcast of his act; he simply sought compensation for the broadcast in the form of damages. . . .

The broadcast of a film of petitioner's entire act poses a substantial threat to the economic value of that performance. As the Ohio court recognized, this act is the product of petitioner's own talents and energy, the end result of much time, effort, and expense. Much of its economic value lies in the "right of exclusive control over the publicity given to his performance"; if the public can see the act free on television, it will be less willing to pay to see it at the fair. The effect of a public broadcast of the performance is similar to preventing petitioner from charging an admission fee. "The rationale for [protecting the right of publicity] is the straight-forward one of preventing unjust enrichment by the theft of good will. No social purpose is served by having the defendant get free some aspect of the plaintiff that would have market value and for which he would normally pay." Kalven, *Privacy in Tort Law — Were Warren and Brandeis Wrong?*, 31 Law & Contemp. Prob. 326, 331 (1966). Moreover, the broadcast of petitioner's entire performance, unlike the unauthorized use of another's name for purposes of trade or the incidental use of a name or picture by the press, goes to the heart of petitioner's ability to earn a living as an entertainer. Thus, in this case, Ohio has recognized what may be the strongest case for a "right of publicity" involving, not the appropriation of an entertainer's reputation to enhance the attractiveness of a commercial product, but the appropriation of the very activity by which the entertainer acquired his reputation in the first place. . . .

There is no doubt that entertainment, as well as news, enjoys First Amendment protection. It is also true that entertainment itself can be important news. *Time, Inc. v. Hill.* But it is important to note that neither the public nor respondent will be deprived of the benefit of petitioner's performance as long as his commercial stake in his act is appropriately recognized. Petitioner does not seek to enjoin the broadcast of his performance; he simply wants to be paid for it. Nor do we think that a state-law damages remedy against respondent would represent a species of liability without fault contrary to the letter or spirit of Gertz v. Robert Welch, Inc., 418 U.S. 323 (1974). Respondent knew that petitioner objected to televising his act but nevertheless displayed the entire film.

We conclude that although the State of Ohio may as a matter of its own law privilege the press in the circumstances of this case, the First and Fourteenth Amendments do not require it to do so.

Reversed.

[Dissenting opinion omitted.]

B. PUBLIC DISCLOSURE OF EMBARRASSING PRIVATE FACTS ABOUT PLAINTIFF

The tort of public disclosure of private facts has been a troubled one. It pits the public's right to information about persons who have been involved in newsworthy events against the right of persons to live their lives quietly and out of the public eye. Some early cases recognized the tort. In Melvin v. Reid, 297 P. 91 (Cal. Ct. App. 1931), a prostitute, who had been tried for murder in 1918 and was acquitted, turned her life around and became a model citizen. She married in 1919 and made friends in a community that did not know of her past. In 1925, the defendant made a movie based on her life entitled *The Red Kimono*. In the movie, the plaintiff was portrayed using her maiden name. The court found that the movie portraying the events of her life was a matter of public record and no action could be based on the story line. The use of the plaintiff's maiden name after she had reformed was not justified and constituted an invasion of her privacy. The plaintiff's claim for damages arising from her loss of reputation and the shunning that followed on the heels of the revelation of her sordid past could be pursued. *See also* Briscoe v. Reader's Digest, 483 P.2d 34 (Cal. 1971) (story in *Reader's Digest* identifying the plaintiff as a hijacker was an invasion of privacy. The incident had taken place 11 years earlier. Plaintiff had rehabilitated his life and become an honorable person. The California court held that the incident could be reported but the identification of the plaintiff by name did not serve the public interest.).

The first major blow to the public disclosure of private facts tort was delivered by the United States Supreme Court in *Cox Broadcasting v. Cohn*. Despite the constitutionalization of the private facts tort, however, plaintiffs occasionally do prevail in these lawsuits, as illustrated by the notorious case following *Cohn*.

COX BROADCASTING CORP. v. COHN
420 U.S. 469 (1975)

WHITE, J.

The issue before us in this case is whether, consistently with the First and Fourteenth Amendments, a State may extend a cause of action for damages for invasion of privacy caused by the publication of the name of a deceased rape victim which was publicly revealed in connection with the prosecution of the crime.

I

In August 1971, appellee's 17-year-old daughter was the victim of a rape and did not survive the incident. Six youths were soon indicted for murder and rape. Although there was substantial press coverage of the crime and of subsequent developments, the identity of the victim was not disclosed pending trial, perhaps because of Ga. Code Ann. § 26-9901 (1972), which makes it a misdemeanor to publish or broadcast the name or identity of a rape victim. In April 1972, some eight months later, the six defendants appeared in court. Five pleaded guilty to rape or attempted rape, the charge of murder having been dropped. The guilty pleas were accepted by the court, and the trial of the defendant pleading not guilty was set for a later date.

In the course of the proceedings that day, appellant Wassell, a reporter covering the incident for his employer, learned the name of the victim from an examination of the indictments which were made available for his inspection in the courtroom. That the name of the victim appears in the indictments and that the indictments were public records available for inspection are not disputed. Later that day, Wassell broadcast over the facilities of station WSB-TV, a television station owned by appellant Cox Broadcasting Corp., a news report concerning the court proceedings. The report named the victim of the crime and was repeated the following day.

In May 1972, appellee brought an action for money damages against appellants, relying on § 26-9901 and claiming that his right to privacy had been invaded by the television broadcasts giving the name of his deceased daughter. Appellants admitted the broadcasts but claimed that they were privileged under both state law and the First and Fourteenth Amendments. The trial court, rejecting appellants' constitutional claims and holding that the Georgia statute gave a civil remedy to those injured by its violation, granted summary judgment to appellee as to liability, with the determination of damages to await trial by jury.

On appeal, the Georgia Supreme Court, in its initial opinion, held that the trial court had erred in construing § 26-9901 to extend a civil cause of action for invasion of privacy and thus found it unnecessary to consider the constitutionality of the statute. . . . 200 S.E.2d 127 (1973). The court went on to rule, however, that the complaint stated a cause of action "for the invasion of the appellee's right of privacy, or for the tort of public disclosure" — a "common law tort exist[ing] in this jurisdiction without the help of the statute that the trial judge in this case relied on." . . . 200 S.E.2d, at 130. Although the privacy invaded was not that of the deceased victim, the father was held to have stated a claim for invasion of his own privacy by reason of the publication of his daughter's name. The court explained, however, that liability did not follow as a matter of law and that summary judgment was improper; whether the public disclosure of the name actually invaded appellee's "zone of privacy," and if so, to what extent, were issues to be determined by the trier of fact. Also, "in formulating such an issue for determination by the fact-finder, it is reasonable to require the appellee to prove that the appellants invaded his privacy with wilful or negligent disregard for the fact that reasonable men would find the invasion highly offensive." . . . 200 S.E.2d, at 131. The Georgia Supreme Court did agree with the trial court, however, that the First and Fourteenth Amendments did not, as a matter of law, require judgment for appellants. The court concurred with the statement in Briscoe v. Reader's Digest Assn., Inc. . . . 483 P.2d 34, 42 (1971), that "the rights guaranteed by the First Amendment do not require total abrogation of the right to privacy. The goals sought by each may be achieved with a minimum of intrusion upon the other." . . .

[W]e do not have at issue here an action for the invasion of privacy involving the appropriation of one's name or photograph, a physical or other tangible intrusion into a private area, or a publication of otherwise private information that is also false although perhaps not defamatory. The version of the privacy tort now before us — termed in Georgia "the tort of public disclosure," . . . is that in which the plaintiff claims the right to be free from unwanted publicity about his private affairs, which, although wholly true, would be offensive to a person of ordinary sensibilities. Because the gravamen of the claimed injury is the publication of information, whether true or not, the dissemination of which is embarrassing or otherwise painful to an individual, it is here that claims of privacy most directly confront the constitutional freedoms of speech and press. The face-off is apparent, and the appellants urge upon us the broad holding that the press may not be made criminally or civilly liable for publishing information that is neither false nor misleading but absolutely accurate, however damaging it may be to reputation or individual sensibilities.

It is true that in defamation actions, where the protected interest is personal reputation, the prevailing view is that truth is a defense; and the message of New York Times Co. v. Sullivan, 376 U.S. 254 . . . and like cases is that the defense of truth is constitutionally required where the subject of the publication is a public official or public figure. What is more, the defamed public official or public figure must prove not only that the publication is false but that it was knowingly so or was circulated with reckless disregard for its truth or falsity. Similarly, where the interest at issue is privacy rather than reputation and the right claimed is to be free from the publication of false or misleading information about one's affairs, the target of the publication must prove knowing or reckless falsehood where the materials published, although assertedly private, are "matters of public interest." Time, Inc. v. Hill . . . 385 U.S., at 387-388.

The Court has nevertheless carefully left open the question whether the First and Fourteenth Amendments require that truth be recognized as a defense in a defamation action brought by a private person as distinguished from a public official or public figure. . . .

Those precedents, as well as other considerations, counsel similar caution here. In this sphere of collision between claims of privacy and those of the free press, the interests on both sides are plainly rooted in the traditions and significant concerns of our society. Rather than address the broader question whether truthful publications may ever be subjected to civil or criminal liability consistently with the First and Fourteenth Amendments, or to put it another way, whether the State may ever define and protect an area of privacy free from unwanted publicity in the press, it is appropriate to focus on the narrower interface between press and privacy that this case presents, namely, whether the State may impose sanctions on the accurate publication of the name of a rape victim obtained from public records — more specifically, from judicial records which are maintained in connection with a public prosecution and which themselves are open to public inspection. We are convinced that the State may not do so.

In the first place, in a society in which each individual has but limited time and resources with which to observe at first hand the operations of his government, he relies necessarily upon the press to bring to him in convenient form the facts of those operations. Great responsibility is accordingly placed upon the news media to report fully and accurately the proceedings of government, and official records and documents open to the public are the basic data of governmental operations. Without the information provided by the press most of us and many of our representatives would be unable to vote intelligently or to register opinions on the administration of government generally. With respect to judicial proceedings in particular, the function of the press serves to guarantee the fairness of trials and to bring to bear the beneficial effects of public scrutiny upon the administration of justice. . . .

The Restatement of Torts, § 867, embraced an action for privacy. Tentative Draft No. 13 of the Second Restatement of Torts, §§ 652A-652E, divides the privacy tort into four branches; and with respect to the wrong of giving unwanted publicity about private life, the commentary to § 652D states: "There is no liability when the defendant merely gives further publicity to information about the plaintiff which is already public. Thus there is no liability for giving publicity to facts about the plaintiff's life which are matters of public record. . . ." The same is true of the separate tort of physically or otherwise intruding upon the seclusion or private affairs of another. Section 652B, Comment *c*, provides that "there is no liability for the examination of a public record concerning the plaintiff, or of documents which the plaintiff is required to keep and make available for public inspection." According to this draft, ascertaining and publishing the contents of public records are simply not within the reach of these kinds of privacy actions.

Thus even the prevailing law of invasion of privacy generally recognizes that the interests in privacy fade when the information involved already appears on the public record. The conclusion is compelling when viewed in terms of the First and Fourteenth Amendments and in light of the public interest in a vigorous press. The Georgia cause of action for invasion of privacy through public disclosure of the name of a rape victim imposes sanctions on pure expression—the content of a publication—and not conduct or a combination of speech and nonspeech elements that might otherwise be open to regulation or prohibition. . . . The publication of truthful information available on the public record contains none of the indicia of those limited categories of expression, such as "fighting" words, which "are no essential part of any exposition of ideas, and are of such slight social value as a step to truth that any benefit that may be derived from them is clearly outweighed by the social interest in order and morality." Chaplinsky v. New Hampshire, 315 U.S. 568. . . .

By placing the information in the public domain on official court records, the State must be presumed to have concluded that the public interest was thereby being served. Public records by their very nature are of interest to those concerned with the administration of government, and a public benefit is performed by the reporting of the true contents of the records by the media. The freedom of the press to publish that information appears to us to be of critical importance to our type of government in which the citizenry is the final judge of the proper conduct of public business. In preserving that form of government the First and Fourteenth Amendments command nothing less than that the States may not impose sanctions on the publication of truthful information contained in official court records open to public inspection. . . .

Appellant Wassell based his televised report upon notes taken during the court proceedings and obtained the name of the victim from the indictments handed to him at his request during a recess in the hearing. Appellee has not contended that the name was obtained in an improper fashion or that it was not on an official court document open to public inspection. Under these circumstances, the protection of freedom of the press provided by the First and Fourteenth Amendments bars the State of Georgia from making appellants' broadcast the basis of civil liability.

Reversed. . . .

Most of the caselaw following *Cox* subordinated the plaintiff's interest in being free from embarrassment or public scrutiny to the broader social interest in access to truthful information about matters of public concern. *See, e.g.,* Ayash v. Dana Farber Cancer Institute, 822 N.E.2d 667 (Mass. 2005) (physician unwillingly became a public figure when a peer review report was disclosed concerning his supervision of other physicians who had inadvertently given lethal chemotherapy doses to patients); Gates v. Discovery Comms., Inc., 101 P.3d 552 (Cal. 2004) (no cause of action for public disclosure of private facts where television documentary published information, obtained from public records, about a person who had served a prison term for being an accessory after the fact to a murder for hire, but who had since "lived an obscure, lawful life and become a respected member of the community"); Hanes v. Alfred A. Knopf Inc., 8 F.3d 1222 (7th Cir. 1993) (denying privacy claim by plaintiff whose life was described in a book about black migration from the South to the North between 1940 and 1970).

A scant five years ago, we would have confidently predicted that the right of privacy is lost for those whose stories are newsworthy in any way. That would leave us with the purely private gossip who knows something embarrassing about a non-newsworthy private person and spreads the true gossip around the neighborhood. This genre of privacy is not subject to constitutional restraints. The media has no interest in publishing this kind of gossip because the public has no interest in such non-public persons. Nonmedia gossips who may indulge in reprehensible gossip are not likely to be solvent defendants worth suing. Thus, even though the branch of privacy that protects against public disclosure of private facts theoretically exists, we are not likely to see much litigation in this area.

But then in 2016 the world of privacy torts was rocked by the jury verdict against an online media company called Gawker. Gawker had published a sex tape featuring Terry Bollea, the professional wrestler known as Hulk Hogan, along with the wife of his best friend, Bubba "The Love Sponge" Clem (you can't make this stuff up). The following state court opinion reverses the trial court's entry of a temporary injunction against the publication of the sex tape as an unconstitutional prior restraint. It considers the balance between the plaintiff's privacy interests and the First Amendment interest in speech on matters of public concern.

GAWKER MEDIA, LLC v. BOLLEA
129 So.3d 1196 (Fla. Dist. Ct. App. 2014)

BLACK, J.

. . .

I. Background

In 2006, Mr. Bollea engaged in extramarital sexual relations with a woman in her home. Allegedly without Mr. Bollea's consent or knowledge, the sexual encounter was videotaped. On or about October 4, 2012, Gawker Media posted a written report about the extramarital affair on its website, including excerpts of the videotaped sexual encounter ("Sex Tape"). Mr. Bollea maintains that he never consented to the Sex Tape's release or publication. Gawker Media maintains that it was not responsible for creating the Sex Tape and that it received a copy of the Sex Tape from an anonymous source for no compensation.

On October 15, 2012, Mr. Bollea initiated an action in federal court by filing a multicount complaint against Gawker Media and others, asserting claims for invasion of privacy, publication of private facts, violation of the right of publicity, and infliction of emotional distress. Additionally, on October 16, 2012, Mr. Bollea filed a motion for preliminary injunction, seeking to enjoin the named defendants from publishing any portion of or any content from the Sex Tape. Following a hearing, the federal court issued an order on November 14, 2012, denying the motion for preliminary injunction. The court found that the requested preliminary injunction would be an unconstitutional prior restraint under the First Amendment and that notwithstanding the First Amendment issue, Mr. Bollea otherwise failed to demonstrate that he was entitled to a preliminary injunction under the applicable injunction standard.

On December 28, 2012, Mr. Bollea voluntarily dismissed the federal action. That same day, Mr. Bollea filed an amended complaint in state circuit court, asserting essentially the same claims that he asserted in federal court. Thereafter and as he did in federal court, Mr. Bollea filed a motion for temporary injunction seeking to enjoin Gawker Media and others not participating in this appeal from publishing and otherwise distributing the video excerpts from the sexual encounter and complementary written report. Following a hearing, the circuit court issued an order on April 25, 2012, granting the motion for temporary injunction. The court did not make any findings at the hearing or in its written order to support its decision. On May 15, 2013, this court stayed the order granting the motion for temporary injunction pending the resolution of this appeal.

II. Applicable Standards

. . . A temporary injunction aimed at speech, as it is here, "is a classic example of prior restraint on speech triggering First Amendment concerns," *Vrasic v. Leibel,* 106 So.3d 485, 486 (Fla. 4th DCA 2013), and as such, it is prohibited in all but the most exceptional cases, *Near v. Minn. ex rel. Olson,* 283 U.S. 697, 716 (1931). Since "prior restraints on speech and publication are the most serious and least tolerable infringement on First Amendment rights," the moving party bears the "heavy burden" of establishing that there are no less extreme measures available to "mitigate the effects of the unrestrained . . . public[ation]" and that the restraint will indeed effectively accomplish its purpose. *Neb. Press Ass'n v. Stuart,* 427 U.S. 539, 558–59, 562 (1976). . . .

III. First Amendment

It is not clear from the hearing transcript, and certainly not from the order, why the circuit court granted the motion for temporary injunction. Based upon the few interjections the court made during the hearing, it appears that the court believed Mr. Bollea's right to privacy was insurmountable and that publishing the content at issue was otherwise impermissible because it was founded upon illegal actions.

A. Privacy

"[W]here matters of purely private significance are at issue, First Amendment protections are often less rigorous." *Snyder v. Phelps*, 131 S. Ct. 1207, 1215 (2011) (citing *Hustler Magazine, Inc. v. Falwell*, 485 U.S. 46, 56 (1988)). On the other hand, "'[s]peech on "matters of public concern" . . . is "at the heart of the First Amendment's protection."'" *Id.* (quoting *Dun & Bradstreet, Inc. v. Greenmoss Builders, Inc.*, 472 U.S. 749, 758–59 (1985) (plurality opinion)).

> Speech deals with matters of public concern when it can be fairly considered as relating to any matter of political, social, or other concern to the community, or when it is a subject of legitimate news interest; that is, a subject of general interest and of value and concern to the public. The arguably inappropriate or controversial character of a statement is irrelevant to the question whether it deals with a matter of public concern.

Id. at 1216 (citations omitted) (internal quotation marks omitted).

Mr. Bollea, better known by his ring name Hulk Hogan, enjoyed the spotlight as a professional wrestler, and he and his family were depicted in a reality television show detailing their personal lives. Mr. Bollea openly discussed an affair he had while married to Linda Bollea in his published autobiography and otherwise discussed his family, marriage, and sex life through various media outlets. Further, prior to the publication at issue in this appeal, there were numerous reports by various media outlets regarding the existence and dissemination of the Sex Tape, some including still shots therefrom. Despite Mr. Bollea's public persona, we do not suggest that every aspect of his private life is a subject of public concern. However, the mere fact that the publication contains arguably inappropriate and otherwise sexually explicit content does not remove it from the realm of legitimate public interest. *See Snyder*, 131 S. Ct. at 1217; *see also Fla. Star v. B.J.F.*, 491 U.S. 524, 525 (1989) (holding that a news article about a rape was a matter of public concern and that the newspaper was not liable for the publication of the victim's identity obtained from a police report released by law enforcement in violation of a Florida statute); *Cape Publ'ns, Inc. v. Hitchner*, 549 So. 2d 1374, 1377 (Fla. 1989) (holding that confidential information regarding a child abuse trial was a matter of legitimate public concern and that thus the newspaper's publication of such did not violate privacy interests). It is clear that as a result of the public controversy surrounding the affair and the Sex Tape, exacerbated in part by Mr. Bollea himself, the report and the related video excerpts address matters of public concern. *See Bartnicki v. Vopper*, 532 U.S. 514, 534 (2001) ("[P]rivacy concerns give way when balanced against the interest in publishing matters of public importance. . . . One of the costs associated with participation in public affairs is an attendant loss of privacy.") . . . *Toffoloni v. LFP Publ'g Grp., LLC*, 572 F.3d 1201, 1213 (11th Cir. 2009) (holding that the publication of nude photographs of a female professional wrestler taken twenty years prior was not protected speech because their publication was not related to the content of the reporting, namely, her murder).

In support of his contention that the report and video excerpts do not qualify as matters of public concern, Mr. Bollea relies on *Michaels v. Internet Entertainment*

Group, Inc., 5 F. Supp. 2d 823 (C.D. Cal. 1998) (*Michaels I*), in which the court enjoined the commercial distribution of an entire sex tape that infringed the plaintiffs' copyrights. However, the court in *Michaels I* found the use of the sex tape to be purely commercial in nature. Specifically, the copyrighted tape was sold via the internet to paying subscribers, and the internet company displayed short segments of the tape as a means of advertisement to increase the number of subscriptions. In contrast, Gawker Media has not attempted to sell the Sex Tape or any of the material creating the instant controversy, for that matter. Rather, Gawker Media reported on Mr. Bollea's extramarital affair and complementary thereto posted excerpts from the video.

The court in *Michaels I* pointed out that although "[t]he plaintiffs are entitled to an injunction against uses of their names or likenesses to sell the [sex tape,] [t]he injunction may not reach the use of their names or likenesses to report or comment on matters of public interest." *Id.* at 838. In accord with this conclusion, the court held in the companion case that the publication of a news report and brief excerpts of the sex tape was not an invasion of privacy and was protected speech. Here, the written report and video excerpts are linked to a matter of public concern — Mr. Bollea's extramarital affair and the video evidence of such — as there was ongoing public discussion about the affair and the Sex Tape, including by Mr. Bollea himself. Therefore, Mr. Bollea failed to meet the heavy burden to overcome the presumption that the temporary injunction is invalid as an unconstitutional prior restraint under the First Amendment. As such, it was within Gawker Media's editorial discretion to publish the written report and video excerpts.

As a matter of First Amendment law, with its strong presumption against prior restraints on publication, this decision was probably correct. Given the court's reasoning that the sex tape was a matter of public concern — due in no small part to Bollea's own publicity-seeking — the logic of *Cox* would suggest that Bollea should have no cause of action against Gawker for public disclosure of private facts. But the trial judge allowed the case to go to the jury, which in March 2016 awarded $115 million in compensatory damages and $25 million in punitive damages to Bollea. The judge denied the defendant's post-trial motions for remittitur or a new trial. *See* Eriq Gardner, "Judge Upholds Hulk Hogan's $140 Million Trial Victory Against Gawker," Hollywood Reporter (May 25, 2016).

Supreme Court cases such as *Florida Star v. B.J.F.*, 491 U.S. 524 (1989), cited by the Florida court in *Bollea*, take an expansive view of the First Amendment's protection for the publication of private facts. *B.J.F.* involved the publication of the name of a rape victim, in violation of a state statute criminalizing the disclosure of such information. The Court emphasized that the information was truthful and had been lawfully obtained (the identity had been inadvertently disclosed). Gawker did not act unlawfully in obtaining the tape, which was delivered anonymously to the organization's offices. Even if it had, however, the First Amendment may protect the disclosure of information obtained unlawfully if it is newsworthy. *See Bartnicki v. Vopper*, 532 U.S. 514 (2001), also cited in *Bollea*. Is the tape of

Bollea having sex with his best friend's wife newsworthy? Bollea certainly talked a great deal in public about his sex life, suggesting there is some interest in the subject. Does that mean that the publication of anything that might conceivably sell newspapers or drive clicks to a website is, by definition, newsworthy?

The general counsel of the *New Yorker* magazine argued that First Amendment protection for publication of this tape may be necessary in order to ensure that the press will not be deterred from publishing other, more newsworthy material:

> "Newsworthy" is not the same as high-minded, and while many publications would not choose to publish a sex tape, the term can conceivably protect one. . . . We have seen many videos that are more newsworthy than this one, and it's even possible to imagine a more newsworthy sex tape. The reported sex tape of John Edwards and Rielle Hunter could have been considered newsworthy, had it been released, and had the former Presidential candidate denied the affair. If the Hogan verdict stands, would a media outlet that published that video be at risk of being put out of business? Would we be worse off if no one were willing to publish such a video? You don't have to be a First Amendment absolutist, in favor of the unlimited publication of sex tapes, to believe that we would.

Fabio Bertoni, "The Stakes in Hulk Hogan's Gawker Lawsuit," New Yorker (Mar. 23, 2016).

What do you think? Is the Hulk Hogan lawsuit a victory for the right of privacy or a threat to a vigorous and free press? Time will tell whether the balance between the privacy interests of individuals and the First Amendment are shifting subtly as courts reckon with new technologies and forms of communication. Time will also tell whether the Florida trial court's decision will be affirmed on appeal. First, however, the defendant may be required to post a $50 million bond as a condition of appealing the verdict. With its entry into bankruptcy, it is uncertain whether Gawker will be able to post the bond. Watch this space, because this is very much a developing story.

IT WASN'T PUBLIC — IT WAS ON MY FACEBOOK PAGE!

We will spare you what could be the painful experience of reading about new technologies in a book written by three people from very different generations. Suffice it to say you know more about social networking than we do, so we can presuppose the facts and ask about the application of privacy torts to online sharing of information. Let's imagine information not contained in public records (as in *Cohn*), pertaining to an incident that is not newsworthy. Suppose, for example, that the plaintiff is a 19-year-old who had too much to drink at a party, took off his clothes, and danced naked on a table. His best friend made a video of the event and sent it to the plaintiff. The plaintiff, thinking the video was hilarious, put it up on his Facebook page, where it was accessible only to those previously deemed online "friends" of the plaintiff. A few of the plaintiff's friends distributed the video further until it ended up in the possession of someone who had a grudge against the plaintiff. This person, whose privacy settings allowed strangers to view anything contained on his page, posted the video with the caption "[Plaintiff] Letting It All Hang Out."

Unfortunately for the plaintiff, he had recently applied for an internship at a corporation in the industry he hoped to work in. The corporation's human resources department routinely runs Google searches on applicants for permanent positions and internships. *See, e.g.*, Carly Brandenburg, *The Newest Way to Screen Job Applicants: A Social Networker's Nightmare*, 60 Fed. Comm. L.J. 597, 600 (2008) (reporting that 10 percent of employers indicate that they review information about applicants posted on social networks); Alan Finder, *When a Risqué Online Persona Undermines a Chance for a Job*, N.Y. Times, June 11, 2006. § 1, at 1, 30. The human resources director watched the video, decided the plaintiff was immature and lacked judgment, and denied his application for the internship. When the plaintiff learned the reason for his denial, he sued the person who had posted the video on a nonprivate page, hoping to recover against that person's parents' homeowners insurance umbrella coverage. The plaintiff's cause of action is stated in Restatement, Second, of Torts § 652D:

> One who gives publicity to a matter concerning the private life of another is subject to liability to the other for invasion of his privacy, if the matter publicized is of a kind that
>> (a) would be highly offensive to a reasonable person, and
>> (b) is not of legitimate concern to the public.

It may be that this sort of litigation will be unusual, but the hypothetical case shows the difficulty involved in adapting century-old common law torts to emerging technologies. *See, e.g.*, Patricia Sánchez Abril, *Recasting Privacy Torts in a Spaceless World*, 21 Harv. J.L. & Tech. 1 (2007). First one might question whether the video is "private" at all. Arguably the plaintiff had a nuanced expectation of privacy in the video. He was willing to share it with his friends—both his "real" friends and his Facebook "friends"—but would not have wanted it disseminated to parents, teachers, and prospective employers. Users of social networks can choose their intended audience, and can customize their privacy settings to control access to information concerning themselves. The plaintiff was harmed relative to his expectations about how the video would be shared, although of course one might question whether he took sufficient care to protect it from unauthorized dissemination (or whether he should have posted it at all).

One commentator has proposed a framework for harmonizing privacy torts and social networking, reflecting developing case law. *See* Abril, *supra*, at 28. Her synthesis of the cases comes down to the following factors:

1. Is the information protected by the First Amendment?
2. What was the overall accessibility of the information when it was disclosed?
3. Did the defendant have malicious intent or motive?
4. Was the plaintiff harmed?
5. Did the victim expressly protect the information via technology, contract, or otherwise?
6. Was the information originally disclosed in the context of a confidential relationship?

On this framework the defendant might be liable if you believe the plaintiff had an expectation of confidentiality in his circle of online "friends." On the other hand, the plaintiff might be said to have tacitly consented to the broader distribution of the video, knowing how easily control over information can be lost on the Internet. The analysis is objective, relying on what a reasonable person would expect in the social networking context. The context arguably requires a certain amount of savvy with respect to the possibility of disclosure of information. The plaintiff let the cat out of the bag by posting the video and sharing it with his Facebook friends, even though he very much wanted to keep it away from potential employers.

C. PLACING THE PLAINTIFF IN A FALSE LIGHT

TIME, INC. v. HILL
385 U.S. 374 (1967)

BRENNAN, J.

The question in this case is whether appellant, publisher of Life Magazine, was denied constitutional protections of speech and press by the application by the New York courts of §§ 50-51 of the New York Civil Rights Law to award appellee damages on allegations that Life falsely reported that a new play portrayed an experience suffered by appellee and his family.

The article appeared in Life in February 1955. It was entitled "True Crime Inspires Tense Play," with the subtitle, "The ordeal of a family trapped by convicts gives Broadway a new thriller, 'The Desperate Hours.'" The text of the article reads as follows:

> Three years ago Americans all over the country read about the desperate ordeal of the James Hill family, who were held prisoners in their home outside Philadelphia by three escaped convicts. Later they read about it in Joseph Hayes's novel, *The Desperate Hours*, inspired by the family's experience. Now they can see the story re-enacted in Hayes's Broadway play based on the book, and next year will see it in his movie, which has been filmed but is being held up until the play has a chance to pay off.
>
> The play, directed by Robert Montgomery and expertly acted, is a heart-stopping account of how a family rose to heroism in a crisis. Life photographed the play during its Philadelphia tryout, transported some of the actors to the actual house where the Hills were besieged. On the next page scenes from the play are re-enacted on the site of the crime.

The pictures on the ensuing two pages included an enactment of the son being "roughed up" by one of the convicts, entitled "brutish convict," a picture of the daughter biting the hand of a convict to make him drop a gun, entitled "daring daughter," and one of the father throwing his gun through the door after a "brave try" to save his family is foiled.

The James Hill referred to in the article is the appellee. He and his wife and five children involuntarily became the subjects of a front-page news story after being held hostage by three escaped convicts in their suburban, Whitemarsh, Pennsylvania, home for 19 hours on September 11-12, 1952. The family was released unharmed. In an interview with newsmen after the convicts departed, appellee stressed that the convicts had treated the family courteously, had not molested them, and had not been at all violent. The convicts were thereafter apprehended in a widely publicized encounter with the police which resulted in the killing of two of the convicts. Shortly thereafter the family moved to Connecticut. The appellee discouraged all efforts to keep them in the public spotlight through magazine articles or appearances on television.

In the spring of 1953, Joseph Hayes' novel, *The Desperate Hours*, was published. The story depicted the experience of a family of four held hostage by three escaped convicts in the family's suburban home. But, unlike Hill's experience, the family of the story suffer violence at the hands of the convicts; the father and son are beaten and the daughter subjected to a verbal sexual insult.

The book was made into a play, also entitled *The Desperate Hours*, and it is Life's article about the play which is the subject of appellee's action. The complaint sought damages under §§ 50-51 on allegations that the Life article was intended to, and did, give the impression that the play mirrored the Hill family's experience, which, to the knowledge of defendant "... was false and untrue." Appellant's defense was that the article was "a subject of legitimate news interest," "a subject of general interest and of value and concern to the public" at the time of publication, and that it was "published in good faith without any malice whatsoever. ..." A motion to dismiss the complaint for substantially these reasons was made at the close of the case and was denied by the trial judge on the ground that the proofs presented a jury question as to the truth of the article.

The jury awarded appellee $50,000 compensatory and $25,000 punitive damages. On appeal the Appellate Division of the Supreme Court ordered a new trial as to damages but sustained the jury verdict of liability. The court said as to liability:

> Although the play was fictionalized, *Life*'s article portrayed it as a re-enactment of the Hills' experience. It is an inescapable conclusion that this was done to advertise and attract further attention to the play, and to increase present and future magazine circulation as well. It is evident that the article cannot be characterized as a mere dissemination of news, nor even an effort to supply legitimate newsworthy information in which the public had, or might have a proper interest. ... 240 N.Y.S.2d 286, 290.

At the new trial on damages, a jury was waived and the court awarded $30,000 compensatory damages without punitive damages.

The New York Court of Appeals affirmed the Appellate Division. ... We reverse and remand the case to the Court of Appeals for further proceedings not inconsistent with this opinion.

Since the reargument, we have had the advantage of an opinion of the Court of Appeals of New York which has materially aided us in our understanding of that court's construction of the statute. It is the opinion of Judge Keating for the court in Spahn v. Julian Messner, Inc. . . . 221 N.E.2d 543 (1966). . . .

. . . *Spahn* was an action under the [privacy] statute brought by the well-known professional baseball pitcher, Warren Spahn. He sought an injunction and damages against the unauthorized publication of what purported to be a biography of his life. The trial judge had found that "the record unequivocally establishes that the book publicizes areas of Warren Spahn's personal and private life, albeit inaccurate and distorted, and consists of a host, a preponderant percentage, of factual errors, distortions and fanciful passages. . . ." The Court of Appeals sustained the holding that in these circumstances the publication was proscribed by § 51 of the Civil Rights Law and was not within the exceptions and restrictions for newsworthy events engrafted onto the statute. The Court of Appeals said: . . .

> But it is erroneous to confuse privacy with "personality" or to assume that privacy, though lost for a certain time or in a certain context, goes forever unprotected. . . . Thus it may be appropriate to say that the plaintiff here, Warren Spahn, is a public personality and that, insofar as his professional career is involved, he is substantially without a right to privacy. That is not to say, however, that his "personality" may be fictionalized and that, as fictionalized, it may be exploited for the defendants' commercial benefit through the medium of an unauthorized biography. *Spahn, supra* . . . 221 N.E.2d, at 545.

As the instant case went to the jury, appellee, too, was regarded to be a newsworthy person "substantially without a right to privacy" insofar as his hostage experience was involved, but to be entitled to his action insofar as that experience was "fictionalized" and "exploited for the defendants' commercial benefit." . . .

The [*Spahn*] opinion goes on to say that the "establishment of minor errors in an otherwise accurate" report does not prove "fictionalization." Material and substantial falsification is the test. However, it is not clear whether proof of knowledge of the falsity or that the article was prepared with reckless disregard for the truth is also required. In New York Times Co. v. Sullivan, 376 U.S. 254 . . . we held that the Constitution delimits a State's power to award damages for libel in actions brought by public officials against critics of their official conduct. Factual error, content defamatory of official reputation, or both, are insufficient for an award of damages for false statements unless actual malice — knowledge that the statements are false or in reckless disregard of the truth — is alleged and proved. The *Spahn* opinion reveals that the defendant in that case relied on *New York Times* as the basis of an argument that application of the statute to the publication of a substantially fictitious biography would run afoul of the constitutional guarantees. The Court of Appeals held that *New York Times* had no application. The court, after distinguishing the cases on the ground that *Spahn* did not deal with public officials or official conduct, then says, "The free speech which is encouraged and essential to the operation of a healthy government is something quite different from an individual's attempt to enjoin the publication of a fictitious biography of him. No public interest is served by protecting the dissemination of the latter. We perceive no constitutional infirmities in this respect." . . . 221 N.E.2d, at 546.

If this is meant to imply that proof of knowing or reckless falsity is not essential to a constitutional application of the statute in these cases, we disagree with the Court of Appeals. We hold that the constitutional protections for speech and press preclude the application of the New York statute to redress false reports of matters of public interest in the absence of proof that the defendant published the report with knowledge of its falsity or in reckless disregard of the truth.

The guarantees for speech and press are not the preserve of political expression or comment upon public affairs, essential as those are to healthy government. One need only pick up any newspaper or magazine to comprehend the vast range of published matter which exposes persons to public view, both private citizens and public officials. Exposure of the self to others in varying degrees is a concomitant of life in a civilized community. The risk of this exposure is an essential incident of life in a society which places a primary value on freedom of speech and of press. "Freedom of discussion, if it would fulfill its historic function in this nation, must embrace all issues about which information is needed or appropriate to enable the members of society to cope with the exigencies of their period." Thornhill v. Alabama, 310 U.S. 88. . . . "No suggestion can be found in the Constitution that the freedom there guaranteed for speech and the press bears an inverse ratio to the timeliness and importance of the ideas seeking expression." Bridges v. California . . . 314 U.S. 252, 269. . . . We have no doubt that the subject of the Life article, the opening of a new play linked to an actual incident, is a matter of public interest. "The line between the informing and the entertaining is too elusive for the protection of . . . [freedom of the press]." Winters v. New York . . . 333 U.S. 507, 510. . . .

In this context, sanctions against either innocent or negligent misstatement would present a grave hazard of discouraging the press from exercising the constitutional guarantees. Those guarantees are not for the benefit of the press so much as for the benefit of all of us. A broadly defined freedom of the press assures the maintenance of our political system and an open society. Fear of large verdicts in damage suits for innocent or merely negligent misstatement, even fear of the expense involved in their defense, must inevitably cause publishers to "steer . . . wider of the unlawful zone," New York Times Co. v. Sullivan, 378 U.S., at 279. . . .

We find applicable here the standard of knowing or reckless falsehood, not through blind application of New York Times Co. v. Sullivan, relating solely to libel actions by public officials, but only upon consideration of the factors which arise in the particular context of the application of the New York statute in cases involving private individuals. This is neither a libel action by a private individual nor a statutory action by a public official. Therefore, although the First Amendment principles pronounced in *New York Times* guide our conclusion, we reach that conclusion only by applying these principles in this discrete context. It therefore serves no purpose to distinguish the facts here from those in *New York Times*. Were this a libel action, the distinction which has been suggested between the relative opportunities of the public official and the private individual to rebut defamatory charges might be germane. And the additional state interest in the protection of the individual against damage to his reputation would be involved. . . . Moreover, a different test might be required in a statutory action by a public official, as opposed to a libel action by a public official or a statutory action by a private individual. Different considerations might arise concerning the degree of "waiver" of the protection the State might afford. But the question whether the same standard should be applicable both to persons voluntarily and involuntarily thrust into the public limelight is not here before us.

II.

Turning to the facts of the present case, the proofs reasonably would support either a jury finding of innocent or merely negligent misstatement by Life, or a finding that Life portrayed the play as a re-enactment of the Hill family's experience reckless of the truth or with actual knowledge that the portrayal was false. . . .

[Justice Breman reviewed the evidence and the jury instructions. He found that the jury instructions did not require a finding that the story was written with knowledge of falsity or reckless disregard of the truth. The judgment was reversed and the case remanded for further proceeding consistent with the opinion.]

[Concurring and dissenting opinions omitted.]

FOOD FOR THOUGHT

The privacy tort that protects people from being portrayed in a false light differs substantially from defamation. The reputation of the plaintiff in *Time, Inc. v. Hill* was not sullied. He would not be held up to shame and ridicule. Instead he felt violated because a harrowing event in the life of his family was falsely portrayed. It was bad enough that they had to go through the ordeal; they need not live with some fictionalized version of the events and presented to the public as an accurate description of what took place. Although the plaintiff in *Time, Inc. v. Hill* brought his action under the New York privacy statute, a large number of states have recognized a common law false light privacy action. Several states have refused to expand their common law to embrace the false light privacy tort. Restatement, Second, of Torts § 652 (1976) sets forth the elements of false light privacy. It provides:

§ 652E. Publicity Placing Person in False Light

One who gives publicity to a matter concerning another that places the other before the public in a false light is subject to liability to the other for invasion of his privacy, if

(a) The false light in which the other was placed would be highly offensive to a reasonable person, and

(b) The actor had knowledge of or acted in reckless disregard as to the falsity of the publicized matter and the false light in which the other would be placed.

Caveat:

The Institute takes no position as to whether there are any circumstances under which recovery can be obtained under this Section if the actor did not know of or act with reckless disregard as to the falsity of the matter publicized and the false light in which the other would be placed but was negligent in regard to these matters.

The Court's decision in *Gertz v. Robert Welch, Inc.*, reproduced in the preceding chapter has cast into doubt the authority of *Time, Inc. v. Hill*. You will recall that in *Gertz* the court held that defamation plaintiffs who are private persons do not have to prove knowledge of falsity or reckless disregard of the truth. They need only prove that the defendant was at fault. Presumably, the plaintiffs in *Time, Inc. v. Hill* were private persons. In Cantrell v. Forest City Publishing Co., 419 U.S. 245 (1974), the Court acknowledged that after *Gertz* the viability of *Time, Inc. v. Hill* was in question. The caveat to § 652E reflects the ambivalence on this issue. When the Supreme Court ultimately faces the question, it will have to take into account the post-*Gertz* case law as well. You will recall that in *Dun & Bradstreet v. Greenmoss Builders, Inc.*, reproduced in the preceding Chapter, the Court appeared to say that *Gertz* might well be limited to cases where the issue was one of public concern. In cases where the issues are not of public concern, plaintiff might not be required to establish fault. If that is a correct reading of *Dun & Bradstreet*, then the courts will have to ask whether the issue in a case such as *Time, Inc. v. Hill* is one of public concern. If it is not, then perhaps plaintiffs need not establish any fault on the part of the defendant.

Our best guess is that newsworthy events, such as took place in *Time, Inc. v. Hill*, will qualify as legitimate issues of public concern. Thus, at the very least, plaintiff will have to establish fault on the part of the defendant in a false light privacy case. Consider your reaction to the Hulk Hogan lawsuit against Gawker in light of *Time, Inc. v. Hill*.

D. INTRUSION UPON THE PLAINTIFF'S SOLITUDE

TOMPKINS v. CYR
995 F. Supp. 664 (N.D. Tex. 1998)

KAPLAN, U.S. Magistrate Judge

Plaintiffs Norman T. Tompkins and Carolyn Tompkins obtained an $8.5 million verdict against eleven abortion protestors after a jury trial. Three motions remain pending before the Court: (1) defendants' renewed motion for judgment as a matter of law; (2) plaintiffs' motion for judgment on the verdict; and (3) plaintiffs' motion for injunctive relief. For the reasons stated herein, defendants' renewed motion for judgment as a matter of law and plaintiffs' motion for judgment on the verdict are granted in part and denied in part. Plaintiffs' motion for injunctive relief is granted, as modified.

I. BACKGROUND

Norman T. Tompkins is a medical doctor who specializes in obstetrics and gynecology. He practiced medicine at various hospitals in the Dallas area for 26 years and served on the faculty of the University of Texas Southwestern Medical School. As a small part of his practice, Dr. Tompkins performed abortions.

Defendants are individuals and organizations who vehemently oppose abortion. Thomas Cyr is the former president of Dallas Pro–Life Action League ("Dallas PLAN"). Phillip Benham is the former director of the Dallas/Fort Worth branch of Operation Rescue. Louis Farinholt is affiliated with an organization called Missionaries to the Pre–Born. The remaining defendants—Richard Blinn, Oldrich Tomanek, Ann Hollacher, Ellen Pavlich, Laura Tellier, and J.R. Dannemiller—all were involved, either formally or informally, with Dallas PLAN.

The acknowledged mission of these pro-life activists was to convince Dallas area doctors to stop providing abortion services. Toward this end, Dallas PLAN devised "Operation John the Baptist." The main thrust of this campaign was to confront doctors who performed abortions and ask them to "repent" for their "sins." Cyr drew up a statement for the doctors to sign. Any doctor refusing to sign this agreement would be "exposed" wherever he went until he agreed to stop performing abortions. This "exposure" took a variety of forms, discussed more fully below. Dallas PLAN compiled a list of twenty physicians to target in this manner. Dr. Tompkins was one of those doctors.

In October 1992, Cyr and Hollacher approached Dr. Tompkins in his driveway as he prepared to leave for work. Dr. Tompkins asked them to make an appointment to come to his office at Presbyterian Hospital. Soon thereafter, Dr. Tompkins met with Cyr and Hollacher. Cyr told Dr. Tompkins that he was a Christian, that he was morally opposed to abortion, and that he wanted Dr. Tompkins to conform his behavior accordingly. Cyr asked Dr. Tompkins to sign the agreement and allow Dallas PLAN to take his picture. Cyr mentioned that he had organized a protest against Clay Alexander, another local physician, until Dr. Alexander finally agreed to stop performing abortions. Daniel Scott, who was present at the meeting, testified that Cyr threatened to "make [Dr. Tompkins'] practice go away" if he did not sign the pledge. Dr. Tompkins refused this ultimatum and the meeting ended.

Dallas PLAN made good on its threat and organized a demonstration at plaintiffs' home. Dr. Tompkins and his wife lived on the corner of Forest Lane, a busy six-lane street, and Forest Lakes, a cul-de-sac. Plaintiffs introduced a videotape of one of the pickets. It showed a group of people standing in the driveway, holding signs and chanting. Mrs. Tompkins testified that the demonstrators often amassed in this small area in front of her garage. The picketers would also "mill around" and march up and down the street. The evidence showed that the protestors held at least eight full neighborhood marches. . . .

Operation John the Baptist was not merely a picketing campaign, however. Dallas PLAN also devised a variety of other tactics to increase the pressure on Dr. Tompkins to stop performing abortions. . . . Dallas PLAN also organized a surveillance of plaintiffs' residence. Several defendants parked their cars in a cul-de-sac that runs behind the house and kept a near-constant watch of plaintiffs inside their home. Cyr, Tomanek, and Farinholt all participated in this surveillance. Plaintiffs' neighbor, Linda Pennington, testified that these defendants often had binoculars and a camera with them while they sat in the car. Tomanek sent several postcards to plaintiffs indicating that he had been watching them.

Cyr, Tomanek, Benham, and Farinholt, alone or in various combinations, routinely followed plaintiffs when they left the house. Cyr took pictures of plaintiffs' license plates for that purpose. Dr. Tompkins often knew he had been followed because he would find a Dallas PLAN pamphlet or flier under the windshield of his car. He said that he was followed nearly every time he left the garage. Mrs. Tompkins was often followed to work. On one occasion, Cyr, Tomanek, and Farinholt followed Dr. Tompkins to a restaurant. They confronted him while he was eating lunch and forced him to leave. Cyr taped this incident and it was shown to the jury. On December 11, 1992, Cyr and Tomanek followed plaintiffs as they were on their way to a party. Plaintiffs tried to elude the defendants and a high speed chase ensued. Cyr and Tomanek were stopped by the police after plaintiffs called for help on their car phone. . . .

These activities continued unabated for ten months and had a profound impact on plaintiffs. Dr. Tompkins and his wife testified that they lost all sense of privacy and security within their own home. They became fearful for their personal safety and hired bodyguards to be with them 24 hours a day. Dr. Tompkins wore a bullet-proof vest when he was out in public and had his car equipped with a bomb detection device. He testified that he feared for his life because he knew what had happened to other doctors and thought he might be next. Plaintiffs told their two grown children not to visit anymore and did not spend the holidays with them. Mrs. Tompkins would not visit her daughter, who lived in Dallas, for fear that the protestors would discover where she lived. Plaintiffs also decided to hold their daughter's wedding out of town and not post an announcement in the paper to avoid attracting attention. Nevertheless, plaintiffs received a letter from Cyr referring to their children. They found this particularly threatening in light of the precautions taken to protect their family. . . .

Plaintiffs experienced mental anguish and emotional distress as a result of the defendants' actions. Dr. Tompkins, once affable and outgoing, is now moody, withdrawn, anxious, and easily angered. He started to have problems with high blood pressure. Dr. Tompkins fears for his life and has a recurring dream about being shot and having his daughter discover his body. He has trouble eating and sleeping. Mrs. Tompkins also has problems sleeping. She no longer feels secure in her home and is afraid to be alone. Mrs. Tompkins is frightened when the phone rings. She becomes depressed, overly emotional, and is easily moved to tears.

Plaintiffs eventually took legal action to end this campaign of harassment and intimidation. They sued defendants in state court for intentional infliction of emotional distress, tortious interference, invasion of privacy, civil conspiracy, and related torts. The state court issued a preliminary injunction limiting the frequency, duration, and nature of the picketing at their home and church. Defendants removed the case to federal court after plaintiffs amended their pleadings to allege a RICO claim.

The case was tried to a jury on October 11-17, 1995. A partial verdict was returned on October 25, 1995. The jury found in favor of plaintiffs on their claims for intentional infliction of emotional distress, invasion of privacy, and civil conspiracy. Plaintiffs were awarded a total of $2,248,000 for intentional infliction of emotional distress and $2,800,000 for invasion of privacy. Ten defendants were order to pay a total of $3,450,000 in exemplary damages. The jury found in favor of all defendants on the claims for tortious interference with a residential sales contract. They were unable to reach a unanimous verdict on the claims for tortious interference with existing or prospective patients and civil RICO. . . .

II. FIRST AMENDMENT ISSUES

Before considering whether the evidence is sufficient to support the jury's verdict as to each claim for relief, the Court must determine whether it may enter *any* judgment in this case consistent with the First Amendment. . . .

B. Time, Place and Manner Regulations

As stated above, otherwise peaceful picketing activity may be regulated as to time, place, and manner. A valid regulation must: (1) be content-neutral; (2) be narrowly tailored to serve a significant government interest; and (3) preserve ample alternative channels of communication.

1. Content–Neutrality

The first question is whether the imposition of tort liability against defendants is content-neutral. A regulation is content-neutral when it is justified without reference to the content of the regulated speech. A regulation that satisfies this standard will be upheld even though it may have incidental effects on some speakers or messages but not others.

The torts of intentional infliction of emotional distress and invasion of privacy are undoubtedly facially content-neutral. They apply equally to any conduct that violates the standards they impose regardless of its First Amendment implications. There are no exemptions or exceptions that might indicate favoritism or hostility toward a particular viewpoint.

Of course, both intentional infliction of emotional distress and invasion of privacy require proof that defendants' behavior was outrageous or offensive. Defendants point out that speech may not be regulated merely because it is offensive, outrageous, or intended to coerce. This is certainly true, but it misses the mark in this case.

Defendants fail to acknowledge that picketing involves both speech *and* conduct. Courts have recognized that:

> [a] communication may be offensive in two different ways. Independently of the message the speaker intends to convey, the form of his communication may be offensive — perhaps because it is too loud or too ugly in a particular setting. Other speeches, even though elegantly phrased in dulcet tones, are offensive simply because the listener disagrees with the speaker's message.

Consolidated Edison Co. of New York, Inc. v. Public Service Commission of New York, 447 U.S. 530, 546-47 (1980) (Stevens, J., concurring in the judgment) (footnotes omitted). A regulation aimed at the offensiveness of the *form* of the communication, rather than the *content* of the message, is content-neutral. The jury was specifically instructed that it could base liability only on defendants' conduct, not the content of their anti-abortion message. The Court must presume that the jurors followed this instruction.

The Court concludes that the jury imposed liability based on the form of defendants' communication, not because they disagreed with their message. The verdict therefore was content-neutral.

2. Narrow Tailoring

The imposition of tort liability must be narrowly tailored to serve an important government interest. It is clear that the torts of intentional infliction of emotional distress and invasion of privacy serve important state interests. The Court further finds that, properly limited to specific forms of proscribed conduct, these torts can be narrowly tailored to further those interests.

a.

The first issue is whether these common law torts further significant government interests. Clearly they do. States have both "the power and duty . . . to take adequate steps to preserve the peace and protect the privacy, the lives, and the property of [their] residents." *Carlson v. California*, 310 U.S. 106, 113 (1940). The Supreme Court has consistently recognized a substantial government interest in protecting individual privacy. *See Cox Broadcasting Corp. v. Cohn*, 420 U.S. 469, 491 (1975) (describing privacy as an interest "plainly rooted in the traditions and significant concerns of our society"); *Rowan v. United States Post Office Dep't*, 397 U.S. 728, 736 (1970) (recognizing the right of every person "to be let alone"). Similarly, citizens have a right to be protected from the kind of "abuse" that the tort of intentional infliction of emotional distress proscribes. *See Farmer v. United Brotherhood of Carpenters and Joiners of America, Local 25*, 430 U.S. 290, 302-03 (1977); *St. Elizabeth Hospital v. Garrard*, 730 S.W.2d 649, 652 (Tex.1987); ("[F]reedom from severe emotional distress is an interest which the law should serve to protect."). . . .

b.

The next issue is whether the torts of intentional infliction of emotional distress and invasion of privacy can be narrowly tailored to further these important interests without unduly burdening free speech. Before addressing that issue, the Court must determine the appropriate legal standard governing its analysis.

(i)

Under the traditional formulation of the time, place, and manner doctrine, a regulation is narrowly tailored when it "targets and eliminates no more than the exact source of the 'evil' it seeks to remedy." Such a regulation need not be the least restrictive or intrusive imaginable alternative. Rather, the regulation is permissible if it is not substantially broader than necessary to achieve the government's interest.

However, the Supreme Court recently fashioned a more rigorous narrow-tailoring standard when the regulation under review is an injunction. *Madsen v. Women's Health Center, Inc.*, 512 U.S. 753 (1994). . . . Based on the rationale of the

Madsen decision, the Court concludes that common law torts are more analogous to statutes of general application and should be governed by the traditional standard of review.

Two principal concerns motivated the adoption of a more rigorous standard in *Madsen*. First, the Court observed that injunctions carry a significant risk of censorship. Injunctions present such risks because they prohibit conduct that has not yet occurred. "It is always difficult to know in advance what an individual will say, and the line between legitimate and illegitimate speech is often so finely drawn that the risks of freewheeling censorship are formidable." *Southeastern Promotions, Ltd. v. Conrad*, 420 U.S. 546, 559, 95 S.Ct. 1239, 1246-47 (1975). As a result, injunctions must be precisely drawn to avoid inordinately chilling potentially protected speech.

Common law torts do not implicate such risks. Rather, they merely provide an aggrieved plaintiff with a remedy for harms that have already occurred. This is entirely consistent with the First Amendment. *Id.* at 1246; *Gertz v. Robert Welch, Inc.*, 418 U.S. 323, 385 (1974). The Supreme Court has long recognized the important distinction between subsequent punishment schemes and so-called prior restraints. Tort liability falls squarely within the sphere of legitimate subsequent punishments.

The second concern expressed in *Madsen* was that injunctions are more likely to be applied in a discriminatory fashion. *Madsen*, 114 S. Ct. at 2524. The Court did not explain why it believed injunctions carry such risks, although this concern likely was related to the larger censorship issues. However, the Court noted that "'there is no more effective practical guaranty [sic] against arbitrary and unreasonable government than to require that the principles of law which officials would impose upon a minority must be imposed generally.'" *Id.* This is precisely how content-neutral tort law operates. The torts of intentional infliction of emotional distress and invasion of privacy apply equally to any defendant and any type of conduct, regardless of their First Amendment implications. This obviates the concerns expressed in *Madsen*.

The Court therefore finds that the more lenient standard of review applies to the regulation in this case. The jury's verdict may be upheld if it is not substantially broader than necessary to accomplish the legitimate objectives of protecting plaintiffs' privacy rights and emotional welfare. . . .

III. POST–VERDICT MOTIONS

Defendants contend that they are entitled to judgment as a matter of law because: (1) their conduct is protected by the First Amendment; and (2) the evidence is insufficient to support the jury's findings of intentional infliction of emotional distress, invasion of privacy, and civil conspiracy. Plaintiffs move for judgment on the verdict. The First Amendment issues have already been addressed. The Court now considers the sufficiency of the evidence. . . .

C. Invasion of Privacy

A plaintiff may recover for invasion of privacy if: (1) the defendant intentionally intruded, physically or otherwise, upon his solitude, seclusion, private affairs

authors' dialogue 41

AARON: Since the Brandeis-Warren article on privacy was published more than a century ago, it has been cited thousands of times in the cases and in the literature. Will history look kindly on their contribution?

JIM: Interestingly enough the privacy tort that they set forth in 1890 was a brilliant and innovative idea, but I think today it is of minor importance.

AARON: What has changed?

JIM: Let's take the four branches of the tort one by one. First, the appropriation of plaintiff's likeness. Today almost nobody uses photographs of unknown persons. The tort almost exclusively protects not privacy but the "right of publicity." It is a purely commercial tort that serves as a common law stand-in for copyright. Second, the public disclosure of private facts is functionally a dead letter today. Except for the rare private gossip case, most public disclosures of private facts are constitutionally protected because they are newsworthy. A celebrity's life is an open book no matter how many years have passed. Third, the false light privacy tort is for the most part covered by the *New York Times* malice standard. On rare occasions plaintiff can make out "knowledge of falsity or reckless disregard of the truth." But for the most part these cases are moribund. Finally, the tort of "intrusion on the plaintiff's private life" has little practical importance. Without this new tort, when the intrusion really gets bad, plaintiff can make out the tort of intentional infliction of emotional distress. Back in 1890 there was no such tort, so the privacy action had some importance.

AARON: Jim, you paint with too broad a brush. At least with regard to "false light" privacy, without the separate tort, plaintiffs would be at the mercy of yellow journalists who could willfully misrepresent their lives to the public. Although the *New York Times* privilege gives the media some breathing room, it does not give irresponsible journalists a free pass. They can and have lost cases on the ground that they published with knowledge of falsity or reckless disregard of the truth. You make an interesting point with regard to "intrusion privacy" but you forget that the elements of intentional infliction of emotion distress are not the same as the element of the privacy tort. The court in *Nader v. General Motors* made a big to-do about that point.

JIM: I'll grant you your point on false light but I think I'm still right on the intrusion tort. I think the New York Court of Appeals in *Nader* made much ado about nothing. I am hard pressed to think of a serious case of intrusion that would not make out a prima facie case for intentional infliction of emotional distress. Almost by definition, such an intrusion is outrageous and if plaintiff is seeking real damages she will, as a practical matter, have to prove that she suffered serious emotional distress.

or concerns; and (2) the intrusion would be highly offensive to a reasonable person. Valenzuela v. Aquino, 853 S.W.2d 512, 513 (Tex.1993); Restatement (Second) of Torts § 652B. The jury found Dallas PLAN, Operation Rescue, Missionaries to the Pre–Born, Thomas Cyr, Phillip Benham, Oldrich Tomanek, Louis Farinholt, Ann Hollacher, Laura Tellier, and J.R. Dannemiller liable for invasion of privacy.

Defendants contest the sufficiency of the evidence as to both elements of this cause of action. First, they claim that there is no evidence of "intrusion" because they did not use intrusive means such as wiretaps. Defendants have provided absolutely no support for this suggested limitation on the right to privacy, and it is not the law. Privacy may be invaded by *any* intrusion, "physical or otherwise." *Valenzuela*, 853 S.W.2d at 513. Cyr, Farinholt, and Tomanek invaded plaintiffs' privacy by watching their house from a car parked on a side street and using binoculars and a camera. *See* Prosser and Keeton on Torts § 117 at 854-44 (5th ed. 1984). Benham used a bull-horn to preach during the demonstrations at plaintiffs' home, which invaded their privacy by creating excessive noise. Cyr and Tomanek made repeated and harassing phone calls to plaintiffs. This invaded their privacy as well. Tomanek invaded plaintiffs' privacy by rattling their gate while they were eating Thanksgiving dinner. . . .

Defendants' renewed motion for judgment as a matter of law and plaintiffs' motion for judgment on the verdict are granted in part and denied in part. Plaintiffs' motion for injunctive relief is granted, as modified. The Court will enter judgment as follows:

. . . 2. Plaintiffs shall recover actual damages in the amount of $2,800,000 for invasion of privacy against Dallas PLAN, Operation Rescue, Thomas Cyr, Phillip Benham, Louis Farinholt, and Oldrich Tomanek, jointly and severally.

INTRUSION: LAST GASP FOR PRIVACY

Having explored the inroads that constitutional law has made on common law privacy actions, it is worth noting that privacy law still has some life. *Tompkins v. Cyr* shows that the intrusion tort sets limits on what would otherwise be core expressive activities. Similarly, placing listening devices into the privacy of bedrooms may support a privacy action, Hamberger v. Eastman, 206 A.2d 239 (N.H. 1964), as will videotaping of sexual encounters. Lewis v. LeGrow, 670 N.W.2d 675 (Mich. Ct. App. 2003). A more difficult question confronted the California court in Shulman v. Group W. Productions, Inc., 955 P.2d 469 (Cal. 1998). Plaintiffs were injured in a serious auto accident and were filmed being extricated from the car in which they were trapped. A nurse accompanied the plaintiffs while being transported to a hospital in a helicopter. A reporter joined them in the helicopter and videotaped the medical care given to the plaintiffs. He also provided the nurse with a small microphone that picked up the conversation between an injured plaintiff and members of the rescue team. The videotape and the conversations were later broadcast on a documentary dealing with emergency rescues. In upholding the denial of summary judgment for intrusion of privacy by the intermediate appellate court, the California Supreme Court agreed that it was a jury question as to whether the recording of plaintiff's conversation would be "highly offensive to a reasonable person." The potential newsworthiness of the accident and its aftermath did not negate the plaintiff's right of privacy.

Where to draw the line between privacy and legitimate investigatory reporting is not easy. Investigatory reporters often pose as customers or as sales representatives to gain entry into a business establishment. Consent to entry is based on a misrepresentation that would otherwise vitiate the consent and constitute a trespass. The reporters thereby become privy to conversations and events that they subsequently broadcast to the world at large. Do these invasions of privacy constitute the tort of intrusion? In a leading opinion, Desnick v. American Broadcasting Cos., Inc., 44 F.3d 1345 (7th Cir. 1995), Judge Richard Posner held that such ruses constitute neither trespass nor invasion of privacy. But other courts have been less solicitous to investigators who have overstepped the boundaries and have reported conversations that were intended to be private in the process of doing their investigations. *See, e.g.,* Food Lion v. Capital Cities/ABC, Inc., 194 F.3d 505 (4th Cir. 1999) (reporters using false resumes were employed by plaintiff who used the ruse to investigate food handling practices and videotaped in nonpublic areas of the store).

A rich literature is developing examining the interface between new technology and privacy. *See, e.g.,* Daniel J. Solove, *A Taxonomy of Privacy*, 154 U. Pa. L. Rev. 477 (2006); Lior J. Strahilevitz, *A Social Networks Theory of Privacy*, 72 U. Chi. L. Rev. 919 (2005); Paul M. Schwartz, *Property, Privacy and Personal Data*, 117 Harv. L. Rev. 2055 (2004); Eugene Volokh, *Freedom of Speech and Information Privacy: The Troubling Implications of a Right to Stop People from Speaking About You*, 52 Stan. L. Rev. 1049 (2000).

Table of Cases

Principal cases are indicated by italics. Alphabetization is letter-by-letter (e.g., "Fordham" precedes "Ford Motor Co.").

Table of Statutes and Other Authorities

RESTATEMENT (THIRD) OF TORTS: APPORTIONMENT OF LIABILITY

RESTATEMENT (THIRD) OF TORTS: INTENTIONAL TORTS TO PERSONS

Index